ABRAHAM LINCOLN,

PRESIDENT OF THE UNITED STATES.

(From a War-time Photograph.)

CAMPFIRE AND BATTLE-FIELD

AN ILLUSTRATED HISTORY OF THE

CAMPAIGNS AND CONFLICTS

OF THE

GREAT CIVIL WAR

BY

ROSSITER JOHNSON

WITH SPECIAL CONTRIBUTIONS BY

GEN. J. T. MORGAN, GEN. O. O. HOWARD, GEN. SELDON CONNOR

HENRY W. B. HOWARD, GEN. JOHN B. GORDON, HON. JAMES TANNER

GEORGE L. KILMER, MRS. L. C. PICKETT

ART EDITORS

FRANK BEARD, GEORGE SPIEL

NEW YORK

BRYAN, TAYLOR & CO.

61 EAST NINTH STREET

REPRINTED 1999 FROM THE 1894 EDITION.

TRIDENT PRESS INTERNATIONAL

ISBN 1-888777-70-2 DELUXE EDITION.

ISBN 1-888777-71-0 STANDARD EDITION.

PRINTED IN SLOVENIA

BEFORE THE BOMBARDMENT.

IN 1865—AFTER ITS REDUCTION BY GENERAL GILLMORE.

FORT SUMTER.

DEFENCES OF WASHINGTON—HEAVY ARTILLERY.

CAMPFIRE AND BATTLEFIELD.

CHAPTER I.

PRELIMINARY EVENTS.

CAUSES OF THE WAR—SLAVERY, STATE RIGHTS, SECTIONAL FEELING—JOHN BROWN—ELECTION OF LINCOLN—SECESSION OF SOUTHERN STATES—"SHOOT HIM ON THE SPOT"—PENSACOLA—MAJOR ROBERT ANDERSON—SUMTER OCCUPIED—THE "STAR OF THE WEST"—SUMTER BOMBARDED AND EVACUATED—THE CALL TO ARMS.

ON the 9th of January, 1861, the *Star of the West*, a vessel which the United States Government had sent to convey supplies to Fort Sumter, was fired on by batteries on Morris Island, in Charleston Harbor, South Carolina, and was compelled to withdraw.

The bombardment of Fort Sumter began on April 12th, the fort was surrendered on the 13th and evacuated on the 14th. On April 19th the Sixth Massachusetts regiment, which had been summoned to the defence of the national capital, was attacked, *en route*, in the streets of Baltimore.

Meanwhile, several Southern States had passed ordinances seceding from the Union, and had formed a new union called the Confederate States of America. Many Government forts, arsenals, and navy yards had been seized by the new Confederacy; and by midsummer a bloody civil war was in progress, which for four years absorbed the energies of the whole American people.

RIVER GUNBOAT (A CONVERTED NEW YORK FERRYBOAT).

What were the causes of this civil war?

The underlying, fundamental cause was African slavery—the determination of the South to perpetuate and extend it, and the determination of the people of the North to limit or abolish it. Originally existing in all the colonies, slavery had been gradually abolished in the Northern States, and was excluded from the new States that came into the Union from the Northwestern Territory. The unprofitableness of slave labor might, in time, have resulted in its abolition in the South; but the invention, at the close of the last century, of Eli Whitney's cotton-gin, transformed the raising of cotton from an almost profitless to the most profitable of the staple industries, and as a result of it the American plantations produced seven-eighths of all the cotton of the world. African labor was necessary to it, and the system of slavery became a fixed and deep-rooted system in the South.

The self-interest thus established led the South, in the face of Northern opposition to slavery which might make an independent government necessary to them, to insist on the sovereignty of the individual States, involving the right to secede from the Union. The Constitution adopted in 1789 did not determine the question as to whether the sovereignty of the States or that of

WILLIAM H. SEWARD,
Secretary of State.

SALMON P. CHASE,
Secretary of the Treasury.

EDWIN M. STANTON,
Secretary of War.

GIDEON WELLES,
Secretary of the Navy.

MONTGOMERY BLAIR,
Postmaster-General.

CALEB B. SMITH,
Secretary of the Interior.

EDWARD BATES,
Attorney-General.

PRESIDENT LINCOLN AND HIS CABINET.

the central government was paramount, but left it open, to be interpreted according to the interests involved, and to be settled in the end by an appeal to the sword. In the earlier history of the country the doctrine of State sovereignty was most advocated in New England; but with the rise of the tariff, which favored the manufacturing East at the expense of the agricultural South, New England passed to the advocacy of national sovereignty, while the people of the South took up the doctrine of State Rights, determined to act on it should a separation seem to be necessary to their independence of action on the issue of slavery.

From this time onward there was constant danger that the slavery question would so imbitter the politics and legislation of the country as to bring about disunion. The danger was imminent at the time of the Missouri agitation of 1820–21, but was temporarily averted by the Missouri Compromise. The Nullification Acts of South Carolina indicated the intention of the South to stand on their State sovereignty when it suited them. The annexation of Texas enlarged the domain of slavery and made the issue a vital one. The aggressiveness of the South appeared in the repeal of the Missouri Compromise in 1854; and the Dred Scott Decision in 1857, giving the slaveholder the right to hold his slaves in a free State, aroused to indignant and determined opposition the anti-slavery sentiment of the North. The

FORT MOULTRIE, CHARLESTON, WITH FORT SUMTER IN THE DISTANCE.

SIEGE GUN BEARING ON SUMTER.
(Showing Carriage rendered useless before Confederate Evacuation, 1864.)

expression in this decision, that the negro had "no rights which the white man was bound to respect," brought squarely before the people the issue of manhood liberty, and afforded a text for preaching effectively the gospel of universal freedom.

The absence of intercourse between the North and the South, and their radically different systems of civilization, made them like two different peoples, estranged, jealous and suspicious. The publication of sectional books fostered animosities and perpetuated misjudgments and misunderstandings; and the interested influence of demagogues, whose purposes would be furthered by sectional hatred, kept alive and intensified the sectional differences.

MAJOR-GENERAL
ROBERT ANDERSON.

There was little feeling of fraternity, then, to stand in the way when the issues involved seemed to require the arbitrament of war, and it was as enemies rather than as quarrelling brothers, that the men of the North and the South rallied to their respective standards.

An episode which occurred about a year before the war, which was inherently of minor importance, brought to the surface the bitter feeling which was preparing the way for the fraternal strife. John Brown, an enthusiastic abolitionist, a man of undoubted courage, but possessing poor judgment, and who had been very prominent in a struggle to make Kansas a free State, in 1859 collected a small company, and, invading the State of Virginia, seized the United States Arsenal at Harper's Ferry. His expectation was that the blacks would flock to his standard, and that, arming them from the arsenal, he could lead a servile insurrection which would result in ending slavery. His project, which was quixotic in the extreme, lacking all justification of possible success, failed miserably, and Brown was hung as a criminal. At the South, his action was taken as an indication of what the abolitionists would do if they secured control of the Government, and the secessionist sentiment was greatly stimulated by his attempt. At the North he became a martyr to the cause of freedom; and although the leaders would not at first call the war for the Union an anti-slavery war, the people knew it was an anti-slavery war, and old

INTERIOR OF FORT SUMTER AFTER THE BOMBARDMENT IN 1863—FROM GOVERNMENT PHOTOGRAPH.

(Presented to participants in Sumter Celebration, April 14, 1865.)

John Brown's wraith hung over every Southern battlefield. The song,

> "John Brown's body lies a-mouldering in the grave,
> His soul is marching on,"

became a battle-cry, sung at every public meeting, sending recruits to the front, and making the echoes ring around the army campfires.

So long as the Democratic party, which was in political alliance with the South, retained control of the Federal Government, there was neither motive nor excuse for secession or rebellion. Had the Free Soil Party elected Frémont in 1856, war would have come then. When the election of 1860, through Democratic dissension and adherence to several candidates, resulted in the election of Abraham Lincoln, the candidate of the Free Soilers, the die was cast, and the South prepared for the struggle it was about to precipitate.

The day after the election, on November 7th, 1860, the Palmetto flag, the ensign of the State of South Carolina, was raised at Charleston, replacing the American flag. High officials in the Government, in sympathy with the Southern cause, had stripped the Northern arsenals of arms and ammunition and had sent them to Southern posts. The little standing army had been so disposed as to leave the city of Washington defenceless, except for a few hundred marines and half a hundred men of ordnance. The outgoing Administration was leaving the national treasury bankrupt, and permitted hostile preparations to go on unchecked, and hostile demonstrations to be made without interference. So little did the people of the North realize that war was impending, that Southern agents found no difficulty in making purchases of military supplies from Northern manufacturers. Except for the purchases made by Raphael Semmes in New England, the Confederacy would have begun the war without percussion caps, which were not manufactured at the South. With every advantage thrown at the outset in favor of the South and against the North, the struggle began.

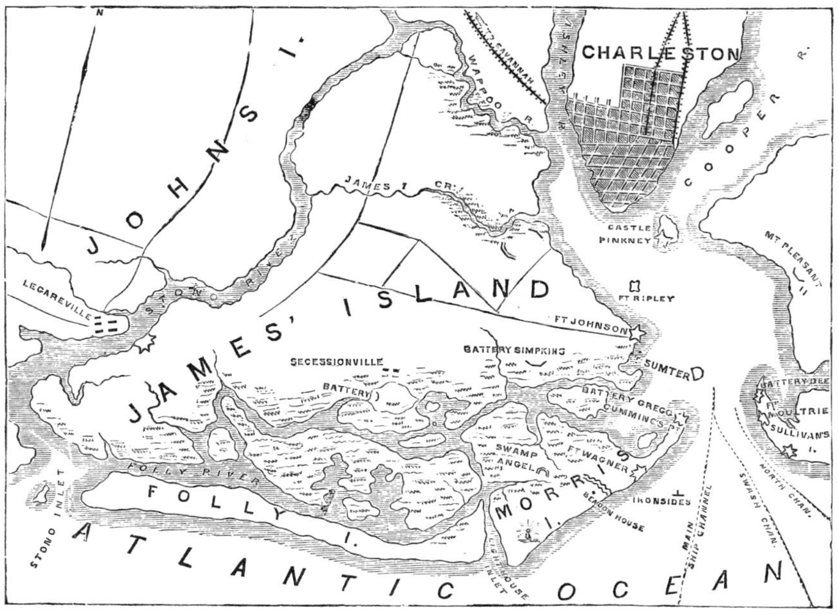

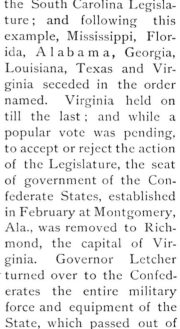

CHARLESTON HARBOR.

THE CONFEDERATE FLAG.

The Southern leaders had been secretly preparing for a long time. During the summer and fall of 1860, John B. Floyd, the Secretary of War, had been sending war material South, and he continued his pernicious activity until, in December, complicity in the theft of some bonds rendered his resignation necessary. About the same time the Secretary of the Treasury, Howell Cobb, the Secretary of the Interior, Jacob Thompson, and the Secretary of State, Lewis Cass, withdrew from the cabinet. On the election of Lincoln, treasonable preparations became more open and more general. These were aided by President Buchanan's message to Congress expressing doubt of the constitutional power of the Government to take offensive action against a State. On December 20, an ordinance of secession was passed by the South Carolina Legislature; and following this example, Mississippi, Florida, Alabama, Georgia, Louisiana, Texas and Virginia seceded in the order named. Virginia held on till the last; and while a popular vote was pending, to accept or reject the action of the Legislature, the seat of government of the Confederate States, established in February at Montgomery, Ala., was removed to Richmond, the capital of Virginia. Governor Letcher turned over to the Confederates the entire military force and equipment of the State, which passed out of the Union without waiting for the verdict of the people. This State was well punished by becoming the centre of the conflict for four years, and by political dismemberment, loyal West Virginia being separated from the original commonwealth and admitted to the Union during the war.

THE PALMETTO FLAG.

During the fall and winter of 1860–61, the Southern leaders committed many acts of treasonable aggression. They seized United States property, acting under the authority of their States, until the formation of the Confederacy, when the central government became their authority. In some of these cases the Federal custodians of the property yielded it in recognition of the right of the State to take it. In some cases they abandoned it, hopeless of being able to hold it against the armed forces that threatened it, and doubtful of support from the Buchanan Administration at Washington. But there were noble exceptions, and brave officers held to their trusts, and either preserved them to the United States Government or released them only when overpowered.

In December, 1860, the rebels seized Castle Pinckney and

A SUMTER CASEMATE DURING THE BOMBARDMENT.

Fort Moultrie in Charleston Harbor, the arsenal at Charleston, and the revenue cutter *William Aiken;* in January, the arsenals at Mount Vernon, Ala., Apalachicola, Fla., Baton Rouge, La., Augusta, Ga., and many forts, hospitals, etc., in Southern ports. By February they had gained such assurance of not being molested in their seizures of Government property, that everything within their reach was taken with impunity. So many of the officers in active service were in sympathy with the South, that it frequently required only a demand for the surrender of a vessel or a fort—sometimes not even that—to secure it. One of these attempted seizures gave rise to an official utterance that did much to cheer the Northern heart. John A. Dix, who in January, 1861, succeeded Cobb as Secretary of the Treasury, sent W. H. Jones, a Treasury clerk, to New Orleans, to save to the Government certain revenue cutters in Southern ports. Jones telegraphed the secretary that the captain of the cutter *McClelland* refused to give her up, and Dix thereupon sent the following memorable despatch :

"Tell Lieutenant Caldwell to arrest Captain Breshwood, assume command of the cutter, and obey the order I gave through you. If Captain Breshwood, after arrest, undertakes to interfere with the command of the cutter, tell Lieutenant Caldwell to consider him as a mutineer and treat him accordingly. If any one attempts to haul down the American flag, shoot him on the spot."

These determined words were among the few that were uttered by Northern officials that gave the friends of the Union any hope of leadership against the aggression of the seceding States ; and they passed among the proverbial expressions of the war, to live as long as American history.

The firmness of Lieutenant Adam J. Slemmer had prevented the surrender of Fort Pickens, in Pensacola Harbor, Florida, on the Gulf of Mexico, when it was demanded with some show of force, in January, 1861.

Meanwhile, an event was preparing, in which the loyalty, courage, and promptness of a United States officer was to bring to an issue the question of "bloodless secession" or war. The seizures of Government property here and there had excited indignation in the loyal North, but no general, effective sentiment of opposition. But at the shot that was fired at Sumter, the North burst into a flame of patriotic, quenchless fury, which did not subside until it had been atoned for on many a battlefield, and the Confederate "stars and bars" fell, never to rise again.

Lieutenant-Colonel Gardner had been in command at Charleston Harbor, S. C., and when he saw the secessionists preparing to seize the forts there, so early as November, 1860, he applied to Washington for reinforcements. Upon this, at the request of Southern members of Congress, Secretary of War Floyd removed him, and sent in his place Major Robert Anderson, evidently supposing that that officer's Kentucky origin would render him faithful to the Southern cause. But his fidelity to the old flag resulted in one of the most dramatic episodes of the war.

On reaching his headquarters at Fort Moultrie, Major Anderson at once applied for improvements, which the Secretary of War was now willing and even eager to make, and he appropriated large sums for the improvement of both Fort Moultrie and Fort Sumter, but would not increase the garrison or the ammunition. It soon became apparent that against a hostile attack Fort Moultrie could not be held, as it was commanded from the house-tops on Sullivan's Island, near by, and Major Anderson decided to move his garrison across the harbor to Fort Sumter, which, unlike Moultrie, was unapproachable by land. The secessionists in Charleston were active and watched suspiciously every movement made by the military, and the latter were constantly on guard to prevent surprise and capture of the fort. The preparations for removal to Sumter were made with the greatest caution. So well had Major Anderson kept his purpose secret, that his second in command, Captain Abner Doubleday, was informed of it only when ordered to have his company ready to go to Fort Sumter in twenty minutes. The families of the officers were sent to Fort Johnson, opposite Charleston, whence they were afterward taken North.

Capt. T. Seymour. 1st Lieut. G. W. Snyder. 1st Lieut. J. C. Davis. 2d Lieut. R. K. Meade. 1st Lieut. T. Talbot.
Capt. A. Doubleday. Major R Anderson. Surg. S. W. Crawford. Capt. J. G. Foster.

MAJOR ANDERSON AND OFFICERS DEFENDING FORT SUMTER.

For the ostensible purpose of removing these non-combatants to a place of safety—a step to which the now well-organized South Carolina militia could make no objection—Anderson's quartermaster, Lieutenant Hall, had chartered three schooners and some barges, which were ultimately used to transport supplies from Moultrie to Sumter. Laden with these supplies, the transports started for Fort Johnson, and there awaited the signal gun which was to direct them to land at Sumter. The guns of Moultrie were trained to bear on the route across the harbor, to be used defensively in case the movement was detected and interfered with.

The preparations completed, at sunset on December 26, the troops, who had equipped themselves in the twenty minutes allowed them, were silently marched out of Fort Moultrie and passed through the little village of Moultrieville, which lay between the fort and the point of embarkation. The march was fortunately made without observation, and the men took their places in rowboats which promptly started on their momentous voyage. After several narrow escapes from being stopped by the omnipresent guard boats, which were deceived into supposing the troop boats to contain only laborers in charge of officers, the party reached Fort Sumter. Here they found crowds of laborers, who were at work, at the Government's expense, preparing Sumter to be handed over to the Southern league. These men, most of them from Baltimore, were nearly all secessionists, and had already refused to man the fort as soldiers for its defence. They showed some opposition to the landing of the troops, but were promptly driven inside the fort at the point of the bayonet, and were presently shipped on board the supply schooners and sent ashore, where they communicated to the secession authorities the news of Major Anderson's clever ruse. The signal gun was fired from Sumter, the supplies were landed, and Fort Sumter was in the hands of the loyal men who were to immortalize their names by their heroic defence of it.

GUSTAVUS V. FOX,
Commanding the Relief Expedition to Fort Sumter; afterward Assistant Secretary of the Navy.

Sixty-one artillerymen and thirteen musicians, under command of seven or eight officers, constituted the slender garrison. Many of these officers subsequently rose to distinction in the service of their country, in which some of them died. Major Anderson became a major-general and served for a while in his native Kentucky, but was soon compelled by failing health to retire. Captains Abner Doubleday, John G. Foster and Truman Seymour, Lieut. Jefferson C. Davis and Dr. S. Wiley Crawford, the surgeon, became major-generals, and were in service throughout the war; Lieut. Norman J. Hall became colonel of the Seventh Michigan Volunteers, and was thrice brevetted in the regular army for gallantry, especially at Gettysburg; Lieuts. George W. Snyder and Theodore Talbot received promotion, but died early in the war; and Edward Moale, a civilian clerk who rendered great assistance, afterward received a commission in the regular army. One only of the defenders of Sumter afterward joined the Confederacy; this was Lieut. Richard K. Meade, who yielded to the tremendous social and family pressure that carried so many reluctant men to the wrong side when the war began. Commissioned in the rebel army, he died in 1862.

At noon on December 27, Major Anderson solemnized his occupancy of Sumter by formally raising the flag of his country, with prayer by the chaplain, Rev. Matthias Harris, and military ceremonies.

The sight of the national ensign on Sumter was quickly observed from a troop ship in the harbor, which hastened to the city with the news, not only that Anderson had moved from Moultrie to Sumter, but also that he was heavily reinforced, the sixty soldiers thronging the parapet making so good a show as to give the impression of a much larger number. At this news Charleston was thrown into a ferment of rage and excitement. South Carolina troops were at once sent, on December 27, to take possession of Castle Pinckney, the seizure of which was perhaps the first overt act of war on the part of the secessionists. This was followed by the rebel occupation of Forts Moultrie and Johnson, which were gotten into readiness for action, and shore batteries, some of them iron clad, were planted near Moultrie and on Cummings Point, an extremity of Morris Island near to Sumter; so that by the time the preparations were completed, Anderson's gallant little band was effectively covered on four different sides.

But the rebels were not relying wholly on measures for reducing Sumter in order to secure it. It was diplomacy rather than war which they expected would place in their hands all the government property in Charleston Harbor. On the very day of Anderson's strategic move across the harbor, three commissioners arrived in Washington for the purpose of negotiating for the peaceable surrender to South Carolina of all the forts and establishments. But the telegraphic news, which reached Washington with the commissioners, that the loyal Anderson was doing his part, met with such patriotic response in the North as effectively to interfere with the commissioners' plans. What Buchanan might have released to them under other circumstances, he could not give them after Major Anderson had taken steps to protect his trust.

Once within the fort, the Sumter garrison set vigorously to work to put it in a defensive condition. The Government work on the fort was not completed, and had the Southerners attacked it at once, as they would have done but for the expectation that the President would order Anderson to return to Moultrie, they could easily have captured it by assault. But they still hoped for "bloodless secession," and deferred offensive action. There were no flanking defences for the fort, and no fire-proof quarters for the officers. There was a great quantity of combustible material in the wooden quarters, which ultimately terminated the defence; for the garrison was rather smoked out by fire, than either starved out or reduced by shot and shell. The engineer officers were driven to all sorts of expedients to make the fort tenable, because there was very little material there out of which to make proper military defences. The workmen had left in the interior of the unfinished fort a confused mass of building material, unmounted guns, gun-carriages, derricks, blocks and tackle. Only two tiers of the fort were in condition for the mounting of heavy artillery—the upper and lower tiers. Although the garrison was severely taxed in performing the excessive guard duty required by their perilous situation, they yet accomplished an enormous amount of work—mounting guns with improvised tackle; carrying by hand to the upper tier shot weighing nearly one hundred and thirty pounds each; protecting the casemates with flag-stones; rigging ten-inch columbiads as mortars in the parade grounds within the fort, to fire on Morris Island; and making their quarters as comfortable as the circumstances admitted. The guns of the fort were carefully aimed at the various objects to be fired at, and the proper elevation marked on each, to avoid errors in aiming when the smoke of action should refract the light.

LIEUTENANT-GENERAL WINFIELD SCOTT,
Commanding U. S. Army, 1861.

To guard against a simultaneous attack from many sides, against which sixty men could make only a feeble defence, mines were planted under the wharf where a landing was most feasible, to blow it up at the proper time. Piles of paving stones with charges of powder under them, to scatter them as deadly missiles among an attacking party, were placed on the esplanade. Metal-lined boxes were placed on the parapet on all sides of the fort, from which musketry-fire and hand-grenades could be thrown down on the invaders directly beneath. Barrels filled

HARPER'S FERRY.

with broken stone, with charges of powder at the centre, were prepared to roll down to the water's edge and there burst. A trial of this device was observed by the rebels, who inferred from it that Sumter was bristling with "infernal machines" and had better be dealt with at long range.

The discomforts and sufferings of the garrison were very great. Quarters were lacking in accommodations; rations were short, and fuel was scanty in midwinter. The transition from the position of friends to that of foes was not immediate, but gradual. After the move to Sumter, the men were still permitted to do their marketing in Charleston; for all that Anderson had then done was to make a displeasing change of base in a harbor where he commanded, and could go where he pleased. Presently market privileges were restricted, and then prohibited altogether; and even when, under the expectation of action at Washington satisfactory to the South, the authorities relaxed their prohibition, the secessionist marketmen would sell nothing to go to the fort. Constant work on salt pork, with limited necessaries and an entire absence of luxuries, made the condition of the garrison very hard, and their conduct worthy of the highest praise.

Anderson has been criticised for permitting the secessionists to build and arm batteries all around him, and coolly take possession of Government property, without his firing a shot to prevent it, as he could easily have done, since the guns of Sumter commanded the waterways all over the harbor. But it is easier now to see what should have been done than it was then to see what should be done. Anderson did not even know that he would be supported by his own Government, in case he took the offensive; and the reluctance to begin hostilities was something he shared with the leaders on both sides, even down to the time of Lincoln's inaugural, in which the President said to the people of the South: "In your hands, my dissatisfied fellow-countrymen, and not in mine, is the momentous issue of civil war. The Government will not assail you. You can have no conflict without being yourselves the aggressors." The fact of Anderson's Southern birth, while it did not interfere with his loyalty, did make him reluctant to precipitate a struggle which he prayed and hoped might be averted. Had the issue of war been declared at the time, freeing him to do what he could, he could have saved Sumter. As it was, the preparations for reducing Sumter went on unmolested.

Instead of yielding to the demand of the South Carolina com-

MAJOR-GENERAL JOHN A. DIX.

missioners for Anderson's return to Moultrie, President Buchanan permitted the organization of an expedition for the relief of Sumter. But instead of sending down a war vessel, a merchant steamer was sent with recruits from Governor's Island, New York. The *Star of the West* arrived off Charleston January 9, and as soon as she attempted to enter the harbor, she was fired on from batteries on Morris Island. Approaching nearer, and coming within gun-shot of Moultrie, she was again fired on. At Sumter, the long roll was beaten and the guns manned, but Anderson would not permit the rebel fire to be returned. The *Star of the West* withdrew and returned to New York. Explanations were demanded by Anderson, with the result of sending Lieutenant Talbot to Washington with a full statement of the affair, there to await instructions. The tacit truce thus established enabled the preparation of Sumter to be completed, but the rebel batteries also were advanced.

Then began a series of demands from Charleston for the surrender of the fort. The secessionists argued with Anderson as to the hopelessness of his case, with the Washington Government going to pieces, and the South determined to have the fort and exterminate the garrison; and still another commission was sent to Washington, to secure there a settlement of the question, which was invariably referred back to Anderson's judgment.

The winter was passed in this sort of diplomacy and in intense activity, within the fort and around it. The garrison shared the general encouragement drawn from the accessions to the cabinet of strong and loyal men, such as John A. Dix and Joseph Holt, to replace the secessionists who had resigned. The Charleston people continued their loud demands for an attack on Sumter. The affair of the *Star of the West*, and the organization of the Confederate Government in February, had greatly stimulated the war spirit of the North, and it was felt that the crisis was approaching. Charleston people began to feel the effects of blockading their own channel with sunken ships, for their commerce all went to other ports.

With the inauguration of Lincoln on March 4, the South learned that they had to deal with an Administration which, however forbearing, was firm as a rock. Indications of a vigorous policy were slow in reaching the anxious garrison of Sumter, for the new President was surrounded with spies, and every order or private despatch was quickly repeated throughout the South, which made him cautious. But the fact that he had determined to reinforce Sumter, and to insist on its defence, did soon become known, both at the fort and in Charleston; and on April 6, Lieutenant Talbot was sent on from Washington to notify Governor Pickens to that effect. This information, received at Charleston April 8, was telegraphed to the Confederate Government at Montgomery, and on the 10th General Beauregard received orders from the rebel Secretary of War to open fire at once on Sumter.

Instantly there was renewed activity everywhere. The garrison, inspired by the prospect of an end to their long and wearisome waiting, were in high spirits. The Confederates suddenly removed a house near Moultrie, disclosing behind it a formidable masked battery which effectually enfiladed the barbette guns at Sumter, which, although the heaviest there were, had to be abandoned. On the afternoon of the 11th, officers came from Beauregard to demand the surrender of the fort, which they learned would have to yield soon for lack of provisions. At

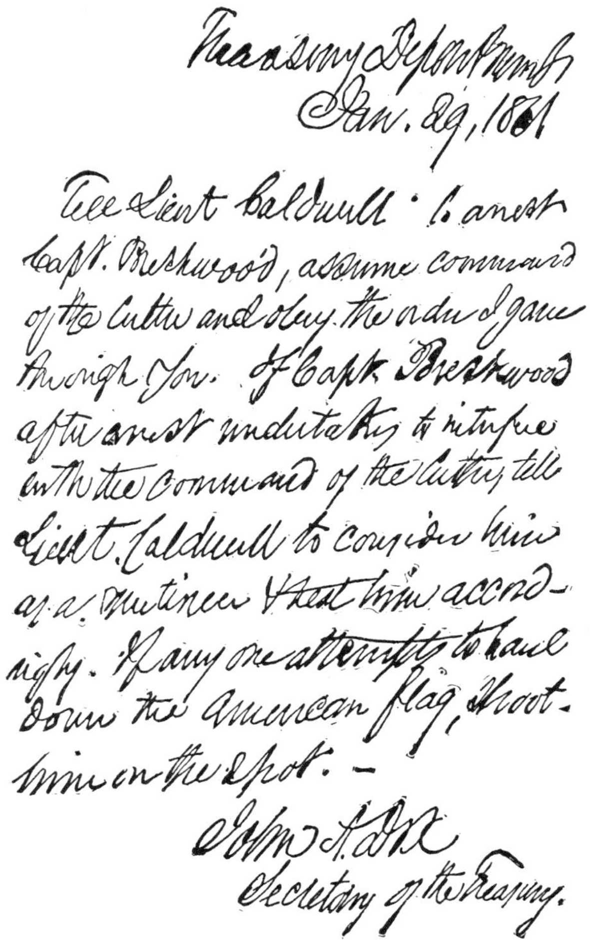

Treasury Department
Jan. 29, 1861

Tell Lieut Caldwell to arrest Capt. Breshwood, assume command of the cutter and obey the order I gave through you. If Capt. Breshwood after arrest undertakes to interfere with the command of the cutter tell Lieut. Caldwell to consider him as a mutineer & treat him accordingly. If any one attempts to haul down the American flag, shoot him on the spot. —

John A. Dix
Secretary of the Treasury.

GENERAL DIX'S FAMOUS DESPATCH.

three A.M. of the 12th, General Beauregard sent word that he would open fire in one hour.

He kept his word. At four o'clock the first gun of the war was fired from the Cummings Point battery on Morris Island, aimed by the venerable Edmund Ruffin, of Virginia, one of the fathers of secession. It was a good shot, the shell penetrating the masonry of the fort and bursting inside. At this signal, instantly the batteries opened on all sides, and the firing became an almost continuous roar.

But, as yet, Sumter made no reply. The artillery duel was not to be a matter of hours, and there was no hurry. Breakfast was served to officers and men, and was eaten amid a continual peppering of the fort with balls and shells from columbiads and mortars. After this refreshment the men were told off into firing parties, and the first detachment was marched to the casemates, where Capt. Abner Doubleday aimed the first gun fired on the Union side against the Southern Confederacy. It was fired appropriately against the Cummings Point battery

LIEUTENANT-GENERAL P. G. T. BEAUREGARD, C. S. A.

which had begun the hostilities; and it struck its mark, but did no damage. The heaviest guns in Sumter being useless, the fort was at a disadvantage throughout the fight, from the lightness of its metal. Notwithstanding Major Anderson's orders that the barbette guns should be abandoned, Sergeant John Carmody, disappointed at the effects produced by the fire of the fort, stole out and fired, one after another, the heavy barbette battery guns. Roughly aimed, they did little mischief; but they scared the enemy, who brought all their weight to bear now on this battery. Captains Doubleday and Seymour directed the firing from Sumter, and were assisted by Lieut. J. C. Davis and Surgeon Crawford, who, having no sick in hospital, volunteered his active services, and hammered away on Fort Moultrie.

By the middle of the morning the vessels of the relieving fleet, sent in pursuance of Lincoln's promise, were sighted outside the bar. Salutes were exchanged, but it was impossible for the vessels to enter the unknown, unmarked channel. This expedition was commanded by Capt. Gustavus V. Fox, afterward Assistant Secretary of the Navy, who had fitted it out with the coöperation of patriotic civilians—G. W. Blunt, William H. Aspinwall,

MAJOR-GENERAL GEORGE B. McCLELLAN.

Russell Sturgis, and others. The vessels arriving on the morning of April 12th were the war ship *Pawnee*, under Commodore Rowan, and the transports *Baltic* and *Harriet Lane*. The *Pocahontas*, Captain Gillis, arrived on the 13th. Knowing in advance the impossibility of entering the harbor with these vessels, a number of launches had been brought, with the intention of running in the reinforcements in these, under cover of night and protected by the guns of Sumter. Except for the delay of the *Pocahontas*, which carried the launches, this would have been attempted on the night of the 12th, when the garrison anxiously expected the new arrivals. Postponed until the 13th, it was then too late, as by that time Sumter had been surrendered.

The expectation of these reinforcements, the fear of a night

AN ALEXANDRIA ANTE-BELLUM RELIC.

assault by the enemy, and the difficulty of deciding whether any boats that might approach would contain friends to be welcomed or enemies to be repulsed, made the night of the 12th a most anxious one for the garrison. But neither friends nor enemies appeared, and after a breakfast of pork and water, on the morning of the 13th, a momentous day's fighting began.

By nine o'clock in the morning fire broke out in the officers' quarters, and it was learned that the hostile batteries were firing red-hot shot. Discovering the flames, the enemy redoubled their firing. It was impossible, even were it desirable, to save the wooden quarters, and, after one or two attempts to quench the flames, they were allowed to burn. Precautions were taken to secure the powder magazines from danger by cutting away the woodwork and spreading wet blankets. Many barrels of powder were rolled out for use. But finally a shot struck the door of the magazine and locked it fast, cutting off further supplies of ammunition. Powder that could not be protected was thrown overboard, but some of it lodging at the base of the fort was ignited by the enemy's shot, and exploded, blowing a heavy gun at the nearest embrasure out of battery. A trench was dug in front of the magazine, and filled with water.

So many of the men were required to attend to these precautions, that the firing from Sumter slackened up almost to cessation, leading the enemy to think they had given up. The fire became intense, driving some of the men outside the fort for air, until the thick-falling missiles drove them in again; and, combined with the bursting shells, all this produced a scene that was terrific. As the fire subsided for want of fuel to burn, the damage was disclosed. A tower at an angle of the fort, in which shells had been stored, had been entirely shattered by the bursting of the shells. The wooden gates at the entrance to the fort were burned through, leaving the way open for assault, and other entrances were now opened in the same way.

Shortly after noon the flag was shot away from its staff. A tremendous amount of ammunition had been wasted by the rebels in the ambitious effort to lower the flag, and at last it was successful. But the exultation of the enemy was cut short by the plucky action of Peter Hart, a servant, who had been allowed to join Major Anderson at the fort on condition that he should remain a non-combatant. Making a temporary flag-staff of a spar, he nailed the flag to it and tied it firmly to the gun-carriages on the parapet, accomplishing his feat under the concentrated fire with which the enemy sought to prevent it.

Supposing the fall of the flag to have been a token of surrender, ex-Senator Wigfall, of Texas, made his appearance at the fort about two P.M., announced himself as an aid to General Beauregard, and requested an interview with Major Anderson. He begged that the bloodshed might cease, and was told that there had been none at Sumter. He offered Anderson honorable terms of evacuation, and then withdrew.

At Wigfall's request, a white flag had been displayed during his presence at the fort, and the firing ceased. Observing this, General Beauregard sent a boat containing Colonels Chestnut, Lee, and Pryor, and Captain Miles, to inquire whether he surrendered. A long parley ensued, during which these officers said that Wigfall had not been in communication with Beauregard; upon which Major Anderson said, "Very well, gentlemen, you can return to your batteries," and announced that he would run up his flag and renew his fire. But at their request he agreed to delay this until they could see General Beauregard, and they withdrew.

LIEUTENANT-GENERAL ROBERT E. LEE, C. S. A.

That evening, another boat-load of officers came, bringing Beauregard's confirmation of the terms of evacuation that had been discussed with Wigfall, although permission to salute the United States flag was granted with much hesitation. It was then arranged that Anderson should leave Fort Sumter on the following day, taking all his men and arms and personal baggage, and saluting the flag.

Early on the morning of Sunday, April 14, all was made ready for the departure. The firing of the salute was a matter of some danger, as there was so much fire still about the fort that it was risky to lay ammunition down, and sparks of fire floated in the air. Fifty guns were fired before the flag was lowered. In reloading one of them, some spark that had lodged in the piece prematurely discharged it, instantly killing the gunner, Daniel Hough. The fire from the muzzle dropping on the cartridges piled below exploded those also, seriously injuring five other men. This was the only life lost at Sumter, and the first life lost in the war; and, with the exception of one man wounded by a bursting shell, these wounded men received the only casualties of the brave little garrison that defended Fort Sumter.

The men were formed in company, banners were flung to the breeze, the drums beat "Yankee Doodle," and the order was given to march through the charred gateway to the transport that lay at the dock in readiness to carry them to the *Baltic,* on which they sailed to New York.

When they reached their destination, they were lionized by their enthusiastic countrymen. Steam whistles and cheers greeted their passage through the harbor; comforts, long a stranger to them, awaited them at Fort Hamilton, where they were greeted in the name of a grateful people by the people's spokesman, Henry Ward Beecher; and the newspapers sang their praises in one harmonious chorus.

When Fort Sumter was evacuated, it presented very much the exterior appearance that it did before the bombardment—a few holes knocked in the masonry were all that the comparatively light artillery then brought to bear on it could accomplish. Occupied by the Confederates after the evacuation, it remained in their hands until the end of the war. When, in 1863, General Q. A. Gillmore bombarded Charleston, Fort Sumter was reduced to a pile of bricks and mortar; but such a quantity of cannon-balls and shells were poured into its débris as to form an almost solid mass of iron, practically impregnable. Sumter never was reduced by artillery fire, and fell into Federal hands again only when Charleston fell before Sherman's march to the sea.

On the conglomerate pile which constituted the ruins of the fort, a dramatic scene of poetic justice occurred on April 14, 1865, the fourth anniversary of the evacuation of Sumter. An expedition was sent by the Government to Charleston Harbor to celebrate the recapture by replacing the national flag on Fort Sumter. The ship *Arago* bore the officials in charge of the ceremony, and many invited guests, among whom were William Lloyd Garrison and the English George Thompson, leading abolitionists. A patriotic oration was pronounced by Henry Ward Beecher; and by the hand of Anderson, now major-general, the same flag which he had lowered in 1861 was drawn to the peak of the flagstaff, while Sumter's guns and those of every battery in the harbor that had fired on that flag fired a national salute of one hundred guns. The flag was riddled with holes, but, as the orator of the day pointed out, as symbolic of the preserved Union, not a single star had been shot away. Peter Hart, the brave man who had reset the flag during the bombardment, was present; and the Rev. Mr. Harris, who read prayers at the first raising, pronounced the benediction on the resurrection of the ensign of the nation.

"WAR GOVERNORS" OF THE NORTHERN STATES.

The shot that was fired on Sumter was the signal for a nation to rise in arms. That Sunday on which Sumter was evacuated was a memorable day to all who witnessed the intense excitement, the patriotic fury of a patient people roused to white-hot indignation. As on a gala day, the American flag suddenly appeared on every public building and from innumerable private residences. Crowds surged through the streets, seeking news and conference. The national flag was thrown to the breeze from nearly every court-house, school-house, college, hotel, engine-house, railway station and public building, from the spires of many churches, and from the windows of innumerable private residences. The fife and drum were heard in the streets, and recruiting offices were opened in vacant stores or in tents hastily pitched in the public squares. All sorts and conditions of men left their business and stepped into the ranks, and in a few days the Government was offered several times as many troops as had been called for. Boys of fifteen sat down and wept because they were not permitted to go, but here and there one dried his tears when he was told that he might be a drummer or an officer's servant. Attentions between young people were suddenly ripened into engagements, and engagements of long date were hastily finished in marriages; for the boys were going, and the girls were proud to have them go, and wanted to send them off in good spirits. Everybody seemed anxious to put forth some expression of loyalty to the national government and the starry flag. In the Ohio senate, on Friday, the 12th, a senator announced that "the secessionists are bombarding Fort Sumter." "Glory to God!" exclaimed a woman in the gallery, breaking the solemn silence which briefly followed the announcement. This was Abby Kelly Foster, an active abolitionist, who discerned that at last the final appeal had been taken on the slavery question—the appeal to the sword—from the triumphant issue of which would come the freedom for which she and her associates had contended, and which they believed could come in no other way.

On Monday, April 15, President Lincoln issued a call for seventy-five thousand militia from the several States "to suppress this combination against the laws, and to cause the laws to be duly executed."

The response to this call was immediate, and within the week some of the troops thus summoned were in Washington.

While forts and arsenals were being seized by the Confederates all over the South, while batteries to reduce Fort Sumter were being constructed and armed, what had been doing at Washington city, the capital of the nation?

ON THE MARCH.

RETURN FROM SKIRMISHING.

CHAPTER II.

PREPARATION FOR CONFLICT.

DEFENCELESS CONDITION OF WASHINGTON—SECESSION SYMPATHIZERS IN OFFICE—VOLUNTEERS IN THE DISTRICT OF COLUMBIA—COL. CHARLES P. STONE—PROTECTION OF PUBLIC OFFICES AND GUARDING OF COMMUNICATIONS—UPRISING OF THE PEOPLE—RESPONSE OF THE MILITIA—THE SIXTH MASSACHUSETTS IN BALTIMORE—THE NEW YORK SEVENTH REACHES WASHINGTON—DEATH OF COLONEL ELLSWORTH—SOUTHERN MILITARY AGGRESSION—HARPER'S FERRY CAPTURED—GOSPORT NAVY YARD BURNED AND EVACUATED.

DURING the interval between the election and the inauguration of President Lincoln, a very alarming condition of affairs existed at the national capital. The administration was in the hands of men who, even those who were not actively disloyal, were not Republicans, and did not desire to assume responsibility for the crisis which the Republican success at the polls had precipitated.

The Government service was honeycombed with secession sentiment, which extended from cabinet officers down to department clerks. Always essentially a city of Southern sympathies, Washington was filled with the advocates of State Rights. The retiring Democratic President, James Buchanan, in addition to a perhaps not unnatural timidity in the face of impending war and a reluctance to embroil his administration in affairs which it properly belonged to the incoming administration to settle, was also torn with conflicting opinions as to the constitutional questions involved, especially as to his power to coerce a sovereign State. Turning to his cabinet for advice, he was easily led to do the things that simplified the Southern preparations to leave the Union.

It has been told that the regular army troops had been sent away from Washington, leaving a mere handful of marines on duty there. It became a problem for loyal men to devise means for the maintenance of order at the seat of Government. It being the policy of the Government at that time to do nothing to provoke hostilities, it was deemed unwise to bring regular troops openly into Washington. There was no regularly organized militia there; only a few independent companies of doubtful, or unascertained, loyalty.

The aged Gen. Winfield Scott was in command of the army in 1860, and appreciating that trouble would come either from continued acquiescence in the aggressions of the South or from a show of force, he advised the President to quietly enroll the loyal people of the District of Columbia for the guardianship of the capital. For this duty he called in Charles P. Stone, a graduate of West Point and a veteran of the Mexican war, who was made Inspector-General of the District of Columbia, with the rank of colonel.

Colonel Stone took measures to ascertain the sentiments of the existing independent military companies. With admirable diplomacy he disarmed such of them as were found to be disloyal. Some of them he found to be in excellent condition of drill and equipment, by connivance of the Secretary of War, John B. Floyd, and they were well aware that it was their destiny to help defend the South against the "coercion" of the Yankees. Opposition from the War Department to Colonel Stone's measures ceased with Floyd's resignation, and under the new Secretary of War, Joseph Holt (afterward Lincoln's Attorney-General), he was able to enroll in a few weeks thirty-three companies of infantry volunteers and two troops of cavalry, under trustworthy leaders. These were recruited from neighborhoods, from among artisans, and from fire companies. All this was done with the discretion required by the strained condition of public feeling, which was such that, as General Scott said to Colonel Stone, "a dog-fight might cause the gutters of the capital to run with blood." As the time for Lincoln's inauguration approached, it became safe to move more openly; and by the 4th of March a company of sappers and miners and a battery had been brought down from West Point, while thirty new companies had been added to the volunteer force of the District.

In the first enthusiasm over the dramatic incidents attending the beginning of hostilities, the great services rendered by these troops were overlooked by the public. Abraham Lincoln's journey to Washington was beset with such danger that the last stage of it was made secretly, in advance of the published programme, and there was great rejoicing when it was announced that the President was "safe in Washington." He could not have been safe there except for the pres-

WASH-DAY IN CAMP--GUARDING THE SUPPLY TRAIN.

John Brown of Ossawatomie, spake on his dying day:
"I will not have to shrive my soul a priest in slavery's pay,
But let some poor slave-mother, whom I have striven to free,
With her children from the gallows stair, put up a prayer for me!"

LAST MOMENTS OF JOHN BROWN.

John Brown of Ossawatomie, they led him out to die:
And lo! a poor slave-mother, with her little child, pressed nigh;
Then the bold blue eye grew tender, and the old harsh face grew mild,
As he stooped between the crowding ranks, and kissed the negro's child!

J. G. Whittier.

LONG BRIDGE—OVER THE POTOMAC, AT WASHINGTON.

The planks were laid loose on the beams, and at night they were taken up, so that the bridge could not be crossed by the Confederate cavalry that hovered about the capital.

ence of Colonel Stone's volunteers. Trouble was apprehended at his inauguration. But the dispositions made by Colonel Stone secured peace and quiet for that ceremonial in a city teeming with traitors and would-be assassins. The advance to Washington of the troops called out by Lincoln's proclamation of April 15 was opposed in Maryland, regiments were attacked in the streets of Baltimore, and communicating railroad bridges were burned in order that no more troops for the subjugation of the South might pass through that border city. The South was flocking to arms, stimulated by the desire of seizing Washington. To a delegation that called on the President to protest against the passage of troops through Baltimore, Mr. Lincoln summed up the situation by saying: "I *must* have troops for the defence of the capital. The Carolinians are marching across Virginia to seize the capital and hang me. What am I to do? I *must* have troops, I say; and as they can neither crawl under Maryland nor fly over it, they must come across it."

During all this troubled time the District volunteers were the only reliance for the security of the public property, for guarding the approaches to the city, and for keeping open the communications for the entrance of the coming troops. They were among the first to be mustered into the United States service, and among the first to advance into Virginia.

To secure the public buildings against a rising among the secessionists living in Washington, the volunteer companies and the regular army batteries were conveniently posted, the bridges and highways leading to the city were guarded, and signals were arranged for the concentration at any given point of the eight thousand men who now constituted the garrison of the capital. Provisions were collected and stored, many of them in the Capitol building, and, to such extent as the force warranted, Washington was considered secure unless a Southern army was marched against it. And this impending danger was daily increasing. On April 17, Jefferson Davis, the President of the Confederacy, had called for thirty-two thousand troops, and had offered letters of marque to vessels to attack American commerce. The arrival of the militia called out by President Lincoln's proclamation was anxiously awaited.

Almost before the boom of the guns that were fired on Sumter had ceased, military preparations were actively under way in nearly every city and village in the North. The uniformed militia regiments were promptly filled up to their full numbers by new enlistments. Home Guards were organized in country towns, to defend their homes should the war be waged in the North, and to man afresh, when necessary, the companies already sent out. To fife and drum, the ununiformed farmers marched up and down the village green, temporarily armed with shot-guns and smooth-bore rifles, acquiring proficiency in "Hardee's Tactics" under the direction of old militia officers who had shone resplendent on former "training days." Neither custom nor regulations prescribing any particular uniforms, the greatest variety of fancy was shown in the equipment of the volunteers. Some adopted the zouave uniform, which had become popular through the then recent war between France and Austria and the memories of Magenta and Solferino. Garibaldi was a popular hero of the day, and the red shirts of his trusty men were another of the uniforms particularly favored. The war enthusiasm extended to the women and children, and sewing circles were organized for the making of many useful, and also many useless, articles for camp and hospital. The "havelocks"—a cap-cover and cape combined—however useful in India, were not wanted in America. Later, when there were sick and wounded to be cared for, these organizations of women were of inestimable service in preparing lint, bandages, and delicacies for the hospitals.

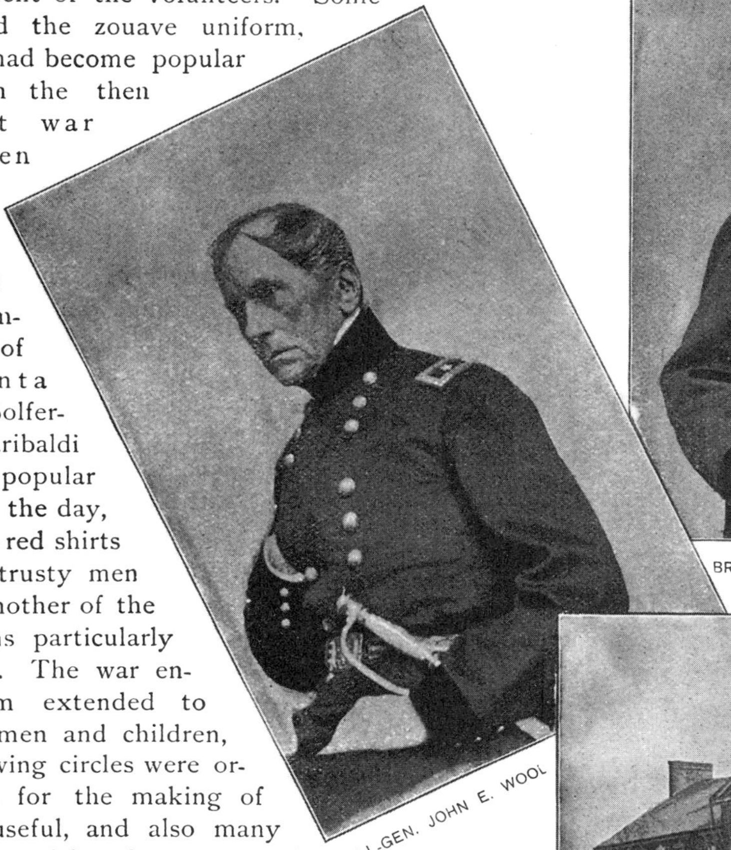

MAJ.-GEN. JOHN E. WOOL

BRIGADIER-GENERAL MONTGOMERY C MEIGS

OLD CAPITOL PRISON, WASHINGTON, D. C.

Prompt to discern the coming appeal to arms, John A. Andrew, the famous "war governor" of Massachusetts, had begun to recruit, arm, and equip his State militia as early as February, 1860, and by the time the call for troops came he had thirteen thousand men ready, not only to go to the front, but to furnish their own camp equipage and rations. Of these, nearly four thousand responded to the first call for three-months' volunteers. The first regiment to start for Washington was the Sixth Militia, Col. Edward F. Jones, which left Boston on April 17, only three days after the fall of Sumter. The passage of the train bearing this regiment was one long ovation from Boston to Philadelphia. At the latter city, as at New York, the men were received with enthusiastic hospitality, welcomed, fed, and plied with good things for their already overstocked haversacks; and it began to seem as though war were one continuous picnic. At least until the defence of Washington should begin, they were under no apprehension of trouble, until, on approaching Baltimore, on April 19, the anniversary of the Revolutionary battle of Lexington, the officers were warned that the passage of the regiment through that city would be forcibly opposed by a mob, which was already collected and marching about the city, following a secession flag. Colonel Jones ordered ammunition to be distributed, and, passing through the cars in person, he warned the men that they were to pay no attention to abuse or even missiles, and that, if it became necessary for them to fire on the mob, they would receive orders to that effect from their commandants.

The passage of trains through Baltimore at that period was by horse power across the city, from one depot to another. The horses being quickly attached as soon as the locomotive was taken off, cars carrying about two-thirds of the regiment were driven rapidly over the route; but to intercept the remaining four companies the mob barricaded the tracks, and it became necessary for these to abandon the cars and cover the remaining distance on foot. At once they became the target for showers of stones thrown by the mob, and in order to lessen the need of armed resistance, the officers gave the order to proceed at the double-quick. It was a mistake, but a common one when citizen soldiers are dealing with a mob; the most merciful as well as the wisest course being to scatter the mob promptly by a warning, followed by the promised volley. The mob thought they had the troops on the run, and were encouraged to believe that they either dared not shoot or that they were without ammunition. The missiles were followed with pistol shots, at which one soldier fell dead. Then the order to fire was given to the troops, and several of the crowd, rioters and spectators, fell. The mayor of Baltimore joined the officers at the head of the column, to give his authority to its progress, and also to tell the officers to

EPISCOPAL CHURCH, ALEXANDRIA, VA.

General George Washington and General Robert Lee attended this church.

PROVOST-MARSHAL'S OFFICE, ALEXANDRIA, VA.

defend themselves. Instead of being faced about to confront the mob, the troops were marched steadily forward, turning about as they advanced and delivering a desultory fire, which, however, did not deter the mob from continuing its attack. At last, Marshal Kane, of the Baltimore police, interposed with a company of policemen between the rear of troops and the rioters, formed a line, and ordered the mob back on penalty of a pistol volley. This was so effective as to practically end the affair, and without further serious disturbance the detachment joined their comrades at the Camden station, and boarded the train that took them to Washington. The regiment's loss was four killed and thirty-six wounded. The men were furious over the affair, and it required all the authority of the colonel to keep them from leaving the cars and taking vengeance on Baltimore for the death of their comrades. Arrived at Washington, the first regiment to come in response to the call of the President, they were quartered in the Senate Chamber.

After this incident, the mayor and police of Baltimore, who had done their duty handsomely, with the approval of the governor destroyed the tracks and railway bridges leading into the city, that there might be no repetition of such scenes; and the troops that followed—the Twenty-seventh Pennsylvania (which, unarmed, had reached Baltimore with the Sixth Massachusetts, but had to turn back), the Eighth Massachusetts under Gen. Benjamin F. Butler, and the famous Seventh New York—had to reach Washington by way of Annapolis. The Seventh, under Colonel Lefferts, was the first home regiment to leave New York City, and nothing could exceed the enthusiasm of the demonstrations that accompanied its march down Broadway. To greet its passage out of the city to the front, all business was suspended, and the population turned *en masse* into the streets. Boxes of cigars and other luxuries were thrust into the hands of the men as they passed down Broadway in a triumphal march such as has never been surpassed in the annals of the city. There was a certain dramatic element, new at the time, and scarcely repeated during the war, in this departure of a regiment composed literally of the flower of a great and wealthy city, representing its best elements, social and commercial. When General (then Major) McDowell mustered them in at Washington, he said to one of the captains: "You have a company of officers, not privates;" and out of the less than one thousand men composing this command, over six hundred, mostly privates, afterward became officers in the Union army. Among these were such names as Abram Duryea, who organized "Duryea's Zouaves;" Egbert L. Viele, Noah L. Farnam, Edward L. Molineux, Alexander Shaler, Louis Fitzgerald, Philip Schuyler, FitzJames O'Brien; Robert G. Shaw, who fell at Fort Wagner, leading to the assault his Massachusetts regiment, which was the first colored regiment to be organized under State authority; and Theodore Winthrop, whose death at Big Bethel, as a brave officer and a man of letters, was one of the conspicuous casualties of the early days of the war.

These troops were taken on transports from Philadelphia to Annapolis, another town of

Southern sympathies, where, except for the hospitality of the United States Naval Academy, they were most unwelcome. From that point they made their way, at first by train, and then, being obstructed by the destruction of railroads and railroad bridges, by forced marches, until they reached Annapolis Junction, where they were met by a regiment sent out from Washington to meet them, and thence proceeded by rail again. The strict discipline of Colonel Lefferts, to which they owed their successful pioneer work in opening the way to the capital, took them in review past President Lincoln at the White House before they breakfasted, and they had no let-up on the hardship of their service until they were quartered in the House of Representatives, where they were subsequently sworn into the service of the Government.

This episode is worth recounting, since it was the determined advance of these troops—the Eighth Massachusetts, under Colonel Hinks, accompanying them—in spite of rumors of a large secessionist force between them and Washington, that made access to the seat of government practicable for the regiments that promptly followed them, including more men from Pennsylvania and Massachusetts, the First Rhode Island, the Sixth, Eighth, Ninth, and Seventy-first New York, the latter regiments reaching Annapolis before the Seventh New York and Eighth Massachusetts left, thus keeping the way open. Had the rumored fifteen thousand rebels actually lain between Annapolis and Washington, it would have gone hard with the Government and the fortunes of the Union.

MARSHALL HOUSE, ALEXANDRIA.
Where Colonel Ellsworth was killed.

THE DEATH OF ELLSWORTH.

Troops continued to pour into Washington, until it really became an embarrassment to know what to do with them. They "bunked" all over the city, were quartered so far as practicable in the Government buildings, and made the national capital festive with the pranks in which they let off the animal spirits they carried into the grand picnic they seemed to have started on. Among them, a regiment of Zouaves, recruited from the New York Fire Department by Col. Elmer E. Ellsworth, was conspicuous. They were the last of the old-time "toughs," and they made things lively in the capital. They swarmed over the Capitol building, scaling its walls and running about its cornices in true fire-laddie fashion, and once they rendered a distinct service to the city of Washington by saving a burning building adjoining Willard's Hotel, displaying a reckless daring that gave the District firemen some new ideas.

COLONEL ELMER E. ELLSWORTH

Ellsworth had attracted much attention in 1860 by the admirable work of a company of Chicago Zouaves, with which he had given exhibition drills in the East, and he was early commissioned a second lieutenant in the regular army. But he resigned this position in order to organize the Fire Zouaves, which he marched down Broadway under escort of the Fire Department, and entered upon active service only to sacrifice his life at the very beginning in a needless but tragic manner. As soon as troops arrived in Washington in sufficient numbers, the Government determined to make Washington secure by seizing its outposts. Among these were Arlington Heights, across the Potomac, on the "sacred soil of Virginia," of which this occupation was termed the first "invasion." Ellsworth's regiment occupied the city of Alexandria; and then, discovering a secession flag flying from the Marshall House, the colonel mounted to the roof in person and tore the flag down. Descending, he was met at the foot of the stairs by Jackson, the proprietor of the hotel, who shot him dead with a shot-gun. Ellsworth's death was promptly avenged by Private Francis E. Brownell, who had accompanied him, and who put a bullet through Jackson's head; but, as the first death of an officer, it created wide-spread excitement

JEFFERSON DAVIS AND HIS CABINET.

JUDAH P. BENJAMIN,
Attorney-General—War—State.

JOHN H. REAGAN,
Postmaster-General.

STEPHEN R. MALLORY,
Secretary of the Navy.

CHRISTOPHER G. MEMMINGER,
Secretary of the Treasury.

ROBERT TOOMBS,
Secretary of State.

LEROY P. WALKER,
Secretary of War.

throughout the North, not excelled by that over the Massachusetts men who fell in Baltimore, and royal honors were shown to his remains. They lay in state in the White House, where he had been a great favorite with the President, and were conveyed to their last resting-place with every military distinction. Perhaps this incident, more than any that had yet occurred, brought home to the people of the North the reality of the war that was upon them. But it only stimulated recruiting; the death of Ellsworth weighing far less with the generous patriotism of the young men who filled up regiment after regiment, than the glory of Ellsworth, and the honor of Private Brownell.

While the levies were coming into Washington, the Southern leaders had not been idle. Response to Jefferson Davis's call for troops was general all over the States, and the week that intervened between Sumter and the riot in Baltimore was a busy one. In Virginia, the Governor took into his own hands measures for the defence of his State. As early as April 15 he caused a number of militia officers to be summoned to Richmond, and he placed in their hands the execution of a movement to capture the United States Arsenal at Harper's Ferry, at the junction of the Potomac and Shenandoah Rivers. Proceeding with a small command through an unfriendly country, these officers, among whom was the afterward famous Confederate general, John D. Imboden, reached their destination in the gray of the early morning of April 18, the day after the Virginia Legislature had passed the ordinance of secession. Instead of the resistance they had looked forward to on information that a Massachusetts regiment was guarding Harper's Ferry, they were welcomed with the sight of buildings in flames, which told them, only too truly, that the United States garrison had abandoned the place on their approach, and had set fire to the arsenal and stores to save them from falling into the hands of the Confederates.

JEFFERSON DAVIS'S RESIDENCE IN RICHMOND.

Early warning of the attempted seizure of Harper's Ferry had been confided to a messenger who had volunteered to acquaint the Government with the impending peril, and word was sent that heavy reinforcements alone would save this property to the United States. But in those formative days, when many earnest men hesitated between loyalty to the Union and loyalty to their State, when officers like Lee abandoned the old service with reluctance under a sense of paramount duty to their State, a man who was loyal one day would conclude overnight to secede with his State. And from some such cause as this, or through fear of the consequences, the messenger never delivered the message to the War Department, and the reinforcements, though anxiously expected, never came. The arsenal had been left in charge of Lieut. Roger Jones, who had been ordered to Harper's Ferry from Carlisle Barracks, Penn., with a small force of forty-five men. Hearing nothing from Washington in response to his request for aid, he made up his mind on the evening of April 17, that the only course open to him was to save his garrison by retreat, and destroy the property thus abandoned. This determination was confirmed by the news brought to him, by a former superintendent of the arsenal, of the coming of the Virginia troops. Although this same man had loyally reported, so long before as January, that an attempt might be made, he now told the workmen engaged at the arsenal that within twenty-four hours the arsenal would be in the hands of the Virginia forces, and advised them to protect the property, cast their lot with the secessionists, and insure to themselves a continuance of work under the new régime.

Lieutenant Jones immediately made secret preparations. He had trains of powder laid through the buildings, and when the force of thirteen hundred Virginians had approached to within a mile of the arsenal, at nine o'clock on the evening of April 17, the torch was applied, and the flames ran through the works, which were quickly burning. Some of the powder trains had been wet by the Southern sympathizers among the workmen, but the result was a practical destruction of nearly all that would have been valuable as munitions of war. The powder that was stored in the buildings exploded from time to time, effectually preventing serious efforts to put out the fire. The garrison was withdrawn

THE CAPITOL AT RICHMOND.

did, when the first considerable struggle of the war came at Bull Run, fifty miles south of them.

Another destruction of Government property by Government officers, about this time, most unnecessary and unfortunate, deprived the Navy Department of ships and material that would have been incalculably precious, and furnished the Confederates with three ships, one of which, the *Merrimac*, was to be heard from later in a signal manner.

At the Gosport Navy Yard, opposite Norfolk, Va., there were, besides many munitions of war, no less than eleven fine war ships, a majority of which were armed and ready for sea. The Government made prompt preparations to secure these after the fall of Sumter; and but for the delay of the commandant, Commodore Charles S. McCauley, in executing his orders, a number of the vessels, with stores, armament, and crews, would have been withdrawn into safe waters. But under the influence of his junior officers, most of whom subsequently joined the Confederacy, he deferred action until better prepared. This delay was fatal; for on April 18 he suddenly was confronted by a hostile force, though small in numbers, under General Taliaferro, which had seized Norfolk and threatened the navy yard. The

across the Potomac and marched back to Carlisle. When the Virginians came up the next morning, they found only the burning arsenal buildings to greet them.

Enough property was rescued from the destruction to make the capture a useful one to the Confederates, however; and the possession of Harper's Ferry gave them command of an important line of communication with Washington, by the Baltimore and Ohio Railroad. Anticipating the use of this line for the transportation of Western troops to Washington, Gen. Kenton Harper, commanding the Virginians, stopped the first train through; but his only capture was the person of Gen. William S. Harney, of the regular army, who was on his way to Washington to resign his commission rather than engage in the civil war. He was made a prisoner and sent to Richmond, whence he was allowed to proceed on his errand. General Harney did not resign, but was presently sent to Missouri to command the Department of the West. But his conciliating method of dealing with the enemy, together with his uncertain loyalty, caused him to be relieved very soon. The strategic value of Harper's Ferry was developed under Col. Thomas J. Jackson (afterward the celebrated "Stonewall"), who was made colonel commandant of all the Virginia forces, superseding all the previously existing militia generals. Robert E. Lee had been given the general command of the State troops, with Jackson as his executive officer, and by a legislative ordinance every militia officer above the grade of captain had been relegated to private life unless reappointed by the governor under the new dispensation.

The bridge at Point of Rocks, a few miles down the Potomac toward Washington, was seized and fortified against a possible attack by General Butler, who was near Baltimore; and by a clever *ruse* a great number of trains on the Baltimore and Ohio Railroad were "bagged," and the cars and engines side-tracked into Strasburg, greatly facilitating the Confederate train service in Virginia. Horses and supplies were secured from the neighboring country, and when Gen. Joseph E. Johnston superseded Jackson a month later at Harper's Ferry, the Confederates were in good shape to confront an advance on their position from Maryland or Pennsylvania, or to send reinforcements, as they

ALEXANDER H. STEPHENS.
Vice-President C. S. A.

action of the latter in waiting one day for expected reinforcements from Richmond, and Commodore McCauley's promise not to move a vessel or fire a shot except in defence, gave the Union commander time to do what he could to destroy the property in his charge; and on April 20 he scuttled every ship in the harbor, sinking them just before the arrival of Capt. Hiram Paulding in the *Pawnee* with orders to relieve McCauley, and to save or destroy the property. Seeing that it would be possible for the enemy to raise the sunken vessels, and that after the ships had been rendered useless he could not hold the place with his small force, Paulding decided to complete the work of destruction as far as possible, and told off his men in detachments for this duty. Ships, ship-houses, barracks, wharves, were at the signal (a rocket) set ablaze, and the display was magnificent as pyrotechnics, and discouraging to the enemy, which had expected to secure a ready-made navy for the taking of it. When to the roar of the flames was added the boom of the loaded guns as the fire reached them, the effect was tremendous. Under cover of all this, the *Pawnee* drew out of the harbor, accompanied by the steam-tug *Yankee* towing the *Cumberland*, which alone of the fleet had not been scuttled, and bearing the loyal garrison and crews. In the haste with which the work of destruction had been undertaken, the result was incomplete. The mine under the dry-dock did not explode; and that most useful appliance, together with many shops, cannon, and provisions, was secured by the Confederates, who also succeeded in raising and using three of the sunken and partially burned vessels—the *Merrimac*, *Raritan*, and *Plymouth*, under the guns of the first of which, from behind its armored sides, the *Cumberland* afterward came to grief in Hampton Roads.

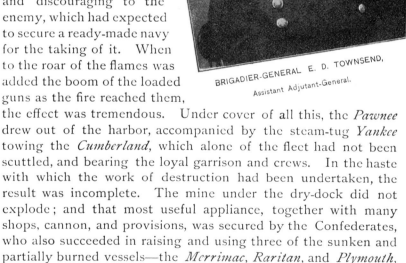

BRIGADIER-GENERAL E. D. TOWNSEND,
Assistant Adjutant-General.

BRIGADIER-GENERAL CHARLES P. STONE.

CHAPTER III.

THE BEGINNING OF BLOODSHED.

LINCOLN'S INAUGURAL ADDRESS—THE STRUGGLE FOR VIRGINIA—OPPOSING VIEWS EXPRESSED BY ALEXANDER H. STEPHENS—THE SLAVE-TRADE OF VIRGINIA—VIRGINIA DRAGOONED—THE FIRST CALL FOR TROOPS—LINCOLN'S FAITH IN THE PEOPLE—ORIGIN OF THE WORD "COPPERHEAD."

ABRAHAM LINCOLN'S inaugural address was one of the ablest state papers recorded in American history. It argued the question of secession in all its aspects—the constitutional right, the reality of the grievance, the sufficiency of the remedy—and so far as law and logic went, it left the secessionists little or nothing to stand on. But neither law nor logic could change in a single day the pre-determined purpose of a powerful combination, or allay the passions that had been roused by years of resentful debate. Some of its sentences read like maxims for statesmen: "The central idea of secession is the essence of anarchy." "Can aliens make treaties easier than friends can make laws?" "Why should there not be a patient confidence in the ultimate justice of the people? Is there any better or equal hope in the world?"

With all its conciliatory messages it expressed a firm and unalterable purpose to maintain the Union at every hazard. "I consider," he said, "that, in view of the Constitution and the laws, the Union is unbroken, and to the extent of my ability I shall take care, as the Constitution itself expressly enjoins upon me, that the laws of the Union be faithfully executed in all the States. Doing this I deem to be only a simple duty on my part; and I shall perform it, so far as practicable, unless my rightful masters, the American people, shall withhold the requisite means, or in some authoritative manner direct the contrary." And in closing he said: "In your hands, my dissatisfied fellow-countrymen, and not in mine, is the momentous issue of civil war. The Government will not assail you. You can have no conflict without being yourselves the aggressors. You have no oath registered in heaven to destroy the Government, while I have the most solemn one to preserve, protect and defend it. . . . We are not enemies, but friends. We must not be enemies. Though passion may have strained, it must not break our bonds of affection. The mystic cords of memory, stretching from every battlefield and patriot grave to every living heart and hearthstone all over this broad land, will yet swell the chorus of the Union when again touched, as surely they will be, by the better angels of our nature."

No such address had ever come from the lips of a Presi-

BRIGADIER-GENERAL WILLIAM S. HARNEY.

Oliver O. Howard. John A. Logan. William B. Hazen. William T. Sherman. Jeff. C. Davis. Henry W. Slocum. J. A. Mower.

SHERMAN AND HIS GENERALS.

GENERAL GRANT'S BODYGUARD

dent before. Pierce and Buchanan had scolded the abolitionists like partisans; Lincoln talked to the secessionists like a brother. The loyal people throughout the country received the address with satisfaction. The secessionists bitterly denounced it. Overlooking all its pacific declarations, and keeping out of sight the fact that a majority of the Congress just chosen was politically opposed to the President, they appealed to the Southern people to say whether they would "submit to abolition rule," and whether they were going to look on and "see gallant little South Carolina crushed under the heel of despotism."

In spite of all such appeals, there was still a strong Union sentiment at the South. This sentiment was admirably expressed by Hon. Alexander H. Stephens in a speech delivered on November 14, 1860, in the following words: "This step of secession, once taken, can never be recalled; and all the baleful and withering consequences that must follow will rest on the convention for all time. . . .

GENERAL ULYSSES S. GRANT, WITH GENERALS RAWLINS AND BOWERS.

What reasons can you give the nations of the earth to justify it? What right has the North assailed? What interest of the South has been invaded? What justice has been denied? And what claim founded in justice and right has been withheld? Can either of you to-day name one governmental act of wrong, deliberately and purposely done by the Government of Washington, of which the South has the right to complain? I challenge the answer. . . . I declare here, as I have often done before, and which has been repeated by the greatest and wisest of statesmen and patriots in this and other lands, that it is the best and freest Government—the most equal in its rights, the most just in its decisions, the most lenient in its measures, and the most inspiring in its principles to elevate the race of men—that the sun of heaven ever shone upon. Now, for you to attempt to overthrow such a Government as this, under which we have lived for more than three-quarters of a century, in which we have gained our wealth, our standing as a nation, our domestic safety while the elements of peril are around us, with peace and tranquillity accompanied with unbounded prosperity and rights unassailed—is the height of madness, folly and wickedness, to which I can neither lend my sanction nor my vote." In a speech by Mr. Stephens delivered in Savannah, March 22, 1861, he expressed entirely different views; in expounding the new constitution, he said: "The prevailing idea entertained by him [Thomas Jefferson] and most of the leading statesmen at the time of the formation of the old Constitution was, that the enslavement of the African was in violation of the laws of nature; that it was wrong in principle, socially, morally and politically. . . . Our new Government is founded upon exactly the opposite idea. Its foundation was laid, and its corner-stone rests, upon the great truth that the negro is not equal to the white man, that slavery, in subordination to the superior race, is his natural and normal condition." Seven slave States had gone out, but eight remained, and the anxiety of the secessionists was to secure these at once, or most of them, before the excitement cooled. The great prize was Virginia, both because of her own power and resources, and because her accession to the Confederacy would necessarily bring North Carolina also. Her governor, John Letcher, professed to be a Unionist; but his conduct after the ordinance of secession had been passed appears to prove that this profession was insincere. In electing delegates to a convention to consider the question of secession, the Unionists cast a majority of sixty thousand votes; and on the 4th of April, when President Lincoln had been in office a month, that convention refused, by a vote of eighty-nine to forty-five, to pass an ordinance of secession. The leading revolutionists of the cotton States were becoming uneasy. Said Mr. Gilchrist, of Alabama, to the Confederate Secretary of War: "You must sprinkle blood in the faces of the people! If you delay two months, Alabama stays in the Union!" Hence the attack on Fort Sumter, out of which the garrison were in peril of being driven by starvation. This certainly had a great popular effect in the South as well as in the North; but Virginia's choice appears to have been determined by a measure that was less spectacular and more coldly significant. The Confederate Constitution provided that Congress should have the power to "prohibit the introduction of slaves from any State not a member of, or Territory not belonging to, this Confederacy," and at the time when Virginia's fate was in the balance it was reported that such an act had been passed by the Congress at Montgomery.* When Virginia heard this, like the young man in Scripture, she went away sorrowful; for in that line of trade she had great possessions. The cultivation of land by slave labor had long since ceased to be profitable in the border States—or at least it was far less profitable than raising slaves for the cotton States—and the acquisition of new territory in Texas had enormously increased the demand. The

THE SIXTH MASSACHUSETTS REGIMENT ATTACKED IN THE STREETS OF BALTIMORE, APRIL 19, 1861.

* It is now impossible to prove positively that such a law was actually passed; for the officially printed volume of "Statutes at Large of the Provisional Government of the Confederate States of America" (Richmond, 1861) was evidently mutilated before being placed in the hands of the compositor. The Acts are numbered, but here and there numbers are missing, and in some of the later Acts there are allusions to previous Acts that cannot be found in the book. It is known that on the 6th of March, 1861, the Judiciary Committee was instructed to inquire into the expediency of such prohibition, and it seems a fair conjecture that one of the missing numbers was an Act of this character. In a later edition (1864) the numbering is made consecutive, but the missing matter is not restored.

DEPARTURE OF THE SEVENTH REGIMENT FROM NEW YORK CITY, APRIL 19, 1861.

COLONEL MARSHALL LEFFERTS,
Commanding Seventh Regiment.

greatest part of this business (sometimes estimated as high as one-half) was Virginia's. It was called "the vigintal crop," as the blacks were ready for market and at their highest value about the age of twenty. As it was an ordinary business of bargain and sale, no statistics were kept; but the lowest estimate of the annual value of the trade in the Old Dominion placed it in the tens of millions of dollars. President Dew, of William and Mary College, in his celebrated pamphlet, wrote: "Virginia is, in fact, a negro-raising State for other States." The New York *Journal of Commerce* of October 12, 1835, contained a letter from a Virginian (vouched for by the editor) in which it was asserted that twenty thousand slaves had been driven south from that State that year. In 1836 the Wheeling (Va.) *Times* estimated the number of slaves exported from that State during the preceding year at forty thousand, valued at twenty-four million dollars. The Baltimore *Register* in 1846 said: "Dealing in slaves has become a large business; establishments are made in several places in Maryland and Virginia, at which they are sold like cattle." The Richmond *Examiner*, before the war, said: "Upon an inside estimate, they [the slaves of Virginia] yield in gross surplus produce, from sales of negroes to go south, ten million dollars." In the United States Senate, just before the war, Hon. Alfred Iverson, of Georgia, replying to Mr. Powell, of Virginia, said Virginia was deeply interested in secession: for if the cotton States seceded, Virginia would find no market for her slaves, without which that State would be ruined.

After Sumter had been fired on, and the Confederate Congress had forbidden this traffic to outsiders, the Virginia Convention again took up the ordinance of secession (April 17) and passed it in secret session by a vote of eighty-eight to fifty-five. It was not to take effect till approved by the people; but the day fixed for their voting upon it was six weeks distant, the last Thursday in May. Long before that date, Governor Letcher, without waiting for the verdict of the people, turned over the entire military force and equipment of the State to the Confederate authorities, and the seat of the Confederate Government was removed from Montgomery to Richmond. David G. Farragut, afterwards the famous admiral, who was in Norfolk, Virginia, at the time, anxiously watching the course of events,

ON PICKET

(Showing photographer's outfit.)

declared that the State "had been dragooned out of the Union," and he refused to be dragooned with her. But Robert E. Lee and other prominent Virginians resigned their commissions in the United States service to enter that of their States or of the Confederacy, and the soil of Virginia was overrun by soldiers from the cotton States. Any other result than a vote for secession was therefore impossible. Arkansas followed with a similar ordinance on the 6th of May, and North Carolina on the 21st, neither being submitted to a popular vote. Kentucky refused to secede. For Tennessee and Missouri there was a prolonged struggle.

GENERAL JOSEPH G. TOTTEN.
Chief of Engineers.

When Fort Sumter was surrendered, the Confederates had already acquired possession of Castle Pinckney and Fort Moultrie in Charleston Harbor, Fort Pulaski at Savannah, Fort Morgan at the entrance of Mobile Bay, Forts Jackson and St. Philip below New Orleans, the navy-yard and Forts McRae and Barrancas at Pensacola, the arsenals at Mount Vernon, Ala., and Little Rock, Ark., and the New Orleans Mint. The largest force of United States regulars was that in Texas, under command of Gen. David E. Twiggs, who surrendered it in February, and turned over to the insurgents one million two hundred and fifty thousand dollars' worth of military property.

GENERAL ABRAM DURYEA.

GENERAL ALEXANDER SHALER.

MAJOR THEODORE WINTHROP.
Killed at Big Bethel.

On the day when Sumter fell, President Lincoln penned a proclamation, issued the next day (Monday, April 15), which declared "that the laws of the United States have been for some time past, and now are, opposed, and the execution thereof obstructed, in the States of South Carolina, Georgia, Alabama, Florida, Mississippi, Louisiana, and Texas, by combinations too powerful to be suppressed by the ordinary course of judicial proceedings or by the powers vested in the marshals by law," and called for militia from the several States of the Union to the number of seventy-five thousand. It also called a special session of Congress, to convene on July 4. He appealed "to all loyal citizens to favor, facilitate, and aid this effort to maintain the honor, the integrity, and existence of our National Union, and the perpetuity of popular government, and to redress wrongs already long enough endured."

With regard to the reception of this celebrated proclamation in the South, Alexander H. Stephens writes as follows, in his History of the war: "The effect of this upon the public mind of the Southern States cannot be described or even estimated. Up to this time, a majority, I think, of even those who favored the policy of secession had done so under the belief and conviction that it was the surest way of securing a redress of grievances, and of bringing the Federal Government back to Constitutional principles. This proclamation dispelled all such hopes. It showed that the party in power intended nothing short of complete centralization. The principles actuating the Washington authorities were those aiming at consolidated power; while the principles controlling the action of the Montgomery authorities were those which enlisted devotion and attachment to the Federative system as established by the Fathers in 1778 and 1787. In short, the cause of the Confederates was States Sovereignty, or the sovereign right of local self-government on the part of the States severally. The cause of their assailants involved the overthrow of this entire fabric, and the erection of a centralized empire in its stead."

The effect of this proclamation in the North has already been referred to. Mr. Lincoln's faith in the people had always been strong; but the response to this proclamation was probably a surprise even to him, as it certainly was to the secessionists, who had assured the Southern people that the Yankees would not fight. The whole North was thrilled with military ardor, and moved almost as one man. The papers were lively with great head-lines and double-leaded editorials; and the local poet filled the spare space—when there was any—with his glowing patriotic effusions. The closing passage of Longfellow's "Building of the Ship," written a dozen years before, beginning:

"Thou, too, sail on, O Ship of State!
Sail on, O Union, strong and great!
Humanity with all its fears,
With all the hopes of future years,
Is hanging breathless on thy fate!"

was in constant demand, and was recited effectively by nearly every orator that addressed a war meeting.

Eminent men of all parties and all professions spoke out for the Union. Stephen A. Douglas, who had long been Lincoln's rival, and had opposed the policy of coercion, went to the White House the day before Sumter fell, had a long interview with the President, and promised a hearty support of the Administration, which was immediately telegraphed over the country, and had a powerful effect. Ex-President Pierce (who had made the direful prediction of blood in Northern streets), ex-President Buchanan (who had failed to find any authority for coercion), Gen. Lewis Cass (a Democratic partisan since the war of 1812), Archbishop Hughes (the highest dignitary of the Roman Catholic Church in America), and numerous others, all "came out for the Union," as the phrase went. The greater portion of the Democratic party, which had opposed Lincoln's election, also, as individuals, sustained the Administration in its determination not to permit a division of the country. These were known as "war Democrats," while those that opposed and reviled the Government were called "Copperheads," in allusion to the snake of that name. Some of the bolder ones attempted to take the edge off the sarcasm by cutting the head of Liberty out of a copper cent and wearing it as a scarf-pin; but all they could say was quickly drowned in the general clamor.

Town halls, schoolhouses, academies, and even churches were turned into temporary barracks. Village greens and city squares were occupied every day by platoons of men, most of them not yet uniformed, marching and wheeling and countermarching, and being drilled in the manual of arms by officers that knew just a little more than they did, by virtue of having bought a handbook of tactics the day before, and sat up all night to study it. There was great scarcity of arms. One regiment was looking dubiously at some ancient muskets that had just been placed in their hands, when the colonel came up and with grim humor assured them that he had seen those weapons used in the Mexican War, and more men were killed in front of them than behind them. The boys had great respect for the colonel, but they wanted to be excused from believing his story.

BURNING OF GOSPORT NAVY YARD, NORFOLK, VA., APRIL 21, 1861.

BURNING OF THE UNITED STATES ARSENAL AT HARPER'S FERRY, VA., APRIL 18, 1861.

CHAPTER IV.

BORDER STATES AND FOREIGN RELATIONS.

GOVERNORS OF CERTAIN STATES REFUSE TROOPS—THE GOVERNOR OF MISSOURI DISLOYAL—EVENTS IN ST. LOUIS—LOYALTY OF GERMANS—BATTLE AT CARTHAGE—THE STRUGGLE FOR KENTUCKY, MARYLAND AND TENNESSEE—ACTIONS IN WEST VIRGINIA—BATTLE OF RICH MOUNTAIN—BATTLE OF BIG BETHEL—HARPER'S FERRY.

THE disposition of the border slave States was one of the most difficult problems with which the Government had to deal. When the President issued his call for seventy-five thousand men, the Governors of Missouri, Kentucky and Tennessee, as well as those of North Carolina and Virginia, returned positive refusals. The Governor of Missouri answered: "It is illegal, unconstitutional, revolutionary, inhuman, diabolical, and cannot

A BATTERY ON DRILL.

be complied with." The Governor of Kentucky said: "Kentucky will furnish no troops for the wicked purpose of subduing her sister Southern States." The Governor of Tennessee: "Tennessee will not furnish a single man for coercion, but fifty thousand, if necessary, for the defence of our rights and those of our brethren." The Governor of North Carolina: "I can be no party to this wicked violation of the laws of the country and to this war upon the liberties of a free people. You can get no troops from North Carolina." The Governor of Virginia: "The militia of Virginia will not be furnished to the powers at Washington for any such use or purpose as they have in view." Every one of these governors was a secessionist, with a strong and aggressive party at his back; and yet in each of these States the secessionists were in a minority. It was a serious matter to increase the hostility that beset the National arms on what in another war would have been called neutral ground, and it was also a serious matter to leave the Union element in the northernmost slave States without a powerful support and protection. The problem was worked out differently in each of the States.

At the winter session of the Missouri Legislature an act had been passed that placed the city of St. Louis under the control of police commissioners to be appointed by the Governor, Claiborne F. Jackson. Four of his appointees were secessionists, and three of these were leaders of bodies of "minute-men," half-secret armed organizations. The mayor of the city, who

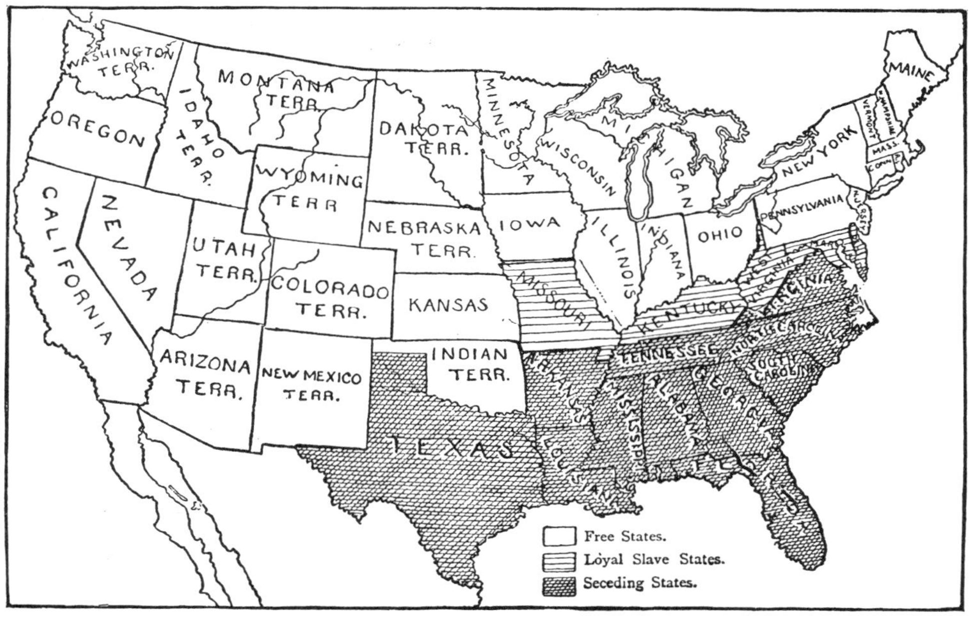

MAP SHOWING LOYAL AND SECEDING STATES.

RECRUITS TO THE FRONT.

was also one of the commissioners, was known as a "conditional Union man." Other acts showed plainly the bent of the Legislature. One made it treason to speak against the authority of the Governor, and gave him enlarged powers, while another appropriated three million dollars for military purposes, taking the entire school fund for the year, and the accumulations that were to have paid the July interest on the public debt.

CAPTAIN NATHANIEL LYON.

(Afterwards Brigadier-General.)

A State convention called to consider the question of secession met in February, and proved to be overwhelmingly in favor of Missouri's remaining in the Union, though it also expressed a general sympathy with slavery, assumed that the South had wrongs, deprecated the employment of military force on either side, and repeated the suggestion that had been made many times in other quarters for a national convention to amend the Constitution so as to satisfy everybody. The State convention made its report in March, and adjourned till December.

This proceeding appeared to be a great disappointment to Governor Jackson; but he failed to take from it any hint to give up his purpose of getting the State out of the Union. On the contrary, he proceeded to try what he could do with the powers at his command. He called an extra session of the Legislature, to convene May 2d, for the purpose of "adopting measures to place the State in a proper attitude of defence," and he called out the militia on the 3d of May, to go into encampment for six days. There was a large store of arms (more than twenty thousand stand) in the St. Louis arsenal; but while he was devising a method and a pretext for seizing them, the greater part of them were suddenly removed, by order from Washington, to Springfield, Illinois. The captain that had them in charge took them on a steamer to Alton, and there called the citizens together by ringing a fire-alarm, told them what he had, and asked their assistance in transferring the cargo to a train for Springfield, as he expected pursuit by a force of secessionists. The many hands that make light work were not wanting, and the train very soon rolled away with its precious freight. The Governor applied to the Confederate Government for assistance, and a quantity of arms and ammunition, including several field-guns, was sent to him in boxes marked "marble." He also ordered a general of the State militia to establish a camp of instruction near the city, and gathered there such volunteer companies as were organized and armed.

General Scott had anticipated all this by sending reinforcements to the little company that held the arsenal, and with them Capt. Nathaniel Lyon, of the regular army, a man that lacked no element of skill, courage, or patriotism necessary for the crisis. The force was also increased by several regiments of loyal home guards, organized mainly by the exertions of Francis P. Blair, Jr., and mustered into the service of the United States.

When the character and purpose of the force that was being concentrated by Jackson became sufficiently evident—from the fact that the streets in the camp were named for prominent Confederate leaders, and other indications—Lyon determined upon prompt and decisive action. This was the more important since the United States arsenal at Liberty had been robbed, and secession troops were being drilled at St. Joseph. With a battalion of regulars and six regiments of the home guard, he marched out in the afternoon of May 10th, surrounded the camp, and trained six pieces of artillery on it, and then demanded an immediate surrender, with no terms but a promise of proper treatment as prisoners of war. The astonished commander, a recreant West Pointer, surrendered promptly; and he and his brigade were disarmed

A VILLAGE COMPANY ON PARADE.

THE BATTLE AT PHILIPPI, JUNE 3, 1861.

and taken into the city. All the "marble" that had come up from Baton Rouge and been hauled out to the camp only two days before was captured and removed to the arsenal, becoming once more the property of the United States.

The outward march had attracted attention, crowds had gathered along the route, and when Lyon's command were returning with their prisoners they had to pass through a throng of people, among whom were not a few that were striving to create a riot. The outbreak came at length; stones were thrown at the troops and pistol-shots fired into the ranks, when one regiment levelled their muskets and poured a volley or two into the crowd. Three or four soldiers and about twenty citizens were killed in this beginning of the conflict at the West. William T. Sherman (the now famous general), walking out with his little son that afternoon, found himself for the first time under fire, and lay down in a gully while the bullets cut the twigs of the trees above him.

Two days later, Gen. William S. Harney arrived in St. Louis and assumed command of the United States forces. He was a veteran of long experience; but ex-Governor Sterling Price, commanding the State forces, entrapped him into a truce that tied his hands, while it left Jackson and Price practically at liberty to pursue their plans for secession. Thereupon the Government removed him, repudiated the truce, and gave the command to Lyon, now made a brigadier-general. After an interview with Lyon in St. Louis (June 11), in which they found it impossible to deceive or swerve him, Price and Jackson went to the capital, Jefferson City, burning railway bridges behind them, and the Governor immediately issued a proclamation declaring that the State had been invaded by United States forces, and calling out fifty thousand of the militia to repel the invasion. Its closing passage is a fair specimen of many proclamations and appeals that were issued that spring and summer: "Your first allegiance is due to your own State, and you are under no obligation whatever to obey the unconstitutional edicts of the military despotism which has introduced itself at Washington, nor submit to the infamous and degrading sway of its wicked minions in this State. No brave-hearted Missourian will obey the one or submit to the other. Rise, then, and drive out ignominiously the invaders who have dared to desecrate the soil which your labors have made fruitful and which is consecrated by your homes."

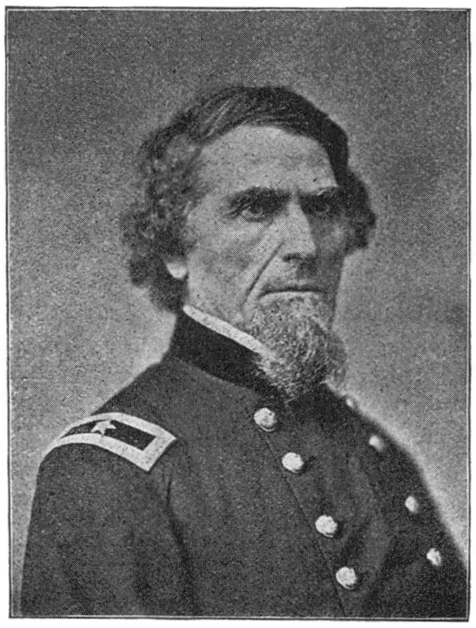

GENERAL B. F. KELLEY.

The very next day Lyon had an expedition in motion, which reached Jefferson City on the 15th, took possession of the place, and raised the National flag over the Capitol. At his approach the Governor fled, carrying with him the great seal of the State. Learning that he was with Price, gathering a force at Booneville, fifty miles farther up Missouri

A BOMB PROOF.

River, Lyon at once reëmbarked the greater part of his command, arrived at Booneville on the morning of the 17th, fought and routed the force there, and captured their guns and supplies. The Governor was now a mere fugitive; and the State convention, assembling again in July, declared the State offices vacant, nullified the secession work of the Legislature, and made Hamilton R. Gamble, a Union man, provisional Governor. Among the citizens whose prompt personal efforts were conspicuous on the Union side were John M. Schofield and Francis P. Blair, Jr. (afterward Generals), B. Gratz Brown (afterward candidate for Vice-President), Rev. Galusha Anderson (afterward President of Chicago University), William McPherson, and Clinton B. Fisk (afterward founder of Fisk University at Nashville).

The puzzling part of the difficulty in Missouri was now over, for the contest was well defined. Most of the people in the northern part of the State, and most of the population of St. Louis (especially the Germans), were loyal to the National Government; but the secessionists were strong in its southern part, where Price succeeded in organizing a considerable force, which was joined by men from Arkansas and Texas, under Gens. Ben. McCulloch and Gideon J. Pillow. Gen. Franz Sigel was sent against them, and at Carthage (July 5) with twelve hundred men encountered five thousand and inflicted a heavy loss upon them, though he was obliged to retreat. His soldierly qualities in this and other actions gave him one of the sudden reputations that were made in the first year of the war, but obscured by the greater events that followed. His hilarious popularity was expressed in the common greeting: "You fights mit Sigel? Den you trinks mit me!" Lyon, marching from Springfield, Mo., defeated McCulloch at Dug Spring, and a week later (August 10) attacked him again at Wilson's Creek, though McCulloch had been heavily reinforced. The national troops, outnumbered three to one, were defeated; and Lyon, who had been twice wounded early in the action, was shot dead while leading a regiment in a desperate charge. Major S. D. Sturgis conducted the retreat, and this ended the campaign. It was found that General Lyon, who was a bachelor, had bequeathed all he possessed (about thirty thousand dollars) to the United States Government, to be used for war purposes.

In the days when personal leadership was more than it can ever be again, while South Carolina was listening to the teachings of John C. Calhoun, which led her to try the experiment of secession, Kentucky was following Henry Clay, who, though a slaveholder, was a strong Unionist. The practical effect was seen when the crisis came, after he had been in his grave nine years. Governor Beriah Magoffin convened the Legislature in January, 1861, and asked it to organize the militia, buy muskets, and put the State in a condition of armed neutrality; all of which it refused to do. After the fall of Fort Sumter he called the Legislature together again, evidently hoping that the popular excitement would bring them over to his scheme. But the utmost that could be accomplished was the passage of a resolution by the lower house (May 16) declaring that Kentucky should occupy "a position of strict neutrality," and approving his refusal to furnish troops for the national army. Thereupon he issued a proclamation (May 20) in which he "notified and warned all other States, separate or united, especially the United and Confederate States, that I solemnly forbid any movement upon Kentucky soil." But two days later the Legislature repudiated this interpretation of neutrality, and passed a series of acts intended to prevent any scheme of secession that might be formed. It appropriated one million dollars for arms and ammunition, but placed the disbursement of the money and control of the arms in the hands of commissioners that were all Union men. It amended the militia law so as to require the State Guards to take an oath to support the Constitution of the United States, and finally the Senate passed a resolution declaring that "Kentucky will not sever connection with the National Government, nor take up arms with either belligerent party." Lovell H. Rousseau (afterward a gallant general in the national service), speaking in his place in the Senate, said: "The politicians are having their day; the people will yet have theirs. I have an abiding confidence in the right, and I know that this secession movement is all wrong. There is not a single substantial reason for it; our Government had never oppressed us with a feather's weight." The Rev. Robert J. Breckinridge and other prominent citizens took a similar stand; and a new Legislature, chosen in August, presented a Union majority of three to one. As a last resort, Governor Magoffin addressed a letter to President Lincoln, requesting that Kentucky's neutrality be respected and the national forces removed from the State. Mr. Lincoln, in refusing his request, courteously reminded him that the force consisted exclusively of Kentuckians, and told him that he had not met any Kentuckian, except himself and the messengers that brought his letter, who wanted it removed. To strengthen the first argument, Robert Anderson, of Fort Sumter fame, who was a citizen of Kentucky, was made a general and given the command in the State in September. Two months later, a secession convention met at Russellville, in the southern part of the State, organized a provisional government, and sent a full delegation to the Confederate Congress at Richmond, who found no difficulty in being

CARING FOR THE DEAD AND WOUNDED.

BATTLE OF WILSON'S CREEK, NEAR SPRINGFIELD MO., AUGUST 10, 1861

MAJOR-GENERAL BENJAMIN F. BUTLER AND STAFF.

admitted to seats in that body. Being now firmly supported by the new Legislature, the National Government began to arrest prominent Kentuckians who still advocated secession, whereupon others, including ex-Vice-President John C. Breckinridge, fled southward and entered the service of the Confederacy. Kentucky as a State was saved to the Union, but the line of separation was drawn between her citizens, and she contributed to the ranks of both the great contending armies.

Like the governor of Kentucky, Gov. Thomas H. Hicks, of Maryland, had at first protested against the passage of troops, had dreamed of making the State neutral, and had even gone so far as to suggest to the Administration that the British Minister at Washington be asked to mediate between it and the Confederates. But, unlike Governor Magoffin, he ultimately came out in favor of the Union. The Legislature would not adopt an ordinance of secession, nor call a convention for that purpose; but it passed a bill establishing a board of public safety, giving it extraordinary authority over the military powers of the State, and appointed as such board six secessionists and the governor. A tremendous pressure was brought to bear upon the State. One of her poets, in a ringing rhyme to a popular air, told her that the despot's heel was on her shore, and predicted that she would speedily "spurn the Northern scum," while the Vice-President of the Confederacy felt so sure of her acquisition that in a speech (April 30) he triumphantly announced that she "had resolved, to a man, to stand by the South." But Reverdy Johnson and other prominent Marylanders were quite as bold and active for the national cause. A popular Union Convention was held in Baltimore; General Butler with his troops restored the broken communications and held the important centres; and under a suspension of the writ of *habeas corpus* some of the more violent secessionists were imprisoned. The release of the citizens was demanded by Chief-Justice Taney, of the United States Supreme Court, who declared that the President had no right to suspend the writ; but his demand was refused. In May the Governor called for four regiments of volunteers to fill the requisition of the National Government, but requested that they might be assigned to duty in the State. So Maryland remained in the Union, though a considerable number of her citizens entered the ranks of the Confederate army.

In the mountainous regions of western North Carolina and eastern Tennessee, where few slaves were held, there was a strong Union element. In other portions of those States there were many enthusiastic secessionists. But in each State there was a majority against disunion. North Carolina voted on the question of calling a convention to consider the subject, and by a small majority decided for "no convention." Tennessee, on a similar vote, showed a majority of fifty thousand against calling a convention. After the fall of Sumter Gov. John W. Ellis, of North Carolina, seized the branch mint at Charlotte and the arsenal at Fayetteville, and called an extra session of the Legislature. This Legislature authorized him to tender the military resources of the State to the Confederate Government, and called a convention to meet May 20th, which passed an ordinance

COMMISSARY QUARTERS.

prominent of the Unionists were Andrew Johnson and the Rev. William G. Brownlow.

That portion of the Old Dominion which lay west of the Alleghany Mountains held in 1860 but one-twelfth as many slaves in proportion to its white population as the remainder of the State. And when Virginia passed her ordinance of secession, all but nine of the fifty-five votes against it were cast by delegates from the mountainous western counties. The people of these counties, having little interest in slavery and its products, and great interests in iron, coal and lumber, the market for which was in the free States, while their streams flowed into the Ohio, naturally objected to being dragged into the Confederacy. Like the people of East Tennessee, they wanted to secede from secession, and one of their delegates actually proposed it in the convention. In less than a

of secession by a unanimous vote. The conservative or Union party of Tennessee issued an address on the 18th of April, in which they declared their approval of the Governor's refusal to furnish troops for the national defence, and condemned both secession and coercion, holding that Tennessee should take an independent attitude. This, with the excitement of the time, was enough for the Legislature. In secret session it authorized Gov. Isham G. Harris, who was a strong secessionist, to enter into a military league with the Confederate Government, which he immediately did. It also passed an ordinance of secession, to be submitted to a popular vote on the 8th of June. Before that day came, the State was in the possession of Confederate soldiers, and a majority of over fifty thousand was obtained for secession. East Tennessee had voted heavily against the ordinance; and a convention held at Greenville, June 17, wherein thirty-one of the eastern counties were represented, declared, for certain plainly specified reasons, that it "did not regard the result of the election as expressive of the will of a majority of the freemen of Tennessee." Later, the people of those counties asked to be separated peaceably from the rest of the State and allowed to remain in the Union; but the Confederate authorities did not recognize the principle of secession from secession, and the people of that region were subjected to a bloody and relentless persecution, before which many of them fled from their homes. The most

month (May 13) after the passage of the ordinance, a Union convention was held at Wheeling, in which twenty-five of the western counties were represented; and ten days later, when the election was held, these people voted against seceding. The State authorities sent recruiting officers over the mountains, but they had little success. Some forces were gathered, under the direction of Gen. Robert E. Lee and under the immediate command of Colonel Porterfield, who began burning the bridges

CULINARY DEPARTMENT.

on the Baltimore and Ohio Railroad. Meanwhile Capt. George B. McClellan had been made a general and placed in command of Ohio troops. With four regiments he crossed the Ohio on the 26th and went in pursuit of the enemy. His movement at first was retarded by the burned bridges; but these were repaired, large reinforcements were brought over, and in small but brilliant engagements—at Philippi and at Rich Mountain—he completely routed the Confederates.

At Philippi the Confederates were completely surprised by Colonels Kelley and Dumont, and beat so hasty a retreat that the affair received the local name of the "Philippi races." The victory at Rich Mountain was the first instance of the capture by either side of a military position regularly approached and defended. A pass over this mountain was regarded as so important that all the Confederate troops that could be spared were sent to defend it, under command of Gen. Robert S. Garnett with Colonel Pegram to assist him. The position was so strong that a front attack was avoided, and its speedy capture resulted from a flank attack skilfully planned and successfully executed by Gen. W. S. Rosecrans. On the retreat up the Cheat River Valley General Garnett was killed, and Pegram, with a considerable number of his men, surrendered to McClellan.

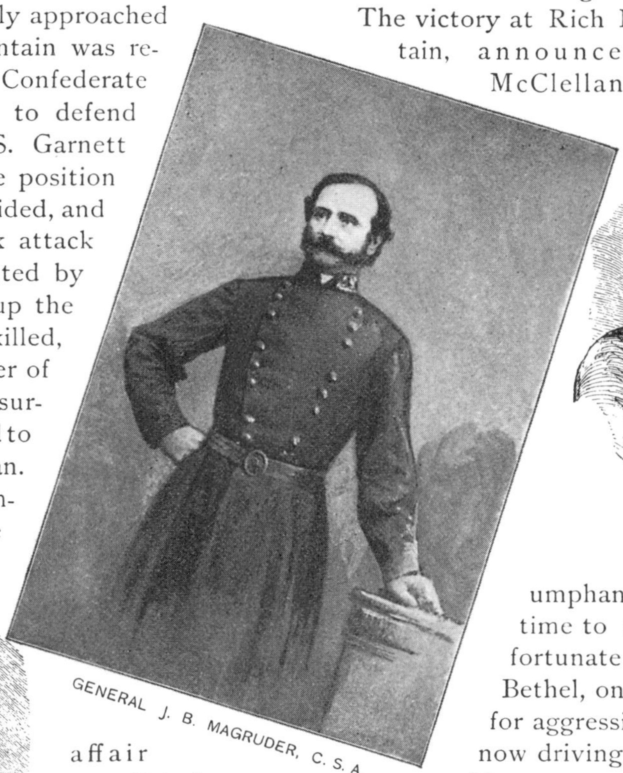
GENERAL J. B. MAGRUDER, C. S. A.

GENERAL BEN McCULLOCH, C. S. A.

The importance of this affair at Rich Mountain was really slight, notwithstanding it was successful in securing to the Union army a footing on this frontier that was not afterward seriously disturbed. But the significance of the action of July 11, and the campaign which it terminated, lies in the instant popularity and prominence it gave to General McClellan. He reported the victory in a Napoleonic despatch, announcing the annihilation of "two armies, commanded by educated and experienced soldiers, intrenched in mountain fastnesses fortified at their leisure;" and concluding, "Our success is complete, and secession is killed in this country." McClellan's failure to accomplish more in this campaign has been indicated by military critics, but at the time nothing obscured the brilliancy of the victory. The people took his own estimate of it, and "Little Mac," the young Napoleon, became a popular hero. The Government also took his view of it; and after the defeat at Bull Run, a few days later, he was given the command of the Army of the Potomac, and in the autumn succeeded to the command of the Armies of the United States.

Delegates from the counties west of the Alleghanies met at Wheeling (June 11), pronounced the acts of the Richmond convention null and void, declared all the State offices vacant, and reorganized the Government, with Francis H. Pierpont as governor. A legislature, consisting of members that had been chosen on the 23d of May, met at Wheeling on the 1st of July, and on the 9th it elected two United States senators. The new State of Kanawha was formally declared created in August. Its constitution was ratified by the people in May, 1862, and in December of that year it was admitted into the Union. But, meanwhile, its original and appropriate name had been exchanged for that of West Virginia.

GENERAL STERLING PRICE, C. S. A.

The victory at Rich Mountain, announced in McClellan's triumphant and resounding words, came in good time to arrest the depression caused by an unfortunate affair of a few weeks before, at Big Bethel, on June 10th; though the popular clamor for aggressive warfare did not cease, but was even now driving the army into a premature advance on Manassas and the battle of Bull Run, for which the preparations were inadequate.

Big Bethel has been called the first battle of the war, though it was subsequent to the affair of the "Philippi races," and at a later day would not have been called a battle at all. But among its few casualties there were numbered the deaths of Major Theodore Winthrop and the youthful Lieut. John T. Greble, and the painful impression caused by these losses converted the affair into a tragic national calamity. The movement was a conception of Gen. B. F. Butler's, who commanded at Fortress Monroe. Annoyed by the aggressions of a body of Confederates, under General Magruder, encamped at Little Bethel, eight miles north of Newport News, he sent an expedition to capture them. It consisted of Col. Abram Duryea's Fifth New York Zouaves, with Lieut.-Col. (afterward General) Gouverneur K. Warren second in command (the Confederates greatly feared these "red-legged devils," as they dubbed them), Col. Frederick Townsend's Third New York, Colonel Bendix's Seventh New York Volunteers, the First and Second New York, and detachments from other regiments, with two field-pieces worked by regulars under Lieutenant Greble; Gen. E. W. Pierce in command. Duryea's Zouaves were sent forward to attack from the rear; but a dreadful mistake of identity led Bendix's men to fire into Townsend's regiment, as these commands approached each other, which brought Duryea back to participate in the supposed engagement in his rear, and destroyed the chance of surprising the rebel camp. The Con-

BATTLE OF BIG BETHEL, VIRGINIA, JUNE 10, 1861

federates abandoned Little Bethel, and took a strong position at Big Bethel, where they easily repulsed the attack that was made, and pursued the retreating Unionists until checked by the Second New York Regiment.

An important preliminary to the battle of Bull Run was the operations about Harper's Ferry in June and July, resulting, as they did, in the release from that point of a strong Confederate reinforcement, which joined Beauregard at Bull Run at a critical time, and turned the fortunes of the day against the Union army.

Harper's Ferry, as we have seen, had been occupied by a Confederate force under Stonewall Jackson, who became subordinate to the superior rank of Gen. Joseph E. Johnston when that officer arrived on the scene. On both sides a sentimental importance was given to the occupation of Harper's Ferry, which was not warranted by its significance as a military stronghold. It did, indeed, afford a control of the Baltimore and Ohio Railroad, so long as the position could be maintained. But it derived its importance in the public mind from the fact that it had been chosen by John Brown as the scene of his projected negro uprising in 1859, and was presumed from that to be a natural fortress, a sort of Gibraltar, which, once gained, could be held forever by a small though determined body of men. The Confederate Government and military staff at Richmond so regarded it, and they warned General Johnston that he must realize, in defending it, that its abandonment would be depressing to the cause of the South. General Patterson, whose army gathered in Pennsylvania was to attack it, impressed on the War Department the paramount importance of a victory, and predicted that the first great battle of the war, the results of which would be decisive in the contest, would be fought at Harper's Ferry. He begged for the means of success, and offered his life as the price of a failure on his part. The Washington authorities, though they did not exact the penalty, took him at his word as to the men and means required, and furnished him with between eighteen and twenty-two thousand men (variously estimated), sending him such commanders as Major-General Sandford, of New York (who generously waived his superior rank, and accepted a subordinate position), Fitz John Porter, George Cadwalader, Charles P. Stone, and others. Both sides, then, prepared for action at Harper's Ferry, as for a mighty struggle over an important strategic position.

The Confederates were the first to realize that this was an error. However desirable it might be to hold Harper's Ferry as the key to the Baltimore and Ohio, and to Maryland, General Johnston quickly discovered that, while it was secure enough against an attack in front, across the Potomac, it was an easy capture for a superior force that should cross the river above or below it, and attack it from the Virginia side. For its defence, his force of six thousand five hundred men would not suffice against Patterson's twenty thousand, and he requested permission to withdraw to Winchester, twenty miles to the southwest. This suggestion was most unpalatable to the Confederate authorities, who understood well that the popular interpretation of the movement would be detrimental to the cause. But the fear that McClellan would join Patterson from West Virginia, and that the loss of an army of six thousand five hundred would be even more depressing than a retreat, they reluctantly consented to Johnston's plan. He destroyed everything at Harper's Ferry that could be destroyed, on June 13th and 14th; and when Patterson, after repeated promptings from Washington, arrived there on the 15th, he found no determined enemy and no mighty battle awaiting him, but only the barren victory of an unopposed occupation of a ruined and deserted camp.

A RAILROAD BATTERY.

CHAPTER V.

ARMY ORGANIZATION NORTH AND SOUTH.

CONFEDERATE ADVANTAGES—THE LEADING GENERAL OFFICERS—GRADUATES OF WEST POINT JOIN THE CONFEDERACY—CAPITAL REMOVED FROM MONTGOMERY—PRESIDENT LINCOLN'S CALL FOR SOLDIERS AND SAILORS—SOUTHERN PRIVATEERS—"ON TO RICHMOND!"

ALTHOUGH up to this time no important engagements between the troops had taken place, the war was actually begun. The Sumter affair had been the signal for both sides to throw away subterfuge and disguise, and it became thenceforth an open struggle for military advantage. The South no longer pleaded State rights, but military necessity, for seizing such Government posts and property as were within reach; the North no longer acted under the restraint of hesitation to commit an open breach, for the peace was broken irrevocably, and whatever it was possible to do, in the way of defence or offence, was now become politic.

The two contending powers were entering on the struggle under very different conditions and with unequal advantages. Before taking up the military operations which ensued, it will be interesting to look at these conditions.

On both sides there were many experienced army and navy officers, who had seen service, had been educated at the United States Military and Naval Academies, and had either remained in the service or, having withdrawn to civil life, were prompt to offer their swords to the side to which they adhered. Assuming the number and quality of these officers to have been equally divided, there were several respects in which the Confederates had the advantage in their preliminary organization, apart from the studied care with which disloyal cabinet officers had scattered the Federal regular army and had stripped Northern posts of supplies and of trustworthy commandants. President Lincoln came on from his Western home without knowledge of war, acquaintance with military men, or familiarity with military matters, and was immediately plunged into emergencies requiring in the Executive an intimate knowledge of all three. He became the titular commander-in-chief of an army already officered, but not only ignorant as to whether he had the right man in the right place, but powerless to make changes even had he known what changes to make, by reason of the law and the traditions governing the *personnel* of the service, in which promotion and personal relations were fixed and established. He found a military establishment that had been running on a peace footing for more than a decade and was not readily adaptable to war conditions; and officers in high command, who, as their States seceded, followed them out of the Union, carrying with them the latest official secrets and leaving behind them vacancies which red-tape and tradition, and not the free choice of the commander-in-chief, were to fill. His near advisers, particularly those in whose hands were the details of military administration, were scarcely better informed than himself, possessing political shrewdness and undoubted loyalty, but none of the professional knowledge of which he stood so sorely in need.

FRANCIS H. PIERPONT,
Governor of West Virginia.

The President of the Southern Confederacy, on the other hand, was Jefferson Davis, a man whose personal instrumentality in bringing about the rebellion gave him both knowledge and authority; an educated soldier and veteran of the Mexican war, in which he held a high command; familiar, through long service as Secretary of War and on the Senate Military Committee, not only with all the details of military administration, but with the points of strength and weakness in the military establishment of the enemy he was about to grapple with. Placed at the head of a new government, with neither army nor navy, nor law nor tradition for their control, he was free to exercise his superior knowledge of military matters for the best possible use of the men at his command in organizing his military establishment. None of the political conditions surrounding him forced on President Davis the appointment of political generals—an unavoidable evil which long postponed the effectiveness of President Lincoln's army administration. Whatever his judgment, guided by his professional military experience, approved of, he was free to do. It was President Lincoln's difficult task to learn something about military matters himself, and then to untie or cut the Gordian knot of hampering conditions; and if, in doing this, an occasional injustice was done to an individual officer, it is a cause for wonder far less significant than that by the exercise of his extraordinary faculty of common-sense he progressed as rapidly as he did toward the right way of accomplishing the ends he had in view.

The beginning of trouble in 1861 found the administration of the War Department in the hands of Secretary Joseph Holt, who had succeeded the secessionist Floyd, and was in turn succeeded by Simon Cameron, the war secretary of Lincoln's first cabinet, who remained there until the appointment of Edwin M. Stanton, the great "war secretary" of the remaining years of the struggle. Cameron was a shrewd politician, but was uninformed on military matters, for advice on which President Lincoln relied principally on other members of the cabinet and on General Scott. The cabinet of 1861 contained also John A. Dix, in the Treasury—whence issued his celebrated "shoot him on the spot" despatch

CAMP OF THE FORTY-FOURTH NEW YORK INFANTRY, NEAR ALEXANDRIA, VA.

—who took a general's commission when he retired in favor of Salmon P. Chase, the Secretary of the Treasury during most of the war. Gideon Welles was Secretary of the Navy.

Among the staff officers of the army were Lorenzo Thomas, Adjutant-General; E. D. Townsend, who as Assistant Adjutant-General was identified with this important office throughout the war; Montgomery C. Meigs, Quartermaster-General; and Joseph G. Totten, Chief of Engineers.

GENERAL SAMUEL P. HEINTZELMAN.

The general in command of the army was Winfield Scott, whose conduct of the Mexican war had made him a conspicuous military and political figure, an able officer and a most loyal Unionist, but already suffering from the infirmities of age, which soon compelled him to relinquish to younger hands the command of the army. But until after the battle of Bull Run, his was the directing mind. His immediate subordinates were Brig.-Gens. John E. Wool, also a veteran in service; William S. Harney, whose reluctance to take part in civil war soon terminated his usefulness; and David E. Twiggs, who surrendered his command to the Confederates in Texas, and going with the South, was replaced by Edwin V. Sumner.

GENERAL GEORGE H. THOMAS.

The command of the main Union force, organized from the volunteers who were pouring into Washington, devolved on Irvin McDowell, a major in the regular army, now promoted to be brigadier-general, who established his headquarters at Alexandria, across the Potomac from Washington, there directing the defence of the capital, and thence advancing to Bull Run. In this command he succeeded Gen. Joseph K. F. Mansfield. Under him, during this campaign, were many officers who rose to eminence during the war. His corps commanders at Bull Run were Gens. Daniel Tyler, David Hunter, Samuel P. Heintzelman, Theodore Runyon, and D. S. Miles; and among the brigade commanders were Gens. Erasmus D. Keyes, Robert C. Schenck, William T. Sherman, Israel B. Richardson, Andrew Porter, Ambrose E. Burnside, William B. Franklin, Oliver O. Howard, Louis Blenker, and Thomas A. Davies. Threatening the approach to Richmond from the lower Chesapeake, was Gen. Benjamin F. Butler, at Fortress Monroe.

MAJOR-GENERAL JOSEPH K. T. MANSFIELD.

Among the Confederate generals who prepared to defend Virginia, were Robert E. Lee, then in command of the Virginia State troops, Samuel Cooper, Joseph E. Johnston, P. G. T. Beauregard, James Longstreet, Jubal A. Early, Richard S. Ewell, Thomas J. ("Stonewall") Jackson, Robert S. Garnett, John C. Pegram, Benjamin Huger, John B. Magruder, and others.

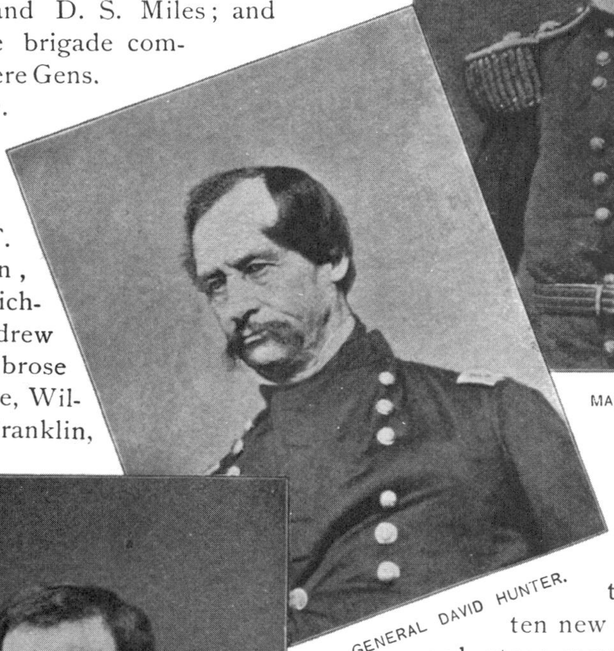

GENERAL DAVID HUNTER.

The seventy-five thousand troops called for in President Lincoln's proclamation of April 15th, were three-months men. On the 3d of May, 1861, he issued another proclamation, calling for forty-two thousand volunteers for three years, and authorizing the raising of ten new regiments for the regular army. He also called for eighteen thousand volunteer seamen for the navy. The ports of the Southern coasts had been already (April 19th) declared in a state of blockade, and it was not only desirable but absolutely necessary to make the blockade effectual. The Confederate Government had issued letters of marque for privateers almost from the first; and its Congress had authorized the raising of an army of one hundred thousand volunteers for one year.

When Congress convened on the 4th of July, President Lincoln asked for four hundred thousand men and four hundred million dollars, to suppress the insurrection; and in response he was authorized to call for five hundred thousand men and spend five hundred million dollars. What he had already done was approved and declared valid; and on the 15th of July the House of Representatives, with but five dissenting votes, passed a resolution (introduced by John A. McClernand, a Democrat) pledging any amount of money and any number of men that might be necessary to restore the authority of the National Government.

The seat of the Confederate Government was removed from Montgomery, Ala., to Richmond, Va., on the 20th of May.

MAJOR-GENERAL W. B FRANKLIN.

BATTLE OF BULL RUN, JULY 21, 1861

BRIGADIER-GENERAL McDOWELL AND STAFF.

CHAPTER VI.

THE BATTLE OF BULL RUN.

THE ADVANCE INTO VIRGINIA—FORTIFICATIONS ON THE POTOMAC—POPULAR DEMAND FOR OFFENSIVE OPERATIONS—CONFEDERATES FORTIFY MANASSAS JUNCTION—THEIR LINE OF DEFENCE AT BULL RUN—McDOWELL'S DEPARTURE FOR BULL RUN—A CHANGE OF PLAN—FIGHTING AT BLACKBURN'S FORD—DETOUR FROM CENTREVILLE AND FLANK ATTACK FROM SUDLEY FORD—UNION SUCCESS IN THE MORNING—DISASTROUS BATTLE OF THE AFTERNOON—LOSS OF THE BATTERIES—A REAR ATTACK—DISORDER AND RETREAT—RESULTS OF THE BATTLE.

THE first serious collision of the opposing armies occurred at Bull Run, in Virginia, on July 18 and 21, 1861. It was a battle between raw troops on both sides, and at a later period in the war a few well-led veterans might have turned it at almost any time into a victory for the losers and a defeat for those who won it. It developed the strength and weakness of the men, the commanders, and the organization of the army. It opened the eyes of the North to what was before them in this conflict, and it gave pause to military operations for a better preparation. Up to Bull Run, the war might have been terminated by a single great battle. After it, the struggle was certain to be a long one.

Up to May 24th, the Union troops had been kept strictly on the Washington side of the Potomac. On that date, Gen. Joseph K. F. Mansfield sent three columns of troops across the river into Virginia, to drive back the Confederate pickets which were within sight of the capital. From Washington to Alexandria, a few miles down the river, a line of fortifications was established, which, with the approaches to Washington from Maryland in Union control, seemed to assure the safety of the city.

Troops from all the loyal States had continued to arrive at Washington. The ninety thousand men who had responded to the first call of the President had enlisted for three months. While these troops predominated in the service it was not the expectation of General Scott to undertake any serious operations. He proposed to utilize these for the defence of Washington; the garrisoning of Fortress Monroe, with possibly the recovery of the Norfolk Navy Yard; the reinforcement of Patterson at Harper's Ferry and of McClellan in the Shenandoah; and the control of the border States. When the half million of three-years men called out in May and July should be equipped with the half billion of dollars voted by Congress, and instructed and drilled during a summer encampment, larger military operations were to ensue; but not before.

But after the mishap to Butler's men at Big Bethel, and the ambushing of a troop train at Vienna, near Washington, there was a public demand for some kind of vigorous action which should retrieve the national honor, tarnished and unavenged since Sumter, and should justify the military establishment, which to the non-military mind seemed already enormous. Brigadiers and gold lace and regiments playing "high jinks" in their camps convenient to the attractions of Washington became a by-word, and "On to Richmond!" became the cry of those who wanted to see some fighting, now there was an army, and wanted to see secession rebuked and rebellion nipped in the bud. Under the stimulus of this public demand, which, however erroneous from a military point of view, could not be ignored, a forward movement was decided on.

The Confederate forces were established on what was known as the "Alexandria line," with its base at Manassas Junction, about thirty miles east of Alexandria. Early in June, General Beauregard, still wearing the laurels of his Sumter victory, was sent in person to command, relieving the Confederate General Bonham. Manassas Junction stood on a high plateau, dropping off toward the east into the valley of the little stream called Bull Run, running from northwest to southeast some three miles distant. The Confederates had begun to intrench and fortify this elevated position; but Beauregard's quick and educated military judgment at once decided that a better defence could be made by moving his line forward to Bull Run, where the stream afforded a natural barrier, except at certain fords, where his men could be posted more effectively. Here he established himself, the right of his line being at Union Mills Ford, nearly due east from Manassas, and his left just above Stone Bridge, by which Bull Run is crossed on the Warrenton Turnpike leading from

FAIRFAX COURT-HOUSE.

Centreville to Gainesville. His commanders (after Johnston's arrival), from left to right, were: Ewell, supported by Holmes; Jones and Longstreet, supported by Early; Bonham, supported by Jackson; Cocke, supported by Bee, each guarding a ford; and, at Stone Bridge, Evans. The Bull Run line of defence requiring a larger force, Beauregard was liberally reinforced from Richmond, so that his army numbered nearly twenty-two thousand men and twenty-nine guns, before he was joined by Johnston with about eight thousand men and twenty-eight guns.

UNITED STATES MILITARY RAILROAD, BULL RUN.

Against this force advanced General McDowell, who had succeeded Mansfield in command of operations south of the Potomac, with something less than twenty-nine thousand men and forty-nine guns. With his army under the commanders already named, he was ready and started from Washington on July 16th, within a week of the date he had planned, notwithstanding the slow operations of the Government's military machinery, rusted by long disuse and not as yet in smooth working order. The departure of his column was a strange spectacle. The novelty of warfare and the general impression that the war was to be ended with one grand, brilliant stroke—an impression largely derived from the confidence at headquarters that the expedition would be successful—turned the march into a sort of festive picnic. Citizens accompanied the column on foot; Congressmen, newspaper correspondents, sight-seers, went along in carriages. There was a tremendous turnout of non-combatants, eager to see the finishing stroke to the rebellion. These were destined to share in the general rout that followed and to come pouring back into the security of Washington, all mixed in with the disorganized and flying troops. One member of Congress, John A. Logan, of Illinois, a veteran of the Mexican War, followed the army from the House of Representatives, armed with a musket, and began as a civilian a participation in the four years' fighting that brought him high rank, great honor, and a distinguished reputation.

GENERAL AMBROSE E. BURNSIDE.

On July 18th the army arrived in front of the enemy at Bull Run. An army of seasoned campaigners, accustomed to self-denial, would have done better, for they would not have stopped along the way to pick blackberries and change stale water for fresh in their canteens at every wayside well and spring. The plan agreed upon by Generals Scott and McDowell had been for an attempt to turn the enemy's right from the south; and to conceal his purpose McDowell ordered an advance, directly along the Warrenton Turnpike, on Centreville, as though that were to be his point of attack. But Washington was full of Confederate spies, and Beauregard was well informed as to what to expect. Tyler, whose division led the way, found Centreville evacuated and the enemy strongly posted along Bull Run, as he could see from his elevated position at Centreville, looking across the Bull Run valley with Manassas looming up beyond. It was McDowell's intention that Tyler should limit himself to making the feint on Centreville, without bringing on any engagement, while diverging to the left behind him the main army attacked Beauregard's right. But neither Tyler nor his men were as yet schooled to find an enemy flying before their advance and not yearn to be after them for a fight. Discovering the position of the enemy across the stream at Blackburn's and Mitchell's fords, he brought up some field pieces and sent forward his skirmishers; and as the enemy continued to retire before his successive increase of both troops and artillery, he presently found that the reconnoissance he had been ordered to make had assumed the proportions of a small engagement with the brigades of Bonham, Longstreet, and Early, which he drove back in confusion, with a loss of about sixty men on each side.

After this engagement, McDowell abandoned his attack from the south in favor of a flank attack from the north, where the roads were better. His

GENERAL LOUIS BLENKER.

army was now concentrated at Centreville, whither the commanders had been attracted by the sound of the engagement at Blackburn's Ford, and there he divulged to his commanders the new plan of attack. Richardson's brigade was continued at Blackburn's Ford to keep up the appearance of an attack in front, and the next two days, Friday and Saturday, July 19th and 20th, were occupied in looking for an undefended crossing of Bull Run north of the Confederate line, in resting the men, and provisioning them from the supply trains, which were slow in reaching the rendezvous at Centreville.

The engineers reported late on Saturday, the 20th, a practicable crossing of the stream at Sudley Ford, accessible by a detour of five or six miles around a bend of Bull Run turning sharply from the west. McDowell determined to send Hunter's and Heintzelman's divisions to make this flank movement over a route which took them north, then west, and brought them upon the enemy's left, as they crossed Bull Run at Sudley Ford and moved due south by the Sudley Road toward Manassas. Meanwhile Tyler was ordered to proceed from Centreville to the Stone Bridge at Bull Run, there to feign attack until he heard Hunter and Heintzelman engaged, when he would cross and join their attack on the Confederate left, or push on to Gainesville, west of Bull Run, and head off Johnston, who McDowell was certain was coming from Winchester, with or without "Patterson on his heels," as General Scott had promised.

But during McDowell's enforced two days of inactivity at Centreville there had been portentous happenings within the Confederate lines. Johnston had already left Winchester on the 18th; one detachment of his army had joined Beauregard on the morning of the 20th; Johnston in person arrived at noon with a second detachment, and the remainder of his force arrived on the 21st in time to take part in the battle, the brunt of which was borne by Johnston's army, which McDowell had hoped not to meet at all! Johnston, as the ranking officer, assumed command, and he and Beauregard turned their attention to defending themselves against the attack now initiated by McDowell.

Hunter and Heintzelman, whose brigades were com-

ON THE ROAD TO BULL RUN.

manded by Cols. Andrew Porter, Ambrose E. Burnside, W. B. Franklin, Orlando B. Willcox, and Oliver O. Howard, reached Sudley Ford after an unexpectedly long march, and crossed it unopposed about nine in the morning. Tyler, who had been expected to hold the Confederate Evans at Stone Bridge by a sharp attack, betrayed the incidental character of his demonstration by the feebleness of his operations; and Evans, suspecting from this an attack from some other direction, was soon rendered certain of it by the clouds of dust which he saw toward the north. Immediately, of his own motion and in the absence of orders from his superiors, he informed his neighboring commander, Cocke, of his intention, and leaving only a few companies to deceive Tyler at Stone Bridge, he turned his command

GENERAL JOSEPH E. JOHNSTON, C. S. A.

to the rear and marched it to a strong position on Young's Branch, where he faced the enemy approaching from his left. This action has commended itself to military critics as the finest tactical movement of the entire battle. Evans was even momentarily successful in repulsing the troops of Burnside's brigade, which he pursued for a short distance. At the outset, General Hunter was severely wounded. Porter came to Burnside's support, and Bee and Bartow, of Johnston's army, aligned their brigades with that of Evans. There was sharp fighting for two hours; but the arrival of fresh supports for Burnside and Porter, including Sykes' regiment of regulars and the regular batteries of Griffin and Ricketts, and the extension of the Union line by Heintzelman's division beyond the Sudley Road, proved too much for the Confederates, who retreated downhill out of the Young's Branch valley before a Union charge down the Sudley Road. But they had checked the advance long enough for Johnston to order a general movement to strengthen the new line of defence which was then formed on a hill half a mile south of Young's Branch, under the direction of Jackson, who with his own brigade of Johnston's army met and rallied the retreating Confederates. It was right here that Stonewall Jackson acquired his *sobriquet*. To encourage his own men to stop and rally, Bee called out to them: "Look at Jackson's brigade! It stands there like a stone wall." And Jackson never was called by his own name again, but only "Stonewall." Tyler did send Keyes' and W. T. Sherman's brigades across Bull Run by the ford above Stone Bridge in time to join in the pursuit, Sherman pushing toward Hunter and Keyes remaining near Bull Run; but Schenck's brigade he did not send across at all.

GENERAL JAMES LONGSTREET, C. S. A.

As a result of the morning's fighting the whole Union line was pushed forward past the Warrenton Turnpike, extending from Keyes' position on Bull Run to where Porter and Willcox were posted, west of the Sudley Road. The Union troops felt not only that they had the advantage, but that they had won the battle; and this confidence, added to the fact that they were weary with marching and fighting, prepared them ill to meet the really serious work of the day, which was still before them.

INTERIOR OF CONFEDERATE FORTIFICATION.

MAJOR-GENERAL ROBERT PATTERSON.

BREVET MAJOR-GENERAL E. B. TYLER.

Johnston and Beauregard came up in person to superintend the dispositions for defence. The line was formed on the edge of a semicircular piece of woods, with the concave side toward the Union advance, on an elevation some distance south of the first position. The Confederate artillery commanded both the Warrenton Turnpike and the Sudley Road (the latter passing through the woods), and the plateau between them was subject to a cross fire. Across this plateau the Union advance had to be made, and it was made under great disadvantages. His effective fighting force reduced by casualties, by the retirement of Burnside's brigade after a hard morning's fighting, and by the separation from the main army of Keyes' brigade, which made an ineffectual attempt to cross Young's Branch and get at the enemy's right, McDowell was no longer superior in numbers, as in the morning. His weary men had not only to fight, but to advance on an enemy in position—to advance over open ground on an enemy concealed in the woods, invisible even while their sharpshooters picked off his gunners at their batteries. The formation of the ground gave him no comprehensive view of the whole field, except such as he got by going to the top of the Henry house, opposite the Confederate centre; nor could his subordinate commanders see what the others were doing, and there was a good deal of independence of action among the Union troops throughout the remainder of the day.

For his afternoon attack on the new Confederate position McDowell had under his immediate control the brigades of Andrew Porter, Franklin, Willcox, and Sherman, with Howard in reserve, back of the Warrenton Turnpike. These commands were not available up to their full strength, for they included a good many regiments and companies that had lost their organization. From their sheltered positions along the sunken turnpike and the valley of Young's Branch he brought them forward for an attack on the centre and left of the enemy. With splendid courage they advanced over the open ground and made a succession of determined assaults, which carried a portion of the position attacked. About the middle of the afternoon the regular batteries of Captains Griffin and Ricketts were brought forward to a position near the Henry house. But though their effectiveness from this point was greatly increased, so also was their danger; and after long and courageous fighting by both infantry and artillery, it was the conflict that surged about these guns that finally gave the victory to the Confederates.

Two regiments had been detailed to support the batteries, but the inexperience of these regiments was such that they were of little service. The batteries had scarcely taken up their advanced position when the gunners began to drop one by one under the fire of sharpshooters concealed in the woods before them. Sticking pluckily to their work, the artillerymen did effective firing, but presently the temptation to secure guns so inefficiently protected by supporting infantry proved strong enough to bring Confederate regiments out from the cover of the woods; and keeping out of the

MAJOR-GENERAL CHARLES GRIFFIN.

MAJOR-GENERAL O. O. HOWARD.

MAJOR-GENERAL JAMES B. RICKETTS.

STONE HOUSE, WARRENTON TURNPIKE, BULL RUN.

THE NEW HENRY HOUSE, BULL RUN.

Showing the Union monument of the first battle.

line of fire, they stole nearer and nearer to the batteries. A Confederate cavalry charge scattered one of the supporting regiments, and a volley from a Confederate regiment, that had gotten up to within seventy yards, sent the other off in confused retreat. So close an approach had been permitted by Captain Griffin under the mistaken impression, communicated to him by the chief of artillery, that the troops approaching so steadily were his own supports. He realized his error too late; and when a volley of musketry had taken off nearly every one of his gunners, had killed Lieutenant Ramsay, and seriously wounded Captain Ricketts, the Confederates rushed in and captured the guns.

They had not as yet become machines, as good soldiers must be. "They were not soldiers," said one officer, "but citizens—independent sovereigns—in uniform." It was impossible, of course, to get strong, concerted action out of such a mass-meeting of individual patriots; and the constant disintegration of regiments and brigades gradually reduced the effectiveness of McDowell's army.

Meanwhile the Confederate reinforcements from the lower fords were arriving. The remainder of Johnston's army from Winchester had already arrived; and though the Union army did not know that they had been fighting the biggest half of Johnston's army all day, they realized that they were dealing

STAND OF THE UNION TROOPS AT THE HENRY HOUSE.

Then ensued a series of captures and recaptures of these same guns, first by one side and then by the other. At the same time there was a general fight all along the line of battle, which did not dislodge the Confederates while it wore out the Union troops. They lacked both the experience and the discipline necessary to keep them together after a repulse. The men lost track of their companies, regiments, brigades, officers, in the confusion, and little by little the army became disorganized, and that at a time when there was still remaining among them both strength and courage enough to have won after all. It has been said that at one time there were twelve thousand individual soldiers wandering about the field of battle who did not know "where they belonged." The strong individuality of the early recruits of the war was in a measure accountable for this.

with Johnston now. During the fight of the day the Union right wing had faced around almost to the east, and the combined attack of the new Johnston brigades and Early's reinforcements from the fords was delivered almost squarely on the rear of its right flank.

A blow so strong and from such an unexpected quarter had a serious effect on the troops that received it. But not as yet was the conviction of defeat general in the Union army. The contest had been waged with such varying results in different parts of the field, one side successful here, another there, and again and again the local advantage turning the other way under some bold movement of an individual command, that neither army realized the full significance of what had happened. The Unionists had begun the afternoon's work

LIEUTENANT-GENERAL JUBAL A. EARLY, C. S. A.

under the impression that the victory was already theirs and that they had only to push on and secure the fruits of it. In some parts of the field their successes were such that it seemed as though the Confederate line was breaking. Many of the Confederates had the same idea of it, and Jefferson Davis, coming up from Manassas on his way from Richmond, full of anxiety for the result, found the roads almost impassable by reason of crowds of Confederates escaping to the rear. His heart sank within him. "Battles are not won," he remarked, "where two or three unhurt men are seen leading away one that is wounded." But he continued on, only to find that the field from which his men were retreating had been already won, and that McDowell's army were in full retreat.

McDowell himself did not know how the retreat had begun. He had not ordered it, for he inferred from the lull in the fighting that his enemy was giving way. But it had dawned on the men, first that their victory was in doubt, then that the Confederates had a fighting chance, and finally that the battle was lost; and by a sort of common consent they began to make their way to the rear in retreat. A curious thing happened which dashed McDowell's hope of making a stand at Stone Bridge. Although the Warrenton Turnpike was open, and Stone Bridge had been freed from the obstructing abattis of trees, offering a straight road from the battlefield to the rendezvous at Centreville, the troops all withdrew from the field by the same directions from which they had approached it in the morning. And so, while the brigades near the Stone Bridge and the ford above it crossed directly over Bull Run, the commands which had made the long detour in the morning made the same detour in retreat, adding many miles to the route they had to travel to reach Centreville.

BRIGADIER-GENERAL BARNARD E. BEE, C. S. A.

McDowell accepted the situation, and made careful dispositions to protect the rear of his retreating army. Stuart's pursuing cavalry found a steady line of defence which they could not break. The rearmost brigades were in such good order that the Confederate infantry dared not strike them. The way over the Stone Bridge was well covered by the reserves east of Bull Run, under Blenker. But now occurred an incident that greatly retarded the orderly retreat and broke it into confusion.

There had been some fighting during the day between the reserves left east of Bull Run and Confederate troops who sallied out from the lower fords. As a result of this a Confederate battery had been posted on an elevation commanding the Warrenton

RUINS OF THE HENRY HOUSE.

Turnpike where it crossed Cub Run, a little stream between Bull Run and Centreville, on a suspension bridge. When the retreating brigades which had made the long detour from Sudley Ford reached this bridge they were met with a shower of fire from this battery. Finally, the horses attached to a wagon were killed, and the wagon was overturned right on the bridge, completely obstructing it. The remainder of the wagon train was reduced to ruin, and the thirteen guns which had been brought safely out of the battle were captured. A panic ensued. Horses were cut from wagons, even from ambulances bearing wounded men, and ridden off. Even while McDowell and his officers were deliberating as to the expediency of making a stand at Centreville, the disorganized men took the decision into their own hands and made a bee-line for Washington.

Portions of the army, however, maintained their organization, and partly successful attempts were made to stop the flight. The Confederates had but little cavalry, and were in no condition to pursue. There was a black-horse regiment from Louisiana that undertook it, but came upon the New York Fire Zouaves, and in a bloody fight lost heavily. The retreat was well conducted; but this was due largely to the fact that the Confederates were too exhausted and too fearful to continue the pursuit. It is not to be denied that on both sides, in the battle of Bull Run, there was displayed much bravery, and not a little skill. Never before, perhaps, was such fighting done by comparatively raw and inexperienced men.

It was a motley crowd that thronged the highway to the capital. Intermixed were soldiers and civilians, privates and members of Congress, worn-out volunteers and panic-stricken non-combatants, "red-legged-devil" Zouaves, gray-coated Westerners, and regular army blue-coats. They pressed right on, fearing the pursuit which, unaccountably, did not follow. Some of the men since morning had marched twenty-five miles, from Centreville and back, and that night they marched twenty miles more to Washington.

All the next day the defeated army straggled into Washington city—bedraggled, foot-sore, wounded, hungry, wet through with the drizzling rain, exhausted. The citizens turned out to receive and succor them, and the city became a vast soup-house and hospital. On the streets, in the shelter of house-areas, under stoops, men dropped down and slept.

FORT LINCOLN, WASHINGTON, D. C.

EXAMINING PASSES AT THE GEORGETOWN FERRY.

CHAPTER VII.

EFFECTS OF THE BATTLE OF BULL RUN.

PARALYSIS OF THE UNION CAUSE—FORTIFYING THE APPROACHES TO THE CAPITAL—WHY THE CONFEDERATES DID NOT ATTEMPT THE CAPTURE OF WASHINGTON—EFFECT OF UNION DEFEAT IN ENGLAND AND FRANCE—SLIDELL AND MASON—CAPTURE OF THE "TRENT"—HENRY WARD BEECHER IN ENGLAND—SYMPATHY OF THE RUSSIAN GOVERNMENT FOR THE NORTH.

THE battle of Bull Run was undertaken with precipitation, fought with much valor on both sides, and terminated with present ruin to the Federal cause. For the moment the Union seemed to stagger under the blow. On the Confederate side there was corresponding exultation; a spirit of defiance flamed up throughout the South.

It is in the nature of things that the initial battle of a war consolidates and crystallizes the sentiments of both the contestants. After Bull Run there was no further hope of peaceable adjustment, but only an increasing and settled purpose to fight out with the sword the great issue which was dividing the Union. For a brief season after the battle there was a paralysis of the Union cause. It was as much as the authorities at Washington could do to make themselves secure against further disaster. Indeed, the Potomac River now gave positive comfort to the Government, since it furnished in some measure a natural barrier to the northward progress of the exultant Confederates. Immediate steps were taken to fortify the approaches to the capital; but while this work was in progress the Government seemed to stand, like an alarmed sentry, on the Long Bridge of the Potomac.

In the South as well as in the North there was much surprise that the Confederates did not pursue the routed Union forces at the battle of Bull Run and capture Washington. Perhaps Gen. Joseph E. Johnston is the best witness on this subject on the Southern side. He says: "All the military conditions, we knew, forbade an attempt on Washington. The Confederate army was more disorganized by victory than that of the United States by defeat. The Southern volunteers believed that the objects of the war had been accomplished by their victory, and that they had achieved all their country required of them. Many, therefore, in ignorance of their military obligations, left the army—not to return. . . . Exaggerated ideas of the victory, prevailing among our troops, cost us more than the Federal army lost by defeat." In writing this passage General Johnston probably took no account of the effect produced in Europe. The early narratives sent there, in which the panic of retreat was made the principal figure, gave the impression that the result arose from constitutional cowardice in Northern men and invincible courage in Southerners. They also gave the impression that the Confederates were altogether superior in generalship; and the effect was deep and long-enduring. The most notable of these was by a correspondent of the London *Times*, who had apparently been sent across the Atlantic for the express purpose of writing down the Republic, writing up the South, and enlisting the sympathies of Englishmen for the rebellion. In his second letter from Charleston (April 30, 1861) he had written that men of all classes in South Carolina declared to him: "If we could only get one of the royal race of England to rule over us, we should be content." "The New Englander must have something to persecute; and as he has hunted down all his Indians, burnt all his witches, persecuted all his opponents to the death, he invented abolitionism

FORT IN FRONT OF WASHINGTON.

as the sole resource left to him for the gratification of his favorite passion. Next to this motive principle is his desire to make money dishonestly, trickily, meanly, and shabbily. He has acted on it in all his relations with the South, and has cheated and plundered her in all his dealings, by villanous tariffs." Many an Englishman, counting his worthless Confederate bonds, and trying to hope that he will yet receive something for them, knows he would never have made that investment but for such writing as this, and the accounts from the same pen of the battle of Bull Run.

At the North the spectacle of McDowell's army streaming back in disorder to the national capital produced first a shock of surprise, then a sense of disgrace, and then a calm determination to begin the war over again. It was well expressed by a Methodist minister at a camp-meeting in Illinois, the Rev. Henry Cox. The news of the battle came while he was preaching, and he closed his sermon with the words: "Brethren, we'd better adjourn this camp-meeting and go home and drill."

THE "SAN JACINTO" STOPPING THE "TRENT."

The effect of this over-discussed battle upon the more confident and boastful of the Southerners was perhaps fairly expressed by an editorial utterance of one of their journals, the Louisville, Ky., *Courier*: "As our Norman kinsmen in England, always a minority, have ruled their Saxon countrymen in political vassalage up to the present day, so have we, the 'slave oligarchs,' governed the Yankees till within a twelvemonth. We framed the Constitution, for seventy years moulded the policy of the government, and placed our own men, or 'Northern men with Southern principles,' in power. On the 6th of November, 1860, the Puritans emancipated themselves, and are now in violent insurrection against their former owners. This insane holiday freak will not last long, however; for, dastards in fight and incapable of self-government, they will inevitably again fall under the control of a superior race. A few more Bull Run thrashings will bring them once more under the yoke, as docile as the most loyal of our Ethiopian chattels."

France and England had made all haste to recognize the Confederates as belligerents, but had not granted them recognition as an established nation, and never did. There was a constant fear, however, that they would; and the Confederate Government did its utmost to bring about such recognition. Messrs. James M. Mason, of Virginia, and John Slidell, of Louisiana, were sent out by that Government, as duly accredited ministers to London and Paris, in 1861. They escaped the blockaders at Charleston, reached Havana, and there embarked on the British mail steamer *Trent* for Europe. But Capt. Charles Wilkes (who had commanded the celebrated exploring expedition in Antarctic waters twenty years before) was on the watch for them with the United States steam frigate *San Jacinto*, overhauled the *Trent* in the Bahama Channel (November 8), took off the Confederate commissioners, and allowed the steamer to proceed on her way. He carried his prisoners to Boston, and they were incarcerated in Fort Warren. This action, for which Wilkes

FORTIFICATION IN FRONT OF WASHINGTON.

received the thanks of Congress, was denounced as an outrage on British neutrality. The entire British public bristled up as one lion, and their Government demanded an apology and the liberation of the prisoners. The American public was unable to see any way out of the dilemma, and was considering whether it would choose humiliation or a foreign war, when our Secretary of State, William H. Seward, solved the problem in a masterly manner. In his formal reply he discussed the whole question with great ability, showing that such detention of a vessel was justified by the laws of war, and there were innumerable British precedents for it; that Captain Wilkes conducted the search in a proper manner; that the commissioners were contraband of war; and that the commander of the *Trent* knew they were contraband of war when he took them as passengers. But as Wilkes had failed to complete the transaction in a legal manner by bringing the *Trent* into port for adjudication in a prize court, it must be repudiated. In other words, by his consideration for the interests and convenience of innocent persons, he had lost his prize. In summing up, Mr. Seward said: "If I declare this case in favor of my own Government, I must disavow its most cherished principles, and reverse and forever abandon its most essential policy. . . . We are asked to do to the British nation just what we have always insisted all nations ought to do to us." The commissioners were released, and sailed for England in January; but the purpose of their mission had been practically thwarted. This was a remarkable instance of eating one's cake and keeping it at the same time.

CHARLES A. DANA, ASSISTANT SECRETARY OF WAR.

But though danger of intervention was thus for the time averted, and the relations between the British Government and our own remained nominally friendly, so far as moral influence and bitterness of feeling could go the Republic had no more determined enemies in the cotton States than in the heart of England. The aristocratic classes rejoiced at anything that threatened to destroy democratic government or make its stability doubtful. They confidently expected to see our country fall into a state of anarchy like that experienced so often by the Spanish-American republics, and were willing to do everything they safely could to bring it about. The foremost English journals had been predicting such a disaster ever since the beginning of the century, had announced it as in progress when a British force burned Washington in 1814, and now were surer of it than ever. Almost our only friends of the London press were the *Daily News* and *Weekly Spectator*. The commercial classes, in a country that had fought so many commercial wars, were of course delighted at the crippling of a commercial rival whom they had so long hated and feared, no matter what it might cost in the shedding of blood and the destruction of social order. Among the working classes, though they suffered heavily when the supply of cotton was diminished, we had many firm and devoted friends, who saw and felt, however imperfectly, that the cause of free labor was their own cause, no matter on which side of the Atlantic the battlefield might lie.

To those who had for years endured the taunts of Englishmen who pointed to American slavery and its tolerance in the American Constitution, while they boasted that no slave could breathe on British soil, it was a strange sight, when our country was at war over the question, to see almost everything that had power

JAMES MURRAY MASON.

CAPTAIN CHARLES WILKES. (Afterward Rear-Admiral.)

JOHN SLIDELL.

and influence in England arrayed on the side of the slaveholders. A few famous Englishmen—notably John Bright and Goldwin Smith—were true to the cause of liberty, and did much to instruct the laboring classes as to the real nature and significance of the conflict. Henry Ward Beecher, then at the height of his powers, went to England and addressed large audiences, enlightening them as to the real nature of American affairs, concerning which most of them were grossly ignorant, and produced an effect that was probably never surpassed by any orator. The Canadians, with the usual narrowness of provincials, blind to their own ultimate interests, were in the main more bitterly hostile than the mother country.

Louis Napoleon, then the despotic ruler of France, was unfriendly to the United States, and did his utmost to persuade the English Government to unite with him in a scheme of intervention that would probably have secured the division of the country. How far his plans went beyond that result, can only be conjectured; but while the war was still in progress (1864) he threw a French force into Mexico, and established there an ephemeral empire with an Austrian archduke at its head. That the possession of Mexico alone was not his object, is suggested by the fact that, when the rebellion was subdued and the secession cause extinct, he withdrew his troops from Mexico and left the archduke to the fate of other filibusters.

The Russian Government was friendly to the United States throughout the struggle. The imperial manifesto for the abolition of serfdom in Russia was issued on March 3, 1861, the day before President Lincoln was inaugurated, and this perhaps created a special bond of sympathy.

FORT MONROE.

MAJOR-GENERAL BENJAMIN F. BUTLER.

COMMODORE S. H. STRINGHAM.
(Afterward Rear-Admiral.)

CHAPTER VIII.

THE FIRST UNION VICTORIES.

FEDERAL NAVY—BLOCKADE-RUNNING—BALLS, POWDER, AND EQUIPMENTS BROUGHT FROM ENGLAND FOR CONFEDERATES—THE FIRST HATTERAS EXPEDITION—CAPTURE OF FORT HATTERAS AND FORT CLARK—CAPTURE OF HILTON HEAD AND PORT ROYAL—GENERAL BURNSIDE'S EXPEDITION TO ROANOKE ISLAND—FEDERAL VICTORY AT MILL SPRINGS, KY.—CAPTURE OF FORT HENRY BY FEDERAL FORCES UNDER GENERAL GRANT—FALL OF FORT DONELSON—BATTLE OF PEA RIDGE.

WHEN the war began, the greater part of the small navy of the United States was in distant waters—off the coast of Africa, in the Mediterranean, on the Asiatic station—and for some of the ships to receive the news and return, many months were required. Twelve vessels were at home—four in Northern and eight in Southern ports. The navy, like the army, lost many Southern officers by resignation or dismissal. About three hundred who had been educated for its service went over to the Confederacy; but none of them took with them the vessels they had commanded. The Government bought all sorts of merchant craft, mounting guns on some and fitting up others as transports, and had gunboats built on ninety-day contracts. It was a most miscellaneous fleet, whose principal strength consisted in the weakness of its adversary. The first purpose was to complete the blockade of Southern ports. Throughout the war this was never made so perfect that no vessels could pass through; but it was gradually rendered more and more effective. The task was simplified as the land forces, little by little, obtained control of the shore, when a few vessels could maintain an effective blockade from within. But an exterior blockade of a port in the hands of the enemy required a large fleet, operating beyond the range of the enemy's fire from the shore, in a line so extended as to offer occasional opportunities for the blockade-runners to slip past. But blockade-running became exceedingly dangerous. Large numbers of the vessels engaged in it were captured or driven ashore and wrecked. The profit on a single cargo that passed either way in safety was very great, and special vessels for blockade-running were built in England. The Confederate Government enacted a law providing that a certain portion of every cargo thus brought into its ports must consist of arms or ammunition, otherwise vessel and all would be confiscated. This insured a constant supply; and though the Southern soldier was often barefoot and ragged, and sometimes hungry, he never lacked for the most improved weapons that English arsenals could produce, nor was he ever defeated for want of powder. A very large part of the bullets that destroyed the lives and limbs of National troops were cast in England and brought over the sea in blockade-runners. Clothing and equipments, too, for the Confederate armies came from the same source. Often when a burial party went out, after a battle, as they turned over one after another of the enemy's slain and saw the name of a Birmingham manufacturer stamped upon his buttons, it seemed that they must have been fighting a foreign foe. To pay for these things, the Confederates sent out cotton, tobacco, rice, and the naval stores produced by North Carolina forests. It was obvious from the first that any movement that would shut off a part of this trade, or render it more hazardous, would strike a blow at the insurrection. Furthermore, Confederate privateers were already out, and before the first expedition sailed sixteen captured merchantmen had been taken into the ports of North Carolina.

ON BOARD THE FIRST BLOCKADE-RUNNER CAPTURED.

Vessels could enter Pamlico or Albemarle Sound by any one of several inlets, and then make the port of Newbern, Washington, or Plymouth; and the first of several naval and military expeditions was fitted out for the purpose of closing the most useful of these openings, Hatteras Inlet, thirteen miles south of Cape Hatteras. Two forts had been erected on the point at the northern side of this inlet, and the project was to capture them; but, so new was everybody to the art of war, it was not at first intended to garrison and hold them.

The expedition, which originated with the Navy Department, was fitted out in Hampton Roads, near Fortress Monroe, and was commanded by Flag-officer Silas H. Stringham. It numbered ten vessels, all told, carrying one hundred and fifty-eight guns. Two were transport steamers, having on board about nine hundred troops commanded by Gen. Benjamin F. Butler,

LAND FORCES STORMING THE FORTIFICATIONS AT FORT CLARK.
(Two views.)

and two were schooners carrying iron surf-boats. It sailed on the 26th of August, 1861, with sealed orders, arrived at its destination before sunset, and anchored off the bar. Early the next morning an attempt was made to land the troops through the surf, at a point three miles from the inlet, whence they might attack the forts in the rear. But it was not very successful. The heavy surf dashed the clumsy iron boats upon the shore, drenching the men, wetting the powder, and endangering everything. About one-third of the troops, however, were landed, with two field-guns, and remained there under protection of the fire from the ships. The forts were garrisoned by about six hundred men, and mounted twenty-five guns; but they were not very strong, and their bomb-proofs were not constructed properly. Stringham's flag-ship, the frigate *Minnesota*, led off in the attack, followed by the *Susquehanna* and *Wabash*, and the guns of the smaller fort were soon silenced. The frigates were at such a distance that they could drop shells into it with their pivot-guns, while the shot from the fort could not reach them. Afterward the larger work, Fort Hatteras, was bombarded, but with no practical effect, though the firing was kept up till sunset. But meanwhile the troops that had landed through the surf had taken possession of the smaller work, Fort Clark. They also threw up a small earthwork, and with their field-pieces fired upon some Confederate vessels that were in the Sound. The next morning (the 28th) the frigates anchored within reach of Fort Hatteras, and began a deliberate and steady bombardment. As before, the shot from the fort fell short of the ships, and neither could that from the smooth-bore broadside guns reach the fort; but the pivot-guns and the rifled pieces of one vessel wrought great havoc. One plunging shell went down through a ventilator and narrowly missed exploding the magazine. At the end of three hours the fort surrendered. Its defenders, who were commanded by Samuel Barron, formerly of the United States navy, had suffered a loss of about fifty in killed and wounded. They had been reinforced in the night, but a steamer was seen taking away a load of troops just before the surrender. The seven hundred prisoners were sent on board the flag-ship and carried to New York. The victors had not lost a man. There had been some intention of destroying the forts and blocking up the channels of the inlet; but it was determined instead to leave a garrison and establish a coaling station for the blockading fleet. Two of the frigates remained in the Sound, and within a fortnight half a dozen blockade-runners entered the inlet and were captured.

FORTS HATTERAS AND CLARK, N. C., CAPTURED ON THE 29th OF AUGUST, 1861.

GUNBOAT "MENDOTA."

COMMANDER C. R. P. RODGERS. (Afterward Rear-Admiral.)

COMMANDER JOHN RODGERS. (Afterward Rear-Admiral.)

A much larger expedition sailed from Hampton Roads on one of the last days of October. It consisted of more than fifty vessels—frigates, gunboats, transports, tugs, steam ferry-boats, and schooners—carrying twenty-two thousand men. The fleet was commanded by Flag-officer Samuel F. Du Pont, the troops by Gen. Thomas W. Sherman (who must not be confounded with Gen. William T. Sherman, famous for his march to the sea). The expedition had been two months in preparation, and though it sailed with sealed orders, and every effort had been made to keep its destination secret, the information leaked out as usual, and while it was on its way the Confederate Secretary of War telegraphed to the Governor of South Carolina and the commander at Hilton Head where to expect it. Bull's Bay, St. Helena, Port Royal, and Fernandina had all been discussed, and the final choice fell upon Port Royal.

A tremendous gale was encountered on the passage; the fleet was scattered, one

BOMBARDMENT OF FORT WALKER, HILTON HEAD, PORT ROYAL HARBOR, S. C., BY UNITED STATES FLEET, NOVEMBER 7, 1861.

transport was completely wrecked, with a loss of seven lives, one gunboat was obliged to throw her broadside battery overboard, a transport threw over her cargo, and one store-ship was lost. When the storm was over, only a single gunboat was in sight from the flag-ship. But the fleet slowly came together again, and was joined by some of the frigates that were blockading Charleston Harbor, these being relieved by others that had come down for the purpose. They arrived off the entrance to Port Royal harbor on the 5th and 6th of November. This entrance was protected by two earthworks—Fort Walker on Hilton Head (the south side), and Fort Beauregard on St. Helena Island (the north side). These forts were about two and a half miles apart, and were garrisoned by South Carolina troops, commanded by Generals Drayton and Ripley. A brother of General Drayton commanded a vessel in the attacking fleet.

On the morning of the 7th the order of battle was formed. The bar was ten miles out from the entrance, and careful soundings had been made by two gunboats, under the fire of three Confederate vessels that ran out from the harbor. The main column consisted of ten vessels, led by the flag-ship *Wabash*, and was ordered to attack Fort Walker. Another column of four vessels was ordered to fire upon Fort Beauregard, pass in, and attack the Confederate craft. All were under way soon after breakfast, and were favored by a tranquil sea. The main column, a ship's length apart, steamed in steadily at the rate of six miles an hour, passing Fort Walker at a distance of eight hundred yards, and delivering a fire of shells and rifled shot. Every gun in the fort that could be brought to bear was worked as rapidly as possible, in a gallant defence. After the line had passed the fort, it turned and steamed out again, passing this time within six hundred yards, and delivering fire from the guns on the other side of the vessels. Three times they thus went around in a long ellipse, each time keeping the fort under fire for about twenty minutes. Then the *Bienville*, which had the heaviest guns, and was commanded by Captain Steadman, a South Carolinian, sailed in closer yet, and delivered a fire that dismounted several guns and wrought dreadful havoc. Meanwhile two or three gunboats had taken a position from which they enfiladed the work, and the flag-ship came to a stand at short range and pounded away steadily. This was more than anything at that stage of the war could endure, and from the mast-head the troops were seen streaming out of the fort and across Hilton Head Island as if in panic. A flag of truce was sent on shore, but there was no one to receive it, and soon after two o'clock the National colors were floating over the fort. The flanking column of vessels had attacked Fort Beauregard; and when the commander of that work saw that Fort Walker was abandoned by its defenders, he also retreated with his force. The Confederate vessels escaped by running up a shallow inlet. The loss in the fleet was eight men killed and twenty-three wounded; that of the Confederates, as reported by their commander, was eleven killed and fifty-two wounded or missing. General Sherman said: "Many bodies were buried in the fort, and twenty or thirty were found half a mile distant." The road across Hilton Head Island to a wharf whence the retreating troops were taken to the mainland was strewn with arms and accoutrements, and two howitzers were abandoned. The surgeon of the fort had been killed by a shell and buried by a falling parapet. The troops were debarked and took possession of both forts, repaired and strengthened the works, formed an intrenched camp, and thus gave the Government a permanent foothold on the soil of South Carolina.

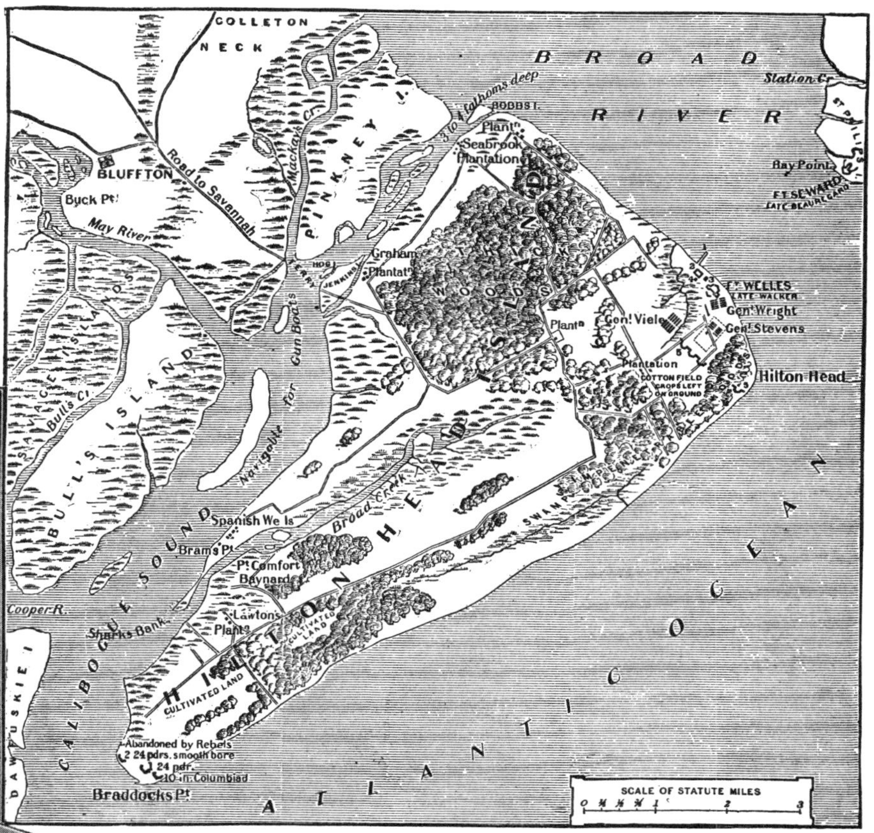

MAP OF HILTON HEAD, SHOWING ITS TOPOGRAPHY.

REAR-ADMIRAL S. F. DU PONT.

BREVET MAJOR-GENERAL T. W. SHERMAN.

Roanoke Island, N. C., lies between Roanoke Sound and Croatan Sound, through which the channels lead to Albemarle Sound, giving access to the interior of the State. This island, therefore, was fortified by the Confederates, in order to command these approaches. The island is about as large as that which is occupied by New York City—ten miles long, and somewhat over two miles wide. In January, 1862, an expedition was fitted out to capture it, and the command was given to Gen.

BRIGADIER-GENERAL T. F. DRAYTON, C. S. A.

Ambrose E. Burnside, who had about fifteen thousand men, with a battery of six guns, carried on forty transports. The naval part of the expedition, consisting of twenty-eight vessels, none of them very large, carrying half a hundred guns, was under the immediate command of Capt. Louis M. Goldsborough. Among his subordinate officers were Stephen C. Rowan and John L. Worden. Burnside's three brigade commanders—all of whom rose to eminence before the war was over—were John G. Foster, Jesse L. Reno, and John G. Parke.

The expedition sailed from Hampton Roads on January 11, and almost immediately encountered a terrific storm, by which the fleet was far scattered, some of the vessels being carried out to sea and others driven ashore. Five were wrecked, and a considerable number of men were lost. By the 28th, all that had weathered the gale passed through Hatteras Inlet into the sounds. The fortifications on the island mounted forty guns; and in Croatan Sound a Confederate naval force of eight vessels lay behind a line of obstructions across the channel.

On February 7th, the National gunboats, advancing in three columns, shelled Fort Bartow—the principal fortification, on the west side of the island—and the Confederate gunboats. The latter were soon driven off, and in four hours the fort was silenced. The transports landed the troops on the west side of the island, two miles south of the fort, and in the morning of the 8th they began their march to the interior, which was made difficult and disagreeable by swamps and a lack of roads, and by a cold storm. On the 9th, the Confederate skirmishers were driven in, and the main line was assaulted, first with artillery, and then by the infantry. The Confederate left wing was turned; and when the national troops had nearly exhausted their ammunition they made a brilliant bayonet charge, led by Hawkins's New York zouave regiment, and stormed the works, which were hastily abandoned by the Confederates, who attempted to reach the northeast shore and cross to Nag's Head, but more than two thousand of them were captured. Fort Bartow still held out, but it was soon taken, its garrison surrendering. In this action the national loss was two hundred and thirty-five men killed or wounded in the army, and twenty-five in the navy.

On the 10th, a part of the fleet, under Captain Rowan, pursued the Confederate fleet up Albemarle Sound, and after a short engagement defeated it. The Confederates set fire to their vessels and deserted them, destroying all but one, which was captured. Rowan then took possession of Elizabeth City and Edenton. The flying Confederates had set fire to the former; but Rowan's men, with the help of the colored people who remained, put out the fire and saved the city.

In this naval battle one of the first medals of honor won in the war was earned by a sailor named John Davis. A shell thrown by the Confederates entered one of the vessels and set fire to it. This was near the magazine, and there was an open barrel of powder from which Davis was serving a gun. He at once sat down on the barrel, and remained there covering it until the fire was put out.

General Burnside next planned an expedition in the opposite direction, to attack Newbern. His forces, numbering about eight thousand men, sailed from Hatteras Inlet in the morning of March 12th, and that evening landed within eighteen miles of Newbern. The next day they marched toward the city, while the gunboats ascended the river and shelled such fortifications and Confederate troops as could be seen. The roads were miry, and the progress of the troops was slow. After removing elaborate obstructions and torpedoes from the channel, the fleet reached and silenced the forts near the city. The land forces then came up and attacked the Confederates, who were about five thousand strong and were commanded by General Branch. After hard fighting, the works were carried, and the enemy fled. They burned the railroad bridge over the Trent River, and set fire to the city; but the sailors succeeded in extinguishing the flames in time to save the greater part of the town. Burnside's loss in this battle was about five hundred and fifty killed or wounded; that of the Confederates, including prisoners, was about the same. Fifty-two guns and two steamers were captured.

Ten days later, Beaufort, N. C., and Morehead City were occupied by the National troops without opposition. Burnside's army was now broken up into comparatively small bodies, holding the various places that had been taken, which greatly diminished the facilities for blockade-running on the North Carolina coast.

The year 1862 opened with indications of lively and decisive

MAJOR-GENERAL AMBROSE E. BURNSIDE.

MAJOR-GENERAL JESSE L. RENO.

MAJOR-GENERAL JOHN G. PARKE.

MAJOR-GENERAL JOHN G. FOSTER.

VICE-ADMIRAL S. C. ROWAN.

REAR-ADMIRAL LOUIS M. GOLDSBOROUGH.

work west of the mountains, and many movements were made that cannot be detailed here. One of the most gallant was in the region of the Big Sandy River in eastern Kentucky, where Humphrey Marshall had gathered a Confederate force of about two thousand five hundred (mostly Kentuckians) at Paintville. Col. James A. Garfield (afterward President), in command of one thousand eight hundred infantry and three hundred cavalry, drove him out of Paintville, pursued him beyond Prestonburg, came up with him at noon of January 10th, and fought him till night, when Marshall retreated under cover of the darkness, leaving his dead on the field.

In the autumn of 1861 a Confederate force, under Gen. Felix K. Zollicoffer, had been pushed forward by way of Knoxville to eastern Kentucky, but was defeated at Camp Wildcat, October 21st, by seven thousand men under General Schoepff, and fell back to Mill Springs at the head of steamboat navigation on the Cumberland. Zollicoffer soon crossed to the northern bank, and fortified a position at Beech Grove, in the angle between the river and Fishing Creek. The National forces in the vicinity were commanded by Gen. George H. Thomas, who watched Zollicoffer so closely that when the latter was told by his superiors he should not have crossed the river, he could only answer that it was now too late to return. As Zollicoffer was only a journalist, with more zeal than military knowledge, Gen. George B. Crittenden was sent to supersede him. Thomas was slowly advancing, through rainy weather, over heavy roads, to drive this force out of the State, and had reached Logan's Cross-roads, within ten miles of the Confederate camp, when Crittenden determined to move out and attack him. The battle began early on the morning of January 19, 1862. Thomas was on the alert, and when his outposts were driven in he rapidly brought up one detachment after another and threw them into line. The attack was directed mainly against the National left, where the fighting was obstinate and bloody, much of the firing being at very close quarters. Here Zollicoffer, thinking the Fourth Kentucky was a Confederate regiment firing upon its friends, rode forward to correct the supposed mistake, and was shot dead by its colonel, Speed S. Fry. When, at length, the right of the Confederate line had been pressed back and broken, a steady fire having been kept up on the centre, the Ninth Ohio Regiment made a bayonet charge on its left flank, and the whole line was broken and routed. The Confederates took refuge in their intrenchments, where Thomas swiftly pursued and closely invested them, expecting to capture them all the next morning. But in the night they managed to cross the river, leaving behind their wounded, twelve guns, all their horses, mules, and wagons, and a large amount of stores. In the further retreat two of the Confederate regiments disbanded and scattered to their homes, while a large number from other regiments deserted individually. The National loss in killed and wounded was two hundred and forty-six; that of the Confederates, four hundred and seventy-one. Thomas received the thanks of the President for his victory. This action is variously called the Battle of Fishing Creek and the Battle of Mill Springs.

When Gen. Henry W. Halleck was placed in command of the Department of Missouri, in November, 1861, he divided it into districts, giving to Gen. Ulysses S. Grant the District of Cairo,

BURNSIDE'S EXPEDITION OFF FORT MONROE.

THE BURNSIDE EXPEDITION CROSSING HATTERAS BAR.

which included Southern Illinois, the counties of Missouri south of Cape Girardeau, and all of Kentucky that lies west of Cumberland River. Where the Tennessee and the Cumberland enter Kentucky from the south they are about ten miles apart, and here the Confederates had erected two considerable works to command the rivers—Fort Henry on the east bank of the Tennessee, and Fort Donelson on the west bank of the Cumberland. They had also fortified the high bluffs at Columbus, on the Mississippi, twenty miles below the mouth of the Ohio, and Bowling Green, on the Big Barren. The general purpose was to establish a military frontier with a strong line of defence from the Alleghany Mountains to the Mississippi.

A fleet of iron-clad gunboats had been prepared by the United States Government for service on the Western rivers, some of them being built new, while others were altered freight-boats.

After a reconnoissance in force by Gen. C. F. Smith, General Grant asked Halleck's permission to capture Fort Henry, and, after considerable delay, received it on the 30th of January. That work was garrisoned by three thousand men under Gen. Lloyd Tilghman. Its position was strong, the ravines through which little tributaries reached the river being filled with slashed timber and rifle-pits, and swampy ground rendering approach from

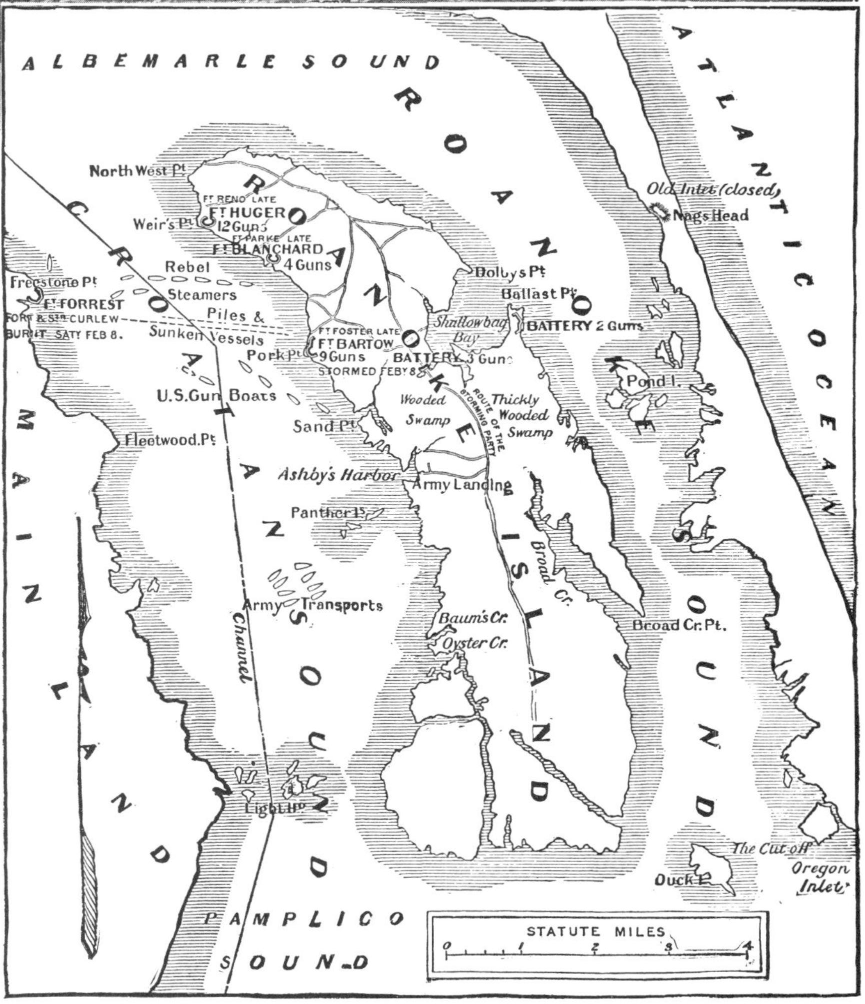

ROANOKE ISLAND, N. C., AND CONFEDERATE FORTS.

the land side difficult. But the work itself was rather poorly built, bags of sand being largely used instead of a solid earth embankment.

On the morning of February 2d the fleet of four iron-clad and two wooden gunboats, commanded by Flag-officer Andrew H. Foote, left Cairo, steamed up the Ohio to Paducah, thence up the Tennessee, and by daylight the next morning were within sight of the fort. Grant's land force was to coöperate by an attack in the rear, but it did not ar-

SIEGE TRAIN, HILTON HEAD.

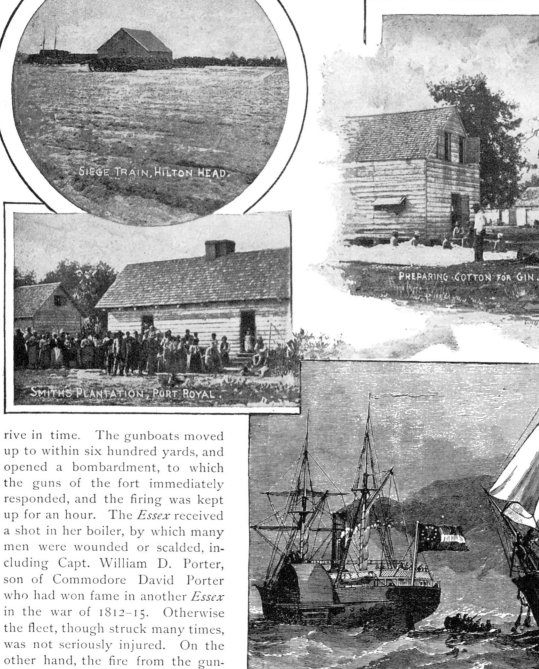

PREPARING COTTON FOR GIN.

SMITH'S PLANTATION, PORT ROYAL.

BURNING OF AMERICAN MERCHANTMAN "HARRY BIRCH" IN BRITISH CHANNEL, BY CONFEDERATE STEAMER "NASHVILLE."

rive in time. The gunboats moved up to within six hundred yards, and opened a bombardment, to which the guns of the fort immediately responded, and the firing was kept up for an hour. The *Essex* received a shot in her boiler, by which many men were wounded or scalded, including Capt. William D. Porter, son of Commodore David Porter who had won fame in another *Essex* in the war of 1812–15. Otherwise the fleet, though struck many times, was not seriously injured. On the other hand, the fire from the gunboats knocked the sand-bags about, dismounted seven guns, brought down the flagstaff, and, together with the bursting of a rifled gun in the fort, created a panic. All but about one hundred of the garrison fled, leaving General Tilghman with the sick and a single company of artillerists; and, after serving a gun with his own hands as long as possible, he ran up a white flag and surrendered. The regret of the victors at the escape of the garrison was more than counterbalanced by their gratification at the behavior of the gunboats in their first serious trial. After the surrender, three of the gunboats proceeded up the Tennessee River to the head of navigation, destroyed the railroad bridge, and captured a large amount of stores.

In consequence of the battle of Mill Springs and the fall of Fort Henry, the Confederate Gen. Simon B. Buckner, who was at Bowling Green with about ten thousand men, abandoned that place and joined his forces to those in Fort Donelson. Gen. Ormsby M. Mitchel, by a forced march, promptly took possession of Bowling Green with National troops; and General Grant immediately made dispositions for the capture of Fort Donelson. This work, situated at a bend of the river, was on high ground, enclosed about a hundred acres, and had also a strong water-battery on the lower river front. The land side was protected by slashed timber and rifle-pits, as well as by the naturally broken ground. The gunboats went down the Tennessee and up the Cumberland, and with them a portion of Grant's force to be used in attacking the water front. The fort contained about twenty thousand men, commanded by Gen. John B. Floyd, who had been President Buchanan's Secretary of War. Grant's main force left the neighborhood of Fort Henry on the morning of February 12th, a portion marching straight on Fort Donelson, while the remainder made a slight detour to the south, to come up on the right, strike the Confederate left, and prevent escape in that

A FEDERAL CAVALRY CHARGE.

direction. They chose positions around the fort unmolested that afternoon, and the next morning the fighting began. After an artillery duel, an attempt was made to storm the works near the centre of the line, but it was a failure and entailed severe loss. The gunboats and the troops with them had not yet come up, and the attack was suspended for the day. A cold storm set in, with sleet and snow, and the assailants spent the night without shelter and with scant rations, while a large part of the defenders, being in the trenches, were equally exposed.

Next morning the fleet appeared, landed the troops and supplies three miles below the fort, and then moved up to attack the batteries. These were not so easily disposed of as Fort Henry had been. It was a desperate fight. The plunging shot from the fort struck the gunboats in their most vulnerable part, and made ugly wounds. But they stood to the work manfully, and had silenced one battery when the steering apparatus of two of the gunboats was shot away, while a gun on another had burst and the flag-officer was wounded. The flag-ship had been struck fifty-nine times, and the others from twenty to forty, when they all dropped down the stream and out of the fight. They had lost fifty-four men killed or wounded. But the naval attack had served to prevent an immediate sortie, and so perhaps ultimately saved the victory for Grant.

That night a council of war was held within the fort, and it was determined to attack the besiegers in the morning with the entire force, in hopes either to defeat them completely or at least to turn back their right wing, and thus open a way for retreat toward the south. The fighting began early in the morning. Grant's right wing, all but surprised, was pressed heavily and borne back, the enemy passing through and plundering McClernand's camps. Buckner sallied out and attacked on the left with much less vigor and with no success but as a diversion, and the fighting extended all along the line, while the Confederate cavalry were endeavoring to gain the National rear. Grant was imperturbable through it all, and when he saw that the attack had reached its height, he ordered a counter attack and recovery of the lost ground on the right, which was executed by the division of Lew Wallace, while that of C. F. Smith stormed the works on the left. Smith rode beside the color-bearer, and, in the face of a murderous fire that struck down four hundred men, his troops rushed forward over every obstruction, brought up field guns and enfiladed the works, drove out the defenders, and took possession.

BRIGADIER-GENERAL FELIX K. ZOLLICOFFER, C. S. A.

COLONEL SPEED S. FRY.

(Afterward Brigadier-General.)

Another bitterly cold night followed, but Grant improved the time to move up reinforcements to the positions he had gained, while the wounded were looked after as well as circumstances would permit. Within the fort another council of war was held. Floyd declared it would not do for him to fall into the

BATTLE OF MILL SPRINGS, LOGAN CROSS ROADS, KENTUCKY, JANUARY 19, 1862.

hands of the Government, as he was accused of defrauding it while in office. So he turned over the command to Gen. Gideon J. Pillow. But that general said he also had strong reasons for not wanting to be a prisoner, so he turned it over to Gen. Simon B. Buckner. With as many of their men as could be taken on two small steamers, Floyd and Pillow embarked in the darkness and went up the river to Nashville. The cavalry, under Gen. N. B. Forrest, also escaped, and a considerable number of men from all the commands managed to steal away unobserved. In the morning Buckner hung out a white flag, and sent a letter to Grant, proposing that commissioners be appointed to arrange terms of capitulation. Grant's answer not only made him famous, but gave an impetus and direction to the whole war: "No terms other than an unconditional and immediate surrender can be accepted. I propose to move immediately upon your works." Buckner, in a petulant and ill-considered note, at once surrendered the fort and his entire command. This numbered about fourteen thousand men; and four hundred that were sent to reinforce him were also captured.

MAJOR-GENERAL HENRY W. HALLECK.

COLONEL JAMES A. GARFIELD

(Afterward Major-General)

General Pillow estimated the Confederate loss in killed and wounded at two thousand. No undisputed figures are attainable on either side. Grant began the siege with about fifteen thousand men, which reinforcements had increased to twenty-seven thousand at the time of the surrender. His losses were about two thousand, and many of the wounded had perished of cold. The long, artificial line of defence, from the mountains to the Mississippi, was now swept away, and the Confederates abandoned Nashville, to which Grant might have advanced immediately, had he not been forbidden by Halleck.

When the news was flashed through the loyal States, and bulletins were posted up with enumeration of prisoners, guns, and small arms captured, salutes were fired, joy-bells were rung, flags were displayed, and people asked one another, "Who is this Grant, and where did he come from?"—for they saw that a new genius had suddenly risen upon the earth.

Both before and after the defeat and death of General Lyon at Wilson's Creek (August, 1861), there was irregular and predatory warfare in Missouri. Especially in the western part of the State half-organized bands of men would come into existence, sometimes make long marches, and on the approach of a strong enemy disappear, some scattering to their homes and others making their way to and joining the bodies of regular troops. In Missouri and northern Arkansas guerilla warfare was extensively carried on for more than a year. Many terrible stories are told of the vengeful spirit with which both sides in this warfare were actuated. It is quite possible these stories were exaggerated, but it is certain that many cold-blooded murders were committed. Very few of the guerillas were Unionists.

MAJOR-GENERAL C. F. SMITH.

Gen. John C. Frémont, who commanded the department, believing that Price was near Springfield, gave orders for the concentration at that place of all the National forces in Missouri. But Price was not there, and in November Frémont was superseded by General Halleck, some of whose subordinate commanders, especially Gen. John Pope, made rapid movements and did good service in capturing newly recruited regiments that were on their way to join Price.

CAPTAIN CUSTER, U. S. A., AND LIEUTENANT WASHINGTON, A CONFEDERATE PRISONER.

Late in December Gen. Samuel R. Curtis took command of twelve thousand National troops at Rolla, and advanced against Price, who retreated before him to the northwestern corner of Arkansas, where his force was joined by that of General McCulloch, and together they took up a position in the Boston Mountains. Curtis crossed the line into Arkansas, chose a strong place on Pea Ridge, in the Ozark Mountains, intrenched, and awaited attack. Because of serious disagreements between Price and McCulloch, Gen. Earl Van Dorn, who ranked them both, was sent to take command of the Confederate force, arriving late in January. There is no authentic statement as to the size of his army. He himself declared that he had but fourteen thousand men, while no other estimate gave fewer than twice that number. Among them was a large body of Cherokee Indians, recruited for the Confederate service by Albert Pike, who thirty years before had won reputation as a poet. On March 5, 1862, Van Dorn moved to attack Curtis, who knew of his coming and formed his line on the bluffs along Sugar Creek, facing southward. His divisions were commanded by Gens. Franz Sigel and Alexander S. Asboth and Cols. Jefferson C. Davis and Eugene A. Carr, and he had somewhat more than ten thousand men in line, with forty-eight guns. The Confederates, finding the position too strong in front, made a night march to the west, with the intention of striking the Nationals on the right flank. But Curtis discovered their movement at dawn, promptly faced his line to the right about, and executed a grand left wheel. His army was looking westward toward the approaching foe, Carr's division being on the right, then Davis, then Asboth, and Sigel on the left. But they were not fairly in position when the blow fell. Carr was struck most heavily, and, though reinforced from time to time, was driven back a mile in the course of the day. Davis, opposed to the corps of McCulloch, was more successful; that general was killed, and his troops were driven from the field. In the night Curtis re-formed and strengthened his lines, and in the morning the battle was renewed. This day Sigel executed some brilliant and characteristic manœuvres. To bring his division into its place on the left wing, he pushed a battery forward, and while it was firing rapidly its infantry supports were brought up to it by a right wheel; this movement was repeated with another battery and its supports to the left of the first, and again, till the whole division had come into line, pressing back the enemy's right. Sigel was now so far advanced that Curtis's whole line made a curve, enclosing the enemy, and by a heavy concentrated artillery fire the Confederates were soon driven to the shelter of the ravines, and finally put to rout. The National loss in this action—killed, wounded, and missing—was over thirteen hundred, Carr and Asboth being among the wounded. The Confederate loss is unknown. Generals McCulloch and McIntosh were killed, and Generals Price and Slack wounded. Owing to the nature of the ground, any effective pursuit of Van Dorn's broken forces was impracticable.

BRIGADIER-GENERAL JOHN B FLOYD, C. S. A.

LIEUTENANT-GENERAL SIMON B. BUCKNER, C. S. A

BRIGADIER-GENERAL G. J. PILLOW, C. S. A.

MAJOR-GENERAL BUSHROD JOHNSON, C. S. A.

The Confederate Government had made a treaty with some of the tribes in the Indian Territory, and had taken into its service more than four thousand Indians, whom the stories of Bull Run and Wilson's Creek had apparently impressed with the belief that they would have little to do but scalp the wounded and rob the dead. At Pea Ridge these red men exhibited their old-time terror of artillery, and though they took a few scalps they were so disgusted at being asked to face half a hundred well-served cannon that they were almost useless to their allies, and thenceforth they took no further part in the war. It is a notable fact that in the wars on this continent the Indians have only been employed on the losing side. In the French and English struggle for the country, which ended in 1763, the French had the friendship of many of the tribes, and employed them against the English settlers and soldiers, but the French were conquered nevertheless. In the Revolution and the war of 1812, the British employed them to some extent against the Americans, but the Americans were victorious. In the great Rebellion, the Confederate Government

MAJOR-GENERAL SAMUEL R. CURTIS.

MAJOR-GENERAL EARL VAN DORN, C. S. A.

BREVET MAJOR-GENERAL A. ASBOTH.

attempted to use them as allies in the West and Southwest, and in that very section the Confederate cause was first defeated. All of which appears to show that though savages may add to the horrors of war, they cannot determine its results for civilized people; nor can irresponsible guerilla bands, of which there were many at the West, nearly all in the service of the Confederacy.

"At the close of Mr. Buchanan's administration nearly all the United States Indian agents in the Indian Territory were secessionists, and the moment the Southern States commenced passing ordinances of secession, these men exerted their influence to get the five tribes committed to the Confederate cause. Occupying territory south of the Arkansas River, and having the secessionists of Arkansas on the east and those of Texas on the south for neighbors, the Choctaws and Chickasaws offered no decided opposition to the scheme. With the Cherokees, the most powerful and most civilized tribes of the Indian Territory, it was different. Their chief, John Ross, was opposed to hasty action, and at first favored neutrality, and in the summer of 1861 issued a proclamation enjoining his people to observe a strictly neutral attitude during the war between the United States and the Southern States. In June, 1861, Albert Pike, a commissioner of the Confederate States, and Gen. Ben. McCulloch, commanding the Confederate forces in Western Arkansas and the Department of Indian Territory, visited Chief Ross, with the view of having him make a treaty with the Confederacy. But he declined to make a treaty, and in the conference expressed himself as wishing to occupy, if possible, a neutral position during the war. A majority of the Cherokees, nearly all of whom were full-bloods, were known as Pin Indians, and were opposed to the South." (*Battles and Leaders*, Vol. I., pp. 335–336.)

After the battle of Wilson's Creek had been fought, General Lyon killed, and the Union army defeated, Chief Ross was easily convinced that the South would succeed, and entered into a treaty with the Confederate authorities.

BATTLE OF PEA RIDGE, MARCH 6, 1862.

GALLANT CHARGE ON OUTWORKS OF FORT DONELSON, FEBRUARY 13, 1862.

THE FRIGATE "CUMBERLAND" RAMMED BY THE "MERRIMAC."

CHAPTER IX.

THE "MONITOR" AND THE "MERRIMAC."

THE CONSTRUCTION OF THE "MONITOR" AND "MERRIMAC"—EFFECT UPON NAVAL ARMAMENTS OF THE WORLD—IDEA OF REVOLVING TOWER NOT ORIGINAL WITH ERICSSON—DESTRUCTION OF THE "CUMBERLAND"—PUBLIC EXCITEMENT AT PROSPECT OF AN ATTACK ON WASHINGTON—THE "MONITOR" SAILS FROM NEW YORK HARBOR MARCH 6TH—GREAT NAVAL BATTLE IN HAMPTON ROADS.

WHILE the great naval expedition was approaching New Orleans, the waters of Hampton Roads, from which it had sailed, were the scene of a battle that revolutionized the naval armaments of the world. When at the outbreak of the war the navy yard at Norfolk, Va., was abandoned, with an attempt at its destruction, the steam frigate *Merrimac* was set on fire at the wharf. Her upper works were burned, and her hull sunk. There had been long hesitation about removing any of the valuable property from this navy yard, because the action of Virginia was uncertain, and it was hoped that a mark of confidence in her people would tend to keep her in the Union. The day that Sumter was fired upon, peremptory orders had been issued for the removal of the *Merrimac* to Philadelphia, and steam was raised and every preparation made for her sailing. But the officer in command, for some unexplained reason, would not permit her to move, and two days later she was burned. Within two months the Confederates were at work upon her. They raised the hull, repaired the machinery, and covered it with a steep roof of wrought iron five inches thick, with a lining of oak seven inches thick. The sides were also plated with iron, and the bow was armed with an iron ram, something like a huge ploughshare. In the water she had the appearance of a house submerged to the eaves, with an immense gun looking out at each of ten dormer windows.

But all this could not be done in a day, especially where skilled workmen were scarce, and it was March, 1862, before she was ready for action. The command was given to Franklin Buchanan, who had resigned a commission in the United States navy. On the 8th of March, accompanied by two gunboats, she went out to raise the blockade of James and Elizabeth Rivers by destroying the wooden war vessels in Hampton Roads. Her first victim was the frigate *Cumberland*, which gave her a broadside that would have riddled a wooden vessel through and through. Some of the shot entered her open ports, killed or wounded nineteen men, and broke two of her guns; but all that struck the armor bounded off like peas. Rifled shot from the *Merrimac* raked the *Cumberland*, and then she ran into her so that her iron prow cut a great gash in the side. The *Cumberland* at once began to settle; but the crew stood by their guns, firing broadside after broadside without producing any impression on the iron monster, and received in return shells and solid shot that made sickening havoc. The commander, Lieutenant Morris, refused to surrender; and at the end of forty-five minutes, when the water was at the gun-deck, the crew leaped overboard and with the help of the boats got ashore, while the frigate heeled over and sank to the bottom. Her topmasts projected above the surface, and her flag was flying. While this was going on, three Confederate steamers came down and attacked the *Congress* with such effect that her commander tried to run her ashore. Having finished the *Cumberland*, the *Merrimac* came up and opened a deliberate attack on the *Congress*, and finally set her on fire, when the crew escaped in their boats. She burned for several hours, and in the night blew up. Of the other National vessels in the Roads, one got aground in water too shallow for the *Merrimac* to approach her, and the others were not drawn into the fight.

JOHN ERICSSON.
Inventor of the "Monitor."

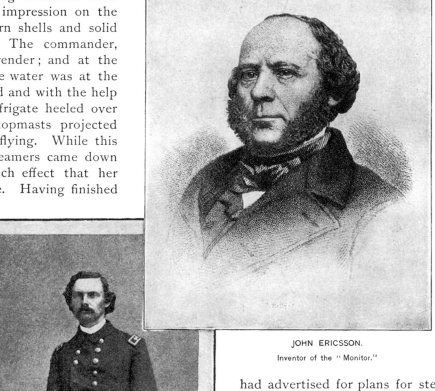

LIEUTENANT G. U. MORRIS.
Commander of the "Cumberland."

REAR-ADMIRAL J. SMITH.
Commander at the Washington Navy Yard.

The next morning the *Merrimac* came down again from Norfolk to finish up the fleet in Hampton Roads, and after that—to do various unheard-of things. The more sanguine expected her to go at once to Philadelphia, New York, and other seaboard cities of the North, and either bombard them or lay them under heavy contribution. The National Administration entertained a corresponding apprehension, and expected to see the *Merrimac* ascend the Potomac and attack Washington first. A part of these expectations were well founded, and the rest were such exaggerations as commonly arise from ignorance. The *Merrimac* could not have reached New York or Philadelphia, because she was not a sea-going vessel. With skilful management and good luck, she might have ascended the Potomac to Washington, but she would have had to run the gantlet of numerous dangers. There is a place in the Potomac called "the kettle-bottoms," where a great many conical mounds, composed of sand and oyster-shells, rise from the channel till their peaks are within a few feet of the surface; and their positions were so imperfectly known at this time that the National vessels frequently ran aground upon them. Several devices were in waiting to make trouble for the iron-clad champion at this point, perhaps the most dangerous of which was that prepared by Captain Love, commanding an armed tugboat. He procured a seine three-quarters of a mile long, took off its floats, and stretched it across the channel in such a way that the *Merrimac* could hardly have passed over it without fouling her propeller, which would have rendered her helpless.

But the dangerous enemy was destined to be disposed of in a more novel and dramatic way. In August, 1861, the Navy Department had advertised for plans for steam batteries, to be iron-clad and capable of fighting the *Merrimac* and other similar armored vessels that the Confederates were known to be constructing. The plan adopted was that presented by Capt. John Ericsson. Its essential features were an iron-clad hull, with an "overhang" to protect the machinery, all of which was below the waterline, surmounted by a round revolving tower or turret, in which were two heavy guns. The idea of a revolving tower was not Ericsson's; it had been put forth by several inventors, especially by Abraham Bloodgood in 1807. But this special adaptation of it, with the application of steam power, was his. The vessel was built in Brooklyn, and was launched January 30, 1862, one hundred days after the laying of the keel. She was named *Monitor*, for the obvious significance of the word. The extreme length of her upper hull was one hundred and seventy-two feet, with a breadth of forty-one feet, while her lower hull was one hundred and twenty-two feet long and thirty-four feet broad. Her depth was eleven feet, and when loaded she drew ten feet of water, her deck thus rising but a single foot above the surface. The turret was twenty feet in diameter and nine feet high. The only conspicuous object on the deck, besides the turret, was a pilot-house about five feet square and four feet high. This was built of solid wrought-iron beams, nine by twelve inches, laid one upon another and bolted together. At a point near the top a slight crack was left between the beams all round, through which the commander and the pilot could see what was going on outside and get their bearings. The guns threw solid shot eleven inches in diameter. The advantage of presenting so small a surface as a target for the enemy, having all the machinery beyond reach of any hostile shot, carrying two large guns, and being able to revolve the turret that contained them, so as to bring them to bear in any direction and keep the ports turned away from danger except at the moment of firing, is apparent.

This novel war-machine sailed from the harbor of New York on March 6, in command of Lieut. John L. Worden, destined for Hampton Roads. She was hardly out at sea when orders came changing her destination to Washington; but fortunately she could not be reached, although a swift tugboat was sent after her. She had a rough passage of three days, the perils of which were largely increased by the fact that her crew did not as yet understand all her peculiarities. They neglected to stop the hawse-hole where the anchor-chain passed out, and large quantities of water came in there, besides what poured down the low smoke-stacks when the waves broke over her.

Outriding all dangers, she arrived in Hampton Roads on Saturday evening, March 8, where the mournful condition of things did not diminish the dispiriting effect of the voyage upon her crew. The *Cumberland* was sunk, the *Congress* was burning, the *Minnesota* was aground, and everybody was dismayed. But Worden seems to have had no lack of confidence in his vessel and his crew. He took on a volunteer pilot, and promptly in the morning went out to his work. He first drove away the wooden vessels that were making for the helpless *Minnesota*, and then steered straight for the *Merrimac*, which was now coming down the channel.

The Confederates had known about the building of the *Monitor* (which they called the *Ericsson*), just as the authorities at Washington had known all about the *Merrimac*. When their men first saw her, they described her as "a cheese-box on a raft," and were surprised at her apparently diminutive size. Buchanan had been seriously wounded in the action of the previous day, and the Confederate iron-clad was now commanded by Lieutenant Jones.

Worden stationed himself in the pilot-house, with the pilot and a quartermaster to man the wheel, while his executive officer, Lieut. Samuel D. Greene, was in the turret, commanding the guns, which were worked by chief engineer Stimers and sixteen men. The total number of men in the *Monitor* was fifty-seven; the *Merrimac* had about three hundred.

The *Merrimac* began firing as soon as the two iron-clads were within long range of each other, but Worden reserved his fire for short range. Then the battle was fairly open, the National vessel firing solid shot, about one in eight minutes, while the Confederates used shells exclusively and fired much more rapidly. The shells struck the turret and made numerous scars, but inflicted no serious damage, except occasionally when a man was leaning against the side at the moment of impact and was injured by the concussion. Worden had his eyes at the sight-hole when a shell struck it and exploded, temporarily blinding him, and injuring him so severely that he turned over the command to Lieutenant Greene and took no further part in the action. Each vessel attempted to ram the other, but always without success. Once when the *Monitor* made a dash at the

BATTLE BETWEEN THE "MONITOR" AND "MERRIMAC," HAMPTON ROADS, VIRGINIA, MARCH 9, 1862.

THE FIGHT OF THE "MONITOR" AND "MERRIMAC," HAMPTON ROADS. FEDERAL FLEET IN THE FOREGROUND.

Merrimac's stern, to disable her steering-gear, the two guns were discharged at once at a distance of only a few yards. The two ponderous shots, striking close together, crushed in the iron plates several inches, and produced a concussion that knocked over the entire crews of the after guns and caused many of them to bleed at the nose and ears. The officers of the *Monitor* had received peremptory orders to use but fifteen pounds of powder at a charge. Experts say that if they had used the normal charge of thirty pounds their shots would undoubtedly have penetrated the *Merrimac* and either sunk her or compelled her surrender. The *Monitor* had an advantage in the fact that she drew but half as much water as the *Merrimac* and could move with much greater celerity. The fight continued for about four hours, and the Confederate iron-clad then returned to Norfolk, and

COMMANDER FRANKLIN BUCHANAN, C. S. N.
Commanding the "Merrimac."

CAPTAIN JOHN L. WORDEN. (Afterward Rear-Admiral.)
Commanding the "Monitor."

she never came down to fight again till the 11th of April, when no battle took place because both vessels had orders to remain on the defensive, each Government being afraid to risk the loss of its only iron-clad in those waters. The indentations on the *Monitor* showed that she had been struck twenty-two times, but she was not in any way disabled. Twenty of her shots struck the *Merrimac,* some of which smashed the outer layers of iron plates. It was claimed that the *Merrimac* would have sunk the *Monitor* by ramming, had she not lost her iron prow when she rammed the *Cumberland* the day before; but a description of the prow, which was only of cast iron and not very large, makes this at least doubtful.

Just what damage the *Merrimac* received in the fight is not known. But it was observed that she went into it with her bow up and her stern down, and went out with her bow down and her stern up; that on withdrawing she was at once surrounded by four tugs, into which her men immediately jumped; and she went into the dry-dock for repairs.

The significance of the battle was not so much in its immediate result as in its effect upon all naval armaments, and because of this it attracted world-wide attention. The London

LIEUTENANT S. DANA GREENE.
Executive Officer of the "Monitor."

Times declared: "There is not now a ship in the English navy, apart from these two [the *Warrior* and the *Ironside*], that it would not be madness to trust to an engagement with that little *Monitor*." The United States Government ordered the building of more monitors, some with two turrets, and they did excellent service, notably in the battle of Mobile Bay.

In May, when Norfolk was captured, an attempt was made to take the *Merrimac* up the James River; but she got aground, and was finally abandoned and blown up. When the Confederates refitted her they rechristened her *Virginia,* but the original name sticks to her in history. In December of that year the *Monitor* attempted to go to Beaufort, N. C., towed by a steamer; but she foundered in a gale off Cape Hatteras and went to the bottom, carrying with her a dozen of the crew.

LOSS OF THE "MONITOR" IN A STORM OFF CAPE HATTERAS, DECEMBER 30, 1862.—GALLANT EFFORTS TO RESCUE THE CREW.

CHAPTER X.

THE CAPTURE OF NEW ORLEANS.

NEW ORLEANS THE LARGEST SOUTHERN CITY—FORTS ON THE MISSISSIPPI—CAPT. DAVID G. FARRAGUT CHOSEN COMMANDER—GEN. BENJAMIN F. BUTLER IN COMMAND OF LAND FORCES—TERRIFIC BOMBARDMENT OF THE FORTS—CUTTING THE CHAIN ACROSS THE MISSISSIPPI—THE GREAT NAVAL BATTLE IN THE NIGHT—ALL THE FORTS AND THE CONFEDERATE FLEET CAPTURED BY FARRAGUT—SURRENDER OF NEW ORLEANS—GENERAL BUTLER'S CELEBRATED "WOMAN ORDER."

THE Crescent City was by far the largest and richest in the Confederacy. In 1860 it had a population of nearly one hundred and seventy thousand, while Richmond, Mobile, and Charleston together had fewer than two-thirds as many. In 1860–61 it shipped twenty-five million dollars' worth of sugar and ninety-two million dollars' worth of cotton, its export trade in these articles being larger than that of any other city in the world. Moreover, its strategic value in that war was greater than that of any other point in the Southern States. The many mouths of the Mississippi, and the frequency of violent gales in the Gulf, rendered it difficult to blockade commerce between that great river and the ocean; but the possession of this lowest commercial point on the stream would shut it off effectively, and would go far toward securing possession all the way to Cairo. This would cut the Confederacy in two, and make it difficult to bring supplies from Texas and Arkansas to feed the armies in Tennessee and Virginia. Moreover, a great city is in itself a serious loss to one belligerent and a capital prize to the other.

As soon as it became evident that war was being waged against the United States in dead earnest, and that it was likely to be prolonged, these considerations presented themselves to the Government, and a plan was matured for capture of the largest city in the territory of the insurgents.

The defences of New Orleans against an enemy approaching from the sea consisted of two forts, on either side of the stream,

PANORAMIC VIEW OF NEW ORLEANS.—FEDERAL FLEET AT ANCHOR IN THE RIVER.

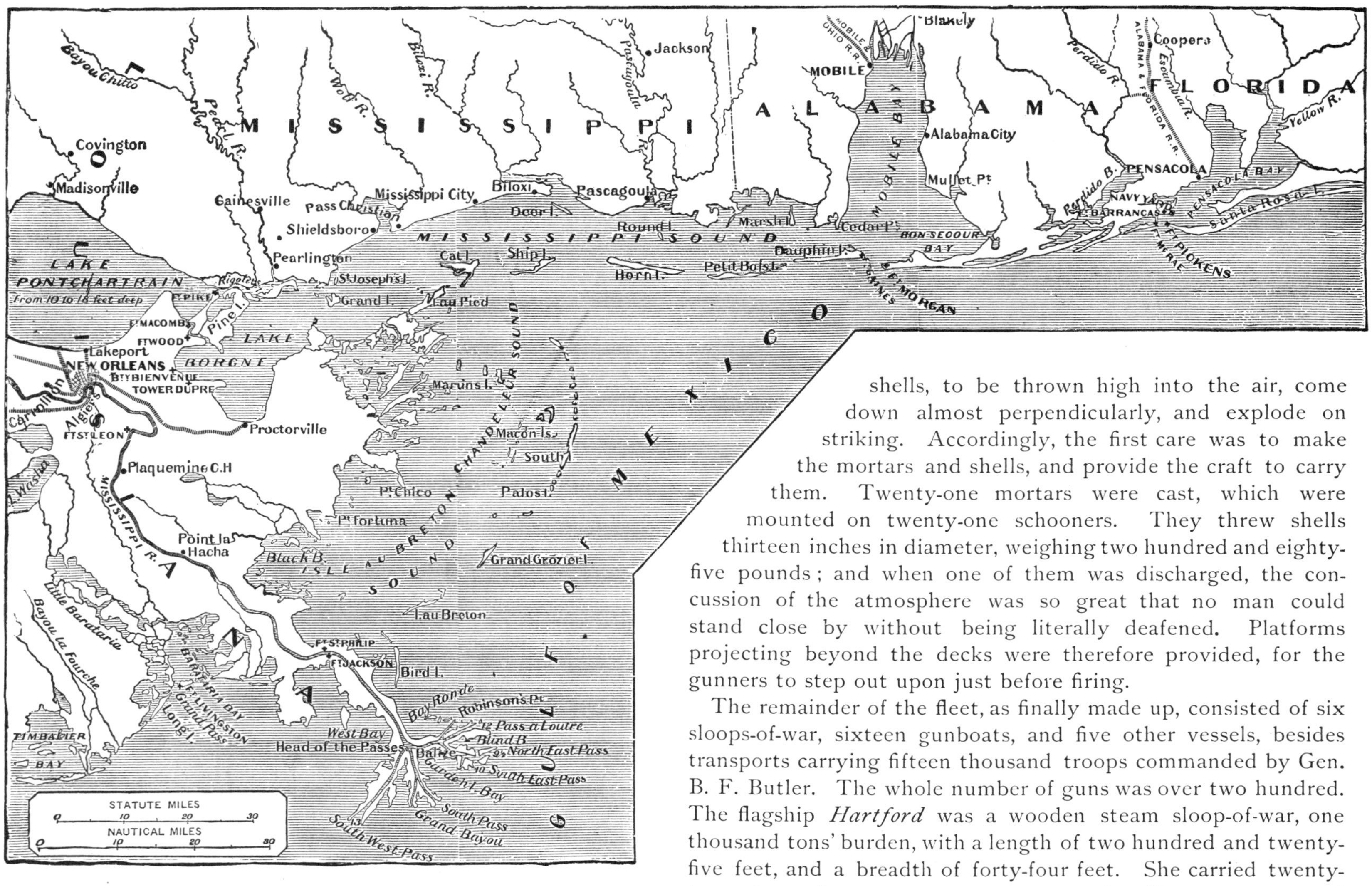

FROM PENSACOLA TO THE MOUTH OF THE MISSISSIPPI.

thirty miles above the head of the five great passes through which it flows to the Gulf. The smaller, Fort St. Philip, on the left bank, was of earth and brick, with flanking batteries, and all its guns were *en barbette*—on the top, in plain sight. These numbered about forty. Fort Jackson, on the right bank, mounted seventy-five guns, fourteen of which were in bomb-proof casemates. Both of these works had been built by the United States Government. They were now garrisoned by about one thousand five hundred Confederate soldiers, commanded by Gen. Johnson K. Duncan. Above them lay a Confederate fleet of fifteen vessels, including an iron-clad ram and a large floating battery that was covered with railroad iron. Just below the forts a heavy chain was stretched across the river—perhaps suggested by the similar device employed to keep the British from sailing up the Hudson during the Revolutionary war. And it had a similar experience; for, at first supported by a row of enormous logs, it was swept away by the next freshet. The logs were then replaced by hulks anchored at intervals across the stream, and the chain ran over their decks, while its ends were fastened to great trees. One thing more completed the defence—two hundred sharp-shooters patrolled the banks between the forts and the head of the passes, to give warning of an approaching foe and fire at any one that might be seen on the decks.

The idea at Washington, probably originated by Commander (now Admiral) David D. Porter, was that the forts could be reduced by raining into them a sufficient shower of enormous shells, to be thrown high into the air, come down almost perpendicularly, and explode on striking. Accordingly, the first care was to make the mortars and shells, and provide the craft to carry them. Twenty-one mortars were cast, which were mounted on twenty-one schooners. They threw shells thirteen inches in diameter, weighing two hundred and eighty-five pounds; and when one of them was discharged, the concussion of the atmosphere was so great that no man could stand close by without being literally deafened. Platforms projecting beyond the decks were therefore provided, for the gunners to step out upon just before firing.

The remainder of the fleet, as finally made up, consisted of six sloops-of-war, sixteen gunboats, and five other vessels, besides transports carrying fifteen thousand troops commanded by Gen. B. F. Butler. The whole number of guns was over two hundred. The flagship *Hartford* was a wooden steam sloop-of-war, one thousand tons' burden, with a length of two hundred and twenty-five feet, and a breadth of forty-four feet. She carried twenty-two nine-inch guns, two twenty-pounder Parrott guns, and a rifled gun on the forecastle, while her fore and main tops were furnished with howitzers and surrounded with boiler iron to protect the gunners. The *Brooklyn*, *Richmond*, *Pensacola*, *Portsmouth*, and *Oneida* were similar to the *Hartford*. The *Colorado* was larger. The *Mississippi* was a large side-wheel steamer.

This was the most powerful expedition that had ever sailed under the American flag, and the man that was chosen to command it, Capt. David G. Farragut, was as unknown to the public as Ulysses S. Grant had been. But he was not unknown to his fellow-officers. Farragut was now sixty years of age, being one of the oldest men that took part in the war, and he had been in the navy half a century. He sailed the Pacific with Commodore Porter years before Grant and Sherman were born, and participated in the bloody encounter of the *Essex* and *Phœbe* in the harbor of Valparaiso. He was

COMMANDER DAVID D. PORTER.

(Afterward Rear-Admiral.)

especially familiar with the Gulf of Mexico, and had pursued pirates through its waters and hunted and fought them on its islands. There was nothing to be done on shipboard that he could not do to perfection, and he could have filled the place of any man in the fleet—except perhaps the surgeon's. He was born in Tennessee, and married twice in Virginia; and if there had been a peaceable separation he would probably have made his home in the South. He was at Norfolk, waiting orders, when Virginia seceded, but he considered that his first duty was to the National Government, which had educated him for its service and given him rank and employment. When he said that "Virginia had been dragooned out of the Union," and that he thought the President was justified in calling for troops after the firing on Sumter, he was told by his angry neighbors that a person holding such sentiments could not live in Norfolk. "Very well, then," said he, "I can live somewhere else." So he made his way North with his little family, and informed the Government that he was ready and anxious for any service that might be assigned to him.

This was in April, 1861; but it was not till January, 1862, that he was appointed to command the New Orleans expedition and the Western gulf blockading squadron. He sailed from Hampton Roads February 2, in the flag-ship *Hartford*. Some sentences from the sailing-orders addressed to him by the Secretary of the Navy, Gideon Welles, are significant and suggestive. "As you have expressed yourself perfectly satisfied with the force given to you, and as many more powerful vessels will be added before you can commence operations, the department and the country require of you success. . . . There are other operations of minor importance which will commend themselves to your judgment and skill, but which must not be allowed to interfere with the great object in view, the certain capture of the city of New Orleans. . . . Destroy the armed barriers which these deluded people have raised up against the power of the United States Government, and shoot down those who war against the Union; but cultivate with cordiality the first returning reason which is sure to follow your success." In a single respect Farragut was not satisfied with his fleet. He had no faith in the mortars, and would rather have gone without them; but they had been ordered before he was consulted, and were under the command of his personal friend Porter. Perhaps his distrust of them arose from his knowledge that, in 1815, a British fleet had unavailingly thrown a thousand shells into a fort at this very turn of the river where he was now to make the attack.

The mortar schooners were to rendezvous first at Key West, and sail then for Ship Island, off Lake Borgne, where the transports were to take the troops and the war-vessels were to meet as soon as possible.

A considerable portion of March was gone before enough of the fleet had reached the rendezvous to begin operations. The first difficulty was to get into the river. The Eads jetties did not then exist, and the shifting mud-banks made constant soundings necessary for large vessels. The mortar schooners went in by Pass à l'Outre without difficulty; but to get the *Brooklyn*, *Mississippi*, and *Pensacola* over the bar at Southwest Pass required immense labor, and occupied two or three weeks. The *Mississippi* was dragged over with her keel ploughing a furrow a foot deep in the river bottom, and the *Colorado* could not be taken over at all.

INGENIOUS METHOD OF DISGUISING COMMANDER PORTER'S MORTAR FLOTILLA.

The masts of the mortar schooners were dressed off with bushes, to render them indistinguishable from the trees on shore near the forts. The schooners were then towed up to a point within range, and moored where the woods hid them, so that they could not be seen from the forts. Lieut. F. H. Gerdes of the Coast Survey had made a careful map of that part of the river and its banks, and elaborate calculations by which the mortars were to be fired with a computed aim, none of the gunners being able to see what they fired at. They opened fire on April

SHIP ISLAND.

18, and kept up the bombardment steadily for six days and nights. Six thousand enormous shells—eight hundred tons of iron—were thrown high into the air, and fell in and around the forts. For nearly a week the garrison saw one of Porter's aërolites dropping upon them every minute and a half. They demolished buildings, they tore up the ground, they cut the levee and let in water, and they killed and mangled men ; but they did not render the forts untenable nor silence their guns. The return fire sank one of the mortar boats and disabled a steamer. Within the forts about fifty men were killed or wounded—one for every sixteen tons of iron thrown.

While the fleet was awaiting the progress of this bombardment, a new danger appeared. The Confederates had prepared several flat-boats loaded with dry wood smeared with tar and turpentine ; and they now set fire to them one after another, and let them float down the stream. But Farragut sent out boats' crews to meet them, who grappled them with hooks, and either towed them ashore or conducted them past the fleet, and let them float down through the passes and out to sea.

In his General Orders, Farragut gave so many minute directions that it would seem as if he must have anticipated every possible contingency. Thus : "Trim your vessel a few inches by the head [that is, place the contents so that she will sink a little deeper at the bow than at the stern], so that if she touches the bottom she will not swing head down the river." "Have light Jacob-ladders made, to throw over the side for the use of the carpenters in stopping shot-holes, who are to be supplied with pieces of inch-board, lined with felt, and ordinary nails." "Have a kedge in the mizzen chains on the quarter, with a hawser bent and leading through in the stern chock, ready for any emergency ; also grapnels in boats, ready to tow off fire-ships." "Have many tubs of water about the decks, both for extinguishing fire and for drinking." "You will have a spare hawser ready, and when ordered to take in tow your next astern do so, keeping the hawser slack so long as the ship can maintain her own position, having a care not to foul the propeller." It was this minute knowledge and forethought, quite as much as his courage and determination, that insured his success. In addition to his own suggestions he called upon his men to exercise their wits for the occasion, and the crews originated many wise precautions. As the attack was to be in the night, they painted the decks white to enable them to find things. They got out all the spare chains, and hung them up and down the sides of the vessels at the places where they would protect the machinery from the enemy's shot. Farragut's plan was to run by the forts, damaging them as much as possible by a rapid fire as he passed, then destroy or capture the Confederate fleet, and proceed up the river and lay the city under his guns.

The time fixed upon for starting was just before moonrise (3:30 o'clock) in the morning of April 24. On the night of the 20th two gunboats went up the river, and a boat's crew from one of them, under Lieut. Charles H. B. Caldwell, boarded one of the hulks and cut the chain, under a heavy fire, making an opening sufficient for the fleet to pass through. Near midnight of the 23d the lieutenant went up again in a gunboat, to make sure that the passage was still open, and this time the enemy not only fired on him, but sent down blazing rafts and lighted enormous piles of wood that they had prepared near the ends of the chain. The question of moonrise was no longer of the slightest importance, since it was as light as day for miles around. Two red lanterns displayed at the peak of the flag-ship at two o'clock gave the signal for action, and at half-past three the whole fleet was in motion.

The sloop *Portsmouth* and Porter's gunboats moved up to a

point where they could engage the water-battery of Fort Jackson while the fleet was going by. The first division of eight vessels, commanded by Capt. Theodorus Bailey, who was almost as old and as salt as Farragut, passed through the opening in deliberate fashion, unmindful of a fire from Fort Jackson, ran over to the east bank, and poured grape and canister into Fort St. Philip as they sailed by, and ten minutes afterward found themselves engaged at close quarters with eleven Confederate vessels. Bailey's flag-ship, the *Cayuga*, was attacked by three at once, all trying to board her. He sent an eleven-inch shot through one of them, and she ran aground and burst into a blaze. With the swivel gun on his forecastle he drove off the second; and he was preparing to board the third when the *Oneida* and *Varuna* came to his assistance. The *Oneida* ran at full speed into one Confederate vessel, cutting it nearly in two, and in an instant making it a shapeless wreck. She fired into others, and then went to the assistance of the *Varuna*, which had been attacked by two, rammed by both of them, and was now at the shore, where she sank in a few minutes. But she had done effective work before she perished, crippling one enemy so that she surrendered to the *Oneida*, driving another ashore, and exploding a shell in the boiler of a third.

CAPTAIN DAVID G. FARRAGUT.
(Afterward Admiral.)

The *Pensacola* steamed slowly by the forts, doing great execution with her rifled guns, and in turn sustaining the heaviest loss in the fleet — thirty-seven men. In an open field men can dodge a cannon-ball; but when it comes bouncing in at a port-hole unannounced, it sometimes destroys a whole gun's-crew in the twinkling of an eye. In such an action men are under the highest possible excitement; every nerve is awake, and every muscle tense; and when a ball strikes one it completely shatters him, as if he were made of glass, and the shreds are scattered over the ship. The *Mississippi* sailed up in handsome style, encountered the Confederate ram *Manassas*, and received a blow that disabled her machinery. But in turn she riddled the ram and set it on fire, so that it drifted away and blew up. The other vessels of this division, with various fortune, passed the forts and participated in the naval battle.

The second division consisted of three sloops of war, the flagship leading. The *Hartford* received and returned a heavy fire from the forts, got aground on a shoal while trying to avoid a fire-raft, and a few minutes later had another raft pushed against her, which set her on fire. A portion of the crew was detailed to extinguish the flames, and all the while her guns were loaded and fired as steadily as if nothing had happened. Presently she was got afloat again, and proceeded up the river, when, suddenly, through the smoke, as it was lighted by the flashes of the guns, she saw a steamer filled with men bearing down upon her, probably with the intention of carrying her by boarding. But a ready gun planted a huge shell in the mysterious stranger, which exploded, and she disappeared—going to the bottom, for aught that anybody knew. The *Brooklyn*, after getting out of her course and running upon one of the hulks, finally got through, met a large Confederate steamer, and gave it a broadside that set it on fire, and then poured such a rain of shot into St. Philip that the bastions were cleared in a minute, and in the flashes the gunners could be seen running to shelter. A Confederate gunboat that attacked her received eleven shells from her, all of which exploded, and it then ran ashore in flames. The *Richmond* sailed through steadily and worked her guns regularly, meeting with small loss, because she was more completely provided with splinter-nettings than her consorts, as well as because she came after them.

COMMANDER C. S. BOGGS.
(Afterward Rear-Admiral.)

CAPTAIN THEODORUS BAILEY.
(Afterward Rear-Admiral.)

Confederate Ram. "Mississippi." Confederate Boat. "Varuna." "Oneida."

PASSAGE OF THE SECOND DIVISION OF THE FEDERAL SQUADRON BY FORTS JACKSON AND ST. PHILIP

The third division consisted of six gunboats. Two of them became entangled among the hulks, and failed to pass. Another received a shot in her boiler, which compelled her to drop down stream and out of the fight. The other three went through in gallant style, both suffering and inflicting considerable loss from continuous firing, and burned two steamboats and drove another ashore before they came up with the advance divisions of the fleet. The entire loss had been thirty-seven killed and one hundred and forty-seven wounded.

Captain Bailey, in the *Cayuga*, still keeping the lead, found a regiment encamped at Quarantine Station, and compelled its surrender. On the morning of the 25th the Chalmette batteries, three miles below the city, were silenced by a fire from the sloops, and a little later the city itself was at the mercy of their guns. At noon Captain Bailey, accompanied only by Lieut. George H. Perkins, with a flag of truce, went ashore, passed through an excited crowd that apparently only needed a word to be turned into a mob, and demanded of the Mayor that the city be surrendered unconditionally and the Louisiana State flag at once hauled down from the staff on the City Hall. Bailey raised the stars and stripes over the Mint; but the Mayor at first refused to strike his colors, and set out upon an elaborate course of letter-writing, which was of no consequence except as it furnished another instance of the fatuity that grasps at a shadow after the substance is gone.

A letter written by Lieutenant Perkins at the time gives a vivid description of this incident, which is interesting in that it exhibits the effect upon the first people of the South who realized the possibility of their being conquered. "Among the crowd were many women and children, and the women were shaking rebel flags and being rude and noisy. As we advanced, the mob followed us in a very excited state. They gave three cheers for Jeff Davis and Beauregard, and three groans for Lincoln. Then they began to throw things at us, and shout, 'Hang them! Hang them!' We reached the City Hall in safety, and there found the Mayor and Council. They seemed in a very solemn state of mind; though I must say, from what they said, they did not impress me as having much mind about anything. The Mayor said he had nothing to do with the city, as it was under martial law, and we were obliged to wait till General Lovell could arrive. In about half an hour this gentleman appeared. He was very pompous in his manner, and silly and airy in his remarks. He had about fifteen thousand troops under his command, and said he would 'never surrender,' but would withdraw his troops from the city as soon as possible, when the city would fall into the hands of the Mayor, and he could do as he pleased with it. The mob outside had by this

CAPTURE OF NEW ORLEANS.

OLD CITY HALL, NEW ORLEANS, WHERE THE SURRENDER OF THE CITY WAS DEMANDED.

time become perfectly infuriated. They kicked at the doors, and swore they would have us out and hang us. Every person about us who had any sense of responsibility was frightened for our safety. As soon as the mob found out that General Lovell was not going to surrender, they swore they would have us out any way; but Pierre Soule and some others went out and made speeches to them, and kept them on one side of the building, while we went out at the other end and were driven to the wharf in a close carriage. The Mayor told the Flag-officer this morning that the city was in the hands of the mob, and was at our mercy, and that he might blow it up or do with it as he chose."

On the night of the 24th, by order of the authorities in the city, the torch was applied to everything, except buildings, that could be of use to the victors. Fifteen thousand bales of cotton, heaps of coal and wood, dry-docks, a dozen steamboats and as many cotton-ships, and an unfinished ironclad ram were all burned. Barrels were rolled out and broken open, the levee ran with molasses, and the poor people carried away the sugar in their baskets and aprons. The Governor called upon the people of the State to burn their cotton, and two hundred and fifty thousand bales were destroyed.

Butler had witnessed the passage of the forts, and he now hurried over his troops and invested St. Philip on the land side, while Porter sent some of his mortar-boats to a bay in the rear of Fort Jackson, and in a few days both works were surrendered. Farragut sent two hundred and fifty marines into the city to take formal possession and guard the public buildings. Butler arrived there with his forces on the 1st of May, and it was then turned over to him, and it remained in Federal possession throughout the war. His administration of the captured city, from May to December, was the subject of much angry controversy; but no one denies that he reduced its turbulence to order, made it cleaner than it had ever been before, and averted a pestilence. He also caused provisions to be issued regularly to many of the needy inhabitants.

The most famous incident of his administration was what became known as "the woman order." Many of the women of New Orleans, even while they were living on food issued to them by the National commissary, took every possible pains to flaunt their disloyalty and to express contempt for the wearers of the blue uniform. If an officer entered a street car, all the women would immediately leave it. If a detachment of soldiers passed through a residence street, many windows were thrown open and "Dixie" or the "Bonny Blue Flag" was loudly played on the piano. If the women met an individual soldier on the side-walk, they drew their skirts closely around them and passed at its extreme edge. And all the while they took every opportunity to display small rebel flags on their bosoms and to proclaim loudly that their city was "captured but not conquered." These things were borne with patience; but when one woman, enraged at the imperturbable calmness of the city's captors, stepped up to two officers in the street and spat in their faces, General Butler judged that the time for putting a stop to such proceedings had come. Accordingly, he issued General Orders No. 28, which read thus:

"As the officers and soldiers of the United States have been subject to repeated insults from the women (calling themselves ladies) of New Orleans, in return for the most scrupulous non-interference and courtesy on our part, it is ordered that hereafter when any female shall, by word, gesture, or movement, insult or show contempt for any officer or soldier of the United States, she shall be regarded and held liable to be treated as a woman of the town plying her avocation."

This immediately produced two effects. It put an end to the annoyances, and it raised an uproar of denunciation based upon the assumption that the commanding officer had ordered his soldiers to insult and assault the ladies of New Orleans. Of course no such thing was intended, or could be implied from any proper construction of the words of the order; but in war, as in politics, it is sometimes considered good strategy to misrepresent an opponent. However honest any Confederate

MAJOR-GENERAL MANSFIELD LOVELL, C. S. A.

THOS. O. MOORE, GOVERNOR OF LOUISIANA.

ON BOARD OF A MORTAR SCHOONER.

citizen or editor may have been in his misconstruction of it, no soldier misunderstood it, and no incivility was offered to the women who were thus subdued by the wit and moral courage of perhaps the most successful man that ever undertook the task of ruling a turbulent city.

One other incident attested the firmness of General Butler's purpose, and assured the citizens of the presence of a power that was not to be trifled with. After Farragut had captured the city and raised the National colors over the Mint, four men were seen to ascend to the roof and tear down the flag, and it was only by a lucky accident that the gunners of the fleet were prevented from instantly discharging a broadside into the streets. The act was exploited in the New Orleans papers, which ostentatiously published the names of the four men and praised their gallantry. General Butler caused the leader of the four, a gambler, to be arrested and tried by a court-martial. He was sentenced to death, and in spite of every solicitation the General refused to pardon him. He was hanged in the presence of an immense crowd of citizens, the gallows being a beam run out from one of the windows of the highest story of the Mint building.

GENERAL BUTLER'S HEADQUARTERS, NEW ORLEANS.

At the first news of this achievement the people of the North hardly appreciated what had been accomplished; many of their newspapers told them that the fleet "had only run by the forts." But as they gradually learned the particulars, and saw that in fighting obstructions, fire-rafts, forts, rams, and fleet, and conquering them all, Farragut had done what neither Nelson nor any other great admiral had ever done before, they felt that the country had produced a worthy companion for the victor of Donelson, and was equal to all emergencies, afloat or ashore.

CAPTURE OF ISLAND No. 10, DURING A VIOLENT HURRICANE, APRIL 1, 1862.

CONSTRUCTING MILITARY ROAD THROUGH SWAMP.

CHAPTER XI.

THE CAMPAIGN OF SHILOH.

OPERATIONS AT ISLAND NO. 10 AND NEW MADRID—NAVAL BATTLE ON THE MISSISSIPPI—THE BLOODIEST BATTLE WEST OF THE ALLEGHANIES—COMMENCEMENT OF BATTLE OF SHILOH, SUNDAY, APRIL 6, 1862—TERRIBLE LOSSES ON BOTH SIDES—TRAGIC DEATH OF GENERAL ALBERT SIDNEY JOHNSTON—GENERALS WALLACE, HINDMAN, AND GLADDEN KILLED—GENERAL GRANT LEADING A REGIMENT—PUBLIC MISUNDERSTANDING REGARDING THIS GREAT BATTLE—INTERESTING INCIDENTS OF THE FIGHT—FATE OF CONFEDERACY DETERMINED AT SHILOH.

WHEN the first line that the Confederates had attempted to establish from the mountains to the Mississippi was broken by the battle of Mill Springs and the fall of Forts Henry and Donelson, their forces at Columbus were withdrawn down the river to the historic latitude of 36° 30′. Here the Mississippi makes a great sigmoid curve. In the first bend is Island No. 10 (the islands are numbered from the mouth of the Ohio southward); and at the second bend, on the Missouri side, is New Madrid. Both of these places were fortified, under the direction of Gen. Leonidas Polk, who had been Bishop of the Protestant Episcopal diocese of Louisiana for twenty years before the war, but entered the military service to give the Confederacy the benefit of his West Point education. A floating dock was brought up from New Orleans, converted into a floating battery, and anchored near the island; and there were also eight gunboats commanded by Commodore George N. Hollins. The works on the island were supplemented by batteries on the Tennessee shore, back of which were impassable swamps. Thus the Mississippi was sealed, and a position established for the left (or western extremity) of a new line of defence.

Early in March, 1862, a National army commanded by Gen. John Pope moved down the west bank of the Mississippi against the position at New Madrid. A reconnoissance in force demonstrated that the place could be carried by storm, but could not be held, since the Confederate gunboats were able (the river being then at high water) to enfilade both the works and the approaches. General Pope went into camp two miles from the river, and sent to Cairo for siege-guns, meanwhile sending three regiments and a battery, under Gen. J. B. Plummer, around to a point below New Madrid, where in the night they sunk trenches for the field-guns and placed sharp-shooters at the edge of the bank, and next day opened a troublesome fire on the passing gunboats and transports. Four guns were forwarded promptly from Cairo, being taken across the Mississippi and over a long stretch of swampy ground where a road had been hastily prepared for the purpose, and arriving at dusk on the 12th. That night Pope's forces crowded back the Confederate pickets, dug trenches, and placed the guns in position. The enemy's first intimation of what was going on was obtained from a bombardment that opened at daylight. The firing was kept up through the day, and some damage was inflicted on both sides; but the next night, in the midst of a heavy storm, New Madrid was evacuated. The National forces took possession, and immediately changed the positions of the guns so as to command the river. On the 16th five Confederate gunboats attacked these batteries; but after one boat had been sunk and some of the others damaged, they drew off. On the 16th and 17th the National fleet of gunboats, under Commodore Andrew H. Foote, engaged the batteries on Island No. 10, and a hundred heavy guns were in action at once. The ramparts in some places had been weakened by the wash of the river, and the great balls went right through them. But the artillerymen stood to their work manfully, many of them in water ankle deep; and though enormous shells exploded within the forts, and one gun burst and another was dismounted, the works were not reduced. A gun that burst in the fleet killed or wounded fourteen men. The attack was renewed from day to day, and one of the batteries was cleared of troops, but with no decisive effect.

At the suggestion of Gen. Schuyler Hamilton, a canal was cut across the peninsula formed by the bend of the river above New Madrid. This task was confided to a regiment of engineers commanded by Col. Josiah W. Bissell, and was completed in nineteen days. The course was somewhat tortuous, and the whole length of the canal was twelve miles. Half of the distance lay through a thick forest standing in deep water; but by an ingenious contrivance the trunks of the trees were sawed off four and a half feet below the surface, and a channel fifty feet wide and four feet deep was secured, through which transports could be passed.

On the night of April 4th the gunboat *Carondelet*, Commander Henry Walke, ran down past the batteries of Island No. 10, escaping serious damage, and in the night of the 6th the *Pittsburg* performed the same feat. With the help of these to silence the batteries on the opposite shore, Pope crossed in force on the 7th, and moved rapidly down the little peninsula. The

SURRENDER OF CONFEDERATE FORCES AFTER RETREAT FROM ISLAND No. 10.

greater part of the Confederate troops that had been holding the island now attempted to escape southward, but were caught between Pope's army and an impassable swamp, and surrendered. General Pope's captures in the entire campaign were three generals, two hundred and seventy-three officers, and six thousand seven hundred men, besides one hundred and fifty-eight guns, seven thousand muskets, one gunboat, a floating battery, six steamers, and a considerable quantity of stores.

On the very day of this bloodless victory, a little log church in southwestern Tennessee gave name to the bloodiest battle that has been fought west of the Alleghanies—Chickamauga being rather *in* the mountains. At Corinth, in northern Mississippi, the Memphis and Charleston Railroad crosses the Mobile and Ohio. This gave that point great strategic importance, and it was fortified accordingly and held by a large Confederate force, which was commanded by Gen. Albert Sidney Johnston (who must not be confounded with the Confederate Gen. Joseph E. Johnston). His lieutenants were Gens. G. T. Beauregard, Braxton Bragg, and William J. Hardee. General Grant, who had nearly forty thousand men under his command, and was about to be joined by Gen. Don Carlos Buell coming from Nashville with as many more, proposed to move against Corinth and capture the place.

REAR-ADMIRAL ANDREW H. FOOTE.

LIEUTENANT-GENERAL LEONIDAS POLK, C. S. A.

On Sunday, April 6th, Grant's main force was at Pittsburg Landing, on the west bank of the Tennessee, twenty miles north of Corinth. One division, under Gen. Lew Wallace, was at Crump's Landing, five miles farther north. The advance division of Buell's army had reached the river, opposite the landings, and the remainder was a march behind. For some days Johnston had been moving northward to attack Grant, and there had been skirmishing between the outposts. Early on the morning of the 6th he came within striking distance, and made a sudden and heavy attack. Grant's line was about two miles long, the left resting on Lick Creek, an impassable stream that flows into the Tennessee above Pittsburg Landing, and the right on Owl Creek, which flows in below. Gen. Benjamin M. Prentiss's division was on the left, Gen. John A. McClernand's in the centre, and Gen. William T. Sherman's on the right. Gen. Stephen A. Hurlbut's was in reserve on the left, and Gen. C. F. Smith's (now commanded by W. H. L. Wallace) on the right. There were no intrenchments. The ground was undulating, with patches of woods alternating with cleared fields, some of which were under cultivation and others abandoned and overgrown with bushes. A ridge, on which stood Shiloh church, formed an important key-point in Sherman's front.

General Grant, in his headquarters at Savannah, down the river, heard the firing while he was at breakfast, and hurried up to Pittsburg Landing. He had expected to be attacked, if at all, at Crump's Landing, and he now ordered Lew Wallace, with his five thousand men, to leave that place and march at once to the right of the line at Shiloh; but Wallace took the wrong road, and did not arrive till dark. Neither did Gen. William Nelson's advance division of General Buell's army cross the river till evening.

The attack began at daybreak, and was made with tremendous force and in full confidence of success. The nature of the ground made regularity of movement impossible, and the battle was rather a series of assaults by separate columns, now at one part of the line and now at another, which were kept up all day with wonderful persistence. Probably no army ever went into action with more perfect confidence in itself and its leaders than Johnston's. Beauregard had told them they should sleep that night in the camps of the enemy, and they did. He also told them that he would water his horse in the Tennessee, but he did not. The heaviest attacks fell upon Sherman and McClernand, whose men stood up to the work with unflinching courage and disputed every inch of ground. But they were driven back by overwhelming numbers, which the Confederate commanders poured upon them without the slightest regard to losses. The Sixth Mississippi regiment lost three hundred men out of its total of four hundred and twenty-five, and the Eighteenth Louisiana lost two hundred and seven. Sherman's men lost their camps in the morning, and retired upon one new line of defence after another, till they had been crowded back more than a mile; but all the while they clung to the road and bridge by which they were expecting Lew Wallace to come to their assistance. General Grant says of an open field on this part of the line, over which repeated charges were made, that it was "so covered with dead that it would have been possible to walk across the clearing in any direction, stepping on dead bodies, without a foot touching the ground. On our side National and Confederate troops were mingled together in about equal proportions; but on the remainder of the field nearly all were Confederates. On one part, which had evidently not been ploughed for several years, bushes had grown up, some to the height of eight or ten feet. Not one of these was left standing unpierced by bullets. The smaller ones were all cut down."

MAJOR-GENERAL SCHUYLER HAMILTON.

BRIGADIER-GENERAL GEORGE W. CULLUM.

Many of the troops were under fire for the first time; but Sherman's wonderful military genius largely made up for this deficiency. One bullet struck Sherman in the hand, another grazed his shoulder, another went through his hat, and several of his horses were killed. A bullet struck and shattered the scabbard of General Grant's sword. Gen. W. H. L. Wallace was mortally wounded. On the other side, Gens. Adley H. Gladden and Thomas C. Hindman were killed; at about half-past two o'clock General Johnston, placing himself at the head of a brigade that was reluctant to attempt another charge, was struck in the leg by a minie-ball. The wound need not have been mortal; but he would not leave the field, and after a time bled to death. The command then devolved upon General Beauregard.

In the afternoon a gap occurred between General Prentiss's division and the rest of the line, and the Confederates were prompt to take advantage of it. Rushing with a heavy force through this gap, and at the same time attacking his left, they doubled up both his flanks, and captured that general and two thousand two hundred of his men. On this part of the field the day was saved by Col. J. D. Webster, of General Grant's staff, who rapidly got twenty guns into position and checked the Confederate advance. They then attempted to come in on the extreme left, along the river, by crossing a ravine. But more guns were brought up, and placed on a ridge that commanded this ravine, and at the same time the gunboats *Tyler* and *Lexington* moved up to a point opposite and enfiladed it with their fire. The result to the Confederates was nothing but a useless display of valor and a heavy loss.

A FEDERAL GUNBOAT.

The uneven texture of Grant's army had been shown when two green colonels led their green regiments from the field at the first fire; and the

FINAL STAND OF THE ARMY OF GENERAL GRANT, APRIL 6, 1862, NEAR PITTSBURG LANDING.

stragglers and deserters, having no opportunity to scatter over the country, necessarily huddled themselves together under the bank of the river at the landing, where they presented a pitiful appearance. General Grant says there were nearly five thousand of them. There was about an equal number of deserters and stragglers from Johnston's army; but the nature of the ground was not such as to concentrate them where the eye could take them all in at one grand review. With the exception of the break when Prentiss was captured, Grant's line of battle was maintained all day, though it was steadily forced back and thirty guns were lost.

Beauregard discontinued the attack at nightfall, when his right was repelled at the ravine, intending to renew it and finish the victory in the morning. He knew that Buell was expected, but did not know that he was so near.

SHILOH LOG CHAPEL, WHERE THE BATTLE OF SHILOH COMMENCED, APRIL 6, 1862.

Lew Wallace was now in position on the right, and Nelson on the left, and all night long the boats were plying back and forth across the Tennessee, bringing over Buell's army. A fire in the woods, which sprang up about dusk, threatened to add to the horrors by roasting many of the wounded alive; but a merciful rain extinguished it, and the two armies lay out that night in the storm. A portion of the Confederates were sheltered by the captured tents, but on the other hand they were annoyed by the shells constantly thrown among them by the gunboats.

At daylight Grant assumed the offensive, the fresh troops on his right and left moving first to the attack. Beauregard now knew that Buell had arrived, and he must have known also that there could be but one result; yet he made a stubborn fight, mainly for the purpose of holding the road that ran by Shiloh church, by which alone he could conduct an orderly retreat. The complete upsetting of the Confederate plans, caused by the death of Johnston, the arrival of Buell, and Grant's promptness in assuming the offensive, is curiously suggested by a passage in the report of one of the Confederate brigade commanders: "I was ordered by General Ruggles to form on the extreme left, and rest my left on Owl Creek. While proceeding to execute this order, I was ordered to move by the rear of the main line to support the extreme right of General Hardee's line. Having taken my position to support General Hardee's right, I was again ordered by General Beauregard to advance and occupy the crest of a ridge in the edge of an old field. My line was just formed in this position when General Polk ordered me forward to support his line. When moving to the support of General Polk, an order reached me from General Beauregard to report to him with my command at his headquarters."

The fighting was of the same general description as on the previous day, except that the advantage was now with the National troops. Sherman was ordered to advance his command and recapture his camps. As these were about Shiloh church, and that was the point that Beauregard was most anxious to hold, the struggle there was intense and bloody. About the same time, early in the afternoon, Grant and Beauregard did the same thing: each led a charge by two regiments that had lost their commanders. Beauregard's charge was not successful; Grant's was, and the two regiments that he launched with a cheer against the Confederate line broke it, and began the rout.

Beauregard posted a rear guard in a strong position, and withdrew his army, leaving his dead on the field, while Grant captured about as many guns on the second day as he had lost on the first. There was no serious attempt at pursuit, owing mainly to the heavy rain and the condition of the roads. The losses on both sides had been enormous. On the National side the official figures are: 1,754 killed, 8,408 wounded, 2,885 missing; total, 13,047. On the Confederate side they are: 1,728 killed, 8,012 wounded, 957 missing; total, 10,699. General Grant says: "This estimate must be incorrect. We buried, by actual count, more of the enemy's dead in front of the divisions of McClernand and Sherman alone than are here reported, and four thousand was the estimate of the burial parties for the whole field." At all events, the loss was large enough to gratify the ill-wishers of the American people, who were looking on with grim satisfaction to see them destroy one another. The losses were the same, in round numbers, as at the historic battle of Blenheim, though the number of men engaged was fewer by one-fourth. If we should read in to-morrow's paper that by some disaster every man, woman, and child in the city of Concord, N. H., had been either killed or injured, and in the next day's paper that the same thing had happened in Montgomery, Ala., the loss of life and limb would only equal what took place on the mournful field of Shiloh.

GENERAL ALBERT SIDNEY JOHNSTON, C. S. A.

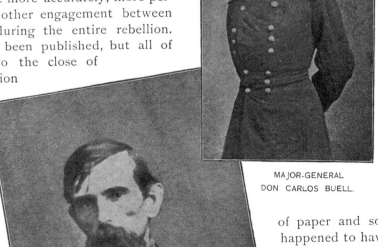

GENERAL BRAXTON BRAGG, C. S. A.

General Grant, in the first article that he ever wrote for publication, remarks that "the battle of Shiloh, or Pittsburg Landing, has been perhaps less understood, or, to state the case more accurately, more persistently misunderstood, than any other engagement between National and Confederate troops during the entire rebellion. Correct reports of the battle have been published, but all of these appeared long subsequent to the close of the rebellion, and after public opinion had been most erroneously formed." No battle is ever fought that it is not for somebody's interest to misrepresent. In the case of Shiloh there were peculiar and complicated reasons both for intentional misrepresentation and for innocent error. The plans of the commanders on both sides were to some extent thwarted and changed by unexpected events. One commander was killed on the first day, and his admirers naturally speculate upon the different results that might have been attained if he had lived. The ground was so broken as to divide the engagement practically into several separate actions, and what was true of one might not be true of another. The peculiarity of the position also brought together in one place, under the river-bank, all who from fright or demoralization fled to the rear of the National army, which produced upon those who saw them an effect altogether different from that of the usual retreating and straggling across the whole breadth of a battle line. Then there was the circumstance of Buell's army coming up at the end of the first day, and not coming up before that, which could hardly fail to give rise to somewhat of jealousy and recrimination. And finally this action encounters to an unusual extent that criticism which reads by the light of after-events, but forgets that this was wanting to the actors whom it criticises.

MAJOR-GENERAL LEW WALLACE.

MAJOR-GENERAL DON CARLOS BUELL.

The point on which popular opinion was perhaps most widely and persistently wrong was, that the defeat of the first day arose from the fact that Grant's army was completely surprised. Public opinion, throughout the war, was formed in advance of the official reports of generals in three ways. There were many press correspondents with every army, and the main purpose of most of them was to construct an interesting story and get it into print as soon as possible. The National Government adopted the wise policy of giving the armies in the field such mail facilities as would keep the soldiers in close touch with their homes, and they wrote millions of letters every year. All that a soldier needed was some scrap of paper and some sort of pen or pencil. If he happened to have no postage stamp, he had only to mark his missive "Soldier's letter," and it would be carried in the mails to its destination, and the postage collected on delivery. After a battle every surviving soldier was especially anxious to let his family know that he had escaped any casualty, and he naturally filled up his letter with such particulars as had most impressed him in that small part of the field that he had seen, and sometimes with such exaggerated accounts as in the first excitement had reached him from other parts. Finally, the journalists were not few who assumed to be accomplished strategists, and talked learnedly in their editorial columns of the errors of generals and the way that battles should have been fought. And some of them had political reasons for writing up certain generals and writing down certain others.

A good instance of innocent misapprehension is probably furnished in what Lieutenant-Colonel Graves, of the Twelfth Michigan, wrote: "On Saturday General Prentiss's division was reviewed. After the review Major Powell, of the Twenty-fifth Missouri, came to me and said he saw Butternuts [Confederate soldiers] looking through the underbrush at the parade—about a dozen. Upon the representation of Major Powell and myself, General Prentiss ordered out one company of the Twelfth Michigan as an advance picket. About 8.30 o'clock Captain Johnson reported from the front that he could see long lines of campfires, hear bugle sounds and drums, which I reported to General Prentiss, and he remarked that the company would be taken if left there; that it was merely a reconnoissance of the enemy in force, and ordered the company in. About ten o'clock I went with Captain Johnson to the tent of General Prentiss, and the captain told him what he saw. The general remarked that we need not be alarmed, that everything was all right. To me it did not appear all right. Major Powell, myself, and several other officers went to the headquarters of Colonel Peabody, commanding our brigade, and related to him what had transpired. He ordered out two companies from the Twelfth Michigan and two from the Twenty-fifth Missouri, under command of Major Powell. About three o'clock in the morning the advance of the enemy came up with this body of men, who fought them till daylight, gradually falling back till they met their regiments, which had advanced about fifty rods. There the regiments met the enemy, and fought till overpowered, when we fell back to our color line and re-formed. General Prentiss was so loath to believe that the enemy was in force, that our division was not organized for defence, but each regiment acted upon its own hook, so far as I was able to observe. The point I wish to make is this: that, had it not been for these four companies which were sent out by Colonel Peabody, our whole division would have been taken in their tents, and the day would have been lost. I shall always think that Colonel Peabody saved the battle of Shiloh."

MAJOR-GENERAL
WILLIAM J. HARDEE, C. S. A.

MAJOR-GENERAL S. A. HURLBUT.

MAJOR-GENERAL B. M. PRENTISS.

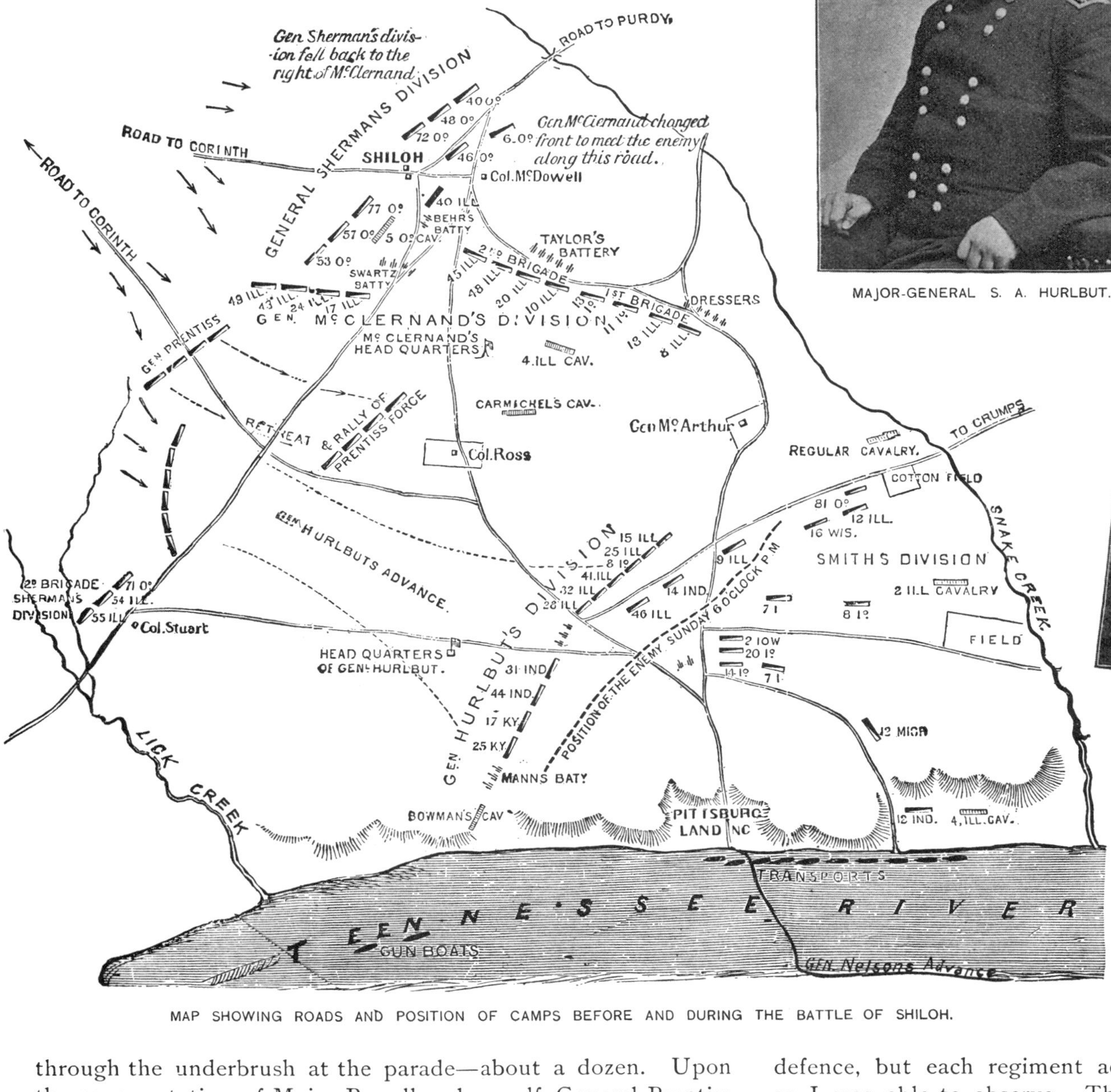

MAP SHOWING ROADS AND POSITION OF CAMPS BEFORE AND DURING THE BATTLE OF SHILOH.

ADVANCE OF THE FEDERAL TROOPS ON CORINTH—GENERAL HURLBUT'S DIVISION FORCING THEIR WAY THROUGH THE MUD.

Such was the testimony and opinion, undoubtedly honest, of an officer of a green regiment which there for the first time participated in a battle. The truth was, the generals of the National forces were not ignorant of the near approach of the enemy. Reconnoissances, especially in Sherman's front, had shown that. They were only waiting for all their forces to come up to make an attack themselves, and when Buell arrived they did make that attack and were successful. General Prentiss's division, so far from being unorganized, kept its lines, received the shock of battle, and stood up manfully to the work before it until the divisions on both sides of it drew back, leaving its flanks exposed, when the Confederates poured through the gaps, struck it on both flanks at once, and captured a large part of it. On the ground along its line and in its front more men were struck down in an hour than on any other spot of equal extent, in the same time, in the whole war.

GENERAL ULYSSES S. GRANT.

The Confederates were successful on the first day, not because of any surprise, but simply because they had the greater number of men and persistently hurled them, regardless of cost, against the National lines. There was also one other reason, which would not have existed later in the war. After the first year no army would occupy any position on the field without intrenching. The soldiers on both sides learned how, in a little while, to throw up a simple breastwork of earth that would stop a large proportion of the bullets that an enemy might fire at them. Grant's army at Shiloh had its flanks well protected by impassable streams, and if it had had a simple breastwork along its front, such as could have been constructed in an hour, the first day's disaster might have been averted. As it was, the men fought in the open field, with no protection but the occasional shelter of a tree trunk, and at one point a slightly sunken road. The habit of Grant's mind was such that he always thought of his army as assuming the offensive and hence having no use for intrenchments, and his green regiments did not as yet appreciate the power of the spade. Shiloh was a severe lesson to them all.

Some of the most interesting incidents of the battle are given by Col. Douglas Putnam, Jr., of the Ninety-second Ohio Infantry, in a paper read before the Ohio Commandery of the Loyal Legion: "With the consent of General Grant, I was permitted to accompany him to the field as a volunteer aid. As we approached Crump's Landing, where the division of Gen. Lew Wallace was stationed, the boat was rounded in and the engines stopped. General Wallace, then standing on the bank, said, 'My division is in line, waiting for orders.' Grant's reply was, that as soon as he got to Pittsburg Landing and learned where the attack was, he would send him orders. . . . After getting a horse, I started with Rawlins to find General Grant; and to my inquiry as to where we would likely find him, Rawlins's reply, characteristic of the man, was, 'We'll find him where the firing is heaviest.' As we proceeded, we met the increasing signs of battle, while the dropping of the bullets about us, on the leaves, led me in my inexperience to ask if it were not raining, to which Rawlins tersely said, 'Those are bullets, Douglas.' When, on meeting a horse through which a cannon-ball had gone, walking along with protruding bowels, I asked permission to shoot him and end his misery, Rawlins said, 'He belongs to the quartermaster's department; better let them attend to it.' We soon found General Grant. He was sending his aids in different directions, as occasion made it necessary, and he himself visited his division commanders one by one. He wore his full uniform, with the major-general's buff sash, which made him very conspicuous both to our own men and to those of the enemy. Lieut.-Col. J. B. McPherson, acting chief of staff, remonstrated with him, as did also Rawlins, for so unnecessarily exposing himself, as he went just in the rear of our line of battle; but he said he wanted to see and know what was going on. About eleven o'clock he met General Sherman on what was called Sherman's drill-ground, near the old peach orchard. The meeting was attended with but few words. Sherman's stock had become pulled around until the part that should have been in front rested under one of his ears, while his whole appearance indicated hard and earnest work. The bullets were plenteous here. Sherman told Grant how many horses he had had killed

A FIELD HOSPITAL.

under him, showing him also the marks of bullets in his clothing. When Grant left Sherman, I think I was the only aid with him. Riding toward the right, the General saw a body of troops coming up from the direction of Crump's Landing, and exclaimed with great delight and satisfaction, 'Now we are all right, all right—there's Wallace.' He was of course mistaken, as the troops he saw were not those he so earnestly looked for, and of whose assistance he was beginning to feel the need. About two o'clock, at one point were gathered General Grant and several of his staff. The group consisted of Grant, McPherson, Rawlins, Webster, and others. This evidently drew the attention of the enemy, and they received rather more than a due share of the fire. Colonel McPherson's horse having been shot under him, I gave him mine, and under directions went to the river on foot. The space under the bank was literally packed by thousands, I suppose, of men who had from inexperience and fright 'lost their grip,' or were both mentally and physically, as we say, let down —however, only temporarily. To them it seemed that the day was lost, that the deluge was upon them. The Tennessee River in front, swamps to the right and swamps to the left, they could go no farther, and there lay down and waited. I remember well seeing a mounted officer, carrying a United States flag, riding back and forth on top of the bank, pleading and entreating in this wise: 'Men, for God's sake, for your country's sake, for your own sake, come up here, form a line, and make one more stand.' The appeal fell on listless ears. No one seemed to respond, and the only reply I heard was some one saying, 'That man talks well, don't he?' But eighteen hours afterward these same men had come to themselves, were refreshed by meeting other troops, and assured that all was not lost, that there was something still left to fight for, and helped also by the magic touch of the elbow, they did valiant service. A group of officers was gathered around General Grant about dusk, at a smouldering fire of hay just on the top of the grade. The rain was falling, atmosphere murky, and ground covered with mud and water. Colonel McPherson rode up, and Grant said, 'Well, Mac, how is it?' He gave him a report of the condition as it seemed to him, which was, in short, that at least one-third of his army was *hors de combat*, and the rest much disheartened. To this the General made no reply, and McPherson continued, 'Well, General Grant, under this condition of affairs, what do you propose to do, sir? Shall I make preparations for retreat?' The reply came quick and short: 'Retreat? No! I propose to attack at daylight, and whip them.'"

MAJOR-GENERAL JONES M. WITHERS, C. S. A.

MAJOR-GENERAL THOMAS L. CRITTENDEN.

MAJOR-GENERAL JOHN A. McCLERNAND.

MAJOR-GENERAL GEORGE B. CRITTENDEN, C. S. A.

The same writer tells of a conversation that he held with General Beauregard some years after the war. "To my query that it had always been a mystery why he stopped the battle when he did Sunday night, when the advantage, on the whole, seemed to be with him, and when he had an hour or more of daylight, General Beauregard replied that there were two reasons: first, his men were, as he put it, 'out of hand,' had been fighting since early morn, were worn out, and also demoralized by the flush of victory in gathering the stores and sutlers' supplies found in our camps. As one man said, 'You fellows went to war with cheese, pigs' feet, dates, pickles—things we rebs had forgotten the sight of.' 'In the second place,' he said, 'I thought I had General Grant just where I wanted him, and could finish him up in the morning.'"

After the battle, General Halleck took command in person, and proceeded to lay siege to Corinth, to capture it by regular approaches. Both he and Beauregard were reinforced, till each had about one hundred thousand men. Halleck gradually closed in about the place, till in the night of May 29th Beauregard evacuated it, and on the morning of the 30th Sherman's soldiers entered the town.

Some military critics hold that the fate of the Confederacy was determined on the field of Shiloh. They point out the fact that after that battle there was nothing to prevent the National armies at the West from going all the way to the Gulf, or—as they ultimately did—to the sea. In homely phrase, the back door of the Confederacy was broken down, and, however stubbornly the front door in Virginia might be defended, it was only a question of time when some great army, coming in by the rear, should cut off the supplies of the troops that held Richmond, and compel their surrender. Those who are disposed to give history a romantic turn narrow it down to the death of General Johnston, declaring that in his fall the possibility of Southern independence was lost, and if he had lived the result would have been reversed. General Grant appears to dispose of their theory when he points out the fact that Johnston was killed while leading a forlorn hope, and remarks that there is no victory for anybody till the battle is ended, and the battle of Shiloh was not ended till the close of the second day. But, indeed, there is no reason why the fatal moment should not be carried back to the time when the line of defence from the mountains to the Mississippi was broken through at Mill Spring and Fort Donelson, or even to the time when the Confederates, because of Kentucky's refusal to leave the Union, were prevented from establishing their frontier at the Ohio. The reason why progress in conquering the Confederacy was more rapid at the West than at the East is not to be found so much in any difference in men as in topography. At the West, the armies moving southward followed the courses of the rivers, and their opponents were obliged to maintain artificial lines of defence; but the Eastern armies were called upon to cross the streams and attack natural lines of defence.

Back of all this, in the logic of the struggle, is the fact that no defensive attitude can be maintained permanently. The belligerent that cannot prevent his own territory from becoming the seat of war must ultimately surrender his cause, no matter how valiant his individual soldiers may be, or how costly he may make it for the invader; or, to state it affirmatively, a belligerent that can carry the war into the enemy's country, and keep it there, will ultimately succeed. In most wars, the side on whose soil the battles were fought has been the losing side; and this is an important lesson to bear in mind when it becomes necessary to determine the great moral question of responsibility for prolonging a hopeless contest.

CHAPTER XII.

MINOR ENGAGEMENTS OF THE FIRST YEAR.

LARGE NUMBER OF BATTLES FOUGHT DURING THE WAR—DISASTER AT BALL'S BLUFF ON THE POTOMAC—SMALL ENGAGEMENTS AT EDWARDS FERRY, VA.—BATTLES AT FALLING WATERS AND BUNKER HILL, VA.—BATTLE AT HARPER'S FERRY—GALLANT BAYONET CHARGE AT DRANESVILLE, VA.—OPERATIONS IN WEST VIRGINIA UNDER GENERAL McCLELLAN—BATTLES AT ROMNEY AND BARBOURSVILLE—EFFORTS TO INDUCE KENTUCKY TO SECEDE—CAMP WILD CAT—ENGAGEMENTS AT HODGESVILLE AND MUMFORDSVILLE AND SACRAMENTO—REASONS WHY MISSOURI DID NOT SECEDE—ENGAGEMENTS AT CHARLESTON, LEXINGTON, AND OTHER PLACES IN THAT STATE—A BRILLIANT CHARGE BY GENERAL FRÉMONT'S BODY GUARD UNDER ZAGONYI—INDIVIDUAL HEROISM—BATTLE OF BELMONT—VAST EXTENT OF TERRITORY COVERED BY WAR OPERATIONS.

THE enormous number of engagements in the civil war, the extent of country over which they were spread, and the magnitude of many of them, have sunk into comparative insignificance many that otherwise would have become historic. The action at Lexington, Mass., in 1775, was nothing whatever in comparison with any one of the several actions at Lexington, Mo., in 1861; yet every schoolboy is familiarized with the one, and many well-read people have scarcely heard of the other. The casualties in the battle of Harlem Heights, N. Y., numbered almost exactly the same as those in the battle of Bolivar Heights, Va.; but no historian of the Revolution would fail to give a full account of the former, while one might read a very fair history of the civil war and find no mention whatever of the latter. In the writing of any history that is not a mere chronicle, it is necessary to observe proportion and perspective; but we may turn aside a little from the main course of our narrative, to recall some of the forgotten actions, in obscure hamlets and at the crossings of sylvan streams, where for a few men and those who were dear to them the call of duty was as stern and the realities of war as relentless as for the thousands at Gettysburg or Chickamauga.

In the State of Virginia, the most disastrous of these minor engagements in 1861 was at Ball's Bluff, on the Potomac, about thirty-five miles above Washington. It has been known also as the battle of Edwards Ferry, Harrison's Island, and Leesburg. At this point there is an island in the river, and opposite, on the Virginia side, the bank rises in a bold bluff seventy feet high. A division of National troops, commanded by Gen. Charles P. Stone, was on the Maryland side, observing the crossings of the river in the vicinity. A Confederate force of unknown strength was known to be at Leesburg, about five miles from the river. McCall's division was at Dranesville, farther toward Washington, reconnoitring and endeavoring to draw out the enemy. At a suggestion of General McClellan to General Stone, that some demonstration on his part might assist McCall, General Stone began a movement that developed into a battle. On the 21st of October he ordered a portion of his command to cross at the island and at Conrad's Ferry, just above. They were Massachusetts troops under Col. Charles Devens, the New York Forty-second (Tammany) regiment, Col. Edward D. Baker's Seventy-first Pennsylvania (called the California regiment), and a Rhode Island battery, in all about two thousand men. The means of crossing—two or three boats—were very inadequate for an advance, and nothing at all for a retreat. Several hours were spent in getting one scow from the canal into the river, and the whole movement was so slow that the Confederates had ample opportunity to learn exactly what was going on and prepare to meet the movement. The battery was dragged up the bluff with great labor. At the top the troops found themselves in an open field of about eight acres, surrounded by woods. Colonel Baker was made commander of all the forces that crossed.

DELIVERING DAILY PAPERS.

The enemy soon appeared, and before the battery had fired more than half a dozen rounds the Confederate sharp-shooters, posted on a hill at the left, within easy range, disabled so many of the gunners that the pieces became useless. Then there was an attack by a heavy force of infantry in front, which, firing from the woods, cut down Baker's men with comparative safety. The National troops stood their ground for two hours and returned the fire as effectively as they could; but the enemy seemed to increase in number, and grew constantly bolder. About six o'clock, wrote Capt. Francis G. Young, "a rebel officer, riding a white horse, came out of the woods and beckoned to us to come forward.

BATTERY WAITING FOR ORDERS.

BREVET MAJOR-GENERAL CHARLES DEVENS.

COLONEL EDWARD D. BAKER.

Colonel Baker thought it was General Johnston, and that the enemy would meet us in open fight. Part of our column charged, Baker cheering us on, when a tremendous onset was made by the rebels. One man rode forward, presented a revolver at Baker, and fired all its charges at him. Our gallant leader fell, and at the same moment all our lines were driven back by the overwhelming force opposed to them. But Captain Beiral, with his company, fought his way back to Colonel Baker's body, rescued it, brought it along to me, and then a general retreat commenced. It was *sauve qui peut*. I got the colonel's body to the island before the worst of the rout, and then, looking to the Virginia shore, saw such a spectacle as no tongue can describe. Our entire forces were retreating—tumbling, rolling, leaping down the steep heights; the enemy following them murdering and taking prisoners. Colonel Devens left his command and swam the river on horseback. The one boat in the Virginia channel was speedily filled and sunk. A thousand men thronged the farther bank. Muskets, coats, and everything were thrown aside, and all were desperately trying to escape. Hundreds plunged into the rapid current, and the shrieks of the drowning added to the horror of sounds and sights. The enemy kept up their fire from the cliff above. A captain of the Fifteenth Massachusetts at one moment charged gallantly up the hill, leading two companies, who still had their arms, against the pursuing foe. A moment later, and the same officer, perceiving the hopelessness of the situation, waved a white handkerchief and surrendered the main body of his command."

Gen. Edward W. Hinks (at that time colonel of the Nineteenth Massachusetts Regiment), who arrived and took command just after the action, wrote in his report: "The means of transportation, for advance in support or for a retreat, were criminally deficient—especially when we consider the facility for creating proper means for such purposes at our disposal. The place for landing on the Virginia shore was most unfortunately selected, being at a point where the shore rose with great abruptness and was entirely studded with trees, being perfectly impassable to artillery or infantry in line. The entire island was also commanded by the enemy's artillery and rifles. Within half a mile, upon either side of the points selected, a landing could have been effected where we could have been placed upon equal terms with the enemy, if it was necessary to effect a landing from the island."

The losses in this action were about a hundred and fifty killed, about two hundred and fifty wounded, and about five hundred captured. Colonel Baker was a lawyer by profession, had been a friend of Lincoln's in Springfield, Ill., had lived in California, then removed to Oregon, and was elected United States senator from that State just before the war began. He was greatly beloved as a man; but though he was brave and patriotic, and had commanded a brigade in the Mexican war, it was evident, from his conduct of the Ball's Bluff affair, that he had little military skill.

Among the other minor engagements was one at Edwards Ferry, Va., June 17th, in which three hundred Pennsylvanians, under Captain Gardner, were attacked by a Confederate force that tried to take possession of the ferry. After a fight of three hours the assailants were driven off with a loss of about thirty men. Captain Gardner lost four.

On July 2d there was an engagement of six hours' duration at Falling Waters, Va., between the brigades of Abercrombie, Thomas, and Negley, and a Confederate force under General Jackson. It was a stubborn fight. The Confederates, who had four regiments of infantry and one of cavalry, with four guns, at length retreated slowly, having lost about ninety men. The National loss was thirteen.

At Bunker Hill, near Martinsburg, on July 15th, General Patterson's division, being on the march, was attacked by a body of about six hundred cavalry, led by Colonel Stuart. When the cavalry charged, the National infantry opened their lines and disclosed a battery, which poured rapid discharges of shells and grape shot into the Confederates, and put them to rout. The Federal cavalry then came up and pursued the fugitives two miles.

In October the Thirteenth Massachusetts Regiment crossed the Potomac at Harper's Ferry, to seize a large quantity of wheat that was stored there for the Confederate Government. A day or two later they were reënforced by three companies of the Third Wisconsin Regiment, four of the Twenty-eighth Pennsylvania, and sections of a New York and a Rhode Island battery. The guns were placed to command approaches of the town, pickets were thrown out, and the wheat was removed. On the 16th the pickets on Bolivar Heights, west of the town, were driven in, and this was followed by an attack from a Confederate force, consisting of three regiments of infantry, one of cavalry, and seven pieces of artillery. Gen. John W. Geary, commanding the National forces, placed one company for the defence of the fords of the Shenandoah, and with the remaining troops met the attack. Three successive charges by the cavalry were repelled; then a rifled gun was brought across the river and directed its fire upon the Confederate battery; and at the same time Geary advanced his right flank, turned the enemy's left, and gained a portion of Bolivar Heights. He then ordered a general forward movement, gained the entire Heights, and drove the enemy across the valley toward Halltown. From lack of cavalry he was unable to pursue; but he planted guns on Bolivar Heights, and soon silenced the Confederate guns on London Heights. Before recrossing the Potomac the troops burned the iron foundry at Shenandoah City. In this action the National loss was four killed, seven wounded, and two captured. The Confederate loss was not ascertained, but it was supposed to be somewhat over a hundred men, besides one gun and a large quantity of ammunition. A member of the Massachusetts regiment, in giving an account of this action, wrote: "There were many side scenes. Stimpson had a hand-to-hand fight with one of the cavalry, whom he bayoneted, illustrating the bayonet drill in which the company had been exercised. Corporal Marshall was chased by a mounted officer while he was assisting one of the wounded Wisconsin boys off. He turned and shot

AN INCIDENT OF CAMP LIFE.—CARD-PLAYING.

BATTLE OF MUMFORDSVILLE, KENTUCKY, SEPTEMBER 14, 1862.

his pursuer through the breast. The officer proved to be Colonel Ashby, commander of the rebels, which accounted for the lull in the battle. We have since learned that he was not killed."

On December 20th Gen. E. O. C. Ord, commanding a brigade, moved westward along the chain-bridge road, toward Dranesville, for the purpose of making a reconnoissance and gathering forage. Near Dranesville, when returning, he was attacked by a Confederate force consisting of five regiments of infantry and one of cavalry, with a battery. The attack came from the south and struck his right flank. Changing front so as to face the enemy, he found advantageous ground for receiving battle, and placed his artillery so as to enfilade the Centreville road on which the enemy's battery was posted. Leaving his cavalry in the shelter of a wooded hill, he got his infantry well in hand and moved steadily forward on the enemy. His guns were handled with skill, and soon exploded a Confederate caisson and drove off the battery. Then he made a bayonet charge, before which the Confederate infantry fled, leaving on the field their dead and wounded, and a large quantity of equipments. His loss was seven killed and sixty wounded. The Confederate loss was about a hundred.

That portion of Virginia west of the Alleghanies (now West Virginia) never was essentially a slaveholding region. The number of slaves held there was very small, as it always must be in a mountainous country; and the interests of the people, with their iron mines, their coal mines, and their forests of valuable timber, and their streams flowing into the Ohio, were allied much more closely with those of the free States than with those of the tide-water portion of their own State. When, therefore, at the beginning of the war, before the people of Virginia had voted on the question of adopting or rejecting the ordinance of secession as passed by their convention, troops from the cotton States were poured into that State to secure it for the Confederacy, they found no such welcome west of the mountains as east of them; and the task of driving them out from the valleys of the Kanawha and the Monongahela was easy in comparison with the work that lay before the National armies on the Potomac and the James. Major-Gen. George B. McClellan, then in his thirty-fifth year, crossed the Ohio with a small army in May, and won several victories that for the time cleared West Virginia of Confederate troops, gained him a vote of thanks in Congress, and made for him a sudden reputation, which resulted in his being called to the head of the army after the disaster at Bull Run. Some of the battles in West Virginia, including Philippi, Cheat River, and Rich Mountain, have already been described. An account of other minor engagements in that State is given in this chapter.

FEDERAL TROOPS FORAGING.

There were several small actions at Romney, in Virginia, the most considerable of which took place on October 26th. General Kelly, with twenty-five hundred men, marched on that place from the west, while Col. Thomas Johns, with seven hundred, approached it from the north. Five miles from Romney, Kelly drove in the Confederate outposts, and nearer the town he met the enemy drawn up in a commanding position, with a rifled twelve-pounder on a hill. They also had intrenchments commanding the bridge. After some artillery firing, Kelly's cavalry forded the river, while his infantry charged across the bridge, whereupon the Confederates retreated precipitately toward Winchester. Kelly captured four hundred prisoners, two hundred horses, three wagon-loads of new rifles, and a large lot of camp equipage. The losses in killed and wounded were small. In this action a Captain Butterfield, of an Ohio regiment, was mounted on an old team horse, which became unmanageable and persisted in getting in front of the field gun that had just been brought up. This embarrassed the gunners, who were ready and anxious to make a telling shot, and finally the captain shouted: "Never mind the old horse, boys. Blaze away!" The shot was then made, which drove off a Confederate battery; and a few minutes later, when the charge was ordered, the old horse, with his tail scorched, wheeled into line and participated in it.

At the same time when General McClellan was operating against the Confederate forces in the northern part of West Virginia, Gen. Jacob D. Cox commanded an expedition that marched from Guyandotte into the valley of the Great Kanawha. His first action was at Barboursville, which he captured. At Scarytown, on the river, a detachment of his Ohio troops, commanded by Colonel Lowe, was defeated by a Confederate force under Captain Patton, and lost nearly sixty men. Cox then marched on Charleston, which was held by a force under General Wise. But Wise retreated, crossed Gauley River and burned the bridge, and continued his flight to Lewisburg. Here he was superseded by General Floyd, who brought reinforcements. Floyd attacked the Seventh Ohio Regiment at Cross Lanes, and defeated it, inflicting a loss of about two hundred men. He then advanced to Carnifex Ferry, endeavoring to flank Cox's force, when General Rosecrans, with ten thousand men, came down from the northern part of the State. Floyd had a strong position on Gauley River, and Rosecrans sent forward a force to reconnoitre. The commander of this, General Benham, pushed it too boldly, and it developed into an engagement (September

10th), wherein he lost about two hundred men, including Colonel Lowe and other valuable officers. Rosecrans made preparations for giving battle in earnest next day; but in the night Floyd retreated, leaving a large portion of his baggage, and took a position thirty miles distant. Soon afterward General Lee arrived with another force and took command of all the Confederate troops, numbering now about twenty thousand, and then in turn Rosecrans retreated. On the way, Lee had made a reconnoissance of a position held by General Reynolds at Cheat Mountain (September 12th), and in the consequent skirmishing he lost about a hundred men, including Col. John A. Washington, of his staff, who was killed. Reynolds's loss was about the same, but Lee found his position too strong to be taken. Early in November, Lee was called to Eastern Virginia, and Rosecrans then planned an attack on Floyd; but it miscarried through failure of the flank movement, which was intrusted to General Benham. But Benham pursued the enemy for fifty miles, defeated the rear guard of cavalry, and killed its leader. On December 12th, General Milroy, who had succeeded General Reynolds, advanced against the Confederates at Buffalo Mountain; but his attack was badly managed, and failed. He was then attacked, in turn, but the enemy had no better success. Three or four hundred men were disabled in these engagements. On the last day of the year Milroy sent eight hundred men of the Twenty-fifth Ohio Regiment, under Major Webster, against a Confederate camp at Huntersville. They drove away the Confederates, burned six buildings filled with provisions, and returned without loss.

MAJOR-GENERAL JACOB D. COX.

BREVET MAJOR-GENERAL EDWARD W. HINKS.

MAJOR-GENERAL WILLIAM S. ROSECRANS.

Through the natural impulses of a large majority of her people, and their material interests, aided by these military operations, small as they were in detail, West Virginia was by this time secured to the Union, and would probably have remained in it even if the war had terminated otherwise.

There never was any serious danger that Kentucky would secede, though her governor refused troops to the National Government and pretended to assume a position of neutrality. Such a position being essentially impossible, such of the young men of that State as believed in the institution of slavery went largely into the Confederate army, while a greater number entered the National service and were among its best soldiers. The Confederate Government was very loath to give up Kentucky, admitted a delegation of Kentucky secessionists to seats in its Congress, and made several attempts to invade the State and occupy it by armed force. The more important actions that were fought there are narrated elsewhere. A few of the minor ones must be mentioned here.

To protect the loyal mountaineers in the eastern part of the State, a fortified camp, called Camp Wild Cat, was established on the road leading to Cumberland Gap. It was at the top of a high cliff, overlooking the road, and was commanded by a heavily-wooded hill a few hundred yards distant. The force there was commanded by Gen. Albin Schoepff. A force of over seven thousand Confederates, commanded by General Zollicoffer, marched upon this camp and attacked it on the same day that the battle of Ball's Bluff was fought, October 21st. The camp had been held by but one Kentucky regiment; but on the approach of the enemy it was reinforced by the Fourteenth and Seventeenth Ohio, the Thirty-third Indiana, and Stannard's battery. After a fight with a battalion of Kentucky cavalry, the Confederate infantry charged up the hill and were met by a withering fire, which drove them back. They advanced again, getting within a few yards of the log breastwork, placed their caps on their bayonets and shouted that they were Union men. This gave them a chance to fire a volley at close range; but it was answered so immediately and so effectively that they broke and fled down the hill. Then the artillery was brought into play and hastened their flight, besides thwarting an attack that had been made by a detachment on the flank. In the afternoon the attempt was repeated, by two detachments directed simultaneously against the flanks of the position; but it was defeated in much the same way that the morning attack had been. Zollicoffer then drew off his forces, and that night their campfires could be seen far down the valley. The National loss was about thirty men, that of the Confederates was estimated at nearly three hundred.

Two days later there were sharp actions at West Liberty and

Hodgesville. A regiment of infantry and a company of cavalry, with one gun, marched thirty-five miles between half-past two and half-past nine P. M., in constant rain, making several fords, one of which, across the Licking, was waist deep. The object was to drive the Confederates out of West Liberty and take possession of the town. In this they were successful, with but one man wounded. The Confederates lost twenty, and half a dozen Union men who had been held as prisoners were released. The greatest benefit resulting from the action was the confidence that it gave to the Unionists in that region. One correspondent wrote: "The people had been taught that the Union soldiers would be guilty of most awful atrocities. Several women made their appearance on Thursday, trembling with cold and fear, and said that they had remained in the woods all night after the fight. The poor creatures had been told that the Abolition troops rejoiced to kill Southern babies, and were in the habit of carrying little children about on their bayonets in the towns which they took; and this was actually believed." A detachment of the Sixth Indiana Regiment made a sudden attack on a Confederate camp near Hodgesville, and after a short, sharp fight drove off the enemy, killing or wounding eight of them, and captured many horses and wagons and a large quantity of powder.

Near Munfordville, on December 17th, a portion of the Thirty-second Indiana Regiment, under Lieutenant-Colonel Trebra, was attacked by two regiments of infantry, a regiment of cavalry, and a battery. They maintained a spirited defence until they were reinforced, and then continued the fight till it ended in the retreat of the enemy. General Buell said in his report: "The attack of the enemy was mainly with his cavalry and artillery. Our troops fought as skirmishers, rallying rapidly into squares when charged by the cavalry—sometimes even defending themselves singly and killing their assailants with the bayonet." The National loss was eight killed and ten wounded; the Confederate, thirty-three killed (including Colonel Terry, commanding) and fifty wounded. A Confederate account said: "All in all, this is one of the most desperate fights of the war. It was hand to hand from first to last. No men could have fought more desperately than the enemy. The Rangers were equally reckless. Colonel Terry, always in the front, discovered a nest of five of the enemy. He leaped in his saddle, waved his hat, and said, 'Come on, boys! Here's another bird's nest.' He fired and killed two of them. The other three fired at him simultaneously. One shot killed his charger; another shot killed him. He fell headlong from his horse without a moan or a groan. At the same time, Paulding Anderson and Dr. Cowan rode up and despatched the remaining three of the enemy. When Colonel Terry's fall was announced it at once prostrated his men with grief. The fight ended here." This action is also known by the name of Rowlett's Station and Woodsonville.

On December 28th a small detachment of cavalry, led by Major Murray, left camp near Calhoun, Ky., for a scout across Green River. Near Sacramento they were surprised and attacked by seven hundred cavalry under Colonel Forrest. They sustained an almost hand-to-hand fight for half an hour, and then, as their ammunition was exhausted, retreated. It is impossible to reconcile the accounts of the losses; but it is certain that Capt. A. G. Bacon was killed on the National side, and Lieutenant-Colonel Meriwether of the Confederates. This closed the first year's fighting in Kentucky.

In Missouri there were special and strong reasons against secession. Her slave population was comparatively small, and her soil and climate were suited to crops that do not require negro labor. She was farthest north of any slave State; and if she had joined the Confederacy, and it had established itself, she would have been bordered on

REVIEW OF CONFEDERATE TROOPS EN ROUTE TO THE FRONT, PASSING PULASKI MONUMENT, SAVANNAH, GA.

SIEGE OF LEXINGTON, MISSOURI.

three sides by foreign territory, with nothing but a surveyed line for the boundary on two of those sides. Moreover, there was a large German element in her population, industrious, opposed to slavery, loving the Union, and belonging, to a considerable extent, to the Republican party. In the presidential election of 1860, 26,430 Republican votes were cast in slave States (all in border States), and of these 17,028 were cast in Missouri. Delaware gave the next highest number—3,815. Of 148,490 Democratic votes cast in Missouri, but 31,317 were for Breckinridge, the extreme pro-slavery candidate. Nevertheless, the secessionists made a strong effort to get Missouri out of the Union. The methods pursued have been described in a previous chapter, together with the results of the first fighting, and the defeat and death of General Lyon in the battle of Wilson's Creek.

COLONEL JAMES A. MULLIGAN.

A Confederate force—or rather the materials for a force, for the men were poorly equipped and hardly drilled at all—commanded by Colonel Hunter, was gathered at Charleston, Mo., in August, encamped about the court-house; and on the 19th Colonel Dougherty, of the Twenty-second Illinois Regiment, set out to capture it. He arrived at Camp Lyon in the evening with three hundred men, learned of the position of the enemy, and said to Captain Abbott, who had made the reconnoissance: "We are going to take Charleston to-night. You stay here and engage the enemy till we come back." Then to his men: "Battalion, right face forward, march!" As they neared the town, double quick was ordered, and the two companies in the advance proceeded rapidly, but the following ones became somehow separated. These two companies drove in the pickets, followed them sharply, and charged into the town, scattering the small detachment of raw cavalry. The second in command then asked of Colonel Dougherty what should be done next. "Take the court-house, or bust," he answered; and at once that building was attacked. The Confederates fired from the windows; but the assailants concentrated a destructive fire upon it, and then rushed in at the doors. Some escaped through the windows, some were shot down while attempting to do so, and many were captured. Later in the day a company of Illinois cavalry pursued the retreating Confederates, and captured forty more, with many horses. In this engagement Lieutenant-Colonel Ransom had a personal encounter with a Confederate officer, who rode up to him and called out: "What do you mean? You are killing our own men."—"I know what I am doing," answered Ransom. "Who are you?"—"I am for Jeff Davis," said the stranger. "Then you are the man I am after," said Ransom, and they drew their pistols. The Confederate fired first, and wounded Ransom in the arm, who then fired and killed his antagonist. The National loss

BURYING THE DEAD.

was one killed and four wounded. The Confederate loss was reported at forty killed; number of wounded, unknown.

Late in August, when it was learned that a movement against Lexington, on Missouri River, was about to be made by a strong Confederate force under General Price, measures were taken to reinforce the small garrison and prevent the place from falling into the hands of the enemy. The Twenty-third Illinois Regiment, Col. James A. Mulligan, which was called "the Irish Brigade," was ordered thither from Jefferson City, and other reinforcements were promised. Mulligan, with his command, set out at once, marched nine days, foraging on the country, and on reaching Lexington found there a regiment of cavalry and one of home guards. The next day the Thirteenth Missouri Regiment, retreating from Warrensburg, joined them. This gave Mulligan a total force of about two thousand eight hundred men, who had forty rounds of ammunition, and he had seven field-guns and a small quantity of provisions. He took possession of the hill east of the town, on which stood the Masonic College, and proceeded to fortify. His lines enclosed about eighteen acres, and he had put but half a day's work on them when, in the evening of September 11th, the enemy appeared. In the morning of the 12th the fighting began, when a part of Mulligan's men drove back the enemy's advance and burned a bridge, which compelled them to make a detour and approach the place by another road. Again Mulligan sent out a detachment to check them while his remaining force worked on the intrenchments, and there was brisk fighting in the cemetery at the edge of the town. In the afternoon there was a lively artillery duel, and the National forces held their own, dismounting a Confederate gun, exploding a caisson, and causing the enemy to withdraw at dusk to a camp two miles away. The next day the garrison fitted up a small foundry, in which they cast shot for their cannon, obtained powder and made cartridges, and continued the work on the intrenchments. The great want was provisions and water. In the next five days the Confederates were heavily reinforced, while the little garrison looked in vain for the promised help.

On the 18th a determined attack in force was made. Colonel Mulligan wrote: "They came as one dark moving mass, their guns beaming in the sun, their banners waving, and their drums beating. Everywhere, as far as we could see, were men, men, men, approaching grandly. Our spies had brought intelligence and had all agreed that it was the intention of the enemy to make a grand rush, overwhelm us, and bury us in the trenches of Lexington." Mulligan's men sustained the shock bravely, and the enemy met such a deadly fire that they could not get to the works. But meanwhile they had interposed a force between the works and the river, shutting off the supply of water, and they kept up a heavy bombardment with sixteen pieces of artillery. They also took possession of a large house outside the lines which was used as a hospital, and filled it with sharpshooters. Mulligan ordered two companies—one of home guards and one from the Fourteenth Missouri—to drive them out, but they refused to undertake so hazardous a task. He then sent a company from his Irish regiment, who rushed gallantly across the intervening space, burst in the doors, took possession of the house, and (under an impression that the laws of war had been violated in thus using a hospital for sharp-shooters) killed every Confederate soldier caught inside. Two hours later the Confederates in turn drove them out and again occupied the building. Firing was kept up through the 19th; and on the 20th the besiegers obtained bales of hemp, wet them, and rolling them along before them as a movable breastwork, were enabled to approach the intrenchments. Bullets would not go through these bales, and red-hot shot would not set them on fire. Yet the fight still continued for some hours, until the ammunition of the garrison was all but exhausted. For five days they had had no water except as they could catch rain when it fell, the provisions were eaten up, and there was no sign of the promised reinforcements. There was nothing to do but surrender. Mulligan had lost one hundred and fifty men killed or wounded; the Confederate report acknowledged a loss of one hundred, which probably was far short of the truth. A correspondent who was present wrote: "Hundreds of the men who fought on the Confederate side were attached to no command. They came in when they pleased, fought or not as they pleased, left when ready, and if killed were buried on the spot—were missed from no muster-roll, and hence would not be reckoned in the aggregate loss. The Confederates vary in their statements. One said they lost sixty killed; another said their loss was at least equal to that of the Federals; while still another admitted to me that the taking of the works cost them a thousand men. I saw one case that shows the Confederate style of fighting. An old Texan, dressed in buckskin and armed with a long rifle, used to go up to the works every morning about seven o'clock, carrying his dinner in a tin pail. Taking a good position, he banged away at the Federals till noon, then rested an hour and ate his dinner, after which he resumed operations till six P. M., when he returned home to supper and a night's sleep." The privates of Mulligan's command were paroled, and the officers held as prisoners.

In October the National troops stationed at Pilot Knob, Mo., commanded by Col. J. B. Plummer, were ordered to march on Fredericktown and attack a Confederate force there, two thousand strong, commanded by Gen. Jeff. Thompson. They arrived at that place in the evening of the 21st, and found that it had just been evacuated. They consisted of Indiana, Illinois, and Wisconsin troops, with cavalry and a battery, and numbered about three thousand five hundred. Three thousand more, commanded by Col. W. P. Carlin, marched from Cape Girardeau and joined them at Fredericktown. About half of the entire force was then sent in pursuit of the enemy, who was found just south of the town. An engagement was at once begun with artillery, and then the Seventeenth Illinois Regiment charged upon the Confederate battery and captured one gun. Then followed a running fight that lasted four hours, the Confederates stopping frequently to make a temporary stand and fire a few rounds from their battery. As these positions were successively charged or flanked, and attacked with artillery and musketry, they retired from them. At five o'clock in the afternoon the pursuit was discontinued, and the National forces returned to Fredericktown. They had lost seven men killed and sixty wounded. They had captured two field-pieces and taken sixty prisoners, and the next day they buried a hundred and sixty Confederate dead. Among the enemy's killed was Colonel Lowe, second in command.

A few days later there was a brilliant affair at Springfield, not far from the scene of General Lyon's defeat and death in August. There was a small, select cavalry organization known as General Frémont's body-guard, commanded by Major Charles Zagonyi, a Hungarian, who had seen service in Europe. On the 24th Zagonyi received orders to take a part of his command, and Major White's battalion of prairie scouts, and march on Springfield, fifty miles distant, with all possible haste. It was supposed that the Confederate troops there numbered four hundred. The order was obeyed with alacrity, and early the next day he neared the town. Here he captured half a dozen Confederate soldiers of a foraging party, and from them and certain Unionists among the inhabitants, he learned that the enemy in the town numbered two thousand instead of four hundred. Undaunted by this, he resolved to push forward. Some of the foraging party who escaped carried the news of his approach, and the Confederates made quick dispositions to receive him. Finding a regiment drawn up beside the road, he avoided it by a detour and came in on another road, but here also the enemy were ready for him. Placing his own command in the advance, with himself at the head, he prepared to charge straight into the midst of the enemy. For some unknown reason, White's command, instead of following directly, counter-marched to the left, and Zagonyi with his one hundred and sixty men went in alone. They began with a trot, and soon increased the pace to a gallop, unmindful of the fire of skirmishers in the woods, which emptied several of their saddles. The enemy, infantry and cavalry, was drawn up in the form of a hollow square, in an open field. Zagonyi's band rode down a lane, jumped a brook, threw down a fence, and then charged right across the field into the midst of their foes, spreading out fan-like as they neared them, and using their pistols and sabres vigorously. The Confederate cavalry gave way and scattered almost at once; the infantry stood a little longer, and then retreated. Major White with his command came up just in time to strike them in the flank, completing the rout. An eye-witness wrote: "Some fled wildly toward the town, pursued by the insatiate guards, who, overtaking them, either cut them down with their sabres or levelled them with shots from their pistols. Some were even chased through the streets of the city and then killed in hand-to-hand encounters with their pursuers." Zagonyi raised the National flag on the court-house, detailed a guard to attend to his wounded, and then retired to Bolivar. His own account of the fight, given in Mrs. Frémont's "Story of the Guard," is quaint and interesting.

FORTIFICATIONS AND INTRENCHMENTS AT PILOT KNOB, MO.

"About four o'clock I arrived on the highest point on the Ozark Mountains. Not seeing any sign of the enemy, I halted my command, made them known that the enemy instead of four hundred is nineteen hundred. But I promised them victory if they will be what I thought and expected them to be. If any of them too much fatigued from the fifty-six miles, or sick, or unwell, to step forward; but nobody was worn out. (Instead of worn out, it is true that every eye was a fist big.) I made them known that this day I want to fight the first and the last hard battle, so that if they meet us again they shall know with who they have to do and remember the Body-Guard. And ordered quick march. Besides, I tell them, whatever we meet, to keep together and look after me; would I fall, not to give up, but to avenge mine death. To leave every ceremonious cuts away in the battlefield and use only right cut and thrust. Being young, I thought they might be confused in the different cuts, and the Hungarian hussars say, 'Never defend yourselves—better make

CHARGE OF FRÉMONT'S BODY-GUARD UNDER MAJOR ZAGONYI, NEAR SPRINGFIELD, MO.

your enemy defend himself and you go in.' I just mention them that you know very well that I promised you that I will lead you shortly to show that we are not a fancy and only guard-doing-duty soldiers, but fighting men. My despatch meant what I will do. In the hour I get the news my mind was settled. I say, Thank God, if I am to fight, it is not four hundred! but nineteen hundred! I halt my men again and say,

PURSUIT OF THE ENEMY.

'Soldiers! When I was to recruit you, I told you you was not parade soldiers, but for war. The enemy is more than we. The enemy is two thousand, and we are but one hundred and fifty. It is possible no man will come back. No man will go that thinks the enemy too many. He can ride back. (I see by the glimpsing of their eye they was mad to be chanced a coward.) The Guard that follow me will take for battle-cry, "Frémont and the Union," and—CHARGE—!' Running down the lane between the cross-fire, the First Company followed close, but the rest stopped for a couple seconds. I had not wondered if none had come—young soldiers and such a tremendous fire, bullets coming like a rain.

MAJOR CHARLES ZAGONYI.

"As I arrived down on the creek I said aloud, 'If I could send somebody back I would give my life for it. We are lost here if they don't follow.' My Adjutant, Majthenyi, hearing, feared that he will be sent back, jumped down from his horse and busy himself opening the fence. I expected to find the enemy on the other end of Springfield, but, unexpectedly coming out of the woods to an open place, I was fired on in front of mine command. Halted for a minute, seeing that, or a bold forward march under a cross-fire, or a doubtful retreat with losing most of my men, I took the first and commanded 'March!' Under a heavy cross-fire (in trot), down the little hill in the lane—two hundred yards—to a creek, where I ordered the fence to be opened—marched in my command—ordered them to form, and with the war-cry of 'Frémont and the Union,' we made the attack. The First Company, forty-seven strong, against five or six hundred infantry, and the rest against the cavalry, was made so successfully, that, in three minutes, the cavalry run in every direction, and the infantry retreated in the thick wood, and their cavalry in every direction. The infantry we were not able to follow in the woods, so that we turned against the running cavalry. With those we had in different places, and in differing numbers, attacked and dispersed—not only in one place, but our men were so much emboldened, that twenty or thirty attacked twenty, thirty times their numbers, and these single-handed attacks, fighting here and there on their own hook, did us more harm than their grand first attack. By them we lost our prisoners. Single-handed they fought bravely, specially one—a lieutenant—who, in a narrow lane, wanted to cut himself through about sixty of us, running in that direction. But he was not able to go very far. Firing two or three times, he ran against me, and put his revolver on my side, but, through the movement of the horse, the shot passed behind me. He was a perfect target—first cut down and after shot. He was a brave man; for that reason I felt some pity to kill him. We went to their encampment, but the ground was deserted, and we returned to the Court-house, raised the company-flag, liberated prisoners, and collected my forces together—which numbered not more, including myself, than seventy men on horseback. The rest—without horses, or wounded, and about thirty who had dispersed in pursuit of the enemy—I could not gather up; and it was midnight before they reached me—and some of them next day. I never was sick in my life, Madame, till what time I find myself leaving Springfield, in the dark, with only sixty-nine men and officers—I was the seventy. I was perfectly sick and disheartened, so I could hardly sit in the saddle, to think of so dear a victory. But it ended so that fifteen is dead—two died after—ten prisoners, who was released, and of the wounded, not one will lose a finger. In all seventeen lost."

"The bugler (Frenchman) I ordered him two three time to put his sword away and take the bugle in his hand, that I shall be able to use him. Hardly I took my eyes down, next minute I seen him, sword in the hand, all bloody; and this he done two or three times. Finally, the mouth of the bugle being shot away, the bugler had excuse for gratifying himself in use of the sword. One had a beautiful wound through the nose. 'My boy,' I told him, 'I would give any thing for that wound.' After twenty-four hours it was beautiful—just the mark enough to show a bullet has passed through; but, poor fellow, he cannot even show it. It healed up so as to leave no mark at all. He had also five on his leg and shoulder, and the fifth wound he only found after six days; he could not move easy, for that reason he was late to find there was two wounds in the legs."

Early in November, General Grant was ordered to make demonstrations on both sides of the Mississippi near Columbus, to prevent the Confederates from sending reinforcements to General Price, in Southern Missouri, and also to prevent them from interfering with the movements of certain detachments of National troops. On the 6th he left Cairo with three thousand men, on five steamers, convoyed by two gunboats, and passed down the river to the vicinity of Columbus. To attack that place would have been hopeless, as it was well fortified and strongly garrisoned. He landed his troops on the Missouri side on the 7th, and put them in motion toward Belmont, opposite Columbus, deploying skirmishers and looking for the enemy. They had not gone far before the enemy was encountered, and then it became a fight through the woods from tree to tree. After two or three miles of this, they arrived at a fortified camp surrounded with abatis. Grant's men charged at once, succeeded in making their way through the obstructions, and soon captured the camp with the artillery and some prisoners. But most of the Confederates escaped and crossed the river in their own boats, or took shelter under the bank. The usual result of capturing a camp was soon seen. The victors laid down their arms and devoted themselves to plundering, while some amused themselves with the captured guns, firing at empty steamers. Meanwhile the defeated men under the bank regained confidence and rallied, and two steamers filled with Confederate soldiers were sent over from Columbus; while the guns there, commanding the western bank, were trained and fired upon the camp. To stop the plundering and bring his men to order, Grant had the camp set on fire and then ordered a retreat. The men formed rapidly, with deployed skirmishers, and retired slowly to the boats, Grant himself being the last one to go on board. Some of the wounded were taken on the transports, others were left on the field. The National loss was 485; the Confederate loss was 642, including 175 carried off as prisoners. The Unionists also spiked four guns and brought off two. Both sides claimed this action as a victory—Grant, because he had accomplished the object for which he set out, preventing reinforcements from being sent to Price; the Confederates, because they were left in possession of the field. But it was generally discussed as a disaster to the National arms. There were many interesting incidents. One man who had both legs shot off was found in the woods singing "The Star Spangled Banner." Another, who was mortally wounded, had propped himself up against a tree and thought to take a smoke. He was found dead with his pipe in one hand, his knife in the other, and the tobacco on his breast. A Confederate correspondent told this story: "When the two columns came face to face, Colonel Walker's regiment was immediately opposed to the Seventh Iowa, and David Vollmer, drawing the attention of a comrade to the stars and stripes that floated over the enemy, avowed his intention of capturing the colors or dying in the attempt. The charge was made, and as the two columns came within a few yards of each other, Vollmer and a young man named Lynch both made a rush for the colors; but Vollmer's bayonet first pierced the breast of the color-bearer, and, grasping the flag, he waved it over his head in triumph. At this moment he and Lynch were both shot dead. Captain Armstrong stepped forth to capture the colors, when he also fell, grasping the flagstaff." Another correspondent wrote: "The Seventh Iowa suffered more severely than any other regiment. It fought continually against fearful odds. Ever pushing onward through the timber, on their hands and knees, they crawled with their standard waving over them until they reached the cornfield on the left of the enemy's encampment, where their cannon was planted, and drove them from their guns, leaving them still unmanned, knowing that other forces were following them up. Their course was still onward until they entered on the camp-ground of the foe and tore down the flag."

Besides those here described, there were many smaller engagements in Missouri—at Piketon, Lancaster, Salem, Black Walnut Creek, Milford, Hudson, and other places. There were also encounters in Florida, in New Mexico, and in Texas; none of them being important, but all together showing that the struggle begun this year had spread over a vast territory and that a long and bloody war was before the people of our country.

ABATIS.

"THE PICKET'S OFF DUTY FOREVER."

WAR SONGS.

IT is probable that war songs are the oldest human compositions. In every nation they have sprung into existence at the very dawning of national life. The first Grecian poems of which we have any record are war songs, chanted to inspire or maintain warlike enthusiasm. Not only did they sing martial melodies as they attacked their enemies, but when the conflict was over, and the victory won, they also sang triumphal odes as they returned to camp. Martial odes that were sung in Gaul by the conquering legions of Julius Cæsar have been handed down to the present time. The student of the history and the literature of Spain finds many traces of the war songs that the all-conquering Romans sang as they marched over the mountains or across the valleys of that then dependent nationality. And long before the time of Cæsar, Servius Tullius ordered that two whole centuriæ should consist of trumpeters, horn-blowers, etc., to sound the charge. In these and subsequent ages, war songs were sung in chorus by a whole army in advancing to the attack. If further proof of the antiquity of military music were needed, a conclusive one is to be found in 2 Chronicles, xx. 21, where it is said that when Jehoshaphat went to battle against the hosts of Ammon "he placed a choir of singers in front of his army."

Wonderful indeed is the war song when studied as to its influence in early times on history. By the power of arms, by the spirit of conquest, did nations arise and continue to exist. The warrior made the nation, and the poet sang and immortalized the warrior's fame; and thus it came to pass that great honor was bestowed upon the poets. Among old Arab tribes, fires were lighted and great rejoicings made by their warriors when a poet had manifested himself among them, for in his songs they anticipated their own glory. In many ancient countries, the bards that sang of battles were regarded as really inspired, and their poetic productions were considered as the language of the gods. Centuries passed before that admiration bestowed upon the singer of war songs was impaired. The ancient literature of many European countries presents numerous indications that the warrior-poets were treated with great consideration; were forgiven by their sovereigns for serious offences on condition that they write a new war song, and were paid what would seem at this day enormous prices for their compositions. It is related that on one occasion King Athelstane, of the Anglo-Saxons, paid a poet sixteen ounces of pure gold for a laudatory song. When the greater value of gold in that distant age is considered, it is probable that no living poet is better paid for his productions than was this old singer whose ballads breathed of bloodshed and slaughter.

The marvellous influence of war songs over the ancient Norsemen is difficult to understand. They were aroused to a high degree of military enthusiasm, almost to madness, by the mere words of certain songs. That it was this influence which frequently drove them onward to great deeds, appears in every chapter of their life history. It was the courage and frenzy aroused by Teutonic war songs that led to the destruction of Rome, and shattered the civilization of southern Europe.

That the influence of the war song over the minds and the hearts of men did not terminate with the long ago past, is apparent to every student of modern history. Garibaldi's warlike Hymn of the Italians, the stirring "Marseillaise" of the light-hearted French, the vigorous "Britannia" of the sturdy English, have inspired determination and aroused courage on many a bloody battlefield. How frequently during our own civil war was retreat checked, and the tide of battle turned, by the singing of "We'll Rally round the Flag, Boys," started at the opportune moment by some brave soldier with a vigorous and melodious voice. It has been said that the Portuguese soldiers in Ceylon, at the siege of Colombo, when pressed with misery and the pangs of hunger, during their marches, derived not only consolation but also encouragement from singing stanzas of their national song.

It is a singular fact that no great national hymn, and no war song that arouses and cheers, was ever written by a distinguished poet. It would seem that a National Hymn is the sort of material that cannot be made to order. Not one of the best-known songs of our own civil war—in the North or in the South—was written by an eminent poet. Five of the greatest American poets were living during the great conflict, and four of them gave expression to its military ardor, determinate zeal, or pathos, but none of them so sung as to touch the popular heart; that is to say, so as to secure the attention of those who do not read poetry. The same is true of the composers of the national anthems and great martial ballads of nearly every other country. The thunder roar of the "Marseillaise," before which all the other military songs of France are dull and weak, was produced by De l'Isle, who lives in the memory of his countrymen and of the world for this alone. The noble measures of "God Save the King" are not the work of any one of the great British poets, but were probably written by Henry Carey; but this is in dispute, and innumerable Englishmen sing the anthem without even attempting to learn the name of the composer.

The Prussian National Anthem was not written by a Goethe, a Schiller, or even a Köner. The name of the writer, Schneckenburger, would not be found in books of reference had he not written "The Watch on the Rhine." The favorite national song of the Italians, known as the "Garibaldian Hymn," is the composition of Mercantini, of whom little is known.

Our own country is especially fortunate in the quality of its great national songs. "The Star Spangled Banner" breathes the loftiest and purest patriotism. The English National Hymn is but a prayer for blessings on the head of the king—the ruler. The "Marseillaise" is calculated to arouse only the spirit of slaughter and bloodshed. Truer than any of these to pure, lofty, and patriotic zeal is our own "Star Spangled Banner."

From our Civil War we have received at least two war songs which, simply as such, are fit to rank with the best of any country—"John Brown's Body" and "Marching through Georgia." The greatest of the Southern war lyrics—"My Maryland"—is equal to these as a powerful lyric. It is said that fully two thousand poems and songs pertaining to the war, both North and South, were written during the first year of this conflict. But most of them are now wholly unknown, except to the special student. Perhaps a score of compositions, the result of the poetic outburst inspired by the Civil War, possess such merit that they will survive through centuries as part of the literary heritage of the nation. Of such we give in this collection about twenty that seem to us the best and most popular.

NORTHERN SONGS.

TRAMP, TRAMP, TRAMP, THE BOYS ARE MARCHING.

THIS is one of the numerous war songs written by Mr. George F. Root. Among his others are "Just before the Battle, Mother," and the "Battle-Cry of Freedom." It is difficult to say which of these three was the most popular. There was a touch of pathos in "Just before the Battle, Mother," which made the words impressive and thrilling to the hearts of men away from home and fireside. Many a brave soldier considered death itself preferable to captivity and incarceration in prison pens. How sad, then, must have been the lot of the soldiers who sat in prison cells and heard the "tramp, tramp, tramp," of the marching boys! Mr. Root was the composer as well as the author of the three great songs mentioned above.

In the prison cell I sit,
Thinking, mother dear, of you,
And our bright and happy home so far away;
And the tears they fill my eyes,
Spite of all that I can do,
Though I try to cheer my comrades and be gay.

CHORUS:

Tramp, tramp, tramp, the boys are marching;
Cheer up, comrades, they will come,
And beneath the starry flag
We shall breathe the air again
Of the free-land in our own beloved home.

In the battle front we stood
When their fiercest charge they made,
And they swept us off a hundred men or more;
But before we reached their lines
They were beaten back dismayed,
And we heard the cry of vict'ry o'er and o'er.

So within the prison cell
We are waiting for the day
That shall come to open wide the iron door;
And the hollow eye grows bright,
And the poor heart almost gay,
As we think of seeing home and friends once more.

ALL QUIET ALONG THE POTOMAC TO-NIGHT.

One cool September morning in 1861, a young woman living in Goshen, Orange County, N. Y., read the familiar announcement from the seat of war near Washington, "All quiet on the Potomac," to which was added in smaller type, "A picket shot." These simple words were the inspiration of a celebrated war song, which is as popular now as when it first appeared. This song was first published in *Harper's Weekly* for November 30, 1861, and it has had many claimants; but after careful investigation, there appears to be no reason whatever for disputing the claim of Mrs. Ethel Lynn Beers. She died in Orange, N. J., October 10, 1879.

"All quiet along the Potomac," they say,
"Except now and then a stray picket
Is shot, as he walks on his beat to and fro,
By a rifleman hid in the thicket.
'Tis nothing—a private or two now and then
Will not count in the news of the battle;
Not an officer lost—only one of the men,
Moaning out, all alone, the death-rattle."

All quiet along the Potomac to-night,
Where the soldiers lie peacefully dreaming;
Their tents in the rays of the clear autumn moon,
Or the light of the watch-fire, are gleaming.
A tremulous sigh of the gentle night-wind
Through the forest leaves softly is creeping;
While stars up above, with their glittering eyes,
Keep guard, for the army is sleeping.

There's only the sound of the lone sentry's tread,
As he tramps from the rock to the fountain,
And thinks of the two in the low trundle-bed
Far away in the cot on the mountain.
His musket falls slack; his face, dark and grim,
Grows gentle with memories tender,
As he mutters a prayer for the children asleep,
For their mother—may Heaven defend her!

The moon seems to shine just as brightly as then,
That night, when the love yet unspoken
Leaped up to his lips—when low-murmured vows
Were pledged to be ever unbroken.
Then drawing his sleeve roughly over his eyes,
He dashes off tears that are welling,
And gathers his gun closer up to its place,
As if to keep down the heart-swelling.

He passes the fountain, the blasted pine-tree—
The footstep is lagging and weary;
Yet onward he goes, through the broad belt of light,
Toward the shade of the forest so dreary.
Hark! was it the night-wind that rustled the leaves?
Was it moonlight so wondrously flashing?
It looked like a rifle . . . "Ha! Mary, good-by!"
The red life-blood is ebbing and plashing.

All quiet along the Potomac to-night;
No sound save the rush of the river;
While soft falls the dew on the face of the dead—
The picket's off duty forever!

THE BATTLE HYMN OF THE REPUBLIC.

PERHAPS the "Battle Hymn of the Republic," by Mrs. Julia Ward Howe, may be considered the most lofty in sentiment and the most elevated in style of the martial songs of American patriotism. During the close of the year 1861, Mrs. Howe with a party of friends visited Washington. While there she attended a review of the Union troops on the Virginia side of the Potomac and not far from the city. During her stay in camp she witnessed a sudden and unexpected attack of the enemy. Thus she had a glimpse of genuine warfare. On the ride back to the city the party sang a number of war songs, including "John Brown's Body." One of the party remarked that the tune was a grand one, and altogether superior to the words of the song. Mrs. Howe responded to the effect that she would endeavor to write other words that might be sung to this stirring melody. That night, while she was lying in a dark room, line after line and verse after verse of the "Battle Hymn of the Republic" was composed. In this way every verse of the song was carefully thought out. Then, springing from the bed, she found a pen and piece of paper and wrote out the words of this rousing patriotic hymn. It was often sung in the course of the war and under a great variety of circumstances.

Mine eyes have seen the glory of the coming of the Lord ;
He is trampling out the vintage where the grapes of wrath are stored ;
He has loosed the fateful lightning of His terrible swift sword ;
His truth is marching on.

I have seen Him in the watch-fires of a hundred circling camps ;
They have builded Him an altar in the evening dews and damps ;
I have read His righteous sentence in the dim and flaring lamps ;
His day is marching on.

I have read a fiery gospel, writ in burnished rows of steel :
"As ye deal with my contemners, so with you my grace shall deal ;"
Let the hero, born of woman, crush the serpent with his heel,
Since God is marching on.

He has sounded forth the trumpet that shall never call retreat ;
He is sifting out the hearts of men before His judgment seat ;
Oh, be swift, my soul, to answer Him ! be jubilant, my feet !
Our God is marching on.

In the beauty of the lilies Christ was born across the sea,
With a glory in His bosom that transfigures you and me ;
As He died to make men holy, let us die to make men free,
While God is marching on.

WHEN THIS CRUEL WAR IS OVER.

WITH the English soldiers a popular song in war times is the well known "Annie Laurie." It is said that during the Crimean War this sentimental ditty was sung by the English forces more frequently than any other melody. Several songs of similar sentimentality were famous on both sides during the civil war. The boys in gray sang "Lorena" at the very beginning of the war, and never stopped till the last musket was stacked, and the last campfire cold. The boys in blue sang "Mother, I've Come Home to Die," "Just before the Battle, Mother," "When this Cruel War is Over," and other songs of sentiment and affection. "When this Cruel War is Over" was written by Charles C. Sawyer, of Brooklyn, N. Y., and was published in the autumn of 1861. More than one million copies of the song have been sold. Some of the other compositions by Mr. Sawyer are "Swinging in the Lane" and "Peeping through the Bars."

Dearest love, do you remember
When we last did meet,
How you told me that you loved me,
Kneeling at my feet ?
Oh, how proud you stood before me,
In your suit of blue,
When you vowed to me and country
Ever to be true !
Weeping, sad and lonely,
Hopes and fears, how vain ;
Yet praying
When this cruel war is over,
Praying that we meet again.

When the summer breeze is sighing
Mournfully along,
Or when autumn leaves are falling,
Sadly breathes the song.
Oft in dreams I see you lying
On the battle-plain,
Lonely, wounded, even dying,
Calling, but in vain.

If, amid the din of battle,
Nobly you should fall,
Far away from those who love you,
None to hear you call,
Who would whisper words of comfort ?
Who would soothe your pain ?
Ah, the many cruel fancies
Ever in my brain !

But our country called you, darling,
Angels cheer your way !
While our nation's sons are fighting,
We can only pray.
Nobly strike for God and liberty,
Let all nations see
How we love the starry banner,
Emblem of the free !

WE ARE COMING, FATHER ABRAHAM.

In the dark days of 1862 President Lincoln issued a proclamation asking for three hundred thousand volunteers to fill the stricken ranks of the army, and to make the cry of "On to Richmond" an accomplished fact. Immediately after this call, Mr. James Sloane Gibbons, a native of Wilmington, Del., living in New York City, wrote:

"We are coming, Father Abraham, three hundred thousand more."

This must have contributed largely to the accomplishment of the military uprising which it relates. The stanzas were first published anonymously in the New York *Evening Post* of July 16, 1862. Owing to this fact, perhaps, its authorship was at first attributed to William C. Bryant. Mr. Gibbons joined the abolition movement when only twenty years of age, and was for a time one of the editors of the *Anti-Slavery Standard*. When the Emancipation Proclamation was issued, he illuminated his residence in New York City. A short time afterward, during the draft riots, he was mobbed, and only by the assistance of friends was he able to save his life by escaping over the roofs of adjoining houses to another street, where a friend had a carriage waiting for him. He died October 17, 1892.

We are coming, Father Abraham, three hundred thousand more,
From Mississippi's winding stream and from New England's shore;
We leave our ploughs and workshops, our wives and children dear,
With hearts too full for utterance, with but a silent tear;
We dare not look behind us, but steadfastly before:
We are coming, Father Abraham, three hundred thousand more!

If you look across the hill-tops that meet the northern sky,
Long moving lines of rising dust your vision may descry;
And now the wind, an instant, tears the cloudy veil aside,
And floats aloft our spangled flag in glory and in pride;
And bayonets in the sunlight gleam, and bands brave music pour:
We are coming, Father Abraham, three hundred thousand more!

If you look all up our valleys where the growing harvests shine,
You may see our sturdy farmer boys fast falling into line;
And children from their mother's knees are pulling at the weeds,
And learning how to reap and sow, against their country's needs;
And a farewell group stands weeping at every cottage door:
We are coming, Father Abraham, three hundred thousand more!

You have called us, and we're coming, by Richmond's bloody tide,
To lay us down, for Freedom's sake, our brothers' bones beside;
Or from foul treason's savage grasp to wrench the murderous blade,
And in the face of foreign foes its fragments to parade.
Six hundred thousand loyal men and true have gone before:
We are coming, Father Abraham, three hundred thousand more!

MARCHING THROUGH GEORGIA.

ALL the great songs of the civil war, with one exception, were written during the first year of the conflict. This exception is "Marching through Georgia." It was written to commemorate one of the most remarkable campaigns of the war. Now that the war has been over for nearly thirty years, and the old soldier has no military duty more serious than fighting his battles o'er again, "Marching through Georgia" has become the song dearest to his heart. At the annual encampments of the Grand Army of the Republic, and at numerous meetings of the members of the Grand Army posts, the writer has heard this sung more frequently than any other. The words were composed by Mr. Henry C. Work, author of many well-known songs. Among the other best known of his patriotic lyrics are "Grafted into the Army" and "Kingdom Come." Mr. Work was born in Middletown, Conn., October 1, 1832. When he was very young his father removed to Illinois. He was an inventor as well as a song writer, and among his successful inventions are a knitting machine, a walking doll, and a rotary engine. He died in Hartford, June 8, 1884.

Bring me the good old bugle, boys! we'll sing another song—
Sing it with that spirit that will start the world along—
Sing it as we used to sing it, fifty thousand strong,
    While we were marching through Georgia.

CHORUS:

"Hurrah, hurrah! we bring the Jubilee!
Hurrah, hurrah! the flag that makes you free!"
So we sang the chorus from Atlanta to the sea,
    While we were marching through Georgia.

How the darkies shouted when they heard the joyful sound!
How the turkeys gobbled which our commissary found!
How the sweet potatoes even started from the ground!
    While we were marching through Georgia.

Yes, and there were Union men who wept with joyful tears,
When they saw the honored flag they hadn't seen for years;
Hardly could they be restrained from breaking out in cheers,
    While we were marching through Georgia.

"Sherman's dashing Yankee boys will never reach the coast!"
So the saucy rebels said, and 'twas a handsome boast;
Had they not forgotten, alas! to reckon with the host,
    While we were marching through Georgia?

So we made a thoroughfare for Freedom and her train,
Sixty miles in latitude—three hundred to the main:
Treason fled before us, for resistance was in vain,
    While we were marching through Georgia.

PRAYER IN "STONEWALL" JACKSON'S CAMP.

SOUTHERN SONGS.

DIXIE.

THE tune "Dixie" was composed in 1859, by Mr. Dan D. Emmett, for Bryant's Minstrels, then performing in New York City. It hit the taste of the New York play-going public, and was adopted at once by various bands of wandering minstrels, who sang it in all parts of the Union. In 1860 it was first sung in New Orleans. In that city the tune was harmonized, set to new words, and, without the authority of the composer, was published. As from Boston "John Brown's Body" spread through the North, so from New Orleans "Dixie" spread through the South; and as Northern poets strove to find fitting words for the one, so Southern poets wrote fiery lines to fill the measures of the other. The only version possessing any literary merit is the one given in this collection. It was written by Gen. Albert Pike, a native of Massachusetts. In early life Mr. Pike moved to Little Rock, Ark., editing a paper and studying law in that city. He served in the Mexican war with distinction, and on the breaking out of the Rebellion enlisted on the Confederate side a force of Cherokee Indians, whom he led at the battle of Pea Ridge. It is said that President Lincoln requested a band in Washington to play "Dixie" in 1865, a short time after the surrender of Appomattox, remarking "that, as we had captured the rebel army, we had captured also the rebel tune."

Southrons, hear your country call you!
Up, lest worse than death befall you!
To arms! To arms! To arms, in Dixie!
Lo! all the beacon-fires are lighted—
Let hearts be now united.
  To arms! To arms! To arms, in Dixie!
    Advance the flag of Dixie!
      Hurrah! hurrah!
For Dixie's land we take our stand,
    And live or die for Dixie!
      To arms! To arms!
    And conquer peace for Dixie!
      To arms! To arms!
    And conquer peace for Dixie!

Hear the Northern thunders mutter!
Northern flags in South winds flutter.
Send them back your fierce defiance;
Stamp upon the accursed alliance.

Fear no danger! Shun no labor!
Lift up rifle, pike, and sabre.
Shoulder pressing close to shoulder,
Let the odds make each heart bolder.

BRIGADIER-GENERAL ALBERT PIKE, C. S. A.

How the South's great heart rejoices
At your cannons' ringing voices!
For faith betrayed, and pledges broken,
Wrongs inflicted, insults spoken.

Strong as lions, swift as eagles,
Back to their kennels hunt these beagles!
Cut the unequal bonds asunder;
Let them hence each other plunder!

Swear upon your country's altar
Never to submit or falter,
Till the spoilers are defeated,
Till the Lord's work is completed.

Halt not till our Federation
Secures among earth's powers its station.
Then at peace, and crowned with glory,
Hear your children tell the story.

If the loved ones weep in sadness,
Victory soon shall bring them gladness,
Exultant pride soon banish sorrow,
Smiles chase tears away to-morrow.

MY MARYLAND.

"MY MARYLAND" is regarded by some as the greatest song inspired by the civil war, and if we consider these songs as poems it is the best. Its burning lines, written early in 1861, helped to fire the Southern heart. Its author, Mr. James Ryder Randall, is a native of Baltimore. He was professor of English literature in Poydras College in Louisiana, a short distance from New Orleans, and there in April, 1861, he read the news of the attack on the Massachusetts troops as they passed through Baltimore. Naturally he was greatly excited on reading this account, and it inspired the song, which was written within twenty-four hours of the time he read of the assault. "My Maryland" is one of a number of songs written by Mr. Randall, but none of the others attained popularity. His "John Pelham," commonly called "The Dead Cannonneer," is a much finer poem. After the war he became editor of the *Constitutionalist*, published in Augusta, Ga., in which city he still resides.

The despot's heel is on thy shore,
      Maryland!
His torch is at thy temple door,
      Maryland!
Avenge the patriotic gore
That flecked the streets of Baltimore,
And be the battle-queen of yore,
      Maryland, my Maryland!

Hark to an exiled son's appeal,
      Maryland!
My Mother State, to thee I kneel,
      Maryland!
For life and death, for woe and weal,
Thy peerless chivalry reveal,
And gird thy beauteous limbs with steel,
      Maryland, my Maryland!

Thou wilt not cower in the dust,
      Maryland!
Thy beaming sword shall never rust,
      Maryland!
Remember Carroll's sacred trust,
Remember Howard's warlike thrust,
And all thy slumberers with the just,
      Maryland, my Maryland!

Come! 'tis the red dawn of the day,
      Maryland!
Come with thy panoplied array,
      Maryland!
With Ringgold's spirit for the fray,
With Watson's blood at Monterey,
With fearless Lowe and dashing May,
      Maryland, my Maryland!

Dear Mother, burst the tyrant's chain,
      Maryland!
Virginia should not call in vain,
      Maryland!

She meets her sisters on the plain,—
"*Sic semper!*" 'tis the proud refrain
That baffles minions back amain,
Maryland!
Arise in majesty again,
Maryland, my Maryland!

Come! for thy shield is bright and strong,
Maryland!
Come! for thy dalliance does thee wrong,
Maryland!
Come to thine own heroic throng
Stalking with Liberty along,
And chant thy dauntless slogan-song,
Maryland, my Maryland!

I see the blush upon thy cheek,
Maryland!
For thou wast ever bravely meek,
Maryland!
But lo! there surges forth a shriek,
From hill to hill, from creek to creek,
Potomac calls to Chesapeake,
Maryland, my Maryland!

Thou wilt not yield the vandal toll,
Maryland!
Thou wilt not crook to his control,
Maryland!
Better the fire upon thee roll,
Better the shot, the blade, the bowl,
Than crucifixion of the soul,
Maryland, my Maryland!

I hear the distant thunder-hum,
Maryland!
The Old Line's bugle, fife, and drum,
Maryland!
She is not dead, nor deaf, nor dumb;
Huzza! she spurns the Northern scum—
She breathes! She burns! She'll come! She'll come!
Maryland, my Maryland!

REBELS.

FIRST published in the Atlanta *Confederacy*. The author is unknown.

Rebels! 'tis a holy name!
The name our fathers bore
When battling in the cause of Right,
Against the tyrant in his might,
In the dark days of yore.

Rebels! 'tis our family name!
Our father, Washington,
Was the arch-rebel in the fight,
And gave the name to us—a right
Of father unto son.

Rebels! 'tis our given name!
Our mother, Liberty,
Received the title with her fame,
In days of grief, of fear, and shame,
When at her breast were we.

Rebels! 'tis our sealèd name!
A baptism of blood!
The war—ay, and the din of strife—
The fearful contest, life for life—
The mingled crimson flood.

Rebels! 'tis a patriot's name!
In struggles it was given;
We bore it then when tyrants raved,
And through their curses 'twas engraved
On the doomsday-book of heaven.

Rebels! 'tis our fighting name!
For peace rules o'er the land
Until they speak of craven woe,
Until our rights receive a blow
From foe's or brother's hand.

Rebels! 'tis our dying name!
For although life is dear,
Yet, freemen born and freemen bred,
We'd rather live as freemen dead,
Than live in slavish fear.

Then call us rebels, if you will—
We glory in the name;
For bending under unjust laws,
And swearing faith to an unjust cause,
We count a greater shame.

CALL ALL.

THIS Southern war song, which was first published in the Rockingham, Va., *Register* in 1861, became quite popular with the boys in gray. It is published here because of its peculiarities rather than on account of its literary merit.

Whoop! the Doodles have broken loose,
Roaring round like the very deuce!
Lice of Egypt, a hungry pack—
After 'em, boys, and drive 'em back.

Bull-dog, terrier, cur, and fice,
Back to the beggarly land of ice;
Worry 'em, bite 'em, scratch and tear
Everybody and everywhere.

Old Kentucky is caved from under,
Tennessee is split asunder,
Alabama awaits attack,
And Georgia bristles up her back.

Old John Brown is dead and gone!
Still his spirit is marching on—
Lantern-jawed, and legs, my boys,
Long as an ape's from Illinois!

Want a weapon? Gather a brick,
Club or cudgel, or stone or stick;
Anything with a blade or butt,
Anything that can cleave or cut;

Anything heavy, or hard, or keen—
Any sort of slaying machine!
Anything with a willing mind
And the steady arm of a man behind.

Want a weapon? Why, capture one!
Every Doodle has got a gun,
Belt, and bayonet, bright and new;
Kill a Doodle, and capture two!

Shoulder to shoulder, son and sire!
All, call all! to the feast of fire!
Mother and maiden, and child and slave,
A common triumph or a single grave.

THE BLACK FLAG.

THE raising of the black flag means death without quarter. It means that prisoners taken should be slaughtered at once. It is contrary to the spirit of modern warfare. General Sherman, in his celebrated letter to the Mayor of Atlanta, says, "War is cruelty, and you cannot refine it." War arouses the fiercest, most tiger-like passions of mankind. Were it not so, the poet who wrote "The Mountain of the Lovers" could never have written "The Black Flag." Paul Hamilton Hayne was born in Charleston, S. C., in 1830. He abandoned the practice of law for literary pursuits. He contributed to the *Southern Literary Messenger*, and for a while edited the Charleston *Literary Gazette*. He entered the Southern army at the outbreak of the civil war, and served until obliged to resign by failing health. His house and all his personal property were destroyed at the bombardment of Charleston. He wrote extensively both in poetry and prose.

Like the roar of the wintry surges on a wild, tempestuous strand,
The voice of the maddened millions comes up from an outraged land;
For the cup of our woe runs over, and the day of our grace is past,
And Mercy has fled to the angels, and Hatred is king at last!

CHORUS:

Then up with the sable banner!
Let it thrill to the War God's breath,
For we march to the watchword—Vengeance!
And we follow the captain—Death!

In the gloom of the gory breaches, on the ramparts wrapped in flame,
'Mid the ruined homesteads, blackened by a hundred deeds of shame;
Wheresoever the vandals rally, and the bands of the alien meet,
We will crush the heads of the hydra with the stamp of our armed feet.

They have taught us a fearful lesson! 'tis burned on our hearts in fire,
And the souls of a host of heroes leap with a fierce desire;
And we swear by all that is sacred, and we swear by all that is pure,
That the crafty and cruel dastards shall ravage our homes no more.

We will roll the billows of battle back, back on the braggart foe,
Till his leaguered and stricken cities shall quake with a coward's throe;
They shall compass the awful meaning of the conflict their lust begun,
When the Northland rings with wailing, and the grand old cause hath won.

LORENA.

THIS doleful and pathetic song of affection was very popular among the Confederate soldiers. It started at the start, and never stopped till the last musket was stacked and the last camp-fire cold. It was, without doubt, the song nearest the Confederate soldier's heart. It was the "Annie Laurie" of the Confederate trenches.

"Each heart recalled a different name,
But all *sang* 'Annie Laurie.'"

The years creep slowly by, Lorena,
The snow is on the grass again;
The sun's low down the sky, Lorena,
And frost gleams where the flowers have been.

But the *heart* throbs on as warmly now
As when the summer days were nigh.
Oh! the sun can never dip so low
Adown *affection's* cloudless sky.

One hundred months have passed, Lorena,
Since last I held that hand in mine;
I felt that pulse beat fast, Lorena,
But mine beat faster still than thine.
One hundred months! 'Twas flowery May,
When up the mountain slope we climbed,
To watch the dying of the day,
And hear the merry church bells chime.

We loved each other then, Lorena,
More than we ever dared to tell;
And what we might have been, Lorena,
Had but our loving prospered well—
But then, 'tis past, the years have flown;
I'll not call up their shadowy forms;
I'll say to them, "Lost years, sleep on—
Sleep on, nor heed life's pelting storms."

It matters little now, Lorena,
The past is the eternal' past;
Our heads will soon lie low, Lorena,
Life's tide is ebbing out so fast.
But there's a future, oh! thank God—
Of life this is so small a part.
'Tis dust to dust beneath the sod;
But *there*, up *there*, 'tis *heart* to *heart*."

STEPHEN COLLINS FOSTER.

"OLD FOLKS AT HOME."

Mr. F. G. de Fontaine, a celebrated Southern war correspondent, writes that the most popular songs with the soldiers of the Confederate armies were negro melodies, such as "Old Folks at Home" and "My Old Kentucky Home." This is our reason for publishing the pacific and kindly words of the most celebrated negro melody, among songs that breathe threatening and slaughter. It is not difficult to understand why such songs were popular with men raised in the South. They would bring forcibly to mind the distant home, and the dear associations of early life on the old plantations. "Old Folks at Home" was written by Stephen Collins Foster. He wrote between two and three hundred popular songs—more than any other American. Among the most familiar of his compositions are "Old Uncle Ned," "Massa's in the Cold, Cold Ground," "Old Dog Tray," and "My Old Kentucky Home." Mr. Foster was finely educated, was proficient in French and German, was an amateur painter of ability, and a talented musician. It is said that he received fifteen thousand dollars for "Old Folks at Home."

Way down upon de Swanee ribber,
  Far, far away,
Dere's wha my heart is turning ebber,
  Dere's wha de old folks stay.

All up and down de whole creation
  Sadly I roam,
Still longing for de old plantation,
  And for de old folks at home.

All round de little farm I wandered
When I was young;
Den many happy days I squandered,
Many de songs I sung.
When I was playing wid my brudder,
Happy was I;
Oh, take me to my kind old mudder!
Dere let me live and die.

CHORUS:

All de world am sad and dreary,
Ebrywhere I roam;
Oh, darkies, how my heart grows weary,
Far from de old folks at home!

One little hut among de bushes,
One dat I love,
Still sadly to my mem'ry rushes,
No matter where I rove.
When will I see de bees a-humming
All round de comb?
When will I hear de banjo tumming,
Down in my good old home?

CHORUS:

All de world am sad and dreary,
Ebrywhere I roam;
Oh, darkies, how my heart grows weary,
Far from de old folks at home!

THE BONNIE BLUE FLAG.

THE most popular war songs of the South were "Dixie" and "The Bonnie Blue Flag." Like "Dixie," the "Bonnie Blue Flag" began its popular career in New Orleans. The words were written by an Irish comedian, Mr. Harry McCarthy, and the song was first sung by his sister, Miss Marion McCarthy, at the Variety Theatre in New Orleans in 1861. The tune is an old and popular Irish melody, "The Irish Jaunting Car." It is said that General Butler, when he was commander of the National forces in New Orleans in 1862, made it very profitable by fining every man, woman, or child, who sang, whistled, or played this tune on any instrument, twenty-five dollars. It has also been said that he arrested the publisher, destroyed the stock of sheet music, and fined him five hundred dollars.

We are a band of brothers, and native to the soil,
Fighting for the property we gained by honest toil;
And when our rights were threatened, the cry rose near and far:
Hurrah for the Bonnie Blue Flag that bears a single star!
Hurrah! hurrah! for the Bonnie Blue Flag
That bears a single star!

As long as the Union was faithful to her trust,
Like friends and like brothers, kind were we and just;
But now when Northern treachery attempts our rights to mar,
We hoist on high the Bonnie Blue Flag that bears a single star.

First, gallant South Carolina nobly made the stand;
Then came Alabama, who took her by the hand;
Next, quickly Mississippi, Georgia, and Florida—
All raised the flag, the Bonnie Blue Flag that bears a single star.

Ye men of valor, gather round the banner of the right;
Texas and fair Louisiana join us in the fight.
Davis, our loved President, and Stephens, statesmen are;
Now rally round the Bonnie Blue Flag that bears a single star.

And here's to brave Virginia! The Old Dominion State
With the young Confederacy at length has linked her fate.
Impelled by her example, now other States prepare
To hoist on high the Bonnie Blue Flag that bears a single star.

Then here's to our Confederacy! Strong we are and brave;
Like patriots of old we'll fight, our heritage to save;
And rather than submit to shame, to die we would prefer.
So cheer for the Bonnie Blue Flag that bears a single star.

Then cheer, boys, cheer, raise the joyous shout,
For Arkansas and North Carolina now have both gone out;
And let another rousing cheer for Tennessee be given.
The single star of the Bonnie Blue Flag has grown to be eleven.
Hurrah! hurrah! for the Bonnie Blue Flag
That bears a single star!

NORTHERN SONGS.

JOHN BROWN'S BODY.

JOHN BROWN was hanged in December, 1859, and a little more than a year after this time the celebrated marching-tune, "John Brown's Body," came into being. It is a singular fact that the composer of the stirring and popular air of this song is unknown. Possibly it had no composer, but, like Topsy, "it was not born, but just growed." This seems to be the most reasonable theory of its origin. The words of the song, as given in this collection, with the exception of the first stanza, were written by Charles S. Hall, of Charlestown, Mass. "John Brown's Body" was the most popular war song among the Northern soldiers on the march and around the campfire. In fact, it became the marching song of the armies of the Nation. It was equally popular in the cities, villages, and homes of the North. The *Pall Mall Gazette*, of October 14, 1865, said: "The street boys of London have decided in favor of 'John Brown's Body' against 'My Maryland' and 'The Bonnie Blue Flag.' The somewhat lugubrious refrain has excited their admiration to a wonderful degree."

John Brown's body lies a-mouldering in the grave;
John Brown's body lies a-mouldering in the grave;
John Brown's body lies a-mouldering in the grave;
His soul is marching on.

Glory, halle—hallelujah! Glory, halle—hallelujah!
Glory, halle—hallelujah!
His soul is marching on!

He's gone to be a soldier in the army of the Lord! (*thrice.*)
His soul is marching on!

John Brown's knapsack is strapped upon his back! (*thrice.*)
His soul is marching on!

His pet lambs will meet him on the way; (*thrice.*)
As they go marching on!

They will hang Jeff Davis to a sour apple tree! (*thrice.*)
As they march along!

Now, three rousing cheers for the Union! (*thrice.*)
As we are marching on!

Glory, halle—hallelujah! Glory, halle—hallelujah!
Glory, halle—hallelujah!
Hip, hip, hip, hip, hurrah!

WHEN JOHNNY COMES MARCHING HOME.

ANOTHER army song that became almost as popular in England as in this country is "When Johnny Comes Marching Home." It was written and composed by Mr. Patrick S. Gilmore, leader of the celebrated Gilmore's Band. The words do not amount to much, but the tune is of that rollicking order which is very catching. Without doubt the author built up the words of this song to suit the air, on the same principle that in Georgia they build a chimney first and erect the house against it. This rattling war song has kept its hold on the ears of the people to the present time. Mr. Gilmore afterward composed an ambitious national hymn which has never attained the popularity of his war song.

When Johnny comes marching home again,
Hurrah! hurrah!
We'll give him a hearty welcome then,
Hurrah! hurrah!
The men will cheer, the boys will shout,
The ladies they will all turn out,
And we'll all feel gay,
When Johnny comes marching home.

The men will cheer, the boys will shout,
The ladies they will all turn out,
And we'll all feel gay,
When Johnny comes marching home.

The old church-bell will peal with joy,
Hurrah! hurrah!
To welcome home our darling boy,
Hurrah! hurrah!

The village lads and lasses say,
With roses they will strew the way;
And we'll all feel gay,
When Johnny comes marching home.

Get ready for the jubilee,
Hurrah! hurrah!
We'll give the hero three times three,
Hurrah! hurrah!
The laurel wreath is ready now
To place upon his loyal brow;
And we'll all feel gay,
When Johnny comes marching home.

Let love and friendship on that day,
Hurrah! hurrah!
Their choicest treasures then display,
Hurrah! hurrah!
And let each one perform some part,
To fill with joy the warrior's heart;
And we'll all feel gay,
When Johnny comes marching home.

The men will cheer, the boys will shout,
The ladies they will all turn out,
And we'll all feel gay,
When Johnny comes marching home.

GRAFTED INTO THE ARMY.

By Henry C. Work.

Our Jimmy has gone to live in a tent,
They have grafted him into the army;
He finally puckered up courage and went,
When they grafted him into the army.
I told them the child was too young—alas!
At the captain's forequarters they said he would pass—
They'd train him up well in the infantry class—
So they grafted him into the army.

CHORUS:

O Jimmy, farewell! Your brothers fell
Way down in Alabarmy;
I thought they would spare a lone widder's heir,
But they grafted him into the army.

Drest up in his unicorn—dear little chap!
They have grafted him into the army;
It seems but a day since he sot on my lap,
But they have grafted him into the army.
And these are the trousies he used to wear—
Them very same buttons—the patch and the tear—
But Uncle Sam gave him a bran new pair
When they grafted him into the army.

Now in my provisions I see him revealed—
They have grafted him into the army;
A picket beside the contented field,
They have grafted him into the army.
He looks kinder sickish—begins to cry—
A big volunteer standing right in his eye!
Oh, what if the duckie should up and die,
Now they've grafted him into the army!

THE BATTLE CRY OF FREEDOM.

GEORGE F. ROOT was born in Sheffield, Mass., August 30, 1820, and he was the founder of the music-publishing firm of Root & Cady. His celebrated "Battle Cry of Freedom" was first sung by the Hutchinson family at a mass meeting in New York City. It is said that during the terrible fight in the Wilderness, on May 6, 1864, a brigade of the Ninth Corps, having broken the enemy's line by an assault, became exposed to a flank attack and was driven back in disorder with heavy loss. They retreated but a few hundred yards, however, re-formed, and again confronted the enemy. Just then some gallant fellows in the ranks of the Forty-fifth Pennsylvania began to sing:

"We'll rally round the flag, boys, rally once again,
Shouting the battle cry of Freedom."

The refrain was caught up instantly by the entire regiment and by the Thirty-sixth Massachusetts, next in line. There the grim ranks stood at bay in the deadly conflict. The air was filled with the smoke and crackle of burning underbrush, the pitiful cries of the wounded, the rattle of musketry, and shouts of men; but above all, over the exultant yells of the enemy, rose the inspiring chorus:

"The Union forever, hurrah! boys, hurrah!
Down with the traitor, up with the star."

This song was often ordered to be sung as the men marched into action. More than once its strains arose on the battlefield. With the humor which never deserts the American, even amid the hardships of camp life and the dangers of battle, the gentle lines of "Mary Had a Little Lamb" were fitted to the tune of the "Battle Cry of Freedom," and many a regiment shortened a weary march, or went gayly into action, singing:

"Mary had a little lamb,
Its fleece was white as snow,
Shouting the battle cry of Freedom.
And everywhere that Mary went,
The lamb was sure to go,
Shouting the battle cry of Freedom."

Yes, we'll rally round the flag, boys, we'll rally once again,
Shouting the battle cry of Freedom;
We will rally from the hillside, we'll gather from the plain,
Shouting the battle cry of Freedom.

The Union forever, hurrah! boys, hurrah!
Down with the traitor, up with the star;
While we rally round the flag, boys, rally once again,
Shouting the battle cry of Freedom.

We are springing to the call of our brothers gone before,
Shouting the battle cry of Freedom;
And we'll fill the vacant ranks with a million freemen more,
Shouting the battle cry of Freedom.

We will welcome to our numbers the loyal true and brave,
Shouting the battle cry of Freedom;
And although they may be poor, not a man shall be a slave,
Shouting the battle cry of Freedom.

So we're springing to the call from the East and from the West,
Shouting the battle cry of Freedom;
And we'll hurl the rebel crew from the land we love the best,
Shouting the battle cry of Freedom.

The Union forever, hurrah! boys, hurrah!
Down with the traitor, up with the star;
While we rally round the flag, boys, rally once again,
Shouting the battle cry of Freedom.

TENTING ON THE OLD CAMP-GROUND.

THE author of "Tenting on the Old Camp-Ground" is Walter Kittridge, who was born in the town of Merrimac, N. H., October 8, 1832. He was a public singer and a composer, as well as a writer of popular songs and ballads. In the first year of the civil war he published a small original "Union Song-Book." In 1862 he was drafted, and while preparing to go to the front he wrote in a few minutes both words and music of "Tenting on the Old Camp-Ground." Like many other good things in literature, this song was at first refused publication. But when it was published, its sale reached hundreds of thousands of copies.

We're tenting to-night on the old camp-ground,
Give us a song to cheer
Our weary hearts, a song of home
And friends we love so dear.

CHORUS:

Many are the hearts that are weary to-night,
Wishing for the war to cease;
Many are the hearts looking for the right,
To see the dawn of peace;
Tenting to-night, tenting to-night,
Tenting on the old camp-ground.

We've been tenting to-night on the old camp-ground,
Thinking of the days gone by;
Of the loved ones at home, that gave us the hand,
And the tear that said, Good-by!

We are tired of war on the old camp-ground;
Many are dead and gone
Of the brave and true who've left their homes;
Others have been wounded long.

We've been fighting to-day on the old camp-ground:
Many are lying near;
Some are dead, and some are dying,
Many are in tears!

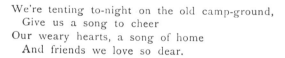

CHAPTER XIII.

THE PENINSULA CAMPAIGN.

COMMAND GIVEN TO McCLELLAN—HIS PLANS—APPOINTMENT OF SECRETARY STANTON — ON THE PENINSULA—BATTLE OF WILLIAMSBURG—ON THE CHICKAHOMINY—THE BATTLE OF FAIR OAKS—EFFECT OF THE SWAMPS—LEE IN COMMAND—STUART'S RAID—NEAREST APPROACH TO RICHMOND—ACTION AT BEAVER DAM CREEK—BATTLE OF GAINES'S MILLS—BATTLE OF SAVAGE'S STATION—BATTLE OF CHARLES CITY CROSS-ROADS—BATTLE OF MALVERN HILL—CRITICISMS OF PENINSULA CAMPAIGN.

WITHIN twenty-four hours after the defeat of McDowell's army at Bull Run (July 21, 1861), the Administration called to Washington the only man that had thus far accomplished much or made any considerable reputation in the field. This was Gen. George B. McClellan. He had been graduated at West Point in 1846, standing second in his class, and had gone at once into the Mexican war, in which he acquitted himself with distinction. After that war the young captain was employed in engineering work till 1855, when the Government sent him to Europe to study the movements of the Crimean war. He wrote a report of his observations, which was published under the title of "The Armies of Europe," and in 1857 resigned his commission and became chief engineer of the Illinois Central Railroad, and afterward president of the St. Louis and Cincinnati. He had done good work in Northwestern Virginia in the early summer, and now, at the age of thirty-five, was commissioned major-general in the regular army of the United States, and given command of all the troops about Washington.

For the work immediately in hand, this was probably the best selection that could have been made. Washington needed to be fortified, and he was a master of engineering; both the army that had just been defeated, and the new recruits that were pouring in, needed organization, and he proved preëminent as an organizer. Three months after he took command of fifty thousand uniformed men at the capital, he had an army of more than one hundred thousand, well organized in regiments, brigades, and divisions, with the proper proportion of artillery, with quartermaster and commissary departments going like clockwork, and the whole fairly drilled and disciplined. Everybody looked on with admiration, and the public impatience that had precipitated the disastrous "On to Richmond" movement was now replaced by a marvellous patience. The summer and autumn months went by, and no movement was made; but McClellan, in taking command, had promised that the war should be "short, sharp, and decisive," and the people thought, if they only allowed him time enough to make thorough preparation, his great army would at length swoop down upon the Confederate capital and finish everything at one blow. At length, however, they began to grow weary of the daily telegram, "All quiet along the Potomac," and the monotonously repeated information that "General McClellan rode out to Fairfax Court-House and back this morning." The Confederacy was daily growing stronger; the Potomac was being closed to navigation by the erection of hostile batteries on its southern bank; the enemy's flag was flying within sight from the capital, and the question of foreign interference was becoming exceedingly grave. On the 1st of November General Scott, then seventy-five years of age, retired, and McClellan succeeded him as General-in-Chief of all the armies.

Soon after this his plans appear, from subsequent revelations, to have undergone important modification. He had undoubtedly intended to attack by moving straight out toward Manassas, where the army that had won the battle of Bull Run was still encamped, and was still commanded by Gen. Joseph E. Johnston. He now began to think of moving against Richmond by some more easterly route, discussing among others the extreme easterly one that he finally took. But, whatever were his thoughts and purposes, his army appeared to be taking root. The people began to murmur, Congress began to question, and the President began to argue and urge. All this did not signify; nothing could move McClellan. He wanted to wait till he could leave

MAJOR-GENERAL GEORGE B. McCLELLAN AND WIFE.

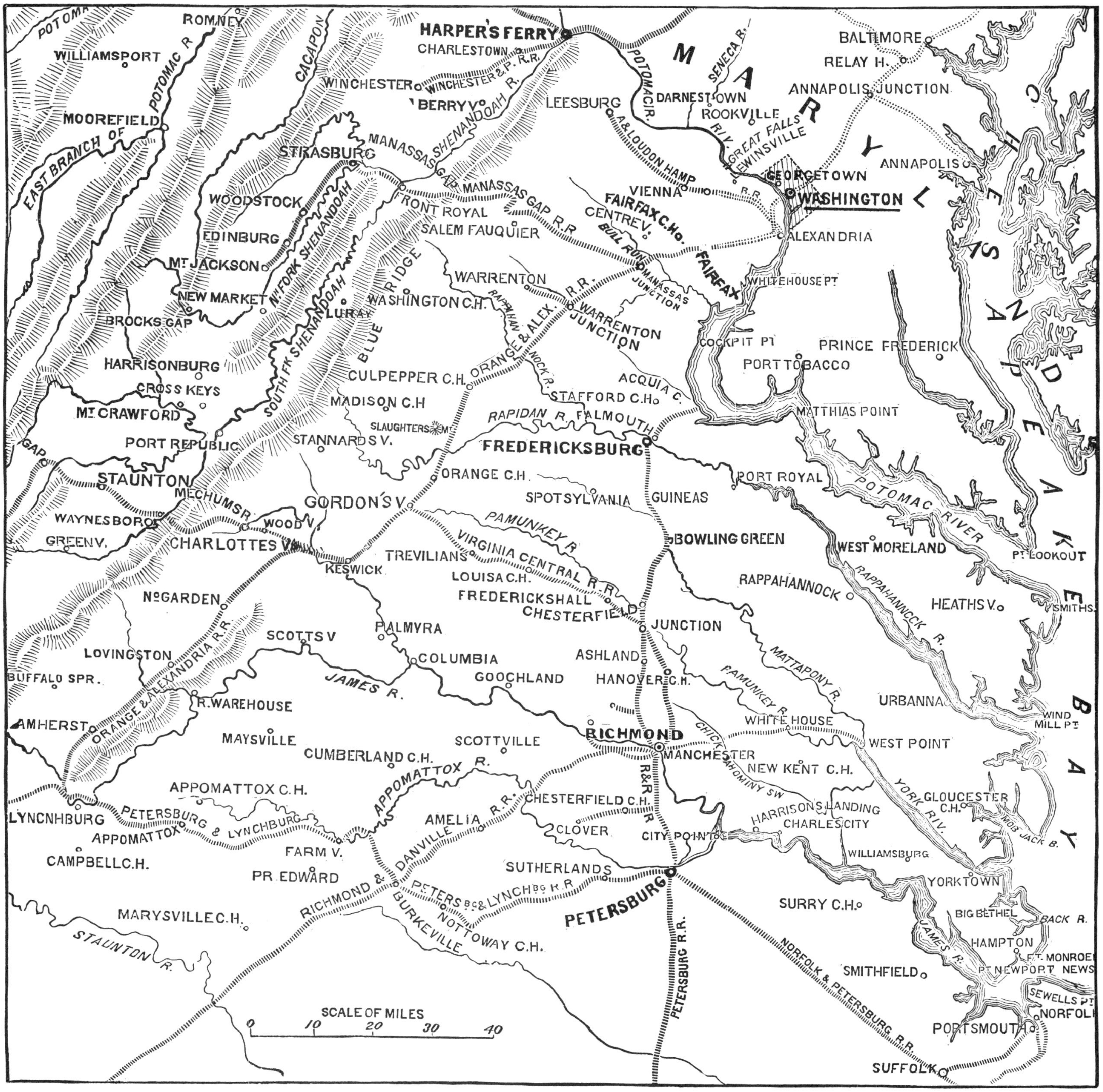

MAP SHOWING THE SEAT OF WAR FROM HARPER'S FERRY TO SUFFOLK, VA.

an enormous garrison in the defences of Washington, place a strong corps of observation along the Potomac, and then move out with a column of one hundred and fifty thousand men against an army that he believed to be as numerous as that, though in truth it was then less than half as large. It is now known that, from the beginning to the end of his career in that war, General McClellan constantly overestimated the force opposed to him. On the 10th of January, 1862, the President held a long consultation with Generals McDowell and Franklin and some members of his cabinet. General McClellan was then confined to his bed by an illness of a month's duration. At this consultation Mr. Lincoln said, according to General McDowell's memorandum: "If something was not soon done, the bottom would be out of the whole affair; and if General McClellan did not want to use the army, he would like to borrow it, provided he could see how it could be made to do something."

Immediately upon McClellan's recovery, the President called him to a similar council, and asked him to disclose his plan for

Captain LeClerc. Comte de Paris. Captain Mohain.
Duc de Chartres. Prince de Joinville.

FOREIGN OFFICERS AND STAFF AT GENERAL McCLELLAN'S HEADQUARTERS.

a campaign, which he declined to do. Finally the President asked him if he had fixed upon any particular time for setting out; and when he said he had, Mr. Lincoln questioned him no further. A few days later, in a letter to the President, he set forth his plan, which was to move his army down the Potomac on transports, land it at or near Fort Monroe, march up the peninsula between York and James rivers, and attack the defences of Richmond on the north and east sides. The President at first disapproved of this plan, largely for the reason that it would require so much time in preparation; but when he found that the highest officers in the army favored it, and considered the probability that any general was likely to fail if sent to execute a plan he did not originate or believe in, he finally gave it his sanction, and once more set himself to the difficult task of inducing McClellan to move at all. And yet the President himself still further retarded the opening of the campaign by delaying the order to collect the means of transportation. Meanwhile General Johnston quietly removed his stores, and on the 8th of March evacuated Centreville and Manassas, and placed his army before Richmond. This reconciled the President to McClellan's plan of campaign, which he had never liked.

The order for the transportation of McClellan's army was issued on the 27th of February, and four hundred vessels were required; for there were actually transported one hundred and twenty-one thousand men, fourteen thousand animals, forty-four batteries, and all the necessary ambulances and baggage-wagons, pontoons and telegraph material. Just before the embarkation, the army was divided into four corps, the commands of which were given to Generals McDowell, Edwin V. Sumner, Samuel P. Heintzelman, and Erasmus D. Keyes. High authorities say this was one of the causes of the failure of the campaign; for the army should have been divided into corps long before, when McClellan could have chosen his own lieutenants instead of having them chosen by the President. General Hooker said it was impossible for him to succeed with such corps commanders. But his near approach to success rather discredits this criticism.

Another element of the highest importance had also entered into the problem with which the nation was struggling. This was the appointment (January 21, 1862) of Edwin M. Stanton to succeed Simon Cameron as Secretary of War. Mr. Stanton, then forty-seven years of age, was a lawyer by profession, a man of great intellect, unfailing nerve, and tremendous energy. He had certain traits that often made him personally disagreeable to his subordinates; but it was impossible to doubt his thorough loyalty, and his determination to find or make a way to bring the war to a successful close as speedily as possible, without the slightest regard to the individual interests of himself or anybody else. He was probably the ablest war minister that ever lived—with the possible exception of Carnot, the man to whom Napoleon said, "I have known you too late." It is indicative of Mr. Lincoln's sagacity and freedom from prejudice, that his first meeting with Mr. Stanton was when he went to Cincinnati, some years before the war, to assist in trying an important case. He found Mr. Stanton in charge of the case as senior counsel, and Stanton was so unendurably disagreeable to him that he threw up the engagement and went home to Springfield. Yet he afterward gave that man the most important place in his cabinet, and found him its strongest member.

One division of the army embarked on the 17th of March, and the others followed in quick succession. General McClellan reached Fort Monroe on the 2d of April, by which time fifty-eight thousand men and one hundred guns had arrived, and immediately moved with this force on Yorktown, the place made famous by the surrender of Cornwallis eighty years before. The Confederates had fortified this point, and thrown a line of earthworks across the narrow peninsula to the deep water of Warwick River. These works were held by General Magruder with thirteen thousand effective men. General Johnston, who was in command of all the troops around Richmond, says he had no expectation of doing more than delaying McClellan at Yorktown till he could strengthen the defences of the capital and collect more men; and that he thought his adversary would use his transports to pass his army around that place by water, after destroying the batteries, and land at some point above.

McClellan, supposing that Johnston's entire army was in the defences of Yorktown, sat down before the place and constructed siege works, approaching the enemy by regular parallels. As the remaining divisions of his army arrived at Fort Monroe, they were added to his besieging force; but McDowell's entire corps and Blenker's division had been detached at the last moment and retained at Washington, from fears on the part of the Administration that the capital was not sufficiently guarded, though McClellan had already left seventy thousand men there or within call. The fears were increased by the threatening movements of Stonewall Jackson in the Shenandoah Valley, where, however, he was defeated by Gen. James Shields near Winchester, March 23.

General Johnston had to contend with precisely the same difficulty that McClellan complained of. He wanted to bring together before Richmond all the troops that were then at Norfolk and in the Carolinas and Georgia, and with the large army thus formed suddenly attack McClellan after he should have marched seventy-five miles up the peninsula from his base at Fort Monroe. But in a council of war General Lee and the Secretary of War opposed this plan, and Mr. Davis adopted their views and rejected it. Johnston therefore undertook the campaign with the army that he had, which he says consisted of fifty thousand effective men.

McClellan spent nearly a month before Yorktown, and when he was ready to open fire with his siege guns and drive out the enemy, May 3d, he found they had quietly departed, leaving "Quaker guns" (wooden logs on wheels) in the embrasures. There was no delay in pursuit, and the National advance came up with the Confederate rear guard near Williamsburg, about twelve miles from Yorktown. Here, May 4th, brisk skirmishing began, which gradually became heavier, till reinforcements were hurried up on the one side, and sent back on the other, and the skirmish was developed into a battle. The place had been well fortified months before. The action on the morning of the 5th was opened by the divisions of Generals Hooker and William F. Smith. They attacked the strongest of the earthworks, pushed forward the batteries, and silenced it. Hooker was then heavily attacked by infantry, with a constant menace on his left wing. He sustained his position alone nearly all day, though losing one thousand seven hundred men and five guns, and was at length relieved by the arrival of Gen. Philip Kearny's division. The delay was due mainly to the deep mud caused by a heavy rain the night before. Later in the day, Hancock's brigade made a wide circuit on the right, discovered some unoccupied redoubts, and took possession of them. When the Confederates advanced their left to the attack, they ran upon these redoubts, which their commanding officers knew nothing about, and were repelled with heavy loss. Hancock's one thousand six hundred men suddenly burst over the crest of the works, and bore down

CAMP OF THE ARMY OF THE POTOMAC AT CUMBERLAND LANDING.

upon the enemy with fixed bayonets, routing and scattering them. McClellan brought up reinforcements, and in the night the Confederates in front of him moved off to join their main army, leaving in Williamsburg four hundred of their wounded, because they had no means of carrying them away, but taking with them about that number of prisoners. The National loss had been about two thousand two hundred, the Confederate about one thousand eight hundred. This battle was fought within five miles of the historic site of Jamestown, where the first permanent English settlement in the United States had been made in 1607, and the first cargo of slaves landed in 1619.

Gen. William B. Franklin's division of McDowell's corps had now been sent to McClellan, and immediately after the battle of Williamsburg he moved it on transports to White House, on the Pamunkey, where it established a base of supplies. As soon as possible, also, the main body of the army was marched from Williamsburg to White House, reaching that place on the 16th of May. From this point he moved westward toward Richmond, expecting to be joined by a column of forty thousand men under McDowell, which was to move from Fredericksburg. On reaching the Chickahominy, McClellan threw his left wing across that stream, and sweeping around with his right fought small battles at Mechanicsville and Hanover Junction, by which he cleared the way for McDowell to join him. But at this critical point of time Stonewall Jackson suddenly made another raid down the Shenandoah Valley, and McDowell was called back to go in pursuit of him.

Johnston resolved to strike the detached left wing of the National army, which had crossed the Chickahominy, and advanced to a point within half a dozen miles of Richmond, and his purpose was seconded by a heavy rain on the night of May 30th, which swelled the stream and swept away some of the bridges, thus hindering reinforcement from the other wing. The attack, May 31st, fell first upon Gen. Silas Casey's division of Keyes's corps, which occupied some half-finished works. It was bravely made and bravely resisted, and the Confederates suffered heavy losses before these works, where they had almost surprised the men with the shovels in their hands. But after a time a Confederate force made a detour and gained a position in the rear of the redoubts, when of course they could no longer be held. Reinforcements were very slow in coming up, and Keyes's men had a long, hard struggle to hold their line at all. They could not have done so if a part of Johnston's plan had not miscarried. He intended to bring in a heavy flanking force between them and the river, but was delayed several hours in getting it in motion. Meanwhile McClellan ordered Sumner to cross the river and join in the battle. Sumner had anticipated such an order as soon as he

NORTH BATTERY OF CONFEDERATES AT SHIPPING POINT, POTOMAC RIVER.

heard the firing, and when the order came it found him with his corps in line, drawn out from camp, and ready to cross instantly. He was the oldest officer there (sixty-six), and the most energetic. There was but one bridge that could be used, many of the supports of this were gone, the approaches were under water, and it was almost a wreck. But he unhesitatingly pushed on his column. The frail structure was steadied by the weight of the men; and though it swayed and undulated with their movement and the rush of water, they all crossed in safety.

Sumner was just in time to meet the flank attack, which was commanded by Johnston in person. The successive charges of the Confederates were all repelled, and at dusk a counter-charge cleared the ground in front and drove off the last of them in confusion. In this fight General Johnston received wounds that compelled him to retire from the field, and laid him up for a long time. The battle—which is called both Fair Oaks and Seven Pines—cost the National army over five thousand men, and the Confederate nearly seven thousand. It was a more destructive battle than any that, up to that time, the Eastern armies had fought. A participant thus describes the after appearance of the field: "Monday, June 2d, we visited the battlefield, and rode from place to place on the scene of conflict. We have often wished that we could efface from our memory the observations of that day. Details were burying the dead in trenches or heaping the ground upon them where they lay. The ground was saturated with gore; the intrenchments, the slashing, the rifle-pits, the thicket, many of the tents, were filled with dead. In the Fair Oaks farmhouse, the dead, the dying, and the severely wounded lay together. Along the Williamsburg road, on each side of it, was one long Confederate grave. An old barn, near where the One Hundred and Fourth Pennsylvania volunteers first formed, was filled with our dead and wounded; and farther to the right, near the station, beside an old building, lay thirteen Michigan soldiers with their blankets over them and their names pinned on their caps. Near the railroad, by a

MAJOR-GENERAL E. W. GANTT, C. S. A.

MAJOR-GENERAL R. E. RODES, C. S. A.

REVIEW IN WASHINGTON, UNDER McCLELLAN, OF EIGHT BATTERIES OF ARTILLERY AND THREE REGIMENTS OF CAVALRY, BY LINCOLN AND HIS CABINET.

PRESIDENT LINCOLN VISITING GENERAL McCLELLAN.

COMTE DE PARIS DUC DE CHARTRES

BRIGADIER-GENERAL CHAS. H. VAN WYCK. (On General McClellan's Staff.)

COLONEL B. S. ALEXANDER (ENGINEER CORPS).

log house, the dead and wounded were packed together. Both were motionless; but you could distinguish them by the livid blackness of the dead. We could trace the path of our regiment, from the wood-pile around by the intrenchments to its camp, by the dead still unburied. Those that died immediately could not be touched, but were covered with ground where they lay; the wounded, who crawled or were carried to the barns, tents, and houses, and who died subsequently, were buried in trenches. Our little tent was still standing, though pierced by several bullets. Beside it lay two dead men of the Ninety-eighth, whom we could not identify; for the sun, rain, and wind had changed their countenances. On the bed lay a dead Confederate. At the left of our camp, in the wood, where the Eighty-first, Eighty-fifth, and Ninety-second New York volunteers and Peck's brigade fought with Huger, the dead were promiscuously mixed together, and lay in sickening and frightful proximity; strong and weak, old and young, officer and private, horse and man—dead, or wounded in the agonies of death, lay where they fell, and furnished, excepting the swaths on the Williamsburg road, the darkest corner on that day's panorama."

Col. William Kreutzer, of the Ninety-eighth New York Regiment, which went into that battle with three hundred and eighty-five men, and lost eighty-five, gives some interesting particulars of the action: "The whole of Company A went to work on the road near the Grapevine bridge. Details were made for men to make abatis and work on the breastworks. Company A left its rifles in

TABBS HOUSE, YORKTOWN.

CONTRABANDS.—AT FOLLER'S HOUSE.

CONWAY LANDING.

camp, and lost them. When it rejoined the regiment, on the 1st of June, it appeared like a company of pioneers, or sappers and miners, carrying axes, shovels, and picks. . . . Soon after one o'clock our pickets begin to come in sight, retiring through the woods and slashing before the enemy. The skirmish line of the enemy pursued them. We could see both parties jumping over the logs and making their way through the brush and bushes, and hear at intervals the sharp report of their rifles. A little later a dense mass of men, about two rods wide, headed by half a dozen horsemen, is seen marching toward us on the Williamsburg road. They move in quick time, carry their arms on their shoulders, have flags and banners, and drummers to beat the step. Our three batteries open simultaneously with all their power. Our regiment pours its volleys into the slashing and into the column as fast as it can load and fire. The One Hundred and Fourth Pennsylvania volunteers aims at the column and at the skirmishers approaching its right front and flank. Unlike us, that regiment has no slashing in its front. The cleared field allowed the enemy to concentrate his fire upon it; too near the approaching column of attack, it interfered with the range and efficiency of our batteries behind. Its position was unfortunate. As the light troops pressed upon it, Colonel Davis ordered it to charge them at the double-quick. The regiment rushed forward with spirit, jumped over a rail fence in its front, with a shout and yell; but it was met so reso-

BATTERY No. 1 IN FRONT OF YORKTOWN.

(FIVE VIEWS.)

lutely and with such a galling fire by the foe, that it fell back in disorder, and did not appear on the field as an organization again during the day. Colonel Davis was wounded, and his 'Ringgold Regiment' fought its first battle as we have seen.

"The One Hundred and Fourth falling back, cleared the field opposite the advancing column, and gave the Ninety-eighth better opportunity to fire upon it as it moved deliberately on. The charging mass staggers, stops, resumes its march again, breaks in two, fills up its gaps; but sure and steady, with its flags and banners, it moves like the tramp of fate. Thinned, scattered, broken, it passes our right, and presses for the batteries. As it advances and passes, we pour our volleys into it with no uncertain aim, no random fire. The gaps we make, the swaths we mow, can be seen in the column, for we are only ten or fifteen rods away. The men behind press on those before. The head finally reaches the redoubt. One of the mounted leaders ascends the parapet and is shot with a pistol by an artillery officer. The whole column, from the fort back, severed, broken, staggers, sinks into the earth. The rifle-pits, breast-works, and the Ninety-eighth have cleared the road.

MAJOR-GENERAL W. B. FRANKLIN.

BREVET BRIGADIER-GENERAL O. H. HART.

"To this time the Ninety-eighth has not lost a man by the enemy; but our batteries behind have killed and wounded of it half a score. There is a lull in the battle,; the coast looks clear; the foe may not appear again. We look at the main road—it is one gray swath of men. Down along the railroad by Fair Oaks station, we hear but a few reports. Smith has had farther to march along the Nine-mile road, and has not struck our right flank yet; on our left, Palmer has not been attacked; Huger is not on time. Casey's division has driven back those of Longstreet and Hill. . . . Our batteries open. High over our heads, around us, beside us, the lead is whistling, and the iron is whizzing, hissing, whirling. Every moment has a new terror, every instant a new horror. Our men are falling fast. We leave the dead and the dying, and send the wounded to the rear. Palmer's regiments have all fallen back; the enemy is on our left and rear. Colonel Durkee tries to move the regiment by the left flank back to the rifle-pits; a part only receive the order. The enemy is getting so near, our experience in battle is so limited, our drill is so imperfect, that many of us will not, cannot, stand upon the order of our going. Durkee passes the rifle-pits with what follows him, and goes to our old camp. The writer rallies a part of the regiment around the flag at the half-deserted intrenchments. There we use, officers and men, the sharp-shooter's practice against the enemy. We can mark the effect of our fire; no rifle was discharged in vain. Many of the men could pick a squirrel from the tallest trees of Wayne and Franklin, and they load and fire with infinite merriment and good-nature."

MAJOR-GENERAL JOSEPH HOOKER.

MAJOR-GENERAL E. D. KEYES.

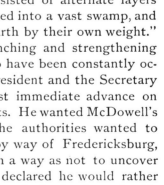

For some time after the battle of Fair Oaks, heavy rains made any movement almost impossible for either of the armies that confronted each other near Richmond. Gen. Alexander S. Webb says: "The ground, which consisted of alternate layers of reddish clay and quicksand, had turned into a vast swamp, and the guns in battery sank into the earth by their own weight." McClellan kept his men at work, intrenching and strengthening his position, while he himself seems to have been constantly occupied in writing despatches to the President and the Secretary of War, alternately promising an almost immediate advance on Richmond, and calling for reinforcements. He wanted McDowell's corps of forty thousand men, and the authorities wanted to give it to him if it could be sent by way of Fredericksburg, and united with his right wing in such a way as not to uncover Washington. But in one despatch he declared he would rather not have it at all unless it could be placed absolutely under his command. In several respects his position was very bad. The Chickahominy was bordered by great swamps, whose malarial influences robbed him of almost as many men as fell by the bullets of the enemy. His base was at White House, on the Pamunkey; and the line thence over which his supplies must come, instead of being at right angles with the line of his front and covered by it, was almost a prolongation of it. It was impossible to maintain permanent bridges over the Chickahominy, and a rain of two or three days was liable at any time to swell the stream so as to sweep away every means of crossing. He could threaten Richmond only by placing a heavy force on the right bank of the river; he could render his own communications secure only by keeping a large force on the left bank. When it first occurred to him that his true base was on the James, or how long he contemplated its removal thither, nobody knows; but he received a startling lesson on the 12th of June, which seems to have determined his apparently indeterminate mind.

When Gen. Joseph E. Johnston was wounded at Fair Oaks, the command devolved upon Gen. G. W. Smith; but two days later Gen. Robert E. Lee was given the command of the Confederate forces in Virginia, which he retained continuously till his surrender brought the war to a close. The plan that he had opposed, and caused Mr. Davis to reject, when Johnston was in command—of bringing large bodies of troops from North Carolina, Georgia, and the Shenandoah Valley, to form a massive army and fall upon McClellan—he now adopted and proceeded at once to carry out. Johnston enumerates reinforcements that were given him aggregating fifty-three thousand men, and says he had then the largest Confederate army that ever fought. The total number is given officially at eighty thousand seven hundred and sixty-two. This probably means the number of men actually carrying muskets, and excludes all officers, teamsters, musicians, and mechanics; for the Confederate returns were generally made in that way.

BATTERY No. 4 IN FRONT OF YORKTOWN.
(Three Views.)

McClellan's total effective force, including every man that drew pay the last week in June, was ninety-two thousand five hundred. His constant expectation of reinforcements by way of Fredericksburg was largely, if not wholly, what kept him in his false position, and it is fair to presume that but for this he would have swung across the peninsula to the new base on the James much sooner and under more favorable circumstances.

Wishing to know the extent of McClellan's earthworks on the right wing, Lee, on June 12th, sent a body of twelve hundred cavalry, with two light guns, to reconnoitre. It was commanded by the dashing Gen. J. E. B. Stuart, commonly called "Jeb Stuart," who used to dress in gay costume, with yellow sash and black plume, wore gold spurs, and rode a white horse. He was only ordered to go as far as Hanover Old Church; but at that point he had a fight with a small body of cavalry, and as he supposed dispositions would be made to cut him off, instead of returning he kept on and made the entire circuit of McClellan's army, rebuilding a bridge to cross the lower Chickahominy, and reached Richmond in safety. The actual amount of damage that he had done was small; but the raid alarmed the National commander for the safety of his communications, and was probably what determined him to change his base. In this expedition Stuart lost but one man. In the encounter at Hanover Old Church a charge was led by the Confederate Captain Latane and received by a detachment commanded by Captain Royall. The two captains

QUAKER GUNS.

fought hand to hand, and Latane was shot dead, while Royall received severe sabre wounds.

Stonewall Jackson, if not Lee's ablest lieutenant, was certainly his swiftest, and the one that threw the most uncertainty into the game by his rapid movements and unexpected appearances. At a later stage of the war his erratic strategy, if persisted in, would probably have brought his famous corps of "foot cavalry" (as they were called from their quick marches) to sudden destruction. An opponent like Sheridan, who knew how to be swift, brilliant, and audacious, without transgressing the fundamental rules of warfare, would have been likely to finish him at a blow. But Jackson did not live to meet such an opponent. At this time the bugbears that haunt imaginations not inured to war were still in force, and the massive thimble-rigging by which he was made to appear before Richmond, and presto! sweeping down the Shenandoah Valley, served to paralyze large forces that might have been added to McClellan's army.

MAJOR-GENERAL SILAS CASEY.

MAJOR-GENERAL E. V. SUMNER.

BRIGADIER-GENERAL JAMES SHIELDS.

The topography of Virginia is favorable to an army menacing Washington, and unfavorable to one menacing Richmond. The fertile valley of the Shenandoah was inviting ground for soldiers. A Confederate force advancing down the valley came at every step nearer to the National capital, while a National force advancing up the valley was carried at every step farther away from the Confederate capital. The Confederates made much of this advantage, and the authorities at Washington were in constant fear of the capture of that city.

Soon after Stuart's raid, Lee began to make his dispositions to attack McClellan and drive him from the peninsula. He wrote to Jackson: "Unless McClellan can be driven out of his intrenchments, he will move by positions, under cover of his

BURNING OF STORES AND MUNITIONS OF WAR AT WHITE HOUSE, VA.—DEPARTURE OF THE FEDERAL FLOTILLA FOR THE JAMES RIVER.

BATTLE OF FAIR OAKS.

heavy guns, within shelling distance of Richmond." To convey the impression that Jackson was to move in force down the valley, Lee drew two brigades from his own army, placed them on the cars in Richmond in plain sight of some prisoners that were about to be exchanged, and sent them off to Jackson. Of course the released prisoners carried home the news. But Jackson returned with these reinforcements and Ewell's division of his corps, joined Lee, and on the 25th of June concerted a plan for immediate attack. Secretary Stanton appears to have been the only one that saw through the game; for he telegraphed to McClellan that while neither Banks nor McDowell nor Frémont could ascertain anything about Jackson's movements, his own belief was that he was going to Richmond. Yet the impression was not strong enough in the mind of the Secretary of War (or else the Secretary could not have his own way) to induce the appropriate counter-move of immediately sending McDowell's whole corps to McClellan. McCall's division of that corps, however, had been forwarded, and on the 18th took a strong position on McClellan's extreme right, near Mechanicsville.

Admiral Phelps, of the navy, then a lieutenant commanding the gunboat *Corwin*, and serving in the waters about the peninsula, writes: "About ten o'clock one evening my emissary notified me that a certain man, who had caused much trouble, would leave Centreville about midnight, in a buggy, with letters for 'Queen Caroline' and Richmond, in violation of orders. Soon after daylight the following morning both man and mail were in my possession. Only one letter in the package was of any value (the others were sent to their destination), and that one—written by an adjutant-general in the Confederate army, informing his father that, 'on a certain night,' mentioning the date, 'one hundred thousand men from Beauregard's army at Shiloh would be in Richmond, after detaching thirty thousand to reinforce Stonewall Jackson, who was doing for the enemy in the mountains'—was placed in General McClellan's hands about five P.M. the following day by one of his aids, to whose care I had intrusted it."

PROFESSOR T. S. C. LOWE, BALLOONIST.

On the 25th McClellan had pushed back the Confederates on his left, taken a new position there, and advanced his outposts to a point only four miles from Richmond. But he began his movements too late, for the Confederates were already in motion. Leaving about thirty thousand men in the immediate defences of Richmond, Lee crossed the Chickahominy with about thirty-five thousand under Generals A. P. Hill, D. H. Hill, and Longstreet, intending to join Jackson's twenty-five thousand, and with this enormous force make a sudden attack on the twenty thousand National troops that were on the north side of the river, commanded by Gen. Fitz-John Porter, destroy them before help could reach them, and seize McClellan's communications with his base. Jackson, who was to have appeared on the field at sunrise of the 26th, was for once behind time. The other Confederate commanders became nervous and impatient; for if the movement were known to McClellan, he could, with a little boldness and some fighting, have captured Richmond that day. Indeed, the inhabitants of the city expected nothing else, and it is said that the archives of the Confederate Government were all packed and ready for instant removal. At midday Gen. A. P. Hill's corps drove the small National force out of Mechanicsville, and advanced to McCall's strong position on Beaver Dam Creek. This they dared not attack in front; but they made desperate attempts on both flanks, and the result was an afternoon of fruitless fighting, in which they were literally mown down by the well-served artillery, and lost upward of three thousand men, while McCall maintained his position at every point and lost fewer than three hundred.

That night, in pursuance of the plan for a change of base, the heavy guns that had thwarted Lee in his first attack were carried across the Chickahominy, together with a large part of the baggage train. On the morning of the 27th Porter fell back somewhat to a position on a range of low hills, where he could keep the enemy in check till the stores were removed to the other side of the river, which was now his only object. McClellan sent him five thousand more men in the course of the day, being afraid to send any greater number, because he believed that the bulk of the Confederate army was in the defences on his left, and a show of activity there still further deceived them.

MAJOR-GENERAL BENJAMIN HUGER, C. S. A

BRIGADIER-GENERAL J. J. PETTIGREW, C. S. A.

ST. PETER'S CHURCH, NEAR WHITE HOUSE.
(George Washington was married in this church.)

On the morning of the 27th Porter had eighteen thousand infantry, two thousand five hundred artillerymen, and a small force of cavalry, with which to meet the attack of at least fifty-five thousand. Longstreet and the Hills had followed the retreat closely, but, warned by the experience of the day before, were not willing to attack until Jackson should join them. The fighting began about two o'clock in the afternoon, when A. P. Hill assaulted the centre of Porter's position, and in a two hours' struggle was driven back with heavy loss. Two attacks on the right met with no better success. The effect on the new troops that had been hurried up from the coast was complete demoralization. The Confederate General Whiting says in his report: "Men were leaving the field in every direction, and in great disorder. Two regiments, one from South Carolina and one from Louisiana, were actually marching back from the fire. Men were skulking from the front in a shameful manner."

But at length Jackson's men arrived, and a determined effort was made on all parts of the line at once. Even then it seemed for a time as if victory might rest with the little army on the hills; and in all probability it would, if they had had such intrenchments as the men afterward learned how to construct very quickly; but their breastworks were only such as could be made from hastily felled trees, a few rails, and heaps of knap-sacks. The Confederates had the advantage of thick woods in which to form and advance. As they emerged and came on in heavy masses, with the Confederate yell, they were answered by the Union cheer. Volley responded to volley, guns were taken and re-taken, and cannoneers that remained after the infantry supports retired were shot down; but it was not till sunset that the National line was fairly disrupted, at the left centre, when the whole gave way and slowly retired. Two regiments were captured, and twenty-two guns fell into the hands of the enemy. In the night Porter crossed the river with his remaining force, and destroyed the bridges. This was called by the Confederates the battle of the Chickahominy; but it takes its better known name from two mills (Gaines's) near the scene of action. The total National loss was six thousand men. The Confederate loss was never properly ascertained, which renders it probable that it was much larger. Some of the wounded lay on the field four days uncared for. This action is sometimes called the first battle of Cold Harbor. The armies under Grant and Lee fought on the same ground two years later.

Lee and Jackson believed that they had been fighting the whole of McClellan's forces, and another mistake that they made secured the safety of that army. They took it for granted that the National commander, driven from his base at White House, would retreat down the peninsula, taking the same route by which he had come. Consequently they remained with their large force on the left bank of the Chickahominy, and even advanced some distance down the stream, which gave McClellan twenty-four hours of precious time to get through the swamp roads with his immense trains. He had five thousand loaded wagons, and two thousand five hundred head of cattle. Gen. Silas Casey's division, in charge of the stores at White House, loaded all they could upon transports, and destroyed the remainder. Trains of cars filled with supplies were put under full speed and run off the tracks into the river. Hundreds of tons of ammunition, and millions of rations, were burned or otherwise destroyed.

Rear Admiral Thomas S. Phelps, United States Navy, gives a vivid description of the scene when the transports and other vessels fled down the river in panic: "Harassing the enemy and protecting the worthy fully occupied my time until the afternoon of June 27, 1862, when Quartermaster-General Ingalls came down the river on a boat provided especially for his use, and after directing an assistant to abandon the Point, immediately continued on his way to Yorktown. Soon afterward the Pamunkey, as far as the eye could reach, appeared crowded with a confused mass of side-wheel boats, propellers, brigs, and schooners, and as they dashed past my vessel there appeared to be as complete a stampede as it has ever been my misfortune to witness. In answer to the hail, 'What is the trouble?' I was greeted with, 'The rebels are coming! The whole country is full of them; go to the mast-head and you will see thousands of them!' Eliciting nothing further of a satisfactory nature, and seeing nothing but empty fields, I directed a count to be made of the fleeing vessels, and by evening's dusk six hundred

BATTLE OF MALVERN HILL.—LEE'S ATTACK.

BATTLE OF CHARLES CITY CROSS-ROADS, JUNE 30, 1862.

and eighty were reported as having passed, not counting several schooners left behind, which on touching the bottom had been abandoned, their crews escaping to more fortunate companions." On the following day the gunboats returned to West Point, towing the derelict schooners which they had floated, and also the half of a regiment which in the hurry of the previous day had been forgotten and left behind. At the last moment Casey embarked his men, and with what he had been able to save steamed down the Pamunkey and York Rivers, and up the James to the new base. At the close of a long despatch to the Secretary of War, on the 28th, General McClellan said: "If I save this army now, I tell you plainly that I owe no thanks to you or to any other persons in Washington. You have done your best to sacrifice this army."

When Gen. John B. Magruder, who had been left in the defences of Richmond, found that the National army was retreating to the James, he moved out to attack it, and struck the rear guard at Allen's farm. His men made three assaults, and were three times repelled. Magruder complained that he lost a victory here because Lee had left him but thirteen thousand men.

LIEUTENANT-GENERAL A. P. HILL, C. S. A.

LIEUTENANT-GENERAL J. E. B. STUART.

BRIGADIER-GENERAL JAS. E. RAINS, C. S. A.
LIEUTENANT-GENERAL D. H. HILL, C. S. A.

The National troops fell back to Savage's Station, where later in the day Magruder attacked them again. He had a rifled cannon mounted on a platform car, with which he expected to do great execution. But there was an ample force to oppose him, and it stood unmoved by his successive charges. About sunset he advanced his whole line with a desperate rush in the face of a continuous fire of cannon and musketry; but it was of no avail, and half an hour later his own line was broken by a counter charge that closed the battle. He admitted a loss of four thousand men. Sumner and Franklin, at a cost of three thousand, had thus maintained the approach to the single road through White Oak Swamp, by which they were to follow the body of the army that had already passed. But it was found necessary to burn another immense quantity of food and clothing that could not be removed, and to leave behind two thousand five hundred sick and wounded men.

Jackson, after spending a day in building bridges, crossed the Chickahominy and attempted to follow McClellan's rear guard through White Oak Swamp; but when he got to the other side he found a necessary bridge destroyed and National batteries commanding its site, so that it was impossible for his forces to emerge from the swamp. But meanwhile Hill and Longstreet had crossed the river farther up stream, marched around the swamp, and struck the retreating army near Charles City Cross-Roads, on the 30th. There was terrific fighting all the afternoon. There were brave charges and bloody repulses, masses of men moving up steadily in the face of batteries that tore great gaps through them at every discharge, crossed bayonets, and clubbed muskets. Only on that part of the line held by McCall did the Confederates, with all their daring, succeed in breaking through. McCall, in his report, describes the successful charge: "A most determined charge was made on Randol's battery by a full brigade, advancing in wedge shape, without order, but in perfect recklessness. Somewhat similar charges had been previously made on Cooper's and Kern's batteries by single regiments, without success, they having recoiled before the storm of canister hurled against them. A like result was anticipated by Randol's battery, and the Fourth Regiment was requested not to fire until the battery had done with them. Its gallant commander did not doubt his ability to repel the attack, and his guns did indeed mow down the advancing host; but still the gaps were closed, and the enemy came in upon a run to the very muzzles of his guns. It was a perfect torrent of men, and they were in his battery before the guns could be removed." General McCall himself, endeavoring to rally his men at this point, was captured and carried off to Richmond. In Kearney's front a similar charge was made three times; but every time a steady musketry fire drove back the enemy that had closed up its gaps made by the artillery. Darkness put an end to the fighting, and that night McClellan's army continued its retreat to Malvern Hill, where

BREVET MAJOR-GENERAL JOHN G. BARNARD.

his advance guard had taken up the strongest position he had yet occupied. The battle just described has several names — Glendale, Frazier's Farm, Charles City Cross-Roads, Newmarket, Nelson's Farm. McClellan here lost ten guns. The losses in men cannot be known exactly, as the reports group the losses of several days together. Longstreet and the two Hills reported a loss of twelve thousand four hundred and fifty-eight in the fighting from the 27th to the 30th.

The last stand made by McClellan for delivering battle was at Malvern Hill. This is a plateau near Turkey Bend of James River, having an elevation of sixty feet, and an extent of about a mile and a half in one direction and a mile in the other. It is so bordered by streams and swamps as to leave no practicable approach except by the narrow northwest face. Here McClellan had his entire army in position when his pursuers came up. It was disposed in the form of a semicircle, with the right wing "refused" (swung back) and prolonged to Haxall's Landing, on the James. His position was peculiarly favorable for the use of artillery, and his whole front bristled with it. There were no intrenchments to speak of, but the natural inequalities of the ground afforded considerable shelter for the men and the guns. It was as complete a trap as could be set for an army, and Lee walked straight into it. Under ordinary circumstances, both commander and men would properly hesitate to attack an enemy so posted. But to the confidence with which the Southerners began the war was now added the peculiar elation produced by a week's pursuit of a retreating army; and apparently it did not occur to them that they were all mortal.

In the first contact seven thousand Confederates, with six guns, struck the left of the position. They boldly advanced their artillery to within eight hundred yards of the cliff; but before they could get at work, a fire of twenty or thirty guns was concentrated upon their battery, which knocked it to pieces in a few minutes; and at the same time some huge shells from a gunboat fell among a small detachment of cavalry, threw it into confusion, and turned it back upon the infantry, breaking up the whole attack.

BREVET BRIGADIER-GENERAL J. J. ABERCROMBIE.

Lee was not ready to assault with his whole army till the afternoon of July 1st. An artillery duel was kept up during the forenoon, but the Confederate commander did not succeed in destroying the National batteries, as he hoped to; on the contrary, he saw his own disabled, one after another. The signal for the infantry attack was to be the usual yell, raised by Armistead's division on the right and taken up by the successive divisions along the line. But the Confederate line was separated by thick woods; there was long waiting for the signal; some of the generals thought they heard it, and some advanced without hearing it. The consequence was a series of separate attacks, some of them repeated three or four times, and every time a concentrated fire on the attacking column and a bloody repulse. The men themselves began to see the hopelessness of it, while their officers were still urging them to renewed efforts. "Come on, come on, my men," said one Confederate colonel, with the grim humor of a soldier; "do you want to live forever?" There were some brief counter-charges, in one of which the colors were taken from a North Carolina regiment; but in general the National troops only maintained their ground, and though fighting was kept up till nine o'clock in the evening, the line—as Gen-

BRIGADIER-GENERAL L. C. HUNT.

BRIGADIER-GENERAL HENRY M. NAGLEE.

BREVET MAJOR-GENERAL INNIS N. PALMER.

eral Webb, then assistant chief of artillery, tells us—was never for one instant broken or the guns in danger. This battle cost Lee five thousand men, and at its close he gave up the pursuit. The National loss was less than one-third as great. That night McClellan withdrew his army to Harrison's Landing, on the James, where he had fixed his base of supplies and where the gunboats could protect his position. This retreat is known as the Seven Days, and the losses are figured up at fifteen thousand two hundred and forty-nine on the National side, and somewhat over nineteen thousand on the Confederate.

GRAPEVINE BRIDGE.

From that time there was an angry controversy as to the military abilities of General McClellan and the responsibility for the failure of the campaign, and partisanship was never more violent than over this question. The General had won the highest personal regard of his soldiers, and they were mostly unwilling or unable to look at the matter in the cold light of the criticism that simply asks, What was required? and What was accomplished? The truth appears to be, that General McClellan, like most men, possessed some virtues and lacked others. He organized a great army, and to the end of its days it felt the benefit of the discipline with which he endowed it. But with that army in hand he did not secure the purpose of its creation. He was an accomplished engineer, and a gigantic adjutant, but hardly the general to be sent against an army that could move and a commander that could think. There can be no doubt that the Administration was over-anxious about the movements in the Shenandoah, and should have sent McDowell's corps to McClellan at once; but neither can there be much doubt that if Little Mac, the Young Napoleon, as he was fondly called, had been a general of the highest order, he would have destroyed Lee's army and captured the Confederate capital with the ample forces that he had. It was not General McClellan alone that was in a false position when his army was astride the Chickahominy, but the Administration and the people of the loyal States as well. Their grand strategy was radically vicious, for they stood astride of the great central question of the war itself.

To a student of the art of war, this disastrous campaign and the many criticisms that it evoked are exceedingly interesting. Nearly every military problem was in some way presented in it. Two or three quotations from the best sources will indicate its importance and the complicated questions that it involved. General McClellan himself says in his report: "It may be asked why, after the concentration of our forces on the right bank of the Chickahominy, with a large part of the enemy drawn away from Richmond, upon the opposite side, I did not, instead of striking for James River fifteen miles below that place, at once march directly on Richmond. It will be remembered that at this juncture the enemy was on our rear, and there was every reason

GENERAL McCLELLAN'S ARMY BETWEEN BIG BETHEL AND YORKTOWN.

to believe that he would sever our communications with our supply depot at the White House. We had on hand but a limited amount of rations, and if we had advanced directly on Richmond it would have required considerable time to carry the strong works around that place, during which our men would have been destitute of food; and even if Richmond had fallen before our arms, the enemy could still have occupied our supply communications between that place and the gunboats, and turned their disaster into victory. If, on the other hand, the enemy had concentrated all his forces at Richmond during the progress of our attack, and we had been defeated, we must in all probability have lost our trains before reaching the flotilla. The battles which continued day after day in the progress of our flank movement to the James, with the exception of the one at Gaines's Mill, were successes to our arms, and the closing engagement at Malvern Hill was the most decisive of all."

One of General McClellan's severest critics, Gen. John G. Barnard, in an elaborate review of the campaign, wrote: "It was a blunder unparalleled to expose Porter's corps to fight a battle by itself on the 27th against overwhelming forces of the enemy. With perfect ease that corps might have been brought over on the night of the 26th, and, if nothing more brilliant could have been thought of, the movement to the James might have been in full tide of execution on the 27th. A more propitious moment could not have been chosen, for, besides Jackson's own forces, A. P. Hill's and Longstreet's corps were on the left bank of the Chickahominy on the night of the 26th. Such a movement need not have been discovered to the enemy till far enough advanced to insure success. At any rate, he could have done no better in preventing it than he actually did afterward. . . . He has spent weeks in building bridges which establish a close connection between the wings of his army, and then fights a great battle with a smaller fraction of his army than when he had a single available bridge, and that remote. He, with great labor, constructs 'defensive works' in order that he 'may bring the greatest possible numbers into action,' and again exhibits his ability to utilize his means by keeping sixty-five thousand men idle behind them, while thirty-five thousand, unaided by 'defensive works' of any kind, fight the bulk of his adversary's forces, and are, of course, overwhelmed by 'superior numbers.' We believe there were few commanding officers of the Army of the Potomac who did not expect to be led offensively against the enemy on the 26th or 27th. Had such a movement been made, it is not improbable that, if energetically led, we should have gone into Richmond. Jackson and A. P. Hill could not have got back in time to succor Magruder's command, if measures of most obvious propriety had been taken to prevent them. We might have beaten or driven Magruder's twenty-five thousand men and entered Richmond, and then, reinforced by the great moral acquisition of strength this success would have given, have fought Lee and reëstablished our communications. At any rate, something of this kind was worth trying. . . . Our army is now concentrated on the James; but we have another day's fighting before us, and this day we may expect the concentrated attack of Lee's whole army. We know not at what hour it will come—possibly late, for it requires time to find out our new position and to bring together the attacking columns—yet we know not when it will come. Where, this day, is the commanding general? Off, with Captain Rodgers, to select 'the final positions of the army and its depots.' He does not tell us that it was on a gunboat, and that this day not even 'signals' would keep him in communication with his army, for his journey was ten or fifteen miles down the river; and he was thus absent till late in the afternoon. This is the first time we ever had reason to believe that the highest and first duty of a general, on the day of battle, was separating himself from his army to reconnoitre a place of retreat! . . . If the enemy had two hundred thousand men, it was to be seriously apprehended that, leaving fifty thousand behind the 'strong works' of Richmond, he would march at once with one hundred and fifty thousand men on Washington. Why should he not? General McClellan and his eulogists have held up as highly meritorious strategy the leaving of Washington defended by less than fifty thousand men, with the enemy in its front estimated to be one hundred and twenty thousand to one hundred and fifty thousand strong, and moving off to take an eccentric line of operations against Richmond; and now the reverse case is presented, but with an important difference. The enemy at Manassas, on learning General McClellan's movement, could either fly to the defence of Richmond or attack Washington. General McClellan says that this latter course was not to be feared. McClellan on the James, on learning that Lee with one hundred and fifty thousand men is marching on Washington, can only attack Richmond; by no possibility can he fly to the defence of Washington. Besides, he is inferior in numbers (according to his own estimate) even to Lee's marching army. Here, in a nutshell, is the demonstration of the folly of the grand strategic movement on Richmond, as given by its own projector."

An English military critic thus analyzes the great campaign: "As regards the value of the plan, in a merely military point of view, three faults may be enumerated: It was too rash; it violated the principles of war; its application was too timid. (1) An army of one hundred and thirty thousand volunteers should not be moved about as if it were a single division. (2) The choice of Fort Monroe as a secondary basis involved the necessity of leaving Washington, or the fixed basis, to be threatened, morally at least, by the enemy. The communications also between these two places were open to an attack from the *Merrimac*, an iron-plated ship, which lay at Norfolk, on the south side of Hampton Roads. The first movement to Fort Monroe was the stride of a giant. The second, in the direction of Richmond, was that of a dwarf. When the army arrived in front of the lines at Yorktown, it numbered, probably, one hundred thousand men, and here there was no timid President to interfere with the command; nevertheless, McClellan suffered himself to be stopped in the middle of an offensive campaign by Magruder and twelve thousand men. . . . The hour of his arrival in front of the lines should have been the hour of his attack upon them. Two overwhelming masses, to which life and energy had been communicated, should have been hurled on separate points. Magruder not only defeated but destroyed! The *morale* of the Federal army raised! The result of the campaign, although it might not have been decisive, would have been more honorable."

On the Confederate side the criticism was almost as severe, because, while claiming the result of the six days as a Confederate success, it was also claimed that the campaign should have resulted in the complete destruction of McClellan's army.

The use of balloons for reconnoitring the enemy's position formed a picturesque feature of this campaign. T. S. C. Lowe, J. H. Stiner, and other aëronauts were at the National headquarters with their balloons, and several officers of high rank accompanied them in numerous ascents. But it seems to have been demonstrated that the balloon was of little practical value.

MAJOR-GENERAL JOHN POPE.

CHAPTER XIV.

POPE'S CAMPAIGN.

FORMATION OF THE ARMY OF VIRGINIA—HALLECK MADE GENERAL-IN-CHIEF — McCLELLAN LEAVES THE PENINSULA — BATTLE OF CEDAR MOUNTAIN — POPE AND LEE MANŒUVRE — BATTLE OF GROVETON—THE SECOND BULL RUN—BATTLE OF CHANTILLY—THE PORTER DISPUTE—GENERAL GRANT'S OPINION—COMPLICATED MOVEMENTS OF THE CAMPAIGN—INTERESTING INCIDENTS.

WHILE McClellan was before Richmond, it was determined to consolidate in one command the corps of Banks, Frémont, and McDowell, which were moving about in an independent and ineffectual way between Washington and the Shenandoah Valley. Gen. John Pope, who had won considerable reputation by his capture of Island No. 10, was called from the West and given command (June 26, 1862) of the new organization, which was called the Army of Virginia. Frémont declined to serve under a commander who had once been his subordinate, and consequently his corps was given to General Sigel. General Pope, on taking command of this force, which numbered all told about thirty-eight thousand men, and also of the troops in the fortifications around Washington, had the bad taste to issue a general order that had three capital defects: it boasted of his own prowess at the West, it underrated his enemy, and it contained a bit of sarcasm pointed at General McClellan, the commander of the army with which his own was to coöperate. Pope says, in his report, that he wrote a cordial letter to McClellan, asking for his views as to the best plan of campaign, and offering to render him any needed assistance; and that he received but a cold and indefinite reply. It is likely enough that a courteous man and careful soldier like McClellan would be in no mood to fall in with the suggestions of a commander that entered upon his work with a gratuitous piece of bombast, and seemed to have no conception of the serious nature of the task. When it became evident that these two commanders could not act sufficiently in harmony, the President called Gen. Henry W. Halleck from the West to be General-in-Chief, with headquarters at Washington, and command them both. Halleck had perhaps more military learning than any other man in the country, and his patriotic intentions were unquestionably good; but in practical warfare he proved to be little more than a great obstructor. He had been the bane of the Western armies, preventing them from following up their victories, and had almost driven Grant out of the service; and from the day he took command at Washington (July 12) the troubles in the East became more complicated than ever.

McClellan held a strong position at Harrison's Landing, where, if he accomplished nothing else, he was a standing menace to Richmond, so that Lee dared not withdraw his army from its defence. He wanted to be heavily reinforced, cross the James, and strike at Richmond's southern communications, just as Grant actually did two years later; and he was promised reinforcements from the troops of Burnside and Hunter, on the coast of North and South Carolina. Lee's anxiety was to get McClellan off from the peninsula, so that he could strike out toward Washington. He first sent a detachment to bombard McClellan's camp from the opposite side of the James; but McClellan crossed the river with a sufficient force and easily swept it out of the way. Then Lee sent Jackson to make a demonstration against Pope, holding the main body of his army ready to follow as soon as some erratic and energetic movements of Jackson had caused a sufficient alarm at Washington to determine the withdrawal of McClellan. The unwitting Halleck was all too swift to coöperate with his enemy, and had already determined upon that withdrawal. Burnside's troops, coming up on transports, were not even landed, but were forwarded up the Potomac and sent to Pope. McClellan marched his army to Fort Monroe, and there embarked it by divisions for the same destination.

Pope's intention was to push southward, strike Lee's western and northwestern communications, and cut them off from the Shenandoah Valley. He first ordered Banks (July 14) to push his whole cavalry force to Gordonsville, and destroy the railroads and bridges in that vicinity. But the cavalry commander, General Hatch, took with him infantry, artillery, and a wagon train, and consequently did not move at cavalry speed. Before he could get to Gordonsville, Jackson's advance reached it, and his movement was frustrated. He was relieved of his command, and it was given to Gen. John Buford, an able cavalry leader.

As soon as Jackson came in contact with Pope's advance, he called upon Lee for reinforcements, and promptly received them. On the 8th of August he crossed the Rapidan, and moved toward Culpeper. Pope, who had but recently taken the field in person, having remained in Washington till July 29th, attempted to concentrate the corps of Banks and Sigel at Culpeper. Banks arrived there promptly on the 8th; but Sigel sent a note from Sperryville in the afternoon, asking by what road he should march. "As there was but one road between those two points," says Pope, "and that a broad stone turnpike, I was at a loss to understand how General Sigel could entertain any doubt as to the road by which he should march." On the morning of the 9th Banks's corps went out alone to meet the enemy at Cedar Mountain. Banks had eight thousand men (Pope says he had supposed that corps numbered fourteen thousand), and attacked an enemy twice as strong. He first struck Jackson's right wing, and afterward furiously attacked the left, rolled up the flank, opened a fire in the rear, and threw Jackson's whole line into confusion. It was as if the two commanders had changed characters, and Banks had suddenly assumed the part that, according to the popular idea, Jackson was always supposed to play. If Sigel had only known what road to take, that might have been the last of Jackson. But Banks's force had become somewhat broken in its advance through the woods, and at the same time the Confederates were reinforced, so that Jackson was able to rally his men and check the movement. Banks in turn was forced back a short distance, where he took up a strong position.

Sigel's corps arrived in the evening, relieved Banks's corps, and made immediate preparations for a renewal of the fight in the morning. The dead were buried, the wounded carried forth, and through the night trains were moving and everything being put in readiness, but at daylight it was discovered that the enemy had fallen back two miles to a new position. Partly because of the strong position held by each, and partly because of the very hot weather, there was little further disposition to renew the fight, and two days later Jackson fell still further back to Gordonsville. In this action, which for the numbers engaged was one of the fiercest and most rapid of the war, the Confederates lost about thirteen hundred men and the National army about eighteen hundred. "Besides which," says General Pope, "fully one thousand men straggled back to Culpeper Court House and beyond, and never entirely returned to their commands." On the other hand, the cavalry under Buford and Bayard pursued the enemy and captured many stragglers. The Confederate Gen. Charles S. Winder was struck by a shell and killed while leading his division.

POPE'S BAGGAGE-TRAIN IN THE MUD.

VIEW IN CULPEPER.

Immediately after this action the cavalry resumed its former position along the Rapidan from Raccoon Ford to the mountains. On the 14th of August General Pope was reinforced by eight thousand men under General Reno, whereupon he pushed his whole force forward toward the Rapidan, and took up a position with his right on Robertson's River, his centre on the slopes of Cedar Mountain and his left near Raccoon Ford. From this point he sent out cavalry expeditions to destroy the enemy's communications with Richmond, and one of these captured General Stuart's adjutant, with a letter from Lee to General Stuart, dated August 15th, which to a large extent revealed Lee's plans. The incident that resulted in this important capture is thus related by Stuart's biographer, Major H. B. McClellan: "Stuart reached Verdiersville on the evening of the 17th, and hearing nothing from Fitz Lee, sent his adjutant, Major Norman R. Fitz Hugh, to meet him and ascertain his position. A body of the enemy's cavalry had, however, started on a reconnoissance on the previous day, and in the darkness of the night Major Fitz Hugh rode into this party and was captured. On his person was found an autograph letter from the commanding general to Stuart which disclosed to General Pope the design of turning his left flank. The fact that Fitz Hugh did not return aroused no apprehension, and Stuart and his staff imprudently passed the night on the porch of an old house on the Plank Road. At daybreak he was aroused by the noise of approaching horsemen, and sending Mosby and Gibson, two of his aides, to ascertain who was coming, he himself walked out to the front gate, bareheaded, to greet Fitz Lee, as he supposed. The result did not justify his expectations. In another instant pistol shots were heard, and Mosby and Gibson were seen running back, pursued by a party of the enemy. Stuart, Von Borcke, and Dabney had their horses inside of the inclosure of the yard. Von Borcke gained the gate and the

HENRY AND ROBINSON HOUSES, BULL RUN.
(From photograph taken in 1884.)

CONFEDERATE DEAD LAID OUT FOR BURIAL.

road, and escaped unhurt after a long and hard run. Stuart and Dabney were compelled to leap the yard fence and take across the fields to the nearest woods. They were pursued but a short distance. Returning to a post of observation, Stuart saw the enemy depart in triumph with his hat and cloak, which he had been compelled to leave on the porch where he had slept. He bore this mortification with good nature. In a letter of about that date he writes: 'I am greeted on all sides with congratulations and "Where's your hat?" I intend to make the Yankees pay for that hat.' And Pope did cancel the debt a few nights afterward at Catlett's Station."

The captured despatch revealed to Pope the fact that Lee intended to fall upon him with his entire army and crush him before he could be reinforced from the Army of the Potomac. Pope says: "I held on to my position, thus far to the front, for the purpose of affording all time possible for the arrival of the Army of the Potomac at Acquia and Alexandria, and to embarrass and delay the movements of the enemy as far as practicable. On the 18th of August it became apparent to me that this advanced position, with the small force under my command, was no longer tenable in the face of the overwhelming forces of the enemy. I determined, accordingly, to withdraw behind the Rappahannock with all speed, and, as I had been instructed, to defend, as far as practicable, the line of that river. I directed Major-General Reno to send back his trains, on the morning of the 18th, by the way of Stevensburg, to Kelly's or Burnett's Ford, and, as soon as the trains had gotten several hours in advance, to follow them with his whole corps, and take post behind the Rappahannock,

MAJOR-GENERAL G. W. C. LEE.
GENERAL ROBERT E. LEE, C. S. A.
COLONEL WALTER TAYLOR.

JOHN LETCHER.
Governor of Virginia.

leaving all his cavalry in the neighborhood of Raccoon Ford to cover this movement. General Banks's corps, which had been ordered, on the 12th, to take position at Culpeper Court House, I directed, with its trains preceding it, to cross the Rappahannock at the point where the Orange and Alexandria railroad crosses that river. General McDowell's train was ordered to pursue the same route, while the train of General Sigel was directed through Jefferson, to cross the Rappahannock at Warrenton Sulphur Springs. So soon as these trains had been sufficiently advanced, McDowell's corps was directed to take the route from Culpeper to Rappahannock Ford, whilst General Sigel, who was on the right and front, was instructed to follow the movements of his train to Sulphur Springs. These movements were executed during the day and night of the 18th, and the day of the 19th, by which time the whole army, with its trains, had safely recrossed the Rappahannock and was posted behind that stream, with its left at Kelly's Ford and its right about three miles above Rappahannock Station." The Confederates followed rapidly, and on the 20th confronted Pope at Kelly's Ford, but with the river between. For two days they made strenuous efforts to cross, but a powerful artillery fire, which was kept up continuously for seven or eight miles along the river, made any crossing in force impossible. Lee therefore sent Jackson to make a flank march westward along that stream, cross it at Sulphur Springs, and come down upon Pope's right. But when Jackson arrived at the crossing, he found a heavy force occupying Sulphur Springs and ready to meet him. Meanwhile Gen. James E. B. Stuart, with fifteen hundred cavalrymen, in the dark and stormy night of August 22d, had ridden around to the rear of Pope's position, to cut the railroad. He struck Pope's headquarters at Catlett's Station, captured three hundred prisoners and all the personal baggage and papers of the commander, and got back in safety. These papers informed Lee of Pope's plans and dispositions.

Jackson, being thwarted at Sulphur Springs, moved still farther up the south bank of the Rappahannock, crossed the headwaters, and turned Pope's right. He passed through Thoroughfare Gap in the Bull Run Mountains on the 26th, destroyed Bristoe Station on the Orange and Alexandria railroad, and sent out Stuart to Manassas Junction, where prisoners were taken and a large amount of commissary stores fell into his hands.

Pope knew exactly the size of Jackson's force, and the direction it had taken in its flank march; for Col. J. S. Clark, of Banks's staff, had spent a day where he had a plain view of the enemy's moving columns, and carefully counted the regiments and batteries. But from this point the National commander, who had hitherto done reasonably well, seemed suddenly to become bewildered.

He explains in his report that his force was too small to enable him to extend his right any further without too greatly weakening his line, and says he telegraphed the facts repeatedly to Washington, saying that he could not extend further West without losing his connections with Fredericksburg. He declares he was assured on the 21st, that if he could hold the line of the river two days longer he should be heavily reinforced, but that this promise was not kept, the only troops that were added to his army during the next four days being seven thousand men under Generals Reynolds and Kearny.

Lee, whose grand strategy was correct, had here blundered seriously in his manœuvres, dividing his army so that the two parts were not within supporting distance of each other, and the united enemy was between. An ordinarily good general, standing in Pope's boots, would naturally have fallen in force upon Jackson, and could have completely destroyed or captured him. But Pope out-blundered Lee, and gave the victory to the Confederates.

He began by sending forty thousand men under McDowell, on the 27th, toward Thoroughfare Gap, to occupy the road by which Lee with Longstreet's division was marching to join Jackson; and at the same time he moved with the remainder of his army to strike Jackson at Bristoe Station. This was a good beginning, but was immediately ruined by his own lack of steadiness. The advance guard had an engagement at that place

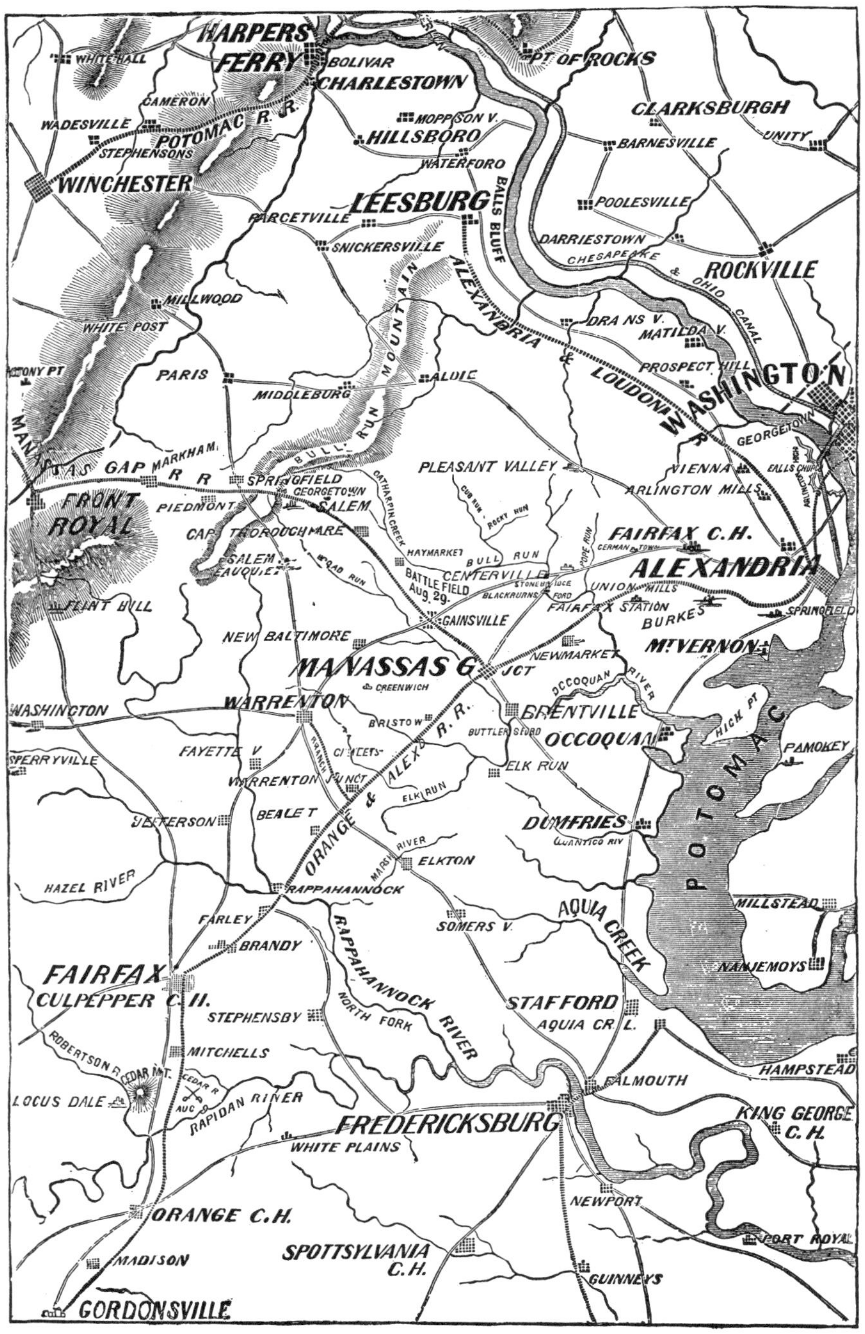

THE SEAT OF MILITARY OPERATIONS IN AUGUST AND SEPTEMBER, 1862.

DAM ACROSS BULL RUN, NEAR BLACKBURN'S FORD.

BRIGADIER-GENERAL HERMANN HAUPT.

BREVET MAJOR-GENERAL GEO. H. GORDON.

with Jackson's rear guard, while his main body retired to Manassas Junction. Pope became elated at the prospect of a great success, and ordered a retrograde movement by McDowell, telling him to march eastward on the 28th, adding: "If you will march promptly and rapidly at the earliest dawn upon Manassas Junction, we shall bag the whole crowd." McDowell obeyed, the way was thus left open for Jackson to move out to meet his friends, and Jackson promptly took advantage of the opportunity and planted himself on the high land around Groveton, near the battlefield of Bull Run. Here King's division of McDowell's corps came suddenly in contact with the enemy, and a sharp fight, with severe loss on either side, ensued. Among the Confederate wounded was Gen. Richard S. Ewell, one of their best commanders, who lost a leg. In the night, King's men fell back to Manassas; and Ricketts's division, which McDowell had left to delay Longstreet when he should attempt to pass through Thoroughfare Gap, was also retired.

All apprehensions on the part of the lucky Jackson were now at an end. His enemies had removed every obstruction, and he was in possession of the Warrenton Turnpike, the road by which Longstreet was to join him. The cut of an abandoned railroad formed a strong, ready-made intrenchment, and along this he placed his troops, his right flank being on the turnpike and his left at Sudley Mill.

General Pope says of his forces at this time: "From the 18th of August until the morning of the 27th the troops under my command had been continuously marching and fighting night and day, and during the whole of that time there was scarcely an interval of an hour without the roar of artillery. The men had had little sleep, were greatly worn down with fatigue, had had little time to get proper food or to eat it, had been engaged in constant battles and skirmishes, and had performed services laborious, dangerous, and excessive beyond any previous experience in this country. As was to be expected under such circumstances, the numbers of the army under my command have been greatly reduced by deaths, by wounds, by sickness, and by fatigue, so that on the morning of the 27th of August I estimated my whole effective force (and I

BREVET BRIGADIER-GENERAL GEO. W. GILL.

think the estimate was large) as follows: Sigel's corps, nine thousand men; Banks's corps, five thousand men; McDowell's corps, including Reynolds's division, fifteen thousand five hundred men; Reno's corps, seven thousand men; the corps of Heintzelman and Porter (the freshest by far in that army), about eighteen thousand men—making in all fifty-four thousand five hundred men. Our cavalry numbered on paper about four thousand men; but their horses were completely broken down, and there were not five hundred men, all told, capable of doing such service as should be expected from cavalry. The corps of Heintzelman had reached Warrenton Junction, but it was without wagons, without artillery, with only forty rounds of ammunition to the man, and without even horses for the general and field officers. The corps of Porter had also reached Warrenton Junction with a very small supply of provisions, and but forty rounds of ammunition for each man."

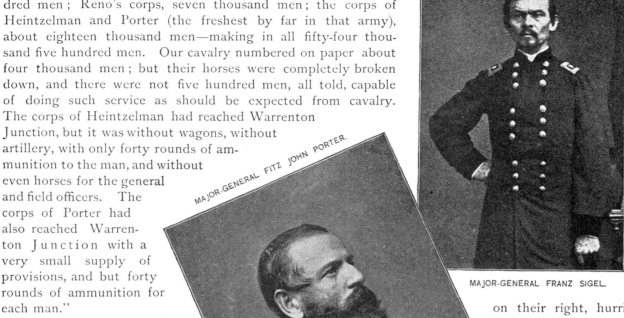

MAJOR-GENERAL FITZ JOHN PORTER.

Longstreet reached the field in the forenoon of the 29th, and took position at Jackson's right, on the other side of the turnpike, covering also the Manassas Gap railroad. He was confronted by Fitz John Porter's corps. McDowell says he ordered Porter to move out and attack Longstreet; Porter says he ordered him simply to hold the ground where he was. At three o'clock in the afternoon Pope ordered Hooker to attack Jackson directly in front. Hooker, who was never loath to fight where there was a prospect of success, remonstrated; but Pope insisted, and the attack was made. Hooker's men charged with the bayonet, had a terrific hand-to-hand fight in the cut, and actually ruptured Jackson's seemingly impregnable line; but reinforcements were brought up, and the assailants were at length driven back. Kearny's division was sent to support Hooker, but too late, and it also was repelled. An hour or two later, Pope, who did not know that Longstreet had arrived on the field, sent orders to Fitz John Porter to attack Jackson's right, supposing that was the right of the whole Confederate line. There is a dispute as to the hour at which this order reached Porter. But it was impossible for him to obey it, since he could not move upon Jackson's

MAJOR-GENERAL FRANZ SIGEL.

flank without exposing his own flank to Longstreet. About six o'clock, when he imagined Porter's attack must have begun, Pope ordered another attack on the Confederate left. It was gallantly made, and in the first rush was successful. Jackson's extreme left was doubled up and broken by Kearny's men, who seized the cut and held it for a time. At this point a Confederate regiment that had exhausted its ammunition fought with stones. There were plenty of fragments of rock at hand, and several men were killed by them. Again the Confederates, undisturbed on their right, hurried across reinforcements to their imperilled left; and Kearny's division, too small to hold what it had gained, was driven back. This day's action is properly called the battle of Groveton.

Pope's forces had been considerably cut up and scattered, but he got them together that night, re-formed his lines, and prepared to renew the attack the next day. Lee at the same time drew back his left somewhat, advanced and strengthened his right, and prepared to take the offensive. Each intended to attack the other's left flank.

When Pope moved out the next day (August 30th) to strike Lee's left, and found it withdrawn, he imagined that the enemy was in retreat, and immediately ordered McDowell to follow it up and "press the enemy vigorously the whole day." Porter's corps—the advance of McDowell's force—had no sooner begun this movement than it struck the foe in a strong position, and was subjected to a heavy artillery fire. Then a cloud of dust was seen to the south, and it was evident that Lee was pushing a force around on the flank. McDowell sent Reynolds to meet and check it. Porter then attempted to obey his orders. He advanced against Jackson's right in charge after charge, but was met by a fire that repelled him every time with bloody loss. Moreover, Longstreet found an eminence that commanded a part of his line, promptly took advantage of it by placing a battery there, and threw in an enfilading fire. It was impossible for anything to withstand this, and Porter's corps in a few minutes fell back defeated. The whole Confederate line was

MAJOR-GENERAL PHILIP KEARNY.

MILL AND HOTEL AT SUDLEY SPRINGS.

advanced, and an attempt was made, by still further extending their right, to cut off retreat; but key-points were firmly held by Warren's brigade and the brigades of Meade and Seymour, and the army was withdrawn in order from the field whence it had retired so precipitously a year before. After dark it crossed the stone bridge over Bull Run, and encamped on the heights around Centreville.

The corps of Sumner and Franklin here joined Pope, and the whole army fell back still further, taking a position around Fairfax Court House and Germantown. Lee meanwhile ordered Jackson to make another of the flank marches that he was so fond of, with a view of striking Pope's right and perhaps interrupting his communication with Washington. It was the evening of September 1st when he fell heavily upon Pope's flank. He was stoutly resisted, and finally repelled by the commands of Hooker and Reno, and a part of those of McDowell and Kearny. General Stevens, of Reno's corps, was killed, and his men, having used up their ammunition, fell back. General Kearny sent Birney's brigade into the gap, and brought up a battery. He then rode forward to reconnoitre, came suddenly upon a squad of Confederates, and in attempting to ride away was shot dead. Kearny was one of the most experienced and efficient soldiers in the service. He had lost an arm in the Mexican war, was with Napoleon III. at Solferino and Magenta, and had just passed through the peninsula campaign with McClellan.

Lee made no further attempt upon Pope's army, and on September 2d, by Halleck's orders, it was withdrawn to the fortifications of Washington, where it was merged in the Army of the Potomac. In this campaign, both the numbers engaged on either side and the respective losses are in dispute, and the exact truth never will be known. Lee claimed that he had captured nine thousand prisoners and thirty guns, and it is probable that Pope's total loss numbered at least fifteen thousand. Pope maintained that he would have won the battle of Groveton and made a successful campaign if General Porter had obeyed his orders. Porter, for this supposed disobedience, was court-martialed in January, 1863, and was condemned and dismissed from the service, and forever disqualified from holding any office of trust or profit under the Government of the United States. Thousands of pages have been written and printed to prove or

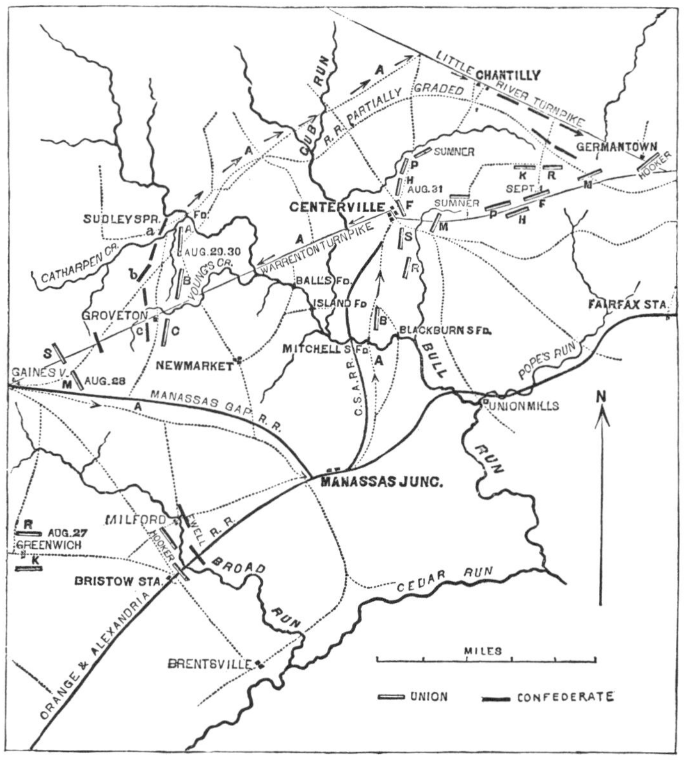

MAP OF SECOND BATTLE OF BULL RUN, SHOWING IMPORTANT POSITIONS OCCUPIED FROM AUGUST 27th TO SEPTEMBER 1st.

SECOND BATTLE
(From a

disprove his innocence, and the evidence has been reviewed again and again. It appears to be established at last that he did not disobey any order that it was possible for him to obey, and that he was blameless—except, perhaps, in having exhibited a spirit of personal hostility to General Pope, who was then his superior officer. A bill to relieve him of the penalty was passed by the Forty-sixth Congress, but was vetoed by President Arthur. Substantially the same bill was passed in 1886 and was signed by President Cleveland. It restored him to his place as colonel in the regular army, and retired him with that rank, but with no compensation for the intervening years.

General Grant, reviewing the case in 1882, came to the conclusion that Porter was innocent, and gave his reasons for it in a magazine article, significantly remarking that "if he was guilty, the punishment awarded was not commensurate with the offence committed." But some other military authorities still believe that his sentence was just. Grant seems to make the question perfectly clear by drawing two simple diagrams. This, he says, is what Pope supposed to be the position of the armies when he ordered Porter to attack:

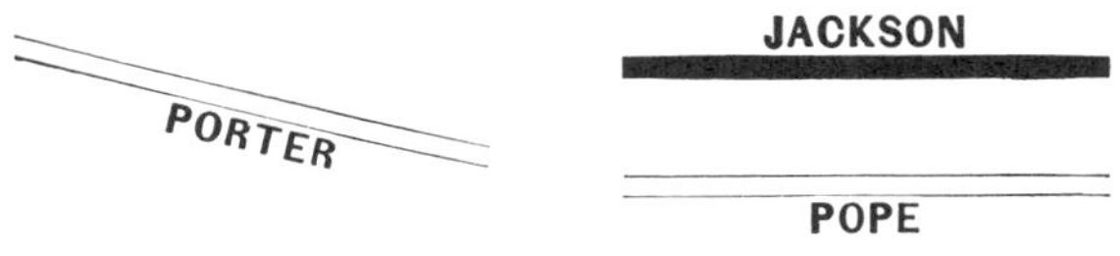

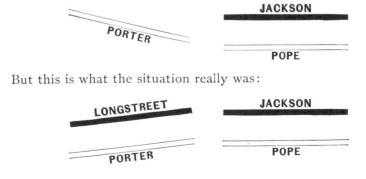

But this is what the situation really was:

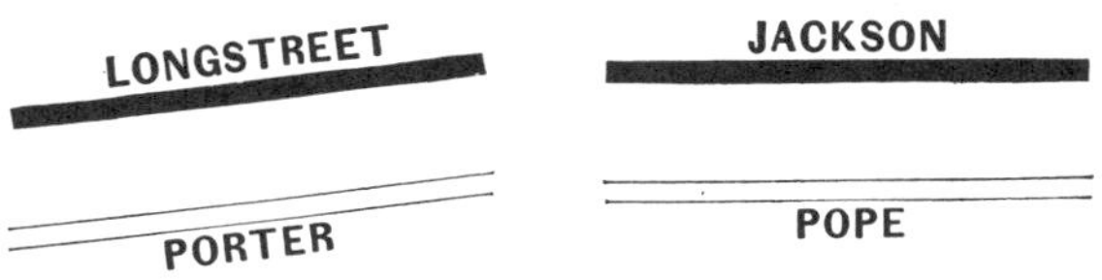

The movements of this campaign were more complicated than those of any other during the war, and it appears to have been

OF BULL RUN.
War-Time Sketch.)

carried on with less of definite plan and connected purpose on either side. It is not probable that its merits, if it had any merits, will ever be satisfactorily agreed upon. On the part of Pope's army, whether by his fault or not, it was a disastrous failure. On the part of Lee's, while it resulted in tactical successes, it did not seriously menace the safety of Washington, and it led him on to his first great failure in an attempted invasion of the North. It is only fair to give General Pope's last word on the subject, which we quote from his article in "Battles and Leaders of the Civil War." "At no time could I have hoped to fight a successful battle with the superior forces of the enemy which confronted me, and which were able at any time to out-flank and bear my small army to the dust. It was only by constant movement, incessant watchfulness, and hazardous skirmishes and battles, that the forces under my command were saved from destruction, and that the enemy was embarrassed and delayed in his advance until the army of General McClellan was at length assembled for the defence of Washington. I did hope that in the course of these operations the enemy might commit some imprudence, or leave some opening of which I could take such advantage as to gain at least a partial success. This opportunity was presented by the advance of Jackson on Manassas Junction; but although the best dispositions possible in my view were made, the object was frustrated by causes which could not have been foreseen, and which perhaps are not yet completely known to the country."

From Capt. Henry N. Blake, of the Eleventh Massachusetts regiment, we have these interesting incidents of the campaign:

"Matches were very scarce upon this campaign, and a private who intended to light one gave public notice to the crowd, who surrounded him with slips of paper and pipes in their hands. Some soldiers were in a destitute condition, and suffered from blistered feet, as they had no shoes, and others required a pair of pants or a blouse; but all gladly pursued Jackson, and his capture was considered a certain event. The column cheered General Pope when he rode along, accompanied by a vast body-guard, and he responded: 'I am glad to see you in such good spirits to-day.' . . . The stream was forded, and the graves and bones of the dead, the rusty fragments of iron, and the weather-beaten *débris* of that contest reminded the men that they were again in the midst of the familiar scenes of the first battle of Bull Run. The cannonading was brisk at intervals during the day. Large tracts of the field were black and smoking from the effect of the burning grass which the shells ignited, and a small force was occasionally engaged upon the right, but there was no general conflict. The brigade took the position assigned to it, upon a slope of a hill, to support a battery which was attached to Sigel's corps, and no infantry was visible in any direction, although the land was open and objects within the distance of half a mile were readily seen. There was no firing, with the exception of the time when the troops debouched from the road in the morning, and the soldiers rested until four P.M. At this moment the enemy opened with solid shot upon the battery, which did not discharge one piece in response. The drivers mounted their horses; all rushed pell-mell through the ranks of the fearless and enraged support, and did not halt within the range of the artillery from which they had so cowardly fled. A member of the staff, dressed like an officer of the day, immediately arrived and gave a verbal order to the brigade commander, after which the regiments were formed and marched, unmindful of the cannon-balls, toward the right of the line, and halted in the border of a thick forest in which many skirmishes had taken place. 'What does the general want me to do now?' General Grover asked the aide who again rode up to the brigade. 'Go into the woods and charge,' was the answer. 'Where is my support?' the commander wisely inquired, for there were no troops near the position. 'It is coming.' After waiting fifteen minutes for this body to appear, the officer returned and said that 'the general was much displeased' because the charge had not been made, and the order was at once issued: 'Fix bayonets.' Each man was inspired by these magical words; great enthusiasm arose when this command was 'passed' from company to company, and the soldiers, led by their brave general, advanced upon a hidden foe through tangled woods which constantly interfered with the formation of the ranks. 'Colonel, do you know what we are going to charge on?' a private inquired. 'Yes; a good dinner.' The rebel skirmishers were driven in upon their reserve behind the bank of an unfinished railroad, and detachments from

RUINS OF THE STONE BRIDGE ON THE WARRENTON TURNPIKE.

(From a War Department photograph.)

five brigades were massed in three lines, under the command of Ewell, to resist the onset of the inferior force that menaced them. The awful volleys did not impede the storming party that pressed on over the bodies of the dead and dying; while the thousands of bullets which flew through the air seemed to create a breeze that made the leaves upon the trees rustle, and a shower of small boughs and twigs fell upon the ground. The balls penetrated the barrels and shattered the stocks of many muskets; but the soldiers who carried them picked up those that had been dropped upon the ground by helpless comrades, and allowed no slight accident of this character to interrupt them in the noble work. The railroad bank was gained, and the column with cheers passed over it, and advanced over the groups of the slain and mangled rebels who had rolled down the declivity when they lost their strength. The second line was broken; both were scattered through the woods, and victory appeared to be certain until the last support, that had rested upon their breasts on the ground, suddenly rose up and delivered a destructive volley which forced the brigade, that had already lost more than one-third of its number in killed and wounded, to retreat. Ewell, suffering from his shattered knee, was borne to the rear in a blanket, and his leg was amputated. The horse of General Grover was shot upon the railroad bank while he was encouraging the men to go forward, and he had barely time to dismount before the animal, mad with pain, dashed into the ranks of the enemy. The woods always concealed the movements of the troops, and at one point a portion of the foe fell back while the others remained. The forces sometimes met face to face, and the bayonet and sword—weapons that do not pierce soldiers in nine-tenths of the battles that are fought —were used with deadly effect in several instances. A corporal exclaimed in the din of this combat, 'Dish ish no place for de mens,' and fled to the rear with the speed of the mythical Flying Dutchman. In one company of the regiment a son was killed by the side of his father, who continued to perform his duty with the firmness of a stoic, and remarked to his amazed comrades, in a tone which showed how a strong patriotic ardor can triumph over the deepest emotion of affection: 'I had rather see him shot dead as he was than see him run away.' . . . The victors rallied the fugitives after this repulse, and their superior force enabled them to assault in front and upon both flanks the line which had been contracted by the severe losses in the charge, and the brigade fell back to the first position under a fire of grape and canister which was added to the musketry. The regimental flag was torn from the staff by unfriendly limbs in passing through the forest, and the eagle that surmounted it was cut off in the contest. The commander of the color-company saved these precious emblems, and earnestly shouted, when the lines were re-formed: 'Eleventh, rally round the pole!' which was then, if possible, more honored than when it was bedecked in folds of bunting. General Grover, who displayed the gallantry throughout this action that he had exhibited upon the peninsula, waved his hat upon the point of his sword to animate his brigade and prepare for a renewal of the fight. Many were scarcely able to speak on account of hoarseness caused by intense cheering, and some officers blistered the palms of their hands by waving swords when they charged with their commands."

GATHERING UP DÉBRIS OF POPE'S RETREAT AFTER THE SECOND BATTLE OF BULL RUN.

(From a War Department photograph.)

GENERAL HANCOCK AND FRIENDS.

(From a War-Time photograph.)

HARPER'S FERRY IN POSSESSION OF THE CONFEDERATE FORCES.

AWAITING THE CHARGE.

CHAPTER XV.

THE ANTIETAM CAMPAIGN.

CONFEDERATE ADVANCE INTO MARYLAND—THE ARMY OF THE POTOMAC SENT AGAINST THEM—LEE'S PLANS LEARNED FROM A LOST DESPATCH—CAPTURE OF HARPER'S FERRY—BATTLE OF SOUTH MOUNTAIN—BATTLE OF ANTIETAM—TERRIFIC FIGHTING AT THE DUNKERS' CHURCH AND THE SUNKEN ROAD—PORTER'S INACTION—FIGHTING AT THE BRIDGE—GENERAL CONDUCT OF THE BATTLE—THE RESULTS.

AFTER his success in the second battle of Manassas, and the retirement of Pope's army to the defences of Washington (September 2, 1862), General Lee pushed northward into Maryland with his whole army. His advance arrived at Frederick City on the 8th, and from his camp near that place he issued a proclamation to the people of Maryland, in which he recited the wrongs they had suffered at the hands of the National Government, and told them "the people of the South have long wished to aid you in throwing off this foreign yoke, to enable you again to enjoy the inalienable rights of freemen and restore the independence and sovereignty of your State." At the same time he opened recruiting-offices, and appointed a provost-marshal of Frederick. The reader of the classics will perhaps be reminded of the shrewd advice that Demosthenes gave the Athenians, when he counselled them not to ask the assistance of the Thebans against Philip of Macedon, but to bring about an alliance by offering to help them against him. But the Confederate chieftain was sadly disappointed in the effect of his proclamation and his presence. When his army marched into the State singing "My Maryland," they were received with closed doors, drawn blinds, and the silence of a graveyard. In Frederick all the places of business were shut. The Marylanders did not flock to his recruiting-offices to the extent of more than two or three hundred, while on the other hand he lost many times that number from straggling, as he says in his report. Several reasons have been assigned for the failure of the people to respond to his appeal, in each of which there is probably some truth. One was, that it had always been easy enough for Marylanders to go to the Confederate armies, and those of them that wished to enlist there had done so already. Another—and probably the principal one—was, that Maryland was largely true to the Union, especially in the western counties; and she furnished many excellent soldiers to its armies—almost fifty thousand. Another was, that the appearance of the Southern veterans was not calculated either to entice the men or to arouse the enthusiasm of the women. The Confederate General Jones says: "Never had the army been so dirty, ragged, and ill-provided for as on this march." General Lee complained especially of their want of shoes. It is difficult to understand why an army that claimed to have captured such immense supplies late in August should have been so destitute early in September.

On the 2d of September the President went to General McClellan's house in Washington, asked him to take command again of the Army of the Potomac, in which Pope's army had now been merged, and verbally authorized him to do so at once. The first thing that McClellan wanted was the withdrawal of Miles's force, eleven thousand men, from Harper's Ferry—where, he said, it was useless and helpless—and its addition to his own force. All authorities agree that in this he was obviously and unquestionably right, for Harper's Ferry had no strategic value whatever; but the marplot hand of Halleck intervened, and Miles was ordered to hold the place. Halleck's principal reason appeared to be a reluctance to abandon a place where so much expense had been laid out. Miles, a worthy subordinate for such a chief, interpreted Halleck's orders with absolute literalness, and remained in the town, instead of holding it by placing his force on the heights that command it.

As soon as it was known that Lee was in Maryland, McClellan set his army in motion northward, to cover Washington and Baltimore and find an opportunity for a decisive battle. He arrived with his advance in Frederick on the 12th, and met with a reception in striking contrast to that accorded to the army that had left the town two days before. Nearly every house displayed the National flag, the streets were thronged with people, all the business places were open, and everybody welcomed the Boys in Blue.

But this flattering reception was not the best fortune that befell the Union army in Frederick. On his arrival in the town, General McClellan came into possession of a copy of General Lee's order, dated three days before, in which the whole campaign was laid out. By this order, Jackson was directed to march through Sharpsburg, cross the Potomac, capture the force at Martinsburg, and assist in the capture of that at Harper's Ferry; Longstreet was directed to halt at Boonsborough with the trains; McLaws was to march to Harper's Ferry, take possession of the heights commanding it, and capture the force there as speedily as possible; Walker was to invest that place from the other side and assist McLaws; D. H. Hill's division was to form the rear guard. All the forces were to be united again at Boonsborough or Hagerstown. General Lee had taken it for granted that Martinsburg and Harper's Ferry would be evacuated at his approach (as they should have been); and when he found they were not, he had so far changed or suspended the plan with which he set out as to send back a large part of his army to capture those places and not leave a hostile force in his rear.

THE TWENTY-SECOND NEW YORK NEAR HARPER'S FERRY.

On the approach of Jackson's corps General White evacuated Martinsburg, and with his garrison of two thousand men joined Miles at Harper's Ferry. That town, in the fork of the Potomac and Shenandoah rivers, can be bombarded with the greatest ease from the heights on the opposite sides of those streams. Miles, instead of taking possession of the heights with all his men, sent a feeble detachment to those on the north side of the Potomac, and stupidly remained in the trap with the rest. McLaws sent a heavy force to climb the mountain at a point three or four miles north, whence it marched along the crest through the woods, and attacked three or four regiments that Miles had posted there. This force was soon driven away, while Jackson was approaching the town from the other side, and a bombardment the next day compelled a surrender when Jackson was about to attack. General Miles was mortally wounded by one of the last shots. About eleven thousand men were included in the capitulation, with seventy-three guns and a considerable amount of camp equipage. A body of two thousand cavalry, commanded by Colonel Davis, had been with Miles, but had escaped the night before, crossed the Potomac, and by morning reached Greencastle, Pa. On the way they captured Longstreet's ammunition train of fifty wagons. Jackson, leaving the arrangements for the surrender to A. P. Hill, hurried with the greater part of his force to rejoin Lee, and reached Sharpsburg on the morning of the 16th.

The range known as the South Mountain, which is a continuation of the Blue Ridge north of the Potomac, is about a thousand feet high. The two principal gaps are Turner's and Crampton's, each about four hundred feet high, with the hills towering six hundred feet above it.

When McClellan learned the plans of the Confederate commander, he set his army in motion to thwart them. He ordered Franklin's corps to pass through Crampton's Gap and press on to relieve Harper's Ferry; the corps of Reno and Hooker, under command of Burnside, he moved to Turner's Gap. The movement was quick for McClellan, but not quite quick enough for the emergency. He might have passed through the Gaps on the 13th with little or no opposition, and would then have had his whole army between Lee's divided forces, and could hardly have failed to defeat them disastrously and perhaps conclusively. But he did not arrive at the passes till the morning of the 14th; and by that time Lee had learned of his movement and recalled Hill and Longstreet, from Boonsborough and beyond, to defend Turner's Gap, while he ordered McLaws to look out for Crampton's.

BREVET BRIGADIER-GENERAL J. C. KELTON.

(Adjutant-General to General Halleck.)

Turner's Gap was flanked by two old roads that crossed the mountain a mile north and south of it; and using these, and scrambling up from rock to rock, the National troops worked their way slowly to the crests, opposed at every step by the Confederate riflemen behind the trees and ledges. Reno assaulted the southern crest, and Hooker the northern, while Gibbon's brigade gradually pushed along up the turnpike into the Gap itself. Reno was opposed by the Confederate brigade of Garland, and both these commanders were killed. There was stubborn and bloody fighting all day, with the Union forces slowly but constantly gaining ground, and at dark the field was won. The Confederates withdrew during the night, and in the morning the victorious columns passed through to the western side of the mountain. This battle cost McClellan fifteen hundred men, killed or wounded. Among the wounded was the lieutenant-colonel in command of the Twenty-third Ohio regiment—Rutherford B. Hayes, afterward President—who was struck in the arm by a rifle-ball. The Confederate loss in killed and wounded was about fifteen hundred, and in addition fifteen hundred were made prisoners. The fight at Crampton's Gap—to defend which McLaws had sent back a part of his force from Harper's Ferry—was quite similar to that at Turner's, and had a similar result. Franklin reached the crests after a fight of three hours, losing five hundred and thirty-two men, inflicting an equal loss upon the enemy, and capturing four hundred prisoners, one gun, and three battle-flags. These two actions (fought September 14, 1862) are generally designated as the battle of South Mountain, but are sometimes called the battle of Boonsborough. In that the enemy was driven away, the ground held, and the passes used, it was a victory, and a brilliant one, for McClellan. But in that Lee, by delaying the advance of his enemy a whole day, thereby gained time to bring together his own scattered forces, it was strategically a victory, though a costly one, for him. But then again it might be argued that if Lee could have kept the four thousand good troops that McClellan deprived him of at South Mountain, it might have fared better with him in the struggle at Antietam three days later.

When Lee retired his left wing from Turner's Gap, he withdrew across the Antietam, and took up a position on high ground between that stream and the village of Sharpsburg. His right, under McLaws, after detaining Franklin till Harper's Ferry was surrendered, crossed the Potomac at that place, recrossed it at Shepherdstown, and came promptly into position. Lee now had his army together and strongly posted. But it had been so reduced by losses in battle and straggling, that it numbered but little over forty thousand combatants. The effect upon the army itself of invading a rich country with troops so poorly supplied had probably not been anticipated. Lee complained bitterly that his army was "ruined by straggling," and General Hill wrote in his report: "Had all our stragglers been up, McClellan's army would have been completely crushed or annihilated. Thousands of thievish poltroons had kept away from sheer cowardice." General Hill, in his anger, probably overestimates the effect; for McClellan had somewhat over seventy thousand men, and though he used but little more than half of them in his attacks, there is no reason to suppose he would not have used them all in a defence. The men that Lee did have, however, were those exclusively that had been able to stand the hard marching and resist the temptation to straggle, and were consequently the flower of his army; and they now awaited, in a chosen position, a battle that they knew would be decisive of the campaign, if not of the war.

MAJOR-GENERAL HOWELL COBB, C. S. A.

MAJOR-GENERAL JOHN G. WALKER, C. S. A.

MAJOR-GENERAL LAFAYETTE McLAWS, C. S. A.

The ground occupied by the Confederate army, with one flank resting on the Potomac, and the other on the Antietam, which flowed in front, was advantageous. The creek was crossed by four stone bridges and a ford, and all except the northernmost bridge were strongly guarded. The land was occupied by meadows, cornfields, and patches of forest, and was much broken by outcropping ledges. McClellan only reconnoitred the position on the 15th. On the 16th he developed his plan of attack, which was simply to throw his right wing across the Antietam by the upper and unguarded bridge, assail the Confederate left, and when this had sufficiently engaged the enemy's attention and drawn his strength to that flank, to force the bridges and cross with his left and centre. Indeed, this was obviously almost the only practicable plan. All day long an artillery duel was kept up, in which, as General Hill says, the Confederate batteries proved no match for their opponents. It was late in the afternoon when Hooker's corps crossed by the upper bridge, advanced through the woods, and struck the left flank, which was held by two brigades of Hood's men. Scarcely more than a skirmish ensued, when darkness came on, and the lines rested for the night where they were. If Lee could have been in any doubt before, he was now told plainly what was to be the form of the contest, and he had all night to make his dispositions for it. The only change he thought it necessary to make was to put Jackson's fresh troops in the position on his left. Before morning McClellan sent Mansfield's corps across the Antietam to join Hooker, and had Sumner's in readiness to follow at an early hour. Meanwhile, all but two thousand of Lee's forces had come up. So the 17th of September dawned in that peaceful little corner of the world with everything in readiness for a great struggle in which there could be no surprises, and which was to be scarcely anything more than wounds for wounds and death for death.

In the vicinity of the little Dunker church, the road running northward from Sharpsburg to Hagerstown was bordered on both sides by woods, and in these woods the battle began when Hooker assaulted Jackson at sunrise. There was hard fighting for an hour, during which Jackson's lines were not only heavily pressed by Hooker in front, but at length enfiladed by a fire from the batteries on the eastern side of the Antietam. This broke them and drove them back; but when Hooker attempted to advance his lines far enough to hold the road and seize the woods west of it, he in turn was met by fresh masses of troops and a heavy artillery fire, and was checked. Mansfield's corps was moving up to his support when its commander was mortally wounded. Nevertheless it moved on, got a position in the woods west of the road, and held it, though at heavy cost. At this moment General Hooker was seriously wounded and borne from the field, while Sumner crossed the stream and came up with his corps. His men drove back the defeated divisions of the enemy without much difficulty, and occupied the ground around the church. His whole line was advancing to apparent victory, when two fresh divisions were brought over from the Confederate right, and were immediately thrust into a wide gap in Sumner's line. Sedgwick, whose division formed the right of the line, was thus flanked on his left, and was easily driven back out of the woods, across the clearing, and into the eastern woods, after which the Confederates retired to their own position. Fighting of this sort went on all the forenoon, one of the episodes being a race between the Fifth New Hampshire Regiment and a Confederate force for a commanding point of ground, the two marching in parallel lines and firing at each other as they went along. The New Hampshire men got there first, and, assisted by the Eighty-first Pennsylvania Regiment, from that eminence threw a destructive fire into the ranks of the regiment they had out-run. The fighting around the Dunker church was so fierce, and so much artillery fire was concentrated upon that spot, that when the woods were cut down, years afterward, and the logs sent to a saw-mill, the saws were completely torn to pieces by the metal that had penetrated the wood and been overgrown.

A short distance south and east of the Dunker church there was a slightly sunken road which crossed the Confederate line at one point and was parallel with it for a certain distance at other points. A strong Confederate force was posted in this sunken road, and when the National troops approached it there was destructive work on both sides; but the heaviest loss here fell upon the Confederates, because some batteries on the high ground east of the Antietam enfiladed portions of the road. This sunken road, which was henceforth called Bloody Lane, has made some confusion in many accounts of the battle, which is explained by the fact that it is not a straight road, but is made up of several parts running at different angles.

THE CHARGE ACROSS THE BURNSIDE BRIDGE.

While this great struggle was in progress on McClellan's right, his centre and left, under Porter and Burnside, did not make any movement to assist. Porter's inaction is explained by the fact that his troops were kept as the reserves, which McClellan refused to send forward even when portions of his line were most urgently calling for assistance. He and Porter agreed in clinging to the idea that the reserves must under no circumstances be pushed forward to take part in the actual battle. This conduct was in marked contrast to that of the Confederate commander, who in this action had no reserves whatever.

At noon Franklin arrived from Crampton's Gap, and was sent over to help Hooker and Sumner, being just in time to check a new advance by more troops brought over from the Confederate right.

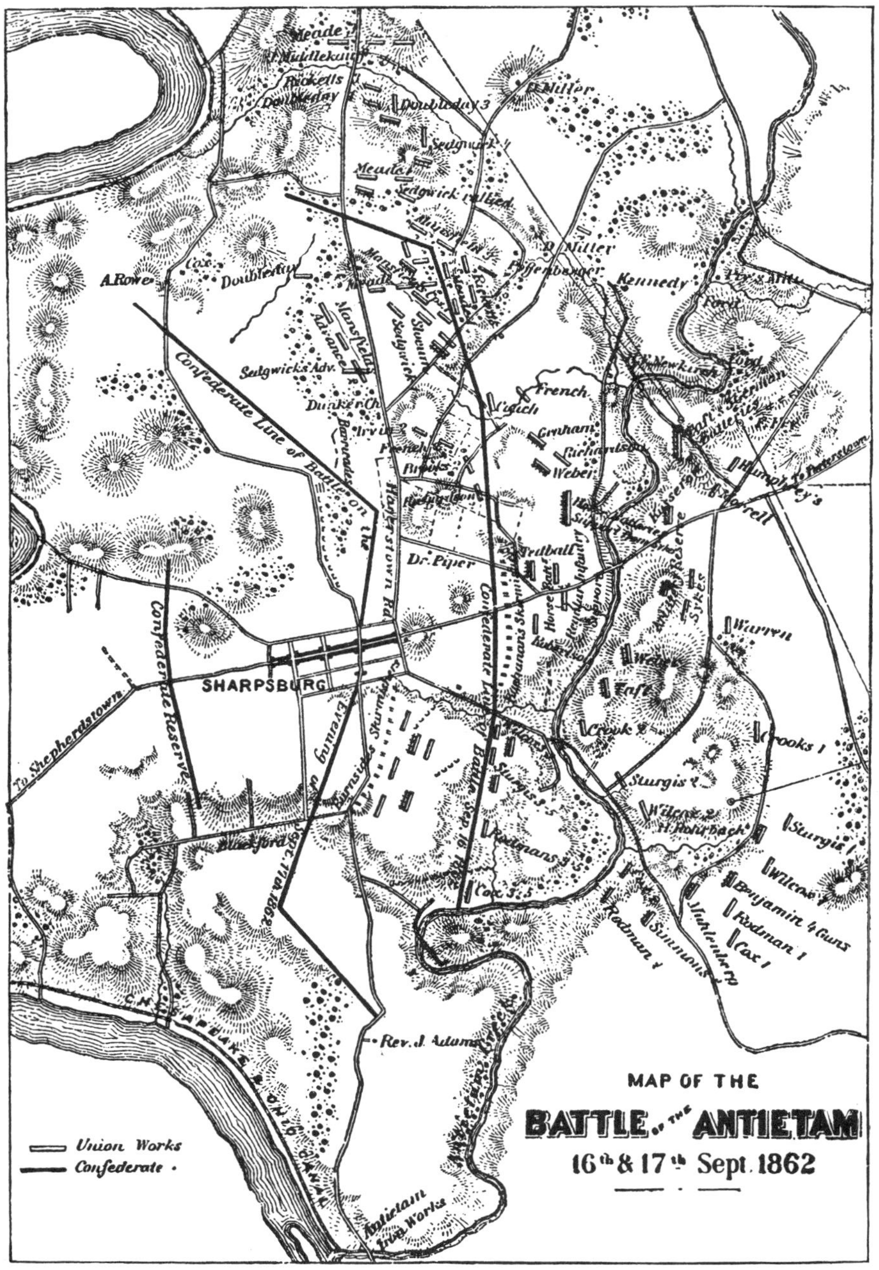

At seven o'clock in the morning Burnside was ordered to have his corps in readiness for carrying the bridge in his front, crossing the stream, and attacking the Confederate right, which order he promptly obeyed. An hour later the order for this movement was issued by McClellan, but it did not reach Burnside till nine o'clock. The task before him was more difficult than his commander realized or than would be supposed from most descriptions of the action. The bridge is of stone, having three arches, with low stone parapets, and not very wide. On the eastern side of the stream, where Burnside's corps was, the land is comparatively low. The road that crosses the bridge, when it reaches the western bank has to turn immediately at a right angle and run nearly parallel with the stream, because the land there is high and overhangs it. As a matter of course, the bridge was commanded by Confederate guns advantageously placed on the heights. The problem before Burnside was therefore exceedingly difficult, and the achievement expected of him certain in any case to be costly. The task of first crossing the bridge fell upon Crook's brigade, which moved forward, mistook its way, and struck the stream some distance above the bridge, where it immediately found itself under a heavy fire. Then the Second Maryland and Sixth New Hampshire regiments were ordered to charge at the double quick and carry the bridge. But the fire that swept it was more than they could stand, and they were obliged to retire unsuccessful. Then another attempt was made by a new storming party, consisting of the Fifty-first New York and Fifty-first Pennsylvania regiments, led by Col. Robert B. Potter and Col. John F. Hartranft. By this time two heavy guns had been got into position where they could play upon the Confederates who defended the bridge, and with this protection and assistance the two regiments just named succeeded in crossing it and driving away the immediate opposing force, and were immediately followed by Sturgis's division and Crook's brigade. The fighting at the bridge cost Burnside about five hundred men. The Fifty-first New York lost eighty-seven, and the Fifty-first Pennsylvania one hundred and twenty. At the same time other troops crossed by a ford below the bridge, which had to be searched for, but was at length found. These operations occupied four hours, being completed about one o'clock P.M. Could they have been accomplished in an hour or two, the destruction or capture of Lee's army must have resulted. But by the time that Burnside had crossed the stream, captured a battery, and occupied the heights overlooking Sharpsburg, the fighting on McClellan's right was over. This left Lee at liberty to strengthen his imperilled right by bringing troops across the short interior line from his left, which he promptly did. At the same time the last division of his forces (A. P. Hill's), two thousand strong, arrived from Harper's Ferry; and these fresh men, together with those brought over from the left, assumed the offensive, drove Burnside from the crest, and retook the battery.

Here ended the battle; not because the day was closed or any apparent victory had been achieved, but because both sides had been so severely punished that neither was inclined to resume the fight. Every man of Lee's force had been actively engaged, but not more than two-thirds of McClellan's. The reason why the Confederate army was not annihilated or captured must be plain to any intelligent reader. It was not because Lee, with his army divided for three days in presence of his enemy, had not invited destruction; nor because the seventy thousand, acting in concert, could not have overwhelmed the forty thousand even when they were united. It was not for any lack of courage, or men, or arms, or opportunity, or daylight. It was simply because the attack was made in driblets, instead of by heavy masses on both wings simultaneously; so that at any point of actual contact Lee was almost always able to present as strong a force as that which assailed him. In a letter written to General Franklin the evening before the battle of South Mountain, General McClellan, having then received the lost despatch that revealed Lee's plans and situation, set forth with much particularity his

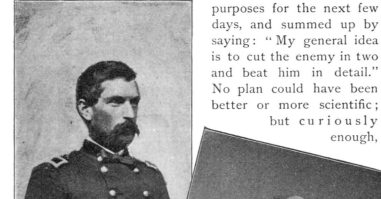

MAJOR-GENERAL JOHN GIBBON.

purposes for the next few days, and summed up by saying: "My general idea is to cut the enemy in two and beat him in detail." No plan could have been better or more scientific; but curiously enough, when it came to actual battle General McClellan's conduct was the exact opposite of this. By unnecessary and unaccountable delays he first gave the enemy time to concentrate his forces, and then made his attacks piecemeal, so that the enemy could fight *him* in detail.

BREVET MAJOR-GENERAL MARSENA R. PATRICK.

Whatever had been the straggling on the march, none of the commanders complained of any flinching after the fight began. They saw veterans taking, relinquishing, and retaking ground that was soaked with blood and covered with dead; and they saw green regiments "go to their graves like beds." There had been a call for more troops by the National Administration after the battles on the peninsula, which was responded to with the greatest alacrity; men of all classes rushing to the recruiting-offices to enroll themselves. It was a common thing for a regiment of a thousand men to be raised, equipped, and sent to the front in two or three weeks. Some of those new regiments were suddenly introduced to the realties of war at Antietam, and suffered frightfully. For example, the Sixteenth Connecticut, which there fired its muskets for the first time, went in with 940 men, and lost 432. On the other side, Lawton's Confederate brigade went in with 1,150 men, and lost 554, including five out of its six regimental commanders, while Hays's lost 323 out of 550, including every regimental commander and all the staff officers. An officer of the Fiftieth Georgia Regiment said in a published letter: "The Fiftieth were posted in a narrow path, washed out into a regular gully, and were fired into by the enemy from the front, rear, and left flank. The men stood their ground nobly, returning their fire until nearly two-thirds of their number lay dead or wounded in that lane. Out of 210 carried into the fight, over 125 were killed and wounded in less than twenty minutes. The slaughter was horrible! When ordered to retreat, I could hardly extricate myself from the dead and wounded around me. A man could have walked from the head of our line to the foot on their bodies. The survivors of the regiment retreated very orderly back to where General Anderson's brigade rested. The brigade suffered terribly. James's South Carolina battalion was nearly annihilated. The Fiftieth Georgia lost nearly all their commissioned officers." The First South Carolina Regiment, which went into the fight with 106 men, had but fifteen men and one officer when it was over. A Confederate battery, being largely disabled by the work of sharp-shooters, was worked for a time, at the crisis of the fight, by General Longstreet and members of his staff acting as gunners. Three generals on each side were killed. Those on the National side were Generals Joseph K. Mansfield, Israel B. Richardson, and Isaac P. Rodman; those on the Confederate side were Generals George B. Anderson, L. O'B. Branch, and William E. Starke. The wounded generals included on the one side Hooker, Sedgwick, Dana, Crawford, and Meagher; on the other side, R. H. Anderson, Wright, Lawton, Armistead, Ripley, Ransom, Rhodes, Gregg, and Toombs.

MAJOR-GENERAL G. W. MORELL.

General McClellan reported his entire loss at 12,469, of whom 2,010 were killed. General Lee reported his total loss in the Maryland battles as 1,567 killed and 8,724 wounded, saying nothing of the missing; but the figures given by his division commanders foot up 1,842 killed, 9,399 wounded, and 2,292 missing—total, 13,533. If McClellan's report is correct, even this statement falls short of the truth. He says: "About 2,700 of the enemy's dead were counted and buried upon the battlefield of Antietam. A portion of their dead had been previously buried by the enemy." If the wounded were in the usual proportion, this would indicate Confederate casualties to the extent of at least 15,000 on that field alone. But whatever the exact number may have been, the battle was bloody enough to produce mourning and lamentation from Maine to Louisiana. It was the bloodiest day's work of the whole war. The battles of Shiloh, Chancellorsville, Gettysburg, Chickamauga, the Wilderness, and Spottsylvania were each more costly, but none of them was fought in a single day.

Nothing was done on the 18th, and when McClellan determined to renew the attack on the 19th he found that his enemy had withdrawn from the field and crossed to Virginia by the ford at Shepherdstown. The National commander reported the capture of more than six thousand prisoners, thirteen guns, and thirty-nine battle-flags, and that he had not lost a gun or a color. As he was also in possession of the field, where the enemy left all their dead and two thousand of their wounded, and had rendered Lee's invasion fruitless of anything but the prisoners carried off from Harper's Ferry, the victory was his.

THE PRIMARY CAUSES OF THE WAR—THE NEGRO AND COTTON.

CHAPTER XVI.

EMANCIPATION.

This Chapter is illustrated with portraits of early abolitionists, and Virginia officials at the time of the celebrated John Brown Raid.

LINCOLN'S ATTITUDE TOWARD SLAVERY—McCLELLAN'S ATTITUDE—THE DEMOCRATIC PARTY'S ATTITUDE—PREDICTIONS BY THE POETS—SLAVES DECLARED CONTRABAND—ACTION OF FRÉMONT—HUNTER'S PROCLAMATION—BLACKS FIRST ENLISTED—DIVISION OF SENTIMENT IN THE ARMY—MARYLAND ABOLISHES SLAVERY—THE PRESIDENT AND HORACE GREELEY CORRESPOND ON THE SUBJECT—EMANCIPATION PROCLAIMED—AUTUMN ELECTIONS—ABOLITION OF SLAVERY IN DELAWARE, KENTUCKY, AND MISSOURI—THE FINAL PROCLAMATION—THE RIGHT OF THE PRESIDENT TO DECLARE THE SLAVES FREE.

THE war had now (September, 1862) been in progress almost a year and a half; and nearly twenty thousand men had been shot dead on the battlefield, and upward of eighty thousand wounded, while an unknown number had died of disease contracted in the service, or been carried away into captivity. The money that had been spent by the United States Government alone amounted to about one billion dollars. All this time there was not an intelligent man in the country but knew the cause of the war, and yet more than a hundred thousand American citizens were killed or mangled before a single blow was delivered directly at that cause. General Frémont had aimed at it; General Hunter had aimed at it; but in each case the arm was struck up by the Administration. One would naturally suppose, from the thoroughness with which the slavery question had been discussed for thirty years, that when the time came for action there would be little doubt or hesitation on either side. On the Confederate side there was neither doubt nor hesitation. On the National side there was both doubt and hesitation, and it took a long time to arrive at a determination to destroy slavery in order to preserve the Union. The old habit of compromise and conciliation half paralyzed the arm of war, and thousands of well-meaning citizens were unable to comprehend the fact that we were dealing with a question that it was useless to compromise and a force that it was impossible to conciliate.

JOHN BROWN.

Mr. Lincoln had hated slavery ever since, when a young man, he made a trip on a flat-boat to New Orleans, and there saw it in some of its more hideous aspects. That he realized its nature and force as an organized institution and a power in politics, appears from one of his celebrated speeches, delivered in 1858, wherein he declared that as a house divided against itself cannot stand, so our Government could not endure permanently half slave and half free. "Either the opponents of slavery will arrest the further spread of it, and place it where the public mind shall rest in the belief that it is in the course of ultimate extinction, or its advocates will push it forward till it shall become alike lawful in all the States, old as well as new, North as well as South." Why, then, hating slavery personally, and understanding it politically, and knowing it to be the cause of the war, did he not sooner declare it abolished?

On the one hand, he was not, like some of our chief magistrates, under the impression that he had been placed in office to carry out irresponsibly a personal policy of his own; and, on the other, he was shrewd enough to know that it would be as futile for a President to place himself far in advance of his people on a great question, as for a general to precede his troops on the battlefield. Hence he turned over and over, and presented again and again, the idea that the war might be stopped and the question settled by paying for the slaves and liberating them. It looked like a very simple calculation to figure out the cost of purchased emancipation and compare it with the probable cost of the war. The comparison seemed to present an unanswerable argument, and in the end the money cost of the war was more than one thousand dollars for every slave emancipated, while in the most profitable days of the institution the blacks, young and old together, had not been worth half that price. The fallacy of the argument lay in its blindness to the fact that the Confederates were not fighting to retain possession of their actual slaves, but to perpetuate the institution itself. The unthrift of slavery as an economic system had been many times demonstrated, notably in Helper's "Impending Crisis," but these demonstrations, instead of inducing the slaveholders to seek to get rid of it on the best attainable terms, appeared only to excite their anger. And it ought to have been seen that a proud people with arms in their hands, either flushed with victory or confident in their own prowess, no matter where their real interests may lie, can never be reasoned with except through the syllogisms of lead and steel. Perhaps Mr. Lincoln did know it, but was waiting for his people to find it out.

The Louisville (Ky.) *Courier*, in a paragraph quoted on page 63 of this volume, had told a great deal of bitter and shameful truth; but when it entered upon the prophecy that the North would soon resume the yoke of the slaveholders, it was not so happy. And yet it had strong grounds for its confident prediction. Not only had a great Peace Convention been held in February, 1861, which strove to prevent secession by offering new guaranties for the protection of slavery, but the chief anxiety of a large number of Northern citizens and officers in the military service appeared to be to manifest their desire that the institution should not be harmed.

The most eminent of the Federal generals, McClellan, when he first took the field in West Virginia, issued a proclamation to the Unionists, in which he said: "Notwithstanding all that has been said by the traitors to induce you to believe our advent among you will be signalized by an interference with your slaves, understand one thing clearly: not only will we abstain from all such interference, but we will, on the contrary, with an iron hand crush any attempt at insurrection on their part." In pursuance of this, he returned to their owners all slaves that escaped and sought refuge within his lines. It was an every-day occurrence for slaveholders who were in active rebellion against the Government that he was serving, to come into his camps under flag of truce and demand and receive their runaway slaves. The Hutchinsons, a family of popular singers, by permission of the Secretary of War, visited his camp in the winter of 1861–62, to sing to the soldiers. But when the general found them singing some stanzas of Whittier's that spoke of slavery as a curse to be abolished, he forthwith issued an order that their pass should be revoked and they should not sing any more to the troops. And even after his retreat on the peninsula, McClellan wrote a long letter of advice to the President, in the course of which he said: "Neither confiscation of property . . . nor forcible abolition of slavery should be contemplated for a moment. . . . Military power should not be allowed to interfere with the relations of servitude, either by supporting or impairing the authority of the master, except for repressing disorder."

In all this General McClellan was only clinging blindly and tenaciously to the idea that had underlain the whole administration of the government while it was in the hands of his party: that the perpetuation of slavery, whether against political opposition or against the growth of civilization and the logic of political economy, was the first purpose of the Constitution and the most imperative duty of the Government. Democratic politicians had never formulated this rule, but Democratic Presidents had always followed it. President Polk had obeyed it when with one hand he secured the slave State of Texas at the cost of the Mexican War, and with the other relinquished to Great Britain the portion of Oregon north of the forty-ninth parallel, but for which we should now possess every harbor on the Pacific coast. President Pierce had obeyed it when he sent troops to Kansas to assist the invaders from Missouri and overawe the free-State settlers. President Buchanan had obeyed it when he vetoed the Homestead Bill, which would have accelerated the development of the northern Territories into States. And innumerable other instances might be cited. The existence of this party in the North was the most serious embarrassment with which the Administration had to contend in the conduct of the war—not even excepting the border States. As individuals, its members were undoubtedly loyal to the Constitution and Government as they understood them, though they wofully misunderstood them. As a party, it was placed in a singular dilemma. It did not want the Union dissolved; for without the vote of the slave States it would be in a hopeless minority in Congress and at every Presidential election; but neither did it wish to see its strongest cohesive element overthrown, or its natural leaders defeated and exiled. What it wanted was "the Union as it was," and for this it continued to clamor long after it had become as plain as daylight that the Union as it was could never again exist.

ANDREW HUNTER.
Prosecuting Attorney at the trial of John Brown.

HON. H. A. WISE.
Governor of Virginia.

Whenever the National armies met with a reverse, if an election was pending, this party was the gainer thereby; if they won a victory, it became weaker. Whenever a new measure was proposed, Congress and the President were obliged to consider not only what would be its legitimate effect, but whether in any way the Democratic press could use it as a weapon against them. Hence the idea of emancipation, though not altogether slow in conception—for many of the ablest minds had leaped at it from the beginning—was tardy in execution.

As early as 1836 John Quincy Adams, speaking in Congress, had said: "From the instant that your slaveholding States become the theatre of war, from that instant the war-powers of the Constitution extend to interference with the institution of slavery in every way in which it can be interfered with." And in 1842 he had expressed the idea more strongly and fully: "Whether the war be civil, servile, or foreign, I lay this down as the law of nations—I say that the military authority takes for the time the place of all municipal institutions, slavery among the rest. Under that state of things, so far from its being true that the States where slavery exists have the exclusive management of the subject, not only the President of the United States, but the commander of the army has power to order the universal emancipation of the slaves." The poets, wiser than the politicians, had long foretold the great struggle and its results. James Russell Lowell, before he was thirty years of age, wrote:

COLONEL ROBERT E. LEE.
Commanding Virginia troops that captured John Brown.

> "Out from the land of bondage 'tis decreed our slaves shall go,
> And signs to us are offered, as erst to Pharaoh;
> If we are blind, their exodus, like Israel's of yore,
> Through a Red Sea is doomed to be, whose surges are of gore."

Twenty years later he saw his prediction fulfilled. But generally the anticipation was that the institution would be extinguished through a general rising of the slaves themselves. Thus Henry W. Longfellow wrote in 1841:

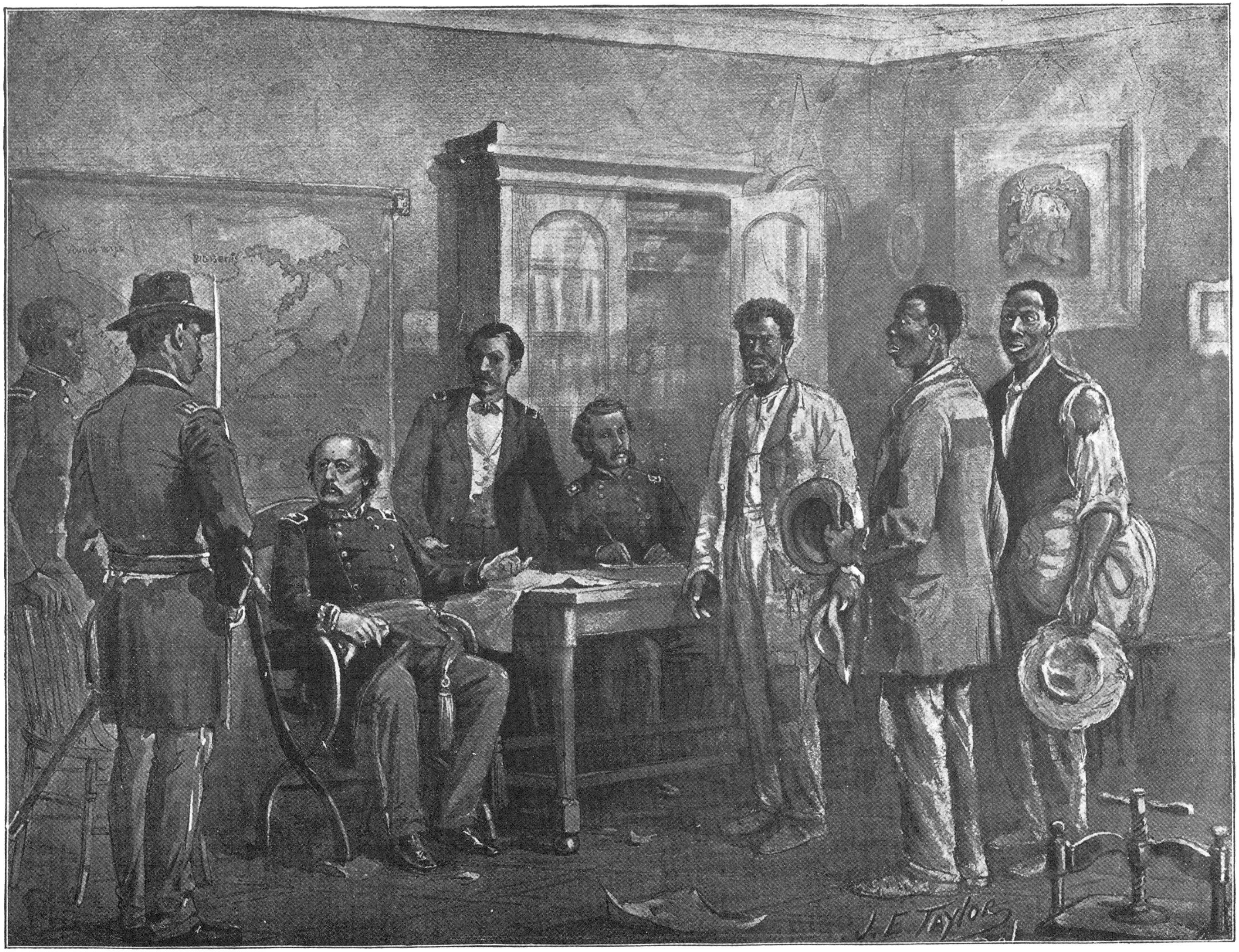

ORIGIN OF THE WORDS, "CONTRABAND OF WAR," APPLIED TO SLAVES—FIRST USED BY GENERAL BUTLER

"There is a poor, blind Samson in this land,
Shorn of his strength, and bound in bonds of steel,
Who may, in some grim revel, raise his hand,
And shake the pillars of this commonweal,
Till the vast temple of our liberties
A shapeless mass of wreck and rubbish lies."

It seems a singular fact that throughout the war there was no insurrection of the slaves. They were all anxious enough for liberty, and ran away from bondage whenever they could; but, except by regular enlistment in the National army, there never was any movement among them to assist in the emancipation of their race.

The first refusal to return fugitive slaves was made as early as May 26, 1861, by Gen. B. F. Butler, commanding at Fort Monroe. Three slaves, who had belonged to Colonel Mallory, commanding the Confederate forces near Hampton, came within Butler's lines that day, saying they had run away because they were about to be sent South. Colonel Mallory sent by flag of truce to claim their rendition under the Fugitive Slave Law, but was informed by General Butler, that, as slaves could be made very useful to a belligerent in working on fortifications and other labor, they were contraband of war, like lead or powder or any other war material, and therefore could not and would not be delivered up. He offered, however, to return these three if Colonel Mallory would come to his headquarters and take an oath to obey the laws of the United States. This declaration—at once a witticism, a correct legal point, and sound common sense—was the first practical blow that was struck at the institution; and it gave us a new word, for from that time fugitive slaves were commonly spoken of as "contrabands." They came into the National camps by thousands, and commanding officers and correspondents frequently questioned the more intelligent of them, in the hope of eliciting valuable information as to the movements of the enemy; but so many apocryphal stories were thus originated that at length "intelligent contraband" became solely a term of derision.

The next step was the passage of a law by Congress (approved August 6, 1861), wherein it was enacted that property, including slaves, actually employed in the service of the rebellion with the knowledge and consent of the owner, should be confiscated, and might be seized by the National forces wherever found. But it cautiously provided that slaves thus confiscated were not to be manumitted at once, but to be held subject to some future decision of the United States courts or action of Congress.

Gen. John C. Frémont, the first Republican candidate for the Presidency (1856), who has had a romantic life, and in whose administration, instead of Lincoln's, the war would have occurred if he had been elected, was in Europe in 1861, and did the Government a timely service in the purchase of arms. Hastening home, he was made a major-general, and given command in Missouri. On the 30th of August he issued a proclamation placing the whole State under martial law, confiscating the property of all citizens who should take up arms against the United States, or assist its enemies by burning bridges, cutting wires, etc., and adding, "their slaves, if any they have, are hereby declared free men." The President called General Frémont's attention to the fact that the clause relating to slaves was not in conformity with the act of Congress, and requested him to modify it; to which Frémont replied by asking for an open order to that effect—in plain words, that the President should modify it himself, which Mr. Lincoln did.

On the 6th of March, 1862, the President, in a special message to Congress, recommended the adoption of a joint resolution to the effect that the United States ought to coöperate with, and render pecuniary aid to, any State that should enter upon a gradual abolition of slavery; and Congress passed such a resolution by a large majority.

Gen. David Hunter, who commanded the National forces on the coast of South Carolina, with headquarters at Hilton Head, issued a general order on April 12, 1862, that all slaves in Fort Pulaski and on Cockspur Island should be confiscated and thenceforth free. On the 9th of May he issued another order, wherein, after mentioning that the three States in his department—Georgia, Florida, and South Carolina—had been declared under martial law, he proceeded to say: "Slavery and martial law, in a free country, are altogether incompatible. The persons in these three States heretofore held as slaves are therefore declared forever free." On the 19th of the same month the President issued a proclamation annulling General Hunter's order, and adding that the question of emancipation was one that he reserved to himself and could not feel justified in leaving to the decision of commanders in the field. General Hunter also organized a regiment of black troops, designated as the First South Carolina Volunteers, which was the first body of negro soldiers mustered into the National service during the war. This proceeding, which now seems the most natural and sensible thing the general could have done, created serious alarm in Congress. A representative from Kentucky introduced a resolution asking for information concerning the "regiment of fugitive slaves," and the Secretary of War referred the inquiry to General Hunter, who promptly answered: "No regiment of fugitive slaves has been or is being organized in this department. There is, however, a fine regiment of persons whose late masters are fugitive rebels, men who everywhere fly before the appearance of the National flag, leaving their servants behind them to shift as best they can for themselves. In the absence of any fugitive-master law, the deserted slaves would be wholly without remedy, had not their crime of treason given the slaves the right to pursue, capture, and bring back these persons of whose protection they have been so suddenly bereft."

Frémont's and Hunter's attempts at emancipation created a great excitement, the Democratic journals declaring that the struggle was being "turned into an abolition war," and many Union men in the border States expressing the gravest apprehensions as to the consequences. The commanders were by no means of one mind on the subject. Gen. Thomas Williams, commanding in the Department of the Gulf, ordered that all fugitive slaves should be expelled from his camps and sent beyond the lines; and Col. Halbert E. Paine, of the Fourth Wisconsin Regiment, who refused to obey the order, on the ground that it was a "violation of law for the purpose of returning fugitives to rebels," was deprived of his command and placed under arrest. Col. Daniel R. Anthony, of the Seventh Kansas Regiment, serving in Tennessee, ordered that men coming in and demanding the privilege of searching for fugitive slaves should be turned out of the camp, and that no officer or soldier in his regiment should engage in the arrest and delivery of fugitives to their masters; and for this Colonel Anthony received from his superior officer the same treatment that had been accorded to Colonel Paine. The division of sentiment ran through the entire army. Soldiers that would rob a granary, or cut down trees, or reduce fences to firewood, without the slightest compunction, still recognized

HORACE GREELEY.

the ancient taboo, and expressed the nicest scruples in regard to property in slaves.

On the 14th of July the President recommended to Congress the passage of a bill for the payment, in United States interest-bearing bonds, to any State that should abolish slavery, of an amount equal to the value of all slaves within its borders according to the census of 1860; and at the same time he asked the Congressional representatives of the border States to use their influence with their constituents to bring about such action in those States. The answer was not very favorable; but Maryland did abolish slavery before the close of the war, in October, 1864. On the very day in which the popular vote of that State decided to adopt a new constitution without slavery, October 12th, died Roger B. Taney, a native of Maryland, Chief Justice of the United States Supreme Court, who had been appointed by the first distinctly pro-slavery President, and from that bench had handed down the Dred-Scott decision, which was calculated to render forever impossible any amelioration of the condition of the negro race.

On July 22, 1862, all the National commanders were ordered to employ as many negroes as could be used advantageously for military and naval purposes, paying them for their labor and keeping a record as to their ownership, "as a basis on which compensation could be made in proper cases."

Thus events were creeping along toward a true statement of the great problem, without which it could never be solved, when Horace Greeley, through the columns of his *Tribune*, addressed an open letter to the President (August 19), entitling it "The Prayer of Twenty Millions." It exhorted Mr. Lincoln, not to general emancipation, but to such an execution of the existing laws as would free immense numbers of slaves belonging to men in arms against the Government. It was impassioned and powerful; a single passage will show its character: "On the face of this wide earth, Mr. President, there is not one disinterested, determined, intelligent champion of the Union cause who does not feel that all attempts to put down the rebellion, and at the same time uphold its exciting cause, are preposterous and futile; that the rebellion, if crushed out to-morrow, would be renewed within a year if slavery were left in full vigor; that army officers who remain to this day devoted to slavery can at best be but half-way loyal to the Union; and that every hour of deference to slavery is an hour of added and deepened peril to the Union."

Any one less a genius than Mr. Lincoln would have found it difficult to answer Mr. Greeley at all, and his answer was not one in the sense of being a refutation, but it exhibited his view of the question, and is perhaps as fine a piece of literature as was ever penned by any one in an official capacity: "If there be perceptible in it [Mr. Greeley's letter] an impatient and dictatorial tone, I waive it in deference to an old friend whose heart I have always supposed to be right. . . . As to the policy I 'seem to be pursuing,' as you say, I have not meant to leave any one in doubt. . . . My paramount object is to save the Union, and not either to save or destroy slavery. If I could save the Union without freeing any slave, I would do it; if I could save it by freeing all the slaves, I would do it; and if I could do it by freeing some and leaving others alone, I would also do that. I have here stated my purpose according to my views of official duty; and I intend no modification of my oft-expressed personal wish that all men everywhere could be free."

In truth, the President was already contemplating emancipation as a war measure, and about this time he prepared his preliminary proclamation; but he did not wish to issue it till it could follow a triumph of the National arms. Pope's defeat in Virginia in August set it back; but McClellan's success at Antietam, though not the decisive victory that was wanted, appeared to be as good an opportunity as was likely soon to present itself, and five days later (September 22, 1862) the proclamation was issued. It declared that the President would,

REV. HENRY WARD BEECHER.

at the next session, renew his suggestion to Congress of pecuniary aid to the States disposed to abolish slavery gradually or otherwise, and gave notice that on the 1st of January, 1863, he would declare forever free all persons held as slaves within any State, or designated part of a State, the people whereof should then be in rebellion against the United States. On that day he issued the final and decisive proclamation, as promised, in which he also announced that black men would be received into the military and naval service of the United States, as follows :

JAMES G. BIRNEY.

" Whereas, on the twenty-second day of September, in the year of our Lord 1862, a proclamation was issued by the President of the United States, containing, among other things, the following, to wit :

" ' That on the first day of January, in the year of our Lord 1863, all persons held as slaves within any State or designated part of a State, the people whereof shall then be in rebellion against the United States, shall be then, thenceforward, and forever free ; and the Executive Government of the United States, including the military and naval authority thereof, will recognize and maintain the freedom of such persons, and will do no act or acts to repress such persons, or any of them, in any efforts they may make for their actual freedom.'

THE SALE OF A SLAVE.

" ' That the Executive will, on the first day of January aforesaid, by proclamation, designate the States and parts of States, if any, in which the people thereof respectively shall then be in rebellion against the United States; and the fact that any State, or the people thereof, shall on that day be in good faith represented in the Congress of the United States, by members chosen thereto at elections wherein a majority of the qualified voters of such State shall have participated, shall, in the absence of strong countervailing testimony, be deemed conclusive evidence that such State, and the people thereof, are not then in rebellion against the United States.'

" Now, therefore, I, Abraham Lincoln, President of the United States, by virtue of the power in me vested as commander-in-chief of the army and navy of the United States in time of actual armed rebellion against the authority and government of the United States, and as a fit and necessary war measure for suppressing said rebellion, do, on this first day of January, in the year of our Lord one thousand eight hundred and sixty-three, and in accordance with my purpose so to do, publicly proclaimed for the full period of one hundred days from the day first above mentioned, order and designate as the States and parts of States wherein the people thereof respectively are this day in rebellion against the United States, the following, to wit :

" Arkansas, Texas, Louisiana (except the parishes of St. Bernard, Plaquemine, Jefferson, St. John, St. Charles, St. James, Ascension, Assumption, Terre Bonne, Lafourche, St. Mary, St. Martin, and Orleans, including the city of New Orleans), Mississippi, Alabama, Florida, Georgia, South Carolina, North Carolina, and Virginia (except the forty-eight counties designated as West Virginia, and also the counties of Berkeley, Accomac, Northampton, Elizabeth City, York, Princess Anne, and Norfolk, including the cities of Nor-

THE BROKEN SHACKLES.

ALLEGORICAL PICTURE, FROM AN ORIGINAL DRAWING BY JAMES E. TAYLOR.

HARRIET BEECHER STOWE.

folk and Portsmouth), and which excepted parts are, for the present, left precisely as if this proclamation were not issued.

"And, by virtue of the power and for the purpose aforesaid, I do order and declare that all persons held as slaves within said designated States and parts of States are and henceforward shall be free; and that the Executive Government of the United States, including the military and naval authorities thereof, will recognize and maintain the freedom of said persons.

"And I hereby enjoin upon the people so declared to be free to abstain from all violence, unless in necessary self-defence; and I recommend to them that, in all cases when allowed, they labor faithfully for reasonable wages.

"And I further declare and make known that such persons, of suitable condition, will be received into the armed service of the United States to garrison forts, positions, stations, and other places, and to man vessels of all sorts in said service.

"And upon this act, sincerely believed to be an act of justice, warranted by the Constitution upon military necessity, I invoke the considerate judgment of mankind, and the gracious favor of Almighty God.

"In testimony whereof, I have hereunto set my name, and caused the seal of the United States to be affixed.

(L.S.) "Done at the city of Washington, this first day of January, in the year of our Lord 1863, and of the Independence of the United States the 87th.

"By the President: ABRAHAM LINCOLN.
"WILLIAM H. SEWARD, Secretary of State."

The immediate effect of this action was what had been expected. The friends of liberty, and supporters of the Administration generally, rejoiced at it, believing that the true line of combat had been drawn at last. Robert Dale Owen probably expressed the opinion of most of them when he wrote, "The true and fit question is whether, without a flagrant violation of official duty, the President had the right to refrain from doing it." The effect in Europe is said to have been decisive of the question whether the Confederacy should be recognized as an established nation; but as to this there is some uncertainty. It is certain, however, that much friendship for the Union was won in England, where it had been withheld on account of our attitude on the slavery question. In Manchester, December 31, a mass-meeting of factory operatives was held, and resolutions of sympathy with the Union, and an address to President Lincoln, were voted. The full significance of this can only be understood when it is remembered that these men were largely out of work for want of the cotton that the blockade prevented the South from exporting. The Confederate journals chose to interpret the proclamation as nothing more than an attempt to excite a servile insurrection. The Democratic editors of the North assailed Mr. Lincoln with every verbal weapon of which they were masters, though these had been somewhat blunted by previous use, for he had already been freely called a usurper, a despot, a destroyer of the Constitution, and a keeper of Bastiles. They declared with horror (doubtless in some cases perfectly sincere) that the proclamation had changed the whole character of the war. And this was true, though not in the sense in which they meant it. When begun, it was a war for a temporary peace; the proclamation converted it into a war for a permanent peace. But the autumn elections showed how near Mr. Lincoln came to being ahead of his people after all; for they went largely against the Administration, and even in the States that the Democrats did not carry there was a falling off in the Republican majorities; though the result was partly due to the failure of the peninsula campaign, and the escape of Lee's army after Antietam. Yet this did not shake the great emancipator's faith in the justice and wisdom of what he had done. He said on New Year's evening to a knot of callers: "The signature looks a little tremulous, for my hand was tired, but my resolution was firm. I told them in September, if they did not return to their allegiance and cease murdering our soldiers, I would strike at this pillar of their strength. And now the promise shall be kept, and not one word of it will I ever recall."

If we wonder at the slowness with which that great struggle arrived at its true theme and issue, we shall do well to note that it has a close parallel in our own history. The first battle of the Revolution was fought in April, 1775, but the Declaration of Independence was not made till July, 1776—a period of nearly fifteen months. The first battle in the war of secession took place in April, 1861, and the Emancipation Proclamation was issued in September, 1862—seven-

CHARLES SUMNER.

teen months. In the one case, as in the other, the interval was filled with doubt, hesitation, and divided counsels; and Lincoln's reluctance finds its match in Washington's confession that when he took command of the army (after Lexington, Concord, and Bunker Hill had been fought) he still abhorred the idea of independence. And again, as the great Proclamation was preceded by the attempts of Frémont and Hunter, so the great Declaration had been preceded by those of Mendon, Mass., Chester, Penn., and Mecklenburg, N. C., which anticipated its essential propositions by two or three years. A period of fifteen or seventeen months, however slow for an individual, is perhaps for an entire people as rapid development of a radical purpose as we could have any reason to expect.

WENDELL PHILLIPS.

WILLIAM LLOYD GARRISON AND DAUGHTER.

JOHN G. WHITTIER.

HENRY W. LONGFELLOW.

In the District of Columbia there were three thousand slaves at the time the war began. In December, 1861, Henry Wilson, senator from Massachusetts, afterward Vice-President, introduced in the Senate a bill for the immediate emancipation of these slaves, with a provision for paying to such owners as were loyal an average compensation of three hundred dollars for each slave. The bill was opposed violently by senators and representatives from Kentucky and Maryland, and by some others, conspicuous among whom was Mr. Vallandigham. Nevertheless, it passed both houses, and the President signed it April 16, 1862.

In Delaware, Kentucky, and Missouri slavery continued until it was abolished by the Thirteenth Amendment to the National Constitution, which in December, 1865, was declared ratified by three-fourths of the States, and consequently a part of the fundamental law of the land.

The President's right to proclaim the slaves free, as a war measure, was questioned not only by his violent political opponents, but also by a considerable number who were friendly to him, or at least to the cause of the Union, but whose knowledge of international law and war powers was limited. Among these were Congressman Crittenden and Wickliffe, of Kentucky, who were stanch supporters of the Union, and Mr. Wickliffe offered resolutions declaring that the President has no right whatever to interfere with slavery even during a rebellion. The whole subject was treated in a masterly way by the Hon. William Whiting in his book entitled "War Powers under the Constitution of the United States." He says: "The liberation of slaves is looked upon as a means of embarrassing or weakening the enemy, or of strengthening the military power of our army. If slaves be treated as contraband of war, on the ground that they may be used by their masters to aid in prosecuting war, as employees upon military works, or as laborers furnishing by their industry the means of carrying on hostilities; or if they be treated as, in law, belligerents, following the legal condition of their owners; or if they be deemed loyal subjects having a just claim upon the Government to be released from their obligations to give aid and service to disloyal and belligerent masters, in order that they may be free to perform their higher duty of allegiance and loyalty to the United States; or if they be regarded as subjects of the United States, liable to do military duty; or if they be made citizens of the United States, and soldiers; or if the authority of the masters over their slaves is the means of aiding and comforting the enemy, or of throwing impediments in the way of the Government, or depriving it of such aid and assistance, in successful prosecution of the war, as slaves would and could afford if released from the control of the enemy; or if releasing the slaves would embarrass the enemy, and make it more difficult for them to collect and maintain large armies; in either of these cases, the taking away of these slaves from the 'aid and service' of the enemy, and putting them to the aid and service of the United States, is justifiable as an act of war. The ordinary way of depriving the enemy of slaves is by declaring emancipation."

He then cites abundant precedents and authorities from British, French, South American, and other sources, one of the most striking of which is this quotation from Thomas Jefferson's letter to Dr. Gordon, complaining of the injury done to his estates by Cornwallis: "He destroyed all my growing crops and tobacco; he burned all my barns, containing the same articles of last year. Having first taken what corn he wanted, he used, as was to be expected, all my stock of cattle, sheep, and hogs for the sustenance of his army, and carried off all the horses capable of service. He carried off also about thirty slaves. Had this been to give them freedom, he would have done right. From an estimate made at the time on the best information I could collect, I suppose the State of Virginia lost, under Lord Cornwallis's hands, that year, about thirty thousand slaves." Whiting says in conclusion: "It has thus been proved, by the law and usage of modern civilized nations, confirmed by the judgment of eminent statesmen, and by the former practice of this Government, that the President, as commander-in-chief, has the authority, as an act of war, to liberate the slaves of the enemy; that the United States have in former times sanctioned the liberation of slaves—even of loyal citizens—by military commanders, in time of war, without compensation therefor, and have deemed slaves captured in war from belligerent subjects as entitled to their freedom."

MAJOR-GENERAL AMBROSE E. BURNSIDE AND STAFF.

CHAPTER XVII.

BURNSIDE'S CAMPAIGN.

McCLELLAN'S INACTION—VISIT AND LETTERS OF LINCOLN TO HIM—SUPERSEDED BY BURNSIDE—THE POSITION AT FREDERICKSBURG—ATTACK UPON THE HEIGHTS—THE RESULT—GENERAL BURNSIDE'S LACK OF JUDGMENT—PRESIDENT LINCOLN'S NATURAL APTITUDE FOR STRATEGY—BRAVERY OF THE SOLDIERS—THRILLING INCIDENTS OF THE BATTLE—GALLANTRY OF THE IRISH BRIGADE.

AFTER the battle of the Antietam, Lee withdrew to the neighborhood of Winchester, where he was reinforced, till at the end of a month he had about sixty-eight thousand men. McClellan followed as far as the Potomac, and there seemed to plant his army, as if he expected it to sprout and increase itself like a field of corn. Ten days after he defeated Lee on the Antietam, he wrote to the President that he intended to stay where he was, and attack the enemy if they attempted to recross into Maryland! At the same time, he constantly called for unlimited reinforcements, and declared that, even if the city of Washington should be captured, it would not be a disaster so serious as the defeat of his army. Apparently it did not occur to General McClellan that these two contingencies were logically the same. For if Lee could have defeated that army, he could then have marched into Washington; or if he could have captured Washington without fighting the army whose business it was to defend it, the army would thereby be substantially defeated.

On the 1st of October the President visited General McClellan at his headquarters, and made himself acquainted with the condition of the army. Five days later he ordered McClellan to "cross the Potomac, and give battle to the enemy, or drive him south." The despatch added, "Your army must move now, while the roads are good. If you cross the river between the enemy and Washington, and cover the latter by your operation, you can be reinforced with thirty thousand men." Nevertheless, McClellan did not stir. Instead of obeying the order, he inquired what sort of troops they were that would be sent to him, and how many tents he could have, and said his army could not move without fresh supplies of shoes and clothing. While he was thus paltering, the Confederate General Stuart, who had ridden around his army on the peninsula, with a small body of cavalry rode entirely around it again, eluding all efforts for his capture. On the 13th the President wrote a long, friendly letter to General McClellan, in which he gave him much excellent advice that he, as a trained soldier, ought not to have needed. A sentence or two will suggest the drift of it: "Are you not over-cautious when you assume that you cannot do what the enemy is constantly doing? . . . In coming to us, he [the enemy] tenders us an advantage which we should not waive. We should not so operate as to merely drive him away. . . . It is all easy if our troops march as well as the enemy, and it is unmanly to say they cannot do it." The letter had outlined a plan of campaign, but it closed with the words, characteristic of Lincoln's modesty in military matters, "This letter is in no sense an order." Twelve days more of fine weather were frittered away in renewed complaints, and such inquiries as whether the President wished him to move at once or wait for fresh horses, for the general said his horses were fatigued and had sore tongue. Here the President began to show some impatience, and wrote: "Will you pardon me for asking what the horses of your army have done since the battle of Antietam that fatigues anything?" The general replied that they had been scouting, picketing, and making reconnoissances, and that the President had done injustice to the cavalry. Whereupon Mr. Lincoln wrote again: "Most certainly I intend no injustice to any, and if I have done any I deeply regret it. To be told, after more than five weeks' total inaction of the army, and during which period we had sent to that army every fresh horse we possibly could, amounting in the whole to 7,918, that the cavalry horses were too much fatigued to move, presented a very cheerless, almost hopeless, prospect for the future, and it may have forced something of impatience into my despatches." That day, October 26, McClellan began to cross the Potomac; but it was ten days (partly owing to heavy rains) before his army was all on the south side of the river, and meanwhile he had brought up new questions for discussion and invented new excuses for delay. He wanted to know to what extent the line of the Potomac was to be guarded; he wanted to leave strong garrisons at certain points, to prevent the army he was driving southward before him from rushing northward into Maryland again; he discussed the position of General Bragg's (Confederate) army, which was four hundred miles away beyond the mountains; he said the old regiments of his command must be filled up with recruits before they could go into action.

MAJOR-GENERAL JOHN NEWTON.

MAJOR-GENERAL E. V. SUMNER.

BREVET MAJOR-GENERAL J. J. BARTLETT.

McClellan was a sore puzzle to the people of the loyal States. But large numbers of his men still believed in him, and—as is usual in such cases—intensified their personal devotion in proportion as the distrust of the people at large was increased. After crossing the Potomac, he left a corps at Harper's Ferry, and was moving southward on the eastern side of the Blue Ridge, while Lee moved in the same direction on the western

CONFEDERATE SHARP-SHOOTERS ON THE HEIGHTS OF FREDERICKSBURG.

side, when, on November 7, the President solved the riddle that had vexed the country, by relieving him of the command.

The successor of General McClellan was Ambrose E. Burnside, then in his thirty-ninth year, who was graduated at West Point fifteen years before, had commanded cavalry during the Mexican war, had invented a breech-loading rifle which was commercially unsuccessful, and at the breaking out of the rebellion was treasurer of the Illinois Central Railroad. When the First Rhode Island Regiment went to Washington, four days after the President's first call for troops, Burnside was its colonel. He commanded a brigade at the first battle of Bull Run; led an expedition that captured Roanoke Island, New Berne, and Beaufort, N. C., in January, 1862; and commanded one wing of McClellan's army at South Mountain and Antietam. Whether he was blameworthy for not crossing the Antietam early in the day and effecting a crushing defeat of Lee's army, is a disputed question. It might be worth while to discuss it, were it not that he afterward accepted a heavier responsibility and incurred a more serious accusation. The command of the Army of the Potomac had been offered to him twice before, but he had refused it, saying that he "was not competent to command such a large army." When the order came relieving McClellan and appointing him, he consulted with that general and with his staff officers, making the same objection; but they took the ground that as a soldier he was bound to obey without question, and so he accepted the place, as he says, "in the midst of a violent snow-storm, with the army in a position that I knew little of."

ATTACK ON FREDERICKSBURG, DECEMBER, 1862.

These two generals were warm personal friends, and McClellan remained a few days to put Burnside in possession, as far as possible, of the essential facts in relation to the position and condition of the forces.

At this time the right wing of Lee's army, under Longstreet, was near Culpeper, and the left, under Jackson, was in the Shenandoah Valley. Their separation was such that it would require two days for one to march to the other. McClellan said he intended to endeavor to get between them and either beat them in detail or force them to unite as far south as Gordonsville. Burnside not only did not continue this plan, but gave up the idea that the Confederate army was his true objective, assumed the city of Richmond to be such, and set out for that place by way of the north bank of the Rappahannock and the city of Fredericksburg, after consuming ten days in reorganizing his army into three grand divisions, under Sumner, Hooker, and Franklin. On the 15th of November he began the march from Warrenton; the head of his first column reached Falmouth on the 17th, and by the 20th the whole army was there. By some blunder (it is uncertain whose) the pontoon train that was to have met the army at this point, and afforded an immediate crossing of the river, did not arrive till a week later; and by this time Lee, who chose to cover his own capital and cross the path of his enemy, rather than strike at his communications, had placed his army on the heights south and west of Fredericksburg, and at once began to fortify them. His line was about five and a half miles long, and was as strong as a good natural

THE STONE WALL UNDER MARYE'S HEIGHTS.

FROM A WAR DEPARTMENT PHOTOGRAPH.

position, earthworks, and an abundance of artillery could make it. He could not prevent Burnside from crossing the river; for the heights on the left bank rose close to the stream, commanding the intermediate plain, and on these heights Burnside had one hundred and forty-seven guns. What with waiting for the pontoons and establishing his base of supplies at Acquia Creek, it was the 10th of December before the National commander was ready to attempt the passage of the stream. He planned to lay down five bridges—three opposite the city and the others two miles below—and depended upon his artillery to protect the engineers.

Before daybreak on the morning of the 11th, in a thick fog, the work was begun; but the bridges had not spanned more than half the distance when the sun had risen and the fog lifted sufficiently to reveal what was going on. A detachment of Mississippi riflemen had been posted in cellars, behind stone walls, and at every point where a man could be sheltered on the south bank; and now the incessant crack of their weapons was heard, picking off the men that were laying the bridges. One after another of the blue-coats reeled with a bullet in his brain, fell into the water, and was carried down by the current, till the losses were so serious that it was impossible to continue the work. At the lower bridges the sharp-shooters, who there had no shelter but rifle-pits in the open field, were dislodged after a time, and by noon those bridges were completed. But along the front of the town they had better shelter, the National guns could not be depressed enough to shell them, and the work on the three upper bridges came to a standstill. Burnside tried bombarding the town, threw seventy tons of iron into it, and set it on fire; but still the sharp-shooters clung to their hiding places, and when the engineers tried to renew their task on the bridges, under cover of the bombardment, they were destroyed by the same murderous fire.

LIEUTENANT-GENERAL RICHARD H. ANDERSON, C. S. A.

At last General Hunt, chief of artillery, suggested a solution of the difficulty. Three regiments that volunteered for the service—the Seventh Michigan, and the Nineteenth and Twentieth Massachusetts—crossed the river in pontoon boats, under the fire of the sharp-shooters, landed quickly, and drove them out of their fastness, capturing a hundred of them, while the remainder escaped to the hills. The bridges were then completed, and the crossing was begun; but it was evening of the 12th before the entire army was on the Fredericksburg side of the river.

On the morning of the 13th Burnside was ready to attack, and Lee was more than ready to be attacked. He had concentrated his whole army on the fortified heights, Longstreet's corps forming his left wing and Jackson's his right, with every gun in position, and every man ready and knowing what to expect. The weak point of the line, if it had any, was on the right, where the ground was not so high, and there was plenty of room for the deployment of the attacking force. Here Franklin commanded, with about half of the National army; and here, according to Burnside's first plan, the principal assault was to be made. But there appears to have been a sudden and unaccountable change in the plan; and when the hour for action arrived Franklin was ordered to send forward a division or two, and hold the remainder of his force ready for "a rapid movement down the old Richmond road," while Sumner on the right was ordered to send out two divisions to seize the heights back of the city. Exactly what Burnside expected to do next, if these movements had been successful, nobody appears to know.

BRIGADIER-GENERAL CADMUS M. WILCOX, C. S. A.

The division chosen to lead Franklin's attack was Meade's. This advanced rapidly, preceded by a heavy skirmish line, while his batteries firing over the heads of the troops shelled the heights vigorously. Meade's men crossed the railroad under a heavy fire, that had been withheld till they were within close range, penetrated between two divisions of the first Confederate line, doubling back the flanks of both and taking many prisoners and some battle-flags, scaled the heights, and came upon the second line. By this time the momentum of the attack was spent, and the fire of the second line, delivered on the flanks as well as in front, drove them back. The divisions of Gibbon and Doubleday had followed in support, which relieved the pressure upon Meade; and when all three were returning unsuccessful and in considerable confusion, Birney's moved out and stopped the pursuing enemy.

MAJOR-GENERAL ROBERT RANSOM, JR., C. S. A.

Sumner's attack was made with the divisions of French and Hancock, which moved through the town and deployed in columns under the fire of the Confederate batteries. This was very destructive, but was not the deadliest thing that the men had to meet. Marye's Hill was skirted near its base by an old sunken road, at the outer edge of which was a stone wall; and in this road were two brigades of Confederate infantry. It could hardly be seen, at a little distance, that there was a road at all. When French's charging columns had rushed across the open ground under an artillery fire that ploughed through and through their ranks, they suddenly confronted a sheet of flame and lead from the rifles in the sunken road. The Confederates here were so numerous that each one at the wall had two or three behind to load muskets and hand them to him, while he had only to lay them flat across the wall and fire them as rapidly as possible, exposing scarcely more than his head. Nearly half of French's men were shot down, and the remainder fell back. Hancock's five thousand charged in the same manner, and some of them approached within twenty yards of the wall; but within a quarter of an hour they also fell back a part of the distance, leaving two thousand of their number on the field. Three other divisions advanced to the attack, but with no better result; and all of them remained in a position where they were just out of reach of the rifles in the sunken road, but were still played upon by the Confederate artillery.

Burnside now grew frantic, and ordered Hooker to attack. That officer moved out with three divisions, made a reconnoissance, and went back to tell Burnside it was useless and persuade him to give up the attempt. But the commander insisted, and so Hooker's four thousand rushed forward with fixed bayonets, and presently came back like the rest, leaving seventeen hundred dead or wounded on the field.

The entire National loss in this battle was twelve thousand six hundred and fifty-three in killed, wounded, or missing, though some of the missing afterward rejoined their commands. Hancock's division lost one hundred and fifty-six officers, and one of his regiments lost two-thirds of its men. The Confederate loss was five thousand three hundred and seventy-seven. Four brigadier-generals were killed in this battle; on the National side, Generals George D. Bayard and Conrad F. Jackson; on the Confederate, Generals Thomas R. R. Cobb and Maxcy Gregg. In the night the Union troops brought in their wounded and buried some of their dead. Severe as his losses had been, Burnside planned to make a fresh attempt the next day, with the Ninth Corps (his old command), which he proposed to lead in person; but General Sumner dissuaded him, though with difficulty. In the night of the 15th, in the midst of a storm, the army was withdrawn to the north bank of the Rappahannock, and the sorry campaign was ended.

COLONEL ROBERT NUGENT.
(Afterward Brevet Brigadier-General.)

BRIGADIER-GENERAL T. F. MEAGHER.

If it had been at all necessary to prove the courage and discipline of the National troops, Fredericksburg proved it abundantly. There were few among them that December morning who did not look upon it as hopeless to assault those fortified slopes; yet they obeyed their orders, and moved out to the work as if they expected victory, suffering such frightful losses as bodies of troops are seldom called upon to endure, and retiring with little disorder and no panic. The English correspondent of the London *Times*, writing from Lee's headquarters, exultingly predicted the speedy decline and fall of the American Republic. If he had been shrewd enough to see what was indicated, rather than what he hoped for, he would have written that with such courage and discipline as the Army of the Potomac had displayed, and superior resources, the final victory was certain to be theirs, however they might first suffer from incompetent commanders; that the Republic that had set such an army in the field, and had the material for several more, was likely to contain somewhere a general worthy to lead it, and was not likely to be overthrown by any insurrection of a minority of its people.

BREVET BRIGADIER-GENERAL G. A. DE RUSSEY.

There never was any question of the gallantry or patriotism of General Burnside, but his woful lack of judgment in the conduct of the battle of Fredericksburg (or perhaps it should be said, in fighting a battle at that point at all) has ever remained inexplicable. His own attempt to explain it, in his official report, is brief, and is at least manly in the frankness with which he puts the entire blame upon himself. He wrote: "During my preparations for crossing at the place I had first selected, I discovered that the enemy had thrown a large portion of his force down the river and elsewhere, thus weakening his defences in front, and also thought I discovered that he did not anticipate the crossing of our whole force at Fredericksburg; and I hoped by rapidly throwing the whole command over at that place to separate, by a vigorous attack, the forces of the enemy on the river below from the forces behind and on the crest in the rear of the town, in which case we could fight him with great advantage in our favor. To do this we had to gain a height on the extreme right of the crest, which height commanded a new road lately made by the enemy for purposes of more rapid communication along his lines, which point gained, his positions along the crest would have been scarcely tenable, and he could have been driven from them easily by an attack on his front in connection with a movement in the rear of the crest. . . . Failing in accomplishing the main object, we remained in order of battle two days—long enough to decide that the enemy would not come out of his strongholds to fight us with infantry—after which we recrossed to this side of the river unmolested, without the loss of men or property. As the day broke, our long lines of troops were seen marching to their different positions as if going on parade—not the least demoralization or disorganization existed. To the brave officers and soldiers who accomplished the feat of thus recrossing the river in the face of the enemy, I owe everything. For the failure in the attack I am responsible, as the extreme gallantry, courage, and endurance shown by them was never exceeded, and would have carried the points had it been possible. The fact that I decided to move from Warrenton on to this line rather against the opinion of the President, Secretary of War, and yourself, and that you left the whole movement in my hands, without giving me orders, makes me the only one responsible."

A HASTY MEAL.

When Burnside's plan was submitted to the President and General Halleck, there was considerable opposition to it, and when finally Halleck informed Burnside that the President consented to that plan, he added significantly: "He thinks it will succeed if you move rapidly; otherwise, not." Though Mr. Lincoln was not a soldier, his natural aptitude for strategy has been much discussed, and it is therefore interesting to remember this saving clause in his consent to the experiment of Fredericksburg. How near the National troops, with all their terrible disadvantages, came to piercing the lines of the enemy on Marye's Hill, we know from the testimony of General Longstreet, who says: "General Lee became uneasy when he saw the attacks so promptly renewed and pushed forward with such persistence, and feared the Federals might break through our lines. After the third charge he said to me, 'General, they are massing very heavily, and will break your line, I am afraid.'" Longstreet represents himself as having no such fears whatever, but it further appears from his testimony that when in the night they captured an officer on whom they found an order for renewal of the battle the next day, General Lee immediately gave orders for the construction of a new line of rifle-pits and the placing of more guns in position.

RELIEF FOR THE WOUNDED.

General Lee, instead of following up his good fortune by counter attack, went off to Richmond to suggest other operations. No such fierce criticism for not reaping the fruits of victories has ever been expended upon him as some of the National commanders have had to endure for this fault, though many of his and their opportunities were closely parallel. In Richmond he was told by Mr. Davis that the Administration considered the war virtually over, but he knew better.

The story of the battle, so far as its strictly military aspect is concerned, is extremely simple, and makes but a short though dreadful chapter in the history of the great struggle. But it was full of incidents, though mostly of the mournful kind, and the reader would fail to get any adequate conception of what was done and suffered on that field without some accounts written at the time by participants. General Meagher, commanding the Irish brigade, made an interesting report, in which he pictured graphically the manner in which that organization went into the action and the treatment that it received. A few extracts will include the most interesting passages. "The brigade never was in finer spirits and condition. The arms and accoutrements were in perfect order. The required amount of ammunition was on hand. Both officers and men were comfortably clad, and it would be difficult to say whether those who were to lead or those who were to follow were the better prepared or the more eager to discharge their duty. A few minutes after four o'clock P.M., word was conveyed to me that a gallant body of volunteers had crossed the river in boats and taken possession of the city of Fredericksburg. Immediately on the receipt of this news, an order reached me from Brigadier-General Hancock to move forward the brigade and take up a position closer to the river. In this new position we remained all night. At seven o'clock the following morning we were under arms, and in less than two hours the head of the brigade presented itself on the opposite bank of the river. Passing along the edge of the river to the lower bridge, the brigade halted, countermarched, stacked arms, and in this position, ankle-deep in mud, and with little or nothing to contribute to their comfort, in complete subordination and good heart, awaited further orders. An order promulgated by Major-General Couch, commanding the corps, prohibited fires after nightfall. This order was uncomplainingly and manfully obeyed by the brigade. Officers and men lay down and slept that night in the mud and frost, and without a murmur, with heroic hearts, composed themselves as best they could for the eventualities of the coming day. A little before eight o'clock A.M., Saturday, the 13th inst., we received orders to fall in and prepare instantly to take the field. The brigade being in line, I addressed, separately, to each regiment a few words, reminding it of its duty, and exhorting it to acquit itself of that duty bravely and nobly to the last. Immediately after, the column swept up the street toward the scene of action, headed by Col. Robert Nugent, of the Sixty-ninth, and his veteran regiment—every officer and man of the brigade wearing a sprig of evergreen in his hat, in memory of the land of his birth. The advance was firmly and brilliantly made through this street under a continuous discharge of shot and shell, several men falling from the effects of both. Even whilst I was addressing the Sixty-ninth, which was on the right of the brigade, three men of the Sixty-third were knocked over, and before I had spoken my last words of encouragement the mangled remains of the poor fellows—mere masses of torn flesh and rags—were borne along the line to the hospital of French's division. Emerging from the street, having nothing whatever to protect it, the brigade encountered the full force and fury of the enemy's fire, and, unable to resist or reply to it, had to push on to the mill-race, which may be described as the first of the hostile de-

ZOUAVE COLOR-BEARER AT FREDERICKSBURG.

fences. Crossing this mill-race by means of a single bridge, the brigade, diverging to the right, had to deploy into line of battle. This movement necessarily took some time to execute. The Sixty-ninth, under Colonel Nugent, being on the right, had to stand its ground until the rest of the brigade came up and formed. I myself, accompanied by Lieutenant Emmet of my staff, crossed the mill-race on foot from the head of the street through which the column had debouched. Trudging up the ploughed field as well as my lameness would permit me, to the muddy crest along which the brigade was to form in line of battle, I reached the fence on which the right of the Sixty-ninth rested. I directed Colonel Nugent to throw out two companies of his regiment as skirmishers on the right flank. This order was being carried out, when the other regiments of the brigade, coming up with a brisk step and deploying in line of battle, drew down upon themselves a terrific fire. Nevertheless the line was beautifully and rapidly formed, and boldly advanced, Colonel Nugent leading on the right, Col. Patrick Kelly, commanding the Eighty-eighth, being next in line, both displaying a courageous soldiership which I have no words, even with all my partiality for them, adequately to describe. Thus formed, under the unabating tempest and deluge of shot and shell, the Irish brigade advanced against the rifle-pits, the breastworks, and batteries of the enemy. . . . The next day, a little after sunrise, every officer and man of the brigade able again to take the field, by order of Brigadier-General Hancock, recrossed to Fredericksburg and took up the same position, on the street nearest the river, which we had occupied previous to the advance, prepared and eager, notwithstanding their exhausted numbers and condition, to support the Ninth Corps in the renewal of the assault of the previous day, that renewal having been determined on by the general-in-chief. Of the one thousand two hundred I had led into action the day before, two hundred and eighty only appeared on that ground that morning. This remnant of the Irish brigade, still full of heart, still wearing the evergreen, inspired by a glowing sense of duty, sorrowful for their comrades, but emboldened and elated by the thought that they had fallen with the proud bravery they did—this noble little remnant awaited the order that was once more to precipitate them against the batteries of the enemy."

Gen. Aaron F. Stevens (afterward member of Congress), who at that time commanded the Thirteenth New Hampshire Regiment, made an interesting report, in the course of which he said: "Just after dark we moved to the river, and crossed without opposition the pontoon-bridge near the lower end of the city. My regiment took up its position for the night in Caroline Street, one of the principal streets of the city, and threw out two companies as pickets toward the enemy. At an early hour on Saturday morning, the eventful and disastrous day of the battle, we took up our position with the brigade under the hill on the bank of the river, just below the bridge which we crossed on Thursday night. Here we remained under arms the entire day, our position being about a mile distant from the line of the enemy's batteries. Occasionally, during the day, fragments of shell from his guns reached us or passed over us, falling in the river and beyond, doing but little damage. One of our own guns, however, on the opposite bank of the river, which threw shells over us toward the enemy, was so unfortunately handled as to kill two men and wound several others in our brigade. As yet all the accounts which I have seen or read, from Union or rebel sources, approach not in delineation the truthful and terrible panorama of that bloody day. Twice during the day I rode up Caroline Street to the centre of the city toward the point where our brave legions were struggling against the terrible combination of the enemy's artillery and infantry, whose unremitting fire shook the earth and filled the plain in rear of the city with the deadly missiles of war. I saw the struggling hosts of freedom stretched along the plain, their ranks ploughed by the merciless fire of the foe. I saw the dead and wounded, among them some of New Hampshire's gallant sons, borne back on the shoulders of their comrades in battle, and laid tenderly down in the hospitals prepared for their reception, in the houses on either side of the street as far as human habitations extended. I listened to the roar of battle and the groans of the wounded and dying. I saw in the crowded hospitals the desolation of war; but I heard from our brave soldiers no note of triumph, no word of encouragement, no syllable of hope that for us a field was to be won. In the stubborn, unyielding resistance of the enemy I could see no point of pressure likely to yield to the repeated assaults of our brave soldiers, and so I returned to my command to wait patiently for the hour when we might be called to share in the duty and danger of our brave brethren engaged in the contest. By stepping forward to the brow of the hill which covered us, a distance of ten yards, we were in full view of the rebel stronghold—the batteries along the crest of the ridge called Stansbury Hill and skirting Hazel Run. For three-fourths of an hour before we were ordered into action, I stood in front of my regiment on the brow of the hill and watched the fire of the rebel batteries as they poured shot and shell from sixteen different points upon our devoted men on the plains below. It was a sight magnificently terrible. Every discharge of enemy's artillery and every explosion of his shells were visible in the dusky twilight of that smoke-crowned hill. There his direct and enfilading batteries, with the vividness, intensity, and almost the rapidity, of lightning, hurled the messengers of death in the midst of our brave ranks, vainly struggling through the murderous fire to gain the hills and the guns of the enemy. Nor was it any straggling or ill-directed fire. The arrangement of the enemy's guns was such that they could pour their concentrated and incessant fire upon any point occupied by our assailing troops, and all of them were plied with the greatest skill and animation. During all this time the rattle of musketry was incessant.

"About sunset there was a pause in the cannonading and musketry, and orders came for our brigade to fall in. Silently but unflinchingly the men moved out from under their cover, and, when they reached the ground, quickened their pace to a run. As the head of the column came in sight of the enemy, at a distance of about three-fourths of a mile from their batteries, when close to Slaughter's house, it was saluted with a shower of shell from the enemy's guns on the crest of the hill. It moved on by the flank down the hill into the plain beyond, crossing a small stream which passes through the city and empties into Hazel Run, then over another hill to the line of railroad. We moved at so rapid a pace that many of the men relieved themselves of their blankets and haversacks, and in some instances of their great-coats, which in most cases were lost. By countermarch, we extended our line along the railroad, the right resting toward the city, and the left near Hazel Run. The words, 'Forward, charge!' ran along the lines. The men sprang forward, and moved at a run, crossed the railroad into a low muddy swamp on the left, which reaches down to Hazel Run, the right moving over higher and less muddy ground, all the time the batteries of the enemy concentrating their terrible fire and pouring it upon the advancing lines. Suddenly the cannonading and musketry of the enemy ceased. The shouts of our men also were hushed, and nothing was heard along the line save the command: 'Forward, men—steady—close up.' In this way we moved forward, until within about twenty yards of the celebrated stone wall. Before we reached the point of which I have been speaking, we came to an irregular ravine or gully, into which, in the darkness of night, the lines plunged, but immediately gained the opposite side, and were advancing along the level ground toward the stone wall. Behind that wall, and in rifle-pits on its flanks, were posted the enemy's infantry—according to their statements—four ranks deep; and on the hill, a few yards above, lay in ominous silence their death-dealing artillery. It was while we were moving steadily forward that, with one startling crash, with one simultaneous sheet of fire and flame, they hurled on our advancing lines the whole terrible force of their infantry and artillery. The powder from their musketry burned in our very faces, and the breath of their artillery was hot upon our cheeks. The 'leaden rain and iron hail' in an instant forced back the advancing lines upon those who were close to them in the rear; and before the men could be rallied to renew the charge, the lines had been hurled back by the irresistible fire of the enemy to the cover of the ravine or gully which they had just passed. The enemy swept the ground with his guns, killing and wounding many—our men in the meantime keeping up a spirited fire upon the unseen foe."

GENERAL GRANT DIRECTING THE DISPOSITION OF TROOPS.

MARCHING THROUGH TENNESSEE.

CHAPTER XVIII.

WAR IN THE WEST.

CONSCRIPTION ACT PASSED BY CONFEDERATE CONGRESS — GENERAL BRAGGS'S OPERATIONS IN KENTUCKY AND EAST TENNESSEE—BATTLE OF PERRYVILLE — GRAPHIC DESCRIPTION OF THE CONFEDERATE CHARGE—BATTLE OF IUKA—BATTLE OF STONE RIVER, OR MURFREESBORO'—ESTRANGEMENT BETWEEN GRANT AND ROSECRANS—BATTLE OF CORINTH—CONFEDERATE RETREAT—HEAVY LOSSES ON BOTH SIDES.

THE Confederate Congress in 1862 passed a sweeping conscription act, forcing into the ranks every man of military age. Even boys of sixteen were taken out of school and sent to camps of instruction. This largely increased their forces in the field, and at the West especially they exhibited a corresponding activity. General Beauregard, whose health had failed, was succeeded by Gen. Braxton Bragg, a man of more energy than ability, who, with forty thousand men, marched northward into eastern Kentucky, defeating a National force near Richmond, and another at Munfordville. He then assumed that Kentucky was a State of the Confederacy, appointed a provisional governor, forced Kentuckians into his army, and robbed the farmers not only of their stock and provisions, but of their wagons for carrying away the plunder, paying them in worthless Confederate money. He carried with him twenty thousand muskets, expecting to find that number of Kentuckians who would enroll themselves in his command; but he confessed afterward that he did not even secure enough recruits to take up the arms that fell from the hands of his dead and wounded. With the supplies collected by his army of "liberators," as he called them, in a wagon-train said to have been forty miles long, he was moving slowly back into Tennessee, when General Buell, with about fifty-eight thousand men (one-third of them new recruits), marched in pursuit.

Bragg turned and gave battle at Perryville (October 8), and the fight lasted nearly all day. At some points it was desperate, with hand-to-hand fighting, and troops charging upon batteries where the gunners stood to their pieces and blew them from the very muzzles. The National left, composed entirely of raw troops, was crushed by a heavy onset; but the next portion of the line, commanded by Gen. Philip H. Sheridan, not only held its ground and repelled the assault, but followed up the retiring enemy with a counter attack. Gooding's brigade (National) lost five hundred and forty-nine men out of fourteen hundred and twenty-three, and its commander became a prisoner. When night fell, the Confederates had been repelled at all points, and a portion of them had been driven through Perryville, losing many wagons and prisoners. Buell prepared to attack at daylight, but found that Bragg had moved off in the night with his whole army, continuing his retreat to East Tennessee, leaving a thousand of his wounded on the ground. He also abandoned twelve hundred of his men in hospital at Harrodsburg, with large quantities of his plunder, some of which he burned, and made all haste to get away. Buell reported his loss in the battle as forty-three hundred and forty-eight, which included Gens. James S. Jackson and William R. Terrill killed. Bragg's loss was probably larger, though he gave considerably smaller figures.

The battle of Perryville is more noteworthy for its fierce fighting and numerous instances of determined gallantry than for any importance in its bearing on the campaign. It was especially notable for the work of the artillery, and the struggles to capture or preserve the various batteries. One National battery of eight guns was commanded by Capt. Charles C. Parsons, and the Confederates making a fierce charge upon it captured seven of the pieces, but not without the most desperate hand-to-hand fighting, in the course of which Parsons at one time was lying on his back under the guns and firing his revolver at the assailants. Sixteen years afterward this man, who in the meantime had become a clergyman, sacrificed his life in attending to the victims of yellow fever on the Mississippi. When Sheridan was heavily pressed by the enemy and his right was in special danger, the brigade of Colonel Carlin was sent to his relief. Carlin's men, reaching the brow of a hill, discovered the advancing enemy, and immediately charged at the double quick with such impetuosity that they not only drove back the Confederates, but passed entirely through their lines where they were in momentary danger of being captured *en masse*. But, during the confusion which they caused, they skilfully fell back, carrying with them a heavily loaded ammunition train which they had captured with its guard. Pinney's Fifth Wisconsin battery was worked to its utmost capacity for three hours without supports, and withstood several charges, piling its front with the bodies of the slain. In the Third Ohio Regiment six color sergeants were shot in succession, but the flag was never allowed to touch the earth. That regiment lost two hundred out of five hundred men. A correspondent of the *Cincinnati Gazette*, who was on the field, thus relates one of the many interesting incidents of the battle: "The Tenth Ohio were lying upon their faces to the left of the Third, near the summit of the same hill, and upon the other side of a lane. The retreat of the Third Ohio and Fifteenth Kentucky had left the right wing of the Tenth uncovered, and a whole brigade of the enemy, forming in mass, advanced toward them over ground of such a nature that if the Tenth did not receive warning from some source the rebel column would be upon them, and annihilate them before they could rise from their faces and change front. Colonel Lytle was expecting the enemy to appear in his front, over the crest of the hill, and had intended to have the gallant Tenth charge them with the bayonet. And they still lay upon their faces while the enemy was advancing upon their flank, stealthily as a cat steals upon her prey. Nearer and nearer they come. Great heavens! Will no one tell the Tenth of their fearful peril? Where is the eagle eye which ought to overlook the field and send swift-footed couriers to save this illustrious band from destruction? Alas, there is none! The heroes of Carnifex are doomed. The mass of Confederates, which a rising ground just to the right of the tent has hitherto concealed from view, rush upon the hapless regiment, and from the distance of a hundred yards pour into it an annihilating fire even while the men are still upon their faces. Overwhelmed and confounded, they leap to their feet and vainly endeavor to change front to meet the enemy. It is impossible to do it beneath that withering, murderous fire; and for the first time in its history the Tenth Regiment turns its back upon the enemy. They will not run; they only walk away, and they are mowed down by scores as they go. The noble, gifted, generous Lytle was pierced with bullets and fell where the storm was fiercest. One of his sergeants lifted him in his arms, and was endeavoring to carry him from the field. 'You may do some good yet,' said the hero; 'I can do no more; let me die here.' He was left there, and fell into the hands of the enemy."

On hearing of this disaster to the Tenth Ohio Regiment, which formed the right of Lytle's Seventeenth Brigade, General Rousseau immediately rode to the scene of it. He says in his report: "Whilst near the Fifteenth Kentucky, I saw a heavy force of the enemy advancing upon our right, the same that had turned Lytle's right flank. It was moving steadily up in full view of where General Gilbert's army corps had been during the day, the left flank of which was not more than four hundred yards from it. On approaching, the Fifteenth Kentucky, though broken and shattered, rose to its feet and cheered, and as one man moved to the top of the hill where it could see the enemy, and I ordered it to lie down. I then rode up to Loomis's battery, and directed him to open upon the enemy. He replied he was ordered by General McCook to reserve what ammunition he had for close work. Pointing to the enemy advancing, I said it was close enough, and would be closer in a moment. He at once opened fire with alacrity, and made fearful havoc upon the ranks of the enemy. It was admirably done, but the enemy moved straight ahead. His ranks were raked by the battery, and terribly thinned by the musketry of the Seventeenth Brigade; but he scarcely faltered, and finally, hearing that reinforcements were approaching, the brigade was ordered to retire and give place to them, which it did in good order. The reinforcements

BATTLE OF STONE RIVER—THE DECISIVE CHARGE OF THE FEDERAL TROOPS ACROSS THE RIVER.

were from Mitchell's division, as I understood, and were Pea Ridge men. I wish I knew who commanded the brigade, that I might do him justice; I can only say that the brigade moved directly into the fight, like true soldiers, and opened a terrific fire and drove back the enemy. After repulsing the enemy, they retired a few hundred yards into a piece of woods to encamp in, and during the night the enemy advanced his pickets in the woods on our left front and captured a good many of our men who went there believing we still held the woods."

MAJOR-GENERAL PHILIP H. SHERIDAN.

General Halleck, at Washington, now planned for Buell's army a campaign in East Tennessee; but as that was more than two hundred miles away, and the communications were not provided for, Buell declined to execute it. For this reason, and also on the ground that if he had moved more rapidly and struck more vigorously he might have destroyed Bragg's army, he was removed from command, and Gen. William S. Rosecrans succeeded him.

In September, when Bragg had first moved northward, a Confederate army of about forty thousand men, under Generals Price and Van Dorn, had crossed from Arkansas into Mississippi with the purpose of capturing Grant's position at Corinth, and thus breaking the National line of defence and coöperating with Bragg. Price seized Iuka, southeast of Corinth, and Grant sent out against him a force under Rosecrans, consisting of about nine thousand men, which included the divisions of Gens. David S. Stanley and Charles S. Hamilton, and the cavalry under Col. John K. Mizner. It was Grant's intention that while this force moved toward Iuka from the south, Gen. E. O. C. Ord's command, consisting of eight thousand men, should move upon it from the west. There are two roads running south from Iuka, about two miles apart, and Grant intended that Rosecrans should approach by both of these roads, so as to cut off the enemy's retreat. But Rosecrans marched only by the westernmost road, leaving the eastern, known as the Fulton road, open. Hamilton's division was in advance, and at four o'clock in the afternoon, at a point two miles from Iuka, the head of his column, ascending a long hill, found the enemy deployed across the road and in the woods a few hundred yards beyond its crest. Hamilton had thrown out a heavy skirmish line, which for four or five miles had kept up a running fight with sharp-shooters. The enemy, in force, occupied a strong line along a deep ravine, from which they moved forward to attack as soon as Hamilton's men appeared on the crest. Hamilton himself, being close to the skirmish line, saw the situation with its dangers and its advantages, and made haste to prepare for what was coming. He deployed his infantry along the crest, got a battery into position under heavy fire where it could command the road in front, placed every regiment personally, and gave each regimental commander orders to hold his ground at all hazards. As the remainder of his forces came up, he placed them so as to extend his flanks and prevent them from being turned. But while he was doing this, the enemy was advancing and the battle was becoming very serious. The enemy came on in heavy masses against his centre, charging steadily up to his guns, which fired canister into them at short range, until nearly every man and horse in the battery was disabled, and it was captured. Brig.-Gen. Jeremiah C. Sullivan then gathered a portion of the right wing, which had been thrown into some disorder, and retook the battery, driving the Confederates back to their line; but rallying in turn they captured it a second time, and a second time it was recaptured. General Stanley's division was now brought up to the assistance of Hamilton's, and the Confederates were driven back once more. They then made an attempt by march-

COLONEL WILLIAM P. CARLIN.

(Afterward Brevet Major-General.)

ing through a ravine to fall upon the National left in heavy force; but their movement was discovered, and the Tenth Iowa Regiment, together with part of a battery, met them with such a reception that they quickly withdrew. The front on which the troops could be deployed was not long enough to permit more than three thousand men of the Nationals to be in action at once; but along this line the fighting was kept up until dark, when the enemy retired, and in the morning, when Rosecrans prepared to attack him, it was found that he was gone. The losses in the National army in this battle were 141 killed, 613 wounded, and 36 missing. On the Confederate side, where not many more men could be engaged at once than on the National, the losses were reported as 85 killed, 410 wounded, and 40 missing, the killed including Brig.-Gen. Henry Little. But these figures are probably altogether too small. General Hamilton reported that 263 Confederates were buried on the field.

General Rosecrans, in a congratulatory order to his troops a few days later, said: "You may well be proud of the battle of Iuka. On the 18th you concentrated at Jacinto; on the 19th you marched twenty miles, driving in the rebel outposts for the last eight; reached the front of Price's army, advantageously posted in unknown woods, and opened the action by four P.M. On a narrow front, intersected by ravines and covered by dense undergrowths, with a single battery, Hamilton's division went into action against the combined rebel hosts. On that unequal ground, which permitted the enemy to outnumber them three to one, they fought a glorious battle, mowing down the rebel hordes, until, night closing in, they rested on their arms on the battleground, from which the enemy retired during the night, leaving us masters of the field. The general commanding bears cheerful testimony to the fiery alacrity with which the troops of Stanley's division moved up, cheering, to support the third division, and took their places to give them an opportunity to replenish their ammunition; and to the magnificent fighting of the Eleventh Missouri under the gallant Mower. To all the regiments who participated in the fight, he presents congratulations on their bravery and good conduct. He deems it an especial duty to signalize the Forty-eighth Indiana, which, posted on the left, held its ground until the brave Eddy fell, and a whole brigade of Texans came in through a ravine on the little band, and even then only yielded a hundred yards until relieved. The Sixteenth Iowa, amid the roar of battle, the rush of wounded artillery horses, the charge of the rebel brigade, and a storm of grape, canister, and musketry, stood like a rock, holding the centre; while the glorious Fifth Iowa, under the brave and distinguished Matthias, sustained by Boomer with part of his noble little Twenty-sixth Missouri, bore the thrice defeated charges and cross-fires of the rebel left and centre with a valor and determination seldom equalled, never excelled, by the most veteran soldiery. . . . The unexpected accident which alone prevented us from cutting off the retreat and capturing Price and his army only shows how much success depends on Him in whose hands are the accidents as well as the laws of life."

MAJOR-GENERAL
WILLIAM S. ROSECRANS.

As the conduct of this battle began a series of causes that resulted in an unfortunate estrangement between Grant and Rosecrans, the bitterness of which was exhibited by the latter in his place in Congress even when Grant was in his dying days, it is interesting to note what Grant says of it. In his official report, written the day after the battle, he said: "I cannot speak too highly of the energy and skill displayed by General Rosecrans in the attack, and of the endurance of the troops under him." In his "Memoirs" he wrote: "General Rosecrans had previously had his headquarters at Iuka. While there he had a most excellent map prepared, showing all the roads and streams in the surrounding country. He was also personally familiar with the ground, so that I deferred very much to him in my plans for the approach. . . . Ord was on the northwest, and even if a rebel movement had been possible in that direction it could have brought only temporary relief, for it would have carried Price's army to the rear of the National forces and isolated it from all support. It looked to me that, if Price would remain in Iuka until we could get there, his annihilation was inevitable. On the morning of the 18th of September General Ord moved by rail to Burnsville, and there left the cars and moved to perform his part of the programme. He was to get as near the enemy as possible during the day and intrench himself so as to hold his position until the next morning. Rosecrans was to be up by the morning of the 19th on the two roads, and the attack was to be from all three quarters simultaneously. . . . I remained at Burnsville with a detachment of nine hundred men from Ord's command and communicated with my two wings by courier. Ord met the advance of the enemy soon after leaving Burnsville. Quite a sharp engagement ensued, but he drove the rebels back with considerable loss, including one general officer killed. He maintained his position and was ready to attack by daylight the next morning. I was very much disappointed at receiving a despatch from Rosecrans after midnight from Jacinto, twenty miles from Iuka, saying that some of his command had been delayed, and that the rear of his column was not yet up as far as Jacinto. He said, however, that he would still be at Iuka by two o'clock the next day. I did not believe this possible, because of the distance and condition of the roads. I immediately sent Ord a copy of Rosecrans's despatch and ordered him to

MAJOR-GENERAL JOHN PEGRAM, C. S. A.

be in readiness to attack the moment he heard the sound of guns to the south or southeast. During the 19th the wind blew in the wrong direction to transmit sound, either toward the point where Ord was or to Burnsville where I remained. [This appears to be the "unexpected accident" to which General Rosecrans refers in his congratulatory order.] A couple of hours before dark, on the 19th, Rosecrans arrived with the head of his column at Barnets. He here turned north without sending any troops to the Fulton road. While still moving in column up the Jacinto road, he met a force of the enemy and had his advance badly beaten and driven back upon the main road. In this short engagement his loss was considerable for the number engaged, and one battery was taken from him. The wind was still blowing hard, and in the wrong direction to transmit sound toward either Ord or me. Neither he nor I nor any one in either command heard a gun that was fired upon the battlefield. After the engagement Rosecrans sent me a despatch announcing the result. The courier bearing the message was compelled to move west nearly to Jacinto before he found a road leading to Burnsville. This made it a late hour of the night before I learned of the battle that had taken place during the afternoon. I at once notified Ord of the fact and ordered him to attack early in the morning. The next morning Rosecrans himself renewed the attack and went into Iuka with but little resistance. Ord also went in according to orders, without hearing a gun from the south of the town, but supposing the troops coming from the southwest must be up before that time. Rosecrans, however, had put no troops upon the Fulton road, and the enemy had taken advantage of this neglect and retreated by that road during the night. I rode into town and found that the enemy was not being pursued even by the cavalry. I ordered pursuit by the whole of Rosecrans's command, and went on with him a few miles in person. He followed only a few miles after I left him, and then went into camp, and the pursuit was continued no further. I was disappointed at the result of the battle of Iuka, but I had so high an opinion of General Rosecrans that I found no fault at the time." General Grant says that the plan of the battle, which included the occupation of the Fulton road, was suggested by Rosecrans himself.

BRIGADIER-GENERAL ROBERT B. MITCHELL.

MAJOR-GENERAL ALEXANDER McDOWELL McCOOK.

MAJOR-GENERAL LOVELL H. ROUSSEAU.

LOOMIS'S BATTERY IN ACTION.

A Confederate soldier, who participated in the engagement, gave a graphic account of it in a letter, a few extracts from which are interesting and suggestive. "I wrote you a short communication from Iuka, announcing its peaceable capture on the 4th, by the army under General Price. I believe I was a little congratulatory in my remarks, and spread out on the rich fruits of the bloodless capture. Indeed, it was a sight to gladden the heart of a poor soldier whose only diet for some time had been unsalted beef and white leather hoe-cake—the stacks of cheese, crackers, preserves, mackerel, coffee, and other good things that line the shelves of the sutlers' shops, and fill the commissary stores of the Yankee army. But, alas! The good things which should have been distributed to the brave men who won them were held in reserve for what purpose I know not, unless to sweeten the teeth of those higher in authority (whilst the men were fed on husks), and I suppose were devoured by the flames on the day of our retreat. We held peaceable possession of Iuka one day, and on the next day were alarmed by the booming of cannon, and called out to spend the evening in battle array in the woods. How on earth, with the woods full of our cavalry, they could have approached so near our lines, is a mystery! They had planted a battery sufficiently near to shell General Price's headquarters, and were cracking away at the Third Brigade in line of battle under General Herbert when our brigade (the Fourth) came up at a double quick and formed on their left. And then for two hours and fifteen minutes was kept up the most terrific fire of musketry that ever dinned my ears. There was one continuous roar of small arms, while grape and canister howled in fearful concert above our heads and through our ranks. General Little, our division commander, whose bravery and kindness had endeared him to the men under his command, was shot through the head early in the action, and fell from his horse dead. He was sitting by General Price and conversing with him at the time. The Third Brigade was in the hottest of the fire. They charged and took the battery, which was doing so much damage, after a desperate struggle, piling the ground with dead. The Third Louisiana Regiment, of this brigade, entered the fight with two hundred and thirty-eight men, and lost one hundred and eight in killed and wounded. The Third Texas fared about as badly. The troops against which we were contending were Western men, the battery manned by Iowa troops, who fought bravely and well. I know this, that the events of that evening have considerably increased my appetite for peace, and if the Yankees will not shoot at us any more I shall be perfectly satisfied to let them alone. All night could be heard the groans of the wounded and dying of both armies, forming a sequel of horror and agony to the deadly struggle over which night had kindly thrown its mantle. Saddest of all, our dead were left unburied, and many of the wounded on the battlefield to be taken in charge by the enemy. . . . During the entire retreat we lost but four or five wagons, which broke down on the road and were left. Acts of vandalism disgraceful to the army were, however, perpetrated along the road, which made me blush to own such men as my countrymen. Cornfields were laid waste, potato-patches robbed, barn-yards and smoke-houses despoiled, hogs killed, and all kinds of outrages perpetrated in broad daylight and in full view of officers. I doubted, on the march up and on the retreat, whether I was in an army of brave men fighting for their country, or merely following a band of armed marauders who are as terrible to their friends as foes. The settlements through which we passed were made to pay heavy tribute to the rapacity of our soldiers. This plunder, too, was without excuse, for rations were regularly issued every night."

Early in October the combined forces of Price and Van Dorn attempted the capture of Corinth, which had been abandoned by Beauregard in May, and from that time had been held by Grant's forces. Grant was now in Jackson, Tenn., where he had been ordered to make his headquarters, and Rosecrans was in immediate command at Corinth with about twenty thousand men. The place was especially tempting to the Confederates because of the enormous amount of supplies in store there, and also for other reasons, which are well stated in Van Dorn's report made after the battle: "Surveying the whole field of operations before me, the conclusion forced itself irresistibly upon my mind, that the taking of Corinth was a condition precedent to the accomplishment of anything of importance in West Tennessee. To take Memphis would be to destroy an immense amount of property without any adequate military advantage, even admitting that it could be held without heavy guns against the enemy's gun and mortar boats. The line of fortifications around Bolivar is intersected by the Hatchie River, rendering it impossible to take the place by quick assault. It was clear to my mind that if a successful attack could be made upon Corinth from the west and northwest, the forces there driven back on the Tennessee and cut off, Bolivar and Jackson would easily fall, and then, upon the arrival of the exchanged prisoners of war (about nine thousand), West Tennessee would soon be in our possession, and communication with General Bragg effected through middle Tennessee. I determined to attempt Corinth. I had a reasonable hope of success. Field returns at Ripley showed my strength to be about twenty-two thousand men. Rosecrans at Corinth had about fifteen thousand, with about eight thousand additional men at outposts from twelve to fifteen miles distant. I might surprise him and carry the place before these troops could be brought in. It was necessary that this blow should be sudden and decisive. The troops were in fine spirits, and the whole Army of West Tennessee seemed eager to emulate the armies of the Potomac and Kentucky. No army ever marched to battle with prouder steps, more hopeful countenances, or with more courage, than marched the Army of West Tennessee out of Ripley on the morning of September 29th, on its way to Corinth."

Rosecrans had several days' notice of the attack, and had placed the main body of the troops in an inner line of intrenchments nearer the town than the old Confederate fortifications. Skirmishing began on the 3d of October, when the Confederates approached from the north and west. The skirmishers were soon driven in, and the advance troops, under McArthur and Oliver, made a more determined resistance than Rosecrans had intended; his idea in thrusting them forward being that they should merely develop the enemy's purpose, find out what point he intended to attack, and then fall back on the main body. In the afternoon this advanced detachment had been pushed back to the main line, and there the fighting became very obstinate and bloody. General Hamilton's division was on the right, Davies's next, Stanley's in reserve, and McKean on the left. The force of the first heavy blow fell upon McKean and Davies. As the Confederates overlapped Davies a little on his right, General Rosecrans ordered Hamilton to move up his left and connect with Davies, then to swing his right around the enemy's left and get in his rear. Hamilton asked for more definite instructions than he had received verbally from the staff officer, and Rosecrans sent him a written order, which he received at five o'clock. Hamilton says: "A simple order to attack the enemy in flank could have reached me by courier from General Rosecrans any time after two P. M. in fifteen minutes. I construed it [the written order] as an order for attack, and at once proceeded to carry it out." A somewhat similar misunderstanding arose between General Hamilton and his brigade commanders, in consequence of which Buford's brigade went astray and a precious hour was lost. During that time the battle was apparently going in favor of the Confederates, although they were purchasing their advantages at heavy cost. Each commander believed that if he could have had an hour more of sunlight the victory would have been his that day. In the evening Rosecrans assembled his division commanders and made his dispositions for a renewal of the battle on the morrow.

At half-past four o'clock in the morning the Confederates opened the fight with their artillery, to which that of Rosecrans promptly replied, and extended their infantry lines farther to the north of the town. Here, on their extreme left, they formed behind a low hill, and then suddenly advanced in line of battle only three hundred yards distant from the National intrenchments. They were soon subjected to a cross-fire from the batteries, their line was broken, and only fragments of it reached the edge of the town, from which they were soon driven away by the reserves. Rosecrans then sent forward one of Hamilton's brigades to attack the broken enemy, which prevented them from re-forming and drove them into the woods. At the most advanced point of the National line, which was a small work called Battery Robinett, the heaviest fighting of the day took place. Here for more than two hours the roar of artillery and small arms was incessant and the smoke was in thick clouds. Through this heavy smoke the Confederates made three determined charges upon Battery Robinett, and the troops on either side of it, all of which were repelled. The heavy assaulting columns were raked through and through by the shot, but they persistently closed up and moved forward until, in one instance, a colonel carrying the colors actually planted them on the edge of the ditch, and then was immediately shot. After this the Confederates gave up the fight and slowly withdrew. At sunset General McPherson arrived from Jackson with reinforcements for the Nationals, and General Hurlbut was on the way with more. General Rosecrans says: "Our pursuit of the enemy was immediate and vigorous, but the darkness of the night and the roughness of the country, covered with woods and thickets, made movement impracticable by night, and slow and difficult by day. General McPherson's brigade of fresh troops with a battery was ordered to start at daylight and follow the enemy over the Chewalla road, and Stanley's and Davies's divisions to support him. McArthur, with all of McKean's division except Crocker's brigade, and with a good battery and a battalion of cavalry, took the route south of the railroad toward Pocahontas; McKean followed on this route with the rest of his division and Ingersoll's cavalry; Hamilton followed McKean with his entire force." But General Grant says in his "Memoirs": "General Rosecrans, however, failed to follow up the victory, although I had given specific orders in advance of the battle for him to pursue the moment the enemy was repelled. He did not do so, and I repeated the order after the battle. In the first order he was notified that the force of four thousand men which was going to his assistance would be in great peril if the enemy was not pursued. General Ord had joined Hurlbut on the 4th, and, being senior, took command of his troops. This force encountered the head of Van Dorn's retreating column just as it was crossing the Hatchie by a bridge some ten miles out from Corinth. The bottom land here was swampy and bad for the operations of troops, making a good place to get an enemy into. Ord attacked the troops that had crossed the bridge and drove them back in a panic. Many were killed, and others were drowned by being pushed off the bridge in their hurried retreat. Ord followed, and met the main force. He was too weak in numbers to assault, but he held the bridge and compelled the enemy to resume his retreat by another bridge higher up the stream. Ord was wounded in this engagement, and the command devolved on Hurlbut. Rosecrans did not start in pursuit till the morning of the 5th, and then took the wrong road. Moving in the enemy's country, he travelled with a wagon train to carry his provisions and munitions of war. His march was therefore slower than that of the enemy, who was moving toward his supplies. Two or three hours' pursuit on the day of battle, without anything except what the men carried on their persons, would have been worth more than any pursuit commenced the next day could have possibly been. Even when he did start, if Rosecrans had followed the route taken by the enemy, he would have come upon Van Dorn in a swamp, with a stream in front and Ord holding the only bridge; but he took the road leading north and toward Chewalla instead of west, and, after having marched as far as the enemy had moved to

MAJOR-GENERAL EDWARD O. C. ORD AND STAFF.

THE PURSUIT.

(FROM A PAINTING BY WILLIAM T. TREGO.)

get to the Hatchie, he was as far from battle as when he started. Hurlbut had not the numbers to meet any such force as Van Dorn's if they had been in any mood for fighting, and he might have been in great peril. I now regarded the time to accomplish anything by pursuit as past, and after Rosecrans reached Jonesboro' I ordered him to return."

General Grant considered that General Rosecrans had made the same serious mistake twice, at Iuka and at Corinth; and for this reason Rosecrans was soon relieved from further service in that department. The Confederate authorities also were dissatisfied with their general, for they accounted the defeat at Corinth a heavy disaster, and Van Dorn was soon superseded by Gen. John C. Pemberton.

Rosecrans superseded Buell October 24th, when his army—thenceforth called the Army of the Cumberland—was at Bowling Green, slowly pursuing Bragg. Rosecrans sent a portion of it to the relief of Nashville, which was besieged by a Confederate force, and employed the remainder in repairing the railroad from Louisville, over which his supplies must come. This done, about the end of November he united his forces at Nashville. At the same time Bragg was ordered to move forward again, and went as far as Murfreesboro', forty miles from Nashville, where he fortified a strong position on Stone River, a shallow stream fordable at nearly all points. There was high festivity among the secessionists in Murfreesboro' that winter, for Bragg had brought much plunder from Kentucky. No one dreamed that Rosecrans would attack the place before spring, and several roving bands of guerilla cavalry were very active, and performed some exciting if not important exploits. The leader of one of these, John H. Morgan, was married in Murfreesboro', the ceremony being performed by Bishop and Gen. Leonidas Polk, and Jefferson Davis being present. It is said that the floor was carpeted with a United States flag, on which the company danced, to signify that they had put its authority under their feet.

The revelry was rudely interrupted when Rosecrans, leaving Nashville with forty-three thousand men, in a rain-storm, the day after Christmas, encamped on the 30th within sight of Bragg's intrenchments.

A correspondent of the Louisville *Journal*, who went over the ground at the time and witnessed the battle, gave a careful description of its peculiarities, which is necessary to a complete understanding of the action: "As the road from Nashville to Murfreesboro' approaches the latter place, it suddenly finds itself parallel to Stone River. The stream flowing east crosses the road a mile this [west] side of Murfreesboro'. Abruptly changing its course, it flows north along the road, and not more than four hundred yards distant, for more than two miles. It is a considerable stream, but fordable in many places at low water. The narrow tongue of land between the turnpike road and the river is divided by the Nashville and Chattanooga Railroad, which, running down the centre of the wedge-like tract, bisects the turnpike half a mile this side of where the latter crosses the river.

CHARGE OF THE FEDERALS AT CORINTH.

Just in rear of the spot where the third milestone from Murfreesboro' stands, the turnpike and railroad—at that point about sixty yards apart—run through a slight cut, and this a few rods farther on is succeeded by a slight fill. The result is to convert both railroad and turnpike for a distance of two or three hundred yards into a natural rifle-pit. On each side of the road at this point there are open fields. That on the left extends to a curtain of timber which fringes the river, and also half a mile to the front along the road, where it gives place to an oak wood of no great density or extent. To the left and front, however, it opens out into a large open plain, which flanks the wood just mentioned, and extends up the river in the direction of Murfreesboro' for a mile. In the field on the left of the railroad there is a hill of no great height sloping down to the railroad and commanding all the ground to the front and right. It was here that Guenther's and Loomis's batteries were posted in the terrible conflict of Wednesday. The open field on the right of the turnpike road, three hundred yards wide, is bounded on the west by an almost impenetrable cedar forest. Just in rear of the forest, and marking its extreme northern limit, is a long, narrow opening, containing about ten acres. There is a swell in the field on the right of the road, corresponding with the one on the left. The crest of this hill is curiously concave. From its beginning point at the corner of the cedars, the northern end of the crest curves back upon itself, so that after fortifying the front of the position it renders the right flank well-nigh impregnable."

Rosecrans intended to attack the next day; but Bragg anticipated him, crossed the river before sunrise, concealed by a thick fog, reached the woods on the right of the National line, and burst out upon the bank in overwhelming force. McCook's command, on the extreme right, was crumbled and thrown back, losing several guns and many prisoners. Sheridan's command, next in line, made a stubborn fight till its ammunition was nearly exhausted, and then slowly retired. General Thomas's command, which formed the centre, now held the enemy back till Rosecrans established a new line, nearly at right angles to the first, with artillery advantageously posted, when Thomas fell back to this and maintained his ground. Through the forenoon the Confederates had seemed to have everything their own way, and they had inflicted grievous loss upon Rosecrans, besides sending their restless cavalry to annoy his army in the rear. But here, as usual, the tide was turned. The first impetuous rush of the Southern soldier had spent itself, and the superior staying qualities of his Northern opponent began to tell. Bragg hurled his men again and again upon the new line; but as they left the cedar thickets and charged across the open field they were mercilessly swept down by artillery and musketry fire, and every effort was fruitless. Even when seven thousand fresh men were drawn over from Bragg's right and thrown against the National centre, the result was still the same. The day ended with Rosecrans immovable in his position; but he had been driven from half of the ground that he held in the morning, and had lost twenty-eight guns and many men, while the enemy's cavalry was upon his communications. Finding that he had ammunition enough for another battle, he determined to remain where he was and sustain another assault. His men slept on their arms that night, and the next day there was no evidence of any disposition on either side to attack. Both sides were correcting their lines, constructing rifle-pits, caring for their wounded, and preparing for a renewal of the fight.

BRIGADIER-GENERAL FRANK C. ARMSTRONG, C. S. A.

MAJOR-GENERAL JAMES B. McPHERSON.

This came on the second day of the new year, when there was some desultory fighting, and Rosecrans advanced a division across the stream to strike at Bragg's communications. Breckenridge's command was sent to attack this division, and drove it back to the river, when Breckenridge suddenly found himself subjected to a terrible artillery fire, and lost two thousand men in twenty minutes. Following this, a charge by National infantry drove him back with a loss of four guns and many prisoners, and this ended the great battle of Stone River, or Murfreesboro'. After the repulse of Breckenridge, Rosecrans advanced his left again, and that night occupied with some of his batteries high ground, from which Murfreesboro' could be shelled. The next day there was a heavy rain-storm, and in the ensuing night the Confederate army quietly retreated, leaving Murfreesboro' to its fate. Rosecrans reported his loss in killed and wounded as eight thousand seven hundred and seventy-eight, and in prisoners as somewhat fewer than twenty-eight hundred. Bragg acknowledged a loss of over ten thousand, and claimed that he had taken over six thousand prisoners.

The number of men engaged on the National side was about forty-three thousand, and on the Confederate about thirty-eight thousand, according to the reports, which are not always reliable.

The losses on the National side included Brig.-Gens. Joshua W. Sill and Edward N. Kirk among the killed, while on the Confederate side Brig.-Gens. James E. Rains and Roger W. Hanson were killed.

The incidents of this great and complicated battle were very numerous, and have been related at great length by different correspondents and participants. The cavalry fighting that preceded the infantry engagement was severe, and in some respects brilliant. This arm of the service was commanded on the National side by Gen. David S. Stanley, and on the Confederate by Gen. Joseph Wheeler. Col. R. H. G. Minty, commanding the First Brigade of the National cavalry, says in his account of the first day's battle: "Crossing Overall's Creek, I took up position parallel to and about three-quarters of a mile from the Murfreesboro' and Nashville pike; the Fourth Michigan forming a line of dismounted skirmishers close to the edge of the woods. My entire force at this time numbered nine hundred and fifty men. The enemy advanced rapidly with twenty-five hundred cavalry; mounted and dismounted, and three pieces of artillery. They drove back the Fourth Michigan, and then attacked the Seventh Pennsylvania with great fury, but met with a determined resistance. I went forward to the line of dismounted skirmishers, and endeavored to move them to the right to strengthen the Seventh Pennsylvania; but the moment the right of the line showed itself from behind the fence where they were posted, the whole of the enemy's fire was directed on it, turning it completely round. At this moment the Fifteenth Pennsylvania gave way and retreated rapidly, leaving the battalion of the Seventh Pennsylvania no alternative but to retreat. I fell back a couple of fields and re-formed in the rear of a rising ground. The rebel cavalry followed us up promptly into the open ground, and now menaced us with three strong lines. General Stanley ordered a charge, and he himself led two companies of the Fourth Michigan, with about fifty men of the Fifteenth Pennsylvania, against the line in front of our left. He routed the enemy, and captured one stand of colors. At the same time I charged the first line in our front with the Fourth Michigan and First Tennessee, and drove them from the field. The second line was formed on the far side of a lane with a partially destroyed fence on each side, and still stood their ground. I re-formed my men and again charged. The enemy again broke and were driven from the field in the wildest confusion."

BRIGADIER-GENERAL JOHN H. MORGAN, C. S. A., AND WIFE.

A correspondent of the Cincinnati *Commercial*, in an account of the battle written on the field, says: "Colonel Innes with the Ninth Michigan engineers, posted at La Vergne to protect the road, had just been reinforced by several companies of the Tenth Ohio, when Wheeler's cavalry brigade made a strong dash at that position. Colonel Innes had protected himself by a stockade of brush, and fought securely. The enemy charged several times with great fury, but were murderously repulsed. About fifty rebels were dismounted, and nearly a hundred of the horses were killed. Wheeler finally withdrew, and sent in a flag of truce demanding surrender. Colonel Innes replied, 'We don't surrender much.' Wheeler then asked permission to bury his dead, which was granted. . . . General Rosecrans, as usual, was in the midst of the fray, directing the movement of troops and the range of batteries."

Some of the things that soldiers have to endure, which are not often mentioned among the stirring events of the field, are indicated in the report of Col. Jason Marsh of the Seventy-fourth Illinois Regiment. He says: "My command was formed in line of battle close behind a narrow strip of cedar thicket, nearly covering our front, and skirting a strip of open level ground about twenty rods wide to the cornfield occupied by the enemy's pickets. Being thus satisfied of the close proximity of the enemy in strong force, and apprehending an attack at any moment, I deemed it

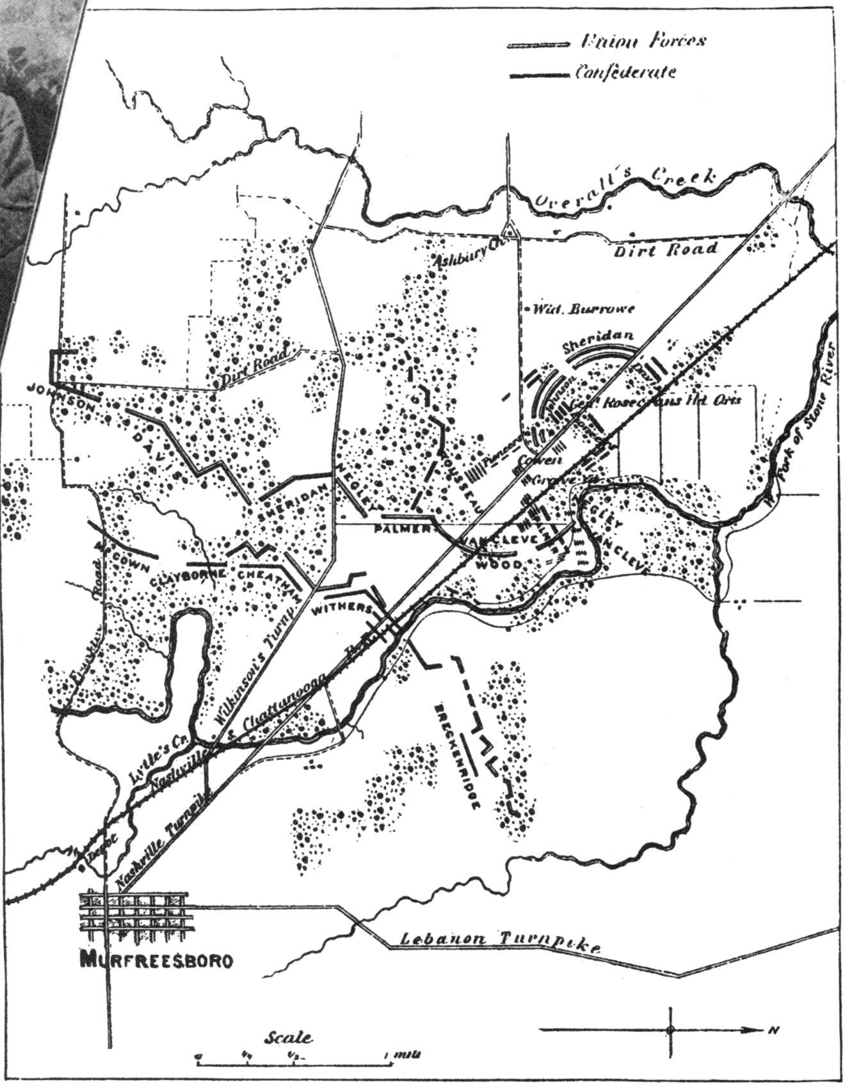

MAP OF THE BATTLEFIELDS OF STONE RIVER, OR MURFREESBORO'.

BREVET MAJOR-GENERAL D. S. STANLEY.

necessary to use the utmost precaution against surprise, and, in addition to general instructions to bivouac without fires, and to maintain a cautious, quiet vigilance, I ordered my command to stack arms, and each man to rest at the butt of his musket without using his shelter tent. Although the night was dark, chilly, and somewhat rainy, and the men cold, wet, weary, and hungry, I deemed it objectionable to use their shelter tents, not only because of the hindrance in case of a sudden attack, but even in a dark night they would be some guide to the enemy to trace our line. At a little before four o'clock A. M., our men were quietly waked up, formed into line, and remained standing at their arms until moved by subsequent orders. As soon as it became sufficiently light to observe objects at a distance, I could plainly discern the enemy moving in three heavy columns across my front, one column striking out of the cornfield and moving defiantly along the edge of the open ground not more than eighty rods from my line. It was plainly to be seen that the fire of my skirmishers took effect in their ranks, and in emptying their saddles; to which, however, the enemy seemed to pay no attention."

Some of the most stubborn fighting of the day was done by Palmer's division, and especially by Hazen's brigade of that division, on the National left, in the angle between the railroad and the turnpike. When the right of Rosecrans's army had been driven back, heavy columns of the Confederates were directed against the exposed flank of his left, which was also subjected to a fierce artillery fire. Palmer's men formed along the railroad and in the woods to the right of the pike, with Cruft's brigade nearest to the enemy, and several batteries were hastily brought up to check the advancing tide. The Confederates moved steadily onward, apparently sure of a victory, overpowered Cruft and drove him back, and were still advancing against Hazen, some of whose regiments had expended their ammunition and were simply waiting with fixed bayonets, when Grose's brigade came to the relief of Hazen, and all stood firm and met the enemy with a terrific and unceasing fire of musketry, to which Parsons's remarkable battery added a rain of shells and canister. The ranks of the Confederates were thinned so rapidly that one regiment after another gave up and fell back, until a single regiment was left advancing and came within three hundred yards of the National line. At this point, when every one of its officers and half its men had been struck down, the remainder threw themselves flat upon the ground, and were unable either to go forward any farther or to retreat. In the afternoon the Confederates made two more similar attempts, but were met in the same way and achieved no success.

Rousseau's division, which had been held in reserve, was brought into action when the fight became critical, and performed some of the most gallant work of the day. A participant has given a vivid description of some of the scenes in Rousseau's front: "The broken and dispirited battalions of our right wing, retreating by the flank, were pouring out of the cornfields and through the skirts of the woods, while from the far end of the field rose the indescribable crackle and slowly curling smoke of the enemy's fire. The line of fire now grew rapidly nearer and nearer, seeming to close in slowly, but with fatal certainty, around our front and flank; and presently the long gray lines of the enemy, three or four deep, could be seen through the cornstalks vomiting flame on the retreating host. The right of Rousseau's division opened its lines and let our brave but unfortunate columns pass through. The gallant and invincible legion came through in this way with fearfully decimated ranks, drawing away by hand two pieces of our artillery. When all the horses belonging to the battery, and all the other guns, had been disabled, the brave boys refused to leave these two behind, and drew them two miles through fields and thickets to a place of safety. It was a most touching sight to see these brave men, in that perilous hour, flocking around Rousseau like children, with acclamations of delight, and every token of love, as soon as they recognized him, embracing his horse, his legs, his clothes. Flying back to the open ground which was now to be the scene of so terrific a conflict, Rousseau galloped rapidly across it, and read with a single eagle glance all of its advantages. Guenther's and Loomis's batteries were ordered to take position on the hill on the left of the railroad, and Stokes's Chicago battery, which had got with our division, was placed there also. History furnishes but few spectacles to be compared with that which now ensued. The rebels pressed up to the edge of the cedar forest and swarmed out into the open field. I saw the first few gray suits that dotted the dark green line of the cedars with their contrasted color thicken into a line of battle, and the bright glitter of their steel flashed like an endless chain of lightning amid the thick and heavy green of the thicket. This I saw before our fire, opening on them around the whole extent of our line, engirdled them with a belt of flame and smoke. After that I saw them no more, nor will any human eye ever see them more. Guenther, Loomis, and Stokes, with peal after peal, too rapid to be counted, mowed them down with double-shotted canister; the left of our line of infantry poured a

LIEUTENANT-GENERAL JOSEPH WHEELER, C. S. A.

continuous sheet of flame into their front, while the right of our line, posted in its remarkable position by the genius of Rousseau, enveloped their left flank and swept their entire line with an enfilading fire. Thick smoke settled down upon the scene; the rim of the hill on which our batteries stood

BURYING A COMRADE.

seemed to be surrounded by a wall of living fire; the turnpike road and the crest of the hill on the right were wrapped in an unending blaze; flames seemed to leap out of the earth and dance through the air. No troops on earth could withstand such a fire as that. One regiment of rebels, the boldest of their line, advanced to within seventy-five yards of our line, but there it was blown out of existence. It was utterly destroyed; and the rest of the rebel line, broken and decimated, fled like sheep into the depths of the woods. The terrific firing ceased, the smoke quickly rolled away, and the sun shone out bright and clear on the scene that was lately so shrouded in smoke and mortal gloom. How still everything was! Everybody seemed to be holding his breath. As soon as the firing ceased, General Rousseau and his staff galloped forward to the ground the rebels had advanced over. Their dead lay there in frightful heaps, some with the life-blood not yet all flowed from their mortal wounds, some propped upon their elbows and gasping their last. The flag of the Arkansas regiment lay there on the ground beside its dead bearer. Every depression in the field was full of wounded, who had crawled thither to screen themselves from the fire, and a large number of prisoners came out of a little copse in the middle of the field and surrendered themselves to General Rousseau in person. Among them was one captain. They were all that were left alive of the bold Arkansas regiment that had undertaken to charge our line."

There was great disappointment and dissatisfaction among the secessionists at the failure of Lee's invasion of Maryland and Bragg's of Kentucky. Pollard, the Southern historian, wrote, "No subject was at once more dispiriting and perplexing to the South than the cautious and unmanly reception given to our armies both in Kentucky and Maryland." They seemed unable to comprehend how there could be such a thing as a slave State that did not want to break up the Union. Pollard, in his account of the response of the people of Maryland to Lee's proclamation, says, "Instead of the twenty or thirty thousand recruits which he had believed he would obtain on the soil of Maryland, he found the people content to gaze with wonder on his ragged and poorly equipped army, but with little disposition to join his ranks."

BRIGADIER-GENERAL ROBERT B. VANCE, C. S. A.

MAJOR-GENERAL JOHN C. BRECKINRIDGE, C. S. A.

DELAWARE INDIANS ACTING AS SCOUTS FOR THE FEDERAL ARMY IN THE WEST.

A SUTLER'S CABIN.

CHAPTER XIX.

MINOR EVENTS OF THE SECOND YEAR.

LARGE ARMIES IN THE FIELD—BOMBARDMENT AND CAPTURE OF FORT PULASKI—BATTLE OF BLUE'S GAP, VA.—MARCHING OVER THE SNOW—OPERATIONS IN THE SHENANDOAH VALLEY—BATTLES OF WINCHESTER AND McDOWELL—CAPTURE OF NORFOLK, VA., BY GEN. JOHN E. WOOL—WEST VIRGINIA CLEAR OF CONFEDERATES—FIGHTING WITH BUSHWHACKERS—OPERATIONS UNDER GENERAL BURNSIDE ON THE NORTH CAROLINA COAST—UNSUCCESSFUL ATTEMPT TO CAPTURE CHARLESTON—ENGAGEMENTS IN EASTERN KENTUCKY—GUERILLA RAID UNDER THE COMMAND OF GEN. JOHN H. MORGAN—EAST TENNESSEEANS LOYAL TO THE UNION—OPERATIONS IN EAST TENNESSEE UNDER GENERAL NEGLEY AND COLONEL BUFORD—RAPID AND DARING RAIDS BY GENERAL FOREST—BATTLES AROUND NASHVILLE—FIGHTING GUERILLAS IN MISSOURI—FIGHTING IN NEW MEXICO—INDIAN OPERATIONS IN THE NORTHWEST.

In the second year of the war, though the struggle did not then culminate, some of the largest armies were gathered and some of the greatest battles fought. At the East, McClellan made his Peninsula campaign with Williamsburg, Fair Oaks, and the Seven Days, and Pope his short and unfortunate campaign known as the Second Bull Run, followed by the moderate victory of Antietam and the horror of Fredericksburg. At the West, with smaller armies, the results were more brilliant and satisfactory. Grant had electrified the country when he captured Fort Donelson and received the first surrender of a Confederate army; and this was followed in April by the battle of Shiloh, which was a reverse on the first day and a victory on the second, and still later by the capture of Corinth. Thomas had gained his first victory at Mill Springs, and Buell had fought the fierce battle of Perryville, where the genius of Sheridan first shone forth. Two great and novel naval engagements had taken place—the fight of the iron-clads in Hampton Roads, and Farragut's passage of the forts and capture of New Orleans. Amid all this there were hundreds of minor engagements, subsidiary expeditions and skirmishes, all costing something in destruction of life and property. Some of them were properly a portion of the great campaigns; others were separate actions, and still others were merely raids of Confederate guerillas, which had become very numerous, especially at the West. This chapter will be devoted to brief accounts of the more important and interesting of these, generally omitting those occurring in the course and as a part of any great campaign. While they had little to do with the results of the struggle, some account of them is necessary to any adequate idea of the condition of the country and the sufferings of that generation of our people.

On the 6th of January a force of about 2,500, principally Ohio and Indiana troops, was sent out by General Kelly, under command of Colonel Dunning, to attack a Confederate force of about 1,800 men strongly posted at Blue's Gap, near Romney, Va. They marched over the snow in a brilliant moonlight night, and as they neared the Gap fired upon a small detachment that was attempting to destroy the bridge over the stream that runs through it. The Gap is a natural opening between high hills with very precipitous sides, and was defended with two howitzers and rifle-pits. There were also entrenchments on the hills. The Fourth Ohio Regiment was ordered to carry those on the one hill, and the Fifth Ohio those on the other, which they did with a rush. The advance then ran down the hills on the other side and quickly captured the two pieces of artillery. After this the soldiers burned Blue's house and mill, and also a few other houses, on the ground that they had been used to shelter the enemy, who had fired at them from the windows. In this affair the Confederates lost nearly 40 men killed and about the same number captured. There was no loss on the other side. The fertile Shenandoah Valley, between the Blue Ridge and the Alleghenies, was important to both sides, strategetically, and to the Confederates especially as a source of supplies. In 1861 Gen. Thomas J. Jackson (commonly called "Stonewall Jackson") was given command there with a Confederate force of about 11,000 men. But he did nothing of consequence during the autumn and winter. The National forces there were commanded at first by General Frémont, and afterward by General Banks. The first serious conflict was at Winchester, March 23, 1862. Winchester was important for military purposes because it was at the junction of several highroads. Jackson's army during the winter and spring had been reduced about one-half, but when he learned that the opposing force was also being reduced by the withdrawal of troops to aid General McClellan, he resolved to make an attack upon the force of General Shields at Winchester. His cavalry, under Turner Ashby, a brilliant leader who fell a few months later, opened the engagement with an attack on Shields's cavalry aided by other troops, and was driven back with considerable loss. In this engagement General Shields was painfully wounded by a fragment of shell. The next day at sunrise the battle was renewed at Kernstown, a short distance south of Winchester, and lasted till noon. About 6,000 men were engaged on the Confederate side, and somewhat more than that on the National. The Confederates were driven back half a mile by a brilliant charge, and there took a strong position and posted their artillery advantageously. Other charges followed, with destructive fighting, when they retired, slowly at first, and afterward in complete rout, losing three guns. They were pursued and shelled by a detachment under Colonel Kimball until they had passed Newtown. The National loss in this action was nearly 600; the Confederate, a little over 700.

The next important engagement in this campaign took place, May 8th, near McDowell. After a slow retreat by the Confederates, which was followed by the National forces under General Schenck, the former turned to give battle, and in heavy force, probably about 6,000, attacked General Milroy's brigade and the Eighty-second Ohio Regiment, numbering in all about 2,300. Milroy's advance retired slowly, one battery shelling the advancing enemy upon his main body, and the next day it was discovered that the Confederates had posted themselves on a ridge in the Bull Pasture Mountain. Milroy's force went out to attack him, and when two-thirds of the way up the mountain began the battle. It was soon found that this was only the advance of the Confederates, which slowly fell back upon the main body posted in a depression at the top of the mountain. One regiment after another was pushed forward, and the fighting was pretty sharp for two or three hours, when Milroy's men gave up the contest as hopeless and fell back. An incident of this fight that illustrates the humors of war is told of Lieut.-Col. Francis W. Thompson of the Third West Virginia Regiment in Milroy's command. He was writing a message, holding the paper against the trunk of a tree, when a bullet struck it and fastened it to the bark. "Thank you," said he; "I am not posting advertisements, and if I were I would prefer tacks." The National loss in this action was reported at 256, and the Confederate at 499. General Frémont's army, moving up the valley, reached Harrisonburg June 6th, and there was a spirited action between a portion of his cavalry and that of the Confederates. The fight fell principally upon the First New Jersey cavalry regiment, which, after apparently driving the enemy a short distance, fell into an ambuscade, where infantry suddenly appeared on both sides of the road, protected by the stone walls, and fired into the regiment, which sustained considerable loss, including the capture of Colonel Wyndham. Other forces, under Colonel Cluseret and General Bayard, were then pushed forward, and the enemy, which was the rear guard of Jackson's army, commanded by Gen. Turner Ashby, was driven from the field. During this action each side successively suffered from an enfilading fire, and General Ashby was killed. Three Confederate color sergeants were shot, and a considerable number of officers either fell or were captured. Capt. Thomas Haines of the New Jersey cavalry, who was one of the last to retire from the ambush, was approached and shot by a Virginia officer in a long gray coat, who sat upon a handsome horse; and the next moment a comrade of the captain's, rising in his saddle, turned upon the foe shouting, "Stop," and shot the Virginian.

While Frémont's force was thus following up Jackson directly, General Shields's division was moving southward on the eastern flank of the Shenandoah, expecting to intercept him. Jackson's purpose was rather to get away than to fight, for by this time he was very much wanted before Richmond. Two days after the affair at Harrisonburg, Frémont overtook, at Cross Keys, Ewell's division, which Jackson had left there to delay Frémont's advance, while he should prepare to cross the Shenandoah with his whole force. Frémont attacked promptly and met a spirited resistance, which he gradually overcame, although at considerable loss. Stahel's brigade, on his left, was the heaviest sufferer. At the close of the action Ewell retired, and Frémont's troops slept on the field. Frémont had lost nearly 700 men. The Confederate loss is unknown. The next day Shields, coming up east of the river, encountered Jackson's main force at Port Republic, and was attacked by it in overwhelming numbers. His men, however, stood their ground and made a brilliant fight, even capturing one gun and a considerable number of prisoners, but were finally routed, and lost several of their own guns. Frémont was prevented from crossing to the aid of Shields by the fact that Jackson had promptly burned the bridge. In this engagement Shields lost about 1,000 men, half of whom were captured. Jackson's loss in the two engagements together was reported at 1,150, and his loss in the entire campaign at about 1,900. After this battle he hurried away to join Lee before Richmond, while Frémont and Shields received orders from Washington to give up the pursuit, and thus ended the campaign in the valley.

On the 10th of May, Gen. John E. Wool, with 5,000 men, landed at Willoughby's Point, Va., and marched on Norfolk.

UNITED STATES MILITARY TELEGRAPH.

As he approached the city he was met by the mayor and a portion of the Common Council, who formally surrendered it. On taking possession, he appointed Gen. Egbert L. Viele military governor, and a little later he occupied Norfolk and Portsmouth. His capture of Norfolk caused the destruction of the *Merrimac*, which the Confederates blew up on the 11th. The navy yard, with its workshops, storehouses, and other buildings, was in ruins; but General Wool's captures included 200 cannon and a large amount of shot and shell. The Norfolk *Day Book*, a violent secession journal, was permitted to continue publication until it assailed Union citizens who took the oath of allegiance, and then it was suppressed.

West Virginia had been pretty effectively cleared of Confederates during the first year of the war, but a few minor engagements took place on her soil during the second year. One of the most brilliant of these was an expedition to Blooming Gap under Gen. Frederick W. Lander, in February. General Lander crossed the Potomac with 4,000 men, marched southward, and bridged the Great Cacapon River. This bridge was one hundred and eighty feet long, and was built in four hours in the night. It was made by placing twenty wagons in the stream, using them as piers, and putting planks across them. General Lander then, with his cavalry, pushed forward seven miles to Blooming Gap, expecting to cut off the retreat of a strong Confederate force that was posted there and hold it until his infantry could come up. He found that they had already taken the alarm and moved out beyond the Gap, but by swift riding he came up with a portion of them. Bringing up the Eighth Ohio and Seventh Virginia regiments of infantry for a support, he ordered a charge, which he lead in person, against a sharp fire. With a few followers he overtook a group of Confederate officers, cut off their retreat, and then dismounted, greeted them with, "Surrender, gentlemen," and held out his hand to receive the sword of the leader. Five of the officers surrendered to him, and

MAJOR-GENERAL ROBERT H. MILROY.

MAJOR-GENERAL ROBERT C. SCHENCK.

four to members of his staff. Meanwhile the Confederate infantry had rallied and made a stand. At this point Lander's cavalry became demoralized and would not face the fire; but he now advanced his infantry, which cleared the road, captured many prisoners, and pursued the flying enemy eight miles. The total Confederate loss was near 100. The National loss was seven killed and wounded. Among the latter was Fitz-James O'Brien, the brilliant poet and story writer, who died of his wound two months later. The Eighth Ohio Regiment was commanded by Col. Samuel S. Carroll, who received special praise for his gallantry in this affair, and two years later, at the request of General Grant, was promoted to a brigadier-generalship for his brilliant services in the Wilderness. General Lander, who was especially complimented for this affair in a letter from President Lincoln, died in March from the effects of a wound received the previous year. He was one of the most patriotic and earnest men and promising officers in the service, and, like his staff officer who fell here, was himself somewhat of a poet.

MAJOR-GENERAL JOHN C. FREMONT.

There were many little bands of bushwhackers in the mountainous portions of the territory covered by the seat of war. Commonly they occupied themselves only in seeking opportunities for murder and robbery of Union citizens, but occasionally they made a stand and showed fight when the bluecoats appeared. Early in May one company of the Twenty-third Ohio infantry had a fight with such a band at Clark's Hollow, W. Va. Under command of Lieutenant Bottsford they scouted the hills until they found the camp of the bushwhackers, which had just been abandoned. Resting for the night at the only house in the hollow, Bottsford's men were attacked at daybreak by the gang they had been hunting, who outnumbered them about five to one. They took possession of the house, made loop-holes in the chinking between the logs, and, being all sharp-shooters, were able to keep the enemy at bay. The leader of the bushwhackers called to his men to follow him in a charge upon the house, assuring them that the Yankees would quickly surrender; but as he immediately fell, and three of his men, endeavoring to get to him, had the same fate, the remainder retreated. Soon afterward the rest of the regiment, commanded by Lieut.-Col. Rutherford B. Hayes, came up and made pursuit. The flying bushwhackers set fire to the little village of Princeton and disappeared over the mountain. In this affair the National loss was one killed and 21 wounded; of the bushwhackers, 16 were killed and 67 wounded.

On the 10th of September, at Fayetteville, the Thirty-fourth Ohio Regiment, under command of Col. John T. Toland, looking for the enemy near Fayetteville, W. Va., found more of him than they wanted. The Confederates were in heavy force, commanded by Gen. William W. Loring, and were posted in the woods on the summit of a steep hill. After three hours of fighting Toland was unable to gain the woods or to flank the enemy, and was obliged to retire, while the Confederates fired upon him from the heights as he passed. He had lost, in killed, wounded, and missing, 109 men. The loss of the Confederates was not ascertained, but was probably very slight.

COLONEL PERCY WYNDHAM.

MAJOR-GENERAL JULIUS H. STAHEL.

After Burnside had established a basis of operations on the North Carolina coast there were numerous small expeditions thence to the interior. These were partly for the purpose of foraging, partly for observation to detect any movements of large bodies of Confederate troops, and partly to give protection and encouragement to Union citizens, of whom were many in that State. On June 5th a reconnoissance in force was made from Washington, N. C., for the purpose of testing the report that a considerable force of cavalry and infantry had been gathered near Pactolus. The expedition was commanded by Colonel Potter of the First North Carolina (National) volunteers, and was accompanied by Lieutenant Avery of the Marine artillery with three boat-howitzers. The day was oppressively hot, and the march laborious. All along the route slaves came from their work in the field, leaned upon the fences, and gave the soldiers welcome in their characteristic way. The enemy were first found at Hodge's Mills, where they were strongly posted between two swamps with the additional protection from two mills. They had cut away the flooring of the mill flumes to prevent the cavalry from reaching them, and on the approach of the National advance they opened fire. The artillery was at once ordered forward within half musket range, and opened such a sharp and accurate fire that in forty-five minutes it completely riddled the buildings and brought down many Confederate sharp-shooters from the trees. When the main body of the troops rushed forward to charge the position, it was found that the Confederates had disappeared. The National loss was 16 men killed or wounded; the Confederate loss was unknown, but was supposed to be nearly a hundred, including the colonel commanding. In their flight they left behind them large numbers of weapons and accoutrements. This action is known as the battle of Tranter's Creek.

On the 2d of September it became known to the commander of the Federal force occupying Plymouth, N. C., that a detachment of about 1,400 Confederates was marching on that town with the avowed intention of burning it. Hastily bringing together a company of Hawkins's Zouaves, a company of loyal North Carolinians, and a few civilians who were willing to fight in defence of their homes, making in all about 300 men, the captain in command sent them out under the charge of Orderly-Sergeant Green. Three miles from the town they met the enemy, which consisted of infantry and cavalry commanded by Colonel Garrett. They were bivouacked in the woods, and Green's force, making a sudden dash, surprised them and fought the whole force for an hour, when they broke and fled. Colonel Garrett and 40 of his men were captured, and about 70 were killed or wounded. Green lost three men. The civilians who had joined the expedition proved to be among the most efficient of the volunteers.

Four days later (September 6th) the Confederates attempted a similar enterprise against Washington, N. C. Early in the morning three companies of the National cavalry, with three guns, had gone out on the road toward Plymouth, when the Confederate cavalry dashed in at the other end of the town, followed by a body of about 400 infantry. The troops remaining in the town were surprised in their barracks, and a special effort was made to capture the loyal North Carolinians. But the men quickly rallied, the Confederate cavalry was driven back, and a slow street fight ensued. The troops that had gone toward Plymouth were recalled, and guns were planted where they could sweep the streets. The National gunboats attempted to aid the land forces, but were largely deterred by a heavy fog. When, however, they got the range of the houses behind which the Confederates were sheltered, the latter quickly retreated, carrying off with them four pieces of artillery. During the fight the gunboat *Picket* was destroyed by the explosion of her magazine. The National loss was about 30, and the Confederate considerably larger.

Throughout the war there was a strong desire to capture or punish the city of Charleston, which was looked upon as the cradle of secession, and also to close its harbor to blockade runners. Elaborate and costly operations on the seaward side were maintained for a long time, but never with any real success. The lowlands that stretch out ten or twelve miles south of the harbor are cut by many winding rivers and inlets, and broken frequently by swamps. At a point a little more than four miles south of the city was the little village of Secessionville, which was used as a summer resort by a few planters. It is on comparatively high ground, and borders on a deep creek on the one side and a shallow one on the other. Across the neck of land between the two was an earthwork about two hundred yards long, known as Battery Lamar. There were similar works at other similar points in the region between Secessionville and the southern shore of the harbor. The National forces on these islands in 1862 were commanded by Gen. H. W. Benham, who in June planned an advance for the purpose of carrying the works at Secessionville and getting within striking distance of the city. The division of Gen. Isaac I. Stevens was to form the assaulting column, and Wright's division and Williams's brigade to act as its support. The movement was made on June 16th, at daybreak. The orders were that the advance should be made in silence, with no firing that could be avoided. Stevens's men pushed forward, captured the Confederate picket, and approached the works through an open field. But the enemy were not surprised, and a heavy fire of musketry and artillery was opened upon them almost from the first. It was found that the front presented by the work was too narrow for proper deployment of much more than a regiment, and the assailants suffered accordingly. There was also a line of abatis to be broken through, and a deep ditch; and yet a portion of the assaulting forces actually reached the parapet, but, of course, found it impossible to carry the works. The Eighth Michigan, which was in the advance, lost 182 men out of 534, including 12 of its 22 officers. Col. William M. Fenton, who commanded this regiment, says: "The order not to fire, but use the bayonet, was obeyed, and the advance companies reached the parapet of the works at the angle on our right and front, engaging the enemy at the point of the bayonet. During our advance the enemy opened upon our lines an exceedingly destructive fire of grape, canister, and musketry, and yet the regiment pushed on as veterans, divided only to the right and left by a sweeping torrent from the enemy's main gun in front. The enemy's fire proved so galling and destructive that our men on the parapet were obliged to retire under its cover. The field was furrowed across with cotton ridges, and many of the men lay there, loading and firing as deliberately as though on their hunting grounds at home." Even had they been able to carry the work, they could not have held it long, for its whole interior was commanded by elaborate rifle-pits in the rear. Artillery was brought up and well served, but made no real impression upon the enemy. When it became evident that no success was possible, General Stevens withdrew his command in a slow and orderly manner. General Beauregard says: "The point attacked by Generals Benham and I. I. Stevens was the strongest one of the whole line, which was then unfinished and was designed to be some five miles in length. The two Federal commanders might have overcome the obstacles in their front had they proceeded farther up the Stone. Even as it was, the fight at Secessionville was lost, in a great measure, by lack of tenacity on the part of Generals Benham and Stevens. It was saved by the skin of our teeth." The National loss in this action was 683 men, out of about 3,500 actually engaged. The Confederates, who were commanded by Gen. N. G. Evans, lost about 200.

LIEUTENANT-COLONEL RUTHERFORD B. HAYES.

(Afterward Brevet Major-General.)

BREVET MAJOR-GENERAL JAMES SHIELDS.

In October an expedition was planned to set out from Hilton Head, S. C., go up Broad River to the Coosahatchie and destroy the railroad and bridges in that vicinity, in order to sever the communications between Charleston and Savannah. It was under the command of Brig.-Gen. J. M. Brannan, and included about 4,500 men. Ascending Broad River on gunboats and transports, October 22d, they landed at the junction of the Pocotaligo and Tullafiny, and immediately pushed inland toward Pocotaligo bridge. They marched about five miles before they encountered any resistance, but from that point were fired upon by batteries placed in commanding positions. As one after another of these was bombarded or flanked, the Confederates retired to the next, burning the bridges behind them, and in some places the pursuing forces were obliged to wade through swamps and streams nearly shoulder deep. At the Pocotaligo there was a heavy Confederate force well posted behind a swamp, with artillery, commanded by General Walker, and here Brannan's artillery ammunition gave out. As the day was now nearly spent, and there seemed no probability of reaching the railroad, Brannan slowly retired and returned to Hilton Head. A detachment which he had sent out under Col. William B. Barton, of the Forty-eighth New York Regiment, had marched directly to the Coosahatchie and poured a destructive fire into a train that was filled with Confederate soldiers coming from Savannah to the assistance of General Walker. He then tore up the railroad for a considerable distance, and pushed on toward the town, but there found the enemy in a position too strong to be carried, and, after exchanging a few rounds, retired to his boats. The National loss in this expedition was about 300; that of the Confederates was probably equal.

NEGRO QUARTERS, HILTON HEAD.

The situation of Fort Pulaski relatively to Savannah was quite similar to that of Fort Sumter relatively to Charleston. It stood on an island in the mouth of Savannah River and protected the entrance to the harbor. Just one year after the bombardment and reduction of Sumter by the Confederate forces, Fort Pulaski was bombarded and reduced by the National forces. This work was of similar construction with Fort Sumter, having brick walls seven and a half feet thick and twenty-five feet high. It was on Cockspur Island, which is a mile long by half a mile wide, and commanded all the channels leading up to the harbor. At the opening of the war it was seized by the Confederate authorities, and it was garrisoned by 385 men, under command of Col. Charles H. Olmstead. It mounted forty heavy guns, which protected blockade-runners and kept out National vessels. Soon after the capture of Port Royal, Gen. Quincy A. Gillmore was ordered to make a reconnoissance of this work and the ground on Tybee Island southeast of it, with a view to its reduction. He reported that it was possible to plant batteries of rifled guns and mortars on Tybee Island, and also on Jones Island, with which he believed the work could be reduced. Jones Island is northwest of Cockspur Island. The Forty-sixth New York Regiment, commanded by Colonel Rosa, was sent to occupy Tybee Island, and a passage was opened between the islands and the mainland north of Savannah, so that guns could be brought through and placed on Jones Island. This was done with tremendous labor, the mortars weighing more than eight tons each and having to be dragged over deep mud on plank platforms, most of the work being done at night. The Seventh Connecticut Regiment was now sent to join the Forty-sixth New York on Tybee, and the construction of batteries and magazines

A NORTH CAROLINA SWAMP.

BATTLE OF SECESSIONVILLE, JAMES ISLAND, S. C.

on that island was begun. Here, also, the guns had to be carried across spongy ground, 250 men being required for the slow movement of each piece, and all the work being done at night and in silence; for the batteries were to be erected within easy reach of the guns of the fort. Their construction occupied about two months, and screens of bushes were contrived to conceal from the Confederates what was going on. There were eleven batteries ranged along the northern edge of Tybee Island, mounting twenty heavy guns and sixteen thirteen-inch mortars. When all was ready, the fort was summoned to surrender by Gen. David Hunter, who had recently been placed in command of the department. Colonel Olmstead replied: "I can only say that I am here to defend the fort, not to surrender it." Thereupon the batteries opened fire upon the fort, and a bombardment of thirty hours ensued—April 10 and 11. At the end of that time ten of the fort's guns were dismounted, and, as the fire of the rifled guns was rapidly reducing its masonry to ruins, it was evident that it could not hold out much longer; whereupon Colonel Olmstead surrendered. The only casualties were one man killed on the National side, and three wounded in the fort. It was found that the mortars had produced very little effect, the real work being done by the rifled guns. General Hunter said in his report: "The result of this bombardment must cause, I am convinced, a change in the construction of fortifications as radical as that foreshadowed in naval architecture by the conflict between the *Monitor* and the *Merrimac*. No works of stone or brick can resist the impact of rifled artillery of heavy calibre." And General Gillmore said: "Mortars are unavailable for the reduction of works of small area like Fort Pulaski. They cannot be fired with sufficient accuracy to crush the casemate arches." A fortnight later, the attempt to reduce Forts Jackson and St. Philip led Farragut to the same conclusion concerning the use of mortars.

One who participated in the bombardment relates an amusing incident. The batteries were under the immediate command of Lieut. (afterward General) Horace Porter, who went around to every gun to ascertain whether its captain was provided with everything that would be necessary when the firing should begin. At one mortar battery fuse plugs were wanting, and the officer was in despair. This battery had the position nearest to the fort, and its four mortars were useless without the plugs. Finally he remembered that there was a Yankee regiment on the island, and remarked, "All Yankees are whittlers. If this regiment could be turned out to-night, they might whittle enough fuse plugs before morning to fire a thousand rounds." Thereupon he rode out in the darkness to the camp of that regiment, which was immediately ordered out to whittle, and provided all the fuse plugs that were needed. The first gun was fired by Lieut. P. H. O'Rourke, who afterward fell at the head of his regiment at Gettysburg. It is said that the first gun against Sumter had been fired by a classmate of his. One who was in the fort says: "At the close of the fight all the parapet guns were dismounted except three. Every casemate gun in the southeast section of the fort was dismounted, and the casemate walls breached in almost every instance to the top of the arch. The moat was so filled with brick and mortar that one could have passed over dry shod. The parapet walls on the Tybee side were all gone. The protection to the magazine in the northwest angle of the fort had all been shot away, the entire corner of the magazine was shot off, and the powder exposed. Such was the condition of affairs when Colonel Olmstead called a council of officers in the casemate, and they all acquiesced in the necessity of a capitulation in order to save the garrison from destruction by an explosion, which was momentarily threatened."

BRIGADIER-GENERAL EGBERT L. VIELE.

On the 16th of April the Eighth Michigan Regiment, Col. William M. Fenton, with a detachment of Rhode Island artillery, was

FORT PULASKI DURING BOMBARDMENT, APRIL 11, 1862

sent from Tybee Island, Ga., to make a reconnoissance of Wilmington Island. On landing, they marched inland by three different roads, and soon discovered the enemy in some force. They took up a position for defence and were attacked by the Thirteenth Georgia Regiment. When Colonel Fenton ordered the bugler to sound the charge for his main body, his advance mistook it for retreat, fell back, and threw his line into confusion. At this moment the enemy advanced and began firing. Order was soon restored, and through the vigorous efforts of Lieut. C. H. Wilson one company was carried to the right, through the woods, and made a flank attack upon the enemy's left. Thereupon the Confederates slowly retired, leaving their dead and wounded on the field. The National loss was 45 men; Confederate loss, unknown.

On the 10th of January an expedition consisting of 5,000 men —infantry, cavalry, and artillery—set out from Cairo to make an extended reconnoissance in the neighborhood of Columbus, Ky., and in the direction of Mayfield. It was led by John A. McClernand, who was temporarily in command of that district. Nearly every point of any consequence within fifteen or twenty miles was visited, roads were discovered that had not been laid down on any map, the position of the enemy at Columbus was correctly ascertained, and much information was obtained regarding the disposition of the inhabitants toward the Government. The march of about one hundred and forty miles was made over icy and miry roads with considerable difficulty, and proved useful for future operations, although it was not enlivened by any conflict.

On the 15th of February Bowling Green, which had been considered an important point in the line of defence that was first broken by General Grant at Fort Henry, was evacuated by the Confederates, who went to join their comrades at Fort Donelson. The National troops under General Buell, marching forty miles in twenty-eight hours, took possession of the place in the afternoon.

Many of the gaps in the Alleghenies were strategically important because they were the natural places for the crossing of the road that connected the States east and west of that range, and there were frequent expeditions and small actions at these gaps by which one side or the other sought to clear them of the enemy. One of these took place in March, 1862, when it was discovered that a somewhat irregular Confederate force of about 500 men had taken possession of Pound Gap, Eastern Kentucky, built huts, and gathered supplies for a permanent occupation. A road to Abingdon, Va., passes through this gap. General James A. Garfield, whose defeat of Humphrey Marshall on the Big Sandy has been recorded in an earlier chapter, set out a month later, March 13th, with a force of 900 men to clear the Gap. It was a laborious march of two days in snow and rain and mud, with roads obstructed by felled trees, and streams whose bridges had been destroyed. Arriving at Elkton Creek, two miles below the Gap, Garfield sent out his cavalry to reconnoitre the position of the enemy, and himself with the infantry climbed the mountain a mile or two below the Gap, and thence moved along the summit to attack them in the flank. When this force arrived at the Gap, the enemy were found deployed on the summit at its opposite side. Garfield deployed his own force down the eastern slope, and then ordered them to charge through the ravine and up the hill held by the enemy, which they promptly did. But before they could ascend the southern slope the whole Confederate force disappeared. Nothing was left for the National troops to do but to ransack the captured camp, pack up what they could of the large quantity of supplies, burn the remainder, and return whence they came.

When Kentucky was invaded by the Confederate forces of Bragg, Humphrey Marshall, and Kirby Smith, the movement was accompanied and assisted by a raid from a large band of guerillas, or partisan rangers as they called themselves, led by a bold rider named John H. Morgan. The principal resistance to Morgan was at Cynthiana, July 17th, about fifty miles south of Cincinnati. The National troops occupying that town were commanded by Lieut.-Col. J. J. Landrum, and numbered about 340, a part of them being home guards not very well armed or disciplined, with one field gun. Morgan's men approached the town suddenly, drove in the pickets, and began shelling the place without giving any notice for the women and children to be removed. Landrum immediately placed his one gun in the public square, where it could be turned so as to sweep almost any of the roads entering the town, and posted all of his force except the artillery in the outskirts where he supposed the enemy were approaching, putting most of them at the bridge overlooking. But to his surprise Morgan's force was very large in comparison with his own, and entered the town from a different direction. In a little while Landrum's men found themselves practically surrounded, and subjected to a sharp fire both front and rear, the guerillas having the shelter of the houses. The artillerymen in the square were subjected to so hot a fire from the riflemen that they were obliged to abandon their gun. Colonel Landrum writes: "I rode along the railroad to Rankin's Hotel to ascertain what position the enemy was taking. Here I met an officer of the rebel band, aid to Colonel Morgan, who demanded my surrender. I replied, 'I never surrender,' and instantly discharged three shots at him, two of which took effect in his breast. He fell from his horse, and I thought him dead; but he is still living, and will probably recover, notwithstanding two balls passed through his body." A portion of Landrum's force, posted north of the town, was overpowered and forced to surrender. With another portion he attempted to drive the enemy from the bridge and take their battery, but found them so strong there as to render this hopeless, while all the time he was subjected to a fire from the rear. Finally he determined with the remainder of his men to cut his way through and escape. He emerged from the town in a southeast direction, met and routed a small detachment of the enemy, and was pursued by another detachment when he made a stand, posting his men behind the fences, and for a considerable time held them in check. When his ammunition was exhausted he gave orders for every man to save himself as he could, and thus his command was dispersed. In this affair the National forces lost about 70 men killed or wounded. The loss of the guerillas is unknown, but they left behind them a considerable number of wounded, and the capture of the town must have cost them about 100 men. In this raid Morgan is said to have commanded from 900 to 1,200 men, to have ridden over 1,000 miles, captured 17 towns, and paroled nearly 1,200 prisoners.

The smaller guerilla raids in Kentucky that year were more numerous than any popular history could find space to record. Some of them, however, were spiritedly met and severely punished. On the 29th of July a band of over 200 attacked the village of Mt. Sterling. The provost-marshal of the place, Capt. J. J. Evans, at once put every able-bodied man in the village under arms, and posted them on both sides of the street by which the guerillas were about to enter. He had hardly done this when in came the enemy, yelling wildly and demanding their surrender. The answer was a well-aimed volley which brought down the whole of their front rank, and which was rapidly followed by other volleys that soon put them to flight. In their retreat they met a detachment of the Eighteenth Kentucky Regiment, under Major Bracht, which had been in pursuit of them, and when these troops charged upon them they scattered in the fields and woods, leaving horses, rifles, and other material. Their loss was about 100.

On the 23d of August the Seventh Kentucky cavalry, a new regiment commanded by Col. Leonidas Metcalfe, had a fight with Confederate troops at Big Hill, about fifteen miles from Richmond. With 400 of his men he set out to attack the enemy, and near the top of the hill dismounted to fight on foot. He says: "We moved forward amid a shower of bullets and shells, which so terrified my raw, undisciplined recruits, that I could not bring more than 100 of them in sight of the enemy. The great majority mounted their horses and fled, without even getting a look at the foe. It was impossible to rally them, and they continued their flight some distance north of Richmond." The hundred men who stood their ground fought the enemy for an hour and a half and finally compelled them to fall back. Soon afterward a new attack was made upon Metcalfe's men by about 100 Confederates who dashed down the road expecting to capture them. But he had placed 200 men of a Tennessee infantry regiment in the bushes by the roadside, and their fire brought down many of the enemy and dispersed the remainder. A few minutes later still another attack was made by another detachment, and, as before, the Tennesseeans met it with a steady fire and drove them off. Metcalfe's men then retired to Richmond, whither the Confederates pursued them and demanded a surrender of the town. Metcalfe replied that he would not surrender but would fight it out, and, as he presently received reinforcements, the enemy departed. He lost in this affair about 50 men. The Confederate loss is unknown.

On the same days when the great battle of Groveton or second Bull Run was fought in Virginia (August 29th and 30th, 1862), one of the severest of the engagements consequent upon Kirby Smith's invasion took place at Richmond, Ky. The National forces numbered about 6,500, largely new troops, and were commanded by Brig.-Gen. M. D. Manson. Kirby Smith had a force at least twice as large. Early in the afternoon of the 29th the Confederates drove in Manson's outpost, and he, having had early information of their approach, marched out to meet them. About two miles from the town he took possession of a high ridge commanding the turnpike, and formed his line of battle with artillery on the flank. The enemy soon attacked in some force, and were driven off by the fire from the guns. Manson then advanced another mile, where he bivouacked, and sent out his cavalry to reconnoitre. Early in the morning of the 30th the enemy advanced again, when Manson's men drove them back and formed on a piece of high wooded ground near Rogersville. Here the enemy attacked him in earnest and in great force, attempting to turn his left flank, which faced about and fought stubbornly. More of his forces were now brought to the front and placed in line, and the battle became quite severe. At length the enemy, with largely superior numbers, succeeded in breaking his left wing, which retreated in disorder. "Up to this time," says General Manson, "I had maintained my first position for three hours and forty minutes, during all of which time the artillery, under command of Lieutenant Lamphere, had kept up a constant fire, except for a very short time when the ammunition had become exhausted. The Fifty-fifth Indiana, the Sixteenth Indiana, the Sixty-ninth Indiana, and the Seventy-first Indiana occupied prominent and exposed positions from the commencement of the engagement, and contended against the enemy with a determina-

A WOUNDED ZOUAVE.

(From a War Department photograph.)

tion and bravery worthy of older soldiers. The three remaining regiments of General Cruft's brigade arrived just at the time when our troops were in full retreat and the rout had become general. The Eighteenth Kentucky was immediately deployed into line, and made a desperate effort to check the advance in the enemy, and contended with him, single-handed and alone, for twenty minutes, when after a severe loss they were compelled to give away before overwhelming numbers." Deploying his cavalry as a rear guard, and placing one gun to command the road, Manson retreated to his position of the evening before and again formed line of battle. Here the enemy soon attacked him again, advancing through the open fields in great force. At this moment he received an order from his superior, General Nelson, directing him to retire if the enemy advanced in force; but it was then too late to obey, for within five minutes the battle was in progress along the whole line. The right of the Confederates was crushed by Manson's artillery fire, and the enemy then made a determined effort to crush Manson's right, which, after being several times gallantly repelled, they at length succeeded in doing. General Nelson now appeared upon the field, and by his orders Manson's men fell back and took up a new position very near the town. Here they sustained another attack for half an hour, and then were broken and once more driven back in confusion. Manson succeeded in organizing a rear guard which assisted the escape of his main force, but was itself defeated and broken to pieces in a later encounter. Manson, attempting to escape through the enemy's lines, was fired upon, and his horse was killed, he being soon afterward taken prisoner. His loss in this engagement was about 900 killed or wounded, besides many prisoners. The Confederate loss was reported at about 700.

BRIGADIER-GENERAL
HUMPHREY MARSHALL, C. S. A.

On the 9th of October a National force, commanded by Col. E. A. Parrott, marched out and met the enemy at a place called Dogwalk, near Lawrenceburg. Parrott placed his men in an advantageous position, with two pieces of artillery, and soon saw the Confederate skirmishers advancing toward it. He sent out his own skirmishers to meet them, and placed his guns to command the road. The artillery was used very effectively, especially in driving the enemy from a dwelling-house where they had opened a severe fire on the line of skirmishers, and after a fight that lasted from eight A. M. till afternoon the Confederates retired, leaving a portion of their dead and wounded on the field. Parrott lost fourteen men.

GENERAL E. KIRBY SMITH, C. S. A.

On the 18th of December a force of Confederate cavalry, under Gen. N. B. Forrest, captured Lexington, Tenn. The town was defended by the Eleventh Illinois cavalry, commanded by Col. Robert G. Ingersoll, which withstood the enemy in a fight of three hours, and was then compelled to retreat, leaving two guns in the hands of the Confederates, who had lost about 40 men.

The State of Tennessee, like some others of the Southern States, had its mountain region and its lowland; and, as was generally true in such cases in the Confederacy, the people of the mountain regions were more inclined to be true to the Union, while those of the lowlands favored secession. This fact, together with the position it occupied, made Tennessee a debatable ground almost throughout the war. Besides the great battles that were fought on her soil —Shiloh, Chickamauga, Chattanooga, Franklin, and Nashville— there were innumerable minor engagements of varying severity and importance.

On the 24th of March, 1862, a regiment of loyal Tennesseeans, commanded by Col. James Carter, left their camp at Cumberland Ford and made a march of forty miles through the mountains to Big Creek Gap, where they fought and defeated a body of Confederate cavalry, and captured a considerable supply of tents, arms, provisions, wagons, and horses.

Union City, Tenn., was a small village at the junction of the railroads from Columbus and Hickman, and on the 30th of March an expedition was sent out from Island No. 10, under Col. Abram Buford, to make a reconnoissance there. Buford had four regiments of infantry, with two companies of cavalry and a detachment of artillery. They made a forced march of twenty-four hours, and discovered a body of Confederate troops drawn in line of battle across the road near the town. The flanks of the Confederate line were protected by woods, and Buford sent off his cavalry to make a detour and get in their rear. In a wheat field at the right of the road he found an eminence suitable for his artillery, and it went into position at a gallop. Almost in one moment the Confederates were subjected to a fire from rifle-guns, saw a line of bayonets coming straight at them in front, and discovered that hostile horsemen with drawn sabres were in their rear. Naturally (and perhaps properly) they immediately turned and fled without firing a gun. They numbered about 1,000 men, infantry and cavalry. A few prisoners were taken, together with the camp and all that it contained. The tents and

MAJOR-GENERAL JOHN M. PALMER.

barracks were now burned, and the National forces marched to Hickman.

Early in June an expedition commanded by Brig.-Gen. James S. Negley, setting out from Columbia, marched eastward and southward toward Chattanooga, for the purpose of reconnoitring and threatening that place, bringing some relief to the persecuted Unionists of East Tennessee, and ascertaining the truth of a report that the Confederates were about to make a strong movement to recapture Nashville. Their first capture was at Winchester, of a squad of cavalrymen, including a man who was at once a clergyman, principal of a female seminary, and captain in the Confederate service. This man had made himself notorious by capturing and bringing in Union men to the town, where they were given the alternative of enlisting as Confederate soldiers or being hanged. Andrew Johnson, military governor of Tennessee, who had himself suffered much persecution at the hands of the secessionists, and was very bitter toward them, had declared that rich rebels should be made to pay for the depredations of the roving Confederate bands upon Union men. In accordance with this, General Negley arrested a considerable number of well-known secessionists in Marion County and assessed them two hundred dollars apiece, appropriating the money to the relief of Union people in that part of the State. Crossing the mountains to the Sequatchie Valley, the expedition first met the enemy at Sweeden's Cove. They were soon put to flight, however, by Negley's guns, and were then pursued by his cavalry, who overtook them after a chase of two or three miles, rode among them, and used their sabres freely until the Confederates were dispersed. The next day the expedition proceeded toward Chattanooga, where they found a large Confederate force with intrenchments and several guns in position. In the afternoon the Confederates opened fire with rifles and artillery, to which Neg-

MAJOR-GENERAL WILLIAM NELSON.

MAJOR-GENERAL JAMES S. NEGLEY.

ley's guns made reply, and the cannonading was kept up for two hours, during which the National gunners exhibited the greater skill and finally silenced the enemy's batteries. These were repaired during the ensuing night, and the next day were bombarded again, until it was discovered that the town had been evacuated. It is related that during this fight a man appeared on the Confederate intrenchments displaying a black flag, and was instantly shot down. In his report General Negley said: "The Union people in East Tennessee are wild with joy. They meet us along the road by hundreds. I shall send you a number of their principal persecutors from the Sequatchie valley."

About this time the roving Confederate cavalry, commanded by Gen. N. B. Forrest, who two years later obtained such an unenviable reputation for his conduct at Fort Pillow, began to attract special attention by the rapidity and daring of its movements. On the 13th of July he made an attack on Murfreesboro' at the head of about 3,000 men. The town was garrisoned by about 800, not very skilfully disposed or very well disciplined. The attack fell principally on the Ninth Michigan Regiment, which fought courageously hand to hand for twenty minutes and put the enemy to flight, losing about 90 men. The attack was soon renewed by a larger force, and finally resulted in the defeat of the Michigan men. Meanwhile another portion of Forrest's command had attacked the court-house, where a portion of the garrison took shelter and kept up a destructive fire from the windows. Being unable to drive them out, the

Confederates set fire to the building, when the garrison were, of course, compelled to retire. The Confederates captured and paroled most of the garrison, packed up and carried off what they could of plunder, and burned a large quantity of camp equipage and clothing. The garrison was commanded by Brig.-Gen. Thomas L. Crittenden, who was severely censured for the mismanagement that made the disaster possible.

ANDREW JOHNSON.
Military Governor of Tennessee, afterward President.

Early in August Colonel De Courcey went out with his brigade from Cumberland Gap southward toward Tazewell on a foraging expedition. Near that town they were attacked by four Confederate regiments under Colonel Rains, and the advance regiment of De Courcey's force was immediately deployed across the road with artillery on the flank. The enemy charged in columns, and was received in silence until he had approached within two hundred and fifty yards, when a terrible fire was opened upon him and threw him into disorder. In the meanwhile a battery of six guns, unobserved by the Confederates, had gained an eminence in their rear, and when it began firing they at once turned and fled. The National loss in this short but brilliant action was 68, 50 of whom were prisoners, being two companies who were out on detached service and were suddenly surrounded. The Confederate loss was about 200.

Brig.-Gen. R. W. Johnson, setting out with a force of infantry, cavalry, and artillery to pursue the raider Morgan and his men, found them (August 21st) at Galletin, and ordered an attack. All seemed to be going well for a time, until confusion began to appear in his command, and soon a panic arose and half of his men ran away. He and some of his officers tried in vain to rally them, and finally he was obliged to order a retreat of such of his men as had stood their ground. He then marched for Cairo on the Cumberland, but, before reaching that place, found the enemy pressing so closely in his rear that he was obliged to form line of battle to receive them. Again, when the firing became brisk, most of his men broke and fled, while with the remainder of his command he held the enemy in check until the fugitives were enabled to cross the river, when he and his little band were surrounded and captured. He had lost 30 men killed, and 50 wounded, and 75 were made prisoners.

A SONG AROUND THE CAMPFIRE.

On the 31st of August there was a severe skirmish near Bolivar, between two regiments of infantry and two detachments of cavalry, and a large Confederate force, which lasted about seven hours, and was brought to a close by an artillery fire and a gallant charge from the National troops. In this charge Lieutenant-Colonel Hogg, of the Second Illinois cavalry, fell in a hand-to-hand fight with Colonel McCullough. The next day, two regiments of infantry, with two companies of cavalry and a battery, commanded by Colonel Dennis, moving to attack this Confederate force in the rear, encountered them at Britton's Lane, near Denmark. Dennis, who had about 800 men, selected a strong position and awaited attack in a large grove surrounded by cornfields. The Confederates, commanded by Brigadier-General Armstrong, numbered at least 5,000, and were able merely to surround the little band. They soon captured the transportation train and two guns, but before the fight was over Dennis's men recaptured them. For four hours the Confederates persisted in making successive charges, all of which were gallantly repelled, when they retired, leaving Dennis in possession of the field. Their loss in killed and wounded was about 400. Dennis lost 60 men.

In October General Negley, commanding at Nashville, learning that a considerable Confederate force under Generals Anderson, Harris, and Forrest was being concentrated at La Vergne, fifteen miles eastward, for the purpose of assaulting the city, sent out a force of about 2,500 men, under command of Gen. John M. Palmer, to attack them. A portion of this force marched directly by the Murfreesboro' road, while the remainder made a detour to the south. The Confederate pickets and videttes were on the alert, and made a skirmish for several miles, enabling the main body to prepare for the attack. The battle was opened by fire of the Confederate artillery, but this was soon silenced when a shell exploded their ammunition chest. Almost at the same moment the detachment that had made a detour came up and struck the Confederates on the flank, at the same time deploying skilfully so as to cut off their retreat. In this difficult situation the Confederates held their ground and fought for half an hour before they broke and retreated in confusion. They had lost about 80 men killed or wounded, and 175 were captured, besides three

GOING TO THE FRONT—REGIMENTS PASSING THE ASTOR HOUSE, NEW YORK.

guns, a considerable amount of stores, stand of colors, etc. General Palmer lost 18 men.

On the 18th of November 200 men of the Eighth Kentucky Regiment, under Lieutenant-Colonel May, was guarding a supply train bivouacked on an old camp-meeting ground at Rural Hills, seventeen miles southeast of Nashville. While they were at breakfast the next morning the crack of rifles was heard, and in a moment two columns of Confederate cavalry were seen rushing upon them from their front and their right. The boys in blue seized their muskets, fell into line, and in a moment met the enemy with a sharp and continuous fire. Presently a section of National artillery was brought into action, and not only played upon the enemy immediately in front, but also upon a larger body that was discovered somewhat more than a mile away. This was answered by two or three Confederate guns, and the fight was continued for half an hour, when the assailants withdrew, leaving a dozen dead men on the field. Colonel May lost no men.

A similar affair took place on the 6th of December, at Lebanon, where the Ninety-third Ohio Regiment, under Col. Charles Anderson, was guarding a forage train. Seeing an enemy in front, who were evidently preparing to intercept the train, he marched his regiment in double-quick time through the fields skirting the road, in order to get ahead of the train and prevent an attack upon it. By the time he got there the Confederates were in position to receive him, and a sharp fight ensued, which ended in the flight of the Confederates. In these little affairs there was often displayed a dash and courage by individual soldiers, which in a war of less gigantic dimensions would have immortalized them. Every historian of the Revolutionary war thinks it necessary to record anew the fact that when the flagstaff of Fort Moultrie was shot away Sergeant Jasper leaped down from the parapet and recovered it under fire. Without disparaging his exploit, it may be said that it was surpassed in hundreds of instances by men on both sides in the civil war. In the little action just described, William C. Stewart, a color-bearer, was under fire for the first time in his life. Colonel Anderson says he "stood out in front of his company and of the regiment with his tall person and our glorious flag elevated to their highest reach; nor could he be persuaded to seek cover or to lower his colors."

At Hartsville on the Cumberland, about forty miles from Murfreesboro', 1,900 National troops, under command of Col. Absalom B. Moore, were encamped in a position which would have been very strong if held by a larger force, but was dangerous for one so small. Against this place Morgan the raider, at the head of 4,000 men, marched on the 7th of December. He crossed the river seven miles from Hartsville, at a point where nobody supposed it could be crossed by any such force, on account of the steepness of the banks. With a little digging he made a slope, down which he slid his horses, and at the water's edge his men remounted. Coming up unexpectedly by a byroad, they captured all the National pickets except one, who gave the alarm and ran into the camp. The Nationals formed quickly in line of battle, but at the first fire the One Hundred and Eighth Ohio broke, leaving the flank exposed. The Confederates saw their advantage, seized it, and quickly poured in a cross-fire, which compelled the remainder of Moore's forces to fall back, though they did not do it without first making a stubborn fight. Soon afterward Colonel Moore, considering it sufficiently evident that further resistance was useless, raised a white flag and surrendered his entire command.

A similar surrender took place at Trenton, December 20th, when Forrest's cavalry attacked that place for the purpose of breaking the railroad and cutting off General Grant's supplies. Col. Jacob Fry, who was in command there, had been notified by Grant to look out for Forrest, as he was moving in that direction. He got together what force he could, consisting largely of convalescents and fugitives, and numbering but 250 in all, and prepared to make a defence. He had a few sharp-shooters, whom he placed on two buildings commanding two of the principal streets, and when in the afternoon the enemy appeared, charging in two columns, they were met by so severe a fire from these men that they quickly moved out of range. Forrest then planted a battery of six guns where it could command the position held by the Nationals, and opened fire with shells. Colonel Fry says: "Seeing that we were completely in their power, and had done all the damage to them we could, I called a council of officers. They were unanimous for surrender. . . . The terms of the surrender were unconditional; but General Forrest admitted us to our paroles the next morning, sending the Tennessee troops immediately home, and others to Columbus under a flag of truce."

Thus far in his raiding operations General Forrest had had things mainly his own way, but in the closing engagement he was not so fortunate. While he was marching toward Lexington a force of 1,500 men, commanded by Col. C. L. Dunham, was sent out to intercept him, and came upon a portion of his troops at Parker's Cross Roads, five miles south of Clarksburg, on the 30th of December. After some preliminary skirmishes Dunham, seeing that he was soon to be attacked, placed his men in readiness, and with two pieces of artillery opened fire. This was replied to by the Confederates with six guns, and Dunham then retreated some distance to a good position on the crest of a ridge, placing his wagon train in the rear. The enemy in heavy column soon emerged from the woods, and made a movement evidently intended to gain his flank and rear; whereupon he promptly changed his position to face them, and opened fire. But the Confederate artillery gained a position where it could enfilade his lines, and at the same time he was attacked in the rear by a detachment of dismounted cavalry. Again he promptly changed his position, facing to the rear, and drove off the enemy with a considerable loss, completing their rout by a brilliant bayonet charge. A detachment of cavalry also made two charges upon him from another direction, and both times was repelled. This was the end of the principal fighting of the day. A few minutes later Forrest sent in a flag of truce demanding an unconditional surrender, to which Colonel Dunham replied: "You will get away with that flag very quickly, and bring me no more such messages. Give my compliments to the general, and tell him I never surrender. If he thinks he can take me, come and try." In the course of the battle Dunham's wagon train was captured, and he now called for volunteers to retake it. A company of the Thirty-ninth Iowa offered themselves for this task and quickly accomplished it, not only recapturing the train but bringing in also several prisoners, including Forrest's adjutant-general and three other officers. Reinforcements for Dunham now approached, and the Confederates departed. The National loss, in killed, wounded, and missing, was 220. The Confederate loss is unknown. Another instance of peculiar individual gallantry is here mentioned by the colonel in his report. "As our line faced about and pressed back in their engagement of the enemy in our rear, one of the guns of the battery was left behind in the edge of the woods. All the

BRIGADIER-GENERAL JUSTUS McKINSTRY

horses belonging to it had been killed but two. After everybody had passed and left it, Private E. A. Topliff, fearing that the enemy might capture it, alone and under a smart fire disengaged the two horses, hitched them to the piece, and took it safely out."

Although the struggle to determine whether Missouri should remain in the Union or go out of it had been decided in the first year of the war, her soil was by no means free from contention and bloodshed in the second year. The earliest conflict took place in Randolph County, January 8th, where 1,000 Confederates, under Colonel Poindexter, took up a strong position at Roan's Tanyard, on Silver Creek, seven miles south of Huntsville. Here they were attacked by about 500 men under Majors Torrence and Hubbard, and after half an hour's fighting were completely routed. Their defeat was owing mainly to the inefficiency of their commander. The victors burned the camp and a considerable amount of stores.

In February Captain Nolen, of the Seventh Illinois cavalry, with 64 men, while reconnoitring near Charleston, struck a small detachment of Confederate cavalry under Jeff Thompson. Nolen pursued them for some distance, and when Thompson made a stand and brought up his battery to command the road, the Illinois men promptly charged upon it, captured four guns, and put the Confederates to flight.

The most infamous of all the guerilla leaders was one Quantrell, who seemed to take delight in murdering prisoners, whether they were combatants or non-combatants. His band moved with the usual celerity of such, and, like the others, was exceedingly difficult to capture, or even find, when any considerable force set out to attack it. On the 22d of March a detachment of the Sixth Kansas Regiment overtook Quantrell near Independence, killed seven of his men, and caused the remainder to retreat precipitately, except eleven of them who were captured.

Another encounter with Quantrell's guerilla band was had at Warrensburg, March 26, where he attacked a detachment of a Missouri regiment commanded by Major Emery Foster. Although Quantrell had 200 men, and Foster but 60, the latter, skilfully using a thick plank fence for protection, succeeded in inflicting so much loss upon the guerillas that they at length retired. Nine of them were killed and 17 wounded. The National loss was 13, including Major Foster wounded. The same night about 500 guerillas attacked four companies of militia at Humonsville, but were defeated and driven off with a loss of 15 killed and a large number wounded.

On the 26th of April the Confederate general John S. Marmaduke attacked the town of Cape Girardeau, but after a smart action was driven off, with considerable loss, by the garrison, under Gen. John McNeil. In the evening of the next day the cavalry force that formed the advance guard on his retreat was surprised and attacked near Jackson by the First Iowa cavalry and other troops. Two howitzers, loaded with musket balls, were fired at them when they were not more than thirty yards away, and the next instant the Iowa cavalry swooped down upon them in a spirited charge, from which not one of the Confederates escaped. All that were not killed were captured, together with a few guns, horses, etc.

One of the most desperate fights with guerillas took place near Memphis, Mo., on the 18th of July. A band of 600 had chosen a strong position for their camp, partly concealed

A MILITARY PONTOON BRIDGE.

by heavy brush and timber, when they were attacked by a force of cavalry and militia, commanded by Major John Y. Clopper. Clopper first knew their location when they fired from concealment upon his advance guard, and he immediately made dispositions for an attack. His men made five successive charges across open ground, and were five times repelled; but, nothing disheartened, and having now learned the exact position of the concealed enemy, they advanced in a sixth charge, and engaged him hand to hand. The result of the fight was the complete defeat of the guerillas, who fled, leaving their dead and wounded on the field and in the woods. Clopper lost 83 men.

MAJOR-GENERAL JOHN S. MARMADUKE, C. S. A.

In these affairs the guerillas were by no means always defeated. When in August a band of 800 had been gathered by one Hughes, it was determined to make an attack upon the small National garrison at Independence, principally for the purpose of obtaining additional arms. The guerillas surprised, captured, and murdered the picket before they could give an alarm, and then entered the town by two roads, and attacked the various buildings where detachments of the garrison were stationed. A gallant resistance was made at every possible point; but as the guerillas outnumbered the defenders two to one, and there was no prospect of any relief, Lieut.-Col. J. T. Buell, commanding the town, finally surrendered. Hughes and many of his men had been killed. Several of the buildings were riddled with balls, and 26 of the garrison lost their lives.

BRIGADIER-GENERAL JEFF M. THOMPSON, C. S. A.

place on the 29th of October, near Butler, in Bates County. A band of them, who had been committing depredations, and were threatening several towns, were pursued by 220 men of the First Kansas colored regiment, commanded by white officers. The guerillas in superior force attacked them near Osage Island, charging upon them and making every demonstration of special hatred for the blacks; but the colored men stood their ground like any other good soldiers, and dealt out severe punishment to the guerillas. When, finally, the cavalrymen succeeded in riding in among the colored troops, many desperate hand-to-hand encounters ensued. Not a colored soldier would surrender; and one of the leaders of the guerillas, in describing the action, said that "the black devils fought like tigers." The character of much of the guerilla fighting may be seen from a few incidents of this battle. While Lieutenant Gardner was lying wounded and insensible, a guerilla approached him, cut his revolver from the belt, and fired it at his head. Fortunately the ball only grazed the skull, and the next instant a wounded colored soldier near by raised himself sufficiently to level his musket and shoot the miscreant dead. Captain Crew had been killed, and a guerilla was rifling his pockets, when another wounded colored soldier summoned strength enough to get to his feet and despatch the guerilla with his bayonet. On the approach of reinforcements for the little band, the guerillas retreated. The National force lost about 20 men.

BRIGADIER-GENERAL H. H. SIBLEY, C. S. A.

Again, at Lone Jack, Mo., five days later (August 16th), the guerillas were successful in a fight with the State militia. Major Foster at the head of 600 militiamen was hunting guerillas, when he suddenly found more than he wanted to see at one time. They were estimated at 4,000, and on the approach of Foster's little force they turned and attacked him. Foster's men fought gallantly for four hours, and were not overpowered until they had lost 160 men, the loss of the guerillas being about equal. On the approach of National reinforcements the guerillas retreated.

A month later, at Shirley's Ford on Spring River, the Third Indiana Regiment, commanded by Colonel Ritchie, attacked and defeated a force of 600 guerillas, including about 100 Cherokee Indians, 60 of whom were killed or wounded before they retreated.

One more desperate fight with guerillas in that State took

Northern Arkansas, as well as southern Missouri, was infested by bands of Confederate guerillas, though it was not so rich a field for their operations, as the number of Unionists in that State was comparatively small.

In February, the First Missouri cavalry, hunting guerillas there, were fired upon from ambush at Sugar Creek, and 18 men fell. The regiment immediately formed for action, and artillery was brought up and the woods were shelled, but with no result except the unseen retreat of the enemy.

At Searcy Landing, on Little Red River, 150 men of the National force had a fight with about twice their number of Confederates, whom they routed with a loss of nearly 100 men.

On the 22d of October, Brig.-Gen. James G. Blunt, commanding a division of the Army of the Frontier, set out from Pea Ridge with two brigades. After a toilsome march of thirty

PRACTICE BATTERY, NAVAL ACADEMY, ANNAPOLIS, MD.

miles he came upon a Confederate force at Old Fort Wayne, near Maysville, which consisted of two Texas regiments and other troops, numbering about 5,000 in all. He found them in position to receive battle, but believing that they intended to retreat he made haste to attack them with his advance guard and shell them with two howitzers. The enemy promptly answered the artillery fire and showed no signs of retreating, but on the contrary attempted to overwhelm the little force. General Blunt hurried forward the main body of his troops and flanked the enemy upon both wings, then making a charge upon their centre and capturing their artillery. This completely broke them up, and they fled in disorder, being pursued for seven miles. Blunt lost about a dozen men, and found 50 of the enemy's dead on the field.

On the 26th of November General Blunt learned that Marmaduke's Confederate command was at Cane Hill, and immediately set out to attack it with 5,000 men and 30 guns. After a march of thirty-five miles he sent spies into the enemy's camp to learn its exact location and condition, who discovered that on one of the approaches there were no pickets out. He therefore made his dispositions for an attack on that side, and was not discovered until he was within half a mile of their lines, when they opened upon him with artillery. He replied with one battery, and kept up a brisk fire while he sent back to hurry up the main body of his troops. Placing guns on an eminence, he shelled the enemy very effectively, and then formed his command in line for an advance, expecting a desperate resistance, but found to his surprise that they had quietly retreated. They made a stand a few miles distant at the base of the Boston Mountains, and there he attacked them again, when they retired to a lofty position on the mountain side, with artillery on the crest. The Second and Eleventh Kansas and Third Cherokee regiments stormed this position and carried it, when the enemy fled in disorder and was pursued for three miles through the woods. Here another stand was made by their rear guard, which was promptly charged by Blunt's cavalry. But the position defended was in a defile, and the cavalry suffered severely. Bringing up his guns, Blunt was about to shell them out, when they sent in a flag of truce with a request for permission to remove their dead and wounded. General Blunt granted this, but it proved that the flag of truce was only a trick of Marmaduke's to obtain time to escape with his command. Darkness now came on, and the pursuit was abandoned. Blunt had lost about 40 men, and Marmaduke about 100.

A much more important action than of those just recorded took place at Prairie Grove on the 7th of December. Learning that General Hindman's forces had joined those of General Marmaduke, making an army of about 25,000 men, General Blunt, fearing an attack, ordered the divisions commanded by Gen. F. J. Herron to join him at once. Herron obeyed the order promptly; but the Confederates, learning of this movement, made an advance for the purpose of interposing between Blunt and Herron. They attacked Herron first, who drove back their advance and then found them in position on a ridge commanding the ford across Illinois Creek. Herron sent a detachment of his men to cut a road through the woods and come in upon their flank, thus drawing their fire in that direction and enabling his main force to cross the ford. This movement was successful, and in a short time his command had crossed and brought its guns to bear upon the enemy's position. He then pushed forward his infantry in several charges, one of which captured a battery, but all of which were finally repelled. The Confederates then made a grand charge in return and came within a hundred yards of Herron's guns, but the fire of artillery and musketry was too much for them, and they retired in disorder. Again, in his turn, Herron charged with two regiments, again captured a battery, and again was forced to retire. While this action was in progress Blunt was pressing forward to the relief of Herron with his command, and now came in on the right, joined in the fight and defeated the enemy, who repeated their trick with a flag of truce and escaped in the night. In this battle the total National loss, killed, wounded, and missing, was 1,148. The Confederate loss is not exactly known, but was much larger, and included General Stein among the killed.

The great war extended not only over the Southern States, but into some of the Territories. In the summer of 1861 the Confederate government commanded Gen. H. H. Sibley to organize a brigade in Texas and march northward into New Mexico for the conquest of that Territory. He moved up the Rio Grande in January, 1862, and early in February came within striking distance of Fort Craig, on the western bank of the river, which was the headquarters of Col. (afterward Gen.) E. R. S. Canby, who commanded the National forces in New Mexico. Canby planned to attack him, and began by sending a force of cavalry with two batteries to cut off the Texans from their supply of water at the river. In that vicinity, on account of the steep banks, there was only one point where the stream could be reached. This detachment, however, was a little too late, as the Confederates had already gained the water. Colonel Roberts, in command of the detachment, fired upon them with his batteries, dismounted one of their guns, and drove them off. Roberts then crossed to the eastern bank, and the fight was renewed with varying success, until the Confederates charged upon and captured some of his guns. Colonel Canby then came upon the field with more of his forces and ordered an advance to attack the enemy where he appeared to be lurking in the edge of a wood. But the Confederates did not wait to be attacked. After a sharp musketry fire on the right flank, they made desperate charges to capture Canby's two batteries. The one against Hall's battery was made by cavalry, and the horsemen were struck down so rapidly by the fire of the guns that they could not reach it. The other was made by infantry, armed principally with revolvers. The guns, commanded by Captain McRae, were served rapidly and skilfully, and made awful slaughter of the Texans; but they continually closed up the gaps in their ranks and steadily pushed forward until the battery was theirs. The infantry supports, who should have prevented this capture, miserably failed in their duty and finally ran away from the field. McRae and his men remained at their guns till the last minute, and most of them, including Captain McRae, were killed. With the loss of the battery, hope of victory was gone, and the National troops retired to the fort. Canby had in this fight about 1,500 men, and lost about 200. The Confederates numbered about 2,000, and their loss is unknown.

ALLAN PINKERTON AND SECRET SERVICE OFFICERS.

Another fight in this territory took place at Apache Cañon, twenty miles from Santa Fé, on the 28th of March, where Major Chivington with 1,300 men and six guns overtook and attacked a force of about 2,000 Texans. The first shots were fired by a small party of the Texans in ambush, who were immediately rushed upon and disposed of by the advance guard of the Nationals. Chivington then pressed forward, surprised and captured the pickets, and about noon attacked the main force of the enemy. The battle lasted four hours, and Chivington with his six guns had a great advantage over the Texans, who had but one. The result was a complete defeat of the Confederates and capture of their entire train

CONSTRUCTING WINTER QUARTERS.

HEADQUARTER GUARD, ARMY OF THE POTOMAC.

consisting of sixty-four wagons. The Texans had made four attempts to capture Chivington's guns, as they had captured Canby's, but only met with heavy loss. The total Confederate loss was over 300 killed or wounded, and about 100 taken prisoners. Chivington's loss was 150.

In obedience to an Act of Congress, Lieut.-Com. Thomas S. Phelps, in command of the steamer *Corwin*, was detached from the North Atlantic blockading squadron and ordered to make a regular survey of the Potomac River, to facilitate the operations of the army, no survey of this river ever having been made. He began the work in July, 1862, and rapidly pushed it to its completion in March, 1863, most of the time opposed by the artillery and cavalry of the Confederates. During the winter months it was frequently necessary to break the ice in order to prosecute the work. While thus engaged, he assisted materially in the blockade of the river and in breaking up the haunts of the contrabandists. The magnitude of the work may be imagined from the fact that on the Kettle-bottoms alone, a section of the river about ten miles in length by an average of four miles in width, more than six hundred miles of soundings were run, necessitated by the immense number of small shoals on this ground which were dangerous to navigation. The length of river surveyed was ninety-seven miles.

BRINGING IN A PRISONER.

Enraged by real or fancied wrongs in the failure of payment of annuities, the Sioux Indians took the opportunity when the Government, as they supposed, had all it could do to grapple with the rebellion, to indulge in a general uprising in the Northwest. In August they attacked several frontier towns of Minnesota and committed horrible atrocities. The village of New Ulm was almost destroyed, and more than 100 of its citizens—men, women, and children—were massacred. They also destroyed the agencies at Redwood and Yellow Medicine, and attacked the villages of Hutchinson and Forest City, but from these latter were driven off. They besieged Fort Ridgley, but did not succeed in capturing it. Altogether they committed about 1,000 murders. Col. H. H. Sibley with a strong force was sent against them, and in September overtook several bodies of the Sioux, all of whom he defeated. In the principal battle two cannon, of which the Indians have always been in mortal terror, were used upon them with great effect. The Indians asked for a truce to rescue their wounded and bury their dead, but Sibley declined to grant any truce until they should return the prisoners whom they had carried off. Ultimately about 1,000 Indians were captured. Many of them were tried and condemned, and 39 were hanged.

CHAPTER XX.

EMPLOYMENT OF COLORED SOLDIERS.

ENLISTMENT OF COLORED SOLDIERS DENOUNCED IN THE SOUTH—NEGRO ASSISTANTS IN CONFEDERATE ARMIES—CONFEDERATE THREATS AGAINST NEGRO SOLDIERS AND THOSE WHO LED THEM—DEMOCRATIC JOURNALS IN THE NORTH DENOUNCE THE ENLISTMENT OF COLORED SOLDIERS—INTENSITY OF FEELING ON THE SUBJECT OF SLAVERY—INTERESTING CRITICISMS BY COUNT GUROWSKI—BLACK SOLDIERS IN THE REVOLUTIONARY WAR—BRAVERY OF COLORED TROOPS—OPINION OF COL. THOMAS W. HIGGINSON—AN INTERESTING STORY—NEGRO SENTINELS IN CONFEDERATE ARMIES.

THE COOK.

THE year 1863 began with several events of the first importance. On December 31st and January 2d there was a great battle in the West, which has just been described. On New Year's Day the final proclamation of emancipation was issued, and measures were taken for the immediate enlistment of black troops. On that day, also, in the State of New York, which furnished one-sixth of all the men called into the National service, the executive power passed into hands unfriendly to the Administration.

The part of President Lincoln's proclamation that created most excitement at the South was not that which declared the freedom of the blacks—for the secessionists professed to be amused at this as a papal bull against a comet—but that which announced that negroes would thenceforth be received into the military service of the United States. Whatever might be said of the powerlessness of the Government to liberate slaves that were within the Confederate lines, it was plain enough that a determination to enlist colored troops brought in a large resource hitherto untouched. Military men in Europe, having only statistical knowledge of our negro population, and not understanding the peculiar prejudices that hedged it about, had looked on at first in amazement, and finally in contempt, at its careful exclusion from military service. The Confederates had no special scruples about negro assistance on their own side; for they not only constantly employed immense numbers of blacks in building fortifications and in camp drudgery, but had even armed and equipped a few of them for service as soldiers. In a review of Confederate troops at New Orleans, in the first year of the war, appeared a regiment of free negroes, and early the next year the legislature of Virginia provided for the enrolment of the same class.

But the idea that emancipated slaves should be employed to fight against their late masters and for the enfranchisement of their own race, appeared to be new, startling, and unwelcome; and the Confederates, both officially and unofficially, threatened the direst penalties against all who should lead black soldiers, as well as against such soldiers themselves. General Beauregard wrote to a friend in the Congress at Richmond: "Has the bill for the execution of Abolition prisoners, after January next, been passed? Do it, and England will be stirred into action. It is high time to proclaim the black flag after that period. Let the execution be with the garrote." Mr. Davis, late in December, 1862, issued a proclamation outlawing General Butler and all commissioned officers in his command, and directing that whenever captured they should be reserved for execution, and added, "That all negro slaves captured in arms be at once delivered over to the executive authorities of the respective States to which they belong, to be dealt with according to the laws of said States," and, "That the like orders be executed with respect to all commissioned officers of the United States, when found serving in company with said slaves." The Confederate Congress passed a series of resolutions in which it was provided that on the capture of any white commissioned officer who had

EVENING AT A NEGRO CABIN.

armed, organized, or led negro troops against the Confederacy, he should be tried by a military court and put to death or otherwise punished.

Democratic journalists and Congressmen at the North were hardly less violent in their opposition to the enlistment of black men. They denounced the barbarity of the proceeding, declared that white soldiers would be disgraced if they fought on the same field with blacks, and anon demonstrated the utter incapacity of negroes for war, and laughed at the idea that they would ever face an enemy. Most of the Democratic senators and representatives voted against the appropriation bills, or supported amendments providing that " no part of the moneys shall be applied to the raising, arming, equipping, or paying of negro soldiers," and the more eloquent of them drew pitiful pictures of the ruin and anarchy that were to ensue. Representative Samuel S. Cox, then of Ohio, said: " Every man along the border will tell you that the Union is forever rendered hopeless if you pursue this policy of taking the slaves from the masters and arming them in this civil strife."

It is impossible at this distance of time, and after the question of slavery in our country has been so thoroughly settled that nobody disputes the righteousness and wisdom of its abolition, to convey to younger readers an adequate idea either of the diversity of opinion or the intensity of feeling on the subject, when it was still under discussion and was complicated with great military and political problems. Not only before the Emancipation Proclamation was issued, but for a considerable time afterward, these opinions were tenaciously held and these feelings expressed. The so-called conservatives of the Northern States constantly affirmed that abolitionists of whatever degree, and active secessionists, were equally wrong and blameworthy; that the latter had no right to break up the Union for any cause, and that the former had no right to emancipate the slaves even to save the Union. They assumed that the Constitution of the United States was perpetual, perfect, and infallible for all time, and ignored the natural antagonism between the systems of slave labor and free labor. In June, 1862, the conservative members of Congress held a meeting, and adopted a declaration of principles which included the following: " At the call of the Government a mighty army, the noblest and most patriotic ever known, sprung at once into the field, and is bleeding and conquering in defence of its Government. Under these circumstances it would, in our opinion, be most unjust and ungenerous to give any new character or direction to the war, for the accomplishment of any other than the first great purpose, and especially for the accomplishment of any mere party or sectional scheme. The doctrines of the secessionists and abolitionists, as the latter are now represented in Congress, are alike false to the Constitution and irreconcilable to the peace and unity of the country. The first have already involved us in a cruel civil war, and the others—the abolitionists—will leave the country but little hope of the speedy restoration of the Union or peace, if the schemes of confiscation, emancipation, and other unconstitutional measures which they have lately carried, and attempted to carry, through the House of Representatives, shall be enacted into the form of laws and remain unrebuked by the people. It is no justification of such acts that the crimes committed in the prosecution of the rebellion are of unexampled atrocity, nor is there any such justification as State necessity known to our government or laws."

On the other hand, at a great mass meeting held in Union Square, New York City, July 15, 1862, a series of resolutions was adopted which included the following:

" That we are for the union of the States, the integrity of the country, and the maintenance of this Government without any condition or qualification whatever, and at every necessary sacrifice of life or treasure.

" That we urge upon the Government the exercise of its utmost skill and vigor in the prosecution of this war, unity of design, comprehensiveness of plan, a uniform policy, and the stringent use of all the means within its reach consistent with the usages of civilized warfare.

" That we acknowledge but two divisions of the people of the United States in this crisis—those who are loyal to its Constitution and every inch of its soil and are ready to make every sacrifice for the integrity of the Union and the maintenance of civil liberty within it, and those who openly or covertly endeavor to sever our country or to yield to the insolent demand of its enemies; that we fraternize with the former and detest the latter; and that, forgetting all former party names and distinctions, we call upon all patriotic citizens to rally for one undivided country, one flag, one destiny."

The extreme of opinion in favor of immediate and unqualified emancipation, and of employment of colored troops, with impatience at all delay in adopting such a policy, was represented picturesquely, if not altogether justly, by Count Gurowski. Adam Gurowski was a Pole who had been exiled for participating in revolutionary demonstrations, and after a varied career had come to the United States, where he engaged in literary pursuits, and from 1861 to 1863 was employed as a translator in the state department at Washington. He was now between fifty and sixty years of age, and was a keen observer and merciless critic of what was going on around him. He had published several books in Europe, and his diary kept while he was in the state department has also been put into print. It is exceedingly outspoken in every direction; and though it is often unjust, and represents hardly more than his own exaggerated eccentricity, yet in many respects he struck at once into the heart of important truths which slower minds comprehended less readily or less willingly. The following extracts are suggestive and interesting. Their dates range from April, 1862, to April, 1863.

" Mr. Blair [Montgomery Blair, Postmaster-General] worse and worse; is more hot in support of McClellan, more determined to upset Stanton; and I heard him demand the return of a poor fugitive slave woman to some of Blair's Maryland friends. Every day I am confirmed in my creed that whoever had slavery for mammy is never serious in the effort to destroy it. Whatever such men as Mr. Lincoln and Mr. Blair will do against slavery will never be radical by their own choice or conviction, but will be done reluctantly, and when under the unavoidable pressure of events. . . . Mr. Lincoln is forced out again from one of his pro-slavery intrenchments; he was obliged to yield, and to sign the hard-fought bill for emancipation in the District of Columbia. But how reluctantly, with what bad grace he signed it! Good boy; he wishes not to strike his mammy. And to think that the friends of humanity in Europe will credit this emancipation not where it is due, not to the noble pressure exercised by the high-minded Northern masses! Mr. Lincoln, his friends assert, does not wish to hurt the feelings of any one with whom he has to deal. Exceedingly amiable quality in a private individual, but at times turning almost to be a vice in a man intrusted with the destinies of a nation. So he never could decide to hurt the feelings of McClellan, and this after all

PLANTER'S RESIDENCE IN LOUISIANA.

A "CONTRABAND."

NEGRO CABIN ON SOUTHERN PLANTATION.

the numerous proofs of his incapacity. But Mr. Lincoln hurts thereby, and in the most sensible manner, the interests, nay, the lives of the twenty millions of people. . . . The last draft could be averted from the North if the four millions of loyal Africo-Americans were called to arms. But Mr. Lincoln, with the Sewards, the Blairs, and others, will rather see every Northern man shot than to touch the palladium of the rebels. . . . Proclamation *conditionally* abolishing slavery from 1863. The *conditional* is the last desperate effort made by Mr. Lincoln and by Mr. Seward to save slavery. The two statesmen found out that it was dangerous longer to resist the decided, authoritative will of the masses. But if the rebellion is crushed before January 1st, 1863, what then? If the rebels turn loyal before that term? Then the people of the North will be cheated. The proclamation is written in the meanest and the most dry routine style; not a word to evoke a generous thrill, not a word reflecting the warm and lofty comprehension and feelings of the immense majority of the people on this question of emancipation. Nothing for humanity, nothing to humanity. How differently Stanton would have spoken! General Wadsworth truly says that never a noble subject was more belittled by the form in which it was uttered. . . . The proclamation of September 22d may not produce in Europe the effect and the enthusiasm which it might have evoked if issued a year ago, as an act of justice and of self-conscientious force, as an utterance of the lofty, pure, and ardent aspirations and will of a high-minded people. Europe may see now in the proclamation an action of despair made in the duress of events. . . . Every time an Africo-American regiment is armed or created, Mr. Lincoln seems as though making an effort, or making a gracious concession in permitting the increase of our forces. It seems as if Mr. Lincoln were ready to exhaust all the resources of the country before he boldly strikes the Africo-American vein."

One hundred and seventy thousand negroes were enlisted, and many of them performed notable service, displaying, at Fort Wagner, Olustee, and elsewhere, quite as much steadiness and courage as any white troops. If the expressions of doubt as to the military value of the colored race were sincere, they argued inexcusable ignorance; for black soldiers had fought in the ranks of our Revolutionary armies, and Perry's victory on Lake Erie in 1813—which, with the battle of the Thames, secured us the great Northwest—was largely the work of colored sailors.

The President recognized the obligation of the Government to protect all its servants by every means in its power, and issued a proclamation directing that "for every soldier of the United States killed in violation of the laws of war, a rebel soldier shall be executed; and for every one enslaved by the enemy or sold into slavery, a rebel soldier shall be placed at hard labor on the public works." But such retaliation was never resorted to.

Before the war it had been a constant complaint of the Southerners, that the discussion of schemes for the abolition of slavery, and the scattering of documents that argued the right of every man to liberty, were likely to excite bloody insurrection among the slaves. And many students of this piece of history have expressed surprise that when the war broke out the blacks did not at once become mutinous all over the South, and make it impossible to put Confederate armies in the field. But it must be remembered, that although the struggle resulted in their liberation, yet when it was begun no intention was expressed on the part of the Government except a determination to save the Union, and the war had been in progress a year and a half before the blacks had any reason to suppose it would benefit them whichever way it might turn. They were often possessed of more shrewdness than they were credited with. Their sentiments up to the time of the Emancipation Proclamation were perhaps fairly represented by one who was an officer's servant in an Illinois regiment, and was at the battle of Fort Donelson. A gentleman who afterward met him on the deck of a steamer, and was curious to know what he thought of the struggle that was going on, questioned him with the following result:

"Were you in the fight?"

"Had a little taste of it, sa."

"Stood your ground, did you?"

"No, sa; I runs."

"Run at the first fire, did you?"

"Yes, sa; and would ha' run soona had I know'd it war comin'."

"Why, that wasn't very creditable to your courage."

"Dat isn't in my line, sa; cookin's my perfeshun."

"Well, but have you no regard for your reputation?"

"Refutation's nuffin by de side ob life."

"Do you consider your life worth more than other people's?"

"It's worth more to me, sa."

"Then you must value it very highly?"

"Yes, sa, I does; more dan all dis wuld; more dan a million of dollars, sa: for what would dat be wuf to a man wid de bref out of him? Self-perserbashum am de fust law wid me."

"But why should you act upon a different rule from other men?"

"Because different men set different values upon dar lives: mine is not in de market."

"But if you lost it, you would have the satisfaction of knowing that you died for your country."

"What satisfaction would dat be to me when de power ob feelin' was gone?"

"Then patriotism and honor are nothing to you?"

"Nuffin whatever, sa: I regard dem as among de vanities; and den de Gobernment don't know me; I hab no rights; may be sold like old hoss any day, and dat's all."

COLONEL ROBERT G. SHAW.
(Commanding the Fifty-fourth Massachusetts Colored Regiment.)

"If our old soldiers were like you, traitors might have broken up the Government without resistance."

"Yes, sa; dar would hab been no help for it. I wouldn't put my life in de scale 'ginst any gobernment dat ever existed; for no gobernment could replace de loss to me."

"Do you think any of your company would have missed you if you had been killed?"

"May be not, sa; a dead white man ain't much to dese sogers, let alone a dead nigga; but I'd a missed myself, and dat was de pint wid me."

Incidents like this were eagerly reported by journals that chose to argue that the colored men would not fight in any case, and such assertions were kept up and repeated by them long after they had fought most gallantly on several fields. Somebody in describing one of these battles used the expression, "The colored troops fought nobly," and this was seized upon and repeated sneeringly in hundreds of head-lines and editorials, always with an implication that it was buncombe, until the readers of those journals were made to believe that such troops did not fight at all. The fact was that their percentage of losses on the whole number that went into the service was slightly greater than that of the white troops; and when we consider that they fought with a prospect of being either murdered or sold into slavery, if they fell into the hands of the enemy, it must be acknowledged that they were entitled to a full measure of credit. Immediately after the proclamation of emancipation was issued, Lorenzo Thomas, adjutant-general of the army, was sent to Louisiana, where he explained his mission in a speech to the soldiers, in the course of which he said:

"Look along the river, and see the multitude of deserted plantations upon its banks. These are the places for these freedmen, where they can be self-sustaining and self-supporting. All of you will some day be on picket-duty; and I charge you all, if any of this unfortunate race come within your lines, that you do not turn them away, but receive them kindly and cordially. They are to be encouraged to come to us; they are to be received with open arms; they are to be fed and clothed; they are to be armed. This is the policy that has been fully determined upon. I am here to say that I am authorized to raise as many regiments of blacks as I can. I am authorized to give commissions, from the highest to the lowest; and I desire those persons who are earnest in this work to take hold of it. I desire only those whose hearts are in it, and to them alone will I give commissions. I don't care who they are, or what their present rank may be. I do not hesitate to say, that all proper persons will receive commissions.

"While I am authorized thus in the name of the Secretary of War, I have the fullest authority to dismiss from the army any man, be his rank what it may, whom I find maltreating the freedmen. This part of my duty I will most assuredly perform if any case comes before me. I would rather do that than give commissions, because such men are unworthy the name of soldiers. This, fellow soldiers, is the determined policy of the Administration. You all know, full well, when the President of the United States, though said to be slow in coming to a determination, once puts his foot down, it is there; and he is not going to take it up. He has put his foot down. I am here to assure you that my official influence shall be given that he shall not raise it."

Major-Gen. B. M. Prentiss then made a speech, in which he said, that "from the time he was a prisoner, and a negro sentinel, with firm step, beat in front of his cell, and with firmer voice commanded silence within, he prayed God for the day of revenge; and he now thanked God that it had come."

General Prentiss, it will be remembered, had been captured at the battle of Shiloh, and from this incidental testimony it appears that he found the Confederates had negroes doing duty as sentinels at least.

Col. Thomas W. Higginson, who saw much service in General Saxton's department on the coast of South Carolina, and who there raised and commanded a regiment of colored troops, wrote: "It needs but a few days to show up the absurdity of distrusting the military availability of these people. They have quite as much average comprehension as whites of the need of the thing, as much courage I doubt not, as much previous knowledge of the gun, and, above all, a readiness of ear and imitation which for purposes of drill counterbalances any defect of mental training. As to camp life, they have little to sacrifice; they are better fed, housed, and clothed than ever in their lives before, and they appear to have fewer inconvenient vices. They are simple, docile, and affectionate almost to the point of absurdity. The same men who stood fire in open field with perfect coolness, on the late expedition, have come to me blubbering in the most irresistibly ludicrous manner on being transferred from one company in the regiment to another. This morning I wandered about where different companies were target shooting, and their glee was contagious. Such exulting shouts of 'Ki! ole man,' when some steady old turkey-shooter brought his gun down for an instant's aim and unerringly hit the mark; and then, when some unwary youth fired his piece into the ground at half cock, such infinite guffawing and delight, such rolling over and over on the grass, such dances of ecstasy, as made the Ethiopian minstrelsy of the stage appear a feeble imitation."

COLORED INFANTRY AT FORT LINCOLN.

The first regiment of colored troops raised at the North was the Fifty-fourth Massachusetts, commanded by Col. Robert G. Shaw, who fell at their head in the desperate assault on Fort Wagner. The whole-heartedness with which, when once permitted to enlist, the colored soldiers entered into the war, is indicated by the fact that their enthusiasm added not only to the muskets in the field, but also to the music and poetry in the air. A private in the regiment just mentioned produced a song which, whatever its defects as poetry, can hardly be criticised for its sentiments.

Frémont told them, when the war it first begun,
How to save the Union, and the way it should be done;
But Kentucky swore so hard, and Old Abe he had his fears,
Till every hope was lost but the colored volunteers.

CHORUS.

Oh, give us a flag all free without a slave!
We'll fight to defend it as our fathers did so brave.
The gallant Comp'ny A will make the rebels dance;
And we'll stand by the Union, if we only have a chance.

McClellan went to Richmond with two hundred thousand brave;
He said, "Keep back the niggers," and the Union he would save.
Little Mac he had his way, still the Union is in tears:
Now they call for the help of the colored volunteers.
Cho.—Oh, give us a flag, etc.

Old Jeff says he'll hang us if we dare to meet him armed—
A very big thing, but we are not at all alarmed;
For he first has got to catch us before the way is clear,
And "that's what's the matter" with the colored volunteer.
Cho.—Oh, give us a flag, etc.

So rally, boys, rally! let us never mind the past.
We had a hard road to travel, but our day is coming fast;
For God is for the right, and we have no need to fear;
The Union must be saved by the colored volunteer.
Cho.—Oh, give us a flag, etc.

How many of them Jeff Davis did hang, or otherwise murder, will never be known; but it is certain that many of those captured were disposed of in some manner not in accordance with the laws of war. At the surrender of Port Hudson not a single colored man was found alive, although it was known that thirty-five had been taken prisoners by the Confederates during the siege. It is no wonder that when they did go into battle they fought with desperation. The first regular engagement in which they took part was the battle of Milliken's Bend, La., June 7, 1863; concerning which an eye-witness wrote:

THE "INTELLIGENT CONTRABAND."

"A force of about five hundred negroes, and two hundred men of the Twenty-third Iowa, belonging to the Second Brigade, Carr's division (the Twenty-third Iowa had been up the river with prisoners, and was on its way back to this place), was surprised in camp by a rebel force of about two thousand men. The first intimation that the commanding officer received was from one of the black men, who went into the colonel's tent, and said, 'Massa, the secesh are in camp.' The colonel ordered him to have the men load their guns at once. He instantly replied: 'We have done did that now, massa.' Before the colonel was ready, the men were in line, ready for action. As before stated, the rebels drove our force toward the gunboats, taking colored men prisoners and murdering them. This so enraged them that they rallied, and charged the enemy more heroically and desperately than has been recorded during the war. It was a genuine bayonet charge, a hand-to-hand fight, that has never occurred to any extent during this prolonged conflict. Upon both sides men were killed with the butts of muskets. White and black men were lying side by side, pierced by bayonets, and in some instances transfixed to the earth. In one instance, two men—one white and the other black—were found dead, side by side, each having the other's bayonet through his body. If facts prove to be what they are now represented, this engagement of Sunday morning will be recorded as the most desperate of this war. Broken limbs, broken heads, the mangling of bodies, all prove that it was a contest between enraged men—on the one side, from hatred to a race; and on the other, desire for self-preservation, revenge for past grievances and the inhuman murder of their comrades. One brave man took his former master prisoner, and brought him into camp with great gusto. A rebel prisoner made a particular request that his own negroes should not be placed over him as a guard."

Capt. M. M. Miller, who commanded a colored company in that action, said: "I went into the fight with thirty-three men, and had sixteen killed, eleven badly wounded, and four slightly. The enemy charged us so close that we fought with our bayonets hand to hand. I have six broken bayonets to show how bravely my men fought. The enemy cried, 'No quarter!' but some of them were very glad to take it when made prisoners. Not one of my men offered to leave his place until ordered to fall back. No negro was ever found alive that was taken a prisoner by the rebels in this fight."

MAJOR-GENERAL JOSEPH HOOKER.

CHAPTER XXI.

CHANCELLORSVILLE.

"FIGHTING JOE HOOKER"—LETTER FROM PRESIDENT LINCOLN—RESTORING THE DISCIPLINE OF THE ARMY—CAPTURING THE HEIGHTS OF FREDERICKSBURG—SKILLFUL MOVEMENT BY "STONEWALL" JACKSON—HEROIC CHARGE OF CAVALRY COMMANDED BY MAJOR PETER KEENAN—ACCIDENTAL SHOOTING OF GENERAL JACKSON—DEFEAT OF THE NATIONAL FORCES—GENERAL HOOKER'S EXPLANATION OF HIS FAILURE—NUMEROUS INTERESTING INCIDENTS.

AFTER Burnside's failure at Fredericksburg, he was superseded, January 25, 1863, by General Joseph Hooker, who had commanded one of his grand divisions. Hooker, now forty-eight years old, was a graduate of West Point, had seen service in the Florida and Mexican wars, had been through the peninsula campaign with McClellan, was one of our best corps commanders, and was a favorite with the soldiers, who called him "Fighting Joe Hooker." In giving the command to General Hooker, President Lincoln accompanied it with a remarkable letter, which not only exhibits his own peculiar genius, but suggests some of the complicated difficulties of the military and political situation. He wrote: "I have placed you at the head of the Army of the Potomac. Of course I have done this upon what appear to me sufficient reasons, and yet I think it best for you to know there are some things in regard to which I am not quite satisfied with you. I believe you to be a brave and skilful soldier, which of course I like. I also believe you do not mix politics with your profession, in which you are right. You have confidence in yourself, which is a valuable if not indispensable quality. You are ambitious, which, within reasonable bounds, does good rather than harm; but I think that during General Burnside's command of the army you have taken counsel of your ambition, and thwarted him as much as you could, in which you did a great wrong to the country, and to a most meritorious and honorable brother officer. I have heard, in such a way as to believe it, of your recently saying, that both the army and the government needed a dictator. Of course it was not for this, but in spite of it, that I have given you the command. Only those generals who gain successes can set up dictators. What I now ask of you is military success, and I will risk the dictatorship. The Government will support you to the utmost of its ability, which is neither more nor less than it has done and will do for all commanders. I much fear that the spirit which you have aided to infuse into the army, of criticising their commander, and withholding confidence from him, will now turn upon you. I shall assist you as far as I can to put it down. Neither you nor Napoleon, were he alive again, could get any good out of any army while such a spirit prevails in it. And now, beware of rashness! Beware of rashness! But with energy and sleepless vigilance go forward and give us victories."

Hooker restored the discipline of the Army of the Potomac, which had been greatly relaxed, reorganized it in corps, and opened the spring campaign with every promise of success. The army was still on the Rappahannock, opposite Fredericksburg, and he planned to cross over and strike Lee's left. Making a demonstration with Sedgwick's corps below the town, he moved a large part of his army up-stream, crossed quickly, and had forty-six thousand men at Chancellorsville before Lee guessed what he was about. This "ville" was only a single house, named from its owner. Eastward, between it and Fredericksburg, there was open country; west of it was the great thicket known as the Wilderness, in the depths of which, a year later, a bloody battle was fought.

Instead of advancing into the open country at once, and striking the enemy's flank, Hooker lost a day in inaction, which gave Lee time to learn what was going on and to make dispositions to meet the emergency. Leaving a small force to check Sedgwick, who had carried the heights of Fredericksburg, he moved toward Hooker with nearly all his army, May 1st, and attacked at various points, endeavoring to ascertain Hooker's exact position. By nightfall of this same day, Hooker appears to have lost confidence in the plans with which he set out, and been deserted by his old-time audacity; for instead of maintaining a tactical offensive, he drew back from some of his more advanced positions, formed his army in a semicircle, and awaited attack. His left and his centre were strongly posted and to some extent intrenched; but his right, consisting of Howard's corps, was "in the air," and, moreover, it faced the Wilderness. When this weak spot was discovered by the enemy, on the morning of the 2d, Lee sent Jackson with twenty-six thousand men to make a long detour, pass into the Wilderness, and, emerging suddenly from its eastern edge, take Howard by surprise. Jackson's men were seen and counted as they passed over the crest of a hill; they were even attacked by detachments from Sickles's corps; and Hooker sent orders to Howard to strengthen his position, advance his pickets, and not allow himself to be surprised. But Howard appears to have disregarded all precautions, and in the afternoon the enemy came down upon him, preceded by a rush of frightened wild animals driven from their cover in the woods by the advancing battle-line. Howard's corps was doubled up, thrown into confusion, and completely routed. The enemy was coming on exultingly, when General Sickles sent Gen. Alfred Pleasonton with two regiments of cavalry and a battery to occupy an advantageous position at Hazel Grove, which was the key-point of this part of the battlefield. Pleasonton arrived just in time to see that the Confederates were making toward the same point and were likely to secure it. There was but one way to save the army, and Pleasonton quickly comprehended it. He ordered Major Peter Keenan, with the Eighth Pennsylvania cavalry regiment, about four hundred strong, to charge immediately upon the ten thousand Confederate infantry. "It is the same as saying we must be killed," said Keenan, "but we'll do it." This charge, in which Keenan and most of his command were slain, astonished the enemy and stopped their onset, for they believed there must be some more formidable force behind it. *

In the precious minutes thus gained, Pleasonton brought together twenty-two guns, loaded them with double charges of canister, and had them depressed enough to make the shot strike the ground half-way between his own line and the edge of the woods where the enemy must emerge. When the Confederates resumed their charge, they were struck by such a storm of iron as nothing human could withstand; other troops were brought up to the support of the guns, and what little artillery the Confederates had advanced to the front was knocked to pieces.

Here, about dusk, General Jackson rode to the front to reconnoitre. As he rode back again with his staff, some of his own men, mistaking the horsemen for National cavalry, fired a volley at them, by which several were killed. Another volley inflicted three wounds upon Jackson; and as his frightened horse dashed into the woods, the general was thrown violently against the limb of a tree and injured still more. Afterward, when his men were bearing him off, a National battery opened fire down the road, one of the men was struck, and the general fell heavily to the ground. He finally reached the hospital, and his arm was amputated, but he died at the end of a week. Jackson's corps renewed its attack, under Gen. A. P. Hill, but without success, and Hill was wounded and borne from the field.

BREVET MAJOR-GENERAL D. N. COUCH.

MAJOR-GENERAL JOHN SEDGWICK.

The next morning, May 3d, it was renewed again under Stuart, the cavalry leader, and at the same time Lee attacked in front with his entire force. The Confederates had sustained a serious disaster the evening before, in the loss of Lee's ablest lieutenant; but now a more serious one befell the National army, for General Hooker was rendered insensible by the shock from a cannon-ball that struck a pillar of the Chancellor house, against which he was leaning. After this there was no plan or organization to the battle on the National side—though each corps commander held his own as well as he could, and the men fought valiantly—while Lee was at his best. The line was forced back to some strong intrenchments that had been prepared the night before, when Lee learned that Sedgwick had defeated the force opposed to him, captured Fredericksburg heights, and was promptly advancing upon the Confederate rear. Trusting that the force in his front would not advance upon him, Lee drew off a large detachment of his army and turned upon Sedgwick, who after a heavy fight was stopped, and with some difficulty succeeded in crossing the river after nightfall. Lee then turned again upon Hooker; but a great storm suspended operations for twenty-four hours, and the next night the National army all recrossed the Rappahannock, leaving on the field fourteen guns, thousands of small-arms, all their dead, and many of their wounded. In this battle or series of battles, the National loss was about seventeen thousand men, the Confederate about thirteen thousand. Hooker had commanded about one hundred and thirteen thousand five hundred, to Lee's sixty-two thousand (disregarding the different methods of counting in the two armies); but as usual they were not in action simultaneously; many were hardly in the fight at all, and at every point of actual contact, with the exception of Sedgwick's first engagement, the Confederates were superior in numbers.

Three general officers were killed in this battle. On the National side, Major-Gens. Hiram G. Berry and Amiel W. Whipple; on the Confederate side, Brig.-Gen. E. F. Paxton.

* This is the story of Keenan's charge as told by General Pleasonton, and generally accepted, which has been made the theme of much comment and several poems. Nobody questions that the charge was gallantly made, and resulted in heavy loss to the intrepid riders; but several participants have recorded their testimony that it did not take place by order of General Pleasonton or in any such manner as he relates—in fact, that it was rather an unexpected encounter with the enemy when the regiment was obeying orders to cross over from a point near Hazel Grove to the aid of General Howard. Among these is Gen. Pennock Huey, who was the senior major in command of the regiment, and was one of the few officers that survived the charge.

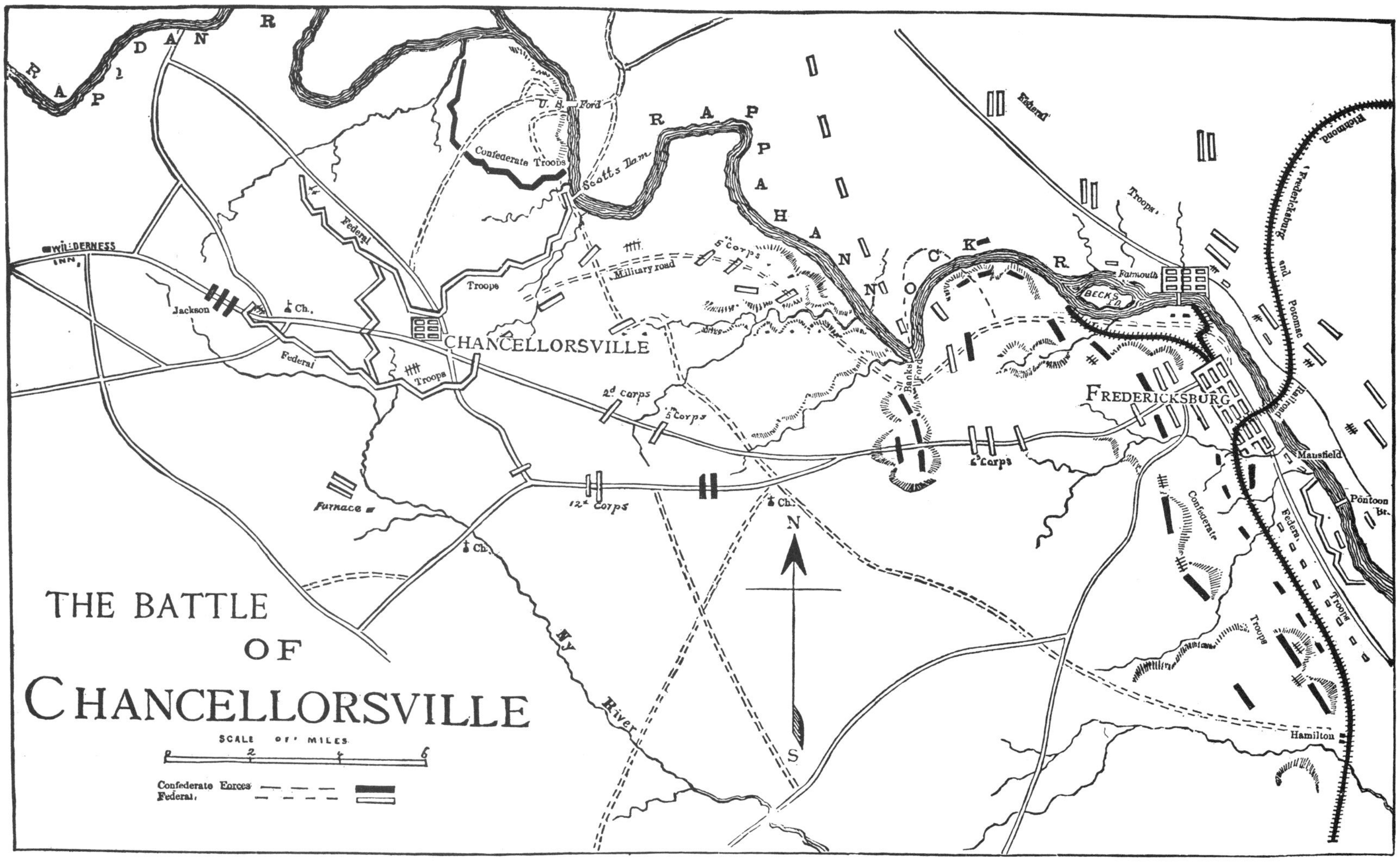

General Jackson, as already mentioned, was mortally wounded, and several others were hurt, some of them severely.

Sedgwick's part of this engagement is sometimes called the battle of Salem Heights, and sometimes the second battle of Fredericksburg.

Two coincidences are noticeable in this action. First, each commander made a powerful flank movement against his opponent's right, and neither of these movements was completely successful, although they were most gallantly and skilfully made. Second, each commander, in his after explanations accounting for his failure to push the fight any farther, declared that he could not conscientiously order his men to assail the strong intrenchments of the enemy.

General Hooker's explanation of his failure, so far as it could be explained, was given in a conversation with Samuel P. Bates, his literary executor, who visited the ground with him in 1876. Mr. Bates says: "Upon our arrival at the broad, open, rolling fields opposite Banks's Ford, three or four miles up the stream, General Hooker explained, waving his hand significantly: 'Here on this open ground I intended to fight my battle. But the trouble was to get my army on it, as the banks of the stream are, as you see, rugged and precipitous, and the few fords were strongly fortified and guarded by the enemy. By making a powerful demonstration in front of and below the town of Fredericksburg with a part of my army, I was able, unobserved, to withdraw the remainder, and, marching nearly thirty miles up the stream, to cross the Rappahannock and the Rapidan unopposed, and in four days' time to arrive at Chancellorsville, within five miles of this coveted ground. . . . But at midnight General Lee had moved out with his whole army, and by sunrise was in firm possession of Jackson's Ford, had thrown up this line of breastworks, which you can still follow with the eyes, and it was bristling with cannon from one end to the other. Before I had proceeded two miles the heads of my columns, while still upon the narrow roads in these interminable forests, where it was impossible to manœuvre my forces, were met by Jackson with a full two-thirds of the entire Confederate army. I had no alternative but to turn back, as I had only a fragment of my command in hand, and take up the position about Chancellorsville which I had occupied during the night, as I was being rapidly outflanked upon my right, the enemy having open ground on which to operate. . . . Very early on the first day of the battle I rode along the whole line and examined every part, suggesting some changes and counselling extreme vigilance. Upon my return to headquarters I was informed that a continuous column of the enemy had been marching past my front since early in the morning. This put an entirely new phase upon the problem, and filled me with apprehension for the safety of my right wing, which was posted to meet a front attack from the south, but was in no condition for a flank attack from the west. I immediately dictated a despatch to Generals Slocum and Howard, saying that I had good reason to believe that the enemy was moving to our right, and that they must be ready to meet an attack from the west. . . . The failure of Howard to hold his ground cost us our position, and I was forced, in the presence of the enemy, to take up a new one.'" *

* "Battles and Leaders of the Civil War," vol. iii. p. 217, *et seq.*

BATTLE OF CHANCELLORSVILLE, SUNDAY, MAY 3, 1863.—REPELLING ATTACK OF CONFEDERATES.

General Howard says he did not receive that despatch, and in his report he gave the following reasons for the disaster that overtook his corps: "I. Though constantly threatened and apprised of the moving of the enemy, yet the woods were so dense that he was able to mass a large force, whose exact whereabouts neither patrols, reconnoissances, nor scouts ascertained. He succeeded in forming a column opposite to and outflanking my right. II. By the panic produced by the enemy's reverse fire, regiments and artillery were thrown suddenly upon those in position. III. The absence of General Barlow's brigade, which I had previously located in reserve and *en echelon* with Colonel Von Gilsa's, so as to cover his right flank. This was the only general reserve I had."

Every such battle has its interesting incidents, generally enough to fill a volume, and they are seldom repeated. Some of the most interesting incidents of Chancellorsville are told by Capt. Henry N. Blake, of the Eleventh Massachusetts Regiment. Here are a few of them:

"A man who was loading his musket threw away the cartridge, with a fearful oath about government contractors; and I noticed that the paper was filled with fine grains of dry earth instead of gunpowder. In the thickest of the firing an officer seized an excited soldier—who discharged his piece with trembling hands near the ears, and endangered the lives, of his comrades—and kicked him into the centre of the road. Trade prospered throughout the day, and the United States sharp-shooters were constantly exchanging their dark green caps for the regulation hats which were worn by the regiment. The captain of one of the companies of skirmishers was posted near a brook at the base of a slight ascent upon which the enemy was massed, and there was a scattering fire of bullets which cautioned all to 'lie down.' While he was rectifying the alignment he perceived with amazement one of his men, who sat astride a log and washed his hands and face, and then cleansed the towel with a piece of soap which he carried. One sharp-shooter shielded himself behind a blanket; and another concealed himself behind an empty cracker-box, the sides of which were half an inch in thickness, exposed his person as little as possible, and felt as secure as the ostrich with his head buried in the sand.

LIEUTENANT-GENERAL THOMAS J. ("STONEWALL") JACKSON, C. S. A.

MAJOR PETER KEENAN.

MAJOR-GENERAL HIRAM G. BERRY.

"The ominous silence of the sharp-shooters in front was a sure indication that the main force was approaching; and a rebel officer, upon the left, brought every man into his place in the ranks by exclaiming to his command: 'Forward, double-quick, march! Guide left!' The hideous yells once more disclosed their position in the dark woods; but the volleys of buck and ball, and the recollection of the previous repulse, quickly hushed their outcries, and they were again vanquished. The conflict upon the left still continued, and the defeated soldiers began to reinforce the troops that were striving by desperate efforts to pierce the line, until a company swept the road with its fire and checked the movement, and only one or two rebels at intervals leaped across the deadly chasm. A demand for ammunition was now heard—the most fearful cry of distress in a battle—and every man upon the right contributed a few cartridges, which were carried to the scene of action in the hats of the donors. The forty rounds which fill the magazines are sufficient for any combat, unless the troops are protected by earthworks or a natural barrier; and the extra cartridges, which must be placed in the pockets and knapsacks, are seldom used.

"It was after sunset; but the flashes of the rifles in the darkness were the targets at which the guns were fired, until the enemy retired at nine P.M., and the din of musketry was succeeded by the groans of the wounded. The song of the whippoorwills increased the gloom that pervaded the forest; and the pickets carefully listened to them, because the hostile skirmishers might signal to each other by imitating the mournful notes. The rebels gave a yell as soon as they were beyond the range of Union bullets, and repeated it in tones which grew more distinct when they had retreated a great distance and considered themselves safe. The abatis upon the extreme left was set on fire in this prolonged struggle; and a gallant sergeant—who fell at Gettysburg—sprang over the work, and averted the most serious results by pouring water from the canteens of his comrades until the flames were extinguished. The skirmishers began to exchange shots at daybreak upon May 3d, and a bullet penetrated the head of a lieutenant who was asleep in the adjoining company, and he never moved. There was a ceaseless roll of musketry; at half-past five A.M. the batteries emitted destructive charges of canister, and most of the men in the ranks of the support crouched upon the ground while the balls passed over them. For two hours the hordes of Jackson, encouraged by their easy victory upon May 2d, screamed like fiends, assailed the troops that defended the plank road, and succeeded in turning their left, and compelling them to retire through the forest, and re-form their shattered lines. There was no running: the soldiers fell back slowly, company after company, and wished for some directing mind to select a new position. Unfortunately the National cause had lost General Berry, the brave commander of the division; the ranking brigadier, General Mott, was wounded; another brigadier was an arrant coward; and the largest part of nine regiments were marched three miles to the rear by one of the generals without any orders. The regiments of the brigade, under the supervision of their field and line officers, rallied in the open field near the Chancellor house, which was the focus upon which Lee concentrated his batteries, until the shells ignited it; and the flames consumed some of the wounded who were helpless, and three women that remained in the cellar for safety barely escaped from the ruins. The brigade was aligned upon the road to the United States ford at nine A.M., and the men recovered their knapsacks in the midst of a heavy cannonading which still continued. No symptoms of fear were manifested, although the artillery was planted upon the left, in the rear and the front, from which point most of the shells were hurled; and the force was threatened with capture. A rebel and a member of the brigade rested together near an oak, and mutually assisted each other to fight the fire in the forest, that began raging while the battle was in progress; and joyfully clasped their scorched and aching hands in friendship when it was quelled. Colors were captured, and hundreds of the foe threw down their arms and retreated with the Union forces; and happy squads without any guard were walking upon the road, and inquiring the way to the rear. Three batteries lost most of their horses, and a large proportion of their men, by the concentration of Lee's artillery, and the bullets of the sharp-shooters, who were specially instructed to pick off the animals before they shot the gunners. Several pieces, including one without wheels, which had been demolished, were drawn from the field by details from the infantry. Some of those who were slightly injured returned to their commands after their wounds had been dressed, and fought again. One cannon-ball killed a cavalryman and his horse; and a shell tore the clothing from an aid, but inflicted no personal hurt, and he returned, after a brief absence, to search for his porte-monnaie, which he carried in the pocket that had been so suddenly wrested from him.

"The corps color was always waving in the front; and General Sickles, smoking a cigar, stood a few feet from the regiment, in the road up which the troops had marched from the Chancellor house; and aids and orderlies were riding to and fro, one of whom reported that his steed had been killed. 'Captain, the Government will furnish you with another horse,' he complacently replied.

"A rebel officer of high rank, who had been captured, stopped

JACKSON'S ATTACK ON RIGHT WING AT CHANCELLORSVILLE.

near the general, and sought to open a conversation, with the following result:

"'General, I have met you in New York.'

"'Move forward that battery.'

"'General, I have seen you before.'

"'The brigade must advance to the woods.

"'General, don't you remember'—

"'Go to the rear, sir; my troops are now in position.'

"There were few, if any, stretcher bearers at the front, and wounded men that had lost a leg or an arm dragged themselves to the field-hospital; and the surgeons of some regiments which had not been engaged in the battle sat upon a log in idleness, and refused, with a great display of dignity, to assist the suffering who were brought to them, because they did not belong to their commands. This shameful conduct, which I often witnessed, exasperated the officers and soldiers; and they compelled the surgeons to discharge their duty in a number of cases by threatening to shoot them. The heat was very severe; many cannoneers divested themselves of their uniforms while they were working; and a number of the skirmishers, who were posted in the open field, and obliged to lie low without any shelter, were sometimes afflicted by sunstroke. 'I will win a star or a coffin in this battle,' remarked a colonel as he was riding to the scene of conflict in which a bullet checked his noble military aspirations. 'To take a soldier without ambition is to pull off his spurs.' 'I have got my leave of absence now,' gladly said an officer, whose application had always been refused at headquarters, when he left the regiment to go to the hospital. The appearance of a rabbit causes an excitement and a chase upon all occasions, and one ran in front of the line as the action commenced; and the birds were flying wildly among the trees, as if they anticipated a storm; and a soldier shouted, 'Stop him, stop him! I could make a good meal if I had him.' 'This is English neutrality,' an intelligent metal moulder remarked, in examining the fragment of a shell, and explaining the process of its manufacture to the company; while the rebel batteries every minute added some specimens to his collection. The officials in Richmond published at this time an order, directing that the clothing should be taken from the bodies of their dead and issued to the living. They always stripped the dead and the dying upon every field; and I noticed that one man who had been stunned, and afterward effected his escape, wore merely a shirt and hat when he entered the lines. An officer who was going the rounds in the night was surprised to find one of his most faithful men who returned no answer to his inquiries; and supposing that he had been overcome by fatigue, and fallen asleep, grasped his hands to awaken him: but they were cold with death. The soldier, killed upon his post of duty, rested in the extreme front, with his musket by his side, and face toward the enemies of his country. General Whipple, the able commander of the third division of the corps, was mortally wounded by a sharp-shooter who was one-third of a mile from him; and a priest administered the last rites of the Roman Catholic Church upon the spot where he fell, in the presence of his weeping staff and soldiers, by whom he was greatly beloved. A brigade made a reconnoissance in the forest at one P.M., and captured forty sharp-shooters who were perched upon the limbs of lofty oaks, and could not descend and escape before this force advanced.

"The rebels ascertained the location of the trains upon the north bank of the Rappahannock, opened a battery upon them, and a squad of three hundred prisoners uttered a yell of joy when they saw a cannon-ball enter a large tent which was crowded with the dying and disabled. The direction of the firing was changed, and caused utter dismay when some of the number were killed by the missiles that were hurled by their comrades in the army of Lee."

BRIGADIER-GENERAL J. H. VAN ALLEN.
(Aide-de-Camp to General Hooker.)

OFFICERS SETTING OUT TO MAKE CALLS OF CEREMONY ON THEIR GENERALS.

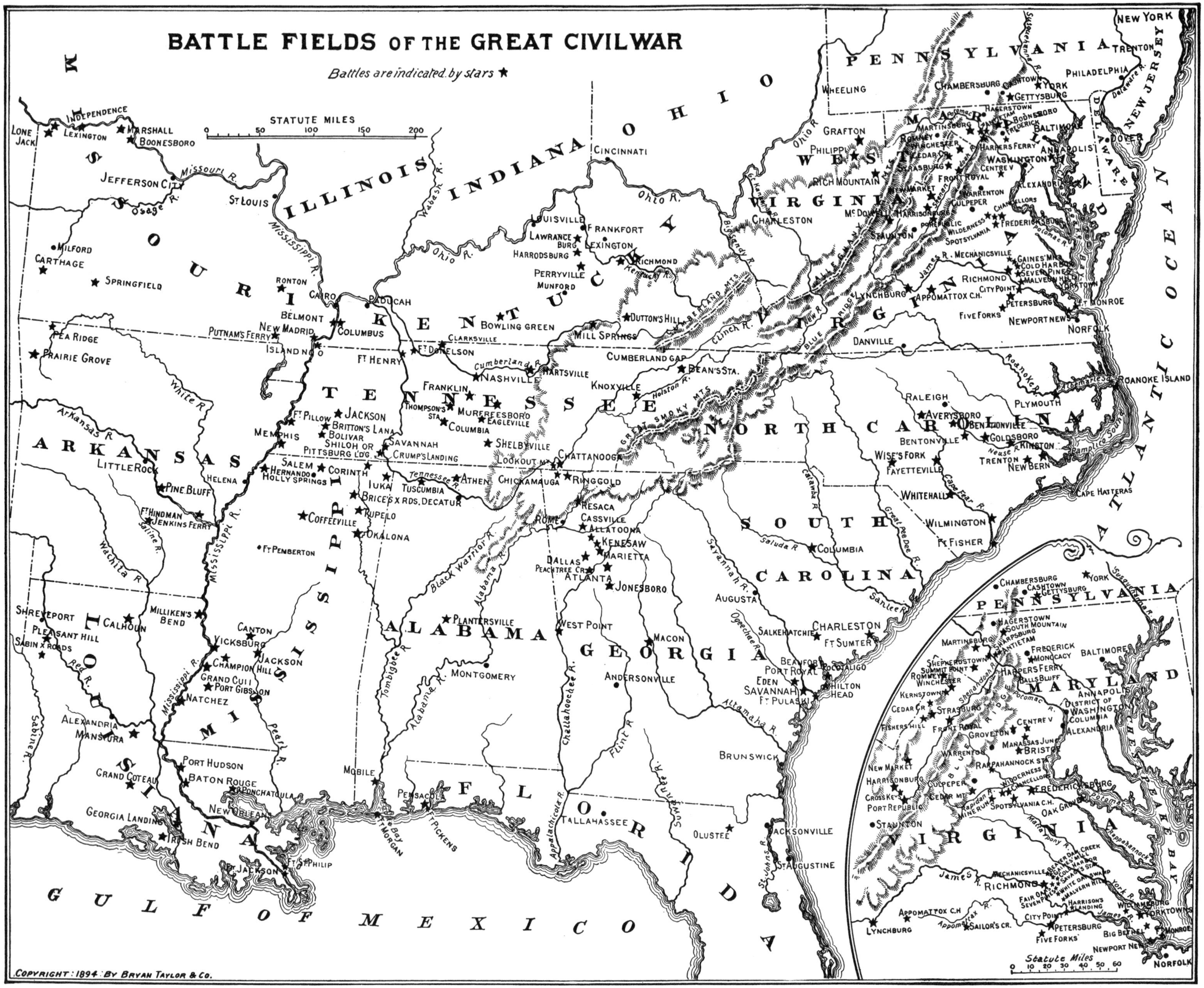
BATTLE FIELDS OF THE GREAT CIVIL WAR
Battles are indicated by stars ★
STATUTE MILES
0 50 100 150 200
MISSOURI
ILLINOIS
INDIANA
OHIO
KENTUCKY
TENNESSEE
ARKANSAS
LOUISIANA
MISSISSIPPI
ALABAMA
GEORGIA
FLORIDA
SOUTH CAROLINA
NORTH CAROLINA
VIRGINIA
WEST VIRGINIA
PENNSYLVANIA
MARYLAND
DELAWARE
NEW JERSEY
NEW YORK
ATLANTIC OCEAN
GULF OF MEXICO
LONE JACK
INDEPENDENCE
LEXINGTON
MARSHALL
BOONESBORO
JEFFERSON CITY
ST. LOUIS
MILFORD
CARTHAGE
SPRINGFIELD
PEA RIDGE
PRAIRIE GROVE
RONTON
CAIRO
BELMONT
NEW MADRID
COLUMBUS
PUTNAM'S FERRY
ISLAND NO. 10
PADUCAH
CINCINNATI
LOUISVILLE
FRANKFORT
LEXINGTON
LAWRENCE BURG
HARRODSBURG
RICHMOND
PERRYVILLE
MUNFORD
BOWLING GREEN
DUTTON'S HILL
MILL SPRINGS
CLARKSVILLE
FT. DONELSON
FT. HENRY
CUMBERLAND GAP
BEAN'S STA.
HARTSVILLE
NASHVILLE
FRANKLIN
KNOXVILLE
THOMPSON'S STA.
MURFREESBORO
EAGLEVILLE
COLUMBIA
SHELBYVILLE
FT. PILLOW
JACKSON
BRITTON'S LANA
BOLIVAR
MEMPHIS
SHILOH OR PITTSBURG LDG.
SAVANNAH
CRUMP'S LANDING
SALEM
HERNANDO
HOLLY SPRINGS
CORINTH
IUKA
TUSCUMBIA
ATHENS
BRICE'S X RDS.
DECATUR
TUPELO
OKALONA
COFFEEVILLE
FT. PEMBERTON
CHATTANOOGA
LOOKOUT MT.
CHICKAMAUGA
RINGGOLD
RESACA
CASSVILLE
ROME
ALLATOONA
KENESAW
MARIETTA
DALLAS
PEACHTREE CR.
ATLANTA
JONESBORO
LITTLE ROCK
PINE BLUFF
HELENA
FT. HINDMAN
JENKINS FERRY
SHREVEPORT
PLEASANT HILL
SABIN X ROADS
CALHOUN
MILLIKEN'S BEND
CANTON
VICKSBURG
CHAMPION HILL
JACKSON
GRAND GULF
PORT GIBSON
NATCHEZ
ALEXANDRIA
MANSURA
PORT HUDSON
BATON ROUGE
GRAND COTEAU
PONCHATOULA
NEW ORLEANS
GEORGIA LANDING
IRISH BEND
FT. JACKSON
FT. ST. PHILIP
MOBILE
FT. MORGAN
PENSACOLA
FT. PICKENS
PLANTERSVILLE
MONTGOMERY
WEST POINT
MACON
ANDERSONVILLE
TALLAHASSEE
OLUSTEE
JACKSONVILLE
ST. AUGUSTINE
BRUNSWICK
AUGUSTA
SAVANNAH
EDEN
FT. PULASKI
PORT ROYAL
BEAUFORT
POCOTALIGO
HILTON HEAD
SALKEHATCHIE
CHARLESTON
FT. SUMTER
COLUMBIA
WILMINGTON
FT. FISHER
WHITEHALL
WISE'S FORK
FAYETTEVILLE
BENTONVILLE
GOLDSBORO
KINSTON
TRENTON
NEW BERN
RALEIGH
AVERYSBORO
PLYMOUTH
ROANOKE ISLAND
CAPE HATTERAS
DANVILLE
WHEELING
GRAFTON
PHILIPPI
RICH MOUNTAIN
CHARLESTON
McDOWELL
STAUNTON
LYNCHBURG
APPOMATTOX C.H.
FIVE FORKS
PETERSBURG
CITY POINT
RICHMOND
MALVERN HILL
SEVEN PINES
COLD HARBOR
GAINES' MILL
MECHANICSVILLE
NEWPORT NEWS
NORFOLK
FT. MONROE
YORKTOWN
FREDERICKSBURG
CHANCELLORSVILLE
WILDERNESS
SPOTSYLVANIA
WARRENTON
CULPEPER
FRONT ROYAL
WINCHESTER
MARTINSBURG
HARPERS FERRY
WASHINGTON
ANNAPOLIS
BALTIMORE
FREDERICK
BOONESBORO
HAGERSTOWN
CHAMBERSBURG
CASHTOWN
GETTYSBURG
YORK
PHILADELPHIA
TRENTON
DOVER
Mississippi R.
Missouri R.
Osage R.
Ohio R.
Wabash R.
Tennessee R.
Cumberland R.
Kentucky R.
Big Sandy R.
Gt. Kanawha R.
Clinch R.
Holston R.
New R.
James R.
Roanoke R.
Neuse R.
Cape Fear R.
Great Pee Dee R.
Santee R.
Catawba R.
Saluda R.
Savannah R.
Ogeechee R.
Altamaha R.
Flint R.
Chattahoochee R.
Apalachicola R.
Suwanee R.
St. Johns R.
Alabama R.
Tombigbee R.
Black Warrior R.
Pearl R.
Red R.
Wachita R.
Saline R.
Arkansas R.
White R.
Sabine R.
Susquehanna R.
Delaware R.
Potomac R.
BLUE RIDGE
ALLEGHANY MTS.
CUMBERLAND MTS.
GREAT SMOKY MTS.
PENNSYLVANIA
MARYLAND
VIRGINIA
CHESAPEAKE BAY
DISTRICT OF COLUMBIA
WASHINGTON
ALEXANDRIA
SOUTH MOUNTAIN
ANTIETAM
MONOCACY
SHEPHERDSTOWN
SUMMIT POINT
ROMNEY
KERNSTOWN
CEDAR CR.
STRASBURG
FISHERS HILL
NEW MARKET
HARRISONBURG
CROSS KEYS
PORT REPUBLIC
CEDAR MT.
GROVETON
MANASSAS JUN.
BRISTOE
CENTREVILLE
BALLS BLUFF
RAPPAHANNOCK STA.
MINE RUN
SPOTSYLVANIA C.H.
OAK GROVE
SAILOR'S CR.
HARRISON'S LANDING
WILLIAMSBURG
BIG BETHEL
Statute Miles
0 10 20 30 40 50 60
COPYRIGHT: 1894: BY BRYAN TAYLOR & CO.

CEMETERY GATE.

CHAPTER XXII.

GETTYSBURG.

INVASION OF THE NORTH DETERMINED ON—CAVALRY SKIRMISH AT FLEETWOOD, WHICH MARKS A TURNING POINT IN THAT SERVICE—HOOKER'S PLANS—HE ASKS TO BE RELIEVED—MEADE IN COMMAND—BATTLE OF GETTYSBURG—POSITION OF CONFEDERATE FORCES—NUMBER OF MEN ENGAGED ON EACH SIDE—SURFACE OF THE COUNTRY ABOUT GETTYSBURG—BLOODY FIGHTING ON THE RIGHT—GENERAL HANCOCK SUPERSEDES GENERAL HOWARD—RAPID CONCENTRATION OF THE ARMIES—TERRIFIC FIGHTING IN THE PEACH ORCHARD—DRAMATIC CHARGE OF THE LOUISIANA TIGERS—THE CHARGE OF PICKETT'S BRIGADE—ROMANTIC AND PATHETIC INCIDENTS OF THE BATTLE—RETREAT OF THE CONFEDERATE ARMIES—VICTORY DUE TO DETERMINATION AND COURAGE OF THE COMMON SOLDIERS—EFFECT OF THE CONFEDERATE DEFEAT IN EUROPE—GREAT NATIONAL CEMETERY ON THE BATTLEFIELD—LINCOLN'S GETTYSBURG ADDRESS.

AFTER the battles of Fredericksburg and Chancellorsville, public opinion in the South began to demand that the army under Lee should invade the North, or at least make a bold movement toward Washington. Public opinion is not often very discriminating in an exciting crisis; and on this occasion public opinion failed to discriminate between the comparative ease with which an army in a strong position may repel a faultily planned or badly managed attack, and the difficulties that must beset the same army when it leaves its base, launches forth into the enemy's country, and is obliged to maintain a constantly lengthening line of communication. The Southern public could not see why, since the Army of Northern Virginia had won two victories on the Rappahannock, it might not march forward at once, lay New York and Philadelphia under contribution, and dictate peace and Southern independence in the Capitol at Washington. Whether the Confederate Government shared this feeling or not, it acted in accordance with it; and whether Lee approved it or not, he was obliged to obey. Yet, in the largest consideration of the problem, this demand for an invasion of the North was correct, though the result proved disastrous. For experience shows that purely defensive warfare will not accomplish anything. Lee's army had received a heavy reinforcement by the arrival of Longstreet's corps, its regiments had been filled up with conscripts, it had unbounded confidence in itself, and this was the time, if ever, to put the plan for independence to the crucial test of offensive warfare. Many subsidiary considerations strengthened the argument. About thirty thousand of Hooker's men had been enlisted in the spring of 1861, for two years, and their term was now expiring. Vicksburg was besieged by Grant, before whom nothing had stood as yet; and its fall would open the Mississippi and cut the Confederacy in two, which might seal the fate of the new Government unless the shock were neutralized by a great victory in the East. Volunteering had fallen off in the North, conscription was resorted to, the Democratic party there had become more hostile to the Government and loudly abusive of President Lincoln and his advisers, and there were signs of riotous resistance to a draft. Finally, the Confederate agents in Europe reported that anything like a great Confederate victory would secure immediate recognition, if not armed intervention, from England and France.

Hooker, who had lost a golden opportunity by his aberration or his accident at Chancellorsville, had come to his senses again, and was alert, active, and clear-headed. As early as May 28, 1863, he informed the President that something was stirring in the camp on the other side of the river, and that a northward movement might be expected. On the 3d of June, Lee began his movement, and by the 8th two of his three corps (those of Ewell and Longstreet) were at Culpeper, while A. P. Hill's corps still held the lines on the Rappahannock.

It was known that the entire Confederate cavalry, under Stuart, was at Culpeper; and Hooker sent all his cavalry, under Pleasonton, with two brigades of infantry, to attack it there. The assault was to be made in two converging columns, under Buford and Gregg; but this plan was disconcerted by the fact that the enemy's cavalry, intent upon masking the movement of the great body of infantry and protecting its flank, had advanced to Brandy Station. Here it was struck first by Buford and afterward by Gregg, and there was bloody fighting, with the advantage at first in favor of the National troops; but the two columns failed to unite during the action, and finally withdrew. The loss was over five hundred men on each side, including among the killed Col. B. F. Davis, of the Eighth New York cavalry, and Colonel Hampton, commanding a Confederate brigade. Both sides claimed to have accomplished their object—Pleasonton to have ascertained the movements of Lee's army, and Stuart to have driven back his opponent. Some of the heaviest fighting was for possession of a height known as Fleetwood Hill, and the Confederates name the action the battle of Fleetwood. It is of special interest as marking the turning-point in cavalry service during the war. Up to that time the Confederate cavalry had been generally superior to the National. This action—a cavalry fight in the proper sense of the term, between the entire mounted forces of the two armies—was a drawn battle; and thenceforth the National cavalry exhibited superiority in an accelerating ratio, till finally nothing mounted on Southern horses could stand before the magnificent squadrons led by Sheridan, Custer, Kilpatrick, and Wilson.

Hooker now knew that the movement he had anticipated was in progress, and he was very decided in his opinion as to what should be done. By the 13th of June, Lee had advanced Ewell's corps beyond the Blue Ridge, and it was marching down the Shenandoah Valley, while Hill's was still in the intrenchments on the Rapidan, and Longstreet's was midway between, at Culpeper. Hooker asked to be allowed to interpose his whole army between these widely separated parts of its antagonist and defeat them in detail; but with a man like Halleck for military adviser at Washington, it was useless to propose any bold or brilliant stroke. Hooker was forbidden to do this, and ordered to keep his army between the enemy and the capital. He therefore left

MAJOR-GENERAL JOHN BUFORD.

MAJOR-GENERAL ALFRED PLEASONTON.

MAJOR-GENERAL J. F. REYNOLDS.

his position on the Rappahannock, and moved toward Washington, along the line of the Orange and Alexandria Railroad. Ewell moved rapidly down the Shenandoah Valley, and attacked Winchester, which was held by General Milroy with about ten thousand men. Milroy made a gallant defence; but after a stubborn fight his force was broken and defeated, and about four thousand of them became prisoners. The survivors escaped to Harper's Ferry.

The corps of Hill and Longstreet now moved, Hill following Ewell into the Shenandoah Valley, and Longstreet skirting the Blue Ridge along its eastern base. Pleasonton's cavalry, reconnoitring these movements, met Stuart's again at Aldie, near a gap in the Bull Run Mountains, and had a sharp fight; and there were also cavalry actions at Middleburg and Upperville. Other Confederate cavalry had already crossed the Potomac, made a raid as far as Chambersburg, and returned with supplies to Ewell. On the 22d, Ewell's corps crossed at Shepherdstown and Williamsport, and moved up the Cumberland Valley to Chambersburg. A panic ensued among the inhabitants of that region, who hastened to drive off their cattle and horses, to save them from seizure. The governors of New York and Pennsylvania were called upon for militia, and forwarded several regiments, to be interposed between the enemy's advance and Philadelphia and Harrisburg. The other two corps of Lee's army crossed the Potomac on the 24th and 25th, where Ewell had crossed; and Hooker, moving on a line nearer Washington, crossed with his whole army at Edward's Ferry, on the 25th and 26th, marching thence to Frederick. He now proposed to send Slocum's corps to the western side of the South Mountain range, have it unite with a force of eleven thousand men under French, that lay useless at Harper's Ferry, and throw a powerful column upon Lee's communications, capture his trains, and attack his army in the rear. But again he came into collision with the stubborn Halleck, who would not consent to the abandonment, even temporarily, of Harper's Ferry, though the experience of the Antietam campaign, when he attempted to hold it in the same way and lost its whole garrison, should have taught him better. This new cause of trouble, added to previous disagreements, was more than Hooker could stand, and on the 27th he asked to be relieved from command of the army. His request was promptly complied with, and the next morning the command was given to General Meade, only five days before a great battle.

George Gordon Meade, then in his forty-ninth year, was a graduate of West Point, had served through the Mexican war, had done engineer duty in the survey of the Great Lakes, had been with McClellan on the peninsula, and had commanded a corps in the Army of the Potomac at Antietam, at Fredericksburg, and at Chancellorsville. The first thing he did on assuming command was what Hooker had been forbidden to do: he ordered the evacuation of Harper's Ferry, and the movement of its garrison to Frederick as a reserve.

At this time, June 28th, one portion of Lee's army was at Chambersburg, or between that place and Gettysburg, another at York and Carlisle, and a part of his cavalry was within sight of the spires of Harrisburg. The main body of the cavalry had gone off on a raid, Stuart having an ambition to ride a third time around the Army of the Potomac. This absence of his cavalry left Lee in ignorance of the movements of his adversary, whom he appears to have expected to remain quietly on the south side of the Potomac. When suddenly he found his communications in danger, he called back Ewell from York and Carlisle, and ordered the concentration of all his forces at Gettysburg. Many converging roads lead into that town, and its convenience for such concentration was obvious. Meade was also advancing his army toward Gettysburg, though with a more certain step—as was necessary, since his object was to find Lee's army and fight it, wherever it might go. His cavalry, under Pleasonton, was doing good service; and that general advanced a division under Buford on the 29th to Gettysburg, with orders to delay the enemy till the army could come up. Meade had some expectation of bringing on the great battle at Pipe Creek, southeast of Gettysburg, where he marked out a good defensive line; but the First Corps, under Gen. John F. Reynolds, advanced rapidly to Gettysburg, and on the 1st of July encountered west of the town a portion of the enemy coming in from Chambersburg. Lee had about seventy-three thousand five hundred men (infantry and artillery), and Meade about eighty-two thousand, while the cavalry numbered about eleven thousand on each side, and both armies had more cannon than they could use.*

When Reynolds advanced his own corps (the First) and determined to hold Gettysburg, he ordered the Eleventh (Howard's) to come up to its support. The country about Gettysburg is broken into ridges, mainly parallel, and running north and south. On the first ridge west of the village stood a theological seminary, which gave it the name of Seminary Ridge. Between this and the next is a small stream called Willoughby Run, and here the first day's battle was fought. Buford held the ridges till the infantry arrived, climbing in the belfry of the seminary and looking anxiously for their coming. The Confederates were advancing by two roads that met in a point at the edge of the village, and Reynolds disposed his troops, as fast as they arrived, so as to dispute the passage on both roads. The key-point was a piece of high ground, partly covered with woods, between the roads, and the advance of both sides rushed for it. Here General Reynolds, going forward to survey the ground, was shot by a sharp-shooter and fell dead. He was one of the ablest corps commanders that the Army of the Potomac ever had. The command devolved upon Gen. Abner Doubleday, who was an experienced soldier, having served through the Mexican war, been second in command under Anderson at Fort Sumter, and seen almost constant service with the Army of the Potomac. The Confederate force contending for the woods was Archer's brigade; the National was Meredith's "Iron Brigade." Archer's men had been told that they would meet nothing but Pennsylvania militia, which they expected to brush out of the way with little trouble; but when they saw the Iron Brigade, some of them were heard saying: "'Taint no militia; there are the —— black-hatted fellows again; it's the Army of the Potomac!" The result here was that Meredith's men not only secured the woods, but captured General Archer and a large part of his brigade, and then advanced to the ridge west of the run.

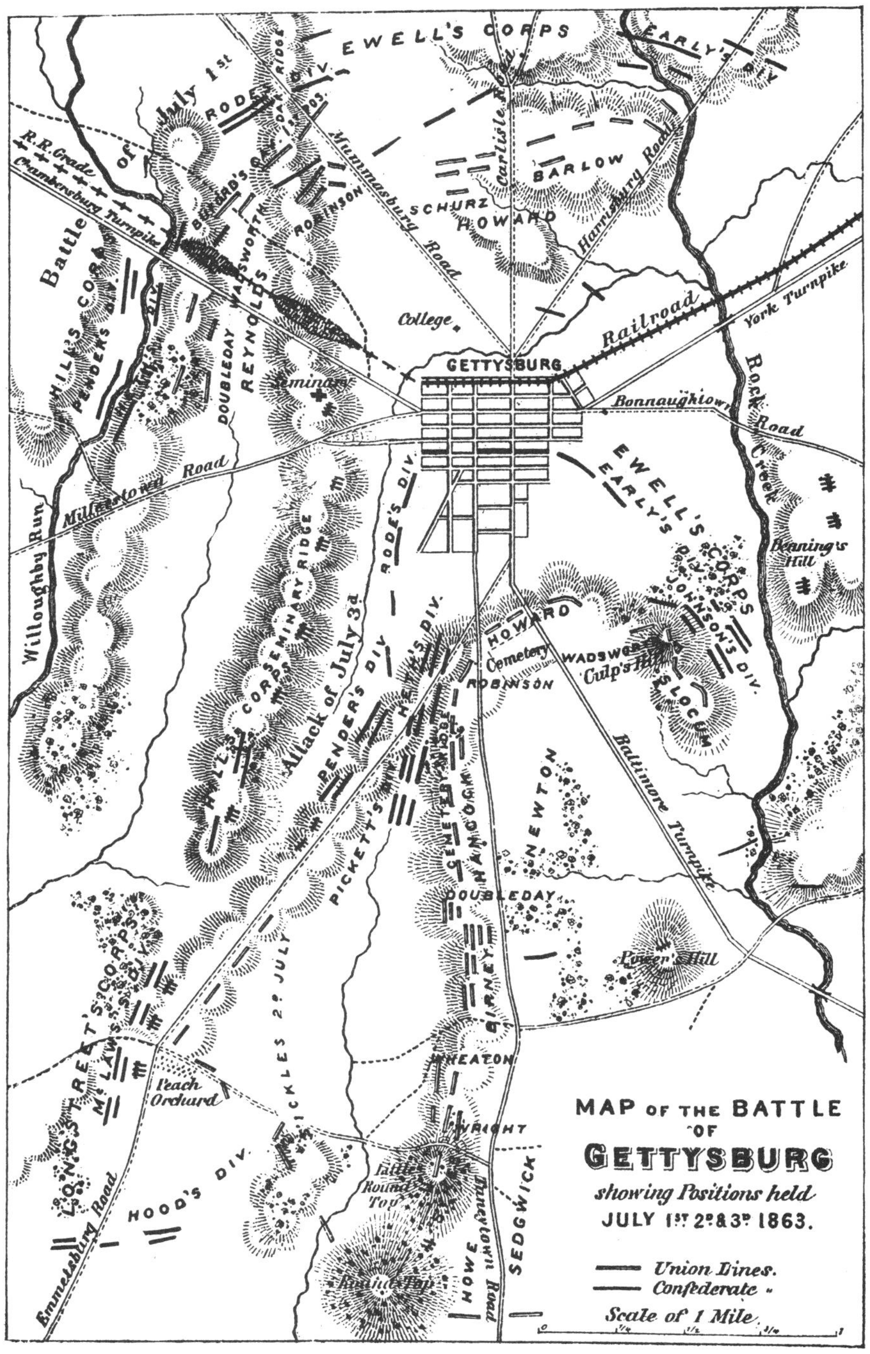

Reproduced by permission of Dick & Fitzgerald, N. Y., from "Twelve Decisive Battles of the War."

On the right of the line there had been bloody fighting, with unsatisfactory results, owing to the careless posting of regiments and a want of concert in action. Two National regiments were driven from the field, and a gun was lost; while on the other hand a Confederate force was driven into a railroad cut for shelter, and then subjected to an enfilading fire through the cut, so that a large portion were captured and the remainder dispersed.

Whether any commander on either side intended to bring on a battle at this point, is doubtful. But both sides were rapidly and heavily reinforced, and both fought with determination. The struggle for the Chambersburg road was obstinate, especially after the Confederates had planted several guns to sweep it. "We have come to stay," said Roy Stone's brigade, as they came into line under the fire of these guns to support a battery of their own; and "the battle afterward became so severe that

* Various figures and estimates are given as representing the strength of the two armies, some of which take account of detachments absent on special duty, and some do not. The figures here given denote very nearly the forces actually available for the battle.

the greater portion did stay," says General Doubleday. A division of Ewell's corps soon arrived from Carlisle, wheeled into position, and struck the right of the National line. Robinson's division, resting on Seminary Ridge, was promptly brought forward to meet this new peril, and was so skilfully handled that it presently captured three North Carolina regiments.

Gen. Oliver O. Howard, being the ranking officer, assumed command when he arrived on this part of the field; and when his own corps (the Eleventh) came up, about one o'clock, he placed it in position on the right, prolonging the line of battle far around to the north of the town. This great extension made it weak at many points; and as fresh divisions of Confederate troops were constantly arriving, under Lee's general order to concentrate on the town, they finally became powerful enough to break through the centre, rolling back the right flank of the First Corps and the left of the Eleventh, and throwing into confusion everything except the left of the First Corps, which retired in good order, protecting artillery and ambulances. Of the fugitives that swarmed through the town, about five thousand were made prisoners. But this had been effected only at heavy cost to the Confederates. At one point Iverson's Georgia brigade had rushed up to a stone fence behind which Baxter's brigade was sheltered, when Baxter's men suddenly rose and delivered a volley that struck down five hundred of Iverson's in an instant, while the remainder, who were subjected also to a cross-fire, immediately surrendered—all but one regiment, which escaped by raising a white flag.

In the midst of the confusion, Gen. Winfield S. Hancock arrived, under orders from General Meade to supersede Howard in the command of that wing of the army. He had been instructed also to choose a position for the army to meet the great shock of battle, if he should find a better one than the line of Pike Creek. Hancock's first duty was to rally the fugitives and restore order and confidence. Steinwehr's division was in reserve on Cemetery Ridge, and Buford's cavalry was on the plain between the town and the ridge; and with these standing fast he stopped the retreat and rapidly formed a line along that crest.

The ridge begins in Round Top, a high, rocky hill; next north of this is Little Round Top, smaller, but still bold and rugged; and thence it is continued at a less elevation, with gentler slopes, northward to within half a mile of the town, where it curves around to the east and ends at Rock Creek. The whole length is about three miles. Seminary Ridge is a mile west of this, and nearly parallel with its central portion. Hancock without hesitation chose this line, placed all the available troops in position, and then hurried back to headquarters at Taneytown. Meade at once accepted his plan, and sent forward the remaining corps. The Third Corps, commanded by General Sickles, being already on the march, arrived at sunset. The Second (Hancock's) marched thirteen miles and went into position. The Fifth (Sykes's) was twenty-three miles away, but marched all night and arrived in the morning. The Sixth (Sedgwick's) was thirty-six miles away, but was put in motion at once. At the same time, Lee was urging the various divisions of his army to make the concentration as rapidly as possible, not wishing to attack the heights till his forces were all up.

MAJOR-GENERAL GEORGE G. MEADE.

It is said by General Longstreet that Lee had promised his corps commanders not to fight a battle during this expedition, unless he could take a position and stand on the defensive; but the excitement and confidence of his soldiers, who felt themselves invincible, compelled him. While he was waiting for his divisions to arrive, forming his lines, and perfecting a plan of attack, Sedgwick's corps arrived on the other side, and the National troops were busy constructing rude breastworks.

Between the two great ridges there is another ridge, situated somewhat like the diagonal portion of a capital N. The order of the corps, beginning at the right, was this: Slocum's, Howard's, Hancock's, Sickles's, with Sykes's in reserve on the left, and Sedgwick's on the right. Sickles, thinking to occupy more advantageous ground, instead of remaining in line, advanced to the diagonal ridge, and on this hinged the whole battle of the second day. For there was nothing on which to rest his left flank, and he was obliged to "refuse" it—turn it sharply back toward Round Top. This presented a salient angle (always a weak point) to the enemy; and here, when the action opened at four o'clock in the afternoon, the blow fell. The angle was at a peach orchard, and the refused line stretched back through a wheat-field; General Birney's division occupying this ground, while the right of Sickles's line was held by Humphreys.

Longstreet's men attacked the salient vigorously, and his extreme right, composed of Hood's division, stretched out toward Little Round Top, where it narrowly missed winning a position that would have enabled it to enfilade the whole National line. Little Round Top had been occupied only by signal men, when General Warren saw the danger, detached Vincent's brigade from

GENERAL HANCOCK AND STAFF NEAR LITTLE ROUND TOP.

FIELD HOSPITAL.—HEADQUARTERS.

(From the Panorama of Gettysburg, at Chicago.)

a division that was going out to reinforce Sickles, and ordered it to occupy the hill at once. One regiment of Weed's brigade (the 140th New York) also went up, dragging and lifting the guns of Hazlett's battery up the rocky slope; and the whole brigade soon followed. They were just in time to meet the advance of Hood's Texans, and engage in one of the bloodiest hand-to-hand conflicts of the war, and at length the Texans were hurled back and the position secured. But dead or wounded soldiers, in blue and in gray, lay everywhere among the rocks. General Weed was mortally wounded; General Vincent was killed; Col. Patrick H. O'Rorke, of the 140th, a recent graduate of West Point, of brilliant promise, was shot dead at the head of his men; and Lieut. Charles E. Hazlett was killed as he leaned over General Weed to catch his last words. "I would rather die here," said Weed, "than that the rebels should gain an inch of this ground!" Hood's men made one more attempt, by creeping up the ravine between the two Round Tops, but were repelled by a bayonet charge, executed by Chamberlain's Twentieth Maine Regiment; and five hundred of them, with seventeen officers, were made prisoners. The peculiarity of Chamberlain's charge, which was one of the most brilliant manœuvres ever executed on a battlefield, consisted in pushing the regiment forward in such a manner that the centre moved more rapidly than the flanks, which gradually brought it into the shape of a wedge that penetrated the Confederate line and cut off the five hundred men from their comrades.

MAJOR-GENERAL CARL SCHURZ.

MAJOR-GENERAL ABNER DOUBLEDAY.

Meanwhile terrific fighting was going on at the salient in the peach orchard. Several batteries were in play on both sides, and made destructive work; a single shell from one of the National guns killed or wounded thirty men in a company of thirty-seven. Here General Zook was killed, Colonel Cross was killed, General Sickles lost a leg, and the Confederate General Barksdale was mortally wounded and died a prisoner. There were repeated charges and counter-charges, and numerous bloody incidents; for Sickles was constantly reinforced, and Lee, being under the impression that this was the flank of the main line, kept hammering at it till his men finally possessed the peach orchard, advanced their lines, assailed the left flank of Humphreys, and finally drove back the National line, only to find that they had forced it into its true position, from which they could not dislodge it by any direct attack, while the guns and troops that now crowned the two Round Tops showed any flank movement to be impossible. About sunset Ewell's corps assailed the Union right, and at heavy cost gained a portion of the works near Rock Creek.

One of the most dramatic incidents of this day was a charge on Cemetery Hill by two Confederate brigades led by an organization known as the Louisiana Tigers. It was made just at dusk, and the charging column immediately became a target for the batteries of Wiedrick, Stevens, and Ricketts, which fired grape and canister, each gun making four discharges a minute. But the Tigers had the reputation of never having failed in a charge, and in spite of the frightful gaps made by the artillery and by volleys of musketry, they kept on till they reached the guns, and made a hand-to-hand fight for them. Friend and foe were fast becoming mingled, when Carroll's brigade came to the rescue of the guns, and the remnants of the Confederate column fled down the hill in the gathering darkness, hastened by a double-shotted fire from Ricketts's battery. Of the seventeen hundred Tigers, twelve hundred had been struck down, and that famous organization was never heard of again.

Many exciting incidents of this twilight battle are told. When the Confederates charged on Wiedrick's battery, there was a difficulty in depressing the guns sufficiently, or they probably never would have reached it; and when they did reach it the gunners stood by and fought them with pistols, handspikes, rammers,

BREVET MAJOR-GENERAL HENRY BAXTER.

BRIGADIER-GENERAL ADOLPH VON STEINWEHR.

and stones; for they had received orders not to limber up under any circumstances, but to fight the battery to the last, and they obeyed their orders literally and nobly. Nearly all of them, however, were beaten down by the Confederate infantrymen, and the battery was captured entire; but the victorious assailants were now subjected to a flank fire from Stevens's battery, which poured in double-shotted canister at point-blank range, before the arrival of Carroll's brigade completed their destruction. At Ricketts's battery a Confederate lieutenant sprang forward and seized the guidon, when its bearer, Private Riggen, shot him dead with his revolver. The next moment a bullet cut the staff of the guidon, and another killed Riggen, who fell across the body of the lieutenant. Another Confederate lieutenant, rushing into the battery, laid his hand upon a gun and demanded its surrender; his answer was a blow from a handspike that dashed out his brains. At another gun a Confederate sergeant, with his rifle in his hand, confronted Sergeant Stafford with a demand for the surrender of the piece; whereupon Lieutenant Brockway threw a stone that knocked him down, and Stafford, catching his rifle, fired it at him and wounded him seriously. Sergeant Geible, of the One Hundred and Seventh Ohio, sprang upon the low stone wall when the Confederates were charging, and defiantly waved the regimental colors, but was immediately shot, and the flag fell outside. Adjutant Young then jumped over the wall and rescued it, while at the same time the color-sergeant of the Eighth Louisiana was rushing up at the head of his regiment and waving his flag. Young sprang upon him, seized the flag, and shot the sergeant; but he also received a bullet which passed through his arm and into his lung, and at the same time a Confederate officer aimed a heavy blow at his head, which was parried by a comrade. Clinging tenaciously to the captured flag, Young managed to get back into his own lines, and sank fainting from loss of blood; but his life was saved, and he was promoted for his gallantry.

While the actions of the first two days were complicated, that of the third was extremely simple. Lee had tried both flanks, and failed. He now determined to attempt piercing the centre of Meade's line. Longstreet, wiser than his chief, protested, but in vain. On the other hand, Meade had held a council of war the night before, and in accordance with the vote of his corps commanders determined to stay where he was and fight it out.

Whether General Meade contemplated a retreat, has been disputed. On the one hand, he testified before the Committee on the Conduct of the War that he never thought of such a thing; on the other, General Doubleday, in his "Chancellorsville and Gettysburg," presents

BRIGADIER-GENERAL FRANCIS C. BARLOW.
MAJOR-GENERAL DAVID B. BIRNEY.
BRIGADIER-GENERAL JOHN GIBBON.
MAJOR-GENERAL WINFIELD S. HANCOCK.

testimony that seems to leave no reasonable doubt. There is nothing intrinsically improbable in the story. Meade's service in that war had all been with the Army of the Potomac, and it was the custom of that army to retreat after a great battle. The only exception thus far had been Antietam; and two great battles, with the usual retreat, had been fought since Antietam. Meade had been in command of the entire army but a few days, and he cannot be said to have been, in the ordinary sense of the term, the master-spirit at Gettysburg. It was Reynolds who went out to meet the enemy, and stayed his advance, on the first day; it was Hancock who selected the advantageous position for the second day; it was Warren who secured the neglected key-point. The fact of calling a council of war at all implies doubt in the mind of the commander. But, after all, the question is hardly important, so far at least as it concerns Meade's place in history. He is likely to be less blamed for contemplating retreat at the end of two days' fighting when he had the worst of it, than for not contemplating pursuit at the end of the third day when the enemy was defeated. There are some considerations, however, which must give Meade's conduct of this battle a very high place for generalship. He seemed to know how to trust his subordinates, and to be uninfluenced by that weakness which attacks so many commanders with a fear lest something shall be done for which they themselves shall not receive the credit. He unhesitatingly accepted Hancock's judgment as to the propriety of receiving battle on Cemetery Hill, and showed every disposition to do all that would tend to secure the great purpose, without the slightest reference to its bearing on anybody's reputation. Furthermore, he had, what brilliant soldiers often lack, a complete comprehension of the entire situation, as regarded the war, and appreciated the importance of the action in which he was about to engage. This is proved by the following circular, which he issued on the 30th of June, one day before the battle, to his subordinates:

"The commanding general requests that, previous to the engagement soon expected with the enemy, corps and all other commanding officers will address their troops, explaining to them briefly the immense issues involved in this struggle. The enemy are on our soil. The whole country now looks anxiously to this army to deliver it from the presence of the foe. Our failure to do so will leave us no such welcome as the swelling of millions of hearts with pride and joy at our success would give to every soldier in the army. Homes, firesides, and domestic altars are involved. The army has fought well heretofore. It is believed that it will fight more desperately and bravely than ever if it is addressed in fitting terms. Corps and other commanders are authorized to order the instant death of any soldier who fails in his duty at this hour."

Lee's first intended movement was to push the success gained at the close of the second day by Ewell on the National right; but Meade anticipated him, attacking early in the morning and driving Ewell out of his works. In preparation for a grand charge, Lee placed more than one hundred guns in position on Seminary Ridge, converging their fire on the left centre of Meade's line, where he intended to send his storming column. Eighty guns (all there was room for) were placed in position on Cemetery Ridge to reply, and at one o'clock the firing

ARTILLERY COMING INTO ACTION.

(From the Panorama of Gettysburg, at Chicago.)

MAJOR-GENERAL GOUVERNEUR K. WARREN.

DEVIL'S DEN.
Position occupied by Confederate Sharp-shooters, the point from which they shot at Union Officers on Little Round Top.
From photograph by W. H. Tipton, Gettysburg.

began. This was one of the most terrific artillery duels ever witnessed. There was a continuous and deafening roar, which was heard forty miles away. The shot and shells ploughed up the ground, shattered gravestones in the cemetery, and sent their fragments flying among the troops, exploded caissons, and dismounted guns. A house used for Meade's headquarters, in the rear of the line, was completely riddled. Many artillerists and horses were killed; but the casualties among the infantry were not numerous, for the men lay flat upon the ground, taking advantage of every shelter, and waited for the more serious work that all knew was to follow. At the end of two hours Gen. Henry J. Hunt, Meade's chief of artillery, ordered the firing to cease, both to cool the guns and to save the ammunition for use in repelling the infantry charge. Lee supposed that his object—which was to demoralize his enemy and cause him to exhaust his artillery—had been effected. Fourteen thousand of his best troops—including Pickett's division, which had not arrived in time for the previous day's fighting—now came out of the woods, formed in heavy columns, and moved forward steadily to the charge. Instantly the National guns reopened fire, and the Confederate ranks were ploughed through and through; but the gaps were closed up, and the columns did not halt. There was a mile of open ground for them to traverse, and every step was taken under heavy fire. As they drew nearer, the batteries used grape and canister, and an infantry force posted in advance of the main line rose to its feet and fired volleys of musketry into the right flank. Now the columns began visibly to break up and melt away; and the left wing of the force changed its direction somewhat, so that it parted from the right, making an interval and exposing a new flank, which the National troops promptly took advantage of. But Pickett's diminishing ranks still pushed on, till they passed over the outer lines, fought hand to hand at the main line, and even leaped the breastworks and thought to capture the batteries. The point where they penetrated was marked by a clump of small trees on the edge of the hill, at that portion of the line held by the brigade of Gen. Alexander S. Webb, who was wounded; but his men stood firm against the shock, and, from the eagerness of all to join in the contest, men rushed from every side to the point assailed, mixing up all commands, but making a front that no such remnant as Pickett's could break. Gen. Lewis A. Armistead, who led the charge and leaped over the wall, was shot down as he laid his hand on a gun, and his surviving soldiers surrendered themselves. On the slope of the hill many of the assailants had thrown themselves upon the ground and held up their hands for quarter; and an immediate sally from the National lines brought in a large number of prisoners and battle-flags. Of that magnificent column which had been launched out so proudly, only a broken fragment ever returned. Nearly every officer in it, except Pickett, had been either killed or wounded. Armistead, a prisoner and dying, said to an officer who was bending over him, "Tell Hancock I have wronged him and have wronged my country." He had been opposed to secession, but the pressure of his friends and relatives

BRIGADIER-GENERAL GABRIEL R. PAUL.

BRIGADIER GENERAL ALFRED N. DUFFIÉ.

AN HEROIC INCIDENT—COLOR SERGEANT BENJAMIN CRIPPEN REFUSES TO SURRENDER THE FLAG had at length forced him into the service. Hancock had been wounded and borne from the field, and among the other wounded on the National side were Generals Doubleday, Gibbon, Warren, Butterfield, Stannard, Barnes, and Brook; General Farnsworth was killed, and Gen. Gabriel R. Paul lost both eyes. Among the killed on the Confederate side, besides those already mentioned, were Generals Garnett, Pender, and Semmes; and among the wounded, Generals Hampton, Jenkins, Kemper, Scales, J. M. Jones, and G. T. Anderson.

While this movement was in progress, Kilpatrick with his cavalry rode around the mountain and attempted to pass the Confederate right and capture the trains, while Stuart with his cavalry made a simultaneous attempt on the National right. Each had a bloody fight, but neither was successful. This closed the battle. Hancock urged that a great return charge should be made immediately with Sedgwick's corps, which had not participated, and Lee expected such a movement as a matter of course. But it was not done.

That night Lee made preparations for retreat, and the next day—which was the 4th of July—the retreat was begun. General Imboden, who conducted the trains and the ambulances, describes it as one of the most pitiful and heart-rending scenes ever witnessed. A heavy storm had come up, the roads were in bad condition, few of the wounded had been properly cared for, and as they were jolted along in agony they were groaning, cursing, babbling of their homes, and calling upon their friends to kill them and put them out of misery. But there could be no halt, for the Potomac was rising, and an attack was hourly expected from the enemy in the rear.

Meade, however, did not pursue for several days, and then to no purpose; so that Lee's crippled army escaped into Virginia, but it was disabled from ever doing anything more than prolonging the contest. Gettysburg was essentially the Waterloo of the war, and there is a striking parallel in the losses. The numbers engaged were very nearly the same in the one battle as in the other. At Waterloo the victors lost twenty-three thousand one hundred and eighty-five men, and the vanquished, in round numbers, thirty thousand. At Gettysburg the National loss was twenty-three thousand one hundred and ninety—killed, wounded, and missing. The Confederate losses were never officially reported, but estimates place them at nearly thirty thousand. Lee left seven thousand of his wounded among the unburied dead, and twenty-seven thousand muskets were picked up on the field.

The romantic and pathetic incidents of this great battle are innumerable. John Burns, a resident of Gettysburg, seventy years old, had served in the War of 1812, being one of Miller's men at Lundy's Lane, and in the Mexican war, and had tried to enlist at the breaking out of the Rebellion, but was rejected as too old. When the armies approached the town, he joined the Seventh Wisconsin Regiment and displayed wonderful skill as a sharp-shooter; but he was wounded in the afternoon, fell into the hands of the Confederates, told some plausible story to account for his lack of a uniform, and was finally carried to his own house. Jennie Wade was baking bread for Union soldiers when the advance of the Confederate line surrounded her house with enemies; but she kept on at her work in spite of orders to desist, until a stray bullet struck her dead. An unknown Confederate officer lay mortally wounded within the Union lines, and one of the commanders sent to ask his name and rank. "Tell him," said the dying man, "that I shall soon be where there is no rank;" and he was never identified. Lieut. Alonzo H. Cushing commanded a battery on General Webb's line, and in the cannonade preceding the great charge on the third day all his guns but one were disabled, and he was mortally wounded. When the charging column approached, he exclaimed, "Webb, I will give them one more shot!" ran his gun forward to the stone wall, fired it, said "Good-by!" and fell dead. Barksdale, of Mississippi, had been an extreme secessionist, and had done much to bring on the war. At that part of the line where he fell, the Union commander was Gen. David B. Birney, son of a slaveholder that had emancipated his slaves, had been mobbed for his abolitionism, and had twice been the presidential candidate of the Liberty party. A general of the National army, who was present, remarks that Barksdale died "like a brave man, with dignity and resignation." On that field perished also the cause that he represented; and as Americans we may all be proud to say that, so far as manly courage

MAJOR-GENERAL DANIEL BUTTERFIELD.

(Chief of Staft to Geheral Meade.)

GENERAL MEADE'S HEADQUARTERS.

PART OF THE BATTLEFIELD OF GETTYSBURG.
(From a War Department photograph.)

could go, it died with dignity if not with resignation.

Gen. Rufus R. Dawes, who was colonel of the Sixth Wisconsin Regiment, gives some particulars of the fight at the railroad cut on the first day: "The only commands I gave, as we advanced, were, 'Align on the colors! Close up on that color!' The regiment was being broken up so that this order alone could hold the body together. Meanwhile the colors were down upon the ground several times, but were raised at once by the heroes of the color-guard. Not one of the guard escaped, every man being killed or wounded. Four hundred and twenty men started as a regiment from the turnpike fence, of whom two hundred and forty reached the railroad cut. Years afterward I found the distance passed over to be one hundred and seventy-five paces. Every officer proved himself brave, true, and heroic in encouraging the men to breast this deadly storm; but the real impetus was the eager, determined valor of our men who carried muskets in the ranks. The rebel color could be seen waving defiantly just above the edge of the railroad cut. A heroic ambition to capture it took possession of several of our men. Corporal Eggleston, a mere boy, sprang forward to seize it, and was shot dead the moment his hand touched the color. Private Anderson, furious at the killing of his brave young comrade, recked little for the rebel color; but he swung aloft his musket, and with a terrific blow split the skull of the rebel who had shot young Eggleston. Lieutenant Remington was severely wounded in the shoulder while reaching for the colors. Into this deadly mélée rushed Corporal Francis A. Waller, who seized and held the rebel battle-flag. It was the flag of the Second Mississippi Regiment. . . . Corporal James Kelly turned from the ranks and stepped beside me as we both moved hurriedly forward on the charge. He pulled open his woollen shirt, and a mark where the deadly minié-ball had entered his breast was visible. He said: 'Colonel, won't you please write to my folks that I died a soldier?'"

BRIGADIER-GENERAL FRANCIS T. NICHOLLS, C. S. A.

The story of the critical struggle for the possession of Little Round Top, or at least of an important portion of it, has been graphically related by Adjutant Porter Farley, of the One Hundred and Fortieth New York Regiment, which went up at the same time with Hazlett's battery. Captain Farley writes:

"Just at that moment our former brigadier, Gen. G. K. Warren, chief engineer of the army, with an orderly and one or two officers, rode down toward the head of our regiment. He came from the direction of the hill-top. His speed and manner indicated unusual excitement. Before he reached us he called out to O'Rorke to lead his regiment that way up the hill. O'Rorke answered him that General Weed had gone ahead and expected this regiment to follow him. 'Never mind that,' answered Warren, 'I'll take the responsibility.' Warren's words and manner carried conviction of the importance of the thing he asked. Accepting his assurance of full justification, O'Rorke turned the head of the regiment to the left, and, following one of the officers who had been with Warren, led it diagonally up the eastern slope of Little Round Top. Warren rode off, evidently bent upon securing other troops. The staff officer who rode with us, by his impatient gestures, urged us to our greatest speed. Some of the guns of Hazlett's battery broke through our files

BRIGADIER-GENERAL ELON J. FARNSWORTH.

COLONEL P. H. O'RORKE.

COLONEL A. VAN HORNE ELLIS.

BRIGADIER-GENERAL S. K. ZOOK.

before we reached the hill-top amid the frantic efforts of the horses, lashed by the drivers, to pull their heavy pieces up that steep acclivity. A few seconds later the head of our regiment reached the summit of the ridge, war's wild panorama spread before us, and we found ourselves upon the verge of battle. It was a moment which called for leadership. There was no time for tactical formation. Delay was ruin. Hesitation was destruction. Well was it for the cause he served that the man who led our regiment that day was one prompt to decide and brave to execute. The bullets flew in among the men the moment the leading company mounted the ridge; and as not a musket was loaded, the natural impulse was to halt and load them. But O'Rorke permitted no such delay. Springing from his horse, he threw the reins to the sergeant-major; his sword flashed from its scabbard into the sunlight, and calling, 'This way, boys,' he led the charge over the rocks, down the hillside, till he came abreast the men of Vincent's brigade, who were posted in the ravine to our left. Joining them, an irregular line was formed, such as the confusion of the rocks lying thereabout permitted; and this line grew and was extended toward the right as the successive rearward companies came upon the scene of action. There, while some were partly sheltered by the rocks and others stood in the open, a fierce fight went on with an enemy among the trees and underbrush. Flushed with the excitement of battle, and bravely led, they pushed up close to our line. The steadfastness and valor displayed on both sides made the result for some few minutes doubtful; but a struggle so desperate and bloody could not be a long one. The enemy fell back; a short lull was succeeded by another onslaught, which was again repelled.

"When that struggle was over, the exultation of victory was soon chilled by the dejection which oppressed us as we counted and realized the cost of all that had been won. Of our regiment eighty-five enlisted men and six officers had been wounded. Besides these, twenty-six of the comrades who had marched with us that afternoon had fallen dead before the fire of the enemy. Grouped by companies, a row of inanimate forms lay side by side beneath the trees upon the eastern slope. No funeral ceremony, and only shallow graves, could be accorded them. In the darkness of the night, silently and with bitter dejection, each company buried its dead. O'Rorke was among the dead. Shot through the neck, he had fallen without a groan, and we may hope without a pang. The supreme effort of his life was consummated by a death heroic in its surroundings and undisturbed by pain."

It has been well said that Gettysburg was the common soldier's battle; that its great results were due, not so much to any generalship either in strategy or in tactics, as to the intelligent courage and magnificent staying powers of the Northern soldier. If any one man was more than another the hero of the fight, it was General Hancock, who for his services on that field received the thanks of Congress. Senator Washburn, who saw him the next year at the Wilderness, remarked: "He was the finest-looking man above ground; he was the very impersonation of war." Hancock not only chose the ground for the battle and set things in order for the conflict of the second day, but seemed to be everywhere present, animating the men with the spirit of his own valor and enthusiasm. He was especially conspicuous during the terrific cannonade that preceded the great charge of the third day, riding slowly up and down the lines. It is said that when he began this ride he was accompanied by thirty men, and when he finished it there was but one man with him—the horseman who carried his corps flag. All the others had either been struck down by the missiles of the enemy, or been called to imperative duty on different parts of the line. As he rode slowly along, he stopped frequently to speak to the men who were lying upon the ground to avoid the shells and balls, and clutching their rifles ready to spring up and meet the charge which they knew would follow as soon as the artillery fire ceased. While this famous charge was in progress, Hancock rode down to speak to General Stannard, whose Vermonters were to move forward and strike the charging column in flank, and at this moment he was most grievously wounded. A rifle ball struck the pommel of his saddle, tearing out and twisting a nail from it, and both bullet and nail entered his thigh. Two of General Stannard's aids caught him as he fell from his horse, and put him into an ambulance. Here he wrote a note to General Meade

BREVET MAJOR-GENERAL PHILIP R. DE TROBRIAND.

MAJOR-GENERAL DANIEL SICKLES. MAJOR-GENERAL SAMUEL P. HEINTZELMAN.

BREVET MAJOR-GENERAL HENRY J. HUNT.

urgently advising that, as soon as the Confederate charge was over, a return charge be made with the comparatively fresh troops of the Sixth Corps. Some think that if this had been done the Army of Northern Virginia would have found the end of its career then and there, instead of at Appomattox a year and a half later. But General Longstreet says he expected such a charge and was prepared for it, and that if it had been made Sedgwick's men would have fared as badly as Pickett's.

It is a little difficult to understand why so much has been made in literature of this charge of Pickett's, unless, perhaps, it is owing to the picturesque circumstances. It was at the close of the greatest battle of the war; it was heralded by the mightiest cannonade of the war; it was witnessed by two great armies; it was made in the middle of the afternoon of a summer day, on a gentle slope, with the sun at the backs of the assailants, the best possible arrangement for a grand display; it exhibited magnificent courage and confidence on the part of the soldiers that made it, and quite as great courage and confidence on the part of those who met and thwarted it. It is, perhaps, for these reasons that it has been made unduly famous; for, after all, it was a blunder and a failure. There were other charges in the war that tested quite as much the devotion and endurance of soldiers, and they were not all failures. The charge of Hooker's and Thomas's men up the heights of Lookout Mountain and Mission Ridge was even more picturesque, and was a grand success. The National position at Gettysburg is always represented as being along a ridge, and this, in a general way, is true; but near the centre the ridge is so low that it almost dies away into the plain, and Pickett's men, being directed toward this point, had only the very gentlest of slopes to ascend. Gen. Alexander S. Webb, whose command was at this point, said in conversation: "We had no intrenchments there, not a sod was turned." "But why did you not intrench?" "Because we never supposed that anybody would be fool enough to charge up there." The peril to the charging column was more from the cross-fire of the batteries on the higher ground to the right and left, than from the direct fire in front.

"I WILL GIVE THEM ONE MORE SHOT!"

General Sickles has been criticised somewhat severely for the erroneous position taken by his corps on the second day of the battle, which resulted in the great slaughter at the peach orchard and the wheat-field. On a subsequent visit to Gettysburg he gave this explanation of his action:

"It was quite early when I rode to General Meade's headquarters for orders. The general told me that he did not think we would be attacked, as he believed the enemy was in no condition to renew the fight. I freely expressed to him my belief that the enemy would not only force a battle at Gettysburg, but would do so soon. From General Meade's conversation, and from his manner, I concluded he did not intend to fight the battle at Gettysburg if he could avoid it. General Butterfield, his chief of staff, told me that orders were being then prepared for a change of position to Pipe Clay Creek. After waiting some time for a decision as to what was to be done, I said to General Meade that I should put my command in position with a view to meet any emergency along my front, and at the same time asked him to send General Butterfield with me to look over the field and inspect the position I had decided to occupy. 'Butterfield is busy,' said he, and he suggested that I use my own judgment. I again replied that I should prefer to have some one of his staff officers sent with me, and asked that General Hunt, chief of the artillery, be sent. General Meade assented, and Hunt and I rode away. Carefully we surveyed the ground in my front. I expressed the opinion that the high ground running from the Emmetsburg road to Round Top was the most advantageous position. Hunt agreed with me.

"'Then I understand that I am to take this position, and you, as General Meade's representative, so order.' 'I do not care,' said he, 'to take the responsibility of ordering you to take that position, but as soon as I can ride to General Meade's headquarters you will receive his orders to do so.'

"He rode away, but before he reached headquarters, or I received orders, my danger became imminent, and I was forced to go into line of battle. Just after I had taken position on the high ground selected, with Humphrey on the right, within and beyond the peach orchard, and Birney on the left toward Round Top, I received an order from General Meade to report at his headquarters. There was vigorous skirmishing on my front, and I returned word to the general that I was about to be attacked and could not leave the field. It was not long before I received a peremptory order to report at once to headquarters, as General Meade was going to hold an important conference of corps commanders. I sent for Birney, put him in command, and rode rapidly to Meade's headquarters. As I rode along I could hear the increasing fire along the line, and felt very solicitous for my command. As I came up to headquarters at a rapid gait, Meade came out hurriedly and said: 'Don't dismount, don't dismount; I fear your whole line is engaged; return to your command, and in a few moments I will join you on the field.' I rode back with all possible speed, reaching my corps before the enemy had made his first furious assault. General Meade soon joined me, as he had promised, and together we inspected

MAJOR-GENERAL GEORGE E. PICKETT, C. S. A.

BATTLE OF GETTYSBURG, THIRD DAY.

GROUP OF CONFEDERATE PRISONERS BEING MARCHED TO THE REAR UNDER GUARD.

(From the Panorama of Gettysburg, at Chicago.)

the position I had taken. 'Isn't your line too much extended?' said he. 'It is,' I replied; 'but I haven't the Army of the Potomac, and have a wide space to cover. Reserves should at once be sent up. My dependence will have to be upon my artillery until support comes, and I need more guns.' 'Send to Hunt for what you want,' said he, and he glanced over the slender line of infantry that stretched toward Round Top. Just before he left I said to him: 'Does my position suit you? If it does not, I will change it.' 'No, no!' he replied quickly; 'I'll send up the Fifth Corps, and Hancock will give any other supports you may require.'

LIEUTENANT-GENERAL JAMES LONGSTREET, C. S. A.

"He rode away, and soon after the battle began. The terrific struggle along the whole line, and especially in the peach orchard and the wheat-field on the right and left of my line, respectively, need not be gone over. It is matter of history. I sent to Hunt, when Meade had gone, for forty pieces of artillery, which, added to the sixty I had, gave me the guns to keep up the fighting while I waited for reinforcements. Warren, who was then an engineer officer, was on Round Top sending urgent appeals to me to send troops to hold that important position. One brigade sent to me I immediately despatched him. As the fighting went on and increased in intensity, I looked for the Fifth Corps again and again, and sent an aid several times to hurry them up. Sykes was slow, and, finding the needs of the hour growing greater and greater every moment, I sent to Hancock for help. Hancock was always prompt and generous, and with eager haste pushed forward his best troops to the assistance of the struggling Third Corps. But the moments I waited for reinforcements that day were as long to me as an eternity, and the brave boys who wore the diamond during all this time were obliged to stand the shock of as furious an assault as was ever dealt against troops on any battlefield of modern times. The struggle in that now peaceful peach-orchard was then fierce as death. The wheat-field yonder was like the winepress with the dead and dying. Men fought there, hand to hand, I think, as never they grappled before. Onward and over against each other they bent again and again. Now the Confederates would drive madly into the conflict. Now our boys would push them back again at the point of the bayonet. Graham's and the Excelsior Brigades, that I organized and commanded during the first of the war, were in that section of the field, and hundreds of them lay down to sleep under the shade of the peach trees that hot July day."

MAJOR-GENERAL FITZHUGH LEE, C. S. A.

BRIGADIER-GENERAL E. P. ALEXANDER, C. S. A.

BRIGADIER-GENERAL RICHARD L. T. BEALL, C. S. A.

One who participated in the bloody struggle of the wheat-field on the second day writes:

"General Birney rode up and ordered a forward movement, and directed that the largest regiment of the brigade be sent double-quick to prolong the line on the left, so as to fill in the intervening gap to the foot of Round Top, for the occupation of which both forces were now engaged in a deadly struggle. General de Trobriand designated the Fortieth New York for this duty, and ordered me to conduct it to its assigned position, and, if necessary, to remain there with it. We proceeded. The air was filled with smoke and the interchanging fires of artillery and musketry. The shouts of both armies were almost deafening, but I succeeded in placing the regiment where it was ordered, and decided to remain with it.

"The enemy had us at a disadvantage. They were on higher ground, and were pouring a terrific fire into our front. I trust in God I may never again be called to look upon such scenes as I there beheld. Col. Thomas W. Egan, the commander of the regiment, one of the bravest men I ever knew, was charging with his command, when a ball from the enemy pierced the heart of his mare, who sank

LIEUTENANT-GENERAL R. S. EWELL, C. S. A.

under him. Major Warner of the same regiment was borne past me for dead, but was only terribly wounded. He afterward recovered. His horse came dashing by a few moments afterward, and my own having been disabled from wounds and rendered unfit for use, I caught and mounted him. The poor brute that I was riding had two minie balls buried in him—one in the shoulders, the other in the hip—and was so frantic with pain that he had wellnigh broken my neck in his violent fall. My sword was pitched a dozen yards from me, and was picked up by one of the men and returned to me that night.

"Col. A. V. H. Ellis, of the One Hundred and Twenty-fourth New York, one of the most chivalrous spirits that ever breathed, had received his mortal wound. He was riding at the head of his regiment, waving his sword in the air, and shouting to his men—his orange blossoms, as he called them, the regiment having been raised in Orange County, New York—when a bullet struck him in the forehead. He was borne to the rear, his face covered with blood, and the froth spirting from his mouth. He died in a few moments. Major Cromwell, also of that regiment, was killed almost at the same instant by a shot in the breast. He died without a groan or struggle. The adjutant of the regiment was killed by a shot through the heart as it was moving off the field. He had fought bravely for hours, and it seemed hard that one so young and hopeful should be thus stricken down by a chance shot after having faced the thickest of the fight unharmed. I learned afterward that the noble young soldier was engaged to be married to a beautiful young lady in his native State.

"It happened by the merest accident that I was within a few feet of General Sickles when he received the wound by which he lost his leg. When our command fell back after being relieved by General Sykes, I hastened to find General De Trobriand, and, seeing a knot of officers near the brick house into which General Sickles was so soon to be taken, I rode up to see whether he (De Trobriand) was among them. The knot of officers proved to be General Sickles and his staff. I saluted him and was just asking for General De Trobriand, when a terrific explosion seemed to shake the very earth. This was instantly followed by another equally stunning, and the horses all began to jump. I instantly noticed that General Sickles's pants and drawers at the knee were torn clear off to the leg, which was swinging loose. The jumping of the horse was fortunate for him, as he turned just in time for him to alight on the upper side of the slope of the hill. As he attempted to dismount he seemed to lose strength, and half fell to the ground. He was very pale, and evidently in most fearful pain, as he exclaimed excitedly, 'Quick, quick! get something and tie it up before I bleed to death.' These were his exact words, and I shall never forget the scene as long as I live, for we all loved General Sickles, who commanded our corps. He was carried from the field to the house I have mentioned, coolly smoking a cigar, quietly remarking to a Catholic priest, a chaplain to one of the regiments in his command, 'Man proposes and God disposes.' His leg was amputated within less than half an hour after his receiving the wound."

Major Joseph G. Rosengarten says of General Reynolds: "In all the intrigues of the army, and the interference of the politicians in its management, he silently set aside the tempting offers to take part, and served his successive commanders with un-

THE STONE WALL.—GENERAL O. O. HOWARD'S POSITION NEAR CEMETERY HILL.

(From the Panorama of Gettysburg, at Chicago.)

swerving loyalty and zeal and faith. In the full flush of life and health, vigorously leading on the troops in hand, and energetically summoning up the rest of his command, watching and even leading the attack of a comparatively small body, a glorious picture of the best type of military leader, superbly mounted, and horse and man sharing in the excitement of the shock of battle, Reynolds was, of course, a shining mark to the enemy's sharp-shooters. He had taken his troops into a heavy growth of timber on the slope of a hill-side, and, under their regimental and brigade commanders, the men did their work well and promptly. Returning to rejoin the expected divisions, he was struck by a minie-ball fired by a sharp-shooter hidden in the branches of a tree almost overhead, and was killed at once. His horse bore him to the little clump of trees, where a cairn of

RESIDENCE OF JOHN BURNS, THE OLD HERO OF GETTYSBURG.

stones and a rude mark on the bark, now almost overgrown, still tell the fatal spot. At the moment that his body was taken to the rear, for his death was instantaneous, two of his most gallant staff officers, Captains Riddle and Wadsworth, in pursuance of his directions, effected a slight movement, which made prisoners of Archer's brigade, so that the rebel prisoners went to the rear almost at the same time, and their respectful conduct was in itself the highest tribute they could pay to him who had thus fallen."

Gen. D. McM. Gregg, who commanded one of the two cavalry divisions of the Army of the Potomac, while Gen. John Buford commanded the other, in a rapid review of the part taken by the cavalry in the campaign, writes: "The two divisions were put in motion toward the Potomac, but did not take exactly the same route, and the Army of the Potomac followed their lead. The advance of Stuart's Confederate cavalry command had reached Aldie, and here, on June 17th, began a series of skirmishes or engagements between the two cavalry forces, all of which were decided successes for us, and terminated in driving Stuart's cavalry through the gap at Paris. Kilpatrick's brigade, moving in the advance of the second division, fell upon the enemy at Aldie, and there ensued an engagement of the most obstinate character, in which several brilliant mounted charges were made, terminating in the retreat of the enemy. On June 19th, the division advanced to Middleburg, where a part of Stuart's force was posted, and was attacked by Col. Irvin Gregg's brigade. Here, as at Aldie, the fight was very obstinate. The enemy had carefully selected the most defensible position, from which he had to be driven step by step, and this work had to be done by dismounted skirmishers, owing to the unfavorable character of the country for mounted service. On the 19th, Gregg's division moved on the turnpike from Middleburg in the direction of Upperville, and soon encountered the enemy's cavalry in great force. The attack was promptly made, the enemy offering the most stubborn resistance. The long lines of stone fences, which are so common in that region, were so many lines of defence to a force in retreat; these could be held until our advancing skirmishers were almost upon them, but then there would be no escape for those behind; it was either to surrender or attempt escape across the open fields to fall before the deadly fire of the carbines of the pursuers. Later in the day General Buford's division came in on the right, and took the enemy in flank. Then our entire force, under General Pleasonton, supported by a column of infantry, moved forward and dealt the finishing blow. Through Upperville the pursuit was continued at a run, the enemy flying in the greatest

MISS JENNIE WADE, THE ONLY WOMAN KILLED AT GETTYSBURG.

confusion; nor were they permitted to re-form until night put a stop to further pursuit at the mouth of the gap. Our losses in the fighting of these three days amounted to five hundred in killed, wounded, and missing; of the latter there were but few. The enemy's loss was much greater, particularly in prisoners. Our captures also included light guns, flags, and small arms. These successful engagements of our cavalry left our infantry free to march, without the loss of an hour, to the field of Gettysburg. At Frederick, Md., the addition of the cavalry, formerly commanded by General Stahl, made it necessary to organize a third division, the command of which was given to General Kilpatrick. Buford, with his division in advance of our army, on July 1st, first encountered the enemy in the vicinity of Gettysburg. How well his brigades of regulars and volunteers resisted the advance of that invading host, yielding so slowly as to give ample time for our infantry to go to his support, is well known. Kilpatrick's division marched from Frederick well to the right, at Hanover engaged the enemy's cavalry in a sharp skirmish, and reached Gettysburg on the 1st. On the left of our line, on the 3d, one of his brigades, led by General Farnsworth, gallantly charged the enemy's infantry and protected that flank from any attack, with the assistance of General Merritt's regular brigade. Gregg's division crossed the Potomac at Edward's Ferry and reached Gettysburg on the morning of the 2d, taking position on the right of our line. On the 3d, during that terrific fire of artillery, it was discovered that Stuart's cavalry was moving to our right, with the evident intention of passing to the rear to make a simultaneous attack there. When opposite our right, Stuart was met by General Gregg with two of his brigades and Custer's brigade of the Third Division, and on a fair field there was another trial between two cavalry forces, in which most of the fighting was done in the saddle, and with the trooper's favorite weapon, the sabre. Stuart advanced not a pace beyond where he was met; but after a severe struggle, which was only terminated by the darkness of night, he withdrew, and on the morrow, with the defeated army of Lee, was in retreat to the Potomac.

The obstinate blindness of English partisanship in our great struggle was curiously illustrated by an incident on the field of Gettysburg. One Fremantle, a lieutenant-colonel in the British army, had come over to visit the seat of war, and published his observations upon it in *Blackwood's Magazine*. He was near General Longstreet when Pickett's charge was made. Standing there with his back to the sun, and witnessing the operation on the great slope before him, he, although a soldier by profession, was so thoroughly possessed with the wish and the expectation that the Confederate cause might succeed, that he mistook Pickett's awful defeat for a glorious success, and rushing up to General Longstreet, congratulated him upon it, and told him how glad he was to be there and see it. "Are you, indeed?" said Longsteet, surprised. "I am not."

About a month after the battle, General Lee wrote a letter to Jefferson Davis, President of the Confederacy, in which he said:

"We must expect reverses, even defeats. They are sent to teach us wisdom and prudence, to call forth greater energies, and to prevent our falling into greater disasters. Our people have only to be true and united, to bear manfully the misfortunes incident to war, and all will come right in the end. I know how prone we are to censure, and how ready to blame others for the non-fulfilment of our expectations. This is unbecoming in a generous people, and I grieve to see its expression. The general remedy for the want of success in a military commander is his removal. This is natural, and in many instances proper; for, no matter what may be the ability of the officer, if he loses the confidence of his troops, disaster must, sooner or later, ensue. I have been prompted by these reflections more than once since my return from Pennsylvania to propose to your Excellency the propriety of selecting another commander for this army. I have seen and heard of expressions of discontent in the public journals at the result of the expedition. I do not know how far this feeling extends in the army. My brother officers have been too kind to report it, and so far the troops have been too generous to exhibit it. It is fair, however, to suppose that it does exist, and success is so necessary to us that nothing should be risked to secure it. I, therefore, in all sincerity, request your Excellency to take measures to supply my place." Mr. Davis declined to relieve General Lee from his command of the Army of Northern Virginia, and, consequently, he retained it until he surrendered himself and that army as prisoners of war in the spring of 1865.

MAJOR-GENERAL GEORGE G. MEADE AND OFFICERS.

The effect that the news of Gettysburg produced in Europe is said to have been the absolute termination of all hope for a recognition of the Confederacy as an independent power. A writer in the *London Morning Advertiser* says: "Mr. Disraeli, although never committing himself, as Mr. Gladstone and Lord John Russell did, to the principles for which the Southern Confederacy was fighting, always regarded recognition as a possible card to play, and was quite prepared, at the proper moment, to play it. The moment seemed to have come when General Lee invaded the Federal States. At that time it was notorious that the bulk of the Tory party and more than half of the Ministerialists were prepared for such a step. I had frequent conversations with Mr. Disraeli on the subject, and I perfectly recollect his saying to me that the time had now come for moving in the matter. 'But,' he said, 'it is of great importance that, if the move is to be made, it should not assume a party character, and it is of equal importance that the initiative should come from our (the Conservative) side. If the thing is to be done, I must do it myself; and then, from all I hear and know, the resolution will be carried, Lord Palmerston being quite disposed to accept the declaration by Parliament in favor of a policy which he personally approves. But I cannot speak without more knowledge of the subject than I now possess, and I should be glad if you could give me a brief, furnishing the necessary statistics of the population, the institutions, the commercial and political prospects of the Southern States, in order that when the moment comes I may be fully armed.' I procured the necessary information and placed it in his hands. Every day seemed to bring the moment for its use nearer, and the general feeling in the House of Commons was perfectly ripe for the motion in favor of recognition, when the news of the battle of Gettysburg came like a thunder-clap upon the country. General Meade defeated Lee, and saved the Union, and from that day not another word was heard in Parliament about recognition. A few days afterward I saw Mr. Disraeli, and his exact words were, 'We nearly put our foot in it.'"

A great national cemetery was laid out on the battlefield, and the remains of three thousand five hundred and sixty soldiers of the National army who had fallen in that campaign were placed in it, arranged in the order of their States. This was dedicated on the 19th of November in the year of the battle, 1863; and this occasion furnished a striking instance of the difference between natural genius and artificial reputation. The orator of the day was Edward Everett, who, by long cultivation and unlimited advertising, had attained the nominal place of first orator in the country; but he was by no means entitled to speak for the men who had there laid down their lives in the cause of universal liberty; for, through all his political life, until the breaking out of the war, he had been a strong pro-slavery man. President Lincoln was invited to be present, as a matter of course, and was informed that he would be expected to say a little something. Mr. Everett delivered a long address, prepared in his usual elaborate and artificial style, which was forgotten by every hearer within twenty-four hours. Mr. Lincoln, on his way from Washington, jotted down an idea or two on the back of an old envelope, by way of memorandum, and when he was called upon, rose and delivered a speech of fewer than three hundred words, which very soon took its place among the world's immortal orations. Some time after the delivery of the address, Mr. Lincoln, at the request of friends, carefully wrote it and affixed his signature. This copy is here reproduced in such a way as to give an exact fac-simile of his writing.

Address delivered at the dedication of the Cemetery at Gettysburg.

Four score and seven years ago our fathers brought forth on this continent, a new nation, conceived in Liberty, and dedicated to the proposition that all men are created equal.

Now we are engaged in a great civil war, testing whether that nation, or any nation so conceived and so dedicated, can long endure. We are met on a great battle field of that war. We have come to dedicate a portion of that field, as a final resting place for those who here gave their lives that that nation might live. It is altogether fitting and proper that we should do this.

But, in a larger sense, we can not dedicate—we can not consecrate—we can not hallow—this ground. The brave men, living and dead, who struggled here have consecrated it, far above our poor power to add or detract. The world will little note, nor long remember what we say here, but it can never forget what they did here. It is for us the living, rather, to be dedicated here to the unfinished work which they who fought here have thus far so nobly advanced. It is rather for us to be here dedicated to the great task remaining before us—that from these honored dead we take increased devotion to that cause for which they gave the last full measure of devotion—that we here highly resolve that these dead shall not have died in vain—that this nation, under God, shall have a new birth of freedom—and that government of the people, by the people, for the people, shall not perish from the earth.

Abraham Lincoln.

November 19. 1863.

COMMUNICATING WITH THE FLOTILLA.

CHAPTER XXIII.

THE VICKSBURG CAMPAIGN.

OPERATIONS ON THE MISSISSIPPI—GRANT PLACED IN COMMAND—PLANS THE CAMPAIGN—LOSS AT HOLLY SPRINGS—SHERMAN AND PORTER DESCEND THE RIVER—SHERMAN'S ATTEMPT ON THE YAZOO—AT HAINES'S BLUFF—CAPTURE OF ARKANSAS POST—CUTTING A CANAL—YAZOO PASS ATTEMPTED—STEELE'S BAYOU—GRANT CROSSES THE MISSISSIPPI—GRIERSON'S RAID—ACTION AT RAYMOND—CAPTURE OF JACKSON—BATTLE OF CHAMPION'S HILL—PEMBERTON IN VICKSBURG—SIEGE OF THE CITY BEGUN—SURRENDER—OPERATIONS OF GUNBOAT ON THE RIVER—A DUMMY GUNBOAT—INTERESTING INCIDENTS DURING THE SIEGE.

IN the autumn of 1862, after the battles of Iuka and Corinth, the National commanders in the West naturally began to think of further movements southward into the State of Mississippi, and of opening the great river and securing unobstructed navigation from Cairo to the Gulf. The project was slow in execution, principally from division of authority, and doubt as to what general would ultimately have the command. John A. McClernand, who had been a Democratic member of Congress from Illinois, and was what was known as a "political general," spent some time in Washington, urging the plan upon the President (who was an old acquaintance and personal friend), of course in the expectation that he would be intrusted with its execution. But he found little favor with General Halleck. At this time General Grant hardly knew what were the limits of his command, or whether, indeed, he really had any command at all.

Vicksburg is on a high bluff overlooking the Mississippi, where it makes a sharp bend enclosing a long, narrow peninsula. The railroad from Shreveport, La., reaches the river at this point, and connects by ferry with the railroad running east from Vicksburg through Jackson, the State capital. The distance between the two cities is forty-five miles. About a hundred miles below Vicksburg is Port Hudson, similarly situated as to river and railways. Between these two points the great Red River, coming from the borders of Texas, Arkansas, and Louisiana, flows into the Mississippi. As the Confederates drew a large part of their supplies from Texas and the country watered by the Red River, it was of the first importance to them to retain control of the Mississippi between Vicksburg and Port Hudson, especially after they had lost New Orleans, Baton Rouge, and Memphis.

After taking New Orleans, in April, 1862, Farragut had gone up the river with some of his ships, in May, and demanded the surrender of Vicksburg; but, though the place was then but slightly fortified, the demand was refused, and without a land force he could not take the city, as it was too high to be damaged by his guns. He ran by the batteries in June, and communicated with the river fleet of Capt. Charles H. Davis. But all the while new batteries were being planted on the bluffs, and after a time it became exceedingly hazardous for any sort of craft to run the gantlet under their plunging fire. In August, a Confederate force, under Gen. John C. Breckinridge, attempted the capture of Baton Rouge, expecting to be assisted in the assault by an immense iron-clad ram, the *Arkansas*, which was coming down the river. The city was occupied by a force under Gen. Thomas Williams, who made a stubborn and bloody fight, driving off the enemy. General Williams was killed, as were also the Confederate General Clarke and numerous officers of lower rank on either side, and more than six hundred men in all were killed or wounded. The ram failed to take part in the fight, because her machinery broke down. She was attacked next day by two or three vessels, commanded by Captain (now Admiral) David D. Porter, and when she had been disabled her crew abandoned her and set her on fire, and she was blown into a thousand fragments. After this defeat, General Breckinridge turned his attention

FLAG OFFICER CHARLES HENRY DAVIS.
(Afterward Rear-Admiral and Chief of Bureau of Navigation.)

COMMODORE W. D. PORTER.

to the fortification of Port Hudson, which was made almost as strong as Vicksburg.

On the 12th of November, 1862, General Grant received a despatch from General Halleck placing him in command of all troops sent to his department, and telling him to fight the enemy where he pleased. Four days later Grant and Sherman had a conference at Columbus, and a plan was arranged and afterward modified, by which Grant (who then had about thirty thousand men under his personal command) was to move southward and confront an equal force, commanded by Gen. John C. Pemberton, on the Tallahatchie; while Sherman, with thirty thousand, was to move from Memphis down the eastern bank of the Mississippi, and, assisted by Porter and his gunboats, attempt the capture of Vicksburg from the rear. If Pemberton moved toward that city, Grant was to follow and engage him as soon as possible.

Sherman and Porter, with their usual energy, went to work with all speed to carry out their part of the programme. Grant moved more slowly, because he did not wish to force his enemy back upon Vicksburg, but to hold him as far north as possible. He established his dépôt of supplies at Holly Springs, and waited for Sherman's movement. But the whole scheme was ruined by the activity of two Confederate cavalry detachments under Generals Van Dorn and Forrest. On the 20th of December Van Dorn made a dash at Holly Springs, which was held by fifteen hundred men under a Colonel Murphy, and captured the place and its garrison. Grant had more than two million dollars' worth of supplies there, and as Van Dorn could not remove them he burned them all, together with the storehouses and railroad buildings. Forrest, making a wide detour, tore up a portion of the railroad between Jackson, Tenn., and Columbus, Ky., so that Grant's army was cut off from all communication with the North for more than a week. It had not yet occurred to anybody that a large army could leave its communications and subsist on supplies gathered in the enemy's country; so Grant gave up this part of his plan and moved back toward Memphis.

But Sherman and Porter, not hearing of the disaster at Holly Springs, had proceeded with their preparations, embarked the troops, and gone down the river in a long procession, the gunboats being placed at intervals in the line of transports. Sherman says: "We manœuvred by divisions and brigades when in motion, and it was a magnificent sight. What few of the inhabitants remained at the plantations on the river bank were unfriendly, except the slaves. Some few guerilla parties infested the banks, but did not dare to molest so strong a force as I then commanded." The guerilla bands alluded to had been a serious annoyance to the boats patrolling the river. Besides the sharp-shooters with their rifles, small parties would suddenly appear at one point or another with a field gun, fire at a passing boat, and disappear before any force could be landed to pursue them. Farragut had been obliged to destroy the town of Donaldsonville, in order to punish and break up this practice on the lower reaches of the river.

The expedition arrived at Milliken's Bend on Christmas, where a division was left, and whence a brigade was sent to break the railroad from Shreveport. The next day the boats, with the three remaining divisions, ascended the Yazoo thirteen miles to a point opposite the bluffs north of Vicksburg, where the troops were landed. They were here on the low bottom-land, which was crossed by numerous bayous, some parts of it heavily wooded, the clearings being abandoned cotton plantations. The bluffs were crowned with artillery, and along their base was a deserted bed of the Yazoo. Most of the bridges were destroyed, and the whole district was subject to inundation. It was ugly ground for the operations of an army; but Sherman, confident that Grant was holding Pemberton, felt sure there could not be a heavy force on the heights, and resolved to capture them without delay. The 27th and 28th were spent in reconnoitring, selecting points for attack, and placing the troops. On the 29th, while the gunboats made a diversion at Haines's Bluff, and a part of Steele's division made a feint on the right, near Vicksburg, the main force crossed the intervening bayous at two points and attacked the centre of the position. The battle was begun by a heavy artillery fire, followed by musketry, and then the rush of the men. They had to face guns, at the foot of the bluff,

By permission of Dick & Fitzgerald, N. Y., from "Twelve Decisive Battles of the War."

that swept the narrow approaches, and at the same time endure a cross-fire from the heights. Blair's brigade reached the base of the hills, but was not properly supported by Morgan's, and had to fall back again, leaving five hundred of its men behind. The Sixth Missouri Regiment, at another point, had also gone forward unsupported, reached the bluff, and could not return. The men quickly scooped niches in the bank with their hands and sheltered themselves in them, while many of the enemy came to the edge of the hill, held out their muskets vertically at arm's-length, and fired down at them. These men were not able to get back to their lines till nightfall. This assault cost Sherman eighteen hundred and forty-eight men, and inflicted upon the Confederates a loss of but two hundred. He made arrangements to send a heavy force on the transports to Haines's Bluff in the night of December 30, to be debarked at dawn, and storm the works there, while the rest of the troops were to advance as soon as the defences had been thus taken in reverse. But a heavy fog prevented the boats from moving, and the next day a rain set in. Sherman observed the water-marks on the trees ten feet above his head, and a great deal more then ten feet above his head in the other direction he saw whole brigades of reinforcements marching into the enemy's intrenchments. He knew then that something must have gone wrong with Grant's co-operating force, and so he wisely re-embarked his men and munitions, and steamed down to the mouth of the Yazoo.

On the 4th of January, 1863, General McClernand assumed command of the two corps that were commanded by Generals Sherman and George W. Morgan. A fortnight before, a Confederate boat had come out of Arkansas River and captured a mail boat, and it was known that there was a Confederate garrison of five thousand men at Fort Hindman, or Arkansas Post, on the Arkansas. It occurred to Sherman that there could be no safety for boats on the Mississippi near the mouth of the Arkansas till this post was captured or broken up; and accordingly he asked McClernand to let him attack it with his corps, assisted by some of the gunboats. McClernand concluded to go himself with the entire army, and Porter also accompanied in person. They landed on the 10th, below the fort, and drove in the pickets. That night the Confederates toiled all night to throw up a line of works reaching from the fort northward to an impassable swamp. On the 11th the whole National force moved forward simultaneously to the attack, the gunboats steaming up close to the fort and sweeping its bastions with their fire, while Morgan's corps moved against its eastern face, and Sherman's against the new line of works. The ground to be passed over was level, with little shelter save a few trees and logs; but the men advanced steadily, lying down behind every little projection, and so annoying the artillerymen with their sharp-shooting that the guns could not be well served. When the gunboats arrived abreast of the fort and enfiladed it, the gunners ran down into

GUNBOATS PASSING VICKSBURG IN THE NIGHT.

the ditch, a man with a white flag appeared on the parapet, and presently white flags and rags were fluttering all along the line. Firing was stopped at once, and the fort was surrendered by its commander, General Churchill. About one hundred and fifty of the garrison had been killed, and the remainder, numbering forty-eight hundred, were made prisoners. The National loss was about one thousand. The fort was dismantled and destroyed, and the stores taken on board the fleet. McClernand conceived a vague project for ascending the river farther, but on peremptory orders from Grant the expedition returned to the Mississippi, steaming down the Arkansas in a heavy snow-storm.

In accordance with instructions from Washington, Grant now took personal command of the operations on the Mississippi, dividing his entire force into four corps, to be commanded by Generals McClernand, Sherman, Stephen A. Hurlbut, and James B. McPherson. Hurlbut's corps was left to hold the lines east of Memphis, while the other troops, with reinforcements from the North, were united in the river expedition.

McClernand and Sherman went down the peninsula enclosed in the bend of the river opposite Vicksburg, and with immense labor dug a canal across it. Much was hoped from this, but it proved a failure, for the river would not flow through it. Furthermore, there were bluffs commanding the river below Vicksburg, and the Confederates had already begun to fortify them ; so that if the canal had succeeded, navigation of the stream would have been as much obstructed as before. Still the work was continued till the 7th of March, when the river suddenly rose and overflowed the peninsula, and Sherman's men barely escaped drowning by regiments.

Grant was surveying the country in every direction, for some feasible approach to the flanks of his enemy. One scheme was to move through Lake Providence and the bayous west of the Mississippi, from a point far above Vicksburg to one far below. This involved the cutting of another canal, from the Mississippi to one of the bayous, and McPherson's corps spent a large part of the month of March in digging and dredging ; but this also was a failure. On the eastern side of the Mississippi there had once been an opening, known as Yazoo Pass, by which boats from Memphis made their way into Coldwater River, thence into the Tallahatchie, and thence into the Yazoo above Yazoo City ; but the pass had been closed by a levee or embankment. Grant blew up the levee, and tried this approach. But the Confederates had information of every movement, and took prompt measures to thwart it. The banks of the streams where his boats had to pass were heavily wooded, and great trees were felled across the channel. Worse than this, after the boats had passed in and removed many of the obstructions, it was found that the enemy were felling trees across the channel behind them, so that they might not get out again. Earthworks also were thrown up at the point where the Yallabusha and Tallahatchie unite to form the Yazoo, and heavily manned. Here the advance division of the expedition had a slight engagement, with no result. Reinforcements arrived under Gen. Isaac F. Quinby, who assumed command, and began operations for crossing the Yallabusha and rendering the Confederate fortification useless, when he was recalled by Grant, who had found that the necessary light-draught boats for carrying his whole force through to that point could not be had.

REAR-ADMIRAL HENRY WALKE.

(Commander of the "Tyler" and "Carondelet.")

One more attempt in this direction was made before the effort to flank Vicksburg on the north was given up. It was proposed to ascend the Yazoo a short distance from its mouth, turn into Steele's bayou, ascend this, and by certain passes that had been discovered get into Big Sunflower River, and then descend that stream into the Yazoo above Haines's Bluff. Porter and Sherman took the lead in this expedition, and encountered all the difficulties of the Yazoo Pass project, magnified several times—the narrow channels, the felled trees, the want of solid ground on which troops could be manœuvred, the horrible swamps and canebrakes, through some of which they picked their way with lighted candles, and the annoyance from unseen sharp-shooters that swarmed through the whole region. Porter at one time was on the point of abandoning his boats ; but finally all were extricated, though some of them had to back out through the narrow pass for a distance of thirty miles.

In March, Farragut with his flagship and one gunboat had run by the batteries at Port Hudson, but the remainder of his fleet had failed to pass. Several boats had run by the batteries at Vicksburg ; and Grant now turned his attention to a project for moving an army by transports through bayous west of the Mississippi to a point below the city, where Porter, after running by the batteries with his iron-clads, was to meet him and ferry the troops across to the eastern bank. The use of the bayous was finally given up, and the army marched by the roads. The fleet ran by the batteries on the night of April 16. As soon as it was discovered approaching, the Confederates set fire to immense piles of wood that they had prepared on the bank, the whole scene became as light as day, and for an hour and a half the fleet was under a heavy fire, which it returned as it steadily steamed by; but beyond the destruction of one transport there was no serious loss.

Bridges had to be built over bayous, and a suitable place discovered for crossing the Mississippi. New Carthage was tried, but found impracticable, as it was nearly surrounded by water. Grand Gulf was strongly fortified, and on the 29th of April seven of Porter's gunboats attacked it. They fired five hundred shots an hour for five hours, and damaged the works somewhat, but only killed or wounded eighteen men, while the fleet lost twenty-six men, and one boat was seriously disabled. Grant therefore gave up the project of crossing here, moved his transports down stream under cover of darkness, and at daylight on the 30th began the crossing at Bruinsburg. McClernand's corps was in the advance, and marched on Port Gibson that night. At dawn the enemy was found in a strong position three miles west of that place. There was sharp fighting all day, the Confederate force numbering about eight thousand, and contesting every foot of the ground; but the line was finally disrupted, and at night-fall they made an orderly retreat, burning bridges behind them. The National loss had been eight hundred and forty-nine men, killed, wounded, or missing; the Confederate, about one thousand. Grant's movements at this time were greatly assisted by one of the most effective cavalry raids of the war. This was conducted by Col. Benjamin H. Grierson, who with seventeen hundred men set out from La Grange, Tenn., on the 17th of April, and rode southward through the whole State of Mississippi, tearing up railroads, burning bridges, destroying supplies, eluding every strong force that was sent out to stop him, defeating several small ones, floundering through swamps, swimming rivers, spreading consternation by the celerity and uncertainty of his movements, and finally riding into Baton Rouge at the end of sixteen days with half his men asleep in their saddles. He had lost but twenty-seven.

LIEUTENANT-COLONEL CHARLES RIVERS-ELLET.

LAKE PROVIDENCE.

LIEUTENANT E. M. KING.

The fortifications at Grand Gulf were abandoned, Porter took possession of them, and Grant established his base there. A bridge had to be rebuilt at Port Gibson, and then Crocker's division pushed on in pursuit of the retreating Confederates, saved a burning bridge at Bayou Pierre, came up with them at Willow Springs, and after a slight engagement drove them across the Big Black at Hankinson's Ferry, and saved the bridge. There was a slight delay, for Sherman's corps and the supplies to arrive, and then Grant pressed on resolutely with his whole army. He had with him about forty-one thousand men, subsequently increased to forty-five thousand; and Pemberton at this time had about fifty thousand.

Grant moved northeasterly, toward Jackson, and on the 12th of May found a hostile force near Raymond. It numbered but three thousand, and was soon swept away, though not until it had lost five hundred men and inflicted a loss of four hundred and thirty-two upon the National troops. It was the purpose of the Union commander to move swiftly, and beat the enemy as much as possible in detail before the scattered forces could concentrate against him. Believing there was a considerable force at Jackson, which he would not like to leave in his rear, he marched on that place, and the next conflict occurred there, May 14th. Gen. Joseph E. Johnston (whom we took leave of when he was wounded at Seven Pines, nearly a year before) had just been ordered by the Confederate Government to take command of all the forces in Mississippi, and arrived at Jackson in the evening of the 13th, finding there about twelve thousand men subject to his orders. Pemberton was at Edwards Station, thirty miles westward, and Grant was between them. Johnston telegraphed to Richmond that he was too late, but took what measures he could for defence. It rained heavily that night, and the next morning, when the corps of Sherman and McPherson marched against the city, they travelled roads that were a foot under water. McPherson came up on the west, and Sherman on the southwest and south. The enemy was met two miles out, and driven in with heavy skirmishing. While manœuvring was going on before the intrenchments, the Union commanders seeking for a suitable point to assault, it was discovered that the enemy was evacuating the place, and Grant and his men went in at once and hoisted the National colors. They had lost two hundred and ninety men in the skirmishing; the enemy, eight hundred and forty-five, mostly captured. Seventeen guns were taken, but the Confederates burned most of their stores.

LIEUTENANT-GENERAL
J. C. PEMBERTON, C. S. A.

Leaving Sherman at Jackson to destroy the railroad, and the factories that were turning out goods for the Confederacy, which he did very thoroughly, Grant ordered all his other forces to concentrate at Bolton, twenty miles west. Marching thence westward, keeping the corps well together, and ordering Sherman to send forward an ammunition-train—for he knew that a battle must soon be fought—Grant found Pemberton with twenty-three thousand men waiting to receive him at Champion's Hill, on high ground well selected for defence, which covered the three roads leading westward. The battle, May 15th, lasted four hours, and was the bloodiest of the campaign. The brunt of it, on the National side, was borne by the divisions of Hovey, Logan, and Crocker; and Hovey lost more than one-third of his men. Logan's division pushed forward on the right, passed Pemberton's left flank, and held the only road by which the enemy could retreat. But this was not known to the Union commander at the time, and when Hovey, hard pressed, called for help, Logan was drawn back to his assistance, and the road uncovered. A little later Pemberton was in full retreat toward the crossing of the Big Black River, leaving his dead and wounded and thirty guns on the field. Grant's loss in the action—killed, wounded, and missing—was twenty-four hundred and forty-one. Pemberton's was over three thousand killed and wounded (including General Tilghman killed), besides nearly as many more captured in battle or on the retreat.

The enemy was next found at the Big Black River, where he had placed his main line on the high land west of the stream, and stationed his advance (or, properly speaking, his rear guard) along the edge of a bayou that ran through the low ground on the east. This advanced position was attacked vigorously on the 17th, and when Lawler's brigade flanked it on the right, that general leading a charge in his shirt-sleeves, the whole line gave way, and Pemberton resumed his retreat, burning the bridge behind him and leaving his men in the lowland to their fate. Some swam the river, some were drowned, and seventeen hundred and fifty were made prisoners. Eighteen guns were captured here. The National loss was two hundred and seventy-nine.

MAJOR-GENERAL CARTER L. STEVENSON, C. S. A.

Sherman now came up with his corps, and Grant ordered the building of three bridges. One was a floating or raft bridge. One was made by felling trees on both sides of the stream and letting them fall so that their boughs would interlace over the channel, the trunks not being cut entirely through, and so hanging to the stumps. Planks laid crosswise on these trees made a good roadway. The third bridge was made by using cotton bales for pontoons. Sherman's troops made a fourth bridge farther up the stream; and that night he and Grant sat on a log and watched the long procession of blue-coated men with gleaming muskets marching across the swaying structure by the light of pitch-pine torches. All the bridges were finished by morning, and that day, the 18th, the entire army was west of the river.

BRIGADIER-GENERAL
LLOYD TILGHMAN, C. S. A.

Pemberton marched straight into Vicksburg, which had a long line of defences on the land side as well as on the water front, and shut himself up there. Grant, following closely, invested the place on the 19th. Sherman, holding the right of the line, was at Haines's Bluff, occupying the very ground beneath which his men had suffered defeat some months before. Here, on the Yazoo, Grant established a new base for supplies. McPherson's corps was next to Sherman's on the left, and McClernand's next, reaching to the river below the city. Sharp skirmishing went on while the armies were getting into position, and an assault in the afternoon of the 19th gained the National troops some advantage in the advancement of the line to better ground. Grant's army had been living for three weeks on five days' rations, with what they could pick up in the country they passed through, which was

MAJOR-GENERAL RICHARD J. OGLESBY.

not a little; and his first care was to construct roads in the rear of his line, so that supplies could be brought up from the Yazoo rapidly and regularly. He had now about thirty thousand men, the line of defences before him was eight miles long, and he expected an attack from Johnston in the rear. At ten o'clock on the 22d, therefore, he ordered a grand assault, hoping to carry the works by storm. But though the men at several points reached the breastworks and planted their battle-flags on them, it was found impossible to take them. McClernand falsely reported that he had carried two forts at his end of the line, and asked for reinforcements, which were sent to him, and a renewal of the assault was made to help him. This caused additional loss of life, to no purpose, and shortly afterward that general was relieved of his command, which was given to Gen. E. O. C. Ord.

After this assault, which had cost him nearly twenty-five hundred men, Grant settled down to a siege of Vicksburg by regular approaches. The work went on day by day, with the usual incidents of a siege. There was mining and counter-mining, and two large mines were exploded under angles of the Confederate works, but without any practical result. The great guns were booming night and day, throwing thousands of shells into the city, and more than one citizen picked up and threw into a heap hundreds of pounds of the iron fragments that fell into his yard. Caves were dug in the banks where the streets had been cut through the clayey hills, and in these the people found refuge from the shells. A newspaper was issued regularly even to the last day of the siege, but it was printed on the back of wallpaper. Provisions of course became scarce, and mule-meat was eaten. Somebody printed a humorous bill of fare, which consisted entirely of mule-meat in the various forms of soup, roast, stew, etc. All the while the besiegers were digging away, bringing their trenches closer to the defences, till the soldiers of the hostile lines bandied jests across the narrow intervening space. At the end of forty-seven days the works arrived at the point where a grand assault must be the next thing, and at the same time famine threatened, and the National holiday was at hand. After some negotiation General Pemberton unconditionally surrendered the city and his army of thirty-one thousand six hundred men, on the 4th of July, 1863, one day after Lee's defeat at Gettysburg.

Port Hudson, which Banks with twelve thousand men and Farragut with his fleet had besieged for weeks, was surrendered with its garrison of six thousand men, five days after the fall of Vicksburg. The entire Confederate loss in Mississippi, from the time Grant entered the State at Bruinsburg to the surrender, was about fifty thousand; Grant's was about nine thousand. But the great triumph was in the opening of the Mississippi River, which cut the Confederacy completely in two.

By Grant's orders there was no cheering, no firing of salutes, no expression of exultation at the surrender; because the triumph was over our own countrymen, and the object of it all was to establish a permanent Union.

In his correspondence with Pemberton, while demanding an unconditional surrender, Grant had written: "Men who have shown so much endurance and courage as those now in Vicksburg will always challenge the respect of an adversary, and I can assure you will be treated with all the respect due to prisoners of war. I do not favor the proposition of appointing commissioners to arrange the terms of capitulation, because I have no terms other than those indicated above." As soon as the surrender was effected, the famished Confederate army was liberally supplied with food, Grant's men taking it out of their own haversacks. All the prisoners at Vicksburg and Port Hudson were immediately paroled and furnished with transportation and supplies, under the supposition that they would go to their homes and remain there till properly exchanged.

The coöperation of Porter's fleet of river gunboats above the city, and some of Farragut's vessels below it, had been a great assistance during the siege, in cutting off the city from communication across the river. General Grant's thoughtfulness and mastery of details in great military movements are suggested by one of his letters to Farragut at this time. Knowing that Farragut's ships would need a constant supply of coal, he sent him a large cargo, and wrote: "Hearing nothing from Admiral Porter, I have determined to send you a barge of coal from here.

BRIGADIER-GENERAL NEAL DOW.

COLONEL CHARLES W. LE GENDRE.

BREVET BRIGADIER-GENERAL WILLIAM E. STRONG.

BRIGADIER-GENERAL ADAM BADEAU.

The barge will be cast adrift from the upper end of the canal at ten o'clock to-night. Troops on the opposite side of the point will be on the lookout, and, should the barge run into the eddy, will start it adrift again."

One of the most ludicrous incidents of the siege was the career of the dummy monitor, sometimes called the "Black Terror." The *Indianola*, of Porter's fleet, had been attacked by the Confederates and captured in a sinking condition. They were hard at work trying to raise her, when they saw something coming down the river that struck them with terror. Admiral Porter had fitted up an old flat-boat so that, at a little distance, it looked like a monitor. It had mud furnaces and a smokestack made of pork barrels. Fire was built in the furnaces, and she was set adrift on the river without a single person on board. The men at the Vicksburg batteries were startled at the appearance of a monitor in those waters, and opened a furious cannonade, but did not succeed in stopping the stranger, which passed on with the current. In the excitement, orders were given to destroy the *Indianola*, and she was blown up just before the trick was discovered.

A few days after the capture of Vicksburg, President Lincoln wrote this characteristically frank and generous letter to General Grant:

MY DEAR GENERAL: I do not remember that you and I ever met personally. I write this now as a grateful acknowledgment for the almost inestimable service you have done the country. I wish to say further: when you first reached the vicinity of Vicksburg, I thought you should do what you finally did—march the troops across the neck, run the batteries with the transports, and thus go below; and I never had any faith, except a general hope that you knew better than I, that the Yazoo Pass expedition and the like could succeed. When you got below and took Fort Gibson, Grand Gulf and vicinity, I thought you should go down the river and join General Banks; and when you turned northward, east of the Big Black, I feared it was a mistake. I now wish to make a personal acknowledgment that you were right and I was wrong.

Yours very truly,

A. LINCOLN.

After the surrender Grant reorganized his army, issued instructions for the care and government of the blacks who had escaped from slavery and come within his lines, and gave orders for furloughs to be granted freely to those of his soldiers who had been conspicuous for their valor and attention to duty during the campaign. It is said that he also took particular care that no exorbitant prices should be demanded of these soldiers on the steamboats by which they ascended the river in going to their homes. His own modesty and loyalty are exhibited in a letter that he wrote, a month later, when the loyal citizens of Memphis proposed to give him a public dinner. He said: "In accepting this testimonial, which I do at great sacrifice of personal feelings, I simply desire to pay a tribute to the first public exhibition in Memphis of loyalty to the Government which I represent in the Department of the Tennessee. I should dislike to refuse, for considerations of personal convenience, to acknowledge anywhere or in any form the existence of sentiments which I have so long and so ardently desired to see manifested in this department. The stability of this Government and the unity of this nation depends solely on the cordial support and the earnest loyalty of the people."

Of the innumerable incidents of the marches and the siege, in this campaign, some of the most interesting were told by Gen. Manning F. Force in a paper read before the Ohio Commandery of the Loyal Legion, all of them being drawn from his own experience. In that campaign he was colonel of the Twentieth Ohio infantry.

"About the 20th of April I was sent, with the Twentieth Ohio and the Thirtieth Illinois, seven miles out from Milliken's Bend, to build a road across a swamp. When the sun set, the leaves of the forest seemed to exude smoke, and the air became a saturated solution of gnats. When my mess sat down to supper under a tree, the gnats got into our mouths, noses, eyes, and ears. They swarmed upon our necks, seeming to encircle them with bands of hot iron. Tortured and blinded, we could neither eat nor see. We got a quantity of cotton, and made a circle around the group, and set it on fire. The pungent smoke made water stream from our eyes, but drove the gnats away. We then supped in anguish, but in peace. I sent back to camp and got some mosquito netting from a sutler. Covering my

BRIGADIER-GENERAL GABRIEL J. RAINS, C. S. A.

THE ADVANCE ON VICKSBURG.—THE FIFTEENTH CORPS CROSSING THE BIG BLACK RIVER BY NIGHT, MAY 16, 1863.

head with many folds, I slept, waking at intervals to burn a wad of cotton. Many of the men sat by the fire all night, fighting the gnats, and slept next day. In the woods we found stray cattle, sheep, and hogs. A large pond was full of fish. We lived royally.

"On the 25th of April, Logan's division marched. The Twentieth Ohio had just drawn new clothing, but had to leave it behind. Stacking spades and picks in the swamp, they took their place in the column as it appeared, taking with them only the scanty supplies they had there. Six days of plodding brought them over nearly seventy miles, to the shore of the river opposite Bruinsburg. We marched six miles one day, and those six miles by evening were strewn with wrecks of wagons and their loads and half-buried guns. At a halt of some hours the men stood in deep mud, for want of any means of sitting. Yet when we halted at night, every man answered to his name, and went laughing to bed on the sloppy ground.

"On the 12th of May the Seventeenth Corps marched on the road toward Raymond. The Thirtieth Illinois was deployed with a skirmish line in front, on the left of the road; the Twentieth Ohio, in like manner on the right. About noon we halted —the Twentieth Ohio in an open field, bounded by a fence to the front, beyond which was forest and rising ground. An unseen battery on some height beyond the timber began shelling the fields. The Twentieth advanced over the fence into the woods. The First Brigade came up and formed on our right. All at once the woods rang with the shrill rebel yell and a deafening din of musketry. The Twentieth rushed forward to a creek, and used the farther bank as breastworks. The timber beyond the creek and the fence was free from undergrowth. The Twentieth Illinois, the regiment next to the right of the Twentieth Ohio, knelt down in place and returned the fire. The enemy advanced into the creek in its front. I went to the lieutenant-colonel, who was kneeling at the left flank, and asked him why he did not advance into the creek. He said, 'We have no orders.' In a few minutes the colonel of the regiment was killed. It was too late to advance, it was murder to remain, and the lieutenant-colonel withdrew the regiment in order back behind the fence. I cannot tell how long the battle lasted. I remember noticing the forest leaves, cut by rifle-balls, falling in thick eddies, still as snowflakes. At one time the enemy in our front advanced to the border of the creek, and rifles of opposing lines crossed while firing. Men who were shot were burned by the powder of the rifles that sped the balls.

"In eighteen days Grant marched two hundred miles, won five battles, four of them in six days, inflicted a loss of five thousand men, captured eighty-eight pieces of artillery, compelled the abandonment of all outworks, and cooped Pemberton's army within the lines of Vicksburg, while he had opened for himself easy and safe communication with the North. During these eighteen days the men had been without shelter, and had subsisted on five days' rations and scanty supplies picked up on the way. The morning we crossed the Big Black I offered five dollars for a small piece of corn bread, and could not get it. The soldier said bread was worth more to him than money.

"The Twentieth was placed in a road-cut, which was enfiladed by one of the enemy's infantry intrenchments. But when we sat with our backs pressed against the side of the cut toward Vicksburg, the balls whistled by just outside of our knees. At sunset the company cooks were possessed to come to us with hot coffee. They succeeded in running the gantlet, and the garrison could hear the jingling of tin cups and shouts of laughter as the cramped men ate their supper. After dark we were recalled and placed on the slope of a sharp ridge, with orders to remain in place, ready to move at any moment, and with strict injunctions not to allow any man's head to appear above the ridge. There we lay two or three days in line. Coffee was brought to us by the cooks at meal-time. Not a man those two or three days left the line without a special order. The first night Lieutenant Weatherby, commanding the right company, reported that the slope was so steep where he was that the men as soon as they fell asleep began to roll down hill. I had to give him leave to shift his position.

"One day when there was a general bombardment I was told a soldier wished to see me. Under the canopy of exploding shell I found a youth, a boy, lying on his back on the ground. He was pale and speechless; there was a crimson hole in his breast. As I knelt by his side he looked wistfully at me. I said, 'We must all die some time, and the man is happy who meets death in the discharge of duty. You have done your whole duty well.' It was all he wanted. His eyes brightened, a smile flickered on his lips, and I was kneeling beside a corpse.

"One day, when the Twentieth Ohio was in advance, we came, at a turn in the road, upon two old colored people, man and woman, plump and sleek, riding mules, and coming toward us. As they caught sight of the long column of blue-coats, the woman, crossing her hands upon her bosom, rolled up her eyes and cried in ecstasy, 'Bress de Lord! Bress Almighty God! Our friends is come, our friends is come!' On the return, we crossed a plantation where the field-hands were ploughing. The soldiers like mules, and the negroes gladly unharnessed them, and helped the soldiers to mount. I said to one, 'The soldiers are taking your mules.' The quick response was, 'An' dey is welcome to 'em, sar; dey is welcome to 'em.' Men and women looked wistfully at the marching column, and began to talk about joining us. They seemed to wait the determination of a gray-headed darky who was considering. Presently there was a shout, 'Uncle Pete's a-gwine, an' I'm a-gwine, too!' As they flocked after us, one tall, stern woman strode along, carrying a wooden tray and a crockery pitcher as all her effects, looking straight to the front. Some one asked, 'Auntie, where are you going?' She answered, without looking, 'I don't car' whicher way I go, so as I git away from dis place.'

"When the working parties carried the saps to the base of the works, the besieged used to light the fuses of six-pound shells and toss them over the parapet. They would roll down among the working parties and explode, sometimes doing serious damage. A young soldier of the Twentieth Ohio, named Friend, devised wooden mortars. A very small charge of powder in one of these would just lift a shell over the enemy's parapet and drop it within. After the surrender there was much inquiry from the garrison how they were contrived."

Concerning this tossing of the shells, one who had been a private in Grant's army said to the writer: "I was in the trenches one evening when a shell came over without noise, as if thrown by hand. Fortunately it did not explode, or it would have injured a good many of us. This greatly surprised me, and when in a few minutes another came, I was on the watch and noted the point from which it seemed to start. By strange luck this also failed to explode. I then laid my rifle across the breastwork, cocked it, and put my eye to the sight, with the muzzle facing the point from which the shell had come. Presently I saw a man rise in the enemy's trench with a third shell in his hand—but he never threw it."

When the siege began, General Pemberton issued an order that all non-combatants leave the city; but many of them refused to go—some because they had no other home, or means to sustain themselves elsewhere—and a few women and children were among those who remained. One lady, wife of an officer in Pemberton's army, published the next year an account of her life in the city during the siege, which is especially interesting for its picturesque and suggestive details, many of which are not to be found elsewhere. A few passages are here reproduced:

"The cave [of a friend] was an excavation in the earth the size of a large room, high enough for the tallest person to stand perfectly erect, provided with comfortable seats, and altogether quite a large and habitable abode (compared with some of the caves in the city), were it not for the dampness and the constant contact with the soft earthy walls.

SIEGE OF VICKSBURG—SHOWING SOME OF THE FEDERAL INTRENCHMENTS.

"Two negroes were coming with a small trunk between them, and a carpet-bag or two, evidently trying to show others of the profession how careless of danger they were, and how foolish 'niggars' were to run 'dat sort o' way.' A shell came through the air and fell a few yards beyond the braves, when, lo! the trunk was sent tumbling, and landed bottom upward; the carpet-bag followed—one grand somerset; and amid the cloud of dust that arose, I discovered one porter doubled up by the side of the trunk, and the other crouching close by a pile of plank. A shout from the negroes on the cars, and much laughter, brought them on their feet, brushing their knees and giggling, yet looking quite foolish, feeling their former prestige gone. The excitement was intense in the city. Groups of people stood on every available position where a view could be obtained of the distant hills, where the jets of white smoke constantly passed out from among the trees.

"The caves were plainly becoming a necessity, as some persons had been killed on the street by fragments of shells. The room that I had so lately slept in had been struck by a fragment of a shell during the first night, and a large hole made in the ceiling. Terror-stricken, we remained crouched in the cave, while shell after shell followed each other in quick succession. I endeavored by constant prayer to prepare myself for the sudden death I was almost certain awaited me. My heart stood still as we would hear the reports from the guns, and the rushing and fearful sound of the shell as it came toward us. As it neared, the noise became more deafening; the air was full of the rushing sound; pains darted through my temples; my ears were full of the confusing noise; and, as it exploded, the report flashed through my head like an electric shock, leaving me in a quiet state of terror the most painful that I can imagine, cowering in a corner, holding my child to my heart—the only feeling of my life being the choking throbs of my heart, that rendered me almost breathless. I saw one fall in the road without the mouth of the cave, like a flame of fire, making the earth tremble, and, with a low, singing sound, the fragments sped on in their work of death.

"So constantly dropped the shells around the city that the inhabitants all made preparations to live under ground during the siege. M—— sent over and had a cave made in a hill near by. We seized the opportunity one evening, when the gunners were probably at their supper, for we had a few moments of quiet, to go over and take possession.

"Some families had light bread made in large quantities, and subsisted on it with milk (provided their cows were not killed from one milking time to another), without any more cooking, until called on to replenish. Though most of us lived on corn bread and bacon, served three times a day, the only luxury of the meal consisting in its warmth, I had some flour, and frequently had some hard, tough biscuit made from it, there being no soda or yeast to be procured. At this time we could also procure beef. A gentleman friend was kind enough to offer me his camp-bed; another had his tent-fly stretched over the mouth of our residence to shield us from the sun. And so I went regularly to work keeping house under ground. Our new habitation was an excavation made in the earth, and branching six feet from the entrance, forming a cave in the shape of a T. In one of the wings my bed fitted; the other I used as a kind of dressing-room. In this the earth had been cut down a foot or two below the floor of the main cave; I could stand erect here; and when tired of sitting in other portions of my residence I bowed myself into it, and stood impassively resting at full height—one of the variations in the still shell-expectant life.

"We were safe at least from fragments of shell, and they were flying in all directions. We had our roof arched and braced, the supports of the bracing taking up much room in our confined quarters. The earth was about five feet thick above, and seemed hard and compact.

"'Miss M——,' said one of the more timid servants, 'do they want to kill us all dead? Will they keep doing this until we all die?' I said most heartily, 'I hope not.' The servants we had with us seemed to possess more courage than is usually attributed to negroes. They seldom hesitated to cross the street for water at any time. The 'boy' slept at the entrance of the cave, with a pistol I had given him, telling me I need not be 'afeared—dat any one dat come dar would have to go over his body first.' He never refused to carry out any little article to M—— on the battlefield. I laughed heartily at a dilemma he was placed in one day. The mule that he had mounted to ride out to the battlefield took him to a dangerous locality, where the shells were flying thickly, and then, suddenly stopping, through fright, obstinately refused to stir. It was in vain that George kicked and beat him—go he would not; so, clinching his hand, he hit him severely in the head several times, jumped down, ran home, and left him. The mule stood a few minutes rigidly; then, looking round, and seeing George at some distance from him, turned and followed quite demurely.

MAKING GABIONS.

"One morning, after breakfast, the shells began falling so thickly around us, that they seemed aimed at the particular spot on which our cave was located. Two or three fell immediately in the rear of it, exploding a few minutes before reaching the ground, and the fragments went singing over the top of our habitation. I at length became so much alarmed—as the cave trembled excessively—for our safety, that I determined, rather than be buried alive, to stand out from under the earth; so taking my child in my arms, and calling the servants, we ran to a refuge near the roots of a large fig-tree, that branched out over the bank, and served as a protection from the fragments of shells. As we stood trembling there—for the shells were falling all around us—some of my gentleman friends came up to reassure me, telling me that the tree would protect us, and that the range would probably be changed in a short time. While they spoke, a shell, that seemed to be of enormous size, fell, screaming and hissing, immediately before the mouth of our cave, sending up a huge column of smoke and earth, and jarring the ground most sensibly where we stood. What seemed very strange, the earth closed in around the shell, and left only the newly upturned soil to show where it had fallen.

"The cave we inhabited was about five squares from the levee. A great many had been made in a hill immediately beyond us; and near this hill we could see most of the shells fall. Caves were the fashion—the rage—over besieged Vicksburg. Negroes who understood their business hired themselves out to dig them, at from thirty to fifty dollars, according to the size. Many persons, considering different localities unsafe, would sell them to others who had been less fortunate or less provident; and so great was the demand for cave workmen, that a new branch of industry sprang up and became popular—particularly as the personal safety of the workman was secured, and money withal.

"A large trunk was picked up after the sinking of the *Cincinnati*, belonging to a surgeon on board. It contained valu-

BRIGADIER-GENERAL SETH M. BARTON, C. S. A.

BRIGADIER-GENERAL N. G. EVANS, C. S. A.

MAJOR-GENERAL WILLIAM PRESTON, C. S. A.

able surgical instruments that could not be procured in the Confederacy.

"I was sitting near the entrance, about five o'clock, thinking of the pleasant change—oh, bless me!—that to-morrow would bring, when the bombardment commenced more furiously than usual, the shells falling thickly around us, causing vast columns of earth to fly upward, mingled with smoke. I was startled by the shouts of the servants and a most fearful jar and rocking of the earth, followed by a deafening explosion such as I had never heard before. The cave filled instantly with powder, smoke, and dust. I stood with a tingling, prickling sensation in my head, hands, and feet, and with a confused brain. Yet alive!—was the first glad thought that came to me; child, servants, all here, and saved!—from some great danger, I felt. I stepped out, to find a group of persons before my cave, looking anxiously for me; and lying all around, freshly torn, rose-bushes, arbor-vitæ trees, large clods of earth, splinters, pieces of plank, wood, etc. A mortar shell had struck the corner of the cave, fortunately so near the brow of the hill that it had gone obliquely into the earth, exploding as it went, breaking large masses from the side of the hill, tearing away the fence, the shrubbery and flowers, sweeping all like an avalanche down near the entrance of my good refuge.

"A young girl, becoming weary in the confinement of the cave, hastily ran to the house in the interval that elapsed between the slowly falling shells. On returning, an explosion sounded near her—one wild scream, and she ran into her mother's presence, sinking like a wounded dove, the life-blood flowing over the light summer dress in crimson ripples from a death-wound in her side, caused by the shell fragment. A fragment had also struck and broken the arm of a little boy playing near the mouth of his mother's cave. This was one day's account.

"I was distressed to hear of a young Federal lieutenant who had been severely wounded and left on the field by his comrades. He had lived in this condition from Saturday until Monday, lying in the burning sun without water or food; and the men on both sides could witness the agony of the life thus prolonged, without the power to assist him in any way. I was glad, indeed, when I heard the poor man had expired on Monday morning. Another soldier left on the field, badly wounded in the leg, had begged most piteously for water; and lying near the Confederate intrenchments, his cries were all directed to the Confederate soldiers. The firing was heaviest where he lay, and it would have been at the risk of a life to have gone to him; yet a Confederate soldier asked and obtained leave to carry water to him, and stood and fanned him in the midst of the firing, while he eagerly drank from the heroic soldier's canteen.

"One morning George made an important discovery—a newly made stump of sassafras, very near the cave, with large roots extending in every direction, affording us an inexhaustible vein of tea for future use. We had been drinking water with our meals previous to this disclosure; coffee and tea had long since been among the things that were, in the army. We, however, were more fortunate than many of the officers, having access to an excellent cistern near us; while many of our friends used muddy water or river water.

"On another occasion, a gentleman sent me four large slices of ham, having been fortunate enough to procure a small piece himself. Already the men in the rifle-pits were on half rations—flour or meal enough to furnish bread equivalent in quantity to two biscuits in two days. They amused themselves, while lying in the pits, by cutting out little trinkets from the wood of the parapet and the minie-balls that fell around them. Major Fry, from Texas, excelled in skill and ready invention, I think; he sent me one day an armchair that he had cut from a minie-ball—the most minute affair of the kind I ever saw, yet perfectly symmetrical. At another time, he sent me a diminutive plough made from the parapet wood, with traces of lead, and a lead point made from a minie-ball.

"The courier brought many letters to the inhabitants from friends without. His manner of entering the city was singular. Taking a skiff in the Yazoo, he proceeded to its confluence with the Mississippi, where he tied the little boat, entered the woods, and awaited the night. At dark he took off his clothing, placed his despatches securely within them, bound the package firmly to a plank, and, going into the river, he sustained his head above the water by holding to the plank, and in this manner floated in the darkness through the fleet, and on two miles down the river to Vicksburg, where his arrival was hailed as an event of great importance in the still life of the city.

"The hill opposite our cave might be called 'death's point,' from the number of animals that had been killed in eating the grass on the sides and summit. Horses or mules that are tempted to mount the hill by the promise of grass that grows profusely there invariably come limping down wounded, to die at the base, or are brought down dead from the summit.

"A certain number of mules are killed each day by the commissaries, and are issued to the men, all of whom prefer the fresh meat, though it be of mule, to the bacon and salt rations that they have eaten for so long a time without change.

"I was sewing, one day, near one side of the cave, where the bank slopes and lights up the room like a window. Near this opening I was sitting, when I suddenly remembered some little article I wished in another part of the room. Crossing to procure it, I was returning, when a minie-ball came whizzing through the opening, passed my chair, and fell beyond it. Had I been still sitting, I should have stopped it."

CHAPTER XXIV.

THE DRAFT RIOTS.

ATTITUDE OF THE DEMOCRATIC PARTY—VALLANDIGHAM BANISHED—SPEECH OF EX-PRESIDENT PIERCE—SPEECH OF HORATIO SEYMOUR—LAW OF SUBSTITUTES PERSISTENTLY MISINTERPRETED—THE DRAFT IN NEW YORK—THE RIOTS—THE AUTUMN ELECTIONS.

THE second attempt at invasion by Lee had ended at Gettysburg even more disastrously than the first, and he returned to Virginia at the head of hardly more than one-half of the army with which he had set out; on the next day Vicksburg fell, the Mississippi was opened, and Pemberton's entire army stacked their muskets and became prisoners. Then the war should have ended; for the question on which the appeal to arms had been made was practically decided. Four great slave States —Maryland, Kentucky, Tennessee, and Missouri—had never really joined the Confederacy, though some of them were represented in its Congress, and the territory that it actually held was steadily diminishing. The great blockade was daily growing more effective, the largest city in the South had been held by National troops for fifteen months, and the Federal authority was maintained somewhere in every State, with the sole exception of Alabama. The delusion that Southern soldiers would make a better army, man for man, than Northern, had long since been dispelled. The nation had suffered from incompetent commanders; but time and experience had weeded them out, and the really able ones were now coming to the front. The taboo had been removed from the black man, and he was rapidly putting on the blue uniform to fight for the enfranchisement of his race. Lincoln with his proclamation, and Meade and Grant with their victories, had destroyed the last chance of foreign intervention. In the military situation there was nothing to justify any further hope for the Confederacy, or any more destruction of life in the vain endeavor to disrupt the Union. If there was any justification for a continuance of the struggle on the part of the insurgents, it was to be found only in a single circumstance—the attitude of the Democratic party in the Northern States; but it must be confessed that this was such as to give considerable color to their expectation of ultimate success.

The habitual feeling of antagonism to the opposite party, from which few men in a land of popular politics are ever wholly free, was reinforced by a sincere belief on the part of many that the Government, in determining to crush the rebellion, had undertaken a larger task than it could ever accomplish. This belief was born of an ignorance that it was impossible to argue with, because it supposed itself to be enlightened and fortified by great historical facts. Both conscious and unconscious demagogues picked out little shreds of history and formulated phrases and catch-words, which village newspapers and village statesmen confidently repeated as unanswerable arguments from the experience of nations. Thus Pitt's exclamation during the war of American independence, "You cannot conquer America!" was triumphantly quoted thousands of times, as an argument for the impossibility of conquering the South. Assertions were freely made that the despotism of the Administration (in trying to save the National armies from useless slaughter, by arresting spies and traitors at the North) exceeded anything ever done by Cæsar or the Russian Czar. The word "Bastile" was given out, without much explanation, and was echoed all along the line. The war Governors of the free States, and especially the provisional military Governors in Tennessee and Louisiana, were called Lincoln's satraps; and "satraps," with divers pronunciations, became a popular word. The fathers of the Republic were all mentioned with sorrowful reverence, and it was declared that the Constitution they had framed was destroyed—not by the Secessionists, but by Mr. Lincoln and his advisers. Somebody invented a story that Secretary Seward had said he had only to reach forth his hand and ring a bell, and any man in the country whom he might designate would at once be seized and thrown into prison; whereupon "the tinkle of Seward's little bell" became a frequent head-line in the Democratic journals. The army before Vicksburg was pointed at in derision, as besieging a place that could never be taken.

It did not occur to any of these orators and journalists to explain the difference between an ocean three thousand miles wide, and the Rappahannock River; or the difference between an absolute monarch born to the purple, and a president elected by a free vote of the people; or even the difference between a state of peace and a state of war. None of them told their hearers that, only eight years before, the city of Sebastopol had withstood the combined armies of England and France for almost a year, while the city of Vicksburg, when Grant besieged it, fell on the forty-seventh day. Nor did any of them ever appear to consider what the probable result would be if the entire Democratic party in Northern States should give the Administration as hearty support as it received from its own.

It is easy to see the fallacy of all those arguments now, and the unwisdom of the policy from which they sprang; but they were a power in the land at that time, and wrought unmeasured mischief. The most conspicuous opponent of the Government in the West was Clement L. Vallandigham, of Ohio, whose position will be understood most readily from a few of his public utterances. He wrote, in May, 1861: "The audacious usurpation of President Lincoln, for which he deserves impeachment, in daring, against the very letter of the Constitution, and without the shadow of law, to raise and support armies, and to provide and maintain a navy, for three years, by mere executive proclamation, I will not vote to sustain or ratify—

never." Speaking in his place in the House of Representatives in January, 1863, he said: "I have denounced, from the beginning, the usurpations and infractions, one and all, of law and Constitution, by the President and those under him; their repeated and persistent arbitrary arrests, the suspension of *habeas corpus*, the violation of freedom of the mails, of the private house, of the press and of speech, and all the other multiplied wrongs and outrages upon public liberty and private right which have made this country one of the worst despotisms on the earth for the past twenty months. To the record and to time I appeal for my justification." In proposing conciliation and compromise as a substitute for the war, he said, borrowing the language of the Indiana Democratic platform, "In considering terms of settlement, we will look only to the welfare, peace, and safety of the white race, without reference to the effect that settlement may have upon the condition of the African." For these and similar utterances, especially in regard to a military order that forbade the carrying of firearms and other means of disturbing the peace, and for the effect they were having upon his followers, Mr. Vallandigham was arrested in May, 1863, by the military authorities in Ohio, tried by court-martial, and sentenced to imprisonment during the war. The President commuted the sentence to banishment beyond the lines, and the prisoner was taken south through Kentucky and Tennessee, and sent into Confederate territory under a flag of truce. This of course placed him in the light of a martyr, and a few months later it made him the Democratic candidate for Governor of Ohio.

In the East, ex-President Pierce, of New Hampshire, loomed up as a leader of the opposition. On January 6, 1860, he had written to Jefferson Davis (who had been Secretary of War in his cabinet) a letter in which he said: "Without discussing the question of right—of abstract power to secede—I have never believed that actual disruption of the Union can occur without blood; and if through the madness of Northern abolitionists that dire calamity must come, the fighting will not be along Mason and Dixon's line merely. It will be within our own borders, and in our own streets, between the two classes of citizens to whom I have referred. Those who defy law and scout constitutional obligations will, if we ever reach the arbitrament of arms, find occupation enough at home." In an elaborate Fourth-of-July oration at Concord in 1863, he said: "No American citizen was then [before the war] subject to be driven into exile for opinion's sake, or arbitrarily arrested and incarcerated in military bastiles—even as he may now be—not for acts or words of imputed treason, but if he do but mourn in silent sorrow over the desolation of his country. Do we not all know that the cause of our calamities is the vicious intermeddling of too many of the citizens of the Northern States with the constitutional rights of the Southern States, coöperating with the discontents of the people of those States? We have seen, in the experience of the last two years, how futile are all our efforts to maintain the Union by force of arms; but, even had war been carried on by us successfully, the ruinous result would exhibit its utter impracticability for the attainment of the desired end. With or without arms, with or without leaders, we will at least, in the effort to defend our rights as a free people, build up a great mausoleum of hearts, to which men who yearn for liberty will in after years, with bowed heads and reverently, resort, as Christian pilgrims to the sacred shrines of the Holy Land." This was long referred to, by those who heard it, as "the mausoleum-of-hearts speech."

In the great State of New York the Democratic leader was Horatio Seymour, who had been elected Governor in the period of depression that followed the military defeats of 1862. While Pierce was speaking in Concord, Seymour was delivering in New York a carefully written address, in which—like Pierce and Vallandigham—he complained, not of the secessionists for making war at the South, but of the Administration for curtailing the liberty of the Government's enemies at the North. He said: "When I accepted the invitation to speak at this meeting, we were promised the downfall of Vicksburg [the telegraph brought news of it while he was speaking], the opening of the Mississippi, the probable capture of the Confederate capital, and the exhaustion of the rebellion. When the clouds of war overhung our country, we implored those in authority to compromise that difficulty; for we had been told by that great orator and statesman, Burke, that there never yet was a revolution that might not have been prevented by a compromise opportunely and graciously made. Until we have a united North, we can have no successful war; until we have a united, harmonious North, we can have no beneficent peace. Remember this, that the bloody and treasonable and revolutionary doctrine of public necessity can be proclaimed by a mob as well as by a government."

The practical effect of all these protests, in the name of liberty, against arrests of spies and traitors, and suspension of the *habeas corpus*, was to assist the slave-holders in their attempt to make liberty forever impossible for the black race, in pursuance of which they were willing to destroy the liberties of the white race and sacrifice hundreds of thousands of lives, most of which were valuable to their country and to mankind, being lives of men who earned a living by the sweat of their own faces. All the abridgment of the liberties of Northern citizens, in time of war, by President Lincoln's suspension of the writ, and by arbitrary arrests, was not a tithe of what those same citizens had suffered in time of peace from the existence of slavery under the Constitution. Yet neither President Pierce, nor Chief Justice Taney, nor Horatio Seymour, nor Mr. Vallandigham, had ever uttered one word of protest against the denial of free speech in criticism of that institution, or against the systematic rifling of mails at the South, or against the refusal to permit American citizens to sojourn in the slave States unless they believed in the divine right of slavery.

It was no wonder that such utterances as those quoted above by the leaders of a party, at such a time, should be translated by its baser followers into reasons for riot, arson, and butchery. Another exciting cause was found in the persistent misinterpretation of what was meant to be a beneficent provision of the conscription law. Drafts had been ordered in several of the States to fill up quotas that were not forthcoming under the volunteer system. The law provided that a man whose name was drawn, if he did not wish to go into the service himself, might either procure a substitute or pay three hundred dollars to the Government and be released. In the North, where there were no slaves to do the necessary work at home, it was absolutely essential to have some system of substitution; and the three-hundred-dollar clause was introduced, not because the Government wanted money more than it wanted men, but to favor the poor by keeping down the price of substitutes, for it was evident that that price could never rise above the sum necessary for a release. Yet this very clause was attacked by the journals that assumed to champion the cause of the poor, as being a discrimination in favor of the rich! Mr. Vallandigham said in a speech at Dayton: "The three-hundred-dollar provision is a most unjust discrimination against the poor. The Administration says to every man between twenty and forty-five, 'Three hundred dollars or your life.'" When the clause had been repealed, in consequence of the ignorant clamor raised by this persistent misrepresentation, the price of substitutes rapidly went beyond a thousand dollars.

A new levy of three hundred thousand men was called for in April, 1863, with the alternative of a draft if the quotas were not filled by volunteering. The quota of the city of New York was not filled, and a draft was begun there on Saturday, the 11th of July. There had been premonitions of trouble when it was attempted to take the names and addresses of those subject to call, and in the tenement-house districts some of the marshals had narrowly escaped with their lives. On the morning when the draft was to begin, several of the most widely read Democratic journals contained editorials that appeared to be written for the very purpose of inciting a riot. They asserted that any draft at all was unconstitutional and despotic, and that in this case the quota demanded from the city was excessive, and denounced the war as a "mere abolition crusade." It is doubtful if there was any well-formed conspiracy, including any large number of persons, to get up a riot; but the excited state of the public mind, especially among the laboring population, inflammatory handbills displayed in the grog-shops, the presence of the dangerous classes, whose best opportunity for plunder was in time of riot, and the absence of the militia that had been called away to meet the invasion of Pennsylvania, all favored an outbreak. It was unfortunate that the draft was begun on Saturday, and the Sunday papers published long lists of names that were drawn—an instance of the occasional mischievous results of journalistic enterprise. Those interested had all Sunday to talk it over in their accustomed meeting-places, and discuss wild schemes of relief or retaliation; and the insurrection that followed was more truly a popular uprising than the rebellion that it assisted and encouraged.

LIEUTENANT-COLONEL EDWARD JARDINE.
Commanding a detachment of troops for service against the rioters.

CLEMENT L. VALLANDIGHAM.

When the draft was resumed on Monday, the serious work began. One provost-marshal's office was at the corner of Third Avenue and Forty-sixth Street. It was guarded by sixty policemen, and the wheel was set in motion at ten o'clock. The building was surrounded by a dense, angry crowd, who were freely cursing the draft, the police, the National Government, and "the nigger." The drawing had been in progress but a few minutes when there was a shout of "Stop the cars!" and at once the cars were stopped, the horses released, the conductors and passengers driven out, and a tumult created. Then a great human wave was set in motion, which bore down everything before it and rolled into the marshal's office, driving out at the back windows the officials and the policemen, whose clubs, though plied rapidly and knocking down a rioter at every blow, could not dispose of them as fast as they came on. The mob destroyed everything in the office, and then set the building on fire. The firemen came promptly, but were not permitted to throw any water upon the flames. At this moment Superintendent John A. Kennedy, of the police, approaching incautiously and unarmed, was recognized and set upon by the crowd, who gave him half a hundred blows with clubs and stones, and finally threw him face downward into a mud-puddle, with the intention of drowning him. When rescued, he was bruised beyond recognition, and was lifted into a wagon and carried to the police headquarters. The command of the force now devolved upon Commissioner Thomas C. Acton and Inspector Daniel Carpenter, whose management during three fearful days was worthy of the highest praise.

HORATIO SEYMOUR.

Another marshal's office, where the draft was in progress, was at Broadway and Twenty-ninth Street, and here the mob burned the whole block of stores on Broadway between Twenty-eighth and Twenty-ninth Streets. At Third Avenue and Forty-fourth Street there was a battle between a small force of police and a mob, in which the police were defeated, many of them being badly wounded by stones and pistol-shots. Some of them who were knocked down were almost instantly robbed of their clothing. Officer Bennett fell into the hands of the crowd, and was beaten so savagely that no appearance of life was left in him, when he was carried away to the dead-house at St. Luke's Hospital. Here came his wife, who discovered that his heart was still beating; means of restoration were used promptly, and after three days of unconsciousness and a long illness he recovered.

Another officer was stabbed twice by a woman in the crowd; and another, disabled by a blow from an iron bar, was saved by a German woman, who hid him between two mattresses when the pursuing mob was searching her house for him. In the afternoon a small police force held possession of a gun factory in Second Avenue for four hours, and was then compelled to retire before the persistent attacks of the rioters, who hurled stones through the windows and beat in the doors.

Toward evening a riotous procession passed down Broadway, with drums, banners, muskets, pistols, pitchforks, clubs, and boards inscribed "No Draft!" Inspector Carpenter, at the head of two hundred policemen, marched up to meet it. His orders were, "Take no prisoners, but strike quick and hard." The mob was met at the corner of Amity (or West Third) Street. The police charged at once in a compact body, Carpenter knocking down the foremost rioter with a blow that cracked his skull, and in a few minutes the mob scattered and fled, leaving Broadway strewn with their wounded and dying. From this time, the police were victorious in every encounter.

During the next two days there was almost constant rioting, mobs appearing at various points, both up-town and down-town. The rioters set upon every negro that appeared—whether man, woman, or child—and succeeded in murdering eleven of them. One they deliberately hanged to a tree in Thirty-second Street, his only offence being the color of his skin. At another place, seeing three negroes on a roof, they set fire to the house. The victims hung at the edge of the roof a long time, but were obliged to drop before the police could procure ladders. This phase of the outbreak found its worst expression in the sacking and burning of the Colored Orphan Asylum, at Fifth Avenue and Forty-fourth Street. The two hundred helpless children were with great difficulty taken away by the rear doors while the mob were battering at the front. The excitement of the rioters was not so great as to prevent them from coolly robbing the building of everything valuable that could be removed before they set it on fire. Bed-clothing, furniture, and other articles were passed out and borne off (in many cases by the wives and sisters of the rioters) to add to the comfort of their own homes. Several tenement houses that were occupied by negroes were attacked by the mob with a determination to destroy, and were with difficulty protected by the police.

RECRUITING OFFICE IN NEW YORK CITY HALL PARK.

(From an engraving published in "Frank Leslie's Illustrated Weekly," during the war.)

The office of the *Tribune* was especially obnoxious to the rioters, because that paper was foremost in support of the Administration and the war. Crowds approached it, singing

"We'll hang old Greeley on a sour-apple-tree,"

and at one time its counting-room was entered by the mob and a fire was kindled, but the police drove them out and extinguished the flames. The printers were then supplied with a quantity of muskets and bomb-shells, and long board troughs were run out at the windows, so that in case of an attack a shell could be lighted and rolled out, dropping from the end of the trough into the crowd, where its explosion would produce incalculable havoc. Happily the ominous troughs proved a sufficient warning.

A small military force was brought to the aid of the police, and whenever an outbreak was reported, a strong body was sent at once to the spot. The locust clubs, when wielded in earnest, proved a terrible weapon, descending upon the heads of rioters with blows that generally cracked the skull. A surgeon who attended twenty-one men reported that they were all wounded in the head, and all past recovery. One of the most fearful scenes was in Second Avenue, where the police and the soldiers were assailed with stones and pistol-shots from the windows and the roofs. Dividing into squads, they entered the houses, which, amid the cries and curses of the women, they searched from bottom to top. They seized their cowering assailants in the halls, in the dark bedrooms, wherever they were hiding, felled them, bayoneted them, hurled them over the balusters and through the windows, pursued them to the roof, shot them as they dodged behind chimneys, refusing all mercy, and threw the quivering corpses into the street as a warning to the mob. It was like a realization of the imaginary taking of Torquilstone.

One of the saddest incidents of the riot was the murder of Col. Henry J. O'Brien, of the Eleventh New York Volunteers, whose men had dispersed one mob with a deadly volley. An hour or two later the Colonel returned to the spot alone, when he was set upon and beaten and mangled and tortured horribly for several hours, being at last killed by some frenzied women. Page after page might be filled with such incidents. At one time Broadway was strewn with dead men from Bond Street to Union Square. A very young man, dressed in the working-clothes of a mechanic, was observed to be active and daring in leading a crowd of rioters. A blow from a club at length brought him down, and as he fell he was impaled on the picket of an iron fence, which caught him under the chin and killed him. On examination, it was found that under the greasy overalls he wore a costly and fashionable suit, and there were other indications of wealth and refinement, but the body was never identified.

Three days of this vigorous work by the police and the soldiers brought the disturbance to an end. About fifty policemen had been injured, three of whom died; and the whole number of lives destroyed by the rioters was eighteen. The exact number of rioters killed is unknown, but it was more than twelve hundred. The mobs burned about fifty buildings, destroying altogether between two million and three million dollars' worth of property. Governor Seymour incurred odium by a speech to the rioters, in which he addressed them as his friends, and promised to have the draft stopped, and by his communications to the President, in which he complained of the draft, and asked to have it suspended till the question of its constitutionality could be tested in the courts. His opponents interpreted this as a subterfuge to favor the rebellion by preventing the reinforcement of the National armies. The President answered, in substance, that he had no objection to a testing of the question, but he would not imperil the country by suspending operations till a case could be dragged through the courts.

Fourteen of the Northern States had enacted laws enabling the soldiers to vote without going home. In some of the States it was provided that commissioners should go to the camps and take the votes; in others the soldier was authorized to seal up his ballot and send it home to his next friend, who was to present it at the polls and make oath that it was the identical one sent to him. The enactment of such laws had been strenuously opposed by the Democrats, on several grounds, the most plausible of which was, that men under military discipline were not practically free to vote as they pleased. The most curious argument was to this effect: a soldier that sends home his ballot may be killed in battle before that ballot reaches its destination and is counted. Do you want dead men to decide your elections?

These were the darkest days of the war; but the riots reacted upon the party that was supposed to favor them, the people gradually learned the full significance of Gettysburg and Vicksburg, and at the autumn election the State of New York, which a year before had elected Governor Seymour, gave a handsome majority in favor of the Administration. In Ohio, where the Democrats had nominated Vallandigham for Governor, and made a noisy and apparently vigorous canvass, the Republicans nominated John Brough. When the votes were counted, it was found that Mr. Brough had a majority of one hundred thousand, the largest that had ever been given for any candidate in any State where there was a contest. Politically speaking, this buried Mr. Vallandigham out of sight forever, and delivered a heavy blow at the obstructive policy of his party.

OFFICERS OF THE FORTY-FOURTH NEW YORK INFANTRY.

THE ATTACK ON CHARLESTON.

CHAPTER XXV.

THE SIEGE OF CHARLESTON.

BLOCKADE OF THE HARBOR—DU PONT'S ATTACK—DEFEAT—CAPTURE OF THE "ATLANTA"—GILLMORE'S SIEGE—ASSAULT ON FORT WAGNER—ITS CAPTURE—THE SWAMP ANGEL—BOMBARDMENT OF CHARLESTON—ACCURATE FIRING FROM MORTAR GUNS—TURNING NIGHT INTO DAY—STEADY CANNONADING FOR FORTY HOURS.

AS Charleston was the cradle of secession, there was a special desire on the part of the Northern people that it should undergo the heaviest penalties of war. They wanted poetic vengeance to fall upon the very men that had taught disunion, fired upon Sumter, and kindled the flames of civil strife. And there were not a few at the South who shared this sentiment, believing that they had been dragged into ruin by the politicians of South Carolina. Many would have been glad if the whole State could have been pried off from the rest of the Union and slidden into the depths of the sea. But there was a better than sentimental reason for directing vigorous operations against Charleston. Its port was exceedingly useful to the Confederates for shipping their cotton to Europe and receiving in return the army clothing, rifles, and ammunition that were produced for them by English looms and arsenals. Early in the war the Government attempted to close this port with obstructions. Several old whale-ships were loaded with stone, towed into the channel, and sunk, at which there was a great outcry, and the books were searched to see whether this barbarous proceeding, as it was called, was permissible under the laws of war and of nations. In 1854 the harbor of Sebastopol had been obstructed in the same way; but that was done by the Russians, whose harbor it was, to prevent the enemy from coming in. The strong currents at Charleston soon swept away the old hulks or buried them in the sand, and a dozen war vessels had to be sent there to maintain the blockade. This was an exceedingly difficult task. The main channel ran for a long distance near the shore of Morris Island, and was protected by batteries. The westward-bound blockade runners commonly went first to the British port of Nassau, in the West Indies, and thence with a pilot sailed for Charleston. After the main channel had been closed in consequence of the occupation of Morris Island by National troops, steamers of very light draft, built in England for this special service, slipped in by the shallower passes. A great many were captured, for the blockaders

MAJOR-GENERAL QUINCY A. GILLMORE.

REAR-ADMIRAL JOHN A. DAHLGREN AND OFFICERS.

developed remarkable skill in detecting their movements, but the practice was never wholly broken up till the city was occupied by the National forces in February, 1865.

In January, 1863, two Confederate iron-clads steamed out of the harbor, on a hazy morning, and attacked the blockading fleet. Two vessels, by shots through their steam-drums, were disabled, and struck their colors; but the remainder of the fleet came to their assistance, and the iron-clads were driven back into the harbor, leaving their prizes behind. General Beauregard and Captain Ingraham (commanding the military and naval forces of the Confederacy at Charleston) formally proclaimed this affair a victory that had "sunk, dispersed, and driven off or out of sight the entire blockading fleet," and, consequently, raised the blockade of the port. These assertions, repeated in foreign newspapers, threatened for a time to create serious complications with European powers, by raising the question whether the blockade (supposed to be thus broken) must not be re-proclaimed, and notice given to masters of merchant vessels, before it could be reëstablished. But the falsity of the claim was soon shown, and no foreign vessels accepted the invitation to demand free passage into the port of Charleston.

This affair increased the desire to capture the port, put an absolute end to the blockade-running there, and use it as a harbor of refuge for National vessels. Accordingly, a powerful fleet was fitted out for the purpose, and placed under the command of Rear-Admiral S. F. Du Pont, who had reduced the forts of Port Royal in November, 1861. It consisted of seven monitors, an iron-clad frigate, an iron-clad ram, and several wooden gunboats. On the 7th of April, 1863, favored by smooth water, Du Pont steamed in to attack the forts, but most extraordinary precautions had been taken to defend the city. The special desire of the Northern people to capture it was offset by an equally romantic determination on the part of the Secessionists not to part with the cradle in which their pet theory had been rocked for thirty years. Besides the batteries that had been erected for the reduction of Fort Sumter, they had established others, and they occupied that fort itself. All these works had been strengthened, and new guns mounted, including some specially powerful ones of English manufacture. All the channels were obstructed with piles and chains, with innumerable torpedoes, some of which were to be fired by electric wires from the forts, while others were arranged to explode whenever a vessel should run against them. The main channel, between Fort Moultrie and Fort Sumter, was crossed by a heavy cable supported on empty barrels, with which was connected a network of smaller chains. In the south channel there was a tempting opening in the row of piles; but beneath this were some tons of powder waiting for the electric spark.

The monitor *Weehawken* led the way, pushing a raft before her to explode the torpedoes. Not a man was to be seen on any of the decks, and the forts were ominously silent. But when the *Weehawken* had reached the network of chains, and had become somewhat entangled therein with her raft, the batteries opened all around, and she and the other monitors that came to her assistance were the target for a terrible concentric fire of bursting shells and solid bolts. The return fire was directed principally upon Sumter, and was kept up steadily for half an hour, but seemed to have little effect; and after trying both the main and the south channel, the fleet retired. The monitor *Keokuk*, which had made the nearest approach to the enemy, was struck nearly a hundred times. Shots passed through both of her turrets, and there were nineteen holes in her hull. That evening she sank in an inlet. Most of the other vessels were injured, and some of the monitors were unable to revolve their turrets because of the bending of the plates.

Du Pont's defeat was offset two months later, when the Confederate iron-clad *Atlanta* started out on her first cruise. She was originally an English blockade-runner, and as she was unable to get out of the port of Savannah after the fall of Fort Pulaski, the Confederates conceived the idea of iron-plating her after the fashion of the *Merrimac* and sending her out to sink the monitors and raise the blockade of Charleston. It was said that the ladies of Charleston contributed their jewelry to pay the expenses, and after fourteen months of hard labor she was ready for action. But Du Pont had heard the story, and sent two monitors to watch her. On the 17th of June, early in the morning, she dropped down the channel, followed by two steamers loaded with citizens, including many ladies, who anticipated a great deal of pleasure in seeing their powerful iron-clad sink the monitors. These came up to meet her, the *Weehawken*, Captain Rodgers, taking the lead. Rodgers fired just five shots from his enormous eleven-inch and fifteen-inch guns. One struck the shutter of a port-hole and broke it, another knocked off the *Atlanta's* pilot-house, another struck the edge of the deck and opened the seams between the plates, and another penetrated the iron armor, splintered the heavy wooden backing, and disabled forty men. Thereupon the *Atlanta* hung out a white flag and surrendered, while the pleasure-seekers hastened back to Savannah. It is said that the vessel might have been handled better if she had not run aground. She was carrying an immense torpedo at the end of a boom thirty feet long, which projected from her bow under water. She was found to be provisioned for a long cruise, and was taken to Philadelphia and exhibited there as a curiosity.

REAR-ADMIRAL D. M. FAIRFAX.

The city of Charleston, between its two rivers, with its well-fortified harbor, bordered by miles of swampy land, was exceedingly difficult for an enemy to reach. General Quincy A. Gillmore, being sent with a large force to take it, chose the approach by way of Folly and Morris Islands, where the monitors could assist him. Hidden by a fringe of trees, he first erected powerful batteries on Folly Island. On the northernmost point of Morris Island (Cumming's Point) was the Confederate Battery Gregg, the one that had done most damage to Sumter at the opening of the war. South of this was Fort Wagner, and still farther south were other works.

Fort Wagner was a very strong earthwork, measuring on the inside six hundred and thirty feet from east to west, and two hundred and seventy-five feet from north to south. It had a bomb-proof magazine, and a heavy traverse protecting its guns from any possible attack on the land side. Behind the sea-face was a well-constructed bomb-proof, into which no shot ever penetrated. The land-face was constructed with reëntering angles, so that the approaches could all be swept by cross fire, and the work was surrounded by a ditch filled with water, in which was a line of boarding-pikes fastened together with interlaced wire, and there were also pickets at the front of the fort with interwoven wire a slight distance above the ground, to impede the steps of any assaulting force. It was one of the most elaborate works constructed during the war. Its engineer, Captain Cleves, was killed by one of the first shells fired at it.

On the morning of July 10th, Gillmore suddenly cut down the trees in his front and opened fire upon the most southerly works on Morris Island, while at the same time the fleet commanded by Admiral Dahlgren, who had succeeded Du Pont, bombarded Fort Wagner. Under cover of this fire troops were landed, and the earthworks were quickly taken.

The day being terribly hot, the advance on Fort Wagner was postponed till the next morning, and then it was a failure. A week later a determined assault was made with a force of six thousand men, the advance being led by the first regiment of colored troops (the Fifty-fourth Massachusetts) that had been raised under the authorization that accompanied the Emancipation Proclamation. A bombardment of the fort by the land batteries and the fleet was kept up from noon till dusk, and during its last hour there was a heavy thunder-storm. As soon as this was over, the assaulting columns were set in motion. They marched out under a concentrated fire from all the Confederate batteries, then met sheets of musketry fire that blazed out from Wagner, then crossed the ditch waist-deep in water, while hand-grenades were thrown from the parapet to explode among them, and even climbed up to the rampart. But here the surviving remnant met a stout resistance and were hurled back. General Strong, Colonel Chatfield, Colonel Putnam, and Robert G. Shaw, the young commander of the black regiment, were all killed, and a total loss was sustained of fifteen hundred men, while the Confederates lost but about one hundred.

In burying the dead, the Confederates threw the body of Colonel Shaw into the bottom of a trench, and heaped

BREVET BRIGADIER-GENERAL STEWART L. WOODFORD.
(Chief of Staff to General Gillmore.)

BREVET BRIGADIER-GENERAL ALFRED H. TERRY.
(Afterward Major-General.)

upon it the bodies of black soldiers, whose valor, no less than their color, had produced an uncontrollable frenzy in the Confederate mind. When it was inquired for, under flag of truce, word was sent back: "We have buried him with his niggers." Those who thus tried to cast contempt upon the boyish colonel were apparently not aware that he was braver than any of his foes. In advancing along that narrow strip of land, every foot of which was swept by a deadly fire, crossing the ditch and mounting the parapet, Colonel Shaw exhibited a physical courage that it was impossible to surpass; while in organizing and leading men of the despised race that was now struggling toward liberty, he showed a moral courage such as the rebels neither shared nor comprehended.

BATTERY REYNOLDS.—FIVE TEN-INCH MORTARS BEARING ON FORT WAGNER.

HEADQUARTERS OF FIELD OFFICERS ON THE SECOND PARALLEL.

Among those who participated in this sorrowful enterprise was the Rev. Henry Clay Trumbull, chaplain of the Tenth Connecticut Regiment, who was so assiduous in his attentions to the wounded, and remained so long on the field among them, that he was captured by the Confederates, who held him a prisoner for several months. Among those in attendance at the hospital at the first parallel was Clara Barton, who afterward became famous for her humane services.

Gen. Alvin C. Voris, who was seriously wounded in the assault on Fort Wagner, has given a vivid description of his experiences there, from which we quote a few interesting passages:

"All through the night of July 17th I lay with my men, the Sixty-seventh Ohio, within half canister range of the fort. It was very dark, cloudy, and enlivened by an occasional splash of rain and lightning, by which we could see sentinels on beat on the fort. Just before break of day we crawled quietly away, and took a good square breath of relief as we passed behind our first line of intrenchments. There we undertook to rest under a most scorching sun and on burning white sand, which reflected back both light and heat rays with torturing rigor. We were compelled to work night and day, twelve hours on and twelve off, all the while under shot and exploding shell from some quarter. When off duty we tried to rest ourselves under the shelter of the low sand-waves silently thrown up by the wind. Our poor tired bodies became so exhausted under the great pressure upon us that we would stretch out on the burning sands, even when under the greatest danger, and snatch a few hours of fitful, anxious sleep, frequently to be awakened by the explosion of some great shell. The land and sea breezes kept the air full of floating sand, which permeated everything—clothing, eyes, ears, nostrils—and at the height of the wind would fly with such force as to make the face and hands sting with pain.

"Just at dark ten regiments of infantry were formed along the beach, one and a half miles below the fort, and the charge was at once undertaken. Quietly the column marched until its head had passed the line of our field batteries. No sooner had this taken place than one thousand six hundred men in Wagner and Gregg sprang to arms and opened on the advancing columns with shot, shell, and musketry, which called to their immediate assistance the armed energies of Sumter, Moultrie, and Beauregard, and all the batteries on Sullivan's and James's Islands. When we got within canister range of the fort there were added to this awful cataclysm double-shotted charges of canister from eight heavy guns directly raking our approach, each discharge equal to a double pailful of cast-iron bullets, three-fourths of an inch in diameter. Every moment some unfortunate comrade fell, to rise no more, but we closed up our shattered ranks and pressed on with such impetuosity that we scaled the walls and planted our banners on the fort. The Sixty-seventh, with heroic cheers, flung her flag to the midnight breezes on the rampart of Wagner, but only to bring it away riddled to tatters. Seven out of eight of the color-guard were shot down, and Color-Sergeant McDonald, with a broken leg, brought it away. Lieutenant Cochran went alone to headquarters, two thousand five hundred yards to the rear, for reinforcements, assuring General Gillmore that we could hold the fort, and then went back to Wagner and brought off eighteen out of forty men with whom he started in the column in that fatal charge. Two other lieutenants, with a dozen men, held one of the enemy's large guns for nearly two hours, over which they had hand-to-hand contests with the soldiers in charge of the piece.

"I was shot within a hundred and fifty yards of the fort, and so disabled that I could not go forward. . . . Two boys of the Sixty-second Ohio found me and carried me to our first parallel, where had been arranged an extempore hospital. Here a surgeon sent his savage finger-nail into my lacerated side and pronounced the bullet beyond his reach, and said I would not need his further attention. Like a baby I fainted, and, on reviving, laid my poor aching head on a sand-bag to recruit a little strength. That blessed chaplain, Henry Clay Trumbull, found me and poured oil of gladness into my soul and brandy into my mouth, whereat I praised him as a dear good man and cursed that monster of a surgeon, which led the chaplain to think the delirium of death was turning my brain, and he reported me among the dead of Wagner."

General Gillmore now resorted to regular approaches for the reduction of Fort Wagner. The first parallel was soon opened, and siege guns mounted, and the work was pushed as rapidly as the unfavorable nature of the ground would admit. By the 23d of July a second parallel was established, from which fire was opened upon Fort Sumter, two miles distant, and upon the intervening earthworks. As the task proceeded the difficulty increased, for the strip of land grew narrower as Fort Wagner was approached, and the men in the trenches were subjected to cross-fire from a battery on James's Island, as well as from sharp-shooters and from the fort itself. A dozen breaching batteries of enormous rifled guns were established, most of the work being done at night, and on the 17th of August all of them opened fire. The shot and shell were directed mainly against Fort Sumter, and in the course of a week its barbette guns were dismounted, its walls were knocked into a shapeless mass of ruins, and its value as anything but a rude shelter for infantry was gone.

The parallels were still pushed forward toward Wagner, partly through ground so low that high tides washed over it, and finally where mines of torpedoes had been planted. When they had arrived so near that it was impossible for the men to work under ordinary circumstances, the fort was subjected to a bombardment with shells fired from mortars and dropping into it almost vertically, while the great rifled guns were trained upon its bomb-proof at short range, and the iron-clad frigate *New Ironsides* came close in shore and added her quota in the shape of eleven-inch shells fired from eight broadside guns. Powerful calcium lights had been prepared, so that there was no night there, and the bombardment went on incessantly. At the end of two days, three columns of infantry were ready to storm the work, when it was discovered that the Confederates had suddenly abandoned it. Battery Gregg, on Cumming's Point, was also evacuated.

It is easy to tell all this in a few words; but no brief account of that operation can give the reader any adequate idea of the enormous labor it involved, the danger, the anxiety, and the dogged perseverance of the besiegers. It required the efforts of three hundred men to move a single gun up the beach. General Gillmore was one of the most accomplished of military engineers, and we present here a few of the more interesting passages from his admirable official report:

At the second parallel the "Surf Battery" had barely escaped entire destruction, about one-third of it having been carried away by the sea. Its armament had been temporarily removed to await the issue of the storm. The progress of the sap was hotly opposed by the enemy, with the fire of both artillery and sharp-shooters. At one point in particular, about two hundred yards in front of Wagner, there was a ridge, affording the enemy good cover, from which we received an unceasing fire of small-arms, while the guns and sharp-shooters in Wagner opened vigorously at every lull in the fire directed upon it from our batteries and gunboats. The firing from the distant James's Island batteries was steady and accurate. One attempt, on the 21st, to obtain possession of the ridge with infantry having failed, it was determined to advance by establishing another parallel. On the night of August 21st the fourth parallel was opened about one hundred yards from the ridge, partly with the flying sap and partly with the full sap. At the place selected for it the island is about one hundred and sixty yards in width above high water. It was now determined to try and dislodge the enemy from the ridge with light mortars and navy howitzers in the fourth parallel, and with other mortars in rear firing over those in front. The attempt was made on the afternoon of August 26th, but did not succeed. Our mortar practice was not very accurate. Brigadier-General Terry was ordered, on the 26th of August, to carry the ridge at the point of the bayonet, and hold it. This was accomplished, and the fifth parallel established there on the evening of the same day, which brought us to within two hundred and forty yards of Fort Wagner. The intervening space comprised the narrowest and shallowest part of Morris Island. It was simply a flat ridge of sand, scarcely twenty-five yards in width, and not exceeding two feet in depth, over which the sea in rough weather swept entirely across to the marsh on our left. Approaches by the flying sap were at once commenced on this shallow beach, from the right of the fifth parallel, and certain means of defence in the parallel itself were ordered. It was soon ascertained that we had now reached the point where the really formidable, passive, defensive arrangements of the enemy commenced. An elaborate and ingenious system of torpedo mines, to be exploded by the tread of persons walking over them, was encountered, and we were informed by the prisoners taken on the ridge that the entire area of firm ground between us and the fort, as well as the glacis of the latter on its south and east fronts, was thickly filled with these torpedoes. This knowledge brought us a sense of security from sorties, for the mines were a defence to us as well as to the enemy. By daybreak on the 27th of August our sappers had reached, by a rude and unfinished trench, to within one hundred yards of Fort Wagner. The dark and gloomy days of the siege were now upon us. Our daily losses, although not heavy, were on the increase, while our progress became discouragingly slow, and even fearfully uncertain. The converging fire from Wagner alone almost enveloped the head of our sap, delivered, as it was, from a line subtending an angle of nearly ninety degrees, while the flank fire from the James's Island batteries increased in power and accuracy every hour. To push forward the sap in the narrow strip of shallow shifting sand by day was impossible, while the brightness of the prevailing harvest moon rendered the operation almost as hazardous by night. Matters, indeed, seemed at a standstill, and a feeling of despondency began to pervade the rank and file of the command. There seemed to be no adequate return in accomplished results for the daily losses which we suffered, and no means of relief, cheering and encouraging to the soldier, appeared near at hand. In this emergency, although the final result was demonstrably certain, it was determined, in order to sustain the flagging spirits of the men, to commence vigorously and simultaneously two distinct methods of attack, viz., first, to keep Wagner perfectly silent with an overpowering curved fire from siege and coehorn mortars, so that our engineers would have only the more distant batteries of the enemy to annoy them; and, second, to breach the bomb-proof shelter with rifled guns, and thus deprive the enemy of their only secure cover in the work, and, consequently, drive them from it. Accordingly, all the light mortars were moved to the front and placed in battery; the capacity of the fifth parallel and the advanced trenches for sharp-shooters was greatly enlarged and improved; the rifled guns in the left breaching batteries were trained upon the fort and prepared for prolonged action; and powerful calcium lights to aid the night-work of our cannoneers and sharp-shooters, and blind those of the enemy, were got in readiness. The coöperation of the powerful battery of the *New Ironsides*, Captain Rowan, during the daytime, was also secured.

MAJOR-GENERAL WILLIAM B. TALIAFERRO, C. S. A.

These final operations against Fort Wagner were actively inaugurated at break of day on the morning of September 5th. For forty-two consecutive hours the spectacle presented was of surpassing sublimity and grandeur. Seventeen siege and coehorn mortars unceasingly dropped their shells into the work, over the heads of our sappers and the guards of the advanced trenches; thirteen of our heavy Parrott rifles—one hundred, two hundred, and three hundred pounders—pounded away at short though regular intervals, at the southwest corner of the bomb-proof; while during the daytime the *New Ironsides*, with remarkable regularity and precision, kept an almost incessant stream of eleven-inch shells from her eight-gun broadside, ricocheting over the water against the sloping parapet of Wagner, whence, deflected upward with a low remaining velocity, they dropped nearly vertically, exploding within or over the work, and rigorously searching every part of it except the subterranean shelters. The calcium lights turned night into day, and while throwing around our own men an impenetrable obscurity, they brilliantly illuminated every object in front, and brought the minutest details of the fort into sharp relief. In a few hours the fort became practically silent.

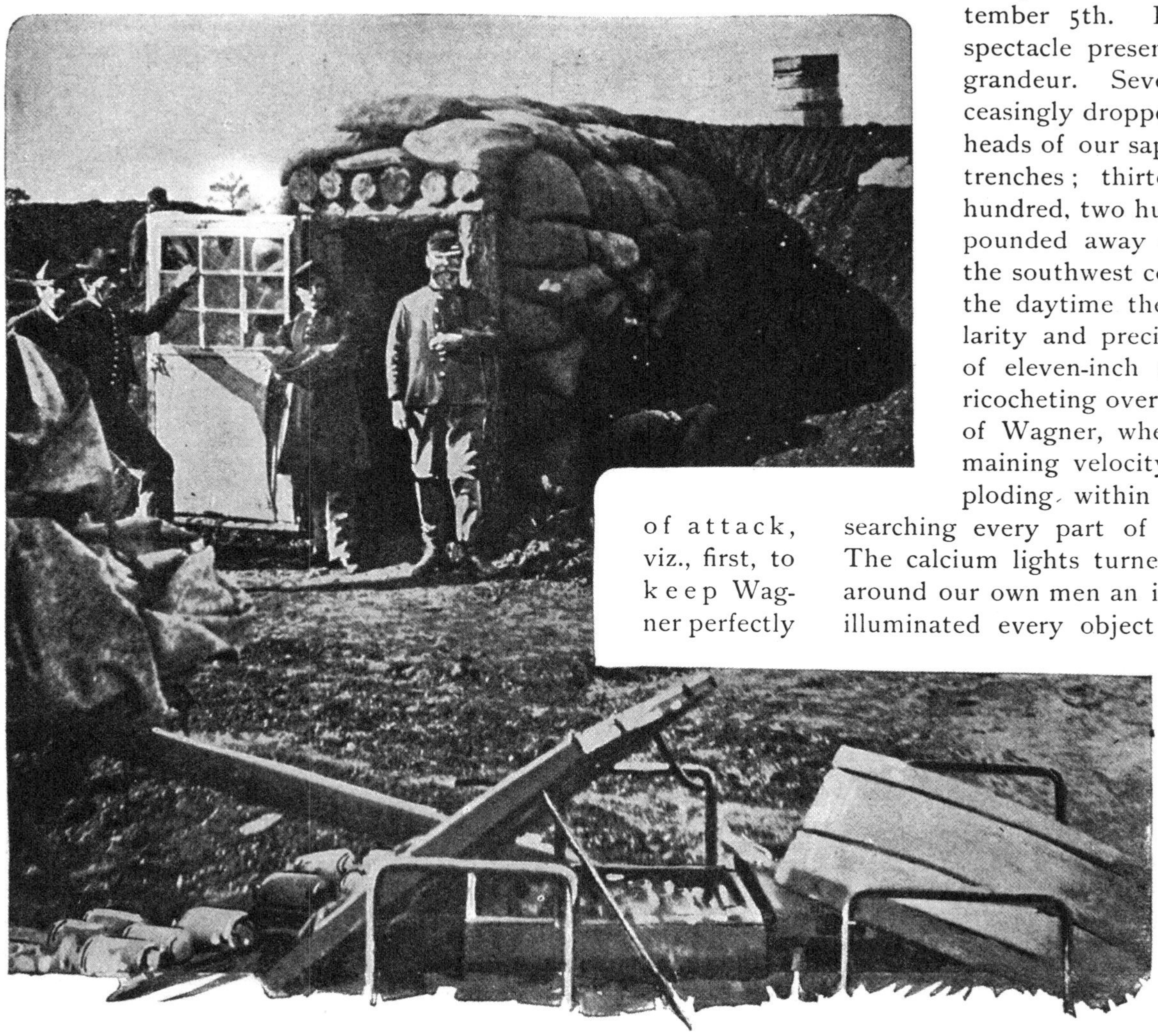

A BOMB PROOF.

The next night, after the capture of Fort Wagner, a few hundred sailors from the fleet went to Fort Sumter in row-boats and attempted its capture. But they found it exceedingly difficult to climb up the ruined wall; most of their boats were knocked to pieces by the Confederate batteries; they met an unexpected fire of musketry and hand-grenades, and two hundred of them were disabled or captured.

While all this work was going on, General Gillmore thought to establish a battery near enough to Charleston to subject the city itself to bombardment. A site was chosen on the western side of Morris Island, and the necessary orders were issued. But the ground was soft mud, sixteen feet deep, and it seemed an impossible task. The captain, a West Pointer, to whom it was assigned, was told that he must not fail, but he might ask for whatever he needed, whereupon he made out a formal requisition for "a hundred men eighteen feet high," and other things in proportion. The jest seems to have been appreciated, but the jester was relieved from the duty, which was then assigned to Col. Edward W. Serrell, a volunteer engineer, who accomplished the work. Piles were driven, a platform was laid upon them, and a parapet was built with bags of sand, fifteen thousand being required. All this had to be done after dark, and occupied fourteen nights. Then, with great labor, an eight-inch rifled gun was dragged across the swamp and mounted on this platform. It was nearly five miles from Charleston, but by firing with a high elevation was able to reach the lower part of the city. The soldiers named this gun the "Swamp Angel." Late in August it was ready for work, and, after giving notice for the removal of non-combatants, General Gillmore opened fire. A few shells fell in the streets and produced great consternation, but at the thirty-sixth discharge the Swamp Angel burst, and it never was replaced.

Gillmore had supposed that when Sumter was silenced the fleet would enter the harbor, but Admiral Dahlgren did not think it wise to risk his vessels among the torpedoes, especially as the batteries of the inner harbor had been greatly strengthened. As Fort Wagner and Battery Gregg were nearer the city by a mile than the Swamp Angel, Gillmore repaired them, turned their guns upon Charleston, and kept up a destructive bombardment for weeks.

As a protection to the city, under the plea that its bombardment was a violation of the rules of war, the Confederate authorities selected from their prisoners fifty officers and placed them in the district reached by the shells. Capt. Willard Glazier, who was there, writes: "When the distant rumbling of the Swamp Angel was heard, and the cry 'Here it comes!' resounded through our prison house, there was a general stir. Sleepers sprang to their feet, the gloomy forgot their sorrows, conversation was hushed, and all started to see where the messenger would fall. At night we traced along the sky a slight stream of fire, similar to the tail of a comet, and followed its course until 'whiz! whiz!' came the little pieces from our mighty two-hundred pounder, scattering themselves all around." By placing an equal number of Confederate officers under fire, the Government compelled the removal of its own.

ST. MICHAEL'S CHURCH, CHARLESTON, S. C.

CHAPTER XXVI.

THE CHATTANOOGA CAMPAIGN AND BATTLE OF CHICKAMAUGA.

ROSECRANS AND BRAGG—FIGHT AT DOVER—AT FRANKLIN—AT MILTON—MORGAN'S RAID IN OHIO—MANŒUVRING FOR CHATTANOOGA—BATTLE AT CHICKAMAUGA—NUMBER OF MEN ENGAGED ON EACH SIDE—OPERATIONS OF THE FIRST DAY—RETREAT OF FEDERAL FORCES AT CHATTANOOGA—NUMBER OF OFFICERS AND MEN KILLED AT CHICKAMAUGA—GENERAL ROSECRANS'S OPINION OF THE GENERAL CONDUCT OF THE BATTLE—INSTANCES OF PERSONAL COURAGE AND GALLANTRY—GENERAL BRAGG'S CRITICISMS OF GENERAL POLK.

WHILE Grant's army was pounding at the gates of Vicksburg, those of Rosecrans and Bragg were watching each other at Murfreesboro', both commanders being unwilling to make any grand movement. General Grant and the Secretary of War wanted Rosecrans to advance upon Bragg, lest Bragg should reinforce Johnston, who was a constant menace in the rear of the army besieging Vicksburg. The only thing Grant feared was, that he might be attacked heavily by Johnston before he could capture the place. But Rosecrans refused to move, on the ground that it was against the principles of military science to fight two decisive battles at once, and that the surest method of holding back Bragg from reinforcing Johnston was by constantly standing ready to attack him, but not attacking. As it happened that Bragg was very much like Rosecrans, and was afraid to stir lest Rosecrans should go to Grant's assistance, the policy of quiet watchfulness proved successful—so far at least as immediate results were concerned. Bragg did not reinforce Johnston, Johnston did not attack Grant; and besiegers and besieged were left, like two brawny champions of two great armies, to fight it out, dig it out, and starve it out, till on the 4th of July the city fell. Whether it afterward fared as well with Rosecrans as it might if he had attacked Bragg when Grant and Stanton wanted him to, is another question.

But though the greater armies were quiescent, both sent out detachments to make destructive raids, and that season witnessed some of the most notable exploits of the guerilla bands that were operating in the West, all through the war, in aid of the Confederacy. Late in January, 1863, a Confederate force of cavalry and artillery, about four thousand men, under Wheeler and Forrest, was sent to capture Dover, contiguous to the site of Fort Donelson, in order to close the navigation of Cumberland River, by which Rosecrans received supplies. The place was held by six hundred men, under command of Col. A. C. Harding, of the Eighty-third Illinois Regiment, who, with the help of gunboats, repelled two determined attempts to storm the works (February 3), and inflicted a loss of seven hundred men, their own loss being one hundred and twenty-six.

Early in March, a detachment of about twenty-five hundred National troops, under Colonels Coburn and Jordan, moving south of Franklin, Tenn., unexpectedly met a force of about ten thousand Confederates under Van Dorn, and the stubborn fight that ensued resulted in the surrounding and capture of Coburn's entire force, after nearly two hundred had been killed or wounded on each side. A few days later, Van Dorn was attacked and driven southward by a force under Gen. Gordon Granger. Still later in the month a detachment of about fourteen hundred men under Colonel Hall went in pursuit of the guerilla band commanded by John Morgan, fought it near Milton, and defeated it, inflicting a loss of nearly four hundred men. Early in April another detachment of National troops, commanded by Gen. David S. Stanley, found Morgan's men at Snow Hill, and defeated and routed them so thoroughly that it was two weeks before the remnants of the band could be brought together again.

In the same month Col. A. D. Streight, with eighteen hundred men, was sent to make a raid around Bragg's army, cut his communications, and destroy supplies. This detachment was pursued by Forrest, who attacked the rear guard at Day's Gap, but was repelled, and lost ten guns and a considerable number of men. Streight kept on his way, with continual skirmishing, destroyed a dépôt of provisions at Gadsden, had another fight at Blount's Farm, in which he drove off Forrest again, and burned the Round Mountain Iron Works, which supplied shot and shell to the Confederates. But on the 3d of May he was confronted by so large a force that he was compelled to surrender.

A PASS IN THE RACCOON RANGE.

MISSIONARY RIDGE, FROM ORCHARD KNOB

(FROM A GOVERNMENT PHOTOGRAPH.)

his men and horses being too jaded to attempt escape.

These are but examples of hundreds of engagements that took place during the war of secession and are scarcely known to the general reader because their fame is overshadowed by the magnitude of the great battles. Had they occurred in any of our previous wars, every schoolboy would know about them. In Washington's celebrated victory at Trenton, the number of Hessians surrendered was fewer than Streight's command captured by Forrest; and in the bloodiest battle of the Mexican war, Buena Vista, the American loss (then considered heavy) was but little greater than the Confederate loss in the action at Dover, related above. The armies surrendered by Burgoyne and Cornwallis, if combined, would constitute a smaller force than the least of the three that surrendered to Grant.

One of these affairs in the West, however, was so bold and startling that it became famous even among the greater and more important events. This was Morgan's raid across the Ohio. In July he entered Kentucky from the south, with a force of three thousand cavalrymen, increased as it went by accessions of Kentucky sympathizers to about four thousand, with ten guns. He captured and robbed the towns of Columbia and Lebanon, reached the Ohio, captured two steamers, and crossed into Indiana. Then marching rapidly toward Cincinnati, he burned mills and bridges, tore up rails, plundered right and left, and spread alarm on every side. But the home guards were gathering to meet him, and the great number of railways in Ohio and Indiana favored their rapid concentration, while farmers felled trees across the roads on hearing of his approach. He passed around Cincinnati, and after much delay reached the Ohio at Buffington's Ford. Here some of his pursuers overtook him, while gunboats and steamboats filled with armed men were patrolling the river, on the watch for him. The gunboats prevented him from using the ford, and he was obliged to turn and give battle. The fight was severe, and resulted in Morgan's defeat. Nearly eight hundred of his men surrendered, and he with the remainder retreated up the river. They next tried to cross at Belleville by swimming their horses; but the gunboats were at hand again, and made such havoc among the troopers that only three hundred got across, while of the others some were shot, some drowned, and the remnant driven back to the Ohio shore. Morgan with two hundred fled still farther up the stream, but at last was compelled to surrender at New Lisbon. He was confined in the Ohio penitentiary, but escaped a few months later by digging under the walls. A pathetic incident of this raid was the death of the venerable Daniel McCook, sixty-five years old. He had given eight sons to the National service, and four of them had become generals. One of these was deliberately murdered by guerillas, while he was ill and riding in an ambulance in Tennessee. The old man, hearing that the murderer was in Morgan's band, took his rifle and went out to join in the fight at Buffington's Ford, where he was mortally wounded.

BRIGADIER-GENERAL J. H. MORGAN, C. S. A.

MAJOR-GENERAL GEORGE L HARTSUFF.

When at last Rosecrans did move, by some of the ablest strategy displayed in the whole war he compelled Bragg to fall back successively from one position to another, all the way from Tullahoma to Chattanooga. This was not done without frequent and heavy skirmishes, however; but the superiority of the National cavalry had now been developed at the West as well as at the East, and they all resulted in one way. Colonel (afterward Senator) John F. Miller was conspicuous in several of these actions, and in that at Liberty Gap one of his eyes was shot out by a rifle-ball.

The purpose of Rosecrans was to get possession of Chattanooga; and when Bragg crossed the Tennessee and occupied that town, he set to work to manœuvre him out of it. To effect this, he moved southwest, as if he were intending to pass around Chattanooga and invade Georgia. This caused Bragg to fall back to Lafayette, and the National troops took

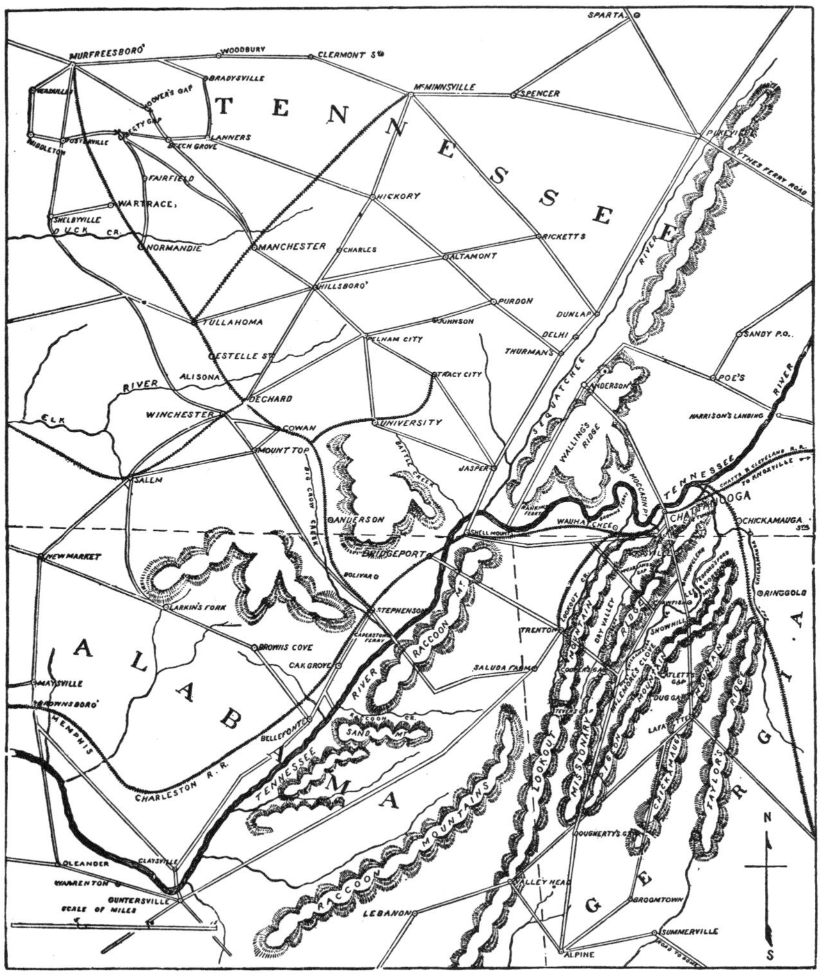

SCENE OF OPERATION OF THE ARMY OF THE CUMBERLAND IN TENNESSEE, GEORGIA, AND ALABAMA.

possession of Chattanooga. But at this time Rosecrans was for a while in a critical situation, where a more skilful general than Bragg would probably have destroyed him; for his three corps — commanded by Thomas, Crittenden, and McCook—were widely separated. The later movements of this campaign had been rendered tediously slow by the heavy rains and the almost impassable nature of the ground; so that although Rosecrans had set out from Murfreesboro in June, it was now the middle of September.

Supposing that Bragg was in full retreat, Rosecrans began to follow him; but Bragg had received large reinforcements, and turned back from Lafayette, intent upon attacking Rosecrans. The two armies, feeling for each other and approaching somewhat cautiously for a week, met at last, and there was fought, September 19 and 20, 1863, a great battle on the banks of a creek, whose Indian name of Chickamauga is said to signify "river of death."

MAJOR-GENERAL GEORGE H. THOMAS.

Rosecrans had about fifty-five thousand men; Bragg, after the arrival of Longstreet at midnight of the 18th, about seventy thousand. The general direction of the lines of battle was with the National troops facing southeast, and the Confederates facing northwest, though these lines were variously bent, broken, and changed in the course of the action. Thomas held the left of Rosecrans's line, Crittenden the centre, and McCook the right. Bragg was the attacking party, and his plan was, while making a feint on the National right, to fall heavily upon the left, flank it, crush it, and seize the roads that led to Chattanooga. If he could do this, it would not only cut off Rosecrans from his base and insure his decisive defeat, but would give Bragg possession of Chattanooga, where he could control the river and the passage through the mountains between the East and the West. The concentration of the National forces in the valley had been witnessed by the Confederates from the mountain height southeast of the creek, who therefore knew what they had to meet and how it was disposed.

The battle of the 19th began at ten o'clock in the forenoon, and lasted all day. The Confederate army crossed the creek without opposition, and moved forward confidently to the attack. But the left of the position—the key-point—was held by the command of Gen. George H. Thomas, who for a slow and stubborn fight was perhaps the best corps commander produced by either side in the whole war. Opposed to him, on the Confederate right, was Gen. (also Bishop) Leonidas Polk. There was less of concerted action in the attack than Bragg had planned for, partly because Thomas unexpectedly struck out with a counter-movement when an opportunity offered; but there was no lack of bloody and persistent fighting. Brigades and divisions moved forward to the charge, were driven back, and charged again. Batteries were taken and re-taken, the horses were killed, and the captains and gunners in some instances, refusing to leave them, were shot down at the wheels. Brigades and regiments were shattered, and on both sides many prisoners were taken. Thomas's line was forced back, but before night he regained his first position, and the day closed with the situation practically unchanged.

During the night both sides corrected their lines and made what preparation they could for a renewal of the struggle. Bragg intended to attack again at daybreak, his plan (now perfectly evident to his opponent) being substantially the same as on the day before. He wanted to crush the National left, force back the centre, and make a grand left wheel with his entire army, placing his right firmly across the path to Chattanooga. But the morning was foggy, Polk was slow, and the fighting did not begin till the middle of the forenoon. Between Polk and Thomas the edge of battle swayed back and forth, and the Confederates could make no permanent impression. Thomas was obliged to call repeatedly for reinforcements, which sometimes reached him and sometimes failed to; but whether they came or not, he held manfully to all the essential portions of his ground.

Rosecrans was constantly uneasy about his right centre, where he knew the line to be weak; and at this point the great disaster of the day began, though in an unexpected manner. It arose from an order that was both miswritten and misinterpreted. This order, addressed to Gen. Thomas J. Wood, who commanded a division, was written by a member of Rosecrans's staff who had not had a military education, and was not sufficiently impressed with the exact meaning of the technical terms. It read: "The general commanding directs that you close up on Reynolds as fast as possible, and support him." It was impossible to obey both clauses of this order; since to "close up" means to bring the ends of the lines together so that there shall be no gap and they shall form one continuous line, while to "support," in the technical military sense, means to take a position in the rear, ready to advance when ordered. The aid that wrote the order evidently used the word "support" only in the general sense of assist, strengthen, protect, encourage, and did not dream of its conflicting with the command to "close up." General Wood, a West Point graduate, instead of sending or going to Rosecrans for better orders, obeyed literally the second clause, and withdrew his command from the line to form it in the rear of Reynolds. Opposite to the wide and fatal opening thus left was Longstreet, the ablest corps commander in the Confederate service, who instantly saw his advantage and promptly poured his men, six divisions of them, through the gap. This cut off McCook's corps from the rest of the army, and it was speedily defeated and routed in confusion. The centre was crumbled, and it looked as if the whole army must be destroyed. Rosecrans, who had been with the defeated right wing, appeared to lose his head completely, and rode back in all haste to Chattanooga to make arrangements for gathering there the fragments of his forces. At nightfall he sent his chief of staff, Gen. James A. Garfield (afterward President), to find what had become of Thomas, and Garfield found Thomas where not even the destruction of three-fifths of the army had moved or daunted him.

When Thomas's right flank was exposed to assault by the disruption of the centre, he swung it back to a position known as Horseshoe Ridge, still covering the road. Longstreet was pressing forward to pass the right of this position, when he was stopped by Gordon Granger, who had been with a reserve at Rossville Gap, but was wiser and bolder than his orders, and, instead of remaining there, moved forward to the support of Thomas. The Confederate commander, when complete victory was apparently so near, seemed reckless of the lives of his men, thrusting them forward again and again in futile charges, where Thomas's batteries literally mowed them down with grape and canister, and a steady fire of musketry increased the bloody harvest. About dusk the ammunition was exhausted, and the last charges of the Confederates were repelled with the bayonet. Thomas had fairly won the title of "the rock of Chickamauga." In the night he fell back in good order to Rossville, leaving the enemy in possession of the field, with all the dead and wounded. Sheridan, who had been on the right of the line and was separated by its disruption, kept his command together, marched around the mountain, and before morning joined Thomas at Rossville, whence they fell back the next day to Chattanooga, where order was quickly restored and the defences strengthened.

The National loss in the two-days' battle of Chickamauga—killed, wounded, and missing—was sixteen thousand three hundred and thirty-six. The Confederate reports are incomplete and unsatisfactory; but estimates of Bragg's loss make it at least eighteen thousand, and some carry it up nearly to twenty-one thousand. With the exception of Gettysburg, this was thus far the most destructive action of the war. Tactically it was a victory for Bragg, who was left in possession of the field; but that which he was fighting for, Chattanooga, he did not get.

Among the killed in this battle were Brig.-Gen. William H. Lytle on the National side, and on the Confederate side Brig.-Gens. Preston Smith, Benjamin H. Helm, and James Deshler; also on the National side, three colonels who were in command of brigades—Cols. Edward A. King of the Sixty-eighth Indiana Regiment, Philemon P. Baldwin of the Sixth Indiana, and Hans C. Heg of the Fifteenth Wisconsin. The number of officers of lower rank who fell, generally when exhibiting notable courage in the performance of their dangerous duties, was very great. Of General Whittaker's staff, numbering seven, three were killed and three wounded. His brigade lost nearly a thousand men, and Colonel Mitchell's brigade of four regiments lost nearly four hundred. The Ninety-sixth Illinois Regiment went into the battle with four

LEE AND GORDON'S MILLS ON THE CHICKAMAUGA.

BATTLE OF CHICKAMAUGA, GA, SEPTEMBER 19th AND 20th, 1863.

hundred and fifteen men, and lost one hundred and sixty-three killed or wounded. Of its twenty-three officers, eleven were either killed or wounded. In the fall of General Lytle we lost another man of great literary promise, though his published writings were not extensive, whose name must be placed on the roll with those of Winthrop, Lander, and O'Brien. He was the author of the popular poem that begins with the line—

"I am dying, Egypt, dying."

Another poet who distinguished himself on this field was Lieut. Richard Realf, of the Eighty-eighth Illinois Regiment, who was honorably mentioned, especially for his services in going back through a heavy fire and bringing up a fresh supply of ammunition when it was sorely needed. Realf was a personal friend of Lytle's, and the bullet that killed Lytle passed through a sheet of paper in his pocket, containing a little poem that Realf had addressed to him a short time before. Some of Realf's war lyrics are among the finest that we have. Here are two stanzas from one:

MAJOR-GENERAL JAMES B. STEEDMAN.

"I think the soul of Cromwell kissed
The soul of Baker when,
With red sword in his bloody fist,
He died among his men.
I think, too, that when Winthrop fell,
His face toward the foe,
John Hampden shouted, 'All is well!'
Above that overthrow.

"And Lyon, making green and fair
The places where he trod;
And Ellsworth, sinking on the stair
Whereby he passed to God;
And those whose names are only writ
In hearts, instead of scrolls,
Still show the dark of earth uplit
With shining human souls."

And here is a sonnet suggested by the loss of many of his comrades on the battlefield:

"Thank God for Liberty's dear slain; they give
Perpetual consecration unto it;
Quickening the clay of our insensitive
Dull natures with the awe of infinite
Sun-crowned transfigurations, such as sit
On the solemn-brooding mountains. Oh, the dead!
How they do shame the living; how they warn
Our little lives that huckster for the bread
Of peace, and tremble at the world's poor scorn,
And pick their steps among the flowers, and tread
Daintily soft where the raised idols are;
Prone with gross dalliance where the feasts are spread,
When most they should stride forth, and flash afar
Light like the streaming of heroic war!"

MAJOR-GENERAL GORDON GRANGER.

General Garfield was distinguished in this action for his judgment and incessant activity. As chief of staff he wrote every order issued by General Rosecrans during the action, except the blundering order that caused the disaster by the withdrawal of Wood's division from the line. He was advanced to the rank of major-general "for gallant and meritorious services at the battle of Chickamauga."

General Rosecrans, in his official report, says of his own personal movements on the field: "At the moment of the repulse of Davis's division [when the Confederates poured through the gap left by Wood] I was standing in rear of his right, waiting the completion of the closing of McCook's corps to the left. Seeing confusion among Van Cleve's troops, and the distance Davis's men were falling back, and the tide of battle surging toward us, the urgency for Sheridan's troops to intervene became imminent, and I hastened in person to the extreme right, to direct Sheridan's movement on the flank of the advancing rebels. It was too late. The crowd of returning troops rolled back, and the enemy advanced. Giving the troops directions to rally behind the ridges west of the Dry Valley road, I passed down it, accompanied by General Garfield, Major McMichael, and Major Bond, of my staff, and a few of the escort, under the shower of grape, canister, and musketry, for two or three hundred yards, and attempted to rejoin General Thomas and the troops sent to his support, by passing to the rear of the broken portion of our line, but found the routed troops far toward the left; and hearing the enemy's advancing musketry and cheers, I became doubtful whether the left had held its ground, and started for Rossville. On consultation and further reflection, however, I determined to send General Garfield there, while I went to Chattanooga to give orders for the security of the pontoon bridges at Battle Creek and Bridgeport, and to make preliminary disposition, either to forward ammunition and supplies should we hold our ground, or to withdraw the troops into good position.

"General Garfield despatched me from Rossville that the left and centre still held its ground. General Granger had gone to its support. General Sheridan had rallied his division, and was advancing toward the same point, and General Davis was going up the Dry Valley road, to our right. General Garfield proceeded to the front, remained there until the close of the fight, and despatched me the triumphant defence our troops there made against the assaults of the enemy."

General Rosecrans says concerning the general conduct of the battle: "The fight on the left, after two P. M., was that of the army. Never, in the history of this war at least, have troops fought with greater energy or determination. Bayonet charges, often heard of but seldom seen, were repeatedly made by brigades and regiments in several of our divisions. After the yielding and severance of the division of the right, the enemy bent all efforts to break the solid portion of our line. Under the pressure of the rebel onset, the flanks of the line were gradually retired until they occupied strong, advantageous ground, giving to the whole a flattened, crescent shape. From one to half-past three o'clock the unequal contest was sustained throughout our line. Then the enemy, in overpowering numbers, flowed around our right, held by General Brannan, and occupied a low gap in the ridge of our defensive position, which commanded our rear. The moment was critical. Twenty minutes more, and our right would have been turned, our position taken in reverse, and probably the army routed. Fortunately Major-General Granger, whose troops had been posted to cover our left and rear, with the instinct of a true soldier and a general, hearing the roar of the battle, and being

BREVET BRIGADIER-GENERAL H. V. N. BOYNTON.

COLONEL B. F. SCRIBNER.
(Afterward Brevet Brigadier-General.)

beyond the reach of orders from the general commanding, moved to its assistance. He soon encountered the enemy's skirmishers, whom he disregarded, well knowing that at that stage of the conflict the battle was not there. Posting Col. Daniel McCook's brigade to take care of anything in that vicinity and beyond our line, he moved the remainder to the scene of action, reporting to General Thomas, who directed him to our suffering right. He discovered at once the peril and the point of danger—the gap—and quick as thought directed his advance brigade upon the enemy. General Steedman, taking a regimental color, led the column. Swift was the charge and terrible the conflict, but the enemy was broken. A thousand of our brave men, killed and wounded, paid for its possession, but we held the gap. Two divisions of Longstreet's corps confronted the position. Determined to take it, they successively came to the assault. A battery of six guns, placed in the gorge, poured death and slaughter into them. They charged to within a few yards of the pieces; but our grape and canister and the leaden hail of our musketry, delivered in sparing but terrible volleys, from cartridges taken, in many instances, from the boxes of their fallen companions, was too much even for Longstreet's men. About sunset they made their last charge, when our men, being out of ammunition, rushed on them with the bayonet, and gave way to return no more."

General Rosecrans adds that: "The battle of Chickamauga was absolutely necessary to secure our concentration and cover Chattanooga. It was fought in a country covered with woods and undergrowth, and wholly unknown to us. Every division came into action opportune-

BREVET MAJOR-GENERAL EMERSON OPDYKE.

ly, and fought squarely on the 19th. We were largely outnumbered, yet we foiled the enemy's flank movement on our left, and secured our own position on the road to Chattanooga."

In this battle the National army expended two million six hundred and fifty thousand rounds of musket cartridges and seven thousand three hundred and twenty-five rounds of artillery ammunition. With figures like these the reader may realize how nearly true is the saying that it requires a man's own weight of metal to kill him in battle. Rosecrans lost thirty-six pieces of artillery and eight thousand four hundred and fifty stand of small arms. He took two thousand prisoners. He says in his report: "A very great meed of praise is due to Capt. Horace Porter, of the Ordnance, for the wise system of arming each regiment with arms of the same calibre, and having the ammunition wagons properly marked, by which most of the difficulties of supplying ammunition where troops had exhausted it in battle were obviated."

Gen. T. J. Wood says in his report, concerning the fight on his part of the line: "A part of the contest was witnessed by that able and distinguished commander Major-General Thomas. I think it must have been two o'clock P.M. when he came to where my command was so hotly engaged. His presence was most welcome. The men saw him, felt they were battling under the eye of a great chieftain, and their courage and resolution received fresh inspiration from this consciousness."

In this terrible two days' struggle there were innumerable instances of the display of special personal courage and timely gallantry. When the One Hundred and Fifteenth Illinois Regiment was struggling to rally after being somewhat broken, General Steedman took the flag from the color-bearer and advanced toward the enemy, saying to the regiment: "Boys, I'll carry your flag if

"DO NOT SKULK HERE——"

you'll defend it." Whereupon they rallied around him and went into the fight once more.

William S. Bean, a quartermaster's sergeant, whose place was at the rear, and who might properly have remained there, went forward to the battle line, and is said to have done almost the work of a general in encouraging the bold and animating the timid. Lieut. C. W. Earle, a mere boy, was left in command of the color company of the Ninety-sixth Ohio Regiment, and stood by his colors unfalteringly throughout the fight, though all but two of the color-guard were struck down and the flag was cut to pieces by the bullets of the enemy. The Twenty-second Michigan Regiment did not participate in the first day's battle, but went in on the second day with five hundred and eighty-four officers and men, and lost three hundred and seventy-two. Its colonel, Heber LeFavour, received high praise for the manner in which he led his regiment in a bayonet charge after their ammunition was exhausted. He was taken prisoner late in the action.

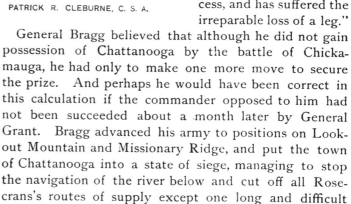

BRIGADIER-GENERAL MARCELLUS A. STOVALL, C. S. A.

General Bragg, in his report of the battle, complains bitterly of General Polk's dilatoriness in obeying orders to attack, and says: "Exhausted by two days' battle, with very limited supply of provisions, and almost destitute of water, some time in daylight was absolutely essential for our troops to supply these necessaries and replenish their ammunition before renewing the contest. Availing myself of this necessary delay to inspect and readjust my lines, I moved, as soon as daylight served, on the 21st. . . . Our cavalry soon came upon the enemy's rear guard where the main road passes through Missionary Ridge. He had availed himself of the night to withdraw from our front, and his main body was already in position within his lines at Chattanooga. Any immediate pursuit by our infantry and artillery would have been fruitless, as it was not deemed practicable, with our weak and exhausted forces, to assail the enemy, now more than double our numbers, behind his intrenchments. Though we had defeated him and driven him from the field with heavy loss in arms, men, and artillery, it had only been done by heavy sacrifices, in repeated, persistent, and most gallant assaults upon superior numbers strongly posted and protected. Our loss was in proportion to the prolonged and obstinate struggle. Two-fifths of our gallant troops had fallen, and the number of general and staff officers stricken down will best show how these troops were led. Major-General Hood, the model soldier and inspiring leader, fell after contributing largely to our success, and has suffered the irreparable loss of a leg."

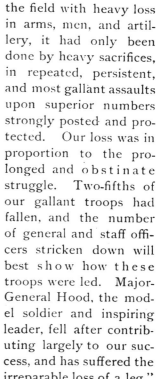

MAJOR-GENERAL PATRICK R. CLEBURNE, C. S. A.

General Bragg believed that although he did not gain possession of Chattanooga by the battle of Chickamauga, he had only to make one more move to secure the prize. And perhaps he would have been correct in this calculation if the commander opposed to him had not been succeeded about a month later by General Grant. Bragg advanced his army to positions on Lookout Mountain and Missionary Ridge, and put the town of Chattanooga into a state of siege, managing to stop the navigation of the river below and cut off all Rosecrans's routes of supply except one long and difficult wagon road. This campaign virtually closed the military career of General Rosecrans. He had shown many fine qualities as a soldier, and had performed some brilliant feats of strategy; but, as with some other commanders, his abilities appeared to stop suddenly short at a point where great successes were within easy reach. It was not more science that was wanted, but more energy. When Grant appeared on the scene, with no more knowledge of the military art than Rosecrans, but with boundless and tireless energy, the conditions quickly changed.

BRIDGE ACROSS TENNESSEE RIVER—CHATTANOOGA AND LOOKOUT MOUNTAIN IN THE DISTANCE.

(FROM A WAR-TIME PHOTOGRAPH.)

GENERAL SHERMAN'S HEADQUARTERS AT CHATTANOOGA.

CHAPTER XXVII.

THE BATTLE OF CHATTANOOGA.

GRANT'S ARRIVAL AT CHATTANOOGA—GENERAL ROSECRANS'S INACTION—OPENING A NEW LINE OF SUPPLY—DESPERATE FIGHTING UNDER GENERAL SHERMAN—PAROLED PRISONERS FORCED INTO THE CONFEDERATE ARMY—FIGHTING AROUND KNOXVILLE—THE BATTLE ABOVE THE CLOUDS—CAPTURE OF MISSIONARY RIDGE—BRAGG'S ARMY COMPLETELY DEFEATED—PICTURESQUE AND ROMANTIC INCIDENTS.

A MONTH after the battle of Chickamauga the National forces in the West were to some extent reorganized. The departments of the Ohio, the Cumberland, and the Tennessee were united under the title of Military Division of the Mississippi, of which General Grant was made commander, and Thomas superseded Rosecrans in command of the Army of the Cumberland. General Hooker, with two corps, was sent to Tennessee. Grant arrived at Chattanooga on the 23d of October, and found affairs in a deplorable condition. It was impossible to supply the troops properly by the one wagon road, and they had been on short rations for some time, while large numbers of the mules and horses were dead.

From the National lines the tents and batteries of the Confederates on Lookout Mountain and Missionary Ridge were in plain sight; their sentinels walked the rounds in a continuous line not a thousand yards away; and from these heights their guns occasionally sent a shot within the lines. When General Sherman, on his arrival, walked out and surveyed the situation, he turned to Grant and exclaimed in surprise, "Why, General, you are besieged." "Yes," said Grant, "it is too true," and pointed out to him a house on Missionary Ridge which was known to be Bragg's headquarters. General Rosecrans, like a similar commander at the East, was able to give most excellent reasons for his prolonged inaction. And so able a soldier as Gen. David S. Stanley, in an article read by him before the Ohio Commandery of the Loyal Legion, seems to justify Rosecrans. The unpleasant and unsatisfactory correspondence of this period, between Rosecrans and the War Department, culminated when the former, having reported the success of an expedition against McMinnville, received a despatch from General Halleck, which said: "The Secretary of War says you always report your successes, but never report your reverses." And Rosecrans replied: "If the Secretary of War says I report my successes, but do not report my reverses, the Secretary of War lies."

It may be that the poor condition of the cavalry, and other discouraging circumstances, were really a proper cause for non-action to a general who was more inclined to study the safety of his own army than the destruction of the enemy; but somehow or other, wherever General Grant appeared, reasons for inactivity seemed to melt away, and the spirit of determined aggression to take their place.

Grant's first care was to open a new and better line of supply. Steamers could come up the river as far as Bridgeport, and he ordered the immediate construction of a road and bridge to reach that point by way of Brown's Ferry, which was done. Within five days the "cracker line," as the soldiers called it, was opened, and thenceforth they had full rations and abundance of everything. The enemy attempted to interrupt the work on the road; but Hooker met them at Wauhatchie, west of Lookout Mountain, and after a three hours' action drove them off.

Chattanooga was now no longer in a state of siege; but it was still seriously menaced by Bragg's army, which held a most singular position. Its flanks were on the northern ends of Lookout Mountain and Missionary Ridge, the crests of which were occupied for some distance, and its centre stretched across Chattanooga Valley. This line was twelve miles long, and most of it was well intrenched.

Grant ordered Sherman to join him with one corps, and Sherman promptly obeyed; but, as he did considerable railroad repairing on the way, he did not reach Chattanooga till the 15th of November. Moreover, he had to fight occasionally, and be ready to fight all the time. At Colliersville he was aroused from a nap in the car by a great noise about the train, and was informed that the pickets had been driven in, and there was every reason to suppose that a large cavalry force would soon make an attack. Sherman immediately got his men out of the train and formed them in a line on a knoll near a railroad cut. Presently a Confederate officer appeared with a flag of truce, and Sherman sent out two officers to meet him, secretly instructing them to keep him in conversation as long as possible. When they returned, it was with the message that General Chalmers demanded the surrender of the place. Sherman ordered his officers to return again to the line and talk as long as possible with the Confederate officer, but finally give him a negative answer. In the little time thus gained he got a telegraph message sent to Memphis and Germantown, ordering Corse's division to hurry forward, and at the same time backed the train into the depot, which was a loopholed brick building, and drew his men into some smaller works that surrounded it. In a few minutes the enemy swooped down, cutting the wires and tearing up the rails on both sides, and then attacked Sherman's little band in their intrenchments. Sherman ordered all the houses that were near enough to shelter the enemy's sharpshooters to be set on fire, and, finding some muskets in the depot, put them into the hands of the clerks and orderlies, making every man available for an active defence. The Confederates had some artillery, with which they knocked his locomotive to pieces, and set fire to the train; but many of Sherman's men were excellent marksmen and trained soldiers, and they not only kept the enemy at bay but managed to put out the fire. This state of things lasted about three hours, when the approach of Corse's division caused the enemy to withdraw. Corse's men had come twenty-six miles on the double quick.

BREVET MAJOR-GENERAL JOHN W. GEARY.

General Sherman, in his graphic "Memoirs," gives many incidents of this march, some of which were not only interesting but significant. Just before he set out, a flag of truce came in one day, borne by a Confederate officer with whom he was acquainted, and escorted by twenty-five men. Sherman invited the officer to take supper with him, and gave orders to his own escort to furnish the Confederate escort with forage and whatever else they wanted during their stay. After supper the conversation turned upon the war, and the Confederate officer said: "What is the use of your persevering? It is simply impossible to subdue eight millions of people. The feeling in the South has become so embittered that a reconciliation is impossible."

DESPATCHES FOR HEADQUARTERS.

Sherman answered: "Sitting as we are here, we appear to be very comfortable, and surely there is no trouble in our becoming friends." "Yes," said the Confederate officer, "that is very true of us; but we are gentlemen of education, and can easily adapt ourselves to any condition of things; but this would not apply equally well to the common people or the common soldiers." Thereupon, General Sherman took him out to the campfires behind the tent and showed him the men of the two escorts mingled together, drinking coffee, and apparently having a happy time. "What do you think of that?" said he. And the Confederate officer admitted that Sherman had the best of the argument. Nevertheless, in spite of the fact that the war had now continued more than two years, that the territory held by the Confederates had steadily diminished, that they had passed the climax of their military resources while those of the North were still abundant, that Gettysburg and Vicksburg had rendered their terrible verdicts, and that all hope of foreign assistance or even recognition was at an end—the opinions expressed by the officer just quoted were very generally held at the South. It is perhaps not wonderful that the ordinary people and the soldiers in the ranks, few of whom understood the philosophy of war in its larger aspects, and to all of whom their generals and their Government continually misrepresented the state of affairs, should have believed that they were invincible. But their educated generals and statesmen ought to have known better; yet either they did not know better, or they concealed their real opinions. Alexander H. Stephens, by many considered the ablest statesman in the Confederacy, late in July of this year (1863), made a speech at Charlotte, N. C., in which he assured his hearers that there was no reason for anything but the most confident hope. He said that the loss of Vicksburg was not as severe a blow as the loss of Fort Pillow, Island No. 10, or New Orleans, and, as the Confederacy had survived those losses, it would also survive this one. He declared that if they were to lose Mobile, Charleston, and Richmond, it would

MAJOR-GENERAL HUGH EWING.

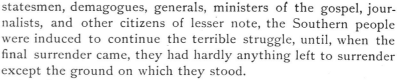

not affect the heart of the Confederacy, which would survive all such losses and finally secure its independence. The enemy, he said, had made two years of unsuccessful war, and thus far had not broken the shell of the Confederacy. He alluded to the fact that during the Revolutionary war the British at one time had possession of North Carolina, South Carolina, New York, and Philadelphia, and yet did not conquer our forefathers; and he added: "In the war of 1812 the British captured the capital of the nation, Washington city, and burned it, yet they did not conquer us; and if we are true to ourselves now, true to our birthright, the Yankee nation will utterly fail to subjugate us. Subjugation would be utter ruin and eternal death to Southern people and all that they hold most dear. Reconstruction would not end the war, but would produce a more horrible war than that in which we are now engaged. The only terms on which we can obtain permanent peace is final and complete separation from the North." With such argument and appeal as this, from statesmen, demagogues, generals, ministers of the gospel, journalists, and other citizens of lesser note, the Southern people were induced to continue the terrible struggle, until, when the final surrender came, they had hardly anything left to surrender except the ground on which they stood.

Another incident of the march was one that gave the Fifteenth Corps its badge. An Irish soldier of that corps one day straggled out and joined a party of the Twelfth Corps at their campfire. Seeing a star marked on every tent, wagon, hat, etc., he asked if they were all brigadier-generals in that corps; and they explained that the star was their corps badge, and then in turn asked him what was the badge of his (the Fifteenth) corps. Now, this corps as yet had not adopted any badge, and the Irishman had never before even heard of a corps badge; but he promptly answered,

BREVET MAJOR-GENERAL ABSALOM BAIRD.

"Forty rounds in the cartridge box and twenty in the pocket." When General Logan heard this story, he adopted the cartridge box and forty rounds as the badge of his corps.

The condition of affairs at this time in that department, and the reasons for it, are set forth with admirable clearness in a letter addressed by General Halleck to General Grant, under date of October 20, 1863:

"It has been the constant desire of the Government, from the beginning of the war, to rescue the loyal inhabitants of East Tennessee from the hands of the rebels, who fully appreciated the importance of continuing their hold upon that country. In addition to the large amount of agricultural products drawn from the upper valley of the Tennessee, they also obtained iron and other materials from the vicinity of Chattanooga. The possession of East Tennessee would cut off one of their most important railroad communications, and threaten their manufactories at Rome, Atlanta, etc.

"When General Buell was ordered into East Tennessee in the summer of 1862, Chattanooga was comparatively unprotected; but Bragg reached there before Buell, and, by threatening his communications, forced him to retreat on Nashville and Louisville. Again, after the battle of Perryville, General Buell was urged to pursue Bragg's defeated army and drive it from East Tennessee. The same was urged upon his successor; but the lateness of the season, or other causes, prevented further operations after the battle of Stone River.

"Last spring, when your movements on the Mississippi River had drawn out of Tennessee a large force of the enemy, I again urged General Rosecrans to take advantage of that opportunity to carry out his projected plan of campaign, General Burnside being ready to coöperate with a diminished but still efficient force. But he could not be persuaded to act in time, preferring to lie still till your campaign should be terminated.

"When General Rosecrans finally determined to advance, he was allowed to select his own lines and plans for carrying out the objects of the expedition. He was directed, however, to report his movements daily, till he crossed the Tennessee, and to connect his left, so far as possible, with General Burnside's right. General Burnside was directed to move simultaneously, connecting his right, as far as possible, with General Rosecrans's left, so that, if the enemy concentrated upon either army, the other could move to its assistance. When General Burnside reached Kingston and Knoxville, and found no considerable number of the enemy in East Tennessee, he was instructed to move down the river and coöperate with General Rosecrans. These instructions were repeated some fifteen times, but were not carried out, General Burnside alleging as an excuse that he believed that Bragg was in retreat, and that General Rosecrans needed no reinforcements. When the latter had gained possession of Chattanooga he was directed not to move on Rome as he proposed, but simply to hold the mountain-passes, so as to prevent the ingress of the rebels into East Tennessee. That object accomplished, I considered the campaign as ended, at least for the present.

"The moment I received reliable information of the departure of Longstreet's corps from the Army of the Potomac, I ordered forward to General Rosecrans every available man in the Department of the Ohio, and again urged General Burnside to move to his assistance. I also telegraphed to Generals Hurlbut, Sherman, and yourself, to forward all available troops in your department. If these forces had been sent to General Rosecrans by Nashville, they could not have been supplied; I therefore directed them to move by Corinth and the Tennessee River. The necessity of this has been proved by the fact that the reinforcements sent to him from the Army of the Potomac have not been able, for the want of railroad transportation, to reach General Rosecrans's army in the field.

"It is now ascertained that the greater part of the prisoners paroled by you at Vicksburg, and General Banks at Port Hudson, were illegally and improperly declared exchanged, and forced into the ranks to swell the rebel numbers at Chickamauga. This outrageous act, in violation of the laws of war, of the cartel entered into by the rebel authorities, and of all sense of honor, gives us a useful lesson in regard to the character of the enemy with whom we are contending. He neither regards the rules of civilized warfare, nor even his most solemn engagements. You may, therefore, expect to meet in arms thousands of unexchanged prisoners released by you and others on parole not to serve again till duly exchanged. Although the enemy, by this disgraceful means, has been able to concentrate in Georgia and Alabama a much larger force than we anticipated, your armies will be abundantly able to defeat him. Your difficulty will not be in the want of men, but in the means of supplying them at this season of the year. A single-track railroad can supply an army of sixty or seventy thousand men, with the usual number of cavalry and artillery; but beyond that number, or with a large mounted force, the difficulty of supply is very great."

Meanwhile, General Longstreet, with about twenty thousand men, was detached from Bragg's army and sent against Burnside at Knoxville, which is about one hundred and thirty miles northeast of Chattanooga. After Sherman's arrival, Grant had about eighty thousand men. He placed Sherman on his left, on the north side of the Tennessee, opposite the head of Missionary Ridge; Thomas in the centre, across Chattanooga valley; and Hooker on his right, around the base of Lookout Mountain. He purposed to have Sherman advance against Bragg's right and capture the heights of Missionary Ridge, while Thomas and Hooker should press the centre and left just enough to prevent any reinforcements from being sent against Sherman. If this were successful, Bragg's key-point being taken, his whole army would be obliged to retreat. Sherman laid two bridges in the night of November 23d, and next day crossed the river and advanced upon the enemy's works; but he met with unexpected difficulties in the nature of the ground, and was only partially successful. Hooker, who had more genius for fighting than for strictly obeying orders, moved around the base of Lookout Mountain, and attacked the seemingly impregnable heights.

General Geary's command led the way, encountering intrenchments and obstructions of all sorts, both in the valley and on the slope of the mountain. Having crossed the Tennessee River below, it moved eastward across Lookout Creek, and thence marched directly up the mountain till its right rested on the palisaded heights. At the same time Grose's brigade advanced farther up stream, drove the Confederates from a bridge, put it into repair, and then moved on. At this moment the Confederates were seen leaving their camps on the mountain and coming down to the rifle-pits and breastworks at its foot to dispute the progress of their enemy. Then another brigade was sent still farther up the stream to make a crossing, and a section of artillery was placed where it could enfilade the position just taken by the Confederates, while another section was established to enfilade the route they had taken in coming down the mountain. All the batteries within range began to play upon the Confederates, and it was made so hot for them that they were glad to abandon their intrenchments in the valley. Then the remainder of Hooker's men were pushed across the stream, and the ascent of the mountain began in earnest. They climbed up over ledges and bowlders directly under the muzzles of the guns on the summit, driving their enemy from one position after another, and following him as closely as possible, in order to make him a shield from the fire of the batteries. The advance had begun at eight o'clock in the morning, and by noon Geary's men had reached the summit of the mountain. Other brigades came up in rapid succession at various points, and on the summit the Confederates found themselves surrounded and subjected to a rapid fire from every direction save one, in which direction (southward along the ridge) all of them who could get away retreated, but many were taken prisoners. At this point the movement of Hooker's men was arrested by darkness. Clouds had been hanging over the summit of the mountain during the morning, and had gradually settled down toward the valley, so that the last of the battle was fought above them, spectators from below seeing the troops go up into those clouds and disappear. Hooker's line was then established on the east side of the mountain, with the left near the mouth of Chattanooga Creek, and the right on the palisades. To prevent the bringing forward of artillery, the Confederates had undermined the road and covered it with felled timber. During the night Hooker's men removed the timber and placed the road in a serviceable condition, while all the time an irregular fire was kept up along the line, and once a serious attack was threatened by the Confederates. But before morning they abandoned the mountain entirely, leaving behind the camp equipage of three brigades. This action is famous as Hooker's "battle above the clouds," and that evening, when the moon rose over the crest of the mountain, a strange spectacle was seen of troops apparently marching across its yellow disk.

The next day, the 25th, Hooker was to pass down the eastern slope of Lookout Mountain, cross Chattanooga valley, and strike the left of Bragg's position, as now held on the crest and western slope of Missionary Ridge. But the destruction of a bridge by the retreating enemy delayed him four hours, and Grant saw that Bragg was weakening his centre to mass troops against Sherman. So, without waiting longer for Hooker, he ordered an advance of the centre held by Thomas. Under the immediate leadership of Generals Sheridan and Wood, Thomas's men crossed the valley, walked right into the line of Confederate works at the base of Missionary Ridge, followed the retreating enemy to a second line halfway up the slope, took this, and still keeping at the very heels of the Confederates, who thus shielded them from the batteries at the top, reached the summit and swept everything before them.

BATTLE OF LOOKOUT MOUNTAIN.

General Sherman advanced, according to orders, against Missionary Ridge, but met with a more determined resistance, and had a much slower fight on the 25th. The enemy massed heavily in his front, and Thomas sent a division to his assistance, when the whole line was pushed forward ; and at length the enemy retired hastily, abandoning the works at the foot of the hill, and were closely followed up the slope to the crest, which was soon captured, with many prisoners and all the guns. Gen. Thomas J. Wood says in his report : "Troops in line and column checkered the broad plain of Chattanooga. In front, plainly to be seen, was the enemy, so soon to be encountered in deadly conflict. My division seemed to drink in the inspiration of the scene, and, when the advance was sounded, moved forward in the perfect order of a holiday parade.

"It has been my good fortune to witness, on the Champs-de-Mars and on Long Champ reviews of all arms of the French service, under the eye of the most remarkable man of the present generation. I once saw a review, followed by a mock battle, of the finest troops of El Re Galantuomo. The pageant was held on the plains near Milan, the queen city of Lombardy, and the troops in the sham conflict were commanded by two of the most distinguished officers of the Piedmontese service—Cialdini, and another whose name I cannot now recall. In none of these dis-

LOOKOUT MOUNTAIN AND TENNESSEE RIVER.

(FROM A PHOTOGRAPH OWNED BY THE UNITED STATES GOVERNMENT.)

plays did I ever see anything to exceed the soldierly bearing and the steadiness of my division, exhibited in the advance on Monday afternoon. There was certainly one striking difference in the circumstances of these grand displays. The French and Italian parades were peaceful pageants; ours involved the exigencies of stern war—certainly an immense difference. I should do injustice to the brave men who thus moved forward to the conflict in such perfect order, were I to omit to record that not one straggler lagged behind to sully the magnificence and perfectness of the grand battle array. . . . As soon as our troops began to move forward, the enemy opened a terrific fire from his batteries on the crest of the ridge. It would not, perhaps, be an exaggeration to say that the enemy had fifty pieces of artillery disposed on the crest of Missionary Ridge. But the rapid firing of all this mass of artillery could not stay the onward movement of our troops. When the first line of intrenchments was carried, the goal for which we had started was won. Our orders carried us no further. We had been instructed to carry the line of intrenchments at the base of the ridge, and then halt. But the enthusiasm and impetuosity of the troops were such that those who first reached the intrenchments at the base of the ridge bounded over them and pressed on up the ascent after the flying enemy. Moreover, the intrenchments were no protection against the enemy's artillery on the ridge. To remain would be destruction; to retire would be both expensive in life and disgraceful. Officers and men all seemed impressed with this truth. In addition, the example of those who commenced to ascend the ridge so soon as the intrenchments were carried was contagious. Without waiting for an order, the vast mass pressed forward in the race of glory, each man eager to be the first on the summit. The enemy's artillery and musketry could not check the impetuous assault. The troops did not halt to fire; to have done so would have been ruinous. Little was left to the immediate commanders of the troops but to cheer on the foremost, to encourage the weaker of limb, and to sustain the very few who seemed to be faint-hearted."

By this brilliant battle, which occupied portions of three days, Bragg's army was completely defeated, and its captured guns were turned upon it as it fled. His men seemed to have lost all respect for him, for when he rode among the fugitives and vainly tried to rally them by shouting, "Here's your commander," he was derisively answered, "Here's your mule," and was obliged to join in the flight. This practically closed his military career. He had been a special favorite of Mr. Davis, who is accused by some Confederate writers of obstinately placing him where it was obvious he should have placed an abler man. He was relieved soon after this battle from command, and called to Richmond as the military adviser of Mr. Davis.

In these battles the National loss was nearly six thousand men. The Confederate loss was about ten thousand (of whom six thousand were prisoners) and forty-two guns. Bragg established the remainder of his army in a fortified camp at Dalton, Ga., and was soon superseded by Gen. Joseph E. Johnston. Granger and Sherman were sent to the relief of Burnside at Knoxville, and Longstreet withdrew to Virginia.

The Chattanooga campaign was perhaps the most picturesque of any in the war, and was full of romantic incidents.

All the armies were followed by correspondents of the great newspapers, some of whom were men of high literary ability and were alive to the inspiration of the great drama they witnessed. Americans may be pardoned for some considerable degree of pride when they consider that in the emergency of that great war they not only had men of sufficient skill and valor for every possible and some seemingly impossible tasks, but also had the resources and the art to manufacture nearly all the arms and material that were called for, and writers capable of putting into dignified and often brilliant literature the rapidly moving story of those terrible days. Among these correspondents was Benjamin F. Taylor, the journalist and poet, who followed the Army of the Cumberland as the representative of the *Chicago Journal*. He witnessed the battles before Chattanooga, and had a son among the blue-coated boys that scaled the mountain. From his description, written very soon after the events, we take the following passages:

"Let me show you a landscape that shall not fade out from 'the lidless eye of time' long after we are all dead. A half mile

COLONEL GREEN B. RAUM.

BREVET BRIGADIER-GENERAL JOHN B. TURCHIN.

BRIGADIER-GENERAL CHARLES R. WOODS.

from the eastern border of Chattanooga is a long swell of land, sparsely sprinkled with houses, flecked thickly with tents, and checkered with two or three graveyards. On its summit stand the red earthworks of Fort Wood, with its great guns frowning from the angles. Mounting the parapet and facing eastward you have a singular panorama. Away to your left is a shining elbow of the Tennessee, a lowland of woods, a long-drawn valley, glimpses of houses. At your right you have wooded undulations with clear intervals extending down and around to the valley at the eastern base of Lookout. From the fort the smooth ground descends rapidly to a little plain, a sort of trough in the sea, then a fringe of oak woods, then an acclivity, sinking down to a second fringe of woods, until full in front of you, and three-fourths of a mile distant, rises Orchard Knob, a conical mound, perhaps a hundred feet high, once wooded, but now bald. Then ledges of rocks, and narrow breadths of timber, and rolling sweeps of open ground for two miles more, until the whole rough and stormy landscape seems to dash against Missionary Ridge, three miles distant, that lifts like a sea-wall eight hundred feet high, wooded, rocky, precipitous, wrinkled with ravines. This is, in truth, the grand feature of the scene, for it extends north as far as you can see, with fields here and there cut down through the woods to the ground, and lying on the hillsides like brown linen to bleach; and you feel, as you look at them, as if they are in danger of slipping down the Ridge into the road at its base. And then it curves to the southwest, just leaving you a way out between it and Lookout Mountain. Altogether the rough, furrowed landscape looks as if the Titans had ploughed and forgotten to harrow it. The thinly fringed summit of the Ridge varies in width from twenty to fifty feet, and houses looking like cigar-boxes are dotted along it. On the top of that wall are rebels and batteries; below the first pitch, three hundred feet down, are more rebels and batteries; and still below are their camps and rifle-pits, sweeping five miles. At your right, and in the rear, is Fort Negley, the old 'Star' fort of Confederate ***régime;*** its next neighbor is Fort King, under the frown of Lookout; yet to the right is the battery of Moccasin Point. Finish out the picture on either hand with Federal earthworks and saucy angles, fancy the embankment of the Charleston and Memphis Railroad drawn diagonally, like an awkward score, across the plain far at your feet, and I think you have the tremendous theatre. . . . At half-past twelve the order came; at one, two divisions of the Fourth Corps made ready to move; at ten minutes before two, twenty-five thousand Federal troops were in line of battle. The line of skirmishers moved lightly out, and swept true as a sword-blade into the edge of the field. You should have seen that splendid line, two miles long, as straight and unwavering as a ray of light. On they went, driving in the pickets before them. Shots of musketry, like the first great drops of summer rain upon a roof, pattered along the line. One fell here, another there, but still, like joyous heralds before a royal progress, the skirmishers passed on. From wood and rifle-pit, from rocky ledge and mountain-top, sixty-five thousand rebels watched these couriers bearing the gift of battle in their hands. The bugle sounded from Fort Wood, and the divisions of Wood and Sheridan began to move; the latter, out from the right, threatened a heavy attack; the former, forth from the left, dashed on into the rough road of the battle. Black rifle-pits were tipped with fire; sheets of flame flashed out of the woods; the spatter of musketry deepened into volleys and rolled like muffled drums; hostile batteries opened from the ledges; the 'Rodmans' joined

WAITING FOR ORDERS.

A DEAD CONFEDERATE IN THE TRENCHES.

in from Fort Wood; bursting shell and gusts of shrapnel filled the air; the echoes roused up and growled back from the mountains; the rattle was a roar—and yet those gallant fellows moved steadily on. Down the slope, through the wood, up the hills, straight for Orchard Knob as the crow flies, moved that glorious wall of blue. The air grew dense and blue, the gray clouds of smoke surged up the sides of the valley. It was a terrible journey they were making, these men of ours; and three-fourths of a mile in sixty minutes was splendid progress. They neared the Knob; the enemy's fire converged; the arc of batteries poured in upon them lines of fire, like the rays they call a 'glory' about the head of the Madonna and Child;—but they went up the rugged altar of Orchard Knob at the double-quick with a cheer; they wrapped like a cloak round an Alabama regiment that defended it, and swept them down on our side of the mound. Prisoners had begun to come in before; they streamed across the field like files of geese. Then on for a second altar, Brush Knob, nearly a half-mile to the northeast, and bristling with a battery; it was swept of foes and garnished with Federal blue in thirty minutes. Perhaps it was eleven o'clock on Tuesday morning when the rumble of artillery came in gusts from the valley to the west of Lookout. Climbing Signal Hill, I could see volumes of smoke rolling to and fro, like clouds from a boiling caldron. The mad surges of tumult lashed the hills till they cried aloud, and roared through the gorges till you might have fancied all the thunders of a long summer tumbled into that valley together. And yet the battle was unseen. It was like hearing voices from the under-world. Meanwhile it began to rain; skirts of mist trailed over the woods and swept down the ravines. But our men trusted in Providence, kept their powder dry, and played on. It was the second day of the drama; it was the second act I was hearing; it was the touch on the enemy's left. The assault upon Lookout had begun! Glancing at the mighty crest crowned with a precipice, and now hung round about, three hundred feet down, with a curtain of clouds, my heart misgave me. It could never be taken. Hooker thundered, and the enemy came down like the Assyrian; while Whittaker on the right, and Colonel Ireland of Geary's command on the left, having moved out from Wauhatchie, some five miles from the mountain, at five in the morning, pushed up to Chattanooga Creek, threw over it a bridge, made for Lookout Point, and there formed the right under the shelf of the mountain, the left resting on the creek. And then the play began; the enemy's camps were seized, his pickets surprised and captured, the strong works on the Point taken, and the Federal front moved on. Charging upon him, they leaped over his works as the wicked twin Roman leaped over his brother's mud wall, the Fortieth Ohio capturing his artillery and taking a Mississippi regiment, and gained the white house. And there they stood, 'twixt heaven and—Chattanooga. But above them, grand and sullen, lifted the precipice; and they were men, and not eagles. The way was strewn with natural fortifications, and from behind rocks and trees they delivered their fire, contesting inch by inch the upward way. The sound of the battle rose and fell; now fiercely renewed, and now dying away. And Hooker thundered on in the valley, and the echoes of his howitzers bounded about the mountains like volleys of musketry. That curtain of cloud was hung around the mountain by the God of battles—even our God. It was the veil of the temple that could not be rent. A captured colonel declared that, had the day been clear, their sharp-shooters would have riddled our advance like pigeons, and left the command without a leader; but friend and foe were wrapped in a seamless mantle, and two hundred will cover the entire Federal loss, while our brave mountaineers strewed Lookout with four hundred dead, and captured a thousand prisoners. Our entire forces bore themselves bravely; not a straggler in the command, they all came splendidly up to the work, and the whole affair was graced with signal instances of personal valor. Lieutenant Smith, of the Fortieth Ohio, leaped over the works, discharged his revolver six times like the ticking of a clock, seized a sturdy foe by the hair, and gave him the heel of the 'Colt' over the head. Colonel Ireland was slightly wounded, and Major Acton, of the Fortieth Ohio, was shot through the heart while leading a bayonet charge. And now, returning to my point of observation, I was waiting in painful suspense to see what should come out of the roaring caldron in the valley, now and then, I confess, casting an eye up to the big gun of Lookout, lest it might toss something my way, over its left shoulder—I, a non-combatant, and bearing no arms but a Faber's pencil 'Number 2'—when something was born out of the mist (I cannot better convey the idea) and appeared on the shorn side of the mountain, below and to the west of the white house. It was the head of the Federal column! And there it held, as if it were riveted to the rock, and the line of blue, a half mile long, swung slowly around from the left, like the index of a mighty dial, and swept up the brown face of the mountain. The bugles of this city of camps were sounding high noon, when in two parallel columns the troops moved up the mountain, in the rear of the enemy's rifle-pits, which they swept at every fire. Ah, I wish you had been here! It needed no glass to see it; it was only just beyond your hand. And there, in the centre of the columns, fluttered the blessed flag. 'My God! what flag is that?' men cried. And up steadily it moved. I could think of nothing but a gallant ship-of-the-line grandly lifting upon the great billows and riding out the storm. It was a scene never to fade out. Pride and pain struggled in my heart for the mastery, but faith carried the day; I believed in the flag, and took courage. Volleys of musketry and crashes of cannon, and then those lulls in a battle even more terrible than the tempest. At four o'clock an aid

MAJOR-GENERAL WILLIAM B. BATE, C. S. A.

MAJOR-GENERAL A. P. STEWART, C. S. A.

came straight down the mountain into the city—the first Federal by that route in many a day. Their ammunition ran low—they wanted powder up on the mountain. He had been two hours descending, and how much longer the return!

"Night was closing rapidly in, and the scene was growing sublime. The battery at Moccasin Point was sweeping the road to the mountain. The brave little fort at its left was playing like a heart in a fever. The cannon upon the top of Lookout were pounding away at their lowest depression. The flash of the guns fairly burned through the clouds; there was an instant of silence, here, there, yonder, and the tardy thunder leaped out after the swift light. For the first time, perhaps, since that mountain began to burn beneath the gold and crimson sandals of the sun, it was in eclipse. The cloud of the summit and the smoke of the battle had met halfway and mingled. Here was Chattanooga, but Lookout had vanished! It was Sinai over again, with its thunderings and lightnings and thick darkness, and the Lord was on our side. Then the storm ceased, and occasional dropping shots told off the evening till half-past nine, and then a crashing volley, and a rebel yell, and a desperate charge. It was their good-night to our boys; good-night to the mountain. They had been met on their own vantage-ground; they had been driven one and a half miles. The Federal foot touched the hill, indeed, but above still towered the precipice.

"At ten o'clock a growing line of lights glittered obliquely across the breast of Lookout. It made our eyes dim to see it. It was the Federal autograph scored along the mountain. They were our campfires. Our wounded lay there all the dreary night of rain, unrepining and content. Our unharmed heroes lay there upon their arms. Our dead lay there, 'and surely they slept well.' At dawn Captain Wilson and fifteen men of the Eighth Kentucky crept up among the rocky clefts, handing their guns one to another—'like them that gather samphire—dreadful trade!'—and stood at length upon the summit. The entire regiment pushed up after them, formed in line, threw out skirmishers, and advanced five miles to Summerton. Artillery and infantry had all fled in the night, nor left a wreck behind.

MAJOR-GENERAL JEREMY F. GILMER, C. S. A.
Chief Engineer Army of the Tennessee.

"If Sherman did not roll the enemy along the Ridge like a carpet, at least he rendered splendid service, for he held a huge ganglion of the foe as firmly on their right as if he had them in the vice of the 'lame Lemnian' who forged the thunderbolts. General Corse's, General Jones's, and Colonel Loomis's brigades led the way, and were drenched with blood. Here Colonel O'Meara, of the Ninetieth Illinois, fell. Here its lieutenant-colonel, Stuart, received a fearful wound. Here its brave young captains knelt at the crimson shrine, and never rose from worshipping. Here one hundred and sixty of its three hundred and seventy heroes were beaten with the bloody rain. The brigades of Generals Mathias and Smith came gallantly up to the work. Fairly blown out of the enemy's guns, and scorched with flame, they were swept down the hill only to stand fast for a new assault. Let no man dare to say they did not acquit themselves well and nobly. To living and dead in the commands of Sherman and Howard who struck a blow that day—out of my heart I utter it—hail and farewell! And as I think it all over, glancing again along that grand, heroic line of the Federal epic—I commit the story with a childlike faith to history, sure that when she gives her clear, calm record of that day's famous work, standing like Ruth among the reapers in the fields that feed the world, she will declare the grandest staple of the Northwest is Man."

A TYPICAL SOUTHERN MANSION.
(From a War-time Photograph.)

PRISONERS IN ANDERSONVILLE STOCKADE.

CHAPTER XXVIII.

THE BLACK CHAPTER.

PERSECUTIONS OF UNION MEN—THE BLACK FLAG—THE GUERILLAS—SECESSION FROM SECESSION—RIOT IN CONCORD, N.H.—MASSACRE AT FORT PILLOW—CARE OF PRISONERS—ANDERSONVILLE—OTHER PRISONS—SUSPENSION OF EXCHANGES—VIOLATION OF PAROLES—PRINCIPLES RELATING TO CAPTURES—CRUELTIES COMMITTED BY UNION SOLDIERS IN VIRGINIA—GENERAL IMBODEN'S STATEMENTS REGARDING FEDERAL ATROCITIES—GENERAL EARLY'S ACCOUNT OF THE BURNING OF CHAMBERSBURG.

So far as the military situation was concerned, the victories at Gettysburg and Vicksburg wrote the doom of the Confederacy, and there the struggle should have ended. That it did not end there, was due partly to a hope that the Democratic party at the North might carry the next presidential election, as well as to the temper of the Southern people, which had been concentrated into an intense personalized hatred. This began before the war, was one of the chief circumstances that made it possible to carry the conspiracy into execution, and seemed to be carefully nursed by Mr. Davis and his ministers.

Gen. Andrew J. Hamilton, who had been attorney-general of Texas, in a speech delivered in New York in 1863, declared that two hundred men were hanged in Texas during the presidential canvass of 1860, because they were suspected of being more loyal to the Union than to slavery. Judge Baldwin, of Texas, speaking in Washington in October, 1864, said: "The wrongs inflicted on the Union men of Texas surpass in cruelty the horrors of the Inquisition. From two to three thousand men have been hanged, in many cases without even the form of a trial, simply and solely because they were Union men and would not give their support to secession. Indeed, it has been, and is, the express determination of the secessionists to take the life of every Union man. Nor are they always particular to ascertain what a man's real sentiments are. It is sufficient for them that a man is a d—d Yankee. One day a secessionist said to the governor of Texas, 'There is Andrew Jackson Hamilton—suppose I kill the d—d Unionist.' Said the governor, 'Kill him or any other Unionist, and you need fear nothing while I am governor.' As I was passing through one place in Texas, I saw three men who had been hanged in the course of the night. When I inquired the cause, I was told in the coolest manner that it was to be presumed they were Union men. In Grayson County, a man named Hillier, who had come from the North, was forced into the Confederate army. Soon afterward his wife was heard to remark that she wished the Union army would advance and take possession of Texas, that her husband might return and provide for his family. This being reported to the provost marshal, he sent six men dressed in women's clothes, who dragged her to the nearest tree and hanged her in the sight of her little children."

In the mountainous portions of Virginia, Tennessee, and North Carolina, where comparatively few slaves were kept, large numbers of the people were opposed to secession, and for their devotion to the Union they suffered such persecution as had never been witnessed in this part of the world. It was perhaps most violent in East Tennessee. Among the numerous deliberate and brutal murders, committed by men in Confederate uniform, were those of the Rev. L. Carter and his son in Bradley County, the Rev. M. Cavander in Van Buren County, the Rev. Mr. Blair of Hamilton County, and the Rev. Mr. Douglas—all for the simple reason that they were Unionists. Many of the outrages upon the wives and children of Union men were such as any writer would shrink from recording. Those who could get away fled northward, often after their homes had been burned and their movable property carried off, and became subjects of charity in the free States.

BRIGADIER-GENERAL A. J. HAMILTON.
(Military Governor of Texas.)

Many secessionists, residing in States that did not secede, had gone unhindered to the Confederate armies, and when such were captured by the National armies they received no different treatment from other prisoners of war. But the Confederate Government professed to look upon all Unionists in the seceded States (and even in some of the States whose secession was at least a doubtful question) as traitors, and numerous orders declaring them such and prescribing their punishment were issued. In one of these, dated November 25, 1861, Judah P. Benjamin, the Confederate Secretary of War, said to a Confederate colonel at Knoxville: "I now proceed to give you the desired instruction in relation to the prisoners of war taken by you among the traitors of East Tennessee. First, all such as can be identified in having been engaged in bridge burning are to be tried summarily by drum-head court-martial, and, if found guilty, executed on the spot by hanging. It would be well to leave the bodies hanging in the vicinity of the burned bridges. Second, all such as have not been so engaged are to be treated as prisoners of war, and sent with an armed guard to Tuscaloosa. . . . In no case is one of the men known to have been up in arms against the Government to be released on any pledge or oath of allegiance. They are all to be held as prisoners of war, and held in jail till the end of the war." The Rev. Thomas W. Humes, in his "Loyal Mountaineers," says that, in consequence of this order, "Two men, Hensie and Fry, were hung at Greenville by Colonel Ledbetter's immediate authority, and without delay. Had not the execution been so hasty, it might have been discovered, in time to save Fry's life, that not he but another person of the same surname was the real offender in the case." Many residents of Knoxville and its vicinity were imprisoned under this order; and the Rev. William G. Brownlow, who was one of them, says that on the lower floor of the jail, where he was kept, the prisoners were so numerous that there was not room for them all to lie down at one time, and that the only article of furniture in the building was a dirty wooden bucket from which the prisoners drank water with a tin cup. The following entries, taken from his diary while he was thus imprisoned, are fair samples of many: "December 17: Brought in a Union man from Campbell County to-day, leaving behind six small children, and their mother dead. This man's offence is holding out for the Union. To-night two brothers named Walker came in from Hawkins County, charged with having 'talked Union talk.'" "December 18: Discharged sixty prisoners to-day, who had been in prison from three to five weeks—taken through mistake, as was said, there being nothing against them." "December 22: Brought in old man Wampler, a Dutchman, seventy years of age, from Green County, charged with being an 'Andrew Johnson man and talking Union talk.'"

In Virginia, Governor Letcher wrote to a man named Fitzgerald, who had been arrested on suspicion of Unionism and asked to be released: "In 1856 you voted for the abolitionist Frémont for President. Ever since the war, you have maintained a sullen silence in regard to its merits. Your son, who, in common with other young men, was called to the defence of his country, has escaped to the enemy, probably by your advice. This is evidence enough to satisfy me that you are a traitor to your country, and I regret that it is not sufficient to justify me in demanding you from the military authorities, to be tried and executed for treason." The Lynchburg *Republican* said, "Our people were greatly surprised, on Saturday morning, to see the black flag waving over the depot of the Virginia and Tennessee Railroad Company. We are for displaying that flag throughout the whole South. We should ask no quarter at the hands of the vandal Yankee invaders, and our motto should be, an entire extermination of every one who has set foot upon our sacred soil." And the Jackson *Mississippian* said, in the summer of 1862, "In addition to pitched battles upon the open field, let us try partisan ranging, bushwhacking, and henceforward, until the close of this war, let our sign be the black flag and no quarter." According to Governor Letcher, as quoted in Pollard's "Secret History of the Confederacy," Stonewall Jackson was, from the beginning of the war, in favor of raising the black flag, and thought that no prisoners should be taken. The same historian is authority for the story that once, when an inferior officer was regretting that some National soldiers had been killed in a display of extraordinary courage, when they might as readily have been captured, Jackson replied curtly, "Shoot them all; I don't want them to be brave."

The rules of civilized warfare forbid the use of explosive bullets, on the ground that when a bullet strikes a soldier it is likely to disable him sufficiently to put him out of the combat; and, therefore, to construct it so that it will explode and kill him after it has entered the flesh, is essentially murder. It has been asserted that in some instances explosive bullets were fired by the Confederates; and it has also been strenuously denied. Gen. Manning F. Force, in his "Personal Recollections of the Vicksburg Campaign," read before the Ohio Commandery of the Loyal Legion, says: "There was much speculation and discussion about certain small explosive sounds that were heard. General Ransom and others maintained they were caused by explosive bullets. General Logan and others scouted the idea. One day one struck the ground and exploded at Ransom's feet. Picking up the exploded shell of a rifle-ball, he settled the question. After the siege, many such explosive rifle-balls, which had not been used, were picked up on the former camp-grounds of the enemy."

The Confederate Congress passed an act, approved April 21, 1862, authorizing the organization of bands of partisan rangers, to be entitled to the same pay, rations, and quarters as other soldiers, and to have the same protection in case of capture. These partisan rangers were popularly known as guerillas, and most of them were irresponsible marauding bands, acting the part of thieves and murderers until captured, and then claiming treatment as prisoners of war, on the ground that they were regularly commissioned and enlisted soldiers of the Confederacy.

Some of the devices that were resorted to for the purpose of intensifying the hatred of Northern people and Unionists now appear ludicrous. Thousands of people in the South were made to believe that Hannibal Hamlin, elected Vice-President on the ticket with Mr. Lincoln, was a mulatto; that Mr. Lincoln himself was a monster of cruelty; and that the National army was made up largely of Irish and German mercenaries.

As Mr. Lincoln predicted, and as every reflecting citizen must have known, those who attempted to carry out the doctrine of secession from the United States were obliged to confront its corollary in a proposal to secede from secession. In North Carolina a convention was held to nominate State officers, with the avowed purpose of asserting North Carolina's sovereignty by withdrawing from the Confederacy—on the ground that it had failed in its duties as agent for the sovereign States composing it—and making peace with the United States. The convention was largely attended, and included many of the most intelligent and wealthy men in the State; but the Confederate Government sent an armed force to break up the meeting and imprison the leaders. In the Confederate Congress there were forty members who always voted in a body, in secret session, as Mr. Davis wanted them to. They were commonly known as "the forty thieves." When the war began to look hopeless, a popular movement in favor of peace resulted in the choice of other men to fill their places. But, before their terms expired, a law was passed which made it treason to use language that could be construed as a declaration that any State had a right to secede from the Confederacy. The people of southwestern North Carolina, like those of eastern Tennessee, were mostly small, industrious farmers, without slaves, living in a secluded valley. They knew almost nothing of the political turmoil that distracted the country, and did not wish to take any part in the war. They had voted against disunion, and asked to be exempted from the Confederate conscription law. When this was denied, they petitioned to be expatriated; and when this also was refused, they resorted to such measures as they could to avoid conscription. Thereupon, the Confederate Government sent North Carolina troops to subdue them; and when these were found to fraternize with the people, troops from other States were sent; and when they also failed to do the required work, a brigade of Cherokee Indians was turned into the valley, who committed such atrocities as might have been expected.*

There were Unionists also in other parts of North Carolina, and against them the Confederate Government appeared to have a special grudge. Some of them entered the National service by regular enlistment, and when the Confederate force, under General Hoke, captured Plymouth, in April, 1864, some of these loyal North Carolinians were among the garrison. Knowing what would be their fate if captured, they had provided themselves with morphine, and when the Confederate sergeants went through the ranks and picked them out, they secretly swallowed the drug. As soon as it was discovered what they had done, each was placed between two Confederate soldiers, who kept him walking and awake until its effects had passed away, in order that the "traitors," as they were called, might die by hanging, and soon afterward they were hanged.

There were instances of intolerance and outrage at the North, but they were comparatively few. One of the most notable occurred in Concord, N. H., in August, 1863, where a newspaper that had been loud in its disloyalty was punished by a mob, mainly of newly recruited soldiers, who gutted the office and threw the type into the street. The sheriff's reading of the Riot Act consisted in climbing a lamp-post, extending his right arm, and saying persuasively to the rioters, "Now, boys, I guess you'd better go home."

The most serious charge made by Confederate writers, with sufficient proof, of violation of the laws of war on the part of National troops or commanders, is that which they bring against Gen. David Hunter for his acts in the Shenandoah Valley, when he commanded there in the summer of 1864. Gen. John D. Imboden has made the most dispassionate and apparently honest statement of these that has been published. He says: "What I write is history—every fact detailed is true, indisputably true, and sustained by evidence, both Confederate and Federal, that no living man can gainsay, and a denial is boldly challenged, with the assurance that I hold the proofs ready for production whenever, wherever, and however required. Perhaps no one now living was in a better position to know, at the time of their occurrence, all the details of these transactions than myself.

"Up to his occupation of Staunton, where his army was so much strengthened by Crook and Averill as to relieve his mind of all apprehension of disaster, his conduct had been soldierly, striking his blows only at armed men. But at Staunton he commenced burning private property, and the passion for house-burning grew upon him, and a new system of warfare was inaugurated that a few weeks afterward culminated in the retaliatory burning of Chambersburg. At Staunton, his incendiary appetite was appeased by the burning of a large woollen mill that gave employment to many poor women and children, and a large steam flouring mill and the railway buildings.

"At the breaking out of the war David S. Creigh, an old man of the highest social position, the father of eleven sons and daughters, beloved by all who knew them for their virtues, and intelligence, resided on his estate, near Lewisburg, in Greenbrier County. His reputation was of the highest order. No man in the large county of Greenbrier was better known or more esteemed; few, if any, had more influence. Besides offices of high public trust in civil life, he was an elder in the Presbyterian church of Lewisburg, one of the largest and most respectable in

EXECUTION OF A PRIVATE SOLDIER FOR DESERTION AND ATTEMPTED COMMUNICATION WITH THE ENEMY.

*See report of a speech by the Hon. C. J. Barlow, of Georgia, delivered in Cooper Institute, New York, October 15, 1864.

the synod of Virginia. In the early part of November, 1863, there being a Federal force near Lewisburg, Mr. Creigh, on entering his house one day, found a drunken and dissolute soldier there using the most insulting language to his wife and daughters, and at the same time breaking open trunks and drawers, and helping himself to their contents. At the moment Mr. Creigh entered, the ruffian was attempting to force the trunk of a young lady teacher in the family. Mr. Creigh asked him to desist, stating that it was the property of a lady under his protection. The villain, rising from the trunk, immediately drew a pistol, cocked it, pointed it at Mr. Creigh, and exclaimed: "Go out of this room. What are you doing here? Bring me the keys." Mr. Creigh attempted to defend himself and family, but a pistol he tried to use for the purpose snapped at the instant the robber fired at him, the ball grazing his face and burying itself in the wall. They then grappled, struggled into the passage, and tumbled downstairs, the robber on top. They rose, and Mr. Creigh attempted to wrest the pistol from the hands of his adversary, when it was accidentally discharged, and the latter wounded. They struggled into the portico, where the ruffian again shot at Mr. Creigh, when a negro woman who saw it all ran up with an axe in her hand, and begged her master to use it. He took it from her and despatched the robber. After consultation and advice with friends, it was decided to bury the body and say nothing about it.

BRIGADIER-GENERAL JOHN S. PRESTON, C. S. A.
(In charge of the Bureau of Conscription.)

BRIGADIER-GENERAL JOHN H WINDER, C. S. A.
(Superintendent of Prisons.)

"The troops left the neighborhood, and did not return till June, 1864, when they were going through to join Hunter. A negro belonging to a neighbor, having heard of the matter, went to their camp and told it. Search was made, the remains found, and Mr. Creigh was arrested. He made a candid statement of the whole matter, and begged to be permitted to introduce witnesses to prove the facts, which was refused, and he was marched off with the army, to be turned over to General Hunter, at Staunton. . . . Mr. Creigh had no trial, no witnesses, no counsel nor friends present, but was ordered to be hanged like a dog for an act of duty to his helpless wife and daughters.

"At Lexington he enlarged upon the burning operations begun at Staunton. On his way, and in the surrounding country, he burnt mills, furnaces, storehouses, granaries, and all farming utensils he could find, besides a great amount of fencing and a large quantity of grain. In the town he burnt the Virginia Military Institute, and all the professors' houses except the superintendent's (General Smith's), where he had his headquarters, and found a portion of the family too sick to be removed. He had the combustibles collected to burn Washington College, the recipient of the benefactions of the Father of his Country by his will; but, yielding to the appeals of the trustees and citizens, spared the building, but destroyed the philosophical and chemical apparatus, libraries, and furniture. He burned the mills and some private stores in the lower part of the town. Captain Towns, an officer in General Hunter's army, took supper with the family of Gov. John Letcher. Mrs. Letcher, having heard threats that her house would be burned, spoke of it to Captain Towns, who said it could not be possible, and remarked that he would go at once to headquarters and let her know. He went, returned in a half hour, and told her that he was directed by General Hunter to assure her that the house would not be destroyed, and she might, therefore, rest easy. After this, she dismissed her fears, not believing it possible that a man occupying Hunter's position would be guilty of wilful and deliberate falsehood to a lady. It, however, turned out otherwise, for the next morning, at half-past eight o'clock, his assistant provost-marshal, accompanied by a portion of his guard, rode up to the door, and Captain Berry dismounted, rang the door-bell, called for Mrs. Letcher, and informed her that General Hunter had ordered him to burn the house. She replied, 'There must be some mistake,' and requested to see the order. He said it was verbal. She asked if its execution could not be delayed till she could see Hunter. He replied: 'The order is peremptory, and you have five minutes to leave the house.' Mrs.

SAMUEL COOPER, C. S. A.
(Adjutant and Inspector-General.)

MAJOR-GENERAL S. B. MAXEY, C. S. A.
(Superintendent of Indian Affairs.)

Letcher then asked if she could be allowed to remove her mother's, her sister's, her own and her children's clothing. This request being refused, she left the house. In a very short time they poured camphene on the parlor floor and ignited it with a match. In the meantime Miss Lizzie Letcher was trying to remove some articles of clothing from the other end of the house, and Berry, finding these in her arms, set fire to them. The wardrobe and bureaus were then fired, and soon the house was enveloped in flames. While Hunter was in Lexington, Capt. Mathew X. White, residing near the town, was arrested, taken about two miles, and, without trial, was shot, on the allegation that he was a bushwhacker. During the first year of the war he commanded the Rockbridge cavalry, and was a young gentleman of generous impulses and good character. The total destruction of private property in Rockbridge County, by Hunter, was estimated and published in the local papers at the time as over two million dollars.

"From Lexington he proceeded to Buchanan, in Botetourt County, and camped on the magnificent estate of Col. John T. Anderson, an elder brother of Gen. Joseph R. Anderson, of the Tredegar Works at Richmond. Colonel Anderson's estate, on the banks of the Upper James, and his mansion, were baronial in character. The house crowned a high, wooded hill, was very large, and furnished in a style to dispense that lavish hospitality which was the pride of so many of the old-time Virginians. It was the seat of luxury and refinement, and in all respects a place to make the owner contented with his lot in this world. Colonel Anderson was old—his head as white as snow—and his wife but a few years his junior. He was in no office, and too old to fight, hence was living on his fine estate strictly the life of a private gentleman. There was no military or public object on God's earth to be gained by ruining such a man. Yet Hunter, after destroying all that could be destroyed on the plantation when he left it, ordered the grand old mansion with all its contents to be laid in ashes.

"It seems that, smarting under the miserable failure of his grand raid on Lynchburg, he came back to the Potomac more implacable than when he left it a month before. His first victim was the Hon. Andrew Hunter, of Charlestown, Jefferson County, his own first cousin, and named after the general's father. Mr. Hunter is a lawyer of great eminence, and a man of deservedly large influence in his county and the State. His home, eight miles from Harper's Ferry, in the suburbs of Charlestown, was the most costly and elegant in the place, and his family as refined and cultivated as any in the State. His offence, in General Hunter's eyes, was that he had gone politically with his State, and was in full sympathy with the Confederate cause. The general sent a squadron of cavalry out from Harper's Ferry, took Mr. Hunter prisoner, and held him a month in the common guard-house of his soldiers, without alleging any offence against him not common to nearly all the people of Virginia, and finally discharged him without trial or explanation, after heaping these indignities on him. Mr. Hunter was an old man, and suffered severely from confinement and exposure. While he was thus a prisoner General Hunter ordered his elegant mansion to be burned to the ground with all its contents, not even permitting Mrs. Hunter and her daughter to save their clothes and family pictures from the flames. His next similar exploit was at Shepherdstown, in the same county, where, on the 19th of July, 1864, he caused to be burned the residence of the Hon. A. R. Boteler. Mrs. Boteler was also a cousin of General Hunter. This homestead was an old colonial house, endeared to the family by a thousand tender memories, and contained a splendid library, many pictures, and an invaluable collection of rare and precious manuscripts, illustrating the early history of that part of Virginia, that Colonel Boteler had collected by years of toil. The only members of the family who were there at the time were Colonel Boteler's eldest and widowed daughter, Mrs. Shepherd, who was an invalid, her three children, the eldest five years old and the youngest eighteen months, and Miss Helen Boteler. Colonel Boteler and his son were in the army, and Mrs. Boteler in Baltimore. The ladies and children were at dinner when informed by the servants that a body of cavalry had turned in at the gate, from the turnpike, and were coming up to the house. It proved to be a small detachment of the First New York cavalry, commanded by a Capt. William F. Martindale, who, on being met at the door by Mrs. Shepherd, coolly told her that he had come to burn the house. She asked him by what authority. He told her by that of General Hunter, and showed her his written order. On reading it, she said: 'The order, I see, sir, is for you to burn the houses of Col. Alexander R. Boteler and Mr. Edmund I. Lee. Now, this is not Colonel Boteler's house, but is the property of my mother, Mrs. Boteler, and therefore must not be destroyed, as you have no authority to burn her house.' 'It's Colonel Boteler's *home*, and that's enough for me,' was Martindale's reply. She then said: 'I have been obliged to remove all my personal effects here, and have several thousand dollars' worth of property stored in the house and outbuildings, which belongs to me and my children. Can I not be permitted to save it?' But Martindale curtly told her that he intended to 'burn everything under roof upon the place.' Meanwhile some of the soldiers were plundering the house of silver spoons, forks, cups, and whatever they fancied, while others piled the parlor furniture on the floors, and others poured kerosene on the piles and floors, which they then set on fire. They had brought the kerosene with them, in canteens strapped to their saddles. Miss Boteler, being devoted to music, pleaded hard for her piano, as it belonged to her, having been a gift from her grandmother, but she was brutally forbidden to save it; whereupon, although the flames were roaring in the adjoining rooms, and the roof all on fire, she quietly went into the house, and seating herself for the last time before the instrument, sang her favorite hymn, 'Thy will be done.' Then shutting down the lid and locking it, she calmly went out upon the lawn, where her sick sister and the frightened little children were sitting under the trees, the only shelter then left for them."

Gen. Jubal A. Early, in his "Memoir of the Last Year of the War," makes briefly the same accusations against General Hunter that have just been quoted from General Imboden's paper, and adds: "A number of towns in the South, as well as private country houses, had been burned by the Federal troops, and the accounts had been heralded forth in some of the Northern papers in terms of exultation, and gloated over by their readers, while they were received with apathy by others. I now came to the conclusion that we had stood this mode of warfare long enough, and that it was time to open the eyes of the people of the North to its enormity, by an example in the way of retaliation. The town of Chambersburg in Pennsylvania was selected as the one on which retaliation should be made, and McCausland was ordered to proceed with his brigade and that of Johnson and a battery of artillery to that place, and demand of the municipal authorities the sum of one hundred thousand dollars in gold, or five hundred thousand dollars in United States currency, as a compensation for the destruction of the houses named and their contents; and, in default of payment, to lay the town in ashes. A written demand to that effect was sent to the municipal authorities, and they were informed what would be the result of a failure or refusal to comply with it. I desired to give the people of Chambersburg an opportunity of saving their town by making compensation for part of the injury done, and hoped that the payment of such a sum would have the desired effect and open the eyes of people of other towns at the North to the necessity of urging upon their Government the adoption of a different policy. McCausland was also directed to proceed from Chambersburg toward Cumberland in Maryland, and levy contributions in money upon that and other towns able to bear them, and, if possible, destroy the machinery at the coal-pits near Cumberland, and the machine shops, depots, and bridges on the Baltimore and Ohio Railroad, as far as practicable. On the 30th of July McCausland reached Chambersburg and made the demand as directed, reading to such of the authorities as presented themselves the paper sent by me. The demand was not complied with, the people stating that they were not afraid of having their town burned, and that a Federal force was approaching. McCausland proceeded to carry out his orders, and the greater part of the town was laid in ashes. For this act I alone am responsible, as the officers engaged in it were executing my orders and had no discretion left them."

LIBBY PRISON—INTERIOR AND EXTERIOR.

The resentment excited by the enlistment of black troops, and the determination not to treat them in accordance with the rules of civilized warfare, were most notably exemplified at the capture of Fort Pillow, April 12, 1864. This work was on the bank of the Mississippi, about forty miles above Memphis, on a high bluff, with a ravine on either side. In the lower ravine were some Government buildings and a little village. The fort, under command of Major L. F. Booth, had a garrison of about five hundred and fifty men, nearly half of whom were colored. The Confederate General Forrest, with about five thousand men, attacked the place at sunrise. The garrison made a gallant defence, aided by the gunboat *New Era*, which enfiladed the ravines, and after half a day's fighting, though the commander of the fort was killed, the besiegers had made no progress. They then resorted to the device of sending in flags of truce, demanding a surrender, and took advantage of the truce to move up into positions near the fort, which they had vainly tried to reach under fire. As soon as the second flag of truce was withdrawn, they made a rush upon the fort, passed over the works, and with a cry of "No quarter!" began an indiscriminate slaughter, though the garrison threw down their arms, and either surrendered or ran down the river-bank. Women and children, as well as men, were deliberately murdered, and the savagery continued for hours after the surrender. The sick and the wounded were butchered in their tents, and in some cases tents and buildings were set on fire after the occupants had been fastened so that they could not escape. In one instance a Confederate officer had taken up a negro child behind him on his horse. When General Chalmers observed this, he ordered the officer to put the child down and shoot him, and the order was obeyed. Major W. F. Bradford, on whom the command of the fort had devolved, was murdered the next day, when he was being marched away as a prisoner. Fewer than a hundred of the garrison were killed in the battle, and about three hundred were butchered after the surrender. Forrest's loss is unknown. His early reports of the affair were exultant. In one he wrote: "We busted the fort at ninerclock and scatered the niggers. The men is still a killanem in the woods. . . . Them as was cotch with spoons and brestpins and sich was killed and the rest of the lot was payrold and told to git." Again he or his adjutant wrote: "The river was dyed with the blood of the slaughtered for two hundred yards. . . . It is hoped that these facts will demonstrate to the Northern people that negro soldiers cannot cope with Southerners." Forrest had been a slave-trader before the war, and did not know that there could be any such thing as cruelty or treachery in dealing with black men. When he found that the civilized world was horrified at what he had done, he attempted to palliate it by saying that the flag at the fort had not been hauled down in token of surrender when his men burst over the works, and that some of the garrison retreating down the river-bank fired at their pursuers. But his argument is vitiated by the fact that, three weeks before, in demanding the surrender of a force at Paducah he notified the commander that if he had to carry the place by storm no quarter need be expected.

There had been from the beginning a difficulty about the care of prisoners in the hands of the Confederates, which arose chiefly from the incompetence and brutality of Commissary-General Northrop. Once when Captain Warner, who had charge of the prisoners in Richmond, was directed to make a requisition on Northrop for subsistence, he was answered, "I know nothing of Yankee prisoners—throw them all into the James River!" "But," said the captain, "at least tell me how I am to keep my accounts for the prisoners' subsistence." "Sir," said Northrop, "I have not the will or the time to speak with you. Chuck the scoundrels into the river!" This man was maintained in the post of commissary-general throughout the war—though his maladministration of the office many times produced a scarcity of food in the Confederate camps—and in the last year the subsistence of prisoners was also intrusted to him.

Of the prisoners captured by the Confederate armies, most of the commissioned officers were confined in the Libby warehouse (thenceforward known as Libby Prison) in Richmond, and at Columbia, S. C. The non-commissioned officers and privates were kept in camps—on Belle Isle, in the James River, at Richmond; at Salisbury, N. C.; at Florence, S. C.; at Tyler, Tex.; and at Andersonville and Millen, Ga. Most of these were simply open stockades, with little or no shelter. That at Andersonville enclosed about twenty acres, afterward enlarged to thirty. The palisade was of pine logs, fifteen feet high, set close together. Outside of this, at a distance of a hundred and twenty feet, was another palisade, and between the two were the guards. Inside of the inner stockade, and about twenty feet from it, was a slight railing known as the "dead line," since any prisoner that passed it, or even approached it too closely, was immediately shot. A small stream flowed sluggishly through the enclosure, and furnished the prisoners their only supply of water for washing, drinking, or cooking. The cook-houses and camp of the guards were placed on this stream, above the stockade. There was plenty of timber in sight from the prison, yet no shelter was furnished inside of the stockade, except such as the prisoners could make with the few blankets they possessed. Their rations were often issued to them uncooked, and they burrowed in the ground for roots with which to make a little fire. The stream was soon polluted, and its banks became a mass of mire and filth. A common exclamation of newly arrived prisoners, as they entered the appalling place, was, "Is this hell?"

It is said that the Confederate general, John H. Winder, under whose direction the stockade was built, was asked to leave a few trees inside of it, and erect some sheds for the shelter of the prisoners, but he answered, "No! I am going to build the pen so as to destroy more Yankees than can be destroyed at the front." Winder's well-known character, the place chosen for the stockade, all its arrangements, and the manner in which it was kept, leave no reasonable doubt that such was the purpose. When Mr. Davis and his cabinet were appealed to by the Confederate inspector of prisons, and others, to replace General Winder by a more humane officer, they answered by promoting Winder to the place of commissary-general of all the prisoners.

MAJOR R. R. TURNER, C. S. A.
(Keeper of Libby Prison.)

"CASTLE THUNDER," RICHMOND, VA.
(In this building Union prisoners were confined.)

One of the prisoners, Robert H. Kellogg, sergeant-major of the Sixteenth Connecticut Regiment, who was taken to Andersonville when it had been in use about two months, says in his diary: "As we entered the place, a spectacle met our eyes that almost froze our blood with horror, and made our hearts within fail us. Before us were forms that had once been active and erect, stalwart men, now nothing but mere walking skeletons, covered with filth and vermin. In the centre was a swamp occupying three or four acres of the narrowed limits, and a part of this marshy place had been used by the prisoners as a sink, and excrement covered the ground, the scent arising from which was suffocating. The ground allotted to our ninety was near the edge of this plague spot, and how we were to live through the warm summer weather in the midst of such fearful surroundings was more than we cared to think of just then. No shelter was provided for us by the rebel authorities, and we therefore went to work to provide for ourselves. Eleven of us combined to form a family. For the small sum of two dollars in greenbacks we purchased eight small saplings, eight or nine feet long. These we bent and made fast in the ground, and, covering them with our blankets, made a tent with an oval roof, about thirteen feet long. We needed the blankets for our protection from the cold at night, but concluded it to be quite as essential to our comfort to shut out the rain. There were ten deaths on our side of the camp that night. The old prisoners called it 'being exchanged,' and truly it was a blessed transformation."

At one time there were thirty-three thousand prisoners in the stockade, which gave a space about four feet square to each man. The whole number sent there was about forty-nine thousand five hundred, of whom nearly thirteen thousand died. At Salisbury prison the deaths were thirteen per cent. a month, and at Florence twelve per cent. Most of the deaths were from disease and starvation, but there were numerous murders. It was said that every sentry, on shooting a prisoner for violation of rules, received a month's furlough; and this was corroborated by the alacrity with which they seized any pretext for firing. In Libby, men were often shot for approaching near enough to a window for the sentry to see their heads. In Andersonville one was shot for crawling out to secure a small piece of wood that lay near the dead-line; and there were many incidents of that kind. Some of the men became deranged or desperate, and

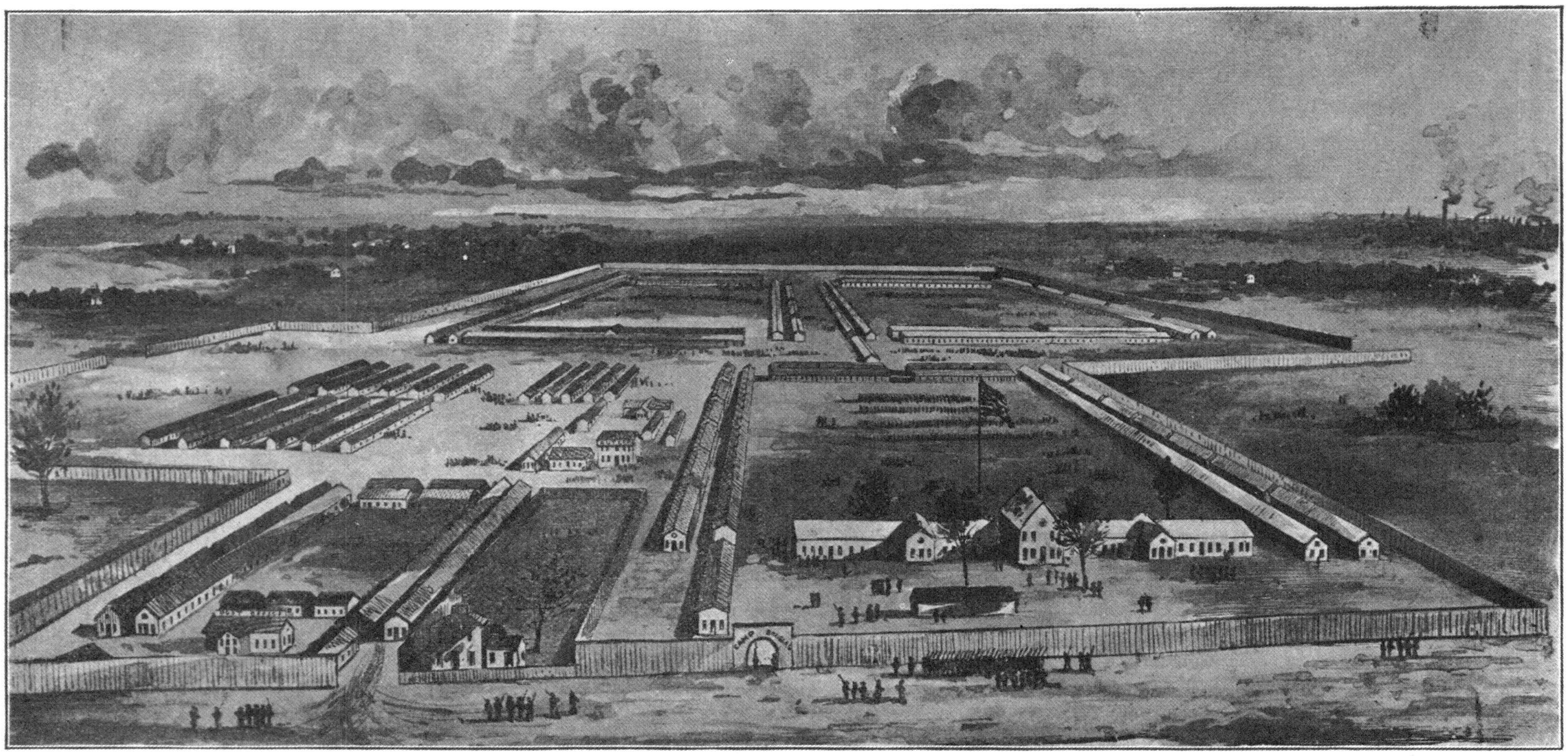

CAMP DOUGLAS, AT CHICAGO. (Confederate prisoners were confined here.)

deliberately walked up to the dead-line for the purpose of being put out of their misery. There were many escapes from these prisons; but the fugitives were generally soon missed, and were followed by fleet horsemen and often tracked by bloodhounds, and though they were always befriended by the negroes, who fed them, concealed them by day, and guided them at night, but few ultimately reached the National lines.

A captain in the Eighty-fifth Pennsylvania Regiment, who was a prisoner in the hands of the Confederates, gives this leaf from his experience: "During the night of July 27, 1864, while several hundred of my brother officers were being transported from Macon to Charleston by rail, Captain Kellogg, of Wisconsin, Ensign Stoner, of New York, Ensign Smith, now of Washington, Lieut. E. P. Brooks, of Washington, Paymaster Billings, of the United States Navy, and myself, jumped from a car and escaped to the swamp, through which we hardly thought an alligator could have followed us. Late in the afternoon of the second day, however, we heard the deep baying of the dogs, and soon we were surrounded with dogs, which we held at bay with stout clubs until the two fiendish hunters had called them off. Before starting on our weary march back to that dread imprisonment, one of our captors took occasion to say: 'It's a good thing for you-uns that our catch-dogs gave out half a mile back, for I reckon they'd a tored you-uns up 'fore we-uns got thare.' He said the dogs that recaptured us were a mixture between the fox-hound and the beagle-dog, but that the large, brutish catch-dogs were a cross between the full South American bloodhound and the bull-dog. He said he kept two large packs of these dogs, with quite a number of catch-dogs, or bloodhounds, at Hamburg, which he hired out for the purpose of hunting escaped Yankee prisoners and runaway niggers. I saw Captain Holmes, of St. Louis, Mo., a prisoner of war at Macon, Ga., in July, 1864, who had been fearfully mangled and torn by a catch-dog in Alabama while he was trying to escape. I frequently saw two large South American bloodhounds outside of the stockade at Macon. At Andersonville they had a large pack of bloodhounds."

The crowded condition of the prisons in 1864 was owing to the fact that exchanges had been discontinued. A cartel for the exchange of prisoners had been in operation for some time; but when it was found that the Confederate authorities had determined not to exchange any black soldiers, or their white officers, captured in battle, the United States Government refused to exchange at all, being bound to protect equally all who had entered its service. Paroling prisoners on the field was also discontinued, because the Confederates could not be trusted to observe their parole. There had been much complaint that Confederate officers and soldiers violated their word in this respect, either because in their intense hatred of the North they could not realize that they were bound by any promise given to it, or because their own Government forced them back into its service. Many of them were captured with arms in their hands, while they were still under parole from a previous capture. All such, by the laws of war, might have been summarily executed, but none of them were. The thirty thousand taken by Grant at Vicksburg, and the six thousand taken by Banks at Port Hudson, in July, 1863, were released on parole, because the cartel designated two points for delivery of prisoners—Vicksburg in the West, and Aiken's Landing, Va., in the East—and Vicksburg, having been captured, was no longer available for this purpose, and Aiken's Landing was too far away. Three months later, the Confederate armies being in want of reinforcements, Colonel Ould, Confederate commissioner of exchange, raised the technical point that the prisoners captured by Grant and Banks had not been delivered at a place mentioned in the cartel, and therefore he declared them all released from their parole, and they were restored to the ranks. At Chattanooga, in November, Grant's army captured large numbers from Bragg's army whom they had captured in July with Pemberton and had released on a solemn promise that they would not take up arms again until properly exchanged.

Other difficulties arose to complicate still further the question of exchanges. At one time the Confederate authorities refused to make any but a general exchange—all held by either side to be liberated—which the National Government declined, since it held an excess of about forty thousand. It was observed, also, when partial exchanges were effected, that the men returning from Southern prisons were nearly all wasted to skeletons and unfit for further service, while the Confederates returning from Northern prisons were well clothed, well fed, and generally in good health. Photographs of the emaciated men from Andersonville and Belle Isle were exhibited throughout the North, and caused more of horror than the report from any battlefield. Engravings from them were published, in the summer of 1864, by newspapers of both parties, for opposite purposes—the Republican, to prove the barbarity of the Confederate authorities and the atrocious spirit of the rebellion; the Democratic, to prove that President Lincoln was a monster of cruelty in that he did not waive all questions at issue and consent to a general exchange. At a later period, the Confederate authorities, being badly in need of men to fill up their depleted armies, offered to give up their point about black soldiers, and exchange man for man—or rather skeleton for man—without regard to color. But as the war was nearing its close, and to do this would have reinforced the Southern armies with some thousands of strong and well-fed troops, and prolonged the struggle, the National Government refused. Efforts were made, both by the Government and by the Sanitary Commission, to send food, clothing, and medical supplies to those confined in the Confederate prisons; but only a small portion of these things ever reached the men for whom they were intended. At Libby Prison, at one time, boxes for the prisoners arrived at the rate of three hundred a week; but instead of being distributed they were piled up in warehouses insight of the hungry and shivering captives, where they were plundered by the guards and by the poorer inhabitants of the city. In one case, a lieutenant among the prisoners saw his own home-made suit of clothes on a prison official, and pointed out his name embroidered on the watch-pocket.*

The total number of soldiers and citizens captured by the Confederate armies during the war was 188,145, and it is estimated that about half of them were actually confined in prisons. The number of deaths in those prisons was 36,401. The number of Confederates captured by the National forces was 476,169, of whom 227,570 were actually confined. The percentage of mortality in the Confederate prisons was over 38; in the National prisons it was 13.3.

There has been much acrimonious controversy over this question of the prisoners, and attempts have been made, by juggling with the figures, to prove that they were as badly treated in Northern as in Southern prisons. The most plausible excuse for the starving of captives at the South is in the assertion that the Confederate army was on short allowance at the same time. It is a sorrowful subject in any aspect, and presents complicated questions; but if it is to be discussed at all, several principles should be kept in view, some of which appear to have been lost sight of. No belligerent is under any obligation to enter into a cartel for the exchange of prisoners. In the war of 1812–15, between the United States and Great Britain, there were no exchanges till the close of the contest. Every belligerent that takes prisoners is bound by the laws of war to treat them well, since they are no longer combatants. A belligerent that has not the means of caring properly for prisoners is in so far without the means of carrying on civilized warfare, and therefore comes so far short of possessing the right to make war at all. Every time a soldier is put out of the combat by being made a prisoner instead of being shot, so much is gained for the cause of humanity; and if all prisoners could be cared for properly, the most humane way of conducting a war would be to make no exchanges, since these reinforce both sides, prolong the contest, and increase the mortality in the field.

Whatever may be said of individual experiences in the prisons, North or South, and whatever may have been the brutality, or the humanity, of this or that keeper, one great fact overtops everything and settles the main question of the treatment of prisoners beyond dispute. The prisons at the South were open stockades, with no building of any kind inside, no tree, no tent, no shelter furnished for the prisoners from sun or rain, not even the simplest sanitary arrangements, and an enormous number of prisoners were crowded into them. At Belle Isle the prisoners were packed so close that when they lay sleeping no one could turn over until the whole line agreed to turn simultaneously. On the other hand, the Northern prisons contained buildings for the shelter of the prisoners, with bunks as comfortable as in any barracks, and stoves to heat them in cold weather, while the sanitary arrangements were carefully looked after, and good rations issued regularly. It is impossible to look upon these contrasted pictures and not say that it was the intention of the one Government that its prisoners should suffer as much as possible, and the intention of the other Government that its prisoners should be made as comfortable as prisoners in large numbers ever can be.

* See "Narrative of Privations and Sufferings of United States Officers and Soldiers while Prisoners of War in the Hands of the Rebel Authorities. Being the Report of a Commission of Inquiry Appointed by the United States Sanitary Commission. With an Appendix containing the Testimony." (1864.) Valentine Mott, M.D., was chairman of the commission.

CHAPTER XXIX.

THE SANITARY AND CHRISTIAN COMMISSIONS.

WOMEN IN THE WAR—SANITARY COMMISSION FORMED—THE PUBLIC IDEA ABOUT IT—WORK OF THE COMMISSION—SANITARY FAIRS—THE CHRISTIAN COMMISSION—VOLUNTARY NURSES—THE VAST AMOUNT OF WORK DONE BY WOMEN IN HOSPITALS—MISS DOROTHEA L. DIX, MISS ALCOTT, AND MANY OTHERS.

THE ancient sarcasm, that women have caused many of the bloodiest of wars, was largely disarmed by the part they played in the war of secession. Their contribution to the comfort and efficiency of the armies in the field, and to the care of the sick and wounded soldiers, was on the same vast scale as the war itself. Their attempts to assist the cause began with the first call for volunteers, and were as awkward and unskilled as the green regiments that they equipped and encouraged. But as their brothers learned the art of war, they kept even pace in learning the arts that alleviate its sufferings. When the President issued the first call for troops, in April, 1861, the women in many places held meetings to confer as to the best methods by which they could assist, and to organize their efforts and resources. The statement of the objects of one of these organizations suggests some conception of the contingencies of war in a country that for nearly half a century had known almost unbroken peace: "To supply nurses for the sick; to bring them home when practicable; to purchase clothing, provisions, and matters of comfort not supplied by Government regulations; to send books and newspapers to the camps; and to hold constant communication with the officers of the regiments, in order that the people may be kept informed of the condition of their friends."

SISTER OF MERCY.

On one of the last days in April, the Rev. Dr. Henry W. Bellows and Dr. Elisha Harris met casually in the street in New York, and fell into conversation concerning the evident need of sanitary measures for the armies that were then mustering. They agreed to attend a meeting of women that had been called to discuss that subject, and from that meeting a call was issued to all the existing organizations of women for a general meeting to be held in Cooper Union. This invitation, which furnished the basis on which the Sanitary Commission was afterward formed, was signed by ninety-two women. The hall was crowded, and the Women's Central Association of Relief was organized, under a constitution written by Dr. Bellows, who was chosen its president. A committee was sent to Washington to offer the services of the organization to the Government, and learn in what way they could be most effective. This committee, consisting of Dr. Bellows and three eminent physicians—Drs. Van Buren, Harsen, and Harris—presented to the War Department an address whose suggestions were based largely upon the experience of the British forces in the Crimean war of 1854–55. Being sent by women who were overflowing with patriotic enthusiasm, to officials who were jealous and distrustful of everything outside of the regulations, they had a difficult and delicate task. The Government was already embarrassed somewhat in the adjustment of authority between regular and volunteer officers, and dreaded a further complication if a third element of civilian authority should be introduced. Even Mr. Lincoln is said to have spoken slightingly of their proposition as a fifth wheel to a coach. General Scott received the committee kindly, but was not willing to give the proposed commission any authority. He would, however, consent to their acting in an advisory capacity, provided the head of the medical bureau agreed. After an interview with Acting Surgeon-General Wood, they obtained his consent to the formation of a "commission of inquiry and advice in respect to the sanitary interests of the United States forces," and he also wrote a letter commending the project to the other officers whose consent was necessary. Most of these officers looked upon the project with distrust and suspicion, and at length the committee were asked to "tell outright what they really did want, under this benevolent disguise." After fighting their way through these obstacles, the committee met with a misfortune in the death of Surgeon-General Lawson. His successor, Dr. Clement A. Finley, frowned upon the whole matter, but after a long struggle was induced to tolerate a commission that should not be clothed with any authority, and should act only in connection with officers of the volunteer army.

MISS LOUISA M. ALCOTT.

Finally, on June 13, 1861, the committee received from President Lincoln and Secretary of War Simon Cameron an order authorizing them to form an association for "inquiry and advice in respect to the sanitary interests of the United States." Their first work was to bring about a re-inspection of the volunteer forces, which resulted in the discharge of many boys and physically unsound men who had been accepted and mustered in through carelessness. When the committee returned to New York, the fact that there was a wide popular demand for the establishment of such an organization as they had proposed was made evident through articles in the newspapers, opinions of physicians, and a multitude of letters from all parts of the country. Dr. Bellows was made president of the Commission, Frederick Law Olmsted secretary, and George T. Strong treasurer, and with them were associated a score of well-known men, including several eminent physicians. In the organization, the first division of the duties of the Commission was into two departments—those of Inquiry and Advice. The Department of Inquiry was subdivided into three—the first, to have charge of such immediate aid and obvious recommendations as an ordinary knowledge of the principles of sanitary science would enable the board to urge upon the authorities; the second, to have charge of the inspection of recruiting stations, transports, camps, and hospitals, and to consult with military officers as to the condition and wants of their men; the third, to investigate questions of cleanliness, cooking, clothing, surgical dressings, malaria, climate, etc. The Department of Advice was also subdivided. The general object was "to get the opinions and conclusions of the Commission approved by the Medical Bureau, ordered by the War Department, and acted upon by officers and men." One sub-committee was in direct communication with the War Department, another with army officers, and a third with the State governments and the local associations.

The popular idea of the Sanitary Commission seemed to be that its chief purpose was to form dépôts for receiving supplies of clothing, medicines, and delicacies for the camps and hospitals, and forwarding them safely and speedily. And this part of the work soon grew to proportions that had never been contemplated. The Commission issued an address "to the loyal women of America," urging the formation of local societies for providing these articles, and in response more than seven thousand such societies were organized. They were managed entirely by women, and were all tributary to the Sanitary Commission. Of the fifteen million dollars' worth of articles received and distributed, more than four-fifths came from these local societies. The Commission was managed as nearly as possible in accordance with military ideas of discipline and precision. Every request that the stores furnished by a State or city might be conveyed to its own regiments was met with the answer that all was for the nation and must be turned in to the general store. The Commission rapidly disarmed prejudice, and won the admiration of everybody in the military service. It employed skilled men to coöperate with the regimental surgeons in choosing sites for camps, regulating the drainage, and inspecting the cooking. It constructed model pavilion hospitals, to prevent the spread of contagion. It established a system of soldiers' homes, where the sick and the convalescent could be provided for on their way back and forth between their homes and the front, and where whole regiments were sometimes fed when their own commissariat failed them. It fitted up hospital steamers on the Mississippi and its tributaries, with surgeons and nurses on board, to ply between the seat of war and the points from which Northern hospitals could be reached. Dr. Elisha Harris, of the Commission, invented a hospital car, in which the stretcher on which a wounded man was brought from the field could be suspended and thus become a sort of hammock. The cars were built with extra springs, to diminish the jolting as much as possible, and trains of them were run regularly, with physicians and stores on board, until the plan was adopted by the Government Medical Bureau. Supplies were constantly furnished in abundance, and the Commission established dépôts at convenient points, where the articles were assorted and labelled, and the army officials were kept constantly informed that such and such things, in such and such quantities, were subject to their requisition. When it was found difficult to transport fresh vegetables from distant points, the Commission laid out gardens of its own, where vegetables were raised for the use of the soldiers in the field. The Commission also had its own horses and wagons, which followed the armies to the battlefield, carrying supplies that were often welcome when those of the medical department were exhausted or had gone astray. After the battle of the Antietam, when ten thousand wounded lay on the field, the train containing the medical stores was blocked near Baltimore; but the wagon-train of the Sanitary Commission had been following the army, and for four days the only supplies were those that it furnished. On this occasion it issued over twenty-eight thousand shirts, towels, pillows, etc., thirty barrels of lint and bandages, over three thousand pounds of farina, over two thousand pounds of condensed milk, five thousand pounds of beef stock and canned meats, three thousand bottles of wine and cordial, several tons of lemons, and crackers, tea, sugar, rubber cloth, tin cups, and other conveniences. In the course of the war, the Commission furnished four million five hundred thousand meals to sick and hungry soldiers. In many instances, notably at the second battle of Bull Run and at the assault on Fort Wagner, the agents of the Commission were on the actual battlefield with their supplies, and were close at the front rescuing the wounded. At Fort Wagner they followed up the storming party to the moat.

A large part of the money and supplies was raised by means of fairs held in nearly every city, and the generosity exhibited in a thousand different ways was something for the nation to be forever proud of. Those who could not give cash gave all sorts of things—horses, cows, carriages, watches, diamonds, books, pictures, curiosities, and every conceivable article. The managers would be informed that a farmer was at the door with a cow, which he wished to give, and some person would be deputed to take the cow and find a stable for her until she could be sold. Another would appear with a portion of his crops. Men and women of note were asked to furnish their autographs for sale, and papers were printed, made up of original contributions by well-known authors. The sales were largely by auction, and rich men would bid off articles at high prices, and then give them back to be sold over again. The amount of cash received by the Commission was over four million nine hundred thousand dollars. The State of California, which was farthest from the seat of war, and contributed but few men to the armies, sent more than one million three hundred thousand dollars. The value of articles received by the Commission was estimated at fifteen million dollars. It established convalescent camps, which were afterward taken by the Government, and a system of hospital directories, and a pension bureau and claim agency, by which soldiers' claims were prosecuted free of charge. From beginning to end there was never a deficit or irregularity of any kind in its finances.

At the beginning of the war, many of the volunteers were members of the Young Men's Christian Association, and through these an especial solicitude was felt in that organization for the spiritual needs of the soldiers. Almost as soon as the first call for troops was made, measures were taken to supply every regiment with religious reading-matter, prayer-meetings were held at the recruiting stations, and a soldiers' hymn-book was compiled and printed by thousands. When the army began to move, men volunteered to go with it, at their own expense, and continue this work. One of these was Vincent Colyer, the artist, who, after spending ten weeks in the field, wrote to the chairman of the national committee of the Association, urging the formation of a Christian Commission to carry on the work systematically. As a result, such a commission was organized on November 14, 1861. The approval of the President and the War Department was obtained more readily than in the case of the Sanitary Commission, but the appeal to the people did not elicit any immediate enthusiasm. Even the religious press was in some instances distrustful and discouraging. For nearly a year the means of the Commission were limited, and its work was feeble. In May, 1862, after an earnest address to the public, it was enabled to equip and send out fourteen delegates, as they were called, ten of whom were clergymen. By the end of that year, they had sent four hundred to the army, and had more than a thousand engaged in the home work. They had distributed in the armies more than a hundred thousand Bibles, as many hymn-books, tens of thousands of other books, ten million leaflets, and hundreds of thousands of papers and magazines; they had formed twenty-three libraries, expended over a hundred and forty thousand dollars in money, and distributed an equal value in stores.

OFFICERS OF THE SANITARY COMMISSION.

(From a War-time Photograph.)

REV. DR. HENRY W. BELLOWS.

(President of the Sanitary Commission.)

At the close of the second year the Commission had one hundred and eleven auxiliary associations, and the work in the field was more perfectly organized. General Grant, then in command in the West, issued a special order giving the Commission every opportunity for the prosecution of its work, and tried, but in vain, to obtain permission for its delegates to visit the National soldiers in Confederate prisons. George H. Stuart, of Philadelphia, was chairman of the executive committee, Joseph Patterson treasurer, and Lemuel Moss secretary. The work increased rapidly. Chapel tents and chapel roofs were furnished to the armies, diet kitchens were established in the hospitals, the service called "individual relief" was extended, and schools were opened for children of colored soldiers. Thousands of letters were written for disabled men in the hospitals, and thousands of packages forwarded to the camps. Jacob Dunton, of Philadelphia, invented a "coffee wagon" and presented it to the Commission. Coffee could be made in it in large quantities, as it was driven along. Like the Sanitary Commission, the Christian Commission had its own teams, and followed the armies with medical supplies. In the course of its existence, it sent out in all six thousand delegates, none of whom received any pay. One hundred and twenty of these were women employed mainly in the diet kitchens.

There were also many women in the service of the Government as volunteer nurses. The first of these was Miss Dorothea L. Dix, who offered her services eight days after the call for troops in April, 1861, and was accepted by the Surgeon-General, who requested that all women wishing to act as nurses report to her. Miss Dix served through the war. Miss Amy Bradley, besides having charge of a large camp for convalescents near Alexandria, Va., assisted twenty-two hundred men in collecting arrears of pay due them, amounting to over two hundred thousand dollars. Arabella Griffith Barlow, wife of the gallant General Francis C. Barlow, spent three years in hospitals at the front, and died in the service. Miss Clara Barton entered upon hospital work at the beginning of the war, had charge of the hospitals of the Army of the James during its last year, and after the war undertook the search for the missing men of the National armies. Miss Louisa M. Alcott, author of "Little Women," served as a nurse, and published her experiences in a volume entitled "Hospital Sketches." Many other women, less noted, performed long and arduous service, which in some cases cost them their lives, for which they live in the grateful remembrance of those who came under their care.

Among these was Miss Helen L. Gilson, a teacher in Boston, who gave this answer to an inquiry as to how she succeeded in getting into the work: "When I reached White House Landing I saw the transport *Wilson Small* in the offing, and knew that it was full of wounded men; so, calling a boatman, and directing him to row me to the vessel, I went on board. A poor fellow was undergoing an amputation, and, seeing that the surgeon wanted help, I took hold of the limb and held it for him. The surgeon looked up, at first surprised, then said, 'Thank you,' and I stayed and helped him. Then I went on with him to the next case; he made no objection, and from that time I never had any difficulty there."

HEADQUARTERS OF THE SANITARY COMMISSION, ARMY OF THE POTOMAC.

(From a War-time Photograph.)

Dr. Bellows, president of the Sanitary Commission, writing of his experiences on the field of Gettysburg, said: "I went out to the field hospital of the Third Corps, where two thousand four hundred men lay in their tents, a vast camp of mutilated humanity. One woman [Miss Gilson], young and fair, but grave and earnest, clothed in purity and mercy—the only woman on that whole vast camp—moved in and out of the hospital tent, speaking some tender word, giving some restoring cordial, holding the hand of a dying boy, or receiving the last words of a husband for his widowed wife. I can never forget how, amid scenes which under ordinary circumstances no woman could have appeared in without gross indecorum, the holy pity and purity of this angel of mercy made her presence seem as fit as though she had indeed dropped out of heaven. The men themselves, sick or well, all seemed awed and purified by such a resident among them." Miss Gilson continued her labors unremittingly through the war, and died about two years after its close, probably from the effects of her arduous work, at the age of thirty-two.

Besides the labors of such women in the field hospitals, a vast amount of similar and quite as useful work was done by a great number of women in the hospitals at various points in the Northern States, whither the wounded were sent as soon as they could be removed. A peculiarly sad and romantic case was that of Margaret Augusta Peterson, a young lady of brilliant promise, who entered upon service in a large hospital at Rochester, N. Y., refused to leave it when there was an outbreak of small-pox, saying she was then needed more than ever, and lost her life, at the age of twenty-three, from some dreadful mistake in the vaccination. Her story, which had other romantic elements, is told literally in this poem:

Margaret Augusta Peterson.

Through the sombre arch of that gateway tower
  Where my humblest townsman rides at last,
You may spy the bells of a nodding flower,
  On a double mound that is thickly grassed.

And between the spring and the summer time,
  Or ever the lilac's bloom is shed,
When they come with banners and wreaths and
    rhyme,
  To deck the tombs of the nation's dead,

They find there a little flag in the grass,
  And fling a handful of roses down,
And pause a moment before they pass
  To the captain's grave with the gilded crown.

But if perchance they seek to recall
  What name, what deeds, these honors declare,
They cannot tell, they are silent all
  As the noiseless harebell nodding there.

She was tall, with an almost manly grace;
  And young, with strange wisdom for one so young;
And fair, with more than a woman's face;
  With dark, deep eyes, and a mirthful tongue.

The poor and the fatherless knew her smile;
  The friend in sorrow had seen her tears;
She had studied the ways of the rough world's guile,
  And read the romance of historic years.

What she might have been in these times of ours,
  At once it is easy and hard to guess;
For always a riddle are half-used powers,
  And always a power is lovingness.

But her fortunes fell upon evil days—
  If days are evil when evil dies—
And she was not one who could stand at gaze
  Where the hopes of humanity fall and rise.

Nor could she dance to the viol's tune,
  When the drum was throbbing throughout the land,
Or dream in the light of the summer moon,
  When Treason was clinching his mailèd hand.

Through the long, gray hospital's corridor
  She journeyed many a mournful league,
And her light foot fell on the oaken floor
  As if it never could know fatigue.

She stood by the good old surgeon's side,
  And the sufferers smiled as they saw her stand;
She wrote, and the mothers marvelled and cried
  At their darling soldiers' feminine hand.

She was last in the ward when the lights burned low,
  And Sleep called a truce to his foeman Pain;
At the midnight cry she was first to go,
  To bind up the bleeding wound again.

For sometimes the wreck of a man would rise,
  Weird and gaunt in the watch-lamp's gleam,
And tear away bandage and splints and ties,
  Fighting the battle all o'er in his dream.

No wonder the youngest surgeon felt
  A charm in the presence of that brave soul,
Through weary weeks, as she nightly knelt
  With the letter from home or the doctor's dole.

He heard her called, and he heard her blessed,
  With many a patriot's parting breath;
And ere his soul to itself confessed,
  Love leaped to life in those vigils of death.

"Oh, fly to your home!" came a whisper dread,
  "For now the pestilence walks by night."
"The greater the need of me here," she said,
  And bared her arm for the lancet's bite.

Was there death, green death, in the atmosphere?
  Was the bright steel poisoned? Who can tell?
Her weeping friends gathered beside her bier,
  And the clergyman told them all was well.

Well—alas that it should be so!
  When a nation's debt reaches reckoning-day—
Well for it to be able, but woe
  To the generation that's called to pay!

Down from the long, gray hospital came
  Every boy in blue who could walk the floor;
The sick and the wounded, the blind and lame,
  Formed two long files from her father's door.

There was grief in many a manly breast,
  While men's tears fell as the coffin passed;
And thus she went to the world of rest,
  Martial and maidenly up to the last.

And that youngest surgeon, was he to blame?—
  He held the lancet—Heaven only knows.
No matter; his heart broke all the same,
  And he laid him down, and never arose.

So Death received, in his greedy hand,
  Two precious coins of the awful price
That purchased freedom for this dear land—
  For master and bondman—yea, bought it twice.

Such fates too often such women are for!
  God grant the Republic a large increase,
To match the heroes in time of war,
  And mother the children in time of peace.

UNION SCOUTS.

A GROCERY STORE IN SOUTHERN VIRGINIA.

CHAPTER XXX.

MINOR EVENTS OF THE THIRD YEAR.

BANDS OF GUERILLAS IN VIRGINIA AND THE EAST—UNSUCCESSFUL ATTEMPTS TO CAPTURE MOSBY—IMPORTANT ACTION AT WAPPING HEIGHTS—NUMEROUS ENGAGEMENTS IN THE SHENANDOAH VALLEY AND ON THE SLOPES OF THE BLUE RIDGE—MINOR ENGAGEMENTS IN CONNECTION WITH THE PURSUIT OF LEE'S ARMY AFTER GETTYSBURG—MINOR ENGAGEMENTS IN WEST VIRGINIA—INVASION OF KENTUCKY BY CONFEDERATES UNDER GENERAL PEGRAM—THE CONFEDERATES' ATTEMPT TO RECAPTURE FORT DONELSON—NUMEROUS SMALL BATTLES IN TENNESSEE—LOYALTY OF THE PEOPLE OF EASTERN TENNESSEE AND WESTERN NORTH CAROLINA—BATTLES AT FAYETTEVILLE, BATESVILLE, AND HELENA, ARK.—OPERATIONS UNDER THE CONFEDERATE GENERAL MARMADUKE IN MISSOURI—SACKING AND BURNING OF LAWRENCE, KAN.—CRUELTIES PRACTISED BY CONFEDERATE GUERILLAS UNDER QUANTRELL AND OTHERS—CAPTURE OF GALVESTON, TEXAS, BY THE CONFEDERATES—MILITARY OPERATIONS AGAINST THE INDIANS.

SOME of the smaller engagements of the year 1863 were so closely connected with the great movements that they have been described in the chapters devoted to those campaigns. Others were isolated from any such connection, and the more notable of them are here grouped in a chapter by themselves.

Suffolk, Va., on Nansemont River, southwest of Portsmouth, was held by a National force that included the Eighty-ninth and One Hundred and Twelfth New York Regiments, and the Eighth and Sixteenth Connecticut. An amusing story is told in the "History of the Sixteenth Connecticut," of its adventures when it first reached Suffolk. It arrived in a dark night, the men not knowing which way to go, or what they would find when they stepped out of the train, and most of their officers having been left behind by accident. Setting out through the darkness, they first tumbled down a steep embankment, then into a deep brook, and finally brought up against a rail fence. Tearing this down, they found themselves in a field, and set about hunting fuel for a fire. Some of them, groping in the darkness, came upon a house which they supposed to be uninhabited, and, beginning at the bottom, pulled off all the clapboards as high as they could reach. When daylight came they discovered that it was a handsome white house inhabited by the owner and his family, who presently appeared on the scene and produced a tableau. In the darkness one of the men had bored a hole into a barrel of coffee, which he supposed was whiskey, and was found shaking it violently and wondering why it did not run. Sunlight showed them that they were on the outskirts of the town, and immediately the One Hundred and Twelfth New York came to their relief with hot coffee, etc. Suffolk really had very little military importance, and yet it was the subject of considerable fighting. Gen. John J. Peck commanded the National forces, and was subjected to much elaborate ridicule for the extent to which he fortified the place. In January the Confederates made an attack, and after some fighting were driven off, and, with the assistance of the gunboats, six guns and two hundred of their men were captured. In April a siege was begun by General Longstreet, who failed in an attempt to carry the place by surprise, and then constructed earthworks, intending to bombard it; but, as soon as he opened fire from them, his guns were silenced by the gunboats on the river and the heavy artillery in the National works. Early in May he was needed to assist General Lee in the impending conflict of Chancellorsville, and slowly drew off his men from Suffolk,

BATTLE OF VERMILION BAYOU, LA.

when Generals Getty and Harland sallied out from that place with a column of seven thousand men and attacked his powerful rear guard. A sharp action ensued, which resulted in no immediate advantage to either side, but in the night the Confederates left the field. Some stragglers were captured, but otherwise there was no definite result except that the siege was raised.

Guerilla bands, so numerous at the West, were few at the East, the most noted being one led by John S. Mosby. In March he made a daring midnight raid with a few of his men on Fairfax Court House, Va., and captured and carried off Brigadier-General Stoughton, two captains, and thirty men, with about sixty horses. In May he approached Warrenton Junction with about three hundred men and attacked a small cavalry force there. The National soldiers were feeding their horses and did not have time to mount, but made a gallant resistance on foot, until they were overcome by numbers. The Fifth New York cavalry then came up, and, sabre in hand, charging upon the guerillas, killed and scattered many, and wounded the rest, except a few whom they captured. Among the killed was a Confederate spy who had just come from Washington and had in his possession many important documents. Again, at Kettle Run, Mosby attacked a railway train that was loaded with forage. When the firing was heard, the Fifth and First Vermont cavalry set out from Fairfax Court House and soon came up with the enemy. His one howitzer was captured in a gallant charge, and a considerable number of his men were killed. It was said that as fast as the band was depleted by the casualties of battle it was filled up with picked men sent from the Confederate army.

Several attempts were made to capture Mosby, but although there was an occasional fight with his band, and a considerable number of his followers fell, he himself eluded captivity till the end of the war, when he issued an order announcing to his men that he was no longer their commander, and they dispersed. The difficulty of capturing a small mounted force, which is irresponsible and has no mission but to roam in a lawless way over a country like that of Virginia, must be always exceedingly great; but there was one opportunity to capture Mosby and his band which would have been successful had the affair not been disgracefully mismanaged. In April, 1863, one hundred and fifty men of the First Vermont cavalry, under Captain Flint, set out to capture them, and found them at a farm-house unprepared to fight. Flint took his men through the gate, fired a volley at Mosby's men, and then charged with the sabre, which would have been correct enough if Flint had kept his command together; but he made the mistake of dividing it and sending a portion around to the rear, in fear that the guerillas would escape. Mosby quickly took advantage of this, ordered a charge upon the detachment headed by Captain Flint, and succeeded in cutting his way through, Flint and some of his men being killed. Of the affair near Warrenton, in May, Mosby, in his somewhat boastful "Reminiscences," gives this highly colored account:

"On May 2, seventy or eighty men assembled at my call. I had information that Stoneman's cavalry had left Warrenton and gone south, which indicated that the campaign had opened. My plan now was to strike Hooker.

"Before we had gone very far, an infantry soldier was caught, who informed me that I was marching right into the camp of an infantry brigade. I found out that there was some cavalry on the railroad at another point, and so I made for that. These troops had just been sent up to replace Stoneman's. I committed a great error in allowing myself to be diverted by their presence from the purpose of my expedition. They were perfectly harmless where they were, and could not help Hooker in the great battle then raging. I should at least have endeavored to avoid a fight by marching around them.

"Just as we debouched from the woods in sight of Warrenton Junction, I saw, about three hundred yards in front of us, a body of cavalry in the open field. It was a bright, warm morning; and the men were lounging on the grass, while their horses, with nothing but their halters on, had been turned loose to graze on the young clover. They were enjoying the music of the great battle, and had no dream that danger was near. Not a single patrol or picket had been put out. At first they mistook us for their own men, and had no suspicion as to who we were until I ordered a charge and the men raised a yell. The shouting and firing stampeded the horses, and they scattered over a field of several hundred acres, while their riders took shelter in some houses near by. We very soon got all out of two houses; but the main body took refuge in a large frame building just by the railroad. I did not take time to dismount my men, but ordered a charge on the house; I did not want to give them time to recover from their panic. I came up just in front of two windows by the chimney, from which a hot fire was poured that brought down several men by my side. But I paid them back with interest when I got to the window, into which I emptied two Colt's revolvers. The house was as densely packed as a sardine box, and it was almost impossible to fire into it without hitting somebody. The doors had been shut from the inside; but the Rev. Sam Chapman dismounted, and burst through, followed by John Debutts, Mountjoy, and Harry Sweeting. The soldiers in the lower rooms immediately surrendered; but those above held out. There was a haystack near by; and I ordered some of the hay to be brought into the house, and fire to be set to it. Not being willing to be burned alive as martyrs to the Union, the men above now held out a white flag from the window. The house was densely filled with smoke, and the floor covered with the blood of the wounded. The commanding officer, Major Steel, had received a mortal wound; and there were many others in the same condition. All who were able now came out of the house.

"After a severe fight I had taken three times my own number prisoners, together with all their horses, arms, and equipments. Most of my men then dispersed over the field in pursuit of the frightened horses which had run away. I was sitting on my horse near the house, giving directions for getting ready to leave with the prisoners and spoil, when one of my men, named Wild, who had chased a horse some distance down the railroad, came at full speed, and reported a heavy column of cavalry coming up. I turned to one of my men and said to him, '*Now we will whip them.*' I had hardly spoken the words when I saw a large body of Union cavalry, not over two hundred or three hundred yards off, rapidly advancing. Most of my command had scattered over the field, and the enemy was so close there was no time to rally and re-form before they got upon us. In attempting to do so, I remained on the ground until they were within fifty yards of me, and was nearly captured. So there was nothing to do but for every man to take care of himself. The command I had at this time was a mere aggregation of men casually gathered, belonging to many different regiments, who happened to be in the country. Of course, such a body has none of the cohesion and discipline that springs from organization, no matter how brave the men may be individually. Men never fought better than they did at the house, while the defenders were inspired to greater resistance, knowing that relief was near. We had defeated and captured three times our own

Colonel John S. Mosby, C. S. A.

A GROUP OF MOSBY'S RAIDERS.

number, and now had to give up the fruits of victory, and in turn to fly to prevent capture. My men fled in every direction, taking off about fifty horses and a number of prisoners. Only one of my men, Templeman, was killed, but I lost about twenty captured, nearly all of whom were wounded."

In March General Hooker, learning that a Confederate force, under Stuart, had set out for Fauquier and the adjoining counties to enforce the draft, determined to send out a large cavalry force to intercept them, and at the same time to make a reconnoissance on the south side of the Rappahannock. The troops chosen for this work were the First and Fifth regulars, the Thirty-fourth and Sixteenth Pennsylvania, the First Rhode Island, the Fourth New York, and the Sixth Ohio, with a battery of six guns, all under the command of Gen. William W. Averill. At the close of the first day's march the expedition encamped near Kelly's Ford on the Rapidan, and the next morning, the 17th, on riding down to the ford, found the passage disputed. The Confederates had constructed abatis along the southern bank and were in strong force. Several attempts to cross the stream by separate regiments were ineffectual, until a squadron of the First Rhode Island, led by Lieutenant Brown, plunged boldly through the stream, cut their way through the abatis, charged up the bank, and routed the enemy in their immediate front. The whole force then crossed and formed in line of battle. As they moved on, the Confederates charged upon them, but were met in a counter charge and broken. Rallying, they attempted it again, and again were broken and put to flight. Meanwhile the Pennsylvania regiment struck them on the flank, and the artillery opened upon them. When a point about a mile and a half from the river had been reached, General Averill re-formed his line, which then moved through the woods and fired as it went. The Confederates now, for the first time, brought their artillery into play, of which they had twelve pieces, and the shot fell fast among Averill's men. Following this, the Confederates made another charge, but were broken by the Third Pennsylvania. A participant says: "From the time of crossing the river until now there had been many personal encounters, single horsemen dashing at each other with full speed, and cutting and slashing with their sabres until one or the other was disabled. The wounds received by both friend and foe in these single combats were frightful, such as I trust never to see again." A running fight was now kept up, the Confederates retreating slowly, and occasionally halting to use their artillery, until a point six miles from the river was reached, when General Averill, finding that his artillery ammunition was nearly exhausted, and that there were strong intrenchments not far ahead, ordered a return. The Confederates, who had been retreating, now advanced in their turn, and annoyed the retiring column somewhat with their artillery. General Averill lost nine men killed, thirty-five wounded, and forty captured. The Confederate loss is not exactly known, but Averill's men brought away sixty prisoners, including Major Breckenridge, of the First Virginia cavalry. In this action was killed John Pelham, commander of Stuart's horse artillery, who was called the "Boy Major" and had won high reputation as an artillerist. His fall is the subject of the finest poem produced at the South during the war, written by James R. Randall.

"Just as the spring came laughing through the strife
With all its gorgeous cheer,
In the bright April of historic life,
Fell the great cannoneer.

The wondrous lulling of a hero's breath
His bleeding country weeps;
Hushed in the alabaster arms of Death
Our young Marcellus sleeps.

Nobler and grander than the child of Rome,
Curbing his chariot steeds,
The knightly scion of a Southern home
Dazzled the land with deeds.

Gentlest and bravest in the battle-brunt,
The champion of the truth,
He bore his banner to the very front
Of our immortal youth.

A clang of sabres 'mid Virginian snow,
The fiery pang of shells—
And there's a wail of immemorial woe
In Alabama dells.

The pennon drops that led the sacred band
Along the crimson field;
The meteor blade sinks from the nerveless hand
Over the spotless shield.

We gazed and gazed upon that beauteous face;
While round the lips and eyes,
Couched in their marble slumber, flashed the grace
Of a divine surprise.

O mother of a blessed soul on high,
Thy tears may soon be shed!
Think of thy boy with princes of the sky,
Among the Southern dead!

How must he smile on this dull world beneath,
Fevered with swift renown—
He, with the martyr's amaranthine wreath
Twining the victor's crown!"

When Lee, after Gettysburg, retreated southward up the Shenandoah Valley, Meade pursued on the eastern side of the Blue Ridge in a parallel line, taking possession of the passes as far southward as Manassas Gap. On the 22d of April, he learned that a Confederate corps was near the western end of that gap, which was held by Buford's division of cavalry alone. The Third Corps, then guarding Ashby's Gap, was thereupon ordered down to Manassas Gap, and made a prompt and swift march, reaching Buford at midnight. The next day, from a lofty point on the mountains, the movements of a large part of the Confederate army could be seen. One immense column was in plain sight, consisting, first, of several thousand infantry, followed by disabled soldiers mounted on horses that had been taken in Pennsylvania, the rear being brought up by a large body of cavalry, while the wagon trains were moving on a parallel road further west, and all were pushing southward as rapidly as possible. It was thought that a movement through the gap might cut the Confederate column in two, and this was accordingly ordered. Berdan's sharp-shooters, the Twentieth Indiana, the Sixty-third Pennsylvania, and the Third and Fourth Maine Regiments, of high reputation as skirmishers, were pushed forward, and soon brushed away the small Confederate force that occupied its western end. This fell back upon a supporting force posted on a lofty hill. Here the sharp-shooters kept the attention of the Confederates while the Maine regiments silently crept up the face of the hill, unobserved from its summit, delivered a volley, and then made a rapid charge which cleared the hill of all Confederates except those that were disabled or made prisoners. It was then discovered that the main body of the Confederate force that was intended to dispute the passage of the gap was on another line of hill, still farther to the west, and strongly fortified. The Excelsior brigade, commanded by General Spinola, was now brought forward to dislodge the enemy. Passing through the line of skirmishers, the men of this brigade soon reached the slope of the hill, which was ragged and precipitous and swept by a fire from the crest. Without a minute's hesitation they scrambled up the ascent, which was more than three hundred feet high, grasping at the bushes and points of rock until they reached the summit, when they fired a volley, fixed their bayonets, gave a shout, and rushed upon the enemy, who immediately fled in confusion. General Spinola was twice wounded in this assault, and the command devolved upon Colonel Farnum, who immediately re-formed the line and set out to carry in a similar manner another crest, which he succeeded in doing, and took a considerable number of prisoners. At this point of time, General Meade, having learned that a Confederate corps was moving down the valley to take part in this action, ordered the troops to discontinue their advance and hold the points already gained. At the same time he brought up the bulk of his army in anticipation of the battle the next day. But when the sun next arose the Confederates had all disappeared. By this movement General Meade lost two days in the race of the armies southward, which enabled the Confederates to get back to their old ground, south of the Rappahannock, before he could reach it. This action is known as the battle of Wapping Heights. The National loss was one hundred and ten men, killed or wounded; the Confederate loss is unknown.

In August, General Averell's cavalry command made an expedition through the counties of Hardy, Pendleton, Highland, Bath, Green Briar, and Pocahontas. They destroyed saltpetre works and burned a camp with a large amount of equipments and stores. They had numerous skirmishes with a Confederate cavalry force, commanded by Gen. Samuel Jones, and at Rocky Gap, near Sulphur Springs, a serious engagement. This battle lasted two days. On the first day the Confederates opened the fire with artillery, which was answered by Averell's guns, and a somewhat destructive duel ensued. The Confederates attempted to capture Averell's battery by charging across an open field, but were repelled by its steady fire. On the other hand, similar charges were made seven times in succession by a portion of Averell's men, and not one of them was successful. When, finally, Averell's ammunition was nearly exhausted, and he learned that the enemy was about to be reinforced, he withdrew from the field in good order. The loss in this engagement was about two hundred on each side.

In an irregular and unsatisfactory campaign of manœuvres between Meade and Lee, along the slopes of the Blue Ridge, after the battle of Gettysburg, but before the retirement to winter quarters, there were some engagements which would have been notable had not the whole campaign resulted in nothing. One of these was at Bristoe Station, three miles west of Manassas Junction, October 14th, when Meade was making retrograde movements, and Lee attacked his rear guard with A. P. Hill's corps. The Second Corps formed the rear of Meade's line, and marched to Bristoe on the south side of the track of the Orange and Alexandria Railroad, with flankers well out on both sides, and skirmishers deployed. About noon, the advance of this corps, which was Gen. Alexander S. Webb's division, reached the eastern edge of woods that look out toward Broad Run. The rear of the Fifth Corps, which preceded the Second on the march, had just crossed the Run. Suddenly they were fired upon by artillery which emerged from the woods by an obscure road, and then a line of Confederate skirmishers appeared on the hill north of the railroad. Immediately General Webb's division was thrown forward in a line south of the railroad, with its right resting on Broad Run, and General Hays's division took position at Webb's left, while Caldwell's faced the railroad, and a section of Brown's Rhode Island battery was put in position on the other side of Broad Run where it could enfilade the enemy's skirmishing line, and the remainder was placed on a hill west of the Run. Arnold's famous battery was also put in a commanding position. Very soon Confederates opened a furious fire of artillery and musketry from the edge of the wood; but when the National battery began its work their batteries were very soon silenced, and their skirmishing line melted away. General Warren ordered a detail of ten men from each regiment in that part of the Fifth Corps which had participated in the fight, to rush forward and bring off the Confederate guns, which, for the minute, seemed to have been deserted. With a cheer the men crossed the railroad track, climbed the hill, wheeled pieces into position, and fired them at the retreating Confederates, and then dragged them away. But they had not gone far when the enemy came out of the wood again and charged upon them. Whereupon they dropped the battery, resumed their small arms, drove back the charge, and then brought off the guns. A participant says, "I have heard some cheering on election nights, but I never heard such a yell of exultation as rent the air when the rebel guns, caissons, and equipments were brought across the railroad track to the line of our infantry." The Confederates now tried the experiment of attacking the Second Corps, and two regiments of North Carolina troops charged upon its right over the railroad. When they reached the track, they were met by two or three deadly volleys, which sent them rapidly back again. They became broken, and hid themselves behind rocks and logs, or came in as prisoners, when the National line was advanced. Still their main body kept up the fight until dark, when they finally retired into the woods, after losing six guns, two battle flags, seven hundred and fifty prisoners, and an unknown number in killed or wounded. Among the Confederate losses in this section was Brig.-Gen. Carnot Posey, mortally wounded.

There was considerable desultory fighting around Charlestown, Va. On the 15th of July a National cavalry force overtook and attacked a Confederate force near that place, and captured about one hundred prisoners, afterward holding the town. On the 18th of October a Confederate cavalry force, under Gen. John J. Imboden, attacked the garrison, finding them in the court-house and other buildings, and demanded the surrender; to which the commander, Colonel Simpson, answered, "Take me if you can." Imboden then opened fire on the court-house with artillery at a distance of less than two hundred yards, and of course soon drove out the occupants. After exchanging a volley or two, most of the National troops surrendered, while some had escaped toward Harper's Ferry. Two hours later a force came up from that place and drove out Imboden's men, who retired slowly toward Berryville, fighting all the way.

In its slow pursuit of the Army of Northern Virginia; the Army of the Potomac, early in November, came up with that army at Rappahannock Station, where the Orange and Alexandria Railroad crosses the Rapidan River. General Lee showed an intention to get into winter quarters here, for the ground was elaborately fortified on both sides of the river, and his men were known to be building huts. General Meade made his dispositions for a serious attack at this point. Lee had a strong force intrenched with artillery on the north side of the river to prevent any crossing, and works extended thence for a considerable distance in each direction, while the main body of his army was on the south side of the river and also intrenched. General Meade placed the Fifth and Sixth Corps under the command of General Sedgwick, fronting Rappahannock Station. General French was placed in command of the First, Second, and Third Corps, and ordered to move to Kelly's Ford, four miles below Rappahannock Station, cross the river, carry the heights on the south side, and then move toward the enemy's rear at Rappahannock to

BREVET MAJOR-GENERAL R. S. FOSTER, AND STAFF.

assist General Sedgwick's column in its front attack. General Buford's cavalry was to cross the Rappahannock above these positions, and General Kilpatrick's below. Sedgwick's column arrived within a mile and a half of the river at noon, on the 7th of November, and threw out skirmishers to examine the enemy's works. At the same hour, French's column arrived at Kelly's Ford. General French promptly opened the battle with his artillery, sent a brigade across the river which captured many prisoners in the rifle trenches, and an hour later crossed the division and began the laying of pontoon bridges, so that his entire command crossed before night. General Lee, believing that the demonstration at Rappahannock Station was a feint and that at Kelly's Ford the real movement, heavily reinforced his troops at the Ford. Those on the north side of the river at Rappahannock Station were also reinforced. Sedgwick's plan of attack was to have the Fifth Corps get possession of the river bank on the left, and the Sixth Corps on the right, and plant his batteries on high ground, from which he could compel evacuation of the works. This movement was made, and the batteries opened their fire, but the Confederates did not leave the works. In the edge of evening it was determined to make an assault in heavy force. The artillery kept up a rapid fire, until the assaulting column, led by Gen. David A. Russell, had moved forward and approached near to the works. This movement appears to have been a surprise to the Confederates, and it was carried out so systematically and rapidly that the storming party, led by the Fifth Wisconsin and the Sixth Maine Regiments, carried the works in a few minutes. The Forty-ninth and One Hundred and Nineteenth Pennsylvania were close after them, and the Fifth Maine and One Hundred and Twenty-first New York at the same time carried the rifle-pits on the right, while the One Hundred and Twenty-fifth New York and the Twentieth Maine, which had been on picket duty, promptly joined in the assault. This gallant affair was a complete success, and General Wright remarked at the time that it was the first instance during the war in which an important intrenched position had been carried at the first assault. The National loss in killed and wounded was three hundred and seventy-one men. The Confederate loss, killed, wounded, and missing, was nearly seventeen hundred, including thirteen hundred captured. The captures also included seven battle-flags, twelve hundred stands of small arms, and four guns. When the Confederate commander learned of the disaster, he burned his pontoon bridge, and in the night fled back to Mount Roan, from which position the next day he withdrew to his old camps south of the Rapidan. A heavy fog on the 8th prevented the National commander from pursuing in time to effect anything.

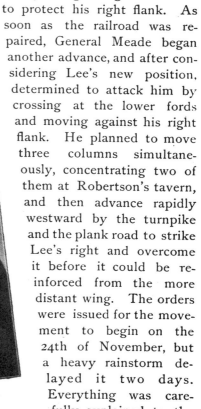

BREVET MAJOR-GENERAL WILLIAM W. AVERELL.

MAJOR-GENERAL SAMUEL JONES, C. S. A.

BRIGADIER-GENERAL HENRY PRINCE.

When the Army of Northern Virginia retired from the action at Rappahannock Station to the south side of the Rapidan, it took up an intrenched position stretching nearly twenty miles along the river, from Barnett's Ford above the railroad crossing to Morton's Ford below. The cavalry were thrown out to watch the fords above and below this position. Lee then constructed a new intrenched line, nearly at right angles with the main line, to protect his right flank. As soon as the railroad was repaired, General Meade began another advance, and after considering Lee's new position, determined to attack him by crossing at the lower fords and moving against his right flank. He planned to move three columns simultaneously, concentrating two of them at Robertson's tavern, and then advance rapidly westward by the turnpike and the plank road to strike Lee's right and overcome it before it could be reinforced from the more distant wing. The orders were issued for the movement to begin on the 24th of November, but a heavy rainstorm delayed it two days. Everything was carefully explained to the corps commanders, and all possible pains were taken to make the different parts of the great machine move harmoniously. The Third and Sixth Corps were to cross at Jacob's Ford and move to Robertson's Tavern, through wood roads which were not known except through inquiry. The ground to be moved over was a part of the so-called Wilderness, which was made famous when Grant began his overland campaign the next spring. The Second Corps, crossing at Germanna Ford, was also to move to Robertson's Tavern. The First and Fifth Corps were to cross at Culpeper Mine Ford, and move to the plank road at Parker's Store, advancing thence to New Hope Church, where a road comes in from Robertson's Tavern. Gregg's cavalry division was to cross at Ely's Ford, covering the left flank, while the other division, under Custer, was to guard the fords above, facing the main line of the enemy. Merritt's cavalry was to protect the trains. Every experienced soldier knows how difficult it is to bring about simultaneous and concentric movements of large bodies of troops separated by any considerable distance, and moving by different routes. Any one of many contingencies may stop the progress of any column or send it astray, and very few such plans have ever succeeded. This one of General Meade's was devised with the utmost care, and every possible provision against miscarriage seemed to have been made. Yet at the very outset, on the morning of the 26th, there was a delay of two hours in crossing the river, because the Third Corps was not up in time, and then there was a further serious loss of time because the bridges for Jacob's Ford and Germanna Ford were found to be a little too short, lacking only one pontoon each. The river banks here on the south side are more than one hundred feet high, and very steep, so that it was only with great labor that the wagons and the guns could be taken up. The artillery of two corps had to be taken to another ford than that by which the infantry of this corps crossed. It happened, therefore, that when the day was spent the heads of the column, instead of being at Robertson's Tavern, were only about three miles from the river, while the tavern is six or seven miles from the river by the road. These fords had all been watched by Confederate cavalry, and the movements of the Army of the Potomac were by this time well known at the Confederate headquarters. They had been inferred still earlier when the Confederate signal men saw the troops and trains moving in the morning. One thing, however, General Lee did not know—whether it was Meade's intention to attack his army where it was, or to move eastward toward Richmond and draw it out of its intrenchments. In the night of the 26th Lee drew his army out of its lines and put it in motion ready to act in accordance with either of these movements of Meade, as the event might determine.

BRIGADIER-GENERAL MICHAEL CORCORAN.

COLONEL HIRAM BERDAN.

Thus affairs were in a state likely to produce exactly such a conflict in the Wilderness as actually was produced when Grant crossed the Rapidan in the spring of 1864, but there was this difference, that it was Meade's intention to turn westward and attack Lee where he was, while it was Grant's intention to move eastward, get out of the Wilderness if possible, plant himself across Lee's communications, and compel him to leave his intrenchments. In the afternoon of the 27th, the leading division of the Fifth Corps, commanded by Gen. Alexander Hays, came into collision with the leading division of Early's Confederate corps, and drove back his skirmishers on the turnpike, while Webb's division to the right, with Rodes's Confederate division in its front, promptly deployed, and drove back his skirmishers toward Raccoon Ford. The National troops in deploying possessed themselves of a strong position, and the Confederate commanders were not willing to attack until reinforced, but their reinforcements were delayed near Bartlett's Mills by being fired upon by the Third Corps pickets, and the expectation of an attack at that point. General French, commanding the Third Corps, appears to have blundered as to the road he was to take, and at the forks took the right hand instead of the left, which not only threw his corps nearer the enemy, but prevented him from appearing where he was expected at Robertson's Tavern at the same hour when the Second Corps arrived there. He then blundered still further by halting and sending word that he was waiting for the Fifth Corps, when in fact the Fifth was waiting for him. By the time that orders had passed back and forth explaining his error, the enemy had begun to throw out a large infantry force upon his right flank. The plan of action was then necessarily so far changed, as that General French was ordered to attack the enemy in his front at once, which he did, the divisions engaged being those of Carr, Prince, and Birney. The heaviest fighting fell upon Carr's division, and there were charges and countercharges, the lines swaying back and forth several times. General Meade, unwilling to bring on a general engagement until he could get his army together, had been holding the First and Fifth Corps in their positions waiting for French's corps to join them, and there was a little fighting in front of the Fifth when the enemy came close to its lines. General Lee was quite as reluctant to attack in force as was General Meade, and that night he drew back his army within its intrenchments. A hard storm the next day delayed all movements, and when, toward evening, Meade advanced to the eastern bank of Mine Run, he found that the Confederate intrenchments on the western bank were altogether too strong to justify an assault. Sending the Fifth Corps, in the night of the 28th, to threaten the Confederate right flank in the

BRIGADIER-GENERAL JOHN S. WILLIAMS, C. S. A.

morning, and turn it if possible, Meade directed his other corps commanders to search for possible weak points in the enemy's lines. One was found on the extreme Confederate left and another near the centre, while the First and Fifth Corps commanders reported that there was no weak spot whatever in their front. A simultaneous assault on these points was arranged for

FORAGING PARTY.

BREVET MAJOR-GENERAL EDWARD HATCH.

the morning of the 30th, to be covered, as usual, by a heavy artillery fire. The guns opened promptly at the designated hour, and were as promptly replied to by the Confederate artillery; but before the assault began, General Warren sent word to General Meade that he found the enemy had so strengthened the works on their right, as to make an assault there hopeless. General Meade, therefore, gave orders to suspend the attacks that were already begun at the other points, and here the campaign virtually ended. There was no other possible movement, except to march around the right of the Confederate position, and for this it would have been necessary first to bring over the trains which had been left on the north side of the river. Further, the weather was very severe; some of the pickets had been frozen to death, and the roads were rapidly becoming impassable. General Meade, therefore, withdrew his army to the north side of the Rapidan in the night of December 1st. In this unfortunate and altogether unsatisfactory affair, Meade lost about a thousand men, most of them in the Third Corps; the Confederate losses were reported at about six hundred.

Early in the morning of January 3d, a strong Confederate cavalry force made a dash upon Moorefield, W. Va., and, after a contest of several hours with the garrison, was driven off. The Confederates, however, carried away sixty-five prisoners and some arms and horses.

In April a Confederate force of five hundred men descended the Kanawha on flat-boats and attacked Point Pleasant, which was garrisoned by fifty men under Captain Carter of the Thirteenth Virginia (National) Regiment. A fight of four hours ensued, the garrison successfully defending themselves in the court house, and refusing to surrender even when the Confederates threatened to burn the town. After the assailants had lost about seventy men, and inflicted a loss on the garrison of nearly a dozen, they withdrew, and their retreat was hastened by some well-directed shots from a Government transport in the river.

The most considerable engagement that resulted from an expedition under General Jones was near Fairmount, where the Baltimore and Ohio Railroad crosses the Monongahela River. The defensive forces here consisted of only three hundred men, while the Confederates numbered several thousands. At their approach, a company of militia and armed citizens went out on the hills to meet them, and made such good preparations for disputing their passage by the turnpike, that a force was sent around the slopes to drive them off, which was accomplished after some fighting. As the Confederates approached the suspension bridge, a part of the defensive force made a gallant stand, taking shelter in a foundry and firing with great effect upon the Confederate skirmishers and sharp-shooters. After a time, this little force fell back, and the Confederates crossed by the suspension bridge and advanced toward the railroad bridge. At the latter there was a similar attack and defence, until the detachments that had crossed at the suspension bridge came up in the rear of those who defended the railroad bridge, and the little band was summoned to surrender. This, however, they did not do until they were completely surrounded and could fight no longer, when they raised a white flag and the firing ceased. Hardly had this taken place, when a detachment of National troops came up the railroad with two guns, and shelled the Confederates on the west side of the river. The Confederates then set about destroying the railroad bridge, which at that time was the finest in the United States. It was of iron, supported on tubular columns of cast iron, which rested on massive

BRIDGE BUILT BY UNITED STATES TROOPS, WHITESIDE, TENN.

(FROM A GOVERNMENT PHOTOGRAPH TAKEN DURING THE WAR.)

stone piers, and had cost about half a million dollars. They poured powder by the kegful into the hollow iron column and exploded it, blowing the whole structure into the river. They had lost in the fight nearly a hundred men, while the National loss was but half a dozen. After robbing every store in the town, and destroying much private property, including the law and private libraries of Governor Pierpont, which they carried into the street and burned, the Confederates departed.

MAJOR-GENERAL W. H. FRENCH.

On the 13th of July a cavalry expedition of two regiments, commanded by Col. John Toland, set out to cut the railroad at Wytheville, Va. They crossed Lens Mountain, reached Coal River, and moved along that stream toward Raleigh Court House, where they began to meet with resistance. They then ascended the Guyan Mountain, and descended on the other side into an almost unknown valley, where, writes one of the officers, "The few inhabitants obtained a livelihood largely by digging ginseng and other roots. They live in huts that the Esquimaux would scorn to be invited into. Long, dirty, tobacco-dried, sallow-complexioned women stare at you as you pass. Ask them a question, they answer you, giving what information they possess, but it is so little as to render you no assistance. Here stands a small, dirty tavern, with two or three half-starved old men gazing upon the Yankees as they march by." The expedition crossed the Tug Mountains, and descended to Abb's Valley. Here they captured a small Confederate camp with thirty-six men. The writer just quoted says of Abb's Valley: "The scenery beggars description for beauty. As far as the eye can reach, stretch hills and vales in every direction. The country is rich, owned principally by wealthy citizens who were very influential in bringing about the rebellion, living in luxury and ease. They little dreamed that they, living in so remote a place, should be made to feel the weight of the hand of war." The expedition then marched to Clinch River, and crossed Rich Mountain. "The people had heard much and seen little of Yankee soldiers, and the white population looked upon us with fear, ready to give all when attacked. On the other hand, the negroes assembled in groups, threw themselves in every conceivable form, jumping, singing, dancing, yelling, and giving signs that the year of jubilee had come. The white men fled as we approached, leaving their homes at our mercy, which were not molested, except those that had been used in some way to benefit the rebel army; in such cases, they were always destroyed." The next march was across Garden Mountain, Rich Valley, and Walker's Mountain, to the vicinity of Wytheville. Here the Confederate pickets were encountered, and skirmishing began. When the whole body of the expedition charged upon the town, they found the Confederates not in line of battle, but in buildings commanding the principal streets, from which they opened fire upon the advancing column. This firing from the houses was participated in by citizens, and also to some extent by women, and was very effective. The three companies that first rode into the town discovered two pieces of artillery in position, and made a dash and captured them. Colonel Toland hurried up with the remainder of his force, and, finding that the enemy could not otherwise be dislodged from the buildings, gave orders to burn the town. The officers were the special mark of the sharp-shooters, and in ten minutes the colonel fell dead, when the command devolved upon Colonel Powell, who also was struck and had to be carried off, seriously wounded. Reinforcements were sent to the Confederates from various points, but before they arrived the town was laid in ashes, and the expedition fell back, burning a bridge behind them. They then slowly retraced their line of march, with occasional skirmishes on the way, but finding their chief hardships in the lack of food and the exhaustion of the horses. "We ascended Blue Stone Mountain by file. The road was very steep, and ere we reached the top twenty-three horses lay stretched across the road, having fallen from exhaustion. The descent was terrible, cliffs ten to thirty-one feet, down which the smooth-footed horse would slip with scarce life enough to arrest his progress, except it be stopped by contact with a tree or some other obstacle." They at length reached Raleigh, N. C., where provisions were forwarded to them from Fayetteville. They had been absent eleven days, and had ridden about five hundred miles. Their loss was eighty-five men and three hundred horses.

An invasion of Kentucky by the Confederate General Pegram, with about two thousand six hundred men, in March, came to a sudden end at Somerset, in the central part of the State. General Gillmore, with twelve hundred mounted men, set out from that town to attack him, and found him in a strong position at Dutton's Hill, twelve miles from Somerset. Gillmore drew up in line of battle, placed his guns in the centre, and, in an artillery fight of an hour and a half, dismounted three of the enemy's pieces. He then ordered his wings to advance, which they did in the face of a brisk fire. But, disregarding this, they pressed on up the hill rapidly until the enemy broke and fled. A body of Confederate cavalry, led by Scott and Ashby, were then detected in a flank movement. This was promptly met, and, after a short conflict, sixty of them were made prisoners and the remainder were put to flight. Three miles from Somerset the Confederates made a stand, but here again they were routed, and

BREVET MAJOR-GENERAL EDWARD FERRERO.

in the night they crossed the river, where it was said many of them were drowned. The Confederate loss was nearly a hundred killed or wounded, besides many prisoners. Gillmore's loss was about forty. They placed a battery on the river bank in the morning, but Gillmore's artillery soon knocked it to pieces, and in another dash four hundred cattle that they had taken were recaptured. His men captured the flags of a Louisiana and a Tennessee cavalry regiment. A participant wrote: "Wolford himself pursued the rebel leader, Colonel Scott, so closely that when within thirty paces of him, with levelled pistol he called upon him to die or surrender. At the moment, Wolford's horse was shot, and Scott escaped. When McIntire arrived, cheering his men forward on foot, the rebels broke in confusion and fled. Wolford halted for ammunition, but McIntire, with seventy-two men yelling like a thousand, followed across an open field and into the woods, and here began the most extraordinary flight and pursuit, I venture to assert, that has been recorded during the war. The rebel panic increased with every rod passed over in their terrific flight over hill and valley, brook and rock, tangled brush and fallen timber. Any one to review the field to-day would pronounce such a race over such ground impossible. At the base of a precipitous hill, and embarrassed by the contracting valley, high fences, and a complication of lanes, the rebels were evidently about to turn at bay in very desperation, when additional reinforcements, under Colonel Sanders, appeared dashing along at their left. This completed their consternation, and they again broke, every man for himself."

Early in January Gen. Stephen A. Hurlbut, commanding the district of Tennessee, issued a proclamation at Memphis, in which he warned the resident sympathizers with the Confederate cause that they must expect to suffer if the guerilla operations, which had become very frequent and annoying in that State, were continued. He alluded especially to the threat to tear up the railroads, and declared that for every such raid he would select ten families from the wealthiest and most noted secessionists in Memphis and send them South.

A detachment of Confederates, commanded by Lieutenant-Colonel Dawson, made a raid into Tennessee in January, and busied themselves especially in burning all the cotton they could find. But on the 8th a detachment of the Twentieth Illinois cavalry, under Captain Moore, surprised Dawson's camp, near Ripley, at sunrise, and, without losing a man, killed eight of the Confederates, wounded twenty, and captured forty-six, while the remainder escaped.

On the last day of January a scouting party of National cavalry, setting out from Nashville, came unexpectedly upon a portion of Wheeler's cavalry at the little village of Rover, and immediately attacked them. A hand-to-hand sabre fight ensued, which resulted in the complete defeat of the Confederates, who had thus been taken unawares. About twenty-five of them were disabled, and three hundred made prisoners.

Fort Donelson, which Grant's army had captured in February, 1862, was now held by six hundred men under Col. A. C. Harding, and on February 3, 1863, was attacked by a force of five thousand under Generals Wheeler and Forrest. At the approach of the enemy Harding sent out his cavalry to reconnoitre, but they were all captured. At the same time his telegraph lines were cut, and he sent out mounted messengers to bring up a gunboat that was down the river. He had hardly placed his little command in position for defence, when the Confederates sent in a flag of truce and demanded a surrender, which he declined. The enemy then opened upon him with eight guns, and he replied steadily with five, called in his skirmishers, and strengthened his line as much as possible. The fight continued from noon till evening, when surrender was again demanded and again refused. The Confederates now made arrangements for an assault, and Harding placed his men in the rifle-pits with fixed bayonets to await the onset. A distant gun told him that help was coming, and very soon the black hull of the *Lexington* was seen moving up the river. The garrison began to cheer, and when her shells were sent over their heads and fell among the enemy, the siege was raised at once and the Confederates quickly fled away. In a charge made at the moment when they broke, Harding took some prisoners. He had lost about seventy-five men, killed or wounded, and the Confederates over four hundred.

Learning that a Confederate cavalry force was foraging, plundering, and conscripting, near Bradyville, twelve miles from Murfreesboro', General Stanley set out (March 1st) with sixteen hundred men in search of it. He found it strongly posted near the village, and at once attacked and drove it through the town. The Confederates took up a new position half a mile distant, where a ledge of rocks gave them good shelter. Stanley then sent a squadron around their left flank, and another to their right, while he made a show of attacking in front. The Confederates stood their ground until they found themselves subjected to two enfilading fires, when they at once gave way, and Stanley's men rode in among them and used their sabres and pistols. They were pursued three miles and completely disorganized. About thirty of them were disabled, and a hundred taken prisoners.

Three days later a similar expedition, under Col. John Coburn, set out from Franklin in search of a similar party of Confederates. They found them near Thompson's Station, and were attacked by riflemen hidden behind a stone wall near the depot. A few minutes later two batteries opened upon them, and the enemy advanced in line of battle. Coburn's infantry stood their ground bravely, but his artillery was badly managed, and his cavalry retired instead of advancing. When his ammunition failed, at the end of three hours, Coburn was obliged to surrender with such of his forces as had not escaped. He lost four hundred men, killed or wounded, and about twelve hundred captured. About six hundred of the Confederates were disabled.

Still another of these expeditions left Murfreesboro', March 18, in search of marauding bands of Confederates. It was commanded by Col. A. S. Hall. At Statesville he encountered and quickly defeated a small body of Confederate cavalry. At Auburn he discovered that a Confederate force, superior to his own, was moving up to attack him, whereupon he drew back to Vaught's Hill, near Milton, and formed his line. One of his two guns began the fight by throwing shells over the little village and into the advance guard of the enemy. The Confederates, consisting of eleven regiments, commanded by Generals Wheeler and Morgan, promptly attacked along the whole line. Hall's guns were advantageously placed, and raked the lines of the enemy as they advanced, while his infantry were very skillfuly managed, and held their ground against determined attacks on both flanks. A detachment of cavalry which had passed around the right flank, and was attempting to get into the rear, was met by such a deadly fire that it immediately withdrew in confusion. The Confederates, enraged at the execution of one of Hall's guns, concentrated a large force and made a desperate rush for its capture. Hall's men allowed them to come within forty yards, and then opened upon them with a fire of musketry so destructive that they soon broke and fled in confusion. The assailants now drew off and contented themselves with cannonading at a distance, which was kept up until one of Hall's skilfully managed guns sent a shot which dismounted one of theirs, and then they withdrew altogether. The Confederate loss in this action was about four hundred, killed or wounded ; the National loss was about forty.

Again, in April, General Stanley set out with a brigade of infantry and two thousand cavalry to attack Morgan's and Wharton's Confederate force at Snow Hill. After some preliminary skirmishes and desultory fighting two regiments of Stanley's cavalry succeeded in getting into the rear of the enemy, when they broke and fled, losing more than a hundred men disabled or captured.

The Confederate General Van Dorn, who had been for some time threatening to attack the garrison of Franklin, commanded by Gen. Gordon Granger, appeared before the town on the 10th of April, with a heavy force, and drove in the outposts. He then formed a strong skirmish line, and behind this a line of battle ready for an immediate charge. Granger's advance troops, consisting of the Fortieth Ohio Regiment, commanded by Capt. Charles G. Matchett, were quickly placed in a critical position, having both flanks menaced at the same time that the enemy was advancing in front. Captain Matchett gave the order to fall back at a double quick, and was, as he expected to be, followed closely by the enemy's mounted skirmishers. Suddenly he halted his regiment, faced them about, and gave the pursuers a volley that drove them back from their main line, when he continued his retreat. This manœuvre was repeated several times in admirable style, the front company each time retiring on the double quick to the rear of the other companies, when they faced about and delivered their fire. In this manner they reached the town, took advantage of the houses and other defences, and checked any further pursuit. The Confederates now opened fire with their batteries, which was replied to by the siege guns in the fortifications, and by field batteries, which drove them off. Meanwhile, a force under General Stanley had moved out and struck the flank of the Confederates, capturing six guns and two hundred prisoners. The National loss was about one hundred men ; the Confederate loss is unknown.

BRIGADIER-GENERAL THOMAS M. SCOTT, C. S. A.

BRIGADIER-GENERAL POWELL CLAYTON.

On the 7th of September a Confederate force of four regiments, which had fortified Cumberland Gap and occupied it nearly a year, surrendered to a National force under General Shackleford without firing a gun.

MAJOR-GENERAL JAMES P. FAGAN, C. S. A.

General Shackleford, undertaking to drive the various bands of Confederates out of East Tennessee, in September, found one near Bristol, fought it, pursued it, and fought it again, until it made a decided stand at Blountville, September 22. Here he opened fire upon them, and the fight lasted from one o'clock till dusk, when the Confederates were defeated, and fled, closely pursued by Colonel Carter's command. They were ultimately dispersed, some of them taking to the mountains, and the others returning to their homes.

The position of General Burnside was peculiar, and probably was more influenced by a feeling of personal regard than that of any other commander on the National side. His enthusiastic loyalty, his bravery, his hearty and manly conduct among his fellow patriots, and his personal modesty were all perfectly evident. His capacity for a large independent command was at least doubtful. Early in the war he had led a successful expedition through many dangers of wind and wave on the coast of North Carolina. Later he had made two notable failures—as a corps commander at Antietam, and as commander of the army at Fredericksburg. But he had never aspired to the chief command, which really was thrust upon him, and he so frankly assumed the responsibility and blame for his errors, that the feeling toward him was much the same as that in the South toward Lee after his disastrous failure at Gettysburg. Although he was not retained in command of the Army of the Potomac, he was, in March, 1863, given command of the Department of the Ohio, and his old corps, the Ninth, was sent to him with the intention of having him go through eastern Kentucky and Tennessee, and relieve the Union people there from the Confederate oppression and outrages that they were suffering. This plan was delayed by the necessity of sending his corps to reinforce Grant at Vicksburg, and Burnside was practically idle through the summer. But late in August, with twenty thousand men, he set out from Richmond, Ky., and moved southward into East Tennessee, where he met with a most enthusiastic reception from the inhabitants. The stars and stripes, which had been hidden away during the presence of Confederate forces, were now waving from nearly every house, and supplies of all kinds were freely brought to his forces. His coming, however, was not the only reason for the withdrawal of the various Confederate bands that had infested that region; these were being united to Bragg's army to strengthen it for his contemplated movement on Chattanooga. Meanwhile, Longstreet, with his corps, had been detached from Lee's army and sent to Bragg's, and had played an important part, as we have seen, in the battle of Chickamauga. Various detachments of Burnside's forces had encountered the enemy, and some of these actions have already been described in this chapter.

The next important movement made by the Confederates was designed to destroy Burnside's force, or drive it out of East Tennessee. That mountainous region, with its sturdily loyal people, lying between the disloyal portions of Virginia and North Carolina on the one hand, and those of Tennessee on the other, was a constant source of discomfort to the Confederate Government, and would evidently be a standing menace to the Confederacy should its independence ever be established. Hence their anxiety to clear it of Union sentiment, by whatever means. About twenty thousand men, under the command of General Longstreet, were detached from Bragg's army and sent out upon this errand. Burnside had scattered his own forces pretty widely, and some of his detachments were obliged to fight the enemy at various points before they were all concentrated again. One of these actions was at the village of Philadelphia, where two thousand men, under Col. F. T. Wolford, were attacked by three times their number of Confederates, and, after a gallant resistance, escaped with the loss of their artillery and wagons, and managed to carry away half a hundred prisoners. Reinforcements coming up, the train was recaptured and the enemy driven in turn. About a hundred men were killed or wounded on each side. Longstreet's general plan and purpose being now evident, Burnside began the concentration of his forces, and, being joined by his Ninth Corps again, had about the same number of men as Longstreet. He chose an advantageous position at Campbell's Station, a dozen miles southwest of Knoxville, and gave battle. He had no difficulty in holding his own against the enemy, although their line was more extended than his, for his artillery was in place while theirs had not yet come up. But when, late in the day, they brought their guns to the front, he was obliged to fall back to another strong position, which he held until his trains were safely under way, and in the night fell back still farther to the defences of Knoxville. In the action at Campbell's Station he had lost about three hundred men; the Confederate loss is unknown. Longstreet followed him slowly, and on the 17th of November sat down before the city. The place was strongly fortified, and although the Confederates by a quick assault carried a position on the right of Burnside's line, they did not materially impair his defences. In this affair Burnside lost about a hundred men, including Brig.-Gen. William P. Sanders killed. Longstreet's men skirmished and bombarded for ten days, at the end of which time, having been reinforced, he determined upon the experiment of a heavy assault. On the 28th of November he hurled three of his best brigades against an unfinished portion of the works on Burnside's left, where Gen. Edward Ferrero was in command. The assault was gallantly delivered, but was quite as gallantly met, and proved a failure, Longstreet losing about eight hundred men, including two colonels killed, while the defenders of the works lost but one hundred. A few days later Grant, having thoroughly defeated Bragg at Chattanooga, sent a force under Sherman to the relief of Knoxville, and Longstreet was obliged to abandon the siege, and returned to Virginia.

BREVET BRIGADIER-GENERAL CHRISTOPHER CARSON.
(Kit Carson.)

When, in June, it was learned that a Confederate force was about to make a raid upon the railroad in Northern Mississippi and destroy the bridges, Lieutenant-Colonel Phillips, of the Ninth Illinois Cavalry, was sent out to meet them with his own regiment and parts of the Fifth Ohio and Eighteenth Missouri. At Rocky Crossing, on the Tallahatchie, he encountered a Confederate force of two thousand men, infantry, cavalry, and artillery, under General Ruggles, and, although he had but six hundred men and no guns, he at once gave battle, and his men fought so spiritedly and skilfully that they drove off the enemy, inflicting a loss of one hundred and thirty-five in killed and wounded, and captured thirty prisoners, themselves losing about thirty-five men.

On the 16th of July, Jackson, capital of Mississippi, which had been besieged by Sherman's forces since the fall of Vicksburg, was evacuated by Johnston, who quietly moved away to the eastward, and the National troops took possession of the town. During the investment there had been no serious fighting, except on the 12th, when General Lauman's division, on Sherman's extreme right, attempted to make an advance and was repelled with heavy loss.

On the same day when Jackson was evacuated, Col. Cyrus Bussey, Sherman's chief of cavalry, was sent out with a thousand horsemen and a brigade of infantry to attack Jackson's cavalry, which was known to be near Canton. The enemy was discovered within two miles of that place, on the west side of Bear Creek, in a position to receive battle. Colonel Bussey immediately deployed his forces and attacked. The Confederates made several attempts to get by his flank and capture his train, but all were thwarted, and, after a somewhat stubborn fight, the whole body of Confederates was driven back through the woods and crossed the creek, destroying the bridge behind them. The next day Bussey moved into the town, and destroyed the forges and machinery that had long been employed in furnishing the Confederates with war materials. He also burned the railroad buildings, with all their contents, thirteen large machine shops, fifty cars, and other property. The retiring force of Confederates had already burned the depot and six hundred bales of cotton. Before the expedition returned it destroyed about forty miles of the railroad that was used by the Confederates for bringing supplies from the west.

On the 13th of October a National cavalry force, commanded by Colonel Hatch, consisting of twenty-five hundred men with eight guns, appeared before the town of Wyatt's, on the Tallahatchie, which was fortified and held by a strong Confederate force. The Confederates began in the afternoon with an attack on the National left, which was not successful. They then massed their forces and made a desperate attempt to break the centre, but were again foiled. Colonel Hatch slowly advanced his line, keeping up a wary fight until evening, when the Confederates retired under cover of darkness and crossed the river. Colonel Hatch lost about forty men and captured seventy-five prisoners, the Confederate loss in killed and wounded being unknown.

Arkansas was still the scene of occasional fighting, though always on a small scale. It furnished supplies to the Confederacy, and was in some respects a tempting field for foraging. Early in February a detachment of cavalry, commanded by Col. George E. Waring, Jr., made a raid in Arkansas and rode suddenly into the town of Batesville, attacked the Confederate force there, defeated it, and drove it out of the town. The Confederates fled in such haste that those who could not crowd into the boats swam the river. Colonel Waring then remounted his men with horses from the surrounding country.

On the 15th of the same month there was a fight at Arkadelphia between a small party of National troops and one of Confederates, in which about twenty men were disabled on each side.

On the 18th of April a Confederate force of cavalry, with a section of artillery and a considerable number of guerillas, made a night march from the Boston Mountains and attacked the

BRIGADIER-GENERAL WILLIAM DWIGHT COMMANDING AT THE BATTLE OF VERMILION BAYOU, LA.

(From an original drawing by James E. Taylor.)

National force at Fayetteville, Ark., commanded by Col. M. L. Harrison, of the First Arkansas cavalry. They charged up a deep ravine and made a desperate attempt to capture Colonel Harrison's headquarters; but he had had some intimation of their coming, and had promptly thrown his men into line for defence, so that every charge was gallantly repelled. The Confederates then tried an artillery fire without doing much damage, and finally a desperate cavalry charge upon Harrison's right wing, which was met by a most destructive fire that caused them to recoil and then to retreat in disorder to the woods. Harrison then sent out two companies, which went within rifle-range of the enemy's artillery and compelled them to withdraw their battery. Their wings were soon broken, but their centre still made a stubborn fight, until about noon that too gave way, and the whole force retreated. Harrison's loss was thirty-five men. That of the enemy was unknown, except that about sixty were captured and a considerable number were left dead or wounded on the field.

Helena, Ark., on the Mississippi, one hundred and fifty miles above Vicksburg, was held by a National force, under Gen. B. M. Prentiss, when on the 4th of July it was attacked by about nine thousand Confederates, under command of Generals Price and Holmes. Learning of their coming, General Prentiss drew his entire force within the fortifications. By a sudden rush, a detachment of the Confederates captured a battery, drove some of the infantry out of the rifle-pits, and were advancing into the town. But a portion of Prentiss's force was boldly pushed forward to check them, and those in possession of the battery were soon subjected to so severe a fire that they were glad to surrender. The Confederates had now planted guns upon commanding positions, with which they opened fire upon the works, but at the same time the gunboat *Tyler* had moved up to the scene and soon began sending its broadsides along the slopes and through the ravines that they occupied. Their batteries were ultimately silenced by this fire, and their infantry lost heavily. A heavy fog settling down caused a cessation of the engagement for some time, and when it lifted the fighting was resumed, the Confederates making desperate assaults upon the works and subjecting themselves to the terrible fire of the heavy guns. After several hours of this reckless work, they were drawn off, leaving their dead and wounded on the field and many prisoners. Prentiss's loss was two hundred and thirty; that of the Confederates, nearly two thousand, including the numerous prisoners. An incident is told that illustrates the character of the fighting. One assaulting column was led by a lieutenant-colonel who preceded his men, and was standing on a log waving his sword and yelling wildly, when the captain of the battery called out to him, "What do you keep swinging that sword for? why don't you surrender?" "By what authority do you demand my surrender?" said the Confederate officer. "By authority of my twelve-pound howitzer," replied the captain. The Confederate looked about him, saw that his command had melted away, and then held out his sword saying, "Very well, sir, I surrender."

On the 1st day of September there was a fight at a place called Devil's Backbone, sixteen miles from Fort Smith, between a portion of General Blunt's forces, under Colonel Cloud, and a Confederate force under Colonel Cabell, in which the latter was defeated and routed with a loss of about sixty men, the National loss being fourteen. This was an incident of the advance of General Blunt to Fort Smith, which place he occupied on the 10th. It had been in the possession of the Confederates since the beginning of the war.

The garrison at Pine Bluff, Ark., commanded by Col. Powell Clayton, was attacked on the 25th of October by a Confederate force under General Marmaduke. The Confederate skirmishers came forward with a flag of truce, met Lieutenant Clark of the Fifth Kansas cavalry outside of the town, and demanded a surrender. Clark replied, "Colonel Clayton never surrenders, but is always anxious for you to come and take him; and you must get to your command immediately, or I will order my men to fire on you." Clayton sent out skirmishers to delay the advance of the enemy, and then set three hundred negroes at work rolling out cotton bales and barricading the streets, while he placed nine guns in position to command every approach to the square. His sharp-shooters were posted in the houses, and he then set the negroes at work bringing water from the river and filling all the barrels they could find, so that, if necessary, he might sustain a siege. The enemy opened upon him with twelve guns, and in the course of two hours succeeded in setting fire to several buildings, some of which were destroyed before the flames were extinguished by the work of the negroes. Meanwhile, Clayton's sharp-shooters had fired at every Confederate that came within range, and succeeded in killing or wounding about one hundred and thirty of them. Finding that he could not set fire to the town, and could not assault the barricades without heavy loss, Marmaduke retired from the field. Whereupon Clayton sent out a pursuing force and captured some prisoners. Thirty-nine of Clayton's men and seventeen of the negroes were killed or wounded.

Missouri, a slave State almost surrounded by free territory, was still a ground of contention for small armed bands, although it had long since become evident that it could not be taken out of the Union.

The garrison at Springfield, commanded by Gen. E. B. Brown, was attacked by about five thousand men, under Marmaduke on the 8th of January. Outposts at Lawrence Mills and Ozark were driven in by the advancing enemy, while General Brown called in small reinforcements from various stations and made hasty preparation to defend the place. The convalescents in the hospitals were brought out and armed, and three guns were made ready in the night. The Confederates advanced slowly across the prairie, coming up in line of battle with three pieces of artillery and cavalry on the wings. General Brown ordered the burning of several houses south of the fort, to prevent their use by the enemy, and opened with his guns as soon as the Confederates came within range. Within an hour there was brisk fighting all along the line, with several charges and counter-charges, in one of which the Confederates captured a gun after a desperate fight. At the same time a detachment of them took possession of an unfinished stockade. The Confederates massed against the centre and the right wing successively, and gained possession of several houses, from one of which a sharp-shooter shot General Brown, wounding him so that he was carried from the field, when the command devolved upon Colonel Crabb. The fighting was kept up steadily with varying fortune, but with no decisive result, till dark, when the Confederates withdrew. The National loss in this action was one hundred and sixty-two men; the Confederate loss is unknown.

Three days later Marmaduke came into collision at Hartsville with a force of eight hundred men, commanded by Colonel Merrill, which was on the march for Springfield. Early in the morning Merrill learned of the approach of the Confederates, and threw his little command into line of battle. The Confederates came up and fought them for an hour, and then unaccountably fell back. Finding that they were moving on Hartsville by another road, Merrill moved to intercept them, and took another position close to the town. Here he was attacked about noon, first with artillery, and then in a cavalry charge. His infantry lay flat upon the ground until the Confederate horsemen were within easy range, when they rose and fired with such accuracy as to throw them all into confusion. For three hours the Confederates continued to attack in small bodies at a time, every one of which was repelled. In the afternoon, they slowly gave up the attempt and fell back, and at night they disappeared. Merrill lost about seventy-five men; the Confederates nearly three hundred. The credit of the victory was given largely to the artillery, which was served with great skill.

LIEUTENANT W. T. CLARK.

(Afterward Brigadier-General.)

One of the most horrible occurrences of the war was the sacking and burning of Lawrence, Kan., on the 21st of August, by the notorious band of Confederate guerillas led by Quantrell. They rode suddenly into the town, shooting right and left, indiscriminately, at whatever citizens they happened to meet, and then, spreading through the place, began systematic plunder. Where they could not get the keys of safes, they blew them open with powder. They took possession of the hotels and robbed the guests of everything valuable, even their finger-rings. Unarmed people, who gave up their money and surrendered, were in numerous instances wantonly shot. The guerillas appeared to have a special animosity against Germans and negroes, and murdered all of these that they could find. The only soldiers there were twenty-two men at a recruiting station, and eighteen of these were shot. After thoroughly sacking the town, the guerillas set many buildings on fire, and a large portion of it was destroyed. It was estimated that their plunder included about three hundred thousand dollars in cash.

The first action of the year in Louisiana was by a combined naval and land force, under Gen. Godfrey Weitzel and Commander McKean Buchanan, against the obstructions in Bayou Teche. It was found that the Confederates had a steam vessel of war, called the *J. A. Cotton*, there, that they had erected many batteries, and that they were now collecting forces above Donaldsonville. General Weitzel set out, with five regiments and three batteries, on the 11th of January, with the gunboats *Calhoun*, *Diana*, *Kinsman*, and *Estrella*, the cavalry and artillery going by land. They proceeded up the Atchafalaya, and on the 14th found the enemy. The gunboats steamed up to a point near the batteries and opened fire upon them, and received a fire in return, but without any special effect. Here a torpedo exploded under the *Kinsman* and lifted her violently out of water, yet without doing serious damage. Commander Buchanan then steamed ahead in his flagship, the *Diana*, when he was subjected to a fire from rifle-pits, and he was the first to fall, shot through the head. At this point the bayou was very narrow, so that the longest of the gunboats could hardly turn around in the channel. Meanwhile, the land forces had been put ashore on the side of the river where the batteries were located, and while one regiment gained the rear of the rifle-pits and drove out the Confederates, taking about forty prisoners, the three batteries passed around a piece of forest and took an advantageous position, from which they opened fire upon the steamer *Cotton*. This craft made a vain effort to fight these batteries, and was raked from stem to stern. She finally retired up the bayou and gave it up, and the next morning she floated down stream in flames. The expedition before returning captured a large number of cattle, but the obstructions to navigation of the bayou were not removed.

BRIGADIER-GENERAL JAMES CRAIG.

When Banks marched out to invest Port Hudson, a portion of his forces, under Gen. Godfrey Weitzel, made a long detour to the west from New Orleans and thence northward. At Franklin, on the Atchafalaya, a strong force of the enemy was found, and Weitzel at once attacked it, April 12th. There was spirited fighting with both infantry and artillery through the day, but with no decisive result, and at night the Confederates retreated toward Irish Bend. Here they met Grover's division, which had been sent there to cut off their retreat, and on the 14th there was another battle. The Twenty-fifth Connecticut Regiment, thrown out as a skirmish line, advanced to the edge of the woods, when they were met with a sharp musketry fire, and also came within range of the Confederate battery and the Confederate gunboat *Diana*. It was the first time that this regiment had been under fire, but the men stood to the work like veterans, and very soon a brigade, under Gen. Henry W. Birge, came to their support. Two guns were brought up, which answered the artillery fire of the enemy; but still the advance troops were suffering from a cross-fire, which was increased by the appearance of two Confederate

THE BATTLE OF INDIAN BEND. LA.

regiments on the right flank. One regiment was moved to the left, and advanced rapidly upon the battery, firing as it went, when the guns were soon whirled away to save them from capture. This regiment did capture the battery's flag, and was just resting in supposed victory, when another Confederate force came upon its flank, and it was hastily withdrawn. A second brigade was now sent to the assistance of the first, and the whole made a grand charge, before which the Confederates fled in disorder; and when a third brigade came up and threatened the capture of the gunboat *Diana*, her crew abandoned her and blew her up. Sixty prisoners were taken, and some artillery horses and many small arms. Out of three hundred and fifty men of the Twenty-fifth Connecticut Regiment, which took the leading part in this action, eighty-six were killed or wounded, and ten were missing. The Thirteenth Connecticut lost seven killed and forty-six wounded. Many instances of peculiar valor in this small but destructive battle are recorded. Of Lieut. Daniel P. Dewey, who was killed at the point where the hostile lines came nearest together, the adjutant wrote: "I saw him then, and the sight I shall never forget—waving his sword above his head, calling to his men, 'Remember you are Company A,' his whole bearing so brave and heroic that it seemed almost impossible for any enemy to avoid marking him. Standing unmoved in a rain of bullets, he had a word of encouragement for every man near him, kindly greeting for a friend, and even a merry quotation from a favorite song to fling after a shell that went shrieking by. So I last saw him, so I shall always remember him." Lieutenant Dewey had left his studies in Trinity College, Hartford, to enlist.

AN ENCOUNTER BETWEEN A UNION AND A CONFEDERATE SOLDIER.

COLONEL H. G. GIBSON.

BREVET BRIGADIER-GENERAL S. J. CRAWFORD.

At Vermilion Bayou there were several slight actions, the most considerable of which took place October 10th. The Confederates being discovered here to the number of six or seven thousand, together with two batteries and a cavalry force, the Nineteenth Corps advanced to take them. After cavalry skirmishing a line of battle was formed, and the Confederates were driven across the bayou. Three batteries of rifled guns were then brought up, and they were diligently shelled wherever there was any appearance of them on the shore or in the woods. The cavalry found a ford, and the infantry improvised a pontoon bridge, which was partly supported by the burned portions of the bridge that the enemy had used. The whole force then crossed the bayou, but was not able to overtake the flying Confederates. A report says: "The conduct of all concerned in this affair was excellent, and the most conspicuous of all was the gallant General Weitzel on his war-horse, riding boldly to the front, whither he had forbidden any other going on horseback. His appearance inspired the troops with the wildest enthusiasm, and the firing, which was warm and rapid before, seemed to redouble as he rode along the line."

In April, another expedition, commanded by Col. O. P. Gooding, consisting of one brigade, marched against the Confederate works on the Bayou Teche. As soon as they arrived in sight of the batteries, on the 13th, they were met by an artillery fire, which they returned at the same time that a large part of the infantry crossed the bayou and gained a position partly in the rear. Here they were met by a heavy skirmish line, which they gradually drove back into the works. A portion of the intrenchments were then carried by assault, when darkness put an end to the fight. In the morning it was found that the enemy had fled. One hundred and thirty of them had been made prisoners. Colonel Gooding's loss was seventy-two men, killed or wounded. One of the many instances of personal daring and skill that occurred in this great war is specially mentioned in the colonel's report. In the course of the fight Private Patrick Smith, of the Thirty-eighth Massachusetts Regiment, came suddenly upon three Confederate soldiers in the woods. He shot one, and compelled the other two to surrender, and brought them in as prisoners.

Galveston, Tex., had been occupied by National forces, and its harbor closed to blockade-running, in October, 1862. On the first day of January, 1863, a strong Confederate force, under Gen. John B. Magruder, attacked the fleet and the garrison, and succeeded in retaking the town and raising the blockade. The naval force there consisted of six gunboats, under Commander W. B. Renshaw. Three Confederate steamers were discovered in the bay by the bright moonlight of the preceding night, and very early in the morning they came down to attack the gunboats, while at the same time the land force attacked the garrison. The gunboat *Harriet Lane* was set upon by two Confederate steamers, which were barricaded with cotton bales, and carried rifled guns, besides a large number of sharp-shooters on the decks. The *Harriet Lane* made a gallant fight, and was rammed by one of the steamers, which so injured itself in the collision that it ran for the shore and sank. The other steamer then ran into the *Harriet Lane*, made fast to her, sent volleys of musketry across her deck, and boarded her. She was quickly captured; but her commander, J. M. Wainwright, refused to surrender, and defended himself with his revolver until he was killed. The first lieutenant and five of the crew also fell. The *Owasco*, going to the assistance of the *Harriet Lane*, got aground several times, and finally, seeing that the guns of the *Harriet Lane* were turned upon her, drew off, but continued the engagement with the enemy on shore. The other gunboats had a similar ill-fortune, and when some of them finally arrived within range of the *Harriet Lane* they were prevented from firing upon her by the fact that the Confederates exposed her captured crew on deck. Flags of truce, demanding surrender, were now sent in by the Confederates, who used the opportunity while operations were thus suspended to capture the garrison on shore, and get artillery into position to fire upon the gunboats. Commander Renshaw declined to surrender, and ordered his executive officer to blow up the *Westfield*, in case she could not be got afloat. Arrangements for this were made, and the explosion took place prematurely, killing Commander Renshaw, two other officers, and a dozen of the crew. The remaining gunboats escaped and abandoned the blockade. General Magruder then issued a proclamation declaring the port opened to commerce.

The minor events of the third year included a few naval affairs of some importance in their way. On the 14th of January guerillas captured the steamer *Forest Queen* at Commerce, Miss., and destroyed her. The privateer *Nashville* had been for some time blockaded by Du Pont's vessels, where she lay under the guns of Fort McAllister, Ga. She made several unsuccessful attempts to get to sea, and finally, on the 27th of February, Commander John L. Worden, perceiving that she had grounded, moved up rapidly with the iron-clad *Montauk*, and at twelve hundred yards fired into her with eleven-inch and fifteen-inch shells. Several of these exploded inside of the *Nashville* and set her on fire. She burned until the flames reached her magazine, when she was blown into fragments. Worden had been assisted by three wooden vessels of the blockading fleet, which kept down the fire of the battery. On the Nansemond River, Va., in April, one of the National gunboats, the *Mount Washington*, being disabled, the Confederate gunboats came down to attack her, using both artillery and sharp-shooters. Lieut. William B. Cushing, commanding the *Barney*, went to her assistance, and after a sharp fight drove off the Confederate boats and brought away the *Mount Washington* in tow. Three of his men were killed and seven wounded. He says in his report: "It is only requisite to look at the *Mount Washington* to see with what desperate gallantry Lieutenant Lampson fought his vessel."

The troubles with Indians, which reached their height in the Minnesota massacres of 1862, continued to some extent through 1863. In July a body of troops, commanded by Lieut.-Col. William R. Marshall, had a severe fight with them at a place called Big Mound, in Dakota. The Indians were posted among the rocky ridges and ravines of the summit range, and Marshall was obliged to make several detours to flank them as he drove them successively from one ridge to another. At the same time a detachment under Major Bradley had fought them on another ridge, and finally, in a desultory fight that lasted from four o'clock in the morning till nine o'clock at night, the Indians were completely routed and scattered. Colonel Marshall lost eight men, including a surgeon who was murdered before the fight, and killed or wounded about one hundred of the Indians. In September there were several other engagements of the usual character with the Indians, in Dakota, the most considerable of them taking place at Whitestone Hill. Here Gen. Alfred Sully's command attacked a party of Indians who had been murdering and plundering, and not only defeated them and put them to flight, but captured much of the property of the Indians, including dogs, tents, and a large quantity of dried buffalo meat, all of which he burned. He took more than one hundred Indians prisoners. On the 8th of July there was a fight near Fort Halleck, Idaho, between the garrison of the fort and a party of Ute Indians. The engagement had lasted two hours, when the soldiers, led by Lieutenant Williams, made a charge that finished the battle, and the Indians fled to the mountains. Sixty of the Indians had been killed or wounded, and half a dozen of the soldiers.

One of the incidents of this year well illustrates the true method of dealing with a contingency that arises in nearly every war. General Burnside had ordered the execution of two Confederate officers who were detected in recruiting for their army within his lines—in other words, inducing his men to desert. In this action he followed strictly the laws of war. When it became known to the Confederate authorities, they ordered that two captains should be selected by lot from among the prisoners held in Libby, for execution in retaliation. The order was transmitted to the keepers of the prison, who proceeded to carry it out, and three chaplains among the prisoners were appointed to conduct the drawing. The lot fell upon Capt. Henry W. Sawyer, of the Second New Jersey cavalry, and Captain Flynn, of the Fifty-first Indiana Regiment. The Richmond *Despatch* said in its report: "Sawyer heard the decision with no apparent emotion, remarking that some one had to be drawn, and he could stand it as well as any one else. Flynn was very white and much depressed." The two condemned men were conveyed to the headquarters of General Winder, who warned them not to be deluded by any hope of escape, as the retaliatory punishment would certainly be inflicted eight days from that time. Captain Sawyer obtained permission to write to his wife, on condition, of course, that the letter should be read by the prison authorities. In this letter, after telling what had been done, he wrote: "The Provost-General, J. H. Winder, assures me that the Secretary of War of the Southern Confederacy will permit yourself and my dear children to visit me before I am executed. You will be permitted to bring an attendant. Captain Whilldin, or uncle W. W. Ware, or Dan, had better come with you. My situation is hard to be borne, and I cannot think of dying without seeing you and the children. I am resigned to whatever is in store for me, with the consolation that I die without having committed any crime. I have no trial, no jury, nor am I charged with any crime, but it fell to my lot. You will proceed to Washington. My Government will give you transportation to Fortress Monroe, and you will get here by a flag of truce, and return the same way." Sawyer and Flynn were then placed in close confinement in a dungeon under ground, where they were fed on corn-bread and water, the dungeon being so damp that their clothing mildewed. Captain Sawyer's letter had precisely the effect that he intended—his wife immediately went to Washington with it, and laid it before the President and the Secretary of War. It happened at this time, that among the Confederate officers who were held as prisoners by the National authorities were a son of General Lee and a son of General Winder, and Secretary Stanton immediately ordered that these officers be placed in close confinement, as hostages for the safety of Sawyer and Flynn, while notification was sent by flag of truce to the Confederate Government, that, immediately upon receiving information of the execution of Sawyer and Flynn, Lee and Winder would be likewise executed. The result was what it always is when prompt and sufficient retaliation is prepared for in such cases—none of the men were executed, and within three weeks Captains Flynn and Sawyer were placed again on the same footing as other prisoners in Libby. During the war, whenever there was a proposal of retaliation for an outrage, there was always an outcry against it, on the ground that it would only result in double murders. Those who made such outcries could not have read history very attentively, or they would have known that the result has always been exactly the opposite of that.

CHAIN BRIDGE OVER THE POTOMAC RIVER, NEAR WASHINGTON.

(From a War-time Photograph.)

CONSTRUCTING WINTER QUARTERS, ARMY OF THE POTOMAC.

CHAPTER XXXI.

THE OVERLAND CAMPAIGN.

GRANT MADE LIEUTENANT-GENERAL WITH COMMAND OF ALL THE ARMIES—HEADQUARTERS WITH THE ARMY OF THE POTOMAC—PLAN OF THE CAMPAIGN—POSITION OF THE ARMIES—RELATIVE NUMBERS—A GREAT ARMY IN WINTER QUARTERS—PICTURESQUE AND INTERESTING DETAILS OF CAMP LIFE—GRANT CROSSES THE RAPIDAN—BATTLE OF THE WILDERNESS—BATTLE OF SPOTTSYLVANIA—BATTLE OF COLD HARBOR—THE LOSSES OF BOTH SIDES—GRANT CROSSES THE JAMES—CAVALRY OPERATIONS—CRITICISMS OF GENERAL GRANT—GENERAL LONGSTREET WOUNDED—EWELL SEES THE END.

AT the close of the third year of the war—the winter of 1863–4—it was evident to all thoughtful citizens that something was lacking in its conduct. To those who understood military operations on a large scale this had been apparent long before. It was true that there had been great successes as well as great failures. Both of Lee's attempts at invasion of the North had resulted disastrously to him—the one at the Antietam, the other at Gettysburg; and when he recrossed the Potomac the second time, with half of his army disabled, it was morally certain that he would invade no more. Grant, first coming into notice as the captor of an army in February, 1862, had captured another, more than twice as large, in the summer of 1863, thus securing the stronghold of Vicksburg, and enabling the Mississippi, as Lincoln expressed it, to flow unvexed to the sea. Later in the same year he had won a brilliant victory over Bragg at Chattanooga, securing that important point and relieving East Tennessee. New Orleans, by far the largest city in the South, had been firmly held by the National forces ever since Farragut captured it, in April, 1862. There were also numerous points on the coast of the Carolinas, Georgia, and Florida where the Stars and Stripes floated every day in assertion of the nation's claim to supreme authority. Missouri, Kentucky, Maryland, West Virginia, and Tennessee—all confidently counted upon by the Confederates at the outset—were now hopelessly lost to them. Though it had seemed, from the reports of the great battles, and the manner in which they were discussed, that the Confederates must be making headway, yet a glance at the map showed that the territory covered by Confederate authority had been steadily diminishing. Only one recapture of any consequence had taken place, and that was in Texas. Faulty though it was, if the military process thus far pursued by the Administration had been kept up, it must ultimately have destroyed the Confederacy. And there was no military reason (using the word in its narrow sense) why it could not be kept up; for the resources of the North, in men and material, were not seriously impaired. All the farms were tilled, all the workshops were busy, the colleges had almost their usual number of students; and there were not nearly so many young women keeping books or standing behind counters as now. Moreover, the ports of the North were all open, and the markets of the world accessible. It is true that the currency and the national securities were at a discount, and it was certain that their value would be diminished still further by the prolongation of the war; but this was not fatal so long as our own country produced everything essential, and it was equally certain that with a restored Union the national credit would be so high that we could take

POPLAR GROVE CHURCH.

(Built by the United States Military Engineer Corps.)

our own time about paying the debt, distributing the burden over as many generations as we chose.

The necessity for a swifter process was more political than military. There was a half-informed populace to be satisfied, and a half-loyal party to be silenced. The subtlest foe was in our own household; and the approach of the Presidential and Congressional elections, unless great National victories should intervene, might bring its opportunity and seal the fate of the Republic.

IN WINTER QUARTERS.

The one thing required was a single supreme military head for all the armies in the field. The faulty disposition by which, in many of the great battles, the several parts of an army had struck the enemy successively instead of all at once, existed also on the grander scale. There was no concert of action between the armies of the East, the West, and the Southwest; so that large detachments of the Confederate forces were sent back and forth on their shorter interior lines, to fight wherever they were most needed. Thus Longstreet's powerful corps was at one time engaged in Pennsylvania, a little later besieging Burnside in Tennessee, and again with Lee in Virginia. Not only was the need for a supreme commander apparent, but it was now no longer possible to doubt who was the man. We had one general that from the first had gone directly for the most important objects in his department, and thus far had secured everything he went for. Accordingly Congress passed a bill reviving the grade of lieutenant-general in February, 1864, and President Lincoln promptly conferred that rank upon General Ulysses S. Grant. Only Washington and Scott had previously borne this commission in the United States service, and through three years of the war we had nothing higher than a major-general in the field. Rank was cheaper in the Confederacy, where there were not only lieutenant-generals, but several full generals. The corps commanders in Lee's army, at the head of ten thousand or fifteen thousand men, had nominally the same rank (lieutenant-general) as Grant when he assumed command of all the National forces in the field. When Lincoln handed Grant his commission, they met for the first time. A year and a month later the war was ended, Grant was the foremost soldier in the world, and Lincoln was in his grave. When the question of headquarters arose, General Sherman, who was one of the warmest of Grant's personal friends as well as his ablest lieutenant, besought him to remain in the West, for he feared the Washington influences that had always been most heavily felt in the army covering the capital. General Sherman, never afraid of anything else, was always in mortal terror of politicians. Grant appears not to have feared even the politicians; for he promptly fixed his headquarters with the Army of the Potomac, thus placing himself where, on the one hand, he could withstand interference that might thwart the operations of a subordinate, and where, on the other, he would personally conduct the campaign against the strongest army of the Confederacy and its most trusted leader.

PICKETS EXAMINING PASSES.

He planned a campaign in which he considered the Army of the Potomac his centre; the Army of the James, under General Butler, his left wing; the Western armies, now commanded by Sherman, his right wing; and the army under Banks in Louisiana, a force operating in the rear of the enemy. In its great feat-

WHARF AT BELLE PLAIN, VA.

ures, the plan was this: that all should move simultaneously—Butler against Petersburg, to seize the southern communications of the Confederate capital; Sherman against Johnston's army (then at Dalton, Ga.), to defeat and destroy it if possible, or at least to force it back and capture Atlanta with its workshops and important communications; Banks to set out on an expedition toward Mobile, to capture that city and close its harbor to blockade-runners; Sigel to drive back the Confederate force in the Shenandoah valley, and prevent that fertile region from being used any longer as a Confederate granary; while the Army of the Potomac, taking Lee's army for its objective, should follow it wherever it went, fighting and flanking it until it should be captured or dispersed.

South of the Rapidan is a peculiar region twelve or fifteen miles square, known as the Wilderness. Some of the earliest iron-works in the country were here, and much of the ground was dug over for the ore, while the woods were cut off to supply fuel for the furnaces. A thick second growth sprang up, with tangled underbrush; the mines were deserted, the furnaces went to decay, and the whole region was desolate, save a roadside tavern or two, and here and there a little clearing. Chancellorsville, where a great battle was fought in May, 1863, was upon the eastern edge of this Wilderness. The bulk of Lee's army was now (May, 1864) upon its western edge, with a line of observation along the Rapidan, and headquarters at Orange Court-House. The Army of the Potomac was north of the Rapidan, opposite the Wilderness, where it had lain since November, when it had crossed to the south side with the purpose of attacking the Army of Northern Virginia (as narrated in a previous chapter), but found it too strongly intrenched along Mile Run, and so recrossed and went into winter quarters.

The conduct of affairs where a great army lies in winter quarters, making a peculiar sort of community by itself, has its picturesque and interesting details and incidents, as well as its general dulness. The reader may get a suggestive glimpse of the camp on the north side of the Rapidan that winter, if he will look at it through the eyes of Captain Blake:

"The army steadily advanced in successive years from river to river, and erected its winter quarters upon the banks of the Potomac, the Rappahannock, and the Rapidan. The headquarters were established at the same point that had been occupied by Lee, and the staff which he left in his hasty flight was unadorned; while the American flag daily ascended and descended the high pole when the call 'to the color' was sounded at sunrise and sunset. The telegraph office in the town was occupied by the same operator for the fifth time in the various changes that had taken place in the position of the army—the rebels always possessed it for a similar purpose as soon as it was abandoned; and both parties used the same table, and several miles of the same wire. Operations against the enemy, and drills, were suspended during the inclement season; and details to guard the trains, the camps, and the picket-lines, and labor upon the roads, comprised the routine of duty. Courts-martial assembled frequently to determine the nature and punishment of military crimes; and one tribunal, of which the author was judge-advocate, tried about forty men for misconduct in skulking from Mine Run; and a chaplain was found guilty of stealing a horse, and dismissed from the service by order of the President.

"The face of the country soon assumed the barren aspect of Falmouth; and the pickets of the brigade, for a month, made their fires of the woodwork of corn-shelling, threshing, and the numerous other machines with which a large farm was supplied; and iron rods, bolts, ploughshares, cranks, and cogwheels were sprinkled upon the ground in the vicinity of the posts. The fifteen hundred inhabitants that lived in Culpeper before the Rebellion had been reduced to only eighty persons, who were chiefly dependent upon the Government for the means of sustenance. The court-house and slave-pen had been gutted, and were used as places of confinement for rebel prisoners. The fences that enclosed the cemeteries which were attached to the churches had been torn down and burned; and sinks, booths, stables for horses, and the fires of the cooks were scattered in the midst of the gravestones and tombs. The state of destitution that prevailed may be illustrated more clearly by quoting the remark of a young woman who resided in the place: 'My father was worth three hundred thousand dollars; but all his people, except a small boy, ran away with your folks; his large house was burned by your cavalry; we eat your pork and bread; and, just think of it, I haven't had a new dress or bonnet since the war began!' The refugees and their families constantly entered the lines; and one of them said that he was assisted by a friend, who gave him his horse, and manifested much indignation and declared that the animal had been stolen, to mislead the neighbors, when he received the news of his successful escape. Deserters exhausted their ingenuity in finding ways to reach the cavalry videttes; and some gladly swam across the Rappahannock in the coldest nights of the year.

"The old residents asserted that the ground upon which the division had encamped was always submerged in winter, and it would be impossible for the men to remain there until spring: but the barracks were never swept away by any inundation; and they explained the matter by saying that it was the dryest season that had existed for thirty years. The results of one severe rain, that deluged the plain, showed that, if they were often repeated, all persons would perceive the wisdom of the warning. The river rose and overflowed the swamp so suddenly that the members of seven posts which were located near it were obliged to climb trees to avoid the unlooked-for danger of drowning; and the brief tour of picket duty was extended many hours. Squads that were not stationed in the forest found themselves upon an island, and waded through the deep water a long distance; and some were compelled to swim to reach the reserve upon what was the mainland. A small stream was enlarged to the dimensions of a lake one-fourth of a mile in width; and a part of the cavalry provost-camp was submerged, and an officer discovered that the rushing water was two feet deep in his tent when he awoke. The weather-wisers always glanced at the mountains; and the voices of experience uttered the following precept—that there would be rain once in every two days as long as the snow crowned the crests of the Blue Ridge.

"During this period the enemy did not attempt to make any movement, although a long line of railroad conveyed supplies from Alexandria; and the troops of Lee labored unceasingly, and constructed miles of earthworks upon the bluffs that had been fortified by nature; while the Union forces rested in their camps, and relied for defence upon the strong arm and loyal heart. A number of false alarms occurred, and the soldiers were sometimes ordered to be in readiness to march at a second's notice to resist an advance.

"The number of officers' wives and other ladies that were present in the camps was much larger than at any previous period; and balls and similar festivities relieved the monotony of many winter quarters. Large details, that sometimes comprised a thousand men, were ordered to report at certain headquarters for the purpose of constructing suitable halls of logs on the 'sacred soil' of Virginia. A chapel was built within the limits of the brigade by the soldiers, who daily labored upon it for three weeks; and many of the officers contributed money to purchase whatever appeared to be required for it. An agent of the Christian Commission furnished a capacious tent, which formed the roof; and religious, temperance, and Masonic meetings were frequently held, until this apostle, who employed most of his time in writing long letters for the press, that portrayed in vivid colors the 'good work' which he was accomplishing, removed the canvas because an innocent social assembly occupied it during one evening. The enlisted men, who rarely enjoyed the benefit of these structures which they erected, originated dances of a singular character. By searching the cabins and houses of the natives, and borrowing apparel, and a liberal use of pieces of shelter tents and the hoops of barrels, one-half of the soldiers were arrayed as women, and filled the places of the seemingly indispensable partners of the gentler sex. The resemblance in the features of some of these persons were so perfect that a stranger would be unable to distinguish between the assumed and the genuine characters.

IN THE WILDERNESS

"Thousands of crows rendered good service by devouring the entrails of animals which had been slaughtered by the butchers, and the carcasses of dead horses and mules. They were never shot, because the citizens had no guns, and the soldiers would be punished if they wasted ammunition; and they grew tame and fat in opposition to the well-known saying, and propagated so rapidly that their immense numbers blackened acres of ground in the vicinity of the camps. One noticeable event was a fire which swept over the field of Cedar Mountain, and caused the explosion of shells that had remained there nearly two years after the battle.

"The ordinary preparations for active operations were made as soon as the roads became dry and hard: the ladies were notified to leave the camps previous to a specified date; surplus baggage resumed its annual visit to the storehouses in the rear; and reviews, inspections, and target-practice daily took place."

The Army of the Potomac was now organized in three infantry corps, the Second, Fifth, and Sixth—commanded respectively by Gens. Winfield S. Hancock, Gouverneur K. Warren, and John Sedgwick—and a cavalry corps commanded by Gen. Philip H. Sheridan; Gen. George G. Meade being still in command of the whole. Burnside's corps, the Ninth, nearly twenty thousand strong, was at Annapolis, and nobody but General Grant knew its destination. President Lincoln and his Cabinet thought it was to be sent on some duty down the coast; and so perhaps did the enemy. Grant knew too well that there was a leak somewhere in Washington, through which every Government secret escaped to the Confederates; and he therefore delayed till the last moment the movement of Burnside's corps to a point from which it could follow the Army of the Potomac across the Rapidan within twenty-four hours.

The Army of Northern Virginia consisted of two infantry corps, commanded by Gens. Richard S. Ewell and Ambrose P. Hill, with a cavalry corps commanded by Gen. James E. B. Stuart; the whole commanded by Gen. Robert E. Lee; while, as an offset to Burnside's corps, Gen. James Longstreet's was within call. The exact number of men in either army cannot be told, as reports and authorities differ; nor can the approximate numbers be mentioned fairly, unless with an explanation. The method of counting for the official reports was different in the two armies. In the National army, a report that a certain number of men were present for duty included every man that was borne on the pay-rolls, whether officer, soldier, musician, teamster, cook, or mechanic, and also all that had been sent away on special duty, guarding trains and the like. This was necessary, because they were all paid regularly, and the money had to be accounted for. In the Confederate army there was no pay worth speaking of, and the principal object of a morning report was to show the exact effective force available that day; accordingly, the Confederate reports included only the men actually bearing muskets or sabres, or handling the artillery. Counted in this way, Lee had sixty thousand, or perhaps sixty-five thousand, men—for exact reports are wanting, even on that basis. If counted after the fashion in the National army, his men numbered about eighty thousand. Grant puts his own numbers, everything included, at one hundred and sixteen thousand, and thinks the preponderance was fully offset by the fact that the enemy was on the defensive, seldom leaving his intrenchments, in a country admirably suited for defence, and with the population friendly to him. As each side received reinforcements from time to time about equal to its losses, the two armies may be considered as having, throughout the campaign from the Rapidan to the James, the strength just stated.

It was clearly set forth by General Grant at the outset that the true objective was the Army of Northern Virginia. In that lay the chief strength of the Confederacy; while that stood, the Confederacy would stand, whether in Richmond or out of it; when that fell, the Confederacy would fall. To follow that army wherever it went, fight it, and destroy it, was the task that lay before the Army of the Potomac; and every man in the army, as well as most men in the country, knew it was a task that could be accomplished only through immense labor and loss of life, hard marching, heavy fighting, and all manner of suffering.

The intention was to have the simultaneous movement of all the armies begin as near the 1st of May as possible. It actually began at midnight of the 3d, when the Army of the Potomac was set in motion and crossed the Rapidan, which is there about two hundred feet wide, on five pontoon bridges near Germania, Culpeper Mine, and Ely's fords. On crossing, it plunged at once into the Wilderness, which is here traversed from north to south by two roads, a mile or two apart. And these roads are crossed by two—the Orange turnpike and Orange plank road—running nearly east and west. Besides these, there are numerous cross-roads and wood-paths. It would have been easy for the army to pass through this wooded tract in a very few hours, and deploy in the open country; but the supply and ammunition train consisted of four thousand wagons, and the reserve artillery of more than one hundred guns—all of which must be protected by keeping the army between them and the enemy. Consequently the troops remained in the Wilderness during the whole of the 4th, while the long procession was filing across the bridges and stretching away on the easternmost roads. And after this the bridges themselves were taken up. Grant's headquarters that night were at the old Wilderness Tavern, on the Orange turnpike, near the intersection of the road from Germania Ford. It had been supposed that Lee would either dispute the passage of the river, or (as he had done on previous occasions) await attack on some chosen ground that was suitable for fighting. As he had not disputed the passage, the army now expected to march out of the Wilderness the next day, thus turning the enemy's right flank, and placing itself between him and his capital.

But Grant kept pickets out on all the roads to the west; and it cannot be said that he was surprised, though he was probably disappointed, when he found his lines attacked on the morning of the 5th. The movement was believed at first to be only a feint, intended to keep the Army of the Potomac in the Wilderness, while the bulk of the enemy should slip by to the south and take up a position covering the approach to Richmond. But it was developed rapidly, and it soon became evident that the Confederate commander had resorted to the bold device of launching his whole army down the two parallel roads, with the purpose of striking the Army of the Potomac when it was ill-prepared to receive battle. Under some circumstances he would thus have gained a great advantage; as it was, the army was clear of the river, with all its trains safe in the rear, was reasonably well together, had had a night's rest, and was not in any proper sense surprised. Hancock's corps, which had the lead and was marching out of the Wilderness, was quickly recalled, Burnside's was hurried up from the rear, and a line of battle was formed—so far as there could be any line of battle in a jungle. Neither artillery nor cavalry could be used to any extent by either side, and the contest was little more than a murdering-match between two bodies of men, each individual having a musket in his hand, and being unable to see more than a few of his nearest neighbors. This went on all day, increasing hourly as more of the troops came into position, with no real advantage to either side when night fell upon the gloomy forest, already darkened by smoke that there was no breeze to waft away. Lee's attack had been vigorous on his left, but imperfect on his right, where Longstreet's corps did not get up in time to participate in the fighting that day. No sooner had the battle ended than both sides began to intrench for the struggle of the morrow, and they would hear the sound of each other's axes, only a few rods distant, as they worked through the night, cutting down trees, piling up logs for breastworks, and digging the customary trench.

Grant intended to take the initiative on the morning of the 6th, and gave orders for an attack at five o'clock. But Lee, who did not want the real battle of the day to begin till Longstreet's corps should be in place on his right, attacked

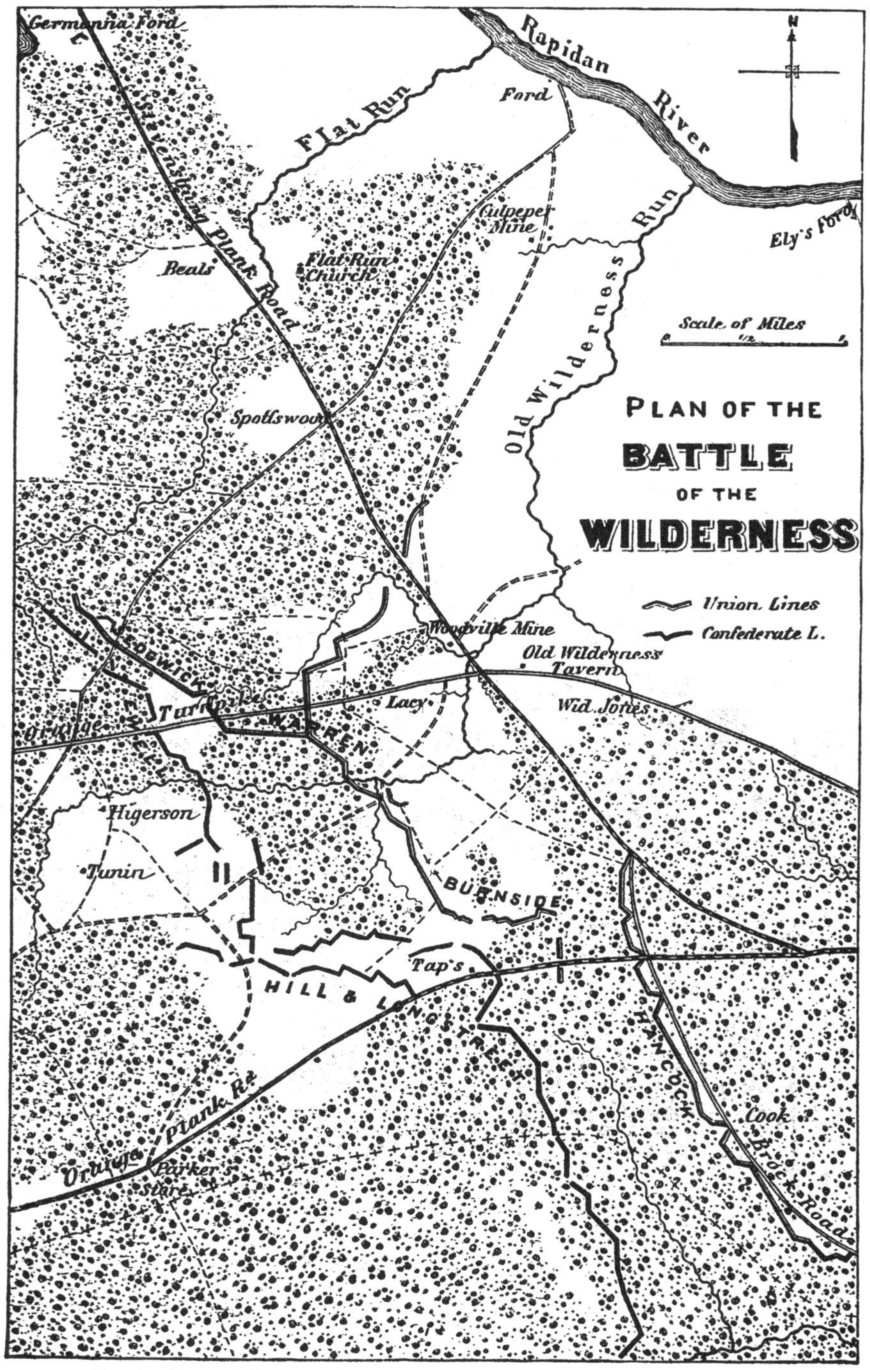

Reproduced by permission of Dick & Fitzgerald, N. Y., from "Twelve Decisive Battles of the War."

with his left at a still earlier hour. Grant recognized this as a feint, and went on with his purpose of attacking the enemy's right before Longstreet should come up. This work devolved upon Hancock's corps, which, as usual, was ready to advance at the hour named; but just then came rumors of a flank movement by Longstreet, and Hancock, detaching troops to meet it, greatly weakened the blow he was ordered to deliver. This was all a mistake, as there was no enemy in that direction, save Rosser's Confederate cavalry, which Sheridan's defeated that day in three encounters. But Hancock's advance was powerful enough to drive the enemy before him for more than a mile. At that juncture Longstreet came up, the broken Confederate line rallied on his corps, and Hancock was driven back in turn. Here the fighting was stubborn, and the losses heavy. Gen. James S. Wadsworth, one of the most patriotic men in the service, was mortally wounded, and died within the Confederate lines. The Confederate General Jenkins was killed, and Longstreet was seriously wounded in almost exactly the same way that Stonewall Jackson had been, a year and three days before, on nearly the same ground. As he was returning from the front with his staff, some of his own men mistook them for National cavalry and fired upon them. Longstreet was shot through the neck and shoulder, and had to be carried from the field. His men had been thrown into great confusion, and General Lee, who now took command of them in person, found it impossible to rally them for an attack on Hancock's intrenchments, or at least deferred the attack that had been planned. But late in the afternoon such an assault was made, and met with a little temporary success.

LIEUTENANT-GENERAL ULYSSES S. GRANT.

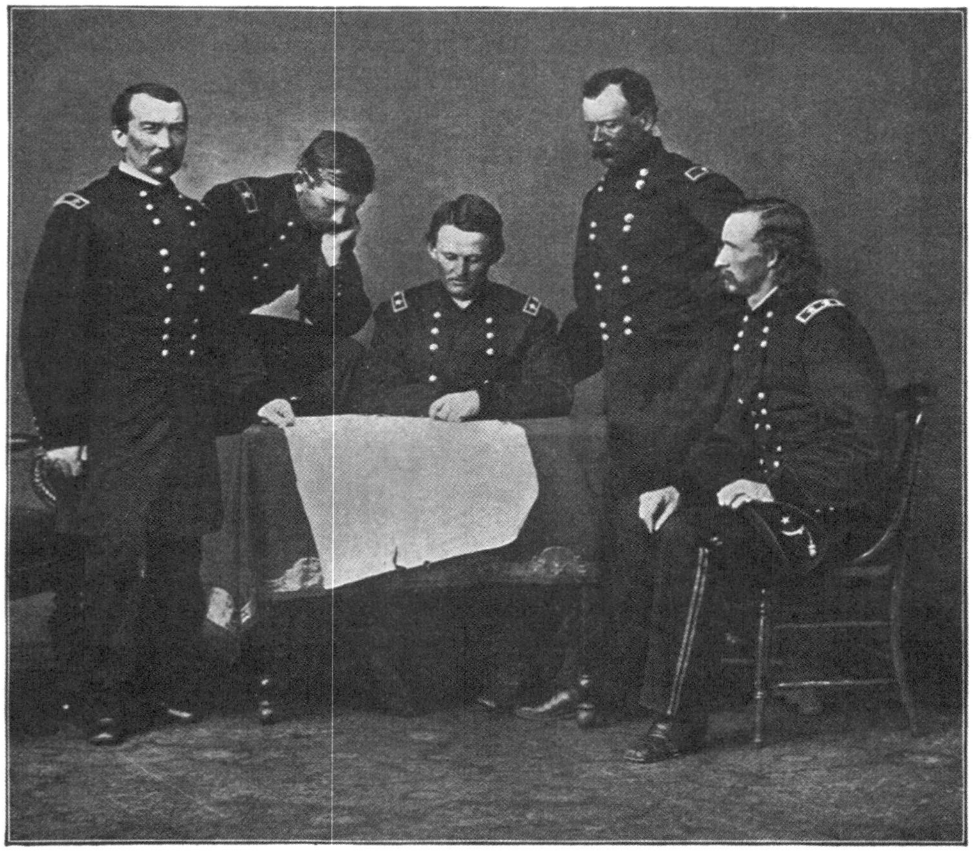

MAJOR-GENERAL PHILIP H. SHERIDAN. BRIGADIER-GENERAL THOMAS C. DEVIN.
BRIGADIER-GENERAL J. I. GREGG. BREVET MAJOR-GENERAL GEORGE A. CUSTER.
MAJOR-GENERAL WESLEY MERRITT.

The Confederates burst through the line at one point, but were soon driven back again with heavy loss. At this time a fire broke out in Hancock's front, and soon his log breastworks were burning. His men were forced back by the heat, but continued firing at their enemy through the flame. Large numbers of the dead and wounded were still lying where they fell, scattered over the belt of ground, nearly a mile wide, where the tide of battle had swayed back and forth, and an unknown number of the wounded perished by the fire and smoke. Burnside had come into line during the day, and fighting had been kept up along the entire front, but it was nowhere so fierce as on the left or southern end of the line, where each commander was trying to double up the other's flank. At night the Confederates withdrew to their intrenchments, and from that time till the end of the campaign they seldom showed a disposition to leave them.

The terrible tangle of the Wilderness in which this great battle was fought is indicated by the fact that in several instances squads from either army, who were guarding prisoners and intending to take them to the rear, lost their way and carried them into their opponents' lines, where the guards in turn became prisoners. A participant says of the fighting on the National right, where the Confederates gained some ground the first day: "The extreme heat of the day increased the fatigue, and tears were shed by some who overrated the results of the disaster. The slaughter in many regiments had been large, and at one point the bodies of the killed defined with terrible exactness the position held by the Union troops, and a long line of rebel corpses was extended in front of it. One of the flag-staffs of the regiment was severed by a bullet, and each hand of the bearer grasped a piece of it." The same participant says of the fighting on his part of the line during the second day:

"The division was posted once more behind the slight breastwork which had been erected upon the Germania-Ford road; the skirmishers were deployed in its front at four P.M., and the author commanded the detachment from the regiment. The groups were properly aligned within the next ten minutes, when the tramp of a heavy force resounded through the woods. Orders were excitedly repeated—'Forward!' 'Guide right!' 'Close up those intervals!'—and finally a voice shouted: 'Now, men, for the love of God and your country, forward!' The legions of Longstreet advanced without skirmishers; the muskets of the feeble line were discharged to alarm the reserve; the men upon the outposts rushed to the main body; and thousands of glistening gun-barrels which were resting upon the works opened, and the fusillade began. The soldiers crouched upon the ground, loaded their pieces with the utmost celerity, rose, fired, and then reloaded behind the shelter; so that the loss was very slight; while the enemy suffered severely, as the trees were small, and there was no protection. The only artillery that was used in the afternoon was planted upon the left of the brigade, and consisted of four cannons, which hurled canister, shell, and solid shot until their ammunition was exhausted. Unfortunately, the dry logs of which the breastwork was formed were only partially covered with earth; and the flames, ignited by the burning wadding during the conflict (an enemy that could not be resisted as easily as the myrmidons of Longstreet), destroyed them, and every second of time widened the breaches. The undaunted men crowded together until they formed fourteen or sixteen ranks; and those who were in the front discharged the guns which were constantly passed to them by their comrades that were in the rear and could not aim with accuracy or safety. The fingers of many men were blistered by the muskets, which became hot from the rapid firing. The fire triumphed when it flashed along the entire barrier of wood, reduced it to ashes, and forced the defenders, who had withstood to the last its intolerable heat, to retire to the rifle-pits a short distance in the rear. The shattered rebel columns cautiously approached the road; but the impartial flames which had caused the discomfiture of the division became an obstacle that they could not surmount. The same misfortune followed the Union forces, and no exertions could check the consuming element; and the second line was burned like the first. The conflagration in the road had nearly ceased at this time; the enemy yelled with exultation; the odious colors were distinctly seen when the smoke slowly disappeared; a general charge was made, which resulted in the capture of the original position; and the pickets were stationed half of a mile in the advance at sunset without opposition. Many were eating their dinners when the assault commenced; and an officer hurriedly rushed to the works with a spoon in one hand and a fork in the other."

COLONEL WILLIAM H. MORRIS.

BREVET BRIGADIER-GENERAL THOMAS A. SMYTH.

BRIGADIER-GENERAL JOSHUA J. OWENS.

The losses in this great two-days' battle cannot be stated accurately. The best authorities vary as to the National loss, from fewer than fourteen thousand—killed, wounded, and missing—to about fifteen thousand four hundred. As to the Confederate loss, the figures can only be made up from partial reports, estimates, and inferences. According to these, it did not differ materially from the National loss, and in the circumstances of the battle there was no reason for thinking it would. Among the officers lost, besides those already mentioned, were, on the National side, Gen. Alexander Hays killed; Generals Getty, Baxter, and McAllister, and Colonels Carroll and Keifer wounded; and Generals Seymour and Shaler captured; on the Confederate side, Generals Pegram and Benning wounded.

If General Lee supposed that the Army of the Potomac, after a sudden blow and a bloody battle, would turn about and go home to repair damages—as it had been in the habit of doing—he omitted from his calculation the fact that it was now led by a soldier who never did anything of the sort. Indeed, he is reported to have said to his lieutenants, after this costly experiment: "Gentlemen, at last the Army of the Potomac has a head." Tactically, it had been a drawn battle. Grant accounts it a victory, which he says "consisted in having successfully crossed a formidable stream, almost in the face of an enemy, and in getting the army together as a unit." It was also a National victory in a certain dismal sense, from the fact that—in changing off man for man to the extent of twelve or fifteen thousand—that had been done which the enemy could least afford.

There was no fighting on the 7th except a cavalry engagement at Todd's Tavern, by which Sheridan cleared the road for the southward movement of the army; and in the afternoon Grant gave the order to move by the left flank toward Spottsylvania. Gen. William T. Sherman says in a private letter: "It was then probably that General Grant best displayed his greatness. Forward by the left flank!—that settled that campaign." That the same opinion was held by a large part of the army itself at the time, is shown by the testimony of various men who were there. Frank Wilkeson writes: "Grant's military standing with the enlisted men this day hung on the direction we turned at the Chancellorsville House. If to the left, he was to be rated with Meade and Hooker and Burnside and Pope—the generals who preceded him. At the Chancellorsville House we turned to the right. Instantly all of us heard a sigh of relief. Our spirits rose. We marched free. The men began to sing. The enlisted men understood the flanking movement That night we were happy."

WOUNDING OF GENERAL LONGSTREET BY HIS OWN MEN.

Grant's general purpose was to place his army between the enemy and Richmond, interfering with the communications and compelling Lee to fight at disadvantage. The immediate purpose was a rapid march to Spottsylvania Court-House, fifteen miles southeast of the Wilderness battle-field, and a dozen miles southwest of Fredericksburg, to take a strong position covering the roads that radiate from that point. Warren's corps was to take the advance, marching by the Brock road, to be followed by Hancock's on the same road. Sedgwick's and Burnside's were to take a route farther north, through Chancellorsville. The trains were put in motion on Saturday, May 7th, and Warren began his march at nine o'clock that evening. To withdraw an army in this manner, in the presence of a powerful enemy, and send it forward to a new position, is a difficult and delicate task, as it may be attacked after it has left the old position and before it has gained the new. The method adopted by General Grant was repeated in each of his flanking movements between the Wilderness and the James. It consisted in withdrawing the corps that held his right flank, and passing it behind the others while they maintained their position. Four small rivers rise in this region—the Mat, the Ta, the Po, and the Ny—which unite to form the Mattapony. Spottsylvania Court-House is on the ridge between the Po and the Ny. The country around it is heavily wooded, and somewhat broken by ravines.

The distances that the two armies had to march to reach Spottsylvania Court-House were very nearly the same; if there was any difference, it favored the National; but two unforeseen circumstances determined the race and the form of the ensuing battle. The Brock road was occupied by a detachment of Confederate cavalry, and Warren's corps stood still while the National cavalry undertook to clear the way. This was not done easily, and the road was further obstructed where the Confederates had felled trees across it. After precious time had been lost Warren's corps went forward and cleared the way for itself. The other circumstance was more purely fortuitous. Anderson's division of Longstreet's corps led the Confederate advance, and Anderson had his orders to begin the march early on Sunday morning, the 8th. But from the burning of the woods he found no suitable ground for bivouac, and consequently marched all night. The National cavalry were in Spottsylvania Court-House Sunday morning, and found there but a slight force of cavalry, easily brushed away; but they had to retire before the Confederate infantry when Anderson came down the road. Consequently, when Warren came within sight of the Court-House, he found the same old foe intrenched in his front. Still, if Hancock had come up promptly, the works might have been carried by a rapid movement, and held till the army should be where Grant wanted it, in position between the enemy and their capital. But Hancock had been held back, because of apprehensions that the Confederates would make a heavy attack upon the rear of the moving columns. So the remainder of Longstreet's corps, and finally all of Lee's troops, poured into the rude sylvan fortress, and once more the Army of Northern Virginia stood at bay.

At this point of time, May 8th, Grant sent Sheridan with his cavalry to do to the Confederate army what in previous campaigns its cavalry had twice done to the Army of the Potomac—to ride entirely around it, tearing up railroads, destroying bridges and depots, and capturing trains. Sheridan set out to execute his orders with the energy and skill for which he was becoming famous. He destroyed ten miles of railroad and several trains of cars, cut all the telegraph wires, and recaptured four hundred prisoners who had been taken in the battle of the Wilderness and were on their way to Richmond. As soon as it was known which way he had gone, the Confederate cavalry set out to intercept him, and by hard riding got between him and Richmond. Sheridan's troops met them at Yellow Tavern, seven miles north of the city, and after a hard fight defeated and dispersed them, Gen. J. E. B. Stuart, the ablest cavalry leader in the Confederacy, being mortally wounded. Sheridan dashed through the outer defences of Richmond and took some prisoners, but found the inner ones too strong for him. He then crossed the Chickahominy, and rejoined the army on the 25th.

As the National army came into position before the intrenchments of Spottsylvania, Hancock's corps had the extreme right or western end of the line; then came Warren's, then Sedgwick's, and on the extreme left Burnside's. While Sedgwick's men were placing their batteries, they were annoyed by sharpshooters, one of whom, apparently posted in a tree, seemed to be an unerring marksman. He is said to have destroyed twenty lives that day. The men naturally shrank back from their work, when General Sedgwick, coming up, expostulated with them, remarking that "they couldn't hit an elephant at this distance." As he stepped forward to the works, a bullet struck him in the face, and he fell dead. In his fall the army lost one of its best soldiers, and the country one of its purest patriots. Sedgwick had been offered higher command than he held, but had firmly declined it, from a modest estimate of his own powers. Gen. Horatio G. Wright succeeded him in the command of the Sixth Corps.

On the evening of the 9th Hancock's corps moved to the right, with a view to flanking and attacking the Confederate left, and made a reconnoissance at the point where the road from Shady Grove church crosses the Po on a wooden bridge. A brigade of Barlow's division laid down bridges and crossed the stream, but was confronted by intrenchments manned by a portion of Early's corps. It was now seen that the Confederate left rested on the stream at a point above, so that Hancock by crossing would only have isolated himself from the rest of the army and invited destruction. But before he could withdraw Barlow, the enemy sallied out from their intrenchments and attacked that brigade in heavy force. The assault was met with steady courage and repelled, with considerable loss to Barlow, but with much greater loss to the assailants. After a short interval the experiment was renewed, with precisely the same result; and Barlow then recrossed, under cover of a supporting column, and took up his bridges.

The weak point in the Confederate line was the salient at the northern point of their intrenchment. A salient is weak because almost any fire directed against it becomes an enfilading fire for one or another part of it. But the National army were not up in balloons, looking down upon the earth as a map; and they could only learn the shape of the Confederate intrenchments after traversing thick woods, following out by-paths and scrambling through dark ravines. As soon as the salient was discovered, preparations were made for assaulting it. The storming party consisted of twelve regiments of Wright's corps, commanded by Col. Emory Upton, and was to be supported by Mott's division of Hancock's, while at the same time the remainder of Wright's and all of Warren's corps were to advance and take advantage of any opportunity that should be made for them. While a heavy battery was firing rapidly at the salient and enfilading one of its sides, Upton's men formed under cover of the woods, near the enemy's line, and the instant the battery ceased firing, about six o'clock in the evening, burst out with a cheer, swept over the works after a short hand-to-hand fight, and captured more than a thousand prisoners, and a few guns. Mott, forming in open ground, did not move so promptly, suffered more from the fire of the enemy, and effected nothing. Warren's corps moved forward, but was driven back with heavy loss. In a second assault, they reached the breastworks and captured them after fierce fighting, but were not able to hold them when strong Confederate reinforcements came up, and retired again. Upton, who had broken through a second line of intrenchments, seemed to have opened a way for the destruction of the Confederate army; but the difficulties of the ground and the lateness of the hour made it impracticable to follow up the advantage by pouring a whole corps through the gap and taking everything in reverse. After dark, Upton's men withdrew, bringing the prisoners and the captured battle-flags, but leaving the guns behind. For this exploit, in which he was severely wounded, Colonel Upton was made a brigadier-general on the field. While this was going on, Burnside, at the extreme left of the line, had obtained a good position, from which he could have assaulted advantageously the Confederate right, which he overlapped. But this was not perceived, and as there was a dangerous gap between his corps and Wright's, he was drawn back in the night, and the advantage was lost.

On the 11th it rained heavily, and there was no fighting; but there were reconnoissances and preparations for a renewal of the battle on the next day. Grant determined to make a heavier and more persistent assault upon the tempting salient, and moved Hancock's corps by a wood-road, after dark, to a point opposite the apex. The morning of the 12th was foggy, but by half-past four o'clock it was light enough, and Hancock's men advanced, some of them passing through thickets of dead pines. When they were half-way across the open ground in front of the salient, they burst into a wild cheer and rushed for the works. Here they were met by a brave and determined resistance on the part of the half-surprised Confederates, who fought irregularly with clubbed muskets. But nothing could resist the impetus of Hancock's corps, which was over the breastworks in a few seconds. Large numbers of Confederates were killed, mostly with the bayonet. So sudden was Hancock's irruption into the enemy's works, that he captured Gen. Edward Johnson's entire division of nearly four thousand men, with its commander and also Brigadier-General Steuart. "How are you, Steuart?" said Hancock, recognizing in his prisoner an old army friend, and extending his hand. "I am General Steuart, of the Confederate army," was the reply, "and under the circumstances I decline to take your hand." "Under any other circumstances," said Hancock quietly, "I should not have offered it." Hancock's men had also captured twenty guns, with their horses and caissons, thousands of small arms, and thirty battle-flags. The guns were immediately turned upon the enemy, who was followed through the woods toward Spottsylvania Court-House till the pursuers ran up against another line of intrenchments, which had been constructed in the night across the base of the salient. At the same time that Hancock assaulted at the apex,

FALL OF GENERAL JOHN SEDGWICK, AT SPOTTSYLVANIA.

Warren and Burnside had assaulted at the sides, but with less success, though their men reached the breastworks.

Lee understood too well the danger of having his line thus ruptured at the centre, and poured his men into the salient with a determination to retake it, for which some of his critics have censured him. Hancock's men, when the pressure became too great for them, fell back slowly to the outer intrenchments, and turning, used them as their own. Five times the Confederates attacked these in heavy masses, and five times they were repelled with bloody loss. Before, they had been at disadvantage from defending a salient, and now they were at equal disadvantage in assailing a reëntrant angle. To add to the slaughter, Hancock had established several batteries on high ground, where they could fire over the heads of his own men and strike the enemy beyond. Here and along the west face of the angle the fighting was kept up all day, and was most desperate and destructive. Field guns were run up close to the works and fired into the masses of Confederate troops within the salient, creating terrible havoc; but in turn the horses and gunners were certain to be shot down. There was hand-to-hand fighting over the breast. works, and finally the men of the two armies were crouching on either side of them, shooting and stabbing through the crevices between the logs. Sometimes one would mount upon the works and have loaded muskets passed up to him rapidly, which he would fire in quick succession till the certain bullet came that was to end his career, and he tumbled into the ditch. In several instances men were pulled over the breastworks and made prisoners. One doughty but diminutive Georgian officer nearly died of mortification when a huge Wisconsin colonel reached over, seized him by the collar, and in a twinkling jerked him out of the jurisdiction of the Confederacy and into that of the United States. The fighting around the "death-angle," as the soldiers called it, was kept up till past midnight, when the Confederates finally withdrew to their interior line. The dead were not only literally piled in heaps, but their bodies were terribly torn and mangled by the shot. Every tree and bush was cut down or killed by the balls, and in one instance the body of an oak tree nearly two feet in diameter was completely cut through by bullets, and in falling injured several men of a South Carolina regiment. Not even Sickles' salient at Gettysburg had been so fatal as this. If courage were all that a nation required, there was courage enough at Spottsylvania, on either side of the intrenchments, to have made a nation out of every State in the Union.

BRIGADIER-GENERAL JOHN M. JONES, C. S. A.
Killed at the Wilderness.

It was extremely difficult for either side to rescue or care for any of the wounded. A note from Col. Leander W. Cogswell, of the Ninth New Hampshire Regiment, gives a suggestive incident: "During the night of the 13th, as officer of the day, I was ordered to take a detail of men from our brigade, and, if possible, find the dead bodies of members of the Ninth Regiment. We went over the intrenchments and into that terrible darkness, under orders 'to strike not a match, nor speak above a whisper. When near the spot where they fell, we crawled upon our hands and knees, and felt for the dead ones, and in this manner succeeded in finding upwards of twenty, and conveyed them within our lines, where, with a few others, they were buried the next morning in one trench."

BRIGADIER-GENERAL ALEXANDER HAYS.
Killed at the Wilderness.

Thus far we have looked only at what was going on in front. A few sentences from the diary of Chaplain Alanson A. Haines, of the Fifteenth New Jersey Regiment, will give the reader an idea of the rear at Spottsylvania: "With Dr. Hall, our good and brave surgeon, I found a place in the rear, a little hollow with grass and a spring of water, where we made hasty preparations to receive the coming wounded. Those that could walk soon began to find their way in of themselves, and some few were helped in by their comrades as soon as the charge was over and a portion withdrawn. It was a terrible thing to lay some of our best and truest men in a long row on the blankets, waiting their turn for the surgeon's care. Some came with body wounds, and arms shattered, and hands dangling. At ten o'clock, with the drum corps, I sought the regiment to take off any of our wounded we could find. On my way, met some men carrying Orderly-Sergeant Van Gilder, mortally wounded, in a blanket. With his hand all blood, he seized mine, saying, 'Chaplain, I am going. Tell my wife I am happy.' At two o'clock A.M. I lay down amid a great throng of poor, bleeding sufferers, whose moans and cries for water kept me awake. At four o'clock got up and had coffee made, and, going around among the wounded, found a Pennsylvanian who had lain at my feet, dead. At noon the regiment moved off to the right. I retained five drummers to bury Sergeants Schenck and Rubadeau. A number of men from several regiments were filling their canteens at the spring. I asked them if they could come for a few moments around a soldier's grave. Most of them came, and uncovered their heads. I repeated some passages of Scripture, and offered a short prayer. Drum-Sergeant Kline filled up the grave, nailing to two posts which he planted a piece of cracker-box, on which I cut the names of the dead. While he was doing this, with my other men I gathered the muskets and accoutrements left by the wounded. Laying the muskets with the muzzle on a stump, one heavy stamp of the foot bent the barrel, broke the stock, and made the piece useless. The accoutrements we heaped together and threw on the fire, and with hasty steps sought the regiment."

The National losses in the fighting around Spottsylvania, from the 8th to the 21st of May, were thirteen thousand six hundred —killed, wounded, and missing. Somewhat over half of this loss occurred on the 12th. There are no exact statistics of the Confederate loss; but it appears to have been ten thousand on the 12th, and was probably about equal in the aggregate to the National loss. The losses were heavy in general officers. In the National army, besides Sedgwick, Gens. T. G. Stevenson and J. C. Rice were killed, and Gens. H. G. Wright and Alexander S. Webb and Col. Samuel S. Carroll were wounded; the last named being promoted to brigadier-general on the field. Of the Confederates, Generals Daniel and Perrin were killed; Gens. R. D. Johnston, McGowan, Ramseur, and Walker wounded, and Gens. Edward Johnston and Steuart captured.

BREVET BRIGADIER-GENERAL WILLIAM DE LACEY.

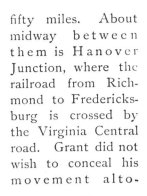

BRIGADIER-GENERAL WILLIAM H. SEWARD.

General Grant had written to Halleck on the 11th: "We have now ended the sixth day of very hard fighting. The result up to this time is much in our favor. But our losses have been heavy, as well as those of the enemy. . . . I am now sending back to Belle Plain all my wagons for a fresh supply of provisions and ammunition, and purpose to fight it out on this line if it takes all summer." A week was spent in manœuvring to find a new point of attack that promised success, but without avail, and at the end of that time it was determined to move again by the left flank. The movement was to the North Anna River; again it was a race, and this time the Confederates had the shorter line.

BREVET BRIGADIER-GENERAL GRIFFIN A. STEDMAN, JR.

BREVET MAJOR-GENERAL R. O. TYLER.

The distance from Spottsylvania Court House to Richmond is a little more than fifty miles. About midway between them is Hanover Junction, where the railroad from Richmond to Fredericksburg is crossed by the Virginia Central road. Grant did not wish to conceal his movement altogether. He was anxious to induce the enemy to fight without the enormous advantage of intrenchments. So he planned to send one corps toward Richmond, hoping that Lee would be tempted to attack it with all his army, whereupon the other corps might follow up sharply and attack the Confederates before they had time to intrench. When the movement was begun, Lee, instead of moving at once in the same direction, sent Ewell's corps to attack the National right. It happened that six thousand raw recruits, under Gen. R. O. Tyler, were on their way to reinforce the Army of the Potomac, and had not quite reached their place in line when they were struck by Ewell's flank movement. Grant says they maintained their position in a manner worthy of veterans, till they were reinforced by the divisions of Birney and Crawford, which promptly moved up to the right and left, and Ewell was then quickly driven back with heavy loss. This was on the 19th of May.

The corps thrown forward as a bait was Hancock's, and it marched on the night of the 20th, going easterly to Guinea Station, and then southerly to Milford. Warren's corps followed twelve hours later, and twelve hours later still the corps of Burnside and Wright. Some trifling resistance was met by the advance; but the Confederates had no notion of taking any risk. They made a reconnoissance to their left, to be sure that Grant had not kept a corps at Spottsylvania to fall upon their rear, and then set out by a shorter line than his to interpose themselves once more between him and their capital.

The new position that was taken up after some tentative movements was one of the strongest that could have been devised. The Confederate left stretched in a straight line, a mile and a half long, from Little River to the North Anna at Oxford. Here, bending at a right angle, the line followed the North Anna down stream for three quarters of a mile, thence continuing in a straight line southeastward, to and around Hanover Junction. The North Anna here makes a bend to the south, and on the most southerly point of the bend the Confederate line touched and held it. If we imagine a ring cut in halves, and the halves placed back to back, in contact, and call one the line of Confederate intrenchments and the other the river, we shall have a fair representation of the essential features of the situation. It is evident that any enemy approaching from the north, and attempting to envelop this position, would have his own line twice divided by the river, so that his army would be in three parts. Any reinforcements passing from one wing to the other would have to cross the stream twice, and, long before they could reach their destination, the army h o l d i n g the intrenchments could strengthen its threatened wing. The obvious point to assail in such a position would be the apex of the salient line where it touched the river; and Burnside was ordered to force a passage at that point. But the banks were high and steep, and the passage was covered by artillery. Moreover, an enfilading fire from the north bank was thwarted by traverses—intrenchments at right angles to the main line. Wright's corps crossed the river above the Confederate position, and destroyed some miles of the Virginia Central Railroad; while Hancock's crossed below, and destroyed a large section of the road to Fredericksburg. By this time they had learned the effective method of not only tearing up the track, but piling up the ties and setting them on fire, heating the rails, and bending and twisting them so that they could not be used again. These operations were not carried on without frequent sharp fighting, which cost each side about two thousand men; but there was no general battle on the North Anna.

Before the next flank movement was made by the Army of the Potomac, Gen. James H. Wilson's cavalry division was sent to make a demonstration on the right, to give the enemy the impression that this time the turning movement would be in that direction. In the night of May 26, which was very dark, the army withdrew to the north bank of the North Anna, took up its pontoon bridges, destroyed all the others, and was put in motion again by the left flank. Sheridan's cavalry led the way and guarded the crossings of the Pamunkey, which is formed by the junction of the North and South Anna Rivers. The Sixth Corps was the advance of the infantry, followed by the Second, while the Fifth and Ninth moved by roads farther north. The direction was southeast, and the distance about thirty miles to a point at which the army would cross the Pamunkey and move southwest toward Richmond, the crossing being about twenty miles from that city. But between lie the swamps of the Chickahominy. In the morning of the 28th the cavalry moved out on the most direct road to Richmond, and at a cross-roads known as Hawes's Shop encountered a strong force of Confederate cavalry, which was d i s m o u n t e d and intrenched. After a bloody fight of some hours' duration, the divisions commanded by Gens. David M. Gregg and George A. Custer broke over the intrenchments and forced back the enemy; the other divisions came up promptly, and the position was held.

BREVET MAJOR-GENERAL JOHN C. ROBINSON.

A member of the First New Jersey cavalry, which participated in this action, writes: "One company being sent on each flank, mounted, Captain Robbins with four companies, dismounted, moved forward and occupied a position on the right of the road, opening a rapid fire from their carbines on the line of the enemy, which was forming for attack. The remainder of the regiment was moved to the left of the road, and having been dismounted, was ordered to the support of the First Pennsylvania, which was hotly engaged. Robbins, as usual, moved with a rush to the assault, and soon cleared his immediate front of the rebels, chasing them across the open ground beyond the wood in which they had taken cover. In this field there was a double ditch, lined by fencing, with another of the same character facing it, only forty or fifty paces distant. As Captain Beekman, heading his men, sprang across the first fence at charging speed, they were met by a desperate volley from the second line of the rebels lying in the other cover. Instinctively, as they saw the flash, the men threw themselves upon the ground, and now Beekman, rolling into the ditch, called his troops there beside him. From the two covers there was kept up a tremendous fire—our men sometimes charging toward the hostile ditch, but in each case falling back, and the fight going on, both parties holding their own, but neither gaining ground upon the other. Meanwhile Captain Robbins, on the right of the

BRIGADIER-GENERAL HARRY T. HAYS, C. S. A.

PONTOON BRIDGE AT DEEP BOTTOM ON THE JAMES RIVER.

road, was being sorely pressed. Major Janeway was sent with two squadrons to his relief, and the fight redoubled in intensity. The ammunition of the men giving out, a supply was brought from the rear and distributed along the line itself by the officers, several of whom fell while engaged in the service. Captain Beekman was shot through both hands as he stretched them forth full of ammunition. Lieutenant Bellis was almost at the same moment mortally wounded, as was also Lieutenant Stewart. Captain Robbins was wounded severely in the shoulder, Lieutenant Shaw severely in the head, Lieutenant Wynkoop fearfully in the foot. Lieutenant Bowne was the only officer of the first battalion on the field who was untouched, and he had several narrow escapes. Major Janeway also had a narrow escape, a ball passing so close to his forehead as to redden the skin. As Lieutenant Brooks was manœuvring the fifth squadron under fire, a ball fired close at hand struck him near his belt-clasp, slightly penetrating the skin in two places, and, doubling him up, sent him rolling headlong for thirty feet across the road. As he recovered steadiness, he saw his whole squadron hurrying to pick him up, and, in the excitement, losing all sensation of pain, he ordered them again forward, and walked after them half-way to the front. There he was obliged to drop upon the ground, and was carried from the field. Lieutenant Craig also, of the same squadron, was badly bruised by some missile that struck him in the breast, but, though suffering severely from the blow, he did not leave the field. Still the men bravely held their own. And now Custer, coming up with his Michigan brigade, charged down the road, the whole body of the First Jersey skirmishers simultaneously springing from their cover and dashing upon the enemy, sweeping him from the field, and pursuing him until the whole mass had melted into disordered rout. Meanwhile the fighting on the left of the road had been of the severest character. Malsbury received a mortal wound; Dye was killed instantly; Cox was hit in the back, but remained the only officer with the squadron till, toward the close of the action, he received a wound which disabled him. The total loss of the nine companies of the First New Jersey engaged, in killed and wounded, was sixty-four, eleven being officers."

Soon after noon of that day three-fourths of the army had crossed the Pamunkey, and the remaining corps crossed that night. Here were several roads leading to the Confederate capital; but the Confederate army, as soon as it found the enemy gone from its front, had moved in the same direction, by a somewhat shorter route, and had quickly taken up a strong position across all these roads, with flanks on Beaver Dam and Totopotomoy creeks. Moreover, at this time it was heavily reinforced by troops that were drawn from the defences east of Richmond.

The next day the opposing forces were in close proximity, each trying to find out what the other was about, and all day the crack of the skirmisher's rifle was heard. Near Bethesda church there was a small but bloody engagement, where a portion of Early's corps made an attack on the National left and gained a brief advantage, but was soon driven back, with a brigade commander and two regimental commanders among its killed. At dusk, one brigade of Barlow's division made a sudden rush and carried a line of Confederate rifle-pits. But it was ascertained that the position offered no chance of success in a serious assault. Furthermore, Grant was expecting reinforcements from Butler's Army of the James, to come by way of White House, at the head of navigation on York River, and he feared that Lee would move out with a large part of his army to interpose between him and his reinforcements and overwhelm them. So he extended his left toward Cold Harbor, sending Sheridan with cavalry and artillery to secure that place. Sheridan was heavily attacked there on the morning of June 1st, but held his ground, and twice drove back the assailants. In the course of the day he was relieved by the Sixth corps, to which the ten thousand reinforcements under Gen. William F. Smith were added. At the same time the Confederate line had been extended in the same direction, so as still to cover all roads leading to Richmond. The Army of the Potomac, in its movement down the streams, was now at the highest point that it had reached in its movement up the peninsula, when led by McClellan two years before.

At six o'clock in the evening, Smith's and Wright's corps attacked the Confederate intrenchments. Along most of the front they were obliged to cross open ground that was swept by artillery and musketry; but they moved forward steadily, in spite of their rapid losses, and everywhere carried the first line of works, taking some hundreds of prisoners, but were stopped by the second. They intrenched and held their advanced position; but it had been dearly bought, since more than two thousand of their men were killed or wounded, including many officers.

When the other corps had followed the Sixth, and the entire army was in its new position at Cold Harbor, eight or ten miles from Richmond, with its enemy but a little distance in front of it, an attack was planned for the morning of the 3d. The Confederate position was very strong. The line was from three to six miles from the outer defences of Richmond, the right resting on the Chickahominy, and the left protected by the woods and swamps about the head-waters of several small streams. The Chickahominy was between it and Richmond, but the water was low and everywhere fordable. The only chance for attack was in front, and it remained to be demonstrated by experiment whether anything could be done there. If Lee's line could be disrupted at the centre, and a strong force thrust through, it would for the time being disorganize his army, though a large part of it would undoubtedly escape across the river and rally in the intrenchments nearer the city.

At half-past four o'clock on the morning of the 3d, the Second, Sixth, and Eighteenth (Smith's) corps began the attack as planned. They moved forward as rapidly and regularly as the nature of the ground would admit, under a destructive fire of artillery and musketry, till they carried the first line of intrenchments. Barlow's division of Hancock's corps struck a salient, and, after a desperate hand-to-hand contest, captured it, taking nearly three hundred prisoners and three guns, which were at once turned upon the enemy. But every assaulting column, on reaching the enemy's first line, found itself subjected to cross-fires from the enemy's skilfully placed artillery, and not one of them could go any farther. Most of them fell back speedily, leaving large numbers prisoners or bleeding on the ground, and took up positions midway between the lines, where they rapidly dug trenches and protected themselves. General Grant had given orders to General Meade to suspend the attack the moment it should appear hopeless, and the heavy fighting did not last more than an hour, though firing was kept up all day. A counter-attack by Early's corps was as unsuccessful as those of the National troops had been; and one or two lighter attacks by the Confederates, later in the day, were also repelled.

The Ninety-eighth New York regiment was among the troops that were brought up from the Army of the James and joined the Army of the Potomac two or three days before the battle of Cold Harbor. Its colonel, William Kreutzer, writes a graphic account of the regiment's experience during those first three days of June:

"After ten o'clock, Devens, putting the Ninety-eighth in charge of one of his staff, sent it, marching by the right flank, through the wood to support one of his regiments. Soon the rattling of the men among the brush and trees attracted some one's attention in front, and he poured a volley down along our line lengthwise. We stop; the ground rises before us, and the aim of the firing is too high. Staff-officer says: 'These are our men, there is some mistake; wait awhile, and the firing will stop.' Firing does not stop, and the aim is better. Staff-officer goes to report, hastens for orders and instructions, and never comes back. Our position is terribly embarrassing, frightfully uncomfortable. Our ignorance of the place, the darkness, the wood, the uncertainty whether the firing is from friend or foe, increase the horrors of that night's battle. The writer walked from the centre to the head of the regiment and asked Colonel Wead what the firing meant. Wead replied: 'We are the victims of some one's blunder.' We suggested: 'Let us withdraw the regiment, or fire at the enemy in front. We can't stay here and make no reply. Our men are being killed or wounded fast.' Wead remarked: 'I have no orders to do either; they may be our men in front. I am here by direction of General Devens, and one of his staff has gone to report the facts to him. He will return in a short time. If we are all killed, I don't see that I can prevent it, or am to blame for it.'

"We asked Colonel Wead to have the men lie down. The order, 'Lie down,' was passed along the line, and we returned to our position by the colors. Subsequently, Colonel Wead joined us there. The firing continued; the range became lower; the men lying down were wounded fast. We all lay down. Colonel Wead was struck a glancing blow on the shoulder-strap by a rifle-ball, and, after lying senseless for a moment, said to the writer, 'I am wounded; take the command.' We arose immediately, walked along the line, and quietly withdrew the men to the lower edge of the wood where we had entered. In that night's blunder the regiment lost forty-two men, killed and wounded. During the night and early morning, Colonel Wead and the wounded crawled back to the regiment. The more severely wounded were carried back half a mile farther to an old barn, where their wounds were dressed and whence they were taken in ambulances to White House. Nothing could equal the horrors of that night's battle; the blundering march into the enemy's intrenchments, his merciless fire, the cries of our

INTRENCHMENTS AT KENESAW MOUNTAIN, GA.

wounded and dying, the irresolute stupidity and want of sagacity of the conducting officer, deepen the plot and color the picture.

"At 4 A.M. of the 3d, the Eighteenth Corps was formed for the charge in three lines; first, a heavy skirmish line; second, a line consisting of regiments deployed; third, a line formed of regiments in solid column doubled on the centre. The Ninety-eighth was in the third line. The whole army advanced together at sunrise. Within twenty minutes after the order to advance had been given, one of the most sanguinary battles of the war, quick, sharp, and decisive, had taken place. By this battle the Army of the Potomac gained nothing, but the Eighteenth Corps captured and held a projecting portion of the enemy's breastwork in front. The Ninety-eighth knew well the ground that it helped to capture, for there lay its dead left on the night of the 1st.

BREVET MAJOR-GENERAL EMORY UPTON.

MAJOR MARTIN T. McMAHON.
(Afterward Brevet Major-General.)

"The men at once began the construction of a breastwork, using their hands, tin cups, and bayonets. Later they procured picks and shovels. They laid the dead in line and covered them over, and to build the breastwork used rails, logs, limbs, leaves, and dirt. The enemy's shells, solid shot and rifle-balls all the while showered upon them, and hit every limb and twig about or above them. Nothing saved us but a slight elevation of the ground in front. A limb cut by a solid shot felled General Marston to the ground. Three boyish soldiers, thinking to do the State service, picked him up, and were hurrying him to the rear, when he recovered his consciousness and compelled them to drop himself. In a short time he walked slowly back to the front. In this advance and during the day our regimental flag received fifty-two bullet-holes, and the regiment lost, killed and wounded, sixty-one. Colonel Wead rose to his feet an instant on the captured line, when a rifle-ball pierced his neck and cut the subclavian vein. He was carried back to the barn beside the road, where he died the same day. . . .

"On the night of the 4th the Ninety-eighth moved from the second line through the approach to the front line, and relieved the One Hundred and Eighteenth New York and the Tenth New Hampshire. It had barely time to take its position when the Confederates made a night attack along our whole front. For twenty minutes before, the rain of shells and balls was terrific; the missiles tore and screamed and sang and howled along the air. Every branch and leaf was struck; every inch of the trees and breastworks was pierced. Then the firing ceased along his line for a few minutes, while the enemy crossed his breastworks and formed for the charge, when,

'At once there rose so wild a yell,
As all the fiends from heaven that fell
Had pealed the banner cry of hell.'

COLONEL SAMUEL S. CARROLL.
(Afterward Brevet Major-General.)

But no living thing could face that 'rattling shower' of ball and shell which poured from our lines upon them. They fell to the ground, they crept away, they hushed the yell of battle. The horrors of that night assault baffle description."

The entire loss of the National Army at Cold Harbor in the first twelve days of June—including the battles just described and the almost constant skirmishing and minor engagements—was ten thousand and eighty-eight; and among the dead and wounded were many valuable officers. General Tyler and Colonel Brooke were wounded, and Colonels Porter, Morris, Meade, and Byrnes were killed.*

* The lines of the two armies were so close to each other that it was impossible to care for the wounded that lay between them, except by a cessation of hostilities. As the National forces had been the assailants, most of the wounded were theirs. General Grant made an immediate effort to obtain a cessation for this humane purpose, but General Lee delayed it with various trivial excuses for forty-eight hours, and at the end of that time all but two of the wounded were dead. See a part of the correspondence in Grant's "Memoirs," Vol. II., pp. 273 *et seq.* As to the losses here and at Spottsylvania, authorities differ. The figures given above are from a statement compiled in the Adjutant-General's office.

BREVET MAJOR-GENERAL P. ST. GEORGE COOKE.

The Confederate loss—which included Brigadier-General Doles among the killed, and Brigadier-Generals Kirkland, Lane, Law, and Finnegan among the wounded—is unknown; but it was much smaller than the National. The attack of June 3d is recognized as the most serious error in Grant's military career. He himself says, in his "Memoirs," that he always regretted it was ever made. It was as useless, and almost as costly, as Lee's assault upon Meade's centre at Gettysburg. But we do not read that any of Grant's lieutenants protested against it, as Longstreet protested against the attack on Cemetery Ridge.

For some days Grant held his army as close to the enemy as possible, to prevent the Confederates from detaching a force to operate against Hunter in the Shenandoah Valley.

General Halleck now proposed that the Army of the Potomac should invest Richmond on the north. This might have prevented any possibility of Lee's launching out toward Washington, but it could hardly have effected anything else. The Confederate lines of supply would have been left untouched, while the National troops would have perished between impregnable intrenchments on the one side and malarious swamps on the other. Grant determined to move once more by the left flank, swing his army across the James, and invest the city from the south. A direct investment of the Confederate capital on that side was out of the question, because the south bank of the James is lower than the city; and the movement would, therefore, resolve itself into a struggle for Petersburg, thirty miles south of Richmond, which was its railroad centre.

To withdraw an army from so close contact with the enemy, march it fifty miles, cross two rivers, and bring it into a new position, was a very delicate and hazardous task, and Grant performed it with consummate skill. He sent a part of his cavalry to make a demonstration on the James above Richmond and destroy portions of Lee's line of supplies from the Shenandoah; he had a line of intrenchments constructed along the north bank of the Chickahominy, from his position at Cold Harbor down to the point where he expected to cross; and directed General Butler to send two vessels loaded with stone to be sunk in the channel of the James as far up-stream as possible, so that the Confederate gunboats could not come down and attack the army while it was crossing. A large number of vessels had been collected at Fort Monroe, to be used as ferry-boats when the army should reach the James. The so-called "bridges" on the Chickahominy were now only names of geographical points, for all the bridges had been destroyed; but each column was to carry its pontoon train.

The march began in the evening of June 12th, and at midday of the 13th a pontoon was thrown across at Long Bridge, fifteen miles below the Cold Harbor position, and Wilson's cavalry crossed and immediately moved out a short distance on the roads toward Richmond, to watch the movements of the enemy and prevent a surprise. The Fifth corps followed quickly, and took a position covering these roads till the remainder of the army could cross. The Second, Sixth, and Ninth corps crossed the Chickahominy a few miles farther down; while the Eighteenth had embarked at White House, to be sent around by water. In the evening of the 13th, the Fifth reached Wilcox's Landing on the James, ten miles below Haxall's, where McClellan had reached the river at the close of his peninsula campaign. The other corps reached the landing on the 14th. The river there is more than two thousand feet wide; but between four o'clock, P.M., and midnight a pontoon was laid, and the crossing began. The artillery and trains were sent over first, and the infantry followed in a long procession that occupied forty-eight hours, the rear guard of the Sixth corps passing over at midnight of the 16th. Thus an army of more than one hundred thousand men was taken from a line of trenches within a few yards of the enemy, marched fifty miles, and, with all its paraphernalia, carried across two rivers and placed in a position threatening that enemy's capital, without a serious collision or disaster. General Ewell said that when the National army got across the James River he knew that the Confederate cause was lost, and it was the duty of their authorities to make

BREVET BRIGADIER-GENERAL JAMES A. BEAVER.

BREVET MAJOR-GENERAL ISAAC S. CATLIN.

the best terms they could while they still had a right to claim concessions.

Most critics of this campaign have persistently proceeded on the assumption that Grant's objective was the city of Richmond, and have accordingly condemned his plan of marching overland, and with apparent conclusiveness have pointed to his heavy losses and to the fact that Richmond was still uncaptured, and then asked the question, which has been wearisomely repeated, why he might not as well have carried his army by water in the first place to a position before Richmond, without loss, as McClellan had done two years before, instead of getting there along a bloody overland trail at such heavy cost. These critics should know, even if Grant himself had not distinctly declared it at the outset, that his objective was not the city of Richmond; that it was Lee's army, which it was his business to follow and fight until he destroyed it. The same critics appear to think also that he ought to have found a way to accomplish his purpose without bloodshed, and that because he did not he was no general, but a mere "butcher," as some of them boldly call him. If they were asked to name a general who had won great victories without himself losing men by the thousand, they would find it difficult to do so, for no such general figures in the pages of history. If there ever was a chance to defeat the Army of Northern Virginia and destroy the Confederacy by anything but hard fighting, it was when McClellan planted his army on the peninsula; but McClellan's timidity was not the quality necessary for a bold and brilliant stroke. Nearly the whole State of Virginia is admirably adapted for defence against an invading army; and by the time that Grant set out on his overland campaign every position where Lee's army could make a stand was thoroughly known, and most of them were fortified; furthermore, the men of his army were now veterans and understood how to use every one of their advantages, while Lee as a general had only to move his army over ground that it had already traversed several times, and manœuvre for a constant defence. Under these circumstances, nothing but hard and continuous fighting could have conquered such an army. The same criticism that finds fault with General Grant for not transporting his army by water to the front of Richmond instead of fighting his way thither overland, must also condemn General Lee for not surrendering in the Wilderness instead of fighting all the way to Appomattox and then surrendering at last.

NEWSPAPER HEADQUARTERS AT THE FRONT.

(From a War-time Photograph.)

COMMANDER ROBERT W. SHUFELDT.
REAR-ADMIRAL HIRAM PAULDING.
COMMANDER S. L. BREESE.

LIEUTENANT-COMMANDER HENRY ERBEN.
COMMANDER E. T. NICHOLS.
COMMANDER NAPOLEON COLLINS.

COMMODORE GEORGE HENRY PREBLE.
CAPTAIN JOHN FAUNCE.
REAR-ADMIRAL H. K. HOFF.

A GROUP OF NAVAL OFFICERS, U. S. N.

Capt. J. A. Winslow.

CAPTAIN JOHN A. WINSLOW AND OFFICERS ON THE DECK OF THE "KEARSARGE."

(From a Government photograph.)

CHAPTER XXXII.

THE CONFEDERATE CRUISERS.

THE "ALABAMA" SUNK BY THE "KEARSARGE"—THE "SUMTER" AND OTHER CRUISERS—PROTEST OF OUR GOVERNMENT TO THE BRITISH GOVERNMENT—SECRETARY SEWARD'S DESPATCHES—PRIVATEERING—WHY ENGLAND DID NOT INTERFERE—ARBITRATION AND AMOUNT OF DAMAGE OBTAINED FROM THE BRITISH GOVERNMENT.

WHILE the Army of the Potomac was putting itself in fighting trim after its change of base, a decisive battle of the war took place three thousand miles away. A vessel known in the builders' yard as the "290," and afterward famous as the *Alabama*, had been built for the Confederate Government in 1862, at Birkenhead, opposite Liverpool. She was of wood, a fast sailer, having both steam and canvas, was two hundred and twenty feet long, and rated at one thousand and forty tons. She was thoroughly fitted in every respect, and cost nearly a quarter of a million dollars. The American minister at London notified the British Government that such a ship was being built in an English yard, in violation of the neutrality laws, and demanded that she be prevented from leaving the Mersey. But, either through design or stupidity, the Government moved too slowly, and the cruiser escaped to sea. She went to Fayal, in the Azores, and there took on board her guns and coal, sent out to her in a merchant ship from London. Her commander was Raphael Semmes, who had served in the United States navy. Her crew were mainly Englishmen. For nearly two years she roamed the seas, traversing the Atlantic and Indian Oceans and the Gulf of Mexico, and captured sixty-nine American merchantmen, most of which were burned at sea. Their crews were sent away on passing vessels, or put ashore at some convenient port. Several war-vessels were sent out in search of the *Alabama*, but they were at constant disadvantage from the rule that when two hostile vessels are in a neutral port, the first that leaves must have been gone twenty-four hours before the other is permitted to follow. In French, and especially in British ports, the *Alabama* was always welcome, and enjoyed every possible facility, because she was destroying American commerce.

In June, 1864, she was in the harbor of Cherbourg, France. The United States man-of-war *Kearsarge*, commanded by John

A. Winslow, found her there, and lay off the port, watching her. By not going into the harbor, Winslow escaped the twenty-four-hour rule. Semmes sent a note to Winslow, asking him not to go away, as he was coming out to fight; but no such challenge was called for, as the *Kearsarge* had come for that purpose, and was patiently waiting for her prey. She was almost exactly the size of the *Alabama*, and the armaments were so nearly alike as to make a very fair match. But her crew were altogether superior in gun-practice, and she had protected her boilers by chains, "stoppered" up and down the side amidships, as had been done in the fights at New Orleans and elsewhere. On Sunday morning, June 19th, the *Alabama* steamed out of the harbor amid the plaudits of thousands of Englishmen and Frenchmen, who had not a doubt that she was going to certain victory. The *Kearsarge* steamed away as she approached, and drew her off to a distance of seven or eight miles from the coast. Winslow then turned and closed with his enemy. The two vessels steamed around on opposite sides of a circle half a mile in diameter, firing their starboard guns. The practice on the *Alabama* was very bad; she began firing first, discharged her guns rapidly, and produced little or no effect, though a dozen of her shots struck her antagonist. But when the *Kearsarge* began firing there was war in earnest. Her guns were handled with great skill, and every shot told. One of them cut the mizzenmast so that it fell. Another exploded a shell among the crew of the *Alabama's* pivot gun, killing half of them and dismounting the piece. Balls rolled in at the port-holes and swept away the gunners; and several pierced the hull below the water line, making the ship tremble from stem to stern, and letting in floods of water. The vessels had described seven circles, and the *Alabama's* deck was strewn with the dead, when at the end of an hour she was found to be sinking, her colors were struck, and her officers, with a keen sense of chivalry, threw into the sea the swords that were no longer their own. The *Kearsarge* lowered boats to take off the crew; but suddenly the stern settled, the bow was thrown up into the air, and down went the *Alabama* to the bottom of the British Channel, carrying an unknown number of her men. An English yacht picked up Semmes and about forty sailors, and steamed away to Southampton with them; others were rescued by the boats of the *Kearsarge*, and still others were drowned.

CAPTAIN RAPHAEL SEMMES.

In January, 1863, the *Alabama* had fought the side-wheel steamer *Hatteras*, of the United States Navy, off Galveston, Tex., and injured her so that she sank soon after surrendering. The remainder of the *Alabama's* career, till she met the *Kearsarge*, had been spent in capturing merchant vessels and either burning them or releasing them under bonds. Before Captain Semmes received command of the *Alabama*, he had cruised in the *Sumter* on a similar mission, capturing eighteen vessels, when her course was ended in the harbor of Gibraltar, in February, 1862, where she was blockaded by the United States steamers *Kearsarge* and *Tuscarora*, and, as there was no probability that she could escape to sea, her captain and crew abandoned her.

A score of other Confederate cruisers roamed the seas, to prey upon United States commerce, but none of them became quite so famous as the *Sumter* and the *Alabama*. They included the *Shenandoah*, which made thirty-eight captures; the *Florida*, which made thirty-six; the *Tallahassee*, which made twenty-seven; the *Tacony*, which made fifteen; and the *Georgia*, which made ten. The *Florida* was captured in the harbor of Bahia, Brazil, in October, 1864, by a United States man-of-war, in violation of the neutrality of the port. For this the United States Government apologized to Brazil, and ordered the restoration of the *Florida* to the harbor where she was captured. But in Hampton Roads she met with an accident and sank. It was generally believed that the apparent accident was contrived with the connivance, if not by direct order, of the Government.

Most of these cruisers were built in British shipyards; and whenever they touched at British ports, to obtain supplies and land prisoners, their commanders were ostentatiously welcomed and lionized by the British merchants and officials.

The English builders were proceeding to construct several swift iron-clad cruisers for the Confederate Government, when the United States Government protested so vigorously that the British Government prevented them from leaving port. One or two passages from Secretary Seward's despatches to Charles Francis Adams, the American minister at London, contain the whole argument that was afterward elaborated before a high court of arbitration, and secured a verdict against England. More than this, these passages contain what probably was the controlling reason that determined England not to try the experiment of intervention. Secretary Seward wrote, under date of October 5–6, 1863:

CAPTAIN JOHN A. WINSLOW.

(Afterward Rear-Admiral.)

"I have had the honor to receive and submit to the President your despatch of the 17th of September, which relates to the iron-clad vessels built at Laird's shipyards for war against the United States, which is accompanied by a very interesting correspondence between yourself and Earl Russell. The positions you have taken in this correspondence are approved. It is indeed a cause of profound concern, that, notwithstanding an engagement which the President has accepted as final, there still remains a doubt whether those vessels will be prevented from coming out, according to the original hostile purposes of the enemies of the United States residing in Great Britain.

"Earl Russell remarks that her Majesty's Government, having

proclaimed neutrality, have in good faith exerted themselves to maintain it. I have not to say now for the first time, that, however satisfactory that position may be to the British nation, it does not at all relieve the gravity of the question in the United States. The proclamation of neutrality was a concession of belligerent rights to the insurgents, and was deemed by this Government as unnecessary, and in effect as unfriendly, as it has since proved injurious, to this country. The successive preparations of hostile naval expeditions in Great Britain are regarded here as fruits of that injurious proclamation. . . . It is hardly necessary to say that the United States stand upon what war broke out, we distinctly confessed that we knew what great temptations it offered to foreign intervention and aggression, and that in no event could such intervention or aggression be endured. It was apparent that such aggression, if it should come, must travel over the seas, and therefore must be met and encountered, if at all, by maritime resistance. We addressed ourselves to prepare the means of such resistance. We have now a navy, not, indeed, as ample as we proposed, but yet one which we feel assured is not altogether inadequate to the purposes of self-defence, and it is yet rapidly increasing in men, material, and engines of war. Besides this regular naval force,

OPENING OF THE FIGHT BETWEEN THE "KEARSARGE" AND THE "ALABAMA."

they think impregnable ground, when they refuse to be derogated, by any act of British Government, from their position as a sovereign nation in amity with Great Britain, and placed upon a footing of equality with domestic insurgents who have risen up in resistance against their authority.

"It does not remain for us even to indicate to Great Britain the serious consequences which must ensue if the iron-clads shall come forth upon their work of destruction. They have been fully revealed to yourself, and you have made them known to Earl Russell, within the restraints which an honest and habitual respect for the Government and the people of Great Britain imposes. It seems to me that her Majesty's Government might be expected to perceive and appreciate them, even if we were henceforth silent upon the subject. When our unhappy civil the President has asked, and Congress has given him, authority to convert the mercantile marine into armed squadrons, by the issue of letters of marque and reprisal. All the world might see, if it would, that the great arm of naval defence has not been thus invigorated for the mere purpose of maintaining a blockade, or enforcing our authority against the insurgents; for practically they have never had an open port, or built and armed, nor could they from their own resources build and arm, a single ship-of-war.

"Thus the world is left free to understand that our measures of maritime war are intended to resist maritime aggression, which is constantly threatened from abroad and even more constantly apprehended at home. That it would be employed for that purpose, if such aggression should be attempted, would seem certain, unless, indeed, there should be reason to suppose that the people do not in this respect approve of the policy and sympathize with the sentiments of the executive Government. But the resistance of foreign aggression by all the means in our power, and at the hazard, if need be, of the National life itself, is the one point of policy on which the American people seem to be unanimous and in complete harmony with the President.

"The United States understand that the *Alabama* is a pirate ship-of-war, roving over the seas, capturing, burning, sinking, and destroying American vessels, without any lawful authority from the British Government or from any other sovereign power, in violation of the law of nations, and contemptuously defying all judicial tribunals equally of Great Britain and all other states. The United States understand that she was purposely built for war against the United States, by British subjects, in a British port, and prepared there to be armed and equipped with a specified armament adapted to her construction for the very piratical career which she is now pursuing; that her armament and equipment, duly adapted to this ship-of-war and no other, were simultaneously prepared by the same British subjects, in a British port, to be placed on board to complete her preparation for that career; that when she was ready, and her armament and equipment were equally ready, she was clandestinely and by connivance sent by her British holders, and the armament and equipment were at the same time clandestinely sent through the same connivance by the British subjects who had prepared them, to a common port outside of British waters, and there the armament and equipment of the *Alabama* as a ship-of-war were completed, and she was sent forth on her work of destruction with a crew chiefly of British subjects, enlisted in and proceeding from a British port, in fraud of the laws of Great Britain and in violation of the peace and sovereignty of the United States.

"The United States understand that the purpose of the building, armament and equipment, and expedition of the vessel was one single criminal intent, running equally through the building and the equipment and the expedition, and fully completed and executed when the *Alabama* was finally despatched; and that this intent brought the whole transaction of building, armament, and equipment within the lawful jurisdiction of Great Britain, where the main features of the crime were executed. The United States understand that they gave sufficient and adequate notice to the British Government that this wrongful enterprise was begun and was being carried out to its completion; and that upon receiving this notice her Majesty's Government were bound by treaty obligations and by the law of nations to prevent its execution, and that if the diligence which was due had been exercised by the British Government the expedition of the *Alabama* would have been prevented, and the wrongful enterprise of British subjects would have been defeated. The United States confess that some effort was made by her Majesty's Government, but it was put forth too late and was too soon abandoned. Upon these principles of law and these assumptions of fact, the United States do insist, and must continue to insist, that the British Government is justly responsible for the damages which the peaceful, law-abiding citizens of the United States sustain by the depredations of the *Alabama*.

"Though indulging a confident belief in the correctness of our positions in regard to the claims in question, and others, we shall be willing at all times hereafter, as well as now, to consider the evidence and the arguments which her Majesty's Government may offer, to show that they are invalid; and if we shall not be convinced, there is no fair and just form of conventional arbitrament or reference to which we shall not be willing to submit them."

In 1856 the great powers of Europe signed at Paris a treaty by which they relinquished the right of privateering, and some of the lesser powers afterward accepted a general invitation to join in it. The United States offered to sign it, on condition that a clause be inserted declaring that private property on the high seas, if not contraband of war, should be exempt from seizure by the public armed vessels of an enemy, as well as by private ones. The powers that had negotiated the treaty declined to make this amendment, and therefore the United States did not become a party to it. When the war of secession began, and the Confederate authorities proclaimed their readiness to issue letters of marque for private vessels to prey upon American commerce, the United States Government offered to accept the treaty without amendment; but England and France declined to permit our Government to join in the treaty then, if its provisions against privateering were to be understood as applying to vessels sent out under Confederate authority. There the subject was dropped, and while the insurgents were thus left at liberty to do whatever damage they could upon the high seas, the United States Government was also left free to send not only its own cruisers but an unlimited number of privateers against the commerce of any nation with which it might become involved in war. When at the beginning of President Lincoln's administration Mr. Adams was sent out as minister at London, he carried instructions that included this passage: "If, as the President does not at all apprehend, you shall unhappily find her Majesty's Government tolerating the application of the so-called seceding States, or wavering about it, you will not leave them to suppose for a moment that they can grant that application and remain the friends of the United States. You may even assure them promptly, in that case, that if they determine to recognize, they may at the same time prepare to enter into alliance with the enemies of this Republic."

England had had a costly experience of American privateering under sail in the war of 1812–15, and she now saw what privateering could become under steam power. While she was rejoicing at the destruction of American merchantmen, she knew what might happen to her own. Let her become involved in war with the United States, and not only a hundred war-ships but a vast fleet of privateers would at once set sail from American ports, and in a few months her commerce would be swept from every sea. The fisherman on the coast of Maine would carpet his hut with Persian rugs, and the ship-carpenter's children would play with baubles intended to decorate the Court of St. James.* The navies of England and France combined could not blockade the harbors of New England; and from those harbors, where every material is at hand, might have sailed a fleet whose operations would not only have impoverished the merchants of London, but called out the wail of famine from her populace. Other considerations were discussed; but it was doubtless this contingency that furnished the controlling reason why the British Government resisted the tempting offers of cotton and free trade, re-

* See lists of goods captured by American privateers in the war of 1812: "Eighteen bales of Turkish carpets, 43 bales of raw silk, 20 boxes of gums, 160 dozen swan-skins, 6 tons of ivory, $40,000 in gold dust, $80,000 in specie, $20,000 worth of indigo, $60,000 in bullion, $500,000 worth of dry goods, 700 tons of mahogany," etc. In Coggeshall's "History of American Privateers."

sisted the importunities of Louis Napoleon, resisted the clamor of its more reckless subjects, resisted its own prejudice against republican institutions, and refused to recognize the Southern Confederacy as an independent nation. It may have been this consideration also that induced it, after the war was over, to agree to exactly that settlement by arbitration which was suggested by Secretary Seward in the despatch quoted above. In 1872 the international court of arbitration, sitting in Geneva, Switzerland, decided that the position taken by the United States Government in regard to responsibility for the Confederate cruisers was right; and that the British Government, for failing to prevent their escape from its ports, must pay the United States fifteen and a half million dollars. So far as settlement of the principle was concerned, the award gave Americans all the satisfaction they could desire; but the sum named fell far short of the damage that had been wrought. Charles Sumner, speaking in his place in the Senate, had contended with great force for the exaction of what were called "consequential damages," which would have swelled the amount to hundreds of millions; but in this he was overruled.

CHAPTER XXXIII.

PRELIMINARY OPERATIONS IN THE WEST.

GENERAL SHERMAN CAPTURES MERIDIAN, MISS.—DESTRUCTION OF RAILROADS AND SUPPLIES—GENERAL BANKS ATTEMPTS TO CAPTURE SHREVEPORT, LA.—BATTLE OF SABINE CROSS-ROADS—TEMPORARY ROUT AND DEFEAT OF THE UNION FORCES—DEFEAT OF THE CONFEDERATES AT PLEASANT HILL—INCIDENTS OF HEROISM ON BOTH SIDES—BUILDING OF DAMS IN THE RED RIVER—SUCCESSFUL PASSAGE OF THE RAPIDS BY GUNBOATS—LOSSES AND INCIDENTS OF THE EXPEDITION.

THE first important movements at the West in 1864 were for the purpose of securing the Mississippi River, possession of which had been won by the victories of Farragut at New Orleans and Grant at Vicksburg, and setting free the large garrisons that were required to hold the important places on its banks. On the 3d of February Gen. William T. Sherman set out from Vicksburg with a force of somewhat more than twenty thousand men, in two columns, commanded respectively by Generals McPherson and Hurlbut. Their destination was Meridian, over one hundred miles east of Vicksburg, where the Mobile and Ohio Railroad is crossed by that from Jackson to Selma. The march was made in eleven days, without notable incident, except that General Sherman narrowly escaped capture at Decatur. He had stopped for the night at a log house, Hurlbut's column had passed on to encamp four miles beyond the town, and McPherson's had not yet come up. A few straggling wagons of Hurlbut's train were attacked at the cross-roads by a detachment of Confederate cavalry, and Sherman ran out of the house to see wagons and horsemen mingled in a cloud of dust, with pistol bullets flying in every direction. With the few orderlies and clerks that belonged to headquarters, he was preparing to barricade a corn-crib where they could defend themselves, when an infantry regiment was brought back from Hurlbut's corps and quickly cleared the ground. General Grant had an equally narrow escape from capture just before he set out on his Virginia campaign. A special train that was taking him to the front reached Warrenton Junction just after a detachment of Confederate cavalry, still in sight, had crossed the track at that point.

General Leonidas Polk, who was in command at Meridian, marched out at the approach of Sherman's columns, and retreated into Alabama—perhaps deceived by the report Sherman had caused to be spread that the destination of the expedition was Mobile. The National troops entered the town on the 14th, and at once began a thorough destruction of the arsenal and storehouses, the machine-shops, the station, and especially the railroads. Miles of the track were torn up, the ties burned, and the rails heated and then bent and twisted, or wound around trees. These were popularly called "Jeff Davis's neckties" and "Sherman's hairpins." Wherever the columns passed they destroyed the mills and factories and stations, leaving untouched only the dwelling-houses. Sherman was determined to disable those railroads so completely that the Confederates could not use them again, and in this he succeeded, as he did in everything he undertook personally. But another enterprise, intended to be carried out at the same time, was not so fortunate. He sent Gen. W. Sooy Smith with a cavalry force to destroy Forrest's Confederate cavalry, which was very audacious in its frequent raids, and liable at any time to dash upon the National railroad communication in middle Tennessee. Smith had about seven thousand men, and was to leave Memphis on the 1st of February and go straight to Meridian, Sherman telling him he would be sure to encounter Forrest on the way, and how he must manage the fight. But Smith did not leave Memphis till the 11th, and, instead of defeating Forrest, allowed Forrest to defeat him and drive him back to Memphis; so that Sherman waited at Meridian till the 20th, and then returned with his expedition to Vicksburg, followed by thousands of negroes of all ages, who could not and would not be turned back, but pressed close upon the army, in their firm belief that its mission was their deliverance.

While the gap that had been made in the Confederacy by the seizure of the Mississippi was thus widened by destruction of railroads east of that river, General Banks, in command at New Orleans, attempted to perform a somewhat similar service west of it. With about fifteen thousand men he set out in March for Shreveport, at the head of steam navigation on Red River, to be joined at Alexandria by ten thousand men under Gen. A. J. Smith (loaned for the occasion by Sherman from the force at Vicksburg) and by Commodore David D. Porter with a fleet of gunboats and transports. Smith and Porter arrived promptly at the rendezvous, captured Fort de Russey below Alexandria, and waited for Banks. After his arrival, the army moved by roads parallel with the river, and the gunboats kept even pace with them, though with great difficulty because of low water. Small bodies of Confederate troops appeared frequently, but were easily brushed aside by the army, while the fire from the gunboats destroyed a great many who were foolhardy enough

LANDING OF FEDERAL FORCES AT INDIAN BEND, LA., APRIL, 1863.

to attack them with musketry and field guns. So used had the troops become to this proceeding, that common precautions were relaxed, and the army jogged along strung out for twenty miles on a single road, with a small cavalry force in the advance, then the wagon-trains, and then the infantry.

As they approached Sabine Cross Roads, April 8, they were confronted by a strong Confederate force commanded by Gen. Richard Taylor, and suddenly there was a battle, though neither commander intended it. Taylor, before camping for the night, had sent out troops merely to drive back the advance guard of the expedition. But the men on both sides became excited, and the Nationals fought persistently to save their trains, while trains became frightened, broke loose, and dashed wildly through the lines of the infantry; and, amid the increasing confusion, the Confederates pressed closer to follow up their advantage. General Banks, General Franklin, and others of the commanders, were in the thick of the fray endeavoring to rally the men and hold them up to the fight. Two horses were killed under General Franklin, and one member of his staff lost both feet by a cannon shot. When the battle had been in progress an hour and a half the line suddenly gave way, and the cavalry and teamsters rushed back in a disorderly mass, followed closely by the victorious enemy. Banks's personal efforts to rally them were useless, and he was borne away by the tide. Three miles in the rear the Nineteenth Corps was drawn up in line, and here the rout was stayed. The Confederates attacked this line, but could not break it, and at nightfall retired. Banks had lost over three thousand men, nineteen guns, and a large amount of stores.

GENERAL BANKS'S ARMY IN THE ADVANCE ON SHREVEPORT, LA., CROSSING CANE RIVER, MARCH 31, 1864.

Banks tried to bring forward his infantry, but in vain, because his wagons blocked the road.

When the skirmish line was driven back on the main body, the Confederates advanced in heavy force, and for a time there was very fierce fighting. Several of the National batteries were pushed forward, and fought most gallantly. On the left was Nim's battery, which was doing terrible execution, when the enemy prepared to make a charge upon it in great force. General Stone, observing this, ordered that the battery be withdrawn to save it from capture; but it was found that this was impossible, because nearly all the horses had been killed. The gunners continued to fire double charges of grape and canister into the advancing enemy, and struck down a great many of them, including Gen. Alfred Mouton, who was leading the charge. But this did not stop the assailants, who rapidly closed up their ranks and pushed on, capturing four of the guns, while the other two were hauled off by hand. Many of the horses of the wagon

A participant in this battle, writing an account of it at the time, said: "General Banks personally directed the fight. Everything that man could do he did. Occupying a position so exposed that nearly every horse ridden by his staff was wounded, and many killed, he constantly disregarded the entreaties of those around, who begged that he would retire to some less exposed position. General Stone, his chief of staff, with his sad, earnest face, that seemed to wear an unusual expression, was constantly at the front, and by his reckless bravery did much to encourage the men. And so the fight raged. The enemy were pushing a temporary advantage. Our army was merely forming into position to make a sure battle. Then came one of those unaccountable events that no genius or courage can control. The battle was progressing vigorously. The musketry firing was loud and continuous, and having recovered from the danger experienced by Ransom's division, we felt secure of the position. I was slowly riding along the edge of a wood, conversing with a friend who had just ridden up about the events and prospects of the day. We had drawn into the side of the wood to allow an ammunition-wagon to pass, and although many were observed going to the rear, some on foot and some on horseback, we regarded it as an occurrence familiar to every battle, and it occasioned nothing but a passing remark. Suddenly there was a rush, a shout, the crashing of trees, the breaking down of rails, the rush and scamper of men. It was as sudden as though a thunder-bolt had fallen among us and set the pines on fire. What caused it, or when it commenced, no one knew. I turned to my companion to inquire the reason of this extraordinary proceeding, but before he had the chance to reply, we found ourselves swallowed up, as it were, in a hissing, seething, bubbling whirlpool of agitated men. We could not avoid the current; we could not stem it; and if we hoped to live in that mad company, we must ride with the rest of them. Our line of battle had given way. General Banks took off his hat and implored his men to remain; his staff-officers did the same, but it was of no avail. Then the general drew his sabre and endeavored to rally his men, but they would not listen. Behind him the rebels were shouting and advancing. Their musket-balls filled the air with that strange file-rasping sound that war has made familiar to our fighting men. The teams were abandoned by the drivers, the traces cut, and the animals ridden off by the frightened men. Bareheaded riders rode with agony in their faces, and for at least ten minutes it seemed as if we were going to destruction together. It was my fortune to see the first battle of Bull Run, and to be among those who made that celebrated midnight retreat toward Washington. The retreat of the fourth division was as much a rout as that of the first Federal army, with the exception that fewer men were engaged, and our men fought here with a valor that was not shown on that serious, sad, mock-heroic day in July. We rode nearly two miles in this madcap way, until, on the edge of a ravine, which might formerly have been a bayou, we found Emory's division drawn up in line. Our retreating men fell beyond this line, and Emory prepared to meet the rebels. They came with a rush, and, as the shades of night crept over the tree-tops, they encountered our men. Emory fired three rounds, and the rebels retreated. This ended the fight, leaving the Federals masters. Night, and the paralyzing effect of the stampede upon our army, made pursuit impossible. The enemy fell back, taking with them some of the wagons that were left, and a number of the guns that were abandoned."

MAJOR-GENERAL NATHANIEL P. BANKS.

BREVET MAJOR-GENERAL CUVIER GROVER.

BREVET MAJOR-GENERAL THOMAS KILBY SMITH.

That night Banks fell back fifteen miles to Pleasant Hill, General Emory's command burying the dead and caring for the wounded before following as the rear-guard. Here General Smith's command joined him, making his full force about fifteen thousand men, and he formed a strong line of battle and waited to be attacked again. The line was stretched across the main road, with its left resting on the slight eminence known as Pleasant Hill. The Confederates spent a large part of the day in gathering up plunder and slowly advancing with skirmishing until about four o'clock in the afternoon. At that hour they advanced their lines in heavy charging columns against the centre, which fought stubbornly for a while and then fell back slowly upon the reserves. The Confederates then pressed upon the right wing, when the reserves were pushed forward and charged them vigorously in turn, while the centre was rallied and re-formed and advanced so as to strike them in the flank. What took place at this time is well described by an eye-witness: "This fighting was terrific—old soldiers say it never was surpassed for desperation. Notwithstanding the terrible havoc in their ranks, the enemy pressed fiercely on, slowly pushing the men of the Nineteenth Corps back, up the hill, but not breaking their line of battle. A sudden and bold dash of the rebels on the right gave them possession of Taylor's battery, and forced our line still further back. Now came the grand *coup de main*. The Nineteenth, on arriving at the top of the hill, suddenly filed off over the hill and passed through the lines of General Smith. The rebels were now in but two lines of battle, the first having been almost annihilated by General Emory, what remained being forced back into the second line. But these two lines came on exultant and sure of victory. The first passed over the knoll, and, all heedless of the long line of cannons and crouching forms of as brave men as ever trod Mother Earth, pressed on. The second line appeared on the crest, and the death-signal was sounded. Words cannot describe the awful effect of this discharge. Seven thousand rifles, and several batteries of artillery, each gun loaded to the muzzle with grape and canister, were fired simultaneously, and the whole centre of the rebel line was crushed down as a field of ripe wheat through which a tornado had passed. It is estimated that one thousand men were hurried into eternity or frightfully mangled by this one discharge. No time was given them to recover their good order, but General Smith ordered a charge, and his men dashed rapidly forward, the boys of the Nineteenth joining in.

The rebels fought boldly and desperately back to the timber, on reaching which, a large portion broke and fled, fully two thousand throwing aside their arms."

After being thus routed, the Confederates were pursued nearly three miles. Their losses this day included Gen. Thomas Green, killed. The Confederate general, E. Kirby Smith, who commanded that department, says: "Our repulse at Pleasant Hill was so complete, and our command was so disorganized, that, had Banks followed up his success vigorously, he would have met but feeble opposition to his advance on Shreveport. . . . Assuming command, I was consulting with General Taylor when some stragglers from the battlefield, where our wounded were still lying, brought the intelligence that Banks had precipitously retreated after the battle, converting a victory which he might have claimed into a defeat."

General Banks, in his official report, gives the reasons why he retreated to Grand Ecore immediately after his brilliant victory at Pleasant Hill: "At the close of the engagement the victorious party found itself without rations and water. To clear the field for the fight, the train had been sent to the rear upon the single line of communication through the woods, and could not be brought to the front during the night. There was water neither for man nor beast, except such as the now exhausted wells had afforded during the day, for miles around. Previous to the movement of the army from Natchitoches, orders had been given to the transport fleet, with a portion of the Sixteenth Corps, under the command of Gen. Kilby Smith, to move up the river, if it was found practicable, to some point near Springfield Landing, with a view of effecting a junction with the army at that point on the river. The surplus ammunition and supplies were on board these transports. It was impossible to ascertain whether the fleet had been able to reach the point designated. The rapidly falling river and the increased difficulties of navigation made it appear almost certain that it would not be able to attain the point proposed. A squadron of cavalry sent down to the river, accompanied by Mr. Young, of the Engineer Corps, who was thoroughly acquainted with the country, reported, on the day of the battle, that no tidings of the fleet could be obtained on the river. These considerations, the absolute deprivation of water for man or beast, the exhaustion of rations, and the failure to effect a connection with the fleet on the river, made it necessary for the army, although victorious in the terrible struggle through which it had just passed, to retreat to a point where it would be certain of communicating with the fleet, and where it would have an opportunity of reorganization."

Another reason for Banks's retreat was that he had been ordered to return Smith's borrowed troops immediately.

The principal hero of this battle was Gen. Andrew Jackson Smith, whose prompt arrival with his command Friday night, together with his energy and good generalship in the battle of the ensuing day, probably saved Banks's army from a second defeat. With him was the gallant Gen. Joseph A. Mower, hardly less conspicuous in the fighting. So far as energy and valor were concerned, however, every officer there rose to his full duty. General Banks was under fire much of the time, and a bullet passed through his coat. General Franklin exhibited great skill in manœuvring his troops. A staff officer was riding down the line with an order, when a cannon shot took off his horse's head. Col. W. F. Lynch, at the head of a small detachment pursuing the enemy, captured three caissons filled with ammunition. As he was attempting to jump his horse over a ditch, a bullet whistled past his ear, and turning, he saw that it had been fired by a wounded Confederate soldier in the ditch, who was just preparing to take a second and more careful shot at him. The colonel drew his revolver and prevented any further mischief from that quarter. Col. Lewis Benedict was wounded early in the fight, but refused to leave the field, and remained with his brigade until he fell at its head, of a mortal wound. Col. W. T. Shaw, commanding a brigade, observed preparations for a cavalry charge intended to break his line, and ordered his men to reserve their fire until the enemy should be within thirty yards. This order was obeyed, and as the Confederate horsemen rode up at a gallop, each infantryman selected his mark, and when the volley was fired, nearly every one of the four hundred saddles was instantly emptied. It was said that not more than ten of the cavalrymen escaped. A participant says: "In the very thickest of the fight, on our left and centre, rode the patriarchal-looking warrior, Gen. Andrew Jackson Smith, whose troops received an increased inspiration of heroism from his presence. Wherever he rode, cheer after cheer greeted him." The same writer says: "There was something more than solemn grandeur in the scene at Pleasant Hill, at sunset, on Saturday, April 9th. Standing on a slight eminence which overlooked the left and centre of our line, I could see the terrible struggle between our well-disciplined troops and the enemy. The sun shone directly in the faces of our men, while the wind blew back the smoke of both the enemy's fire and that of our own gallant men into our ranks, rendering it almost impossible at times to distinguish the enemy in the dense clouds of smoke. All of a sudden, our whole front seemed to gather renewed strength, and they swept the rebels before them like chaff."

The Forty-ninth Illinois Regiment, led by Major Morgan, charged a Confederate battery and captured two guns and a hundred prisoners. A brigade, consisting of the Fifty-eighth and One Hundred and Nineteenth Illinois, and the Eighty-ninth Indiana, being a part of the force that struck the Confederates in the flank, retook one of the batteries that had been lost the day before, and with it four hundred prisoners.

It was said that one reason for the recklessness with which the Confederates threw away their lives in hopeless charges was that they had found a large quantity of whiskey among the captures of the previous day. The writer last quoted gives a vivid description of the appearance of the field after the battle. He says: "On Sunday morning, at daybreak, I took occasion to visit the scenes of Saturday's bloody conflict, and a more ghastly spectacle I have not witnessed. Over the field and upon the Shreveport road were scattered dead horses, broken muskets, and cartridge-boxes stained with blood, while all around, as far as the eye could reach, were mingled the inanimate forms of patriot and traitor, side by side. Here were a great many rebels badly wounded, unable to move, dying for want of water, and not a drop within two miles, and no one to get it for them. Their groans and piteous appeals for 'Water! water! water!' were heart-rending, and sent a shudder to the most stony heart. I saw one sweet face, that of a young patriot, and upon his icy features there lingered a heavenly smile, speaking of calmness and resignation. The youth was probably not more than nineteen, with a full blue eye beaming, even in death, with meekness. The morning wind lifted his auburn locks from off his marble face, exposing to view a noble forehead, which was bathed with the heavy dew of Saturday night. I dismounted for a moment, hoping to be able to find some trace of the hero's name, but the chivalry had stripped his body of every article of value. The fatal ball had pierced his heart. Not twenty feet from this

BAILEY'S DAM, RED RIVER.

dreary picture lay prostrate the mutilated body of an old man. His cap lay by the side of his head, in a pool of blood, while his long flowing gray beard was dyed with his blood. A shell had fearfully lacerated his right leg, while his belt was pierced in two places. In front of the long belt of woods which skirted the open field, and from which the rebels emerged so boldly, was a deep ditch, and at this point the slaughter among the rebels was terrific. In many places the enemy's dead were piled up in groups, intermixed with our dead."

Banks's loss in the three days, April 7–9, was three thousand nine hundred and sixty-nine men, of whom about two thousand were prisoners. The Confederate loss never was reported; but there is reason to believe that it was even larger than Banks's.

LIEUTENANT-GENERAL RICHARD TAYLOR, C. S. A.

When the army and the fleet were once more together at Grand Ecore, a new difficulty arose. There was a rapid in the river about a mile long, and the fleet in ascending had been taken over it with great difficulty. The water had now fallen, bringing to view many ragged rocks, and leaving it impossible to find any channel of sufficient depth for the boats to descend. They were in imminent danger of being captured, and it was seriously proposed to abandon or destroy them. Admiral Porter says: "I saw nothing before me but the destruction of the best part of the Mississippi squadron." But he adds: "There seemed to have been an especial Providence looking out for us, in providing a man equal to the emergency." This man was Lieut.-Col. Joseph Bailey, engineer of the Nineteenth Corps, who had foreseen the difficulty and proposed its remedy just before the battle of Pleasant Hill. His proposition, which was to build a dam or dams and raise the water sufficiently to float the boats down over the rapid, was ridiculed by the regular engineers. But it had the sanction of General Banks; and with three thousand men he set to work. Two regiments of Maine lumbermen began the felling of trees, while three hundred teams were set in motion bringing in stone and logs, and quarries were opened, and flat-boats were hastily constructed to bring material down the stream. Admiral Porter says: "Every man seemed to be working with a vigor I have seldom seen equalled, while perhaps not one in fifty believed in the success of the undertaking." Bailey first constructed a dam three hundred feet long, reaching from the left bank of the river straight out into the stream. It was made of the heaviest timbers he could get, cross-tied, and filled with stone. Four barges were floated down to the end of it, and then filled with brick and stone until they sank. From the right bank a similar dam was run out until it nearly met the barges. At the end of eight days the water had risen sufficiently to allow the smaller gunboats to go down, and it was expected that in another day it would be deep enough for all; but the pressure was too much, and two of the barges were swept away. This accident threatened to diminish the accumulated water so rapidly that none of the boats could be saved, when Admiral Porter ordered that one of the larger vessels, the *Lexington*, be brought down to attempt the passage. This was done; and he says: "She steered directly for the opening in the dam, through which the water was rushing so furiously that it seemed as if nothing but destruction awaited her. Thousands of beating hearts looked on, anxious for the result. The silence was so great as the *Lexington* approached the dam, that a pin might almost be heard to fall. She entered the gap with a full head of steam on, pitched down the roaring torrent, made two or three spasmodic rolls, hung for a moment on the rocks below, was then swept into deep water by the current, and rounded-to safely into the bank. Thirty thousand voices rose in one deafening cheer, and universal joy seemed to pervade the face of every man present. The *Neosho* followed next; all her hatches battened down, and every precaution taken against accident. She did not fare as well as the *Lexington*, her pilot having become frightened as he approached the abyss, and stopped her engine when I particularly ordered a full head of steam to be carried; the result was that for a moment her hull disappeared from sight under the water. Every one thought she was lost. She rose, however, swept along over the rocks with the current, and fortunately escaped with only one hole in her bottom, which was stopped in the course of an hour." Two more of the boats then passed through safely.

A LOUISIANA SUGAR PLANTATION.

This partial success filled everybody with enthusiasm, and the soldiers, who had been working like beavers for eight days, some of them up to their necks in water, set to work with a will to repair the dams, and in three days had done this, and also constructed a series of wing dams on the upper falls. The six large vessels then passed down safely without any serious accident, and a few hours later the whole fleet was ready to go down the river with the transports under convoy. Admiral Porter says, in his report: "The highest honors that the Government can bestow on Colonel Bailey can never repay him for the service he has rendered the country. He has saved to the Union a valuable fleet, worth nearly two million dollars, and he has deprived the enemy of a triumph which would have emboldened them to carry on this war a year or two longer; for the intended departure of the army was a fixed fact, and there was nothing left for me to do, in case that occurred, but to destroy every part of the vessels, so that the rebels could make nothing of them."

In this expedition the fleet lost two small gunboats and a quartermaster's boat, which they were convoying with four hundred troops on board. At Dunn's Bayou, three hundred miles below Alexandria, a powerful land force, with a series of batteries, attacked these boats, pierced their boilers with shot, and killed or wounded many of the soldiers with rifle-balls. The crews fought their vessels as long as possible, but at length were obliged to give up the contest, and one of the gunboats was abandoned and burned, while the other was surrendered because her commander would not set fire to her when she had so many wounded men on her decks.

MAJOR-GENERAL WILLIAM H. EMORY.

E. C. Williams, who was an ensign in the fleet on this expedition, says, in the course of his "Recollections," read before the Ohio Commandery of the Loyal Legion: "Our station for coaling was at Fort Butler, a small earthwork at the mouth of Bayou Lafourche, occupied by a small garrison from Banks's army. The garrison had erected a very tall flag-staff, reaching far above the fog-bank that in that latitude usually shut out all view of the land in the early fall and spring mornings. From our boat it was a sight of rare beauty to watch the flag as it was each morning unfurled over the little fort. Shut out from all view of the surrounding country by the impenetrable fog as completely as though we had been in mid-ocean, our attention would be first attracted to the fort by the shrill notes of the fife and the rattle of the drum as they sounded the color salute, when, watching the top of the staff, which was usually visible above the bank of fog that covered the lowlands from our view, we would see the flag rise to the peak; and as the last shrill note of the fife was sounded, accompanied by the roll of the drum, the halyards were cleared, and the flag, full and free, floated out in the heavens over us, far above the clouds, and the mists, and the gloom with which we were surrounded. Officers, at their own request, were repeatedly called from their sleep to see the sight which I have so faintly portrayed.

"It was part of our duty—at least we made it so—to take on board all escaped slaves that sought our protection, and turn them over to the nearest army garrison. Many affecting incidents occurred in connection with these poor people seeking the freedom vouchsafed them by Uncle Sam under Lincoln's proclamation. I remember one day when we were in a part of the river peculiarly infested with marauding bands of the rebel forces, a hail from shore was reported. Under cover of our guns, a boat was sent off to see what was wanted, and, returning, reported that a large number of slaves were near at hand, concealed in the dense cotton-wood brush. They had been hiding in the woods for several days, fearing re-capture by some of the roving bands of the enemy, and a scouting party was even then hard upon them, from which they could not hope to escape unless we gave them protection by taking them on board. We at once made for the designated spot, not far distant, and, running inshore, taking all precaution against a surprise, threw open a gangway, and, as the slaves showed themselves, ran out a long plank, and called to them to hurry on board. On they came—a great motley crowd of them, of both sexes and all ages, from babies in arms to gray-headed old patriarchs. One of the latter—and who was evidently the leader of the party—stood at the foot of the plank encouraging the timid and assisting the weak as they hurried on board, and, when he had seen all the others safely on, stepped on the plank himself; and as he reached the guard before coming on board, little heeding our orders to hurry, he dropped on his knees, and, reverently uncovering his head, pressed his lips fervently to the cold iron casemates, and with uplifted eyes, and hands raised to heaven, broke out with, 'Bress God and Massa Lincum's gunboats! We's free! We's free!'"

COLONEL ALBERT L. LEE.

(Afterward Brigadier-General.)

There was much speculation as to the real or ulterior object of this Red River expedition. Some writers spoke of it flippantly as a mere cotton-stealing enterprise, while others imagined they discovered a deep design to push our arms as far as possible toward the borders of Mexico, because a small French army had recently been thrown into that country, and was supposed to be a menace to our Republic.

GENERAL JOSEPH E. JOHNSTON, C. S. A.

GENERAL JOHN B. HOOD, C. S. A.

CHAPTER XXXIV.

THE ATLANTA CAMPAIGN.

SHERMAN AND JOHNSTON—SHERMAN BEGINS THE CAMPAIGN—JOHNSTON ABANDONS RESACA—FIGHTING AT NEW HOPE CHURCH—THE POSITION AT PINE MOUNTAIN—JOHNSTON AT KENESAW—FALL OF GENERAL POLK—SHERMAN EMPLOYS NEGROES—BATTLE OF KENESAW—CROSSING THE CHATTAHOOCHEE—HOOD SUPERSEDES JOHNSTON—ACTION AT PEACH TREE CREEK—BATTLE OF ATLANTA—DEATH OF GENERAL McPHERSON—THE LOSSES—CAVALRY EXPEDITIONS—STONEMAN'S RAID—FALL OF ATLANTA.

THE expeditions described in the foregoing chapter were preliminary to the great campaign that General Grant had designed for an army under Sherman, simultaneous with that conducted by himself in Virginia, and almost equal to it in difficulty and importance. The object was to move southward from Chattanooga, cutting into the heart of the Confederacy where as yet it had been untouched, and reach and capture Atlanta, which was important as a railroad centre and for its manufactures of military supplies. This involved conflict with the army under Gen. Joseph E. Johnston, by some esteemed the ablest general in the Confederate service. If he was not the ablest in all respects, he was certainly equal to the conducting of a defensive campaign with great skill. There could be no running over an army commanded by him ; it must be approached cautiously and fought valiantly. The distance from Chattanooga to Atlanta, in a straight line, is a hundred miles, through a country of hills and streams, with a great many naturally strong defensive positions. Johnston was at Dalton, with an army which he sums up at about forty-three thousand, infantry, cavalry, and artillery. But this (according to the Confederate method of counting) means only the men actually carrying muskets or sabres or handling the guns, excluding all officers, musicians, teamsters, etc. If counted after the ordinary method, his army probably numbered not fewer than fifty-five thousand.

To contend with this force, Sherman had about a hundred thousand men, consisting of the Army of the Cumberland commanded by Gen. George H. Thomas, the Army of the Tennessee commanded by Gen. James B. McPherson, and the Army of the Ohio commanded by Gen. John M. Schofield. The discrepancy in numbers seems very great, until we consider that Sherman was not only to take the offensive, but must constantly leave detachments to guard his communications ; for he drew all his supplies from Nashville, over one single-track railroad, and it was liable to be broken at any time by guerilla raids. As he advanced into the enemy's country, this line would become longer, and the danger of its being broken still greater. Johnston, on the contrary, had nothing to fear in the rear, for he was fighting on his own ground, and could bring his entire force to the front at every emergency. All things considered, it was pretty nearly an even match. In one respect, however, Sherman had a decided advantage ; he possessed the confidence of the Government that he served, while Johnston did not. At least, Johnston complains that Mr. Davis did not trust him as he should, and thwarted him in many ways ; and in this the general appears to be corroborated by the circumstances of the campaign.

When Sherman concentrated his forces at Chattanooga, and considered the means of supply, he found that about one hundred and thirty cars loaded with provisions must arrive at that point every day. But that railroad had not cars and locomotives enough for such a task, and so he sent orders to Louisville for the seizure of trains arriving there from the North, and soon had rolling-stock in great abundance and variety. While he thus provided liberally for necessary supplies, he excluded all luxuries. Tents were taken only for the sick and wounded. The sole exception to this was made in favor of General Thomas, who needed a tent and a small wagon-train, which the soldiers immediately christened "Thomas's Circus." Sherman had no tent or train. Every man, whether officer or private, carried provisions for five days.

Thus equipped and disciplined, the army set out from Chattanooga on the 5th of May (the day on which Grant entered the Wilderness), following the line of the railroad south toward Atlanta. A direct approach to Dalton was impossible, because of Johnston's fortifications at Tunnel Hill. So Sherman made a feint of attacking there, and sent McPherson southward to march through the gap in the mountains, strike Resaca, and cut the railroad over which Johnston drew all his supplies. Here at the very outset was the brilliant opportunity of the campaign, not to occur again. McPherson reached Resaca, but found fortifications and an opposing force there, and just lacked the necessary boldness to attack promptly and vigorously, thrusting his army into a position where it would have made the destruction of Johnston's almost certain. Instead of this, he fell back to the gap, and waited for the remainder of the army to join him there. But this enabled Johnston to learn what was going on, and when Sherman had passed down to the gap with his entire

THE BATTLE OF ATLANTA, GA., JULY 22, 1864.

army, he found, of course, that his antagonist had fallen back to Resaca and concentrated his forces there in a strong position.

General Sherman says of this error of McPherson's: "McPherson had startled Johnston in his fancied security, but had not done the full measure of his work. He had in hand twenty-three thousand of the best men of the army, and could have walked into Resaca (then held only by a small brigade), or he could have placed his whole force astride the railroad above Resaca, and there have easily withstood the attack of all of Johnston's army, with the knowledge that Thomas and Schofield were on his heels. Had he done so, I am certain that Johnston would not have ventured to attack him in position, but would have retreated eastward by Spring Place, and we should have captured half his army and all his artillery and wagons at the very beginning of the campaign. But at the critical moment McPherson seems to have been a little cautious. Still he was perfectly justified by his orders, and fell back and assumed an unassailable defensive position in Sugar Valley, on the Resaca side of Snake Creek Gap. As soon as informed of this, I determined to pass the whole army through Snake Creek Gap, and to move on Resaca with the main army."

MAJOR-GENERAL JOHN M. SCHOFIELD.

On the 14th of May, Sherman's army was in position around Resaca on the north and west, and on that and the next day there was continual skirmishing and artillery firing, though nothing like a great battle. Neither general was willing to fight at disadvantage; Sherman would not attack the intrenchments, and Johnston would not come out of them. McPherson, on the right, advanced his line of battle till he gained an elevated position from which his guns could destroy the railroad bridge over the Oostenaula in the Confederate rear, and all attempts to drive him out of this position ended only in bloody repulse. On the left of the line, Hooker exhibited something of his usual dash by capturing a small portion of the enemy's intrenchments, with four guns and some prisoners. Meanwhile, Sherman had thrown two pontoon bridges across the river three miles below the town, so that he could send over a detachment to break the railroad, and had also sent a division of cavalry down the river, to cross at some lower point for the same purpose. Johnston, therefore, seeing his communications threatened so seriously, and having no good roads by which he could retreat eastward, did not wait to be cooped up in Resaca, but in the night of the 15th retired southward across the river, following the railroad, and burned the bridges behind him. Sherman thus came into possession of Resaca; but Resaca was not what he wanted, and without the slightest delay he started his entire army in pursuit of the enemy. Hooker crossed the river by fords and ferries above the town; Thomas and Schofield repaired the half-burned bridges and used them; McPherson crossed by the pontoons.

The enemy was found, on the 19th, in position at Cassville, just east of Kingston, and apparently ready to fight; but when Sherman's columns converged on the place the Confederates, after some sharp skirmishing, retreated again in the night of the 20th, and crossed Etowah River. Johnston had really intended to fight here, and he explains his refusal to do so by saying that Hood and Polk told him their corps could not hold their positions, as a portion of each was enfiladed by the National artillery. Hood's version of the mysterious retreat is to the effect that he wanted to assume the offensive, marching out with his own corps and a part of Polk's to overwhelm Schofield, who was separated from the remainder of the National army.

Here Sherman halted for a few days, to get his army well together, re-provision it, and repair the railroad in his rear. Twenty years before, when he was a young lieutenant, he had ridden through the country from Charleston, S. C., to northwestern Georgia, and he still retained a good recollection of the topography. Knowing that Allatoona Pass, through which runs the railroad south of Kingston, was very strong and would probably be held by Johnston, he diverged from the railroad at Kingston, passing considerably west of it, and directed his columns toward Dallas; his purpose being to threaten Marietta and Atlanta so as to cause Johnston to withdraw from Allatoona and release his hold on the railroad, which became more and more necessary to the invading army as it advanced into the country. Johnston understood this manœuvre, and moved westward to meet it. The armies, in an irregular way—for each was somewhat scattered and uncertain of the other's exact position—came into collision at the cross-roads by New Hope Church. Around this place for six days there was continuous fighting, sometimes mere skirmishing, and sometimes an attack by a heavy detachment of one party or the other; but all such attacks, on either side, were costly and fruitless. The general advantage, however, was with Sherman; for as he gradually got his lines into proper order, he strengthened his right, and then reached out with his left toward the railroad, secured all the wagon-roads from Allatoona, and sent out a strong force of cavalry to occupy that pass and repair the railroad. Johnston then left his position at New Hope Church, and took up a new one.

Thus ended the month of May in this campaign, where each commander exercised the utmost skill, neither was guilty of anything rash, and the results were such as would naturally follow from the military conditions with which it began. The losses on each side, thus far, were fewer than ten thousand men—killed, wounded, and missing; but strong positions had been successively taken up, turned, abandoned; and Sherman was steadily drawing nearer to his goal.

Johnston's new position was on the slopes of Kenesaw, Pine, and Lost Mountains, thus crossing the railroad above Marietta. It had the advantage of a height from which everything done by Sherman's approaching army could be seen; but it had the disadvantage of a line ten miles long, and so disposed that one part could not readily reinforce another. Though heavy rains were falling, the National army kept close to its antagonist, and intrenched at every advance. The railroad was repaired behind it, and the trains that brought its supplies ran up almost to its front. In one instance, an engineer detached his locomotive and ran forward to a tank, where he quietly took in the necessary supply of water, while a Confederate battery on the mountain fired several shots, but none of them quite hit the locomotive, which woke the echoes with its shrill whistling as it ran back out of range.

When the rain was over, Sherman occupied a strongly intrenched line that followed the contour of Johnston's, and was at

BRIGADIER-GENERAL J. S. ROBINSON.

BREVET MAJOR-GENERAL T. H. RUGER.

BRIGADIER-GENERAL W. F. BARTLETT.

BREVET MAJOR-GENERAL W. Q. GRESHAM.

nearly all points close to it. Both sides maintained skirmish lines that were almost as strong as lines of battle, and occupied rifle-pits. From these the roar of musketry was almost unceasing, and there was a steady loss of men. On June 14, while General Sherman was reconnoitring the enemy's position, he observed a battery on the crest of Pine Mountain, and near it a group of officers with field-glasses. Ordering a battery to fire two or three volleys at them, he rode on. A few hours later, his signal officer told him that the Confederates had signalled from Pine Mountain to Marietta, "Send an ambulance for General Polk's body." The group on the mountain had consisted of Generals Johnston, Hardee, and Polk, and a few soldiers that had gathered around them. One of the cannon-balls had struck General Polk in the chest and cut him in two. He was fifty-eight years old at the time of his death, had been educated at West Point, but afterward studied theology, and at the outbreak of the war had been for twenty years the Protestant Episcopal Bishop of Louisiana.

The next day Sherman advanced his lines, intending to attack between Kenesaw and Pine Mountain, but found that Johnston had withdrawn from Pine Mountain, taking up a shorter line, from Kenesaw to Lost Mountain. Sherman promptly occupied the ground, and gathered in a large number of prisoners, including the Fourteenth Alabama Regiment entire. The next day he pressed forward again, only to find that the enemy had still further contracted his lines, abandoning Lost Mountain, but still occupying Kenesaw, and covering Marietta and the roads to Atlanta with the extension of his left wing. The successive positions to which Johnston's army had fallen back were prepared beforehand by gangs of slaves impressed for the purpose, so that his soldiers had little digging to do, and could save their strength for fighting. After a time Sherman adopted a similar policy, by setting at work the crowds of negroes that flocked to his camp, feeding them from the army supplies, and promising them ten dollars a month, as he was authorized to do by an act of Congress. The fortifications consisted of a sort of framework of rails and logs, covered with earth thrown up from a ditch on each side. When there was opportunity, they were finished with a heavy head-log laid along the top, which rested in notches cut in other logs that extended back at right angles and formed an inclined plane down which the head-log could roll harmlessly if knocked out of place by a cannon-shot. Miles of such works were often constructed in a single night; and they were absolutely necessary, when veteran armies were facing each other with weapons of precision in their hands.

Sherman was now facing a little south of east, and kept pressing his lines closer up to Johnston's, with rifle and artillery firing going on all the time. On the 21st the divisions of Generals Wood and Stanley gained new positions, on the southern flank of Kenesaw, where several determined assaults failed to dislodge them; and the next day the troops of Hooker and Schofield pressed forward to within three miles of Marietta, and withstood an attack by Hood's corps, inflicting upon him a loss of a thousand men. As the National line was now lengthened quite as far as seemed prudent, and still the Confederate communications were not severed, Sherman determined upon the hazardous experiment of attacking the enemy in his intrenchments. He chose two points for assault, about a mile apart, and on the morning of the 27th launched heavy columns against them, while firing was at the same time kept up all along the line. He expected to break the centre, and with half of his army take half of Johnston's in reverse, while with the remainder of his troops he held the other half so close that it could not go to the rescue. But his columns wasted away before the fire from the intrenchments, and as in Pickett's charge at Gettysburg, and Grant's assault at Cold Harbor, only a remnant reached the enemy's works, there to be killed or captured. Among those sacrificed were Brig.-Gens. Daniel McCook and Charles G. Harker, both of whom died of their wounds. This experiment cost Sherman over two thousand five hundred men, while Johnston's loss was but little over eight hundred.

It was evident that any repetition would be useless, and the approved principles of warfare seemed to supply no alternative. What General Sherman therefore did was to disregard the maxim that an army must always hold fast to its communications; and by doing the same thing on a grander scale six months later he won his largest fame. He determined to let go of the railroad north of Kenesaw, take ten days' provisions in wagons, and move his whole army southward to seize the road below Marietta. This would compel Johnston either to fall back farther toward Atlanta, or come out and fight him in his intrenchments—which, as both commanders well knew, was almost certain destruction to the assaulting party. In the night of July 2, McPherson's troops, who had the left or north of the line, drew out of their works and marched southward, passing behind the lines held by Thomas and Schofield. This was the same manœuvre as that by which Grant had carried his army to its successive positions between the Wilderness and the James River, except that he moved by the left flank and Sherman by the right, and Grant never had to let go of his communications, being supplied by lines of wagons from various points on the Potomac.

When Johnston saw what Sherman was doing he promptly abandoned his strong position at Kenesaw, and fell back to the Chattahoochee; but he did not, as Sherman hoped, attempt to cross the stream at once. Intrenchments had been prepared for him on the north bank, and here he stopped. Sherman, expecting to catch his enemy in the confusion of crossing a stream, pressed on rapidly with his whole army, and ran up against what he says was one of the strongest pieces of field fortification he had ever seen. A thousand slaves had been at work on it for a month. And yet, like many other things in the costly business of war, it was an enormous outlay to serve a very brief purpose. For Sherman not only occupied ground that overlooked it, but held the river for miles above and below, and was thus able to cross over and turn the position. Johnston must have known this when the fortifications were in process of construction, and their only use was to protect his army from assault while it was crossing the river. On the 9th of July, Schofield's army crossed above the Confederate position, laying two pontoon bridges, and intrenched itself in a strong position on the left bank. Johnston, thus compelled to surrender the stream, crossed that night with his entire army, and burned the railroad and other bridges behind him. Sherman was almost as cautious in the pursuit, wherever there was any serious danger, as Johnston was in the retreat; and he not only chose an upper crossing, farther from Atlanta, but spent a week in preparations to prevent disaster, before he threw over his entire army. This he did on the 17th, and the next day moved it by a grand right wheel toward the city of Atlanta.

The Chattahoochee was the last great obstruction before the fortifications of the Gate City were reached, and on the day that Sherman crossed it something else took place, which, in the opinion of many military critics, was even more disastrous to the fortunes of the Confederacy. This was the supersession of the careful and skilful Johnston by Gen. John B. Hood, an impetuous and sometimes reckless fighter, but no strategist. The controversy over the wisdom of this action on the part of the Confederate Government will probably never be satisfactorily closed. The merits of it can be sufficiently indicated by two brief extracts. The telegram conveying the orders of the War Department said: "As you have failed to arrest the advance of the enemy to the vicinity of Atlanta, far in the interior of Georgia, and express no confidence that you can defeat or repel him, you are hereby relieved from the command of the Army and Department of Tennessee, which you will immediately turn over to General Hood." General Johnston said in his reply: "As to the alleged cause of my removal, I assert that Sherman's army is much stronger compared with that of Tennessee than Grant's compared with that of Northern Virginia. Yet the enemy has been compelled to advance much more slowly to the vicinity of Atlanta than to that of Richmond and Petersburg, and penetrated much deeper into Virginia than into Georgia. Confident language by a military commander is not usually regarded as evidence of competence."

Within twenty-four hours the National army learned that its antagonist had a new commander, and there was eager inquiry as to Hood's character as a soldier. Schofield and McPherson had been his classmates at West Point, and from their testimony and the career of Hood as a corps commander it was easily inferred that a new policy might be looked for, very different from Johnston's. Sherman warned his army to be constantly prepared for sallies of the enemy, and his prediction did not wait long for fulfilment. On the 20th, at noonday, as his army was slowly closing in upon the city, the Confederates left the intrenchments that Johnston had prepared for them along the line of Peach Tree Creek, where he would have awaited attack, and made a heavy assault upon Thomas, who held the right of the National line. The weight of the blow fell mainly upon Hooker's corps, and the attack was so furious and reckless that in many places friend and foe were intermingled, fighting hand to hand. A heavy column of Confederates attempted to fall upon an exposed flank of the Fourth Corps; but Thomas promptly brought several batteries to play upon it, and at the end of two hours the enemy was driven back to his intrenchments, leaving hundreds of dead on the field. Hooker also lost heavily, because his men fought without intrenchments or cover of any kind.

The Confederates now abandoned the line of works along Peach Tree Creek, and fell back to the immediate defences of the city. It was seen that one point in their line was an eminence—then called Bald Hill, but since known as Leggett's Hill—from which, if it could be occupied, the city could be shelled. After a consultation between Generals Blair and McPherson on the afternoon of the 20th, it was agreed that this hill ought to be captured, and the task was assigned to Gen. Mortimer D. Leg-

FALL OF GENERAL JAMES B McPHERSON, NEAR ATLANTA.

gett's division. Leggett accordingly said to Gen. M. F. Force, who commanded his first brigade: "I want you to carry that hill. Move as soon as it is light enough to move. I will support your left and rear with the rest of the division, and the fourth division will make a demonstration as you go up to distract the attention of the enemy in their front." Accordingly, at daylight, Leggett's skirmish line cautiously went forward, and got as near as possible to the Confederate works without alarming the enemy. After some little delay, caused by waiting for the fourth division, General Force gave the order for the assault. What then followed is told by Col. Gilbert D. Munson, of the Seventy-eighth Ohio Regiment: "The skirmish line sprang forward; the brigade debouched from its concealment in the wood. In the front line on came the Twelfth and Sixteenth Wisconsin, close supported by the Twentieth, Thirtieth, and Thirty-first Illinois—the second line of battle; flags flying, bayonets fixed; arms right shoulder shift and unloaded; Force and his aid, Adams, just in rear of the Wisconsin regiments, and his adjutant-general, Capt. J. Bryant Walker, and another aid, Evans, with the Illinois boys—mounted; all regimental officers on foot. The skirmishers, for a moment, distracted the enemy by their rapid advance and firing; then the brigade received and enveloped them as it reached the crest of the hill, and exposed its full front to the steady fire of Cleburne's rifles. Our men fell in bunches; still came the charging column on; faster and faster it pressed forward. 'Close up! close up!' the command, and each regiment closed on its colors, and over the barricades went the first line, handsomely, eagerly, and well aligned. Then began our firing and our fun. Into the gray-coats the Sixteenth Wisconsin poured a rattling

COLONEL CHARLES CANDY.
(Afterward Brigadier-General.)

BREVET MAJOR-GENERAL EDWARD M. McCOOK.

fire, as they scattered and ran along the level ground, down the slope of the hill, and on toward Atlanta. I joined General Force after the skirmish line was merged in his line of battle, and was with him when it came to and went over the barricades. 'Our orders are to carry this hill, General; the Sixteenth are away beyond, where, I understand, we are to go.' Force said something about being able to take the next hill, too, but immediately sent Captain Walker after Colonel Fairchild, and his 'Right about, march,' brought the regiment back. Captain Walker then reported the capture of the hill to General Leggett, who was with the rest of the division. Walker said to me, on his return, that, having a message for Gen. Giles A. Smith, commanding the fourth division, he told him the hill was won and held by Force, but Smith would hardly believe him: he thought he was joking. It seemed doubtful to him that such an important point had been won so quickly."

BRIGADIER-GENERAL GEORGE H. GORDON.

The fourth division, on the right of Force's brigade, met with a stubborn resistance, but finally overcame it, and other troops were brought up, and after a little the place was firmly held. This hill was the key-point of the line, and its capture was what caused Hood to come out and give battle the next day. He found that Sherman's left flank, which crossed the line of railroad to Augusta, was without proper protection, and consequently he moved to the attack at that point. He marched by a road parallel with the railroad, and the contour of the ground and the forests hid him until his men burst in upon the rear of Sherman's extreme left, seized a battery that was moving through the woods, and took possession of some of the camps. But McPherson's veterans were probably in expectation of such a movement, and under the direction of Generals Logan, Charles R. Wood, and Morgan L. Smith, quickly formed to meet it. That flank of the army was "refused"—turned back at a right angle with the main line—and met the onsets of the Confederates with steady courage from noon till night. Seven heavy assaults were made, resulting in seven bloody repulses, guns were taken and retaken, and finally a counter attack was made on the Confederate flank by Wood's division, assisted by twenty guns that fired over the heads of Wood's men as they advanced, which drove back the enemy, who retired slowly to their defences, carrying with them some of the captured guns. It had been intended that Wheeler's Confederate cavalry should capture McPherson's supply-trains, which were at Decatur; but the troopers were fought off till the trains could be drawn back to a place of safety, and Wheeler only secured a very few wagons. The National loss in this battle was thirty-five hundred and twenty-one men killed, wounded, and missing, and ten guns. The total Confederate loss is unknown, but it was very heavy; General Logan reported thirty-two hundred and twenty dead in front of his lines, and two thousand prisoners, half of whom were wounded. The most grievous loss to Sherman was General McPherson, who rode off into the woods at the first sounds of battle, almost alone. His horse soon came back, bleeding and riderless, and an hour later the general's dead body was brought to headquarters. McPherson was a favorite in the army. He was but thirty-four years old, and with the exception of his error at the outset of the campaign, by which Johnston was allowed to escape from Dalton, he had a brilliant military record. Gen. Oliver O. Howard, who had lost an arm at Fair Oaks and was now in command of the Fourth Corps, was promoted to McPherson's place in command of the Army of the Tennessee; whereupon General Hooker, commanding the Twentieth Corps, who believed that the promotion properly belonged to him, asked to be relieved, and left the army. His corps was given to Gen. Henry W. Slocum.

Sherman now repeated his former manœuvre, of moving by the right flank to strike the enemy's communications and compel him either to retreat again or fight at a disadvantage. The Army of the Tennessee was withdrawn from the left on the 27th, and marched behind the Army of the Cumberland to the extreme right, with the intention of extending the flank far enough to cross the railroad south of Atlanta. The movement was but partially performed when Hood made a heavy attack on that flank, and for four or five hours on the 28th there was bloody fighting. Logan's men hastily threw up a slight breastwork, from which they repelled six charges in quick succession, and later in the day several other charges by the Confederates broke against the immovable lines of the Fifteenth Corps. Meanwhile Sherman sent Gen. Jefferson C. Davis's division to make a detour, and come up into position where it could strike the Confederate flank in turn; but Davis lost his way and failed to appear in time. In this battle Logan's corps lost five hundred and seventy-two men; while they captured five battle-flags and buried about six hundred of the enemy's dead. The total Confederate losses during July, in killed and wounded, were reported by the surgeon-general at eighty-eight hundred and forty-one, to which Sherman adds two thousand prisoners. Sherman reports his own losses during that month—killed, wounded, and missing—at ninety-seven hundred and nineteen; but this does not include the cavalry. Johnston's estimate of Sherman's losses is so enormous that if it had been correct his government would have been clearly justified when it censured him for not driving the National army out of the State.

Sherman had sent out several cavalry expeditions to break the railroads south of Atlanta, but with no satisfactory results. They tore up a few miles of track each time, but the damage was quickly repaired. The marvellous facility with which both sides mended broken railroads and replaced burned bridges is illustrated by many anecdotes. Sherman had duplicates of the important bridges on the road that brought his supplies, and whenever the guerillas destroyed one, he had only to order the duplicate to be set up. On the 26th Gen. George Stoneman had set out with a cavalry force to break up the railroad at Jonesboro', with the intention of pushing on rapidly to Macon and Andersonville, and releasing a large number of prisoners that were confined there in stockades; while at the same time another cavalry force, under McCook, was sent around by the right to join Stoneman at Jonesboro'. They destroyed two miles of track, burned two trains of cars and five hundred wagons, killed eight hundred mules, and took three or four hundred prisoners. But McCook was surrounded by the enemy at Newnan, and only escaped with a loss of six hundred men; while Stoneman destroyed seventeen locomotives and a hundred cars, and threw a few shells into Macon, but was surrounded at Clifton, where he allowed himself and seven hundred of his men to be captured in order to facilitate the escape of the remainder of his command.

BREVET MAJOR-GENERAL MANNING F. FORCE.

Perhaps it was quite as well that he did not reach Andersonville, for General Winder, in command there, had issued this order on July 27th: "The officers on duty and in charge of battery of Florida artillery will, on receiving notice that the enemy has approached within seven miles of this post, open fire on the stockade with grape-shot, without reference to the situation beyond this line of defence." The conduct of those on guard duty at the prison leaves little doubt that this order would have been obeyed with alacrity.

Two or three weeks later, Wheeler's Confederate cavalry passed to the rear of Sherman's army, captured a large drove of cattle, and broke up two miles of railroad; and about the same time Kilpatrick's cavalry rode entirely round Atlanta, fought and defeated a combined cavalry and infantry force, and inflicted upon the railroad such damage as he thought it would take ten days to repair; but within twenty-four hours trains were again running into the city.

Finding that cavalry raids could effect nothing, Sherman posted Slocum's corps at the railroad bridge over the Chattahoochee, and, moving again by the right, rapidly but cautiously, concealing the movement as far as possible, he swung all the remainder of his army into position south of Atlanta, where they tore up the railroads, burning the ties and twisting the rails, and then advanced toward the city. There was some fighting, and Govan's Confederate brigade was captured entire, with ten guns; but the greater part of Hood's forces escaped eastward in the night of September 1st. They destroyed a large part of the Government property that night, and the sound of the explosions caused Slocum to move down from the bridge, when he soon found that he had nothing to do but walk into Atlanta. A few days later Sherman made his headquarters there, disposed his army in and around the city, and prepared for permanent possession.

CHAPTER XXXV.

THE BATTLE OF MOBILE BAY.

DEFENCES — ADMIRAL FARRAGUT'S PREPARATIONS — PASSING THE FORTS—LOSS OF THE "TECUMSEH"—FIGHT WITH THE RAM "TENNESSEE"—COST OF THE VICTORY—CRAVEN'S CHIVALRY—OFFICIAL REPORT OF ADMIRAL FARRAGUT—POETIC DESCRIPTION OF THE BATTLE BY A POET WHO PARTICIPATED IN THE CONFLICT.

THE capture of Mobile had long been desired, both because of its importance as a base of operations, whence expeditions could move inland, and communication be maintained with the fleet, and because blockade-running at that port could not be entirely prevented by the vessels outside. Grant and Sherman had planned to have the city taken by forces moving east from New Orleans and Port Hudson; but everything had gone wrong in that quarter.

REAR-ADMIRAL DAVID G. FARRAGUT.

The principal defences of Mobile Bay were Fort Morgan on Mobile Point, and Fort Gaines, three miles northwest of it, on the extremity of Dauphin Island. The passage between these two works was obstructed by innumerable piles for two miles out from Fort Gaines, and from that point nearly to Fort Morgan by a line of torpedoes. The eastern end of this line was marked by a red buoy, and from that point to Fort Morgan the channel was open, to admit blockade-runners.

Farragut's fleet had been for a long time preparing to pass these forts, fight the Confederate fleet inside (which included a powerful iron-clad ram), and take possession of the bay. But he wanted the coöperation of a military force to capture the forts. This was at last furnished, under Gen. Gordon Granger, and landed on Dauphin Island, August 4th. Farragut had made careful preparations, and, as at New Orleans, had given minute instructions to his captains. The attacking column consisted of four iron-clad monitors and seven wooden sloops-of-war. To each sloop was lashed a gunboat on the port (or left) side, to help her out in case she were disabled. The heaviest fire was expected from Fort Morgan, on the right, or starboard, side. Before six o'clock in the morning of the 5th all were under way, the monitors forming a line abreast of the wooden ships and to the right of them. The *Brooklyn* headed the line of the wooden vessels, because she had an apparatus for picking up torpedoes. They steamed along in beautiful style, coming up into close order as they neared the fort, so that there were spaces of but a few yards from the stern of one vessel to the bow of the next. The forts and the Confederate fleet, which lay just inside of the line of torpedoes, opened fire upon them half an hour before they could bring their guns to answer. They made the *Hartford*, Farragut's flagship, their especial target, lodged a hundred-and-twenty-pound ball in her mainmast, sent great splinters flying across her deck, more dangerous than shot, and killed or wounded many of her crew. One ball from a Confederate gunboat killed ten men and wounded five. The other wooden vessels suffered in like manner as they approached; but when they came abreast of the fort they poured in rapid broadsides of grape-shot, shrapnel, and shells, which quickly cleared the bastions and silenced the batteries.

The captains had been warned to pass to the east of the red buoy; but Captain T. A. M. Craven, of the monitor *Tecumseh*, eager to engage the Confederate ram *Tennessee*, which was behind the line of torpedoes, made straight for her. The consequence was that his vessel struck a torpedo, which exploded, and she went down in a few seconds, carrying with her the captain and most of the crew. The *Brooklyn* stopped when she found torpedoes, and began to back. This threatened to throw the whole line into confusion while under fire, and defeat the project; but Farragut instantly ordered more steam on his own vessel and her consort, drew ahead of the *Brooklyn*, and led the line to victory. All this time he was in the rigging of the *Hartford*, and a quartermaster had gone up and tied him to one of the shrouds, so that if wounded he should not fall to the deck. As the fleet passed into the bay, several of the larger vessels were attacked by the ram *Tennessee* and considerably damaged, while their shot seemed to have little effect on her heavy iron mail. At length she withdrew to her anchorage, and the order was given from the flagship, "Gunboats chase enemy's gunboats," whereupon the lashings were cut and the National gunboats were off in a flash. In a little while they had destroyed or captured all the Confederate vessels save one, which escaped up the bay, where the water was too shallow for them to follow her.

But as the fleet was coming to anchor, in the belief that the fight was over, the *Tennessee* left her anchorage and steamed boldly into the midst of her enemies, firing in every direction and attempting to ram them. The wooden vessels stood to the fight in the most gallant manner, throwing useless broadsides against the monster, avoiding her blows by skilful manœuvring, and trying to run her down till some of them hammered their bows to splinters. The three monitors pounded at her to more purpose. They fired one fifteen-inch solid shot that penetrated her armor; they jammed some of her shutters so that the port-holes could not be opened; they shot away her steering-gear, and knocked off her smoke-stack, so that life on board of her became intolerable, and she surrendered. Her commander, Franklin Buchanan, formerly of the United States navy, had been seriously wounded.

This victory cost Farragut's fleet fifty-two men killed and one hundred and seventy wounded, besides one hundred and thirteen that went down in the *Tecumseh*. Knowles, the same old quartermaster that had tied Farragut in the rigging, says he saw the admiral coming on deck as the twenty-five dead sailors of the *Hartford* were being laid out, "and it was the only time I ever saw the old gentleman cry, but the tears came into his eyes like a little child." The Confederate fleet lost ten men killed, sixteen wounded, and two hundred and eighty prisoners. The loss in the forts is unknown. They were surrendered soon afterward to the land forces, with a thousand men.

Of the four iron-clads that went into this fight, two—the *Tecumseh* and the *Manhattan*—had come from the Atlantic coast, while the *Chickasaw* and the *Winnebago*, which had been built at St. Louis by James B. Eads, came down the Mississippi. Much doubt had been expressed as to the ability of these two river-built monitors to stand the rough weather of the Gulf, and Captain Eads had visited the Navy Department, and offered to bear all the expenses in case they failed. It is agreed by all authorities, that in the fight with the ram *Tennessee*, which was a much more serious affair than passing the forts, the best work was done by the monitor *Chickasaw*. The commander of this vessel, George H. Perkins, and his lieutenant, William Hamilton, had received leave of absence and were about to go North, when they learned that the battle was soon to take place, and volunteered to remain and take part in it. They were then at New Orleans and were assigned to the *Chickasaw*. As this vessel passed thence down the Mississippi on her way to Mobile, she took a pilot for the navigation of the river. It often happened that the National vessels were obliged to take Southern men as pilots in the Southern waters, and they were not always to be trusted. In this instance, Captain Perkins, being called away from the pilot-house for a few minutes, observed that his vessel's course was at once changed and she was heading for a wreck. Rushing back to the pilot-house, he seized the wheel and gave her the proper direction, after which he drew his pistol and told the pilot that if the ship touched ground or ran into anything, he would instantly blow out his brains. The pilot muttered something about the bottom of the river being lumpy, and the best pilots not always being able to avoid the lumps. But Captain Perkins told him he could not consider any such excuse, and if he touched a single lump he would instantly lose his life. There was no more trouble about the piloting.

BREVET MAJOR-GENERAL W. P. BENTON.

The *Chickasaw* was a double-turreted monitor, carrying two eleven-inch guns in each turret, and she was the only iron-clad that remained in perfect condition throughout the fight. This, perhaps, was owing to the fact that Captain Perkins, who was young, enthusiastic, and ambitious, personally inspected everything on the ship while she was in preparation and before she went into action. The place of the ships in line was determined by the rank of their commanders, and the *Chickasaw* came last of the monitors. In the fight with the *Tennessee*, she fired solid shot, most of them striking her about the stern. The pilot of the *Tennessee* said after the battle: "The *Chickasaw* hung close under our stern; move where we would, she was always there, firing the two eleven-inch guns in her forward turret like pocket pistols, so that she soon had the plates flying in the air." Captain Perkins himself says: "When the *Tennessee* passed my ship first, it was on my port side. After that she steered toward Fort Morgan. Some of our vessels anchored, others kept under way, and when the *Tennessee* approached the fleet again, she was at once attacked by the wooden vessels, but they made no impression upon her. An order was now brought from Admiral Farragut to the iron-clads, by Dr. Palmer, directing them to attack the *Tennessee*; but when they approached her, she moved off toward the fort again. I followed straight after her with the *Chickasaw*, and, overtaking her, I poured solid shot into her as fast as I could, and after a short engagement forced her to surrender, having shot away her smoke-stack, destroyed her steering-gear, and jammed her after-ports, rendering her guns useless, while one of my shots wounded Admiral Buchanan. I followed her close, my guns and turrets continuing in perfect order in spite of the strain upon them. When Johnston came on the roof of the *Tennessee*, and showed the white flag as signal of surrender, no vessel of our fleet, except the *Chickasaw*, was within a quarter of a mile. But the *Ossipee* was approaching, and her captain was much older than myself. I was wet with perspiration, begrimed with powder, and exhausted with constant and violent exertion; so I drew back and allowed Captain LeRoy to receive the surrender, though my first lieutenant, Mr. Hamilton, said at the time, 'Captain Perkins, you are making a mistake.'"

BRIGADIER-GENERAL F. M. COCKRELL, C. S. A.

Admiral Farragut says in his official report: "As I had an elevated position in the main rigging near the top, I was able to overlook not only the deck of the *Hartford*, but the other vessels of the fleet. I witnessed the terrible effects of the enemy's shot, and the good conduct of the men at their guns; and although no doubt their hearts sickened, as mine did, when their shipmates were struck down beside them, yet there was not a moment's hesitation to lay their comrades aside, and spring again to their deadly work. . . . I must not omit to call the attention of the department to the conduct of Acting Ensign Henry C. Nields, of the *Metacomet*, who had charge of the boat sent from that vessel, when the *Tecumseh* sunk. He took her under one of the most galling fires I ever saw, and succeeded in rescuing from death ten of her crew within six hundred yards of the fort." Commodore Foxhall A. Parker, in his very accurate account of this battle, describes more particularly the exploit of Ensign Nields: "Starting from the port quarter of the *Metacomet*, and steering the boat himself, this mere boy pulled directly under the battery of the *Hartford*, and around the *Brooklyn*, to within a few hundred yards of the fort, exposed to the fire of both friends and foes. After he had gone a little distance from his vessel, he seemed suddenly to reflect that he had no flag flying, when he dropped the yoke-ropes, picked up a small ensign from the bottom of the boat, and unfurling it from its staff, which he shipped in a socket made for it in the stern-sheets, he threw it full to the breeze, amid the loud cheers of his men. 'I can hardly describe,' says an officer of the *Tennessee*, 'how I felt at witnessing this most gallant act. The muzzle of our gun was slowly raised, and the bolt intended for the *Tecumseh* flew harmlessly over the heads of that glorious boat's crew, far down in the line of our foes.' After saving Ensign Zelitch, eight men, and the pilot, Nields turned, and, pulling for the fleet, succeeded in reaching the *Oneida*, where he remained until the close of the action."

In a memorandum discovered among Admiral Farragut's papers he said: "General orders required the vessels to pass inside the buoys next to Fort Morgan. When the *Tecumseh* reached that point, it looked so close that poor Craven said to the pilot, 'The admiral ordered me to go inside that buoy, but it must be a mistake.' He ran just his breadth of beam too far westward, struck a torpedo, and went down in two minutes. Alden saw the buoys ahead, and stopped his ship. This liked to have proved fatal to all of us. I saw the difficulty, and ordered the *Hartford* ahead, and the fleet to follow. Allowing the *Brooklyn* to go ahead was a great error. It lost not only the *Tecumseh*, but many valuable lives, by keeping us under the fire of the forts for thirty minutes; whereas, had I led, as I intended to do, I would have gone inside the buoys, and all would have followed me. The officers and crews of all the ships did their duty like men. There was but one man who showed fear, and he was allowed to resign. This was the most desperate battle I ever fought since the days of the old *Essex*."

CAPTAIN TUNIS A. M. CRAVEN.

The thorough discipline and devotion of the crews is illustrated by an incident on the *Oneida*. A shot penetrated her starboard boiler, and the escaping steam scalded thirteen men. At this one gun's-crew shrank back for a moment, but when Captain Mullany shouted, "Back to your quarters, men!" they instantly returned to their guns. Soon afterward, Captain Mullany lost an arm and received six other wounds. Craven's chief engineer in the *Tecumseh*, C. Farron, was an invalid in the hospital at Pensacola when the orders were given to sail for Mobile, but he insisted on leaving his bed and going with his ship, with which he was lost.

A Confederate officer who was in the water battery at Fort Morgan expressed unbounded admiration at the manœuvring of the vessels when the *Brooklyn* stopped and the *Hartford* drew ahead and took the lead. "At first," he says, "they appeared to be in inextricable confusion, and at the mercy of our guns; but when the *Hartford* dashed forward, we realized that the grand tactical movement had been accomplished."

An officer of the *Hartford* wrote in his private journal: "The order was, to go slowly, slowly, and receive the fire of Fort Morgan. At six minutes past seven the fort opened, having allowed us to get into such short range that we apprehended some snare; in fact, I heard the order passed for our guns to be elevated for fourteen hundred yards some time before one was fired. The calmness of the scene was sublime. No impatience, no irritation, no anxiety, except for the fort to open; and, after it did open, full five minutes elapsed before we answered. In the mean time the guns were trained as if at a target, and all the sounds I could hear were, 'Steady, boys, steady! Left tackle a little—so! so!' Then the roar of a broadside, and an eager cheer as the enemy were driven from their water battery. Don't imagine they were frightened; no man could stand under that iron shower; and the brave fellows returned to their guns as soon as it lulled, only to be driven away again."

CAPTAIN PERCIVAL DRAYTON.

Farragut, who was a man of deep religious convictions, fully realized the perils of the enterprise upon which he was entering, and did not half expect to survive it. In a letter to his wife, written the evening before the battle, he said: "I am going into Mobile Bay in the morning, if God is my leader, as I hope he is, and in him I place my trust. If he think it is the proper place for me to die, I am ready to submit to his will in that as in all other things." In spite of the universal sailor superstition, he fought this battle on Friday.

REAR-ADMIRAL
THORNTON A. JENKINS.

One incident of this battle suggests the thought that many of the famous deeds of Old-World chivalry have been paralleled in American history. When the *Tecumseh* was going down, Captain Craven and his pilot met at the foot of the ladder that afforded the only escape, and the pilot stepped aside. "After you, pilot," said Craven, drawing back, for he knew it was by his own fault, not the pilot's, that the vessel was struck. "There was nothing after me," said the pilot, in telling the story; "for the moment I reached the deck the vessel seemed to drop from under me, and went to the bottom."

ON BOARD THE "HARTFORD," BATTLE OF MOBILE BAY.

(FROM A PAINTING BY W. H. OVEREND.)

In all the literature of our language there is but one instance of the poetical description of a battle by a genuine poet who was a participator in the conflict. This instance is Brownell's "Bay Fight." Drayton's fine "Ballad of Agincourt" has long been famous, but that battle was fought a century and a half before Drayton was born. Campbell witnessed the battle of Hohenlinden, famous through his familiar poem, but only from the distant tower of a convent. Byron's description of the battle of Waterloo is justly admired, but Byron was not at Waterloo. Tennyson's "Charge of the Light Brigade at Balaklava," which every schoolboy knows, is another hearsay poem, for Tennyson was never within a thousand miles of Balaklava. Henry Howard Brownell, a native of Providence, R. I., when a young man taught a school in Mobile, Ala. Afterward he practised law in Hartford, Conn., but left it for literature, and at the age of twenty-seven published a volume of poems that attracted no attention. During the war he made numerous poetical contributions to periodicals, some of which were widely copied. One of these, a poetical version of Farragut's General Orders at New Orleans, attracted the admiral's attention and led to a correspondence. Brownell wrote that he had always wanted to witness a sea-fight, and Farragut, answering that he would give him an opportunity, procured his appointment as acting ensign on board the *Hartford*. During the battle of Mobile, Brownell was on deck attending to his duties, for which he was honorably mentioned in the admiral's report, and at the same time taking notes of the picturesque incidents. The outcome was his unique and powerful poem entitled "The Bay Fight." Oliver Wendell Holmes, in an article in the *Atlantic Monthly*, said: "New modes of warfare thundered their demand for a new poet to describe them; and Nature has answered in the voice of our battle laureate, Henry Howard Brownell." From Mr. Brownell's poem we take the following stanzas:

"Three days through sapphire seas we sailed;
  The steady trade blew strong and free,
The northern light his banners paled,
The ocean stream our channels wet.
  We rounded low Canaveral's lee,
And passed the isles of emerald set
  In blue Bahama's turquoise sea.

By reef and shoal obscurely mapped,
  And hauntings of the gray sea-wolf,
The palmy Western Key lay lapped
  In the warm washing of the gulf.

GUN PRACTICE ON A NATIONAL WAR-SHIP.

(From a War-time Photograph.)

But weary to the hearts of all
The burning glare, the barren reach
Of Santa Rosa's withered beach,
And Pensacola's ruined wall.

And weary was the long patrol,
The thousand miles of shapeless strand,
From Brazos to San Blas, that roll
Their drifting dunes of desert sand.

Yet, coast-wise as we cruised or lay,
The land-breeze still at nightfall bore,
By beach and fortress-guarded bay,
Sweet odors from the enemy's shore,

Fresh from the forest solitudes,
Unchallenged of his sentry lines—
The bursting of his cypress buds,
And the warm fragrance of his pines.

Our lofty spars were down,
To bide the battle's frown,
(Wont of old renown)—
But every ship was drest
In her bravest and her best,
As if for a July day.
Sixty flags and three,
As we floated up the bay;
Every peak and mast-head flew
The brave red, white, and blue—
We were eighteen ships that day.

On, in the whirling shade
Of the cannon's sulphury breath,
We drew to the line of death
That our devilish foe had laid—
Meshed in a horrible net,
And baited villanous well,
Right in our path were set
Three hundred traps of hell!

And there, O sight forlorn!
There, while the cannon
Hurtled and thundered—
(Ah! what ill raven
Flapped o'er the ship that morn!)—
Caught by the under-death,
In the drawing of a breath,
Down went dauntless Craven,
He and his hundred!

A moment we saw her turret,
A little heel she gave,
And a thin white spray went o'er it,
Like the crest of a breaking wave.
In that great iron coffin,
The channel for their grave,
The fort their monument,
(Seen afar in the offing),
Ten fathom deep lie Craven,
And the bravest of our brave.

Trust me, our berth was hot;
Ah, wickedly well they shot!
How their death-bolts howled and stung!
And their water batteries played
With their deadly cannonade
Till the air around us rung.
So the battle raged and roared—
Ah! had you been aboard
To have seen the fight we made!

Never a nerve that failed,
Never a cheek that paled,
Not a tinge of gloom or pallor.
There was bold Kentucky's grit,
And the old Virginian valor,
And the daring Yankee wit.

There were blue eyes from turfy Shannon,
There were black orbs from palmy Niger;
But there, alongside the cannon,
Each man fought like a tiger.

And now, as we looked ahead,
All for'ard, the long white deck
Was growing a strange dull red;
But soon, as once and again
Fore and aft we sped
(The firing to guide or check),
You could hardly choose but tread
On the ghastly human wreck,
(Dreadful gobbet and shred
That a minute ago were men)!

Red, from main-mast to bitts!
Red, on bulwark and wale—
Red, by combing and hatch—
Red, o'er netting and rail!

And ever, with steady con,
The ship forged slowly by;
And ever the crew fought on,
And their cheers rang loud and high.

Fear? A forgotten form!
Death? A dream of the eyes!
We were atoms in God's great storm
That roared through the angry skies.

A league from the fort we lay,
And deemed that the end must lag;
When lo! looking down the bay,
There flaunted the rebel rag—
The ram is again under way
And heading dead for the flag!

Steering up with the stream,
Boldly his course he lay,
Though the fleet all answered his fire,
And, as he still drew nigher,
Ever on bow and beam
Our monitors pounded away—
How the *Chickasaw* hammered away!

Quickly breasting the wave,
Eager the prize to win,
First of us all the brave
Monongahela went in,
Under full head of steam—
Twice she struck him abeam,
Till her stem was a sorry work.
(She might have run on a crag!)
The *Lackawanna* hit fair—
He flung her aside like cork,
And still he held for the flag.

Heading square at the hulk,
Full on his beam we bore;
But the spine of the huge sea-hog
Lay on the tide like a log
He vomited flame no more.

By this he had found it hot.
Half the fleet, in an angry ring,
Closed round the hideous thing,
Hammering with solid shot,
And bearing down, bow on bow—
He has but a minute to choose;
Life or renown?—which now
Will the rebel admiral lose?

Cruel, haughty, and cold,
He ever was strong and bold—
Shall he shrink from a wooden stem?
He will think of that brave band
He sank in the *Cumberland*—
Ay, he will sink like them!

Nothing left but to fight
Boldly his last sea-fight!
Can he strike? By Heaven, 'tis true!
Down comes the traitor blue,
And up goes the captive white!

Ended the mighty noise,
Thunder of forts and ships,
Down we went to the hold—
Oh, our dear dying boys!
How we pressed their poor brave lips
(Ah, so pallid and cold!)
And held their hands to the last
(Those that had hands to hold)!

O motherland, this weary life
We led, we lead, is 'long of thee!
Thine the strong agony of strife,
And thine the lonely sea.

Thine the long decks all slaughter-sprent,
The weary rows of cots that lie
With wrecks of strong men, marred and rent,
'Neath Pensacola's sky.

And thine the iron caves and dens
Wherein the flame our war-fleet drives—
The fiery vaults, whose breath is men's
Most dear and precious lives.

Ah, ever when with storm sublime
Dread Nature clears our murky air,
Thus in the crash of falling crime
Some lesser guilt must share!

To-day the Dahlgren and the drum
Are dread apostles of His name;
His kingdom here can only come
By chrism of blood and flame.

Be strong! already slants the gold
Athwart these wild and stormy skies;
From out this blackened waste behold
What happy homes shall rise!

And never fear a victor foe—
Thy children's hearts are strong and high;
Nor mourn too fondly—well they know
On deck or field to die.

Nor shalt thou want one willing breath,
Though, ever smiling round the brave,
The blue sea bear us on to death,
The green were one wide grave.

CHAPTER XXXVI.

THE ADVANCE ON PETERSBURG.

ADVANCE ON PETERSBURG—GENERAL BUTLER'S MOVEMENT—BEAUREGARD'S COUNTER-MOVEMENT—ADVANCE FORCES UNDER GENERAL SMITH—HANCOCK'S ATTACK—CUTTING OFF THE RAILROADS—THE FIGHT AT WELDON ROAD—BURNSIDE'S MINE—EXPLOSION AND THE SLAUGHTER AT THE CRATER—FIGHTING AT DEEP BOTTOM—THE CONSTRUCTION OF AN ARMY RAILROAD—SIEGE OF PETERSBURG BEGUN.

It had been a part of Grant's plan, in opening the campaign of 1864, that Gen. B. F. Butler, with a force that was called the Army of the James, should march against Richmond and Petersburg. He moved promptly, at the same time with the armies led by Grant and Sherman, embarking his forces on transports at Fort Monroe, and first making a feint of steaming up York River. In the night the vessel turned back and steamed up the James. Early the next day, May 6th, the troops were landed at City Point, at the junction of the James and the Appomattox, and intrenchments were thrown up. Detachments were sent out to cut the railroads south of Petersburg, and between that city and Richmond; but no effective work was done. General Butler was ordered to secure a position as far up the James as possible, and advanced to Drury's Bluff, where he was attacked by a force under General Beauregard and driven back to Bermuda Hundred. At the point where the curves of the James and the Appomattox bring those two streams within less than three miles of each other, Butler threw up a line of intrenchments, with his right resting on the James at Dutch Gap, and his left on the Appomattox at Point of Rocks. The position was very strong, and it would be hopeless for the Confederates to assault it. The disadvantage was, that Beauregard had only to throw up a parallel line of intrenchments across the same neck of land, and Butler could not advance a step. What he had secured, however, was afterward valuable as a protection for City Point, when Grant swung the Army of the Potomac across the James, which became thenceforth the landing-place for supplies.

Grant had reinforced Butler with troops under Gen. William F. Smith, and planned to have an immediate advance on Petersburg while the Army of the Potomac was crossing the James (June 14, 1864). The work was intrusted to Smith, who was to get close to the Confederate intrenchments in the night, and carry them at daybreak. He unexpectedly came upon the enemy fortified between City Point and Petersburg, and had a fight in which he was successful, but it caused a loss of precious time. Grant hurried Hancock's troops over the river, to follow Smith. But this corps was delayed several hours waiting for rations, and finally went on without them. It appears that Hancock's instructions were defective, and he did not know that he was expected to take Petersburg till he received a note from Smith urging him to hurry forward. Smith spent nearly the whole of the 15th in reconnoitring the defences of Petersburg, which were but lightly manned, and in the evening carried a portion of them by assault, the work being done by colored troops under Gen. Edward W. Hincks. In the morning of the 16th Hancock's men captured a small additional portion of the works; but here that general had to be relieved for ten days, because of the breaking out of the grievous wound that he had received at Gettysburg. Gen. David B. Birney succeeded him in the command of the corps. General Meade came upon the ground, ordered another assault, and carried another portion. But by this time Beauregard had thrown more men into the fortifications, and the fighting was stubborn and bloody. It was continued through the 17th, with no apparent result, except that at night the Confederates fell back to an inner line, and in the morning the National line was correspondingly advanced. In these preliminary operations against Petersburg, the National loss was nearly ten thousand men. There is no official statement of the Confederate loss, but the indications were that it was about the same.

When Lee found where Grant was going, he moved east and south of Richmond, crossing the James at Drury's Bluff, and presently confronting his enemy in the trenches east and

CITY POINT—A FEDERAL SUPPLY STATION.

south of Petersburg. The country is well adapted for defence, and the works were extensive and very strong. Seeing that the city itself could not be immediately captured, Grant endeavored to sever its important communications. The Norfolk Railroad was easily cut off; and the Army of the Potomac, which for some time had hardly known any difference between day and night, was allowed a few days of rest and comparative quiet. But the most important line was the Weldon Railroad, which brought up Confederate supplies from the South, and Grant and Meade made an early attempt to seize it. On the 21st and 22d Birney's corps was pushed to the left, extending south of the city, while Wright's was sent by a route further south to strike directly at the railroad. Wright came into a position nearly at right angles with Birney, facing west toward the railroad, while Birney faced north toward the city. They were not in connection, however, and did not sufficiently guard their flanks. A heavy Confederate force under Gen. A. P. Hill, coming out to meet the movement, drove straight into the gap, turned the left flank of the Second Corps, threw it into confusion, and captured seventeen hundred men and four guns. The fighting was not severe; but the movement against the railroad was arrested. Hill withdrew to his intrenchments in the evening, the Second Corps reëstablished its line, and the Sixth intrenched itself in a position facing the railroad and about a mile and a half from it. On this flank, affairs remained substantially in this condition till the middle of August.

BREVET MAJOR-GENERAL J. J. BARTLETT.

BRIGADIER-GENERAL LYSANDER CUTLER.

But meanwhile something that promised great results was going on near the centre of the line, in front of Burnside's corps. A regiment composed largely of Pennsylvania miners dug a tunnel under the nearest point of the Confederate works. These works consisted of forts or redans at intervals, with connecting lines of rifle-pits, and the tunnel was directed under one of the forts. The digging was begun in a ravine, to be out of sight of the enemy, and the earth was carried out in barrows made of cracker-boxes, and hidden under brushwood. The Confederates learned what was being done, and the location of the tunnel, but did not succeed in striking it by countermining. They came to have vague and exaggerated fears of it, and many people in Petersburg believed that the whole city was undermined. The work occupied nearly a month, and when finished it consisted of a straight tunnel five hundred feet long, ending in a cross-gallery seventy feet long. In this gallery was placed eight thousand pounds of powder, with slow-matches. The day fixed for the explosion was the 30th of July. To distract attention from it, and diminish if possible the force that held the lines immediately around Petersburg, Hancock was sent across the James at Deep Bottom, where an intrenched camp was held by a force under Gen. John G. Foster, to make a feint against the works north of the river. This had the desired effect, as Lee, anxious for the safety of Richmond, hurried a large part of his army across at Drury's Bluff to confront Hancock. With this exception, the arrangements for the enterprise were all bad. The explosion of the mine alone would do little or no good; but it was expected to make such a breach in the enemy's line that a strong column could be thrust through and take the works in reverse. For such a task the best of troops are required; but Burnside's corps was by no means the best in the army, and the choice of a divi-

BREVET MAJOR-GENERAL RUFUS INGALLS.

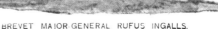

MAJOR-GENERAL W. H. F. LEE, C. S. A.

MAJOR-GENERAL HENRY HETH, C. S. A.

BRIGADIER-GENERAL R. E. COLSTON, C. S. A.

sion to lead, being determined by lot, fell upon Gen. James H. Ledlie's, which was probably the worst, and certainly the worst commanded. Furthermore, the obstructions were not properly cleared away to permit the rapid deployment of a large force between the lines.

A few minutes before five o'clock in the morning, the mine was exploded. A vast mass of earth, surrounded by smoke, with the flames of burning powder playing through it, rose two hundred feet into the air, seemed to poise there for a moment, and then fell. The fort with its guns and garrison—about three hundred men of a South Carolina regiment — was completely destroyed, and in place of it was a crater about thirty feet deep and nearly two hundred feet long. At the same moment the heavy batteries in the National line opened upon the enemy, to protect the assaulting column from artillery fire. Ledlie's division pushed forward into the crater, and there stopped. General Ledlie himself did not accompany the men, and there seemed to be no one to direct them. Thirty golden minutes passed, during which the Confederates, who had run away in terror from the neighboring intrenchments, made no effort to drive out the assailants. At the end of that they began to rally to their guns, and presently directed a heavy fire upon the men in the crater. Burnside tried to remedy the difficulty by pushing out more troops, and at

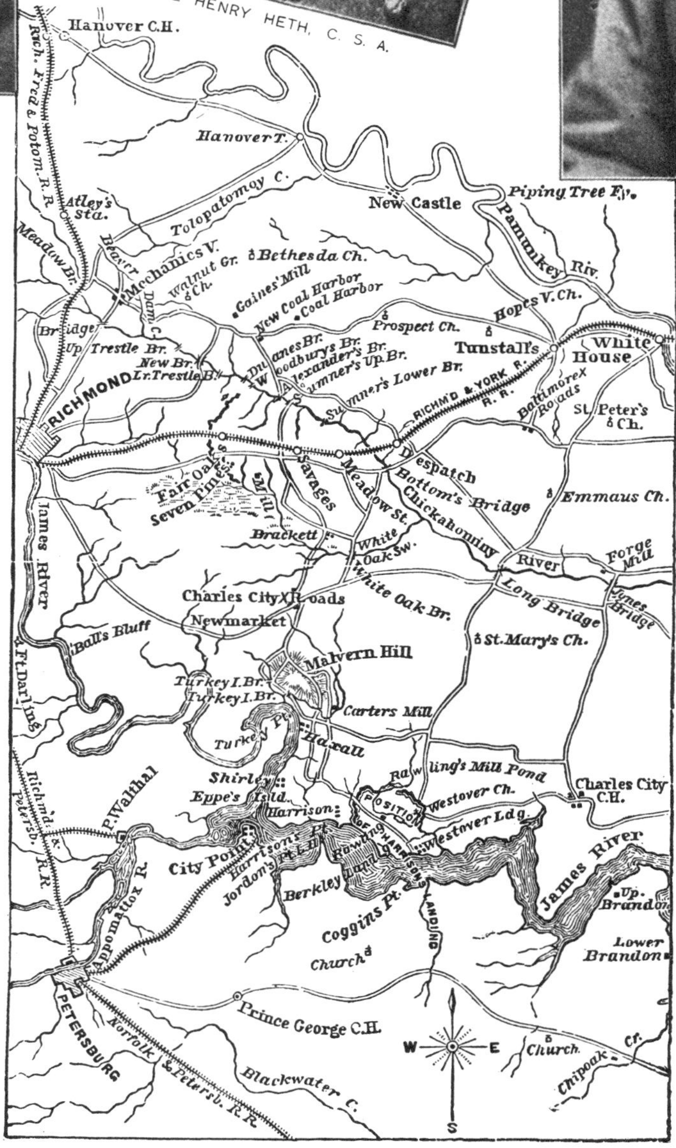

PETERSBURG, RICHMOND, AND VICINITY.

length sent his black division, which charged through the crater and up the slope beyond, but was there met by a fire before which it recoiled; for the Confederates had constructed an inner line of breastworks commanding the front along which the explosion had been expected. Finally, both musketry and artillery were concentrated upon the disorganized mass of troops huddled in the crater, while shells were lighted and rolled down its sloping sides, till those who were left alive scrambled out and got away as best they could. This affair cost the National army about four thousand men—many of them prisoners — while the Confederate loss was hardly a thousand. Soon after this General Burnside was relieved, at his own request, and the command of his corps was given to Gen. John G. Parke. General Grant had never had much faith in the success of the mine, and had given only a reluctant consent to the experiment. Perhaps this was because he had witnessed two similar ones at Vicksburg, both of which were failures. He could hardly escape the criticism, however, that it was his duty either to forbid it altogether or to give it every element of success, including especially a competent leader for the assault.

On the 13th of August, Hancock made another and more serious demonstration from Deep Bottom toward Richmond.

He assaulted the defences of the city, and fighting was kept up for several days. He gained nothing, for Lee threw a strong force into the intrenchments and repelled his attacks. But there was great gain at the other end of the line; for Grant took advantage of the weakening of Lee's right to seize the Weldon Railroad. Warren's corps was moved out to the road on the 18th, took a position across it at a point about four miles from Petersburg, and intrenched. On the 19th, and again on the 21st, Lee made determined attacks on this position, but was repelled with heavy loss. Warren clung to his line, and made such dispositions as at length enabled him to meet any assault with but little loss to himself. A day or two later, Hancock returned from the north side of the James, and was rapidly marched to the extreme left, to pass beyond Warren and destroy some miles of the Weldon Railroad. He tore up the track and completely disabled it to a point three miles south of Reams Station, and on the 25th sent out Gibbon's division to the work some miles farther. But the approach of a heavy Confederate force under Gen. A. P. Hill caused it to fall back to Reams Station, where with Miles's division (six thousand men in all) and two thousand cavalry it held a line of intrenchments. Three assaults upon this line were repelled, with bloody loss to the Confederates. General Hill then ordered Heth's division to make another assault and carry the works at all hazards. Heth found a place from which a part of the National line could be enfiladed by artillery, and after a brisk bombardment assaulted, carried the works, and captured three batteries. Miles's men were rallied, retook a part of the line and one of the batteries, and formed a new line, which they held, assisted by the dismounted cavalry, who poured an effective fire into the flank of the advancing Confederates. At night both sides withdrew from the field. Hancock had lost twenty-four hundred men, seventeen hundred of whom were prisoners. The Confederate loss is unknown, but it was severe.

From that time Grant held possession of the Weldon Railroad, and whatever supplies came to the Confederate army by that route had to be hauled thirty miles in wagons. The National army constructed for its own use a railroad in the rear of and parallel with its long line of intrenchments, running from City Point to the extreme left flank. This road was not particular about grades and curves, but simply followed the natural contour of the ground. Then began what is called the siege of Petersburg, which was not a siege in the proper sense of the word, because the Confederate communications were open; but the military preparations and processes were identical with those known as siege operations, and every possible appliance, mechanical or military, that could assist in the work was brought here.

EXPLOSION OF THE MINE BEFORE PETERSBURG.

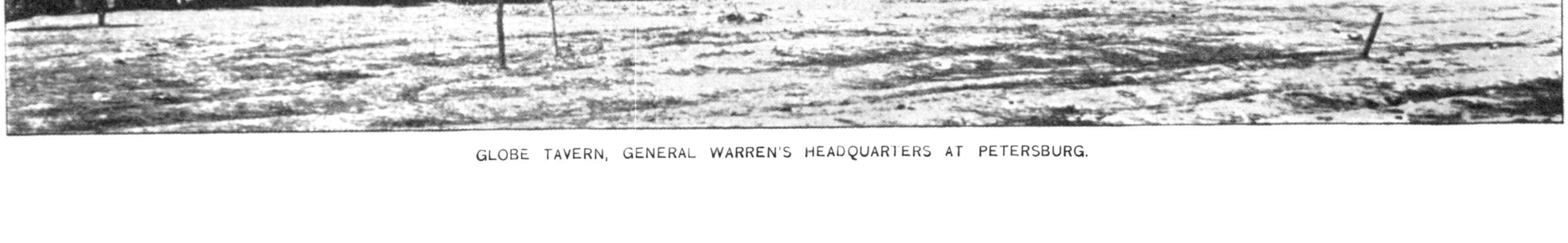
GLOBE TAVERN, GENERAL WARREN'S HEADQUARTERS AT PETERSBURG.

MAJOR-GENERAL JOHN G. FOSTER.

BRIGADIER-GENERAL H. H. HEATH.

MAJOR-GENERAL ROBERT B. POTTER AND STAFF.

GENERAL DAVID B. BIRNEY.

BRIGADIER-GENERAL WILLIAM HAYS.

BRIGADIER-GENERAL ORLANDO B. WILCOX.

(Afterward Major-General.)

BRIGADIER-GENERAL SIMON G. GRIFFIN.

INTERIOR OF A FORT—PART OF THE DEFENCES OF WASHINGTON.
(From a Government photograph.)

CHAPTER XXXVII.

WASHINGTON IN DANGER.

CONFEDERATE FORCES THREATEN THE NATIONAL CAPITAL — GENERAL GRANT SENDS TROOPS TO ITS DEFENCE—BATTERIES AND INTRENCHMENTS AROUND WASHINGTON—CONFEDERATE FORCES IN SIGHT OF THE DOME OF THE CAPITOL—PRESIDENT LINCOLN EXPOSED TO THE FIRE OF CONFEDERATE SHARP-SHOOTERS—GENERAL EARLY'S RETREAT UP THE SHENANDOAH VALLEY.

ABRAHAM LINCOLN.

PARTLY to check the movements of General Hunter in the Shenandoah Valley, and partly with the hope that an attack on Washington would cause Grant to withdraw from before Richmond and Petersburg, Lee sent Early's corps into the valley. Hunter, being out of ammunition, was obliged to retire before the Confederates, and Early marched down the Potomac unopposed, and threatened the National capital. Serious fears were entertained that he would actually enter the city, and all sorts of hurried preparations were made to prevent him, department clerks being under arms, and every available man pressed into the service.

The defences of Washington, which had been in course of construction ever since the war began, consisted of sixty-eight enclosed forts or batteries, connected by lines of intrenchments, forming a circle about that city and Alexandria, and being on an average four miles from the centre of the city. These mounted about eight hundred guns and one hundred mortars, and, with their connecting works, were calculated to give fighting room for thirty-five thousand men. But at this time they were manned by not more than thirteen thousand. Some of these were members of the invalid corps, which was formed of soldiers who had been wounded so as to be unfit for the hard duty at the front; others were hundred-day men. There was great excitement in Washington, and serious fears that the Confederates might succeed in marching into the capital.

Gen. Lew Wallace, in command at Baltimore, gathered a body of recruits and went out to meet Early, not with the hope of defeating him, but only of delaying him till a sufficient force could be sent from the Army of the Potomac. Ricketts's division of the Sixth Corps had already set out for Baltimore, and on arriving there immediately followed Wallace. They met the enemy at the Monocacy, thirty-five miles from Washington, July 9, and took up a position on the left bank of the stream, covering the roads to the capital. Wallace had six field guns and a small force of cavalry, and disposed his line so as to hold the bridges and fords as long as possible. The Confederates attacked at first in front, with a strong skirmish line and sixteen guns, and there was bloody fighting at one of the bridges. Then they changed their tactics, marched a heavy force down stream, crossed at a ford out of range of the National artillery, and then marched up stream again to strike Wallace's left flank. That part of the line was held by Ricketts, who changed front to meet the attack, and was promptly reinforced from Wallace's scanty resources. Two assaults in line of battle were repelled, after some destructive fighting, and Wallace determined still to hold his ground, as he was hourly expecting three additional regiments. But the afternoon wore away without any appearance of assistance, and when he saw preparations for another and heavier assault he determined to retreat. While the left was being withdrawn, the right, under General Tyler, was ordered to prevent the remaining Confederate force from crossing at the bridges. The wooden bridge was burned, and the stone bridge was held to the last possible moment, when Tyler also retreated. The missing regiments were met on the road, and there was no pursuit. This action was not important from its magnitude; but in that it probably saved the city of Washington from pillage and destruction, it was of the first importance. Wallace has received high praise for his promptness and energy in fighting a battle of great strategic value when he knew that the immediate result must be the defeat of his own force. He lost about fourteen hundred men, half of whom were prisoners. The Confederates admitted a loss of six hundred.

Early now marched on Washington, and on the 12th was within a few miles of it, where some heavy skirmishing took place with a force sent out by Gen. Christopher C. Augur. His nearest approach was at Fort Stevens, directly north of the city. General Early says in his memoir: "I rode ahead of the infantry and arrived in sight of Fort Stevens a short time after noon, when I discovered that the works were but feebly manned. Rodes, whose division was in front, was immediately ordered to bring it into line as rapidly as possible, and move into the works if he could." This is supposed to have been Early's golden opportunity, which he somehow missed, for the capture of Washington. His own explanation is this: "My whole column was then moving by flank, which was the only practicable mode of marching on the road we were on; and before Rodes's division could be brought up we saw a cloud of dust in the rear of the works toward Washington, and soon a column of the enemy filed into them on the right and left, and skirmishers were thrown out in front, while an artillery fire was opened on us from a number of batteries. This defeated our hopes of getting possession of the works by surprise, and it became necessary to reconnoitre. Rodes's skirmishers were thrown to the front, driving those of the enemy to the cover of the works, and we proceeded to examine the fortifications in order to ascertain if it was practicable to carry them by assault. They were found to be exceedingly strong. The timber had been felled within cannon range all round, and left on the ground, making a formidable obstacle, and every possible approach was raked by artillery. On the right was Rock Creek, running through a deep ravine, which had been rendered impassable by the felling of the timber on each side, and beyond were the works on the Georgetown pike, which had been reported to be the strongest of all. On the left, as far as the eye could reach, the works appeared to be of the same impregnable character. This reconnoissance consumed the balance of the day. The rapid marching, which had broken a number of the men who were weakened by previous exposure, and had been left in the valley and directed to be collected at Winchester, and the losses in killed and wounded at Harper's Ferry, Maryland Heights, and Monocacy, had reduced my infantry to about eight thousand muskets. Of those remaining, a very large number were greatly exhausted by the last two days' marching, some having fallen by sunstroke; and I was satisfied, when we arrived in front of the fortifications, that not more than one-third of my force could have been carried into action. After dark on the 11th, I held a consultation with Major-Generals Breckenridge, Rodes, Gordon, and Ramseur, in which I stated to them the danger of remaining where we were, and the necessity of doing something immediately, as the probability was that the passes of the South Mountain and the fords of the upper Potomac would soon be closed against us. After interchanging views with them, being very reluctant to abandon the project of capturing Washington, I determined to make an assault at daylight next morning. During the night a despatch was received from Gen. Bradley Johnson, from near Baltimore, informing me that two corps had arrived from General Grant's army, and that his whole army was probably in motion. As soon as it was light enough to see, I rode to the front and found the parapets lined with troops. I had, therefore, reluctantly to give up all hopes of capturing Washington, after I had arrived in sight of the dome of the Capitol."

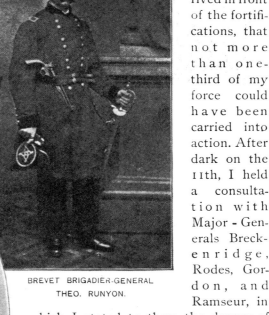

BREVET BRIGADIER-GENERAL C. G. SAWTELLE.

BREVET BRIGADIER-GENERAL THEO. RUNYON.

BRIGADIER-GENERAL ANDREW PORTER.

BRIGADIER-GENERAL J. A. HASKIN.

Early's information was correct, as Grant had sent to Washington the remainder of the Sixth Corps, and also the Nineteenth Corps, which had just arrived from Louisiana.

JOHN CABIN BRIDGE NEAR WASHINGTON.

During the fighting at Fort Stevens, President Lincoln was in the fort, and was exposed to the fire of the Confederate sharp-shooters. General Wright had the greatest difficulty in persuading him to leave his dangerous position, and could not do so until an officer standing near the President had been struck down by a shot from the enemy. Even then, Mr. Lincoln persisted in looking over the parapet to see what was going on, and when finally the Sixth Corps men drove back the enemy he was as excited and jubilant in the cheering as any of those around him.

AN EARNEST REQUEST FOR A FURLOUGH.

Early retreated up the valley, carrying with him considerable plunder, and was followed some distance until the pursuing force was withdrawn. The Sixth and Nineteenth Corps were ordered to rejoin Grant's army, and were on their way to it when it was learned that Early was again advancing. Grant now determined to finish him and clear the valley, and accordingly sent General Sheridan to command in that quarter, in August. Meanwhile, a part of Early's force had been struck at Winchester by a force under General Averell, who defeated it and captured four guns and about four hundred men. Three days later, Early defeated a force under Gen. George Crook, and drove it across the Potomac, after which he sent his cavalry, under Generals McCausland and Bradley T. Johnson, to make a raid into Pennsylvania. McCausland, in the course of his raid, burned Chambersburgh, the particulars of which have been given in another chapter.

This raid created a panic among the inhabitants of western Maryland and southern Pennsylvania, many of whom fled from their homes, driving off their cattle and carrying whatever they could.

CHAPTER XXXVIII.

SHERIDAN IN THE SHENANDOAH.

IMPORTANCE OF THE VALLEY—HUNTER ASKS TO BE RELIEVED—SHERIDAN'S CAREER—GRANT'S INSTRUCTIONS—INTERFERENCE AT WASHINGTON—LINCOLN GIVES GRANT A HINT—SHERIDAN MARCHES ON WINCHESTER—MINOR ENGAGEMENTS—SHERIDAN'S OPPORTUNITY—BATTLE OF THE OPEQUAN—EARLY GOES WHIRLING THROUGH WINCHESTER—BATTLE OF FISHER'S HILL—DESTRUCTION IN THE VALLEY—ACTION AT TOM'S BROOK—BATTLE OF CEDAR CREEK.

IT had become plainly evident that something must be done to cancel the whole Shenandoah Valley from the map of the theatre of war. The mountains that flanked it made it a secure lane down which a Confederate force could be sent at almost any time to the very door of Washington; while the crops that were harvested in its fertile fields were a constant temptation to those who had to provide for the necessities of an army. General Grant took the matter in hand in earnest after Early's raid and the burning of Chambersburg. His first care was to have the separate military departments in that section consolidated, his next to find a suitable commander, and finally to send an adequate force. He would have been satisfied with General Hunter, who was already the ranking officer there; but Hunter had been badly hampered in his movements by constant interference from Washington, and knowing that he had not the confidence of General Halleck, he asked to be relieved, since he did not wish to embarrass the cause. In this, Grant says, Hunter "showed a patriotism that was none too common in the army. There were not many major-generals who would voluntarily have asked to have the command of a department taken from them on the supposition that for some particular reason, or for any reason, the service would be better performed." Grant accepted his offer, and telegraphed for General Sheridan to come and take command of the new department. Sheridan was on hand promptly, and was placed at the head of about thirty thousand troops, including eight thousand cavalry, who were named the Army of the Shenandoah.

MAJOR-GENERAL H. G. WRIGHT.

BREVET MAJOR-GENERAL A. T. A. TORBERT.

Sheridan was now in his thirty-fourth year; and Secretary Stanton, with a wise caution, made some objection, on the ground that he was very young for a command so important. He had not stood remarkably high at West Point, being ranked thirty-fourth in his class when the whole number was fifty-two; but he had already made a brilliant record in the war, winning his brigadier-generalship by a victory at Booneville, Mo., and conspicuous for his gallantry and skill at Perryville, Murfreesboro', Chickamauga, and Missionary Ridge, and for his bold riding around Lee's army in the spring campaign of 1864. Under him and Custer, Crook, Merritt, and Kilpatrick, the cavalry arm of the National service, weak and inefficient at the opening of the war, had become a swift and sure weapon against the now declining but still defiant Confederacy. It had been noted by everybody that Grant exhibited an almost unerring judgment in the choice of his lieutenants.

In his instructions, which were at first written out for Hunter and afterward transferred to Sheridan, Grant said: "In pushing up the Shenandoah Valley, where it is expected you will have to go first or last, it is desirable that nothing should be left to invite the enemy to return. Take all provisions, forage, and stock wanted for the use of your command. Such as cannot be consumed, destroy. It is not desirable that the buildings should be destroyed—they should rather be protected; but the people should be informed that so long as an army can subsist among them recurrences of these raids must be expected, and we are determined to stop them at all hazards."

The condition of things at Washington—where Halleck always, and Stanton sometimes, interfered with orders passing that way—is vividly suggested by a despatch sent in cipher to Grant at this time, August 3. Mr. Lincoln wrote: "I have seen your despatch, in which you say, 'I want Sheridan put in command of all the troops in the field, with instructions to put himself south of the enemy and follow him to the death. Wherever the enemy goes, let our troops go also.' This I think is exactly right, as to how our forces should move. But please look over the despatches you may have received from here, even since you made that order, and discover, if you can, that there is any idea in the head of any one here of 'putting our army south of the enemy,' or of 'following him to the death' in any direction. I repeat to you, it will neither be done nor attempted unless you watch it every day and hour, and force it." This caused Grant to go at once to Maryland and put things in train for the vigorous campaign that he had planned in the valley of the Shenandoah. Perhaps Mr. Lincoln had found a way to give Halleck also an impressive hint; for the very next day that general telegraphed to Grant: "I await your orders, and shall strictly carry them out, whatever they may be."

Grant, who had all confidence in Sheridan, wrote to him: "Do not hesitate to give command to officers in whom you repose confidence, without regard to claims of others on account of rank. If you deem Torbert the best man to command the cavalry, place him in command, and give Averell some other command, or relieve him from the expedition and order him to report to General Hunter. What we want is prompt and active movements after the enemy, in accordance with the instructions you have already had. I feel every confidence that you will do the very best, and will leave you, as far as possible, to act on your judgment, and not embarrass you with orders and instructions." In accordance with this, Torbert was made Sheridan's chief of cavalry, and Merritt was given command of Torbert's division. When Grant visited Sheridan, before the battle of the Opequan, he carried a plan of battle in his pocket; but he says he found Sheridan so thoroughly ready to move, with so perfect a plan, and so confident of success, that he did not even show him his plan or give him any orders, except authority to move.

BREVET BRIGADIER-GENERAL LOUIS H. PELOUZE.

Early, whose main force was on the south bank of the Potomac, above Harper's Ferry, still had a large part of his cavalry in Maryland, where they were loading their wagons with wheat on the battlefield of Antietam, and seizing all the cattle that the farmers had not driven off beyond their reach. But these were now recalled. As soon as Sheridan could get his force well in hand, he moved it skilfully southward toward Winchester, in order to threaten Early's communications and draw him into a battle. Early at once moved his army into a position to cover Winchester, but was unwilling to fight without the reinforcements that were on the way to him from Lee's army; so he retreated as far as Fisher's Hill to meet them, and was followed by Sheridan, who was about to attack there when warned by Grant to be cautious, as the enemy was too strong for him. He therefore withdrew to his former position on Opequan Creek, facing west toward Winchester and covering Snicker's Gap, through which reinforcements were to come to him. Here he was attacked, August 21, and after a fight in which two hundred and sixty men on the National side were killed or wounded, he drew back to a stronger position at Halltown. He had complained, in a letter to Grant, that there was not a good military position in the whole valley south of the Potomac. In his retrograde movement, as he reported, he "destroyed everything eatable south of Winchester."

Early reconnoitred the position at Halltown and found it too strong to be attacked, but for three or four weeks remained with his whole force at the lower end of the valley, threatening raids into Maryland, Pennsylvania, and West Virginia, breaking the Baltimore and Ohio Railroad and the Chesapeake Canal, keeping the authorities at Washington in a constant state of anxiety, and all the time inviting attack from Sheridan. There were frequent minor engagements, mainly by cavalry, with varying results. In one, Custer's division only escaped capture by crossing the Potomac in great haste. In another, a force under Gen. John B. McIntosh captured the Eighth South Carolina infantry entire—though that regiment now consisted of but one hundred and six men. It had probably consisted of a thousand men at the outset, and the wear and tear of three years of constant warfare had reduced it, like many others on either side, to these meagre proportions.

BREVET MAJOR-GENERAL ALFRED GIBBS.

Grant and Sheridan were in perfect accord as to the best policy, and they pursued it steadily, in spite of the uneasiness at Washington, the complaints of the Maryland farmers, and the criticisms of the newspapers. They knew that with the Army of the Potomac constantly busy in his front, feeling out for new positions beyond Petersburg, or massing north of the James in close proximity to Richmond, or threatening to break through his centre, the time must come when Lee would recall a part of the forces that he had sent to the valley, and that would be the moment for Sheridan to spring upon Early. The opportunity arrived on the 19th of September, when Lee had recalled the command of R. H. Anderson, with which he had reinforced Early in August, and Early, as if to double his danger, had sent a large part of his remaining troops to Martinsburg, twenty miles away. Grant's order to Sheridan at this juncture was "Go in," and Sheridan promptly went in.

BREVET BRIGADIER-GENERAL W. H. PENROSE.

The various movements of the two armies had brought them around to substantially the same positions that they held in the engagement of August 21—Early east of and covering Winchester, Sheridan along the line of Opequan Creek, which is about five miles east of the city. Sheridan's plan was to march straight on Winchester with his whole force, and crush Early's right before the left could be withdrawn from Martinsburg to assist it. He set his troops in motion at three o'clock in the morning, to converge toward the Berryville pike, a macadamized

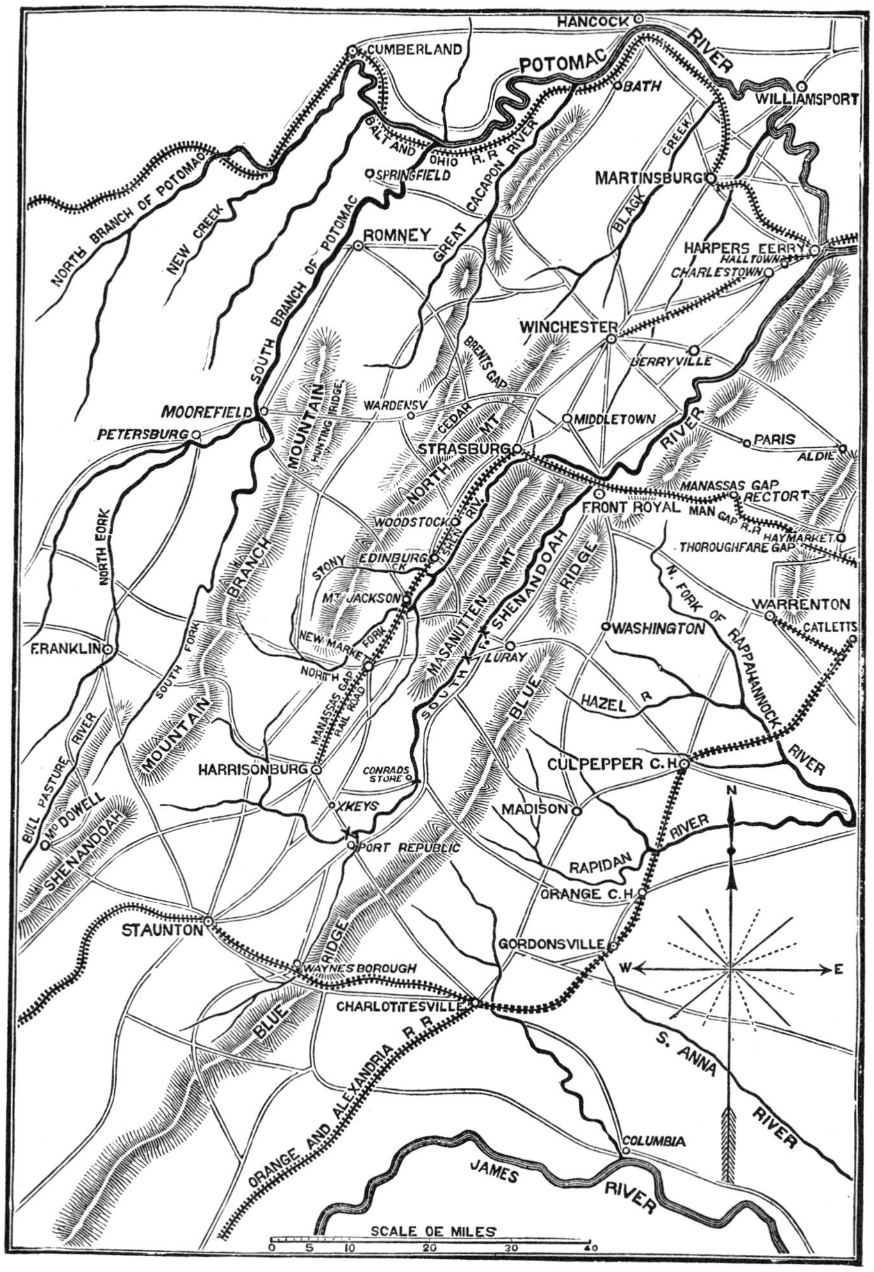

THE SHENANDOAH VALLEY

road crossing the Opequan, passing through a ravine, and leading into Winchester. Wilson's cavalry secured the crossing of the stream, and cleared the way through the ravine for the infantry; but there was, as usual, some difficulty in moving so many troops by a single road, and it was midday before the battle began. This delay gave Early an opportunity to bring back his troops from Martinsburg and unite his whole force in front of Winchester. Sheridan's infantry deployed under a heavy artillery fire from Early's right wing, and advanced to the attack, when the battle began almost simultaneously along the whole line, and was kept up till dark. There were no field-works, the only shelter being such as was afforded by patches of woodland and rolling ground, and the fighting was obstinate and bloody. The usual difficulty of preserving the line intact while advancing over broken ground was met, and wherever a gap appeared it was promptly taken advantage of. In one instance, a Confederate force led by Gen. Robert E. Rodes drove in between the Sixth and Nineteenth Corps, crumbled their flanks, and turned to take the Nineteenth in reverse; but at this juncture a division of the Sixth Corps under Gen. David A. Russell, coming forward to fill the gap, struck the flank of the intruding Confederate force in turn, enfiladed it with a rapid fire of canister from the Fifth Maine battery, and sent it back in confusion, capturing a large number of prisoners. In this movement Generals Rodes and Russell were both killed. On the National right the fighting was at first in favor of the Confederates, and that wing was temporarily borne back some distance.

Sheridan now brought up his reserves, which he had intended to move south of Winchester to cut off retreat, and sent them into the fight on his right flank, while the cavalry divisions of Merritt and Averell, under Torbert, came in by a detour and struck Early's left, pushing back his cavalry and getting into the rear of a portion of his infantry. From this time Sheridan drove everything before him. The Confederates found some shelter in a line of field-works near the town, but were soon driven out, and fled through the streets in complete rout and confusion. But darkness favored them, and most of them escaped up the valley. Their severely wounded were left in Winchester. The National loss was nearly five thousand men. The Confederates lost about four thousand—including two generals, Rodes and Godwin—with five guns and nine battle-flags. Early established a strong rear guard, and managed to save his trains.

This battle, which in proportion to the numbers engaged was one of the most destructive of the war, had its many curious and valorous incidents. Near its close General Russell received a bullet in his breast, but did not mention it even to his staff officer, and continued urging forward and encouraging the troops. A little later, in the very moment of victory, a fragment of shell tore through his heart. Lieut. Morton L. Hawkins, of the Thirty-fourth Ohio Regiment, writes: "Here fell badly wounded our gallant division commander, Gen. I. H. Duval; and while crossing a cornfield, and just before reaching the edge of the sanguinary Red Bud, the chivalrous and manly Carter, at the head of Company D, my old regiment, fell dead at my feet, struck in the forehead with a musket ball; but never faltering, with our eyes fixed on the enemy, who at that time were advancing to the opposite side of the Red Bud, we pushed on, amid a shower of musketry that was simply murderous. Emerging on the opposite bank, we ascended the elevation and met them face to face. Then ensued a hand-to-hand contest. The ranks of Union and Confederate regiments mingled indiscriminately, the colors of both floating in the breeze together, the blue and the gray, man to man. Duval had been carried to the rear with a musket ball in his thigh, but Col. R. B. Hayes, since President of the United States, assumed the command of the division, and by his presence in the battle wreck encouraged his men to deeds of daring. Cool and vigilant, he sat upon his horse amid that leaden rain, while scores of veterans on either side went down around him. Finally the tide turned in our favor. Down the hill, hotly pressed by the Union men, went that valiant band of rebels. The day was won. The flag of the old Thirty-fourth never looked so beautiful, nor was borne so proudly, as on that glorious day, when in the thickest of the fight its shadow fell on its brave defenders."

In contrast with this is the entry in the journal of a Confederate officer who was wounded and captured: "I never saw our

MAJOR-GENERAL PHILIP H. SHERIDAN AND STAFF.

troops in such confusion before. Night found Sheridan's hosts in full and exultant possession of much-abused, beloved Winchester. The hotel hospital was full of desperately wounded and dying Confederates. The entire building was shrouded in darkness during the dreadful night, and sleep was impossible, as the groans, sighs, shrieks, prayers, and oaths of the wretched sufferers, combined with my own severe pain, banished all thought of rest. Our scattered troops, closely followed by the large army of pursuers, retreated rapidly and in disorder through the city. It was a sad, humiliating sight."

General Early attributes his defeat largely to the fact that his cavalry was inferior in both numbers and equipments to the National cavalry that opposed it.

The news of this battle was received with unmeasured enthusiasm in the Army of the Potomac, in Washington, and at the North, where every newspaper repeated in its bold head-lines Sheridan's expression that he had "sent Early whirling through Winchester."

BRIGADIER-GENERAL N. P. CHIPMAN.

President Lincoln telegraphed to General Sheridan: "Have just heard of your great victory. God bless you all, officers and men. Strongly inclined to come up and see you." General Grant telegraphed: "I congratulate you and the army serving under you for the great victory just achieved. It has been most opportune in point of time and effect. It will open again to the Government and to the public the very important line from Baltimore to the Ohio, and also the Chesapeake Canal. Better still, it wipes out much of the stain upon our arms by previous disasters in that locality. May your good work continue, is now the prayer of all loyal men."

For this brilliant success, Sheridan was advanced to the grade of brigadier-general in the regular army.

When Early retreated southward after this battle of the Opequan (or battle of Winchester as the Confederates called it), he took up a position at Fisher's Hill, where the valley is but four miles wide. As Sheridan had said, there was no really good military position in the valley, unless for a much larger army than either he or Early commanded. At Fisher's Hill, the Confederate right rested on the North Fork of the Shenandoah, and was sufficiently protected by it; but for the left there was no natural protection. Early's men set to work vigorously constructing intrenchments and preparing abatis. Sheridan followed promptly, his advance guard skirmishing with the Confederate pickets and driving them through Strasburg. There was an eminence overlooking the Confederate intrenchments, and after a sharp fight this was gained by the National troops, who at once began to cut down the trees and plant batteries. When Sheridan had thoroughly reconnoitred the position, he planned to send the greater part of his cavalry through the Luray Valley to get into the rear of the Confederates and cut off retreat; then to attack in front with the Sixth and Nineteenth Corps, while Crook, with the Eighth Corps, should make a detour and come in on the enemy's left flank. The ground was so broken that the manœuvres were necessarily slow, and it was almost sunset when Crook reached Early's flank. But the little daylight that remained was used to the utmost advantage. Crook came out of the woods so suddenly and silently that the Confederates at that end of the line were simply astounded. Their works were taken in reverse, and their dismounted cavalry was literally overrun. The forward movement of the troops in front was prompt, the right of the Sixth Corps joining properly with the left of Crook's, and everywhere Sheridan and his lieutenants were with the men, repeating the command to push forward constantly, without stopping for anything. The result was a complete rout of the Confederates, who fled in confusion once more up the valley, leaving sixteen of their guns behind. But Sheridan's plan for their capture was foiled because his cavalry, meeting a stout resistance from Early's cavalry, failed to get through to their rear. Pursuit was made in the night, but to no purpose. In this battle, which was fought on the 22d of September, the National loss was about four hundred; the Confederate, about fourteen hundred.

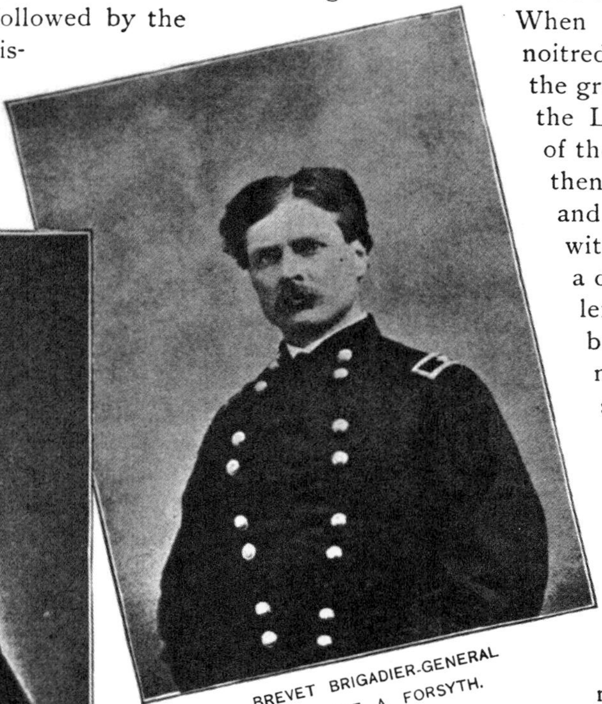

BREVET BRIGADIER-GENERAL GEORGE A. FORSYTH.

BREVET BRIGADIER-GENERAL NICHOLAS DAY.

For the next three days the retreat was continued, Sheridan's whole force following rapidly, and often being near enough to engage the skirmishers or exchange shots with the artillery. Early went to Port Republic to meet reinforcements that were on the way to him from Lee's army, and there stopped. Sheridan halted his infantry at Harrisonburg, but sent his cavalry still farther up the valley. The column under Torbert reached Staunton, where it destroyed a large quantity of arms, ammunition, and provisions, and then tore up the track of the Virginia Central Railroad eastward to Waynesboro', and pulled down the iron bridge over the stream at that point. Here it was attacked in force, and retired. Grant wanted the movement continued to Charlottesville; but Sheridan found serious difficulties in his lack of supplies and transportation so far from his base. He adopted the alternative of rendering the valley untenable for any army that could not bring its provisions with it, and Grant had repeated his early instructions, saying, "Leave nothing for the subsistence of an army on any ground you abandon to the enemy." On the 5th of October the march down the valley was begun. The infantry went first, and the cavalry followed, being stretched entirely across the valley, burning and destroying, as it went, everything except the dwellings. Sheridan said in his report: "I have destroyed over two thousand barns filled with wheat, hay, and farming implements; over seventy mills filled with flour and wheat; have driven in front of the army over four thousand head of stock, and have killed and issued to the troops not less than three thousand sheep."

Early, being reinforced, now turned and pursued Sheridan. At Tom's Brook, on the 7th, the National cavalry under Torbert, Merritt, and Custer engaged the Confederate cavalry under Rosser and Lamont. After a spirited engagement Rosser was driven back twenty-five miles, and Torbert captured over three hundred prisoners, eleven guns, and a large number of wagons—or, as was said in the report, "everything they had on wheels."

Sheridan halted at Cedar Creek, north of Strasburg, and put his army into camp there, while he was summoned to Washington for conference as to the continuation of the campaign, leaving General Wright in command. Early, finding nothing in the valley for his men and horses to eat, was obliged to do one thing or another without delay—advance and capture provisions from the stores of his enemy, or retreat and give up the ground. He chose to assume the offensive, and in the night of the 18th moved silently around the left of the National line, taking the precaution to leave behind even the soldiers' canteens, which might have made a clatter. In the misty dawn of the 19th the Confederates burst upon the flank held by Crook's corps, with such suddenness and vehemence that it was at once thrown into confusion and routed. They were among the tents before anybody knew they were coming, and many of Crook's men were shot or stabbed before they could fairly awake from their sleep. The Nineteenth Corps was also routed, but the Sixth stood firm, and the Confederates themselves became somewhat broken and demoralized by the eagerness of the men to plunder the camps. Wright's Sixth Corps covered the retreat; and when Sheridan, hearing of the battle and riding with all speed from Winchester, met the stream of fugitives, he deployed some cavalry to stop them, and inspired his men with a short and oft-repeated oration, which is reported as, "Face the other way, boys! We are going back to our camps! We are going to lick them out of their boots!" This actually turned the tide; a new line was quickly formed and intrenched, and when Early attacked it he met with a costly repulse. In the afternoon Sheridan advanced to attack in turn, sending his irresistible cavalry around both flanks, and after some fighting the whole Confederate line was broken up and driven in confusion, with the cavalry close upon its heels. All the guns lost in the morning were retaken, and twenty-four besides. In this double battle the Confederate loss was about thirty-one hundred; the National, fifty-seven hundred and sixty-four, of whom seventeen hundred were prisoners taken in the morning and hurried away toward Richmond. Among the losses in this battle on the National side were Brig.-Gens. Daniel D. Bidwell, Charles R. Lowell, J. H. Hitching, and George D. Welles, and Col. Joseph Thoburn, all killed; on the Confederate side, Major-Gen. Stephen D. Ramseur, killed.

A VIEW ON GOOSE CREEK, VIRGINIA.

(From a War-time Photograph.)

The explanation of Early's well-planned attack upon the camp is found in the fact that the Confederates had a signal station on Massanutten Mountain from which everything in Sheridan's army could be seen. On the day before the battle Gen. John B. Gordon climbed to that signal station, where with his field-glass he says, "I could distinctly see the red cuffs of the artillerymen. In front of the Belle Grove mansion I could see members of Sheridan's staff coming and going. I could not imagine a better opportunity for making out an enemy's position and strength. I could even count the men who were there. I marked the position of the guns, and the pickets walking to and fro, and observed where the cavalry was placed." The explanation of the surprise is, that the Confederates by careful approach captured a picket and obtained the countersign. They then proceeded to capture more of the pickets, exchanged clothes with them and put their own men on guard. This, of course, enabled them to open the door of the camp, so to speak, in perfect silence for their approaching army.

BRIGADIER-GENERAL
BRADLEY T. JOHNSON, C. S. A.

The story of Sheridan's return, and how he changed the defeat into a victory, as here told, is that which is generally received. But some of his soldiers say it is more dramatic than strictly truthful. They say that when he arrived General Wright already had restored order, and had the Sixth Corps in perfect condition for an advance movement. Still there is no doubt that the presence of Sheridan brought with it an inspiration, and gave vigor to the movement when it was made. Col. Moses M. Granger, of the One Hundred and Twenty-second Ohio Regiment, which was in the Sixth Corps, says: "When Sheridan arrived, the line in position consisted of the cavalry, with its right on the pike; the second division, Sixth Corps, with its left on the pike; then Hayes, with part of the Army of West Virginia; and next to him our Second Brigade, third division, Sixth Corps. I had no watch with me, but at the time, I supposed that we connected with Getty not far from ten o'clock in the forenoon. As our breakfast had been very early and hasty, we now advanced the dinner hour, made coffee, and soon felt refreshed—ready for anything. While we were in this state of good feeling, General Sheridan, attended by Major A. J. Smith, came riding along the line. Just in my rear, as I was sitting on a stump, he drew rein, returned our salute, gave a quick look at the men, and said: 'You look all right, boys! We'll whip 'em like —— before night!' At this, hearty cheers broke out, and he rode on, passing from the rear to the front of our line, through the right wing of my regiment, and thence westward, followed ever by cheers. Instantly all thought of merely defeating an attack upon us ended. In its stead was a conviction that we were to attack and defeat them that very afternoon. . . . Thus before Sheridan arrived Wright had given orders for the establishment of a strong and well-manned line, and made it certain that the rebel advance must there stop. What Wright might or would have done if Sheridan had remained at Winchester, I cannot tell. Called from his bed to fight an enemy already on his flank and rear and partly within his lines, his promptness and decision enabled him to withdraw from Early's grasp almost all that was not in his hands before Wright's eager haste brought him from bed to battle. When his black horse brought Sheridan to our lines on that October forenoon, Wright turned over to him an army ready, eager, and competent to win success that afternoon."

MAJOR-GENERAL R. E. RODES, C. S. A.
Killed at Winchester, Va.

BREVET MAJOR-GENERAL DAVID A. RUSSELL.
Killed at Winchester, Va.

Sheridan's campaign in the Valley of the Shenandoah was now practically ended, and the people of the loyal North were no longer obliged to call it the Valley of Humiliation.

An incident of this campaign inspired one of the most vigorous and popular of the war poems, entitled "Sheridan's Ride." We quote two stanzas:

"But there is a road from Winchester town,
A good broad highway leading down;
And there, through the flash of the morning light,
A steed as black as the steeds of night
Was seen to pass, as with eagle flight,
As if he knew the terrible need;
He stretched away with the utmost speed;
Hills rose and fell—but his heart was gay,
With Sheridan fifteen miles away.

. . . . . .

"Hurrah! hurrah for Sheridan!
Hurrah! hurrah for horse and man!
And when their statues are placed on high,
Under the dome of the Union sky,
The American soldier's Temple of Fame,
There, with the glorious general's name,
Be it said, in letters both bold and bright:
'Here is the steed that saved the day
By carrying Sheridan into the fight
From Winchester—twenty miles away!'"

CHAPTER XXXIX.

THE PRESIDENTIAL ELECTION.

EFFORTS TOWARD PEACE—THE FRÉMONT CONVENTION—THE REPUBLICAN CONVENTION—NOMINATION OF LINCOLN AND JOHNSON—THE DEMOCRATIC CONVENTION—ITS DENUNCIATION OF THE WAR—NOMINATION OF McCLELLAN AND PENDLETON—FRÉMONT WITHDRAWS—CHARACTER OF THE CANVASS—THE HOPE OF THE CONFEDERATES—THE ISSUE AS POPULARLY UNDERSTOOD—ELECTION OF LINCOLN—MARYLAND ABOLISHES SLAVERY—THE HIGHEST ACHIEVEMENT OF THE AMERICAN PEOPLE.

THE length of time that the war had continued, the drain upon the resources of both belligerents, and especially the rapidity and destructiveness of the battles in the summer of 1864, had naturally suggested the question whether there were not some possibility of a satisfactory peace without further fighting. In each section there was a party, or at least there were people, who believed that such a peace was possible; and the loud expression of this opinion led to several efforts at negotiation, as it also shaped the policy of a great political party. In July Col. James F. Jacques, of the Seventy-third Illinois Regiment, accompanied by James R. Gillmore (known in literature by his delineations of Southern life just before the war, under the pen-name of "Edmund Kirke"), went to Richmond under flag of truce, where they were admitted to a long interview with the chief officers of the Confederate Government. They had gone with Mr. Lincoln's informal sanction, but had no definite terms to offer; and if they had, Mr. Davis's remarks show that it would have been in vain. At the close he said: "Say to Mr. Lincoln, from me, that I shall at any time be pleased to receive proposals for peace on the basis of our independence. It will be useless to approach me with any other." In that same month of July, three Southerners of some note created a great sensation by a conference at Niagara Falls, with Horace Greeley, on the subject of peace; but the affair came to nothing.

The first Presidential convention of the year met at Cleveland, O., on the last day of May, in response to a call addressed "to the radical men of the nation." The platform declared, among other things, "that the rebellion must be suppressed by force of arms, and without compromise; that the rebellion has destroyed slavery, and the Federal Constitution should be amended to prohibit its reëstablishment; that the question of the reconstruction of the rebellious States belongs to the people, through their representatives in Congress, and not to the Executive; and that confiscation of the lands of the rebels, and their distribution among the soldiers and actual settlers, is a measure of justice." Gen. John C. Frémont was nominated for the Presidency, and Gen. John Cochrane for the Vice-Presidency. Though this was the least of the conventions, yet in all the points here quoted from its platform, with the exception of the last, it indicated the policy that was ultimately pursued by the nation; and it is a singular fact that the exceptional plank (confiscation) was objected to by both candidates in their letters of acceptance.

The Republican National Convention met in Baltimore on the 7th of June. It dropped the word "Republican" for the time being, and simply called itself a Union Convention, to accommodate the war Democrats, who were now acting with the Republican party. Not only the free States were represented, but some that had been claimed by the Confederacy and had been partially or wholly recovered from it, including Tennessee, Louisiana, and Arkansas. The platform, reported by Henry J. Raymond, one of the ablest of American journalists, was probably written largely, if not entirely, by him. Its most significant passages were these:

"That we approve the determination of the Government of the United States not to compromise with the rebels, nor to offer them any terms of peace except such as may be based upon an unconditional surrender of their hostility and a return to their full allegiance to the Constitution and the laws of the United States.

"That as slavery was the cause and now constitutes the strength of this rebellion, and as it must be always and everywhere hostile to the principles of republican government, justice and the national safety demand its utter and complete extirpation from the soil of the Republic. . . . We are in favor, furthermore, of such an amendment to the Constitution, to be made by the people in conformity with its provisions, as shall terminate and forever prohibit the existence of slavery within the limits of the jurisdiction of the United States.

"That we approve and applaud the practical wisdom, the unselfish patriotism, and unswerving fidelity to the Constitution and the principles of American liberty, with which Abraham Lincoln has discharged, under circumstances of unparalleled difficulty, the great duties and responsibilities of the presidential office; that we approve and indorse, as demanded by the emergency and essential to the preservation of the nation, and as within the Constitution, the measures and acts which he has adopted to defend the nation against its open and secret foes; that we approve especially the Proclamation of Emancipation, and the employment as Union soldiers of men heretofore held in slavery.

"That the National faith, pledged for the redemption of the public debt, must be kept inviolate; that it is the duty of every loyal State to sustain the credit and promote the use of the National currency."

On the first ballot, all the delegations voted for Mr. Lincoln, except that from Missouri, whose vote was given to General Grant. According to the official report of the proceedings, the first ballot for a candidate for Vice-President resulted in two hundred votes for Andrew Johnson, one hundred and eight for Daniel S. Dickinson (a war Democrat), one hundred and fifty for Hannibal Hamlin (who then held the office), and fifty-nine scattering; several delegations changed their votes to Johnson, and he was almost unanimously nominated. But according to the testimony of one who was on the floor as a delegate, the nomination of Mr. Lincoln was immediately followed by an outburst of cheering, yelling, and the wildest excitement, and in the confusion and uproar it was declared that Mr. Johnson had somehow been nominated. He had been a poor white in the South, and a life-long Democrat, but had done some brave things in withstanding secession, and some bitter things in thwarting the slave-holders. Mr. Lincoln had appointed him military governor of Tennessee in March, 1862, and he was still acting in that capacity. Whatever may have been the wisdom of nominating a war Democrat when the war was so near its close, the Republican party found reason in the next four years to repent its choice of Andrew Johnson as bitterly as its predecessor, the Whig party, had repented the choice of John Tyler, a life-long Democrat, in 1840. But the nominating conventions that have sufficiently considered the contingent importance of the Vice-Presidency have been exceedingly few.

The Democratic National Convention, called to meet in Chicago, did not convene till nearly three months after the Republican, August 29. In the meantime, the hard fighting around Richmond, and on Sherman's road to Atlanta, the fruits of which were not yet evident, the appearance of Confederate forces at the gates of Washington, and the delay of Sheridan's movements in the Shenandoah Valley, had produced a more gloomy feeling than had been experienced before since the war began; and this feeling, as was to be expected, operated in favor of whatever opposed the National administration. The suffering and the discontented are always prone to cry out for a change, without defining what sort of change they want, or considering what any change is likely to bring. Seizing upon this advantage, the Democratic convention made a very clear and bold issue with the Republican. It was presided over by Horatio Seymour, then governor of New York, while Clement L. Vallandigham was a member of the committee on resolutions, and is supposed to have written the most significant of them. The platform presented these propositions:

"That this Convention does explicitly declare, as the sense of the American people, that, after four years of failure to restore the Union by the experiment of war, during which, under the pretence of military necessity of a war power higher than the Constitution, the Constitution itself has been disregarded in every part, and public liberty and private right alike trodden down, and the material prosperity of the country essentially impaired—justice, humanity, liberty, and the public welfare demand that immediate efforts be made for a cessation of hostilities, with a view to an ultimate convention of all the States, or other peaceable means, to the end that, at the earliest practicable moment, peace may be restored on the basis of the Federal Union of the States.

"That the aim and object of the Democratic party is to preserve the Federal Union and the rights of the States unimpaired."

On the first ballot, Gen. George B. McClellan was nominated for President, receiving two hundred and two and a half votes, against twenty-three and a half for Thomas H. Seymour, of Connecticut. George H. Pendleton, of Ohio, an ultra-peace man, was nominated for Vice-President. General McClellan, in his letter of acceptance, virtually set aside a portion of the platform, and said: "The reëstablishment of the Union, in all its integrity, is and must continue to be the indispensable condition in any settlement. . . . No peace can be permanent without Union."

The declaration that the war had been a failure received a crushing comment the day after the convention adjourned; for on that day Sherman's army marched into Atlanta. And this success was followed by others—notably Sheridan's brilliant movements in the valley—all of which, when heralded in the Republican journals, were accompanied by the quotation from the Democratic platform declaring the war a failure. General Frémont withdrew from the contest in September, saying in his published letter:

"The policy of the Democratic party signifies either separation or reëstablishment with slavery. The Chicago platform is simply separation; General McClellan's letter of acceptance is reëstablishment with slavery. The Republican candidate is, on the contrary, pledged to the reëstablishment of the Union without slavery; and, however hesitating his policy may be, the pressure of his party will, we may hope, force him to it. Between these issues, I think no man of the Liberal party can remain in doubt; and I believe I am consistent with my antecedents and my principles in withdrawing—not to aid in the triumph of Mr. Lincoln, but to do my part toward preventing the election of the Democratic candidate."

The canvass was exceedingly bitter, especially in the abuse heaped upon Mr. Lincoln. The undignified and disgraceful epithets that were applied to him by journals of high standing were not such as would make any American proud of his country. This course had its culmination in the publication of certain ghastly pictures of returned prisoners, to show what Lincoln—the usurper, despot, and tyrant, as they freely called him—was doing by not disregarding "nigger soldiers" and continuing the exchange of whites. They constantly repeated the assertion with which they had greeted the Emancipation Proclamation, that the war had been wickedly changed from one for the preservation of the Union into one for the abolition of slavery. On the other hand, the Republican press freely accused the Democratic party of desiring the success of secession—which was not true. Aside from all patriotic considerations, that party had the strongest reasons for wishing to perpetuate the Union, because without the Southern vote it was in a minority. There were many members of that party, however, who, while they by no means desired the destruction of the Union, believed it was inevitable, and thought the sooner the necessity was acknowledged the better.

One of the most effective arguments of the canvass was furnished in a condensed form by one of Mr. Lincoln's famous little stories, and in that form was repeated thousands of times. Answering the address of a delegation of the Union League, a day or two after his nomination, he said: "I have not permitted myself to conclude that I am the best man in the country; but I am reminded in this connection of the story of an old Dutch farmer, who once remarked to a companion that 'it was not best to swap horses when crossing streams.'" There was singing in the canvass, too, and some of the songs rendered by glee-clubs every evening before large political meetings were very effective. One of the most notable had been written in response to the President's call for three hundred thousand volunteers, and bore the refrain,

"We are coming, Father Abraham, three hundred thousand more!"

Much of the popular parlor music of the time consisted of songs relating to the great struggle, prominent among which were "Tenting on the Old Camp-Ground" and "When this Cruel War is over." At the South, as at the North, there had been an outburst of lyric enthusiasm at the beginning of the war, which found expression in "My Maryland," the "Bonnie Blue Flag," and "Dixie;" but the spirit that inspires such poems seems to have died out there after the war had been in progress two or three years, when its terrible privations were increasing every day.

The Confederates were now looking eagerly for the result of the Presidential election as a possible solution of the great question in their favor. John B. Jones, who was a clerk in the Confederate War Department, recorded in his published diary that Mr. Vallandigham, when banished to the South, had assured the officers of the Government at Richmond that "if we [the Confederates] can only hold out this year, the peace party of the North would sweep the Lincoln dynasty out of political existence." This was now their strongest hope; and it was common talk

BRIGADIER-GENERAL GEORGE D. RAMSAY.

BREVET MAJOR-GENERAL RUFUS SAXTON.

BRIGADIER-GENERAL
F. T. DENT.

BRIGADIER-GENERAL C. P. BUCKINGHAM.

BREVET BRIGADIER-GENERAL
WILLIAM P. RICHARDSON.

BREVET MAJOR-GENERAL J. K. BARNES.

BRIGADIER-GENERAL WILLIAM A. HAMMOND.

BRIGADIER-GENERAL
HENRY A. BARNUM.

BREVET MAJOR-GENERAL AMOS B. EATON.

MAJOR-GENERAL MORTIMER LEGGETT AND STAFF.

across the lines, between the pickets, that in the event of McClellan's election the Confederates expected a speedy cessation of hostilities and ultimately their independence. And such is the unaccountable elasticity of the human mind, in dealing with facts and principles, that a large number of the bravest and most devoted soldiers in the National service, knowing this, were preparing to cast their ballots in a way to give the utmost assistance and encouragement to the very enemy into the muzzles of whose guns they were looking.

Whether General Frémont's arraignment of the Administration as "politically, militarily, and financially a failure" was just or unjust, whether it was true or not that the triumph of General McClellan and his party would result in a final disruption of the country, before the canvass was over the land had settled down to the belief that the only way to secure the continuance of the war to a successful termination was to reëlect Mr. Lincoln, while a vote for General McClellan meant something else—nobody knew exactly what. The solemnity of the occasion appeared to be universally appreciated, and though a heavy vote was polled the election was the quietest that had ever been held. The citizens were dealing with a question that, in most of its aspects at least, they by this time thoroughly understood. When they sprang to arms in 1861, they did not know what war was; but now they had had three years of constant schooling to its burdens and its horrors. They had seen regiment after regiment march away to the music of drum and fife, with a thousand men in the ranks, and come back at the end of two years' service with perhaps two hundred bronzed veterans to be mustered out. They had read in their newspapers, after every great battle, the long lists of killed and wounded, which the telegraph was quick to report. Every city had its fair for the relief of the widows and orphans, every hamlet its two or three crippled soldiers hobbling about in their faded blue overcoats, almost every house its incurable sorrow. They had seen the wheel turning in the provost-marshal's office, in places where volunteering was not sufficiently rapid, and knew that their own names might be the next to be drawn for service at the front. They knew how many graves there were at Gettysburg, how many at Shiloh, how many at Stone River; they knew what was to be seen in the hospitals of every Northern city, and something of the unspeakable horrors of captivity. They saw the price of gold go beyond two hundred, while the Government was spending between two and three millions of dollars a day, piling up a national debt in undreamed-of proportions, for which they were already heavily taxed, and which must some day be paid in solid coin.

Seeing and understanding all this, and having the privilege of a secret and unquestioned ballot, they quietly walked up to the polls and voted for a vigorous prosecution of the war, reëlecting Mr. Lincoln by a popular majority of more than four hundred thousand, and giving him the votes of all the States excepting Delaware, New Jersey, and Kentucky—two hundred and twelve against twenty-one. The vote of the soldiers in the field, so far as it could be counted separately (for in some States it was sent home sealed, and mingled with the other ballots in the boxes), showed about one hundred and nineteen thousand for Lincoln, and about thirty-four thousand for McClellan. The soldiers confined in some of the Confederate prisons held an election at the suggestion of their keepers, who were exceedingly curious to see how the prisoners would vote. Sergeant Robert H. Kellogg tells us that in the stockade at Florence, S. C., where he was confined, two empty bags were hung up, and the prisoners were furnished with black and white beans and marched past in single file, each depositing a black bean for Lincoln, or a white one for McClellan. The result was in the proportion of two and a half for Lincoln to one for McClellan. In the prison at Millen, Ga., Sergeant W. Goodyear tells us, the vote was three thousand and fourteen for Lincoln, and one thousand and fifty for McClellan. In Congress, the number of Republican members was increased from one hundred and six to one hundred and forty-three, and the number of Democratic members reduced from seventy-seven to forty-one.

Meanwhile, in October, Maryland had adopted a new constitution, in which slavery was prohibited. In answer to serenades after the election, Mr. Lincoln made some of his best impromptu speeches, saying in one: "While I am duly sensible to the high compliment of a reëlection, and duly grateful, as I trust, to Almighty God for having directed my countrymen to a right conclusion, as I think, for their good, it adds nothing to my satisfaction that any other man may be disappointed by the result. May I ask those who have not differed with me to join with me in this same spirit toward those who have?"

If there is any one act of the American people that above all others, in the sober pages of history, reflects credit upon them for correct judgment, determined purpose, courage in present difficulties, and care for future interests, that act, it seems to me, was the reëlection of President Lincoln.

CHAPTER XL.

THE NATIONAL FINANCES.

AN EMPTY TREASURY—BORROWING MONEY AT TWELVE PER CENT.—SALMON P. CHASE MADE SECRETARY OF THE TREASURY—THE DIRECT-TAX BILL—ISSUE OF DEMAND NOTES—CHASE'S COURAGE—THE BANKS FORM SYNDICATE—ISSUE OF BONDS—AMOUNT OF COIN IN CIRCULATION—SUSPENSION OF SPECIE PAYMENTS—PAY OF SOLDIERS—GREENBACKS—CHASE'S PLAN FOR A NATIONAL BANKING SYSTEM—THE FRACTIONAL CURRENCY—FLUCTUATIONS OF GOLD—THE COST OF THE WAR.

WHEN President Lincoln came into office he found the treasury empty, and the public debt somewhat over seventy-six million dollars. In the last days of President Buchanan's administration the Government had been borrowing money at twelve per cent. per annum. In December, 1860, Congress passed a bill for the issue of ten million dollars in one-year treasury notes. Half of this amount was advertised, and offers were received for a small portion, at rates of discount varying from twelve to thirty-six per cent. The twelve per cent. offers were accepted, and subsequently a syndicate of bankers took the remainder of the five millions at that figure. The other five millions were taken a month later at eleven per cent. discount. In February, 1861, Congress authorized a loan of twenty-five millions, to bear interest at six per cent., and to be paid in not less than ten nor more than twenty years. The Secretary succeeded in negotiating one-third of the amount at rates from ninety to ninety-six.

In Mr. Lincoln's cabinet, Salmon P. Chase (formerly governor of Ohio, and then United States senator) was made Secretary of the Treasury. Under the existing acts he borrowed eight millions in March at ninety-four and upward—rejecting all offers under ninety-four—and early in April issued at par nearly five millions in two-year treasury notes, receivable for public dues and also convertible into six-per-cent. stocks. On the 12th of that month the war was begun by the firing on Fort Sumter. In May seven millions more of the six-per-cent. loan were issued at rates from eighty-five to ninety-three, and two and a half millions in treasury notes at par. These transactions were looked upon as remarkably successful, for many considered it questionable whether the Government would survive the blow that was aimed at its life, and be able to redeem any of its securities. The existing tariff, which was low, produced an annual income of not more than thirty millions.

Congress met, at the call of the President, on the 4th of July, 1861, and on the 17th passed a bill (with but five dissenting votes in the House of Representatives) for the issue of bonds and treasury notes to the amount of two hundred and fifty millions. It also increased the duties on many articles, passed an act for the confiscation of the property of rebels, and levied a direct tax of twenty millions, apportioned among the States and Territories. The States that were in rebellion of course did not pay. All the others paid except Delaware, Colorado, Utah, Oregon, and the District of Columbia. The law provided for collection by United States officers in such States as should not formally assume and pay the tax themselves. In some of the seceding States, lands worth about seven hundred thousand dollars were seized and sold for non-payment.

In August the first demand notes were issued as currency, being paid to clerks in the departments for their salaries. Though these were convertible into gold, there was at first great reluctance to receive them, but after a little time they became popular, and in five months about thirty-three millions were issued.

In August also Mr. Chase held a conference with the principal bankers of New York, Boston, and Philadelphia, to negotiate a national loan on the basis of the recent acts of Congress. Most of them expressed their desire to sustain the Government, but they made some objections to the terms and rates of interest. When it looked as if the negotiation might fail, the Secretary assured the bankers that if they were not able to take the loan on his terms, he would return to Washington and issue notes for circulation, "for it is certain that the war must go on until the rebellion is put down, if we have to put out paper until it takes a thousand dollars to buy a breakfast." The banks agreed to form a syndicate to lend the Government fifty million dollars in coin, to pay which the Secretary was to issue three-year notes bearing seven and three-tenths per cent. interest, convertible into six-per-cent. twenty-year bonds. These were popularly known as "seven-thirties." The peculiar rate of interest was made both as a special inducement and for ease of calculation, the interest being two cents a day on each hundred dollars. They were issued in denominations as low as fifty dollars, so that people of limited means could take them, and were very popular. The coupon and registered bonds that were to run not less than five years nor more than twenty were popularly known as "five-twenties." Subscription-books were opened in every city, and the people responded so promptly that the Government was soon enabled to repay the banks and make another loan on similar terms. But a third loan was refused, and Secretary Chase then issued fifty millions in "five-twenties," bearing interest at six per cent., but sold at such a discount as to make a seven-per-cent. investment. Of all the agents employed to dispose of these bonds, Jay Cooke, of Philadelphia, was the most successful. They were paid one-fifth of one per cent. for the first hundred thousand dollars, and one-eighth of one per cent. for all in excess of that sum.

The amount of coin in circulation in the United States at this time was estimated at about two hundred and ten million dollars. Before the war had been in progress one year, the operations of the Government had become so vast that this did not furnish a sufficient volume of currency for the transactions. On December 30, 1861, the banks suspended specie payments, and the Government was then obliged to do likewise. There were now over half a million men in the field, and the navy had been increased from forty-two vessels to two hundred and sixty-four. The pay of a private soldier was thirteen dollars a month, with food and clothing. The total cost to the Government for each soldier maintained in the field was about a thousand dollars a year—two and a half times the cost of a British soldier, and twelve times the cost of a French soldier.

Early in 1862 even the smallest coins disappeared from circulation, and some kinds of business were almost paralyzed for want of change. Tokens and fractional notes were issued by private firms, and various expedients were resorted to, a favorite one being the enclosure of specified amounts of postage-stamps in small envelopes properly labelled. Thaddeus Stevens, member of Congress from Pennsylvania, proposed that the Government should issue notes for circulation, to any amount that might be required, and make them legal tender for all debts, public and private. Secretary Chase opposed this, and proposed instead a national banking system, which should embrace an issue of notes bearing a common impression and a common authority, the redemption of these notes by the institutions to which the Government should deliver them for issue, and a pledge of United States stocks as security for such redemption. This scheme was opposed by the State banks, and Mr. Chase gave a reluctant consent to the legal-tender measure, which was then carried through Congress, and the "greenbacks" became payable for everything except duties on imports. Subsequently Mr. Chase's plan for a national banking system was also adopted, substantially as we have it now. In the loyal States the greenbacks were popular from the first, and the large amount in circulation led to general extravagance in expenditures. In the insurrectionary States they were at first refused with scorn. But when the secessionists found that these notes had a purchasing power vastly superior to those of their own Government, they soon became reconciled to them. When soldiers of the National army were made prisoners of war, they were almost immediately requested by their captors to exchange any greenbacks they might have for Confederate money, and some show of fairness was made by the allowance of a heavy discount, seldom less than seven for one. The Confederate currency was redeemable "six months after the ratification of a treaty of peace with the United States." The Government supplemented the greenbacks with fractional paper currency in denominations of fifty, twenty-five, ten, and five cents; and in this money the war bills were paid and all business transacted, except at the custom-houses.

The daily quotations of gold were looked to as an indication of the prospects of the war. Gold itself did not materially change in value, but the premium on it represented the depreciation of the greenbacks with which it was purchased. At the beginning of 1862 there was a premium of about two per cent. on gold. This fluctuated from day to day, but the general tendency was upward, till at the end of that year the premium was thirty-three. By the end of 1863 gold had risen to one hundred and fifty-one; and on June 21, 1864, just after the Army of the Potomac crossed the James, it touched two hundred. In other words, the United States paper dollar was then worth half a dollar. On the 11th of July, 1864, gold reached its highest point, two hundred and eighty-five. Confederate paper money had been at par until November, 1861; but from that time its value diminished steadily and rapidly, until, at the close of 1864, five hundred paper dollars were worth but one dollar in gold, and three months later six hundred.

Most of the funded debt of the United States was represented by five-twenty bonds. An act was passed authorizing the issue of ten-forties, but they were not popular, and comparatively few were taken. The total assessed value of all the property in the United States, real and personal, by the census of 1860, was somewhat over sixteen thousand million dollars. The cost of the war to the Government has been nearly, if not quite, half that amount—or about equal to the value in 1860 of all the real estate in the loyal States. The amount of the Confederate debt is unknown. If that and the incidental losses could be ascertained, the cost of the war would probably make a grand total almost equivalent to a wiping out of all values in the country as they were estimated in the year of its beginning. The fourteenth amendment to the Constitution—proposed in 1866, and declared in force in 1868—provides, on the one hand, that the validity of the public debt shall not be questioned, and, on the other, that neither the United States nor any State shall ever pay any debt or obligation that has been incurred in aid of insurrection against the United States.

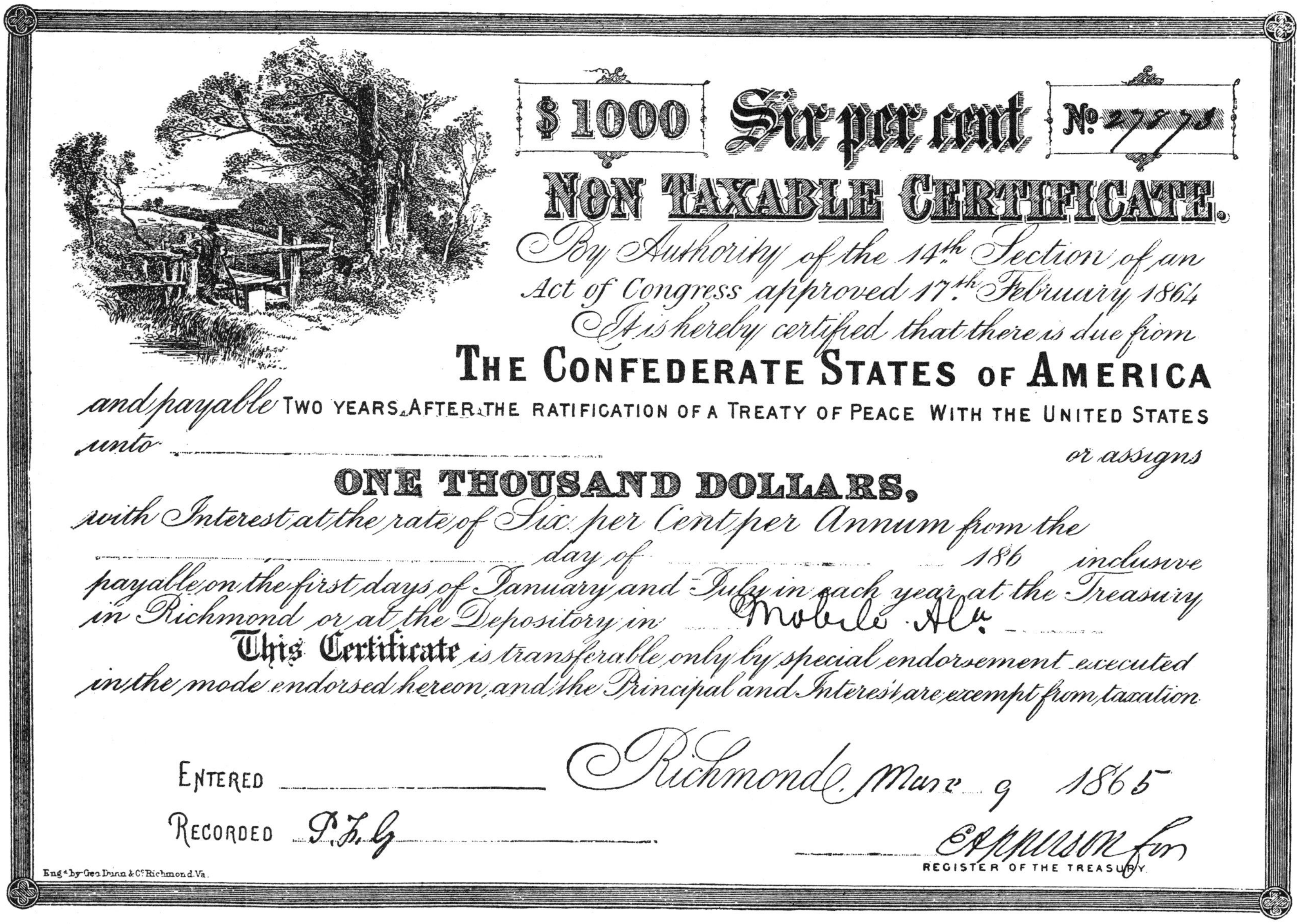
$1000 Six per cent No. 27575

NON TAXABLE CERTIFICATE.

By Authority of the 14th Section of an Act of Congress approved 17th February 1864

It is hereby certified that there is due from

THE CONFEDERATE STATES OF AMERICA

and payable TWO YEARS AFTER THE RATIFICATION OF A TREATY OF PEACE WITH THE UNITED STATES unto ________ or assigns

ONE THOUSAND DOLLARS,

with Interest at the rate of Six per Cent per Annum from the ________ day of ________ 186__ inclusive payable on the first days of January and July in each year at the Treasury in Richmond or at the Depository in Mobile Ala.

This Certificate is transferable only by special endorsement executed in the mode endorsed hereon, and the Principal and Interest are exempt from taxation.

ENTERED ________ Richmond, Mar. 9 1865

RECORDED P. F. G. ________

________ for REGISTER OF THE TREASURY.

Eng.d by Geo. Dunn & Co. Richmond Va.

FAC-SIMILE OF A CONFEDERATE BOND.

BRIGADIER-GENERAL W. E. STRONG GENERAL McPHERSON'S INSPECTOR-GENERAL, ORDERING A COLONEL TO PLACE HIS COMMAND IN ACTION.

CHAPTER XLI.

THE MARCH TO THE SEA.

SHERMAN MAKES ATLANTA A MILITARY DEPOT—HIS PECULIAR POSITION—DISAFFECTION IN THE CONFEDERACY—HOOD ATTACKS THE COMMUNICATIONS—DEFENCE OF ALLATOONA—THOMAS ORGANIZES AN ARMY—SHERMAN DETERMINES TO GO DOWN TO THE SEA—DESTRUCTION IN ATLANTA—THE ORDER OF MARCH—SHERMAN'S INSTRUCTIONS—THE ROUTE—INCIDENTS—DESTRUCTION OF THE RAILROAD—KILLING THE BLOODHOUNDS—THE BUMMERS—CAPTURE OF FORT McALLISTER—HARDEE EVACUATES SAVANNAH, AND SHERMAN OFFERS IT AS A CHRISTMAS PRESENT TO THE PRESIDENT—BATTLE OF FRANKLIN—BATTLE OF NASHVILLE—HOOD'S ARMY DESTROYED.

BEFORE Sherman's army had been a week in Atlanta he determined to send away all the inhabitants of the city, giving each the choice whether to go South or North, and furnishing transportation for a certain distance. His reason for this measure is given briefly in his own words: "I was resolved to make Atlanta a pure military garrison or dépôt, with no civil population to influence military measures. I had seen Memphis, Vicksburg, Natchez, and New Orleans, all captured from the enemy, and each at once was garrisoned by a full division of troops, if not more, so that success was actually crippling our armies in the field by detachments to guard and protect the interests of a hostile population." Of course this action met with a vigorous protest from the people themselves, from the city authorities, and from General Hood, between whom and General Sherman there was a sharp correspondence discussing the humanity of the measure and to some extent the issues of the war.

General Sherman also received a letter signed by the mayor and two of the councilmen, in which they set forth the difficulties and sufferings that the people would encounter, and asked him to reconsider his order for their removal. This he answered at length, presenting a broad view, not of Atlanta only, but of the entire country, and the state of the war, and the effect that this would have upon it. There were few generals on either side who understood the entire aspect, military, political, moral, and economical, as thoroughly, or describe it as clearly, as Sherman. He said: "I give full credit to your statements of the distress that will be occasioned, and yet shall not revoke my orders, because they were not designed to meet the humanities of the case, but to prepare for the future struggles in which millions of good people outside of Atlanta have a deep interest. We must have peace, not only at Atlanta, but in all America. To secure this, we must stop the war that now desolates our once happy and favored country. To stop war, we must defeat the rebel armies which are arrayed against the laws and Constitution that all must respect and obey. To defeat those armies, we must prepare the way to reach them in their recesses, provided with the arms and instruments which enable us to accomplish our purpose. Now, I know the vindictive nature of our enemy, that we may have many years of military operations from this quarter, and therefore deem it wise and prudent to prepare in time. The use of Atlanta for warlike purposes is inconsistent with its character as a home for families. There will be no manufactures, commerce, or agriculture here, for the maintenance of families, and sooner or later want will compel the inhabitants to go. Why not go now, when all the arrangements are completed for the transfer, instead of waiting till the plunging shot of contending armies will renew the scenes of the past month? Of course I do not apprehend any such thing at this moment, but you do not suppose this army will be here until the war is over. I cannot discuss this subject with you fairly, because I cannot impart to you what we propose to do; but I assert that our military plans make it necessary for the inhabitants to go away, and I can only renew my offer of services to make their exodus in any direction as easy and comfortable as possible.

"You cannot qualify war in harsher terms than I will. War is cruelty, and you cannot refine it; and those who brought war into our country deserve all the curses and maledictions a people can pour out. I know I had no hand in making this war, and I know I will make more sacrifices to-day than any of you to secure peace. But you cannot have peace and a division of our country. If the United States submits to a division now, it will not stop, but will go on until we reap the fate of Mexico, which is eternal war. The United States does and must assert its authority wherever it once had power; for, if it relaxes one bit to pressure, it is gone, and I believe that such is the national feeling. This feeling assumes various shapes, but always comes back to that of Union. Once admit the Union, once more acknowledge the authority of the National Government, and, instead of devoting your houses and streets and roads to the dread uses of war, I and this army become at once your protectors and supporters, shielding you from danger, let it come from what quarter it may. I know that a few individuals cannot resist a torrent of error and passion, such as swept the South into rebellion; but you can point out, so that we may know those who desire a government, and those who insist on war and its desolation.

"You might as well appeal against the thunder-storm as against these terrible hardships of war. They are inevitable; and the only way the people of Atlanta can hope once more to live in peace and quiet at home, is to stop the war, which can only be done admitting that it began in error and is perpetuated in pride. We don't want your negroes, or your horses, or your houses, or your lands, or anything that you have, but we do want and will have a just obedience to the laws of the United States. That we will have, and, if it involves the destruction of your improvements, we cannot help it. You have heretofore read public sentiment in your newspapers, that live by falsehood and excitement; and the quicker you seek for truth in other quarters, the better. I repeat, then, that, by the original compact of government, the United States had certain rights in Georgia, which have never been reliquished and never will be; that the South began war by seizing forts, arsenals, mints, custom-houses, etc., long before Mr. Lincoln was installed, and before the South had one jot or tittle of provocation. I myself have seen in Missouri, Kentucky, Tennessee, and Mississippi, hundreds and thousands of women and children fleeing from your armies and desperadoes, hungry and with bleeding feet. In Memphis, Vicksburg, and Mississippi, we fed thousands upon thousands of the families of rebel soldiers left on our hands, and whom we could not see starve. Now that war comes home to you, you feel very different. You deprecate its horrors, but did not feel them when you sent car-loads of soldiers and ammunition, and moulded shells and shot, to carry war into Kentucky and Tennessee, to desolate the homes of hundreds and thousands of good people who only asked to live in peace at their old homes and under the government of their inheritance. But, my dear sirs, when peace does come,

HON. JOSEPH E. BROWN,

Governor of Georgia.

you may call on me for anything. Then I will share with you the last cracker, and watch with you to shield your homes and families against danger from every quarter."

Among the considerations that influenced General Sherman's action at that time, two appear to have been paramount—one a hope, the other a fear. The fear was, that some portion of Hood's army would make a serious break in his communications by destroying portions of the long, single-track railroad over which he drew all his supplies from Chattanooga. The hope was, that Georgia, seeing any further prosecution of the war to be useless, would withdraw her troops from the Confederate armies and practically secede from the Confederacy. Some color was given to this from the fact that Gov. Joseph E. Brown had recalled the Georgia militia from Hood's army, while Mr. Davis, on a flying visit to that army, had made a speech in which he threw the blame for the recent disasters upon General Johnston and Governor Brown, and told the soldiers they were about to set out on a campaign that would carry them to Tennessee and Kentucky. Sherman sent word to Governor Brown that if Georgia's troops were withdrawn from the Confederate service, he would pass across the State as harmlessly as possible, and pay for all the corn and fodder that he took; but if not, he would devastate the State through its whole length and breadth.

In North Carolina there had been a strong movement for peace this year, the only difference of opinion being as to the method in which peace should be sought. The governor, Zebulon B. Vance, as a candidate for reëlection, represented those who held that the State should only act in coöperation with the other States that were engaged with her in the war. The other party, whose candidate was William W. Holden, held that North Carolina should assert her sovereignty and negotiate peace directly and alone with the United States. Governor Vance probably presented the decisive argument when he said: "Secession from the Confederacy will involve us in a new war, a bloodier conflict than that which we now deplore. So soon as you announce to the world that you are a sovereign and independent nation, as a matter of course the Confederate Government has a right to declare war against you, and President Davis will make the whole State a field of battle and blood. Old Abe would send his troops here also, because we would no longer be neutral; and so, if you will pardon the expression, we would catch the devil on all sides." At the election in August, Governor Vance received fifty-four thousand votes, against twenty thousand for Mr. Holden.

Georgia did not secede from the Confederacy, but Hood did attack the communications. At every important point on the railroad there was a strong guard, and at the bridges there were block-houses with small but well-appointed garrisons. About the 1st of October Hood crossed the Chattahoochee, going northward to strike the railroad. Sherman hurried after him, and on the 5th looked down from Kenesaw Mountain upon the fires that were burning the ties and heating the rails of a dozen miles of his road. Anticipating an attack on Allatoona, which was held by a small brigade under command of Lieut.-Col. John E. Tourtellotte, he signalled over the heads of the enemy a message to Allatoona conveying an order for Gen. John M. Corse, then at Rome, to go to the relief of Tourtellotte with a strong force. Corse obeyed promptly, going down with all the men he could obtain transportation for, and arriving at midnight. In the morning the garrison, now nearly two thousand strong, were summoned to surrender immediately, to avoid a needless effusion of blood. General Corse answered, "We are prepared for the needless effusion of blood whenever it is agreeable to you," and at once his men were attacked from all sides. They were driven into their redoubts, and there made so determined a resistance that after five hours of desperate fighting the Confederates withdrew, leaving their dead and wounded on the field. Corse had lost seven hundred and seven men out of his nineteen hundred and forty-four, including Colonel Redfield, of the Thirty-ninth Iowa, killed, and had himself suffered the loss of an ear and a cheek-bone. The total Confederate loss is unknown; but Corse reported burying two hundred and thirty-one of their dead, and taking four hundred and eleven prisoners, which would indicate a total loss of sixteen hundred. This successful defence of Allatoona was one of the most gallant affairs of the kind in history.

General Thomas had previously been sent to Nashville with two divisions, General Slocum was left in Atlanta with the Twentieth Corps, and with the remainder of his forces Sherman pursued Hood through the country between Rome and Chattanooga and westward of that region. But he could not bring the Confederates to battle, and had little expectation of overtaking them. He thinks he conceived of the march to the sea some time in September; the first definite proposal of it was in a telegram to General Thomas, on the 9th of October, in which he said: "I want to destroy all the road below Chattanooga, including Atlanta, and to make for the sea-coast. We cannot defend this long line of road." In various despatches between that date and the 2d of November, Sherman proposed the great march to Grant and to the President.

ALLATOONA PASS, LOOKING NORTH.

(From a War-time Photograph.)

Grant thought Hood's army should be destroyed first, but finally said: "I do not see that you can withdraw from where you are, to follow Hood, without giving up all we have gained in territory. I say, then, go on as you propose." This was on the understanding, suggested by Sherman, that Thomas would be left with force enough to take care of Hood. Sherman sent him the Fourth and Twenty-third Corps, commanded by Generals Stanley and Schofield, and further reinforced him with troops that had been garrisoning various places on the railroad, while he also received two divisions from Missouri and some recruits from the North. These, when properly organized, made up a very strong force; and, with Thomas at its head, neither Sherman nor Grant felt any hesitation about leaving it to take care of Tennessee.

Sherman rapidly sent North all his sick and disabled men, and all baggage that could be spared. Commissioners came and took the votes of the soldiers for the Presidential election, and departed. Paymasters came and paid off the troops, and went back again. Wagon trains were put in trim and loaded for a march. Every detachment of the army had its exact orders what to do; and as the last trains whirled over the road to Chattanooga, the track was taken up and destroyed, the bridges burned, the wires torn down, and all the troops that had not been ordered to join Thomas concentrated in Atlanta. From the 12th of November nothing more was heard from Sherman till Christmas.

The depot, machine-shops, and locomotive-house in Atlanta were all torn down, and fire was set to the ruins. The shops had been used for the manufacture of Confederate ammunition,

MAJOR-GENERAL JOHN M. CORSE.

and all night the shells were exploding in the midst of the ruin, while the fire spread to a block of stores, and finally burned out the heart of the city. With every unsound man and every useless article sent to the rear, General Sherman now had fifty-five thousand three hundred and twenty-nine infantrymen, five thousand and sixty-three cavalrymen, and eighteen hundred and twelve artillerymen, with sixty-five guns. There were four teams of horses to each gun, with its caisson and forge; six hundred ambulances, each drawn by two horses; and twenty-five hundred wagons, with six mules to each. Every soldier carried forty rounds of ammunition, while the wagons contained an abundant additional supply and twelve hundred thousand rations, with oats and corn enough to last five days. Probably a more thoroughly appointed army was never seen, and it is difficult to imagine one of equal numbers more effective. Every man in it was a veteran, was proud to be there, and felt the most perfect confidence that under the leadership of "Uncle Billy" it would be impossible to go wrong.

On the 15th of November they set out on the march to the sea, nearly three hundred miles distant. The infantry consisted of four corps. The Fifteenth and Seventeenth formed the right wing, commanded by Gen. Oliver O. Howard; the Fourteenth and Twentieth the left, commanded by Gen. Henry W. Slocum. The cavalry was under the command of Gen. Judson Kilpatrick. The two wings marched by parallel routes, generally a few miles apart, each corps having its own proportion of the artillery and trains. General Sherman issued minute orders as to the conduct of the march, which were systematically carried out. Some of the instructions were these:

"The habitual order of march will be, wherever practicable, by four roads, as nearly parallel as possible. The separate columns will start habitually at seven A.M., and make about fifteen miles a day. Behind each regiment should follow one wagon and one ambulance. Army commanders should practise the habit of giving the artillery and wagons the road, marching the troops on one side. The army will forage liberally on the country during the march. To this end, each brigade commander will organize a good and sufficient foraging party, who will gather corn or forage of any kind, meat of any kind, vegetables, corn meal, or whatever is needed by the command, aiming at all times to keep in the wagons at least ten days' provisions. Soldiers must not enter dwellings or commit any trespass; but, during a halt or camp, they may be permitted to gather turnips, potatoes, and other vegetables, and to drive in stock in sight of their camp. To corps commanders alone is intrusted the power to destroy mills, houses, cotton-gins, etc. Where the army is unmolested, no destruction of such property should be permitted; but should guerillas or bushwhackers molest our march, or should the inhabitants burn bridges, obstruct roads, or otherwise manifest local hostility, then army commanders should order and enforce a devastation more or less relentless, according to the measure of such hostility. As for horses, mules, wagons, etc., belonging to the inhabitants, the cavalry and artillery may appropriate freely and without limit; discriminating, however, between the rich, who are usually hostile, and the poor and industrious, usually neutral or friendly. In all foraging, the parties engaged will endeavor to leave with each family a reasonable portion for their maintenance."

Thus equipped and thus instructed, the great army moved steadily, day after day, cutting a mighty swath, from forty to sixty miles wide, through the very heart of the Confederacy. The columns passed through Rough and Ready, Jonesboro', Covington, McDonough, Macon, Milledgeville, Gibson, Louisville, Millen, Springfield, and many smaller places. The wealthier inhabitants fled at the approach of the troops. The negroes in great numbers swarmed after the army, believing the long-promised day of jubilee had come. Some of them seemed to have an intelligent idea that the success of the National forces meant destruction of slavery, while most of them had but the vaguest notions as to the whole movement. One woman, with a child in her arms, walking along among the cattle and horses, was accosted by an officer, who asked her, "Where are you going, aunty?" "I'se gwine whar you's gwine, massa." One party of black men, who had fallen into line, called out to another who seemed to be asking too many questions, "Stick in dar! It's all right. We'se gwine along; we'se free." Major George Ward Nichols describes an aged couple whom he saw in a hut near Milledgeville. The old negress, pointing her long finger at the old man, who was in the corner of the fireplace, hissed out, "What fer you sit dar? You s'pose I wait sixty years for nutten? Don't yer see de door open? I'se follow my child; I not stay; I walks till I drop in my tracks."

The army destroyed nearly the whole of the Georgia Central Railroad, burning the ties, and heating and twisting the rails. As they had learned that a rail merely bent could be straightened and used again, a special tool was invented with which a

BRIGADIER-GENERAL NATHAN KIMBALL

BRIGADIER-GENERAL N. C. McLEAN.

red-hot rail could be quickly twisted like an auger, and rendered forever useless. They also had special appliances for tearing up the track methodically and rapidly. All the depot buildings were in flames as soon as the column reached them. As the bloodhounds had been used to track escaped prisoners, the men killed all that they could find.

The foraging parties—or "bummers," as they were popularly called—went out for miles on each side, starting in advance of the organizations to which they belonged, gathered immense quantities of provisions, and brought them to the line of march, where each stood guard over his pile till his own brigade came along. The progress of the column was not allowed to be interrupted for the reception of the forage, everything being loaded upon the wagons as they moved. The "flankers" were thrown out on either side, passing in thin lines through the woods to prevent any surprise by the enemy, while the mounted officers went through the fields to give the road to the troops and trains.

MAJOR-GENERAL PETER J. OSTERHAUS.

The only serious opposition came from Wheeler's Confederate cavalry, which hung on the flanks of the army and burned some bridges, but was well taken care of by Kilpatrick's, who generally defeated it when brought to an encounter. There was great hope that Kilpatrick would be able to release the prisoners of war confined in Millen, but when he arrived there he found that they had been removed to some other part of the Confederacy. When the advance guard was within a few miles of Savannah there was some fighting with infantry, and a pause before the defences of the city.

Fort McAllister, which stood in the way of communication with the blockading fleet, was elaborately protected with ditches, palisades, and *chevaux-de-frise;* but Gen. William B. Hazen's division made short work with it, going straight over everything and capturing the fort on the 13th of December, losing ninety-two men in the assault, and killing or wounding about fifty of the garrison. That night General Sherman, with a few officers, pulled down the river in a yawl and visited a gunboat of the fleet in Ossabaw Sound. Four days later, having established full communication, Sherman demanded the surrender of the city of Savannah, which Gen. William J. Hardee, who was in command there with a considerable force, refused. Sherman then took measures to make its investment complete; but on the morning of the 21st it was found to be evacuated by Hardee's forces, and Gen. John W. Geary's division of the Twentieth Corps marched in. The next day Sherman wrote to the President: "I beg to present you as a Christmas gift the city of Savannah, with one hundred and fifty heavy guns and plenty of ammunition, also about twenty-five thousand bales of cotton." Sherman's entire loss in the march had been seven hundred and sixty-four men.

That phase of war which reaches behind the armies in the field and strikes directly at the sources of supply, bringing home its burdens and its hardships to men who are urging on the conflict without participating in it, was never exhibited on a grander scale or conducted with more complete success. This, in fact, is the most humane kind of war, since it accomplishes the purpose with the least destruction of life and limb. Sherman's movement across Georgia naturally brings to mind another famous march to the sea; but that was a retreat of ten thousand, while this was a victorious advance of sixty thousand; and it was only in their shout of welcome, *Thalatta! thalatta!* ("The sea! the sea!") that the weary and disheartened Greeks resembled Sherman's triumphant legions.

The condition of affairs in Georgia, as seen by the residents, just before and at the time of Sherman's great march, has been vividly described by the Rev. J. Ryland Kendrick, who was pastor of a church in Charleston when the war broke out, and two years later removed to Madison, Ga. He says:

"In passing from South Carolina to Georgia one could hardly fail to be immediately conscious of breathing a somewhat larger and freer atmosphere. The great mass of the people in the latter State were perhaps no less ardent in their zeal for the

BRIGADIER-GENERAL BENJAMIN HARRISON. BREVET MAJOR-GENERAL WILLIAM T. WARD. COLONEL DANIEL DUSTIN. BREVET BRIGADIER-GENERAL WILLIAM COGGSWELL.

CONFEDERATE WORKS BEFORE ATLANTA.

(FROM A GOVERNMENT PHOTOGRAPH.)

Confederate cause than those of the former, but still there was among them more latitude of opinion, and criticisms on the political and military status were not so rigorously repressed. Owing to her greater extent of territory, her less aristocratic civil institutions, and her more composite population, Georgia had long been characterized by a broader spirit of tolerance than South Carolina, and she manifested that spirit during the war. Not a few might be found in almost any community who had no heart in the pending conflict, and little faith in its successful issue. Besides, her governor, Joseph E. Brown, early showed a disposition to do his own thinking, and to take ground which was not always pleasing to the autocratic will of Jefferson Davis. This naturally encouraged freedom of thought and utterance among the people at large.

"At the beginning of 1863 I received a call to the pastorate of the Baptist church in Madison, a village on the Georgia railroad, and made my home there for the remainder of the war. It was an ideal refuge amidst the storm and stress of the time, especially for a man with my peculiar convictions. The village was one of the pleasantest and most attractive in the State, comprising in its population a considerable number of wealthy, educated, and refined families, a large share of which belonged to my church. In the ante-bellum days it had been distinguished as an educational centre for girls, with two flourishing seminaries—one Baptist, the other Methodist. When I went there the war had closed both of them. Just on the line which divides the upper from the lower country, Madison was as remote from the alarms of war as any place in the war-girdled South could well be, and fairly promised to be about the last spot which the invaders would strike. To its various attractions Madison added, for me, one other, which at the time was not generally esteemed an attraction at all, but rather a serious reproach. I refer to its reputation for somewhat lax loyalty to the Confederacy. It was known throughout the State as a town much given to croaking and criticism, with a suspicion of decided disaffection on the part of some of its leading citizens. Foremost among these sullen and recalcitrant Madisonians was Col. Joshua Hill, familiarly known as 'Josh Hill,' confessedly the most prominent man in the community, and about as much at odds with the Confederate Government as one could well be without provoking the stroke of its iron hand. He had been a member of the United States Congress when the secession fury began, and having stuck to his post as long as possible finally retired from it in a regular and honorable way.

"Preaching as I did only on Sunday mornings, I often availed myself of the opportunity to attend, in the after-part of that day, the religious services of the colored people; sometimes preaching to them myself, but more commonly listening to the preachers of their own race. While, as might be expected, there was a sad lack of any real instruction in their pulpit performances, there was superabundance of fervor and not a little of genuine oratorical effectiveness.

"It interested me especially, in these meetings of the colored people, to watch their attitude toward the pending war, in whose issues they had so great a stake, and by which they were placed in an extremely delicate relation to their masters. Their shrewdness was simply amazing Their policy was one of reserve and silence. They rarely referred to the war in their sermons or prayers, and when they did mention it they used broad terms which meant little and compromised nobody. Of course they could not betray sympathy for the invaders, but they certainly exhibited none for the other side. To any keen observer their silence was significant enough, but nobody cared to evoke their real sentiments. The subtlest sagacity could not have dictated a more prudent line of conduct than that which their instincts chose. Indeed, the conduct of the colored people through the whole war, whose import they vaguely but truly divined, was admirable, and such as to merit the eternal gratitude of the Southern whites. Under the most tempting opportunities, outrages upon women and children were never fewer, petty crimes were not increased, and of insurrectionary movements, so far as I knew, there were absolutely none, while the soil was never tilled with more patient and faithful industry. No doubt their conduct was largely determined by a shrewd comprehension of the situation, as well as by their essential kindliness of nature. They understood that bodies of soldiery were never far away, and that any uprising would be speedily and remorselessly crushed. They knew, too, that it was wiser to wait for the coming of 'Massa Linkum's' legions, whose slow approach could not be concealed from them.

"If the colored people dimly saw that their deliverance was approaching with the advance of the Federal armies, the faith of the whites in the perpetuity of the divine institution lingered long and died hard. It seemed to them impossible that this institution should come to an end. Indeed, there was manifested on the part of some very good and devout people a disposition to hazard their faith in the veracity of God and the Bible on the success of the Southern arms. The Bible, they argued, distinctly sanctioned slavery, and if slavery should be overthrown by the failure of the South the Bible would be fatally discredited.

"In those trying days some few compensations came to us for the deprivations inflicted by the blockade. For one thing, the tyranny of fashion was greatly abated. Style was little thought of, and fine ladies were made happy by the possession of an English or French calico gown. For another thing, cut off from magazines, reviews, and cheap yellow-covered literature, and with newspapers so curtailed of their ordinary proportions that they were taken in at a *coup d'œil*, we were driven back upon old standard books. I suspect that among the stay-at-homes a larger amount of really good, solid reading was done during the war than in the previous decade. Now and then a contraband volume slipped through the blockade, and was eagerly sought after. Somehow, a copy of Buckle's 'History of Civilization' got into my neighborhood, and had a wide circulation. Victor Hugo's 'Les Misérables' appeared among us in a shocking edition, printed, I think, in New Orleans.

"The ever-beginning, never-ending topic of conversation was the war, with its incidents and prospects. We breakfasted, dined, and supped on startling reports of victories or defeats, and vague hints of prodigious things shortly to occur. It is noteworthy that our reports were almost uniformly of victories, frequently qualified by the slow and reluctant admission that, having won a brilliant success, the Confederate forces at last fell back. This trick of disguising defeat came, after a while, to be so well understood, that 'to conquer and fall back' was tossed about as a grim jest.

"As the tide of war surged southward, and at last reached Chattanooga, our village, like nearly all others on railway lines, became a hospital station, and the large academy was appropriated to the sick and wounded.

"After the battle of Chickamauga great trains of cars came lumbering through our town, crowded with Union captives. They were a sad sight to look upon. Standing one day by the track as such a train was slowly passing, the irrepressible prisoners shouted to me, 'Old Rosey will be along here soon!' 'Old Rosey' never came, but 'Uncle Billy' in due time put in an unmistakable appearance, which more than fulfilled what at the moment seemed the prediction of mere reckless bravado.

"During the summer of 1864 our secluded little village was rudely shaken by its first experience in the way of invasion. After steadily pushing back the Confederate columns, Sherman had at last reached Atlanta, and his hosts were in fact only about seventy miles away from us. In certain conditions of the atmosphere we could hear the dull, heavy thunder of his guns. Yet, strangely enough, this proximity of war in its sternest form created no panic among us. In fact, a kind of paralysis now benumbed the sensibilities of the people. The back of the Confederacy had been definitely broken in the preceding summer by the battle of Gettysburg. Nearly all discerning persons were conscious of this, and but for the foreordained and blind obstinacy of Jefferson Davis and his satellites efforts would have been made to save the South from utter wreck. Alexander H. Stephens was understood to entertain very definite ideas as to the hopeless and disastrous course of events under Davis's policy.

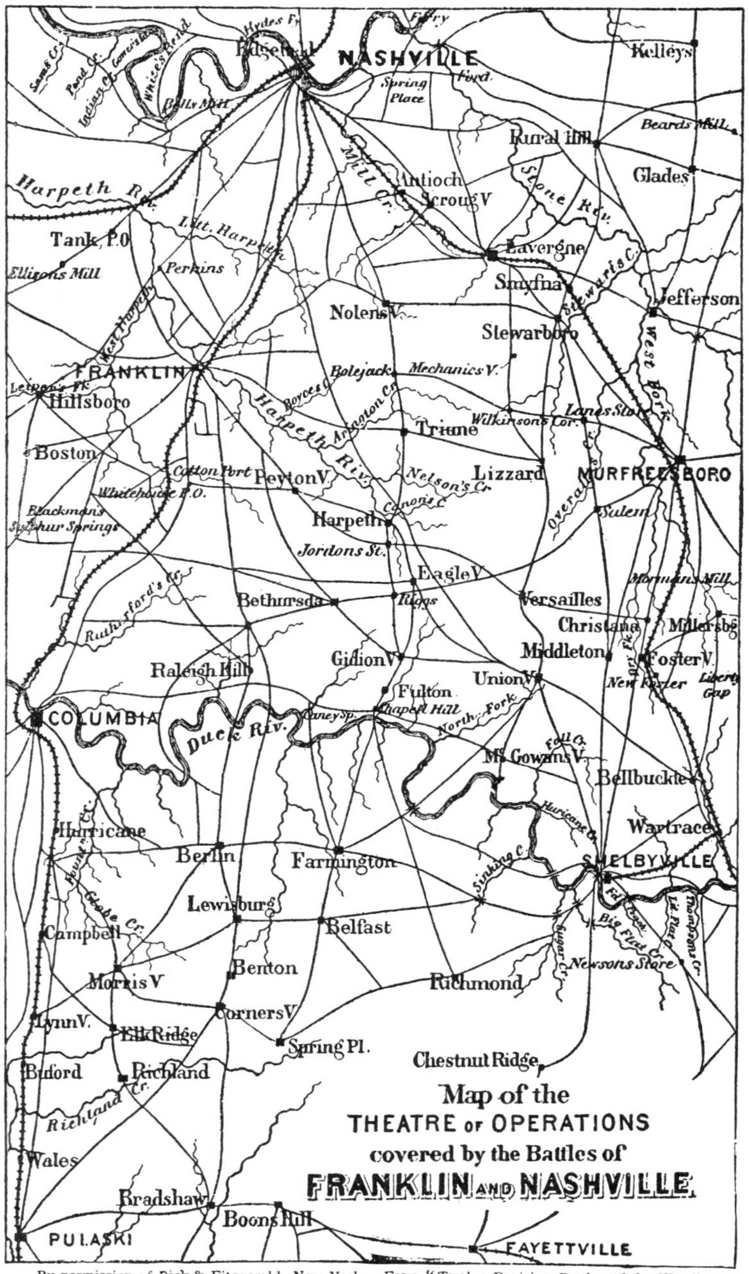

By permission of Dick & Fitzgerald, New York. From "Twelve Decisive Battles of the War."

"On a hot July morning I was sitting, Southern fashion, with a number of gentlemen before a store just outside of the public square. We were canvassing a strange rumor which had just reached us, to the effect that Yankee soldiers had been seen not far from the town. At that moment a man from the country rode up to our group, and, hearing the topic of conversation, generously offered to 'eat all the Union soldiers within ten miles of Madison.' Scarcely had he uttered these reassuring words when a man in uniform galloped into the square. Now, we said, we shall get trustworthy information, thinking that this was a Confederate scout. In a moment, however, another cavalryman dashed around the corner, and fired a pistol at a fugitive clad in Confederate gray. The truth instantly flashed upon us, and with a cry of '*Yankees!*' we all sprang to our feet. Not much alarmed myself, I called to my friends, 'Don't run!' but the most of them, disregarding my advice, took themselves off in remarkably quick time. The strange intruders, coming upon us as suddenly as if they had dropped out of the summer sky, now poured into the square and overflowed all the streets. Boldly standing my ground, I approached the first officer I could make out, and requested permission to go at once to my home on the outskirts of the village. He informed me that I must wait until the arrival of the colonel in command. So it was that for a space of five or ten minutes I may be said to have been a prisoner under the flag of my country. The colonel soon rode up, a stalwart, square-built, kindly-faced Kentuckian—Colonel Adams, as I afterward learned—who promptly granted my request, and directed an officer to see me safe through the crowd of soldiers. At my gate I found two or three soldiers, quietly behaved, and simply asking for food. Gratefully receiving such as we could give them, they departed, leaving us quite unharmed.

"In November an important ministerial service called me to southwestern Georgia, and, as all seemed quiet about Atlanta, I hesitatingly ventured, accompanied by my wife, upon the journey. Starting homeward after a few days, we reached Forsyth, and paused there on the edge of the desert. For a desert it was that stretched for some sixty miles between us and Madison, a *terra incognita*, over which no adventurous explorer had passed since Sherman's legions had blotted out all knowledge of it. Only wild rumors filled the air. At last a friend took the serious risk of letting us have his carriage, with a pair of mules and a negro driver, for the perilous journey. Having crossed the Ocmulgee, we at once struck the track of Sherman's army, his right, under Howard, having kept near the river. In that day's ride we met on the road but one human being—a negro on horseback. A white woman rushed frantically from her little cabin to inquire if any more Yankees were coming, a question which I ventured to answer with a very confident negative. Rather late in the afternoon, as we were passing a pleasant farm-house, a gentleman came out to our carriage and with a very solemn voice and manner warned us against going any further. He had just been informed that ten thousand Yankee soldiers were at somebody's mills, not far away, and he declared that we were *driving* straight into their ranks. This staggered me for a *moment*. But a little reflection convinced me of the violent improbability of the rumor, and a little further reflection determined me to go on. From that moment to the evening hour when we drew up before a planter's house to spend the night, we saw not a human being, scarcely a living thing. Indeed, the wide, dead silence was the most marked sign that we were in the path over which a few days before a great army had passed. The road here and there was considerably cut up, showing that heavy wagons had recently gone over it. Fences were frequently down or missing, and two or three heaps of blackened ruins, surmounted by solitary chimneys, denoted that the torch had done some destructive work. The next day, in passing through Monticello, I saw the charred remains of the county jail, but the signs of conflagration were surprisingly few.

"The family with whom we spent the night had had the strange experience of being for a while in the midst of an encamped army. The soldiers, they informed us, had swarmed about them like bees, but had behaved as well as soldiers commonly do. The planter's horses and cattle had been freely appropriated, and as much of his corn and vegetables as were needed; but there was no complaint of violence or rudeness, and an ample supply of the necessaries of life was left for his household. Indeed, from my observations in this trip across the line of Sherman's march, that march, so far from having been signalized by wanton destruction, was decidedly merciful. No doubt bummers and camp followers committed many atrocities, but the progress of the army proper was attended by no unusual incidents of severity. The year had been one of exceptional bounty, and there was no want in Sherman's rear. Such was the plenty that I believe he might have retraced his steps and subsisted his army on the country.

"On reaching Madison we found the place substantially intact. Not a house had been destroyed, not a citizen harmed or insulted. The greatest sufferers from the invasion were the turkeys and chickens. The country was thickly strewn with the feathers of these slaughtered innocents. When I expressed to a friend some doubt as to Sherman's ability to reach the sea, he replied, 'If you had been here and seen the sort of men composing his cohorts, you would not question that they could go wherever they had a mind to.'

MAJOR-GENERAL GUSTAVUS W. SMITH, C. S. A.

"Our life between the time of Sherman's march and Lee's surrender, with the scenes and incidents that attended and followed that surrender, was as strange and abnormal as a bad dream. We had, indeed, an abundance of the necessary articles of food and clothing. I have hardly ever lived in more physical comfort than during the last year of the war. The few fowls that had escaped the voracious appetites of the invaders soon provided a fresh supply of chickens and eggs. Coffee at twenty-five dollars a pound (Confederate money), and sugar at not much less cost, were attainable, and I managed to keep a fair supply of them for my little family. But though our physical conditions were tolerable, life was subject to a painful strain of uncertainty and anxiety, relieved only by the conviction that the war, of which all were weary and sick unto death, was nearly over. When the end came, confusion was confounded in a jumble so bewildering as scarcely to be credited with reality. The town streets and country roads were full of negroes, wandering about idle and aimless, going they knew not whither—a pitiful spectacle of enfranchised slaves dazed by their recent boon of liberty. Presently Union soldiers were everywhere. A German colonel, lately a New York broker, moved among us in the spick-and-span bravery of his uniform, the sovereign arbiter of our destinies. The world had rarely presented such a topsy-turvy condition of things, half tragical, half comical.

"As soon as matters had sufficiently quieted down to warrant it, I resolved on a visit to my Northern friends, toward whom my heart yearned. My point of departure was Atlanta, still a desolation of falling walls, blackened chimneys, and almost undistinguishable streets. How queer it was to be again in the great world! How splendid Nashville, Louisville, and Cincinnati appeared, with their brilliant gaslights, crowded thoroughfares, showy shop windows, and fashionably dressed people! Evidently war here, whatever it had meant of sorrow and deprivation, had not been war as we had known it in the beleaguered, invaded, blockaded South. This prosperity was all but incredible when contrasted with Southern poverty, distress, and desolation." *

MAJOR-GENERAL BENJAMIN F. CHEATHAM, C. S. A.

BRIGADIER-GENERAL JOHN T. MORGAN, C. S. A.

When Hood found that he could not lure Sherman away from Atlanta, or make him loose his hold upon that prize of his long campaign, he turned toward Nashville, under orders from Richmond, hoping to destroy the army that Thomas was organizing. He was hindered by heavy rains, and it was late in November when he arrived at Duck River, about forty miles south of the city. Here he found a force, under Gen. John M. Schofield, which was easily flanked by crossing the river, whereupon Schofield fell back to Franklin, on Harpeth River, eighteen miles from Nashville, intrenched a line south and west of the town, with both flanks resting on bends of the river, and got his artillery and trains across the stream, placing the guns where they could play upon any attacking force. Schofield had about twenty-five thousand men, and Hood over forty thousand. In the afternoon of November 30 the attack was made. Schofield's rear guard, consisting of Wagner's brigade, instead of falling back to the main body, as ordered, so as to permit the fire of the whole line to be poured into the advancing enemy, attempted to withstand the Confederate onset. Of course it was quickly swept back,

* *Atlantic Monthly* for October, 1889.

POTTER HOUSE, ATLANTA—SHOWING EFFECT OF ARTILLERY FIRE.

(FROM A GOVERNMENT PHOTOGRAPH.)

and as the men rushed in confusion into the lines they were closely followed by the enemy, who captured a portion of the intrenchments. From a part of the line thus seized they were driven in turn, but they clung tenaciously to the remainder, and Schofield established a new line a few rods in the rear.

Hood's orders to his corps and division commanders were that they were to drive the National army into Harpeth River, while Forrest's cavalry was to cross the river above, sweep down upon the trains, and destroy or capture whatever remnant should have succeeded in crossing the stream. General Schofield did not believe that the attack upon so strong a position would be made in front; he looked for a flank movement, and accordingly, when the battle took place, he was on the north side of the river making arrangements for an adequate means of crossing in case of such movement. But he gave Hood credit for more generalship than he ever possessed. Hood never seemed to have a conception of any method of conducting a battle except by driving his men straight up against the guns and intrenchments of the enemy. In this instance, although he possessed an abundance of artillery, only two batteries were with him. Schofield's line was about a mile and a half long, running through the suburbs of the little town which lay in the bend of the river. The town was approached by three roads, from the southeast, south, and southwest, and along these converging roads Hood pushed the twenty-two thousand men that he brought into the fight. The immediate commander on the field of the National forces was Gen. Jacob D. Cox, who showed himself a masterly tactician and inspiring leader. The works were well planned and very strong, and as the reckless Hood pushed his doomed men up against them they were swept down by front-fire and cross-fire, musketry and artillery, in ghastly heaps along the whole line. When the advanced line was driven back and the centre temporarily broken, the exultant Confederates imagined they were to have everything their own way; and as their divisions came in on converging lines they were crowded together in great masses, through which the fire of the artillery from right and left, as well as the musketry, played with terrible effect. Two companies of one Kentucky regiment were armed with repeating rifles, and their fire alone was equal to that of five hundred ordinary infantrymen. A participant describing the scene at this time says: "From Stiles's and Casement's brigades a blaze of fire leaped from the breastworks and played so incessantly that it appeared to those who saw it as if it had formed a solid plane upon which a man might walk;" and a Confederate staff officer describes it as "a continuous living fringe of flame." Lieutenant Speed, of the Twelfth Kentucky Regiment, says: "The artillery in the line played incessantly, hurling double charges of grape over the field. From Casement and Stiles to the left there was an unabated roar of musketry, which now was continued with intensified fury along Reilly's line up to the pike, and swelled with terrific grandeur along the front all the way to Carter's Creek pike. Along Reilly's line it was a desperate hand-to-hand conflict. Sometimes it seemed that the masses of the assailants would overwhelm all opposition. The struggle was across and over the breastworks. The standards of both armies were upon them at the same time. Muskets flashed in men's faces. Officers fought with the men, musket in hand. The Confederates were at a disadvantage on account of the ditch outside the works, which they could not cross under the blinding storm of lead. Bewildered and confused, they, who had a moment before shouted the cry of victory, could now only receive death and destruction in the most appalling form. In this immediate front the Confederate loss was heavier than at any other point. Here Cleburne fell, almost up to the works; also Granberry and Quarles. The ditch outside the works was filled with killed and wounded men. Confederate officers who witnessed their removal next morning have stated that in places they were piled five deep." The Confederates made in rapid succession so many charges against the new line of works where they had broken the first line, that witnesses differed as to their number. Some counted fourteen, and none counted fewer than ten. But all were in vain. In this action the National troops expended a hundred wagon loads of ammunition, and as the smoke did not rise readily it seemed as if the darkness

CAPTAIN JOSEPH B. FORAKER.

(Afterward Governor of Ohio.)

BREVET BRIGADIER-GENERAL JOSEPH W. FISHER.

of night were coming on prematurely. No doubt this circumstance contributed largely to the terrible losses of the Confederates. Forrest's cavalry, which was expected to cross the river and capture Schofield's trains, did not accomplish anything. The reason given for its inaction was lack of ammunition. In this brief and bloody encounter Hood lost more than one-third of his men engaged. His killed numbered one thousand seven hundred and fifty. The number of his wounded can only be computed, but it is not probable that they were fewer than seven thousand. Major Sanders, of the Confederate army, estimates the loss in two of the brigades at sixty-five per cent. These losses included Major-Gen. Patrick R. Cleburne and Brig.-Gens. John Adams, Oscar F. Strahl, S. R. Gist, and H. B. Granberry, all killed; also six general officers wounded and one captured; and more than thirty colonels and lieutenant-colonels were killed or wounded. Schofield lost two thousand five hundred men, and his army took seven hundred prisoners and thirty-three stands of colors. At midnight Schofield crossed the river and retreated to Nashville. Hood followed him, and there confronted the whole of Thomas's army. Schofield has been criticised for thus retreating after his victory; but if he had remained at Franklin the conditions for a battle the next day would have been materially changed. Hood brought up all his artillery in the night, intending to open upon the works in the morning, and it is not probable that Forrest's vigorous cavalry would have remained inactive another day.

Everybody complained of Thomas's slowness, and he was in imminent danger of being superseded; but he would not assume the offensive till he felt that his army was prepared to make sure work. When all was ready, he still had to delay because of bad weather; but on the 15th of December (one day after Sherman reached the sea) the long-meditated blow was given. Thomas's army advanced against Hood's, striking it simultaneously in front and on the left flank. The weight of the attack fell upon the flank, which was completely crushed, and a part of the intrenchments with their guns fell into the hands of the National forces. In the night Hood retreated a mile or two, to another line on the hills, made some new dispositions, and awaited attack. He was seriously embarrassed by the absence of a large part of Forrest's cavalry, which should have been protecting his flanks. In the afternoon of the 16th, Thomas, having sent Wilson's cavalry around the enemy's left flank, attacked with his whole force. He made no headway against Hood's right, but again he crushed the left flank, and followed up the advantage so promptly and vigorously that all organization in the Confederate army was lost, and what was left of it fled in wild confusion toward Franklin, pursued by Wilson's cavalry. Thomas captured all their artillery and took forty-five hundred prisoners. The number of their killed and wounded was never reported. His own loss was about three thousand. Brig.-Gen. Sylvester G. Hill was among the killed.

SHERMAN'S FORAGERS ON A GEORGIA PLANTATION.

CHAPTER XLII.

MINOR EVENTS OF THE FOURTH YEAR.

DESPERATE CONDITION OF THE CONFEDERACY—THE EXPORTATION OF COTTON, TOBACCO, AND SUGAR PROHIBITED—THE THREATENED SECESSION OF NORTH CAROLINA FROM THE CONFEDERACY—SWEEPING CONSCRIPTION ACTS—FORCES UNDER GENERAL BUTLER ATTEMPT TO CAPTURE RICHMOND—NUMEROUS MINOR ENGAGEMENTS IN THE SHENANDOAH VALLEY—BATTLE BETWEEN CAVALRY FORCES AT TREVILIAN STATION—PLYMOUTH, N. C., CAPTURED BY THE CONFEDERATES—BLACK FLAG RAISED AND NEGRO PRISONERS SHOT — THE DESTRUCTION OF THE RAM "ALBEMARLE" BY A FORCE UNDER LIEUTENANT CUSHING —DEFEAT OF FEDERAL FORCE AT OLUSTEE—ENGAGEMENTS AT DAND RIDGE AND FAIR GARDENS, TENN. — OPERATIONS IN LOUISIANA AND MISSISSIPPI.

WITH the dawn of the fourth year of the war the statesmen and journalists of the Confederacy showed by their utterances that they knew how desperate were its straits, and how much its prospects had waned since the victories of the first and second years. The *Richmond Whig* said: "The utmost nerve, the firmest front, the most undaunted courage, will be required during the coming twelve months from all who are charged with the management of affairs in our country, or whose position gives them any influence in forming or guiding public sentiment." The *Wilmington* (N. C.) *Journal* said: "Moral courage, the power to resist the approaches of despondency, and the faculty of communicating this power to others, will need greatly to be called into exercise; for we have reached that point in our revolution—which is inevitably reached in all revolutions—when gloom and depression take the place of hope and enthusiasm, when despair is fatal, and despondency is even more to be dreaded than defeat. Whether a crisis be upon us or not, there can be in the mind of no one, who looks at the map of Georgia and considers her geographical relations to the rest of the Confederacy, a single doubt that much of our future is involved in the result of the next spring campaign in upper Georgia." The Confederate Congress passed, in secret session, a bill to prohibit exportation of cotton, tobacco, naval stores, molasses, sugar, or rice, and one to prohibit importation of luxuries into the Confederacy, both of which bills were promptly signed by Mr. Davis. At Huntsville, Ala., a meeting of citizens was held, at which resolutions were passed deprecating the action of the South, and calling upon the Government to convene the legislature, that it might call a convention to provide some mode for the restoration of peace and the rights and liberties of the people. The legislature of Georgia, in March, adopted resolutions, declaring that the Confederate Government ought, after every success of the Confederate arms, to make to the United States Government an official offer to treat for peace. The *Richmond Examiner* said: "People and army, one soul and one body, feel alike, in their inmost hearts, that when the clash comes it will be a struggle for life or death. So far we feel sure of the issue. All else is mystery and uncertainty. Where the first blow will fall, when the two armies of Northern Virginia meet each other face to face, how Grant will try to hold his own against the master-spirit of Lee, we cannot yet surmise; but it is clear to the experienced eye that the approaching campaign will bring into action two new elements not known heretofore in military history, which may not unlikely decide the fate of the gigantic crusade. The enemy will array against us his new iron-clads by sea and his colored troops by land." In the western districts of North Carolina the execution of the Confederate conscription law created great excitement, and several public meetings were held to consider the action of separating from the Confederacy and returning to the Union. The *Raleigh Standard* declared boldly, that, if the measures proposed by the Confederate Government were carried out, the people of North Carolina would take their affairs into their own hands and proceed, in convention assembled, to vindicate their liberties and privileges.

A FEDERAL SIGNAL STATION NEAR WASHINGTON.

As the war pro-

CHARGE OF CONFEDERATE CAVALRY AT TREVILIAN STATION, VIRGINIA.

gressed, and the Confederate armies were depleted by the casualties of battle and the illness attendant upon the hardships of the camp, the conscription became more sweeping, and at last it was made to embrace every man in the Confederacy between eighteen and forty-five years of age. This almost emptied the colleges, until some of them reduced the age of admission to sixteen years, when they were rapidly filled up again. But even these boys were held subject to military call in case of necessity, and in some of the battles of the last year cadets of the Virginia Military Institute took part, and many of them were killed. Another noticeable effect was the diminution in the number of small and detached military operations, because the waning resources of the Confederacy were concentrated more and more in its principal armies.

On the first day of the year a detachment of seventy-five men, commanded by Major Henry A. Cole, being on the scout near Harper's Ferry, suddenly encountered, near Rectortown, a portion of General Rosser's Confederate command, and a stubborn fight ensued. The result was that fifty-seven of Cole's men were either killed or captured, and the remainder made their escape. Two days later a Confederate force, under Gen. Sam Jones, suddenly attacked an Illinois regiment, commanded by Major Beers, near Jonesville, and after a desperate fight compelled them to surrender.

On the 6th of February, an expedition, organized by General Butler for the purpose of dashing into Richmond and releasing the prisoners there, marched from Yorktown by way of New-Kent Court House. They failed in their purpose to surprise the enemy at Bottom's Bridge, where they were to cross the Chickahominy, because, as a Richmond newspaper said, "a Yankee deserter gave information in Richmond of the intended movement." The Confederates had felled a great number of trees across the roads and made it impossible for the cavalry to pass. There was great consternation in Richmond, however, and in the evening of the 7th the bells were rung, and men rushed through the streets crying, "To arms, to arms! the Yankees are coming." The home guard was called out, and the women and children ran about seeking places of safety.

Early in May, General Crook, with about seven thousand men, moving from the mouth of New River through Raleigh Court House and Princeton toward Newbern, met a Confederate force, under Albert G. Jenkins, on Cloyd's Mountain, on the 9th. In the engagement that ensued, the Confederates were defeated and General Jenkins was killed. The next day a cavalry force under General Averell was met at Crockett's Cove by one under General Morgan, and was defeated. General Crook, after the battle of Cloyd's Mountain, destroyed the bridge over New River and a considerable section of the Virginia and Tennessee railroad.

On the 15th of May, General Sigel's force in the Shenandoah Valley being in the northern outskirts of the town of Newmarket, General Breckenridge moved up from the south to attack him. The town is divided by a ravine running at right angles to the Shenandoah, and in the beginning the contest was mainly an artillery battle, both sides firing over the town. Then General Breckenridge's cavalry, with one or two batteries, made a detour to the right, and obtained a position on a hill where they could enfilade the left of Sigel's line, and drove back his cavalry on that wing. At the same time Breckenridge advanced his infantry and pushed back Sigel's whole line about half a mile. Later in the day, repeating the same tactics, he pushed Sigel back a mile farther, but did not accomplish this without severe fighting. One notable incident was the capture of an unsupported battery on the right of Sigel's line, which had been playing with terrible effect upon Breckenridge's left. One regiment of veterans and the cadets of the Military Institute were sent to capture it, which they did at terrible cost. Of the five hundred and fifty men in the regiment, two hundred and forty-one were either killed or wounded, nearly all of them falling in the last three hundred yards before they reached the battery. Of the two hundred and twenty-five boys from the Institute, fifty-four were killed or wounded. When night fell, Sigel crossed the river and burned the bridge behind him. General Imboden, who commanded Breckenridge's cavalry in this action, says: "If Sigel had beaten Breckenridge, General Lee could not have spared the men to check his progress (as he did that of Hunter, a month later) without exposing Richmond to immediate and almost inevitable capture. The necessities of General Lee were such that on the day after the battle he ordered Breckenridge to join him near Richmond with the brigades of Echols and Wharton."

Early in June General Sheridan was sent out with the cavalry of the Army of the Potomac, about eight thousand strong, to strike the Virginia Central Railroad near Charlotteville, where it was expected he would meet the force under General Hunter moving through the Shenandoah Valley. He intended to break the main line at Trevilian Station, and the Lynchburg branch at Charlotteville. He encountered the enemy's cavalry near Trevilian Station on the morning of the 11th. Sending Custer's brigade to the left, and Torbert with the remainder of his division to the right, Sheridan moved directly forward with his main body. The enemy was found dismounted in the edge of the forest, his line stretching across the road. Sheridan's men also dismounted, and promptly attacked. Sharp fighting ensued, in the course of which the enemy was driven back two miles with a heavy loss. Williston's battery was then brought up, and with great skill sent its shells into the mass of fleeing Confederates, whose retreat was turned into a wild rout. A portion of the defeated force, retreating toward Louisa Court House, was struck by Custer's brigade, which defeated them, and captured about three hundred and fifty men. But a little later Fitz Lee's Confederate cavalry came up in the rear of Custer, and captured his wagon-train and headquarters baggage. One of his guns also was captured, but was recaptured in a charge that he led in person. Custer and his whole command came so near being captured when the enemy closed around them, that, when his color-bearer was killed, he tore the flag from the staff and hid it in his bosom. That night the remainder of the enemy retired toward Gordonsville. The next day Sheridan's men destroyed about five miles of the railroad. In the afternoon Torbert advanced toward Gordonsville, and found the Confederates in position across the railroad, facing east. Here they attacked them again, chiefly on their left wing, and again bringing forward Williston's battery, punished them severely, but not so as to drive them from their position before dark. In these actions Sheridan lost about six hundred men. The Confederate loss is not fully known, but it was probably larger. Sheridan now learned that Hunter would not conclude to meet him, and that he was likely instead to encounter Ewell's corps. He therefore turned back, and recrossed the North Anna.

Plymouth, N. C., had been held for some months by a garrison of sixteen hundred men, under General Wessells, when it was attacked on April 17, 1864, by the Confederate General Hoke, with about five thousand men. Skirmishing and artillery firing began early in the morning, and very soon the National camps

BRIGADIER-GENERAL WILLIAMS C. WICKHAM, C. S. A.

BRIGADIER-GENERAL H. B. LYON, C. S. A.

were riddled by shot from the guns. The skirmishers retired within their works, and the Confederates pressed up to these in heavy masses, and were shot down in great numbers. One of the forts, which stood some distance in front of the general line of fortifications, was supplied with hand grenades, and these were used with great effect. But at last this work was captured. The next day the attack was renewed, and a most gallant defence was made. General Hoke, who had been promised a promotion in case of his capturing the place, was determined to do it at whatever cost. Three times he demanded its surrender, and three times he was refused, when he said: "I will fill your citadel full of iron; I will compel your surrender if I have to fight to the last man." It is doubtful, however, if he would have succeeded but for the assistance of the ram *Albemarle*, which came down the river and got into the rear of the National position. Lieutenant Blakeslee, of the Sixteenth Connecticut Regiment, says: "There was a force of five or six thousand in line about six hundred yards in front of our works. At this hour a rocket was sent up as the signal for the attack, and a more furious charge we never witnessed. Instantly over our heads came a peal of thunder from the ram. Up rose a curling wreath of smoke—the batteries had opened, and quickly flashed fierce forks of flame—loud and earth-shaking roars in quick succession. Lines of men came forth from the woods—the battle had begun. We on the skirmish line fell back and entered Coneby redoubt, properly barred the gates and manned the works. The enemy, with yells, charged on the works in heavy column, jumped into the ditch, climbed the parapet, and for fifteen murderous minutes were shot down like mown grass. The conflict was bloody, short, and decisive. The enemy were in such numbers that we had to yield. The gate had been crushed down by a rebel shot, and the enemy poured in, to the number of five or six hundred, with thousands on the outside. Great confusion then ensued; guns were spiked, musket barrels bent, and all sorts of mischief practised by the Union soldiers, while the enemy were swearing at a terrible rate because we would not take off equipments and inform them if the guns could be turned on the town, and in trying to reorganize their troops, who were badly mixed, to take the next work. We were prisoners, and as we marched out of the fort, we could see at what a fearful cost it was to them. Of the eighty-two men in this fort, but one was wounded." The Confederates then worked their way from one redoubt to another, each of which was obstinately defended, but finally captured, until all were taken, and Plymouth was theirs. Lieutenant Blakeslee says: "The rebels raised the black flag against the negroes found in uniform, and mercilessly shot them down. The shooting in cold blood of three or four hundred negroes and two companies of North Carolina troops, who had joined our army, and even murdering peaceable citizens, were scenes of which the Confederates make no mention, except the hanging of one person, but of which many of us were eyewitnesses." The loss of the garrison in the fighting was fifteen killed and about one hundred wounded. The Confederate loss is not exactly known, but it appears to have been well nigh two thousand.

When the iron-clad ram *Albemarle* came down the Roanoke to assist General Hoke in the capture of Plymouth, she not only bombarded the garrison, but attacked the National flotilla there and destroyed or scattered it. She wrecked the *Southfield* by ramming, and when the wooden gunboat *Miami* gallantly stood up to the work and fired

BRIGADIER-GENERAL JOHN D. IMBODEN, C. S. A.

BREVET MAJOR-GENERAL DAVID McM. GREGG AND STAFF.

its broadsides against her iron walls, the shot simply rebounded or rolled off, and one of these returning shots struck and killed Lieut. C. W. Flusser who was in command of the *Miama*.

In the autumn, Lieut. William B. Cushing, of the United States navy, who had performed many gallant exploits, and whose brother was killed beside his gun at Gettysburg, formed a plan for the destruction of the *Albemarle*. He obtained the sanction of his superior officer for the experiment, which Cushing himself considered so hazardous that he asked leave to make a visit to his home before carrying it out. On his return he fitted up an open launch about thirty feet long with a small engine, a twelve-pound howitzer in the bow, and a boom fourteen feet long swinging at the bow by a hinge. This boom carried a torpedo at the end, so arranged that it could be lowered into the water, pushed under a vessel, and then detached from the boom before being exploded. With fifteen picked men in this little craft, in the night of October 27th, Cushing steamed off in the darkness and found the ram at her mooring at Plymouth. When he drew near he was discovered and sharply challenged, whereupon he ordered on all steam and steered straight for the ram. He was fired upon, but in the darkness the shot failed of its mark. Then a large fire was lighted on the bank, and this revealed to him the fact that the *Albemarle* was protected by a circle or boom of logs. Without hesitation, he drew back about a hundred yards, and then under full headway drove straight at them, trusting to make his launch slip over them into the enclosed space where the ram lay. In this he was successful. By this time the crew of the ram were thoroughly alarmed, and as Cushing stood on the bow with the exploding line in his hand he could hear every word of command on the ram, and his clothing was perforated with bullets. He now ordered the boom to be lowered until the motion of the launch pushed the torpedo under the ram's overhang. Then he pulled the detaching line, and, after waiting a little for the torpedo to rise in the water and rest under the hull, he pulled the exploding line. The result to the ram was that a hole was torn in her hull which caused her to keel over and sink. At the same instant a discharge of grape shot from one of her guns tore the launch to pieces, and a large part of the mass of water that was lifted by the torpedo came down upon her little crew. Cushing commanded his men to save themselves, and throwing off his sword, revolver, shoes, and coat, jumped into the water and swam for the opposite shore. Making his way through swamps, and finding a skiff, Lieutenant Cushing at last, almost exhausted, reached the National fleet. One of his crew also escaped, two were drowned, and the remainder were captured. The *Albemarle* was of no further use.

MAJOR-GENERAL GEORGE CROOK

BRIGADIER-GENERAL CHARLES T. EWING.

During the early days of the year a constant fire was kept up upon Charleston, and sometimes as many as twenty shells, loaded with Greek fire, were thrown into the city in a day. The Charleston *Courier* said: "The damage being done is extraordinarily small in comparison with the number of shot and weight of metal fired. The whizzing of shells overhead has become a matter of so little interest as to excite scarcely any attention from passers-by."

In Savannah, April 17th, there was a riot of women who marched through the streets in procession, demanding bread or blood, many of them carrying arms. They seized food wherever they could find it. After a time soldiers were called out, and the leaders of the riot were arrested and put into jail.

Early in February, Gen. Truman Seymour, by order of General Gillmore, left Hilton Head with five thousand five hundred men for Jacksonville, Fla., accompanied by five gunboats under Admiral Dahlgren. The object of the expedition was to penetrate the country west of Jacksonville for the purpose of making an outlet for cotton and lumber, cutting off one source of the enemy's supplies, obtaining recruits for black regiments, and taking measures to protect any citizens who might be disposed to bring the State back into the Union. It was unfortunate that the immediate commander of the expedition, General Seymour, did not altogether believe in its objects. Marching inland, he dispersed some small detachments of Confederate soldiers and captured some guns. He then pushed forward for Suwanee River to destroy the bridges and the railroad, and prevent communication between East and West Florida. Meanwhile the Confederate general, Joseph Finegan, had been collecting troops to oppose the expedition, concentrating them at Lake City, and got together a force about equal to Seymour's. On the 20th of February Seymour moved out from his camp on St.

A UNION TRANSPORT ON THE SUWANEE RIVER.

BREVET BRIGADIER-GENERAL GUY V. HENRY.

REAR-ADMIRAL JOHN A. DAHLGREN.

Mary's River to engage the enemy, who threw forward some troops to meet him. They met near Olustee, and a battle ensued, which was fought on level ground largely covered with open pine forests. Seymour massed his artillery in the centre, and opened from it a fierce fire which was very effective. He then endeavored to push forth his infantry on both flanks, and at the same time the whole Confederate line was advanced. The Seventh New Hampshire and Eighth United States colored regiment, being subjected to a very severe fire, gave way. The fire of the Confederates was then concentrated largely on the artillery, and so many men and horses fell in the short time that five of the guns had to be abandoned. The Confederate reserves were then brought up to a point where they could put in a cross-fire on the National right, and at the same time the whole Confederate line was advanced again. The National line now slowly gave way, and at length was in full retreat; but there was no pursuit. The Confederate loss was nine hundred and forty men; the National loss was one thousand eight hundred and sixty-one.

An escort of eight hundred men, who had charge of the wagon train with commissary stores for the garrison at Petersburg, was suddenly attacked, January 29th, near Williamsport, by several detachments of Confederates who rushed in from different directions. There was a stubborn fight, which lasted from three o'clock in the afternoon until dark. When at last the Confederates, after several repulses, succeeded, they had lost about one hundred men killed and wounded, and the Nationals had lost eighty.

On the 17th of January, a Confederate force made a sudden and determined assault upon the National lines near Dandridge, Tenn. But the Nationals, though surprised, stubbornly stood their ground, and a division of cavalry under Col. D. N. McCook charged the enemy and decided the fate of the conquest. The National loss in this affair was about one hundred and fifty men, nearly half of which fell upon the First Wisconsin Regiment.

A body of National cavalry, commanded by General Sturgis, attacked the Confederate force on January 27th, near Fair Gardens, ten miles east of Sevierville. The fight lasted from daylight until four o'clock in the afternoon, the Confederates being slowly pushed back, when finally the National cavalry drew their sabres and charged with a yell, completely routing the enemy, and capturing two guns and more than one hundred prisoners.

Early in February, a detachment of the Seventh Indiana Regiment entered Bolivar under the supposition that it was still occupied by National troops, and were surprised to find there a large detachment of Confederates. When they learned that these were Mississippi troops, the Indianians, shouting, "Remember Jeff Davis," made a furious attack and drove out the Confederates in confusion, killing, wounded, or capturing a large number of them.

At Powell's River bridge, February 22d, there was an engagement between five hundred Confederates and two companies of the Thirty-fourth Kentucky infantry. The Confederates made four successful charges upon the bridge, and were repelled every time. Finally they were driven off, leaving many horses, arms, saddles, etc., on the field. A participant says: "The attack was made by the infantry, while the cavalry prepared for a charge. The cavalry was soon in line moving on the bridge. On they came in a steady solid column, covered by the fire of their infantry. In a moment the Nationals saw their perilous position, and Lieutenant Slater called for a volunteer to tear up the boards and prevent their crossing. There was some hesitation, and in a moment all would have been lost had not William Goss leaped from the intrenchments, and running to the bridge, under the fire of about four hundred guns, thrown ten boards off into the river, and returned unhurt. This prevented the capture of the whole force."

BRIGADIER-GENERAL S. D. STURGIS.

BRIGADIER-GENERAL W. L. McMILLEN.

Shelby's Confederate force was attacked on January 19th at a point on the Monticello Railroad, twenty miles from Pine Bluff, by a National force under Colonel Clayton, which in course of two hours drove the Confederates seven miles and completely routed them. Clayton's men had marched sixty miles in twenty-four hours.

An expedition commanded by Col. C. C. Andrews of the Third Minnesota infantry ascended White River and marched thirty miles to Augusta, from which place he set out April 1st in search of a Confederate force under Colonel McCrae. It proved that McCrae's forces were divided into scattered detachments, which were successively overtaken and defeated by Colonel Andrews. At Fitzhugh's Woods, however, a large force of the enemy was concentrated, and attacked Colonel Andrews's men in a sharp fight that lasted more than two hours. Andrews took a good position, and thwarted every effort of the enemy to carry it or flank it, when at last they gave up and retired. He lost about thirty men, and estimated the enemy's loss at a hundred.

In the middle of February, the Confederates made a determined attempt to capture the fort at Waterproof, La. First, about eight hundred cavalry drove in the pickets and assaulted the garrison, who might have been overcome but for the assistance of the gunboat *Forest Rose*, Captain Johnson, which with its rapid fire sent many shells into the ranks of the Confederates, and after a time drove them away. This proceeding was repeated later in the day with the same result. Next day the Confederates, largely reinforced, tried it again. Before the fight was over the ram *Switzerland* arrived and took part in it, and the result was the same as on the previous day.

SLAVES GOING TO JOIN THE FEDERAL ARMY.

"THE COUNTERSIGN."

"'Halt! Who goes there?' My challenge cry,
It rings along the watchful line:
'Relief!' I hear a voice reply.
'Advance and give the Countersign!'"

MAJOR-GENERAL ALFRED H. TERRY.

A BOMB PROOF, FORT FISHER.

CHAPTER XLIII.

THE FINAL BATTLES.

SHERMAN MARCHES THROUGH THE CAROLINAS—JOHNSTON RESTORED TO COMMAND—COLUMBIA BURNED—CHARLESTON EVACUATED—CAPTURE OF FORT FISHER—BATTLE OF AVERYSBORO—BATTLE OF BENTONVILLE—SCHOFIELD JOINS SHERMAN—A PEACE CONFERENCE—BATTLE OF WAYNESBORO—SHERIDAN'S RAID ON THE UPPER JAMES—LEE PLANS TO ESCAPE—FIGHTING BEFORE PETERSBURG—BATTLE OF FIVE FORKS—LEE'S LINES BROKEN—RICHMOND EVACUATED—LEE'S RETREAT—HIS SURRENDER—GRANT'S GENEROUS TERMS—SURRENDER OF THE OTHER CONFEDERATE ARMIES.

AFTER Sherman's army had marched through Georgia and captured Savannah, he and General Grant at first contemplated removing it by water to the James, and placing it where it could act in immediate connection with the Army of the Potomac against Petersburg and Richmond. But several considerations soon led to a different plan. One was, the difficulty of getting together enough transports to carry sixty-five thousand men and all their equipage without too much delay. A still stronger one was the fact that in a march through the Carolinas General Sherman's army could probably do more to help Grant's and bring the war to a speedy close than if it were suddenly set down beside it in Virginia. The question of supplies, always a vital one for an army, had become very serious in the military affairs of the Confederacy. The trans-Mississippi region had been cut off long ago, the blockade of the seaports had been growing more stringent, Sheridan had desolated the Shenandoah Valley, Sherman had eaten out the heart of Georgia. And now if that same army, with its increased experience and confidence, should go through South and North Carolina, living on the country, Lee's position in the defences of Richmond would soon become untenable for mere lack of something for his army to eat. Sherman's military instinct never failed him; and, after tarrying at Savannah three weeks, he gathered up his forces for another stride toward the final victory. Turning over the city on January 18, 1865, to Gen. John G. Foster, who was in command on the coast, he issued orders on the 19th for the movement of his whole army.

The right wing was concentrated at Pocotaligo, about forty miles north of Savannah, and the left at Robertsville, twenty miles west of Pocotaligo. After some delay caused by the weather and the necessity for final preparations, the northward march was begun on the 1st of February. Sherman had sent out rumors that represented both Charleston and Augusta as his immediate goal; but instead of turning aside for either of those cities, he pushed straight northward, on a route midway between them, toward Columbia.

This march, though not so romantic as that through Georgia, where a great army was for several weeks hidden from all its friends, was really much more difficult and dangerous, and required greater skill. In the march from Atlanta to the sea, the army moved parallel with the courses of the rivers, and found highways between them that it was not easy for any but a large force to obstruct or destroy. But in the march through the Carolinas, all the streams, and some of them were rivers, had to be crossed. A single man could burn a bridge and stop an army for several hours. Moreover, after the disasters that befell General Hood at Franklin and Nashville, public sentiment in the Confederacy had demanded the reinstatement of Gen. Joseph E. Johnston, and that able soldier had been placed in command of whatever remained of Hood's army, to which were added all the scattered detachments and garrisons that were available, and with this force he took the field against his old antagonist. Of course he was not able now to meet Sherman in anything like a pitched battle; but there was no telling how a sudden blow

BREVET MAJOR-GENERAL N. M. CURTIS.

BREVET MAJOR-GENERAL ADELBERT AMES AND STAFF.

might fall upon an army on the march. Another danger, which was seriously contemplated by Sherman, was that Lee, instead of remaining in his intrenchments while his source of supply was being cut off, might with his whole army slip away from Grant and come down to strike Sherman somewhere between Columbia and Raleigh. With a caution that admirably balanced his boldness, Sherman arranged to have the fleet coöperate with him along the coast, watching his progress and establishing points where supplies could be reached and refuge taken if necessary. He even sent engineers to repair the railroads that, starting from the ports of Wilmington and Newbern, unite at Goldsboro', and to collect rolling-stock there. He intended, when once under way, to push through to Goldsboro', four hundred and twenty-five miles, as rapidly as possible.

BREVET BRIGADIER-GENERAL NATHAN GOFF, JR.

BREVET BRIGADIER-GENERAL ALBERT M. BLACKMAN.

Wheeler's cavalry had been considerably reduced by its constant efforts to delay the march through Georgia, and Wade Hampton's, heretofore with the Army of Northern Virginia, was now sent down to its assistance. They felled trees in the roads, and attempted to make a stand at Salkehatchie River; but Sherman's men made nothing of picking up the trees and casting them one side, while the force at the river was quickly brushed away. The South Carolina Railroad was soon reached, and the track was destroyed for miles. Then all the columns pushed on for Columbia. Sherman expected to meet serious opposition there, for it was the capital of the State; but the Confederate leaders were holding their forces at Charleston and Augusta, confidently expecting those cities to be attacked, and nothing but Hampton's cavalry was left to take care of Columbia. The main difficulty was at the rivers, where the Confederates had burned the bridges, which Sherman's men rapidly rebuilt, and on the 17th the National troops entered the city as Hampton's cavalry left it. Bales of cotton piled up in the streets were on fire, there was a high wind, and the flakes of cotton were flying through the air like a snow-storm. In spite of all efforts of the soldiers, the fire persistently spread at night, several buildings burst into a blaze, and before morning the heart of the city was a heap of ruins. There has been an acrimonious dispute as to the responsibility for this fire. It seems probable that Hampton's soldiers set fire to the cotton, perhaps without orders, and it seems improbable that any one would purposely set fire to the city. At all events, Sherman's men did their utmost to extinguish the flames, and that general gave the citizens five hundred head of cattle, and did what he could to shelter them. He did destroy the arsenal purposely, and tons of powder, shot, and shell were taken out of it, hauled to the river, and sunk in deep water. He also destroyed the foundries and the establishment in which the Confederacy's paper money was printed, large quantities of which were found and carried away by the soldiers.

That same day, the 18th, Charleston was evacuated by the Confederate forces under General Hardee, and a brigade of National troops commanded by General Schimmelpfennig promptly took possession of it.

On the 20th, leaving Columbia, Sherman's army bore away for Fayetteville, the right wing going through Cheraw, and the left through Lancaster and Sneedsboro', and threatening

BREVET BRIGADIER-GENERAL JOSEPH C. ABBOTT.

Charlotte and Salisbury. The most serious difficulty was met at Catawba River, where the bridges were destroyed, the floods interfered with the building of new ones, and there was a delay of nearly a week. In Cheraw was stored a large amount of valuable personal property, including fine furniture and costly wines, which had been sent from Charleston for safe-keeping. Most of this fell into the hands of the invading army. Here also were found a large number of arms and thirty-six hundred barrels of powder; and here, as at Columbia, lives were lost by the carelessness of a soldier in exploding the powder.

Fayetteville was reached on the 11th of March, and here communication was opened with Gen. Alfred H. Terry, whose men had captured Fort Fisher, below Wilmington, after a gallant fight, in January, and later the city itself, thus closing that harbor to blockade-runners. In taking the fort, Terry's men had fought their way from traverse to traverse, and the stubborn garrison had only yielded when they literally reached the last ditch. All this time the Confederate forces, somewhat scattered, had hung on the flanks of Sherman's column or disposed themselves to protect the points that were threatened. But now they knew he was going to Goldsboro', and accordingly they concentrated in his front, between Fayetteville and that place.

At Averysboro', thirty-five miles south of Raleigh, on the 16th of March, the left wing suddenly came upon Hardee's forces intrenched across its path. The left flank of the Confederates was soon turned, and they fell back to a stronger position. Here a direct attack was made, but without success, and Kilpatrick's cavalry was roughly handled by a division of Confederate infantry. General Slocum then began a movement to turn the flank again, and in the night Hardee retreated. Each side had lost five hundred men.

MAJOR-GENERAL EDWARD O. C. ORD.

BREVET MAJOR-GENERAL GEORGE A. CUSTER.

Averysboro' is about forty miles west of Goldsboro'. Midway between is Bentonville, where on the 19th the left wing again found the enemy intrenched across the way, this time in greater force, and commanded by General Johnston. Thickets of blackjack protected the flanks, and it was ugly ground for fighting over. Slocum's men attacked the position in force as soon as they came upon it. They quickly broke the Confederate right flank, drove it back, and planted batteries to command that part of the field. On the other flank the thickets interfered more with the organization of both sides, the National troops threw up intrenchments, both combatants attacked alternately, and the fighting was very bloody. After nightfall the Confederates withdrew toward Raleigh, and the road was then open for Sherman to march into Goldsboro'. At Bentonville, the last battle fought by this army, the National loss was sixteen hundred and four men, the Confederate twenty-three hundred and forty-two. At Goldsboro' Sherman was joined by Schofield's corps, which had been transferred thither from Thomas's army.

Several attempts to negotiate a peace were made during the winter of 1864–65, the most notable of which took place early in February, when Alexander H. Stephens, Vice-President of the Confederacy, accompanied by John A. Campbell and Robert M. T. Hunter, applied for permission to pass through Grant's lines for the purpose. They were conducted to Fort Monroe, met President Lincoln and Secretary Seward on a steamer in Hampton Roads, and had a long and free discussion. The Confederate commissioners proposed an armistice, with the hope that after a time, if trade and friendly relations were resumed, some sort of settlement or compromise could be reached without more fighting. But Mr. Lincoln would consent to no peace or armistice of any kind, except on condition of the immediate disband-

GENERAL WILLIAM T. SHERMAN.

head." The Confederate commissioners were not authorized to concede the restoration of the Union, and thus the conference ended with no practical result.

Late in February General Sheridan, at the head of ten thousand cavalry, moved far up the Shenandoah Valley, and at Waynesboro' his third division, commanded by General Custer, met Early's force on the 2d of March. In the engagements that ensued, Early was completely defeated, and about fifteen hundred of his men were captured, together with every gun he had, and all his trains. Sheridan then ruined the locks in the James River Canal, destroyed portions of the railroads toward Lynchburg and Gordonsville, and rode down the peninsula to White House, crossed over to the James and joined Grant, taking post on the left of the army, and occupying Dinwiddie Court House on the 29th.

Grant and Lee had both been waiting impatiently for the roads to dry, so that wagons and guns could be moved—Lee, because he saw that Richmond could not be held any longer, and was anxious to get away; Grant, because he was anxious to begin the final campaign and prevent Lee from getting away. The only chance for Lee to escape was by slipping past Grant's left, and either joining Johnston in North Carolina or taking a position in the mountainous country to the west. But Grant's left extended too far westward to permit of this without great hazard. To compel him to contract his lines, drawing in his left, Lee planned a bold attack on his right, which was executed in the night of the 24th. Large numbers of deserters had recently left the Confed-

ment of the Confederate armies and government, the restoration of the Union, and the abolition of slavery. With these points secured, he was willing to concede everything else. Mr. Stephens, trying to convince Mr. Lincoln that he might properly recognize the Confederacy, cited the example of Charles I. of England negotiating with his rebellious subjects. "I am not strong on history," said Lincoln; "I depend mainly on Secretary Seward for that. All I remember about Charles is, that he lost his

BREVET MAJOR-GENERAL ROMEYN B. AYRES.

BREVET MAJOR GENERAL HENRY E. DAVIES, JR.

erate army and walked across to Grant's lines, bringing their arms with them, and this circumstance was now used for a ruse. At a point where the hostile lines were not more than a hundred yards apart, some of General Gordon's men walked out to the National picket-line as if they were deserters, seized the pickets, and sent them back as prisoners. Then a column charged through the gap, surprised the men in the main line, and captured a section of the works. But General Parke, commanding the Ninth Corps, where the assault was delivered, promptly made dispositions to check it. The Confederates were headed off in both directions, and a large number of guns were soon planted where they could sweep the ground that had been captured. A line of intrenchments was thrown up in the rear, and the survivors of the charging column found themselves where they could neither go forward, nor retreat, nor be reinforced. Consequently they were all made prisoners. This affair cost the Confederates about four thousand men, and inflicted a loss of two thousand upon the National army.

Grant, instead of contracting his lines, was making dispositions to extend them. Three divisions under Gen. E. O. C. Ord were brought from his right, before Richmond, in the night of the 27th, and placed on his extreme left, while a movement was planned for the 29th by which that wing was to be pushed out to the Southside Railroad. When the day appointed for the movement arrived, heavy rains had made the ground so soft that the roads had to be corduroyed before the artillery could be dragged over them. But the army was used to this sort of work, and performed it with marvellous quickness. Small trees were cut down, and rail fences disappeared in a twinkling, while the rude flooring thus constructed stretched out over the sodden road and kept the wheels of the guns from sinking hopelessly in the mire and quicksands.

Grant's extreme left, where the critical movement was to be made, was now held by his most energetic lieutenant, General Sheridan, with his magnificent cavalry. By Grant's orders, Sheridan made a march through Dinwiddie Court House, to come in upon the extreme Confederate right at Five Forks, which he struck on the 31st. He had no difficulty in driving away the Confederate cavalry; but when a strong infantry force was encountered he was himself driven back, and called upon Grant for help. Grant sent the Fifth Corps to his assistance; but it was unusually slow in moving, and was stopped by the loss of a bridge at Gravelly Run, so that it was midday of April 1st before Sheridan began to get it in hand. Lee had strengthened the force holding Five Forks; but Sheridan was determined to capture the place, and when his troops were all up, late in the afternoon, he opened the battle on a well-conceived plan.

BRIGADIER-GENERAL AUGUST V. KAUTZ.
MAJOR-GENERAL GODFREY WEITZEL.

SHERIDAN AND HIS GENERALS RECONNOITRING AT FIVE FORKS (DINWIDDIE COURT-HOUSE).

Engaging the enemy with his cavalry in front, he used the Fifth Corps as if it were his immense right arm, swinging it around so as to embrace and crush the Confederate force. With bloody but brief fighting the manœuvre was successful; Five Forks was secured, and more than five thousand prisoners were taken. Sheridan's loss was about one thousand. In the hour of victory came orders from Sheridan relieving Warren of his command, because of that officer's slowness in bringing his corps to the attack. Whether this harsh action was justified or not, it threw a blight upon the career of one of the best corps commanders that the Army of the Potomac ever had, and excited the regret, if not the indignation, of every man that had served under him.

Judging that Lee must have drawn forces from other parts of his line to strengthen his right, Grant followed up the advantage by attacking Lee's centre at daybreak the next morning, Sunday, April 2d, with the corps of Wright and Parke, the Sixth and Ninth. Both of these broke through the Confederate lines in the face of a musketry fire, took large portions of them in reverse, and captured three or four thousand prisoners and several guns. The Second Corps, under Gen. Andrew A. Humphreys, and three divisions under General Ord, made a similar movement, with similar success; Sheridan moved up on the left, and the outer defences of Petersburg were now in the possession of the National forces, who encircled the city with a continuous line from a point on the Appomattox River above to one below. Two strong earthworks, Forts Gregg and Whitworth, salient to the inner Confederate line, still held out. But Foster's division of the Twenty-fourth Corps carried Fort Gregg after a costly assault, and Fort Whitworth then surrendered. In the fighting of this day the Confederate general A. P. Hill was killed.

BRIGADIER-GENERAL STEPHEN ELLIOTT, JR., C. S. A.

BRIGADIER-GENERAL A. H. COLQUITT C. S. A.

LIEUTENANT-GENERAL JOHN B. GORDON.

LIEUTENANT-GENERAL WADE HAMPTON, C. S. A.

MAJOR-GENERAL G. W. C. LEE, C. S. A.

MAJOR-GENERAL WILLIAM MAHONE, C. S. A.

General Lee now sent a telegram to Richmond, saying that both cities must be evacuated. It was received in church by Mr. Davis, who quietly withdrew without waiting for the service to be finished. As the signs of evacuation became evident to the people, there was a general rush for means of conveyance, and property of all sorts was brought into the streets in confused masses. Committees appointed by the city council attempted to destroy all the liquor, and hundreds of barrelfuls were poured into the gutters. The great tobacco warehouses were set on fire, under military orders, and the iron-clad rams in the river blown up; while a party of drunken soldiers began a course of pillaging, which became contagious and threw everything into the wildest confusion. The next morning a detachment of black troops from Gen. Godfrey Weitzel's command marched into the city, and the flag of the Twelfth Maine Regiment was hoisted over the Capitol.

When Lee, with the remnant of his army, withdrew from Richmond and Petersburg, he fled westward, still keeping up the organization, though his numbers were constantly diminishing by desertion, straggling, and capture. Grant was in close pursuit, striving to head him off, and determined not to let him escape. He moved mainly on a parallel route south of Lee's, attacking vigorously whenever any portion of the hostile forces approached near enough. Some of these engagements were very sharply contested; and as the men on both sides had attained the highest perfection of destructive skill, and were not sheltered by intrenchments, the losses were severe, and the seventy miles of the race was a long track of blood. There were collisions at Jetersville, Detonville, Deep Creek, Sailor's Creek, Paine's Cross Roads, and Farmville; the most important being that at Sailor's Creek, where Custer broke the Confederate line, capturing four hundred wagons, sixteen guns, and many prisoners, and then the Sixth Corps came up and captured the whole of Ewell's corps, including Ewell himself and four other generals. Lee was stopped by the loss of a provision train, and spent a day in trying to collect from the surrounding country something for his famished soldiers to eat.

DEFENCE OF FORT GREGG, PETERSBURG.

When he arrived at Appomattox Court House, April 9th, a week from the day he set out, he found Sheridan's dismounted cavalry in line across his path, and his infantry advanced confidently to brush them away. But the cavalrymen drew off to the right, and disclosed a heavy line of blue-coated infantry and gleaming steel. Before this the weary Confederates recoiled, and just as Sheridan was preparing to charge upon their flank with his cavalry a white flag was sent out and hostilities were suspended on information that negotiations for a surrender were in progress. Grant had first demanded Lee's surrender in a note written on the afternoon of the 7th. Three or four other notes had passed between them, and on the 9th the two commanders met at a house in the village, where they wrote and exchanged two brief letters by which the surrender of the Army of Northern Virginia was effected; the terms being simply that the men were to lay down their arms and return to their homes, not to be molested so long as they did not again take up arms against the United States. The exceeding generosity of these terms, to an army that had exacted almost the last life it had power to destroy, was a surprise to many who remembered the unconditional surrender that General Grant had demanded at Vicksburg and Fort Donelson. But he considered that the war was over, and thought the defeated insurgents would at once return to their homes and become good citizens of the United States. In pursuance of this idea, he ordered that they be permitted to take their horses with them, as they "would need them for the ploughing." The starving Confederates were immediately fed by their captors; and, by General Grant's orders, cheering, firing of salutes, and other demonstrations of exultation over the great and decisive victory were immediately stopped. The number of officers and men paroled, according to the terms of the surrender, was twenty-eight thousand three hundred and sixty-five.

The next day General Lee issued, in the form of a general order, a farewell address to his army in which he lauded them in unmeasured terms, to the implied disparagement of their conquerors, and assured them of his "unceasing admiration of their constancy and devotion to their country." It seems not to have occurred to the general that he had no army, for it had been taken away from him, and no right to issue a military document of any kind, for he was a prisoner of war; and he certainly must have forgotten that the costly court of last resort, to which he and they had appealed, had just decided that their country as he defined it had no existence.

General Johnston, who was confronting Sherman in North Carolina, surrendered his army to that commander at Durham Station, near Raleigh, on the 26th of April, receiving the same terms that had been granted to Lee; and the surrender of all the other Confederate armies soon followed, the last being the command of Gen. E. Kirby Smith, at Shreveport, La., on the 26th of May. The number of Johnston's immediate command surrendered and paroled was thirty-six thousand eight hundred and seventeen, to whom were added fifty-two thousand four hundred and fifty-three in Georgia and Florida.

THE McLEAN HOUSE WHERE GENERAL LEE SURRENDERED TO GENERAL GRANT.

THE SURRENDER OF GENERAL LEE.

CHAPTER XLIV.

PEACE.

THE WAR GOVERNORS—CIVILIAN PATRIOTS—THE SUDDEN FALL OF THE CONFEDERACY—CAPTURE OF MR. DAVIS—CHARACTER OF THE INSURRECTION—MAGNANIMITY OF THE VICTORS—THE ASSASSINATION CONSPIRACY—LINCOLN'S SECOND INAUGURAL ADDRESS—LINCOLN IN RICHMOND—THE GRAND REVIEW—THE HOME-COMING—LESSONS OF THE WAR.

NO account of the war, however brief, can properly be closed without some mention of the forces other than military that contributed to its success. The assistance and influence of the "war governors," as they were called—including John A. Andrew of Massachusetts, William A. Buckingham of Connecticut, Edwin D. Morgan of New York, William Dennison of Ohio, and Oliver P. Morton of Indiana—was vital to the cause, and was acknowledged as generously as it was given. There was also a class of citizens who, by reason of age or other disability, did not go to the front, and would not have been permitted to, but found a way to assist the Government perhaps even more efficiently. They were thoughtful and scholarly men, who brought out and placed at the service of their country every lesson that could be drawn from history; practical and experienced men, whose hard sense and knowledge of affairs made them natural leaders in the councils of the people; men of fervid eloquence, whose arguments and appeals aroused all there was of latent patriotism in their younger and hardier countrymen, and contributed wonderfully to the rapidity with which quotas were filled and regiments forwarded to the seat of war. There were great numbers of devoted women, who performed uncomplainingly the hardest hospital service, and managed great fairs and relief societies with an enthusiasm that never wearied. And there were the Sanitary and Christian Commissions, whose agents went everywhere between the dépôt in the rear and the skirmish-line in front, carrying not only whatever was needed to alleviate the sufferings of the sick and wounded, but also many things to beguile the tedious hours in camp and diminish the serious evil of homesickness.

It was a common remark, at the time, that the Confederacy crumbled more suddenly in 1865 than it had risen in 1861. It seemed like an empty shell, which, when fairly broken through, had no more stability, and instantly fell to ruins. It was fortunate that when the end came Lee's army was the first to surrender, since all the other commanders felt justified in following his example. To some on the Confederate side, especially in Virginia, the surrender was a surprise, and came like a personal and irreparable grief. But people in other parts of the South, especially those who had seen Sherman's legions marching by their doors, knew that the end was coming. Longstreet had pronounced the cause lost by Lee's want of generalship at Gettysburg; Ewell had said there was no use in fighting longer when Grant had swung his army across the James; Johnston and his lieutenants declared it wrong to keep up the hopeless struggle after the capital had been abandoned and the Army of Northern Virginia had laid down its weapons, and so expressed themselves to Mr. Davis when he stopped to confer with them, in North Carolina, on his flight southward. He said their fortunes might still be retrieved, and independence established, if those who were absent from the armies without leave would but return to their places. He probably understood the situation as well as General Johnston did, and may have spoken not so much from judgment as from a consciousness of greater responsibility, a feeling that as he was the first citizen of the Confederacy he was the last that had any right to despair of it.

Nevertheless, he continued his flight through the Carolinas into Georgia; his cabinet officers, most of whom had set out with him from Richmond, leaving him one after another. When he had arrived at Irwinsville, Ga., accompanied by his family and Postmaster-General Reagan, their little encampment in the woods was surprised, on the morning of May 11th, by two detachments of Wilson's cavalry, and they were all taken prisoners. In the gray of the morning the two detachments, approaching from different sides, fired into each other before they discovered that they were friends, and two soldiers were killed and several wounded. Mr. Davis was taken to Savannah, and thence to Fort Monroe, where he was a prisoner for two years, after which he was released on bail—his bondsmen being Cornelius Vanderbilt, Horace Greeley, and Gerrit Smith, a life-long abolitionist. He was never tried.

The secession movement had been proved to be a rebellion and nothing else—although the mightiest of all rebellions. It never rose to the character of a revolution; for it never had possession of the capital or the public archives, never stopped the wheels of the Government for a single day, was suppressed in the end, and attained none of its objects. But although it was clearly a rebellion, and although its armed struggle had been maintained after all prospect of success had disappeared, such was the magnanimity of the National Government and the Northern people that its leaders escaped the usual fate of rebels. Except by temporary political disabilities, not one of them was punished—neither Mr. Davis nor Mr. Stephens, nor any member of the Confederate cabinet or congress; neither Lee nor Johnston, nor any of their lieutenants, not even Beauregard who advocated the black flag, nor Forrest who massacred his prisoners at Fort Pillow. Most of the officers of high rank in the Confederate army were graduates of the Military Academy at West Point, and had used their military education in an attempt to destroy the very government that gave it to them, and to which they had solemnly sworn allegiance. Some of them, notably General Lee, had rushed into the rebel service without waiting for the United States War Department to accept their resignations. But all such ugly facts were suppressed or forgotten, in the extreme anxiety of the victors lest they should not be sufficiently magnanimous toward the vanquished. There was but a single act of capital punishment. The keeper of the Andersonville stockade was tried, convicted, and executed for cruelty to prisoners. His more guilty superior, General Winder, died two months before the surrender. Two months after that event, the secessionist that had sought the privilege of firing the first gun at the flag of his country, committed suicide rather than live under its protection. The popular cry that soon arose was, "Universal amnesty and universal suffrage!"

No such exhibition of mercy has been seen before or since. Four years previous to this war, there was a rebellion against the authority of the British Government; six years after it, there was one against the French Government; and in both instances the conquered insurgents were punished with the utmost severity. In our own country there had been several minor insurrections preceding the great one. In such of these as were aimed against the institution of slavery—Vesey's, Turner's, and Brown's

—the offenders suffered the extreme penalty of the law ; in the others—Fries's, Shays's, Dorr's, and the whiskey war—they were punished very lightly or not at all.

The general feeling in the country was of relief that the war was ended—hardly less at the South than at the North. After the surrender of the various armies, the soldiers so recently in arms against each other behaved more like brothers than like enemies. The Confederates were fed liberally from the abundant supplies of the National commissariat, and many of them were furnished with transportation to their homes in distant States. Some of them had been absent from their families during the whole war.

THE LAST MEETING OF THE CONFEDERATE CABINET.

If the people of the North had any disposition to be boisterous over the final victory, it was completely quelled by the shadow of a great sorrow that suddenly fell upon them. A conspiracy had been in progress for a long time among a few half-crazy secessionists in and about the capital. It culminated on the night of Good Friday, April 14, 1865. One of the conspirators forced his way into Secretary Seward's house and attacked the Secretary with a knife, but did not succeed in killing him. Mr. Seward had been thrown from a carriage a few days before, and was lying in bed with his jaws encased in a metallic frame-work, which probably saved his life. The chief conspirator, an obscure actor, made his way into the box at Ford's Theatre where the President and his wife were sitting, witnessing the comedy of "Our American Cousin," shot Mr. Lincoln in the back of the head, jumped from the box to the stage with a flourish of bravado shouting "*Sic semper tyrannis!*" and escaped behind the scenes and out at the stage door. The dying President was carried to a house across the street, where he expired the next morning. As the principal Confederate army had already surrendered, it was impossible for any one to suppose that the killing of the President could affect the result of the war. Furthermore, Mr. Lincoln had long been in the habit of going to the War Department in the evening, and returning to the White House, unattended, late at night ; so that an assassin who merely wished to put him out of the way had abundant opportunities for doing so, with good chances of escaping and concealing his own identity. It was therefore perfectly obvious that the murderer's principal motive was the same as that of the youth who set fire to the temple of Diana at Ephesus. And the newspapers did their utmost to give him the notoriety that he craved, displaying his name in large type at the head of their columns, and repeating about him every anecdote that could be recalled or manufactured. The consequence was that sixteen years later the country was disgraced by another Presidential assassination, mainly from the same motive ; and, as the journalists repeated their folly on that occasion, we

JEFFERSON DAVIS.

(From a photograph taken in 1881.)

shall perhaps have still another by and by.

Mr. Lincoln had grown steadily in the affections and admiration of the people. His state papers were the most remarkable in American annals; his firmness where firmness was required, and kind-heartedness where kindness was practicable, were almost unfailing; and as the successive events of the war called forth his powers, it was seen that he had unlimited shrewdness and tact, statesmanship of the broadest kind, and that honesty of purpose which is the highest wisdom. Moreover, his lack of all vindictive feeling toward the insurgents, and his steady endeavor to make the restored Union a genuine republic of equal rights, gave tone to the feelings of the whole nation, and at the last won many admirers among his foes in arms. In his second inaugural address, a month before his death, he seemed to speak with that insight and calm judgment which we only look for in the studious historian in aftertimes. "Neither party expected for the war the magnitude or the duration which it has already attained. Neither anticipated that the cause of the conflict might cease with, or even before, the conflict itself should cease. Each looked for an easier triumph and a result less fundamental and astounding. Both read the same Bible, and pray to the same God, and each invokes his aid against the other. It may seem strange that any men should dare to ask a just God's assistance in wringing their bread from the sweat of other men's faces. But let us judge not, that we be not judged. The prayer of both could not be answered; that of neither has been answered fully. If we shall suppose that American slavery is one of those offences which, in the providence of God, must needs come, but which, having continued through his appointed time, he now wills to remove, and that he gives to both North and South this terrible war as the woe due to those by whom the offence came, shall we discern therein any departure from those divine attributes which the believers in a loving God always ascribe to him? Fondly do we hope, fervently do we pray, that this mighty scourge of war may speedily pass away. Yet if God wills that it continue until all the wealth piled by the bondman's two hundred and fifty years of unrequited toil shall be sunk, and until every drop of blood drawn with the lash shall be paid by another drawn with the sword, as was said three thousand years ago, so still it must be said, 'The judgments of the Lord are true and righteous altogether.' With malice toward none, with charity for all, with firmness in the right as God gives us to see the right, let us strive to finish the work we are in, to bind up the nation's wounds, to care for him who shall have borne the battle, and for his widow and his orphan, to do all which may achieve and cherish a just and a lasting peace among ourselves and with all nations."

JEFFERSON DAVIS'S BODYGUARD.

A day or two after the evacuation of Richmond, Mr. Lincoln walked through its smoking and disordered streets, where the negroes crowded about him and called down all sorts of uncouth but sincere blessings on his head. He had lived to enter the enemy's capital, lived to see the authority of the United States restored over the whole country, and then was snatched away, when the people were as much as ever in need of his genius for the solution of new problems that suddenly confronted them.

The funeral train retraced the same route over which Mr. Lincoln had gone to Washington from his home in Springfield, Ill., four years before; and to the sorrowful crowds that were gathered at every station, and even along the track in the country, it seemed as if the light of the nation had gone out forever.

The armies returning from the field were brought to Washington for a grand review before being mustered out of service. The city was decorated with flags, mottoes, and floral designs, and the streets were thronged with people, many of whom carried wreaths and bouquets. The Army of the Potomac was reviewed on May 23d, and Sherman's army on the 24th, the troops marching in close column around the Capitol and down Pennsylvania Avenue to the music of their bands. As they passed the grand stand at the White House, where President Johnson and his cabinet reviewed them, the officers saluted with their swords, and commanders of divisions dismounted and went upon the stand.

The armies were quickly disbanded, and each regiment, on its arrival home, was given a public reception and a fitting welcome. The men were well dressed and well fed, but their bronzed faces and their tattered and smoky battle-flags told where they had been. It was computed that the loss of life in the Confederate service was about equal to that in the National. Their losses in battle, as they were generally on the defensive, were smaller, but their means of caring for the wounded were inferior. Thus it cost us nearly six hundred thousand lives and more than six thousand million dollars to destroy the doctrine of State sovereignty, abolish the system of slavery, and begin the career of the United States as a nation.

The home-coming at the North was almost as sorrowful as at the South, because of those that came not. In all the festivities and rejoicings there was hardly a participator whose joy was not saddened by missing some well-known face and form now numbered with the silent three hundred thousand. Grant was there, the commander that had never taken a step backward; and Farragut was there, the sailor without an equal; and the unfailing Sherman, and the patient Thomas, and the intrepid Hancock, and the fiery Sheridan, and the brilliant Custer, and many of lesser rank, who in a smaller theatre of conflict would have won a larger fame. But where was young Ellsworth?—shot dead as soon as he crossed the Potomac. And Winthrop—killed in the first battle, with his best books unwritten. And Lyon—fallen at the head of his little army in Missouri, the first summer of the war. And Baker—sacrificed at Ball's Bluff. And Kearny at Chantilly, and Reno at South Mountain, and Mansfield at Antietam, and Reynolds at Gettysburg, and Wadsworth in the Wilderness, and Sedgwick at Spottsylvania, and McPherson before Atlanta, and Craven in his monitor at the bottom of the sea, and thousands of others, the best and bravest—all gone—all, like Latour, the immortal captain, dead on the field of honor, but none the less dead and a loss to their mourning country. The hackneyed allegory of Curtius had been given a startling illustration and a new significance. The South, too, had lost heavily of her foremost citizens in the great struggle—Bee and Bartow, at Bull Run; Albert Sidney Johnston, leading a desperate charge at Shiloh; Zollicoffer, soldier and journalist, at Mill Spring; Stonewall Jackson, Lee's right arm, at Chancellorsville; Polk, priest and warrior, at Lost Mountain; Armistead, wavering between two allegiances and fighting alternately for each, and Barksdale and Garnett—all at Gettysburg; Hill, at Petersburg; and the dashing Stuart, and Daniel, and Perrin, and Dearing, and Doles, and numberless others. The sudden hush and sense of awe that impresses a child when he steps upon a single grave, may well overcome the strongest man when he looks upon the face of his country scarred with battlefields like these, and considers what blood of manhood was rudely wasted there. And the slain were mostly young, unmarried men, whose native virtues fill no living veins, and will not shine again on any field.

It is poor business measuring the mouldered ramparts and counting the silent guns, marking the deserted battlefields and decorating the grassy graves, unless we can learn from it all some nobler lesson than to destroy. Men write of this, as of other wars, as if the only thing necessary to be impressed upon the rising generation were the virtue of physical courage and contempt of death. It seems to me that is the last thing that we need to teach; for since the days of John Smith in Virginia and the men of the *Mayflower* in Massachusetts, no generation of Americans has shown any lack of it. From Louisburg to

RICHMOND AFTER THE EVACUATION—SHOWING THE EFFECT OF THE FIRE.

(From a War Department Photograph.)

GRAND REVIEW OF THE ARMY, WASHINGTON, MAY 23–24, 1865.

Petersburg—a hundred and twenty years, the full span of four generations—they have stood to their guns and been shot down in greater comparative numbers than any other race on earth. In the war of secession there was not a State, not a county, probably not a town, between the great lakes and the gulf, that was not represented on fields where all that men could do with powder and steel was done, and valor was exhibited at its highest pitch. It was a common saying in the Army of the Potomac that courage was the cheapest thing there; and it might have been said of all the other armies as well. There is not the slightest necessity for lauding American bravery or impressing it upon American youth. But there is the gravest necessity for teaching them respect for law, and reverence for human life, and regard for the rights of their fellow-men, and all that is significant in the history of our country—lest their feet run to evil and they make haste to shed innocent blood. I would be glad to convince my compatriots that it is not enough to think they are right, but they are bound to know they are right, before they rush into any experiments that are to cost the lives of men and the tears of orphans, in their own land or in any other. I would warn them to beware of provincial conceit. I would have them comprehend that one may fight bravely, and still be a perjured felon; that one may die humbly, and still be a patriot whom his country cannot afford to lose; that as might does not make right, so neither do rags and bare feet necessarily argue a noble cause. I would teach them that it is criminal either to hide the truth or to refuse assent to that which they see must follow logically from ascertained truth. I would show them that a political lie is as despicable as a personal lie, whether uttered in an editorial, or a platform, or a President's message, or a colored cartoon, or a disingenuous ballot; and that political chicanery, when long persisted in, is liable to settle its shameful account in a stoppage of civilization and a spilling of life. These are simple lessons, yet they are not taught in a day, and some whom we call educated go through life without mastering them at all.

It may be useful to learn from one war how to conduct another; but it is infinitely better to learn how to avert another. I am doubly anxious to impress this consideration upon my readers, because history seems to show us that armed conflicts have a tendency to come in pairs, with an interval of a few years, and because I think I see, in certain circumstances now existing within our beloved Republic, the elements of a second civil war. No American citizen should lightly repeat that the result is worth all it cost, unless he has considered how heavy was the cost, and is doing his utmost to perpetuate the result. To strive to forget the great war, for the sake of sentimental politics, is to cast away our dearest experience and invite, in some troubled future, the destruction we so hardly escaped in the past. There can be remembrance without animosity, but there cannot be oblivion without peril.

AN EXPLODED GUN IN THE DEFENCE OF RICHMOND.

THE FIRST UNITED STATES FLAG RAISED IN RICHMOND AFTER THE WAR.

BY MRS. LASALLE CORBELL PICKETT,

Wife of Major-General George E. Pickett, C. S. A.

THE first knell of the evacuation of Richmond sounded on Sunday morning while we were on our knees in St. Paul's Church, invoking God's protecting care for our absent loved ones, and blessings on our cause.

The intense excitement, the tolling of the bells, the hasty parting, the knowledge that all communication would be cut off between us and our loved ones, and the dread, undefined fear in our helplessness and desertion, make a nightmare memory.

General Ewell had orders for the destruction of the public buildings, which orders our Secretary of War, Gen. J. C. Breckenridge, strove earnestly but without avail to have countermanded. The order, alas! was obeyed beyond "the letter of the law."

The terrible conflagration was kindled by the Confederate authorities, who applied the torch to the Shockoe warehouse, it, too, being classed among the public buildings because of the tobacco belonging to France and England stored in it. A fresh breeze was blowing from the south; the fire swept on in its haste and fury over a great area in an almost incredibly short time, and by noon the flames had transformed into a desert waste all the city bounded by Seventh and Fifteenth Streets, and Main Street and the river. One thousand houses were destroyed. The streets were filled with furniture and every description of wares, dashed down to be trampled in the mud or buried where they lay.

At night a saturnalia began. About dark, the Government commissary began the destruction of its stores. Soldiers and citizens gathered in front, catching the liquor in basins and pitchers; some with their hats and some with their boots. It took but a short time for this to make a manifestation as dread as the flames. The crowd became a howling mob, so frenzied that the officers of the law had to flee for their lives, reviving memories of 1781, when the British under Arnold rode down Richmond Hill, and, invading the city, broke open the stores and emptied the provisions and liquors into the gutters, making even the uninitiated cows and hogs drunk for days.

All through the night, crowds of men, women, and children traversed the streets, loading themselves with supplies and plunder. At midnight, soldiers drunk with vile liquor, followed by a reckless crowd as drunk as themselves, dashed in the plate-glass windows of the stores, and made a wreck of everything.

About nine o'clock on Monday morning, terrific shell explosions, rapid and continuous, added to the terror of the scene, and gave the impression that the city was being shelled by the retreating Confederate army from the south side. But the explosions were soon found to proceed from the Government arsenal and laboratory, then in flames. Later in the morning, a merciful Providence caused a lull in the breeze. The terrific explosion of the laboratory and of the arsenal caused every window in our home to break. The old plate-glass mirrors, built in the walls, were cracked and shattered.

Fort Darling was blown up, and later on the rams, It was eight o'clock when the Federal troops entered the city. It required the greatest effort to tame down the riotous, crazed mob, and induce them to take part in the struggle to save their own. The firemen, afraid of the soldiers who had obeyed the orders to light the torch, would not listen to any appeals or entreaties, and so the flames were under full headway, fanned by a southern breeze, when the Union soldiers came to the rescue.

The flouring mills caught fire from the tobacco houses, communicating it to Cary and Main Streets. Every bank was destroyed. The War Department was a mass of ruins; the *Enquirer* and *Dispatch* offices were in ashes; and the county court-house, the American Hotel, and most of the finest stores of the city were ruined.

Libby Prison and the Presbyterian church escaped. Such a reign of terror and pillage, fire and flame, fear and despair! The yelling and howling and swearing and weeping and wailing beggar description. Families houseless and homeless under the open sky!

I shall never forget General Weitzel's command, composed exclusively of colored troops, as I saw them through the dense black columns of smoke. General Weitzel had for some time been stationed on the north side of the James River, but a few miles from Richmond, and he had only to march in and take possession. He despatched Major A. H. Stevens of the Fourth Massachusetts cavalry, and Major E. E. Graves of his staff, with about a hundred mounted men, to reconnoitre the roads and works leading to Richmond. They had gone but a little distance into the Confederate lines, when they saw a shabby, old-fashioned carriage, drawn by a pair of lean, lank horses, the occupants waving a white flag. They met this flag-of-truce party at the line of fortifications, just beyond the junction of the Osborne turnpike and New Market road. The carriage contained the mayor of Richmond—Colonel Mayo—Judge Meredith of the Supreme Court, and Judge Lyons. The fourth worthy I cannot recall. Judge Lyons, our former minister to England, and one of the representative men of Virginia, made the introductions in his own characteristic way, and then Colonel Mayo, who was in command of the flag-of-truce party, handed to Major Stevens a small slip of wall paper, on which was written the following: "It is proper to formally surrender to the Federal authorities the city of Richmond, hitherto capital of the Confederate States of America, and the defences protecting it up to this time." That was all. The document was approved of, and Major Stevens most courteously accepted the terms for his commanding general, to whom it was at once transmitted, and moved his column upon the evacuated city, taking possession and saving it from ashes.

His first order was to sound the alarm bells and to take command at once of the fire department, which consisted of fourteen substitute men, those who were exempt from service because of disease, two steam fire engines, four worthless hand engines, and a large amount of hose, destroyed by the retreating half-crazed Confederates. His next order was to raise the stars and stripes over the Capitol. Quick as thought, two soldiers, one from Company E and one from Company H of the Fourth Massachusetts cavalry, crept to the summit and planted the flag of the nation. Two bright, tasteful guidons were hoisted by the halyards in place of the red cross. The living colors of the Union were greeted, while our "Warriors' banner took its flight to meet the warrior's soul."

That flag, whose design has been accredited alike to both George Washington and John Adams, was raised over Virginia by Massachusetts, in place of the one whose kinship and likeness had not, even after renewed effort, been entirely destroyed. For by the adoption of the stars and bars (three horizontal bars of equal width—the middle one white, the others red—with a blue union of nine stars in a circle) by the Confederate Congress in March, 1861, the Confederate flag was made so akin and so similar to that of the nation, as to cause confusion; so in 1863 the stars and bars was supplanted by a flag with a white field, having the battle flag (a red field charged with a blue saltier, on which were thirteen stars) for a union. This, having been mistaken for a flag of truce, was altered by covering the outer half of the field beyond the union with a vertical red bar. This was the last flag of the Confederacy.

Richmond will testify that the soldiers of Massachusetts were worthy of the honor of raising the first United States flag over her Capitol—the Capitol of the Confederacy—and also to the unvarying courtesy of Major Stevens, and the fidelity with which he kept his trust.

HUMOROUS INCIDENTS OF THE WAR.

The illustrations of this chapter are exact reproductions of cartoons published during the war in various newspapers and periodicals.

FUN FROM ENLISTMENT TO HONORABLE DISCHARGE—RECRUITS' EXCUSES—BULL RUN PLEASANTRIES—GREENHORNS IN CAMP—FUN WITH THE AWKWARD SQUAD—OFFICERS LEARNING THEIR BUSINESS—SENTRIES AND SHOULDER STRAPS—STORIES OF GRANT, LINCOLN, BUTLER, SHERMAN, ETC.—DUTCH, IRISH, AND DARKY COMEDY—EXPEDIENTS OF THE HOMESICK—ARMY CHAPLAINS—HOSPITAL HUMOR—GRANT'S "PIE ORDER"—"THROUGH VIRGINIA"—YANKEE GOOD NATURE AND PLUCK A BETTER STIMULANT THAN WHISKEY.

THE hardships of campaigning, the sufferings of the hospital, the horrors of actual combat — none of these sufficed to keep down the irrepressible spirit of fun in the American soldier. From the day of his enlistment to the day of his discharge he did not cease to look upon the funny side of every situation, and the veterans of to-day talk more about the humor of the war than of privations and pitched battles. Wits in and out of the army said and did clever things, some of which have passed into the proverbs and idioms of the American people; and more than one distinguished "American humorist" laid the foundation of his reputation in connection with the war.

Humorous situations began at the very recruiting office, or the citizens' meeting which stimulated recruiting, and continued to the end of the service. It was at one of the meetings held in a New England village that the wife of a spirited citizen, whose patriotism consisted in brave words, said to him: "I thought you said you were going to enlist to-night." Well, he had thought better of it. "Take off those breeches, then, and give them to me, and I will go myself." There was not much prospect of "peace" for him in a life at home after that; so he went to the front. Countless excuses were offered by candidates for the draft in the hope of proving themselves physically disqualified for service. The man who had one leg too short was let off; but the man behind him, who pleaded that he had "both legs too short," failed to prove a double incapacity, and he wore the blue, and that creditably.

Officers who tarried too long in Washington on their way to the front were not seldom rendered uncomfortable by the remarks made to them or in their hearing. One who was eager for news from the first battle of Bull Run bought an "extra" of a newsboy who was calling, "All about the battle!" Glancing over it, he shouted after the boy: "Here! I don't see any battle in this paper." "Don't you?" said the boy. "Well, you won't see any battle if you loaf around this hotel *all* the time." It was of the battle of Bull Run that a wit said, it was so popular it had to be repeated the very next year, to satisfy the public demand for it. And one of the participants in this first experience of the new army said: "At Bull Run we were told that the eyes of Washington were upon us; when we knew very well that what we were most anxious about was to get our eyes on Washington." It was said of the soldiers on both sides in that battle, that their guns trembled in their hands, so that if the enemy was dodging he was almost certain to be hit, and that the conclusion arrived at by the rearward experiments of both armies was that a soldier may retreat successfully from almost any position if only he starts in time. Thus the pleasantry of the day turned to account the "baptism of fire" of some of the bravest troops that ever wore blue or gray.

Once in camp, the school-boy spirit revelled in larks of every description. A few weeks of experience developed military manners and prepared the recruit to enjoy the greenness of the newer comers. On drill, a new recruit was sure to get his toes exactly where a "vet" wanted to drop the butt of his musket as he ordered arms, and if there was a mud-puddle within a yard of him he was sure to "dress" into it. The new men were sent to the officers' quarters on the most absurd errands, usually in quest of some luxury which, fresh from the comforts of home, they still regarded as a necessity. The drilling of the awkward squad was a never-ending source of amusement; for some men are constitutionally incapable of moving in a machine-like harmony with others, and these were continually out of

MANAGER LINCOLN. "Ladies and Gentlemen, I regret to say that the Tragedy, entitled *The Army of the Potomac*, has been withdrawn on account of Quarrels among the leading Performers, and I have substituted three new and striking Farces or Burlesques, one, entitled *The Repulse at Vicksburg*, by the well-known, popular favorite, E. M. STANTON, Esq., and the others, *The Loss of the Harriet Lane* and *The Exploits of the Alabama*—a very sweet thing in Farces, I assure you—by the Veteran Composer, GIDEON WELLES."
(*Unbounded Applause by the* COPPERHEADS.)

place. One of them was a loose-jointed fellow from, say, Nantucket, who was so thorough a patriot that he was always longing for home, and he met every hardship and discouragement with a sigh and the wish that he was back in Nantucket. He was exceedingly awkward at drill. He seemed to make every movement on the "bias." One day, in responding to a command, he figured it out so badly as to find himself all alone, several yards away from the rest of the squad. All at sea, he said: "Captain, where ought I to be now?" The captain, thoroughly out of patience, shouted back: "Why, *back in Nantucket*, gol darn you!" There was the Irishman who said he had spent two years in the cavalry learning to turn his toes *in*, and two years in the infantry learning to turn his toes *out*. "Divil take such a sarvice," said he; "there's no plazing the blackguards, anyhow."

The drill jokes were not all on the men. The officers, who at the beginning were non-military citizens like their soldiers, had their business to learn. Indeed, it was not an easy matter at first to preserve thorough discipline, because of the frequent equality, in military knowledge, between the officers and the men. It was said that the American soldier was perfectly willing to endure hardships, to fight, and if necessary to die, for his country; but the hardest thing for him to submit to was to be bossed around by his superior officer, who might, like enough, be his next-door neighbor at home. One captain, who had abandoned railroading for the war, in his excitement over the necessity of halting his men suddenly, true to his former calling, shouted out, "Down brakes!" And another, who had forgotten the command for breaking ranks, dismissed his company with the order, "Adjourn for rations!" It was a Georgian commandant of a Home Guard who, while showing his men off before a visiting officer, invented his own tactics on the basis of "common sense." His first order after falling in was, "In two ranks, git!" It was not long before he had his men pretty well mixed up; but, equal to the occasion, he shouted, "Disentangle to the front, march!" which was as effective as anything in "Hardee's Tactics." Drill sergeants were often peremptory fellows, and they

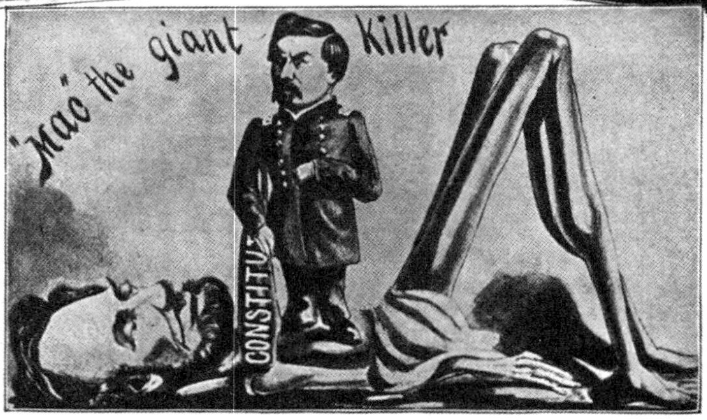

sometimes called on their men to perform difficult feats. One under-sized sergeant had much trouble with an Irish recruit, whose enormous height had given him the habit of looking *down*, and he could not keep his chin up to the military angle. Finally the sergeant reached up to the Irishman's chin (for which he had to stand on tip-toe) and poked it up, saying, "That's the place for it; now don't let us see your head down again."—"Am I always to be like this, sergeant?" asked the recruit. "Yes, sir."—"Then I'll say good by to yez, sergeant, for I'll niver see yez again." It was a very fresh recruit who was found on his sentry post sitting down and cleaning his gun, which he had taken entirely to pieces. The officer who discovered him rebuked him sternly and asked, "Are you the sentinel here?"—"Well, I'm a sort of a sentinel."—"Well, I'm a sort of officer of the day."—"All right," said the undismayed recruit, "just hold on till I get my gun together, and I'll give you a sort of a salute."

The military rule that a sentry must challenge everybody, and not pass unchallenged even those whom he knew to be all right, was often as slow in taking possession of the officers' minds as those of the least experienced of the men. A full-uniformed lieutenant, much disgusted at the "Who goes there?" of one of his own company on guard, expressed his sentiments by indignantly exclaiming, "Ass!" To which the sentry promptly responded, "Advance, Ass, and give the countersign!" Not infrequently general officers and high dignitaries had experiences with the guards of their own camps. It is said that every great general in history has been halted by a guard, the approach of a well-known superior officer giving the sentry an opportunity of showing off his discipline. General McClellan was not only halted on a certain occasion, but forced to dismount and call up the officer of the guard before a sentry would let him pass. General Sherman, who used to see for himself what was going on among his men, under the incognito afforded by a rather unmilitary dress, once interfered with a teamster who was pounding a mule, and told him who he was. "Oh, that's played out!" said the mule driver; "every man that comes along here with an old brown coat and a stove-pipe hat claims to be General Sherman." This suggests the story of a mule driver in the army who was swearing at and kicking a span of balky mules, when the general, who was annoyed at his profanity, ordered him to stop. "Who are you?" said the mule driver. "I'm the commander of the brigade," said the general. "I'm the commander of these mules, and I'll do as I please, or resign, and you can take my place!" The general passed on. Even the President of the United States had his encounter with a guard, and was for a short time kept waiting outside General Grant's tent under the order, suggested by his somewhat clerical appearance, "No sanitary folks allowed inside!"

Lincoln always made friends among the soldiers. On one occasion he came on some men hewing logs for a hospital, and remarking, with a reminiscence of his rail-splitting days, that he "used to be pretty good on the chop," made the chips fly for a while like a veteran lumberman. The President's half-pathetic saying, that he had "no influence with this administration," has passed into history; but less familiar is his remark, when some one applied to him for a pass to go into Richmond, and he said, "I don't know about that; I have given passes to about two hundred and fifty thousand men to go there during the last two years, and not one of them has got there yet."

GENERAL POPE.

Ben Butler was credited with a lawyer-like disinclination to be cross-questioned when he gave orders. Word was brought to him that his favorite horse, "Almond-eye," had fallen into a ravine and been killed, and he called an orderly and told him to go to the ravine and skin the horse. "What, is Almond-eye dead?" asked the man. "Never you mind whether he is or not," said the general, "you obey orders." The man came back in about two hours and reported that he had finished. "Has it taken you all this time to skin a horse?" asked Butler. "Oh, no; it took me half an hour to catch him," was the reply. "You don't mean to say you killed him?" shouted the irate general. "My orders were to skin him," said the soldier, "and I obeyed them without asking any questions."

Officers and men alike showed much wit in their way of dealing with impossible or unwelcome orders. A lieutenant protested against an order to take a squad of men across a swamp where he knew the depth was enough to drown every man of them. He was sternly rebuked by his superior, who ordered him peremptorily to make the crossing, telling him that his requisition would be honored for whatever he might require for the purpose. So he made a requisition for "twenty men eighteen feet long to cross a swamp fifteen feet deep."

We will give another of the many similar stories. After a long march a captain ordered, as a sanitary precaution, that the men should change their under-shirts. The orderly sergeant suggested that half of the men had only one shirt each. The captain hesitated a moment and then said: "Military orders must be obeyed. Let the men, then, change with each other."

Orders against unauthorized foraging were very strict. A youthful soldier was stopped on his way into camp with a fine goose slung over his shoulder, and he was required to account for it. "Well," said he, "I was coming through the village whistling 'Yankee Doodle,' and this confounded rebel of a goose came out and hissed me; so I shot it."

"Where did you get that turkey?" said the colonel of the —— Texas regiment to one of his amiable recruits that came into camp with a fine bird.

"Stole it," was the laconic reply.

"Ah!" said the colonel, triumphantly, to a bystander, "you see my boys may steal, but they won't lie."

During a battle the interest in the work was so intense as to leave small room for fear, either of the enemy or of superior officers. An Irish private was ordered to take up the colors when the color-bearer was shot down. "By the holy St. Patrick, colonel," said he, "there's so much good shooting here, I haven't a minute's time to waste fooling with that thing."

The desire to get home for a few days developed much ingenuity among the enlisted men. "What do you want, Pat?" asked General Rosecrans, as he rode along the line, inquiring into the wants of his men. "A furlough!" said Pat. "How long has your sister been dead?" asked a sympathetic comrade of a soldier who had obtained a leave on account of the family trouble. "About ten years," was the cool reply. General Thomas asked a man who applied for leave to go and see his wife how long it was since he had seen her. "Over three months," was the answer. "Three months!" exclaimed the general; "why, I haven't seen my wife for three *years!*" "That may be," said the soldier, "but you see, general, me and my wife ain't o' that sort."

The "intelligent contraband," the irrepressible darky, is one of the few types of mankind that furnish as much fun in real life as on the stage. He was a source of constant amusement in the army. A colored refugee from the Confederate lines brought word, as the only news worth mentioning (referring to himself), that "a man in Culpeper lost a mighty valuable nigger this mornin'." The driver of a commissary wagon exemplified the general non-combativeness of his race, when, in describing his emotions during an attack on the train, he said he felt "like every hair of his head was a bugle, an' dey was all a-playin' 'Home, Sweet Home.'" An officer tried to induce his servant, who was a refugee, to enlist, saying he must trust the Lord to keep him safe. "Well," he said, "I *did* trust de Lord when I was tryin' to get into de Union lines, but I dun dare resk Him again!"

The army chaplain now and then ran against the rough soldier wit. One of them, who took a practical view of his responsibility for the souls of his regiment, welcomed some recruits with the suggestion that, having joined the army of their country, they should now also join the army of the Lord. "What bounty does He give?" was the irreverent rejoinder. Even in hospital the disposition to look on the humorous side of life—or of death—never forsook men. One who had lost three fingers held up the maimed member and sorrowfully regretted that he "never could hold a full hand again." A pale-faced sufferer in a hospital near a large city was asked by a visiting lady if she could not do something for him. No. Could she not bathe his head? "You may if you want to very much," he replied; "but if you do, you will be the fourteenth lady that has bathed my head this morning." It was an Irish surgeon who remarked that "the man who has lost his finger makes more noise about it than the man who has lost his head." A nurse was shocked one morning to find two attendants noisily hammering and sawing at one end of a ward where a very sick man was lying. In reply to her questions, they said they were making a coffin. "Who for?" "Him"—pointing to the sick man. "Is he going to die?" she asked, much distressed. "The doctor says he is, an' *I guess he knows what he give him!*" It was a Confederate guerilla who comforted himself, while lying on his hospital cot, with the reflection, "I reckon I killed as many of them as they did of me."

FUN IN CAMP.

A soldier was wounded by a shell at Fort Wagner. He was going to the rear. "Wounded by a shell?" some one asked. "Yes," he coolly answered. "I was right under the durned thing when the bottom dropped out."

The occurrences in the enemy's country, and stories that originated there, furnished no small portion of the humor that was current during the war. "Where does this road lead to?" asked the lieutenant in command of a reconnoitering party. "It leads to h——!" was the surly reply of the unregenerate rebel thus interrogated. "Well, by the appearance of the inhabitants of this country, I should judge that I'm most there," was the retort. An old man in Georgia was called upon to declare which side he took, and, uncertain as to the identity of his captors, he said: "I ain't took no side; but both sides hev took me!" It must have been his wife who said: "I ain't neither Secesh nor Union—jest Baptist."

The devotion of Southern women to the Confederacy has often been remarked. One of the minor officers of the army, who marched with Sherman to the sea, and who states that he tramped, all told, at least two thousand miles during the war through the South, says that he saw many Southern men who were loyal to the Union, and who regretted the secession of their respective States, but he saw only one Southern woman whom he even suspected to be Union in sentiment. He saw this woman during a foraging expedition in connection with the march to the sea. He had charge of a squad of thirteen men who had marched through the woods some distance away from the army. As they rounded a sharp curve in the road, they suddenly came upon a house almost covered with foliage. In front of the house, and only a few yards from the men, was a woman picking up chips. Her back was toward the soldiers, and she had not noticed their approach. The commanding officer motioned to his men to stop, and, tip-toeing up to the side of the woman, he put his arm around her waist and kissed her. Stepping back a pace or two, he waited for the bitter denunciation and abuse that he was sure would come. The woman, however, straightened herself up, looked at the officer for a moment, and then said slowly: "You'll find me right here every morning a-picking up chips." The officer said he strongly suspected that she was disloyal to the South.

A military peculiarity of General Bragg's was touched on in the remark that, when he died and approached the gate of heaven and was invited in, the first thing he'd do would be to "fall back." Gen. W. T. Sherman never seemed to suit the Confederates, no matter what he did. One of the prisoners who fell into the hands of his army gave the following graphic expression of the Southern idea of the general: "Sherman gits on a hill, flops his wings and crows; then he yells out: 'Attention, creation! by kingdoms, right wheel, *march!*' And then we git!" It was a solitary relic left behind after one of Sherman's advances, that, communing with himself, said: "Well, I'm badly whipped and somewhat demoralized, but no man can say I am scattered."

Among the humorous miscellanies of the war, General Grant's "pie order" must have an immortal place. It was during Grant's early campaign in Eastern Missouri that a lieutenant in command of the advance guard inspired the mistress of a wayside house with exceptional alacrity in supplying the wants of himself and men by announcing himself to be Brigadier-General Grant. Later in the day the general himself came to the same house and was turned away with the information that General Grant and staff had been there that morning and eaten everything in the house but one pumpkin pie. Giving her half a dollar, he told her to keep that pie till he sent for it. That evening the army went into camp some miles beyond this place, and at the dress parade that was ordered, the following special order was published:

"HEADQUARTERS, ARMY IN THE FIELD.

"SPECIAL ORDERS, NO. —.

"Lieutenant Wickfield, of the —th Indiana Cavalry, having on this day eaten everything in Mrs. Selvidge's house, at the crossing of the Ironton and Pocahontas and Black River and Cape Girardeau roads, except one pumpkin pie, Lieutenant Wickfield is hereby ordered to return with an escort of one hundred cavalry and eat that pie also.

"U. S. GRANT,

"*Brigadier-General Commanding.*"

Virginia mud and Virginia swamps were celebrated by the invention of the response to the question, "Did you go through Virginia?" "Yes—in a number of places;" and the exclamation of the trooper who was fording a stream flanked by miles of swamp on either side: "Blowed if I don't think we have struck this stream lengthwise."

It is impossible here to attempt more than a suggestion of the combination of good nature and pluck that, all through the dreadful days of the war, rendered hardships endurable, lent courage to the faint-hearted, and cheered the low-spirited. "The humor of the war" was no mere ebullition of school-boy fun: it was as potent a factor in accomplishing the results of the war as powder and shot—a stimulant that carried men over hard places better than whiskey.

WAR HUMOR IN THE SOUTH

THE BADINAGE OF THE ARMY—NO RESPECTER OF PERSONS—"PICKIN' A CHUNE" FROM A BASS DRUM—SWEARING THAT WAS "PLUM NIGH LIKE PREACHIN'"—WHAT IS A "BEE-LINE"?—FUN AMONG THE NEGROES—STONEWALL JACKSON'S BODY-SERVANT—WOMEN IN SEWING SOCIETIES AND AT THE BEDSIDES OF THE WOUNDED.

SOUTHERN soldiers, like their Northern opponents, soon found that humor was a safety valve—a diversion from the graver thoughts that, in their lonely hours, lingered around the wife, mother, and children in the distant home. Withal, it was a spontaneous good humor, such as Washington Irving calls the "oil and wine of a merry meeting," where the companionship was contagious and the jokes small, but the jollity was abundant. It might not have been as polished as that of Uncle Toby or Corporal Trim, nor as philosophical as Dickens makes the observations of the elder Mr. Weller and his son "Sam," but it exemplified human nature in the rough, and overflowed harmlessly.

Those who have had occasion to make the comparison have, without doubt, observed salient points of difference between the styles of badinage prevalent in the Northern and Southern armies. Your Southerner was no respecter of persons. He seized on any feature of an individuality that presented a ludicrous side. If a stranger was unusually long or short, or lean or fat, he was sure to be a target for ridicule.

Passing through Frederick in the first Maryland campaign (1862), a good-natured-looking citizen, who evidently had not been able to tie his shoestrings for a number of years, stood on his doorstep watching us as we passed. "Hi, there! Hog-killing time, boys," suddenly astonished his ears, and was the signal for an instant fire of playful chaff. "Aint he swelled powerful?" "Must have swallowed a bass drum." "I say, stranger, buttermilk or corn-fed?" "Does it hurt much?" "What hurt?" ventured the fat man, quizzically. "Why, totin' them rations around with yer all day." In a minute or two the old gentleman, very red in the face, carried his abdominal rotundity into the house, but quickly reappeared with a demijohn in each hand. "Here, boys!" he exclaimed, "wash your mouths out with some of this applejack, and have a bit of mercy on a fat man." It is needless to say that the boys promptly cheered their vote of thanks.

GENERAL HOOKER.

The colonel of a South Carolina regiment, having returned from his furlough with a pair of high top boots—boots were then worth seven or eight hundred

THE OLD JOHN ROSS HOUSE, NEAR RINGGOLD, GA.—MISSIONARY RIDGE ON THE RIGHT.

(FROM A GOVERNMENT PHOTOGRAPH.)

GENERAL BEAUREGARD.

dollars—had the temerity to run the gauntlet of a neighboring brigade, and heard comments like these: "I say, mister, better git out'r them smokestacks; know you're in thar 'cause we kin see yer head stickin' out." "Boys, the kern'l 's gone into winter quarters." "What mout be the price o' them nail kags?" etc. An officer wearing noticeably bushy whiskers was unfeelingly invited to "come out from behind that bunch of har! 'Taint no use t' say yer aint in thar, 'cause yer ears is workin' monstrous powerful." It was rarely safe, under these circumstances, to answer with either wit or abuse.

Our soldiers had little respect for what were known as "bombproofs"—the fellows who had easy positions in the rear. On one occasion a smartly dressed young officer belonging to this kindred cantered up to a depot where a regiment of men were awaiting transfer. As soon as they saw him they began whooping: "Oh, my! aint he pooty!" "Say, mister, whar'd ye git that biled shut?" "Does yer grease that har with ham fat, or how?" And so they plied the poor fellow with all manner of questions concerning his age, occupation, religious and political convictions, that were calculated to make a man feel uncomfortable. One feather, however, broke the camel's back. A long, cadaverous specimen of humanity, who had evidently been making a comical survey of the victim—his handsome uniform, and well-polished boots—taking a step or two forward as if to show his intense interest, solemnly drawled out: "Was yer ra-a-ly born so, or did they put yer together by corntract? Strikes me yer must have got yere in a drove or ben picked afore you was ripe." Then somebody suggested that "sich a nice-lookin' rooster ought to git down and scratch for a wurrum"; and amid the laughter that followed, he was glad to put spurs to his horse and gallop out of hearing.

Cavalrymen were called by the infantry "buttermilk rangers," and the musicians came in for more than their share of good-natured chaff. Rather than be tormented, the latter would sometimes leave the line of march and go through the fields, thus avoiding the frequent invitation to "give us a toot on yer old funnel," or "brace up with yer blow-pipe." One day a bass drummer, plodding along, was attracted by a pitiful voice coming from a group of men resting by the roadside: "Mister, oh, mister, please come yere?" Turning in the direction, he found it proceeded from a woe-begone-looking Mississippian, whose sickly appearance was well calculated to arouse the sympathy of a tender-hearted musician. "Well, what can I do for you?" said the man with the drum. "Oh, a heap, a heap. I've got a powerful misery, and I thought as how you mout set down yere and pick a chune for a sick man on that ar thing you tote around on your stomach." Shouts of laughter told him that he was "sold," and he never heard the last of the applications for the soothing tones of "that ar thing."

This drollery of expression cropped out even amid the turmoil and excitement of the battlefield. The story is told of a young fellow who was under fire at Manassas for the first time, one of those hundreds of thousands on both sides behind whose inexperience was too much pride of character to permit them to show the white feather, and whose fear of the contempt of their comrades, as well as of the disgrace at home, made them good fighters. He had become pretty well warmed up and was doing excellent service when suddenly he caught sight of a rabbit loping across the field between the lines. Dropping his gun, as he was about to shoot, he looked dolefully at the little animal for an instant and then yelled with honest pathos: "Go it, cotton tail, go it. I'm ez skeered ez you be, an' ef I hadn't a reputation to lose I'd run too."

GENERAL McDOWELL.

At the battle of Kinston, N. C., Gen. N. E. Evans, of South Carolina, familiarly known in the old army as "Shanks," posted a body of raw militia at the crossing of a creek, but they were met by a severe fire and forced to give way. In the disorder that followed, the general caught one of the fugitives and with a number of emphatic adjectives demanded: "What are you running away for, you blank, blank coward? You ought to be ashamed of yourself." "I ain't runnin' away, gineral, I'm jes' skeered. Why, them fellers over thar are shootin' bullets at us big

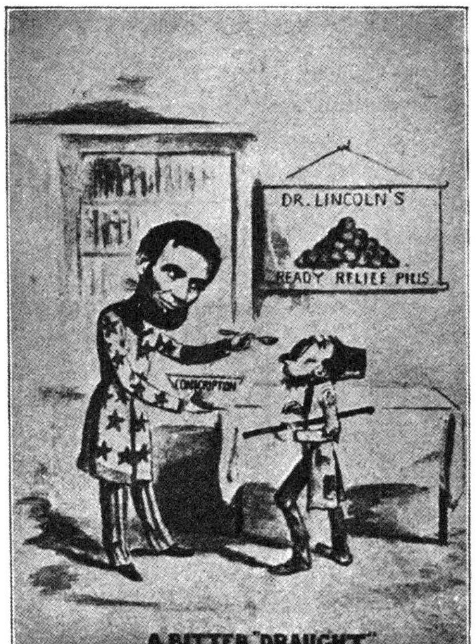

A BITTER DRAUGHT.

as watermillions, boo-hoo-hoo! One on 'em went right peerst my head—right peerst—an' I want ter go home."

"Well, why didn't you shoot back, sir? You are crying like a baby."

"I know it, gineral, I know it, boo-hoo! and I wish I was a baby, and a gal baby too, and then I wouldn't have ben cornscripted."

This reminds us of another North Carolina story. During the Rebellion the staff of General Wise was riding through a rather forlorn part of that State, and a young Virginian of the staff concluded to have a little fun at the expense of a long-legged specimen of the genus *homo* who wore a very shabby gray uniform and bestrode a worm fence at the roadside. Reining in his horse, he accosted him with "How are you, North Carolina?"

"How are you, Virginia?" was the ready response.

TRIBUNE—HERALD—TIMES.

The staff officer continued: "The blockade on turpentine makes you rather hard up, don't it? No sale for tar now?"

"Well—yes—" was the slow response. "We sell all our tar to Jeff Davis now."

"The thunder you do! What on earth does the President want of your tar?"

North Carolina answered, "He puts it on the heels of Virginians to make them stick on the battlefield."

The staff rode on.

Speaking of General Evans, an incident is recalled concerning his brother-in-law, Gen. Mart Gary, who succeeded Wade Hampton in the command of the Hampton Legion. Gary employed many phrases, especially in battle, that are not often heard in polite society. His old body-servant, commenting on this habit, gave the following description of the manner in which his master stormed and swore at some disobedience of orders during one of the fights.

"I golly, massa, but de way de ole man moub about dat day was 'scrutiatin'. He went dis away an' he went dat away wabin his sword like a scythe blade. He went yere and he went dar; but to hear de ole man open battery on de hard wuds in de langidge and jes' frow um aroun'—frow um aroun' loose—I declar, boss, it were plum nigh like preachin'."

At first, the necessity for discipline was not recognized by the raw Southern volunteers, and instances of the verdancy which prevailed were common. When a picket guard at Harper's Ferry, where our first troops assembled, was being detailed for duty, one of the men stoutly protested against any such arrangement, because, as he remarked, "What's the use of gwine out thar t' keep ev'rybody off? We've all kim here t' hev a fight with the Yankees, and ef yer keep fellers out thar t' skeer 'em off, how in thunder are we gwine to hev a scrimmage?"

An officer, while inspecting the sentinel lines one day, asked a picket what he would do if he saw a body of men coming. "Halt 'em, and demand the countersign, sir!" "But suppose they wouldn't halt?" "Then I'd shoot." "Suppose they didn't stop then, what would you do?" "I reckon I'd form a line, sir." "A line? What kind of a line?" "A bee-line straight for camp, and run like thunder!"

LINCOLN SIGNING THE EMANCIPATION PROCLAMATION.—FROM A SOUTHERN WAR ETCHING.

A young lieutenant, fresh from a country drill ground and sadly ignorant of the tactics of Hardee or Scott, didn't know exactly what to do when the commanding officer ordered him one morning to "mount guard." He marched off with his squad of men, however, and about an hour afterwards was found sitting under a tree and talking to some one in the branches. "Well, lieutenant, have you mounted guard?" "Oh, yes, sir," was the cool reply; "got 'lev'n up this tree and t'others 'r' over yander roost'n' in another."

The Southern negroes also furnished abundant humor of their peculiar kind. During the occupation of Yorktown, Va., a shell entering camp made a muddle of a lot of pots and kettles. Mingo, the cook, at once started off for a safe place in the rear. On the way he was met by one of his brother servants, who inquired: "Wot's de matter, Mingo? Whar's yo' gwine wid such a hurrification?"

"'Ain't gwine nowhar p't'c'lar; jis' gittin' outen de way dem waggin hubs dey's t'rowin' at us."

"Eh, eh, Mingo, I 'spects dat's a sign you's a wicked nigger, for ef yo' was a good Chrishun yo' nebber be skeer by dem shell. Ef yo' listen to de Good Book, yo' find dat Massa up yander am pintin' eb'ry one ob em, an' know 'zactly whar to drap um!"

"Da' mebbe so, mebbe so; but yo' can't fool dis chile. Hear me, Jupiter. Dar's too much powder in dem t'ings for the good Lor' to meddle wid 'em, and dis chile ain't gwine ter bu'n hisself, needer. And dar's dem Minnie bullets, too. When dey come flyin' troo de air singin' de chune, whar is yer, whar is yer? I ain't gwine for to stop and say whar I is fur de bessest cotton patch in the lan'. I'se a twenty-two-hundred-dollar nigger, Jupiter, an' I'se gwine t' tek keer ob what b'long t' massa."

It is said that the body-servant of Stonewall Jackson always knew when he was about to engage in a battle. Some one asked him how he came to be so much in the confidence of his master. "Lor', sir," was the reply, "de gin'rul nebber tell me nuffin'. De way I know is dis: massa say he prayer twice a day—mornin' an' night; but w'en he git up two or t'ree time in de night to pray, den I begin to pack de haversack de fus' t'ing, ca'se I know dere'll be de ole boy to pay right away."

UNIVERSAL ADVICE TO ABRAHAM: "DROP 'EM!"

In the early part of the war there was much equality between the officers and privates. Many of the latter were socially and intellectually superior to the former. In the course of an altercation one day, a subordinate made an irritating remark, when his captain exclaimed: "If you repeat that, I'll lay down my rank and fight you." "Lay down your rank!" was the indignant response. "That won't make you a gentleman. A coward ought to fight with straps on his shoulders, but it takes a gentleman to fight for eleven dollars a month!"

GENERAL JOHNSTON.

The women of the South furnished what may be called the nerve-force of the war. From the very beginning they made it disgraceful for any man of fighting age to stay at home without sufficient cause. Their earliest associations were soldiers' sewing societies. Yet not all of the ladies were at first adepts in fashioning men's attire, and sometimes comical results followed. Stockings failed to match, and buttons would be sewed on the wrong side of a man's shirt or breeches. In one instance a friend of the writer turned over to the matron president of her society in Charleston a pair of trousers with one leg. "Why, what in the world did you make that thing for?" was asked by the old lady. "Oh—er—er, why, that's for a one-legged soldier, of course," gasped the young patriot in her confusion. "That's all right, Miss Georgia; very thoughtful, very thoughtful. But," looking at them quizzically through her spectacles, "Miss Georgia, you've got 'em buttoned up behind."

After the battle of Leesburg, Va., a group of ladies visited the wounded, and seeing one of the latter prone upon his stomach, the sympathetic question was asked, as would be quite natural: "Where are you hurt?" The man, an Irishman, pretended not to hear, and replied: "Purthy well, I thank ye, mum." "But where were you wounded?" again fired away one of the ladies. "Faith, it's nothing at all, at all, that I want, leddies. I think I'll be on me way to Richmond in about tin days," again answered Pat, with a peculiarly distressed look, as if he wished to avoid further conversation on a delicate subject.

Thinking that he was deaf, an old lady, who had remained in the background, now put her mouth down to his ear and shouted: "We—want—to—know—where—you—are—hurt—where—you—are—wounded—so—we—can—do—something—for—you!"

Pat, evidently finding that if the bombardment continued much longer he would have to strike his flag, concluded to do so at once, and with a face as rosy as a boiled lobster and a humorous twinkle in his eye replied: "Sure, leddies, it's not deaf that I am; but since ye're determined to know where I've been hurted, it's—it's where I can't sit down to take my males. The rascally bullet entered the behind o' me coat!"

Sudden locomotion followed, and the story circulated among the fair sex like quicksilver on a plate of glass; but while Paddy had plenty of sympathy, they pestered him with no more questions of "Where are you hurt?"

HENRY W. B. HOWARD.

INDIVIDUAL HEROISM AND THRILLING INCIDENTS.

KINDNESS TO FEDERAL PRISONERS BY MEMBERS OF THE FIFTY-FOURTH VIRGINIA REGIMENT—AN ORATION ON PATRIOTISM—THE LAST WORDS OF AN HEROIC SOLDIER—HE DIES FOR US—MATCHING GALLANT AND CHIVALROUS DEEDS OF PREVIOUS WARS—AN INCIDENT OF GETTYSBURG—HOW GENERAL JOHN B. GORDON GAVE AID AND COMFORT TO HIS ENEMY, GENERAL BARLOW—WOMEN WHO DARED AND SUFFERED FOR THE FLAG—MRS. BROMWELL, A BRAVE COLOR-BEARER IN TIME OF DANGER—A MODERN ANDRÉ—THE SULTANA DISASTER—THE HERO OF BURNSIDE'S MINE.

AN ORATION ON PATRIOTISM.

I HAVE listened to the best speakers our country has possessed in the thirty years which have elapsed since the war, but not one of them has made the impression on my mind which a few words, falling from the lips of a private soldier, did away back in 1862.

It was the night of the 30th of August, 1862, and I, with others, was lying in the Van Pelt farmhouse, on the field of the Second Bull Run. The time of night I do not know. I had been semi-unconscious from the joint effect of chloroform and amputations. The room in the old farmhouse in which I lay was crowded with desperately wounded men, or boys, for some of us were not nineteen years of age—one hundred and seventy odd men in and around the house. With returned consciousness, sometime in the night, I became aware of voices near me.

I turned my head as I lay on the floor, and next beyond me I saw the dim light of a kerosene lamp on the floor. I soon made out that some one was kneeling by a wounded man and examining his wounds. I heard the injunction given, "Tell me honestly, doctor, what my chance is." He had been shot in the abdomen, and all too soon came the verdict, "My poor fellow, you will not see another sunrise." I heard his teeth grate as he struggled to control himself, and then he spoke: "Doctor, will you do me a favor?"—"Certainly," was the response; "what is it?"—"Make a memorandum of my wife's address and write her a line telling her how and when and where I die." Out came the surgeon's pencil and memorandum book, and made note of the name and address. I did not remember them the next day, or since. I only recall it was some town in Michigan.

It appeared that the dying soldier was a man of some property, and in the clearest manner he stated his advice to his wife as to the best way to handle it. All this was noted down, and then he paused; and the surgeon, anxious, it is to be presumed, to get along to others who so sorely needed his aid, said, "Is that all, my friend?"—"No," he replied falteringly; "that is not all. I have two little boys. Oh, my God!" Just this one outburst from an agonized heart, and then, mastering his emotion, he drew himself hastily up, resting on his elbows, and said: "Tell my wife, doctor, that with my dying breath I charge her to so rear our boys that if, when they shall have come to years of manhood, their country shall need their services, even unto death, they will give them as fully as, I trust under God, their father gives his life this night." That was all. He sank back, exhausted, and the surgeon passed along. In the gray of the morning, when I roused enough to be aware of what was transpiring around me, I glanced toward him. A cloth was over his face, and soon his silent form was carried out. I repeat, I have heard the best speakers of my time, but after all these years I still

WE DRANK FROM THE SAME CANTEEN.

pronounce the dying utterances of that unknown soldier as the grandest oration on patriotism I have ever listened to.

HE DIED FOR US.

As I stir the memories of those days, there comes to mind one experience which, even after the lapse of all these years, stirs me deeply. For over three hundred years English history has been enriched by the recital of the chivalrous act of Sir Philip Sidney, who, stricken with a mortal wound at Zutphen, and being offered a drink of water, took the cup, but, when about to raise it to his lips, saw the eyes of a wounded private soldier fixed longingly thereon. With all the grace and courtliness which had at any time characterized him when treading the salon of Queen Elizabeth, the gallant knight handed him the refreshing draught, saying, "Friend, thy necessities are greater than mine, drink." The private drank, and the knight died.

I have a pride in the belief that in our four years of bloody strife we matched the most gallant, chivalrous deeds that previous history has recorded. It was my good fortune to meet and participate in the beneficence of a lineal descendant, in spirit, if not in blood, of Sir Philip Sidney, albeit he was garbed in the uniform of a private soldier of the Union army. Some of us who were lying there in the Van Pelt farmhouse, after the battle of the Second Bull Run, and who had suffered amputations, were carried out of the house and placed in a little tent in the yard. There were six of us in the tent, and we six had had seven legs amputated. Our condition was horrible in the extreme. Several of us were as innocent of clothing as the hour we were born. Between our mangled bodies and the rough surface of the board floor there was a thin rubber blanket. To cover our nakedness, another blanket. I was favored above the others in that I had a short piece of board set up slanting for a pillow. Between us and the fierce heat of that Virginia sun there was but the poor protection of the thin tent-cloth. There were plenty of flies to pester us and irritate our wounds. Our bodies became afflicted with loathsome sores, and, horror indescribable! maggots found lodging in wounds and sores, and we were helpless. Cremation made converts in those hours.

A very few attendants had been detailed to stay behind with us when it was apparent we must fall into the enemy's hands, but they were entirely inadequate in point of numbers to minister to our wants. Heat and fever superinduced an awful thirst, and our moans were for water, water, and very often there was none to give us water.

We lay there one day when there was none to answer our cry; but outside of our tent the ground was strewn with wounded men, one among whom was Christ-like in his humanitarianism. Sorely wounded in his left side, torn by a piece of a shell, he could not rise and go and get us drink, but it always seemed to us that, like his prototype of more than three centuries ago, he said in the depths of his great heart, "Their necessities are greater than mine," for he could crawl and we could not. Some little distance across the grass he saw where some apples had fallen down from the branches overhead. Every motion must have been agony to him, yet he deliberately clutched at the grass, dragged himself along until he was in reach of the apples, some of which he put in the pockets of his army blouse, and then turning, and keeping his bleeding side uppermost, he dragged himself back to our tent and handed out the apples.

As I lay nearest, I took them from him one by one and passed them along till we each had one, and I had just set my teeth in the last one he handed in, and it tasted as delicious as nectar, when, hearing an agonizing moan at my right, I turned my head on my board pillow, and saw our unknown benefactor, his hands clutched, his eyes fixed in the glare of death; a tremor shook his figure, and the eternal peace of death was his.

This was all we ever knew of him. His name and condition in life were a sealed book to us. I saw that he was unkempt of hair, unshaven of beard; his clothes were soiled with dirt and stained with blood—not at all such a figure as you would welcome in your parlor or at your dinner table; but this I thought as I gazed at the humble tenement of clay from which the great soul had fled, that in that last act of his he had exhibited so much of the purely Christ-like attribute in the effort to reach out and help poor suffering humanity, that in the last day when we shall be judged for what we have been and not for what we may have pretended to have been, I had rather take that man's chance at the judgment bar of God than that of many a gentleman in my circle of acquaintance of much greater pretensions.

AN INCIDENT OF GETTYSBURG.*

Though never a war was fought with more earnestness than our own late war between the North and the South, never a war was marked by more deeds of noble kindness between the men, officers and privates, of the contending sides. Serving at the front during the entire war as a captain of engineers of the Confederate army, many such deeds came under my own personal attention, and many have been related to me by eye-witnesses. Here is one especially worthy of record:

The advance of the Confederate line of battle commenced early on the morning of July 1, 1863, at Gettysburg. The infantry division commanded by Major-Gen. John B. Gordon, of Georgia, was among the first to attack. Its objective point was the left of the Second Corps of the Union army. The daring commander of that corps occupied a position so far advanced beyond the main line of the Federal army, that, while it invited attack, it placed him beyond the reach of ready support when the crisis of battle came to him in the rush of charging lines more extended than his own. The Confederate advance was steady, and it was bravely met by the Union troops, who for the first time found themselves engaged in battle on the soil of the North, which until then had been virgin to the war. It was "a far cry" from Richmond to Gettysburg, yet Lee was in their front, and they seemed resolved to welcome their Southern visitors "with bloody hands to hospitable graves." But the Federal flanks rested in air, and, being turned, the line was badly broken, and, despite a bravely resolute defence against the well-ordered attack of the Confederate veterans, was forced to fall back.

Gordon's division was in motion at a double quick, to seize and hold the vantage ground in his front from which the opposing line had retreated, when he saw directly in his path the apparently dead body of a Union officer. He checked his horse, and then observed, from the motion of the eyes and lips, that the officer was still living. He at once dismounted, and, seeing that the head of his wounded foeman was lying in a depression

* The account here given of this interesting incident is taken from an article by Capt. T. J. Mackey, of the Confederate army, recently published in *McClure's Magazine*.

CONFEDERATE INTRENCHMENTS ON THE BATTLEFIELD OF NEW HOPE CHURCH, GA.

(FROM A WAR-DEPARTMENT PHOTOGRAPH.)

in the ground, placed under it a near-by knapsack. While raising him at the shoulders for that purpose, he saw that the blood was trickling from a bullet-hole in the back, and then knew that the officer had been shot through the breast. He then gave him a drink from a flask of brandy and water, and, as the man revived, said, while bending over him, "I am very sorry to see you in this condition. I am General Gordon. Please tell me who you are. I wish to aid you all I can."

The answer came in feeble tones: "Thank you, general. I am Brigadier-General Barlow, of New York. You can do nothing for me; I am dying." Then, after a pause, he said, "Yes, you can. My wife is at the headquarters of General Meade. If you survive the battle, please let her know that I died doing my duty."

General Gordon replied: "Your message, if I live, shall surely be given to your wife. Can I do nothing more for you?"

After a brief pause, General Barlow responded: "May God bless you! Only one thing more. Feel in the breast pocket of my coat—the left breast—and take out a packet of letters."

As General Gordon unbuttoned the blood-soaked coat, and took out the packet, the seemingly dying soldier said: "Now please take out one, and read it to me. They are from my wife. I wish that her words shall be the last I hear in this world."

Resting on one knee at his side, General Gordon, in clear tones, but with tearful eyes, read the letter. It was the missive of a noble woman to her worthy husband, whom she knew to be in daily peril of his life, and with pious fervor breathed a prayer for his safety, and commended him to the care of the God of battles. As the reading of the letter ended, General Barlow said: "Thank you. Now please tear them all up. I would not have them read by others."

General Gordon tore them into fragments and scattered them on the field "shot-sown and bladed thick with steel." Then, pressing General Barlow's hand, General Gordon bade him good-by, and, mounting his horse, quickly joined his command.

RETREAT OF LEE'S ARMY AFTER GETTYSBURG.

He hastily penned a note on the pommel of his saddle, giving General Barlow's message to his wife, but stated that he was still living, though seriously wounded, and informing her where he lay. Addressing the note to "Mrs. General Barlow, at General Meade's headquarters," he handed it to one of his staff, and told him to place a white handkerchief upon his sword, and ride in a gallop toward the enemy's line, and deliver the note to Mrs. Barlow. The officer promptly obeyed the order. He was not fired upon, and, on being met by a Union officer who advanced to learn his business, he presented the note, which was received and read, with the assurance that it should be delivered instantly.

Let us turn from Gettysburg to the capital, Washington, where, eleven years later, General Gordon held with honor, as now, a seat as senator of the United States, and was present at a dinner party given by Orlando B. Potter, a representative in Congress from the State of New York.

Upon Mr. Potter's introducing to him a gentleman with the title of General Barlow, General Gordon remarked: "Are you a relative of the General Barlow, a gallant soldier, who was killed at Gettysburg?"

The answer was: "I am the General Barlow who was killed at Gettysburg, and you are the General Gordon who succored me!" The meeting was worthy of two such brave men—every inch American soldiers.

I should add, that, on receiving her husband's note, which had been speedily delivered, Mrs. Barlow hastened to the field, though not without danger to her person, for the battle was still in progress. She soon found her husband, and had him borne to where he could receive surgical attendance.

Through her devoted ministrations he was enabled to resume his command of the "Excelsior Brigade," and add to the splendid reputation which it had achieved under General Sickles, its first commander.

AN INTERESTING INCIDENT.

It was a curious fact during the war, that, however savage and hostile the armies and the troops might be in action, there was a certain friendly relation subsisting between individuals on the

COURT HOUSE, PETERSBURG, VA.

opposing sides, and even between special commands. The semi-intercourse between the picket lines is a familiar story; it was based principally on an agreement that the popping over of an occasional poor devil who happened to be exposed was not compensated for by any material military gain, so the pickets were generally suffered to perform their lonesome vigil without being shot like squirrels. But there was also a touch of the common humanity in this intercourse, which went beyond mere military conventions. A pleasant episode of warfare in Tennessee marked the kindly relation that sometimes was established between regiments. The Third Ohio Regiment were among the prisoners after a certain engagement, and when they entered a Tennessee town, on their way to the prisons in Richmond, they were visited, through curiosity, by a number of the Fifty-fourth Virginia, who wanted to see how the Yankees liked it to be hungry and tired and hopeless. The melancholy picture that met their gaze was enough to touch their hearts, and it did so. They ran back to their camp, and soon returned reinforced by others of their regiment, all bringing coffee (and kettles to boil it in), corn-bread, and bacon; and with these refreshments, which were all they had themselves, they regaled the hungry prisoners, mingling with them and doing all they could to relieve their distress, and the next morning the prisoners departed on their weary way, deeply grateful for the kindness of their enemies, and vowing never to forget it. It was not long before the opportunity came to them to show that they remembered it. In due time they were exchanged, and, returning to service, they found themselves encamped near Kelly's Ferry, on the Tennessee River. When Missionary Ridge was stormed, a lot of prisoners were taken from the Confederates, and among the number was the Fifty-fourth Virginia, and they were marched nine miles to Kelly's Ferry. It happened that at the landing there were some of the Third Ohio, and they asked what regiment this was. The answer, "The Fifty-fourth Virginia," had a most surprising effect on them. They left the spot on the run, and rushing up to their camp they shouted out to the boys, "The Fifty-fourth Virginia is at the ferry!" If they had announced the appearance of a hostile army in force, they could not have started up a greater or a quicker activity in the camp. The men ran about like mad, loaded themselves up with every eatable thing they could lay their hands on—coffee, bacon, sugar, beef, preserved fruits, everything—and started with a yell for the ferry, where they surrounded and hugged the Virginians like so many reunited college-mates, and spread before them the biggest feast they had seen since the Old Dominion seceded from the Union.

THE "SULTANA" DISASTER.

The Mississippi steamer *Sultana* called at Vicksburg, April 25, 1865, on her journey from New Orleans to St. Louis, receiving on board nineteen hundred and sixty-four Union prisoners from Columbia, Salisbury, Andersonville, and elsewhere, who had been exchanged in regular manner, or set free through the surrender or flight of their jailers.

Being anxious to proceed North, the poor fellows gave little heed to the fact that the *Sultana* was already carrying a heavy load of passengers and freight, and that workmen were busy repairing her boilers as she lay at the wharf. So great was the swarm that when they came to lie down for sleep every foot of available space on all the decks, and even the tops of the cabins and the wheel-house, was occupied by a soldier wrapped in his blanket, and making light of his uncomfortable berth in anticipation of a speedy arrival home.

From Vicksburg the *Sultana* steamed to Memphis, and there took on coal, leaving the wharf at one A. M. on the 27th. The next news of her received at that port came from the lips of survivors snatched from the rushing current of the river. When about eight miles above Memphis, one of her boilers had blown up, with frightful effect. To add to the horror, the woodwork around the engines had been set on fire by the accident, and the steamer burned to the water's edge, compelling all who had been spared by the explosion to leap overboard for safety.

The force of the explosion hurled hundreds of the sleeping soldiers into the air, killing many, mangling others; while others again, terribly scalded, fell into the water and were swallowed up by the resistless tide, never again to rise. The few survivors

JAMES RIVER, BELOW DUTCH GAP.

who had escaped all these perils finally reached the Arkansas shore, which, owing to the unusual high waters, was a long distance from the channel.

Among the soldiers on board were thirty commissioned officers, of whom only three were rescued. The dead at the scene of the accident numbered fifteen hundred, nearly all of them soldiers belonging to Western States. The heaviest loss in any one regiment fell to the One Hundred and Fifteenth Ohio, which numbered eighty-three victims on the list. The One Hundred and Second Ohio counted seventy, and the Ninth Indiana cavalry was represented by seventy-eight.

A catastrophe of similar character, not quite so appalling in results, had occurred on the Atlantic coast only three weeks previous. The steamer *General Lyon*, from Wilmington, bound for Fortress Monroe, burned to the water's edge off Cape Hatteras, on the night of March 31st. Out of five hundred on board, over four hundred of them soldiers, only twenty escaped. Among the lost were eleven officers and one hundred and ninety-five men belonging to the Fifty-sixth Illinois, with nearly two hundred released Union prisoners.

"CROW'S NEST," AN ARMY OBSERVATORY, NEAR PETERSBURG.

(From a War Department photograph.)

THE HERO OF BURNSIDE'S MINE

In the ranks of the Forty-eighth Pennsylvania, the regiment which placed the powder magazine of Burnside's mine, at Petersburg, underneath the doomed Confederate fort, was a sergeant known as Harry Reese.

He had been the first to propose the mine seriously. Permission to construct it having been granted at headquarters, he, with a score of his fellows, all experienced coal miners, set to work with their ordinary camp tools, and, under cover of night, in one month excavated, concealed from the enemy's eyes, eighteen thousand cubic feet of earth, creating a tunnel nearly six hundred feet long. On two occasions Reese, by personal effort, saved the enterprise from failure; once when the shaft opened into a bed of quicksand, and again when the army engineers through faulty measurements located the powder-chamber outside the limits of the fort to be destroyed, instead of directly under it.

Finally came the hour for the explosion. The troops stood ready to charge into the breach, and the long fuse was ignited by Reese, who, with a group of his mining companions, stayed at the mouth of the shaft, awaiting the result. Generals and aids anxiously studied their watch-dials, that would show the flight of moments beyond the appointed time. Grant telegraphed from army headquarters over his special field-wire: "Is there any difficulty in exploding the mine?" and again: "The commanding general directs, if your mine has failed, that your troops assault at once."

The mine had failed. Daylight was spreading over the trenches, and the enemy were alert even to the point of expecting an assault.

Reese drew his soldier's clasp dirk, and, turning to a comrade, said: "I am going into the mine. If it don't blow up, give me time to reach the splice in the fuse, and then come to me with fresh fuse and twine." He creeps into the shaft with resolute caution, following up the tell-tale streak of black ashes, which shows that the fuse has surely burned its way toward the powder-cells in the chamber beyond. It may reach there any second, and then! At last, just ahead of him, the brave miner sees a stretch of fuse outwardly uncharred. A fine thread of flame may be eating through its core, nevertheless, one spark of which is enough to set the terrible train ablaze. Reese knows this, for a man accustomed to handling powder cannot for an instant lose consciousness of its quick and awful violence when the connecting flash is struck. He knows his peril, yet presses on, and with his blade severs the fuse beyond the charred streak. Danger for that moment is over.

The delay had been caused by a splice wound so tightly that the fire could not eat through freely. He made a new short fuse, relit the flashing string, and escaped to the mouth of the tunnel, just as the magazine chambers exploded, spreading a mass of ruins where the armament of Lee had stood grim and threatening in the morning light but a moment before.

The fort thus destroyed was occupied by Capt. R. G. Pegram's Virginia battery, and the trenches—which means the system of walled ditches, bomb proofs, and other shelter for troops on both sides of the battery—by the Eighteenth and Seventy-second South Carolina infantry. These men, numbering several hundred, lay sound asleep, all except the sentinels. The battery and the sections of work adjoining were hoisted into the air, and two hundred and eighty-eight officers and soldiers were buried in the débris, while their comrades who escaped injury fled in confusion, leaving a defenceless gap in the line twenty or thirty rods wide, into which Burnside's corps charged without a moment's hesitation.

The Union advance was promptly met by a sharp fire from the Confederate reserves, and the fight which ensued in the breach is known as the battle of the Crater.

THE ARKANSAS BOY SPY.

When the Confederate army abandoned Little Rock in 1863, one of its military operators, David O. Dodd, stayed back and lived some time in the Union lines. He was a lad of seventeen. Shortly after the town was Unionized he left there, ostensibly to go to Mississippi, but returned in a few days and lingered about in his old haunts. A second time he passed out of the picket lines, unrestrained until he reached the outposts, where the guards, searching him, discovered some curious pencil marks in a memorandum book carried openly in his pocket.

He was arrested, and at headquarters the marks were shown to be telegraphic dots and dashes that gave a full description of the Union fortifications and the distribution of forces about the city. His act was that of a spy, and his life was the forfeit. Having admitted that he had accomplices, he was offered pardon if he would betray them. A last appeal was made at the scaffold by his friends and relatives, but he firmly put the temptation aside and signalled the executioner to do his duty. Then the drop fell, carrying him and his secret to another world. My informant, who witnessed the hanging, declared that the lad met his doom with the coolness of a stoic, while the spectators, chiefly soldiers, wept like children.

WOMEN WHO DARED AND SUFFERED FOR THE FLAG.

War calls women to weep, not to take up the sword in battle, yet to such lengths does their devotion run that the place of danger finds them on hand unasked. On the Union side in the civil war military heroines came from every class and from every stage of civilization. Of those who put on uniforms the record is hard to trace, but their dead and mangled forms on countless battlefields proved that the American amazon was no myth. Not to speak of these, there were women who openly faced all the terrors and hardships of war. Michigan seems to have eclipsed the record in this class of heroines.

When the Second Michigan volunteers started for the seat of war in 1861, Annie Etheridge, a young woman just out of her teens, volunteered as daughter of the regiment. Her dress was a riding habit, and she wore a military cap as a badge of her calling. A pair of pistols rested in her holsters for use in emergencies. Annie served four years, part of the time with the Fifth Michigan, and always in the Army of the Potomac. Her service was the relief of wounded on the field, which means under fire. General Kearny presented her with the "Kearny badge" for her devotion to his wounded at Fair Oaks. Once while bandaging a wound for a New York boy a Confederate shell killed him under her hands.

Though not called on to fight, Annie had spirit enough to make a battle hero. At Chancellorsville she went to the outposts with the skirmishers, and was ordered back to the lines. The enemy was already shooting at the pickets. On the way back she passed a line of low trenches where the Union soldiers lay concealed, and spurning the thought that the affair must end in a retreat, she turned her face to the front and called out to the men, "Boys, do your duty and whip those fellows!" A hearty cheer was the response, and "those fellows" poured a volley into the hidden trenches. Annie was hit in the hand, her skirt was riddled, and her horse wounded. At Spottsylvania she turned a party of retreating soldiers back to their place in the ranks by offering to lead them into battle. No one but a miscreant could spurn that call.

The other Michigan heroines were Bridget Divers, of the First cavalry, an unknown in the Eighth and in the Twenty-fifth regiments who passed as Frank Martin, and Miss Seelye who served in the Second as Frank Thompson. "Thompson" and "Martin" wore men's disguise. Bridget Divers was the wife of a soldier, and performed deeds of daring in bringing wounded from the field, under fire.

Two Pennsylvania regiments carried women into battle in men's disguise—Charles D. Fuller, of the Forty-sixth, and Sergt. Frank Mayne, of the One Hundred and Twenty-sixth. "Mayne" was killed. The Fifth Rhode Island Regiment produced a heroine in Mrs. Kady Brownell, wife of a sergeant. She is credited with having been a skilful shooter with a rifle and also a brave color-bearer in time of danger. The wives of officers were accorded great freedom of action at the front, and many a gallant and noble deed was called forth by devotion to husband first and incidentally to the cause. Madame Turchin, wife of the Illinois general, went into battle and rescued wounded men, besides cheering and inspiring the soldiers of the general's command. Gen. Francis C. Barlow, of New York, was accompanied by his wife, who attended the wounded on the field. This devoted woman served at the front until 1864, and died of fever contracted in the hospitals at Petersburg.

A MODERN ANDRÉ.

Lieut. S. B. Davis, of the Confederate service, probably came the nearest of any officer on either side to playing the rôle of the André of the Rebellion. He did not, it is true, lose his life in an attempt to nogotiate for the surrender of an enemy's fortress, as did the noted British spy; but he was sentenced to be

A COMPANY OF SHERMAN'S VETERANS.

hanged for complicity, under disguise, in negotiations between citizens of the United States and Confederate officials in Richmond and in Canada for the delivery of the States of Ohio, Illinois, and Indiana, and certain military positions on the lakes, into the power of organized and armed emissaries of the South, led by Confederate officers.

Lieutenant Davis was but twenty-four, a native of Delaware, a State that did not secede, and entered into the part he played on his own motion; that is, he volunteered to act as a messenger between Richmond and Canada. He was provided with a British passport under an assumed name, had his hair dyed, and put on citizen's dress. The regular route of communication between Richmond and Canada was by steamer, viâ Bermuda; but for some reason never yet explained Davis went from Richmond to Baltimore, and from there to Columbus, O., where he certainly communicated with people of suspicious character at the time.

From Columbus he went to Detroit, and from there to Windsor, Canada, where he met the notorious Jacob Thompson and other Confederate emissaries.

There were many points about the young man to give him peculiar fitness for his work; there was also a fatally weak spot in his harness. He was well bred and of prepossessing appearance. A native of Delaware, he could mingle with Northern people without arousing suspicion. He was a distant relative of Jefferson Davis, and had the respect and confidence of the Confederate chieftains. Too young to have attained prominence before the war, and never having served in the regular army, his personality was not likely to be known on the Union side of the lines. But he had served a long time on the staff of General Winder, commander at Andersonville prison, where many Union soldiers had seen him often.

Fortune favored him in his daring enterprise until his arrival, on what proved to be his final trip southward from Canada, at Newark, O. He was travelling in the passenger cars of the Baltimore and Ohio railroad; had passed safely through Columbus and other public centres most dangerous to him.

At Newark two Union soldiers entered the car where the disguised Confederate sat. They had been in Andersonville prison, and after eying their fellow passenger for a time one ex-prisoner whispered in his comrade's ear, "There is Lieutenant Davis, of Andersonville!"

Both arose, and, approaching Davis, one called out bluntly to the stranger, "Aren't you Lieutenant Davis?"

"No, sir; my name is Stewart," was the prompt reply.

"Yes, you are Lieutenant Davis, and you had charge of the prison when I was in Andersonville," persisted the soldier. A crowd of passengers quickly surrounded the parties, and seeing that his stubborn cross-questioners would not be convinced, the Confederate yielded, and said:

"Well, boys, you've got me. I am Lieutenant Davis."

The provost marshal of Newark was summoned, and the prisoner was speedily hurried to the common jail. A search of his person failed to disclose any secret papers, and he was left in the main room with a number of ordinary county criminals. Soon after the military had left the place the stranger was seen to remove from inside his coat-lining a number of despatches and drawings upon white silk, and to burn them in the fire which was blazing in an open stove. The link that would have removed all doubt as to his purposes and condemned him to the gallows was thus hopelessly destroyed; but a court martial held that his presence in the Union lines in disguise constituted the offence for which the penalty is death. When the evidence was all in and the case clear against him, the prisoner rose, facing the officers and witnesses, every one wearing the colors of his mortal enemies, and some of them scarred with the conflicts in which he and his own had been pitted against them. There was no reason to expect mercy, and he did not ask it.

After stating his case briefly, he looked over his accusers and judges, and said: "I do not fear to die. I am young and would like to live, but I deem him unworthy who should ask pity of his foemen. Some of you have wounds and scars; I can show them, too. You are serving your country as best you may; I have done the same. I can look to God with a clear conscience:

and whenever the chief magistrate of this nation shall say, 'Go,' whether upon the scaffold or by the bullets of your soldiery, I will show you how to die."

The sentence was that he be confined in the military prison at Johnson Island, in Lake Erie, until the 17th of February, 1865, then "to be hung by the neck until he is dead."

During the night of the 16th of February, when all preparations had been made, and Davis had, as he believed, beheld the last sunset on earth, a reprieve came from President Lincoln. He was placed in a dungeon at Fort Warren, Boston Harbor, and before the reprieve ended the war closed. Then the authorities permitted him to go free. To the end he kept the secret of his mission to Ohio.

THE BATTLE FLAGS AND MARKERS OF THE FOURTEENTH REGIMENT NEW YORK ARTILLERY.

ENGAGEMENTS IN WHICH THE REGIMENT, WITH THESE FLAGS, TOOK PART.

Wilderness, Va.,	May 5–7, 1864.
Spottsylvania C. H.,	May 10–19, 1864.
North Anna River, Va.,	May 23–26, 1864.
Tocopotomy Creek, Va.,	May 30, 1864.
Bethesda Church, Va.,	May 31, 1864.
Shady Grove Road, Va.,	June 2, 1864.
Cold Harbor, Va.,	June 3–12, 1864.
Petersburg Front, Va.,	June 16–18, 1864.
Siege of Petersburg, First,	June 19 to August 19, 1864.
Crater, Va.,	July 30, 1864.
Bliell's Station, Va.,	August 19, 1864.
Weldon Railroad, Va.,	August 21, 1864.
Peebles Farm, Va.,	September 29, 1864.
Poplar Springs Church, Va.,	September 30, 1864.
Siege of Petersburg, Second,	November 29, 1864, to April 3, 1865.
Fort Haskell, Va.,	March 25, 1865.
Fort Steadman, Va.,	March 25, 1865.
Capture of Petersburg, Va.,	April 3, 1865.
Appomattox, Va.,	April 9, 1865, Surrender of Lee and his Army of Northern Virginia.

REMINISCENCES OF THE BATTLE OF BULL RUN.

BY GENERAL JOHN T. MORGAN, C. S. A.

THE battle of Bull Run—the first battle of Manassas—was a great and decided victory for the Confederate army, and aroused the pride and enthusiasm of the Southern people as no other event ever did. Yet there is a painful recollection in every mind that it was the first act in an awful drama, the first great field upon which the hosts of the North and the South measured arms and opened the series of great tragedies of the civil war, in which millions of men perished.

If that had been the last battle of the war instead of the first, and if it had been accepted as the final arbitrament of the questions that could not have been settled otherwise, I would still recall its incidents with pride, but also with sadness. But the glory of it would have scarcely compensated for its sacrifices.

I doubt if any humane person can recall without pain even the most gratifying victories of a great war in which he was a participant. The excessive toil and anxiety are only made tolerable, and the suffering and waste of human life can only be endured, for the sake of our interest in the cause that demands such victims for the altar of sacrifice.

Yet war, like other intense passions, often becomes a consuming desire, as the hope of victory verges upon the recklessness of despair. My earlier impressions of civil war may be illustrated by a few personal incidents connected with the first battle of Manassas.

With the exception of a few "regulars" in either army, every experience of actual warfare was then entirely new to the soldiery, and not a man in any position failed to seriously question his heart as to its fortitude in the approaching crisis of battle. None, perhaps, were about to march upon that great and open field who did not overdraw the pictures of danger and distress that he would be called to meet. It was a relief from this excessive tension that enabled men of highly nervous condition to quiet their emotions and to engage in battle like trained veterans, when its realities were found to be less harrowing than they expected.

It is probable that no two armies of trained soldiers ever confronted each other with a less daunted spirit than the hundred thousand proud men who, in almost full view of the extended lines of each army, marched steadily into action across the open fields about Manassas. For many miles the view was uninterrupted.

The approaches of the martial hosts, in line after line of supporting columns, under the fire of artillery that covered the field with the bluish haze of battle, were marked with an air of firm defiance, which spoke of the cause at stake, and of a contest for principles which, as they were felt to be involved, commanded the devotion of each army. It was not a flag or a government for which either army was fighting, but a dispute about rights under the Constitution of a common country. War under such circumstances is always desperate, and too often becomes ferocious. When men make war as political or religious partisans, they often forget the honorable zeal of the true soldier and lend themselves as the instruments of vengeance. We had not then reached that stage of hostility. On this field there met in battle many thousands of the best and most enlightened men of a great nation, all Americans, and all inspired with the love of a common country, and many in the opposing ranks were of the same families. They were gallant and chivalric men, and their fierce onsets left the field thickly strewn with dead and wounded. Almost every man who fell had some personal history in which whole communities felt a proud and grateful interest. The survivors in such armies could not be cruel.

As the incidents of the battle were narrated in the camps of the victors, and by parties returning from the pursuit of McDowell's shattered forces, it was clearly manifested that it was political antagonism and not sectional animosity that had brought on the war.

When the death or capture of some leading Federal officer was announced, respectful silence was observed and personal sympathy was manifested with sincerity; but, when the capture of a leading politician or of a member of Congress was announced, the wildest rejoicing was heard in the crowds of delighted listeners.

That was a grand field of battle, and it was occupied by armies that were all the more eager for war because they did not then realize its terrible significance.

Few strategic surprises were possible on such a field, and none were attempted. An approaching column could be seen, as it was headed toward a point of attack, when it was miles away; and the clouds of dust, rolling up in vast volume, indicated its strength. Then, suddenly, arose the opposing cloud, and presently both were illumined with flashes of artillery, and roared with the spiteful din of musketry, in their quickened dash, and were clamorous with hoarse cheers from thousands of sturdy men. A few crashing volleys; the swaying back and forth of the lines, as repeated charges were met and repulsed—and the field was won and lost by some impulse, in which all seemed to share at the same moment, that was as much a mystery to the victors as it was to the vanquished. It was what is called "a square stand-up fight" in an open field, without military defences; and the result was a notable victory of the soldiers engaged, not a victory won by superior strategy or gallant leadership. The battle ended late in the afternoon, and by nightfall, the successful army was in bivouac, while the beaten army was in flight for Washington, unpursued. The rain began to fall in floods as the night came on, adding to the misery of the wounded of both armies, who were treated with every possible kindness. To a novice in warfare, the battlefield was a fearful scene, as the bright morning of the next day dawned upon it, with the dead scattered over it, lying beside dead horses, broken artillery, muskets, wagons, and shattered trees. It was the silent reproach of havoc and death upon the fierce injustice of a resort to war as the arbiter of differences of opinion as to civil government, which had been exaggerated to such awful conclusions, and could not, after all, be in any wise settled by such means. Peace and wiser judgment finally came out of the thousand succeeding conflicts, but were not created by them. They were only made possible by the failure of war to convince anybody of errors.

Taking a half-dozen cavalry and a brother officer along, we moved, at daylight, under orders given to me to follow and reconnoitre the army that had moved off in column at the close of the battle, but was supposed to have camped not far away. We soon found that nothing remained of that army but the evidences of panic which had overtaken almost every command. The wounded had, in some cases, been left to their own resources, and, at bridges that were broken, there were piled in wild confusion, dead men and horses, guns and caissons, wagons and sutlers' goods, tents, muskets, drums, ambulances, spring wagons, and the lighter vehicles that had brought the picnic parties from Congress to witness the consummation of their "policy." It was to them a sudden and frightful adjournment, *sine die*.

As we rode over the field, gray-haired fathers and mothers from the nearer homes in Virginia were already there looking for their dead or wounded sons. All was silent save the moanings of the sufferers, and the subdued chirrup of little wrens as they sought for their mates. The birds seemed as sad as the venerable seekers for their loved ones. The dead seemed to preserve their personal characteristics, and the tense strain of the conflict was settled upon their features. In most cases, death on the battlefield is instantaneous and painless, and the latest thoughts seem to linger on the faces of the dead.

As we rode along the farm lanes where the rail fences had

AQUEDUCT BRIDGE, POTOMAC RIVER.

been torn away as they were crossed and recrossed by charging columns, we found, not widely separated, the victims of the bayonet. Several had fallen in this close combat.

One of them was a very handsome man, clean-shaven, and dressed in a neat uniform as a private in the Federal army. He was about thirty years old. On his shirt bosom there was a single spot of blood. He sat almost erect, his back propped in a corner of the fence, with his blue eyes wide open, and his mouth was firmly closed, and his gun and hat near by him. His form and face were majestic, and his pallid brow, with the hair gracefully swept back, was a splendid picture of the serenity of death, almost as expressive as life, and the most earnest plea for peace that I had ever contemplated.

On the opposite side of the lane was a Confederate soldier—an Irishman—whom a ball had killed. Evidently he had received a mortal wound, and had sat down to die in an angle of the fence, and rested on a small log he found there. He was also leaning against the fence, which held him up in a position that seemed very life-like. His hat was on his head and sheltered his face which was slightly bowed to the front. In his mouth he held his pipe, with a very short stem, in a way that was quite natural and suggestive of his race. His wound was in the thigh, and while he was bleeding to death, he had doubtless sought comfort in his pipe.

A beautiful photograph was in the side pocket of the Federal soldier, near the fatal blood-spot on his shirt bosom. We thought we could readily trace his dying thoughts to that dear friend. We left him with his friend's picture where we found it, to find, in another spot, a mile distant, a living proof that it is love and not hatred that survives death, and commands the heart's last tribute of devotion.

The body of an oak tree that was heavily clad in foliage had been cut through with cannon shot until the top had fallen over and formed a thick mass of branches and leaves on the ground. There was a copse of undergrowth near by, into which we saw a man dart like an arrow as we rode up. From the tree-top came low moanings, as from one who feared discovery, and yet could not stifle his voice when spasms of pain returned upon him. It proved to be a field officer of a New Jersey or Delaware regiment, whose thigh had been crushed by a cannon shot in the battle.

His servant had laid him in the tree-top, with leaves and a horse blanket for a bed, and was guarding him. When the servant saw us halt, he came out timorously from his hiding, and was weeping and pleading for the life of his master. I said to him, "What do you take us for?"—"But be you not rebels?" he said. I answered, "We are called rebels, and yet your kindred."—"Be you Christian men?" I said that was our faith. "And you will be merciful to the major?" I replied, "I am a major, and have no ill-will toward majors, even if they are enemies." The major, hearing our conversation, invited us to dismount and come to him. We went to his hiding-place, and found him pale with loss of blood, and in great anguish.

Seeing that we were Confederate officers, he said, "I wish to give you my parole."—"We need none from you," I replied; "our friendship has been broken, and renewed very suddenly by your wounds, it seems, and you are our guest."—"Are you Virginians?"—"No, we are Alabamians, and this is our home, as it is yours, for we are all Americans."—"A home I have invaded," he said, "and I don't know why. I wish this war had never occurred; but I longed for it, in my thoughtless anger, and here I must meet death."

He said, "I am a lawyer."—"So are we," I replied. "I am a Mason."—"So are we," I replied. "Thank God," he exclaimed, "I may yet see my wife before I die. She came to Washington with me, and I parted with her at Longbridge, three days ago, as we crossed the Potomac."

I assured him that I would inform his wife of his condition, through the first flag of truce that went over the lines, and that she should have safe-conduct to join him. Taking our hands, he prayed God to bless us; and turning to his servant, whose astonishment was now greater than his fear, he said, "Sam, get me the bread and the canteen, and give me some whiskey. Maybe if I eat and take a stimulant, I may live to see her." It was a hard, rough crust of corn-bread, which he munched with energy, and the canteen contained a few spoonfuls of common whiskey, a part of which he drank. I said, "This business is urgent, and we will gallop to your lines with your message."—"Yes," he said, "a race for a life, that has but one hope, that I may see her—my wife—before I die." We soon met a surgeon at a field hospital—a few blankets on which wounded soldiers were stretched—and he went at once to the sufferer in the tree-top. The message was despatched, and the loving wife came to find that, after one last kiss from his conscious lips, she was a widow indeed.

BRIGADIER-GENERAL JOHN T. MORGAN, C. S. A.

The glory of our victory was saddened to my heart by the reflection that the blood that enriched the fields was American, and was poured out from hearts that were alike and equally patriotic. Yet the sacrifice was voluntary, and may have been needed to demonstrate again the devotion of the American people to what they believe to be their duty in the defence of their liberties as they understand them, and in the enforcement of our laws as they are written.

This grand result, which seems to be perfectly assured, and this demonstration of American manhood is worth all that it has cost.

The battle of Bull Run was the last political battle of the civil war. It set Congress to passing vain resolutions to stop the war, and to reconcile the people and the States. After that awful event, war for the sake of war, and not for peace or justice, swept over the land and raged with unheard-of fury, until the sheer power of numbers prevailed, and peace came from exhaustion, but not from a broken spirit.

PICKING UP THE WOUNDED, FIFTY-SEVENTH NEW YORK AMBULANCE CORPS.

BOMBARDMENT OF THE CONFEDERATE LINES BY FORT PICKENS, SANTA ROSA ISLAND, PENSACOLA BAY.

PICKETT'S CHARGE AT GETTYSBURG.

THE MEASURE OF VALOR.

So far as valor is to be measured by dangers voluntarily encountered and losses sustained, the American citizen may justly compare with pride the incidents and statistics of the great civil war with those of any modern conflict in Europe. In our chapter on Gettysburg the close resemblance between that battle and Waterloo—in the numbers engaged on each side and the losses—has been pointed out. When comparison is made of the losses of regiments and other organizations, in particular engagements, the larger figures are with the Americans. The charge of the British Light Brigade, at Balaklava, in 1854, has been celebrated in verse by Tennyson and other poets, and is alluded to over and over again as if it were the most gallant achievement in modern warfare. Every time that some old soldier chooses to say he is one of the survivors of that charge, the newspapers talk about him as a wonder, report his words and publish his portrait. Yet that exploit sinks into insignificance when compared with the charge of the First Minnesota Regiment at Gettysburg. The order for the charge at Balaklava was a blunder, blunderingly obeyed; it accomplished nothing, and the total loss to the Light Brigade was thirty-seven per cent. At Gettysburg, on the second day, General Hancock observed a gap in the National line, and saw that Wilcox's Confederate Brigade was pushing forward with the evident intention of passing through it. He looked about for troops to close the gap, and saw nothing within immediate reach but the First Minnesota, though others could be brought up if a little time could be gained. Riding up to Colonel Colville, he said: "Do you see those colors?" pointing at the Confederate flag. "Take them!" Instantly the regiment dashed forward and charged the brigade; there was a short, fierce fight, and the regiment lost eighty-two per cent. of its numbers in killed and wounded, but the onset of the enemy was stayed, the desired time was gained, and even the colors were captured and brought off. In the Franco-German war of 1870 the heaviest loss sustained by any German regiment in a single battle was a fraction more than forty-nine per cent. In the National service during the civil war there were sixty-four regiments that sustained a loss of over fifty per cent. in some single action, and in the Confederate service there were fifty-three, making a hundred and seventeen American regiments that, in this respect, surpassed the German regiment of highest record.

There were thirteen battles in which one side or the other (in most instances each) lost more than 10,000 men, taking no account of the great capitulations like Fort Donelson and Vicksburg. And in the least of these nearly 1,900 men were shot dead on the field. The greatest losses on both sides were sustained at Gettysburg. Next in order (aggregating the losses on both sides*) come Spottsylvania, 36,800; the Wilderness, 35,300; Chickamauga, 34,600; and Chancellorsville, 30,000. But each of these battles occupied more than one day. The bloodiest single day was September 17, 1862, at the Antietam, where the National army lost 2,108 men killed and 9,549 wounded, with about 800 missing. The Confederate loss cannot be stated with exactness. General Lee's report gives only consolidated figures for the whole campaign, including Harper's Ferry and South Mountain, as well as the main battle; and these figures fall short by a thousand (for killed and wounded alone) of those given by his division commanders, who also report more than 2,000 missing. On the other hand, McClellan says that "about 2,700 of the enemy's dead were counted and buried upon the battle-field of Antietam," while "a portion of their dead had been previously buried by the enemy." Averaging these discrepant figures, and bearing in mind that there were no intrenchments at the Antietam, we may fairly put down the losses as equal on the two sides, which would give a total, on that field in one day, of 4,200 killed and 19,000 wounded. The number of prisoners was not large.

The heaviest actual loss that fell upon any one regiment in the National service in a single engagement was that sustained by the First Maine heavy artillery (acting as infantry) in the assault on the defences of Petersburg, June 18, 1864, when 210 of its men were killed or mortally wounded, the whole number of casualties being 632 out of about 900 men. This regiment was also the one that suffered most in aggregate losses in battle during the war, its killed and wounded amounting to 1,283. Over nineteen per cent. were killed. Another famous fighting regiment was the Fifth New Hampshire infantry, which had 295 men killed or mortally wounded in battle, the greatest loss, 69, occurring at Cold Harbor, June 1, 1864. Its first colonel, Edward E. Cross, was killed while leading it in the thickest of the second day's fight at Gettysburg. Another was the One Hundred and Forty-first Pennsylvania, which lost three-quarters of its men at Gettysburg, and at Chancellorsville lost 235 out of 419. At the second Bull Run (called also Manassas), the One Hundred and First New York lost 124 out of 168; the Nineteenth Indiana lost 259 out of 423; the Fifth New York lost 297 out of 490; the Second Wisconsin lost 298 out of 511; and the First Michigan lost 178 out of 320. At Antietam the Twelfth Massachusetts lost 224 out of 334. It had lost heavily also at Manassas, where Col. Fletcher Webster (only son of Daniel Webster) was killed at its head. It lost, altogether, 18 officers in action. Another famous Massachusetts regiment was the Fifteenth, which at Gettysburg lost 148 men out of 239, and at the Antietam, 318 out of 606, and, out of a total enrolment of 1,701, lost during the war in killed and wounded 879. Another Massachusetts regiment distinguished by hard fighting was the Twentieth, which General Humphreys compliments as "one of the very best in the service." Its greatest loss, in killed (48), was at Fredericksburg, where it was in the brigade that crossed the river in boats, to clear the rifle-pits of the sharp-shooters that

COLONEL G. T. ROBERTS.
Killed at Baton Rouge, La.

LIEUTENANT JOHN T. GREBLE.
Killed at Big Bethel.

COLONEL JAMES H. PERRY.
Died from wounds received at Fort Pulaski.

COLONEL ULRIC DAHLGREN.
Killed at Walkerton, Va.—Kilpatrick's Raid on Richmond.

* As there are discrepancies in all the counts, only the round numbers are given here.

were making it impossible to lay the pontoon bridges. This regiment had the task of clearing the streets of the town, and as it swept through them it was fired upon from windows and house-tops. The other regiments that participated in this exploit were the Seventh Michigan, the Nineteenth Massachusetts, and the Eighty-ninth New York. Some nameless poet has made it the subject of one of the most striking bits of verse produced during the war:

They leaped in the rocking shallops,
  Ten offered, where one could go,
And the breeze was alive with laughter,
  Till the boatmen began to row.
In silence how dread and solemn!
  With courage how grand and true!
Steadily, steadily onward
  The line of the shallops drew.
'Twixt death in the air above them,
  And death in the waves below,
Through ball and grape and shrapnel
  They moved, my God, how slow!
And many a brave, stout fellow,
  Who sprang in the boats with mirth,
Ere they made that fatal crossing
  Was a load of lifeless earth.
And many a brave, stout fellow,
  Whose limbs with strength were rife,
Was torn and crushed and shattered—
  A helpless wreck for life.

The Twentieth lost 44 men killed at Gettysburg, 38 at Ball's Bluff, 36 in the Wilderness, 20 at Spottsylvania, and 20 at the Antietam. During its whole service it had 17 officers killed, including a colonel, a lieutenant-colonel, two majors, an adjutant, and a surgeon. The story that Dr. Holmes tells in "My Hunt after the Captain" relates his adventures in the track of this regiment just after the battle of the Antietam.

Among the Vermont regiments, the one that suffered most in a single action was the Eighth, which at Cedar Creek lost sixty-eight per cent. of its numbers engaged. The First Heavy Artillery from that State, acting most of the time as infantry, with a total enrolment of 2,280, lost in killed and wounded 583. The Second Infantry, with a total enrolment of 1,811, lost 887. Its heaviest loss was at the Wilderness, where, out of 700 engaged, 348 (about half) were disabled, including the colonel and lieutenant-colonel killed. And a week later, at Spottsylvania, nearly half of the remainder (123) were killed or wounded. The Fourth Infantry, at the Wilderness, went into the fight with fewer than 600 men, and lost 268, including seven officers killed and ten wounded. In the fight at Savage Station, the Fifth Vermont walked over a regiment that had thrown itself on the ground and refused to advance any farther, pressed close to the enemy, and was taken by a flank fire of artillery that struck down 44 out of the 59 men in one company. Yet the regiment held its ground, faced about, and silenced the battery. It lost 188 men out of 428.

AFTER THE FIRST DAY'S BATTLE AT GETTYSBURG.

BRIGADIER-GENERAL ROBERT HATTON, C. S. A.
Killed at Stone River.

BRIGADIER-GENERAL R. S. GARNETT, C. S. A.
Killed near Carrick's Ford, Va.

In the second and third years of the war, several regiments of heavy artillery were raised. It was said that they were intended only to garrison the forts, and there was a popular belief that their purpose was to get into the service a large number of men who were not quite willing to subject themselves to the greater risks incurred by infantry of the line. But after a short period of service as heavy artillery, most of them were armed with rifles and sent to the front as infantry, and many of them ranked among the best fighting regiments, and sustained notable losses. The First Maine and First Vermont have been mentioned already. The Second Connecticut heavy artillery, the first time it went into action, stormed the intrenchments at Cold Harbor with the bayonet, and lost 325 men out of 1,400, including the colonel. At the Opequan it lost 138, including the major and five line officers; and at Cedar Creek, 190. The Seventh, Eighth, Ninth, and Fourteenth New York heavy artillery regiments all distinguished themselves similarly. The Seventh, during one hundred days' service in the field as infantry (Grant's overland campaign), lost 1,254 men, only a few of whom were captured. The Eighth lost 207 killed or mortally wounded, at Cold Harbor alone, with more than 200 others wounded. Among the killed were eight officers, including Col. Peter A. Porter (grandson of Col. Peter B. Porter, of the war of 1812), who fell in advance of his men. Its total loss in the war was 1,010 out of an enrolment of 2,575. The Ninth had 64 men killed at Cedar Creek, 51 at the Monocacy, 43 at Cold Harbor, and 22 at the Opequan. Its total loss in killed and wounded was 824 in an enrolment of 3,227. This regiment was commanded, a part of the time, by Col. William H. Seward, Jr. The Fourteenth had 57 men killed in the assault on Petersburg, 43 at Cold Harbor, 30 in the trenches before Petersburg, 26 at Fort Stedman, 22 at the mine explosion, and 16 at Spottsylvania. It led the assault after the mine explosion, and planted its colors on the captured works. Its total loss in killed and wounded was 861, in an enrolment of 2,506. In comparing these with other regiments, it must be remembered that their terms of service were generally shorter, because they were enlisted late in the war. The Fourteenth, for instance, was organized in January, 1864, which gave it but fifteen months of service, and it spent its first three months in the forts of New York harbor; so that its actual experience in the field covered somewhat less than a year. In that time one-third of all the men enrolled in it were disabled; and if it had served through the war at this rate, nothing would have been left of it. This explanation applies equally to several other regiments.

BRIGADIER-GENERAL
PRESTON SMITH, C. S. A.
Killed at Chickamauga.

The State of New York furnished one-sixth of all the men called for by the National Government. Of Fox's "Three Hundred Fighting Regiments" (those that had more than 130 men killed during the war), New York has 59—nine more than its proportion. The Fifth Infantry, known as Duryea's Zouaves, met with its heaviest loss, 297 out of 490, at Manassas, and lost 162 at Gaines's Mill. This regiment was commanded at one time by Gouverneur K. Warren, afterward famous as a corps commander, and General Sykes pronounced it the best volunteer regiment that he had ever seen. The Fortieth had 238 men killed in battle, and lost in all 1,217. Its heaviest losses were in the Seven Days' battles, 100; Fredericksburg, 123; Gettysburg, 150; and the Wilderness, 213. The Forty-second lost 718 out of 1,210 enrolled, its heaviest loss, 181, being at the Antietam. The Forty-third lost 138 at Salem Church, and 198 in the Wilderness, its colonel, lieutenant-colonel, and major all being killed there. The Forty-fourth, originally called "Ellsworth Avengers," was composed of picked men from every county in the State. It lost over 700 out of 1,585 enrolled. At Manassas, out of 148 men in action, it lost 71. It was a part of the force that seized Little Round Top at Gettysburg. The Forty-eighth was raised and commanded by a Methodist minister, James H. Perry, D.D., who had been educated at West Point. He died in the service in 1862. The regiment participated in the assault on Fort Wagner, and lost there 242 men. At Olustee it lost 244. Its total loss was 859 out of an enrolment of 2,173. The Forty-ninth had two colonels, a lieutenant-colonel, and a major killed in action. The Fifty-first New York and Fifty-first Pennsylvania carried the stone bridge at the Antietam, the New York regiment losing 87 men, and the Pennsylvanians 120. The Fifty-second New York lost 122 men at Fair Oaks, 121 in the siege of Petersburg, and 86 at Spottsylvania. It was a German regiment, and two Prussian officers on leave of absence fought with it as line officers at Spottsylvania and were killed in the terrible struggle at the bloody angle. The Fifty-ninth went into the battle of the Antietam with 321 men, fought around the Dunker Church, and lost 224, killed or wounded, including nine officers killed. The Sixty-first lost 110 killed or wounded at Fair Oaks, out of 432; 106 in the siege of Petersburg, and 79 at Glendale. Francis C. Barlow and Nelson A. Miles were two of its four successive colonels. One company was composed entirely of students from Madison University. The Sixty-third, an Irish regiment, lost 173 men at Fair Oaks, 98 at Gettysburg, and 59 at Spottsylvania. The Sixty-ninth, another Irish regiment, lost more men killed and wounded than any other from New York. At the Antietam, where it contended at Bloody Lane, eight color-bearers were shot. The Seventieth lost 666 men in a total enrolment of 1,462. Its heaviest loss, 330, was at Williamsburg. Daniel E. Sickles was its first colonel. The Seventy-sixth lost 234 men out of 375 in thirty minutes at Gettysburg. In the Wilderness it lost 282. The Seventy-ninth was largely composed of Scotchmen. It lost 198 men at Bull Run, where Colonel Cameron (brother of the Secretary of War) fell at its head. At Chantilly six color-bearers were shot down, when General Stevens (who had been formerly its colonel) seized the flag and led the regiment to victory, but was shot dead. The Eighty-first lost 215 men at Cold Harbor, about half the number engaged. The Eighty-second, at the Antietam, lost 128 men out of 339, and at Gettysburg 192 out of 305, including its colonel. The Eighty-third lost 114 men at the Antietam, 125 at Fredericksburg, 115 in the Wilderness, and 128 at Spottsylvania. The Eighty-fourth, a Brooklyn zouave regiment, lost 142 men at Bull Run, 120 at Manassas, and 217 at Gettysburg, where, with the Ninety-fifth, it captured a Mississippi brigade. The Eighty-sixth lost 96 men at Po River, and over 200 in the Wilderness campaign. The Eighty-eighth, an Irish regiment, lost 102 men at the Antietam, and 127 at Fredericksburg. The Ninety-third lost 260 men in the Wilderness, out of 433. The Ninety-seventh at Gettysburg lost 99 men, and captured the colors and 382 men of a North Carolina regiment. The One Hundredth lost 176 men at Fair Oaks, 175 at Fort Wagner, and 259 at Drewry's Bluff. The One Hundred

MAJOR-GENERAL JAMES B. GORDON, C. S. A.
Killed at Yellow Tavern, Va.

and Ninth lost 140 men at Spottsylvania, and 127 in the assault on Petersburg. Benjamin F. Tracy, Secretary of the Navy in President Harrison's cabinet, was its first colonel. The One Hundred and Eleventh lost 249 men at Gettysburg, out of 390, and again at the Wilderness it lost more than half of the number engaged. The One Hundred and Twelfth lost 180 men at Cold Harbor, including its colonel killed, and it lost another colonel in the assault on Fort Fisher. The One Hundred and Twentieth, at Gettysburg, lost 203 men, including seventeen officers killed or wounded. The One Hundred and Twenty-first, at Salem Church, lost 276 out of 453, and at Spottsylvania it lost 155. On both occasions it was led by Emory Upton, afterward general. Its total of killed and wounded in the war was 839, out of an enrolment of 1,426. The One Hundred and Twenty-fourth lost at Chancellorsville 204 out of 550, and at Gettysburg 90 out of 290. The One Hundred and Twenty-sixth lost at Gettysburg 231 men, including the colonel, who was killed, and another colonel was killed before Petersburg. The One Hundred and Thirty-seventh lost 137 at Gettysburg, where it formed a part of the brigade that held Culp's Hill. At Wauhatchie it lost 90, and in the Battle above the Clouds 38 more. The One Hundred and Fortieth lost 133 men at Gettysburg, where it formed part of the force that occupied Little Round Top at the critical moment, and helped to drag up Hazlett's battery. Its colonel was killed in this struggle. In the Wilderness it lost 255, and at Spottsylvania another colonel and the major were killed. The One Hundred and Forty-seventh was in the brigade that opened the battle of Gettysburg, and there lost 301 out of 380 men. The One Hundred and Forty-ninth was one of the regiments that saw service both at the East and the West. It lost 186 men at Chancellorsville, and at Lookout Mountain lost 74 and captured five flags. In the Atlanta campaign it lost 136 out of 380 men. The One Hundred and Sixty-fourth, an Irish regiment, participated in the assault at Cold Harbor and carried the works in its front, but at the cost of 157 men, including the colonel and six other officers killed. The One Hundred and Seventieth, another Irish regiment, lost 99 men at the North Anna and 136 in the early assaults on Petersburg. Its total of killed and wounded during the war was 481 out of 1,002 enrolled.

Thus runs the record to the end. These regiments are not exceptional so far as the State or the section is concerned. Quite as vivid a picture of the perils and the heroism of that great struggle could have been presented with statistics concerning the troops of any other States. Looking over all the records, one discovers no difference in the endurance or fighting qualities of the men from different States. For instance, the Eighth New Jersey lost, at Chancellorsville, 125 men out of 268; and in the same battle the Twelfth New Jersey lost 178; while at Gettysburg less than half of the regiment made a charge on a barn filled with sharp-shooters, and captured 99 men. The Fifteenth New Jersey had 116 men killed, out of 444, at Spottsylvania. The Eleventh Pennsylvania, at Fredericksburg, lost 211 killed or wounded out of 394, and in its whole term of service it had 681 men disabled in an enrolment of 1,179; and the Twenty-eighth lost 266 men at the Antietam. The Forty-ninth Pennsylvania had 736 men disabled, in an enrolment of 1,313, its heaviest loss being at Spottsylvania, where it participated in the charge at the bloody angle and lost 260 men, including its colonel and lieutenant-colonel killed. The Seventy-second lost 237 at the Antietam, and 191 at Gettysburg, where it was in that part of the line aimed at by Pickett's charge. The Eighty-third Pennsylvania suffered heavier losses in action than any other regiment, save one, in the National service. At Gaines's Mill it lost 196, at Malvern Hill 166, at Manassas 97, and at Spottsylvania 164. At Gettysburg it formed part of the force that seized Little Round Top. Its total losses were 971 in an enrolment of 1,808. The Ninety-third, like a regiment previously mentioned, was raised and commanded by a Methodist minister. It rendered specially gallant service at Fair Oaks, the Wilderness, and Spottsylvania. The One Hundred and Nineteenth made a gallant charge at Rappahannock Station, capturing guns, flags, and many prisoners, and losing 43 men. It fought at the bloody angle of Spottsylvania, and there and in the Wilderness lost 231 out of 400, including two

COLONEL FLETCHER WEBSTER.
Only son of Daniel Webster.—Killed at Second Bull Run.

BRIGADIER-GENERAL WILLIAM P. SANDERS.
Killed at Knoxville, Tenn.

BRIGADIER-GENERAL HENRY BOHLEN.
Killed at Freeman's Ford.

CAPTAIN W. N. GREENE, OF THE ONE HUNDRED AND SECOND NEW YORK REGIMENT,

Capturing the Battle Flag of the Twelfth Georgia Regiment at Chancellorsville.

regimental commanders killed. The One Hundred and Fortieth was in the wheat-field at Gettysburg, and there lost 241 men out of 589. Its total killed and wounded numbered 732 in an enrolment of 1,132.

Delaware, a slave State, contributed its quota to the armies that fought for the Union. At the Antietam its First Regiment lost 230 men out of 650. At Gettysburg it was among the troops that met Pickett's charge.

Maryland, another slave State, contributed many good troops to the Union cause. Its Sixth Regiment lost 174 men at Winchester, and 170 in the Wilderness.

The Seventh West Virginia lost 522 men killed or wounded, in an enrolment of 1,008.

The Seventh Ohio lost, at Cedar Mountain, 182 out of 307 men. At Ringgold all its officers except one were either killed or wounded. At Chickamauga the Fourteenth lost 245 men out of 449. At Jonesboro it carried the works in front of it by a brilliant charge, but at heavy loss. The Twenty-third, at South Mountain and Antietam, lost 199 men. Two of its four successive colonels were William S. Rosecrans and Rutherford B. Hayes.

It was not in the famous battles alone that heavy regimental losses were sustained. At Honey Hill, an action seldom mentioned, the Twenty-fifth Ohio had 35 men killed, with the usual proportion of wounded; and at Pickett's Mills, hardly recorded in any history, the Eighty-ninth Illinois lost 154.

The Fifth Kentucky, at Stone River, lost 125 out of 320 men, and at Chickamauga 125. It was commanded by Lovell H. Rousseau, an eminent soldier. Its total loss was 581, in an enrolment of 1,020. The Fifteenth, at Perryville, lost 196 men, including all its field officers killed. Its "boy colonel," James B. Forman, was killed at Stone River. Its total killed and wounded numbered 516, in an enrolment of 952.

The Fourteenth Indiana lost 181 men at the Antietam, out of 320. At Gettysburg it formed part of the brigade that annihilated the Louisiana Tigers. The Nineteenth suffered, during its whole term of service, a loss of 712 killed and wounded, in an enrolment of 1,246. The Twenty-seventh lost 616 from an enrolment of 1,101.

The Eleventh Illinois lost, at Fort Donelson, 339 men out of 500. It was commanded by W. H. L. Wallace, who was after-

SCENE OF MAJOR-GENERAL JAMES B. McPHERSON'S DEATH, ATLANTA, GA., JULY 22, 1864.

(FROM A WAR DEPARTMENT PHOTOGRAPH.)

ward a brigadier-general and fell at Shiloh. The Twenty-first lost 303 men at Stone River, and 238 at Chickamauga. Its first colonel was Ulysses S. Grant. The Thirty-first lost 176 at Fort Donelson. Its first colonel was John A. Logan. The Thirty-sixth lost 212 at Stone River. The Fortieth lost 216 at Shiloh, and gained special credit for keeping its place in the line after its ammunition was exhausted. The Fifty-fifth lost 275 at Shiloh out of 512. The Ninety-third lost 162 at Champion Hill, and 89, including its colonel, at Mission Ridge.

The First Michigan lost, at Manassas, 178 out of 240 men, including the colonel and fifteen other officers. The Fourth lost 164 at Malvern Hill, including its colonel. At Gettysburg it was in the wheat-field, and lost 165 men. Here a Confederate officer seized the regimental colors and was shot by the colonel, who the next moment was bayoneted by a Confederate soldier, who in his turn was instantly killed by the major. This regiment had three colonels killed in action. The Twenty-fourth, at Gettysburg, lost 363 men, including the colonel and twenty-one other officers, out of 496.

The Second Wisconsin lost 112 men at the first Bull Run and 298 at the second, including its colonel killed; and the Seventh had a total loss in killed and wounded of 1,016 from an enrolment of 1,630; and the Twenty-sixth lost 503 from an enrolment of 1,089.

The Fifth Iowa lost 217 men at Iuka, and the Seventh, at Belmont, lost 227 out of 410. At Pea Ridge the Ninth lost 218 out of 560. In the assault on Vicksburg the Twenty-second lost 164, and was the only regiment that gained and held any portion of the works. Of a squad of twenty-one men that leaped inside and waged a hand-to-hand fight, nineteen were killed.

BRIGADIER-GENERAL J. W. SILL.

Killed at Stone River.

The Eleventh Missouri had a total loss of 495 from an enrolment of 945. Its heaviest loss was in the assault on Vicksburg, 92. Joseph A. Mower, afterward eminent as a general, was at one time its colonel. The Twelfth Missouri lost 108 in the assault on Vicksburg, and the Fifteenth lost 100 at Chickamauga. General Osterhaus was the first colonel of the Twelfth.

The First Kansas lost 106 men killed and wounded at Wilson's Creek.

The losses in the cavalry were not so striking as those of the infantry, because they were seldom so heavy in any one engagement. But the cavalry were engaged oftener, sometimes in a constant running fight, and the average aggregate of casualties was about the same as in other arms of the service.

In the artillery there were occasionally heavy losses when the enemy charged upon a battery and the gunners stood by their pieces. At Iuka, Sands's Ohio battery had 105 men, including drivers. It was doing very effective service when two Texas regiments charged it, and 51 of its men were killed or wounded. It was captured and recaptured. Seeley's battery at Chancellorsville lost 45 men, and at Gettysburg 25. Campbell's lost 40 at the Antietam, and Cushing's 38 at Gettysburg. The Fifth Maine battery lost 28 at Chancellorsville, 28 at Cedar Creek, and 23 at Gettysburg.

The colored regiments, which were not taken into the service till the third year of the war, suffered quite as heavily as the white ones. They lost over 2,700 men killed in battle (not including the mortality among their white officers), and, with the usual proportion of wounded, this would make their total of casualties at least 12,000.

COLONEL JOHN W. LOWE.

Killed at Carnifex Ferry.

The regimental losses in the Confederate army were at least equal to those in the National, and were probably greater, for the reason that for them "there was no discharge in that war." Every organization in the National service was enlisted on a distinct contract to serve for a definite term—three months, nine months, two years, or three years—and when the term expired, the men were sent home and mustered out. But when a man was once mustered into the Confederate army, he was there till the end of the war, unless he deserted or was disabled. But no records are available from which complete statistics can be compiled. And in May, 1863, General Lee issued an order forbidding commanders to include in their reports of casualties in battle any wounds except such as disabled the men for further service, and also forbidding them to mention the number of men engaged in an action. This makes any mathematical comparison with the casualties in the National armies impossible; and without information as to the number engaged, the percentage of loss, which is the true test, cannot be computed. Still, there were a considerable number of regiments the statistics of which were recorded and have been preserved. The heaviest loss known in any Confederate regiment was that of the Twenty-sixth North Carolina, at Gettysburg. It went into the fight with somewhat more than 800 men, and lost 588 killed or wounded, besides 120 missing. One company went into the first day's battle with three officers and 84 men, and all but one man were either killed or wounded. Another North Carolina regiment, the Eleventh, went in on the first day with three officers and 38 men, and two of the officers and 34 men were killed or wounded. At Fair Oaks, the Sixth Alabama lost 373 out of 632, and the Fourth North Carolina, 369 out of 687. At Gaines's Mill the First South Carolina lost 319 out of 537; and at Stone River the Eighth Tennessee lost 306 out of 444.

The heaviest percentage of loss, so far as known, was that of the First Texas, at the Antietam, 82 per cent. In that same battle the Sixteenth Mississippi lost 63 per cent.; the Twenty-seventh North Carolina, 61 per cent.; the Eighteenth and Tenth Georgia, each 57 per cent.; the Seventeenth Virginia, 56 per cent.; the Fourth Texas, 53 per cent.; the Seventh South Carolina, 52 per cent.; the Thirty-second Virginia, 45 per cent.; and the Eighteenth Mississippi, 45 per cent. Some of the losses at Chickamauga were equally appalling. The Tenth Tennessee lost 68 per cent.; the Fifth Georgia, 61 per cent.; the Second and Fifteenth Tennessee, 60 per cent.; the Sixteenth Alabama and the Sixth and Ninth Tennessee, each 58 per cent.; the Eighteenth Alabama, 56 per cent.; the Twenty-second Alabama, 55 per cent.; the Twenty-third Tennessee, 54 per cent.; the Twenty-ninth Mississippi and the Fifty-eighth Alabama, each 52 per cent.; the Thirty-seventh Georgia and the Sixty-third Tennessee, each 50 per cent.; the Forty-first Alabama, 49 per cent.; the Twentieth and Thirty-second Tennessee, each 48 per cent.; and the First Arkansas, 45 per cent. And these losses include very few prisoners. At Gettysburg, besides the regiments already mentioned, the heaviest losers among the Confederates were: the Second North Carolina, 64 per cent.; the Ninth Georgia, 55 per cent.; the Fifteenth Georgia, 51 per cent.; and the First Maryland, 48 per cent. At Shiloh the Sixth Mississippi lost 70 per cent. At Manassas the Twenty-first Georgia lost 76 per cent.; the Seventeenth South Carolina, 67 per cent.; the Twenty-third South Carolina, 66 per cent.; the Twelfth South Carolina and the Fourth Virginia, each 54 per cent.; and the Seventeenth Georgia, 50 per cent. At Stone River the Eighth Tennessee lost 68 per cent.; the Twelfth Tennessee, 56 per cent., and the Eighth Mississippi, 47 per cent. At Mechanicsville the Forty-fourth Georgia lost 65 per cent. At Malvern Hill the Third Alabama lost 56 per cent.; the Forty-fourth Georgia, 46 per cent.; and the Twenty-sixth Alabama, 40 per cent.

COLONEL E. E. ELLSWORTH.
Killed at Alexandria, Va.

BRIGADIER-GENERAL GEORGE D. BAYARD.
Killed at Fredericksburg.

LIEUTENANT-COLONEL EDWARD CARROL.
Killed at the Battle of the Wilderness.

LIEUTENANT-COLONEL JOHN H. WHITE.
Killed at Fort Donelson.

COLONEL C. FRED. TAYLOR.
Killed at Gettysburg.

COLONEL EDWARD E. CROSS.
Killed at Gettysburg.

Some writers have asserted that the Confederate troops were better led than the National, and that this is proved by the greater loss of commanding officers. But the statistics do not bear out any such assertion. On each side one army commander was killed—Gen. J. B. McPherson and Gen. Albert Sidney Johnston. On each side three corps commanders were killed—National, Generals Mansfield, Reynolds, and Sedgwick; Confederate, Jackson, Polk, and A. P. Hill. On the National side fourteen division commanders were killed, and on the Confederate, seven. In comparing losses of brigade commanders, it should be explained, that in the Confederate service, as soon as a man was put in command of a brigade he was made a brigadier-general, but the National government was more chary of rank, and often left a colonel for a long time at the head of a brigade. Counting such colonels who actually fell at the head of their brigades as brigadiers, we find that eighty-five brigade-commanders were killed on the National side, and seventy-three on the Confederate.

On any other subject, the figures that crowd this chapter would be "dry statistics," but when we remember that every unit here presented represents a man killed or seriously injured, a citizen lost to the Republic—and not only that, but its loss of the sons that should have been born to these slaughtered men—every paragraph acquires a deep, though mournful interest. We may well be proud of American valor, but we should also feel humiliated by the supreme folly of civil war.

NOTE.—For the statistics of this chapter, we are largely indebted to Col. William F. Fox's admirable compilation of "Regimental Losses in the American Civil War" (Albany, 1893).

LIEUTENANT-COLONEL THOS. S. MARTIN.
Killed at the Second Battle of Bull Run.

MAJOR-GENERAL ISRAEL B. RICHARDSON.
Killed at Antietam.

LAST DAYS OF THE CONFEDERACY.*

BY GEN. JOHN B. GORDON, C. S. A.

I WILL give you from my personal knowledge the history of the struggles that preceded the surrender of General Lee's army, the causes that induced that surrender—as I had them from General Lee—the detailed account of the last assault ever made upon the Federal lines in pursuance of an offensive purpose, and a description of the last scenes of the bloody and terrible civil war. This history has never been published before. No official reports, I believe, were ever made upon the Confederate side; for after the battle of Hare's Hill, as the attack upon Fort Steadman was called, there was not an hour's rest until the surrender. From the 25th of March, 1865, until the 9th day of April, my men did not take their boots off, the roar of cannon and the rattle of musketry was scarcely stilled an instant, and the fighting and marching was continuous. Hence no report of these operations was ever made.

You will remember the situation of affairs in Virginia about the first of March, 1865. The Valley campaign of the previous summer, which was inaugurated for the purpose of effecting a diversion and breaking the tightening lines about Richmond and Petersburg, and from which so much had been expected, had ended in disaster. Grant had massed an enormous army in front of Petersburg and Richmond, and fresh troops were hurrying to his aid. Our army covered a line of over twenty miles, and was in great distress. The men were literally starving. We were not able to issue even half rations. One-sixth of a pound of beef a day, I remember, was at one time the ration of a portion of the army, and the men could not always get even that. I saw men often on their hands and knees, with little sticks, digging the grains of corn from out of the tracks of horses, and washing it and cooking it. The brave fellows were so depleted by the time Grant broke our lines, that the slightest wound often killed them. A scratch on the hand would result in gangrene and prove fatal. The doctors took me to the hospitals and showed me men with a joint on their fingers shot off, and their arms gangrened up to the elbows. "The men are starved," they said, "and we can do little for them."

A TERRIBLE SITUATION.

The sights that I saw as I walked among these poor, emaciated, hungry men, dying of starved and poisoned systems, were simply horrible. Our horses were in no better condition; many of them were hardly able to do service at all. General Lee had gone in person into Petersburg and Richmond, and begged the citizens to divide what little they had with his wretched men. The heroic people did all that they could. Our sole line of supplies was the railroad running into North Carolina and penetrating into "Egypt," as we called Southwest Georgia, which was then the provision ground for our armies. Such was the situation. My corps (Stonewall Jackson's old corps), after severe and heroic work in the Valley campaign, had been ordered back to Petersburg and placed upon the right wing of the army. I had general instructions to protect the flank of the army, prevent General Grant from turning it, and, above all, to protect the slender line of road from which solely we received our scanty supplies. We were almost continually engaged in fighting, making feints, and protecting our skirmish lines, which the enemy were feeling and pressing continually. Before daylight on the morning of the 2d of March, 1865, General Lee sent for me. I mounted my horse at once and rode to the general's headquarters. I reached the house in which he was staying at about four o'clock in the morning. As I entered the room to which I had been directed, I found General Lee alone. I shall never forget the scene. The general was standing at the fireplace, his head on his arm, leaning on the mantelpiece—the first time I ever saw him looking so thoroughly dejected. A dim lamp was burning on a small centre-table. On the table was a mass of official reports. General Lee remained motionless for a moment after I opened the door. He then looked up, greeted me with his usual courtesy, motioned me to the little table, and, drawing up a chair, sat down. I sat opposite him. "I have sent for you, General Gordon," he said, "to make known to you the condition of our affairs and to confer with you as to what we had best do." The night was fearfully cold. The fire and lamp both burned low

* This article was dictated by Gen. John B. Gordon to the late Henry W. Grady, and prepared by him for publication. It appeared originally in the Philadelphia *Times*. It is reprinted here by permission, after revision and correction by General Gordon.

as General Lee went on to give me the details of the situation. "I have here," he said, "reports sent in from my officers to-night. I find, upon careful examination, that I have under my command, of all arms, hardly forty-five thousand men. These men are starving. They are already so weakened as to be hardly efficient. Many of them have become desperate, reckless, and disorderly as they have never been before. It is difficult to control men who are suffering for food. They are breaking open mills, barns, and stores in search of food. Almost crazed from hunger, they are deserting from some commands in large numbers and going home. My horses are in equally bad condition. The supply of horses in the country is exhausted. It has come to be where it is just as bad for me to have a horse killed as a man. I cannot remount a cavalryman whose horse dies. General Grant can mount ten thousand men in ten days, and move around your flank. If he were to send me word to-morrow that I might move out unmolested, I have not enough horses to move my artillery. He is not likely to send this message, however; and yet," smiling, "he sent me word yesterday that he knew what I had for breakfast every morning. I sent him word that I did not think this could be so, for if he did know he would surely send me something better. But, now, let us look at the figures. I have, as I have shown you, not quite 45,000 men. My men are starved, exhausted, sick. His are in the best condition possible. But beyond this there is Hancock, at Winchester, with a force of probably not less than 18,000 men. To oppose this force I have not a solitary vidette. Sheridan, with his terrible cavalry, has marched almost unmolested and unopposed along the James, cutting the railroads and canal. Thomas is approaching from Knoxville with a force I estimate at 30,000, and to oppose him I have a few brigades of badly disciplined cavalry, amounting to probably 3,000 in all. General Sherman is in North Carolina, and, with Schofield's forces, will have 65,000 men. As to what I have to oppose this force, I submit the following telegram from General Johnston. The telegram reads: 'General Beaureguard telegraphed you a few days ago that, with Governor Vance's Home Guards, we could carry 20,000 men into battle. I find, upon close inspection, that we cannot muster over 13,000 men.'" (This, General Gordon said, was, as nearly as he could recollect, General Johnston's telegram.) "So there is the situation. I have here, say, 40,000 men able for duty, though none of my poor fellows are in good condition. They are opposed directly by an army of 160,000 strong and confident men, and converging on my little force four separate armies, numbering, in the aggregate, 130,000 more men. This force, added to General Grant's, makes over a quarter million. To prevent these from uniting for my destruction there are hardly 60,000 men available. My men are growing weaker day by day. Their sufferings are terrible and exhausting. My horses are broken down and impotent. I am apprehensive that General Grant may press around my flank and cut our sole remaining line of supplies. Now, general," he said, looking me straight in the face, "what is to be done?" With this he laid his paper down and leaned back in his chair.

A MORTAR MOUNTED ON A FLAT CAR, UNITED STATES MILITARY RAILROAD.

WHAT IS TO BE DONE?

I replied: "Since you have done me the honor to ask my opinion, I will give it. The situation as you portray it is infinitely worse than I had dreamed it was. I cannot doubt that your information is correct. I am confident of the opinion, therefore, that one of two things should be done, and at once. We must either treat with the United States Government for the best terms possible, or we should concentrate all our strength at one point of Grant's line—selecting some point on the right bank of the Appomattox—assault him, break through his lines, destroy his pontoons, and then turn full upon the flank of his left wing, sweep down it and destroy it if possible, and then join General Johnston in North Carolina by forced marches, and, combining our army with his, fall upon Sherman."

"And what then?"

"If we beat him or succeed in making a considerable battle, then treat at once for terms. I am forced to the conclusion, from what you say, sir, that we have no time for delay."

"So that is your opinion, is it?" he asked, in a tone that sent the blood to my face. I ought to have remembered that it was a way that General Lee had of testing the sincerity of a man's opinion by appearing to discredit it.

"It is, sir," I replied; "but I should not have ventured it, had it not been asked; and since you seem to differ from the opinion I hold, may I ask you what your opinion is?"

At once his manner changed, and, leaning forward, he said, blandly: "I entirely agree with you, general."

"Does President Davis and the Congress know these facts? Have you expressed an opinion as to the propriety of making terms, to President Davis or the Congress?"

General Lee replied to this question: "General Gordon, I am a soldier. It is my duty to obey orders."

"Yes," I replied; "but if you read the papers, General Lee, you can't shut your eyes to the fact that the hopes of the Southern people are centred in and on your army, and if we wait until we are beaten and scattered

LIEUTENANT-GENERAL JOHN B. GORDON, C. S. A.

GENERAL ROBERT E. LEE, C. S. A.

into the mountains before we make an effort at terms, the people will not be satisfied. Besides, we will simply invite the enemy to hunt us down all over the country, devastating it wherever they go."

General Lee said nothing to this for some time, but paced the floor in silence, while I sat gloomily enough, as you may know, at the fearful prospect. He had, doubtless, thought of all I said long before he sent for me. I don't wish you to understand that I am vain enough to believe for a moment that anything I said induced him to go to Richmond the next day. As I said before, he had probably decided on his course before he sent for me, and only feigned a difference of opinion or hesitation in order to see with what pertinacity I held my own. He did go to Richmond, and on his return sent for me again, and in reply to my question as to what had occurred, he said:

"Sir, it is enough to turn a man's hair gray to spend one day in that Congress. The members are patriotic and earnest, but they will neither take the responsibility of acting nor will they clothe me with authority to act. As for Mr. Davis, he is unwilling to do anything short of independence, and feels that it is useless to try to treat on that basis. Indeed, he says that, having failed in one overture of peace at Hampton Roads, he is not disposed to try another."

"Then," said I, "there is nothing left for us but to fight, and the sooner we fight the better, for every day weakens us and strengthens our opponents."

It was these two conferences that led to the desperate and almost hopeless attack I made upon the 25th of March on Grant's lines at Fort Steadman and Hare's Hill, in front of Petersburg. My corps was, as I tell you, at that time on the extreme right of General Lee's army, stretching from Hatcher's Run, southward along the Boydton plank road. He proposed to transfer my corps to lines in and around Petersburg, and have me familiarize myself with the strong and weak points, if there were any *weak* ones, on Grant's line near the bank of the Appomattox River. He ordered my command into Petersburg to replace the troops which were there. I spent a week examining Grant's lines, learning from deserters and men captured the names of the Federal officers and their commands in the front. At last I selected a point which I was sure I could carry by a night assault. I so reported to General Lee. It was in the last degree a desperate undertaking, as you will presently see; but it was the best that could be suggested—better than to stand still. Almost hopeless as it was, it was less so than the certain and rapid disintegration, through starvation and disease and desertion, of the last army we could ever organize. The point on my line from which I decided to make the assault was Colquitt's salient, which had been built by Governor Colquitt and his men and held by them, when, to protect themselves, they had to move under covered ways and sleep burrowed in the ground like Georgia gophers. I selected this point because the main lines here were closest together, being not more than two hundred yards apart, I should say, while the picket lines were so close that the Confederate, and the Federals could easily converse. By a sort of general consent the firing between the pickets nearly ceased during the day, so that I could stand upon my breastworks and examine General Grant's. It is necessary that you should know precisely the situation of the lines and forts, as I can illustrate by a rough diagram:

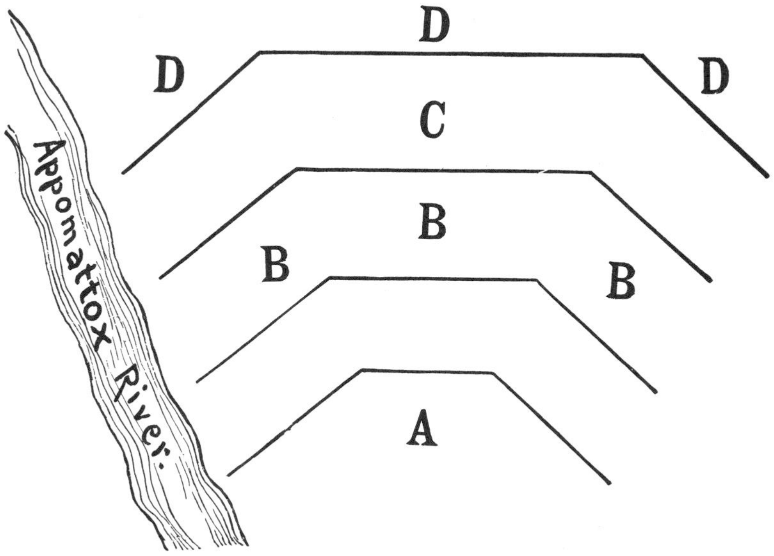

A, Colquitt's salient. *B*, the main line of Federal intrenchment, with Fort Steadman in the centre and two other forts flanking it. *C*, line of Federal reserves to support Fort Steadman and the troops in the main trenches *D*, second line of Federal forts, so arranged as to command Fort Steadman and the main line of intrenchments, should these be broken.

A STRONG POSITION.

You can see at a glance how desperately strong was even this, the weakest point on Grant's line. It was close to Colquitt's salient where the fearful mine was sprung called the Crater. The whole intervening ground between Fort Steadman and Colquitt's salient, over which I had to make the assault, was raked not only by a front fire, but by flank fires from both directions from the forts and trenches of the main line, *B*. An attack, therefore, by daylight would have been simply to have the men butchered, without any possibility of success, so that nothing but a night attack was to be thought of. Between the main line of trenches and forts and the rear line of forts, *D*, was a heavy line of Federal reserves, *C*, and the rear forts were placed with such consummate engineering skill as to command any point on that portion of Grant's line which might be captured. It was, therefore, necessary to capture or break through the reserves and take the rear line of forts as well as the front. This rear line of forts was so protected by abatis in front that the whole of General Lee's army could not have stormed them by a front attack, and the only possibility of securing them was to capture them from the rear, where there was an opening. This could only be done by stratagem, if it could be done at all.

I finally submitted a plan of battle to General Lee, which he approved and ordered executed. It was briefly this: To take Fort Steadman by direct assault at night, then send a separate body of men to each of the rear forts, who, claiming to be Federals, might pass through the Federal reserves and take possession of the rear line of forts as if ordered to do so by the Federal commander; next, then to press with my whole force to the rear of Grant's main line and force him out of the trenches, destroy his pontoons, cut his telegraph wires, and press down his flank. Of course, it was a most desperate and almost hopeless undertaking, and could be justified only by our desperate and hopeless condition if we remained idle. We both recognized it as the forlornest of forlorn hopes. Let me particularize a little more. The obstructions in front of my own lines had to be removed, and removed silently, so as not to attract the attention of the Federal pickets. Grant's obstructions had to be removed from the front of Fort Steadman. These obstructions were of sharpened rails, elevated to about breast high, the other end buried deeply in the ground, the rails resting on a horizontal pole and wrapped with telegraph wire. They could not be mounted or pushed aside, but had to be cut away with axes. This had to be done immediately in front of the guns of Fort Steadman. These guns were at night doubly charged with canister, as I learned from Federal prisoners. The rush across the intervening space between the lines had to be made so silently and swiftly as to take the fort before the gunners could fire. The reserves had to be beaten or passed and the rear line of forts taken before daylight. All this had to be accomplished before my main forces could be moved across and placed in position to move on Grant's flank, or râther left wing.

THE PLAN OF ATTACK.

My preparations were these: I called on my division commanders for a detail of the bravest men in their commands. To rush over the Federal pickets and into the fort and seize the Federal guns, I selected a body of only one hundred men, with empty rifles and fixed bayonets. To precede these, to clear an opening to the fort, I selected fifty of the most stalwart and brave men I could find, and armed them with axes to cut down the obstructions in front of the fort. They were ordered to remove my own abatis, rush upon the Federal obstructions, and cut away a brigade front. The one hundred with empty rifles and fixed bayonets were to follow immediately, and this one hundred and fifty men were not to falter or fire, but to go into Fort Steadman, if they had to do it in the face of the fire from all the forts. Immediately after these axemen and the one hundred had cleared the way and gained the fort, three other squads of one hundred each were to rush across, pass through Fort Steadman, and go pell-mell to the rear, and right through the Federal reserves, crying as they went: "The rebels have carried our lines in front, captured Fort Steadman, and we are ordered by General McLaughlin, Federal commander of Fort Steadman, to go back to the rear forts and hold them against the rebels." I instructed each commander of these last squads as to what particular fort he was to enter; and a guide, who had been raised on the ground, was placed with each of these three squads, or companies, who was to conduct them through the reserves and to the rear of the forts. If they were halted by the Federal reserves, each commander was instructed to pass himself off as one of the Federal officers whose names I had learned. I remember that I named one commander of one of the companies Lieutenant-Colonel Pendergrast, of a Pennsylvania regiment—I think that was the name and regiment of one of the Federal officers in my front. As soon as Fort Steadman should be taken, and these three bodies of one hundred men each had succeeded in entering the rear forts, the main force of infantry and cavalry were to cross over. The cavalry was to gallop to the rear, capture the fugitives, destroy the pontoons, cut down the telegraph wires, and give me constant information, while the infantry was to move rapidly down Grant's lines, attacking and breaking his division in detail, as they moved out of his trenches. Such, I say, was the plan of this most desperate and last aggressive assault ever made by the Confederate army.

General Lee had sent me, in addition to my own corps, a portion of Longstreet's corps (Pickett's division) and a portion of A. P. Hill's and a body of cavalry. During the whole night of the 24th of March I was on horseback, making preparations and disposing of troops. About four o'clock in the morning I called close around me the fifty axemen and four companies, one hundred each, of the brave men who were selected to do this hazardous work. I spoke to them of the character of the undertaking, and of the last hope of the cause, which was about to be confided to them. Around the shoulders of each man was bound a white strip of muslin, which Mrs. Gordon, who sat in a room not far distant listening for the signal gun, had prepared, as a means of recognition of each other. The hour had come, and when everything was ready I stood on the breastworks of Colquitt's salient and ordered two men to my side, with rifles, who were to fire the signal for attack. The noise of moving our own obstructions was going on and attracted the notice of a Federal picket. In the black darkness his voice rang out:

"Hullo there, Johnny Reb! what are you making all that fuss about over there?"

The men were just leaning forward for the start. This sudden call disconcerted me somewhat; but the rifleman on my right came to my assistance by calling out in a cheerful voice:

"Oh! never mind us, Yank; lie down and go to sleep. We are just gathering a little corn; you know rations are mighty short over here."

There was a patch of corn between our lines, some of it still hanging on the stalks. After a few moments there came back the kindly reply of the Yankee picket, which quite reassured me. He said:

"All right, Johnny; go ahead and get your corn. I won't shoot at you."

As I gave the command to forward, the man on my right seemed to have some compunctions of conscience for having stilled the suspicions of the Yankee picket who had answered him so kindly, and who the next moment might be surprised and killed. So he called out to him:

"Look out for yourself now, Yank; we're going to shell the woods."

This exhibition of chivalry and of kindly feelings on both sides, and at such a moment, touched me almost as deeply as any minor incident of the war. I quickly ordered the two men to "Fire."

Bang! Bang! The two shots broke the stillness, and "Forward!" I commanded. The chosen hundred sprang forward, eagerly following the axemen, and for the last time the stars and bars were carried to aggressive assault.

FORT STEADMAN TAKEN.

In a moment the axemen were upon the abatis of the enemy and hewing it down. I shall never know how they whisked this line of wire-fastened obstructions out of the way. The one hundred overpowered the pickets, sent them to the rear, rushed through the gap made by the axemen up the slope of Fort Steadman, and it was ours without the firing of a single gun, and with the loss of but one man. He was killed with a bayonet. The three companies who were to attempt to pass the reserves and go into the rear forts followed and passed on through Fort Steadman. Then came the other troops pouring into the fort, We captured, I think, nine pieces of artillery, eleven mortars, and about six hundred or seven hundred prisoners, among whom was General McLaughlin, who was commanding on that portion of the Federal line. Many were taken in their beds. The prisoners were all sent across to our lines, and other troops of my command were brought to the fort. I now anxiously awaited to learn the fate of the three hundred who had been sent in companies of one hundred each to attempt the capture of the three rear forts. Soon a messenger reached me from two officers commanding two of these chosen bodies, who informed me that they had succeeded in passing right through the line of Federal reserves by representing themselves as Federals, and had certainly gone far enough to the rear for the forts, but that their guides had abandoned them or been lost, and that they did not know in what direction to move. It was afterward discovered, when daylight came, that these men had gone further out than the forts, and could have easily entered and captured them if the guides had not been lost, or had done their duty. Of course, after dawn they were nearly all captured, being entirely behind the Federal reserves.

CITY POINT, VIRGINIA.

(From a War-time Photograph.)

GENERAL ULYSSES S. GRANT.

FAILURE OF THE ATTACK.

In the mean time, the few Federal soldiers who had escaped from the fort and intrenchments we had captured had spread the alarm and aroused the Federal army. The hills in the rear of Grant's lines were soon black with troops. By the time it was fairly daybreak the two forts on the main line flanking Fort Steadman, the three forts in the rear, and the reserves, all opened fire upon my forces. We held Fort Steadman, and the Federal intrenchments to the river, or nearly so. But the guides had been lost, and as a consequence the rear forts had not been captured. Failing to secure these forts, the cavalry could not pass, the pontoons could not be destroyed, and the telegraph wires were not cut. In addition to these mishaps, the trains had been delayed, and Pickett's division and other troops sent me by General Lee had not arrived. The success had been brilliant so far as it had gone, and had been achieved without loss of any consequence to our army; but it had failed in the essentials to a complete success or to a great victory. Every hour was bringing heavy reinforcements to the Federals and rendering my position less and less tenable. After a brief correspondence with General Lee, it was decided to withdraw. My loss, whatever it was, occurred in withdrawing under concentrated fire from forts and infantry. The fighting over the picket lines and main lines from this time to the surrender was too incessant to give me an opportunity to ascertain my loss. It was considerable; and although I had inflicted a heavy loss upon the enemy, I felt, as my troops reëntered Colquitt's salient, that the last hazard had been thrown, and that we had lost.

MAJOR-GENERAL MATTHEW W. RANSOM, C. S. A.

I will give you here the last note I ever received from General Lee, and one of the last he ever wrote in his official capacity. It is as follows:

4.30 P.M., HEADQUARTERS, *March* 24, 1865.

GENERAL: I have received yours of 2.30 P.M., and telegraphed for Pickett's division, but I do not think it will reach here in time; still we will try. If you need more troops, one or both of Heth's brigades can be called to Colquitt's salient, and Wilcox's to the Baxter road. Dispose of the troops as needed. I pray that a merciful God may grant us success, and deliver us from our enemies.

Very truly,

R. E. LEE, *General.*

GEN. J. B. GORDON.

P. S.—The cavalry is ordered to report to you at Halifax Road and Norfolk Railroad (iron bridge) at three A.M. to-morrow. W. F. Lee to be in vicinity of Monk's Corner at six A.M. R. E. L.

THE DEATH STRUGGLE.

I had very little talk with General Lee after our withdrawal. I recognized that the end was approaching, and of course he did. It will be seen from his semi-official note, quoted above, that he became very much interested in the success of our movement. While he had known as well as I that it was a desperate and forlorn hope, still we had hoped that we might cut through and make a glorious dash down the right and seek Johnston in North Carolina. The result of the audacious attempt that had been made upon his line, and its complete success up to the time that it was ruined by a mischance, was to awaken General Grant's forces into more aggressive measures. A sort of respite was had, for a day, after the night attack on Fort Steadman, and then the death-struggle began. Grant hurried his masses upon our starved and broken-down veterans. His main attack was made upon our left, A. P. Hill's corps. Grant's object was to turn our flanks, and get between us and North Carolina. The fighting was fearful and continuous. It was a miracle that we held our lines for a single day. With barely six thousand men I was holding six miles of line. I had just one thousand men to the mile, or about one to every two yards. Hill and Longstreet were in not much better trim, and some part of this thin line was being forced continually. The main fight was on my line and Hill's, as General Longstreet was nearer Richmond. Heavy masses of troops were hurled upon our line, and we would have to rally our forces at a certain point to meet the attack. By the time we would repel it, we would find another point attacked, and would hurry to defend that. Of course, withdrawing men from one part of the line would leave it exposed, and the enemy would rush in. Then we would have to drive them out and reëstablish our line. Thus the battle raged day after day. Our line would bend and twist, and swell and break, and close again, only to be battered against once more. Our people performed prodigies of valor. How they endured through those terrible, hopeless, bloody days, I do not know. They fought desperately and heroically, although they were so weakened through hunger and work that they could scarcely stand upon their feet and totter from one point of assault to another. But they never complained. They fought sternly, grimly, as men who had made up their minds to die. And we held our lines. Somehow or other—God only knows how—we managed day by day to wrest from the Federals the most of our lines. Then the men, dropping in the trenches, would eat their scanty rations, try to forget their hunger, and snatch an hour or two of sleep.

MAJOR-GENERAL THOS. L. ROSSER, C. S. A.

THE EVACUATION OF PETERSBURG.

Our picket lines were attacked somewhere every night. This thing went on till the morning of the 2d of April. Early that day it became evident that the supreme moment had come. The enemy attacked in unusually heavy force, and along the line of mine and Hill's corps. It became absolutely necessary to concentrate a few men at points along my line, in order to make a determined resistance. This left great gaps in my line of breastworks, unprotected by anything save a vidette or two. Of course, the Federals broke through these undefended passes, and established themselves in my breastworks. At length, having repulsed the forces attacking the points I defended, I began reëstablishing my line. My men fought with a valor and a desperate courage that has been rarely equalled, in my opinion, in military annals. We recaptured position after position, and by four o'clock in the afternoon I had reëstablished my whole line except at one point. This was very strongly defended, but I prepared to assault it. I notified General Lee of my purpose and of the situation, when he sent me a message, telling me that Hill's lines had been broken, and that General Hill himself had been killed. He ordered, therefore, that I should make no further fight, but prepare for the evacuation which he had determined to make that night. That night we left Petersburg. Hill's corps, terribly shattered and without its commander, crossed the river first, and I followed, having orders from General Lee to cover the retreat. We spent the night in marching, and early the next morning the enemy rushed upon us. We had to turn and beat them back. Then began the most heroic and desperate struggle ever sustained by troops—a worn and exhausted force of hardly four thousand men, with a vast and victorious army, fresh and strong, pressing upon our heels! We turned upon every hilltop to meet them, and give our wagon-trains and artillery time to get ahead. Instantly they would strike us, we invariably repulsed them. They never broke through my dauntless heroes; but after we had fought for an hour or two, we would find huge masses of men pressing down our flanks, and to keep from being surrounded I would have to withdraw my men. We always retreated in good order, though always under fire. As we retreated we would wheel and fire, or repel a rush, and then stagger on to the next hill-top, or vantage ground, where a new fight would be made. And so on through the entire day. At night my men had no rest. We marched through the night in order to get a little respite from fighting. All night long I would see my poor fellows hobbling along, prying wagons or artillery out of the mud, and supplementing the work of our broken-down horses. At dawn, though, they would be in line ready for battle, and they would fight with the steadiness and valor of the Old Guard.

APPOMATTOX COURT-HOUSE.

(From a War Department Photograph.)

THE LAST COUNCIL OF WAR.

This lasted until the night of the 7th of April. The retreat of Lee's army was lit up with the fire and flash of battle, in which my brave men moved about like demigods for five days and nights. Then we were sent to the front for a rest, and Longstreet was ordered to cover the retreating army. On the evening of the 8th, when I had reached the front, my scout George brought me two men in Confederate uniform, who, he said, he believed to be the enemy, as he had seen them counting our men as they filed past. I had the men brought to my campfire, and examined them. They made a most plausible defence, but George was positive they were spies, and I ordered them searched. He failed to find anything, when I ordered him to examine their boots. In the bottom of one of the boots I found an order from General Grant to General Ord, telling him to move by forced marches toward Lynchburg and cut off General Lee's retreat. The men then confessed that they were spies, and belonged to General Sheridan. They stated that they knew that the penalty of their course was death, but asked that I should not kill them, as the war could only last a few days longer, anyhow. I kept them prisoners, and turned them over to General Sheridan after the surrender. I at once sent the information to General Lee, and a short time afterward received orders to go to his headquarters. That night was held Lee's last council of war. There were present General Lee, General Fitzhugh Lee, as head of the cavalry, and Pendleton, as chief of artillery, and myself. General Longstreet was, I think, too busily engaged to attend. General Lee then exhibited to us the correspondence he had had with General Grant that day, and asked our opinion of the situation. It seemed that surrender was inevitable. The only chance of escape was that I could cut a way for the army through the lines in front of me. General Lee asked me if I could do this. I replied that I did not know what forces were in front of me; that if General Ord had not arrived—as we thought then he had not—with his heavy masses of infantry, I could cut through. I guaranteed that my men would cut a way through all the cavalry that could be massed in front of them. The council finally dissolved with the understanding that the army should be surrendered if I discovered the next morning, after feeling the enemy's line, that the infantry had arrived in such force that I could not cut my way through.

NEARING THE END.

My men were drawn up in the little town of Appomattox that night. I still had about four thousand men under me, as the army had been divided into two commands and given to General Longstreet and myself. Early on the morning of the 9th I prepared for the assault upon the enemy's line, and began the last fighting done in Virginia. My men rushed forward gamely and broke the line of the enemy and captured two pieces of artillery. I was still unable to tell what I was fighting; I did not know whether I was striking infantry or dismounted cavalry. I only knew that my men were driving them back, and were getting further and further through. Just then I had a message from General Lee, telling me a flag of truce was in existence, leaving it to my discretion as to what course to pursue. My men were still pushing their way on. I sent at once to hear from General Longstreet, feeling that, if he was marching toward me, we might still cut through and carry the army forward. I learned that he was about two miles off, with his face just opposite from mine, fighting for his life. I thus saw that the case was hopeless. The further each of us drove the enemy the further we drifted apart, and the more exposed we left our wagon trains and artillery, which were parked between us. Every line either of us broke only opened the gap the wider. I saw plainly that the Federals would soon rush in between us, and then there would have been no army. I, therefore, determined to send a flag of truce. I called Colonel Peyton of my staff to me, and told him that I wanted him to carry a flag of truce forward. He replied:

"General, I have no flag of truce."

I told him to get one. He replied:

"General, we have no flag of truce in our command."

Then said I, "Get your handkerchief, put it on a stick, and go forward."

"I have no handkerchief, General."

"Then borrow one and go forward with it."

He tried, and reported to me that there was no handkerchief in my staff.

"Then, Colonel, use your shirt!"

"You see, General, that we all have on flannel shirts."

At last, I believe, we found a man who had a white shirt. He gave it to us, and I tore off the back and tail, and, tying this to a stick, Colonel Peyton went out toward the enemy's lines. I instructed him to simply say to General Sheridan that General Lee had written me that a flag of truce had been sent from his and Grant's headquarters, and that he could act as he thought best on this information. In a few moments he came back with some one representing General Sheridan. This officer said:

"General Sheridan requested me to present his compliments to you, and to demand the unconditional surrender of your army."

"Major, you will please return my compliments to General Sheridan, and say that I will not surrender."

"But, General, he will annihilate you."

"I am perfectly well aware of my situation. I simply gave General Sheridan some information on which he may or may not desire to act."

THE FLAG OF TRUCE.

He went back to his lines, and in a short time General Sheridan came forward on an immense horse, and attended by a very large staff. Just here an incident occurred that came near having a serious ending. As General Sheridan was approaching I noticed one of my sharp-shooters drawing his rifle down upon him. I at once called to him: "Put down your gun, sir; this is a flag of truce." But he simply settled it to his shoulder and was drawing a bead on Sheridan, when I leaned forward and jerked his gun. He struggled with me, but I finally raised it. I then loosed it, and he started to aim again. I caught it again, when he turned his stern white face, all broken with grief and streaming with tears, up to me, and said: "Well, General, then let him keep on his own side." The fighting had continued up to this point. Indeed, after the flag of truce, a regiment of my men, who had been fighting their way through toward where we were, and who did not know of a flag of truce, fired into some of Sheridan's cavalry. This was speedily stopped, however. I showed General Sheridan General Lee's note, and he determined to await events. He dismounted, and I did the same. Then, for the first time, the men seemed to understand what it all meant, and then the poor fellows broke down. The men cried like children. Worn, starved, and bleeding as they were, they had rather have died than have surrendered. At one word from me they would have hurled themselves on the enemy, and have cut their way through or have fallen to a man with their guns in their hands. But I could not permit it. The great drama had been played to its end. But men are seldom permitted to look upon such a scene as the one presented here. That these men should have wept at surrendering so unequal a fight, at being taken out of this constant carnage and storm, at being sent back to their families;

GENERAL LEE LEAVING THE McLEAN HOUSE AFTER THE SURRENDER.

that they should have wept at having their starved and wasted forms lifted out of the jaws of death and placed once more before their hearthstones, was an exhibition of fortitude and patriotism that might set an example for all time.

THE END.

Ah, sir, every ragged soldier that surrendered that day, from the highest to the lowest, from the old veteran to the beardless boy, every one of them, sir, carried a heart of gold in his breast! It made my heart bleed for them, and sent the tears streaming down my face, as I saw them surrender the poor, riddled, battle-stained flags that they had followed so often, and that had been made sacred with the blood of their comrades. The poor fellows would step forward, give up the scanty rag that they had held so precious through so many long and weary years, and then turn and wring their empty hands together and bend their heads in an agony of grief. Their sobs and the sobs of their comrades could be heard for yards around. Others would tear the flags from the staff and hide the precious rag in their bosoms and hold it there. As General Lee rode down the lines with me, and saw the men crying, and heard them cheering "Uncle Robert" with their simple but pathetic remarks, he turned to me and said, in a broken voice: "Oh, General, if it had only been my lot to have fallen in one of our battles, to have given my life to this cause that we could not save!" I told him that he should not feel that way, that he had done all that mortal man

A SOUTHTERN PLANTER'S RESIDENCE IN RUINS.

could do, and that every man and woman in the South would feel this and would make him feel it. "No, no!" he said, "there will be many who will blame me. But, General, I have the consolation of knowing that my conscience approves what I have done, and that the army sustains me."

In a few hours the army was scattered, and the men went back to their ruined and dismantled homes, many of them walking all the way to Georgia and Alabama, all of them penniless, worn out, and well-nigh heartbroken. Thus passed away Lee's army; thus were its last battles fought, thus was it surrendered, and thus was the great American tragedy closed, let us all hope, forever.

PUNISHMENT INFLICTED FOR MINOR OFFENCES

CAMP LIFE.

BY GENERAL SELDEN CONNOR.

A MAJORITY OF SOLDIERS IN THE UNION ARMY WERE YOUNG MEN—THE WAR A COLOSSAL PICNIC—THE ATTRACTIONS OF CAMP LIFE FOR YOUNG MEN—DRILLING AND GUARD DUTY—STYLES OF TENTS USED IN THE ARMY—LOG HUTS FOR WINTER QUARTERS—A NEW USE FOR WELL-SEASONED FENCE RAILS—RISE AND FALL OF A LIGHT "TOWN OF CANVAS"—GENUINE LOVE FOR HARD-TACK—THE TRIALS AND DANGERS OF AN ARMY SUTLER—DRAMATIC AND MINSTREL ENTERTAINMENTS IN CAMP—HORSE-RACING AND THE "DERBY" OF THE ARMY OF THE POTOMAC—CARD-PLAYING AND OTHER GAMES—CAMPS OF NORTHERN SOLDIERS KEPT IN BETTER CONDITION THAN THOSE OF SOUTHERN SOLDIERS—FENCING, BOXING, AND DRILLING—STUDYING GEOLOGY.

FROM one point of view the war for the Union was a colossal picnic. Not that it was in the spirit of a summer holiday, with pure gayety of heart, that a million of the bravest and best of the country took to the tented field to interpose their lives between their country and all that would do her harm. No soldiers were ever more impressed with the serious nature of the contest for which they had enlisted than were those of '61. But the "men" who composed the Union armies were by far and away a majority very young men; they were then really "the boys" in the sight of all the world, as they are now to each other when veteran comrades meet and "Bill" greets "Joe," and the wrongs of time are forgotten in the vividness of their memories of the time when they wore the blue livery and ate the very hard bread of Uncle Sam. They were real human boys, like those of to-day, and as the boys of '76 very likely were; and so, mingled with the glow of patriotic ardor in their breasts, and the determination to do their duty whatever might betide, there was a keen sense of the novelty of the soldier's life. They had read of wars and soldiers from Cæsar to Zack Taylor, and were filled with the traditional pride of American citizens in the heroism and exploits of the men who achieved independence. The greater number of them had recollections, more or less clear, of cheering for Buena Vista and Resaca de la Palma. But wars were "old, unhappy, far-off things," entirely out of date, inconsistent alike with "the spirit of the times" and "the principles of free popular government." "The American boys of this peaceful age would never be called upon"— But, hark! the drum! Partings were sad, with home, kindred, friends. The old life-plans with all their courses, ambitions, hopes, and dreams, were temporarily turned to the wall. There was no room for regrets or forebodings. Duty called, and their country's flag waved its summons to them. War's dangers were before them; but there were in prospect also the experience of a soldier's life, the zest of the sharp change from the dull monotony of peaceful pursuits to the stir and novelty of the camp. They took up the new life with a kind of "fearful joy." It had its drawbacks, but on the whole it had many and strong attractions to lusty and imaginative youth. "It amuses me," said a veteran of the Mexican war to a company just enlisted in a three-months regiment under the President's first call for troops, "to hear you boys talk about coming home when your term of service is out. When you once follow the drum you are bound to keep on just as long as the music lasts." The boys found that the veteran was right. At the conclusion of their three months' service they reënlisted almost, if not quite, to a man, and most of them became officers.

It did not quite suit the dignity of the young soldiers, as free and independent American citizens, to yield implicit obedience to any man, and especially to be "bossed" by officers who, as their neighbors, had no claim to superiority, and to have all their incomings and outgoings regulated by the tap of the drum. When they realized, as they were not long in doing, that officers as well as men had to obey at their peril, and that good discipline was essential to their well-being and efficiency as soldiers, they accepted the situation, and rendered a ready and dutiful obedience.

The secret of the charm of the soldier's life is not far to seek. The soldier is care-free, absolved from that "pernicious liberty of choice" which makes ordinary life weary and anxious, and his responsibility is limited to his well-defined line of duty. Above all, the bond of sympathy is closer than in any other form of association. To pursue the same routine, to go to bed and rise up at a common call, to be served with the same food, drink, and clothes by a common master, to share the same hardships and perils, to own one leadership, and to be engaged in a common purpose with hundreds of thousands of others, constitutes in the highest degree that unity which Cicero found to be the essence of friendship, the bond of nearness and dearness known to the soldier as "comradeship." Allied to this feeling, and aiding to exalt the soldier's profession, is that "esprit de corps" which fills his heart with pride in his company, his regiment, corps, and army. As a rider feels that he shares the sinewy strength of the steed under him, so the soldier, though a unit among thousands, exults in the dread power and beauty of the bounding column or long line of which he forms a part; in the order and precision which transform a multitude of individuals into one terrible engine. The Roman citizen was not more proud of his country than the Union soldier was of his army. A soldier of the Army of the Potomac writes in a home letter dated April, 1863: "I have just taken a ride of about fifteen miles through the army. It is really a sight worth while to go through this vast army and see how admirably everything is conducted. The discipline is fine, the men look healthy and are in the best possible spirits, and the cleanliness of the camps and grounds is a model for housewives." The delights of the gypsy-like way of living of the soldier had a large part in forming the bright side of the new vocation. It seemed good to turn from the comforts and luxuries of easeful homes, and go back to the simple and nomadic habits of the hardy primitive man; to live more closely with Nature, and be subject to her varying moods; to have the sod for a couch, and the winds for a lullaby, and to be constantly familiar with the changing skies from early morning through the day and the watches of the night. The pork and beef boiled in the kettles hung over the campfire, the beans cooked in Dutch ovens buried in the embers, owed their sweet savor to the picturesque manner of the cooking as well as to uncritical appetites sharpened by living in the open air, and by plenty of exercise, drilling, guard duty, and "fatigue." And what feast could compare with the unpurchased chicken broiled on the coals, sweet potatoes roasted in the ashes—trophies of his "bow and spear" in foraging—and his tin cup of ration coffee; the product of the marauder's own culinary skill, over his private fire, served "à la fourchette" and smoking hot; with perhaps the luxury of a soft hoe-cake, acquired by barter of some "auntie," in lieu of the daily hard bread!

Not least among the fascinations of the soldier's life is the uncertain tenure he has of his camp. He has no local habitation. He may flatter himself that the army is going to remain long enough to make it worth his while to provide the comforts and conveniences within the compass of his resources and ingenuity, and when he has fairly established himself and contemplates his work with complacency, the ruthless order comes to "break camp," and down goes his beautiful home as if it were but a child's house of blocks. He grumbles a little at the sacrifice, but the prospect of fresh scenes and adventures is sufficient solace of his disappointment, and he cheerfully makes himself at home again at the next halt of his regiment.

In the matter of habitation the soldier did not pursue the order of the pioneer who begins with a brush lean-to, then builds a log house, and continues building nobler mansions as his labors prosper and fortune smiles, until, maybe, a brownstone front shelters him. The home of the soldier of the War for the Union was, like the bumble-bee, "the biggest when it was born." In 1861 the volunteer regiments were generally fitted out, before leaving their respective States, with tents, wagons, mess furniture, and all other "impedimenta," according to the requirements of army regulations. The tents commonly furnished for the use of the rank and file were the "A" and the "Sibley" patterns. The "A" was wedge-shaped, as its name indicates, and was supposed to quarter five or six men. The "Sibley" was a simple cone, suggested by the Indian "tepee," with an opening at the apex for ventilation and the exit of the smoke of the fire, for which provision was made in the centre of the tent by the use of a tall iron tripod as a foundation for the pole. It comfortably accommodated fifteen or sixteen men, lying feet to the pole, and radiating thence like the spokes of a wheel. This tent, improved by the addition of a curtain, or wall, is now in use by the regular army, and it is known as the "conical wall tent." Officers were provided with wall tents, canvas houses, two to each field or staff officer above the rank of captain, one to each captain, and one to every two subaltern officers. Each company had a "cook tent," and the cooking was done over a fire in the open. The fires of the cooks of companies from the northern lumbering regions could always be distinguished by the "bean holes," in which the covered iron pot containing the frequent "pork and beans," the favorite and distinctive article of Yankee diet, was buried in hot embers and, barring removal by unauthorized hands, allowed to remain all night. The lumberman and the soldier declare that he who has not eaten them cooked in this manner does not really "know beans." The regimental camp of infantry was arranged according to regulations, with such modifications as the nature of the ground might make desirable. The company "streets" were at right angles with the "color line" or "front" on which the regiment was formed, and began ten paces in rear of it. The tents of the "rank and file" of each company were pitched on both sides of its street. In rear of them, with an interval of twenty paces between the lines, and in successive order, was the line of "kitchens," the line of non-commissioned staff, sutler and police guard, the line of company officers, and the line of field and staff officers. In the rear of the camp were the baggage train and officers' horses.

The first winter of the Army of the Potomac was to a large part of the army one of much suffering from cold. The hills of Virginia, along the Potomac, are anything but tropical in the winter. The frequent light snows and rains, followed by thawy, sunny days, produced a moisture in the air which, combined with winds from the mountains, struck a chill to the very marrow of the bones of even the men from the far North accustomed to a much lower temperature but in a dry atmosphere. The commander of the army gave no encouragement to the building of winter quarters, and the prevailing impression was that the army must remain on the *qui vive*, ready to move on slight notice whenever the commander (or the enemy) might give the word. There was plenty of fine timber in the section of country occupied by the army, and it would have been an easy matter to the skilled axemen and mechanics in which most regiments abounded, and entailing comparatively slight expense, to build log huts that would have housed them in comfort and saved many a stout soldier for the impending days of battle. Some commands, either by special permission or taking the responsibility upon themselves, did build huts, and were snugly and warmly housed for months, while their less fortunate or unenterprising neighbors were shivering under their canvas. The rude fireplaces made of stones, with the tenacious Virginia mud for mortar, having chimneys of sticks and clay, or barrels, served fairly well to heat a well-chinked hut; but their small, sputtering fires could make but little impression on the temperature of a space which had only a thin cotton barrier as a defence against the keen wintry blasts. The unnecessary hardships of such exposure inflicted severe loss on the army, especially in those regiments which had been visited in the autumn by that scourge common to new levies, the measles. That disease, though not dangerous in itself, leaves its subjects in an enfeebled condition for a long time after apparent recovery, and incapable of withstanding exposures and ailments ordinarily regarded as slight. In the camps of regiments which had been afflicted with it, the burial party marching with slow and solemn step to the wail of the dirge was an all too frequent ceremony through the long winter, and far from inspiriting to young soldiers, while the number of the dead was as great as that of the slain in a hard-fought battle. Perhaps the relentless necessities attending the hasty gathering and organization of a great army made it difficult or impossible to bestow upon convalescents the care necessary to preserve their lives; but, leaving aside the question of humanity, an intelligent self-interest should have induced the responsible head of the army to make every effort to guard against such deplorable impairment of the strength of his command as arose from causes which seem to have been preventable. If the men who perished miserably on the bleak hillsides of Virginia, and who never had a chance to strike a blow for the cause that was so dear to them, had been sent where they could have received proper care and treatment, the number of these restored to health and strength would have constituted a powerful reinforcement in the following campaign where the cry for help was raised so lustily.

The mistake of the first winter was not repeated. The fact was recognized that the army must go into winter quarters, and timely and adequate preparations to encounter the rigors of the season were made by the whole army. An officer writing from "Camp near White Oak Church, Virginia," in the winter of 1862–63, says: "We have fixed up our camp so that it is quite comfortable. Each squad of four men has its hut, made by digging into the ground a foot or two and then placing on the ground at the sides several logs, and roofing with their shelter tents. At the side they dig a fireplace, and build a chimney outside with sticks and mud. It is Paddy-like, but much more comfortable than no house at all. My 'house' is very nice; it is built up with split hardwood logs about four feet above the ground, and on this foundation my wall tent is pitched, making

HOSPITAL CORPS—AMBULANCE DRILL.

a room nine by nine, with walls six feet high. At one end there is a fine fireplace, which does not smoke at all. I told Captain C., who was just in, that if I had a cat on the hearth it would be quite domestic." The general style of architecture throughout the army was the same; but there were wide differences in the manner of construction and the details of the work. The huts of some commands were rudely built and without uniformity, giving to the camp a mean and squalid appearance, while other camps were very attractive with their rows of solid and trim-looking structures, as like each other as the houses of a builder in a city addition.

The real soldiering and camping began when, after a period of stripping for the campaign by sending the sick to hospitals and all unnecessary baggage to the rear for storage, of outfitting with all the required clothing, arms, equipments, and ammunition, and of repeated inspections and reviews to make sure that everybody and everything was in readiness, the troops were

A NEW RECRUIT BEING INITIATED.

drawn out of winter quarters and put on the march toward the enemy. Every man had to be his own pack animal and carry upon his shoulders and hips his food—rations for one day or a week, according to the nature of the enterprise in hand and the prospect of making a connection with the wagon trains; drink in his canteen; cartridges—a cartridge box full and oftentimes as many more as could be crowded into knapsacks and pockets; and, lastly, his lodging, a woollen blanket and one of rubber, and the oblong piece of cotton cloth which was his part of the "shelter tent." This tent was invented by the French and had long been in use by them. It is one of the most useful articles of the soldier's equipment. It is but a slight addition to his burden, and a very great one to his comfort. Two or more comrades, by buttoning their several sections together, and the use of a few slight sticks, or sticks and cord, can speedily prepare a very effective protection against the dew, the wind, and "the heaviest of the rain." Generally three comrades joined their sections to form a tent; two sections made the sides and one an end, the other end either remaining open to admit the heat of a fire or being closed by a rubber blanket. When four men tented together, which they could do by "packing close," the extra section was used instead of the rubber blanket, and then the squad was very thoroughly housed.

Schiller's word-picture of a military camp vividly recalls to the soldier one of the most characteristic and impressive pictures of his army life:

"Lo there! the soldier, rapid architect!
Builds his light town of canvas, and at once
The whole scene moves and bustles momently.
With arms and neighing steeds, and mirth and quarrel,
The motley market fills: the roads, the streams,
Are crowded with new freights; trade stirs and hurries.
But on some morrow morn, all suddenly,
The tents drop down, the horde renews its march.
Dreary and solitary as a churchyard
The meadows and down-trodden seed-plot lie,
And the year's harvest is gone utterly."

The rise and fall of "the light towns of canvas," movable cities that attended the progress of the army, seemed wonderful and magical. Imagine a broad plantation stretching its sunny acres from river to forest, a vast and lonely area with no signs of human occupancy anywhere, except, perhaps, the toil-bent figures of a few bondservants of the soil at their tasks in the fields, under the eye of the overseer, lending by the unjoyous monotony of their labor an air of gloom and melancholy to the oppressive loneliness of the scene. Suddenly and quietly from the road at the edge of the forest a few horsemen ride into the open, a banneret bearing some cabalistic device fluttering over them, closely followed by a rapidly moving column of men whose gleaming muskets indicate afar off their trade; and presently, when the centre of the regiment breaks into view and Old Glory appears in all its beauty against the background of dark forest, it announces to all who may behold that one of the grand armies of the Republic is on the march. As the regiment emerges in the easy marching disorder of "route step" and "arms at will," it seems to be a confused tide of men flowing steadily along and filling the whole roadway. A few sharp orders ring out, and the throng is transformed almost instantly to a solid military machine; officers take their posts, "files cover," arms are carried uniformly, the cadence step is taken—"short on the right" that the men may "close up" to the proper distance—and, under the guidance of a staff officer, the regiment marches to its assigned camping-ground, where it is brought to a front, arms are stacked, and ranks broken. With whoops and cries expressing their gratification that the day's march is over and a rest is in prospect, the released soldiers scatter, unstrapping their irksome knapsacks and throwing them off with sighs of relief, and betake themselves to the preparation of their temporary home. If there be any prize which these old campaigners have discovered as with wise prevision and hawk-like ken they surveyed their environment in marching to the camping-ground—a comely fence of well-seasoned rails, for instance—they "make a break" for it on the instant of their deliverance from the restraint of discipline, and with a unanimity and alacrity that give little hope of a share to the slow-footed, and fill the hearts of the incoming regiment, not yet released, with envy and unavailing longing. When the scramble is over, and the foragers have swarmed in like ants, laden with their plunder, each squad with practised skill proceeds to its domestic duties. One man pitches the "dog tent," and utilizes any material that may be at hand for making the couch dry and soft. Another, laden with the canteens, explores the hollows and copses for the cool spring of which he has had tantalizing visions on the dusty march. The rest build the fire, if one is needed for warmth, or for cooking in case the wagons containing the company mess kettles and rations are not with the command or have not come up, and therefore every man is left to boil his coffee and fry his pork to his own taste, and lend a hand whenever needed. Every man is expected to contribute of the best that the country affords, and not to be nice as to the method of acquisition, to eke out the plain fare of the marching ration. Foraging in Virginia, except to the cavalry, was not a very prosperous pursuit after the country had been occupied a few months by the army. There was, however, game almost anywhere for those emancipated from vulgar prejudices in the matter of diet, as De Trobriand's Zouaves appear to have been, for he says of them that they "discovered the nutritive qualities of the black snake." The *menu* including a black snake hash suggests a wide range of possibilities. By the time the first arrivals have leisure to look about them, the plain far and near is covered with tents: the "rapid architect" has done his work, and the "light town" is established.

Perhaps before the next morning's sun was high in the heavens the town had disappeared like a scene conjured up by a magician, leaving the plain to resume its wonted loneliness so strangely interrupted.

The routine of camp-life so absorbed the time of the soldier that there was little left to hang heavy on his hands. The odd minutes between drills, roll-calls, police and fatigue duty, could be well utilized in cleaning his musket and equipments, washing and mending his clothes, darning his stockings, procuring fuel, improving his quarters, writing home, and re-reading old letters. After a hard night's duty on camp guard or picket, with sleep on the instalment plan, it was luxury to lie warm and make up the arrears undisturbed by fear of the dread summons, "Fall in, second relief." Very restful it was, too, to stretch out at full length on the spring bunk, made of barrel staves across poles, with a knapsack for a pillow, and indulge in the fragrant briarwood, conversing with comrades of home and friends, or discussing the gossip of the camp. In spring and summer camps each tent commonly had an arbor of foliage for a porch, and when there swung in its shelter a shapely hammock ingeniously woven of withes and grapevines, attached to spring poles driven into the earth, and filled with the balmy tips of cedar boughs, the extreme of sybaritish appointments was attained. It was always in order to hunt for "something to eat," not perhaps so much to appease absolute hunger as to vary the tiresome monotony of the regulation diet. Desirable articles of food were acquired in all ways recognized by civilized peoples as legitimate: by purchase, by barter, and by—right of discovery. In camp and all accessible places on the march the sutler tempted appetites weary of hard-tack and pork, with dry ginger cakes, cheese, dried fruits, and apples in their season. Sardines, condensed milk, and other tinned food preparations were so expensive that they could not be indulged in to a great extent. The canning industry was then in its infancy. If it had then attained its present development, and all kinds of fruits, vegetables, and meats had been accessible to the soldier, he would have been in full sympathy with the Arizona miner who said to his "pard," as they were consuming the customary flapjacks and bacon, "Tom, I hope I shall strike it rich; I should just like to strike it rich."—"Well, Bill, s'pose you should strike it rich, what then?"—"If I should strike it rich, Tom, I'd live on canned goods *one* six months."

Although the old soldier would growl about his hard-tack and feign to have slight regard for it, the sincerity of his attachment was attested by an incident occurring in a command which halted for a few days, after the battle of Gettysburg, at a rural town in Pennsylvania. It was far from the base of supplies, and the commissary's supplies had become exhausted, and he was obliged to purchase flour and issue it to the companies. Having no facilities for baking, they had their flour made into bread at the farmhouses in their vicinity. The bread was fairly good and there was plenty of it; nevertheless, when the wagons appeared laden with the familiar boxes of veteran "squares," cheers went up all along the line as if for a victory or the return of missing comrades.

THE ARMY OF THE POTOMAC.—FIRST YEAR IN WINTER QUARTERS.

(From a War Department Photograph.)

LANDING REINFORCEMENTS FOR FORT PICKENS, FLORIDA, JUNE, 1861.

The sutler was an institution of the camp not to be overlooked. When transportation was safe and not expensive, he kept a general store of everything that officers and men required or could be tempted to buy, save such articles as were prohibited by the Council of Administration which had the general oversight of his business. Where carriage was difficult and dangerous, a choice of articles had to be made in order to supply those most needed. Tobacco and matches were easily first in order of selection. Soldiers of the Army of the Potomac will remember the blue-ended matches that left such a track behind when struck; they touched nothing they did not adorn.

SOLDIERS' WINTER HUTS—TWO VIEWS.

The sutlers of German-American regiments were expected to accomplish the impossible in order to supply lager, Rhine wine, and bolognas. Whenever a fresh stock of such goods had been received, the crowd around the sutler's tent mustered in far greater numbers than appeared at the parade of the regiment. It was popularly considered very desirable to have a German regiment in a brigade. In one respect the sutler's business was a safe one: he could collect at the paymaster's table the sums due him, if he took care not to give men credit in excess of the proportion of their pay permitted by regulations. On the other hand, his profits were in danger of diminution from many quarters. In camp the sutler and his clerks could not always distinguish, among a crowd of customers coming and going, who paid and who did not; storehouses were slight and penetrable, and marauders were watchful and cunning. Those commands were very exceptional that were in Falstaff's condition, "heinously unprovided with a thief." On the march, dangers to the sutler's stock multiplied. To say nothing of ordinary risks attending carriage over bad roads, and of the watchful guerilla, there was always an uneasy feeling in the breast of the purveyor when most surrounded by men in friendly uniform, that there might be "unguarded moments" when the cry, "Rally on the sutler," would be followed by a speedy division of his goods, leaving him lamenting. Personally the sutler was generally a prudent and tactful man, and gained the goodwill of his customers by an obliging disposition and a readiness to take a joke even if it was a little rough and at his expense. When the command was in the field he made himself especially serviceable as a medium of communication with the "base," and many and various were the commissions he was called upon to execute.

Camp life had its diversions in addition to the many interesting and enjoyable features of the daily round of duties. Military life in itself is necessarily spectacular, abounding in scenes of animation and display. He must be of an unsusceptible nature and void of enthusiasm who is indifferent to the splendid pageantry which attends the business of war; whose senses are not pleased and imagination excited by charging squadrons, batteries dashing across the field with a rumble and clang suggestive of the thunderbolts they bear, and by "heavy and solemn" battalions moving with perfect order and precision to the stormy music of martial airs, with banners flying, rows of bright arms reflecting the rays of the sun in streams of silver light, and horses proudly caracoling in excited enjoyment of the music, the glitter, and the movement.

Such spectacles thrill the breast of the soldier with pride in his profession, and cause him to feel that

"All else to noble hearts is dross,
All else on earth is mean."

The daily ceremonies of "guard mounting" and "dress parade," and the frequent reviews and brigade and division drills, afforded splendid entertainments, entirely gratuitous except the contribution of personal services. Candor compels the admission that the soldier sometimes considered the show dear at the price. When weather and ground were favorable, the men played the game that then passed for "ball"—not so warlike an affair as the present contest by that name—and pitched quoits, using horse-shoes, when attainable, for that purpose. The Virginia winter often afforded material for snowballing, and there were occasions when whole regiments in order of battle were pitted against each other in mimic warfare, filling the air with snowy pellets, and Homeric deeds were done. Theatrical and minstrel entertainments were given by "native talent," and were liberally patronized. The first warm days of spring opened the season of horse-racing. The "Derby" of the Army of the Potomac was St. Patrick's Day. Running and hurdle races were held on a grand scale. The fine horses and their dashing riders, the grand stand filled with generals and staff officers, visiting dignitaries and ladies, the band composed of many regimental bands consolidated for the occasion and pouring forth a perfect Niagara of sound, mounted officers and soldiers in thousands occupying the central space of the track, and General Meagher, in the costume of "a fine old Irish gentleman," presiding as grand patron of the races—all combined, with the military accessories of glittering uniforms and comparisons, to make a scene of unusual animation and brilliancy. For "fireside games" the various inventions played with the well-thumbed pack of cards were greatly in favor. Sometimes it was a simple, innocent game "just to pass away the time." At other times it was a serious contest resulting to the unfortunate in "passing away" all that was left him of his last pay and perhaps an interest in his next stipend. The colored retainers and camp followers were generally votaries of the goddess of chance and were skilled in getting on her blind side. One day Major Blank, a gallant officer of the staff, was showing a friend some tricks with cards. Bob, his colored boy, was apparently very busy brushing up the quarters and setting things to rights, paying no attention to the exhibition. The next day the major saw his retainer counting over a whole fistful of greenbacks. "Why, Bob," said he, "where did you get all that money?" Bob, looking up with a grin and a chuckle: "I'se down ter de cavalry last night, major, and dem fellers down dar didn't know nuffin 'bout dat little trick wid de jacks what you's showin' to de cunnel." Bob had tasted the sweets of philosophy, and proved that "knowledge is power." The colored "boys" who came into camp when the army was in the enemy's country, for the purpose of gazing at the "Linkum" soldiers, or marching along with them in any capacity that would give them rations, gave much entertainment to their hosts by their simplicity, their stolidness, or their accomplishments as whistling, singing, or dancing darkies. The morning after "Williamsburg," half a dozen boys from some plantation in the vicinity came near several officers grouped about a fire. "Good morning, boys," said Captain C., "where did you all come from?"—"We come from Marsa Jones's place, right over yer," said the spokesman. "We h'ar de fightin' goin' on yes'erday, an' we jes come over dis mornin' to see about it and see you all."—"Do you think, boys," resumed the captain, "that it is quite the polite thing to wear such clothes as you have on when you come to visit gentlemen of President Lincoln's army?"—"Dese yer's de bes' close we got," was the earnestly uttered reply. "You must certainly have better hats than those?"—"No! no! no!" came in chorus, "we has only one hat to w'ar."—"It is a shame," said the captain, drawing a memorandum book from his pocket with a business-like air and poising his pencil, "that such good-looking boys as you are should only have one hat, and such bad ones at that; I must send back to Fortress Monroe and have some hats sent up for you. What kind of a hat do you want?" addressing himself to the spokesman. "I wants a low-crowned hat, massa," was the quick and earnest response; and then each boy in turn eagerly expressed his personal preference, "I wants a wide-rimmed hat," "I wants a hat ter fit me," etc., until the order was completed and apparently taken down by the guileful scribe. Their confidence made the deceit so easy as to greatly dull the point of the practical joke. Maybe they never questioned the good faith of their generous friend, and ascribed the non-delivery of the hats to other causes than his neglect.

It was not often that a camp had such a sensational and pleasurable incident as that which occurred to the First Vermont volunteer infantry, a three months' regiment, at Newport News, in the summer of 1861. The Woodstock company formed a part of the detachment of that regiment, which participated in the unfortunate expedition to Big Bethel; and on the return of the company, private Reuben Parker was missing. The company had been somewhat broken up in making an attack in the woods. Several men remembered seeing Parker, who was a brave fellow and a skilled rifleman, somewhat in advance of the rest of the company, busily loading and firing. Some were even quite sure they had seen him fall. Days and weeks having passed without his appearance or any further news of him, there seemed no doubt about his fate, and he was reported "killed in action." Funeral services were held at his hoi in Vermont, and his wife and children put on mourning for the lost husband and father. One day the surprising and joyful report spread swiftly through the camp, that Parker was alive and had returned. He came from Richmond under the escort of two Louisiana "tigers," sent in for exchange. He had been taken prisoner uninjured and carried to Richmond, where he enjoyed the distinction of being the first Yankee captive exhibited in that city, and the first occupant of "the Libby." Parker was the lion of the day for many days after his return to the company, and his accounts of the colloquies he held with curious rebels, and of the insults and revilings he was subjected to in prison, made him in great request among his comrades. His case was the first of the instances occurring in the war when Southern prisons "yawned" and yielded "their dead unto life again."

Mr. H. V. Redfield, whose home in Lower East Tennessee was visited several times by both the Union and the Confederate armies, observed and noted some of the differing characteristics of the two sides. It was the opinion of his neighbors that they would see none of the soldiers throughout the war, because they "could not get their cannon over the mountains." But it was not long before they learned to their cost that mountains offered no insurmountable obstacles to modern armies, or to their artillery either.

The first time that it dawned upon the inhabitants of this section that there was a possible fighting chance for the North, and that one Southern soldier was not necessarily equal to five from the North, was after the Confederate defeat at Mill Spring, Ky., where Zollicoffer was killed. The Confederate panic was so complete and so lasting, that some of the refugees ran fully one hundred and fifty miles from the scene of battle before they dared stop to take their breath and rest. They arrived wild-eyed and in confusion, and not only to the men themselves, but to all the neighborhood, it was an "eye-opener" as to the fact that there was a war on hand that was likely to last until there had been some hard fighting on both sides.

It was not long after this that General Floyd, the disloyal Secretary of War, who had done so much before his resignation to prepare the South for the conflict, came to Lower Tennessee in his flight from Fort Donelson. He sent for the Northern men in the town, and told them, in explanation of his flight from Donelson, that he would "never be captured in this war. I have a long account to settle with the Yankees, and they can settle it in hell!"

The Southern soldiers were always prone to talk back at their officers, lacking the discipline which was quickly established in the Union army; and when they suffered defeat they took it as a personal disappointment, for which they meant to get even with the Yanks after the war; and they also had a bad habit of laying the responsibility for every reverse on the shoulders of their superiors. When General Bragg retreated through Tennessee, his men were greatly cast down, though they insisted that their retreat did not mean that they were whipped, which they insisted they were not. "It is bad enough," said one of the soldiers, "to run when we are whipped; but d——n this way of beating the Yankees and then running away from them!" One of them was asked where they were retreating to. "To Cuba," he said angrily, "if old Bragg can get a bridge built across from Florida." A horse trade was proposed on this retreat, between two soldiers whose horses were pretty well spent, and a farmer who was willing to exchange fresher ones for these and a bonus. One of the soldiers objected to the horse that was offered to him, because it had a white face that the enemy could see for a mile. "Oh, that's no objection," said his companion; "it's the other end of Bragg's cavalry that is always toward the Yankees."

At the beginning of the war the Confederate cavalry was rather the better mounted, because so many of the men owned their own horses; but as the original supply gave out, and the renewing of the mounts became a question of the respective ability of the governments to furnish the best animals, this difference changed in favor of the Northern cavalry. Also, at the beginning the Confederates were by far the best riders, as might be expected of a race of men who spent much time in the saddle before the war. But it was not long before the Union cavalryman learned to ride, too, and then, with better horses, better equipments, and better fodder, the efficiency of the cavalry of the North was superior.

Before the war had gotten very far along, the greater facility of the Union Government for equipping, subsisting, and generally preparing its army, brought about a contrast between the two hostile armies distinctly favorable to that of the North. The Union men were better fed. To be sure, the Confederates had plenty of tobacco, while often the Union troops were rather short of that luxury, and were ready to make trades with the pickets of the enemy in order to secure it. But the Unionists had plenty of coffee, and that good, while coffee was an item that quickly disappeared from the Southern bill of fare. Meat and flour also became scarce, and througn a good many campaigns corn-meal was the staple of the Confederate diet. The advantage of having coffee appeared in some cases to be a distinct military advantage. The story is told of a man who had volunteered in the Confederate army, and had been captured, paroled, and sent home. The Union army presently encamped near his home, and his two boys went down to camp to take a look around; and when some friends whom they met there regaled them with all the crackers and coffee they wanted, they made up their minds to enlist under Uncle Sam just to get an amount and quality of "grub" to which they had long been strangers. The old man was much disturbed, and went down to see what he could do to get the boys out of the scrape. But he found that he himself was like the man who said he could "resist anything except temptation," for his first taste of the Yankee coffee seduced him from his allegiance to the Stars and Bars, and he, too, enlisted for the war. This story is vouched for as a fact, illustrating the seductive power of a good commissariat for the enticement of recruits.

PRESIDENT LINCOLN VISITING CAMP.

The Northern soldier was the best clothed, and the clothing was uniform, which could not be said of that of the Southern soldier, who, although he was supposed to be dressed in gray or butternut, was really dressed in whatever he could pick up, which often did not include overcoats or oil-blankets. Supplied with good materials, and plenty of them, the Northern soldier was expected to take care of them, and he did so. But the Confederate soldier seldom took care to keep his weapons bright and free from dirt and rust. The Confederate lacked thoroughness in his camp housekeeping; he almost never fixed up the little comfortable arrangements that characterized a Union camp, if occupied for any length of time, nor did he "police" his camp carefully, to keep it neat or even clean, the lack of ordinary cleanliness being so marked as really to contribute materially to losses through disease. The way in which the Union soldier made even a temporary camp homelike was well described by an army correspondent, Benjamin F. Taylor: "No matter where or when you halt them, they are at once at home. They know precisely what to do first, and they do it. I have seen them march into a strange region at dark, and almost as soon as the fires would show well they were twinkling all over the field, the Sibley cones rising like the work of enchantment everywhere, and the little dog-tents lying snug to the ground, as if, like the mushrooms, they had grown there, and the aroma of coffee and tortured bacon suggesting creature comforts, and the whole economy of life in canvas cities moving as steadily on as if it had never been intermitted. The movements of regiments are as blind as fate. Nobody can tell to-night where he will be to-morrow, and yet with the first glimmer of morning the camp is astir, and the preparations begin for staying there forever. An axe, a knife, and a will are tools enough for a soldier house-builder. He will make the mansion and all its belongings of red cedar, from the ridge-pole to the forestick, though a couple of dog-tents stretched from wall to wall will make a roof worth thanking the Lord for. Having been mason and joiner, he turns cabinetmaker; there are his table, his chairs, his sideboard; he glides into upholstery, and there is his bed of bamboo, as full of springs and comfort as a patent mattress. He whips out a needle and turns tailor; he is not above the mysteries of the saucepan and camp-kettle; he can cook, if not quite like a Soyer, yet exactly like a soldier, and you may believe that he can eat you hungry when he is in trim for it. Cosey little cabins, neatly fitted, are going up; here is a boy making a fireplace, and quite artistically plastering it with the inevitable red earth; he has found a crane somewhere, and swung up thereon a two-legged dinner-pot; there a fellow is finishing out a chimney with brick from an old kiln of secession proclivities; yonder a bower-house, closely interwoven with evergreen, is almost ready for the occupants; the avenues between the lines of tents are cleared and smoothed—'policed,' in camp phrase; little seats with cedar awnings in front of the tents give a cottage-look, while the interior, in a rude way, has a genuine homelike air. The bit of looking-glass hangs against the cotton wall; a handkerchief of a carpet just before the bunk marks the stepping-off place to the land of dreams; a violin case is strung to a convenient hook, flanked by a gorgeous picture of some hero of somewhere, mounted upon a horse rampant and saltant, 'and what a length of tail behind!'

"The business of living has fairly begun again. There is hardly an idle moment; and save here and there a man brushing up his musket, getting that 'damned spot' off his bayonet, burnishing his revolver, you would not suspect that these men had but one terrible errand. They are tailors, they are tinkers, they are writers; fencing, boxing, cooking, eating, drilling—those who say that camp life is a lazy life know little about it. And then the reconnoissances 'on private account;' every wood, ravine, hill, field, is explored; the productions, animal and vegetable, are inventoried, and one day renders them as thoroughly conversant with the region round about as if they had been dwelling there a lifetime. Soldiers have interrogation points in both eyes. They have tasted water from every spring and well, estimated the corn to the acre, tried the watermelons, bagged the peaches, knocked down the persimmons, milked the cows, roasted the pigs, picked the chickens; they know who lives here and there and yonder, the whereabouts of the native boys, the names of the native girls. If there is a curious cave, a queer tree, a strange rock anywhere about, they know it. You can see them with chisel, hammer, and haversack, tugging up the mountain, or scrambling down the ravine, in a geological passion that would have won the right hand of fellowship from Hugh Miller, and home they come with specimens that would enrich a cabinet. The most exquisite fossil buds just ready to open, beautiful shells, rare minerals, are collected by these rough and dashing naturalists."

In the larger equipments of the army there was again a superiority in those of the North. Their wagon trains were better, the wagons of a uniform style, and they were marked with the name of regiment and brigade, so that there never was any doubt as to where a stray wagon belonged. The Confederate wagons were of all sorts and shapes and sizes, a job lot, ill-matched, ill-kept, and ill-arranged, and the harnesses were patchwork of inferior strength.

Residents of the South observed with pain one distinction between the armies, which reminds one of Henry W. Grady's remark about General Sherman, that he was a smart man, "but mighty careless about fire." Encamped in a Southern community, a Southern army was careful not to forage promiscuously, or appropriate to its own uses the various provisions and live-stock of the non-combatant people who lived near. But the Northern troops had a feeling that they were in the enemy's

AN OLD-FASHIONED TRAINING DAY.

country and that they were entitled to live on it. There were orders against unauthorized foraging; but the temptation to bring into camp an occasional chicken, sundry pigs, cows, vegetables, and in some cases even money and jewelry, is said by Southern residents to have sometimes overcome a soldier here and there; so that the visit of a Northern army was the signal for the good people of the neighborhood to get as much of their belongings out of sight as possible. What was taken in this way was taken without the formality of a request, of payment, or of a receipt given, except when the victim claimed to be a loyal Unionist. The Southern soldiers usually paid for what they took, even if it was in Confederate script; but the Northern pillagers did not do even that. Those who recall and chronicle this habit, admit that it was due in great measure to the foreign element in the Northern army, and to the recruits from the large cities, elements which in the Confederate army were comparatively scarce.

The practical jokes that were played on some of the Southern farmers illustrate the tendency on the part of the Northern soldier to "do" a rebel. One farmer drove into a Union camp with a forty-gallon barrel of cider, which he sold by the quart to the men, over the side of his wagon. He was astonished to find that his barrel was empty after he had sold only about twenty quarts, and on investigating the cause, he discovered that while he was engaged in peddling the cider over the side board, some soldiers had put an auger through the bottom of his wagon and into the barrel, and had drawn the rest off into their canteens. Another trader lost the contents of a barrel of brandy which he had stored in a shanty overnight, in a similar manner; while several farmers concluded that it was in vain to go to the Yankee camp with wagon loads of apples or other fruit, unless they had a detachment to guard every side of the wagon, for while they dealt fair over one side, their stock would disappear over the other. One who had suffered in this way came to the conclusion that "the Yankees could take the shortening out of a gingercake without breaking the crust."

SOUTHERN SPIES AND SCOUTS IN THE WAR.

BY F. G. DE FONTAINE.

THE INGENIOUS DEVICE OF A WOMAN—DESPATCHES CONCEALED UNDER THE HIDE OF A DOG—"DEAF BURKE," THE MAN OF MANY DISGUISES—FREQUENT COMMUNICATIONS BETWEEN THE LINES—BISCUIT A MEDIUM OF CORRESPONDENCE—DEATH OF COON HARRIS AT SHILOH—A BOLD UNION SPY—AN EXECUTION AT FRANKLIN, TENN.

THE secret service or "spy" system of the South did not differ greatly from that of the North. There may have been in that section a lack of available gold with which to pay expenses when desirable information was required, but there was certainly no absence of courage or patriotism on the part of those who were willing to risk their lives or imprisonment in the event of capture. This was especially true of Southern women; and those who are familiar with their achievements in this field of war will bear witness to the shrewdness, persistence, and fidelity with which they often pursued their dangerous investigations.

One or two incidents will illustrate. It was of the utmost importance to General Beauregard, in 1862, to learn the strength of McClellan's army and whatever facts might relate to his suspected designs on Centreville, Va. For this mission a woman was chosen. She was a young widow whose husband had been killed at the second battle of Manassas; a Virginian of gentle birth; prior to the war a resident of Washington, and a frequent visitor in the society circles of Baltimore, Philadelphia, and New York. Making her way across the lines, she promptly entered upon her task, and through trusty agents was soon enabled to obtain a complete roster of the Federal army, together with much valuable information concerning its probable movements. She was absent two months.

Returning at the end of this time, she crossed the Potomac opposite Dumfries, Va., an outpost then under the command of Col. (afterward Gen.) Wade Hampton, and the fair spy was promptly forwarded to the Confederate headquarters at Centreville. Her baggage consisted of a small grip-sack and a tiny Scotch terrier. Warmly welcomed by Beauregard, she proceeded with true womanly volubility to entertain him with a description of her adventures and their result. The general patiently permitted the lingual freshet to flow on without interruption, supposing that when she got tired she would produce the expected despatches from other secret agents in the North. But the little woman's tongue seemed to be hung in the middle and to wag at both ends; moreover, she was too pretty to be abruptly silenced by the polite creole commander.

Finally, unable to restrain his anxiety any longer, he said, "Well, Mrs. M., I shall be glad to see your papers."—"I didn't dare to bring them on my person," was the reply; "it was unsafe. In fact, I have been suspected and searched already, and so I familiarized myself with their contents. You see it is fortunate that I have a good memory." At this remark, Beauregard showed his chagrin, and frankly told the lady he could place but little reliance on her memory of so many figures and details, and therefore that her mission had proved of little use.

Listening to his scolding with a demure air, and looking at him with a mischievous twinkle in her eye, she called her dog: "Here, Floy!" The Skye terrier jumped in her lap. "General, have you a knife about you?" The knife was produced. Then she turned the animal over on its back, and, to the amazement of Beauregard, deliberately proceeded to rip him open. In less time than it takes to tell the story, she held in one hand the precious papers and in the other the skin of the Skye terrier, while prancing about the floor was a diminutive black-and-tan pup overjoyed at his relief from an extra cuticle.

The shrewd woman had sewed the despatches between the two skins in a manner that defied detection, and under the very noses of the Federal outposts had brought through the lines some of the most important information transmitted during the war. It is needless to say that Beauregard was delighted, and it was but a little while after this incident that McClellan advanced on Centreville only to find deserted camps, batteries of "Quaker guns," and the Confederate army falling back toward Richmond and Yorktown.

* * * * *

Combining in his person the qualities of scout, sharp-shooter, dare-devil, and spy, a Texan known as "Deaf Burke" made himself famous among the higher officers of Longstreet's corps during the early part of the war. Like Terry of Texas, afterward notorious in California, Adams of Mississippi, Mason of Virginia (brother of the United States senator who with Slidell of Louisiana, became the subject of international complications with England), and many other daring spirits, he was at first merely a volunteer or independent fighter subject to no orders; but his temerity in passing the lines, mingling in disguise with Union officers and soldiers, and his adroitness in securing valuable information quickly brought him to the notice of Lee and Longstreet. He was about forty-five years of age, a natural mimic and dialectician—could talk to you like a simpleton from the backwoods, or a thoroughbred gentleman—and he never lost his nerve. Not far from the Potomac, the writer met him in the garb of a Quaker, but only recognized him at night when incidentally he became a tent mate. Then it was learned that he had just returned from Washington, where during the preceding three weeks he had mingled among Southern sympathizers and secured the information for which he had been sent. Prior to this, disguised as an old farmer living in Fairfax County, Va., he had driven a load of wood across the Federal lines. In one of the logs were concealed the despatches intended for headquarters. Later in the war, when transferred to the West, he distinguished himself as one of twelve sharp-shooters chosen to handle as many Whitworth rifles that had been imported; and still later was killed in battle among the Texans, of whom it was his pride to be considered one.

The comparative ease with which communications were established between the lines is further illustrated by an incident. General Rosecrans and a portion of his staff, when in Tennessee, occupied a mansion not far from the outposts of the two armies. The hostess, Mrs. Thomas, was the wife of a Confederate colonel whose regiment was but a few miles distant. Her negro cook made excellent biscuit, which had become the subject of frequent comment at the table, the general being especially pleased. Mrs. Thomas taking advantage of this circumstance, and her acquaintance with him, suggested the propriety of sending some of the warm breakfast to their mutual friend—her husband. Rosecrans readily agreed, and under his own flag of truce, and through one of his own orderlies, a package of biscuit was duly forwarded to Colonel Thomas with an open letter from his wife. Two hours later, the Confederate officer was in possession of all the available secrets at Federal headquarters, and for weeks afterward the bake oven was the mute agent of communications, some of which proved important to the Southern commanders. The housewife had enclosed her tissue-written missives in the pastry, and the ruse was not discovered until after the war, when the story was told to mutual friends.

PAULINE CUSHMAN.
(A Federal Spy.)

In the category of Southern women who in one way or another made their way through the lines, might be included many who carried to the Confederacy supplies of quinine and other articles that could be easily concealed on the person. It is safe to say that hundreds passed backward and forward across the borders of Virginia and Maryland, and with but rare exception their native shrewdness enabled them to escape the vigilance of the pickets on guard.

The bravery of Northern spies in the South is a theme not to be forgotten in this connection. Before General Sherman in his "March to the Sea" reached the several cities through which he was to pass, one or more of his secret agents was sure to be found mingling sociably among the residents. In Savannah, a gentleman appeared as a purchaser of the old wines for which that city was once famous, and remained undiscovered until the end came. In Charleston, news was communicated to the Union officers through the medium of two or three whites and of negroes who made their way to the islands on the coast, and there met and delivered to waiting boats' crews the papers consigned to their care. In Columbia, S. C., an officer wearing the uniform of the Confederate navy visited the best families for more than a month; escorted young ladies to fairs held for the benefit of army hospitals and other entertainments, and made himself generally popular. One of these newly made acquaintances was the daughter of the mayor. After Sherman entered, and the conflagration that destroyed the city was in progress, he repaired to her house and tendered his services. Then for the first time she learned the truth of the saying that she had "entertained an angel unawares." He aided materially in saving the property of the family and affording desired protection.

BELL BOYD.
(A Confederate Spy.)

The task of a spy in the army was not so easy. It was full of personal danger. Success meant the praise of his superiors and possible promotion. Failure might mean an ignominious death. After the battle of Shiloh, or Pittsburg Landing as it is sometimes known, one Coon Harris, a Tennesseean, went through the Confederate army without detection, but in a skirmish a few days afterward he was captured while acting as guide to a column moving to attack a weak point in the Confederate lines. Bragg was in command, and the poor fellow had but a short shrift. Tried by a drum-head court martial, he was sentenced to be shot at daylight.

In his calm demeanor he illustrated how a brave man animated by a high principle can die. There was no pageantry, no clergyman with his last rites, no nothing, save a handful of curious spectators following a rude army wagon wherein, on a rough box called by courtesy a coffin, sat unbound a middle-aged farmer in his butternut suit, riding to his death. Not the closest observer could have discovered any difference in coolness between him and a bystander. Arriving at the place of execution he jumped lightly from the wagon, lingered a moment to see his coffin removed, and then sauntered carelessly down the little valley to the tree beneath which he was to meet his fate.

The ceremony was brief. The officer in charge of the shooting squad asked him if he had any final message to leave. "Yes," was the reply; "tell my family that my last thoughts were of them, and that I died doing my duty to my State and country!" Then his arms were pinioned, the faded brown coat was buttoned across his breast, and he sat down upon his coffin. A handkerchief was tied over his eyes, and voluntarily he laid his head back against the tree. Even now, preserving his remarkable self-possession, he called for a piece of tobacco, and, chewing upon it vigorously, occupied several seconds in adjusting his head to the bark of the tree, as one would fit himself to a pillow before going to sleep. Then he quietly said, "Boys, ready!"

A file of eight men stepped forward until within ten paces of the doomed man; the order was given to "Fire!" and with a splash of brains, and a trickling rivulet of blood down his hairy breast, the soul of the brave man passed into the keeping of the Creator.

During the first march of the Confederate army into Maryland, a handsome young fellow, one Charles Mason, who gave his home as Perrysville, Penn., boldly intercepted a courier who was carrying an order. "What division do you belong to?" he inquired. "Longstreet's," was the reply; "what's yours?" asked the courier. "Jackson's." The presence of a gray uniform favored this statement, and the two rode together. The courier, however, observed a disposition on the part of his companion to drop behind, and suddenly was confronted by a pistol and a demand for the delivery of his despatches. Not being promptly forthcoming, the spy fired, secured the papers, and galloped away. The Confederate lived long enough to describe his assailant and make his identification certain.

A few hours afterward the man became a victim to his own daring. Riding up to the head of a column, he said to the general in command: "I am from General Jackson; he desires me to request you to halt and await further orders."—"I am not in the habit of receiving my orders from General Jackson," answered the officer; "what command do you belong to?" Hesitating an instant, the spy said: "To the Hampton Legion." "In whose brigade and division is that?" continued the general. The pretended courier confessed that he had forgotten. Taken into custody, a search revealed his true character. On his person were found shorthand and other notes, a pair of lieutenant's shoulder straps, and other evidences of his calling. A drumhead court martial was promptly convened, and he was sentenced to be hanged then and there. He met his fate stoically, and without other expressed regret save that, since his mission had been a failure, he could not die the death of a soldier.

"On June 9, 1863," wrote a correspondent of the Nashville *Press*, "two strangers rode into the Union camp, at Franklin, Tenn., and boldly presented themselves at Colonel Baird's headquarters. They wore Federal regulation trousers and caps, the latter covered with white flannel havelocks, and carried side arms. Both showed high intelligence. One claimed to be a colonel in the United States army, the other a major, and they represented that they were inspecting the outposts and defences. Official papers purporting to be signed by General Rosecrans, and also from the War Department at Washington, seemed to confirm this statement. So impressive was their manner, in fact, that Colonel Baird, at the request of the elder officer, loaned him fifty dollars, the plea being that they had been overhauled by the enemy and had lost their wardrobe and purses.

"Just before dark they left camp, saying they were going to Nashville, and started in that direction. Suddenly, said Colonel Baird, in describing the occurrence, the thought flashed upon him that they might be spies; and turning to Colonel Watkins, of the Sixth Kentucky cavalry, who was standing near by, he ordered him to go in pursuit. Being overtaken, they were placed under arrest, and General Rosecrans was informed by telegraph. He quickly answered that he knew nothing of the men, and had given no passes of the kind described.

"With this evidence in hand their persons were searched, and various papers still further showing their guilt were found. On the major's sword was found etched the name, 'Lieutenant W. G. Peter, Lieutenant Confederate Army.' They then confessed.

"Colonel Baird at once telegraphed the facts to General Rosecrans, and asked what should be done. The reply was: 'Try them by a drum-head court martial, and if found guilty, hang them immediately.' The court was convened, and before daylight the prisoners knew they must die. A little after nine o'clock that morning the whole garrison was marshalled around the place of execution, the guards, in tribute to their gallantry, being ordered to march with arms reversed. The unfortunate men made no complaint of the severity of their punishment, but regretted, as brave men might do, the ignominy of being hung, and a few hours afterward both were buried in the same grave."

The history of the war on both sides is full of similar instances of daring, and since the curtain has fallen upon the bloody drama, and the voices of passion are hushed amid the anthems of peace, it is no longer in the hearts of true Americans to withhold the honor that belongs to all our heroes, whether they wore the blue or the gray.

NORTHERN SPIES AND SCOUTS IN THE WAR.

BY HENRY W. B. HOWARD.

IS THE RÔLE OF A SPY DISHONORABLE?—THE SPY A NECESSARY ELEMENT IN A CAMPAIGN—REMARKABLE HEROISM—ONE OF GENERAL GRANT'S SPIES—HOW HE ESCAPED BEING BURIED ALIVE—THE FIGHT OF A SPY WITH A BLOODHOUND—THE PERILOUS ADVENTURES OF CAPTAIN LEIGHTON, OF MICHIGAN—THE VARIED AND THRILLING ADVENTURES OF COL. L. C. BAKER—HIS EXPERIENCES AS A YANKEE SPY IN RICHMOND—MISS EMMA EDMONDS, A NOTED NORTHERN SPY—PASSING THROUGH THE CONFEDERATE LINES DISGUISED AS A NEGRO BOY—A FEMALE UNION SPY IN THE CONFEDERATE CAVALRY.

MILITARY writers have not been entirely agreed as to whether the rôle of spy is an honorable part to play in warfare. Much stress has been laid on the necessarily disgraceful nature of a calling that can justly subject one to the hangman. The ignominy of this punishment is held to relieve all soldiers from the *duty* of service as spies, even under orders, and in consequence all spies are necessarily volunteers. But it is agreed, on the other hand, that the death penalty which is inevitable for the detected spy is intended, not as a punishment for the individual, but as a measure of preventing the spy from carrying on his work, so full of danger to his enemy. This lack of personal responsibility is so well understood, that a spy successful in his expedition is not liable to death after its completion, and

BRIGADIER-GENERAL RANDALL LEE GIBSON.

MAJOR-GENERAL ARNOLD ELZEY.

BRIGADIER-GENERAL ROGER A. PRYOR.

BRIGADIER-GENERAL THOMAS L. CLINGMAN.

BRIGADIER-GENERAL EPPA HUNTON.

BRIGADIER-GENERAL A. R. LAWTON.

BRIGADIER-GENERAL M. W. GARY.

LIEUTENANT-GENERAL SIMON B. BUCKNER.

MAJOR-GENERAL PIERCE M. B. YOUNG.

MAJOR-GENERAL HENRY W. ALLEN.

MAJOR-GENERAL WILLIAM SMITH.

A GROUP OF CONFEDERATE OFFICERS.

if subsequently captured in battle may not be executed for having previously been a spy.

But however at variance they may be as to the nature of his calling, all critics are of one mind in regarding the work of the spy an absolutely necessary element in the conduct of a campaign by the commander. Without it, he would be at a loss as to the most essential facts that must govern his movements. The strength of the enemy, the nature and advantages of his position, the best approaches to it, the ground commanded by his batteries, as well as his intentions—all these and many other details must be in some degree known to a commander who would direct his troops with safety or success. Some of this information he can pick up from resident non-combatants; some he can wrest from his unwilling prisoners; some he can purchase from treacherous members of the force opposing him. But for most of it he is absolutely dependent on the brave men in his own command who are willing, for the sake of their cause, to risk the death that awaits the spy caught in the enemy's country.

These men certainly cannot be regarded with the contempt which a commander feels for the mere tools of whose treachery, cupidity, or indifference he avails himself while scorning the instrument. And, if not that, then they must be regarded as heroic even beyond those of their fellows who are as brave as lions on the field of battle. For their mission is a solitary one, and they have none of the cheering companionship and stimulating emulation that bring courage for the charge. Instead of being under fire for a few brief moments or hours, their nerves are on the rack for days and weeks. With no commanding officer to obey as he orders them here or there, they are thrown on their own resources in the most perilous and trying situations. They must avoid dangerous meetings, disarm suspicions, turn aside questions, invent lies by the hundred without having one contradict another. A constant play of quick wits, steady nerves, and, at the right moment, prompt and courageous physical force, elevates the work of a spy to a fine art, in comparison with which the mere enthusiastic bravery of the battlefield is child's play. Darkly threatening throughout all this perilous work is the imminent and ever-present risk of detection, with its certainty of a death, not glorious like that of those who fall in the hand-to-hand conflict, not the ordinary fortune of war like that of the sharp-shooter's victim brought down at long range, not even invested with the pathos of a death, however sudden, among sympathizing comrades—but the death of a dog, promptly dealt out, without a friendly face among the spectators.

A good illustration of the consummate skill, coolness of head, and strength of will and nerve required in this duty was given by a scout named Hancock, attached to General Grant's army in Virginia. He had failed to escape detection, and was sent under guard to Castle Thunder, in Richmond. His situation was most perilous; but this did not prevent his utilizing his innate joviality to lighten the life of his fellow-prisoners, and bringing his wonderful power of facial expression to bear on the great object of his own escape. In the midst of one of his songs in the prison he suddenly threw up his hands with a cry, fell to the ground in a heap, and lay there so obviously dead that the post surgeon—not over-solicitous to keep a Yankee above ground—pronounced him a case for the grave-digger, and he was bundled into a pine coffin and started on his last journey. But when the driver reached the burying-place, the coffin was empty. Hancock had dexterously slid from the wagon, and, it being night, had joined the followers on foot without detection. When the driver reported back to the prison, the trick was suspected, and a sharp lookout was ordered, which he evaded in the most unexpected way. He went direct to the best hotel in Richmond and registered from Georgia, had a good night's rest, and spent the following day, in the character of a government contractor, in learning what he wanted to know about the city. He was twice arrested by the guards, and escaped the first time through the intervention and identification of the hotel clerk. The second time he was returned to the prison, where for seven days he concealed his identity by assuming a squint and a distortion of feature, which he abandoned when he learned that imprisonment was all he had to fear, as by that time the war was virtually over. Ten days later he was set at liberty with his fellow-prisoners.

The peril of a spy's career is not intermittent, like that of active fighting; it is continuous. A moment may give him his liberty or may bring him face to face with death. An unnamed scout of the Army of the Potomac—so many of these heroic men are even to this day unnamed—had collected his intelligence in the enemy's country, and had arrived close to the stream beyond which were the Union lines. In the darkness of the night, with the sense of danger keen within him, he groped his way along the shore, seeking the skiff he had concealed there for his return. To his horror it dawned on him that he had missed his landmark and could not find the boat. There he stood, the evidences of his calling unmistakably on him, knowing that he had been suspected and followed, and realizing that only a few minutes were his in which to complete his escape. Nothing could exceed the mental agony of the next quarter hour. Under stress of danger he had just let himself into the water, determined to attempt to swim the wide stream as a forlorn hope, when suddenly the baying of a bloodhound dashed even this faint hope from him, and presently the crackling of twigs announced the near approach of the savage pursuer. But there were evidences that for the moment the dog was at fault, and in mere desperation the hunted man waded beneath the overhanging banks where he might sell his life as dearly as possible. Something struck against his breast. He could not restrain a cry as he seized what proved to be his missing boat. In an instant he had clambered in and cast off the line, when a sudden gleam of moonlight breaking through the clouds revealed at the other end of the log to which the boat had been moored the crouching figure of the bloodhound, poising for a spring. Simultaneously with the leap of the dog, the skiff darted out into the stream. A blow with the oar aimed at the head of the animal nearly upset the fragile craft and was easily eluded by the dog, which, swimming forward, laid its forepaws on the gunwale and attempted to seize the edge of the boat with his teeth. The situation was desperate. Laying aside his revolver, a shot from which would have drawn a volley from the shore, the brave scout seized his bowie-knife, and with one frenzied stroke cut the throat of the bloodhound, severing its neck clean to the back. The dog sank from sight, and the man was free! A few minutes' quiet pulling landed him on the further shore, whence a brief walk brought him to camp, to tell his adventures and turn in his stock of information.

Perhaps as thrilling an experience as ever was reported was that which fell to the lot of Captain Leighton, formerly of a Michigan battery, but led by the fascination of adventure into scout and spy duty. It was brief, but so charged with peril and nerve-tension that in a few short hours he seemed to have lived days, and needed a long sleep after it, as though he had been awake for a week. In a single afternoon he left his own camp and rode into the enemy's country, passing two pickets, killed a guard, listened to the council of war in the tent of the rebel general, fought his way back through the pickets, who now knew his mission, set off the signal agreed on, and rode to safety on his unusually fleet horse. The first picket he met on his way out was misled by supposing him to be a spy of their own returning with information, and from them he got what sounded like the countersign, but was not, as he discovered when, riding on, he attempted with it to pass the sentry near the rebel general's tent. The sentry pulled trigger on him, but the cap snapped on the musket, there was a hand-to-hand scuffle not a hundred yards from the camp, and the sentry was stabbed to the heart. Clad in the sentry's uniform, under cover of the night, he heard from the very lips of the general and his council the secret he was in search of—that the enemy would mass on the left wing to meet the attack of the morrow—sauntered carelessly about as the council dispersed, and then mounted his superb gray and was off. It was a perilous ride, for every picket he had passed in the afternoon fired on him as he rode through, and it was indeed a charmed life that escaped their bullets. The last picket he had to pass—the same that had mistaken him for a rebel scout—was numerous, and met him with a volley, followed up by a sharp attack with sabres and revolvers. Shooting, stabbing, slashing, and swearing like a fiend, wounded and wounding, he fought his way through them, and then fled onward, reeling in his saddle with excitement and loss of blood, until, arrived at the hollow stump where his rockets were concealed, he set them both off (thus giving the desired information to his own commander). Then, emptying his revolver at his nearest pursuer, he again rode away, unharmed further by the shots that followed him like hail. What added to the bravery of this deed was the fact that he knowingly went out to replace a scout who had been killed the night before on the very same mission.

JOHN WILKES BOOTH.

All spies were not so fortunate as to complete their expeditions in one day. Sometimes, although in comparative safety, they were unable to get out of the enemy's territory for many days. An Illinois private, named Newcomer, who had just missed some important battles, was accustomed to vary the monotony of his camp life in Alabama by making secret trips after information overnight. This work suited him so well that he determined on a more extensive expedition among the guerilla cavalry that he learned from a negro lay some miles below the Union camp. His first bold act was to crawl into a corn-crib where a number of these men lay sleeping, their horses picketed outside, and, feeling around, he calmly drew a good revolver from the belt of one of the unconscious sleepers, having the good luck to wake none of them up. He had provided himself with a forged certificate of discharge from the rebel army, by means of which he was by some unsuspecting Southern sympathizers put in communication with a Southern agent for the purchase of stores, named Radcliffe, who was known to everybody in and about Franklin, Tenn., and who vouched for him throughout his stay among the Confederates. He took on the character of one seeking office in the rebel army, and as a seller of contraband articles obtained from the North. In this guise, turning up at Radcliffe's house as occasion required, he explored the situation and reported back to his superiors at Nashville. Before he got back he had serious trouble in getting away from Shelbyville, for lack of a pass. A good-natured crowd, to whom he had dispensed the contents of his whiskey flask, were willing to help him away, but stuck at telling the provost marshal that they knew him; but it was finally managed by writing his name on the collective pass on which they travelled. Lagging behind them on the road, he turned off in the direction he wanted to go, only to fall into the hands of one of Morgan's bands of scouts, who swore he was a Yankee, and actually had the halter around his neck to hang him on the spot, when he succeeded in persuading them to take him back to Radcliffe for identification, where he was released, and

War Department, Washington, April 20, 1865.

$100,000 REWARD!

THE MURDERER

Of our late beloved President, ABRAHAM LINCOLN,

IS STILL AT LARGE.

$50,000 REWARD!

will be paid by this Department for his apprehension, in addition to any reward offered by Municipal Authorities or State Executives.

$25,000 REWARD!

will be paid for the apprehension of JOHN H. SURRATT, one of Booth's accomplices.

$25,000 REWARD!

will be paid for the apprehension of DANIEL C. HARROLD, another of Booth's accomplices.

LIBERAL REWARDS will be paid for any information that shall conduce to the arrest of either of the above-named criminals, or their accomplices.

All persons harboring or secreting the said persons, or either of them, or aiding or assisting their concealment or escape, will be treated as accomplices in the murder of the President and the attempted assassination of the Secretary of State, and shall be subject to trial before a Military Commission and the punishment of DEATH.

Let the stain of innocent blood be removed from the land by the arrest and punishment of the murderers.

All good citizens are exhorted to aid public justice on this occasion. Every man should consider his own conscience charged with this solemn duty, and rest neither night nor day until it be accomplished.

EDWIN M. STANTON, *Secretary of War.*

DESCRIPTIONS.—BOOTH is 5 feet 7 or 8 inches high, slender build, high forehead, black hair, black eyes, and wears a heavy black moustache.

JOHN H. SURRATT is about 5 feet 9 inches. Hair rather thin and dark; eyes rather light; no beard. Would weigh 145 or 150 pounds. Complexion rather pale and clear, with color in his cheeks. Wore light clothes of fine quality. Shoulders square; cheek bones rather prominent; chin narrow; ears projecting at the top; forehead rather low and square, but broad. Parts his hair on the right side; neck rather long. His lips are firmly set. A slim man.

DANIEL C. HARROLD is 23 years of age, 5 feet 6 or 7 inches high, rather broad shouldered, otherwise light built; dark hair, little (if any) moustache; dark eyes, weighs about 140 pounds.

GEO. F. NESBITT & CO., Printers and Stationers, cor. Pearl and Pine Streets, N. Y.

REDUCED FACSIMILE OF POSTER ISSUED BY THE WAR DEPARTMENT.

then was furnished by Radcliffe with a written voucher on which he succeeded in making his way, after many exciting and perilous adventures, to his commander. He brought him the important news, confided to him by a rebel who took him for a fellow spy, of a projected attack on the Union fleet on the river, and steps were taken that saved the ships.

Perhaps the most varied experience was that of Col. L. C. Baker, who organized the secret service, and performed himself every duty, from that of actual spy to that of chief of the national police, beginning with a personal expedition to Richmond and ending with the capture of Wilkes Booth, the assassin of President Lincoln. His first Richmond trip was made in July, 1861, under cover of a general movement of Southern sympathizers away from the North. General Scott himself sent him to obtain information concerning the strength and disposition of troops in the Confederate capital. His greatest difficulty at the outset was to get through the Northern lines without betraying his errand, and three times he was sent back to General Scott as a Southern spy. Finally he got through, and, armed with letters to prominent residents of Richmond, he was promptly forwarded on his way, but was carefully turned over to Jefferson Davis himself, who kept him under guard while he made up his mind whether the stranger was a spy or the "Mr. Munson" he pretended to be with business in Richmond. Succeeding in getting satisfactorily identified through a sort of "bunco" self-introduction to a man from Knoxville, where he claimed to have lived, he was paroled and turned loose in Richmond. When he had picked up the information he desired, he began his efforts to get back to Washington with his precious news. A pass to visit Fredericksburg enabled him to leave Richmond, but an attempt to go further on the same pass only got him into the hands of a patrol. But he soon not only eluded his sleepy guard, but rode off on the sentry's horse as well. Followed and surrounded in a negro cabin where he had stopped to rest, he managed to hide under a haystack, where he narrowly escaped the searching sabre-thrust of his pursuers, and then made again for the Potomac. Hunger induced him to risk introducing himself to two German pickets guarding the bank on the Confederate side of that river, and they hospitably kept him in their tent overnight, though they watched him closely and made him a semi-prisoner. The watches of the night he consumed in vain endeavors to crawl out of the tent while his captors slept; but they slept "with one eye open," as it were, and it was not until dawn that he managed unobserved to get down to the river-bank, secure the pickets' boat with its single broken oar, and push for liberty out into the stream. The men were quickly after him, however, and he had to shoot one of them to save himself, while the other ran for assistance. The detachment that quickly reached the shore made the water about his craft uncomfortably lively with their bullets; but he fortunately managed to paddle out of range without being hit, and after a row of four miles, which was the width of the river at that point, he reached the Maryland shore and made his way to Washington.

The papers with which Baker had been intrusted at Richmond gave him much information involving Northern traitors who were aiding the Southern cause, and for some time he was engaged in the work of bringing them to justice. But he occasionally returned to special duty, as he did in the autumn of 1863, when, after Pope's defeat by Lee, great solicitude was felt for the safety of Banks's army, the whereabouts of which even was unknown, and in ignorance of Lee's success Banks was supposed to be seeking a junction with Pope. Baker undertook to carry informing despatches to Banks, and to bring that officer's report back to Washington. Mounted on the famous race-horse "Patchen," he succeeded in reaching Banks near Manassas without adventure, but his return trip was full of peril. Conscious of the great importance of haste, he started straight for the rebel lines between himself and Washington, and after riding two miles to the eastward he caught sight of the hostile army near the old Bull Run battlefield. To save time, instead of making a detour to avoid them, he halted and awaited an opportunity of slipping through, availing himself of the detached order of march in which the enemy was proceeding. A break in the column soon gave him this chance, and although he knew that he would become a target for every marksman that saw him, the intrepid Baker nerved himself for a quick and desperate dash and gave spurs to his splendid steed. Lying close to Patchen's neck, he flew like an arrow within thirty feet of a squad of infantry, but had the good luck to bring both himself and his horse through without harm from the bullets that whistled thick about them. A squad of cavalry quickly took up the pursuit; but, tired as he was, Patchen soon distanced all but a few who were particularly well mounted. For nine miles the chase continued, the pursuers dropping off until only three remained, when fatigue began to tell on both horse and rider. Then, turning a low hill, Baker wheeled sharply about and concealed himself in a clump of pines, while his pursuers rode past unconscious of his presence. But they soon discovered that there was no longer any one in front of them. Returning, one of them was apprised of Baker's whereabouts by a slight movement of the latter's horse, and the crisis of the adventure was at hand. Baker shot down one Confederate cavalryman, and then turned sharply off the path to avoid the other two, who were now on their way back. But, although he passed them, it was not without their seeing him, and, firing their carbines, they renewed the pursuit. Spurring Patchen to a final burst of speed, Baker plunged into the swollen waters of Bull Run, hoping to get across before his pursuers could reach the bank and fire at him in mid-stream. This he accomplished, and had even clambered up the almost perpendicular bank beyond by the time the rebels had plunged in to follow him over. Before Baker could fire on them the Union pickets, attracted by the shots, came running to the edge of the bluff. Baker shouted out his errand, and the pickets with a volley emptied one of the Confederate saddles, while the remaining pursuer escaped to tell the tale. This was a pretty close call for Baker, but it was typical of the scout's experience, and illustrated well the many serious chances taken by every successful seeker after information in the enemy's territory.

The spies of the war were not all men. Many women on both sides did effective secret work for the cause they espoused. Perhaps this agency was more common among the Southern than the Northern sympathizers. Residence in the North was free from the necessity of accounting for one's presence and business as rigidly as in the South; and not only in Washington and the border towns, but in all the cities of the North, the rebels had fair emissaries who kept them pretty well informed of passing events. Among the Northern women who did good service during the war, both as spy and nurse, was Miss Emma Edmonds. After spending several months in the hospitals of the Army of the Potomac, she volunteered to take the place of a spy who had been executed at Richmond. Disguised as a colored boy, she soon found herself within the rebel lines, where she joined a gang of negroes who were carrying provisions to the pickets, and afterward working on the fortifications at Yorktown. After doing a man's day's work, she used her evening liberty in making a careful inspection of the defences, counting the guns, etc., and picked up much other information through the free discussion of what was going on, common in the rebel army among both officers and men. Her opportunity to get back to the Union lines came when, on visiting the pickets with their evening meal, she was for a time stationed on the post of a picket who had just been shot; for while the adjacent pickets had their backs turned, she slipped away into the darkness, carrying her valuable information with her. Later on she made another secret expedition, this time in the guise of an Irish female peddler. Her first experience on this trip was the discovery of a wounded and dying Confederate officer in a deserted house, and the mementos and messages for home which he confided to her proved to be her passport to the rebel headquarters. She had already gained from the pickets and the men about the camp the information she was seeking, and was quite ready to return, when she was sent, mounted, to guide a detachment to bring back the dead officer's body from the house near her own lines, and thus was fairly started on her way. The expedition of the detachment was a somewhat perilous one for them, and they sent her farther down the road to watch for Yankees and give them timely warning of the approach of any from the Union side. Not seeing any Yankees in that vicinity, she kept on until she did—and then she was safe back in her own quarters, and the Union troops were soon able to cross the Chickahominy with a pretty fair knowledge of the enemy's dispositions and purposes.

Miss Edmonds had a strange career for a woman. She kept with the Union advance, varying her womanly ministrations in camp and field hospital with occasional duty as an orderly and on secret service. She entered the Confederate lines, now as a contraband, now as a rebel soldier. In the latter character she was impressed into the Confederate cavalry and went into action, where she managed to change sides during the fight and to wound the rebel officer who had conscripted her. After this adventure her secret service had perforce to be confined to the Union lines, for she had become pretty well known in all the disguises she could assume.

CONFEDERATE MONUMENT AND CEMETERY, RICHMOND, VA.

The experiences of all scouts and spies can be well understood from the instances that have now been given. Their work was most important, and their days were filled with thrilling adventure, most fascinating to adventurous spirits. Many of them never lived to tell their story, but received the prompt justice of a drum-head court martial and a short shrift. Their performances rose often to the height of heroism, and their prowess, when they found themselves in close quarters, equalled anything ever done on the battlefield.

IMPORTANT HISTORY SUGGESTED BY A PICTURE GROUP OF SHERMAN AND HIS GENERALS. (See page 30.)

THIS picture was to consist of General Sherman, his two army-commanders, and the four corps-commanders in charge at the close of the war.

It does not, however, contain the portrait of General Blair, who was absent on a short leave. At the time the photograph was taken, I [General Howard] was no longer connected with General Sherman's army. My picture was included for the following reason:

After the army's arrival near Washington, I was assigned to other duty, and General Logan took my place in command of the Army of the Tennessee. When the group was made up, as I had been so long identified with that army, General Sherman desired me to be included. General Logan was seated for the picture where I would have sat, had there been no late change of commanders. In all the field operations from Atlanta to the sea, and from Savannah through the Carolinas to Raleigh, and on to Washington, I was denominated "the right wing commander," and General Slocum "the left wing commander." The division of cavalry under Kilpatrick was sometimes independent of either wing, but usually reported for orders to one wing or the other, as Sherman directed.

MAJOR-GENERAL OLIVER O. HOWARD.

The right wing was the "Army of the Tennessee;" the left wing, the "Army of Georgia." In the field service, from Atlanta on, each wing had two army corps, as follows: the right wing, the Fifteenth and Seventeenth; the left wing, the Fourteenth and Twentieth Corps. When General Logan passed to the charge of the Army of the Tennessee, General Hazen was assigned to command the Fifteenth Corps. Though absent, General Blair retained the Seventeenth Corps. After our march, for some reason—I think for Mower's promotion—Gen. A. S. Williams had been relieved from the Twentieth Corps, and General Mower assigned to his place. The Fourteenth Corps, which Gen. George H. Thomas had so long and so ably commanded, was during all that march under the direction of Gen. Jefferson C. Davis.

It may be of interest, while inspecting this noted picture, to recall something characteristic of the men who compose it. Let us begin with the junior officer of the group.

MAJOR-GENERAL JEFFERSON C. DAVIS.

General Davis, promoted to a volunteer appointment from the regular army, became early conspicuous as a successful commander in Missouri and other Western fields. For example, he captured one thousand prisoners at Milford, repelled Confederate attack upon Sigel's centre at Pea Ridge, commanded a division at Stone River, and took as prisoners one hundred and fourteen of Wheeler's raiders.

In August, 1862, ill-health constrained him to leave the front for a short time, when he visited his home in Clarke County, Ind. The northward movement of the Confederates against Louisville subsequently caused him to hasten to that city and volunteer his services to General Nelson.

This general, William Nelson, a native of Kentucky, was a middle-aged naval officer at the breaking out of the war. His experience in Mexico, his strong character as a loyal Kentuckian, had caused his transfer to the army. Among undisciplined masses of volunteers he had already done wonders. He attained special distinction as a division commander under Buell at the fiercely contested battle of Shiloh; but with all his patriotism, energy, and capability, he was a martinet in discipline, very often giving great offence by his rough language and impatient ways.

MAJOR-GENERAL JEFFERSON C. DAVIS.

Gen. Jefferson C. Davis had hardly come in contact with Nelson when he was subjected to treatment that offended him greatly.

Davis was of slender build, while Nelson was a large and powerful man. Davis endeavored, without success, to get an apology from Nelson for hard words and mistreatment. Abbott, in his History of the Civil War, shows how he was met:

"Here he (Davis) was outrageously insulted by General Nelson, and after demanding an apology and receiving only reiterated abuse, he (Davis) shot him on the stairs of the Galt House. General Nelson died in a few hours. General Davis was arrested, but was soon released, sustained by the almost universal sympathy of the public and of the army."

In subsequent years it was my lot to be on duty with General Davis. He reported to me and was under my command while pursuing the Confederates under Bragg, just after the battle of Missionary Ridge, November 25, 1863. His method of covering his front and flanks with skirmishers, and holding his troops well in hand for the prompt deployment, greatly pleased me. He was one of those officers constantly on the *qui vive*, impossible to surprise, difficult to defeat, and ever ready, at command, effectively to take the offensive. He succeeded to the Fourteenth Corps because Gen. John M. Palmer, offended at a decision of General Sherman, resigned the position. While Davis was a just man, he was strongly prejudiced against negroes, often, in his conversations, declaiming against them. But subsequent to the war, when commanding the State of Kentucky, acting as Assistant Commissioner for Freedmen, he took strong grounds against all lawless white men who sought to do them injury. In 1874, when a confusion of counsels had caused endless complications during the Modoc War in Southern Oregon, General Davis was, as a final resort, selected and despatched to the scene of operations. His unfailing courage and steady action soon ended the war. The Modocs were conquered, taken prisoners, and their savage and treacherous leaders punished.

I had many a conversation with General Davis. He would lead me when we were alone, in a few minutes, according to the bias of his heart, to the subject of his difficulty with Nelson. Though others exculpated him, his own heart never seemed to be at rest. It was more to himself than to others the one cloud in his otherwise unblemished, patriotic career.

MAJOR-GENERAL WILLIAM B. HAZEN

entered the military academy one year after me (1851), so that I was associated with him there for three years. As a young man, he was very thin of flesh, so much so as to cause remark. The first time I saw him after graduation, he was on a visit to West Point, in 1860. He had been in many Indian engagements in Texas and New Mexico, and had been brevetted for gallant conduct in battle; his arm at that time was in a sling, he having been wounded with an arrow.

A most wonderful change had taken place in his personal appearance. Instead of a young man of cadaverous build, he was large, fleshy, handsome. As a cadet he had been very retiring; now quite the opposite—in fact, he soon became remarkable among us for his bold frontier stories and an increased self-esteem.

Such was Hazen at the breaking out of the war. He went to the front in Kentucky, commanding the Forty-first Ohio Volunteers. During the series of operations and battles in which he was engaged, he maintained in his commands unusual neatness of attire and excellent discipline, and received for himself four brevets for gallant and meritorious service; the last being that of major-general in the regular army. Probably his most distinguished effort, one which called the especial attention of General Sherman to his merit, was the taking, under my orders, of Fort McAllister, December 13, 1864. He at that time had charge of a division, assisted in building a long bridge over the Ogeechee, crossed with his men, and, pushing on rapidly southward, completely environed Fort McAllister from sea-shore to sea-shore. General Sherman, with myself, more inland, were watching his operations in plain view from a rice-mill on the other side of the Ogeechee. The sudden and persistent attack, the exploding of numerous torpedoes, the tremendous vigor of the defence, afforded us an exciting scene, which ended in a much-needed victory; for this fort at the mouth of the river was the last obstruction between our army and the supplies which were coming from the sea. This success of Hazen caused me to recommend him for further promotion to the command of the Fifteenth Army Corps; and this was his crowning honor in the great war.

MAJOR-GENERAL WILLIAM B. HAZEN.

MAJOR-GENERAL JOSEPH A. MOWER.

I found General Mower in command of the First Division Sixteenth Army Corps (a little later, of a division in the Seventeenth Army Corps, under General Blair); that was when I came to the Army of the Tennessee at Atlanta. He was already well known in that army. In conversation around campfires staff-officers spoke of him in this way: "Mower is a rough diamond;" "He is rather a hard case in peace;" "He cannot be beaten on the march;" "You ought to see him in battle."

MAJOR-GENERAL J. A. MOWER.

These expressions indicate somewhat the character of the man. About six feet in height, well proportioned and of great muscular strength, probably there was no officer in our picture group who was better fitted in every way for hard campaigning. On one occasion during the march through the Carolinas, as we approached the westernmost branch of the Edisto, all the country had apparently been swept by the inhabitants clean of supplies. The cattle and horses had been driven eastward beyond the river, and all food carried off or hidden. As I approached a house near the river crossing, I saw General Mower and his staff apparently in conversation with the owner, who had, for some purpose, remained behind his fleeing people in his almost empty tenement. Mower was asking him questions; these the man at first evaded, or answered derisively. Then, becoming angry at Mower's persistence, he refused to tell anything. The general, just as I was passing through the gate, said to an orderly, in his deep, strong, decisive voice: "Orderly, fetch a rope!" He did not intimate what he proposed to do with the rope, but one glance at Mower's face was sufficient for the stranger. He immediately became courteous, and gave Mower all the information he desired as to the roads, bridges, and neighboring country. A few days later I was with Mower's division when he fought his way across the main stream near Orangeburgh. His energy in leading his men through swamps, directing them while they were cutting the cypresses, making temporary bridges, wading streams, constructing and carrying the canvas boats, ferrying the river, and appearing with marvellous rapidity upon the enemy's right or left flank on the open fortified bluff of the eastern shore, drew my attention more than ever to Mower's capabilities. I remember when we stood together inside the first captured work, while our men were rushing for the railroad above and below the city, Mower dismounted, and looking at me with his face full of glad triumph, said: "*Fait accompli!* General, *fait accompli!*"

At Bentonville, the 20th and 21st of March, 1865, I saw Mower ride into battle. As he approached the firing, the very sound of it gave him a new inspiration; his muscular limbs gripped his horse, and he leaned forward apparently carrying the animal with him into the conflict. He was the only officer I ever saw who manifested such intense joy for battle. At last, having brought his division through the woods and a little beyond the left flank of the Confederate commander (General Johnston), Mower and one or two of his staff dismounted, so as to work himself with his men through a dense thicket where he could not ride. The point sought in Johnston's left rear was just gained by the indomitable Mower, when General Sherman called us off, saying "that there had been fighting enough." Concerning this event, General Sherman, in his "Memoirs," makes a significant remark:

"The next day (21st) it began to rain again, and we remained quiet till about noon, when General Mower, ever rash, broke through the rebel line, on his extreme left flank, and was pushing straight for Bentonville and the bridge across Mill Creek. I ordered him back, to connect with his own corps; and lest the enemy should concentrate on him, ordered the whole rebel line to be engaged with a strong skirmish fire."

MAJOR-GENERAL FRANCIS PRESTON BLAIR, JR.,

whose biography is in every public library, is too well known to require a detail of introduction.

As early as 1843 he formed a law partnership with his brother Montgomery, in the city of St. Louis, Mo.; here he worked till his health gave way. Requiring a change of climate, he went to New Mexico. While he was there General Kearney, as soon as the Mexican war came on, began operations which ended in his grand march to the Pacific coast. Young Blair was a volunteer aid, and by his intelligence and energy gave that general the effective help which he needed. This short service in the Mexican war was enough to beget in Blair a taste for military reading and study; so that, being in St. Louis at the fever period of the outbreak of the great rebellion in 1861, he was not unprepared for the double part he was soon called upon to play.

Having been elected and sent to Congress in 1858, previously having had a term in the Missouri Legislature, in both as a "Freesoiler," he threw all his political ability and knowledge upon the side of the Union. As a military man, he promptly acted and greatly helped in organizing and raising troops. Probably it is due to his energy more than to anything else that St. Louis and Missouri were kept to the Union. Mr. Lincoln, who had the greatest confidence in Blair, commissioned him a brigadier-general in August, 1862. He performed thereafter no obscure part in all those battles along the Mississippi, which ended in the capture of Vicksburg. He was rapidly advanced from command of a brigade to that of a division and corps in Grant's Army of the Tennessee. His name and able work are identified with both the Fifteenth and Seventeenth Corps.

The first time I saw General Blair was on November 25, 1863; it was in the evening after Sherman's first hot charge up the rough steeps on the north end of Missionary Ridge. Part of my command had participated in the bloody work of the day, and General Grant had detached the remainder of my corps from General Thomas on the straight front, and sent us around to strengthen Sherman. It was an informal council of war in the woods, by a small campfire, where I met for the first time Generals Tom Ewing, Jefferson C. Davis, and Blair. The latter, who was obliged at times to go to civil duties in Congress, had then, as I was told, just returned from Washington. He brought to us the latest messages from Mr. Lincoln. He had on a light blue soldier's overcoat; it was distinguished by a broad, elegant fur collar. In repose and in photograph, Blair's countenance might pass one as ordinary; but as soon as he spoke it was suffused with light and animation. He was five feet ten, and not fleshy. He walked about the fire, and with his ready talk, never too serious, kept Sherman and all the party, for such a sad night, in fair humor; for our best men had been stopped short of the coveted tunnel, and many of them were driven with heavy losses down the rugged slopes. The whole man so impressed me that night, that I never forgot him. During the march to the sea, in skirmish, campaign, and battle, Blair was often with me; many a day's journey we rode side by side.

MAJOR-GENERAL FRANCIS P. BLAIR, JR.

His mind was replete with knowledge. As we, talking together, recalled the battles of the Revolution in the Carolinas, and often differed in discussing them, Blair would say: "Well, general, let us go to Sherman; he never forgets anything!" I may add that the reference was always the settlement of the question, for Sherman's historic knowledge was unfailing. Blair's forte was the law. I knew fairly well the army regulations; but Blair always went back of the regulations to the statute law and

THE BATTLE OF ATLANTA, JULY 22, 1864.—FULLER'S DIVISION RALLYING AFTER BEING FORCED BACK BY THE CONFEDERATES.

the Constitution. His mind was a compendium—one always at hand for me; and it was pleasant to consult him, for he never took advantage in an ungenerous manner of the superiority of his knowledge, but ever, without abating his most loyal service, gave me the information I desired.

During the great march through Georgia and the Carolinas the necessity of "foraging liberally on the country," of destroying property, as cotton in bales, factories of all kinds, storehouses, and other buildings of a public and private nature, troubled General Blair very much. The conduct of bummers, camp-followers, and of many robbers, who preceded or followed in the wake of the armies in their destruction and depredation of private dwellings, vexed him still more. One day in May, 1865, as we were nearing North Carolina, Blair was riding with me for the day. After a period of silence, he said: "General, I am getting weary of all this business. Can't we do something to bring it to a close? All this terrible waste and destruction and bloodshed appear to me now to be useless." I do not remember my reply, but I do recall a visit I made to General Sherman about that time, when I urged him not to destroy the works at Fayetteville Arsenal, N.C. I said: "General, the war will soon be over; this property is ours [that is, the Government's]. Why should we destroy our own property?" The general replied with some little asperity to the effect: "They [meaning the Confederates] haven't given up yet. They shall not have an arsenal here!" In this matter General Blair's sentiment and mine had agreed.

At another time, noticing that Wheeler's (or Hampton's) cavalry were burning the cotton to prevent its falling into our hands, and that we were burning cotton to cripple the Confederate revenue, General Blair remarked: "Both sides are burning cotton; somebody must be making a mistake!"

These growing sentiments in genuine sympathy with the suffering people of the Carolinas, were Blair's thus early, and account, in a measure, for his subsequent political course; for, as Hammersley says:

"Brave and gallant soldier as he was, and uncompromisingly hostile as he was to the enemies of his country, when the war was over, and the Southern army had laid down their arms, he at once arrayed himself against those who were in favor of continuing to treat Southern people as enemies, and with voice and pen constantly urged the adoption of a liberal and humane policy. From this time he united with the Democratic party."

Blair died in July, 1875. He was of a jovial turn and convivial, but I think he enjoyed the relief of fun and frolic more than the pleasures which attend high living. Like his father and his brother, he was a man of marked ability; he had great acquirements; he was a determined enemy, but an unswerving and generous friend. In political life his course seemed to lack consistency; but when judged from an unpartisan bias, his was, we may be sure, the outward manifestation of a persistent, patriotic spirit.

MAJOR-GENERAL JOHN A. LOGAN.

A young man received a musket-shot wound through both thighs; he repaired to the doctor to have his wound dressed, and asked if he could have it dressed at once, so that he might return to the fight. The surgeon told him he was in no condition to admit of his return, but should go to the hospital. The youth remarked that he had fired twenty-two rounds after he was wounded, and thought he could fire as many more if his wound were dressed. Finding it impossible to detain him, the doctor dressed the wound, and the young man returned to his comrades in the struggle, dealing out his ammunition to good account until the day was over, as if nothing had happened to him.

This brave young man afterwards became Gen. John A. Logan. He had such a striking face that, once seen, it was never forgotten.

MAJOR-GENERAL JOHN A. LOGAN.

There was the straight and raven hair, that, thrown back from his forehead, was long enough to cover his ears, and make vertical lines just behind his eyes. There were the broad brow, the firm round chin, and strong neck. There was the broad, well-cut mouth, always crowned by a dark, heavy mustache. But the features first seen, and never forgotten, were those black eyes with brows and lashes to match. At times those eyes were gentle, pleasant, winning; at times they were cold and indifferent; but at the least excitement they would quicken, and under provocation flash fire. Logan's whole figure, not above five feet nine, was closely knit. His true portrait is everywhere caught by the photographer, the caricaturist, the painter; but we seldom meet with a portraiture of the man that animated that splendid tenement. Abbott compares him with McPherson and contrasts him with Hood. He says: "When Logan was McPherson's successor on the field of Atlanta, rivalling his predecessor in bravery, patriotism, and military ability." . . . When speaking of him and Hood, he says: "General Logan was by no means his inferior in impetuous daring, and far his superior in all those intellectual qualities of circumspection, coolness, and judgment requisite to constitute a general."

I hardly think that one who knew both would speak just that way of Hood and Logan. The fact is, the two men were very much alike. Both were impetuous, both brave, and both able generals. Hood was put into the place of General Johnston by Davis with orders to fight desperately; had Logan been sent to Nashville to relieve General Thomas when it was contemplated, he would have done precisely as did Hood—he would have fought, and at once. He might have been defeated—as Thomas was not. Before Sherman threw his forces upon Hood's communications, Logan was greatly depressed concerning the proposed plan. "How can it succeed?" he asked. But when the first battle came on, all his pluck, forethought, energy, Samson-like, came to him. Permit me to repeat my words at the time concerning him, just after that action:

"I wish to express my high gratification with the conduct of the troops engaged. I never saw better conduct in battle.

General Logan, though ill and much worn out, was indefatigable, and the success of the day is as much attributable to him as to any one man. . . ."

As I now estimate General Logan, I think him like Napoleon's Marshal Murat. He was made for battle; the fiercer, the better it seemed to suit his temper; but the study of campaigns and military strategy was not his forte. His personal presence was not only striking, but almost resistless. The power of love and hate belonged to his nature. If a friend, like Andrew Jackson, he was a friend indeed; but if an enemy, it was not comfortable to withstand him. Logan had a good loyal heart; he sincerely loved his country and her institutions. He is justly enrolled as a hero and patriot.

MAJOR-GENERAL HENRY WARNER SLOCUM.

In the very beginning of Slocum's career, one characteristic becomes noticeable from his earliest childhood—he always had a wholesome object in view; so that, when he attained one elevation, he fixed his eye steadily upon another still higher, and bent his energies to attain it.

Early in life he cherished a desire for a cadetship at West Point; this desire was gratified in 1848. Sheridan speaks in his "Memoirs" of his (Slocum's) studious habits and willingness to aid others. I was myself at the academy and remember his strong character when the pro-slavery sentiment at West Point was so great as to lessen the popularity of any one even suspected of entertaining abolition views. He fearlessly and openly expressed himself as an opponent to human slavery.

General Slocum graduated high in his class; saw service in the Seminole wars in Florida, and remained stationed in the South until 1857, when, having studied law, he resigned to practise his profession in Syracuse, N. Y., being a representative at Albany in 1859, and instructor of militia from 1859 to 1861. When Fort Sumter fell he tendered his services, and was given the command of the Twenty-seventh New York Volunteers, which he led in a charge at Bull Run, where he was severely wounded. In August, 1861, he was made brigadier-general of volunteers, and took a brigade in General Franklin's division. When Franklin passed to the command of a corps, Slocum took the division. His work was noticeable on the Peninsula, at Yorktown, West Point, Gaines's Mill, Glendale, and Malvern Hill, and on each occasion he received the praise of his commanders. At South Mountain his division drove the enemy from its position with such a rush as to prevent any chance of rallying, which act brought him still more commendation. It was Slocum who led the advance of Franklin's corps to the field of Antietam, and enabled us to recover and hold much ground that had been taken from us in the first struggle.

MAJOR-GENERAL HENRY WARNER SLOCUM.

By October of 1862 Slocum's manifest ability had given him the Twelfth Corps, with which his name is so closely identified. In the Chancellorsville campaign it was Slocum who made the march around Lee's left, and showed himself the "cool, self-poised, and prompt commander that he had always been, and which made him distinguished even in the brilliant group of generals of which he was a member." It would require the whole history of Gettysburg to fairly portray Slocum's part there. The most impressive incident of that battle to me was Slocum's own battle on the 3d day of July, 1863. For five anxious hours Slocum commanded the field to our right; that dreadful struggle went on until Ewell with Early's and Edward Johnson's large divisions was forced to give up and abandon his prize of the night before. Slocum's resolute insistence, on the 2d, upon leaving Greene and his brigade as a precaution when General Meade ordered the Twelfth Corps to be sent to his (Meade's) left, with Greene's marvellous night battle, and more still, Slocum's organized work and engagement of the following morning, in my judgment prevented Meade losing the battle of Gettysburg.

The disaster at Chickamauga took Slocum's corps from the Rappahannock to Tennessee. Soon after his arrival he was sent to command the district of Vicksburg, where his work consisted of expeditions to break up bridges and railroads and to repel rebel raids. When the death of General McPherson, Slocum's department commander, at Atlanta, caused so many changes, Slocum was brought to that city to command the Twelfth Corps. When, a little later, we swung off on Hood's communications, Slocum being located south of the Atlanta crossing of the Chattahoochee River, it was his quick perception that recognized the significance of the final explosions, and it was he who pushed forward over the intervening six miles and took possession of that citadel of Georgia; and it was his despatch to his watchful commander, thirty miles away, that inspired that brief proclamation, "Atlanta is ours, and fairly won!"

In the march to the sea and through the Carolinas, General Sherman had given to Slocum the left wing, the Army of Georgia. He crossed the Savannah River when the high waters made it most difficult, pushing and fighting through the swamps of the Carolinas. He fought the battle of Averysboro, and later took a leading part at Bentonville, where Johnston, the toughest Confederate of them all, surrendered, and we turned our faces homeward.

At the close of the war General Slocum resigned from the army and engaged in civil pursuits, adding to his magnificent military reputation a civil repute for ability, honesty, and probity in business as well as in political affairs.

GENERAL WILLIAM TECUMSEH SHERMAN.

With regard to the central figure of this group, General Sherman himself, libraries are so full of his characteristic work and worth that I will simply add to the above sketches a few items. Those have been chosen which are the more personal. It is said that when his father gave him the name of the great Indian chief, Tecumseh, he remarked: "Who knows but this child may be a fighter?" It is indeed remarkable how often

names are prophetic. A fighter he was, but one thoroughly equipped with that most valuable weapon to a general, namely, such knowledge of history as to make him an authority to all of us. Any disputed point we carried to him; we relied upon his being able to set us right. Indeed, one of his most marked characteristics was his quick perception and exceedingly retentive memory. This he evidenced in many ways; years after he ascended the Indian River in Florida he remembered with minute distinctness what he saw, from the shape of the inlet to the roosting pelicans along the mangrove islands. Talking with him before the battle of Kenesaw Mountain, I found him so conversant with the Chattahoochee Valley and the roads to and from Marietta, and all the features of that region, that I was astonished, and asked him where he had gotten such valuable information. He said he had gained it twenty years before, when travelling through the country as a member of a board of officers detailed to appraise horses lost in the Florida war. During his service in the South before the war he travelled much, and appears to have remembered ever after, with wonderful distinctness, the features of the country.

Sherman was, above all, pure in his patriotism and free from thought of self. When, from his position at the Military Seminary in Louisiana, he saw the conflict coming, he wrote: "I accepted this position when the motto of the seminary, inserted in marble over the main door, was, 'By the liberality of the General Government of the United States.'—'The Union'—'Este perpetua.' . . . If Louisiana withdraws from the Federal Union, I prefer to maintain my allegiance to the old Constitution as long as a fragment of it survives;" adding, "for on no account will I do any act or think any thought hostile to or in defiance of the old government of the United States." When his clear perception of the magnitude of the struggle before us made him declare to Secretary Cameron that it "was nonsense to carry on a picayune war; that sixty thousand men were needed for immediate work to clear Kentucky and Tennessee; and two hundred thousand men to finish the war in that quarter;" and when the supposed extravagance of his demands led to the suspicion that his mind was unbalanced, thus placing him under a cloud, no selfish thought seems to have occurred to him. Instead of dwelling upon the injustice done him, he devoted all his knowledge, his wonderful energy and skill, to aiding General Grant; and, further, while under this cloud he gathered and sent forward to Grant much-needed supplies and men. He put order among quartermasters and commissaries anew, equipped new commands, and pushed them, never thinking of himself, to the front. This energy and generosity General Grant promptly acknowledged; and it was here, after the battle of Fort Donelson, that the celebrated Army of the Tennessee was born.

General Sherman's organizing powers have been tested by results. Doubtless his brilliant genius gave more or less inspiration to his subordinates, and his magnetic influence lifted up to prominence some very common men; yet, no proof-sustaining bridge can be condemned! He generously gave both confidence and scope to his officers, just as Grant had given confidence and scope to him; and such sunshine develops men and makes them strong. His memory was phenomenal; he had acquired knowledge with intense rapidity, from observation and from books, from childhood to age; and by a thousand tests he showed that he had forgotten nothing that he had once learned. Who could estimate the number of officers and men he knew at the close of the war? And at the time of his death thousands claimed his personal recognition.

He led his quartermasters in their plans and estimates for his army; he was quicker than his chief commissary in figuring the rations for a month's supply; he was equal to the great engineering general in everything that pertains to the construction of railroads and the running of trains; he was more than a match for his Confederate adversaries in field correspondence with them at Atlanta—a correspondence rapid and pungent, which involved laws of war and of nations.

When the Hon. Thomas Ewing, in kindness to General Sherman's family, offered to adopt a child, his choice fell upon Tecumseh. Mr. Ewing's testimony, after a little experience with him as a member of his family, is, "That he was a lad remarkable for accuracy of memory and straightforwardness."

When truthfulness is the corner-stone of a character—all things being equal—we have reason to anticipate a strong superstructure. How this was realized in Sherman, the world knows.

Loyalty to family, loyalty to friends, loyalty to society about him, loyalty to duty and country, he quickly observed in another. And this loyalty was a marked characteristic of his own great soul.

OLIVER OTIS HOWARD,
Major-General U. S. Army.

GOVERNOR'S ISLAND, N. Y., *July* 6, 1894.

LIBBY PRISON, RICHMOND, VA.

(From a War-time Photograph.)

PRISONS AND ESCAPES.

BY GEORGE L. KILMER.

ESCAPE OF THREE WAR CORRESPONDENTS FROM SALISBURY PRISON—SEVENTY PRISONERS ESCAPED, BUT ONLY FIVE REACHED THE NORTH—LONG AND PERILOUS JOURNEY THROUGH THE ENEMY'S COUNTRY—"OUT OF THE JAWS OF DEATH, OUT OF THE MOUTH OF HELL"—A LEAP FOR LIBERTY—FOUR UNION PRISONERS ESCAPED NEAR CHARLESTON, S. C.—JOURNEY THROUGH SWAMPS AND OVER MOUNTAINS TO TENNESSEE—ESCAPES FROM ANDERSONVILLE—TUNNELLING UNDER THE STOCKADE—REMARKABLE ESCAPE OF THE CONFEDERATE GENERAL MORGAN—COLONEL ROSE'S TUNNEL AT LIBBY PRISON.

ALBERT D. RICHARDSON and Junius Henri Brown, war correspondents of the *New York Tribune*, were taken prisoners from a Union vessel that attempted to pass the Confederate batteries at Grand Gulf, Miss. After passing some time in Castle Thunder and Libby Prison, Richmond, they were sent to Salisbury, N. C., as a punishment for endeavoring to escape, and while there, W. T. Davies of the *Cincinnati Gazette* united his fortunes with the *Tribune* men.

Again and again plans to obtain their freedom were frustrated by some trifle, until desperation spurred them to the most daring attempts, but these also ended in failure. One day a body of prisoners, led by Robert E. Boulger of the Twenty-fourth Michigan, rushed upon a guard relief, seized their muskets, and attacked the sentinels on their posts. In their haste, all rushed to one point and attempted to pass the fence; but a couple of field-pieces and the muskets of the reserve guard turned upon that one point, quelled the insurrection in three minutes, killing and wounding one hundred men. A scheme of tunnelling was then proposed and pushed far toward success, but the prison commandant took alarm and posted a second line of guards, one hundred feet outside the stockade, and that rendered egress by tunnels out of the question. After spending ten months in the Salisbury prison, Richardson and his two companions determined to take heavy risks in order to get out and make their way to the mountains of East Tennessee. The outlook, according to the statistics of escapes during their experiences in that prison, was not at all promising, for out of seventy prisoners that had passed the guard, but five had reached the North. The others had been retaken or had been shot in the mountains. By extraordinary good luck the trio passed the guards on the night of December 17, 1864. All three were on duty at the time in the hospital, and Davies and Browne held passes permitting them to go outside the first line of sentinels to a Confederate dispensary for supplies. This privilege had been enjoyed so long that they were allowed to go on sight. The night of the escape, Browne loaned his pass to Richardson, and with Davies walked coolly out to the dispensary. Richardson describes his exit as follows:

"A few minutes later, taking a box filled with the bottles in which the medicines were usually brought, and giving it to a lad who assisted me in my hospital duties, I started to follow them. As if in great haste, we walked rapidly toward the fence. When we reached the gate, I took the box from the boy and said to him, for the benefit of the sentinel, of course: 'I am going outside to get these bottles filled. I shall be back in fifteen minutes, and want you to remain right here to take and distribute them among the hospitals. Do not go away.' The lad, understanding me perfectly, replied, 'Yes, sir,' and I attempted to pass the sentinel by mere assurance. He stopped me with his musket, demanding:

"'Have you a pass, sir?'

"'Certainly I have a pass,' I replied with all the indignation I could assume. 'Have you not seen it often enough to know it by this time?'

"Apparently a little dumbfounded, he modestly replied: 'Perhaps I have; but they are strict with us, and I am not quite sure.'"

The sentinel examined the document which was all right in Browne's hands, but all wrong in Richardson's. But he did not know the difference, and told Richardson to pass on. Once outside he met several Confederate officials who knew him, and knew too that he was out of his place, but the "peculiarly honest and business-like look of that medicine box" threw them off their guard. Instead of entering the dispensary, Richardson hid his box and slipped under a convenient shelter. At dark his friends joined him, and the three passed the outer guard without difficulty. For the *Tribune* men this was the end of twenty months of captivity. The first night and day were passed in the barn of a friendly citizen within one mile of the prison. The second night, a Confederate lieutenant belonging to the Sons of America, an order of Southerners who secretly aided the Union, met them and gave them full directions how and where to reach friends on their journey. Then they set out on their long winter tramp, poorly clad, and weak from long confinement.

The main guide of the refugees was a railroad running west, but they were often obliged to leave the line to avoid crowded settlements, and were frequently lost in making those detours. In such emergencies they relied upon chance friends among the slaves to direct them aright.

On the morning of the seventh day of their escape, they found that they had made fifty miles of their direct journey. December 30th they crossed the Yadkin River, now getting into a region where Union homes were plenty. Communications had to be opened with women, as the men were "lying out" in order to avoid impressment by the hated Confederacy; and, after allaying all suspicion, our refugees found these people of great service.

"The men of the community were walking arsenals. Each had a trusty rifle, one or two navy revolvers, a great bowie-knife, a haversack, and a canteen."

Guided and fed by the friends they found here, the three reached Tennessee early in January; but their perils were not yet over, for the mountains were constantly patrolled by Confederate guerillas. Once they had to pass within a quarter of a mile of a notorious rendezvous, called Little Richmond. An invalid arose from his bed and guided them past the danger at the risk of his life. On another occasion their guide, the celebrated Dan Ellis, aroused the party from sleep with the startling announcement: "We have walked right into a nest of rebels. Several hundred are within a few miles, and eighty in this immediate vicinity!"

They scattered in various directions, Richardson and his party—for others had joined them—being led by a young woman who often performed this service, though her name, Melvina Stephens, was never revealed until the war had closed.

On the 14th of January, 1865, the *Tribune* printed this despatch from its long-lost correspondent:

"KNOXVILLE, TENN., *January* 13, 1865.
"Out of the jaws of death; out of the mouth of hell.
"ALBERT D. RICHARDSON."

He had travelled three hundred and forty miles since leaving the prison, twenty-seven days before.

Of the thousands of prisoners held by either side during the four years of the war, those who escaped and succeeded in reaching their own lines were exceedingly few, although the attempts at escape were numerous, and a good many got away from the prisons only to be brought back captives again in a few days. The most notable adventure of this kind was an escape from Libby Prison by a hundred and eight officers in February, 1864. In that crowded prison, which was an old tobacco warehouse, the prisoners had little to do but play checkers on squares of the floor marked out with their pocket knives, play cards, tell stories, and devise plans for escape. One of them discovered a way of getting into the basement, and, by removing stones, making a hole through the eastern foundation wall. With a few assistants he then proceeded to dig a tunnel across the breadth of the yard. The earth that was taken out was dumped in a dark corner of the cellar where it never attracted attention. The work had to be carried on very secretly, not only to escape the notice of the guards, but even to prevent the knowledge of it from reaching any prisoner who might not be trustworthy. When the tunnel was about ten yards long a slight opening was made to the surface of the ground for light and ventilation; and an old shoe thrown out at this opening in the night, and resting near it upon the surface, enabled the tunnellers, looking from the windows of the prison in the daytime, to get their bearings and determine how much farther they must dig in order to pass under the fence. When all was done the night of February 9th was fixed for the escape. One of the officers who passed through the tunnel says of himself and two companions: "Each man had an entire suit of clothes, a double suit of underclothes, the pair of boots in which he stood on entering the prison, an overcoat, and a cap. In common we possessed a coil of rope, a diminutive hatchet, one pint of brandy, a half pint of extract of Jamaica ginger, two days' scant rations of dried meat and hard bread, one pipe, and a bit of tobacco. The tunnel was about fifty-three feet long, and so small in diameter that in order to pass through it was necessary to lie flat on one's face, propelling with one hand and the feet, the other hand being thrown over the back to diminish the breadth of the shoulders and carry overcoat, rations, etc. Early in the evening, as I was seated at the card table, Randolph tapped me on the shoulder. 'The work is finished,' he said. 'The first party went through soon after dark; there is no time to lose.' Every one knew it then. We possessed only the advantage of being perfectly cool and having a plan agreed upon. The excitement in the prison was of the wildest kind. Parties were formed, plans arranged, farewells exchanged, all in less time than one can describe. We dropped one by one into the cellar. I remember well the instructions: "Feet first; back to the wall; get down on your knees; make a half face to the right, and grasp the spike in the wall below with your right hand; lower yourself down; feel for the knotted rope below with your legs.' Then one had but to

GUARDING CONFEDERATE PRISONERS.

(FROM A WAR DEPARTMENT PHOTOGRAPH.)

drop in the loose straw shaken from hospital beds to be in the cellar. To walk across that foul pit in the dark was no easy matter; but it was soon accomplished, and together we crouched at the entrance of the tunnel. Only one at a time; and as about three minutes were consumed in effecting the passage, progress was quite slow. Of our party Randolph was the first to enter. 'I'm going. Wait till I get through before you start.' It seemed that his long legs would never disappear; but a parting kick in the face, as he wriggled desperately in, quite reassured me. When a cool blast of air drawing through the tunnel gave the welcome assurance that the passage was clear, in I went. So well did the garment of earth fit, that at moments my movements corresponded somewhat to those of a bolt forcing its way through a rifled gun. Breath failed when I was about two-thirds through, but a score or more of vigorous kicks brought me to the earth's surface where Randolph awaited my coming. With sundry whispered instructions about getting out without making undue noise and without breaking my skull against the bottom of a board fence, he then crept away toward the street, keeping in the shadow of a high brick wall, leaving me to assist in turn and instruct the colonel, who could now be heard thundering through the tunnel. Dirty but jubilant, we were soon standing in the shadow of a low brick arch, outside of which a sentinel paced backward and forward, coming sometimes within two yards of our position. One after another stole out of the archway, and we met, as agreed, at the corner of the second street below. Arm in arm, whistling and singing, we turned and struck out, strong and hopeful, for home and liberty." The one hundred and eight men who escaped through this tunnel followed different plans and routes for getting within the National lines, but the greater part of them were recaptured. The party of which the officer just quoted was one, after twelve days of journeying through swamps and by-ways, fed and guided by the friendly negroes, at length reached the National lines on the Pamunkey.

RUINS OF CHARLESTON, S. C.

A LEAP FOR LIBERTY.*

On the morning of October 6, 1864, a party of six hundred captive Union officers were put on board of a train of box-cars to be transported from the jail yard at Charleston to prison quarters at Columbia. Among the number was Capt. J. Madison Drake, of the Ninth New Jersey volunteers, who had been a prisoner of war five months and an inmate during that time of three different prisons—Libby, Macon, Ga., and Charleston. Although he had been foiled in many attempts to escape, he resolved on one more effort, and, having received warning of the trip to Columbia, induced three fellow-prisoners to join him: Capt. H. H. Todd, Eighth New Jersey; Capt. J. E. Lewis, Eleventh Connecticut; and Capt. Alfred Grant, Nineteenth Wisconsin. While the train was crawling slowly on toward Columbia, the bold projector of the scheme managed to remove the gun-caps from the nipples of the muskets of several guards

* Rewritten (by permission) from Captain Drake's narrative as printed in the private history of the Ninth New Jersey Volunteers.

on the car where the four friends were; and as soon as dusk came on, the party at a signal took their daring leap. They landed in a cypress swamp on Congaree River, and found themselves waist deep in water and mud. A volley of shots from all the guards followed the fugitives, but no one was hurt, as the train was running under good headway. A night and a day were passed in the swamp, and although the barking of dogs and shouting of men indicated that pursuers had been sent out, the runaways were not disturbed. The second night a bright new moon arose, and they started on a systematic journey toward the Union lines in Tennessee.

Before leaving Charleston, one of the party had found a school map of South Carolina, and with this guide a course had been studied out. They decided to hug the swamps and woods by day, and at night use the fields and roads, and spend as little time as possible in sleep until the mountains of North Carolina were reached. Their chief guide-mark in South Carolina was the Wateree River.

At the end of a week their rations had all been consumed, and in desperation the wanderers began to think of food to the exclusion of all else. Captain Drake says that in these times they heartily yearned for the government "hard tack" and the contractor's beef they had so often anathematized on the march and in camp.

But fortune will favor the bold, and one night, as they halted on a roadside to debate whether it should be a quest for bread or for a road to liberty, a dark form came shambling along the road, and in the moonlight they saw at a distance that it was an old negro with a basket on his arm. Without ceremony the famished men crowded around the old man, and finding that he had in his basket a "pone" of corn-bread, they seized it and began to devour it ravenously. After a time the situation was explained, and when the negro learned who the highwaymen were, he supplied a quantity of meal and salt, and sent them on their way mentally resolved to cultivate acquaintance with colored folks as often as possible.

Not until several hundred miles had been placed between their fainting feet and Charleston did the hapless fugitives feel a sense of freedom. Often their fears and alarms were causeless, but they suffered loss of vitality all the same. Sometimes seeming misfortunes proved to be blessings. One night a pack of dogs chased them into a crowded village, and they took refuge in a graveyard vault. There Captain Drake found a copy of a local newspaper, warning the people to be on guard for escaped Union prisoners. The escaped prisoners themselves got the benefit of the hint. At another time some Confederate cavalrymen chased them on the high-road, and they escaped by getting into a dense wood, where the horses couldn't follow. While wandering about, they fell in with a loyal mountaineer, who took them to his home, fed them, and directed them to other Unionists.

Many of the men met with in the mountains were of the class known as "lyers out," deserters from the Confederate army, and fugitive conscripts. A hundred or more of these men were persuaded to join Drake's party on their tramp toward the Union lines. Thus reinforced with guides and armed companions, the prospects of the runaway prisoners began to brighten. But they were not out of the woods by a long way, as the sequel proved.

When the fugitives drew near the Union lines the danger of capture increased, for a cordon of mountain rangers patrolled the region to head off any fortunate ones who got thus far on the journey homeward. The mountains were simply barren wastes, the few cabins had to be shunned, and the only food to be obtained was wild game which the rifles of the "lyers out" brought down. In the uplands the poor fellows were hounded by "rangers," and in the valleys mounted Confederates dashed about on all sides.

At length the party reached the vicinity of Bull's Gap, a railway pass through the mountains, and guarded by Union troops as an outpost of Knoxville. The chief scout announced that the gap was fifteen miles from the foot of the hill whence it was first sighted, and that, once reached, the refugees would be safe. The news stimulated the men anew, and they started down the mountain with their eyes riveted on the gap, for fear, as Drake says, it would take wings and flee. Alas! alas! The unexpected happens in war if nowhere else.

The gap didn't exactly take wings and flee, but the ubiquitous General Breckenridge, with an army at his back, fell like a thunderbolt upon the Union garrison at the pass, defeated and routed the entire force and hurled them backward at mounted double-quick pace toward Knoxville; and, presto! the gap was closed in the very faces of the yearning-eyed, broken-bodied pilgrims. Think of it—at the end of those terrible weeks of endurance and suffering, to find a hostile army springing across the path at a bound, and its scouts and patrols beating every byway and bush in the region for the luckless strays of the fleeing enemy!

A young woman of the mountains volunteered to scout toward the gap and bring news to the refugee camp. She simply learned that Breckenridge was sweeping the country of Union troops and marching upon Knoxville.

At the same time it was discovered that a band of Confederate partisans were on the trail of the fugitives, and to escape this new danger they found comparative shelter in a ravine. Two of the men who had leaped from the car with Drake, Captains Todd and Grant, ventured out to obtain rations, which were sadly needed, as they were all living on dry corn. During the night mounted men attacked the bivouac, and the refugees scattered, every man for himself. At the end of a week they fell in with a cavalry patrol, and were once more, after forty-nine days' wandering, under the protection of the Stars and Stripes.

ATTEMPTS AT ESCAPE FROM ANDERSONVILLE.

Escapes from Andersonville, except through the portals of death—that is, complete escape to the Union lines—were exceedingly rare. Hundreds, through one device or another, succeeded in getting outside of the stockade, but the prison was so strongly surrounded with guards and forts and quarters occupied with zealous attendants, that it was difficult for a prisoner to elude the detective on the outside even when he had succeeded in passing the main barrier. Adding to this the existence of the deep swamps and vast forests just beyond the camp precincts, in which a stranger to the locality would be only too sure to lose his way, it will be seen that to enter Andersonville was indeed to leave "all hope behind." The favorite method of attempting escape was by tunnelling, for the great extent of the camp area, some twenty-five acres, and its crowded condition, made the work of excavation, without danger of discovery by the guards and keepers, comparatively easy. Another favorable circumstance was the fact that prisoners were allowed to dig wells to supply drinking water, and the grounds were everywhere dotted with piles of fresh earth that had been thrown up in consequence.

In order to excavate a tunnel, the prisoners contemplating escape would commence a lateral shaft a few feet below the mouth of one of these wells, located near the stockade; and as the work was done at night, the earth thus removed was carried in small quantities and deposited on the piles of fresh earth thrown out from the newly sunken wells. The tools used were of the rudest kind—tin plates, cups, and knives with which to loosen the earth, and bare hands to scoop it into the haversacks, or bags improvised from clothes and pieces of blanket; and in this manner these tunnels were frequently extended, not only beyond the stockade, but even beyond the outer line of prison guards. Yet, although hundreds passed out—as many as one hundred escaped through one tunnel in a single night, late in 1864—they were invariably brought back; sometimes through the treachery of spies, who mingled with the prisoners, and at other times by hunters with their dogs, who were constantly patrolling the vicinity of the camp, and, in fact, the entire region, in search of deserters from the Confederate army and runaway slaves, as well as fugitive prisoners. Not one well-authenticated case of a prisoner getting out through a tunnel, and making his way North, is to be found on record.

Another method of escape from the enclosure was by strolling beyond the sight of the guards when allowed to go out to the forests for wood; some, again, tried hiding in the huge boxes used for bringing prisoners into the camp, and many were missed from their quarters who had succeeded for the time being in misleading their guards, but eventually the fugitives turned up elsewhere; while such as enlisted in the Confederate army, this being their last hope of escape, soon reappeared, either as willing prisoners or deserters.

One tunnel, which had been carried under and beyond the stockade, was broken into by a severe flood, and the stockade undermined, which opened the celebrated "providential spring."

In August, 1864, when prisoners were dying from the use of unwholesome drinking water, a heavy thunder storm flooded the little brook that, running through the enclosure, passed in and out under the stockade. The rushing element not only broke in the roof of the tunnel, but loosened a quantity of earth which, since the construction of the stockade, had dammed up a copious stream of clear, fresh water, its original course passing right through the prison quarters. Some attributed the reopening to the action of lightning, while others looked upon it as a direct interposition of Heaven for their relief. But, whatever the cause, it supplied the prisoners with an abundance of good water through the remainder of their stay, and is still in existence.

NATIONAL CEMETERY, RICHMOND, VA.

MORGAN'S ESCAPE.

The account of the capture and escape of General Morgan as here given is condensed from an article by Samuel B. Taylor, originally published in the Cincinnati *Tribune*.

In the summer of 1863, General Morgan's command made, through Southern Ohio, one of those raids which were the most daring and successful in the history of modern and ancient warfare. In that instance he did not meet with his usual great success, for his raid terminated, in July of that year, with the capture of himself and sixty-eight of his officers and men. By order of General Burnside, he and a number of his officers were confined in the Ohio Penitentiary, at Columbus.

"We were each placed in a separate cell, in the first and second range or tier of cells on the south side of the east wing of the prison. These cells were let into a solid block of masonry, one hundred and sixty feet long and twenty-five feet thick. They opened into a hall twelve feet wide and one hundred and sixty feet in length. Then, as now, the prison buildings and their yard were enclosed by a solid stone wall thirty feet high and four feet in thickness, and level on top.

"We at length became so desperate from confinement that we determined to escape, no matter at what hazard. But how was escape to be effected?

"From five o'clock P.M. till seven A.M. we were locked in our cells, with no means of communication. Through the day we were allowed to roam about the large hall on to which our cells opened and to converse freely with each other, though there was an armed sentry at either end of this hall, through which the regular keepers of the prison passed at frequent and regular intervals. We discussed every possible and impossible plan of escape, as we thought, but could hit upon none that seemed feasible.

"We had been some three months in durance vile, when, in consequence of an insult that was offered to one of our number, Capt. Thomas A. Hines, by the deputy warden, a plan was evolved by which we did finally succeed in making our escape. Captain Hines retired to his cell about eight o'clock A.M., vowing that food should not pass his lips and that sleep should not rest upon his eyelids until he had thought out some plan of escape that should be practicable.

"About a quarter to twelve o'clock he came to me and said that he had hit upon a plan which he thought would do. At all events he was determined to try it. He then informed me that he had noticed that the walls of his cell, instead of being damp, as they naturally would have been from the fact that they were built upon a level with the ground outside, were perfectly dry. From this he concluded that there must be an air chamber beneath. Now, if such should be the case, Captain Hines's plan was to run a tunnel from it through the foundation into the yard, and then to escape over the prison wall.

"The cells were built in five tiers. Some of our party occupied the lowest or ground tier, while others, including General Morgan himself, occupied the second tier. Of course only those in the ground tier could escape by means of Captain Hines's plan, and in order for General Morgan to do so it would be necessary to have him exchange cells with some one in the tier below. The plan of Captain Hines was communicated to General Morgan and the other officers that afternoon, and after being fully discussed, it was decided that not more than seven of those on the lower tier could escape, because the greater the number the greater would be the danger of discovery. We arranged to have the work begin in the cell of Captain Hines, and in order to prevent the usual daily inspection being made of it, he asked permission to thereafter sweep it himself. The permission was granted, and he kept it so scrupulously clean that after a few mornings no inspection was made of it. Work was therefore begun in his cell on the morning of November 4th. With two small table-knives, obtained from sick comrades in the hospital, Captain Hines cut through six inches of cement, removed six layers of brick, concealing them in his bed tick, and came to an air chamber six feet in height. The work was carried on under his cot.

"Having progressed thus far, Captain Hines now mounted guard at the door of his cell, while the work was carried on by the rest of us. He pretended to be deeply engrossed in study, but in reality he was watching every movement of the guards and keepers. If one approached, he gave us warning by a system of taps on the floor. One tap meant to stop work, two to proceed, and three to come out.

"We cut a tunnel at right angles from the air chamber through the foundation wall of the cell block five feet, through twelve feet of grouting to the outer wall of the east wing of the prison, then through this wall six feet in thickness, and then four feet up near the surface of the yard in an unfrequented place. Our tunnel completed, it only remained to make an entrance from the cell of each man who was to escape into the air chamber. This could only be done by working from the air chamber upward.

"To do this we must have something to measure with in order to locate the spots at which to make these holes. We secured a measuring line by involving the warden in a dispute about the length of the hall, Captain Hines abstracting it long enough, after the hall had been measured, to answer our purpose. The chamber being very dark, we obtained matches and candles from our sick comrades in the hospital.

"It was very essential to our purpose that we should have an accurate knowledge of the prison yard and the wall inclosing it, but the windows of the hall were too high to afford us a view. Fortunately the warden ordered the walls and ceiling of the hall to be swept, and a long ladder being brought for that purpose, I offered the warden a wager that I could go hand over hand to its top, rest for a moment, and then descend in the same way. He took me up, and having been famous all my life for feats of strength and agility, I readily won the bet. While resting at the top of the ladder I made a thorough survey of the yard. There was a double gate to the outer wall south of the wing in which we then were and almost at right angles from its eastern end. Of this double gate, the outer portal was solid as the wall itself, while the inner was of wooden uprights four inches apart. By means of this latter gate we might ascend to the top of the prison wall. For that purpose we made a rope of our bed ticking, and fastened it to a grappling iron made out of the poker of the hall stove.

"All our money had been taken by our captors, but we obtained a fresh supply from friends in the South, secreted in the cover of an old book sent through the mail. An old convict, who was often sent into the city on errands by the warden, procured us a newspaper, from which we learned that a train left for Cincinnati—whither we were bound—at 1.15 o'clock A.M. At midnight the guards made a round of the cells, and we determined to start at that hour. I was to descend into the air chamber and notify the others by a tap under the floor of each cell.

"The evening of November 27th being dark and cloudy, we determined to try our luck that night. When we were locked up for the night, General Morgan contrived to change places with his brother, who occupied one of the lower cells, and who greatly resembled him in face and form. Every man arranged the stool, with which each cell was supplied, in his bed to look like a sleeping man when the guard should thrust his lantern through the cell door a few minutes later.

"I had General Morgan's gold watch, and punctually at midnight I broke with my boot-heel the thin layer of cement which separated my cell from the air chamber, and passing along the latter gave a tap under the floor of each of the others, who soon joined me. We crawled through our tunnel, and, breaking the thin layer of earth which separated its end from the surface, we were soon in the prison yard. Over the wooden gate, which I had seen from the ladder, we threw our grappling iron, and by its bed-ticking rope drew ourselves up till we stood on the wing wall, whence we readily passed to the outside wall in full view of freedom.

"The top of the latter wall was so broad as to form a walkway for the guards, who were stationed there during the day, but who at night were placed inside the walls. This walkway was supplied with sentry boxes, and in one of these we divested ourselves of the garments we had soiled in passing through the tunnel, each man having provided for this by wearing two suits. With one of the knives used in tunnelling, General Morgan then cut the rope running along the wall to the warden's office bell. Fastening our grappling iron to the railing running along the edge of the wall, we descended to the ground outside, and were free once more, though at that very moment the prison guards were sitting around a fire not sixty yards away.

"We now separated, and in parties of two and three made our way to the railroad station, and took the train for Cincinnati. During the journey General Morgan sat beside a Federal major in full uniform, and was soon on the best of terms with him. Our route lay directly past the prison whence we had just come, and, as we whizzed by it, the Federal officer said to our leader:

"'That is where the rebel General Morgan is now imprisoned.'

"'Indeed,' said General Morgan; 'I hope they will always keep him as safely as they have him now.'

"At Dayton our train was delayed for over an hour, and this made it unsafe for us to go on to Cincinnati, as we had intended, because we should now be unable to reach the city until long after seven o'clock in the morning, and by that time our escape was certain to be discovered and telegraphed all over the country, and we should be watched for in every large city in which there was any possibility of our going. We therefore alighted from the train as it was passing through Ludlow Ferry, a suburb of the city, and we quickly ferried across the Ohio River into Kentucky. There we found many kind friends, who aided us with hospitality, money, concealment when necessary, horses, and arms. The adventures, the dangers, hardships, hairbreadth escapes from capture, and serious and laughable incidents through which each one of us passed in making our way back into the Confederate lines, would fill an immense volume. For the purposes of this article, it must suffice to say that ultimately we all succeeded in rejoining our comrades at the front, though one or two of our number were recaptured before they could do so, but they again succeeded in escaping.

"What transpired in Columbus after the discovery of our escape we did not learn until long afterward. Then we found that we had created one of the greatest—if not the very greatest—sensations of the war. Our escape had been effected in such a seemingly impossible manner, and was so absolutely without parallel in the history of prison escapes, that the people of the North refused to believe that it had been accomplished without collusion on the part of some of our keepers. It is no wonder that they thought so, for everything in connection with the affair happened so fortunately for us that it really seemed as if we must have had some assistance from some one within the prison. The way in which we obtained the line with which to measure for the holes in the cell floors, the way I obtained a view of the prison yard, the way in which General Morgan and his brother changed cells on the night of our escape, all of which I have detailed before, would certainly seem impossibilities without connivance. Then, when it is considered that the digging of the tunnel consumed over three weeks, and that the keepers were almost constantly passing over where it was going on, it seems incredible that they never became aware of it.

"Nevertheless, there was never any bribery even attempted. It seemed as though fate or Providence or some controlling power had decreed that we were to escape, and directed everything to that end. The only bribery was that practised upon the old convict I have mentioned, to induce him to bring us a newspaper, contrary to the warden's rules, that we might find out about the trains for Cincinnati, and the convict in question had not the slightest idea what we wanted it for. I believe Warden N. L. Merion was perfectly loyal to the Union."

BREVET BRIGADIER-GENERAL O. E. BABCOCK.

MAJOR-GENERAL EDW. R. S. CANBY.

MAJOR-GENERAL C. M. CLAY.

BREVET BRIGADIER-GENERAL ANSON G. McCOOK.

UNION AND CONFEDERATE RAIDS AND RAIDERS.

BY GEORGE L. KILMER.

BEALL, THE LAKE RAIDER—ANDREWS AND HIS DISGUISED RAIDERS—LIEUTENANT CUSHING'S BOAT RAIDS—KILPATRICK'S RAID BY RICHMOND—MORGAN'S KENTUCKY RAID—RAIDING A CITY.

THE secret enterprise which placed Lieutenant Davis in a dungeon cell and nearly cost him his life had a deeply tragic ending for John Y. Beall, the young Virginian, executed at Fort Columbus, New York Harbor, the 24th of February, 1865. Beall was the chief promoter and the leader of the Lake Erie raid in the fall of 1864, but technically the offence for which he suffered was that of a spy. The judge advocate of the court which condemned him spoke of the prisoner as one "whom violent passions had shorn of his nature's elements of manliness, and led him to commit deeds which to have even suspected him of at an earlier stage in his career would have been a calumny and a crime."

Beall had been wounded in the Confederate service early in the conflict. As master in the navy, he had led for a time the daring, reckless life of a "swamp angel" in the lower Potomac, destroying the Union commerce in Chesapeake Bay and its adjacent waters.

While thus engaged, he planned a lake raid, but failed to get his government to sanction the project until 1864, when the Northwestern Confederacy movement made it necessary for Jacob Thompson and his co-conspirators in Canada to have a foothold upon Union soil along the border.

BRIGADIER-GENERAL JUDSON KILPATRICK.
(Afterward Major-General.)

One of Thompson's cherished plans was an uprising of the notorious Sons of Liberty at Chicago, during the Democratic national convention in August, 1864. About this time Beall arrived at Sandusky, O., with authority to proceed on his raiding enterprise. Thompson had prepared the way for him by a careful investigation of the lake defences, through an emissary located at Sandusky—Capt. Charles H. Cole, formerly of Morgan's raiders. Cole was supplied with means to entertain and bribe such Union officials as might be of service to the Confederacy; and he finally concluded that the control of the lakes could be secured by the capture of the gunboat *Michigan*, the sole defender of the waters, and the liberation of the Confederate prisoners at Camp Douglas, Chicago, and at Johnson's Island in Sandusky Bay.

Thompson gave Cole authority to capture the *Michigan*, and appointed Beall to aid him. It was arranged between Cole and Beall that the former would remain in Sandusky and coöperate by bribing some of the men on the *Michigan*, and by preparing the prisoners on Johnson's Island for an outbreak. The *Michigan* lay off the island. The date was fixed for the night of September 19th, and Beall went to Canada to organize a force, hazarding everything, as will be seen, on the success of his confederate, who, at the decisive moment, when Beall's attacking party should arrive off Sandusky, was to make rocket signals from Johnson's Island that the expected aid was a certainty.

Beall secured the services of nineteen Confederate refugees, chiefly escaped prisoners of war harbored in Canada, and the party disguised in civilian dress took passage on a steamer plying between Sandusky and Detroit, carrying in their baggage a supply of revolvers and hatchets. At the proper time, the captain in his office, and the mate at the wheel, were told to vacate their stations, revolvers were suddenly brandished right and left to intimidate the officers and men, and Beall as spokesman declared, "I take possession of this boat in the name of the Confederate States."

Under his direction the vessel was put about and headed for Middle Boss Island, in Ohio waters, where the passengers and regular crew were set ashore.

From the island Beall bore his vessel directly for the gunboat *Michigan*, steamed up within cannon range, and awaited a rocket signal. When the hour passed and no signal came, he decided to risk everything, board the gunboat at all hazards, and strike for Johnson's Island. In his crisis an unlooked-for event dashed his high resolves suddenly to the ground. The crew of the *Philo Parsons* mutinied. The absence of the shore signals was interpreted by them as a warning that the plot had been discovered; and, although Beall argued and pleaded, the men insisted that the death penalty awaited them if captured, and they felt certain that such would be the end of it all. Their boat was then run to the Canada shore, abandoned, and destroyed.

LIEUTENANT-GENERAL NATHAN B. FORREST, C. S. A.

The scene now changes to Union soil. On the night of the 15th of December, 1864, the engineer on an eastern-bound express train on the Erie railroad, between Buffalo and Dunkirk, saw a railroad rail across the track, in front of his engine, just in time to reverse and strike the obstruction at reduced speed without severe damage. The next night two policemen at the New York Central depot, Niagara City, arrested two suspicious men who were about to take the cars for Canada. Beall was one of them, and, though he made some attempt to deny his identity, he was sent to New York City and accused of the lake raid and of the attempt at train wrecking. The clerk of the *Philo Parsons*, and one of the passengers, and also a confederate in the attempt on the train, identified him, and furnished ample evidence for a case.

The train-wrecking enterprise was doubtless a last resort by Beall to secure funds for the prosecution of his plans on the lake. Five men were engaged in it. The party lay hidden near the track when the train struck, and seeing that the damage was only trifling they hastened to Buffalo and secreted themselves. Subsequently the arrest of Beall took place, purely on suspicion.

He was arraigned on two charges—violation of the laws of war and acting as a spy. His defence was that his acts had been justifiable acts of war; and, if confined to his attempt on the gunboat *Michigan* and the Johnson's Island prison, the plea might have had weight. But every circumstance likely to weigh in his favor, his education, his noble bearing, his manly conduct toward the captives on the *Philo Parsons*, was lost sight of in the appalling railroad horror that had been planned with such cool deliberation, and with no purpose evident other than robbery—robbery at the sacrifice of innocent lives.

A most deplorable tragedy brought about by the spy system, or what was analogous to that, and involving the execution of six Ohio soldiers,* also the imprisonment of sixteen others, who barely escaped the gallows, is the story of the Andrews railroad raid, or bridge-burning expedition, in Georgia, in the spring of 1862.

During General Buell's occupancy of Central Tennessee, before the armies marched to Shiloh, he had occasionally employed the services of a spy, named James J. Andrews, who carried on a contraband trade in quinine, and in the course of his travels across the border often managed to pick up information valuable to the Union generals. At his solicitation, Buell permitted a detail from three regiments belonging to General Sill's brigade, the Thirty-third, Twenty-first, and Second Ohio, to set out with him, disguised in civilian's dress. They were to burn the railway bridges east and west of Chattanooga, and thus isolate that important town, possibly insuring its speedy capture. The soldiers were given to understand that they took their lives in their hands, but none declined the dangerous honor. Guided by Andrews, they started from Shelbyville, April 7th, and in five days made their way to Marietta, Ga., losing but two of their number on the road. At Marietta two more disappeared, leaving Andrews with eighteen soldiers and a civilian volunteer to undertake the hazardous work mapped out by the leader, which was to capture an engine with a few cars attached, board them, and speed westward, firing the bridges as they passed. Securing tickets at Marietta, they entered a westbound train as ordinary passengers. At Big Sandy station, where the trainmen took breakfast, these *pseudo* passengers left their seats, and two of them, William Knight and Wilson Brown, professional engineers, leaped into the cab. The coupling bolt of the third car from the tender was pulled, and the remainder of the party scrambled on board as best they could. Off sped the stolen train in full view of scores of astonished bystanders and railroad men. What made the deed doubly risky was the fact that a camp of Confederate soldiers had been established at Big Sandy since Andrews's last visit there, and the station was surrounded by armed men. In fact, a sentinel, musket in hand, stood within a few yards of the engine, watching the whole proceeding, but too dazed to act or sound the alarm. But this amazement was short-lived. The railroad men were prompt to give chase, first with a hand-car, afterward with a chance engine picked up on the road. The raiders were delayed by eastward trains, it being a single-track line; but with singular good fortune ran over half the distance to Chattanooga, having stopped to cut telegraph wires and remove rails, in order to baffle their pursuers. The attempt to fire bridges failed. It was raining, and the would-be incendiaries had provided no combustibles beyond what the train supplied. In the meanwhile their pursuers picked up a car-load of armed men, and came up with the runaway train west of Dalton, where the fuel of the stolen engine gave out, bringing the raiders to a dead stop. Andrews gave the word, "Save who can," and all sprang for the woods, but were captured within a few days. Taken within the enemy's lines in citizen's dress, a court-martial pronounced them spies worthy of death. Andrews, with six of the soldiers, also the citizen volunteer, were executed at Atlanta. The others, including the two Marietta delinquents who had been arrested and identified, were thrown into dungeons; but preferring death in any form to the fate which seemed to await them, they succeeded one day in overpowering their guards, and so escaping to the woods. Eight of the party made their way North, while the other six were recaptured and held until the spring of 1863, when they were exchanged for a like number of Confederate soldiers held by the Union authorities, to answer for a similar offence.

JAMES J. ANDREWS.

Cushing was not picturesque in figure, though marked by strong individual peculiarities. His height was five feet ten inches, his form slender, his face grave and thoughtful. With steps springy and quick, prominent cheek bones, a piercing eye and restless habit, he seemed to his associates like some spirited Indian in the garb of a paleface.

In July, 1862, a lieutenant's straps were given him for acts of bravery performed in his routine duties with the blockading squadron off North Carolina. Four months later, at the age of twenty, he commanded his first expedition, a gunboat raid into New River Inlet, waters wholly in the possession of active enemies. His vessel, the *Ellis*, stranded within range of the Confederate batteries, but he brought his crew and equipments off in schooners captured before the disaster. A few weeks later he entered Little River at night with twenty-five men, in

* George D. Wilson, Marion A. Ross. and Perry G. Shadrack, Second Ohio; Samuel Slavens and Samuel Robinson, Thirty-third Ohio; and John Scott, Twenty-first Ohio.

BREVET BRIGADIER-GENERAL ELY S. PARKER.

BREVET BRIGADIER-GENERAL HORACE CAPRON.

BRIGADIER-GENERAL W. A. GORMAN.

MAJOR-GENERAL CHRISTOPHER C. AUGUR.

BRIGADIER-GENERAL JAMES B. FRY.

BRIGADIER-GENERAL CHARLES K. GRAHAM.

BRIGADIER-GENERAL THOMAS C. DEVIN.

MAJOR-GENERAL NELSON A. MILES.

COLONEL HORACE PORTER.

BRIGADIER-GENERAL GERSHOM MOTT.

LIEUTENANT WILLIAM B. CUSHING.

a cutter, dispersed the gunners of a shore battery by land assault, and got out with the loss of one man. Cushing sometimes volunteered, and at others was chosen, for these fugitive exploits.

In the summer of 1863 it was known on the blockading fleet that the Confederates possessed a couple of rams and some torpedo boats in Cape Fear River around Wilmington; and on the night of June 25 Cushing set out from his ship *Monticello* in a cutter, with two officers and fifteen men, and crossed the bar, passing some forts and the town of Smithville without discovery. On the way his boat nearly collided with a blockade runner putting to sea, and also with a Confederate guard-boat. The night was dark until the cutter was abreast of a fortified bluff known as the Brunswick batteries, when the moon suddenly emerged from a cloud and disclosed the strange craft to the enemy's sentinels on shore. Shots were fired at the cutter, and the garrison was alarmed. Cushing directed his men to pull to the opposite shore and proceed up the river. When within seven miles of Wilmington the boat was hidden in a marsh, and the party lay all next day within sight of passing blockade runners.

After dark the cutter took to the wave and captured two rowboats filled with men, who proved to be fishermen from Wilmington. Cushing impressed them for guides and reconnoitred all the batteries and forts on the river. He discovered that the ram *Raleigh* was a hopeless wreck, the ram *North Carolina* useless because her draught didn't admit of passing the bar to attack the Union blockading fleet, and that the Confederate torpedo boats had been destroyed during a scare. On the way to sea the cutter was headed off by a gunboat and several small boats filled with men. It was night and the moon shone, and Cushing managed to turn and double on his pursuers until he got a start on them, and by vigorous rowing dashed into the breakers at the Carolina shoal, where the enemy dare not follow. The cutter was so heavy that she outrode the breakers and escaped to the fleet. On this raid two days and three nights were spent in the enemy's territory.

In the month of February, 1864, the Administration at Washington proposed a cavalry raid to Richmond. One object was to circulate, within the Confederate lines, the President's amnesty proclamation, offering full pardon and a restoration of rights to any individuals, or to States, that might wish to return to their allegiance. Another was the release of the Union prisoners in Belle Isle and Libby prisons. The expedition was intrusted to Kilpatrick, who was to have a picked force of four thousand cavalrymen and a horse battery.

It was believed in the Union camps that a surprise could be effected, and with this end in view, Kilpatrick set out one Sunday night, the 28th of February, for the lower fords of the Rapidan. Reaching Spottsylvania unmolested, he sent out from here a detachment of five hundred men, under Col. Ulric Dahlgren, toward the Virginia Central Railroad, instructing him to enter Richmond from the south, while he himself should attack from the north. Through the treachery or ignorance of a negro guide engaged by Dahlgren, his column failed to find a ford in the James River, which was a serious drawback, because he had intended to enter Richmond from the rear, the weakest point. On March 1st, Dahlgren was eight miles west of Richmond on the James, and Kilpatrick at Atlee's station, eight miles north, the distance between them being only about twelve miles. Kilpatrick, however, was returning from his raid, and the two forces were destined to remain apart and receive severe handling from enemies now swarming about them.

Kilpatrick had passed the outer defences of Richmond by one o'clock of the 1st, but on approaching the inner line he was met by infantry and artillery. Skirmishing continued for several hours, the object of the Union leader being to prolong the situation until he should hear Dahlgren on the opposite side of the city. Finally, as he saw Confederate troops moving in large bodies, he withdrew to Atlee's to pass the night.

The Confederate cavalry command of Gen. Wade Hampton was strung along the railroad between Lee's army and Richmond, and Gen. Bradley T. Johnson, leading a brigade under him, had learned of Kilpatrick's march and telegraphed to Richmond on the 29th that a raid was abroad. He also had notified the troops all along the line, and both himself and Hampton followed in Kilpatrick's path, about a day behind him. On the night of the 1st Hampton attacked Kilpatrick's camp at Atlee's and drove him out. The following morning Kilpatrick started down the Peninsula toward White House, on the Pamunkey.

On the day of Kilpatrick's farthest advance Dahlgren had drawn to within five miles of the city and then retired. After dark of that day he, too, started to move down the peninsula along the Pamunkey. Placing the main body in reserve, Dahlgren rode on ahead with the advance guard, and on the next night fell into ambush prepared by a number of cavalry officers who were at their homes in the vicinity on recruiting service or leave of absence.

A challenge to halt Dahlgren answered by a threat, and the commander of the Confederate outpost gave the order instantly to fire. At the first volley Dahlgren fell dead. His men were surrounded and held until daylight, when the whole party of survivors surrendered.

The chief victim of this raid, Colonel Dahlgren, was the son of Admiral John A. Dahlgren, and at his death was twenty-two years old. Early in the war he had served as an artillerist with Generals Sigel, Frémont, and Pope in northern Virginia. On the retreat of Lee from Gettysburg toward the Potomac, Dahlgren was at the front under Kilpatrick, leading about one hundred men, and in the encounter with Stuart at Hagarstown, July 6th, he received a wound in the foot that cost him his leg. Having been commissioned colonel in the cavalry service, he returned to the front wearing a cork leg, but was obliged to depend on crutches. He volunteered for the expedition in which he lost his life.

Morgan the raider had given the North an exhibition of his boldness before he entered upon that celebrated ride across Ohio in 1863. On the 13th of July, 1862, President Lincoln telegraphed from Washington to the Union commander in the far West, "They are having a stampede in Kentucky. Please look to it."

The whole trouble was caused by Colonel Morgan, with a couple of cavalry regiments, and a clever telegraph operator named Ellsworth. Ellsworth tapped the wires between Nashville and Louisville, and sent a bogus despatch to the Union authorities in the latter city, stating that Morgan was operating around the former, when, in reality, he was riding northward toward the heart of Kentucky. Moving along the railroad lines, Union operators were everywhere surprised at their keys and compelled to serve the raider's commands, while Ellsworth manipulated the wires. In this way the Union forces ahead on the line of march were ordered out of the road, or drawn off by false alarms, and Morgan was able to get exact knowledge as to the location and numbers of the Union garrisons. At Georgetown, only sixty miles from Cincinnati, he halted for two days, producing, by means of the wires, a terrible scare in Lexington, and drawing all the Union forces to that region. He himself then moved southward to cross into Tennessee, Ellsworth managing to counteract the Union orders for pursuit during the retreat by his bogus telegrams. So the raiders finished their long ride without once encountering an armed foe.

MAJOR-GENERAL WINFIELD S. HANCOCK.

Forrest marched to Memphis on his memorable raid in August, 1864, with a detachment of his choicest cavalry, numbering fifteen hundred men. The leader of the advanced guard was his brother, Captain W. H. Forrest, and into his hands the general gave the difficult task of opening the main road to the town. Captain Forrest approached the outer pickets about daylight on Sunday morning, knocked the challenging vidette senseless with the handle of his sabre, and with ten athletic followers disarmed the reserves on the nearest post. A musket accidentally discharged during the *mêlée* aroused others near by, and the entire main camp of ten thousand soldiers stretching around the city soon caught the alarm.

Nothing daunted, Forrest galloped his men into the heart of the stronghold, bent upon creating a panic for ulterior purposes of his own, and he succeeded. Captain Forrest's band, followed by another detachment, dashed down the main street to the Gayo House, riding over an artillery camp on the way, and leaped their horses up the steps into the office and dining-hall. Still another body, led by Colonel Jesse Forrest, rode to the headquarters of the Union commandant, General Hurlbut, who escaped capture by the merest accident. In a few moments all Memphis was in an uproar; and the raiders, moving in five isolated bodies, were overpowered in detail and compelled to unite before they could cut their way out. But Forrest had effected his purpose, and the glory of the exploit compensated him for the haste with which he was obliged to abandon the hazardous game.

CONFEDERATE ARTILLERY CAPTURED AT ATLANTA.

WOMAN'S CONTRIBUTION TO THE CAUSE.

At the close of the chapter on the Sanitary and Christian Commissions we have given some account of the work of a few of the women whose service was connected with or similar to that of those organizations. It would require many pages to tell the entire story of the contribution of the loyal women to the cause of the Union—a most noble story, however monotonous and repetitious. It is impossible to publish the records of all who served thus, any more than to treat of every citizen who stepped into the ranks and, as a simple private, gave his life for his country. But a specific account of what was done by some of them will give the reader a more vivid idea of the great price that was paid for the unity of our country and the perpetuation of our government than can be conveyed by any general statement. It is the story of women who did not urge their brothers and lovers to go to the field without themselves following as far and as closely as the law would let them, and sharing in the toils, the privations, and sometimes even the peculiar perils, of war. Many of them lost their lives, directly or indirectly, in consequence of their labors.

> "On fields where Strife held riot,
> And Slaughter fed his hounds,
> Where came no sense of quiet,
> Nor any gentle sounds,
> They made their rounds.
>
> "They wrought without repining,
> And, weary watches o'er,
> They passed the bounds confining
> Our green, familiar shore
> Forevermore."

It is claimed for Mrs. Almira Fales, of Washington, that she was the first woman in the United States to perform any work for the comfort of the soldiers during the Rebellion. In December, 1860, when South Carolina had seceded and she saw that war was very probable, if not certain, she began the preparation of lint and hospital stores, in anticipation of the hostilities that did not break out until the next April. Her husband was employed by the Government, and her sons entered the army. During the war she emptied seven thousand boxes of hospital stores, and distributed to the sick and wounded soldiers comforts and delicacies to the value of one hundred and fifty thousand dollars. She spent several months at sea attending to the wounded on hospital ships, and during the seven days' battles she was under fire on the Peninsula. One of her sons was killed in the battle of Chancellorsville. It was said that she was full of a quaint humor, and her visits to the hospitals never failed to awaken smiles and bring about a general air of cheerfulness.

Mrs. Harris, wife of John Harris, M.D., of Philadelphia, was one of the earliest volunteers in the work, and one who had, perhaps, the widest experience in its various branches. She is described as a pale and delicate woman, and yet she endured very hard service in the cause of her country. At the beginning of the war she became corresponding secretary of the Ladies' Aid Society of Philadelphia, but very soon she went to the field as its correspondent and one of its active workers. In the spring of 1862 she accompanied the Army of the Potomac to the Peninsula, and spent several weeks in the hospitals at Fort Monroe. After the battle of Fair Oaks she went on board a transport that was given to the wounded, and she thus describes what she saw there: "There were eight hundred on board. Passage-ways, state-rooms, floors from the dark and fœtid hold to the hurricane deck, were all more than filled; some on mattresses, some on blankets, others on straw; some in the death-struggle, others nearing it, some already beyond human sympathy and help;

some in their blood as they had been brought from the battle-field of the Sabbath previous, and all hungry and thirsty, not having had anything to eat or drink, except hard crackers, for twenty-four hours. When we carried in bread, hands from every quarter were outstretched, and the cry, 'Give me a piece, oh, please! I have had nothing since Monday.' Another, 'Nothing but hard crackers since the fight,' etc. When we had dealt out nearly all the bread, a surgeon came in and cried, 'Do please keep some for the poor fellows in the hold, they are so badly off for everything.' So with the remnant we threaded our way through the suffering crowd, amid such exclamations as, 'Oh! please don't touch my foot!' or, 'For mercy's sake, don't touch my arm!' another, 'Please don't move the blanket, I am so terribly cut up,' down to the hold, in which were not less than one hundred and fifty, nearly all sick, some very sick. It was like plunging into a vapor bath, so hot, close, and full of moisture, and then in this dismal place we distributed our bread, oranges, and pickles, which were seized upon with avidity. And here let me say, at least twenty of them told us next day that the pickles had done them more good than all the medicine they had taken." In the autumn of 1863, just after the battle of Chickamauga, she went to the West and began work at Nashville among the refugees. Afterward, at Chattanooga, she labored in the hospitals until her strength was overtaxed, and for several weeks her life was despaired of. Coming again to the East, in the spring of 1864, she was with the Army of the Potomac in its bloody campaign through the Wilderness, and afterward with the Army of the Shenandoah. In the spring of 1865 she visited North Carolina to care for the released prisoners of Andersonville and Salisbury.

MISS MARGARET E. BRECKENRIDGE.

MRS. CORDELIA A. P. HARVEY.

Mrs. Eliza C. Porter, of Chicago, after her eldest son had enlisted, devoted herself to the work, first taking charge of the Sanitary Commission rooms in that city, and in the spring of 1862 going to the army hospitals. At Cairo, she and other women were accustomed to work from four o'clock in the morning until ten at night. They went to the front at Pittsburgh Landing, and not only labored in the hospitals, but did much for refugees and escaped slaves, and established schools for the blacks. In a letter written from a field hospital near Chattanooga, in January, 1864, she says: "The field hospital was in a forest, about five miles from Chattanooga; wood was abundant, and the camp was warmed by immense burning 'log heaps,' which were the only fire-places or cooking-stoves of the camp or hospitals. Men were detailed to fell the trees and pile the logs to heat the air, which was very wintry. And beside them Mrs. Bickerdyke made soup and toast, tea and coffee, and broiled mutton without a gridiron, often blistering her fingers in the process. A house in due time was demolished to make bunks for the worst cases, and the brick from the chimney was converted into an oven, when Mrs. Bickerdyke made bread, yeast having been found in the Chicago boxes, and flour at a neighboring mill, which had furnished flour to secessionists through the war until now. Great multitudes were fed from these rude kitchens. Companies of hungry soldiers were refreshed before those open fire-places and from those ovens. On one occasion a citizen came and told the men to follow him; he would show them a reserve of beef and sheep which had been provided for General Bragg's army, and about thirty head of cattle and twenty sheep was the prize. Large potash kettles were found, which were used over the huge log fires, and various kitchen utensils for cooking were brought into camp from time to time, almost every day adding to our conveniences. The most harrowing scenes are daily witnessed here. A wife came on yesterday only to learn that her dear husband had died the morning previous. Her lamentations were heart-breaking. 'Why could he not have lived until I came? Why?' In the evening came a sister, whose aged parents had sent her to search for their only son. She also came too late. The brother had gone to the soldier's grave two days previous. One continued wail of sorrow goes up from all parts of this stricken land."

MRS. MARY A. BICKERDYKE.

Mrs. Mary Bickerdyke, mentioned in Mrs. Porter's letter, was a widow in Cleveland, Ohio, at the opening of the war, and immediately gave herself to the work. Leaving her two little boys at home, she went to the front and made herself useful in the hospitals at Savannah, Chattanooga, and other points. She was a woman of great energy and courage, and it is said that, in carrying on her work for the sick and wounded soldiers, she used to violate military rules without the least hesitation, in order to obtain what she wanted. On one occasion, when she found that an assistant surgeon had been off on a drunken spree and had not made out the special diet list for his ward, leaving the men without any breakfast, she not only denounced him to his face but caused him to be discharged from the service. Going to General Sherman to obtain reinstatement, the surgeon was asked: "Who caused your discharge?" "Why," said he, "I suppose it was Mrs. Bickerdyke." "If that is the case," said General Sherman, "I can do nothing for you. She ranks me." Finding great difficulty in obtaining milk, butter, and eggs for her hospital in Memphis, she resolved to establish a dairy of her own. She therefore went to Illinois, and in one of its farming regions obtained stock, by begging, until she had two hundred cows and one thousand hens, which she took to Memphis, where the commanding general gave her an island in the Mississippi, on which she established her dairy. Her clothing was riddled with holes from sparks at the open fires where she cooked for the field hospitals, and some ladies in Chicago sent her a box of clothing for herself, which included two elegant nightdresses trimmed with ruffles and lace. Using only some of the plainest garments, she traded others with secessionist women of the vicinity for delicacies for the hospital. The two nightdresses she reserved to sell in some place where she thought they would bring a higher price; but on the way to Kentucky she found two wounded soldiers in a miserable shanty for whom nothing had been done, and, after attending to their wounds and finding that they had no shirts, she gave them the nightdresses, ruffles, lace, and all.

Miss Margaret Elizabeth Breckenridge was a native of Philadelphia, but was closely related to the well-known Breckenridge family of Kentucky. She entered upon hospital service at the West in the spring of 1862, and served constantly as long as her health and strength permitted. In June, 1864, while she was prostrated by illness, the news came that her brother-in-law, Col. Peter A. Porter, had been killed in the battle of Cold Harbor, and this proved a greater shock than she could bear. She had been especially helpful in cheering up the soldiers in the hospitals and writing letters for them. One very young soldier who lay wounded said to her: "Where do you come from? How could such a lady as you are come down here to take care of us poor, sick, dirty boys?" "I consider it an honor to wait on you," she said, "and wash off the mud you waded through for me." Another man said: "Please write down your name and let me look at it, and take it home, to show my wife who wrote my letters and combed my hair and fed me. I don't believe you're like other people."

Mrs. Stephen Barker, who was a sister of the attorney-general of Massachusetts, and whose husband was chaplain of a regiment from that State, gave nearly the whole four years of the war to hospital duty, mostly in and around Washington, where at one time she had charge of ten hospitals, which she carefully inspected herself with perfect regularity. In her report she says: "I remember no scenes in camp more picturesque than some of our visits have presented. The great open army wagon stands under some shade-tree, with the officer who has volunteered to help, or the regular field agent, standing in the midst of boxes, bales, and bundles. Wheels, sides, and every projecting point are crowded with eager soldiers, to see what the 'Sanitary' has brought for them. By the side of the great wagon stands the light wagon of the lady, with its curtains all rolled up, while she arranges before and around her the supplies she is to distribute. Another eager crowd surrounds her, patient, kind, and respectful as the first, except that a shade more of softness in their look and tone attest the ever-living power of woman over the rough elements of manhood. In these hours of personal communication with the soldier she finds the true meaning of her work. This is her golden opportunity, when by look and tone and movement she may call up, as if by magic, the pure influences of home, which may have been long banished by the hard necessities of war. Quietly and rapidly the supplies are handed out for companies A, B, C, etc., first from one wagon, then the other, and as soon as a regiment is completed the men hurry back to their tents to receive their share, and write letters on the newly received paper, or apply the long-needed comb or mend the gaping seams in their now 'historic garments.' When at last the supplies are exhausted, and sunset reminds us that we are yet many miles from home, we gather up the remnants, bid good-by to the friendly faces, which already seem like old acquaintances, promising to come again to visit new regiments to-morrow, and hurry home to prepare for the next day's work. Every day, from the first to the twentieth day of June, our little band of missionaries has repeated a day's work such as I have now described."

Miss Amy M. Bradley, a native and resident of Maine, who had been for some years a teacher, volunteered as a nurse at the very beginning of the war and went out with the Fifth Maine regiment, many of the soldiers in which had been her pupils. She became noted for the efficiency and good condition of the hospitals over which she presided, and in December, 1862, was sent to what the soldiers called Camp Misery, on the opposite side of the Potomac from Washington, as a special relief agent of the Sanitary Commission. This camp, as its name indicated, was in a deplorable condition; but she immediately instituted reforms which rapidly improved it. She not only obtained supplies for the invalids and others who were there, but brought about a system of transfer by which more than two thousand of them were sent where they could be taken care of more comfortably, and she was especially efficient in setting right the accounts of men who were suffering from informality in their papers. In eight months she procured the reinstatement of one hundred and fifty soldiers who had been unjustly dropped from the rolls as deserters, and secured their arrears of pay for them.

Miss Arabella Griffith was a native of New Jersey, and at the beginning of the war was engaged to Francis C. Barlow, a promising young lawyer. On April 19, 1861, Mr. Barlow enlisted as a private; on the 20th they were married, and on the 21st he went with his regiment to Washington. A week later Mrs. Barlow followed him, and still later she joined in the hospital work of the Sanitary Commission. The day after the battle of Antietam she found her husband badly wounded, and when, in the spring, he went to the field again, she accompanied him. At Gettysburg he was again wounded and was left within the enemy's lines, but she by great effort managed to get him within the Union lines, where she took care not only of him, but many others of the wounded men in that great battle. In the spring of 1864 she was again in the field, hard at work in the hospitals that were nearest the front. A friend who knew her at this time writes: "We call her 'The Raider.' At Fredericksburg she had in some way gained possession of a wretched-looking pony and a small cart, with which she was continually on the move, driving about town or country in search of such provisions or other articles as were needed for the sick and wounded. The surgeon in charge had on one occasion assigned to us the task of preparing a building, which had been taken for a hospital, for a large number of wounded who were expected immediately. It was empty, containing not the slightest furniture, save a large number of bed-sacks, without material to fill them. On requisition a quantity of straw was obtained, but not nearly enough, and we were standing in a mute despair when Mrs. Barlow came in. 'I'll find some more straw,' was her cheerful reply, and in another moment she was urging her tired beast toward another part of the town where she remembered having seen a bale of straw earlier in the day. Half an hour afterward it had been confiscated, loaded upon the little wagon, and brought to the hospital." Her health became so impaired in the field that, in July, 1864, she died. Her husband, meanwhile, had risen to the rank of brigadier-general, and was known as one of the most gallant men in the army. Surgeon W. H. Reed, writing of her, said: "In the open field she toiled with Mr. Marshall and Miss Gilson, under the scorching sun, with no shelter from the pouring rains, with no thought but for those who were suffering and dying all around her. On the battlefield of Petersburg, hardly out of range of the enemy and at night witnessing the blazing lines of fire from right to left, among the wounded, with her sympathies and powers both of mind and body strained to the last degree, neither conscious that she was working beyond her strength nor realizing the extreme exhaustion of her system, she fainted at her work, and found, only when it was too late, that the raging fever was wasting her life away. Yet to the last her sparkling wit, her brilliant intellect, her unfailing good humor, lighted up our moments of rest and recreation."

MRS. MARY MORRIS HUSBAND.

MRS. MARY A. LIVERMORE.

Mrs. Nellie M. Taylor (May Dewey) was a native of Watertown, New York, but settled with her husband in New Orleans. There, on the breaking out of the war, she was subjected to all kinds of persecution because she was a Unionist. On one occasion a mob assembled around her house, where she was watching at the bedside of her dying husband, and the leader said: "Madam, we give you five minutes to decide whether you are for the South or for the North. If at the end of that time you declare yourself for the South, your house shall remain; if for the North, it must come down." "Sir," she answered, "I will say to you and your crowd that I am, always have been, and ever shall be, for the Union. Tear my house down if you choose!" The mob seemed to be a little ashamed of themselves at this answer, and finally dispersed without destroying the house. Seven times before the capture of the city by the National forces her home was searched by self-constituted committees of citizens, who every time found the National flag displayed at the head of her bed; and on one occasion she was actually fired at from a window. Mrs. Taylor gave a large part of her time during the war to hard work in the hospitals, and in addition she spent many of her earnings for the benefit of the sick and wounded soldiers.

In the spring of 1862, Governor Harvey, of Wisconsin, visited General Grant's army with medicines and other supplies for the wounded from his State, and just after the battle of Shiloh he was accidentally drowned there. His widow, Cordelia P. Harvey, devoted herself to the work in which he had lost his life, and served faithfully in the hospitals of that department. One of her most valuable achievements consisted in persuading the government to establish general hospitals in the Northern States, where suffering soldiers might be sent and have a better chance of recovery than if kept in the hospitals further south.

Mrs. Sarah R. Johnston was a native of North Carolina, and at the beginning of the war was teaching at Salisbury, in that State. When the first prisoners were brought to the town for confinement in the stockade there, the secessionist women turned out in carriages to escort them through the town, and greeted them with contemptuous epithets as they filed past. The sight of this determined Mrs. Johnston to devote herself to the work of ameliorating their condition. This subjected her to all sorts of insults from her townspeople and broke up her school; but she persevered, nevertheless, and earned the gratitude of many of the unfortunate men who there suffered from the studied cruelty of the Confederate government. She made up her carpets and spare blankets into moccasins, which she gave to the prisoners as they arrived; and when they stood in front of her house waiting their turn to be mustered into the prison, she supplied them, as far as she could, with bread and water, for in many instances they had been on the railroad forty-eight hours with nothing to eat or drink. The prisoners were not permitted to leave their ranks to assist her in obtaining the water, all of which had to be drawn from a well with an old-fashioned windlass. On one occasion a Confederate sergeant in charge told her that if she attempted to do anything for the Yankees or come outside her gate, he would pin her to the earth with his bayonet. Paying no attention to this, she took a basket of bread in one hand and a bucket of water in the other, and walked past him on her usual errand. The sergeant followed her and touched her upon the shoulder with the point of his bayonet, whereupon she turned and asked him why he did not pin her to the earth, as he had promised to. Some of the Confederate soldiers called out: "Sergeant, you can't make anything out of that woman; you had better leave her alone." And then he desisted.

Mrs. Mary Morris Husband, of Philadelphia, was a granddaughter of Robert Morris of Revolutionary fame. When her son, who had enlisted in the Army of the Potomac, was seriously ill on the Peninsula, she went there to take care of him, and what she saw determined her to give her services to the country as a nurse. She was on one of the hospital transports at Harrison's Landing when the Confederates bombarded it, but kept right on with her work as if she were not under fire. She was at Antietam immediately after the battle, and remained there two months in charge of the wounded, sleeping in a tent in all kinds of weather and attending the hospital with perfect regularity. She contrived an ensign for her tent by cutting out the figure of a bottle in red flannel and sewing it upon a piece of calico, this bottle flag indicating the place where medicines were to be obtained.

In the severe winter of 1862–63 she often left her tent several times in the night and visited the cots of those who were apparently near death, to make sure that the nurses did not neglect them; and when diphtheria appeared in the hospital and many of the nurses left from fear of it, she remained at her post just as if there were no such thing as a contagious disease. It is said that in several instances where she believed a soldier had been unjustly condemned by court-martial, she obtained a pardon or commutation of his sentence by laying the case directly before President Lincoln.

MRS. HENRIETTA L. COLT.

MISS EMILY E. PARSONS.

MRS. R. H. SPENCER.

Miss Katherine P. Wormeley, known of late as a translator of Balzac's works, is a native of England. Her father, born in Virginia, was an officer in the British Navy. Her mother was a native of Boston. At the beginning of the war Miss Wormeley was living at Newport, R. I., and almost at once she enlisted in the work of aid for the soldiers. When the hospital transport service was organized, in the summer of 1862, she was one of the first volunteers for that branch of the service. Later she had charge of a large hospital in Rhode Island, which held two thousand five hundred patients.

Among others who volunteered for the hospital transport service were Mrs. Joseph Howland, whose husband was colonel of the Sixteenth New York regiment, and her sister, Mrs. Robert S. Howland, whose husband was a clergyman working in the hospitals. The latter Mrs. Howland, who died in 1864, was the author of a short poem, entitled "In the Hospital," which has become famous.

> "I lay me down to sleep, with little thought or care
> Whether my waking find me here—or there!
>
> A bowing, burdened head, that only asks to rest,
> Unquestioning, upon a loving breast.
>
> My good right hand forgets its cunning now;
> To march the weary march I know not how.
>
> I am not eager, bold, nor strong—all that is past;
> I am ready not to do at last, at last.
>
> My half-day's work is done, and this is all my part—
> I give a patient God my patient heart;
>
> And grasp His banner still, though all the blue be dim:
> These stripes, as well as stars, lead after Him."

These two ladies had two unmarried sisters, Jane C. and Georgiana M. Woolsey, who also were in the service. Miss Georgiana Woolsey wrote some entertaining letters from the seat of war, in one of which she tells of some women in Gettysburg who, like Jennie Wade, kept at their work of making bread for the soldiers while the battle was going on. One of them had refused to leave the house or go into the cellar until a third shell passed through the room, when, having got the last loaf into the oven, she ran down the stairs. "Why did you not go before?" she was asked. "Oh, you see," she answered, "if I had, the rebels would 'a' come in and daubed the dough all over the place." These ladies were cousins of Miss Sarah C. Woolsey, who is now, under her pen-name of Susan Coolidge, well known as a writer for the young. She also served for some time in the hospitals.

Anna Maria Ross, of Philadelphia, was known as a most energetic worker in the hospitals, chiefly in what was called the Cooper Shop Hospital of Philadelphia, of which she was principal until, from overwork and anxiety, she died in December, 1863.

Miss Mary J. Safford, a native of Vermont, was living in Cairo, Ill., when the war began, and at once enlisted in the work of aid for the soldiers. Immediately after the battle of Shiloh she went to the front with a large supply of hospital stores, and labored there day and night for three weeks, when she came North with a transport loaded with wounded men. She is said to have been the first woman in the West to engage in this work. The hardships that she endured caused a disease of the spine, and at the end of a year and a half she broke down, and had to be sent to Europe for treatment.

Mrs. Annie Wittenmeyer, of Iowa, was appointed sanitary agent for that State, and is said to have been the originator of the diet kitchens attached to the hospitals. The object of these was to have the food for the wounded and sick prepared in a skilful manner and administered according to surgeons' orders, and they were a very efficient branch of the hospital service.

Another Iowa woman who devoted herself to the service was Miss Melcenia Elliott. She served in the hospitals in Tennessee, and afterward in St. Louis had charge of the Home for Refugees. Here she established a school, and instituted many reforms in the direction of cleanliness and industry. It is related that in Memphis, when she was refused admission to one of the hospitals where a neighbor's son was ill, she every night scaled a high fence in the rear of the building and managed to get into the ward where she could attend to the poor boy until he died.

Miss Clara Davis, of Massachusetts, was one of the earliest volunteers, and she was so assiduous in her labors and so cheerful in her manners in the hospital that the soldiers came to look upon her with most profound admiration and affection. One of them was heard to say, "There must be wings hidden beneath her cloak." Her labors were mainly with the Army of the Potomac, and she continued them until an attack of typhoid fever made further work of the kind impossible.

Mrs. R. H. Spencer, of Oswego, N. Y., whose husband enlisted in the One Hundred and Forty-seventh New York regiment, followed that organization to the front, and made herself useful as a nurse and hospital attendant. On the march toward Gettysburg she rode a horse which carried, besides herself, bedding, cooking utensils, clothing, and more than three hundred pounds of supplies for the sick and wounded. While that great battle was in progress, Mrs. Spencer, a part of the time actually under fire, established a field hospital in which sixty wounded men were treated. One day she discovered a townsman of her own who had been shot through the throat, and whose case was pronounced hopeless by the surgeon, as he could swallow nothing. Mrs. Spencer took him in hand, and asked him if he could do without food for a week. The man, who was young and strong, gave signs that he could. "Then," said she, "do as I tell you, and you shall not die." She procured a basin of pure cold water, and directed him to keep the wound continually wet, which he did, until in a few days the inflammation subsided and the edges of the wound could be closed up. After which she began to feed him carefully with broth, and every day brought further improvement until he entirely recovered. When the ammunition barge exploded at City Point a piece of shell struck her in the side, but inflicted only a heavy bruise.

Mrs. Harriet Foote Hawley, wife of Gen. Joseph R. Hawley, of Connecticut, did much work in the hospitals on the Carolina coast, whither she had gone in the first instance to engage in teaching the freedmen. At Wilmington, where typhoid fever broke out, she remained at her post when many others were frightened away. In the last month of the war she was injured on the head by the overturning of an ambulance, and this rendered her an invalid for a long time.

Miss Jessie Home, a native of Scotland, entered the service as a hospital nurse at Washington and continued there for two years, making many friends and doing a vast amount of good, until, from overwork, she was struck down by disease.

Mrs. Sarah P. Edson entered the service during the first year of the war, and was assigned to the general hospital at Winchester, Va. In the spring of 1862 she was with McClellan's army on the Peninsula, and after the battle of Williamsburg, learning that her son was among the wounded, she walked twelve miles to find him, apparently dying, where, with other wounded men, he was greatly in need of care. She worked night and day to alleviate their sufferings, and brought something like cleanliness and order out of the dreadful condition in which she found them. In the ensuing summer she passed through a long and severe illness in consequence of her labors. On her recovery she formed a plan for the training of nurses, and, after her experiment had been tried, an official of the medical department declared "that it was more than a success, it was a triumph."

Miss Maria M. C. Hall, of Washington, was associated with Mrs. Fales in hospital work, and went through the four years of it with unfailing energy and enthusiasm. She finally became general superintendent of the Naval Academy Hospital at Annapolis. After the war she wrote: "I mark my hospital days as my best ones, and thank God for the way in which He led me into the good work, and for the strength which kept me through it all.'

Mrs. A. H. Gibbons was a daughter of Isaac T. Hopper, the famous Quaker philanthropist, and wife of James Sloane Gibbons, who wrote the famous song, "We are coming, Father Abraham, three hundred thousand more." With her eldest daughter (afterward Mrs. Emerson) she went to Washington in the autumn of 1861, and entered upon hospital service. One day they discovered a small hospital near Falls Church, where about forty men were ill of typhoid fever, and one young soldier, who seemed to be at the point of death, appealed to them, saying: "Come and take care of me, and I shall get well; if you do not come, I shall die." Finding that the hospital was in a wretched condition, they got leave to take it in charge, and presently had it in excellent order, with a large number of the patients recovering. These ladies were on duty at Point Lookout for over a year, and there they were obliged to oppose and evade the officers in various ways, in order to assist the escaped slaves, whom these officers were only too ready and anxious to return to slavery. While they were engaged in this work, their home in New York was sacked by the mob in the draft riots.

Mrs. Jerusha R. Small, of Cascade, Iowa, followed her husband, who enlisted at the beginning of the war, and became a nurse in the regimental hospitals. At the battle of Shiloh, the tent in which she was caring for a number of wounded men, among whom was her husband, was struck by shells from the enemy's guns, and she was obliged to get her patients away as fast as she could to an extemporized hospital beyond the range of fire. After the most arduous service, extending over several weeks with no intermission, she was struck down by disease and died. To one who said to her in her last hours, "You did wrong to expose yourself so," she answered, "No, I feel that I have done right. I think I have been the means of saving some lives, and that of my dear husband among the rest; and these I consider of far more value than mine, for now they can go and help our country in its hour of need." She was buried with military honors.

Another lady who accompanied her husband to the field was

the wife of Hermann Canfield, colonel of the Seventy-first Ohio regiment, who was killed in the battle of Shiloh. After taking his body to their home, she returned to the army and continued her hospital service until the close of the war.

When the Rev. Shepard Wells and his wife were driven from East Tennessee because of their loyalty to the government, they went to St. Louis, where he engaged in the work of the Christian Commission, and she entered the hospital and became superintendent of a special diet kitchen, which did an immense amount of work for the cause.

Mrs. E. C. Witherell, of Louisville, Ky., was another of those who devoted themselves to the merciful and patriotic work in the hospitals at the expense of their lives. She was head nurse on a hospital steamer in the Mississippi until she was stricken down with fever and died in July, 1862. Still another of those was Miss Phebe Allen, a daughter of Iowa, who served in a hospital at St. Louis until she died in the summer of 1864. Mrs. Edwin Greble, mother of Lieut. John T. Greble, who was killed in the battle of Big Bethel, and of another son who died in the army, of fever, devoted herself to hospital service and to preparing garments and blankets for the soldiers.

Mrs. Isabella Fogg, of Maine, was another of those who pushed their way into the service before it was organized, and found some difficulty in so doing. But she got there at last, and took part in the hospital transport service in the waters of Chesapeake Bay. After the battle of Chancellorsville, she was serving in a temporary hospital at United States Ford when it was shelled by the Confederates. Her son was in the Army of the Shenandoah, and was badly wounded in the battle of Cedar Creek. While performing her duties on a Western hospital boat, in charge of the diet kitchen, she fell through a hatchway and received injuries that disabled her for life.

Mrs. E. E. George, of Indiana, when she applied for a place in the service, was refused on the ground that she was too old. But in spite of her advanced years she insisted upon enlisting in the good cause, and in Sherman's campaign of 1864 she had charge of the Fifteenth Army Corps hospital, and in the battles before Atlanta she was several times under fire. The next spring she was on duty at Wilmington, N. C., when eleven thousand prisoners released from Salisbury were brought there in the deplorable condition that was common to those who had been in Carolina in Confederate stockades. Her incessant labors in behalf of those unfortunate men prostrated her, and she died.

MISS MARY J. SAFFORD.

Large numbers of the troops raised in the Eastern and Middle States passed through Philadelphia on their way to the seat of war, and some philanthropic ladies of that city established a refreshment saloon where meals were furnished free to soldiers who were either going to the front or going home on furlough or because disabled. Among the most assiduous workers here was Mary B. Wade, widow of a sea captain, who, despite her seventy years, was almost never absent, night or day, through the whole four years.

MRS. MARIANNE F. STRANAHAN.

Another widow who gave herself to the cause was Henrietta L. Colt (*née* Peckham), a native of Albany County, N. Y., whose husband was a well-known lawyer. She labored in the Western hospitals and on the river hospital steamers, looking especially after the Wisconsin men, as she was for some time a resident of Milwaukee. She wrote in one of her letters: "I have visited seventy-two hospitals, and would find it difficult to choose the most remarkable among the many heroisms I every day witnessed. I was more impressed by the gentleness and refinement that seemed to grow up in the men when suffering from horrible wounds than from anything else. It seemed to me that the sacredness of the cause for which they offered up their lives gave them a heroism almost superhuman."

Among the great fairs that were held for the benefit of the Sanitary Commission, that in Brooklyn, N. Y., was one of the most successful. It paid into the treasury of the Commission three hundred thousand dollars and furnished supplies valued at two hundred thousand more. This was the work of the Brooklyn Women's Relief Association, of which Mrs. James S. T. Stranahan was president. Her efforts in this work broke down her health, and she died in the first year after the war.

Miss Hattie A. Dada, of New York, was one of the women who volunteered as nurses immediately after the first battle of Bull Run. From that date she was continually in service till the war closed—her time being about equally divided between the Eastern and Western armies. After General Banks's retreat in the Shenandoah Valley, she and Miss Susan E. Hall, remaining with the wounded, became prisoners to the Confederates and were held about three months. From that time these two ladies were inseparable, their last two years of service being in the scantily furnished hospitals at Murfreesboro, Tenn., one of the most difficult fields for such work.

At the beginning of the war, Miss Emily E. Parsons, daughter of Prof. Theophilus Parsons, of Cambridge, Mass., entered a hospital in Boston as pupil and assistant to educate herself for work among the soldiers. A year and a half later she volunteered and was sent to Fort Schuyler, near New York. Early in 1863 she went to St. Louis, where she served in the hospitals and on the hospital steamers. The Benton Hospital, under her superintendence, became famous for its efficiency and its large percentage of recoveries.

Next after the men who commanded armies, the name of Gen. James B. Ricketts is one of the most familiar in the history of the war. When he was gravely wounded at Bull Run and taken prisoner, his wife managed to make her way to him, sharing his captivity, and by careful nursing saved his life. He was exchanged in December, 1861, and his wife afterward devoted herself to the care of the wounded in the Army of the Potomac.

Mrs. Jane R. Munsell, of Maryland, entered upon the service when she saw the wounded of the battle of Antietam, and devoted both her life and her property to it until she died of the incessant labor.

Besides these women who served in the hospitals, there were others who performed quite as important work in organizing the means of supply—in holding fairs, in obtaining materials and workers and superintending the manufacture of garments and other necessary articles, and forwarding them to the right places at the right time. One of the foremost of these was Mrs. Mary A. Livermore, a native of Boston, who afterward became eminent as a pulpit orator. She organized numerous aid societies in the Northwestern States, made tours of the hospitals in the Mississippi valley, to find out what was needed and how the supplies were being disposed of, and was most active in getting up and carrying through to success the great Northwestern Sanitary Fair in Chicago. There was hardly a city in the North in which one or more similar women did not rise to the occasion and do similar work, though on a smaller scale.

NOTE.—For many of the facts related in this chapter we are indebted to Dr. L. P. Brackett's excellent volume on "Woman's Work in the Civil War."

INTERIOR OF HOSPITAL CONSTRUCTED BY THE SANITARY COMMISSION.

INDEX.

Besides the usual abbreviations for titles and given names of persons, and for names of States, N stands for National or Federal, C for Confederate, port. for portrait, inf. for infantry, cav. for cavalry, art'y for artillery.